ENGLISH SPIRITUALITY

For Anne

ENGLISH SPIRITUALITY

From Earliest Times to 1700

Gordon Mursell

Westminster John Knox Press
LOUISVILLE
LONDON • LEIDEN

Published in Great Britain in 2001 by
Society for Promoting Christian Knowledge
Holy Trinity Church
Marylebone Road
London NW1 4DU

First published in the United States in 2001 by
Westminster John Knox Press
Louisville, KY 40202-1396

Scripture quotations are from the New Revised Standard Version of the Bible,
copyright 1989 by the Division of Christian Education of the National Council of the
Churches of Christ in the USA. Used by permission. All rights reserved.

The author and publisher acknowledge with thanks permission to use extracts
from the following in Volumes 1 and 2:
Philip Larkin, 'Faith Healing', in *Collected Poems*, Marvell and Faber, 1988.
T. S. Eliot, 'Murder in the Cathedral' and 'Choruses from *The Rock*',
in *Poems and Plays*, Faber and Faber, 1936.
R. Hamer, ed. and trans., 'The Seafarer' and 'The Dream of the Rood',
in *A Choice of Anglo-Saxon Verse*, Faber and Faber, 1970.
T. Shippey, trans., *Poems of Wisdom and Learning in Old English*, D.S. Brewer, 1976.

British Library Cataloguing-in-Publication Data
A catalogue record for this book is available from the British Library

ISBN 0-281-05408-8

Library of Congress Cataloging-in-Publication Data is on file at the
Library of Congress, Washington, D.C.

ISBN 0-664-22504-7

Typeset by Kenneth Burnley, Wirral, Cheshire
Printed in Great Britain by Mackays of Chatham

Contents

Acknowledgements

Almost all of this book was researched and written while the author was engaged in a busy parochial ministry. The great weaknesses of attempting such a project in such a context are self-evident. It is to be hoped that there will have been some modest compensations; that the opportunity, for example, to test out theories and ideas in small groups, or in the practice of pastoral ministry, or through engagement in secular society, will have some value in enlarging or shaping the perspective. It certainly means that I owe a particular and immense debt to the clergy and people of the Parish of Stafford, not only for their forbearance and support during eight years of rewarding ministry there, but for their willingness to allow me some sabbatical leave during early 1998 which made possible the completion of the penultimate chapter.

I also wish to thank two Stafford people whose contributions were beyond anything I had a right to expect or deserve. Alison Corden and Dr Kenneth Rose both gave invaluable advice and made critical suggestions in regard to Chapter 1 of Volume 2: without them, that chapter would have been seriously impoverished in scope, and a number of basic errors would have remained undiscovered. The same is true of Canon Reginald Askew, whose critical advice was indispensable in the section on Jeremy Taylor in Chapter 5 of this volume. For the errors that remain, in these chapters and elsewhere, I have no one to blame but myself.

I am grateful to the staff of a number of libraries on whose services I have had to draw extensively during the past ten years: among them, the Bodleian Library at Oxford, the libraries of the Universities of Keele and Birmingham, Dr Williams's Library in London, and the Dean Savage Library at Lichfield have been particularly important. But perhaps the libraries to which I owe the greatest debt have been the local ones, and none more than the main public library of the Borough of Stafford, whose staff have coped with endless requests for inter-library loans of the most obscure kinds, and have responded to every approach with a warmth and enthusiasm which, alas, not all library staffs display.

I am most grateful to Dr R. Hamer for permission to quote from his translation of 'The Seafarer' in Chapter 2.

Two people have acted as readers and critical mentors throughout the writing of this book, and to them I owe a debt of gratitude impossible to articulate – not only for the immense care they have taken and the comments they made, but for their friendship and companionship: the Revd Professor Leslie Houlden, formerly of King's College

London; and the Revd Dr Gordon Wakefield, formerly of Queen's College Birmingham.

Finally, I owe a special debt of gratitude to my wife Anne, who has coped patiently with the demands of this massive project on top of her and my other responsibilities, and who has looked forward with an enthusiasm shared only by me for the day when it would finally be completed. Furthermore her shrewd advice and suggestions, as a psychiatrist of experience and wisdom, have been more valuable than she could ever have imagined.

For the rest, there are only the words of T. S. Eliot:

> What is there to conquer
> By strength and submission, has already been discovered
> Once or twice, or several times, by men whom one cannot hope
> To emulate – but there is no competition –
> There is only the fight to recover what has been lost
> And found and lost again and again: and now, under conditions
> That seem unpropitious. But perhaps neither gain nor loss.
> For us, there is only the trying. The rest is not our business.[1]

GORDON MURSELL
January 2000

1. 'East Coker', from *Four Quartets*, in *The complete poems and plays of T. S. Eliot* (London: Faber & Faber, 1969), p. 182.

Note

The New Revised Standard Version of the Bible is used throughout for biblical texts. Where translations are made from other languages into English, the translator is always acknowledged: where no such acknowledgement is made, the translations are my own.

In writing this book, every effort has been made to offer a coherent and continuous narrative for each chapter. The footnotes are not just references: they are intended to amplify, or comment upon, or suggest ways of exploring further, themes mentioned in the main text.

Each chapter has its own bibliography. All works cited in the bibliographies are works which have been drawn on in the writing of this book, or which enlarge upon some aspect of its contents. Books and articles of specific and very limited relevance to a particular point are cited in the footnotes only.

Abbreviations

Acta SS	*Acta sanctorum* (Lives of the saints, ed. by the Bollandists) (Antwerp, 1634– ; Paris, 1863–8)
BCP	Book of Common Prayer
CCCM	*Corpus Christianorum (Continuatio Medievalis)* (Turnhout: Brepols)
CCSL	*Corpus Christianorum* (Turnhout: Brepols)
CF	Cistercian Fathers (Kalamazoo: Cistercian Publications)
DLT	Darton, Longman & Todd
edn	edition
EETS	Early English Text Society
	e.s. extra series
	o.s. original series
	s.s. supplementary series
EHD	*English historical documents*
ET	English translation
ME	Middle English
MGH	Monumenta Germaniae Historica
n.s.	new series
PG	*Patrologia Graecae*, ed. J.-P. Migne
PL	*Patrologia Latina*, ed. J.-P. Migne
rev.	revised
UP	University Press

1

A Hard and Realistic Devotion

English Spirituality: Context and Background

INTRODUCTION

> There is no country in Christendom in which there is so little false devotion as in England, the national character being too hard and realistic to lend itself easily to ecstatic fervours, and too practical to take much interest in abstract intellectual speculation on religious subjects.[1]

These words were written by the nineteenth-century English writer Dora Greenwell.[2] She went on to observe that England's

> spiritual men are still in an eminent degree her practical men, only practical on a higher level than that of ordinary routine and convention.[3]

The early-twentieth-century prime minister Stanley Baldwin noted another English characteristic: 'a profound sympathy for the under-dog'.[4] In 1932, Sir Stephen Tallents suggested some others:

> In international affairs – *a reputation for disinterestedness.*
> In national affairs – *a tradition of justice, law and order.*
> In national character – *a reputation for coolness.*
> In commerce – *a reputation for fair dealing.*
> In manufacture – *a reputation for quality . . .*
> In sport – *a reputation for fair play.*[5]

These impressionistic reflections could be multiplied many times over, and they certainly do not add up to a coherent summary of the English character. Indeed it is highly unlikely that such a thing as 'the English character' could be authoritatively described anyway. It could tentatively be suggested that the particular mix of Celtic, Roman, Scandinavian, Anglo-Saxon, Norman, and (more recently) Asian and Afro-Caribbean blood which have contributed to that character appear to have imparted a pragmatic combination of eclecticism with a certain stubborn independence of spirit which has inevitably influenced its spirituality. And it could also be suggested that that mix underlines a crucial point, not always acknowledged, let alone celebrated, by the English: that the narrow English Channel has not prevented the country from being in continual contact with other nations and cultures; and that the island of Britain is home to two other states, with their own distinctive spiritual traditions.

1

Dora Greenwell's observations are certainly borne out by some aspects of the exploration of English spirituality undertaken in this book. There is a robust empiricism about much of it, a marked absence of grand systematizing theological schemas in the manner of an Aquinas or a Karl Barth: the very title of Richard Hooker's massive work (*Of the laws of ecclesiastical polity*), perhaps the closest equivalent to St Thomas' *Summa*, makes the English writer's far more precise and specific objective clear. There may be even be some truth in Ronald Knox's exasperated reference to 'the Englishman's incurable dislike of dogma', even though Knox's fellow Catholic G. K. Chesterton set out vigorously to prove him wrong.[6] And there is certainly truth in Martin Thornton's conviction that the 'English school' of spirituality (which for Thornton was supremely represented by the medieval 'English mystics', the Prayer Book, and the seventeenth-century 'Caroline Divines') achieved a striking synthesis of the speculative and the affective, scorning the extremes of both.[7]

Yet all this still brings us little nearer any overall sense of what 'English' spirituality might be expected to denote, still less to define. And even the broadest generalizations such as those noted above require extensive qualification. The passionate spirituality of Richard Rolle; the vigorous heterodoxy of the Lollards; the rich byways of Puritan mysticism; the English Pentecostal tradition – all these, and many more besides them, will reveal, as we explore them in this book, aspects of 'English spirituality' entirely different from what middle-class Church of England figures like Dora Greenwell or Martin Thornton had in mind.

We may therefore do best to content ourselves with a few modest preliminary remarks. First, England is part of an island; and its insularity has undoubtedly been a significant factor in shaping its outlook and character, giving rise to a distinctive combination of self-reliance, suspicion of foreigners, and enterprising fascination with what lay beyond the horizon.[8]

Secondly, the English literary tradition is of an exceptional richness. This is not simply reflected in the astonishing achievement of great writers like Chaucer, Shakespeare, and the compilers of the King James or Authorized Version of the Bible: a love of words, from high literature to crosswords and journalism, appears to be a prominent characteristic of English culture. By contrast, the few outstanding English composers and artists, such as Purcell and Turner, scarcely invite comparison with Bach or Raphael. In part this must be the result of climate: a wildly unpredictable northern European climate may not be most propitious for a highly visual culture. In part, it must be the consequence of the development of the English language into an extraordinarily versatile resource. In part, too, it is the result of history: the Reformation set little store by images, but a great deal by words.

This predilection for words, both spoken and written, goes some way to justifying the overwhelming emphasis placed upon word-based spirituality found in this book. We shall glance at other manifestations of 'the spiritual' as well: jewellery, sculpture, music, paintings, landscape and architecture will all find a place. But there is another, more profound, reason why the word must continue to find a central place in any exploration of Christian spirituality; and that is its formative role in the Bible.

DEFINITIONS OF 'SPIRITUALITY'

Before we explore it, it is worth briefly considering how the word 'spirituality' itself has changed its meaning over time.[9] In *Piers Plowman*, the fourteenth-century writer William Langland uses the word in the context of describing the bitter quarrels between friars and secular clergy:

> I, Wrath, walk with them and tell them of my books.
> Thus they speak of spirituality (*spiritualte*), who each despise one another,
> Till they be both beggars and by my spirituality live,
> Or else all rich and ride about.[10]

For Langland, the term denotes ecclesiastical properties, endowments and income (such as tithes); Wrath is suggesting that by arguing fruitlessly over such things, the warring clergy and friars end up with none of them and have to put up with living off the endowments that Wrath himself provides for them. The same meaning appears in a Lollard text of perhaps a century later, *Of poor preaching priests*, where the writer demands that 'all clerks live cleanly on spiritualte, as Christ and his apostles did'.[11]

The term 'spirituality' came also to refer to the clergy. In the sixteenth century, Sir Thomas More uses the word in this sense, describing the clergy as 'the chiefe of the spiritualty'.[12] And a contemporary Protestant bishop, Hugh Latimer, does the same:

> Further, we pray that the priests, the spirituality, or the churchmen, as they call them, do their duties.[13]

By the seventeenth century, the word is beginning to acquire its twentieth-century meaning. Thus the Puritan Richard Baxter tells his readers to 'be sure to maintain a constant delight in God, and a seriousness and spirituality in all his worship'.[14] His fellow Puritan John Bunyan uses the term to mean the spiritual dimension or nature of something;[15] and their Anglican contemporary Jeremy Taylor uses it similarly:

> This is the verification of that great prophecy which Christ made, that 'in all the world the true worshippers should worship in spirit and in truth;' that is, with a pure mind, with holy desires, for spiritual things, according to the mind of the Spirit, in the imitation of Christ's intercession, with perseverance, with charity or love. That is the Spirit of God, and these are the spiritualities of the Gospel, and the formalities of prayers as they are christian and evangelical.[16]

Elsewhere Taylor explores the nature of Christ's presence in the Eucharist, arguing that we eat his body spiritually, for 'the changing all into spirituality is the greatest increasing of blessing in the world'.[17]

By the eighteenth century, the word is being used as it would be in the twentieth. The poet Samuel Taylor Coleridge may have been among the first explicitly to criticize the older use of the term to denote the exercise or possession of secular power by religious authorities:

> This is a gross *abuse* of the term, spiritual . . . Our great Church dignitaries sit in the Upper House of the Convocation, as *Prelates* of the National Church: and as *Prelates*, may exercise *ecclesiastical* power. In the House of Lords they sit as *barons*, and by virtue of the baronies which, much against the will of those haughty prelates, our kings forced upon them: and as such, they exercise a *Parliamentary* power. As bishops of the Church of Christ only can they possess, or exercise (and God forbid! I should doubt, that as such, many of them do faithfully exercise) a *spiritual* power, which neither king can give, nor King and Parliament take away. As Christian *bishops*, they are spiritual *pastors*, by power of the spirit ruling the flocks committed to their charge; but they are *temporal* peers and prelates.[18]

The Nonconformist Isaac Watts uses the word to denote a concern with spiritual things: 'spirituality and heavenly-mindedness, should run through the whole of this duty [of prayer]'.[19] The Evangelical clergyman John Newton says in a letter that

> To those who have a due sense of the spirituality and ground of the divine precepts, and of what passes in their own hearts, there will never be wanting causes of humiliation and self-abasement on the account of sin.[20]

And Newton's friend, the poet William Cowper, describes the Reverend William Bull (1738–1814), the Independent minister at nearby Newport Pagnell, as a man whose

> eminent spirituallity [*sic*] would recommend him to any man desirous of an edifying Companion.[21]

THE SPIRITUALITY OF THE BIBLE

The Creator Spirit

These usages of the word correspond to much modern use of it (though the under-standing of 'spirituality' as the academic study of prayer, mysticism, and devotion appears only in the twentieth century). In any case, if we are to give the term some positive meaning in regard to the subject of this book, we need to go much further back. The English word 'spirit' comes from the Latin *spiritus*, whose primary meaning is 'breath' or 'breeze'.[22] In this sense it is something physical but invisible: the air we breathe, the odours we smell. But *spiritus* had an important secondary meaning even in classical times: 'inspiration' (a word that literally means 'breathing-in'), perhaps of a poet or a god. So Cicero could speak of a poet being 'inspired as though with a kind of divine spirit' (*poetam divino quodam spiritu inflari*) and Livy of being 'touched by the divine spirit' (*spiritu divino tactus*).[23] The word 'spirit', then, denoted invisible reali-ties, both physical and immaterial, which could not be seen but which exerted a palpable effect on the lives of individuals and communities.

The way in which the Latin word for 'spirit' holds together both a physical and an immaterial meaning is significant; for exactly the same thing happens in the Hebrew and Greek languages of the Bible; and the great cultures from which these languages come – the Jewish, the Greek, and the Roman – form the three primary seedbeds in which early Christian spirituality grew. The Hebrew word *ruach*, like the Greek *pneuma* and the Latin *spiritus*, means both 'breath' and 'spirit'. Hence the rich ambivalence of the opening verses of scripture:

> In the beginning when God created the heavens and the earth, the earth was a formless void and darkness covered the face of the deep, while a wind from God swept over the face of the waters. Then God said, 'Let there be light'; and there was light. And God saw that the light was good; and God separated the light from the darkness. God called the light Day, and the darkness he called Night.[24]

The phrase rendered 'a wind from God' could as easily be translated 'the spirit of God'. Hebrew knows no absolute distinction between the physical, material world, and a wholly separate 'spiritual' one. The spirit, or wind, from God sweeps over the raw primal watery chaos that existed at the dawn of space and time. And God speaks: the word of God is uttered *into* the chaos, drawing forth from it order, identity, pattern, purpose, and meaning – in a word, creation. And the newly-created reality (first light, then everything else) is *separated* from the chaos from which it was summoned. God sees that this new reality is good; and God *names* it.

In these few majestic verses something of the essential nature of 'spirituality' in the Judaeo-Christian tradition is revealed. It is the process by which God created, and continues to create, all that is. The primordial chaos that represents pure potential, for both creation and destruction, is swept over by the wind or breath or spirit of God, and addressed by God's word. God breathes and speaks, and things come to be. God looks upon them, delights in them, separates them from the chaos, and gives them names. The chaos is not destroyed, but penned in;[25] it is tamed, and then used, for if it is not worked on and governed by God's creative word, it becomes destructive: so the inevitable consequence of humanity's endemic wickedness was a reversion to primal chaos, in the story of Noah's flood.[26] Both creation and chaos represent, not only (or even primarily) once-for-all historical events but continuing processes: hence the Psalmist can pray

> Save me, O God,
>   for the waters have come up to my neck.
> I sink in deep mire,
>   where there is no foothold;
> I have come into deep waters,
>   and the flood sweeps over me.[27]

Or, in the terrible despair of the devout person whose memory of past blessings collides painfully with present distress:

> These things I remember,
>   as I pour out my soul:
> how I went with the throng,
>   and led them in procession to the house of God,

with glad shouts and songs of thanksgiving,
    a multitude keeping festival.
Why are you cast down, O my soul . . . ?
My soul is cast down within me;
    therefore I remember you
from the land of Jordan and of Hermon,
    from Mount Mizar.
Deep calls to deep
    at the thunder of your cataracts;
all your waves and your billows have gone over me.[28]

But human sin, and incapacity to co-operate with the Creator Spirit, do not have the last word; and the Psalmist praises the Creator's ultimate victory over the disorder from which all that exists came forth:

Therefore let all who are faithful offer prayer to you;
    at a time of distress, the rush of mighty waters
        shall not reach them.[29]

The floods have lifted up, O LORD,
    the floods have lifted up their voice;
    the floods lift up their roaring.
More majestic than the thunders of mighty waters,
    more majestic than the waves of the sea,
        majestic on high is the LORD!
Your decrees are very sure;
    holiness befits your house,
    O LORD, for evermore.[30]

Note the sharp antithesis of 'sea' and 'decrees' here: it is God's word, spoken into the abyss of chaos, which alone brings meaning and hope. The abyss is sometimes personified as a sea-monster; and in the apocalyptic literature of the Bible (such as the books of Daniel and Revelation) the beasts that threaten all humanity come up from the sea.[31] But the personification should not be misunderstood; there is no dualism here. Rather the image allows the Hebrew scriptures to retain a healthy awareness of the active potential for evil that exists all the time, everywhere that God's creative word is ignored or disobeyed; and in the New Testament vision of the final consummation, the sea gives up its dead, and is no more.[32]

The resonances, for later ages, between the work of the Creator Spirit and the birth of a child, or the processes of psychology and psychotherapy, are clear: as the child is separated from the mother's womb, drawn forth from the waters, so God draws each created thing lovingly into being: 'it was you who took me from my mother's womb'.[33] And the careful work of naming what is otherwise disordered and troubling personal experience anticipates the craft of the spiritual director or therapist. But there is a subversive tone to the work of the Creator Spirit too; for creation begins in a head-on confrontation between God and every kind of disorder. God comes into the story as critic, and his first word is a word of doom to the *status quo*.[34]

In the story of the Exodus, and again in the great prophetic oracles of the Hebrew Bible, that subversive element is made more explicit as the Creator Spirit, roused to action by the cries of oppressed humanity, forces back the chaos again and again. The monumental 78th Psalm describes the process: God acts, humanity thanks – and then forgets, allowing the forces of disorder to triumph again; so humanity cries out to God, who awakes 'as from sleep, like a warrior shouting because of wine' in order to rescue his people.[35] In the great prophecies of Isaiah, the exiled Israelites are told that God regards their enemies as 'chaos': God is the one who

> . . . stretches out the heavens like a curtain,
>   and spreads them like a tent to live in;
> who brings princes to naught,
>   and makes the rulers of the earth as nothing.[36]

The Hebrew word translated 'nothing', *tohu*, is the word used for chaos or void at the beginning of Genesis. Those who claim to take God's place will be thrown down into the chaos from which they came. In another oracle, God explicitly renews the work of creation:

> I will pour water on the thirsty land,
>   and streams on the dry ground;
> I will pour my spirit [*ruach*] upon your descendants,
>   and my blessing on your offspring.
> They shall spring up like a green tamarisk,
>   like willows by flowing streams . . .
> All who make idols are nothing [*tohu*].[37]

Here the water becomes fruitful, and the children of God are like trees planted by flowing streams.[38] And again:

> For thus says the LORD,
> who created the heavens
>   (he is God!),
> who formed the earth and made it
>   (he established it;
> he did not create it a chaos [*tohu*],
>   he formed it to be inhabited!):
> I am the Lord, and there is no other.
> I did not speak in secret,
>   in a land of darkness;
> I did not say to the offspring of Jacob,
>   'Seek me in chaos [*tohu*].'[39]

And there is profound paradox: the awesome power of the Creator Spirit, when it is manifested to the broken and exhausted prophet Elijah, is not present in elemental wind and earthquake, but in a 'sound of sheer silence', or 'still small voice'.[40] God is not seen, but heard; the Hebrews, fearful of the prohibition of graven images, believed that hearing was the primary spiritual sense. John Donne, commenting on the mystical experience of St Paul recorded in 2 Corinthians 12, says

> When S.Paul was carried up *in raptu*, in an extasie, into paradise, that which he gained by this powerfull way of teaching, is not expressed in a *Vidit*, but an *Audivit*, It is not said that he saw, but that he heard unspeakeable [*sic*] things. The eye is the devils doore, before the eare: for, though he doe enter at the eare, by wanton discourse, yet he was at the eye before; we see, before we talke dangerously. But the eare is the Holy Ghosts first doore.[41]

The word that is uttered and heard, that creates and recreates, and that never returns empty to its speaker, is a word at once of intimacy and of power.[42]

Life in the Spirit

That combination of intimacy and power is further developed in the New Testament and the life of the early church. The water comes to be seen as an image both of death and of the new life of baptism, by which we are rescued from the grip of disorder.[43] And the spirit of God that swept over the chaos becomes a living manifestation of God's own presence, bestowing gifts and healing and fostering growth.[44] In the Gospel of John, Jesus declares that 'God is spirit, and those who worship him must worship in spirit and truth.'[45] William Temple comments

> God is not the totality of things – the All; nor is He an immanent principle to which all things conform; He is Spirit – active energy, alive and purposive, but free from the temporal and spatial limitations which are characteristic of matter.[46]

Yet this is not to imply that the material and temporal dimensions are somehow opposed to the spiritual, even though much ancient Greek philosophy did make this assumption. In the letters of St Paul, we encounter a contrast, not between two parts of the self so much as between two different allegiances to which the self could choose to commit itself.[47] Paul, like all the New Testament writers, wrote in Greek; but he wrote as a Jew; and when he distinguished two kinds of life – the one lived 'according to the flesh' and the other 'according to the Spirit' – he was not rejecting material things *tout court*, in the manner of some Greek philosophers.[48] Rather he was contrasting a life lived in a narrowly this-worldly context, without a living faith in God, with a life lived in the perspective of our relationship with God as God is in Jesus, a life in which the fruits of Christ's self-giving on the cross are made available to us.[49] On this view, 'spirituality' becomes just that: all of life, lived in the light of our relationship with God in Christ. It is integrating, relational, Christ-centred. And it is transforming: we live no longer for ourselves, but for Christ; and so if anyone is in Christ, there is a new creation: everything old has passed away; see, everything has become new! All this is from God, who reconciled us to himself through Christ, and has given us the ministry of reconciliation.[50]

For the Christian, then, what began at the dawn of all time and is continued by the Creator Spirit finds its supreme actuality in the gift of faith and the incorporation of the believer into the life of the Spirit in the church. 'Spirituality', on this view, is always primarily corporate and only secondarily an individual affair. And, for St Paul, this is its goal:

Now the Lord is the Spirit, and where the Spirit of the Lord is, there is freedom. And all of us, with unveiled faces, seeing the glory of the Lord as though reflected in a mirror, are being transformed into the same image from one degree of glory to another; for this comes from the Lord, the Spirit . . . We do not proclaim ourselves; we proclaim Jesus Christ as Lord and ourselves as your slaves for Jesus' sake. For it is the God who said, 'Let light shine out of darkness,' who has shone in our hearts to give the light of the knowledge of the glory of God in the face of Jesus Christ.[51]

This dense passage is much controverted.[52] But the way it recapitulates the language of creation seems clear:[53] to the extent to which we are transformed into the likeness of Christ, we reflect that glory in the world; and we become, not just creatures drawn from chaos, but instruments of God's new creation, priests for others too. For Christ *is* the creative Word, made flesh in history, through whose death and resurrection an entirely new relationship between Creator and creatures is opened up. We are still, in Paul's view, caught between life 'in the flesh' and life 'in the Spirit'; and we must live with that tension, the tension between the 'now' and the 'not yet'.[54] True, Paul says that we 'know' the glory of God, in a knowing that passes beyond intellectual understanding to a free and active participation of the will and the whole person.[55] But even this has an in-built tension: 'Now I know only in part; then I will know fully, even as I have been fully known.'[56] Elsewhere Paul expresses that tension thus:

Even though our outer nature is wasting away, our inner nature is being renewed day by day. For this slight momentary affliction is preparing us for an eternal weight of glory beyond all measure, because we look not at what can be seen but at what cannot be seen; for what can be seen is temporary, but what cannot be seen is eternal.[57]

We know that the whole creation has been groaning in labour pains until now; and not only the creation, but we ourselves, who have the first fruits of the Spirit, groan inwardly while we wait for adoption, the redemption of our bodies. For in hope we were saved . . . Likewise the Spirit helps us in our weakness; for we do not know how to pray as we ought, but that very Spirit intercedes with sighs too deep for words. And God, who searches the heart, knows what is the mind of the Spirit, because the Spirit intercedes for the saints according to the will of God.[58]

These texts open up immense issues and areas of debate, well beyond the scope of this book.[59] But at the very least they imply: first, that there is a dynamism about the Christian view of the spiritual life, and a dynamism that is shared with the whole created order as it 'groans in labour pains' and longs for all that lies ahead; secondly, that Christian spirituality is rooted not only in our nature as *creatures* but in our nature as *children*, adopted in Christ and by his free grace; thirdly, that there is no absolute distinction between matter and spirit – we wait for 'the redemption of our bodies', and all of what makes us who we are is destined for transformation into the inconceivable glory that Christ has opened up for us; finally, that prayer is *par excellence* what we are called to do as we wait in hope, a prayer that the Spirit articulates for us and in us and that is always forward-looking, as 'the creation waits with eager longing for the revealing of the children of God'.[60]

One other implication is worth drawing out briefly here. To be adopted as children is to be invited into a new and intimate relationship with God. Jesus says to his disciples: 'unless you change and become like children, you will never enter the kingdom of heaven'.[61] And Paul tells the Romans that 'you did not receive a spirit of slavery to fall back into fear, but you have received a spirit of adoption'.[62] To be adopted, and to be given the hope of eternal life, is also to be given another spiritual gift: boldness, as Paul tells the Corinthians.[63] The Greek word (*parrhesia*) here means literally frankness or freedom of speech; and in classical Greek it was the privilege claimed by citizens in the Athenian democracy.[64] There are clear anticipations of this spiritual virtue in the Hebrew Bible, as the fruits of the covenant relationship between God and the people of Israel;[65] and it is this bold willingness to challenge God which supremely characterizes the great psalms of lament, as well as some of the prophetic literature.[66]

In the New Testament, *parrhesia* is used both with regard to Christians' relationships with God, and with regard to their relationships with their neighbours.[67] To be a child of God is to experience a love strong and unconditional enough to make you bold, both in your relationship with your adopted parent and in your ability to relate to a world which is often hostile.[68] We shall see, in the exploration of English spirituality that follows, how various writers (particularly in the Protestant tradition) deploy the virtue of boldness as a crucial weapon in the Christian's spiritual armoury.

Holiness in the Biblical Tradition

The creation, renewed in the Exodus, challenging the powers of evil and chaos in the prophetic writings, represents the starting-point for what we might call the spirituality of the Bible. Something needs to be said about the process by which the people are called to grow, to respond to and appropriate for themselves the life-giving word. We have already seen that God creates by separating: light from darkness, water above the sky from water below it, male from female. This process of separation is what came to be called *holiness*. The Hebrew *qadosh*, the Greek *hagios*, the Latin *sanctus* all carry overtones of separateness, of being consecrated and set apart.

But set apart from what? In the Hebrew tradition, to be holy is to be set apart (as God is set apart) from what is *unclean*. In the Book of Leviticus, the antithesis of holiness and uncleanness is elaborated on at length; for both holiness and uncleanness were believed to be infectious, attractive even.[69] To be holy is to be set apart for God. But this was far from being a narrowly ritual or liturgical procedure. The nineteenth chapter of Leviticus begins with the solemn words:

> The LORD spoke to Moses, saying: Speak to all the congregation of the people of Israel and say to them: You shall be holy, for I the LORD your God am holy.[70]

As the chapter progresses, it becomes clear that holiness involves ethical and moral probity, reverence for the elderly and the alien, the practice of true justice and above all of love ('you shall love your neighbour as yourself') – as well as a willingness to keep the sabbaths, avoid witchcraft, and not cross-breed cows. Why this strange mix? Because in the Hebrew tradition, holiness means separation, not just of the holy from the unclean, but of the good from the evil.

To belong to the people of Israel is to be summoned to holiness; and the fruits of that holiness are nowhere more eloquently or searchingly reflected upon than in the longest and most intimate of all the Bible's prayers: Psalm 119. In this extraordinary prayer, constructed in a series of 22 sections (one for each letter of the Hebrew alphabet), each consisting of eight mantra-like verses beginning with the same letter of the alphabet), everything extraneous is filtered out. The believer, drawing on a wide range of imagery and affective language, seeks to appropriate for herself or himself the essence of that holiness which constitutes the beauty and integrity of the spiritual life at its fullest. And the *torah* or word of God which is the instrument for attaining that holiness is not simply the inspired scriptures: it is God's providential and practical wisdom for everyday living, 'a lamp to my feet and a light to my path', a jewel of inexhaustible richness and attractiveness:

> Open my eyes, so that I may behold
>   wondrous things out of your law . . .
> I will also speak of your decrees before kings,
>   and shall not be put to shame . . .
> Your statutes have been my songs
>   wherever I make my home.[71]

In the New Testament, this notion of holiness as separation from all that is unclean and evil, so as to be able to live the full radiance of the life to which God calls his people, is further developed. The writer of the First Letter of Peter quotes Leviticus 19:

> As he who called you is holy, be holy yourselves in all your conduct; for it is written, 'You shall be holy, for I am holy.'[72]

In the Gospel of Matthew, Jesus tells his disciples not to give to dogs what is holy – a characteristic example of Levitical teaching.[73] And St Paul takes up the notion of holiness as infectious in his teaching on the church:

> If the part of the dough offered as first fruits is holy, then the whole batch is holy; and if the root is holy, then the branches also are holy.[74]

Similarly 'the unbelieving husband is made holy through his wife'.[75] Holiness belongs to the whole people of God, because it first belonged to Jesus; and as the body of Christ in the world, the Church radiates a holiness that rivals and surpasses that of the great Jerusalem Temple:

> Do you not know that you are God's temple and that God's Spirit dwells in you? If anyone destroys God's temple, God will destroy that person. For God's temple is holy, and you are that temple.[76]

But it is perhaps in the Farewell Discourses of the Gospel of John that this notion of holiness is most movingly articulated. Jesus gives his disciples (whom he calls friends instead of servants because he has opened his heart to them) a new commandment: 'Just as I have loved you, you also should love one another.'[77] Here the great Levitical injunction to love one's neighbour is deepened by the prior gift of God's unconditional love. The Father and the Son will 'make their homes' with those who love them.[78] And, in the great final prayer, Jesus prays not for his friends to be taken *out of* the world, but to be protected *in* the world from the power of the evil one.[79] They are to be separated, not from the world but from the structures of evil that exist within the world. They are to be sanctified in the truth, the truth of the word of God;[80] and that word, which from all eternity was spoken into the abyss and brought forth creation, was made flesh in the form of Jesus Christ.[81] Jesus makes himself holy ('I sanctify myself') for their sake, so that they may be holy too.[82] But he does that by giving up his life for them, not so that they do not have to, but to give them the freedom to do the same.[83] By making their own this extraordinary, self-giving, unconditional love, they share his glory and become one with him, so that through them the world may believe. There is no higher or more luminous embodiment of Christian spirituality than this.

THEMES IN THE SPIRITUALITY OF EARLY CHRISTIANITY

Holiness in the Early Christian Tradition

The biblical understanding of holiness was rooted, as we have seen, in the fundamental notion of *separation* – but separation of the good from the evil, the holy from the unclean. In addition to the cultures and languages of Hebrew and Latin, however, those of classical Greece also exerted a profound and lasting influence on the development of Christian spirituality. And in that tradition, holiness tended to denote, not the separation of the good from the evil, but the separation of the 'spiritual' (i.e. the non-material) from the physical, the soul from the body.[84] In the *Symposium* of Plato, the most influential of all ancient Greek writers on the course of the Christian spiritual tradition, we find this:

> This above all others . . . is the region where a man's life should be spent, in the contemplation of absolute beauty. Once you have seen that, you will not value it in terms of gold or rich clothing or of the beauty of boys and young men . . . Do you think that it will be a poor life that a man leads who

has his gaze fixed in that direction, who contemplates absolute beauty with the appropriate faculty and is in constant union with it? Do you not see that in that region alone where he sees beauty with the faculty capable of seeing it, will he be able to bring forth not mere reflected images of goodness but true goodness, because he will be in contact not with a reflection but with the truth? And having brought forth and nurtured true goodness, he will have the privilege of being beloved of God, and becoming, if ever a man can, immortal himself.[85]

A number of features of that extract may strike the reader at once: the strongly male language and imagery; the close relationship between the three great 'ideas' of beauty, truth, and goodness; the highly visual tone, entirely different from the Hebrew emphasis on hearing; the belief that you are (or can be) transformed by the object of your contemplation, which was to exert a profound influence on later Christian spirituality; the reference to 'immortality'; and the fundamental Platonic principle that the invisible realities (such as truth and beauty) are far more real than their physical manifestations (such as a truthful person or a beautiful thing). These matters have been extensively studied.[86] What is important for our purposes is, first, their enormous influence on subsequent thought and spirituality – and, secondly, the bearing they have on the nature of holiness.

For the Greeks, the human soul was immortal: it came from a pre-existent reality and would return there after it was released from its temporary attachment to a physical body. Holiness therefore came to denote, not the separation of the good from the evil, but the separation of the soul from the body, the spiritual from the material. This notion, quite different from (say) St Paul's belief in the resurrection of the body, came to exert an enormous influence on early Christianity. Negatively, it led to a pervasive depreciation of all things bodily, encouraging a particular kind of anti-material asceticism which found its normative expression in the monastic or eremitic life.[87] Positively, it imparted to Christian spirituality a dynamism, an emphasis on a divinely conferred striving or desire for something that was always above and greater than what could be seen or grasped, which it might otherwise have lacked.

Platonism was not, of course, swallowed neat: too much of it was incompatible with Christianity for that to be possible. There is an interesting text in the writings of the medieval English monastic writer Gilbert of Hoyland, in which he distinguishes between two kinds of 'narrowness' (*brevitas*):

There is a narrowness which knows how to welcome [Christ] alone, and a narrowness which is unable to welcome him fully. The former is characteristic of charity and discipline, but the latter of infirmity and human nature.[88]

Monastic writers were well aware of the difference between an unhealthy false asceticism and one securely grounded on Christian truth.[89] Furthermore, the heart of early Christian ascetic spirituality had a far more positive content than is often supposed. Olivier Clément describes it as 'an awakening from the sleep-walking of daily life', requiring of us above all 'a loving attentiveness', whose purpose is to divest oneself of surplus weight, of spiritual fat. It is to dissolve in the waters of baptism, in the water of tears, all the hardness of the heart, so that it may become an antenna of infinite sensitivity, infinitely vulnerable to the beauty of the world and to the sufferings of human beings, and to God who is Love, who has conquered by the wood of the cross.[90]

Even so, it would be impossible to deny the Platonic element not only in early Christianity but in medieval and later Christianity too. The firm insistence on curbing, repressing or redirecting the desires and urges of the body are deeply influenced by Platonic spirituality. And the difference between that kind of asceticism and that of the Jewish tradition is underlined by the Jewish scholar Gershom Sholem:

> There is . . . one important respect in which Hasidism differs sharply from its Christian contemporaries: it does not enjoin sexual asceticism. On the contrary, the greatest importance is assigned in the *Sefer Hasidim* to the establishment and maintenance of a normal and reasonable marital life. Nowhere is penitence extended to sexual abstinence in marital relations. The asceticism of the typical Hasidic concerns solely his social relations towards women, not the sexual side of his married life.[91]

Early Christian spirituality, then, was heir to two different traditions of holiness: the Hebrew, and the Greek. The tension between them was always there. But it was grounded in the truth of the life, death, and resurrection of Jesus, and the emerging doctrines that articulated and secured that truth.[92] It was also grounded in scripture, which was subjected to close and often allegorical reading which led to the sacred text becoming inseparable from the truth it was believed to proclaim.[93] The eastern Christian tradition tended to take a more optimistic view of human nature and its capacity to be divinized, transformed into the very life of God; the western tradition, with a more negative view of humanity and a larger emphasis on the consequences of the Fall, emphasized this less, and tended to be more introspective.[94] Furthermore, there existed in both east and west two different kinds of theology: *apophatic* theology held that God, always strictly unknowable, could be approached only through the mystery of love, and that the closer we come to God, the less we have to say about it.[95] *Cataphatic* theology took a more affirmative view of human capacity to apprehend the reality of God.[96] Both these exerted immense influence on the western Christian tradition.

Yet patristic writers, however diverse, held to a number of profound and common truths. They believed human beings to have been created in the image of God, following Genesis; they believed that image to have been defaced, but not obliterated, as a result of sin; and they believed that, through a process of divine grace and our free co-operation with that grace, our lost likeness to God could be restored.[97] Above all, perhaps, they believed that authentic Christian spirituality is inconceivable outside the Church: it was within the Church, within its sacramental life and structures, that human longing for the divine could be directed aright, and (so far as the limitations of this world allowed) satisfied.[98] And it is within that context that the whole notion of Christian 'spiritual life' needs to be seen: the New Testament perspective, centred on life in Christ and the expectation of an imminent 'end', allowed little room for any sense of spiritual growth or progress other than in the particular perspectives outlined above. Patristic Christianity begins to enlarge these perspectives, though always in a firmly ecclesial context.

The Influence of St Augustine

English spirituality was shaped, directly and indirectly, by a wide range of continental sources and ideas: indeed the fertile intercourse between England and continental Europe, even in the earliest centuries, is one of the most striking features of the country's spiritual history. But, after the Bible, one person's influence, across many different subject areas and centuries, stood out; indeed that one person may claim to be the single most influential person in the history of Christian thought and spirituality: St Augustine – not the Augustine whom St Gregory the Great sent as an apostle to the English in 597, but the Bishop of Hippo in North Africa, whose death in 430 effectively marked the end of western Roman civilization.[99]

It is worth briefly enumerating some of the principal features of this vastly influential spirituality. First, Augustine attached exceptional importance to the human will.[100] For Augustine, the sin of the first human beings in Eden was above all a misdirection of their wills, a deliberate act of disobedience against God; and in his view, which became increasingly gloomy as he grew older, that act bequeathed to all subsequent human beings a kind of inherent flaw, a predisposition to choose against God – or, more specifically, to choose to live what St Paul had called life 'according to the flesh'.[101] Secondly, and as a consequence of this, Augustine attached exceptional importance to the workings of divine grace, and (again as he grew older) he came to believe that that grace was irresistible: in other words, God predestined some to salvation and others (indeed most) to damnation, and it was the work of divine grace rather than the free choice of the individual concerned that was determinative.[102]

Thirdly, and following from this, Augustine conceived of human beings as caught in a dilemma. On the one hand, we are created in the image of God; and that image is no static thing, but a living, dynamic reality, a restless longing which God alone can satisfy.[103] Our inherited predisposition to choose against God, and to try to satisfy that longing through inappropriate finite means, does not destroy the image of God within us, which is located in the deepest part of our souls: it simply obscures it.[104] What matters for Augustine is our *intention*; we cannot attain God by our own efforts; but we can *want* to attain God, we can want to be loved and saved by God. Hence his famous declaration:

> [Sometimes it is the case that] a person can act cruelly through love and agreeably through wickedness. A father beats his child, and a slave-master is kind to his slave. If you were to choose between the two things, lashes and kindness, who would not choose kindness and flee from lashes? But if you consider the persons [behaving in this way], [you see that it is] love [that] does the beating, [whilst] wickedness is kind. For many things can appear to be good and not proceed from the root of love. Therefore once for all this short command is given to you: 'Love and do what you will.' If

you keep silent, keep silent through love; if you speak, speak through love; if you correct someone, correct them for reasons of love; if you pardon, pardon them through love: let love be rooted in you, and from this root nothing but good can grow.[105]

Finally, Augustine matters because he bequeathed to subsequent generations a vision of 'the good', of the spiritual life, which was profoundly attractive. We are created with a divine longing: 'the whole life of the good Christian', he wrote, 'is a holy desire' (*tota vita Christiani boni, sanctum desiderium est*);[106] and the closer we come to God, the greater our desire for God becomes, transforming us in the process as we grow in a personal union of love, which is the goal of human life.[107] Nothing was, or is, more difficult or challenging for the Christian church than to present, and live by, a vision of 'the good' which is deeply attractive; in articulating such a vision, and notwithstanding the grim pessimism of his last years (which led him grossly to depreciate the natural goodness of sexuality and the body), Augustine entrusted to the western spiritual tradition a rich conflation of Platonism and biblical thought which began in a searching exploration of the nature of the self and culminated in a transcendent vision of the power of love to transform and redeem.

SPIRITUALITY AND METHODOLOGY

Any historical study of spirituality will involve awkward decisions of method and judgement. In his *An essay in aid of a grammar of assent*, John Henry Newman considers these difficulties:

The inquirer has first of all to decide on the point from which he is to start in the presence of the received accounts; on what side, from what quarter he is to approach them; on what principles his discussion is to be conducted; what he is to assume, what opinions or objections he is summarily to put aside as nugatory, what arguments, and when, he is to consider as apposite, what false issues are to be avoided, when the state of his arguments is ripe for a conclusion. Is he to commence with absolutely discarding all that has hitherto been received; or to retain it in outline; or to make selections from it; or to consider and interpret it as mythical, or as allegorical; or to hold so much to be trustworthy, or at least of *prima facie* authority, as he cannot actually disprove; or never to destroy except in proportion as he can construct? Then, as to the kind of arguments suitable or admissible, how far are tradition, analogy, isolated monuments and records, ruins, vague reports, legends, the facts or saying of later times, language, popular proverbs, to tell in the inquiry? what are marks of truth, what of falsehood, what is probable, what suspicious, what promises well for discriminating facts from fictions?

Then, arguments have to be balanced against each other, and then lastly the decision is to be made, whether any conclusion at all can be drawn, or whether any before certain issues are tried and settled, or whether a probable conclusion or a certain. It is plain how incessant will be the call here or there for the exercise of a definitive judgment, how little that judgment will be helped on by logic, and how intimately it will be dependent upon the intellectual complexion of the writer.[108]

But there are other difficulties too. A historical study of spirituality (or indeed of anything else) will also be influenced, consciously or not, by the culture and presuppositions, as well as by the gender, of the person writing it.[109]

The use of the term 'mysticism' or 'mystical' is a good illustration of these considerations. It can be asserted, with some claim to objectivity, that the noun 'mysticism' is relatively modern;[110] that it derives from the Greek word that denoted devotees of pagan 'mystery cults' which attached particular importance to secret truths vouchsafed only to initiates;[111] that in early Christianity 'mystical' referred to the hidden truths or meanings of the Bible, and supremely to the revelation of the hidden and invisible God in the manifest and visible form of Jesus Christ;[112] and that the term is generally used to describe an experience of (or an aspirant after) intimate union with God.

But thereafter the matter becomes more difficult.[113] In an important study, Don Cupitt has argued that the notion of an omnipotent, omnipresent God is explicable only in terms of the parallel notion of an omnipotent, omnipresent nation-state: the two ideas grew symbiotically.[114] People believed in God not because they loved him so much as because they were terrified of what he (or his official representatives) would do if they didn't. In this context, Cupitt argues, mysticism acquires a powerfully subversive role: its language, so often female and sexual, alone challenges the authority of the religious system. Mystics alone write against the omnipotent system or single truth-power.[115] Cupitt's argument is typically provocative, and his theory is questionable in many respects: it is not, for example, at all clear that mystics are *invariably* persecuted, as he claims.[116] But he surely has a point in saying that

> mystical writing of any kind . . . is therapeutic. It seeks to cure the deep feeling of alienation that is produced by perhaps every professional discipline, and by institutionalization.[117]

And his insistence that we cannot, so to speak, step behind the words and language used by mystics to describe their experiences, or separate the words from some 'pure' and wordless experience somehow recoverable centuries later, is surely important.[118]

Other perspectives on what we mean by mysticism are no less important. The American scholar Helen White, writing about William Blake, suggests that any understanding of mysticism which excludes the earthy and childish will be inadequate:

> when man enters with all his being into any enterprise, what is base of him goes in with what is high; what is immature and childish, with what is of fullest stature. Nowhere is this more true than in religion. Where religion forgets the savage and the child in man, she loses her chance to reach the man.[119]

And Robert Alfred Vaughan, a nineteenth-century Protestant historian of mysticism, wrote

Mysticism has no genealogy. It is no tradition conveyed across frontiers or down the course of generations as a ready-made commodity. It is a state of thinking and feeling, to which minds of a certain temperament are liable at any time or place, in occident and orient, whether Romanist or Protestant, Jew, Turk, or Infidel. It is more or less determined by the positive religion with which it is connected. But though conditioned by circumstance or education, its appearance is ever the spontaneous product of a certain crisis in individual or social history. A merely imitative mysticism, as exemplified by some Tractarian ecclesiastics, is an artificial expedient.[120]

Both these insights need to be kept in mind as well. A study of spirituality or mysticism which neglects the social and political context forfeits any right to be taken seriously. And Vaughan's point is vital too: genuine mystical experience does not arise out of the leisured reflections of the comfortable, but out of some 'crisis in individual or social history'. Another nineteenth-century figure, the Roman Catholic George Tyrrell, adds a further interpretative criterion:

it was Christianity, with its conception of God as subsistent righteousness, its recognition of the voice of conscience as the voice of God, that first revealed the two interests – the religious and the moral – as identical, and thereby gave a mystical depth to morality, and a moral earnestness to religion, and brought this world and the Beyond, and our lives in reference to both, into a coherent unity.[121]

Recent feminist scholarship has immensely enlarged our perspective, and sharpened our interpretative criteria, for the study of a subject such as mysticism. Difference of gender *must* create a different perspective when experiencing or writing about such a subject; for a woman to reach out to a loving God, who has throughout Christian history been described in male terms, will be quite different than for a man; and the way we read devotional texts will be profoundly affected by whether or not we are willing to take this into account.[122] Grace Jantzen argues that women were drawn to mysticism and mystical theology in part because these things are based on experience, not authority: hence the importance to the ecclesiastical establishment of ensuring that those (whether men or women) who claimed a special or direct (i.e. 'mystical') knowledge of God were kept firmly under the church's control.[123]

Furthermore, the essence of mysticism is the discovery and experience of a God whose essence is not independence, power and domination so much as love and intimacy.[124] Hence too, though, the importance of first being encouraged to develop a sense of self-worth: you cannot, after all, surrender a sense of self you have never had.[125] Hence as well the vital importance of resisting easy stereotypical judgements of women mystics as emotional, or hysterical or extravagant, and of recalling Simone de Beauvoir's insistence on the relationship between mysticism and sexual love: 'it is not that mystical love always has a sexual character, but that the sexuality of the woman in love is tinged with mysticism.'[126]

Feminist scholarship has also opened up the exploration of the imagery used in spiritual writing, reminding us that much of the language and imagery of ascent is typically male: St John of the Cross's vision was of a mountain to be climbed, where St Teresa's was of an interior castle to be explored.[127] And it has prevented us from separating issues of spirituality from issues of power: as Jantzen points out, 'it is necessary to investigate the ways in which shifts in who counts as a mystic were part of the ongoing struggles for power in the medieval church'.[128] Any historical study will need to be attentive to issues such as this, and in particular to how those who have no power seek to express their spiritual values. Not the least of the reasons for the enduring vitality of biblical spirituality is that so much of it arose out of situations where the participants were *not* in control, or were not where they would like to be.

Finally, none of these interpretative points remove the continuing need for rigorous application of the sober criteria of the historian's trade: by whom, and for whom, was this text or artefact produced, and in what social and theological context? What was it intended to convey, and why? What does it *not* say: what is the author or artist choosing to omit? What was its influence, and by whom was that influence shaped or transmitted? To whom does it speak today, and why? What impact does it have on *me*, and why?[129] Failure to bear in mind that last question implies failure honestly to concede that any historical study, whatever its other faults or strengths, will bear the imprint of its author's peculiar and particular personality, context and story.

Two final quotations are worth including here. The Catholic medieval historian Marie-Dominique Chenu wrote:

> The economy of salvation is not defined exclusively in the reflective and cautiously reasoned understanding of a few licensed thinkers, but also in the concrete decisions, in the states of life embraced, in the ideals of sanctity, in the evangelical work which the church, in its head and members, approves, sets up, promotes – in short, defines.[130]

To that list one might add that the economy of salvation is also defined by the quality of life of a given ecclesial community, its outward-looking and compassionate nature (or lack of it), its concern for those who are not its members. And Robert Alfred Vaughan, the idiosyncratic but shrewd Victorian Nonconformist historian of mysticism, has this to say at the close of his great work:

> There is a considerable class, in these restless, hurrying, striving days, who would be much the better for a measure of spiritual infusion from the Quietism of Madame Guyon . . . The want of leisure, the necessity for utmost exertion, to which most of us are subject, tends to make us too anxious about trifles, presumptuously eager and impatient. We should thank the teacher who aids us to resign ourselves, to be nothing, to wait, to trust. But it is to be feared that such lessons will have the greatest charm for those who need them least – for pensive, retiring contemplatists, who ought rather to be driven out to action and to usefulness.[131]

The final criterion for a history of spirituality is addressed to the reader: what particular individuals, groups, ideas or themes attract *you*, or repel you, and why?

CONCLUSION

We need finally to return to the spirituality of the Bible. There is throughout scripture a tension between structure and spontaneity, between priest and prophet, between the institutional and the charismatic, which all authentic Christian spirituality must reproduce. Two quotations from modern theologians bring this out. The Orthodox writer Olivier Clément, writing about the theology of the patristic period, sets this tension in the perspective of the doctrine of God as Trinity:

> The Spirit comes from the Father in the Son and manifests him. The Son is born of the Father in the Spirit and is manifested by the Spirit. And both reveal the Father. In the Church the same reciprocity and the same mutual service must exist between the priesthood, which bears witness to the sacramental presence of Christ, and prophecy, which reveals the freedom of each conscience in the Holy Spirit.[132]

It is of the very essence of the Church that that tension find expression: without it, there will be no spiritual life worthy of the name. And the German Protestant theologian Johannes Baptist Metz, reflecting on the psalms of lament, writes:

> Speaking about God always stems from speaking to God; theology comes from the language of prayer. That sounds pious and subjects me, in the eyes of those who choose not to understand me in other contexts as well, to the suspicion that I, the political theologian, have made another turn-about, this time to piety and pious submission. But let us make no mistake: the language of prayer is not only more universal, but also more exciting and dramatic, much more rebellious and radical than the language of current theology. It is much more disturbing, much more unconsoled, much less harmonious than that . . . Have we, perhaps, oriented ourselves far too well to the tamed prayer language of church and liturgy, and nourished ourselves on too many one-sided examples from the biblical tradition?[133]

The point is crucial. Spiritual life, the life of the people of God, is supremely conceived of in scripture as a journey. Much of that journey is spent in exile; from the expulsion of Adam and Eve from Eden onwards, individuals and communities constantly find themselves where they would prefer not to be. The life of faith means precisely to do what Abraham did: to 'set out, not knowing where he was going'.[134]

Scripture never pretends that life is fair; and many faithful people will have experienced the puzzled jealousy of St Peter when they appear to have received, as he did, a vocation which did not attract them, and wonder why others have not received it too: 'Lord, what about him?'[135] Furthermore, in the life of exile, there is no going back home: the gates of Eden are barred. So home is always on ahead, always in the future, our experience of it now a transitory one. Hence the tremendous power of the words of God through the prophet Jeremiah to the Jews, exiled at Babylon and doubtless encouraging one another with nostalgic memories of an idealized past:

The days are surely coming, says the LORD, when I will make a new covenant with the house of Israel and the house of Judah. It will not be like the covenant that I made with their ancestors when I took them by the hand to bring them out of the land of Egypt – a covenant that they broke, though I was their husband, says the LORD. But this is the covenant that I will make with the house of Israel after those days, says the LORD: I will put my law within them, and I will write it on their hearts; and I will be their God, and they shall be my people. No longer shall they teach one another, or say to each other, 'Know the LORD,' for they shall all know me, from the least of them to the greatest, says the LORD; for I will forgive their iniquity, and remember their sin no more.[136]

In the Bible, and for those courageous enough to embark upon it, the spiritual journey is always oriented to the future, however unpalatable that appears. For the Christian, unlike the Greek, the soul was eternal, not immortal; there was no 'return' after death to a familiar homeland. The Celestial City that ends the Bible is not at all like the Garden of Eden that begins it. And that gives the journey of those who seek it the character, not of a predetermined routine, but of an adventure. It was and is that quality above all others that imparted to the Christian spiritual tradition a dynamism which even the most terrible suffering or appalling ecclesiastical bigotry could never quite extinguish. Its presence at every turn of the long history of English spirituality is the surest mark of its authenticity, and the best possible reason for studying it.

NOTES

1. '*Christianos ad leones*', in *Essays* (London: Alexander Strahan, 1866), p. 216.
2. For Greenwell, see Volume 2, Chapter 2.
3. *Essays*, p. 218.
4. Baldwin, *On England* (London: Philip Allan, 1926), pp. 4–5.
5. Stephen Tallents, *The projection of England* (London: Faber & Faber, 1932, repr. by The Film Centre, 1955), p. 14. In 1998 Jeremy Paxman agreed with Tallents: 'while the French Revolution invented the Citizen, the English creation is the game' (*The English* (London: Michael Joseph, 1998), p. 194).
6. Knox, *Enthusiasm* (Oxford: Clarendon, 1950), p. 145. For Chesterton, see Volume 2, Chapter 3.
7. Thornton (1963) p. 24.
8. See the remarks of Jeremy Paxman, in *The English* (1998) pp. 29–35.
9. For a succinct overview, see Owen Chadwick, 'Indifference and morality', in P. Brooks (ed.), *Christian spirituality: essays in honour of Gordon Rupp* (London: SCM Press, 1975), p. 205.
10. Langland, *Piers Plowman*, Passus V, lines 147–50.
11. EETS o.s. 74, p. 276.
12. More, *A treatise upon the Passion*, ed. G. E. Haupt, *The complete works of St Thomas More*, vol. 13 (New Haven and London: Yale UP, 1976), p. 73.
13. Sermon 2 on the Lord's Prayer, in *Sermons*, ed. G. E. Corrie (Parker Society) (Cambridge UP, 1844). The word is used frequently by Latimer to denote the clergy or religious establishment.
14. Baxter, Dedication to *The saints everlasting rest*, in *The practical works of the Rev Richard Baxter*, ed. W. Orme (London: James Duncan, 1830), vol. 23, p. 13.
15. As in 'the spirituality of the Law'; Bunyan, *The doctrine of the law and grace unfolded*, in *The*

miscellaneous works of John Bunyan vol. 2, ed. R. L. Greaves (Oxford: Clarendon, 1976), p. 138.

16. Taylor, *A course of sermons* 2.2, in *The whole works of the Right Rev Jeremy Taylor DD*, ed. by R. Heber and rev. by C. P. Eden (London: Brown, Green & Longmans, 1856), vol. 4, p. 345.

17. Taylor, *The worthy communicant*, in *The whole works* (ed. cit. in previous note), vol. 8, p. 417.

18. Coleridge, *On the constitution of church and state*, in *Collected works,* ed. J. Colmer (London: Routledge and Princeton UP, 1976), vol. 10, p. 124.

19. Watts, *A guide to prayer* 3, in *The works of . . . Isaac Watts*, ed. G. Burder (London: Barfield, 1810), vol. 3, p. 162; cf. *Essays on the law and gospel, faith and works* 3, in *Works* vol. 3, p. 637.

20. Newton, *Twenty-six letters to a nobleman* 7, in *Cardiphonia* (in *The works of John Newton* (Edinburgh: Brown and Nelson, 1834)), p. 137.

21. Cowper, Letter of 24 September 1780 to John Newton, in *The letters and prose writings of William Cowper*, ed. J. King and C. Ryskamp (Oxford: Clarendon, 1979–82), vol. 1, p. 393). Elsewhere he speaks of 'that spirituality which once enliven'd all our intercourse' (Letter of 2 October 1787 to John Newton, *Letters and prose writings* vol. 3, p. 37).

22. *Spiritus* itself derives from *spirare*, to breathe or blow.

23. The examples are drawn from Smith and Lockwood's *Chambers Murray Latin–English Dictionary* (Edinburgh and London: Chambers and John Murray, 1933, repr. 1976), and C. T. Lewis and C. Short, *A Latin Dictionary* (Oxford: Clarendon, 1879).

24. Genesis 1.1–5a.

25. Psalm 104.7–9.

26. Genesis 6–9.

27. Psalm 69.1–2. References to the water of chaos, and to God's spoken word as source of creation and healing, abound in the Psalms.

28. Psalm 42.4–7.

29. Psalm 32.6.

30. Psalm 93.3–5.

31. See Daniel 7.3; Revelation 13.1.

32. Revelation 20.13; 21.1.

33. Psalm 71.6; cf. Psalm 22.9–10.

34. Davies (1971) p. 40.

35. Psalm 78.65.

36. Isaiah 40.22–3.

37. Isaiah 44.3–4, 9. Cf. the tremendous theophany of Psalm 18.16–17: 'He reached down from on high . . . he drew me out of mighty waters. He delivered me from my strong enemy'.

38. Cf. Psalm 1.3; Jeremiah 17.8.

39. Isaiah 45.18–19.

40. 'However quietly such a word may come, this is God, for this is what "God" means, the one who provides a perceptible alternative to chaos' (Davies (1971) p. 39).

41. John Donne, Sermon 8.9 (ed. cit. in Bibliography to Chapter 5), p. 228.

42. Cf. Isaiah 55.10–11.

43. See Romans 6.1–11, and countless early Christian liturgical references to 'the waters of death'.

44. Within the English spiritual tradition, see Michael Ramsey, *Holy Spirit* (London: SPCK, 1977).

45. John 4.24.

46. Temple, *Readings in St John's Gospel* (London: Macmillan, 1955), p. 64.

47. In what follows, and in addition to a number of representatives from the English spiritual tradition whose works are cited, the principal theological studies drawn on are Feuillet (1966), Harvey (1996), Murphy-O'Connor (1991), and Segal (1990).

48. Segal (1990), esp. pp. 132, 140 and 147; Kirk (1934) pp. 40–4; John Ziesler, *Paul's Letter to the Romans* (London: SCM Press, 1989), p. 61; John Robinson, *Wrestling with Romans* (London: SCM Press, 1979), pp. 96–9. Segal suggests (p. 38) that Paul is 'undisturbed by Platonic ideas of the soul's immortality'. See also (on the relation of 'spirit' to 'breath' in the

NT) John Macquarrie, *Paths of spirituality* (London: SCM Press, 1972), chapter 4. He notes that (a) both the OT and Hegel, in his sophisticated philosophy of spirit, insist on holding the physical and the spiritual together; and (b) that in both 'spirit', like 'breath', is dynamic, life-giving, powerful; (c) that the 'spiritual' will always be elusive, mysterious, not easily to be comprehended. C. K. Barrett (*The Epistle to the Romans* (London: A. & C. Black, 1957), p. 158) suggests that 'life in the spirit' means for Paul that our lives are directed from a source outside ourselves. Cf. also Michael Ramsey, *Holy Spirit* (London: SPCK, 1977), pp. 52–3, on 1 Corinthians 15 in this context.

49. The seventeenth-century English mystical writer Peter Sterry suggests that by 'flesh' Paul means 'the State of Nature in its highest Principles, and utmost Extent' (*The rise, race and royalty of the kingdom of God in the soul of man* (London: Cockerill, 1683), p. 56.

50. 2 Corinthians 5.17–18.

51. 2 Corinthians 3.17–18; 4.5–6.

52. See, e.g., Feuillet (1966), esp. pp. 141ff; Segal (1990) p. 152; Michael Ramsey, *The glory of God and the transfiguration of Christ* (1967); N. T. Wright, 'Reflected glory: 2 Corinthians 3', in *The climax of the covenant: Christ and the Law in Pauline theology* (Edinburgh: T. & T. Clark, 1991), pp. 175–92.

53. Though this too is much disputed. See A. E. Harvey: 'It was God who created light at the beginning of the world. His creation continues in that supernatural light which now makes it possible to discern the likeness of God in Christ – "the light which is knowledge of the glory of God in the face of Jesus Christ" (2 Cor. 4:6)' (Harvey (1996) p. 54; see also Murphy-O'Connor (1991) p. 43, though Murphy-O'Connor argues that Paul does not have Genesis 1.3 in mind here).

54. Jean-Jacques Suurmond (*Word and Spirit at play: towards a charismatic theology* (London: SCM Press, 1994, p. 169) puts it thus: 'The charismatic tension between the "now already" of our eschatological identity in the Word and the Spirit (the true self) and the "not yet" of our present "flesh" ruled by anxiety (the false self) is generally seen as characteristic of Paul's thought. The division between the true and the false self goes right through the human "I".'

55. See the remarks of McIntosh. He notes that poetic (and sometimes 'mystical') language 'pushes the reader towards a far more participatory and existential kind of "knowing"' than much prose does (1998, p. 132). He cites Augustine in stressing that in *understanding* we not only come to knowledge: we also affirm what we know, and by affirming we respond to what we know. Hence the will becomes involved: willing and knowing are intimately linked (1998, p. 160).

56. 1 Corinthians 13.12b.

57. 2 Corinthians 4.16b–18.

58. Romans 8.22–24a, 26–7.

59. For their relevance to Christian spirituality, see esp. Cullmann (1995). In particular, he stresses the importance of Paul's link between Spirit and creation in the exploration of prayer in Romans 8 (p. 80).

60. Romans 8.19. Cullmann (1995, p. 79) notes that the Greek word used by Paul here – *apokar-odokia*, lit. 'with raised head' – 'expresses a quite particularly intense longing'.

61. Matthew 18.3.

62. Romans 8.15.

63. 'Since, then, we have such a hope, we act with great boldness' (2 Corinthians 3.12).

64. Greek *parrhesia*. The word derives from *pas* (all) and *rheo* (to speak, pour forth). In ancient Greece it could have a negative dimension too. The Cynics (classical Greek philosophical movement) stressed self-sufficiency and freedom, especially *parrhesia*: their biting wit (which gave them their name) was designed precisely to shock people into seeing the futility of social constraint. The word could signify inappropriate rudeness; Plutarch saw it as an art, the art of saying the right thing at the right time (see Frances Young and David F. Ford, *Meaning and truth in 2 Corinthians* (Biblical foundations in theology) (London: SPCK, 1987), p. 95).

65. The nearest equivalent is perhaps *chutzpah*. See especially 2 Samuel 7.18–29, where David in

prayer appears to take charge over Yahweh: he becomes the 'lead partner' in the dance of prayer. For the spirituality of the covenant relationship, see especially Psalm 105. In the Hebrew Bible 'prayer is active, covenantal action in which Israel takes a bold initiative between the partners' (Brueggemann (1995) p. 148). The term *parrhesia* appears in the Greek Septuagint (LXX) version of the Hebrew Bible: see, e.g., Proverbs 1.20 'speaks *openly*'; Wisdom 5.1; Job 22.26; Psalm 11.6. Also Leviticus 26.13 – 'made you walk erect' – the LXX has 'led you out *openly*', *meta parrhesias*. Other refs. in the LXX are: Proverbs 10.10 ('the one who rebukes *boldly*', *meta parrhesias*); Job 27.10; Ecclesiasticus 25.25 ('boldness of speech'); 1 Maccabees 4.18. In the LXX generally, God acts and speaks with *parrhesia*, wisdom speaks with *parrhesia*, and the righteous possess *parrhesia* – they can address God in prayer with joyous *parrhesia* (Job 22.25–6 'if the Almighty is your gold and your precious silver, then you will delight yourself in the Almighty, and lift up your face to God').

66. Notably the Book of Habakkuk. See Gordon Mursell, *Out of the deep: prayer as protest* (London: DLT, 1989).

67. For the use of *parrhesia* with regard to Christians' relationships with God, see esp. Ephesians 3.11–12; Hebrews 3.6; 4.16; 10:19; 1 John 2.28; 3.21; 5.14. For its use with regard to their relationships with others, see esp. Acts 2.29; 4:13, 29, 31 and 1 Timothy 3.13; also (as a verb) Acts 14.3 and 19.8; 1 Timothy 3.13.

68. See Hans Urs von Balthasar, *Prayer* (London: SPCK, 1961), esp. pp. 37ff; S. B. Marrow, '*Parrhesia* and the New Testament', in *Catholic Biblical Quarterly* 44 (1982), pp. 431–46; W. C. van Unnik, 'The Christian's freedom of speech in the New Testament', in *Bulletin of the John Rylands Library* 44 (1962), pp. 466–88; '"With unveiled face", an exegesis of 2 Corinthians 3:12–18', in *Novum Testamentum* 6 (1963), pp. 153–69. For the use of *parrhesia* in the medieval tradition, see Alexander Murray, *Reason and society in the Middle Ages* (Oxford: Clarendon, 1978), pp. 393–9.

69. In Leviticus, what is not *holy* is *common*. What is *common* is subdivided into what is *clean* and what is *unclean*. *Cleanness* is a state between *holiness* and *uncleanness*, and represents the normal condition of most things and people. Sanctification elevates the *clean* into the *holy*, and pollution degrades the *clean* into the *unclean*. And both *holiness* and *uncleanness* can be transmitted by contact. See Leviticus 6.20, 27 and 11.39–40; and Gordon J. Wenham, *The Book of Leviticus* (New international commentary on the Old Testament); Grand Rapids: Eerdmans (1979), esp. pp. 18–20; Mary Douglas, *Purity and danger* (London: Routledge & Kegan Paul, 1966); Mary Douglas, *Leviticus as literature* (Oxford UP, 1999), esp. p. 146; Erhard S. Gerstenberger, *Leviticus: a commentary* (Old Testament library), ET by Douglas W. Scott (Louisville: Westminster John Knox, 1996, esp. pp. 125–6, 281–6; and John F. A. Sawyer (ed.), *Reading Leviticus: a conversation with Mary Douglas* (JSOT Supplement 227) (Sheffield Academic Press, 1996), esp. the articles by Milgrom, Douglas and Maccoby.

70. Leviticus 19.1–2.

71. Psalm 119.105, 18, 46, 54.

72. 1 Peter 1.15–16.

73. Matthew 7.6.

74. Romans 11.16.

75. 1 Corinthians 7.14a.

76. 1 Corinthians 3.16–17.

77. John 15.15; 13.34b.

78. John 14.23b.

79. John 17.15.

80. John 17.17.

81. John 1.14.

82. John 17.19.

83. John 15.13–14.

84. The Hebrew tradition, lacking any developed notion of a body/soul duality, was never able to conceive of holiness in this way.

85. Plato, *Symposium* 211A–212A (speech of Diotima); ET by Hamilton (Harmondsworth: Penguin, 1951), pp. 94–5.
86. See esp. McGinn (1992) for a succinct introduction to Platonic and Neoplatonic mysticism. For the influence of Platonism on English literature and culture, see the series of essays in Baldwin and Hutton (1994).
87. For Plato the whole point of philosophy is to secure our passage to the spiritual world: it is 'practising death' (*Phaedo* 81a; Louth (1981) pp. 7–9).
88. Gilbert of Hoyland, *Sermons on the Song of Songs* 2.1 (ET by Braceland (CF 14) p. 56, slightly altered; Latin text in PL 184:17–18.) Cf. 5.6 'The narrower the streets, the richer and more free is the interior leisure of the mind' (*Quanto magis coangustati sunt vici, tanto uberiora et liberiora sunt intus otia mentis*), CF 14, p. 90, PL 184:35.
89. Even in the earliest Christian centuries, much Christian asceticism 'was grounded in positive, conscious aspirations, not in an alienation from the material world' (Robin Lane Fox, *Pagans and Christians* (London: Viking, 1986), p. 331). Yet, as Lane Fox himself goes on to point out, 'from its very beginnings, Christianity has considered an orderly sex life to be a clear second best to no sex life at all' (p. 355).
90. Clément (1993) p. 131.
91. Gershom G. Sholem, *Major trends in Jewish mysticism* (London: Thames & Hudson, 1955), p. 106.
92. 'The whole of life, the whole universe was interpreted in the light of Christ's death and resurrection, which was the key to understanding all significant processes of change' (Clément (1993) p. 10).
93. See McGinn (1992) pp. 36 (on Philo), 64 and 86: 'scripture, christologically interpreted, was the ground of all Christian thought, including mysticism, especially in the first centuries'.
94. See esp. McGinn (1992) p. 191; Clément (1993); and Louth (1981).
95. *Apophasis* means the 'leap' towards the mystery (Clément, p. 38). Thus it is not simply about negative theology, but about the opening up of an encounter, a revelation which is however strictly unthinkable. It is 'a soaring of the personality towards that personal God who was led by love to assume the condition of a slave and to die on a cross' (Clément, p. 231). See also Vladimir Lossky, *In the image and likeness of God* (London: Mowbray, 1975), chapter 1; and Denys Turner, *The darkness of God: negativity in Christian mysticism* (Cambridge UP, 1995).
96. See Harvey J. Egan SJ, 'Affirmative way', in M. Downey (ed.), *The new dictionary of Catholic spirituality* (Collegeville: Liturgical Press, 1993), pp. 14–17.
97. See Clément (1993) p. 91.
98. McGinn (1992) pp. 183–4.
99. The literature on Augustine is immense. For the purposes of this book, the most useful introductions are: Burnaby (1938) (still unrivalled as an exposition of the central theme of Augustine's thought, the theology of love); Brown (1967 and 1989); Chadwick (1986); Rist (1994). See also the articles in Fitzgerald (1999). For Augustine's understanding of humanity's creation in the image and likeness of God, see R. A. Markus, '*Imago* and *similitudo* in Augustine', in *Revue des Études Augustiniennes* 10 (1964), pp. 125–43 and 13 (1967), and the article 'Image doctrine' by Mary T. Clark in Fitzgerald (1999) pp. 440–1. For his doctrine of desire, see Isabelle Bochet, *Saint Augustin et le désir de Dieu* (Études Augustiniennes) (Paris, 1982); and Gerald Bonner, *The desire for God and the need for grace in Augustine's theology* (Atti del Congresso Internazionale su S. Agostino nel XVI centenario della conversione) (Rome: Institutum Patristicum 'Augustinianum', 1987) (Studia Ephemeridis 'Augustinianum', 24).
100. See the article by Marianne Djuth, 'Will (*voluntas*)', in Fitzgerald (1999) pp. 881–5.
101. For this subject see esp. Augustine's *Confessiones* Book VIII; and Brown (1989) chapter 19, esp. pp. 418ff.
102. For Augustine, 'the state of sin is *involuntary* in the sense that the subject of it cannot escape from it by his own will; and secondly, it is a state which *cannot* be said to arise only as the consequence of the subject's own voluntary activity' (Burnaby (1938) p. 187). In a compelling study, Rist both sets out the heart of Augustine's thought and demonstrates its classical

antecedents: thus he says that

> it is helpful . . . to think of Augustine's account of human weakness in terms of the standard classical descriptions of weakness of will or *acrasia*, above all that of Aristotle in the *Nicomachean Ethics*. Aristotle thinks that some of us are *acratic* some of the time, and a few of us may be *acratic* all the time (at least about something), while Augustine's position is rather that all of us are *acratic* all the time, and that while we may think we have overcome a particular moral weakness, there is always the real possibility that it will return. To this, however, we should add that his identification of the main feature of the morally good act as loving rather than as some sort of knowing makes such an analysis much more convincing. (1994, p. 184)

103. See esp. *Confessiones* Books 6 and 7, and *De Trinitate* Book 11.

104. Augustine, *On the Trinity* (*De Trinitate*) 14.10–11. For Augustine, 'La notion du péché oblige à distinguer entre image et participation de Dieu. *L'image de Dieu est une capacité de Dieu, une possibilité de participer à la divinité*; même difforme, c'est un potentiel' (R. Javelet, *Image et ressemblance au XIIme siècle* (Paris: Letouzey & Ané, 1967), vol. 1, p. 62).

105. Augustine, *On the Letters of St John* (*In Epist. Ioann. tract.*) 7.8.

106. *On the Letters of St John* 4.6.

107. This is not the same as the Greek notion of deification. In a key passage (1938, pp. 177–9), Burnaby differentiates the Greek approach to participation in God from that of Augustine. 'For the Greek mind, immortality meant divinisation: the word *theos* denoted, not the one Creator and Ruler whom Israel worshipped, but a *kind* of being whose most important difference from humanity was freedom from death. The datum of Greek theology was thus the assumed fact that through Christ the individual man becomes *theos* – divine.' Augustine resisted the language of deification in order to safeguard the uniqueness of God. 'The superiority of his understanding of Christianity lies in the sureness of his conviction, first, that "cleaving to God" must be the personal union of love, and second, that this union is neither cause nor effect of a transformation of man's nature, but is itself that transformation.'

108. *A grammar of assent* 9.3, 6th edn (London: Longmans, Green, 1887), pp. 363–4.

109. For this subject, see esp. Cupitt (1998); Jantzen (1995); McIntosh (1998); Sheldrake (1991); and Steggink (1991).

110. Jantzen (1995, p. 27) points out that its first known use was in seventeenth-century France.

111. Jantzen; also L. Bouyer, *The Christian mystery: from pagan myth to Christian mysticism*, ET by Illtyd Trethowan (Edinburgh: T. & T. Clark, 1990).

112. See McIntosh (1998) p. 43; McGinn (1992) p. 86.

113. Martin Thornton (*English spirituality* (1963) p. 19) understandably complains that the 'wretched' word has caused endless confusion, and should be eliminated altogether!

114. Cupitt (1998) pp. 52–3.

115. Cupitt (1998) p. 92.

116. Cupitt (1998) p. 106.

117. Cupitt (1998) p. 133.

118. Cupitt (1998) p. 59. In fact Cupitt goes so far as to argue that 'St John of the Cross did not first have a language-transcending experience and then subsequently try to put it into words. On the contrary, the very composition of the poem was *itself* the mystical experience' (p. 74). Mark McIntosh makes a similar point: 'it remains a fallacy that we can ever "know" his or her interior experiences. What we have is simply that which the mystics themselves laboured over and bequeathed to us: their texts' (1998, p. 121). It is worth recalling a further point made by McIntosh in his excellent book: that interpretation need not be seen as some thin academic affair. Levinas says that the practice of interpretation is akin to responding to a call from the 'other' (see McIntosh (1998) p. 135). In such a context 'the movement of interpretation . . . is not backwards towards a putative experience behind the text, but forwards into reflection on the structure of that new world of divine–human encounter that is being opened up between the text and the reader' (McIntosh, p. 142).

119. Helen C. White, *The mysticism of William Blake* (1927; repr. New York: Russell & Russell, 1964), p. 47.

120. R. A. Vaughan, *Hours with the mystics: a contribution to the history of religious opinion*, 5th edn (London: Gibbings, 1891), vol. 1, p. 54.
121. Tyrrell, *Lex credendi* (London: Longmans, Green, 1907), p. 32.
122. See esp. Miles (1988).
123. Jantzen (1995) p. 2.
124. 'Mysticism helps us learn the great surrender'; so Dorothee Sölle, quoted in King (1993) pp. 109–10.
125. King (1993) p. 222.
126. De Beauvoir (1988) p. 659. She argues that male mysticism is of a highly refined intellectual cast; whereas women who abandon themselves to the joys of the heavenly nuptials are legion, and their experience is of a peculiarly emotional nature. Ultimately she rejects female mysticism:

    > Mystical fervour, like love and even narcissism, can be integrated with a life of activity and independence. But in themselves these attempts at individual salvation are bound to meet with failure: either woman puts herself into relation with an unreality: her double, or God; or she creates an unreal relation with a real being. In both cases she lacks any grasp on the world; she does not escape her subjectivity; her liberty remains frustrated. There is only one way to employ her liberty authentically; and that is to project it through positive action into human society. (p. 687)

127. See Jantzen (1995) p. 147. Modern psychologists, notably Erik Erikson, have noted the male preference for verticality (hierarchies, images of ascent, etc.), compared to the female preference for horizontality (relationships, interiors, etc.). How much of this is cultural and how much genetic remains a matter of much debate.
128. Jantzen (1995) pp. 14–15.
129. Philip Sheldrake notes that 'to enter fruitfully into the unfamiliar one needs a real sense of where one belongs' (1991, p. 210).
130. Chenu, *Nature, man and society in the twelfth century: essays on new theological perspectives in the Latin West*, ed. and ET by J. Taylor and L. K. Little (Chicago and London: Chicago UP, 1968), pp. 202–3.
131. Vaughan, *Hours with the mystics: a contribution to the history of religious opinion*, 5th edn (London: Gibbings, 1891), vol. 2, p. 356.
132. Clément (1993) p. 70.
133. Johannes Baptist Metz, quoted in Erich Zenger, *A God of vengeance? Understanding the Psalms of wrath*, ET by Linda M. Maloney (Louisville: Westminster John Knox, 1996), p. 95.
134. Hebrews 11.8b.
135. John 21.20b.
136. Jeremiah 31.31–4.

BIBLIOGRAPHY

The Nature of the English and English Spirituality

Allchin, A. M., 'Anglican spirituality', in S. Sykes and J. Booty (eds.), *The study of Anglicanism* (London: SPCK; Philadelphia: Fortress, 1988), pp. 313–24
Baldwin, Anna, and Hutton, Sarah (eds.), *Platonism and the English imagination* (Cambridge UP, 1994)
Elton, Geoffrey, *The English* (Oxford: Blackwell, 1992)
Paxman, Jeremy, *The English* (London: Michael Joseph, 1998; repr. Penguin, 1999)
Thornton, Martin, *English spirituality* (London: SPCK, 1963)

The Spirituality of the Bible

Balentine, Samuel E., 'Prayer in the wilderness traditions: in pursuit of divine justice', in *Hebrew Annual Review* 9 (1985), pp. 53–74

Brueggemann, Walter, *The Psalms and the life of faith* (Minneapolis: Fortress, 1995)

Cullmann, O., *Prayer in the New Testament* (London: SCM Press, 1995)

Davies, John, *Beginning now: contemporary experiences of Creation and Fall* (London: Collins, 1971)

Feuillet, A., *Le Christ sagesse de Dieu d'après les Épitres Pauliniennes* (Études bibliques) (Paris: Librairie Lecoffre, 1966)

Harvey, A. E., *Renewal through suffering: a study of 2 Corinthians* (Studies of the New Testament and its world) (Edinburgh: T. & T. Clark, 1996)

Murphy-O'Connor, J., *The theology of the Second Letter to the Corinthians* (New Testament theology) (Cambridge UP, 1991)

Segal, Alan F., *Paul the convert: the apostolate and apostasy of Saul the Pharisee* (Yale UP, 1990)

The Spirituality of the Early Church

Brown, Peter, *Augustine of Hippo* (London: Faber & Faber, 1967)

Brown, Peter, *The body and society: men, women and sexual renunciation in early Christianity* (London: Faber & Faber, 1989)

Burnaby, J., *Amor Dei: a study of the religion of St Augustine* (London: Hodder & Stoughton, 1938)

Chadwick, Henry, *Augustine* (Past Masters) (Oxford UP, 1986)

Clément, Olivier, *The roots of Christian mysticism* (ET by Theodore Berkeley of *Sources* (Paris, 1982)) (London: New City, 1993)

Fitzgerald, Allan D., OSA (ed.), *Augustine through the ages: an encyclopaedia* (Grand Rapids: Eerdmans, 1999)

Fox, Robin Lane, *Pagans and Christians* (London: Viking, 1986)

Kirk, Kenneth E., *The vision of God*, abridged edn (Cambridge: James Clarke, 1934; repr. 1977)

Louth, Andrew, *The origins of the Christian mystical tradition* (Oxford UP, 1981)

McGinn, Bernard, *The foundations of mysticism* (London: SCM Press, 1991)

McGinn, Bernard, *The growth of mysticism* (London: SCM Press, 1994)

Rist, John M., *Augustine: ancient thought baptized* (Cambridge UP, 1994)

Williams, Rowan, *The wound of knowledge* (London: DLT, 1979)

Spirituality and Methodology

Beauvoir, Simone de, *The second sex* (ET by H. M. Parshley of *Le deuxième sexe* (Paris: Gallimard, 1949)) (London: Picador, 1988)

Cupitt, Don, *Mysticism after modernity* (Oxford: Blackwell, 1998)

Jantzen, Grace, *Power, gender and Christian mysticism* (Cambridge studies in ideology and religion 8) (Cambridge UP, 1995)

King, Ursula, *Women and spirituality: voices of protest and promise,* 2nd edn (Basingstoke: Macmillan, 1993)

McIntosh, M., *Mystical theology: the integrity of spirituality and theology* (Oxford: Blackwell, 1998)

Miles, Margaret, *The image and practice of holiness* (London: SCM Press, 1988)

Sheldrake, Philip, *Spirituality and history* (London: SPCK, 1991)

Steggink, Otger, 'Study in spirituality in retrospect: shifts in methodological approach', in *Studies in Spirituality* 1 (1991), pp. 5–23

2

The Seafarer

Anglo-Saxon Spirituality

I sing my own true story, tell my travels,
How I have often suffered times of hardship
In days of toil, and have experienced
Bitter anxiety, my troubled home
On many a ship has been the heaving waves,
Where grim night-watch has often been my lot
At the ship's prow as it beat past the cliffs.
Oppressed by cold my feet were bound by frost
In icy bonds, while worries simmered hot
About my heart, and hunger from within
Tore the sea-worthy spirit. He knows not,
Who lives most easily on land, how I
Have spent my winter on the ice-cold sea,
Wretched and anxious, in the paths of exile,
Lacking dear friends, hung round by icicles,
While hail flew past in showers. There heard I nothing
But the resounding sea, the ice-cold waves.
Sometimes I made the song of the wild swan
My pleasure, or the gannet's call, the cries
Of curlews for the missing mirth of men,
The singing gull instead of mead in hall.
Storms beat the rocky cliffs, and icy-winged
The tern replied, the horn-beaked eagle shrieked.
No patron had I there who might have soothed
My desolate spirit. He can little know
Who, proud and flushed with wine, has spent his time
With all the joys of life among the cities,
Safe from such fearful venturings, how I
Have often suffered weary on the seas.
Night shadows darkened, snow came from the north,
Frost bound the earth and hail fell on the ground,
Coldest of corns. And yet the heart's desires
Incite me now that I myself should go

29

> On towering seas, among the salt waves' play;
> And constantly the heartfelt wishes urge
> The spirit to venture, that I should go forth
> To see the lands of strangers far away.[1]

THE CONTEXT

From Pagan to Christian

So begins 'The seafarer', one of the most famous of all Anglo-Saxon poems. The seafarer evidently misses the warmth and companionship of home; and yet an inner restlessness and longing drives him to embark on his lonely journey. The nostalgia for what he has left behind does not diminish as the poem proceeds, for, as the poet puts it, 'he who goes to sea must ever yearn'. But his longing for what lies beyond the horizon is stronger; and later that longing is given explicitly Christian clothing:

> The cuckoo cries, incites the eager breast
> On to the whale's roads irresistibly,
> Over the wide expanses of the sea,
> Because the joys of God mean more to me
> Than this dead transitory life on land.[2]

The joys of the life to come, however, are not easily to be won; and those in search of them must engage in combat against both external and internal evil:

> For every warrior the best
> Memorial is the praise of living men
> After his death, that ere he must depart
> He shall have done good deeds on earth against
> The malice of his foes, and noble works
> Against the devil . . .
>
> Though a brother
> May strew with gold his brother's grave, and bury
> His corpse among the dead with heaps of treasure,
> Wishing them to go with him, yet can gold
> Bring no help to the soul that's full of sins,
> Against God's wrath.[3]

The stress here on both courageous combat in the manner of a pagan hero and the need for interior sanctification in the manner of the Christian is striking, and suggests that the former has been appropriated in the service of the latter. A more distinctively pagan note may be sounded in what stands between the two excerpts just cited – a nostalgia for the lost glories of the past:

> The great old days have gone, and all the grandeur
> Of earth; there are not Caesars now or kings
> Or patrons such as once there used to be,
> Amongst whom were performed most glorious deeds,
> Who lived in lordliest renown. Gone now
> is all that host, the splendours have departed.
> Weaker men live and occupy the world.

Despite this, however – indeed, precisely because of it – human beings must prepare for the coming judgement:

> Foolish is he who does not fear his Lord,
> For death will come upon him unprepared.[4]

Yet in the end the Christian vision of the life to come has the last, triumphant, word:

> Let us think where we have our real home,
> And then consider how we may come thither;
> And let us labour also, so that we
> May pass into eternal blessedness,
> Where life belongs amid the love of God,
> Hope in the heavens. The Holy One be thanked
> That He has raised us up, the Prince of Glory,
> Lord without end, to all eternity.
>
> > Amen.[5]

Both the origins and the meaning of the poem are much controverted: it is at least possible that it derives from a lost pagan original, orally transmitted and rewritten as a Christian poem of pilgrimage. But it is equally possible, and more probable, that it was written by a Christian, perhaps by a monk or priest, whose concern was precisely to give the great themes and concerns of contemporary pagan culture an unmistakably Christian orientation.[6]

For our purposes what matters is that it sets before us some of the most important themes in Anglo-Saxon spirituality: the dialectic between home and wandering exile, between domestic intimacy and the harsh struggle to survive; a restless inner longing, or desire, both for the experience and uncertain outcome of seafaring, and for the eternal home which forms its ultimate destination; the nostalgia for a lost heroic past; and the need to engage in spiritual combat both internally and externally in view of the imminence of death and judgement. All these themes find their expression in 'The seafarer' in the context of the poet's journey, a journey at once personal and universal, vividly expressing both one person's experience and the essential nature of the human condition. Each of these themes forms vital threads in the fabric of Anglo-Saxon spirituality, and helps to create its distinctive texture and hue.

Whatever its provenance, 'The seafarer' may offer us some useful clues about the Anglo-Saxon world-view. It has been pointed out that one of the striking difference between classical Latin poets and the writers of Anglo-Saxon England consisted in their respective attitudes to nature.[7] Where Virgil or Homer could celebrate its beauty and beneficence, the poet of 'The seafarer' is aware only of its icy hostility.[8] It would be strange if climate, and the relative inhospitality of the landscape, played no part in the formation of Anglo-Saxon spirituality; and it may be no coincidence that most Anglo-Saxon writers stress the menace and foreboding, rather than the beauty, of the natural world.[9] The world is above all strange, mysterious and wild, full of symbols and portents of good and evil which the wise person will do well to discern, as the seafarer does when he responds to the cuckoo's cry calling him to set out.[10] Other Anglo-Saxon writers will contrast the perilous landscapes of this world with the peaceful landscape of paradise.[11] Small wonder, then, if the dialectic of exile and home, of *wraecca* and *cynn*, were so pronounced: journeying abroad, whether literally or allegorically, was a harsh and hazardous affair, not an easy stroll through scenic landscapes.

Of pre-Christian English spirituality there is little that can be said with any certainty. The Roman historian Tacitus speaks of the 'sacred rites and superstitions' of the Gauls as being discernible among the Britons as well.[12] At Fishbourne, near Chichester in Sussex, the remains of a first-century Roman palace probably belonging to a British client-king has been excavated.[13] The main hall may well have been used for rituals connected with worship of the emperor; evidence exists to show that the client-king erected a temple to Neptune and Minerva nearby.[14] But the most interesting feature of all is the remarkable mosaics, some of which were probably the work of imported Roman artists, but one at least of which (dating from the beginning of the second century AD) is more likely to have been created by local ones. Its subject is classical: the mythical Medusa, with her hair full of writhing snakes, forms the centrepiece. But the design as a whole – a profuse and intricate mixture of flowers or rosettes with a rich variety of fantastic motifs, crudely but colourfully executed – suggests a local artist; and the interweaving of nature, myth and imagination may yield a tiny but fascinating insight into the spiritual world of early Roman England.[15]

The origins and nature of the earliest Christian communities in Britain, during the period of the Roman Empire, are largely lost to us. Tertullian, writing in c.208, mentions 'the haunts of the Britons – inaccessible to the Romans, but subjugated to Christ';[16] and certainly by the third century Christianity was an active presence in England.[17] At Lullingstone in Kent there are the remains of a Roman villa whose owner, at some stage in the fourth century, was a Christian: a chapel seems to have been built over the old cellar, and decorated with a painted wall-plaster showing Christians with arms outstretched in a position of prayer.[18] The sixth-century monk Gildas tells of the native Britons, confronted by Anglo-Saxon invaders, praying in despair as they took to their boats, 'singing a psalm that took the place of a shanty "You have given us like sheep for eating and scattered us among the heathen"'.[19]

Something at least of the legacy of these early Christians endured: when the Roman monk and missionary Augustine arrived in Kent in the late sixth century, he encountered the cult of a martyr.[20] The story of the encounter between the Roman mission of Augustine and the Irish Christians who came to Lindisfarne from Iona, an encounter that culminated in 716 with the submission of the northern Christians over the date of Easter, is well known, and derives from the great ecclesiastical history of Bede;[21] but in the telling of it, it is sometimes forgotten that Irish Christians were Romans too, orthodox in theology and with an episcopal and monastic institutional structure that acknowledged the authority of the bishop of Rome.[22]

It is impossible to calculate precisely the nature of the spirituality brought to England by the Irish missionary monks. A number of features of Irish Christian spiritual life are familiar to us, however: a firm, often fierce asceticism;[23] loyalty to Rome, though with abbots exercising more power than bishops;[24] a love of pilgrimage, which led Columba to Iona and Columbanus to Switzerland and Italy;[25] a profound awareness of, and reverence for, the communion of saints, which in turn led to a pervasive sense of awe in the face of the natural world, which they believed to be actively peopled with saints and demons;[26] and a particular devotion to the Psalms.[27] Those features have much in common with contemporary Roman Christianity, controverting the old belief that Irish and Roman missionaries were at loggerheads from the start.[28] And recent scholarship has underlined the importance, even at this early date, of England's relationship with the continent, and particularly with the Frankish church of northern Gaul.[29]

Faced with a renewed Christian evangelism from both north and south, the indigenous Anglo-Saxon population did not overnight abandon its pagan beliefs and customs: the names still given to the days of the week derive from the old Germanic pantheon, and testify to the enduring nature of some at least of these beliefs and customs; and we may reasonably assume that among communities of lay people throughout England pagan practices were insensibly blended with Christian ones.[30] An Anglo-Saxon prescription for a holy salve as a dressing for wounds stipulates that it must consist of butter from a cow that should be all of one colour, mixed with sixty herbs, and stirred with a four-pronged stick with the names of the four evangelists carved on each prong; a blend of Christian and gibberish chants was to be sung over the result to which spittle had been added, before the salve, blessed by a mass-priest, was applied.[31]

Christian spirituality, then, was not created *ex nihilo* from the lifeless ashes of a ruinous or barbaric pagan past. And the relevance of poems like 'The seafarer' or 'Beowulf' to an understanding of Anglo-Saxon spirituality is reflected in the extent to which that spirituality drew upon the themes and images they offered it. The Christians did not suppress pagan culture: they redirected it, thereby ensuring its survival, albeit in a massively altered form.[32] Thus the pagan fondness for gold, precious metals and intricate craftsmanship was swiftly appropriated by the Christians: vivid descriptions of the heavenly Jerusalem, together with a fascination with Old Testament accounts of Moses' tabernacle and Solomon's temple, reflect this love of colour, light and splendour.[33] A seventh-century helmet found at Benty Grange in Derbyshire is embossed with both a silver cross and a delicately-carved silver-and-iron boar, with gilded tusks and glinting, jewelled eyes: both cross and boar may be intended as mascots or talismens, the warrior hedging his bets by invoking both pagan and Christian sources of protection.[34]

The Monasteries

The extent to which 'The seafarer' and other Old English poems contain imagery and develop themes derived from pagan myths and culture is almost impossible to calculate, because almost all the literature that survives was either created or copied in monastic scriptoria. It would be no exaggeration to say that Anglo-Saxon Christianity, whether Irish or Roman in origin, was dominated by the monasteries.[35] Nearly all the written records that survive were created or copied by monks or nuns; and monastic perspectives and preferences colour every aspect of their extant writings on the spiritual life.

This is not to say that Anglo-Saxon spirituality originated in the monasteries: indeed the monks themselves excelled at preserving for posterity much that derived from Irish and patristic, as well as vernacular, culture. But all that they handed on they also interpreted, adjusting it where necessary so as to fit their own theology and grand design. That design was far more than narrow self-interest, for the monasteries were also centres of teaching and evangelism; and their aim was the conversion and salvation of the English people. They also had to show that their shrines and beliefs and holy people were just as powerful as pagan gods had been held to be, and just as capable of offering protection and guidance. Yet the very extent and vastness of their aim helped to ensure, for good or ill, that their influence pervaded every aspect of Anglo-Saxon life.

Many of the contemporary or near-contemporary accounts of early English saints illustrate this point by presenting their subjects as exemplars of monastic spirituality, and suitable models for imitation even by lay people as far as possible.[36] Thus Bede describes St Aidan (d.651), brought from the monastery at Iona in 645 by King Oswald of Northumbria to be Bishop of Lindisfarne, as 'a man of outstanding gentleness, devotion, and moderation'.[37] He commends his generosity to the poor, and tells us that all who accompanied him were to engage in some form of study, that is to say, to occupy themselves either with reading the scriptures or learning the psalms. This was the daily task of Aidan himself and of all who were with him, wherever they went.[38]

Bede also describes how Aidan's holy oil calmed a storm at sea: this emphasis on holiness as exerting power over the forces of nature is not empty rhetoric, for it serves to convey both the Christlike authority of the saint or holy person and the value to the world at large of their ascetic spirituality and lifestyle. In short, Bede presents him to us as in effect a model of the Christian life – an exemplary missionary bishop, whose ministry of itinerant pastoral work interspersed with regular solitary retreats (to the Farne islands) is founded on a monastic simplicity and humility. This presentation may owe a good deal to the portrait of St Martin of Tours drawn by Sulpicius Severus, which exerted a considerable influence on subsequent Christian hagiography; but through it we can still sense something of Aidan's own attractive and compassionate character.[39]

Not all early English monastic saints were men:[40] one of the many who went to Germany in the eighth century to assist St Boniface in the evangelization of pagans was St Leoba (c.700–780), a nun from a double monastery at Wimborne in Dorset.[41] She was a person of formidable intellectual power:[42] her ninth-century biographer describes her as

> deeply aware of the necessity for concentration of mind in prayer and study, and for this reason took care not to go to excess either in watching or in other spiritual exercises.[43]

Her combination of intellectual and spiritual wisdom is reflected in a powerful story from the same source, in which she identifies, through a period of prolonged prayer and rigorous spiritual exercise, the mother of a baby who had been found dead in a nearby pool.[44] Nor is this capacity for supernatural discernment the only respect in which Leoba is the equal of any Anglo-Saxon holy man: like Aidan, she is also described as possessing power over the elements. When a violent thunderstorm threatens the neighbourhood, Leoba is urgently summoned:

> At these words Leoba rose up from prayer and, as if she had been challenged to a contest, flung off the cloak which she was wearing and boldly opened the doors of the church.[45]

She makes the sign of the cross, invokes Mary's intercession; and the storm abates at once. Like some of her male counterparts, Leoba is also granted the gift of healing.[46] Indeed in many respects Leoba could be taken as the classic exemplar of Anglo-Saxon monastic spirituality: she is, first and foremost, a mystic, entirely transparent to the loving wisdom of God. She once dreams that an immense length of purple thread emerges from within her: she rolls it into a ball, and is told that the ball represents the mystery of divine teaching, alternately rolling upwards (through contemplation) and downwards (through compassion for one's neighbour).[47] But she is also a genuinely attractive person, whose spiritual maturity is coupled with (indeed, expressed in) a love that is heedless of class or status:

> She kept open house for all without exception, and even when she was fasting gave banquets and washed the feet of guests with her own hands.[48]

THEMES IN ANGLO-SAXON SPIRITUALITY

Exile and Home

Against this background we may examine the themes of Anglo-Saxon spirituality articulated, or hinted at, in 'The seafarer', and the question of how far they reflect the process whereby pagan culture and piety were both christianized and monasticized, so to speak. The dialectic between wandering exile and home is a universal topic, found in texts as diverse as the Mahabharata, the Odyssey, and the Old Testament. In Old English texts this dialectic is often focused on two contrasting images: the *wraecca,* or exile, and the *cynn* – the tightly-knit community bound to its lord, to its hall, and to its bonds of mutual protection and survival. The seafarer misses the drinking of mead in his hall, and the 'dear friends' he lacks even more – the corporate, sociable aspect of the

Anglo-Saxon's inner landscape is worth noting in passing – but he endures the rigours of exile for the sake of his true home beyond.[49]

The theme appears in much Anglo-Saxon poetry, notably in 'Beowulf', the most famous of all poems from Anglo-Saxon England and one which may itself have been written by a Christian cleric, deliberately drawing on pagan images and themes in order to embed them definitively in a Christian context.[50] Here Beowulf has to leave the warmth of his hall for a dangerous journey over the sea in order to engage the evil monster Grendel in combat: the prominence of the monstrous and the bestial in this poem is much more pronounced than in 'The seafarer' and recurs in much explicitly Christian writing, such as hagiography.[51]

The seemingly pagan context of Beowulf's wandering is explicitly christianized in another poem, 'Christ and Satan'. Here the devil bemoans the fact that 'sorrow-stricken, I must travel the ways of exile, far-flung roads': the wicked spirits have been cast out of heaven and wander in exile, while the Lord sits in his heavenly hall and offers a 'secure home' to the upright.[52] It is possible that this poet, like the author of 'The seafarer', may have been influenced by the spirituality of the desert tradition, in which the loftiest human vocation is the (often solitary) combat against the powers of evil.[53] Here, as in 'The seafarer', exile is a costly but holy state, a necessary rejection of the easy securities of hearth and hall in the search of the only home that endures. And Bede points out that the difference between the elect and the damned in this life is that

> the elect as strangers and exiles now look for a fatherland in the future and are less pleased with the passing joys of the present the more they hope to receive future joys without end.[54]

Thus the pagan monster has become a demon, and the pagan hero a monk: the exile is a journey from an earthly to a heavenly hall. Yet the process is not simply one-way: the resulting Christian texts are suffused with the vivid and fantastic imagery of beasts and heroic combat; and Anglo-Saxon spirituality inherits something of the fierce wildness of lost pagan culture. In this sense 'Beowulf' and 'The seafarer' may offer us clues to the origins of Anglo-Saxon culture more than (say) the writings of Bede, where the untamed northern English mental landscape has been insensibly softened by patristic sophistication.

Longing and Desire

In 'The seafarer', the traveller's inner restlessness and longing for the warmth of the home he has left is in the end outweighed by (or rather transformed into) a greater longing for the goal of his journey.[55] One of the most profound effects of Christian monastic spirituality was to transmute the pagan longing for hall, womenfolk or heroic endeavour on the high seas into the Christian longing for heaven. Anglo-Saxon Christian spirituality has a strongly eschatological tone; and both the fear of hell and the longing for heaven played formative parts in determining its identity. The next world, whatever form it may take, is above all real to them, easily and vividly imaginable.[56] A tenth-century sermon describes heaven as being everything this life is not: youth without age, life without ending, joy without sadness, no hunger or thirst, 'nor wind, nor storm, nor the noise of water' – a very English vision, perhaps.[57] And a tenth-century queen who made generous provision for the poor in her will nonetheless indicated that her motives were as much a concern for her own soul in the next world as for those still living in this one:

> And I wish that half my men in every village be freed for my soul; and that
> half the stock which I have be distributed in each village for my soul.[58]

The achievement of Anglo-Saxon monastic spirituality was to make heaven intensely attractive, infinitely more deserving as an object of human *langung* than hall or heroism. In so doing they availed themselves of the rich Augustinian and Gregorian spirituality of the desire for God, in the process giving that spirituality a distinctively Anglo-Saxon timbre.[59] Two examples are worth citing: the writings of St Aldhelm of Malmesbury; and the eighth-century *Life of St Guthlac*.

Aldhelm was the author of a substantial and influential treatise on virginity (*De virginitate*), addressed to Hildelith, abbess of Barking, and a number of her nuns.[60] Many of these monastic houses counted among their number people, often of noble birth, who had left the world (and often their spouses too) for the monastic life; and it may be that Aldhelm had them particularly in mind when he wrote it.[61] It is certainly not easy to see whom else he might have had in mind in writing, for Aldhelm goes even further than earlier patristic protagonists of virginity (such as St Ambrose, on whose work his own appears to have been based[62]) in commending those who leave their spouses for the religious life. Where Ambrose, Jerome and Augustine each compared the three states of virginity, widowhood and marriage respectively to the hundredfold, sixtyfold and thirtyfold fruits of the parable of the sower, Aldhelm replaces these categories with virginity, chastity (i.e. the state of a married person who subsequently rejects matrimony 'for the sake of the heavenly kingdom'), and marriage itself.[63] Aldhelm does not explicitly debase marriage (though his lack of enthusiasm for it is much in evidence): he simply sees it as silver to virginity's gold.[64]

It would be easy, and understandable, to dismiss Aldhelm's treatise as just another example of monastic propaganda in the flamboyant tradition of St Jerome. Before doing so, however, we should pay attention to the theme of desire that animates his writing. He describes some 'aspirants to the blessed life' who from birth are

> so goaded by the spur of divine love and inflamed by the blazing torch of
> heavenly ardour, that every day they eagerly long to depart from the prison
> of the body, transported from the adversity of this world; and through the
> chariness of their abstemiousness they bring it about that they hasten as
> quickly as possible to the celestial homeland of Paradise, while, with secret
> singing of psalms and salt fountains of tears they fail to dissimulate the
> burning desire of their minds and groan aloud because of the frequent
> sighings of remorse drawn from the deepest recesses of their hearts.[65]

Such extravagant writing could easily be dismissed as propaganda, and derivative at that, influenced as it clearly is by the letters of St Jerome and other patristic exemplars[66] – and doubtless also by Aldhelm's eagerness to please the nuns of Barking. Yet it at least serves to remind us that, for the monastic writers of Anglo-Saxon England, the context and perspective in which they wrote was sharply (almost unimaginably) different from our own.

The desire for heaven, for intimacy with God, and for personal salvation offered a powerful source of purpose and meaning in a life in which suffering and death were everyday companions. And, by encouraging women to prefer the monastic life to marriage, Aldhelm may have been offering them a sense of self-worth unlikely to have been available to many women at the time. At the heart of Aldhelm's spirituality was a subtle ambivalence about the world, a recognition that beauty and decay walked hand in hand, and an implicit conviction that monastic communities offered havens of scholarship and charity that best prepared their members for the delights of paradise. This is what he wrote about the creation in one of his characteristic riddles:

> I am more fragrant than perfumed incense, exuding the scent of ambrosia, and I can surpass the lilies, growing in the earth in combination with ruby-red rose-bushes, through the full sweetness of the redolent nard; and then again I stink with the putrid stench of reeking filth.[67]

No one exemplifies the sheer power exerted by 'the holy' more graphically than St Guthlac (674–715), whose life was written by one Felix only about twenty years after his death. Here the Anglo-Saxon fondness for the otherworldly, the magical and the supernatural referred to earlier is allowed full play; and Felix's work, a sophisticated synthesis of the desert and patristic traditions with vernacular myth and legend, is a brilliant portrayal of Anglo-Saxon monastic spirituality, in which many of the themes adumbrated in 'The seafarer' are vividly illustrated, among them that of longing or desire.[68] In Guthlac's youth, 'a noble desire for command burned in his young breast': he becomes a monk at Repton for two years, after which, on reading about the solitary monks of former ages, 'his heart was enlightened and burned with an eager desire to make his way to the desert'.[69]

Nostalgia for a Heroic Past

Felix's *Life of St Guthlac* illustrates another of the themes found in 'The seafarer': a nostalgia for a glorious past. Before embarking on his spiritual journey, Guthlac 'remembered the valiant deeds of heroes of old'; so he engages in numerous bloody exploits, until one night 'a spiritual flame . . . began to burn in this man's heart': as he reflects on the deaths of the ancient kings of his race, 'in imagination the form of his own death revealed itself to him; and, trembling with anxiety at the inevitable finish of this brief life, he perceived that its course daily moved to that end'.[70] This causes him to become a servant of Christ. The powerful way in which the nostalgia for a glorious past is described as being overtaken by a sudden contemplation of his own death, which in turn radically alters his attitude to his own life, is particularly striking.

The nostalgia for a lost heroic past is even more in evidence in 'Beowulf' than in 'The seafarer'; and in the former it is so strong that it can no longer be regarded simply as nostalgia: it underpins the crucial Anglo-Saxon virtue of loyalty, to one's past and to one's kin, which in turn demands of the characters that they set generosity to their kinsfolk before the pursuit of personal power and greed.[71] After he has defeated

Grendel, Beowulf is gently warned not to follow the example of Heremod, who ignored his obligations to others and ended up as an exile and outcast.[72] This blend of nostalgia and loyalty is less prominent in explicitly Christian writers such as Bede, for whom the Bible provided the appropriate 'past', rather than the family sagas of pre-Christian Europe. But Patrick Wormald has argued that, although Anglo-Saxon aristocracy was prepared to accept a new God, 'it was *not* prepared to jettison the memory of the example of those who had worshipped the old';[73] and poems like 'The seafarer' illustrate the manner in which the Anglo-Saxon spiritual landscape sought to combine the features both of its pagan past and of its Christian future.

Cross and Judgement

But it was in respect of the themes of spiritual combat and of the imminence of judgement that the Christian reclothing of an older pagan *topos* is most striking. In the Christian prospectus, the hero's struggle with fearful beasts becomes the holy man's war against both sin and Satan; and the instrument of victory is not the sword but the Cross. Devotion to the Cross, which perhaps reached Northumbria from Ireland, became increasingly popular throughout Europe after the discovery of a relic of the true Cross during the pontificate of Pope Sergius (686–701):[74] fragments of the Cross were ever more widely disseminated; and in England the process may well have been further enhanced during the seventh century through the influence of Theodore of Tarsus (602–690), Archbishop of Canterbury from 668 to 690.[75] In the poem 'The dream of the Rood', the poet, in a brilliantly imaginative stroke, personalizes the Cross, allowing the reader to enter vividly into the death of Christ by seeing it through the eyes, not of biblical characters, but of the very instrument of his death.[76] Yet this is a victorious death; and Christ is not an involuntary victim but a hero worthy of pagan epics:

> Then the young hero (who was God Almighty)
> Got ready, resolute and strong in heart.
> He climbed onto the lofty gallows-tree,
> Bold in the sight of many watching men.[77]

This is a contest of cosmic proportions:

> I saw the God of hosts stretched grimly out.
> Darkness covered the Ruler's corpse with clouds,
> His shining beauty; shadows passed across,
> Black in the darkness. All creation wept.[78]

But the contest is won at the very moment of apparent defeat: it is 'the Lord of victories' who is laid in the tomb, and his resurrection is only a manifestation of what is already effectively accomplished. The Cross describes itself being decorated with gold and silver; and it becomes a powerful instrument of salvation for those who pray to it. The poem ends with a vivid description of the harrowing of hell, and the return of the hero from exile to his heavenly hall – his home, and now ours too:

> May God be friend to me,
> He who once suffered on the gallows tree
> On earth here for men's sins. Us He redeemed
> And granted us our life and heavenly home.
> Hope was renewed with glory and with bliss
> For those who suffered burning fires in hell.
> The Son was mighty on that expedition,
> Successful and victorious; and when
> The one Almighty Ruler brought with Him
> A multitude of spirits to God's kingdom,
> To bliss among the angels and the souls
> Of all who dwelt already in the heavens
> In glory, then Almighty God had come,
> The Ruler entered into His own land.[79]

Some of the lines that appear in 'The dream of the Rood' were earlier inscribed in runes on a stone cross which has claims to be one of the greatest masterpieces of British art: it now stands in a Scottish parish church, in the gentle landscape of the Solway south of Dumfries, towering improbably above the sober Presbyterian furniture around it.[80] The Ruthwell Cross is an extraordinary and highly sophisticated piece of eighth-century Northumbrian sculpture, whose intricate carvings reflect a coherent, though perhaps not completely recoverable, theological programme.[81] It was not created as a work of art, but as an instrument of conversion, instruction and even of penance, and like many similar crosses of the period might originally have stood at a cross-roads or at some other public meeting-place:[82] at once both a sign of protection from the powers of evil and a summons to conversion of life.[83]

Yet it is also much more than that. The position of Christ's crucifixion is such as to suggest an emphasis on the apocalyptic significance of Christ in Majesty rather than Christ suffering.[84] The Christ of Ruthwell is *Christus victor*,[85] but he is also the Christ of the desert tradition: one panel on the Cross, depicting Christ standing victorious over wild beasts, may be inspired by St Jerome's *Life of Paul the first hermit*, in which a strange animal worships Christ and warns against the dangers of pagan worship; or it may reflect the Irish monastic tradition in stressing that Christ tames even the fiercest of animals, who recognize his divinity.[86] The Ruthwell Cross is both a powerful sign of Christ's victory over pagan gods and wild animals and a subtle summons to embrace the virtues and perspective of the monastic life.[87] This is in no sense disinterested art: its iconography reflects contemporary liturgical innovations, such as the introduction by Pope Sergius of the Agnus Dei; and its devotional perspective is strongly monastic[88] – indeed it may well have been as much intended to foster the private devotion of monks as to propagate the faith and values they espoused.[89]

The sophistication of the Ruthwell Cross is to be found in much Anglo-Saxon religious art.[90] In a major study, Barbara Raw has pointed out that one of the primary functions of such art was to provide a focus for meditation – but that, far from explaining Christian belief in simple terms for the unlettered, it reflects a complex and sophisticated theological programme whose agenda and perspective was that of the monasteries.[91] Indeed, most of it was intended for the use of monks and nuns; and the paintings that decorated churches of the period had a contemplative, rather than catechetical, function.[92]

Such art explored many themes, among the most important of which was eschatology: much decoration of Anglo-Saxon churches related to the theme of the church as a symbol of the heavenly city, encouraging worshippers to see their participation in liturgy as a foretaste of the worship of heaven.[93] In turn this led to an emphasis on the communion of saints, and on the essentially corporate nature of Christian liturgy and spirituality.[94] But it also underlines the way in which the monastic perspective sought to shift the orientation of those who prayed and worshipped from the past to the future, from a nostalgia for the pagan heroes of yesterday to a longing for the heavenly Jerusalem of tomorrow.

It is in this context, too, that the all-pervasive emphasis on the cross, and on Christ's passion, needs to be perceived.[95] For Anglo-Saxon Christians, as has been seen, the cross was a sign of victory: it was Christ's divinity, more than his humanity, which was stressed, though by the tenth and eleventh centuries compassion for his sufferings had become almost equally important. In the parish church of Breamore in Hampshire a Saxon rood survives, much mutilated, from the late tenth or early eleventh century. A medieval wall-painting has been superimposed upon it; but despite the alterations, and the repositioning of the entire rood, the bare silhouette of the bent and crucified Christ, his great arms extended on either side, is profoundly moving. This is still a king, but of a very different kind from earthly monarchs; and his victory, though complete, has been won at great cost.[96] Hence the power of the cross both as a focus for devotion and as a source of continuing protection from present evil and future damnation.[97]

Spiritual Combat

This emphasis on the victory of Christ on the Cross does not at all mean that Christians can, so to speak, sit back and thank God that all the hard work has been done for them. On the contrary: it demands of Christians a willingness to engage in battle in the service of their crucified Lord. Here too monastic spirituality took one of the primary ingredients of contemporary life – physical combat – and internalized it.[98] Aldhelm of Malmesbury warns virgins to avoid all pride, and to see themselves as 'combatants in the monastic army', who like St Guthlac have to engage in spiritual combat against the vices that assail them.[99] And Guthlac himself, after deciding to embrace the full severity of the solitary life, is guided to a remote spot in the Fen country called Crowland, where (as with Farne) no one had been able hitherto to dwell alone 'on account of the phantoms of demons which haunted it'.[100] Here, sustained by the powerful aid of St Bartholomew, who keeps him company,

> he determined with heavenly aid to be a soldier of the true God amid the gloomy thickets of that remote desert. Then, girding himself with spiritual arms against the wiles of the foul foe, he took the shield of faith, the breastplate of hope, the helmet of chastity, the bow of patience, the arrows of

psalmody, making himself strong for the fight. So great in fact was his confidence that, despising the foe, he hurled himself against the torrid troops of Tartarus.[101]

The demons, however, are not easily repelled: they assail Guthlac at night, in the midst of his prayers, when 'he suddenly saw the whole tiny cell filled with horrible troops of foul spirits; for the door was open to them as they approached from every quarter'.[102] St Bartholomew rescues him just before he is carried off into hell. This emphasis on the communion of saints is important, for Guthlac knows he cannot endure his struggle against evil alone, and is only too conscious both of his own sin and of his occasional temptation to despair.[103] The virtue that sustains him most is patience, which in the monastic tradition is more than a placid perseverance: it is a robust synthesis of acute self-knowledge and courageous willingness to endure in sure hope of what is to come. In the end this patience earns Guthlac the respect even of the birds and fishes, who come at his call and take food from his hand. Felix points the moral:

> For if a man faithfully and wholeheartedly serves the Maker of all created things, it is no wonder though all creation should minister to his commands and wishes. But for the most part we lose dominion over the creation which was made subject to us, because we ourselves neglect to serve the Lord and Creator of all things.[104]

This is a vital point: the hermit-monk wrestling with the powers of evil in solitude does more than engage in courageous combat on our behalf. He also helps to restore the lost order of creation established in Eden, where God, human beings and animals lived in intimate harmony.[105] The wild bogs of Crowland become a foretaste of Paradise restored; and the lonely Elijah-figure of the Fen country a sacrament of the ultimate unity of all creation in God: when two swallows enter Guthlac's little house and sing a song, settling on his shoulders and lap, his visitor is astonished; but the saint answers

> Have you not read how if a man is joined to God in purity of spirit all things are united to him in God?[106]

Penance and Spiritual Guidance

One other example of the ubiquitous influence of monasteries on Anglo-Saxon spirituality is to be found in the practice of penance, for no aspect of church life more clearly reflects the monastic concern to impose their ideal on the whole of society.[107] The question of whether true holiness was in practice attainable by a lay person remained uncertain in an age where virginity and priesthood were consistently more highly valued than marriage and the lay state; and, if it were attainable at all, it could only be by the practice of penance and the adoption of a quasi-monastic way of life.[108]

Private penitential practice – that is, the imposition of a penance by a priest on an individual confessing his or her sins as a prerequisite for the granting of absolution – seems to have been a distinctively Irish custom, quite different from the Roman system of public penance: its introduction into England is one example of the extensive Irish influence on Anglo-Saxon religion.[109] In England, as in Ireland, penitentials were produced, detailing the specific penances to be imposed for each sin: the most influential, that of Theodore of Tarsus, became the standard English penitential.[110] But where the Irish penitentials seem to have been primarily intended for those living near monasteries, Theodore's has been described as 'a prescription for social observance intended for all devout Christians'.[111]

The practice of penance, in both Ireland and England, was in itself originally a monastic one: it spread first to very devout lay people concerned to adopt monastic virtues, and only gradually spread to the populace as a whole.[112] And, in doing so, it profoundly influenced spirituality, so that much private prayer appears to have been concerned with protection from the dangers of falling into sin.[113] The lively belief in the reality of judgement, reflected in 'The seafarer', was immensely influential in this regard: penance came to be seen as a form of spiritual medicine helping to inoculate the penitent against the fearsome terrors of hell; and one of the most popular forms of prayer in Anglo-Saxon England, as in Ireland, was the *lorica* (literally 'breastplate'), which may well have become even more widespread during periods of war or epidemic.[114]

The penitentials of Anglo-Saxon England were, then, unquestionably influenced by the perspectives of monastic asceticism: even by the mid-eighth century most of them prescribed substantial periods of sexual abstinence for married people. The Penitential of Theodore indicates that partners were expected to abstain from intercourse for three nights before receiving communion, and for forty days before Easter.[115] Elsewhere it declares that

> He who has sexual relations on the Lord's day shall ask indulgence from
> God and do penance for one or two or three days.[116]

and the general attitude to the body is exemplified in a further injunction which states baldly:

> A husband ought not to see his wife nude.[117]

Furthermore, since the penitentials included injunctions about almsgiving and fasting as well as specific penances for sins, they reflect the slow but inexorable process whereby the church in England extended its control over every aspect of human life.[118] More positively, though, the penitentials reflect a concern with the whole of a person's life and inner integrity; and they reveal a preoccupation with the self that strikingly anticipates the introspection of St Anselm and of other medieval writers. If no aspect of an individual's life was expected to elude the watchful eye and strictures of the priest, the Anglo-Saxon Christian was at least reminded thereby of the intrinsic importance of every aspect of his or her life and inward disposition.[119]

There is also a more positive aspect to this theme. Underlying the emphasis on penance was a concern not simply to save souls, but to assist fellow-Christians to make progress in the spiritual life. Two Anglo-Saxon saints may serve to exemplify this concern: St Wilfrid (633–709), and St Boniface (680–754). Wilfrid was a controversial man, every inch a prince-bishop, and presented by his biographer Stephen of Ripon (Eddius Stephanus) more as an Old Testament prophet than as a Christ-figure.[120] Spiritual power radiates from him, a power so strong that even after his death it provides both protection and punishment: when some evil-doers set fire to the monastery at Oundle where he had died, the flames die out as soon as they reach the saint's room; and all the arsonists are killed other than those who had crossed themselves.[121] Yet the power that is vested in the saint is almost always put to good effect: Bede describes what happens when Wilfrid converts the people of Sussex to Christianity – after three years' drought and famine, during which

> forty or fifty men, wasted with hunger, would go to some precipice or to the sea shore where in their misery they would join hands and leap into the sea, perishing wretchedly either by the fall or by drowning. But on the very day on which the people received the baptism of faith, a gentle but ample rain fell; the earth revived.[122]

Wilfrid did not, however, convert the South Saxons simply by the exercise of sheer miraculous power. He also taught them how to fish, demonstrating a practical concern which helps to justify Patrick Wormald's claim that he was 'the greatest . . . of all the early Anglo-Saxon saints'.[123] Wilfrid might have been both papalist and prophet; but he was also someone of profound pastoral concern, praised by his biographer as a spiritual director: 'to everyone he gave different advice, advice always suitable to the individual character'.[124]

Like Wilfrid, St Boniface was an evangelist: he was born in Crediton but spent most of his life among the peoples of Germany, where he also received a martyr's death.[125] Both his own letters and the near-contemporary biography of him give us some vivid glimpses of the spirituality of an eighth-century English monastic figure whose immediate concerns were the evangelizing and catechizing of pagans with whom he lived and worked.[126] Prayer, for Boniface, is described as a 'laborious exercise', yet a crucial one for someone whose spiritual world-view was strongly eschatological:[127] he twice tells the English people in his letter to them that 'the way of all the earth draws near' – hence the urgent need for their prayers.[128] One of the other letters from his collection describes a vision seen by a monk at Wenlock, in which both purgatory and hell are vividly and extensively described (the former as a fiery river which souls must cross on a log), whereas heaven is said to be a

> place of wondrous beauty wherein a multitude of very handsome people were enjoying extraordinary happiness.[129]

The dialectic of heaven and hell, and the imminent possibility of either, dominates Boniface's spirituality, leading him to denounce both the practices of paganism and a failure on the part of Christians to live what they profess: at Judgement Day, those of high and low degree alike will receive what their sins deserve; and the damned will include abbots and abbesses.[130] Right belief alone, then, is not a sufficient predeterminant of salvation: it must be accompanied by right action; and a spiritual life is one of active moral virtue firmly rooted in eschatological hope. The hope of heaven inspired Boniface to acts of prophetic iconoclasm: he is said to have hewn down the great oak of Thor at Geismar before a scandalized pagan assembly without fear of a retributory thunderbolt.[131] But it also animated his preaching of an exemplary Christian lifestyle, the pattern of this life mattering precisely because that of the next matters more.

It is within this theological context that Boniface's concern for spiritual guidance needs to be seen. This is what he writes to one Nithard, encouraging him to continue his studies:

> Give rein to your natural gifts and abilities; do not stifle your literary talents and your keen spiritual understanding with gross pleasures of the flesh . . . Put aside all harmful obstacles; strive with unflagging zest to pursue your study of the scriptures and thereby acquire that nobility of mind which is divine wisdom [which will] guide you to the shore of an enchanting paradise and the everlasting bliss of the angels.[132]

And Boniface's concerns, like those of Bede before him, extended from the individual to embrace the whole Christian community. In another letter he wrote:

> We [i.e. Boniface et al.] have ordered every priest annually during Lent to render to his bishop an account of his ministry, the state of the Catholic faith, Baptism and every detail of his administration. We have decreed that every bishop shall make an annual visitation of his diocese confirming and instructing the people, seeking out and forbidding pagan rites, divination, fortune-telling, soothsaying, charms, incantations and all Gentile vileness. We have forbidden the servants of God to wear showy or martial dress or to carry arms.[133]

Lay Spirituality and Private Prayer

It will by now be clear that it is virtually impossible to identify distinctive aspects of lay (as opposed to monastic) spirituality in the Anglo-Saxon period: monastic texts, religious art and penitentials tell us a great deal about how lay people were expected to pray, but very little about how they actually did.[134] They can, however give us some modest but useful clues. Consider, for example, this prescription in the Penitential of Theodore:

> If a man is vexed by the devil and can do nothing but run about everywhere, and [if he] slays himself, there may be some reason to pray for him if he was formerly religious. If it was on account of despair, or of some fear, or for unknown reasons, we ought to leave to God the decision of this matter, and we dare not pray for him.[135]

Such guidance may appear grudging to twentieth-century Christians for whom intercessory prayer is both common and world-embracing. But for Anglo-Saxons the focus of such prayer reflects the very different self-understanding on the part of the Church by comparison with what predominates today. The Church was an ark of salvation, standing firmly *contra mundum*; and a prayer such as this for the mentally ill reflects its single overriding concern – to assist its members in attaining eternal life in heaven. If the man concerned were seeking salvation, then perhaps even suicide was justifiable.

More information about the content of Anglo-Saxon prayer can be gained from the collections of private prayers which survive from the period, for here at least we may be able to eavesdrop, so to speak, upon an individual's personal devotions. *Libelli precum* were particularly abundant in Anglo-Saxon England, some dating from as early as the eighth century; and they reflect the emphasis of Irish monasticism on the welfare of the individual soul: where the Rule of St Benedict merely allows for private prayer in cell, the *Regula monachorum* of St Columbanus explicitly requires it.[136] The principal ingredient of such prayer-books was the Psalter; and abbreviated psalters, or florilegia consisting mainly of extracts from it, appear to have become relatively commonplace. One of the ways in which religious communities sought to influence lay piety may well have been by producing devotional anthologies suitable for lay (especially noble) people as well as for monks and nuns; and in due course prayer-books of this kind became common throughout Europe, the normative pattern being a psalter with private prayers interspersed or appended to it.[137]

What was the content of private prayer in eighth- or ninth-century England? The ninth-century *Book of Cerne,* which despite its title probably belonged to a monk or canon regular of Mercia, perhaps associated with Æthelwald of Lichfield,[138] consists of an abridged psalter, extracts from the Passion narratives in the Gospels, hymns and prayers of both Roman and Irish character – in general, the Irish pattern of prayers tended to be more verbose and extravagant, and the Roman more precise but cool – and an apocryphal text describing the harrowing of hell.[139] Two themes predominate in the prayers: a concern for personal protection from evil, and an emphasis on the communion of saints. Thus the sixth prayer in the collection asks that the person's mouth will be protected from secular stories and from cursing, and his eyes from desiring women; and the various other parts of the body deemed to be prone to sin are specifically listed and prayed for.[140] The ensuing prayer for use in the morning illustrates the importance of the saints in Anglo-Saxon piety of this genre:

> May we walk in prosperity in this day of light:
> In the power of the most high God, greatest of the gods,
> In a manner pleasing to Christ,
> In the light of the Holy Spirit,
> In the faith of the patriarchs,
> In the merits of the prophets,
> In the peace of the apostles,
> In the joy of the angels,
> In the splendour of the saints,
> In the works of monks,
> In the power of the just,
> In the martyrdom of the martyrs,
> In the chastity of the virgins,
> In the wisdom of God,
> In much patience,
> In abstinence of flesh,
> In continence of tongue,
> In abundance of peace,

> In praise of the Trinity,
> With our senses alert,
> With constant good works,
> With the spiritual realities [*formae*],
> With divine conversation,
> With blessings,
> In these things is the journey of all labouring for Christ
> who leads his saints after death into eternal joy
> That I may hear the voice of the angels praising God
> and saying Holy, Holy, Holy.[141]

The stress on the communion of saints provides a corporate perspective that complements the self-preoccupation of much Anglo-Saxon piety, a perspective further heightened by the growth during this period of devotion to the Trinity.[142] This corporate emphasis is further reflected in the popularity of litanies of the saints, a form of both public and private prayer whose earliest exemplars were produced in England during the tenth century but which may well have been introduced from the Greek East via Theodore of Tarsus during the seventh century; since Theodore and his companion Hadrian (abbot of the monastery of SS Peter and Paul Canterbury 670–709) were responsible for establishing a school at Canterbury whose productions clearly reflect the influence of Greek Christian scholarship and piety, it is highly likely that they also brought with them from the Christian East patterns of devotion characteristic of Greek spirituality which in turn influenced those of contemporary Anglo-Saxon England.[143] It appears that this genre of prayer was introduced by England to the continent, and that in turn later continental developments influenced the later Anglo-Saxon church:[144] the impact of these will be considered when the nature of personal devotion during the tenth-century monastic reform movement is explored later.

Since almost all the writers whose work is studied in this chapter were monks, it is difficult to glean much about the nature of lay spirituality from them. But there is one exception, even though he can hardly be taken as typical of the mass of his people: King Alfred the Great (849–99).[145] Asser (his biographer) describes the king as a layperson of exceptional religious observance, 'in the invariable habit of listening daily to divine services and Mass, and of participating in certain psalms and prayers and in the day-time and night-time offices' (though we need to remember that monastic biographers frequently described their subjects, even when lay, as proto-monks).[146] Like Augustine of Hippo,[147] Alfred had a gift for friendship: in one of the additions the king made to Boethius' work he wrote, in words that could as easily have come from Augustine's pen:

> One loves a friend sometimes out of affection, sometimes out of trust,
> even though no other return is expected from him.[148]

Alfred stands out among the writers discussed here simply because he was a layman: Asser, perhaps with that disdain for the lay state that occasionally characterizes the monk, describes him as someone who realized he was 'unable to abstain from carnal desire';[149] and to some extent the texts that appear likely to have come from Alfred himself offer us a window into a layperson's (albeit a king's) spiritual world. He writes about God's omnipresence in his translation of Boethius;[150] but elsewhere he says that this does not diminish the need for us consciously to fix our attention on God. Using the nautical imagery of which he seems to have been fond,[151] he tells the soul to:

> look directly with your mind's eye at God, just as directly as the ship's anchor-cable is stretched in a straight line from the ship to the anchor; and fix your mind's eye on God as the anchor is fixed in the ground. Even though the ship is on the waves out at sea, it is safe and sound if the cable holds, because one of its ends is fixed in the ground and the other is fixed to the ship.[152]

The more worldly desires the soul relinquishes, the more anchors it acquires:[153] like Augustine, Alfred was well aware that God knew of the conflict between worldly and heavenly desires deep within himself; and he includes in his translation of the *Soliloquies* the passage in which Augustine says that the very existence within us of a desire to know whence we come and whither we go after death is sure testimony to our own eternal vocation.[154] Alfred's spiritual writing is unequivocally ascetic, in the spirit of those whose works he translated: his contribution to spirituality may be said to consist above all in his appropriation to his own life and interior struggles of some of the primary insights of the patristic writers he loved.[155] Thus, in his translation of the third book of Augustine's *Soliloquies* (perhaps the most original piece of Alfred's writing to have survived), the king uses an analogy drawn from the experience of a secular ruler to stress the creative value of the sufferings of the upright:

> A powerful man in this world may have expelled one of his favourites from him, or against both their wishes the man may have been banished, and the man might then experience many torments and many misfortunes on his journey of exile, and return nevertheless to the same lord with whom he previously had been, and be received there with greater honour than he had formerly been. At that point he will recall the misfortunes which he experienced on his journey of exile, and yet will not be any the more unhappy for that.[156]

He did the same thing with the psalms: in his introductions to each of the fifty psalms he translated he sought to appropriate its subject-matter or theme for himself. At the head of Psalm 3 he wrote:

> David sang this third psalm when he was lamenting Absalom his son, and he bewailed his misery to the Lord. Everyone who sings this psalm does likewise: he laments his tribulations, of either mind or body, to the Lord.[157]

And, at the head of Psalm 13:

> When David sang this thirteenth psalm, he lamented to the Lord in the psalm that in his time there should be so little faith, and so little wisdom should be found in the world. And so does every just man who sings it now: he laments the same thing in his own time.[158]

Alfred's own life and achievements bear witness to the fruit that such lamentation can bear.

INDIVIDUAL STUDIES

The Nature of Holiness: St Cuthbert of Lindisfarne (634–87)

Introduction

Like his predecessor Aidan, Cuthbert belonged to the Irish monastic tradition, brought up at Melrose in southern Scotland: he has been described as having lived and died 'after the manner of the typical Irish monk'.[159] He became prior of Lindisfarne in 664 at the age of 30, and bishop in 685: he died in 687, after having withdrawn to live as a hermit on one of the Farne islands. His background has been charmingly described as that of the 'country gentry';[160] and like Aidan he was both monk and evangelist: Bede describes how he 'sought to convert the neighbouring people far and wide from a life of foolish customs to a love of heavenly joys' – the 'foolish customs' were doubtless pagan practices.[161] Nothing written by him survives; and the anonymous author of the first *Vita sancti Cuthberti* borrowed extensively from earlier hagiography (such as Sulpicius' *Life of St Martin* and Athanasius' *Life of St Antony*) in his presentation of the saint. It is certainly possible that this presentation is motivated in part by a concern to foster the reputation of Lindisfarne as the shrine of a saint.[162]

Even if this is so, however, both the anonymous *Life* and Bede's *Vita sancti Cuthberti* offer us some valuable insights into Anglo-Saxon spirituality. For neither was seeking to produce a bare historical record: each was writing hagiography, and concerned to celebrate Cuthbert as an exemplar of the Christian life.[163] Furthermore, since each was writing from within a firmly monastic context, each offers us a portrayal of the saint which incarnates the chief monastic virtues and values, making them accessible and even imitable by lay people too. This is not to say that the Lives tell us nothing at all about the historical Cuthbert. But it is to say that their primary purpose was both to celebrate his holiness, and to offer his life as a model for others to follow insofar as they could.

The holiness of St Cuthbert

The holiness attributed to St Cuthbert is something palpable, objectively recognizable, and with a powerful effect on the world around him. It is something even the animals recognize, as when two little sea animals lick and warm his bare feet after he has spent part of the night praying while standing in the sea.[164] It comprises, among other things, an acute sensitivity to evil, as when he foresees that the devil will tempt some villagers.[165] It gives him miraculous power over nature, vividly exemplified when the sea provides him with the twelve-foot beam he needed to build his hermitage.[166] It enables him to heal the sick, among them a woman afflicted with insanity (thereby demonstrating Cuthbert's Christlike authority over evil or unclean spirits).[167] It equips him to live, and is itself attained by, a life of exemplary asceticism, which is described in terms clearly borrowed from the lives of the desert fathers.[168] Bede describes his humble service of others in washing their feet, but goes on to tell us that

> once he had put on his boots at Easter, he did not take them off until Easter came round again a year later, and then only for the washing of the feet which takes place on Maundy Thursday.[169]

Cuthbert's holiness not only allows him to remain impervious to the promptings of personal hygiene: it also enables him to remain untroubled by external suffering because of the 'inward consolation of the Holy Spirit'.[170] It bestows upon him an exceptional discernment, as when he sees St Aidan's soul being taken up into heaven;[171] a disarming modesty (Bede charmingly describes Cuthbert's inclination to talk about his spiritual gifts as though they were someone else's[172]); an exemplary humility (manifested in his reluctance to accept episcopal office[173]); and an acute awareness of his own sinfulness (we are told that he could never finish saying Mass without bursting into tears[174]).

Above all, however, holiness is power, a power that is mediated both by the saint's inner life and character and by his clothing and (later) his relics: it is this power which implicitly guarantees the equivalent power of the saint's intercession.[175] Bede tells us how an abbess, and subsequently one of the virgins in her monastery, were healed by touching Cuthbert's girdle (though he goes on to say that the girdle then disappeared lest unworthy people, who would not have deserved healing, disparaged it when they were not healed by it).[176]

Like the desert fathers before him, Cuthbert goes to seek solitude in a remote place (like Aidan, he chooses one of the Farne islands), not in order to escape the powers of evil, but precisely in order to confront them: the island he chooses is peopled by demons which he first has to expel,[177] and which according to Bede prevented anyone from dwelling there before him:[178] there is nothing romantic about the fondness of the writers of this period for wild and solitary places. As with the writer of 'The seafarer', the solitary life is an unremitting struggle; and despite Cuthbert's longing for heaven (which causes him to build a dwelling on the island so designed that only the sky could be seen from it[179]), the approach of death brings him only a yet more severe combat with the devil: 'my adversaries', he says, 'have never persecuted me so frequently, during all the time I have been living on this island, as during these five days'.[180] Yet his physical weakness only enhances the miraculous power wrought by his interior holiness; and he heals a sick brother shortly before his own death.[181]

St Cuthbert and the life of heaven

The terrible dereliction experienced by Cuthbert during his last days may not appear to be a very compelling encouragement to others to embrace the monastic or eremitic life, just as the sufferings of the seafarer might have been expected to dissuade any would-be imitators from attempting a similar journey themselves. But texts of this kind may have had a twofold audience in mind. For the monastic communities from which and for which they were written, they offered a message of hope rooted in stark realism. The glories of heaven can be attained only at enormous cost; and yet the journey towards them will itself be a progressive manifestation of the power of Christ at work within each person who embarks upon it.

And for society as a whole the message is no less compelling. It is as though contemporaries were in effect being told: those like St Cuthbert who leave the world do so not only to save their own souls but also to save yours. They overcome demons so that you can do the same with temptations. They desire heaven, and attain it, so that you can do so too, even though monks and nuns have chosen a more excellent way. Like them, you are made for something more than the uncertainties and transient pleasures of life on earth; and sooner or later you will have to decide whether or not to respond to the innate and restless longing for heaven which exists within you. But (and this is crucial) contemporaries were also being told that the journey of St Cuthbert is quite different from that of the pagan hero, even though both encounter numerous enemies and demonstrate superhuman courage and power.

For Cuthbert's power is not of his creating, or even (despite his spiritual athleticism) of his achieving: it is the power of Christ working in and through him. And, as Benedicta Ward has written, his final illness is a form of Gethsemane experience, 'the last darkness of the saints in their union with Christ'.[182] Understood in this context, the sufferings of Cuthbert become more than just stepping-stones on the road to eternity: they become redemptive for others. The result, irrespective of the extent to which it does or does not approximate to history, is that Cuthbert becomes a figure of extraordinary power and attractiveness, and (as with Christ and the desert fathers before him) both power and attractiveness are manifested in practical pastoral concern:

> Now many came to the man of God, not only from the neighbourhood of Lindisfarne but also from the remoter parts of Britain, having been attracted by the report of his miracles; such people declared to him either the sins they had committed or the temptations of devils to which they were exposed, or else revealed the common troubles of mankind by which they were afflicted, hoping that they would get consolation from a man of such sanctity. Nor did their hope deceive them. For no one went away from him without enjoying his consolation, and no one returned accompanied by that sorrow of mind which he had brought thither.[183]

The Life of the World to Come: The Venerable Bede (673–735)

Introduction

If Aldhelm of Malmesbury was the Jerome of Anglo-Saxon England, Bede comes closest to being the Augustine: the range and variety of his concerns, together with the force of theological originality he brought to bear upon contemporary issues, marks him out from his contemporaries as an outstanding thinker and polymath.[184]Unlike Augustine, however, Bede's life was strikingly uneventful; and he describes it thus:

> I was born in the territory of this monastery.[185] When I was seven years of age I was, by the care of my kinsmen, put into the charge of the reverend Abbot Benedict and then of Ceolfrith, to be educated. From then on I have spent all my life in this monastery, applying myself entirely to the study of the Scriptures; and, amid the daily task of singing in the church, it has always been my delight to learn or to teach or to write.[186]

The monastery in which Bede lived for most of his life was far from being a backwater: it was a centre of learning and culture in the midst of a thriving kingdom; and the reign of Aldfrith (685–705) saw Northumbrian literature, painting, building, and sculpture all flourish.[187] Once entering the monastery, Bede seems never to have travelled further than Lindisfarne to the north and York to the south;[188] and his writings reflect a narrowly focused perspective that is striking even by comparison with near-contemporaries like Alcuin.[189] Yet at the heart of the ascetic spirituality which animated him is this willed renunciation of everything else for the sake of the *unum necessarium*, an uncompromising desire to see this world with the fierce and unblinking gaze of someone already looking forward to the next one; and the spirituality of Bede will make no sense unless that perspective is recognized.

Bede and Rome

Yet if the longing for heaven formed one pole in Bede's spiritual world-view, somewhere very different formed the other: Rome, and specifically the Rome of St Gregory the Great, who had sent Augustine to England in 597.[190] Bede did not ignore the Northumbria of his day; but he saw it, its people and their forebears in a perspective that is catholic in both literal and theological senses of the word.[191] Richard Southern, describing his aim as 'simple, and grand', has expressed it thus:

> to make the raw nation, not yet a nation till he pronounced it one, at home
> in the past – not the past of pagan genealogies, folk-tales and heroic legend
> that he could see all round him, but the past of the Latin learning of the
> Christian Church.[192]

Thus St Cuthbert, in Bede's *Life*, embodies Bede's own vision of the monastic ruler, teacher and preacher – a vision in turn heavily influenced by St Gregory the Great;[193] and the *Ecclesiastical history* that is Bede's most famous work portrays the English people as strikingly similar to the Israelites of the Old Testament, suffering decline and decay after an early monarchical golden age.[194] Bede preferred the cultural perspective of Gregorian Rome, and thereby insensibly softened some of the rough edges of Irish spirituality:[195] not for him a world of Grendels and grotesqueries.[196]

Yet Bede's presentation of saints in the Irish tradition like Aidan and Cuthbert is generous, even though he is clearly more at home with them than with more actively this-worldly figures like Wilfrid.[197] Bede's view of the world is unequivocally monastic; and in Gregory he found a master whose eloquent Latin style, wide learning, and passionate longing for God profoundly influenced the monk of Jarrow.[198] The Rule of St Benedict,[199] and the vision of the monastic community as an anticipation of the heavenly city, exerted a profound influence on Bede's spirituality.

Bede and eschatology

This future-oriented perspective colours the whole of Bede's spirituality; and here as elsewhere the influence of Gregory is pervasive.[200] Bede describes Benedict Biscop, the founder of his monastery, returning from Rome with many paintings (in themselves valuable teaching tools in a largely non-literate age), among them scenes from the Apocalypse with which he decorated the north wall of the monastery church at Jarrow:

> Thus all who entered the church, even those who could not read, were
> able, whichever way they looked, to contemplate the dear face of Christ

and His saints, even if only in a picture, to put themselves more firmly in mind of the Lord's Incarnation and, as they saw the decisive moment of the Last Judgement before their very eyes be brought to examine their conscience with all due severity.[201]

In order to encourage such severity, Bede waxes eloquent about both the joys of heaven and the horrors of hell: thus he vividly describes Fursa's vision of the four fires of judgement, and the devils 'stirring up the fires of war against the just';[202] and later in his *History* he describes with equal immediacy the vision of the layman Drycthelm, who sees the environs of heaven as

> a very broad and pleasant plain, full of . . . a fragrance of growing flowers [and] many companies of happy people.[203]

This description, like that of Fursa, is not rhetorical but didactic: if we are to avoid Fursa's own horrible fate (he is burned for accepting some clothing from a sinner), we are both to imitate the life of austere penitence he lived in terrified remembrance of his vision, and to make our own Drycthelm's 'unwearied longing for heavenly bliss' as he in turn remembered his. Bede's eschatological perspective collapses the barriers between this world and the next, so that the latter interpenetrates the former: our prayers, liturgy, and manner of life directly affect the state of those awaiting entry into heaven after death.[204] In one of his sermons Bede writes:

> There are six ages in this life, punctuated by well-known feasts, in which it is necessary to devote ourselves to labour for God and to work for the sake of obtaining eternal rest. The seventh age is not in this life but in another: it is the life of souls resting until the time of resurrection. But the eighth age is the blessed and unending day of resurrection itself.[205]

We live in the sixth age, in which Christ became incarnate; the seventh age is the intervening repose between death and judgement, the cosmos' Holy Saturday; and the eighth is at once the first and the last age, the endless sabbath day of paradise where we shall live for ever with the saints.[206] The communion of saints is a crucial feature in Bede's spiritual landscape, adding a rich corporateness to his understanding of the human journey.[207] But, for Bede as for the seafarer, that journey is no easy undertaking. He describes Benedict Biscop as someone whose mind 'was constantly fixed on the life of heaven': he commends his virginity and his rejection of country, home, family, and marriage, 'so that he might receive a hundredfold in return and gain eternal life':[208] Benedict's fellow monks, his spiritual sons, represent a far more fruitful chastity than any physical marriage could have offered;[209] and in any case the saints, who keep us company from heaven, are a powerful source of support for us on our earthly journeys. In a striking interpretation of a verse in the Song of Songs, Bede writes:

> But we seek 'the covert of the cliff' (Song 2:14) in a swift flight; in other words, we seek the abundant intercessions for us either of the saints, or of angels, or of human beings in the presence of the mercy of the righteous Maker.[210]

The Christian's spiritual life

This strongly eschatological framework leads Bede to lay great emphasis on two inter-related themes which we have already found to be characteristic of Anglo-Saxon spirituality: a view of life as a costly and difficult journey involving spiritual combat against evil; and the desire for God, which (as with the seafarer) animates the traveller. But in both cases Bede's approach is patristic rather than distinctively Anglo-Saxon. It is true that he describes St Fursa fighting against evil spirits in a manner very similar to that of St Guthlac.[211] But in general his approach reflects the theological sophistication of Augustine or Gregory rather than the pictorial vividness of 'Beowulf'.

It is also worth noting that, in Bede's reflections on the importance of the desert as a metaphor for a vital stage in the spiritual life, it is intimacy with God rather than spiritual combat which he stresses: for Bede, the desert solitude of St John the Baptist is an altogether more appealing experience than it was for St Guthlac or St Antony.[212] His view of the spiritual journey is less pictorial, more theological. Thus in a Lenten sermon he tells his brethren:

> We should rejoice that the solemnity of the Passover is wrought in us when we strive to cross from vices to virtues. Indeed the word 'Passover' (*pascha*) means a crossing-over.[213]

And in his commentary on the Song of Songs he tells his fellow Christians that they of all people should grieve least during the labours of this world's exile, since they are hastening through it towards the vision of eternal peace.[214]

The same point may be made of his treatment of the theme of desire. Like St Augustine of Hippo and St Gregory, he stresses the importance of rightly ordered desire – a desire for God, and a longing for heaven – as the mainspring and dynamic of the Christian's spiritual life. Life is a journey towards perfection; and both love and contemplation are, so to speak, appetizers, pledges of what is yet to come.[215] In his commentary on the seven 'Catholic Epistles', he quotes St Gregory, who says that a longing for earthly things at best induces satiety which in turn leads to disgust; whereas a longing for heavenly things induces an ever-greater desire the more it is satisfied.[216] And in his commentary on St Luke's Gospel, Bede quotes Jesus as saying

> I came into the world to inflame people away from earthly longings towards heavenly desires.[217]

Bede and lay Christian formation

All this is classical ascetic teaching, unmistakably indebted to Augustine and Gregory – and directed above all to a monastic audience. It is true that Bede does not ignore the spiritual needs of lay people outside the monastic enclosure: in his letter to Egbert, he says that catechetical instruction is vital for them if they are 'to fortify and arm themselves against the assaults of unclean spirits';[218] and to this end he also encourages them to repeat the words of the Creed as a 'spiritual antidote', and to devote themselves to assiduous prayer, genuflecting while saying the Lord's Prayer regularly.[219] They are to make the sign of the cross frequently in order to protect themselves and their possessions against unclean spirits, and should receive Holy Communion daily.[220]

Nevertheless Bede follows writers like Jerome and Aldhelm in consistently depreciating marriage and favouring virginity;[221] and in his frequent reflections on the relative merits of the active and contemplative lives, there is no doubt about which is to be preferred. One of his sermons on this theme is worth quoting more fully, for it exposes at once the power and the ascetic perspective of Bede's spirituality:

> [To live] the active life means to persevere as a conscientious servant of Christ by means of just labours, and first to keep oneself unstained by the world; to keep one's hand, tongue and other bodily members from every defilement of tempting fault and always to subjugate them to the service of God; it is also to attend to the necessities of one's neighbour as far as one can, giving food to the hungry, drink to the thirsty, clothing to the cold, receiving the needy and vagrant into one's house, visiting the sick, burying the dead, snatching the weak from the hands of the strong and the needy and poor from the hands of those who oppress them, but also showing the way of truth to the wandering, committing oneself to others in actions of fraternal love, and by striving for justice even unto death. But the contemplative life is when someone who is trained by much experience of good actions, instructed in the sweetness of extended prayer, and habituated by frequent tears of compunction, learns to free himself from all worldly affairs and applies the eye of the mind only to love: he begins to have a foretaste of the joy of perpetual blessedness which he will attain in the life to come by intensely desiring it now, and even by sublimely contemplating (*speculando*) it in mental rapture so far as mortals may. Now this life of divine contemplation admits especially those who after extended instruction in hidden monastic virtue know how to live away from other people, occupying their mind the more freely in heavenly meditation the more it is separated from earthly tumults.[222]

The power of such writing is undeniable: Bede genuinely values the virtues of the active life, and elsewhere describes Christ as incarnating the fullness of both that and the life of contemplation.[223] And his reasons for preferring the contemplative vocation are not self-seeking but eschatological: the active life will end at death, after which no one will need serving any more, whereas the contemplative life begins here but reaches its perfection in heaven.[224] But the very dynamism and élan with which Bede, following Gregory, infuses the monastic life inevitably diminishes the value of any other manner of living; and the result is a spirituality which, for all its intellectual depth and pastoral subtlety, is unambiguously oriented towards the cloister.

Participation in God

Yet this is not to imply that the spirituality of Bede has nothing to offer to those living outside the monastic enclosure. Bede was deeply interested in the task of evangelizing his contemporaries, and encouraged suitable people of all backgrounds to be chosen as teachers of the faith.[225] He believed all Christians had a responsibility to support or instruct, and certainly to love, their neighbours;[226] and he believed they were to practise works of equity and justice.[227] He believed passionately in the unity of the

Church, a unity that surpasses the rich diversity of its members.[228] We might conclude by considering two other aspects of his thought which are of universal application: his understanding of prayer, and the theology which underlies it. In a sermon for Christmas Day, Bede reflects on the image of the Roman emperor found on coins, and then says:

> We should also express in the same coinage of our good manner of life that image of his [Christ's] which he taught us about, saying: 'Be holy for I the Lord your God am holy (Lev. 19:2).' Now this is the image of God in which we were fashioned in the first human being, so that we might be holy for ever by participation in the divine holiness. Hence the psalmist's words: 'You have set upon us the light of your countenance, O Lord (Ps 4:7).' But because humanity lost this light of the divine countenance by sinning, it pleased God to assume the condition of a human countenance by being born in the flesh, so that thereby he might teach us that we should be reborn in the spirit; and it pleased him to appear in the likeness of sinful flesh yet without sin, so that he might cleanse us from every sin and reform in us the clarity of his image.[229]

Participation in the divine holiness (*participatio divinae sanctitatis*): this is a central theme in Bede's spirituality. Later in the same sermon he says that Christ 'descended to earth and was made a sharer (*particeps*) in our nature, and granted to us a share (*participium*) in his grace, so that, as the apostle says, "he might be the first-born of many brothers" (Rom. 8:29)'.[230]

This emphasis on human dignity in virtue of our creation in the image of God and our participation in the divine nature is thoroughly patristic; and Bede's sermons quote frequently from the works of St Augustine and St Leo, among others.[231] We are sharers in the divine life in virtue of our creation in the image of God; and that longing for an ever deeper participation in the nature and holiness of God will, if we yield ourselves to it, lead us to heaven.

The theology and practice of prayer

And the primary means by which we yield to the desire for God which burns within us, rather than to the perilous promptings of the flesh, is the life of prayer. Bede is entirely within the western monastic tradition in seeing prayer not as an occasional exercise but as an entire manner of life, enjoined upon all Christians by St Paul's command to 'pray without ceasing'.[232] In his commentary on the First Book of Samuel, he declares that all the actions of the just person who lives according to the will of God are to be regarded as prayers.[233] In the *De templo*, he describes prayer as 'all the things by which we are united to our Maker through interior compunction';[234] and in his commentary on St Mark, he writes:

> Prayer as a whole consists not only in the words by which we invoke the divine mercy, but also in all the things which we do in the service of our Maker by the devotion of faith . . . For how could anyone invoke the Lord with words in every hour and moment without a break? But we pray

without ceasing when we perform only those works which commend us by
our godliness to our Maker.[235]

In one of his sermons, Bede goes further: he tells his readers that

> the prayers of the saints are like the savour of incense, because whatever
> good people who are wholeheartedly devoted to God do or say certainly
> fulfils the duty of prayer for them, when it directs the devotion of their
> minds to the things of God.[236]

Something of this concern to integrate the practice of prayer into a coherent
manner of life is reflected in what Bede has to say about petitionary prayer. In an East-
ertide sermon, Bede tells his brethren that to make our requests to God in words is not
enough: we must seek to live in such a way that we are worthy of obtaining what we
ask for.[237] But he goes on to say that not all who appear to pray are regarded by God as
doing so: 'they indeed invoke the Lord in truth who do not contradict in their lives
what they say in their prayers'.[238] To pray is to seek God's will for us: if we do that, we
may be sure we are being listened to, even if we do not receive what we asked for.[239]

For Bede prayer is 'a sweet colloquy with the Lord',[240] a firm protection against the
most insidious of sins,[241] and the surest means to perfection for practitioners of both
active and contemplative lives.[242] Yet the very breadth and depth of his theology of
prayer, the way in which he conceives of it as an entire manner of life, leads
inescapably to the conclusion that only those willing to withdraw from the world can
fully make it their own. In some imaginative exegesis of an obscure Old Testament
text, this is what Bede writes about the contemplative life:

> The poles with the ark are concealed in the sanctuary because now are also
> hidden the perfect and those who are elect and who preceded us from the
> world into a hidden place before the face of God far from the confusion of
> humanity; but the tops of the poles are sometimes seen in the open sanctu-
> ary by those who draw near, since he grants to the perfect and to those who
> singlemindedly purify the eye of their hearts something of the ultimate joy
> of the heavenly citizenry for them to contemplate; and this contemplation
> is certainly granted least to those who have withdrawn for the least time,
> because the more they remain with a wandering mind on the outside, the
> less they see the joys which are within.[243]

And, in a marvellous but severely ascetic reading of the Song of Songs:

> And beautifully it is said that he does not remain in these hills, but leaps
> upon them, or leaps over them, because the sweetness of interior contem-
> plation, being something high above us because it apprehends heavenly
> things, is only brief and rare, because of the heaviness of carnal minds still
> oppressed by the things that detain them.[244]

Elsewhere the point is made more explicitly. Citing St Paul's exhortation to married
couples to desist occasionally from conjugal intimacy in order to have leisure for
prayer, Bede comments:

> He [St Paul] mentions . . . that prayers are hindered by the conjugal duty, because as often as I perform what is due my wife I am not able to pray. But if according to another statement of the apostle we must pray without ceasing, I must therefore never gratify my conjugal duty, lest I be hindered at any hour from prayer, in which I am ordered always to persevere.[245]

Conclusion

It will by now be clear that Bede's writing on the spiritual life is founded upon a strong ecclesiology: in a Lent sermon, he offers a rich exegesis of the Old Testament temple in which the lower part of the temple represents the present life of Christians, the upper house represents heaven, and the gate in the middle the means of access from the former to the latter.[246] The interpenetration of the earthly by the heavenly, of the lay by the monastic, of the individual by the corporate, is one of his most distinctive emphases; and the consistent emphasis on love of neighbour which derives from that one of his most attractive ones. Eschatology and ecclesiology together inform his spirituality: we pray for the departed, and our prayer can be powerfully effective – but no more so than their prayer for us.

Bede wrote for monks: the fact that he wrote in Latin in itself rendered his work inaccessible to the vast majority of contemporaries who lived outside the cloister, and doubtless to a substantial number inside too. But he deserves a far wider audience, for the ascetic, monastic and (in the strict sense) otherworldly perspective which colours everything he wrote did not prevent him from bequeathing to subsequent generations a spirituality that is full of what the patristic writers he loved called *philosophia* – wisdom that is not simply understood, but *lived*:

> So by means of the very frequency of his physical appearances [after his res-urrection], the Lord wanted to reveal that in each place he is present by divine providence to the desires of good people. He appeared at the tomb to those weeping: he will also be present to us, who are profitably sorrowful when we call to mind his absence. He went to meet those returning from the tomb so that they might preach the joy they felt at the resurrection; he will also be with us when we rejoice faithfully to announce to our neighbours the good things we know ourselves. He appeared at the breaking of the bread to those who had invited him in as a guest, assuming he was a traveller; he will also come to us when we willingly dispense whatever good things we can to travellers and to the poor. He will be with us too at the breaking of the bread when we take the sacraments of his body, that is of the living bread, with a pure and untroubled conscience. He appeared in disguise to those who were discussing his resurrection: he is also present now to us, by the gift of himself, when we do the same; and he will always be present to us when we come together from external activities to spend time speaking of his grace . . . And may it be that, through the bestowal of his grace, he who remains with us until the end of this life may raise us after this life to see the rewards of heavenly life with him, in which he lives and reigns as God, with the Father, in the unity of the Holy Spirit, for all eternity. Amen.[247]

The Theology of Spiritual Formation: Alcuin (732–804)

Introduction

The eighth century saw an England divided into a number of small kingdoms, whose Christian allegiance was insecure but growing. For the rulers of these kingdoms, that allegiance provided a single and unifying ideology which had the obvious advantage of helping them to maintain or increase their control. For them as well as for their subjects, however, it also had another advantage, though one which on occasions was to prove a two-edged sword: it kept them in contact with the European mainland.

Perhaps the most striking example of the symbiotic relationship with Europe that existed in the eighth century is provided by the life and work of Alcuin, a native of Northumbria and student of the cathedral school at York (of which he later became master): when he met Charlemagne during a visit to Italy in 781, he accepted the Frankish king's invitation to become a member of his court, and spent most of the rest of his life there.[248] He was a deacon but never became a priest, or a monk, which alone makes him exceptional among contemporary writers on the spiritual life. What makes him even more exceptional is the combination of an English intellectual formation with long years of teaching at the court of a king who in 800 had himself crowned as Emperor of the West at Rome. As well as being a teacher, Alcuin was a scholar, a liturgical expert, and a considerable theologian: Charlemagne's biographer Einhard describes him as as 'a man universal in learning' with, it seems, a particular interest in astronomy and arithmetic.[249]

Alcuin as spiritual guide

Alcuin was also, however, a spiritual guide and writer of great wisdom and renown: as a scholar, he played a major part in the transmission of devotional material between England and the continent,[250] was the first person to comment on the seven penitential psalms as a group, and may well have been the first to commend their regular use.[251] One of his last works of spiritual guidance was a *manualis libellus* written for the young men who shared his resident community at the Carolingian court: this includes a short exposition of a number of the psalms, together with guidance on confession for young people.[252] Throughout his life, however, he took a personal interest in fostering individual piety; and a considerable number of his letters survive,[253] most of which date from the last years of his life.[254] These are a delight: they abound with expressions of warm friendship, pastoral guidance and humorous detail.[255]

Many of the letters contain themes which we have seen to be common threads in Anglo-Saxon spirituality, though here as elsewhere Alcuin speaks with a distinctive voice. Thus he often writes about the imminence of death and the hope of heaven, telling one correspondent to imitate 'our fathers in the Lord' so as to be sure of attaining Paradise,[256] and another that

> the nearer the time of our reward, the more careful should we be that he
> who is first to go leaves a friend in the world [to pray for him].[257]

He prays that the life of one ex-pupil, now an archbishop, will be prolonged, and admits that he is not looking forward to his own death; but he tells his addressee that even if he lives to be fifty, he cannot count on doing so. So 'let your bodily weakness make your spirit strong . . . Your alms should be of two kinds, in saving souls and in meeting the bodily needs of the poor.'[258] In a letter written to Charlemagne to console him on the loss of some friends who have died, Alcuin writes:

> For a good man the day he dies is happier than the day he is born, for it is the start of peace, as the latter is of pain. We are born to die; we die to live better. This life is a road to our own country.[259]

The hope of heaven is accompanied by a strong emphasis on the communion of saints and on the power of intercessory prayer, both of the living for the departed and vice versa, as well as of the living for the living:[260] here as in many other respects Alcuin follows the classical monastic tradition, gently but firmly encouraging people 'in the world' to make their own the great monastic virtues, notably those of humility and patience.[261] Alcuin also warns against excessive love of worldly things and commends virginity as a sure route to heaven.[262] But he also follows Bede, whom he greatly admired and studied, in refusing to condemn – indeed, in encouraging – secular learning as a step on the way to 'the high peak of gospel perfection'.[263]

The life of the world to come

Like Bede, Alcuin was heir to the riches of the western patristic tradition, and in particular to the work of St Augustine of Hippo; and the spirituality of Augustine underlies all that he wrote on the spiritual life.[264] Thus he celebrates the beauty of this world as in effect a stepping-stone to the beauty of heaven – here the Augustinian tradition of the Roman West parts company with that of the Anglo-Saxons, for whom the created order was more to be feared than praised. Writing to Bishop Æthelbert of Hexham and his community, Alcuin says:

> Most noble sons of holy fathers, who have succeeded to their honour and venerable life and live in the beautiful place where they lived, follow in their footsteps, that from this beautiful place you may by the grace of God come to share in the eternal joy of those who fathered you for the beauty of the kingdom of heaven.[265]

Alcuin and lay spiritual formation

The influence of Augustine is also to be found in Alcuin's concern for lay spirituality, though here in particular Alcuin speaks with a voice of his own. To some extent, as we have seen, this is a matter of exhorting lay people to embrace the standard monastic virtues as far as they could. Alcuin hopes that lay people as well as clergy will 'learn the gospel',[266] and follows Bede in seeking to provide suitable adaptations of monastic offices for the use of busy lay people.[267] He also tells one Nathanael to 'take no interest in dancing-bears, but in psalm-singing clergy'.[268] But in one letter Alcuin goes further, telling Count Wido:

> Do not be worried about being a layman living in the world, as if you could not enter the gates of heaven in that condition . . . The kingdom of heaven is open to every sex, age and person equally according to his

deserts. There is no distinction there as to who was lay or clergy, rich or poor, young or old, slave or master in the world, but each will be crowned with eternal glory according to his good works.[269]

Alcuin also wrote for Wido the *Liber de virtutibus et vitiis*, which is in effect a practical guide for living the Christian life.[270] This is not to suggest that Alcuin is seeking to create a distinctively lay spirituality: such a thing would probably never have occurred to him. But, both in his writings and in his day-to-day dealings with others, he does reflect a concern to give as much attention to the spiritual formation of lay people as to those living in religious houses. This is simply the pastoral and practical outworking of the theological principles that underlay everything Alcuin wrote on the spiritual life.

Conclusion

Alcuin made very much his own the fundamental Augustinian conviction that all human beings were created in the image of God, telling one lay woman to 'keep the nobility of [God's] image in her', and not to glory in earthly nobility.[271] For Alcuin, as for Augustine, this image is dynamic, not static: it is the source within each of us of an infinite desire, which God alone can satisfy, and which grows stronger the more we respond to it.[272] Alcuin seems, however, to have gone beyond Augustine in arguing that conscious human effort can assist us in attaining to that likeness to God which is the fulfilment of the potential represented by the divine image within us.[273] Indeed Alcuin may be said to have bequeathed to those who followed him a refined Augustinian spirituality free from the dark pessimism of Augustine's own later writing, and combining a sharp awareness of sin with a healthy optimism about the human potential for co-operating with the divine grace in the work of salvation and holiness. The fact that this in turn is combined with both scholarly rigour and pastoral warmth makes him one of the most attractive figures in the English spiritual tradition, and one who deserves to be much better known.

Spirituality in the Tenth and Early Eleventh Centuries: Ælfric, Dunstan, and the Monastic Reform Movement

Introduction

The first half of the tenth century saw a steady consolidation of Alfred's political and cultural achievements.[274] Under Edward the Elder (899–924) and Æthelstan (924–39), royal control extended to nearly the whole of England, especially after the Northumbrians rejected the suzerainty of the Norwegian king Eric Bloodaxe. A number of Æthelstan's relations were married to continental rulers, bringing England into much closer contact with Europe, and thus putting the English church in touch with contemporary monastic and liturgical reforms, particularly with the ninth-century reforms associated with Benedict of Aniane.[275]

The spirituality of the monastic reform movement

These reforms, which involved a return to the strict and uniform observance of the Rule of St Benedict, were supported as enthusiastically by English kings as by continental ones, and for good reason: the development of an integrated network of powerful monastic houses, each enjoying royal patronage, clearly assisted in maintaining royal control, and perhaps in ensuring divine protection against the threat of further Scandinavian invasions.[276] In England the culmination of this process was reached with the *Regularis concordia*, probably compiled by St Æthelwold and promulgated c. 970 with the authority of Edgar: this is in effect a supplement to the Rule of St Benedict; and it emphasizes the bond between monasticism and the state, and the royal protection enjoyed by monks and nuns.[277]

The monastic reforms of the tenth century were, then, closely linked with the endeavours of the monarchy, and this in turn affected the tone of tenth-century monastic spirituality: the monks were there to pray for everyone, but perhaps especially for the rich and powerful, and vicariously to do penance for their sins.[278] Evidence for this can be found in contemporary art: the depiction of St Benedict with a diadem in a mid-eleventh-century copy of the *Regularis concordia* suggests that monks were encouraged to aspire to wear the royal diadem of Christ just as Benedict did. In short, abbot and king came to mirror each other's roles and attributes, each in turn participating in the kingship of Christ.[279] And the remarkable flowering of devotion to the Virgin Mary associated with the monastic reform movement provides further evidence of this: the earliest surviving depiction of the Coronation of the Virgin appears as a miniature in the Benedictional of St Æthelwold; and this emphasis on Mary's royalty may well be linked with the importance of the queen in contemporary Anglo-Saxon England.[280]

The principal figures of the monastic reform movement wrote little of their own that has survived, though their influence on English spiritual and religious life must have been considerable. St Dunstan (909–88), successively Abbot of Glastonbury and Archbishop of Canterbury, is described in his late-tenth-century *vita* as someone who spent as much time as he could in psalmody, vigils and prayer;[281] and while at Glastonbury he taught his monks that 'one should pass the troublesome pathways of this life to the eternal delights of the celestial banquets'.[282] Much of this is hagiographical commonplace, however; and it is difficult to discern the man beneath the stereotype, though his biographer describes him as skilled at handwriting, painting and at playing the harp.

It is similarly difficult to assess accurately the nature of Dunstan's personal contribution to the monastic reform, especially as the extent to which the monasteries had been affected by the Scandinavian invasions, whilst unquestionably considerable, is much disputed.[283] St Æthelwold (908–84) became Bishop of Winchester (963–84) and a formidable supporter of the reform movement, as did St Oswald (d.992), Bishop of Worcester and later Archbishop of York, who like the other two was in regular contact with some of the centres of monastic reform on the continent, such as Fleury and Ghent (Oswald was for a time a monk at the former house).[284]

The piety of noble women

A fascinating insight into the piety of aristocratic women in tenth-century Anglo-Saxon England is provided by the discovery of the will of a wealthy widow, Æthelgifu, which dates from c.980.[285] In the midst of various provisions, she stipulates that

Mann [my] goldsmith is to be freed and his eldest son and the youngest and his wife, and the wife of Wulfric the huntsman and their children, and Ælfwaru their daughter on condition that [each] sing four psalters every week [for the first month after my death] and [one] psalter every week [for the next] twelve months.[286]

This provision, clearly implying that these (hitherto unfree) women were literate, suggests that Æthelgifu had followed a practice that was common among widows at that time, of living a religious life at home, in company with some other women attached to her household, some at least of whom will have taken a vow not to marry or remarry. In the case of a wealthy widow who would make a desirable partner for some aspiring nobleman, this would make much sense; and the practice was encouraged by the church.[287]

St Ælfric (955–1020): the spirituality of the cross

If the greatest figures of the monastic reform movement left relatively little direct evidence of its spirituality, others fortunately supplied the lack. Of these the most substantial is perhaps St Ælfric, a pupil of St Æthelwold and later Abbot of Evesham, who lived long enough to experience the resumption of Viking raids during the reign of Æthelred 'the Unready' (978–1016), an experience which may have sharpened the apocalyptic tone of his writings.[288] The two series of homilies by him which have survived reflect his concern to improve the general level of religious education and spiritual life among clergy and people:[289] they were written in a simple English style.[290] They also reflect many of the primary themes of the monastic reform movement: a high doctrine of the church, and a lofty conception of the king's role, together with a pervasive concern to improve the standards of morality among lay Christians.

Ælfric's influence on English spirituality can be seen in several areas. First, he maintained and developed the strongly apocalyptic tone already found in most earlier writers. Gatch has pointed out that his sermons contain three kinds of eschatological visions: those concerned with individual judgement, designed to exhort people to penance and amendment of life; those providing doctrinal instruction about the nature of life after death; and those designed to show the efficacy of intercession.[291] In one of his sermons, Ælfric says that in heaven our friends await our arrival and are anxious for our safety: they pray for us against the machinations of the devil. The fire of purgatory – Ælfric's belief in this state is noteworthy[292] – punishes those sins which can be atoned for; but its duration can be reduced by the intercession both of those in heaven and of those on earth – of the latter, the prayers of those in orders are especially powerful. The sermon ends with a long section vividly describing the Day of Judgement, when all will be equal, irrespective of rank or class.[293]

The second area of significance in the spirituality of Ælfric is his attitude to the suffering Christ. The Anglo-Saxon emphasis on the triumphant *Christus victor* remains central for him, though Ælfric stresses the Christ of the Last Judgement as much as the victor over death and hell: a large line-drawing of Christ as *iustus iudex* and *rex regum*, probably the work of a monk of Canterbury, forms the frontispiece to an eleventh-century manuscript of his sermons.[294] He enlarges this perspective still further by stressing the part human beings have to play in the drama of redemption, particularly in their devotion to the crucifix: the work of Christ on the cross is an act of love as well as of power, and demands our love and gratitude in response.[295]

Devotion based on the cross and passion of Christ grew steadily during the tenth and eleventh centuries; and many of the prayers on the passion from ninth-century texts such as the Books of Nunnaminster and Cerne were adapted for use in the Good Friday ceremonies of the *Regularis concordia*.[296] But the new and wider perspective associated with Ælfric and others, in which the suffering Christ and the Christ of judgement become as significant as the victorious Christ, represents a significant development, and anticipates the writings of eleventh-century figures such as St Anselm. This development, then, was in effect in two directions – inwardly, as writers stressed the importance of our response to Christ's supreme act of suffering love; and outwardly, as they came increasingly to link the cross with the final judgement, Good Friday with Doomsday.[297]

It is, perhaps, the latter direction that predominates: tenth-century writings still often appear to conceive of Christ as a somewhat distant, glorious but remote figure.[298] Thus one of the tenth-century Blickling Homilies, for Easter Day, shows much more interest in the passion of Christ, the descent into hell, and Doomsday, than in the resurrection.[299] Devotion to the cross remains above all else a means of *protection* from evil, and an assurance of salvation, rather than a means of interior spiritual growth. Thus, the writer of another of the Blickling Homilies declares that all Christians are

> to bless their entire bodies seven times with the sign of Christ's Cross. First in the early morning, the second time at underntide [nine o'clock], the third time at midday, the fourth time at the hour of none [three o'clock], the fifth time in the evening, the sixth time at night, ere he go to rest, the seventh time at dawn.

It is essential that all God's people are taught to do this, 'because God's people ought to know how to shield themselves from devils'.[300]

Finally, both Ælfric and other contemporary writers show great interest in spiritual and pastoral guidance: their eschatology and Christology are designed to change people's lives, not simply instruct them in the faith. It is true that Ælfric, like his near-contemporary St Wulfstan (1009–95), is constantly concerned about the perils of pagan beliefs and customs, reflecting the fact that England was far from fully christianized even in the tenth century.[301] Indeed in one sermon in which he warns against the dangers of diabolical charms Ælfric gives us a glimpse of contemporary superstitious practices:

> Some foolish men . . . say, that there are some kinds of animals which one should not bless; and say that they decline by blessing, and by cursing thrive.[302]

But in general Ælfric shows much more interest in encouraging his hearers to develop a pattern of spiritual life and discipline firmly within the penumbra of the church's teaching and sacraments, and inspired by biblical *exempla*. In a sermon for the third

Sunday after the Epiphany he says that, just as under the 'old law' a leper had to show himself to the priest both when he found himself to be infected and when he was cleansed, those suffering from an interior leprosy (as a result of their sins) should 'go to God's priest, and open his secret to the ghostly leech, and, by his counsel and aid, heal by penance the wounds of his soul'.[303] The writer of one of the Blickling Homilies declares that:

> The priest that is very tardy in driving out the devil from a man, and in speedily ridding the soul with oil and water from the adversary, shall be assigned to the fiery river and the iron hook.[304]

Furthermore, many tenth-century texts encourage regular celebrations of the Eucharist: another of the Blickling Homilies declares that bishops and priests must 'minister daily to God's people', and at least once a week say mass for all Christians who have ever lived; 'and it is God's will that they should intercede for them', while those in heaven in their turn intercede for them.[305] We can see here signs of a more developed institutional spirituality, reflecting in turn the growth of a rudimentary parish system providing catechesis and pastoral care.[306]

Private prayer in the tenth and eleventh centuries

What was the fabric of a person's prayer in the late tenth and early eleventh century? In the case of the monk or nun it was centred on recitation of the psalter;[307] and St Wulfstan of Worcester, like Alcuin before him, expected lay people to recite the canonical offices as far as they were able:[308] most, not being literate, will have had to learn scriptural texts by heart, allowing them to ruminate upon them so that the word of God both informed and collided with everyday experience. But even the prayers of religious were not confined to the psalter; and we may suppose the same to be true of lay people, even though little evidence in this respect regarding them survives. What evidence there is suggests a concern to hold together the spiritual and the secular, the individual and the corporate. There is evidence of the existence of eleventh-century gilds: associations of lay people, often linked with a cathedral or minster church, whose purposes would include paying not only for mass-priests to pray for the souls of the dead but also for hearty communal feasts whose origins probably lie in earlier pagan customs.[309]

An early eleventh-century prayer-book, probably (though not certainly) compiled by a monk and later used by a nun, gives us some further clues about the spiritual concerns of the day.[310] Many of the prayers invoke the prayers of the saints and angels, and in a more sophisticated manner than earlier examples: individual saints are associated with particular virtues.[311] Others reflect the growing emphasis on personal and interior sinfulness, together with a characteristically Gregorian stress on *compunctio cordis*.[312] One prayer contains what may at first sight appear a series of moralizing platitudes:

> Drive away from me, O Lord, greed and give me the virtue of abstinence; make the spirit of fornication flee from me, and give me the ardour of chastity; extinguish in me cupidity, and give me voluntary poverty; con-

strain my anger, and kindle in me a genuine sweetness and love for God and neighbour; cut off from me, O Lord, worldly melancholy, and increase in me spiritual joy; rid me of boastfulness and bestow compunction of heart upon me; lessen my pride, and perfect in me true humility.[313]

In fact it is a careful and precisely constructed set of antitheses, more apparent in the original Latin than in English: the writer prays that a series of vices may be driven out (note that a different verb is associated with each: *repelle, fuga, extingue, coibe, abscide, expelle, minue*), and replaced with its matching virtue: greed with abstinence, fornication with chastity, cupidity with a freely-chosen poverty, and so on. This is a sophisticated prayer of unmistakably patristic style. What is striking about this collection is that prayers such as these sit next to Irish-style prayers of colourful prolixity (such as the prayer of confession in which the writer lists each part of the body and itemizes its sin in turn[314]), and simple but practical prayers (such as the prayer for curing foot ailments[315]), and even Old English medical recipes for restoring the body to health through prayer.[316]

CONCLUSION: WISDOM FOR THE JOURNEY

It is perhaps here, in an obscure eleventh-century prayer-book, that the essential genius of Anglo-Saxon spirituality is most apparent – its vigorous eclecticism.[317] The spiritual journey, in the perspective of a wide range of writers from the author of 'The seafarer' to the homilies of Ælfric, is at once hazardous and unavoidable; and the traveller must expect to be beset by as many adversities as a Boniface in Germany, or a Benedict Biscop en route to Rome. So it is not surprising if those who counselled all who were to embark on the journey drew upon as many sources of guidance and sustenance as were available to them. At its best Anglo-Saxon spirituality blends vernacular imagery and patristic sophistication, Irish exuberance and Roman sobriety, hero and holy man, with extraordinary success; and both its grandest monuments, like the Ruthwell cross or the sermons of Bede, and its more intimate manifestations reflect this adventurous capacity for adapting themes from very diverse backgrounds in the interests of offering guidance for the human journey. The journey itself, however, remained mysterious, not easily charted, irreducibly strange – which is perhaps why, in the end, it is poets like the author of 'The seafarer' who capture its character and rhythm best. An anonymous tenth-century poet may illustrate the point:

> Grief is remarkably hard to shake off. The clouds roll on . . . A hawk must go on a glove, the wild thing stay there. The wolf must be in the forest, wretched and solitary, the boar in the wood with his strong, fixed tusks. A good man must gain honour in his own country. The javelin goes in the hand, the spear that glitters with gold. On a ring a jewel should stand large and prominent. A river must mix in the waves with the sea's current. A ship must have a mast, a standing spar for sails. The splendid iron sword must lie in the lap. A dragon must live in a barrow, old and proud of his treasures. A fish must spawn its kind in the water. In the hall a king must share

out rings. A bear must live on the heath, old and terrifying. A river must run downhill in a grey torrent. The army must keep together, a band of men set on glory. A warrior must show loyalty, a man must have wisdom. On the earth a wood must bear blossoms and fruit. On the land a hill must stand out green. God's place is in heaven, he is the judge of deeds. A hall must have a door, the building's broad mouth. A shield must have a boss, a firm finger-guard. A bird must play, up in the air. In a deep pool the salmon must glide with the trout. Stirred by the wind the shower shall come down to this world from the sky.[318]

NOTES

1. 'The seafarer', ll.1–38; Hamer (1970) pp. 187–9.
2. ll. 62–6.
3. ll. 72ff and 97ff.
4. ll. 105–6.
5. ll. 117–end.
6. For bibliography on the poem, see Anne L. Klinck's article in Lapidge et al. (1999) p. 413. For the identity of the poet, see Whitelock (1950) pp. 259–72; Pope (1974) p. 75; and Bradley (1982) p. 87.
7. Dodwell (1982) p. 25.
8. Hence the references to hail, icicles, &c.: see Owen (1981) pp. 56 and 139–40. Virgil was nonetheless probably the most influential pagan poet in Anglo-Saxon England.
9. See Dodwell (1982) p. 26. This is not, of course, a uniquely Anglo-Saxon view. Biblical writers conceived of the sea as primal, unformed chaos: see, e.g., Genesis 1; Jonah 1–2; W. H. Propp, article 'Water' in B. M. Metzger and M. D. Coogan (eds.), *The Oxford companion to the Bible* (Oxford UP, 1993), pp. 792–3.
10. ll. 53ff and 62ff. See also D. Pearsall and E. Salter, *Landscapes and seasons of the medieval world* (London: Paul Elek, 1973), and Fichtenau (1991) pp. 317–24.
11. See, e.g., the poem 'The Phoenix', an eighth-century reworking of a fourth-century Latin original attributed to Lactantius (trans. S. A. J. Bradley (1982), pp. 286ff); and 'Genesis', another Old English poem in which the writer compares Eden before the Fall ('Nor as yet did dark clouds carry with the wind rainstorms across the spacious plain, but the ground stood covered with crops') with what Adam predicts will happen after their sin ('Dark cloud will loom up, a hailstorm will come pelting from the sky and frost will set in along with it, which will be wickedly cold' (Bradley, pp. 18 and 34)).
12. Tacitus, *Agricola* 11 (and see the Latin ed. cit., p. 177). For the influence of pre-Roman iconography on Roman Britain, see M. J. Green, 'God in man's image: thoughts on the genesis and affiliations of some Romano-British Cult-imagery', in *Britannia* 29 (1998), pp. 17–30.
13. See Cunliffe (1998). The client-king was Tiberius Claudius Togidubnus (or Cogidubnus), whom Tacitus describes as 'a prince who within our own memory continued in perfect fidelity [to Rome]' (*Agricola* 14).
14. Cunliffe (1998) pp. 84 and 107.
15. See Cunliffe (1998) pp. 113–14; Salway (1981) chapter 21 (esp. p. 709); and Thomas (1986) pp. 26–8 (on Roman piety).
16. Tertullian, *Adversus Iudaeos* ('An Answer to the Jews'), 7.
17. The Council of Arles in 314 was attended by three British bishops (of York, London, and somewhere else; Collingwood and Myres (1937) p. 271). Collingwood and Myres argue that

in early centuries it was strongest among the poor, though gradually it worked its way up the social scale (pp. 272–3). By the end of the fourth century it remained a minority faith (p. 273). Christianity's universal offer of salvation, and assurance of a recent founder who was God's son and had overcome death, may well have been crucial ingredients in its appeal (Thomas (1981) pp. 33–4). See also Thomas (1986) pp. 52–7.

18. See Blair (1963) p.129; J. Newman, *West Kent and the Weald* (The buildings of England) (Harmondsworth: Penguin, 1969), p. 374.

19. Gildas, *De excidio Britonum* 25, ET by M. Winterbottom, ed. cit., pp. 27–8; the quotation is from Psalm 44.11. Gildas is a notably unreliable historian; and it is likely that the early Anglo-Saxon invasions of Britain represented, not massive influxes of Germanic peoples, but the appearance of powerful settlers from northern Germany (and perhaps Scandinavia) whose own culture and practices are archaeologically apparent, alongside those of the indigenous peoples, from the fifth century onwards. See James (1999) pp. 109–13.

20. Sims-Williams (1990) p. 62 and n. 34.

21. Bede, *Hist. eccles.* V.22.

22. Chadwick (1961) pp. 64–5; Thomas (1986) pp. 128–35.

23. Chadwick (1961) pp. 90–118. The term 'Celtic' has been largely avoided in this book, partly because it was not used before the sixteenth century and not in common use until well into the eighteenth, but primarily because there remains serious doubt about whether there ever was an invasion of Britain by 'Celtic' people from the continent, and therefore about whether the term has any use in denoting the pre-Roman inhabitants of Ireland and Britain. See esp. James (1999).

24. See G. S. M. Walker, introduction to the works of St Columbanus (*Sancti Columbani opera*) (Dublin: Scriptores Latini Hiberniae II), p. xvi; and Chadwick (1961), esp. chapter 2.

25. See K. Hughes, 'The changing theory and practice of Irish pilgrimage', in *Journal of Ecclesiastical History* 11 (1960), pp. 143–51; Chadwick (1961) pp. 79–84; Tomás Ó Fiaich, 'Irish monks on the continent', in Mackey (1989) pp. 101–39.

26. See O'Dwyer, 'Celtic monks and the Culdee Reform', in Mackey (1989) pp. 140–71. O'Dwyer (p. 152) points out the popularity of the Benedicite in Irish monasticism.

27. See M. McNamara, 'Celtic scriptures: text and commentaries', in Mackey (1989) pp. 414–40; 'The Psalter in early Irish monastic spirituality', in *Monastic Studies* 14 (1983), pp. 179–206; and 'Psalter text and Psalter study in the early Irish Church (AD 600–1200)', in *Proceedings of the Royal Irish Academy* 73C (1973), pp. 201–98.

28. See Ward (1999) pp. 16–22.

29. See Sims-Williams (1990) pp. 109–10 and 273.

30. For this see Owen (1981).

31. Grattan and Singer (1952). See also the leechbook preserved in the British Library (MS Harley 585), which combines Graeco-Roman herb recipes and charms with others from pagan Teutonic lore: the anthology also includes both the 'Lay of the Nine Twigs of Woden', describing how diseases first arose in the world, and the Christian 'Lorica of Gildas', invoking the protection of God and the saints for each part of the supplicant's body (Backhouse, Turner and Webster (1984) no. 163). Sims-Williams (1990, p. 54) cites an eighth-century English prayer for protection which concludes 'I adjure thee, Satan, devil, elf, by the living and True God, and by the terrible Day of Judgment, that it may flee from the man who goes about with this writing with him, in the name of the Father, Son and Holy Ghost.' Laurence Cameron warns of any easy assumption that such prayers and charms imply any deliberate recourse to superstition or magic in the practice of medicine (see his article 'Medical literature and medicine' in Lapidge et al. (1999) pp. 304–5). See also the leechbook quoted in Jolly (1996) p. 149.

32. See Owen (1981) for a discussion of this subject.

33. Dodwell (1982) pp. 27–34. See also Backhouse, Turner and Webster (1984) and (on Anglo-Saxon love of light) Raw (1997) p. 71. It is interesting to note the (very rare) description, in a seventh-century commentary on the Pentateuch produced at the school of Theodore of

Tarsus at Canterbury, of the creation by God (in Genesis 1.3) of a primeval light which in turn gave rise to the light of sun, moon and stars (see the text in Bischoff and Lapidge (1994), p. 305 n. 23, and their remarks on pp. 434–6 and 498; cf. also pp. 387 and 498).

34. See Webster and Backhouse (1991) pp. 22 and 59f.

35. For seventh- and eighth-century English monasteries, see Sims-Williams (1990) pp. 115–43. He points out (p. 170) that there was a blurred dividing line, during much of this period, between the monastic community with its abbot and the parochial 'minster church' devoted to pastoral work.

36. For the saints and angels as exemplars of monastic spirituality, see Henderson (1999) pp. 136–76.

37. Bede, *Hist. eccles.* III.3, pp. 218–19. All references to this are to the edition ed. and trans. by B. Colgrave and R. A. B. Mynors (Oxford UP, 1969).

38. Bede, *Hist. eccles.* III.5, pp. 226–7. The psalms remained one of the bedrocks of Anglo-Saxon spirituality throughout this period: see, e.g., Raw (1997) p. 170; Ward (1999) pp. 34–9.

39. Bede's only complaint about Aidan was that, like all the early Irish monks, he observed Easter on the wrong (i.e. the non-Roman) date (*Hist. eccles.* III.17). In every other respect he commends him. For a fuller assessment of Aidan, see Mayr-Harting (1972) pp. 94–9.

40. See the comments of C. H. Talbot in the introduction to his edition and translation of the *Life of St Leoba* (see following note): 'Never, perhaps, has there been an age in which religious women exercised such great power' (pp. xii–xiii). See also Sims-Williams (1990) pp. 118–20.

41. The principal source of information about Leoba is her Life (the *Vita S.Leobae,* hereafter referred to as VSL), written by Rudolf, a monk of Fulda, c.836 (for details see the Bibliography to this chapter). Talbot describes Rudolf as 'probably the most learned man of his age' (1954, p. 204); though see also the remarks of Brunhölzl on the *Vita* (1991, p. 101). One of Leoba's own letters is preserved, written to St Boniface (no. 29 in the Tangl edition, 17 in the Emerton translation). See also E. McLaughlin, 'Women, power and the pursuit of holiness', in R. Ruether and E. McLaughlin (eds.), *Women of spirit: female leadership in the Jewish and Christian traditions* (New York: Simon & Schuster, 1979), pp. 99–130, esp. pp. 103–8; and Leyser (1995) pp. 28–32.

42. VSL p. 215.

43. VSL p. 215. It may be worth noting at this point that contemporaries attached great importance to the physical aspects of prayer, such as posture: thus the seventh-century penitential canons atributed to Archbishop Theodore explicitly state that 'one ought to pray standing, out of reverence for God' (cited in McNeill and Gamer (1990) p. 217).

44. VSL pp. 216–18.

45. VSL pp. 219–20.

46. VSL pp. 220–1.

47. VSL pp. 212–13. For Bede, purple signifies blood ('quia colorem sanguinis ostendit', *De tabernaculo* 2, quoted in Henderson (1999) pp. 126–7).

48. VSL p. 216.

49. On the theme of exile in 'The seafarer', see John C. Pope, 'Second thoughts on the interpretation of The seafarer', in Clemoes et al. (eds.), *Anglo-Saxon England* 3 (Cambridge UP, 1974), pp. 75–86, esp. 77–8.

50. For the theme of exile in Anglo-Saxon poetry, see esp. S. B. Greenfield, *Hero and exile: the art of Old English poetry,* ed. G. H. Brown (London: Hambledon, 1989), esp. 'The formulaic expression of the theme of "exile" in Anglo-Saxon poetry' (pp. 125–32). For Beowulf see the important article by Patrick Wormald, 'Bede, Beowulf, and the conversion of the Anglo-Saxon aristocracy', in Farrell (1978) pp. 32–95. See also George Jack, art. 'Beowulf' and bibliography, in Lapidge et al. (1999) pp. 61–2. The monks who came with Augustine were of course themselves exiles (a point made by Ward (1999) p. 6).

51. See, e.g., Felix's *Life of St Guthlac,* and L. Jordan, 'Demonic elements in Anglo-Saxon iconography', in Szarmach (1986) pp. 283–318.

52. trans. Bradley (1982) pp. 86–105.

53. See Bradley's introduction to the poem, p. 87.

54. *Commentary on the Seven Catholic Epistles*, ET by D. Hurst (1985) p. 89. The same approach is just as prominent at the end of the Anglo-Saxon period, as can be seen in this extract from one of the tenth-century Blickling Homilies (no. 2, for Quinquagesima, ed. Morris (1874–80), p. 22):

> Therefore it is needful for us to perceive the blindness of our pilgrimage; we are in the foreign land of this world – we are exiles in this world, and so have been ever since the progenitor of the human race brake God's behests, and for that sin we have been sent into banishment, and now we must seek hereafter another kingdom, either in misery or in glory, as we may now choose to merit.

55. 'Whatever unruly desires may once have disturbed him have been, not suppressed, but redirected towards the spiritual joys he now intensely craves' (Pope (1974) p. 78).

56. See, e.g., Letter 23 of St Boniface, the eighth-century English missionary to the Germans, in which he writes: 'I mean not merely heaven and earth which we see with our eyes but the whole extent of space which even the heathens can grasp in their imagination' (ET by C. H. Talbot (1954), p. 76). See also the Old English version of the third-century *Vision of St Paul*, with its vivid descriptions of the experiences of both the righteous and the damned after death: A. di Paolo Healey (ed.), *The Old English Vision of St Paul* (Speculum anniversary monographs 2) (Cambridge, Mass.: The Mediaeval Academy of America, 1978).

57. Blickling Homilies, no. 5 (for the Fifth Sunday of Lent), ed. R. Morris (1874–80), p. 64.

58. Will of Æthelflæd, second wife of King Edmund, c.950; ET of text in Whitelock (1930) p. 37.

59. 'Augustinian' in this context refers to St Augustine of Hippo: for his theology of desire, see Isabelle Bochet, *Saint Augustin et le désir de Dieu* (Études Augustiniennes) (Paris, 1982). For that of St Gregory the Great, see Patrick Catry OSB, 'Amour du monde et amour de Dieu', in *Studia Monastica* 15 (1973) pp. 253–75, repr. in Catry, *Parole de Dieu, amour et Esprit-Saint chez saint Grégoire le Grand* (Vie monastique 17) (Bellefontaine: 1984, pp. 61–84); and Jean Leclercq, *The love of learning and the desire for God*, ET by C. Misrahi (London: SPCK, 1978).

60. For the influence of the *De virginitate*, see Lapidge (1993) p. 112. It may well have had a significant influence on contemporary Carolingian spiritual writers such as Angilbert of Saint-Riquier and Paulinus of Aquileia. See Susan A. Rabe, *Faith, art and politics at Saint-Riquier* (Philadelphia: Pennsylvania UP, 1995), pp. 56–7. For Aldhelm's skill (or serious lack of it) as a poet, see Lapidge (1996i) pp. 248–69. For a summary of his life and a recent bibliography, see Lapidge et al. (1999) pp. 25–7.

61. Lapidge and Herren (1979) p. 52; Leyser (1995) pp. 33–4.

62. Lapidge and Herren (1979) p. 56.

63. *De virginitate* XIX, ed. Lapidge and Herren, p. 75. The use of the parable of the sower to emphasize the priority of virginity is common in Anglo-Saxon spirituality: see, e.g., Bede's *History of the abbots of Wearmouth and Jarrow*, chapter 1 (on St Benedict Biscop).

64. *De virginitate* VIII–IX, p. 65.

65. *De virginitate* XIV, p. 71.

66. See J. Leclercq, 'Lettres de vocation à la vie monastique', in *Analecta Monastica* 3 (Studia Anselmiana 37) (Rome, 1955), pp. 169–97.

67. *Enigmata* 100, p. 93.

68. Felix's work is clearly influenced by St Athanasius' *Life of Antony*, and at several points reflects the influence of patristic theology. See Sims-Williams (1990), esp. chapter 9.

69. Felix, *Vita S. Guthlaci*, pp. 86–7.

70. Felix, *Vita S. Guthlaci* ed. and trans. B. Colgrave as *Felix's Life of St Guthlac* (Cambridge UP, 1956), pp. 80–3.

71. For tenth-century attitudes to family and kin in Europe, see Fichtenau (1991) pp. 81–132.

72. 'Beowulf', ll. 1710–25. The most accessible translations are by Michael Alexander, *Beowulf* (Harmondsworth: Penguin Classics, 1973), and by S. A. J. Bradley, *Anglo-Saxon poetry* (Everyman's library) (London: Dent, 1982), pp. 408–94.

73. Wormald, 'Bede, *Beowulf* and the conversion of the Anglo-Saxon aristocracy', in Farrell (1978) p. 67.

74. See Ludwig Bieler, 'Ireland's contribution to Northumbrian culture', in Bonner (1976) pp. 210–28, esp. p. 220.

75. The commentary on the Pentateuch now known to have been produced at Canterbury at the school of Theodore and his colleague abbot Hadrian interprets some Old Testament texts in the light of the crucifixion of Christ (see the text in Bischoff and Lapidge (1994) p. 323 and their comment on pp. 452–3). For Theodore himself, see esp. Lapidge (1995).

76. Michael D. Cherniss ('The cross as Christ's weapon: the influence of heroic literary tradition on *The Dream of the Rood*', in Clemoes et al. (eds.), *Anglo-Saxon England* 2 (Cambridge UP, 1973), pp. 241–52) suggests that the idea of a speaking cross is derived from vernacular sources both Christian and Anglo-Saxon.

77. trans. Hamer, ll. 35–8. For this approach to the redemptive work of Christ, see the Gospel of St John and also Colossians 2.14–15.

78. ll. 51–4. For possible pagan overtones here, see Owen (1981) p. 28.

79. ll. 144–end. The theme of the harrowing of hell was very popular in Anglo-Saxon prose and verse: see, e.g., Bede (*Hist. eccles.* V.12; *Commentary on the First Epistle of St Peter* 3.19–20); Cynewulf and other poets ('Christ and Satan' ll. 366–664; 'Elene' ll. 179–82, 293–7 and 905–13; 'Phoenix' ll. 417–23; 'Guthlac' ll. 1074–7; 'Credo' ll. 25–32; and esp. 'Christ' ll. 558–85). See also The Blickling Homilies, ed. Morris, pp. 85ff; *The Homilies of the Anglo-Saxon Church*, ed. Thorpe, vol. I, pp. 26–8, 94, 108, 216, 218, 228, 248, 460; vol. II, pp. 80, 606–8.

80. For comments on its original location, strategically set at the far west end of Hadrian's Wall, see Farrell and Karkov (1992): they justly describe its present dwelling as 'specially-built, cannily economical and maddeningly inappropriate' (p. 36), since the cross's principal face is partly obscured. The connection between the cross and the poem is uncertain: 'The dream of the Rood' (the title is modern) appears in an Anglo-Saxon manuscript, Codex 107 of the library at Vercelli Cathedral, Italy, which almost certainly dates from the late tenth century, i.e. about three centuries after the cross. See Farrell and Karkov (1992) pp. 46–7; Swanton, introduction to *The dream of the Rood*, pp. 9–37; Meyvaert (1992) pp. 164–5; and O Carragáin, art. 'Ruthwell Cross' with bibliography, in Lapidge et al. (1999) pp. 403–4. A brief summary of the cross's history and description can be found in J. Gifford, *Dumfries and Galloway* (The buildings of Scotland) (Harmondsworth: Penguin, 1996), pp. 505–6.

81. See Cramp (1978) p. 118. The history of the reconstruction of the Ruthwell Cross by the local Presbyterian minister, Henry Duncan, in 1802, makes fascinating reading; but it is important to remember that the damage it has sustained during its long history is considerable, and must make any detailed analysis of its meaning conjectural, notwithstanding the recently scholarly attention it has received: see Farrell (1986) pp. 357–76, esp. pp. 361–5; Cassidy (1992) pp. 3–34; and Farrell (1992), esp. p. 37. For the date of the cross, see Douglas Mac Lean, 'The date of the Ruthwell Cross', in Cassidy (1992) pp. 49–70. Perhaps the single most convincing and comprehensive analysis of the cross's theological programme, taking fully into account the vicissitudes of its history, is that of Meyvaert (1992), though he too acknowledges the provisionality of this or any other interpretation (p. 165).

82. See Mayr-Harting (1972) p. 261.

83. Mayr-Harting (1972) p. 248; Henderson (1999) pp. 203–14 (esp. pp. 209–10). Paul Meyvaert (1992, p. 106; see also pp. 157–8) offers a fascinating alternative location: within the nave of the original church, one side (representing the church) facing towards the congregation, the other (representing the monastic life) towards the sanctuary where the monks themselves worshipped.

84. Cramp (1978) p. 128. The legs of the crucified Christ are strong and forceful, not broken or frail; and Howlett (1992, p. 72) points out that the crucified Christ stands, rather than hangs, on the cross. See also Meyvaert (1992) pp. 106–8.

85. See Cramp (1965). Northumbrian sculptors lavished most of their efforts on crosses of victory, following the example of Constantine's cross recorded in Eusebius, *Hist. eccl.* IX.9

(Cramp, pp. 4–5). Much of the artwork of these crosses suggests Middle Eastern influence, perhaps via Theodore of Tarsus (Archbishop of Canterbury 668–90), who came from Cilicia.

86. Jerome, *The life of Paul the first hermit*, chapter 8. See Haney (1985), esp. p. 219, and the excellent discussion of this panel in Meyvaert (1992) pp. 125–9.

87. Haney (1985); Meyvaert (1992), esp. pp. 125–47.

88. See the fascinating article by É. O Carrágain (1978). For the influence of Rome on the iconography of the Ruthwell Cross, see Ortenberg (1992) pp. 160–1.

89. See O Carrágain (1986), esp. p. 397.

90. For this subject, see Dodwell (1982) and Gameson (1995).

91. Raw (1990) and Henderson (1999, esp. pp. 17–18). Raw also argues (1997, p. 119) that, where pictures of events invite meditation, portrait-images invite contemplation: the former is primarily something we do, the latter primarily the work of God in us.

92. Raw (1990) p. 38. Elaborate and expensive books of illuminated manuscripts such as the (early tenth-century) Harley Psalter, perhaps produced for a bishop, presuppose an intimacy with the text in order for the illuminations to draw the reader into a profounder understanding of the mystery being pondered. See W. Noel, *The Harley Psalter* (Cambridge UP, 1995), esp. pp. 196 and 198–200.

93. Raw (1990) p. 11.

94. Bede, *Hist. abbat.* VI (ed. Plummer), pp. 369–70; Raw (1990) p. 13.

95. Raw (1990) p. 16.

96. See Raw (1990) pp. 141–2. For the Breamore rood, see E. Coatsworth, 'Late pre-Conquest sculptures with the Crucifixion south of the Humber', in Yorke (1988) pp. 161–93, and W. Rodwell and E. C. Rouse, 'The Anglo-Saxon rood and other features in the south porch of St Mary's Church, Breamore, Hampshire', in *Antiquaries Journal* 64 (1984), pp. 298–325.

97. Early Christians also invoked the power of the cross, not least by making the sign of the cross, when praying for protection from the power of evil: there is an interesting example of a third-century prayer of this kind in A. Hammann, *Early Christian prayers* (ET by W. Mitchell; London: Longmans, 1961), p. 333: 'the sign of the passion is of proven efficacy against the Devil, provided that you make it at the prompting of your faith, in the knowledge that it will protect you like a shield.'

98. Gameson (1995: see esp. p. 19) shows how Anglo-Saxon illuminated psalters and other illustrated texts heightened the sense of the spiritual life in this world as a struggle between good and evil, heaven and hell.

99. *De virginitate* XI, p. 68 (in *Aldhelm: the poetic works*).

100. Felix, *Vita S. Guthlaci*, pp. 88–9.

101. Felix, *Vita S. Guthlaci*, pp. 90–1.

102. Felix, pp. 100–3. There is a similar account in Alcuin's *Poem on the Bishops, Kings, and Saints of the Church of York*, in which he describes the anchorite Balthere, on the Bass Rock off the Scottish coast, where he 'vanquished time and again the hosts of the air that waged war upon him in countless shapes' (ll. 1328–9, ed. Godman, pp. 104–5).

103. Felix, pp. 94–7. It is worth noting that the Old English version of the legend of St Margaret goes much further than the Latin versions do in emphasizing the violence of her struggle with demons: see Clayton and Magennis (1994) p. 45.

104. Felix, pp. 120–1; cf. also Bede, *Vita S. Cuthberti* 21.

105. Felix's writing here reflects a remarkable combination of Augustinian anthropology with Anglo-Saxon imagery. See Augustine's Sermons on the Letters of St John (*Tract. in Epist. Ioann.*) 8.7–8, where he distinguishes the three orders of creation – God, human beings, and beasts. Man is to acknowledge what is above him, so that those beneath him may in their turn acknowledge him. If man despises his superior, he becomes subject to his inferior.

106. Felix, pp. 122–3.

107. See Mayr-Harting (1972) p. 257.

108. Mayr-Harting, pp. 260–1.

109. See Frantzen (1983i and 1983ii and his article 'Penitentials', with bibliography, in Lapidge et

al. (1999) pp. 362–3). In the tenth century, as a result of the ecclesiastical reform movement, Anglo-Saxon England inherited the dual system of penance developed by the Carolingians: private penance for private sins, public penance for public offences (Frantzen 1983i, p. 141).

110. Frantzen (1983) pp. 64–5. Bischoff and Lapidge (1994, pp. 150–1) point out that the penitential is a compilation based on Theodore's opinions, not an original work by the archbishop himself. See also the detailed discussion by T. Charles-Edwards ('The Penitential of Theodore and the *Iudicia Theodori*', in Lapidge (1995) pp. 141–74), which sets this penitential in its Irish context. For the influence of Theodore's penitential on the continent, see also Payer (1984) p. 85.

111. Frantzen (1983) p. 67.

112. Frantzen (1983) p. 201.

113. Mayr-Harting, pp. 182–4.

114. Kathleen Hughes, 'Some aspects of Irish influence on early English private prayer', in *Studia Celtica* (1970), pp. 48–61, esp. pp. 55, 59–60. Many of the prayers in the ninth-century compilation known as the *Book of Cerne* are *loricae*: some of them explicitly pray for protection for those parts of the body that are most prone to sin. See Kuypers (1902), Frantzen (1983) p. 80; and Sims-Williams (1990) chapter 10 (esp. pp. 297–8). In the early medieval period the *lorica* denoted a shirt of iron mail worn by ascetics as a sign of their willingness to engage in spiritual combat with the devil and the flesh: thus the twelfth-century recluse St Wulfric of Haselbury is described by his biographer as beginning to wear a *lorica* soon after embracing the solitary life (John of Ford, *Life of Wulfric* chapter 5, ed. cit. in Bibliography to Chapter 3, pp. 18–19). For the most famous of all *loricae*, the 'breastplate' prayer attributed to St Patrick, see N. D. O'Donoghue, 'St Patrick's Breastplate', in Mackey (1989) pp. 45–63.

115. McNeill and Gamer (1938; repr. 1990) p. 208.

116. Cited in Payer (1984) p. 25.

117. McNeill and Gamer (1938; repr. 1990) p. 211.

118. Frantzen (1983) p. 82.

119. Frantzen (1983) p. 205.

120. See Mayr-Harting (1972) pp. 139ff; S. Coates, 'The role of bishops in the early Anglo-Saxon Church: a reassessment', in *History* 81 (1996), pp. 177–96; and Alan Thacker, art. 'St Wilfrid' (with bibliog.) in Lapidge et al. (1999) pp. 474–6. For Eddius' Life (the *Vita S. Wilfridi*), see *The Life of Bishop Wilfrid by Eddius Stephanus*, ed. and trans. B. Colgrave (Cambridge UP, 1982).

121. Eddius, *Vita S. Wilfridi*, chapter 67. It is not surprising to find prayer described by his biographer as an armoury, when members of Wilfrid's community have urgent recourse to it during the saint's grave illness (chapter 62).

122. Bede, *Hist. eccles.* IV.13, pp. 372–5.

123. Bede, *Hist. eccles.* IV.13; Wormald, 'Bede, *Beowulf* and the conversion of the Anglo-Saxon aristocracy', in Farrell (1978) p. 55.

124. Eddius, *Vita S. Wilfridi*, chapter 12.

125. See Lapidge (1996) pp. 11–12, with the references given there.

126. The biography written by St Willibald c.760 (hereafter cited as VSB): for details, see Bibliography at the end of this chapter.

127. VSB 3 (trans. Talbot, p. 33).

128. Letter to the whole English race (ed. Tangl. no. 46; Emerton pp. 76f; translation quoted from that in EHD vol. I, no. 174, pp. 812–13).

129. Letter 2 (trans. Emerton, p. 28 (trans. slightly altered); no. 2 in the Tangl. edn).

130. See Letter 189 (trans. Emerton, p. 92; no. 115 in the Tangl. edn).

131. VSB 6, pp. 45–6.

132. Letter 1 (trans. Talbot, p. 66; no. 9 in the Tangl. edn).

133. Letter 35 in the Talbot trans. (pp. 130–1; no. 78 in the Tangl. edn).

134. For lay piety in general, see Fichtenau (1991) pp. 301ff.

135. McNeill and Gamer (1938; repr. 1990) p. 207.

136. See T. H. Bestul, 'Continental sources of Anglo-Saxon devotional writing', in Szarmach (1986) pp. 103–26.

137. Bestul, p. 112.

138. Webster and Backhouse (1991) p. 211.

139. For the significance and context of private prayer books of this kind, see Sims-Williams (1990) chapter 10.

140. Latin text in Kuypers (1902).

141. Latin text in Kuypers, pp. 91–2.

142. See Raw (1997), esp. pp. 10, 14, and 168–9 (where she notes the interest on the part of the early eleventh-century Harley Psalter in the mutual love of the persons of the Trinity). See also Gameson (1995) p. 42.

143. See the introduction to Lapidge (1991); Brooks (1984) p. 97; and Bischoff and Lapidge (1994), esp. pp. 168–72.

144. Lapidge (1991) p. 41.

145. For Alfred, see Smyth (1995). For learning and literature in the reign of Alfred, see Lapidge (1993) pp. 5–12.

146. Asser, *Life* §76 (Keynes & Lapidge, p. 91). For a major critique of the authenticity of Asser's *Life*, see Smyth (1995), esp. pp. 149–70 and 200–3; and Simon Lapidge, art. 'Asser' with bibliography, in Lapidge et al. (1999) pp. 48–50.

147. Whose *Soliloquies* Alfred translated.

148. Alfred's translation of Boethius' *Consolation of philosophy* XXIV.3 (ET by Keynes & Lapidge, p. 133).

149. Asser, *Life of Alfred* §74 (Keynes & Lapidge (1983) pp. 88–90).

150. Alfred's translation of Boethius's *Consolation of philosophy* XLII (ET by Keynes & Lapidge (1983), p. 137). For this translation, see Smyth (1995) pp. 534–6.

151. ET by Keynes & Lapidge (1983) p. 300 n. 9.

152. Alfred's translation of St Augustine's *Soliloquies*, ET by Keynes & Lapidge (1983) p. 140. The text cited is an addition to Augustine's text written by Alfred himself.

153. p. 141.

154. pp. 147–8.

155. In his exploration of early medieval Latin literature, Brunhölzl (1996, pp. 440–1) suggests that, whereas the Carolingian intellectual renaissance was essentially *humanist*, concerned with the renewal of learning and culture for its own sake, that of Alfred was essentially *realist*: his aims were educational and practical.

156. Alfred's translation of St Augustine's *Soliloquies*, Book III, ed. cit. pp. 151–2. On the originality of the translation of Book III, see Smyth (1995) pp. 537–8.

157. Alfred's *Prose translation of the Psalter* (ET by Keynes & Lapidge, p. 154). Alfred's introductory reflections to each psalm are drawn from a variety of sources: see the remarks of Keynes and Lapidge, p. 302.

158. p. 158.

159. See Bertram Colgrave's introduction to his *Two Lives of Saint Cuthbert* (1940; repr. 1985), p. 5. For Irish influence on Northumbrian monasticism, see Ludwig Bieler, 'Ireland's contribution to Northumbrian culture', in Bonner (1976) pp. 210–28. For Irish influence on Anglo-Saxon spirituality in general, see Kathleen Hughes, 'Some aspects of Irish influence on early English private prayer', in *Studia Celtica* 5 (1970), pp. 48–61.

160. Bonner, 'Saint Cuthbert – soul friend', in Rollason (1987) p. 31.

161. Bede, *Hist. eccles.* IV.27–32, pp. 432–3.

162. See the articles by D. W. Rollason in *Cuthbert: saint and patron*, pp. 9–22 and 45–59, though some of Rollason's arguments do not carry entire conviction.

163. See G. Bonner (1970) p. 42; Benedicta Ward, 'The spirituality of St Cuthbert', in Bonner (1989) pp. 65–76; Ward (1990) pp. 89–91. For Bede's *Vita*, see Lapidge, 'Bede's metrical *Vita S. Cuthberti*', in Bonner (ed.) (1989) pp. 77–93, repr. in Lapidge (1996) pp. 339–55. This approach to history informs all Bede's historical works; in Christ, the saints and patriarchs of

scripture and church history are our contemporaries, and their every word and deed a source of inspiration for us.

164. *Vita sancti Cuthberti* (hereafter VSC), ed. B. Colgrave, *Two lives of Saint Cuthbert* (ed. cit.), pp. 80–1. The animals were probably otters (Colgrave, p. 319). See also Bonner (1979) p. 10; B. Ward (1989) p. 72. St Jerome relates a similar incident regarding two lions who rushed from the desert and licked the feet of St Antony (*The life of Paul the first hermit*, trans. W. H. Fremantle, in *St Jerome: letters and select works* (Nicene and Post-Nicene Fathers, 2nd series, 6) (Grand Rapids: Eerdmans, repr. 1979), p. 302. There are also many examples of animals recognizing the holiness of the saints in the Anglo-Saxon period, such as the dog that recognizes St Brendan as its master (*The voyage of St Brendan* (early tenth-century Irish), chapter 6). Bede thought Tobit's dog represented Christian teachers who defend the church and its flock from thieves and wild animals (*On Tobit* 6.1, trans. Connolly p. 46; CCSL 119B, p. 8; also 11.9, trans. Connolly p. 57; CCSL 119B, p. 15).

165. VSC, pp. 88–9.

166. VSC, pp. 100–1. Cf.the passage in Alcuin's *Poem on the bishops, kings, and saints of the Church of York* concerning the anchorite Balthere, who fell off a cliff but landed safely on the sea, 'walking on the waves as if stepping in a country field' (l. 1370, ed. Godman, pp. 106–7).

167. VSC, pp. 92–3.

168. Colgrave (1940; repr. 1985) pp. 315–16.

169. Bede, VSC, pp. 218–19. See also Colgrave's comments on p. 350. Bede was clearly seeking to portray Cuthbert as a second St Antony here.

170. Bede, VSC, pp. 210–11.

171. Bede, VSC, pp. 164–7. Alcuin describes an even more remarkable degree of discernment in his description of the anchorite Echa: he says that 'by leading the life of an angel devoutly on earth, [Echa] predicted much of the future like a prophet' (*Poem on the bishops, kings and saints of the Church of York*, ll. 1392–3, ed. Godman, pp. 108–9).

172. Bede, VSC, pp. 178–9.

173. Bede, VSC, pp. 238–9.

174. Bede, VSC, pp. 212–13. Here as elsewhere Bede's presentation of St Cuthbert is strongly influenced by the spirituality of St Gregory the Great. For the gift of tears and its association with sainthood, see A. Vauchez, *Sainthood in the later Middle Ages* (full reference in Bibliography to Chapter 3), pp. 438–9.

175. In one of the Old English versions of the *Life of St Margaret*, God promises the saint, immediately before her death, that 'your body will be honoured among men, so that whoever touches your relics will be healed from that moment on of whatever infirmity he has. Where your relics are [kept] neither evil nor the unclean spirit will approach there' (trans.Clayton and Magennis, ed. cit., pp. 133–5). For tenth-century views of the power of relics, see Fichtenau (1991) pp. 324–32.

176. Bede, VSC, pp. 232–3. Cuthbert seems to have a positive and warm attitude towards women, unlike many continental (and later English) saints – see Colgrave (1940; repr. 1985) pp. 318–19.

177. VSC, pp. 96–7.

178. Bede, VSC, pp. 214–15.

179. Bede, VSC, pp. 216–17.

180. Bede, VSC, pp. 276–7.

181. Bede, VSC, pp. 280–1.

182. B. Ward (1989) p. 73.

183. Bede, VSC, pp. 228–9. For a description of how a similar combination of pastoral concern and sheer power, manifested above all in miracles, appears in the *vitae* and cults of St Martin of Tours and Caesarius of Arles, see W. E. Klingshirn, *Caesarius of Arles: the making of a Christian community in late antique Gaul* (Cambridge studies in medieval life and thought) (Cambridge UP, 1994), pp. 161ff.

184. For Bede's thought, see Bonner (1966, 1970 and 1986) and Ward (1990); for a good brief

summary of his writings, see Lapidge (1996) pp. 14–21.

185. The monastery of SS Peter and Paul at Wearmouth and Jarrow, founded by Benedict Biscop (628–89) at Wearmouth. Jarrow, where Bede spent most of his life, was a well-endowed and thriving monastic centre, accessible from Scotland and Ireland as well as from the south.

186. *Hist. eccles.* V.24, pp. 566–7.

187. For Bede's own reverence for church buildings, see Ward (1999) pp. 33–4.

188. Bonner (1986) p. 223.

189. Donald Nicholl describes Bede's spirituality as that of the technician, 'the man who serves his apprenticeship quietly, steadily and conscientiously mastering the necessary skills and only revealing his consummate achievement in the last decade of his life' ('St Bede', in *The Month* (November 1959), reprinted in *The beatitude of truth* (London: DLT, 1997), p. 15).

190. Ward (1990) p. 6; P. Wormald, 'Bede and Benedict Biscop', in Bonner (1976) pp. 154–5; Ortenberg (1992) p. 181.

191. Cf. the remark of Mary Thomas Aquinas Carroll: 'The key to the equanimity of his character lies perhaps in the wholeness of his view' (Carroll (1946) p. 53).

192. Southern (1970) p. 5.

193. See Thacker (1985).

194. Thacker (1985) pp. 142–3.

195. Cf. Thacker's comparison of Bede's treatment of the vision of Fursa in the *Hist. eccles.* with that of the earlier Gallo-Irish *vita* (Thacker (1985) p. 145).

196. Carroll (1946, p. 17) suggests that Bede 'tended to abstract from evil and even unpleasant situations. Under his peaceful pen, the unsettled times lose much of their brutality, and the impression which remains is of an idyllic society.'

197. See D. Whitelock, 'Bede and his teachers and friends', in Bonner (1976) p. 33.

198. Meyvaert (1964) p. 15.

199. For the influence of the Rule on Bede, see Van der Walt (1986) pp. 367–76.

200. See Bonner (1966).

201. *History of the abbots of Wearmouth and Jarrow* chapter 6, trans. D. H. Farmer, pp. 190–1. See P. Meyvaert, 'Bede and the church paintings at Wearmouth-Jarrow', in Clemoes et al. (eds.), *Anglo-Saxon England* 8 (Cambridge UP, 1979), pp. 63–78. See also Raw (1997) p. 172 on Anglo-Saxon contemplation.

202. *Hist. eccles.* III.19, pp. 272–3. This passage, with its stress on the punishment of evil desires, is classically Gregorian in tone. For the significance of fire in visions during this period, see Sims-Williams (1990) pp. 251–6.

203. *Hist. eccles.* V.12, pp. 492–9; see also Sims-Williams (1990) pp. 259–62.

204. *Hist. eccles.* V.12, pp. 494–5.

205. Hom. I.11 (on the Circumcision of Christ), CCSL 122, p. 77. The same point is made in Hom. I.14, 23, 24; II.7.

206. *De temporum ratione* 71, trans. F. Wallis, pp. 246–9. In 10 (p. 41), Bede says that it is in the seventh age that the souls of the righteous 'will rest forever in another life which will never be blemished by any sorrow, but rather will culminate in the greater glory of the Resurrection'.

207. 'For us [the eighth age] will begin when we deserve to enter into it in order to see it, where the saints, renewed in the blessed immortality of flesh and spirit, are occupied in doing what the Psalmist invokes, who sings to God in praise of His love: Blessed are they who inhabit your house; they shall praise you, world without end' (*De temporum ratione* 71, trans. F. Wallis, p. 249). In his *De templo*, Bede describes the cedar ceilings of Solomon's temple as representing the saints who 'by their intercessions and exhortations . . . keep the spirits of the weak from failing in temptation' (1.8, trans. Connolly, p. 32).

208. *History of the abbots* I (ET by D. H. Farmer), p. 185.

209. See Bede's Hom. I.13, CCSL 122, pp. 88–94, in honour of Benedict Biscop.

210. 'Sed et cavernam maceriae cito volatu petamus . . .' (*In Cant. Cant. alleg. expos.* 3.5, p. 287). Bede goes on to say that priests especially must avidly seek the intercession of angels, saints and others. For the ascetical nature of Bede's commentary on the Song of Songs, see E. Ann

Matter, *The voice of my beloved: the Song of Songs in western medieval Christianity* (Philadelphia: Pennsylvania UP, 1990), pp. 97–101.

211. *Hist. eccles.* III.19, pp. 268–77. For the indebtedness of both Bede and Felix (writer of the *Vita S. Guthlaci*) to the earlier *Vita S. Fursei*, see Sims-Williams (1990) pp. 249–50.

212. See Hom. I.1 (for Advent), CCSL 122, pp. 1–6.

213. Hom. II.1, CCSL 122, p. 186.

214. *In Cant. Cant.* 1.1, p. 195.

215. See Carroll (1946) pp. 234 ff.

216. *In VII epist. cathol.* (on 1 Peter 1.12), Bede cites Gregory's *Hom. in Evang.* II.36, PL 76:1266.

217. *In Luc. evang. expos.* 12.49, CCSL 120, p. 261.

218. *Letter to Egbert* (ET by D. Whitelock), EHD I, p. 801.

219. EHD 1, p. 802.

220. EHD 1, pp. 807–8.

221. See, for example, his comments on the parable of the sower (*In Luc. evang. expos.* 8.15, CCSL 120, p. 177), where he interprets those who bring forth fruit thirtyfold as representing the fruitfulness of marriage, whilst hundredfold represents the crown of virginity: this is of course similar to the interpretation found in Aldhelm's *Carmen de virginitate* (for which see above, p. 37). In one of his sermons (Hom. I.14, CCSL 122, p. 95), Bede curiously contrasts the fecundity of the spiritual marriage between Christ and his church, of which humanity form the offspring, with the superiority of virginity over any form of earthly marriage. See also *De templo* 1.7, where married people form the lowest floor among the faithful, with those who practise continence above them, and virgins higher still.

222. Hom. I.9 (on St John the Evangelist), CCSL 122, pp. 64–5.

223. *In Luc. evang. expos.* II.5, CCSL 120, pp. 118–19.

224. See his magnificent commentary on the story of Martha and Mary (*In Luc. evang. expos.* 10.38 ff, CCSL 120, p. 120), where he describes the active life as giving bread to the hungry, wisdom to the ignorant, correction to the errant, recalling the proud to humility, healing the sick and giving those committed to our charge whatever is needful. The reference to the active life as ending with death is explicitly taken from St Gregory (*Hom. in Ezech.* II.2, PL 76:953–4).

225. 'People are to be sought from the whole Church who, whether by example or word, are competent to build the house of the Lord, and wherever they are found they are to be promoted to the office of teachers without any exception of persons' (*De templo* 1.3, trans. Connolly, p. 9).

226. 'The more each one labours in giving his neighbours support in their needs or in correcting their mistakes, the more surely may he expect in the life to come the rewards whether of peace of soul after death or of blessed immortality of body' (*De templo* 1.3, trans. Connolly, p. 12). References to love of neighbour abound in Bede: cf. e.g. *De templo* 1.15, where he insists that no one can enter the gate of life except through the twofold love of God and neighbour (trans. Connolly, p. 56); and 1.16 (pp. 60–2) and 2.18 (p. 79), where he reflects on the inseparability of the two forms of love. See also Donald Nicholl, 'St Bede' (*The Month*, 1959), repr. in *The beatitude of truth* (London: DLT, 1997), p. 24.

227. *De templo* 2.19, trans. Connolly, p. 90.

228. *De templo* 2.18, trans. Connolly, p. 78.

229. Hom. I.6, CCSL 122, p. 39.

230. Hom. I.6, CCSL 122, p. 41.

231. Raw (1997, p. 62), noting Bede's affirmative view of images, contrasts this with the Carolingians across the Channel, who shared the hostility of the iconoclasts on the matter. She also notes (p. 184) that contemplation, for Bede, is the means by which the divine image is restored in us.

232. '*The prayer of the prophet Habakkuk for his trangressions*, because whatever a holy man utters is wholly and entirely a prayer to God; everything a person does whose honest intention is to please the Lord intercedes for him before the Lord and commends him to the Lord' (*On the Canticle of Habakkuk* 3.16, trans. Connolly, p. 88; CCSL 119B, p. 402). For the significance

of the command to 'pray without ceasing' for the monastic theology of prayer, see Adalbert de Vogüé, 'The Rule of Saint Benedict: a doctrinal and spiritual commentary', in *Cistercian Studies* 54, trans. J. B. Hasbrouck (Kalamazoo: Cistercian Publications, 1983), pp. 127ff.

233. *In I partem Samuhelis* I, CCSL 119, pp. 21–2.

234. *De templo Salomonis* I, CCSL 119A, p. 151.

235. *In Marc. evang. expos.* III, CCSL 120, p. 550. The same point about the nature of unceasing prayer is made in Bede's commentary on St Luke (*In Luc. evang. expos.* V, CCSL 120, p. 322), and in his commentary on the Song of Songs (*In Cant. Cant. alleg. expos.* III, CCSL 119B, p. 261).

236. Hom. II.22, CCSL 122, p. 344. Bede makes the same point in his commentary on the book of Habakkuk (*In Cant. Hab. alleg. expos.*, CCSL 119B, p. 91).

237. Hom. II.14, CCSL 122, p. 272.

238. Hom. II.14, CCSL 122, p. 274.

239. *In VII epist. catholicas* (on 1 John 5.14), CCSL 121, p. 324.

240. *In Marc. evang. expos.* I, CCSL 120, p. 454.

241. 'Where elsewhere he bids us not to manifest our righteousness before other people, in the same text he only unites fasting, almsgiving and prayer, setting them as so many arms of defence against the dart of the enemy, so that carnal concupiscence is driven out by fasting, avarice by almsgiving, and boasting about one's merits by prayers' (*In Luc. evang. expos.* 1, CCSL 120, p. 99).

242. Commenting on the story of Martha and Mary, Bede writes: 'After the story of the sisters who signified the two lives of the Church, it is not in vain that the Lord is described both as praying himself and as teaching the disciples to pray. For the prayer which he taught contains in itself the mystery of both ways of living, and the perfection of the lives themselves is to be obtained not by our strength, but by our prayers' (*In Luc. evang. expos.* III, CCSL 120, p. 226).

243. *In Regum Librum XXX Quest.* 14, CCSL 119, p. 307.

244. *In Cant. Cant. alleg. expos.* 1, CCSL 119B, p. 218.

245. *In epist. VII catholicas* (on 1 Peter 3.7), CCSL 121, p. 244; trans. Hurst (1985) p. 96.

246. Hom. II.1, CCSL 122, p. 191.

247. Hom. II.8, pp. 237–8.

248. For Alcuin see Allott (1974); Lapidge (1996) pp. 21–5 (with refs.); and Mary Garrison, art. 'Alcuin of York' (with bibliography) in Lapidge et al. (1999) pp. 24–5.

249. Einhard, *Vita Karoli Magni*, §25 (Leipzig: MGH, 1911), p. 30. See also A. Murray, *Reason and society in the Middle Ages* (Oxford: Clarendon, 1978), p. 151. For Alcuin's intellectual achievements, see D. A. Bullough (1983); J. Marenbon, *From the circle of Alcuin to the school of Auxerre* (Cambridge UP, 1981); F. Brunhölzl (1991) pp. 29–46 (with extensive bibliography on pp. 267–72). For Alcuin's extensive involvement in Carolingian life and theological concerns, see Susan A. Rabe, *Faith, art and politics at Saint-Riquier* (Philadelphia: Pennsylvania UP, 1995). A measure of his theological competence is seen in his critique of the adoptionist heresy in a short treatise he wrote (*Liber Alcuini contra Haeresim Felicis*, ed. G. B. Blumenshine (Studi et testi 285) (Vatican City: Biblioteca Apostolica Vaticana, 1980) which is crammed with patristic citations but also contains Alcuin's own vigorous exhortation to the addressee to abandon the heresy – see chapter 37, pp. 75–6.

250. Bullough (1983, p. 13) describes Alcuin in this connection as 'responding to new opportunities and new stimuli with *preces privatae* that earn him a distinctive place in a tradition which will lead through Anselm to Lancelot Andrewes'.

251. Bullough (1983) pp. 19–20; Brunhölzl (1991) p. 36.

252. Bullough (1983) pp. 67–9.

253. Latin text, ed. E. Dümmler, MGH, Epistolae vol. IV (1895); ET by Stephen Allott (1974). The translations and numbering cited here are from the Allott translation (the MGH numbers are given in brackets).

254. P. Godman, introduction to Alcuin's *Poem on the bishops, kings, and saints of the Church of York* (Oxford: Clarendon, 1982), pp. xxxviii–xxxix.

255. See, e.g., the exquisite Letter 154 (MGH 26) to Archbishop Riculf of Mainz, thanking him for the gift of a comb.

256. Letter 4 (MGH 47).

257. Letter 3 (MGH 44).

258. Letter 6 (MGH 114).

259. Letter 97 (MGH 198).

260. See, e.g., Letter 6 (MGH 114); Letter 14 (MGH 105); Letter 23 (MGH 3); Letter 27 (MGH 21); and Letter 48 (MGH 17).

261. Letter 1 (MGH 42); Letter 20 (MGH 232).

262. Letter 1 (MGH 42); Letter 44 (MGH 36).

263. Letter 34 (MGH 280). For the influence of Bede on Alcuin, see P. Godman's introduction to his edition of the *Poem on the bishops, kings and saints of the Church of York*, esp. p. lxviii. Godman also lists (p. lxxii) Alcuin's citations of classical Latin poetry in the same poem. Alcuin wrote a 'Compendium on the Song of Songs' (*Compendium in Canticum Canticorum*) which is largely derived from Bede: an extract, with introduction and references to his indebtedness to Bede, appears in Denys Turner, *Eros and allegory: medieval exegesis of the Song of Songs* (Cistercian Studies 156) (Kalamazoo: Cistercian Publications, 1995). See also E. Ann Matter, *The voice of my beloved: the Song of Songs in western medieval Christianity* (Philadelphia: Pennsylvania UP, 1990), pp. 101–2.

264. For Alcuin's indebtedness to Augustine in his use of images, see Mary Carruthers, *The craft of thought* (full ref. in Bibliography to Chapter 3), pp. 118–22.

265. Letter 23 (MGH 31).

266. Letter 66 (MGH 136).

267. See, e.g., Letter 84 (MGH 304).

268. Letter 125 (MGH 244).

269. Letter 161 (MGH 305).

270. Text in PL 101:613–38. See also L. Wallach, 'Alcuin on virtues and vices: a manual for a Carolingian soldier', in *Harvard Theological Review* 48 (1955), pp. 175–95; Brunhölzl (1991) pp. 40–1.

271. Letter 87 (MGH 15).

272. See Letter 67 (MGH 229), where Alcuin says he is now weak and must learn to accept his frailty 'so that the inner man may be daily renewed by the desire for salvation, however much illness and age weary the outer man'.

273. Bullough (1983) pp. 23ff.

274. For learning and literature in this period, see Lapidge (1993) pp. 1–48.

275. For links with the continent during this period, see esp. Ortenberg (1992), and (for Benedict of Aniane and the monastic reform movement in particular) P. Wormald, 'Æthelwold and his continental counterparts: contact, comparison, contrast', in Yorke (1988) pp. 13–42.

276. For a discussion of the prominence of prayers for the king in the *Regularis concordia*, see P. A. Stafford, 'Church and society in the age of Ælfric', in Szarmach and Huppé (1978) p. 15. For the significance of the cults of royal saints in Anglo-Saxon England in this connection, see Ridyard (1988), esp. pp. 234–52.

277. Text ed. and trans. by Dom Thomas Symons (1953). For Æthelwold's authorship, see Lapidge (1993) p. 192. The royal connection gave English monasticism what Dom David Knowles describes as 'a bent quite peculiar to itself by the intimate connection established with the national life' (*The monastic order in England*, 2nd edn (Cambridge UP, 1963), p. 45). On the intimate relationship between St Æthelwold and King Edgar, see Lapidge and Winterbottom's edition of the *Vita S. Æthelwoldi* by Wulfstan of Winchester (1991) pp. xliv–xlv. For continental influence on the *Regularis concordia*, see Ortenberg (1992) pp. 237 and 245.

278. Stafford (cited in n. 276), p. 19.

279. See Deshman (1988). For tenth-century views of sacred kingship in Europe, see Fichtenau (1991) pp. 161–4.

280. See Ridyard (1988) p. 137; Clayton (1990) pp. 164–5; and Gameson (1995) pp. 47–8. Raw

(1997, p. 112) notes how the paintings in the Benedictional 'allow those looking at them to share in the gospel manifestations of the divine'.

281. Text in W. Stubbs (1874) pp. 3–52. There is a partial English translation, quoted here, in EHD, vol. I, no. 234, pp. 897–903. The reference here is to §37, p. 902. For the *vita*, see Lapidge (1993) pp. 279–91. The identity of the author remains unknown.

282. §15, EHD I, pp. 899–900.

283. See Brooks (1984) p. 145.

284. For Æthelwold, see the Lives by Ælfric and Wulfstan of Winchester (details in Bibliography at the end of this chapter), and the essays in Yorke (1988). For Oswald, see the *Vita* by Byrht-ferth (a Benedictine monk from Ramsey), and the essays in Brooks and Cubitt (1996). Lapidge (1996ii) shows convincingly that Byrhtferth presents us with an Oswald who is simply an exemplar of Benedictine monasticism: it tells us almost nothing about Oswald the man, or about his personal piety. See also Lapidge (1996i) pp. 28–30 (with refs.). For Oswald and Fleury, see J. Nightingale, 'Oswald, Fleury and continental reform', in Brooks and Cubitt (1996) pp. 23–45.

285. *The will of Æthelgifu* (1968). For the position of women in Anglo-Saxon England, see Carole Hough, art. 'Women' with bibliography in Lapidge et al. (1999) pp. 485–7; Leyser (1995) chapters 1–4; H. Jewell, *Women in medieval England* (Manchester UP, 1996), pp. 26–56 (esp. pp. 45–51). Jewell suggests (p. 32) that the position of women in the Danelaw of eastern England was better than that of women under indigenous English rule.

286. *The will of Æthelgifu*, pp. 12–13.

287. See the remarks of Dorothy Whitelock, *The will of Æthelgifu*, pp. 33–4.

288. For Viking culture and spirituality, see Owen (1981) pp. 165–77, and R. I. Page, *Chronicles of the Vikings: records, memorials and myths* (London: British Museum, 1995), chapter 9 and pp. 224–5. More generally, see Else Roesdahl, *The Vikings* (originally published as *Vikingernes Verden*, Copenhagen: Gylendal, 1987); ET by S. M. Margeson and K. Williams (Harmondsworth: Penguin, 1991). Viking attitudes to Christianity in England may have been much less antagonistic than is often supposed: the generally pantheistic Vikings may not have found it hard to assimilate the Christian God: see G. F. Jensen, 'The Vikings in England: a review', in Clemoes et al. (eds.), *Anglo-Saxon England* 4 (Cambridge UP, 1975), pp. 181–206, esp. pp. 204–5. For Ælfric, see Raw (1997), who stresses both his originality and his links with Carolingian piety: she also notes (p. 36) the Augustinian nature of his devotion to the Trinity.

289. *The Catholic homilies*: 2 vols. (vol. 1 ed. Thorpe, 1844–6; vol. 2 ed. Godden, 1979). See also Gatch (1977); E. John, 'The World of Abbot Aelfric', in Wormald (1983) pp. 300–16; and Swan (1996).

290. John (see n. 292), p. 302. Brunhölzl (1992/6, p. 448) notes the unusual extent, by comparison with contemporary continental cultures, to which English society in this period exhibited *une préférence marquée* for the vernacular.

291. Gatch (1977), esp. pp. 69–71: he notes (p. 79) the influence of Gregory the Great on Ælfric's apocalypticism.

292. Gatch (1977) pp. 72–3.

293. *Sermo ad populum in octavis Pentecosten dicendus* (c.1002–5): much of it is based on the *Prognosticon futuri saeculi* of Julian of Toledo; ed. J. C. Pope, *Homilies of Aelfric: a supplementary collection*, 2 vols., EETS 259–60 (London, 1967–8), XI; Gatch (1977) pp. 97ff.

294. See Backhouse, Turner and Webster (1984), pp. 78–9. For the ways in which later Anglo-Saxon editors of Ælfric's sermons adapted them to their own theological and pastoral priorities, see Swan (1996), esp. pp. 38–46.

295. *Catholic homilies* II.18. See Raw (1990) p. 65 and n. 134. Raw argues that in such passages 'the two themes kept separate in the early church – the hope of heaven and compassion for Christ's sufferings – come together' (p. 66). See also E. John (1983) pp. 309–12; and F. Wormald, *English drawings of the tenth and eleventh centuries* (London: Faber, 1952).

296. Raw (1990) p. 166; see also Sims-Williams (1990) pp. 275–6. Brunhölzl (1992/6, pp. 443–4) notes the description in the *Regularis* (chapters 46–7 and 51) of the semi-dramatic

representation of the Adoration of the Cross and Burial on Good Friday, for the edification of non-literate worshippers.

297. See S. McEntire, 'The devotional context of the Cross before AD 1000', in Szarmach (1986) pp. 345–56. Clayton and Magennis, editors of the Old English version of the *Life of St Margaret*, note the emphasis in it on a spirituality of love and a personal devotion to God which themselves reflect the changing nature of Anglo-Saxon piety with the advent of the Normans (1994, pp. 70–1).

298. See, e.g., the comments of M. A. Dalbey on the tenth-century Blickling Homilies ('Themes and techniques in the Blickling Lenten Homilies', in Szarmach and Huppé (1978) p. 237).

299. ed. R. Morris (1874–80), Homily 7, pp. 84–94. On the descent into hell, see also Ælfric's *Catholic homily* I.2 (*Sermo de initio creaturae*).

300. Hom. 4 (for the Third Sunday of Lent), ed. cit., p. 46.

301. See, e.g., the 'Canons of Edgar' (1005–7), which formed a central part of Wulfstan's programme of ecclesiastical reform. Canon 16 is against pagan practices, especially witchcraft, superstition, and the worship of natural objects (Fowler (1972) p. 27). The precision with which the penalties are specified reflects the seriousness with which ecclesiastics took pagan practices. See also Wulfstan's own Hom. XII (*De falsis deis*); and (for a study of how pagan charms came to be christianized), Jolly (1996). For Wulfstan see Mason (1990) and Brunhölzl (1992/6) pp. 445–7 (with excellent bibliography on pp. 598–9).

302. *Catholic Homilies* I.6, ed. Thorpe, I pp. 100–1. See also Wulfstan's *Sermo lupi ad Anglos* (c.1014), in which he includes among the sins which have precipitated the coming Doomsday the proliferation of evildoers, including 'wizards and sorceresses' (*valkyries*) (ET in EHD I, no. 240, p. 933); and (for a study of charms in Anglo-Saxon England) Jolly (1996). Jolly (ibid. pp. 143–4) cites one (probably monastic) prayer for use when a horse is shot (i.e. afflicted with an aliment or injury believed to have been the result of an elf attack):

> May the beasts on earth be healed, they are vexed in health; in the name of God the Father and the Son and the Holy Spirit let the Devil be expelled through the imposition of our hands; who shall separate us from the love of Christ; through the invocation of all your saints; through Him who lives and reigns for ever. Amen. [Repeat] 'Lord, wherefore they are increased' [Ps 2] thrice.

Note the mix of petition and command, the use of biblical material from Romans and the Psalms, and the invocation of the saints.

303. *Catholic Homilies* I.8, ed. Thorpe, I pp. 124–5.

304. Hom. 4 (for the Third Sunday of Lent), ed. cit., p. 42.

305. Blickling Homilies, no. 4 (for the Third Sunday of Lent), ed. cit., p. 34. See also the *Regularis concordia*, where devotion to the Eucharist is particularly stressed: Symons (1953, p. xxxix) says that in no other contemporary document is specific mention of daily Holy Communion found.

306. See N. J. G. Pounds, *A history of the English parish* (Cambridge UP, 2000).

307. On St Wulfstan's practice here, see Mason (1990) p. 157. For the psalms in this period, see Gameson (1995) pp. 62–3. For the monastic timetable after the *Regularis concordia*, see Mary Berry's article on Anglo-Saxon liturgical music, in Yorke (1988) pp. 149–60, esp. pp. 150–1.

308. Mason (1990) p. 161.

309. See G. Rosser, 'The Anglo-Saxon gilds', in J. Blair (ed.), *Minsters and parish churches: the local church in transition* (Oxford University archaeology monograph 17) (Oxford, 1988), pp. 31–4.

310. British Library MSS Galba A.xiv and Nero A.ii; edited by B. J. Muir (1988).

311. See no. 19 (prayer to Christ and the Twelve Apostles) in Muir (1988) pp. 48–51.

312. See no. 16 (the prayer of one approaching death) in Muir (1988) p. 42. For Gregory, 'compunction is an act of God in us, an act by which God awakens us, a shock, a blow, a "sting", a sort of burn' (J. Leclercq, *The love of learning and the desire for God* (trans. C. Misrahi) (London: SPCK, 1978), p. 38. Cf. the private prayers in a manuscript which has come to be known as *Ælfwine's Prayerbook* (Ælfwine was an early eleventh-century dean of Winchester),

in one of which (addressed to the Virgin Mary) Ælfwine says 'because there is nothing good in me from which I may become whole, pray especially for me, holy Mary ever-virgin' (*Ælfwine's Prayerbook*, p. 141).

313. Prayer no. 24 (a prayer to the patriarchs and prophets), in Muir (1988) p. 59.
314. Prayer no. 26 in Muir (1988) pp. 70–3.
315. Prayer no. 34 in Muir (1988) p. 89.
316. Prayer no. 70 in Muir (1988) p. 150.
317. On the extent to which the English church in this period both borrowed from, and contributed to, continental Christianity, see Ortenberg (1992).
318. trans. Tom Shippey in *Poems of wisdom and learning in Old English* (Cambridge: D. S. Brewer, 1976), p. 77.

BIBLIOGRAPHY

Primary Works

Ælfric, *The Catholic homilies* Part 1: ed. and trans. Thorpe, 2 vols (London: The Aelfric Society, 1894 & 1896). Part 2: ed. M. Godden, *Ælfric's Catholic homilies: the second series* (EETS s.s. 5) (London, 1979)

Ælfric, *Homilies of Aelfric: a supplementary collection*, ed. J. C. Pope, 2 vols (EETS 259–60) (London, 1967–8)

Ælfwine: Günzel, B. (ed.), *Ælfwine's Prayerbook* (Henry Bradshaw Society 108) (London: Boydell, 1993)

Æthelgifu: *The will of Æthelgifu: a tenth-century Anglo-Saxon manuscript* (with ET by D. Whitelock) (Oxford: Roxburghe Club, 1968)

Æthelwold, *Old English account of King Edgar's establishment of minsters* (ed. and trans. Whitelock et al.), *Councils and synods* (Oxford: Clarendon, 1981), vol. I (871–1204), no. 33, pp. 142–54

[Æthelwold.] *Vita S.Æthelwoldi*, in *Chronicon monasterii de Abingdon* (Rolls Series 2) (London, 1858), pp. 255–66; trans. D. Whitelock, in EHD I, pp. 903–11.

[Æthelwold.] Wulfstan of Winchester, *The Life of St Aethelwold*, ed. M. Lapidge and M. Winterbottom (Oxford: Clarendon, 1991)

Alchfrid, *Letter to Hyglac*: see Levison (under Secondary Works)

Alcuin, *Poem on the bishops, kings and saints of the Church of York (Versus de patribus regibus et sanctis Euboricensis ecclesiae)*, ed. P. Godman (Oxford: Clarendon, 1982)

Alcuin, *Letters*, ed. E. Dümmler, MGH *Epistolae* vol. 4, pp. 1–481; vol. 5, pp. 643–5; ET by Stephen Allott, *Alcuin of York* (York: William Sessions, 1974)

Aldhelm, works: Latin text ed. R. Ehwald, *Aldhelmi opera* (MGH: Auctores Antiquissimi 15) (Berlin, 1919); ET (of prose works) by M. Lapidge and M. Herren, *Aldhelm: the prose works* (Ipswich: Brewer, 1979); ET (of poetic works) by M. Lapidge and J. L. Rosier, *Aldhelm: the poetic works* (Woodbridge: Brewer, 1985)

Alfred the Great: Asser's *Life of King Alfred* and other contemporary sources, ET by S. Keynes and M. Lapidge in *Alfred the Great* (Harmondsworth: Penguin, 1983) (includes extracts from Alfred's own writings)

The Anglo-Saxon Chronicle, ed. D. Dumville and S. Keynes (Cambridge: D. S. Brewer, 1983–)

Anglo-Saxon Litanies of the Saints, ed. M. Lapidge (London: Henry Bradshaw Society, 1991)

Asser: see under Alfred the Great

Bede, *Ecclesiastical History of the English People*, ed. and ET by B. Colgrave and R. A. B. Mynors (Oxford UP, 1969); ET by J. McClure and R. Collins (Oxford UP, 1994)

Bede, *History of the abbots of Wearmouth and Jarrow*, ed. C. Plummer in *Venerabilis Bedae opera historica* (Oxford, 1896), vol. I, pp. 363–87; ET by D. H. Farmer in *The age of Bede* (Harmondsworth: Penguin, 1983; rev. edn 1988)

Bede, *Homilies on the Gospels (Homeliarum evangelii)*, ed. D. Hurst, CCSL 122 (1982); ET by L. T.

Martin and D. Hurst, 2 vols (Cistercian Studies 110–11) (Kalamazoo, 1991)

Bede, *Commentary on the Seven Catholic Epistles (in epistolas VII catholicas)*, ed. D. Hurst, CCSL 121 (1983); ET by D. Hurst (Cistercian Studies 82) (Kalamazoo, 1985)

Bede, *Life of St Cuthbert (Vita S. Cuthberti)*, ed. and ET by B. Colgrave, *Two Lives of Saint Cuthbert* (Cambridge UP, 1940; repr. 1985)

Bede, *Commentary on St Luke's gospel (In Lucae evangelium expositio)*, ed. D. Hurst, CCSL 120 (1960)

Bede, *Commentary on St Mark's gospel (In Marci evangelium expositio)*, ed. D. Hurst, CCSL 120 (1960)

Bede, *Letter to Egbert (Epist. ad Ecberhtum)*, ed. C. Plummer in *Bedae Historia ecclesiastica gentis Anglorum: Venerabilis Bedae opera historica* (Oxford, 1896), vol. I, pp. 405–23; ET by D. Whitelock in EHD I, no. 170

Bede, *On the temple (De templo)*, ed. D. Hurst, CCSL 119A (1969); ET by S. Connolly: *Bede: On the temple* (Translated texts for historians 21) (Liverpool UP, 1995)

Bede, *On the Song of Songs (In Cantica Canticorum)*, ed. D. Hurst, CCSL 119B (1983), pp. 165–375

Bede, *The reckoning of time (De temporum ratione)*, ed. C. W. Jones, CCSL 123B (1977); ET by F. Wallis: *Bede: The reckoning of time* (Translated texts for historians 29) (Liverpool UP, 1999)

Bede, *On Tobit (In Tobiam)*, ed. D. Hurst, CCSL 119B (1983), pp. 1–19

Bede, *On the Canticle of Habakkuk (In Canticum Abacuc prophetae)*, ed. D. Hurst, CCSL 119B (1983), pp. 377–409; ET by S. Connolly, *Bede: On Tobit and On the Canticle of Habakkuk* (Dublin: Four Courts, 1997), pp. 39–64

Beowulf, ET by Michael Alexander (Harmondsworth: Penguin, 1973)

Biblical commentaries from the Canterbury School of Theodore and Hadrian, ed. and ET by B. Bischoff and M. Lapidge (Cambridge studies in Anglo-Saxon England 10) (Cambridge UP, 1994)

The Blickling homilies, ed. R. Morris (EETS o.s. 58, 63 and 73) (London, 1874–80; repr. as one in 1967)

Boniface, *Letters*, ed. M. Tangl, *Die Briefe Bonifatius und Lullus* (MGH: Epistolae Selectae, 1) (Berlin, 1916); ET by E. Emerton, *The letters of Saint Boniface* (New York: Columbia UP, 1940); ET of selected letters in C. H. Talbot, *The Anglo-Saxon missionaries in Germany* (London: Sheed & Ward, 1954)

[Boniface.] Willibald, *Vita S. Bonifatii*, ed. and ET in C. H. Talbot, *The Anglo-Saxon missionaries in Germany* (London: Sheed & Ward, 1954)

[*Book of Cerne.*] *The Prayer Book of Aedeluald the Bishop, commonly called the Book of Cerne*, ed. Dom A. B. Kuypers (Cambridge: C.J. Caly, 1902)

Bradley, S. A. J. (ed. & trans.), *Anglo-Saxon poetry* (Everyman classics) (London: Dent, 1982)

Byrhtferth: see under Oswald.

[Ceolfrid.] *Vita S. Ceolfridi*, ET in EHD I, no. 155, pp. 758–70. Text ed. C. Plummer in *Venerabilis Bedae opera historica* (Oxford, 1896), vol. I, pp. 388–404

[Cuthbert.] *Vita S. Cuthberti*, ed. and ET by B. Colgrave, *Two Lives of Saint Cuthbert* (Cambridge UP, 1940; repr. 1985)

The dream of the Rood, ed. M. Swanton (Exeter medieval English texts and studies) (Exeter UP, 1987); ET by R. Hamer in *A choice of Anglo-Saxon verse* (London: Faber & Faber, 1970), pp. 159–71

[Dunstan.] *Vita S. Dunstanii*, ed. W. Stubbs, *The memorials of Saint Dunstan* (London: Rolls Series, 1874), pp. 3–52; partial ET in EHD I, no. 234, pp. 897–903

Eddius Stephanus: see under Wilfrid.

[Edgar.] *Wulfstan's Canons of Edgar*, ed. R. Fowler (EETS 266) (Oxford UP, 1972)

English historical documents, ed. D. C. Douglas, vol. I (500–1042) (London: Methuen, 1979)

Felix: see under Guthlac.

Gildas, [*De excidio Britonum.*] 'The ruin of Britain' and other documents, ed. and ET by M. Winterbottom (History from the sources: Arthurian period 7) (Chichester: Phillimore, 1978)

[Gregory the Great.] *Liber beati Gregorii papae*, ed. and trans. B. Colgrave, *The earliest Life of Gregory the Great* (Cambridge UP, 1968)

[Guthlac.] *Felix's Life of St Guthlac*, ed. and ET by B. Colgrave (Cambridge UP, 1956)

Hamer, R. (ed. & trans.), *A choice of Anglo-Saxon verse* (London: Faber & Faber, 1970)

[Leoba.] *Vita Leobae abbatissae Biscofesheimensis* [Rudolf's *Vita S.Leobae*] ed. G. Waitz in MGH Scriptores 15:1 (1887), pp. 118–31; ET by C. H. Talbot, *The Anglo-Saxon missionaries in Germany* (London: Sheed & Ward, 1954)

Love, R. C. (ed.), *Three eleventh-century Anglo-Saxon Saints' Lives* (Oxford: Clarendon, 1996)

McNeill, J. T., and Gamer, H. M. (eds. & trans.), *Medieval handbooks of penance* (Records of western civilization) (New York: Columbia UP, 1938; repr. 1990)

[Margaret.] *The Old English Lives of St Margaret*, ed. and ET by M. Clayton and H. Magennis (Cambridge studies in Anglo-Saxon England 9) (Cambridge UP, 1994)

Muir, B. J. (ed.), *A pre-Conquest English prayer-book* (London: Henry Bradshaw Society, 1988)

[Oswald.] Byrhtferth, *Vita S. Oswaldi*, ed. J. Raine, *The historians of the Church of York and its archbishops*, vol. 1 (London: Rolls Series, 1879), pp. 399–475

Regularis concordia, ed. and ET by T. Symons (Nelson medieval classics) (London: Nelson, 1953)

Rudolf: see under Leoba.

Shippey, Tom (ed.), *Poems of wisdom and learning in Old English* (Cambridge: D. S. Brewer, 1976)

Skeat, W. W. (ed.), *Lives of the Saints* (EETS 76, 82, 94, 114) (London, 1881–1900)

Tacitus, *Agricola* (*De vita Iulii Agricolae*), ed. R. M. Ogilvie and Ian Richmond (Oxford: Clarendon, 1967); ET in *The works of Tacitus* (Oxford translation), vol. 2 (London: Bell, 1911), pp. 343–89

Thorpe, B. (ed.), *The homilies of the Anglo-Saxon Church*, 2 vols. (London, 1844–6)

Whitelock, D. (ed. & trans.), *Anglo-Saxon wills* (Cambridge UP, 1930)

[Wilfrid.] *Vita S. Wilfridi*, ed. and ET by B. Colgrave, *The Life of Bishop Wilfrid by Eddius Stephanus* (Cambridge UP, 1982)

Willibald: see under Boniface

Wulfstan of Winchester: see under Æthelwold

Wulfstan of Worcester, *The homilies of Wulfstan*, ed. D. Bethurum (Oxford: Clarendon, 1957)

Wulfstan of Worcester, *Sermo Lupi ad Anglos*: ET in EHD I, no. 240, pp. 928–34

Secondary Works

Backhouse, J., Turner, D. H., and Webster, L. (eds.), *The golden age of Anglo-Saxon art, 966–1066* (London: British Museum, 1984)

Battiscombe, C. F., *The relics of Saint Cuthbert* (Oxford UP, 1956)

Blair, Peter Hunter, *Roman Britain and early England, 55 BC – AD 871*; (London: Nelson, 1963)

Bonner, Gerald, *Saint Bede in the tradition of western apocalyptic commentary* (Jarrow Lecture 1966)

Bonner, Gerald, 'The Christian life in the thought of the Venerable Bede', in *Durham University Journal* 62 (n.s. 32) (1970), pp. 39–55

Bonner, Gerald (ed.), *Famulus Christi: essays in conmmemoration of the thirteenth centenary of the birth of the Venerable Bede* (London: SPCK, 1976)

Bonner, Gerald, 'The Holy Spirit within: St Cuthbert as a western Orthodox saint', in *Sobornost* n.s. 4:2 (1979), pp. 7–22

Bonner, Gerald, 'Bede and his legacy', in *Durham University Journal* 78:2 (n.s. 47:2) (1986), pp. 219–30

Bonner, Gerald, 'Saint Cuthbert – soul friend', in *Cuthbert: saint and patron* (Durham: Dean and Chapter, 1987), pp. 23–44

Bonner, Gerald (ed.), *Saint Cuthbert, his cult and his community to AD 1200* (Woodbridge: Boydell, 1989)

Brooks, Nicholas, *The early history of the church of Canterbury: Christ Church from 597 to 1066* (Leicester UP, 1984)

Brooks, N., and Cubitt, C. (eds.), *St Oswald of Worcester: life and influence* (London: Leicester UP, 1996)

Brunhölzl, F. (French trans. by H. Rochais), *Histoire de la littérature latine du moyen âge* (Turnhout:

Brépols): vol. I.1 *L'époque Merovingienne* (1990); vol. I.2 *L'époque carolingienne* (1991); vol. II *De l'époque carolingienne au milieu du onzième siècle* (1996) (orig. published in German as *Geschichte der lateinischen Literatur des Mittelalters* (München: Wilhelm Fink, 1975–92))

Bullough, Donald A., 'Alcuin and the kingdom of heaven', in U.-R. Blumenthal (ed.), *Carolingian essays* (Washington DC: Catholic University of America, 1983), pp. 1–69

Carroll, Mary Thomas Aquinas, *The Venerable Bede: his spiritual teachings* (Studies in mediaeval history, n.s. 9) (Washington DC: Catholic University of America, 1946)

Cassidy, B. (ed.), *The Ruthwell Cross: papers from the colloquium sponsored by the Index of Christian Art, Princeton University, 8 December 1989* (Princeton UP, 1992)

Chadwick, Nora K., *The age of the saints in the early Celtic Church* (London: Oxford UP, 1961)

Clayton, Mary, *The cult of the Virgin Mary in Anglo-Saxon England* (Cambridge studies in Anglo-Saxon England 2) (Cambridge UP, 1990)

Collingwood, R. G., and Myres, J. N. L., *Roman Britain and the English settlements*, 2nd edn (Oxford: Clarendon, 1937)

Cramp, Rosemary, *Early Northumbrian sculpture* (Jarrow Lecture 1965) (Jarrow, n.d.)

Cramp, Rosemary, 'The evangelist symbols and their parallels in Anglo-Saxon sculpture', in Farrell (1978) pp. 118–30

Cunliffe, Barry, *Fishbourne Roman Palace* (1971; rev. edn Stroud: Tempus, 1998)

Deanesly, Margaret, *The pre-Conquest church in England*, 2nd edn (London: A. & C. Black, 1963)

Deshman, Robert, '"Benedictus monarcha et monachus": early medieval ruler theology and the Anglo-Saxon reform', in *Frühmittelalterliche Studien* 22 (1988), pp. 204–40

Dodwell, E. R., *Anglo-Saxon art: a new perspective* (Manchester studies in the history of art 3) (Manchester UP, 1982), pp. 21–3

Dubuisson, D., 'L'Irlande et la théorie mediévale des "trois ordres"', in *Revue de l'histoire des religions* 188 (1975), pp. 35–63

Farrell, R. T. (ed.), *Bede and Anglo-Saxon England: papers in honour of the 1300th anniversary of the birth of Bede, given at Cornell University in 1973 and 1974* (British Archaeological Reports 46) (Oxford, 1978)

Farrell, R. T., 'Reflections on the iconography of the Ruthwell and Bewcastle Crosses', in Szarmach and Oggins (1986) pp. 357–76

Farrell, R. T. (with C. Karkov), 'The construction, deconstruction, and reconstruction of the Ruthwell Cross: some caveats', in Cassidy (1992), pp. 35–47

Fichtenau, H. (ET by P. J. Geary), *Living in the tenth century: mentalities and social orders* (1984; Chicago UP, 1991)

Frantzen, A. J., *The literature of penance in Anglo-Saxon England* (New Brunswick, NJ: Rutgers UP, 1983) (1983i)

Frantzen, A. J., 'The tradition of penitentials in Anglo-Saxon England', in Clemoes et al. (eds.), *Anglo-Saxon England* 11 (Cambridge UP, 1983), pp. 23–56 (1983ii)

Gameson, Richard, *The role of art in the late Anglo-Saxon church* (Oxford: Clarendon, 1995)

Gatch, M. McC., *Loyalties and traditions* (New York: Pegasus, 1971)

Gatch, M. McC., *Preaching and theology in Anglo-Saxon England: Aelfric and Wulfstan* (Toronto UP, 1977)

Godfrey, John, *The church in Anglo-Saxon England* (Cambridge UP, 1962)

Grattan, J. H. G., and Singer, C., *Anglo-Saxon magic and medicine* (Oxford UP, 1952)

Greenfield, S. B., *Hero and exile: the art of Old English poetry* (ed. G. H. Brown) (London: Hambledon, 1989)

Haney, Kristine Edmondson, 'The Christ and the Beasts panel on the Ruthwell Cross', in *Anglo-Saxon England* 14 (1985), pp. 215–32

Henderson, George, *Vision and image in early Christian England* (Cambridge UP, 1999)

James, Simon, *The Atlantic Celts* (London: British Museum Publications, 1999)

John, E., 'The world of Abbot Aelfric', in P. Wormald (ed.), *Ideal and reality in Frankish and Anglo-Saxon society* (Oxford: Blackwell, 1983), pp. 300–16

Jolly, Karen Louise, *Popular religion in late Saxon England: elf charms in context* (Chapel Hill: North Carolina UP, 1996)

Lapidge, M., *Anglo-Latin literature, 900–1066* (London: Hambledon, 1993)

Lapidge, M. (ed.), *Archbishop Theodore: commemorative studies on his life and influence* (Cambridge UP, 1995)

Lapidge, M., *Anglo-Latin literature, 600–899* (London: Hambledon, 1996) (1996i)

Lapidge, M., 'Byrhtferth and Oswald', in N. Brooks and C. Cubitt (eds.), *St Oswald of Worcester: life and influence* (Leicester UP, 1996), pp. 64–83 (1996ii)

Lapidge, M., and Gneuss, H. (eds.), *Learning and literature in Anglo-Saxon England* (Cambridge UP, 1985)

Lapidge, M., et al. (eds.), *The Blackwell encyclopaedia of Anglo-Saxon England* (Oxford: Blackwell, 1999)

Levison, Wilhelm, *England and the continent in the eighth century* (Oxford UP, 1946)

Leyser, Henrietta, *Medieval women: a social history of women in England, 450–1500* (1995; London: Orion, 1996)

Loyn, H. R., *Anglo-Saxon England and the Norman Conquest* (London: Longmans, Green, 1962)

Mackey, J. P. (ed.), *An introduction to Celtic Christianity* (Edinburgh: T. & T. Clark, 1989)

Mason, Emma, *St Wulfstan of Worcester, c. 1008–1095* (Oxford: Blackwell, 1990)

Mayr-Harting, Henry, *The coming of Christianity to Anglo-Saxon England* (London: Batsford, 1972)

Mayr-Harting, Henry, *The Venerable Bede, the Rule of St Benedict, and social class* (Jarrow Lecture 1976) (Jarrow, n.d.)

Meyvaert, Paul, OSB, *Bede and Gregory the Great* (Jarrow Lecture 1964) (Jarrow: H.Saxby, 1964)

Meyvaert, Paul, OSB, 'A new perspective on Ruthwell Cross: *ecclesia* and *vita monastica*', in Cassidy (1992) pp. 95–166

Nicholson, M. F., 'Celtic theology: Pelagius', in Mackey (1989) pp. 386–413

O Carrágain, Eamonn, 'Liturgical innovations associated with Pope Sergius and the iconography of the Ruthwell and Bewcastle Crosses', in Farrell (1978) pp. 131–47

O Carrágain, Eamonn, 'Christ over the beasts and the Agnus Dei: two multivalent panels on the Ruthwell and Bewcastle Crosses', in Szarmach and Oggins (1986) pp. 376–403

O Carrágain, Eamonn, 'The Ruthwell crucifixion poem in its iconographic and liturgical contexts', in *Peritia* 6–7 (1987–88), pp. 1–71

Ortenberg, Veronica, *The English church and the continent in the tenth and eleventh centuries: cultural, spiritual and artistic exchanges* (Oxford: Clarendon, 1992)

Owen, Gale R., *Rites and religions of the Anglo-Saxons* (Newton Abbot: David & Charles, 1981)

Payer, Pierre J., *Sex and the penitentials: the development of a sexual code, 550–1150* (Toronto UP, 1984)

Pope, John C., 'Second thoughts on the interpretation of *The Seafarer*', in *Anglo-Saxon England* 3 (1974)

Raw, Barbara, *Anglo-Saxon crucifixion Iconography and the art of the monastic revival* (Cambridge studies in Anglo-Saxon England 1) (Cambridge UP, 1990)

Raw, Barbara, *Trinity and incarnation in Anglo-Saxon art and thought* (Cambridge studies in Anglo-Saxon England 21) (Cambridge UP, 1997)

Ridyard, Susan J., *The royal saints of Anglo-Saxon England: a study of West Saxon and East Anglian cults* (Cambridge UP, 1988)

Ritzke-Rutherford, J., 'Anglo-Saxon antecedents of the Middle English mystics', in M. Glasscoe (ed.), *The medieval mystical tradition in England* (Exeter UP, 1980), pp. 216–33

Rollason, D. W., 'Why was St Cuthbert so popular?' in *Cuthbert: saint and patron* (Durham: Dean and Chapter, 1987), pp. 9–22

Rollason, D. W., 'The wanderings of St Cuthbert', in *Cuthbert: saint and patron* (Durham: Dean and Chapter, 1987), pp. 45–59

Saxl, F., 'The Ruthwell Cross', in *Journal of the Warburg and Courtauld Institutes* 6 (1943), pp. 1–19

Schapiro, M., 'The religious meaning of the Ruthwell Cross', in *Art Bulletin* 26 (1944), pp. 232–45

Sims-Williams, Patrick, *Religion and literature in western England 600–800* (Cambridge studies in Anglo-Saxon England 3) (Cambridge UP, 1990)

Smyth, Alfred P., *King Alfred the Great* (Oxford UP, 1995)

Southern, R. W., 'Bede', in *Medieval humanism and other studies* (Oxford: Blackwell, 1970)

Stevens, Clifford, 'Saint Cuthbert: the early years', in *Cistercian Studies* 23 (1988), pp. 3–13

Stevens, Clifford, 'Saint Cuthbert: crisis in Northumbria', in *Cistercian Studies* 24 (1989), pp. 280–92

Swan, Mary, 'Holiness remodelled: theme and technique in Old English composite homilies', in B. M. Kienzle (ed.), *Models of holiness in medieval sermons: proceedings of the International Symposium at Kalamazoo, 4–7 May 1995* (Textes et études des instituts d'études du Moyen Age 5) (Louvain-la-Neuve: Fédération Internationale des Instituts d'Études Médiévales, 1996), pp. 35–46

Szarmach, P. E., and Huppé, B. F., *The Old English homily and its backgrounds* (Albany: New York State UP, 1978)

Szarmach, P. E. and Oggins, V. D. (eds.), *Sources of Anglo-Saxon culture* (Studies in medieval culture 20) (Kalamazoo, 1986)

Talbot, C. H., *The Anglo-Saxon missionaries in Germany* (London: Sheed & Ward, 1954)

Thacker, Alan, 'Bede's ideal of reform', in P. Wormald et al. (eds.), *Ideal and reality in Frankish and Anglo-Saxon society* (Oxford UP, 1985), pp. 130–53

Thomas, Charles, *Christianity in Roman Britain to AD 500* (London: Batsford, 1981)

Thompson, A. Hamilton (ed.), *Bede: his life, times and writings: essays in commemoration of the twelfth centenary of his death* (Oxford: Clarendon 1935)

van der Walt, A. G. P., 'Reflections of the Benedictine Rule in Bede's Homiliary', in *Journal of Ecclesiastical History* 37 (1986), pp. 367–76

Ward, Benedicta, 'The spirituality of St Cuthbert', in G. Bonner et al. (eds.), *St Cuthbert, his cult and his community to AD 1200* (Woodbridge: Boydell, 1989), pp. 65–76

Ward, Benedicta, *The Venerable Bede* (London: Geoffrey Chapman, 1990)

Ward, Benedicta, *High King of Heaven: aspects of early English spirituality* (London: Mowbray, 1999)

Webster, L., and Backhouse, J., *The making of England: Anglo-Saxon art and culture, AD 600–900* (London: British Museum, 1991)

Whitelock, Dorothy, 'The interpretation of *The Seafarer*', in C. Fox and B. Dickins (eds.), *The early cultures of north west Europe* (Cambridge UP, 1950), pp. 259–72

Wormald, P (ed.), *Ideal and reality in Frankish and Anglo-Saxon society: studies presented to J. M. Wallace-Hadrill* (Oxford: Blackwell, 1983)

Wormald, P., 'Bede, *Beowulf* and the conversion of the Anglo-Saxon Aristocracy', in Farrell (1978) pp. 32–95

Yorke, B. (ed.), *Bishop Æthelwold: his career and influence* (Woodbridge: Boydell, 1988)

3

St Godric and the Deer

Medieval Spirituality (1066–1300)

During the time that Rainulf was Bishop of Durham, some of his relatives went out to go hunting: having chosen a particularly splendid stag, they set off in pursuit of it with hounds. Being forced towards capture with shouting and barking, the stag fled to Godric for safety, and by its despairing bellowing appeared to be asking for help. The venerable man went out, saw the beast standing at the door, worn out with exertion and terror, and having pity on it ordered it to stop bellowing, opened the door of his little dwelling and allowed it to enter: in no time the animal lay down at the saint's feet. But the latter, sensing the approach of the hunters, went out, shut the door behind him and sat down in the open air. Meanwhile the hounds, as though mourning the loss of their prey, returned to their masters barking loudly. But they followed the prints of the stag, surrounded the area, made their way through what was an almost inaccessible mass of briars and brambles, cutting a path with swords, and found the man of God clothed in his wretched rags. When they asked him about the stag, he had no wish to betray his guest, and shrewdly replied that God knew where it was. Seeing in his face the beauty of an angel, and respecting the holiness of his religious life, they bowed deeply, begging his forgiveness for their rash request. Afterwards they described with awe what had happened to them, transmitting the memory of it to posterity by repeating it often. Meanwhile the stag stayed with Godric until evening, when he allowed it to leave; and for many years thereafter it used to come and stay with him, lying down at his feet as a way of offering thanks for its rescue.[1]

This charming story appears in an early Life of St Godric of Finchale, written by Geoffrey, a monk of Durham, who knew the saint personally.[2] The more supernatural aspects of the story (such as the way in which the deer instantly obeys the saint's command to enter his dwelling, and the ability of the saint to sense the approach of the hunters) reveal the influence of earlier saints like Cuthbert; and we know that Godric visited Farne Island, where Cuthbert had lived.[3] But if we compare the story as a whole with earlier saints' lives, what is striking is the relative absence of such supernatural material. Godric works no miracles. He calms the deer, and deals with its pursuers, by his own shrewdness: that is, by an authority that derives from his interior wisdom and religious way of life, not by the spectacular exercise of supernatural strength. The outstanding characteristic of his holiness is not power, but beauty; and what he inspires is not fear, but reverence.[4]

Godric was not a priest, nor a scholar, nor even a monk. Unlike a large proportion (perhaps the majority) of recognized medieval saints, Godric was born poor, in rural Lincolnshire.[5] He spent a good deal of his life as a trader in Europe, though as a pilgrim he also visited Rome, Compostela and Jerusalem. When he eventually became an anchorite,[6] he settled at Finchale, a place of exceptional beauty in a thickly wooded loop of the River Wear a few miles north of Durham, on land granted him by Ranulf Flambard, bishop of Durham; and he died there in May 1170.[7] He represents much of what is distinctive in medieval church life: an independent solitary,[8] who had first been an active and much-travelled (and devout) layperson, and who settled in a place of great natural beauty and became famous not so much for the power of his miracles as for the compassion and holiness of his life, a holiness which was palpable and attractive to human beings and animals alike.[9] The story of St Godric and the deer may serve to introduce us to some of the principal themes of English medieval spirituality: the discovery of the self, the theology of love, the rise of lay piety, and the cult of the saints. First, its context needs briefly to be outlined.

THE CONTEXT OF MEDIEVAL SPIRITUALITY

England and Europe

Whatever the effects of the Norman Conquest, it certainly bound England more closely to Europe and to Latin and Western European culture than to Scandinavia, a consequence which now appears inevitable but which at the time might well not have been.[10] And by the time of Henry II (1154–89), England was part of a vast Plantagenet empire that stretched from the Scottish border to the Pyrenees; and significant changes in human and social life (such as improvements in travel, the beginnings of the universities, and the growth of towns) helped first to underpin the structures of a feudal society and later to transform them.[11]

For good or ill, then, England was part of a wider world; and as such it was also profoundly influenced by two major features of western European life in the Middle Ages: the process of social, intellectual, and artistic renewal which was rooted in a desire to recover the ancient truths of the past and which came to be known as the twelfth-century renaissance;[12] and the Gregorian reform movement associated particularly with Pope Gregory VII (1073–85), which sought to make the church free of secular control, improve clerical education and morality, define more sharply the constituent parts of the church, and thus increase the authority of the clergy. In a feudal world, the clergy (and particularly those who had taken religious vows) became an *ordo* in their own right: they were the *oratores*, the ones who prayed, whose function was as clearly recognized as those of the *bellatores* (the warriors), or the *laboratores* (the workers).[13]

Post-Conquest England was not, however, simply an appendage to continental

Europe: it also developed distinctive features of its own. Ranulf (Rainulf) Flambard, whose relatives encountered St Godric at Finchale, was a Norman bishop, appointed to Durham by William Rufus in 1099, and active throughout Rufus' reign as the instrument of his absolute power.[14] The Normans gradually but inexorably dissolved the old Anglo-Saxon pattern of landholding based on kinship, replacing it with one based instead on services, obligations and dues.[15] The influence of secular lords, both local and national, over church life was significantly greater than in much of Europe, and led (as on the continent) to confrontation with Rome over the appointment of bishops (the so-called 'Investiture Contest').[16]

This is not to suggest that life for most (or even many) people in the Middle Ages was either tranquil or optimistic. The economic and social history of the twelfth and thirteenth centuries was one of inexorable and fundamental change. The development of a money economy drew down the condemnation of innumerable medieval religious writers for whom avarice became the most serious of all sins.[17] The author of the *Anglo-Saxon Chronicle* had this to say about the situation in the mid-twelfth century, when England was racked by civil strife:

> Wherever men tilled, the earth bore no grain, for the land was totally ruined [by exploitation and plunder]; and they openly said that Christ and his saints slept. Such and more than we can relate we endured nineteen years for our sins.[18]

In a society in which belonging – to a lord, a piece of land, a court, a religious order, or something else – was what mattered most, outsiders often suffered.[19] Antisemitism steadily increased, as did the number of Jews in England.[20] The twelfth-century monastic chronicler Jocelin of Brakelond records the occasion in Bury St Edmunds when

> the Abbot ordered that all those who from that time forth should receive Jews or harbour them in the town of St Edmund should be solemnly excommunicated in every church and at every altar.[21]

For many the situation did not materially improve even in the long and (relatively) more peaceful reign of Henry III. In the thirteenth century, no contemporary recorded the experience of the mass of the populace more vividly than Matthew Paris (d.1259), a black (i.e. Benedictine) monk of St Albans. Writing of England in 1258, he tells us:

> In this year the north wind blew incessantly for several months, when April, May, and the principal part of June, had passed, and scarcely were there visible any of the small and rare plants, or any shooting buds of flowers; and, in consequence, but small hopes were entertained of the fruit crops. Owing to the scarcity of wheat, a very large number of poor people died; and dead bodies were found in all directions, swollen and livid, lying by fives and sixes in pigsties, on dunghills, and in the muddy streets. Those who had houses did not dare, in their own state of need, to provide house-room for the dying, for fear of contagion. When several corpses were

found, large and spacious holes were dug in the cemeteries, and a great many bodies were laid in them together.[22]

This was England a hundred years before the arrival of the Black Death; and it may serve to remind us that for many in the Middle Ages the rise of the universities, or the growth of the towns, let alone the twelfth-century renaissance, brought no more advantage than satellite television would bring the inhabitants of the Sudan at the close of the twentieth. The point may be illustrated by reference to the history of English art: the twelfth century in England witnessed the increasing popularity of the bestiary, or treatise on beasts. In part this reflects the values of the twelfth-century renaissance: a growing fascination with both the classical and the early Christian past. But it also reflects something of what life was like for many; for the images of wild dragons and terrifying serpents 'are the images of an age hardened to unalleviated pain, to the wearing pangs of undiagnosed disease and its no less agonizing attempted cures, to wounds and blows, to the arrow that flieth by day and the pestilence that walketh in darkness'.[23] Hermits like Godric, freely embracing the imitation of the poor and naked Christ, identified themselves with those who had no option but to do the same.[24]

The Medieval world-view

The process of centralization and enhancement of royal authority that continued throughout the reigns of the first three Norman kings enhanced more than merely the religious mystique of monarchy:[25] it must also have influenced people's perceptions of God; and, as in previous ages, it was significant that the word used to designate him (*dominus*) was also used of the local lord.[26] God was the king's liege lord, the ruler of the world, the fount of all *ordo*, the ultimate protection against chaos. The angels were his principal vassals, the monks his elite troops, the true Christian his faithful follower, doing homage to his heavenly lord as he might to his earthly one: on his knees, bare-headed, with hands clasped.[27]

This view is represented in countless artistic representations of the period, and must have been reinforced by the appearance in England of the great Gothic cathedrals and churches whose soaring vaults and verticality were perfectly suited to this view of God. It is important to stress that it also had a positive aspect: since every feudal relationship was a two-way affair, vassals looked to God to provide the same kind of protection as they expected to receive from their local lord: they also looked forward to a share in paradise, the 'everlasting fief'.[28]

Thus the Anglo-Saxon view of the world, as an alarming and arbitrary place whose potential to revert to primal chaos was held in check only by the exercise of God's absolute power, was gradually changing; and here too the recovery of classical learning was important, for it gave Christian theologians a new interest in the workings of the world around them. God's immediate providence was no longer the sole element in the governance of the universe: divinely ordained natural laws were at work too.[29] Instead of being seen only as a wild and startling place, filled with grotesqueries and dark portents, the medieval feudal world, with its emphasis on *ordo* and hierarchy, came to be seen as possessing a harmony and beauty that bore witness to its Creator: scholars wrote encyclopaedic treatises about the whole range of human knowledge, and masons built cathedrals that were 'encyclopaedias in stone'.[30] The twelfth-century monastic scholar Hugh of St Victor wrote:

> By contemplating what God has made, we realize what we ourselves ought to do. Every nature tells of God; every nature teaches humanity; every nature reproduces its essential form, and nothing in the universe is infecund.[31]

In short, people were no longer satisfied with the knowledge *that* things were the way they were: they wanted to know *why* they were thus. Hence the fascination exerted by marvels both natural and supernatural – eclipses of the sun, miracles at the shrines of saints, and so on.[32] And that interest extended from the innermost psychological workings of the human soul (seen by many medieval writers as a microcosm of the entire cosmos[33]) to the ultimate depths of the life of the Trinity. Where Aelred of Rievaulx, in the twelfth century, concentrated his attention in his 'Mirror of charity' (*Speculum caritatis*) on the inner workings of the human person, Robert Grosseteste in the thirteenth could speak of all created things as mirrors which reflect their Creator.[34] Much of this interest was not new, and could be found above all in Augustine. But whereas Augustine was content (indeed determined) to see the things of this world exclusively as stepping-stones or signposts to the next, twelfth- and thirteenth-century theologians gradually came to bestow upon them a new and deeper significance in their own right. And once that happened, nothing could ever be quite the same again.[35]

Monks, Canons, and Hermits

The two and a half centuries which are explored in this chapter may fairly be said to represent the last and greatest flowering of western Christian monasticism; and the subject has been given the treatment it deserves, both in Europe in general and in England in particular.[36] In a manner not easy for us now to understand, the structures of feudalism and the primary values of monasticism embraced and fulfilled each other: while the *bellatores* fought and the *laboratores* worked, the *oratores* prayed for both. G. K. Chesterton described medieval chivalry as 'the baptism of Feudalism'.[37] But he was wrong: where chivalry touched only one part of society, monasticism reached and baptized it all, embracing its core virtues of warfare, hierarchy, service, and honour, and bringing each to bear as part of an organic Christian vision in which everything had its place *sub specie aeternitatis*. In 1147 Alexander, abbot of Kirkstall, persuaded a group of hermits to join the Cistercian Order,

> pointing out to them the dangers inherent in self-will and lack of numbers, the perils of being disciples without a master, laymen without a priest, persuading them to a greater perfection and better form of religion.[38]

It was a call which not only hermits but medieval women and men in their thousands were to hear and obey: although, at the start of the twelfth century, Benedictines or black monks were numerically the largest group, the century witnessed the arrival and rapid development of a number of other orders – notably the Cistercians, Carthusians, and regular canons;[39] and during the twelfth century itself the opportunities available for women to enter the religious life in England multiplied dramatically, though often (at least initially) in the teeth of opposition from male orders, including the Cistercians.[40]

The Cistercians

Of the 'new' monastic orders of the eleventh and twelfth centuries – the inverted commas are important, for most of the medieval monastic founders saw themselves as rediscovering the original purity of monastic life as adumbrated in St Benedict's Rule, rather than starting new and independent orders – it was that of Cîteaux which was to exert the greatest influence in England, perhaps partly because it was itself founded by an Englishman, St Stephen Harding (in 1098).[41] William of Malmesbury described Cistercian monasticism as 'the surest road to heaven'.[42] The first English Cistercian house was founded at Waverley in Surrey in 1128, soon followed by Rievaulx in Yorkshire in 1131–32; and thereafter its expansion was rapid.[43] The twelfth-century chronicler William of Newburgh gives a vivid impression of the first English Cistercians:

> Twelve or thirteen monks of the convent of York, eager of spirit and scrupulous in conscience, took a closer look at themselves, and noted that they were living the religious life according to the Cluniac or other similar traditions, but were not observing the letter of the blessed Benedict's rule which they professed. So with the intention of living a better and stricter life (for the fame of the recently founded Cistercian Order was now widespread) they left their monastery. The venerable Thurstan [archbishop of York] welcomed their committed zeal . . . and set them in a place of pasture. The place is called Fountains.
>
> A little time before, some monks of Clairvaux had been invited by a nobleman called Walter Espec, and sent by abbot Bernard of happy memory[44] to Yorkshire. They had accepted a lodging in a place now called Rievaulx, which at that time was a dreadful spot in the deserted wilds . . . The two communities [of Fountains and Rievaulx] were separated by place but not in heart . . . The Lord blessed them . . . so that not only did they gather together a numerous crowd in the service of almighty God, but they also had plenty for the distribution of more abundant alms to the poor.[45]

With the exception of Aelred of Rievaulx, no English Cistercian achieved the stature of a Bernard or a William of St Thierry. Yet they played their part in creating a theology of the Cistercian life which might both give expression to their desire to recover what they saw as the authentic spirit of St Benedict, and draw many others in to share it with them. The devotional works of Stephen of Sawley (d.1252), and the sermons of Gilbert of Hoyland (d.1172) and John of Ford (d.1214) on the Song of Songs, express something of the affective and Christ-centred intensity of Cistercian spirituality:

> We have today no lack of those who love Christ and who love to lay hold of every single moment of his life and lavish kisses on it for ever.[46]

The Carthusians

The Carthusian Order, founded by St Bruno of Cologne at the Chartreuse, in the diocese of Grenoble, in 1084, also profoundly influenced English monastic spirituality, though its spread in this country was not nearly as rapid as that of the Cistercians. In part this must have been the result of the exceptional austerity of Carthusian life; but it may also have been affected both by the sheer distance of the Chartreuse from England, and by the development of a distinctively English eremitical tradition between c.1066 and the mid-twelfth century.[47] The development of the order in England has been fully described, as has the life of its most famous exemplar in this country, St Hugh of Lincoln, who was born at Avalon near Grenoble and after becoming a monk at the Chartreuse was made successively prior of Witham in c.1179 and Bishop of Lincoln in 1186.[48]

Hugh exemplifies many of the characteristics of contemporary monasticism, Carthusian and Cistercian, English and continental alike: he was a stout defender of the church in general and of Gregorian reform values in particular; like St Bernard, he saw no conflict between living the life of an enclosed monk and speaking out fiercely on contemporary issues, but unlike Thomas Becket he did not fall foul of the king in so doing. (He did less well, however, with the then archbishop of Canterbury, Hubert Walter: when St Hugh was dying, and the archbishop suggested that he should take the opportunity of repenting of his rudeness to him, Hugh refused, saying that he wished he had been ruder still.[49]) Above all, though, we can see in Adam of Eynsham's *vita* of St Hugh the presentation of a great saint whose holiness combines something of the power and attractiveness of St Cuthbert with the love and compassion of St Bernard or St Francis.

The Canons Regular: Premonstratensians and Gilbertines

Cistercian monks were not the only 'new' order to take fertile root in English soil. Alongside the *ordo monasticus*, which broadly speaking may be said to have embraced a wide variety of monastic orders and houses all generically claiming the Rule of St Benedict as their primary authority, there also existed the *ordo canonicus*, comprising communities of canons regular living under rule, but deriving their own charism from the fifth-century Rule attributed to St Augustine: the principal distinction between monks and canons consisted in the fact that canonical houses were usually in towns or cities, rather than remote from human habitation.[50] These communities provided an opportunity for clergy to live together, holding everything in common, yet able to continue a pastoral or teaching ministry inappropriate to monks. The Gregorian reform movement revitalized the lives of canons even more than that of monks;[51] and the influence of continental reformers like the Italian St Peter Damian was particularly crucial.[52]

The canons regular of the order of Prémontré, or Premonstratensians, founded by St Norbert of Xanten (c.1080–1134), followed the Cistercians in making numerous English foundations in the mid-twelfth century, beginning with Newhouse in Lincolnshire c.1143.[53] It is at least arguable that the distinction between monastic and canonical traditions and spirituality may not then have seemed as significant as it might appear to us with hindsight: the architecture of both, for example, was often strikingly similar.[54]

In 1131 one Gilbert, a parish priest, established a new order on English soil, at Sempringham in Lincolnshire, consisting of enclosed nuns, together with a group of lay sisters, soon followed by lay-brothers (similar to the Cistercian *conversi*) who did the necessary manual work.[55] The order remained exclusively English in its foundations, which increased rapidly;[56] but Gilbert sought affiliation to the Cistercians which, however, was refused.[57] Pope Eugenius III, himself a Cistercian, nonetheless authorized the new foundation, with Gilbert as its master; and on his return from France Gilbert enlarged the community with the addition of some (male) Augustinian canons.[58] The order reflects the rich complexity of medieval monasticism: Gilbert drew from many continental sources (including Cîteaux and the so-called Rule of St Augustine, used by canons regular) for the new order's constitution;[59] and when in the late 1160s the lay-brothers rebelled against Gilbert on account of the severity of their life, it was (among others) the Carthusian bishop of Lincoln, St Hugh, who arbitrated in the matter.[60]

The solitary life

The dramatic increase in the number of individuals embracing the solitary life during the late eleventh and twelfth centuries is one of the most striking features of medieval church life in western Europe. The reasons for this increase are many and varied: it can be seen as a crucial ingredient of the Gregorian reform movement – the ultimate protest against a worldly or lay-led church, or against the growing prosperity and perceived secularity of urban and mercantile life (though without that prosperity the growth of the eremitic movement would have been far less likely: as in the fourth century, such a movement flourished precisely on the margins of a wealthy society[61]). It can also be seen as the reflection of an interior world-weariness, a rejection of contemporary values and an embracing of poverty as a direct attempt to imitate the human Christ:[62] thus Godric's decision to become a hermit is rooted in his response to Christ's call to be perfect, which causes him to give away all he owned.[63] It can be seen, too, as part of the attempt by many to recover the lost integrity of early Christianity, in this case in particular the purity of the early desert anchorites.[64] But it was also, as we shall see, an attempt to articulate some of the central spiritual ideals of the time – particularly the preoccupation with love – and to transfigure them by making them the central dynamic of the Christian life.[65]

It remains a matter of some dispute as to how far the expansion of the eremitic life in medieval England was independent of, or consequent upon, the similar movement that took place on the continent:[66] it is surely better to see it as a part, albeit a remarkably lively one, of the overall continental eremitical movement. What does appear to be distinctive about it is the extent to which in England secular lords (themselves considerably more powerful after 1066 than their continental counterparts) both encouraged and endowed eremitic foundations.[67]

There were more female than male recluses in medieval England:[68] some, like St Godric, lived as anchorites or anchoresses in remote places, others in towns or attached to parish churches.[69] One of these, Christina of Markyate (c.1097–c.1160), became the focus for a religious community, another common feature of contemporary religious life:[70] she was a formidable and talented woman (who refused at the last minute to enter into an unwelcome marriage), a famous embroiderer[71] and spiritual director;[72] and it is clear from the magnificent 'St Albans' Psalter, which was almost certainly made for her, that she conceived of her role as that of a pilgrim in the manner of the disciples of Jesus on the Emmaus road.[73]

Recluses such as Christina, Godric, or Wulfric of Haselbury were crucial figures in the contemporary spiritual landscape: independent, even idiosyncratic, figures who were believed to possess authority not only as healers and prophets but also as arbitrators in local disputes, advisers on all matters from spiritual progress to village gossip, but clearly held in high regard by those among whom they lived.[74] Reginald of Durham describes local people of all ages flocking to Godric's cell at Finchale, though they become very jealous when his attempts at cultivation are vastly more successful than theirs.[75] And Wulfric, on discovering while sitting quietly in his cell one day that a mouse had been nibbling his cloak, angrily declared that it should die: whereupon it did, at his feet. He promptly confessed his sin to a priest, who responded by regretting that the holy man had not killed all the other mice in the neighbourhood as well.[76]

THEMES IN MEDIEVAL SPIRITUALITY

The Discovery of the Self

Against this background we can now explore some of the themes of medieval spirituality introduced to us by the story of St Godric. The description of St Godric's simple but compelling holiness is deceptive: for it reflects a desire on the part of the Church to seek inspiration by returning to its origins, just as philosophy, art, architecture, poetry and jurisprudence (among others) sought theirs in a recovery of classical culture. St Godric was one of many people across Europe who sought to rediscover the purity of early Christianity by embracing the solitary life: in the story of his encounter with the deer we are shown not so much the heroic sanctity of the Anglo-Saxon period as the hidden holiness of the desert fathers. And his intimacy with animals hints at a desire to recover something more ancient still: the pristine perfection of Eden.[77]

This looking backwards caused a new interest in the self, an interest to which many great writers of earlier ages contributed: Latin love poets, Plato and (in the thirteenth century) Aristotle, but supremely Augustine. This interest was tilted in favour of the male: Aristotle's emphatic devaluing of women's physiology further depreciated contemporaries' assessment of women in general.[78]

Nonetheless, the twelfth century has been memorably described as the age which saw 'the discovery of the individual'; and although the accuracy of that description remains a subject of scholarly dispute,[79] it serves to underline a direction in spirituality which was to be of fundamental importance. People no longer simply looked *upwards* to find God: they also looked *inwards*. Medieval spirituality had its own equivalents of the Crusades: many of the great quests or adventure stories of the Middle Ages, such as the legend of the Holy Grail or the Arthurian romances, were as much about a journey within as about anything external; and the values they espoused were far more monastic than courtly.[80] Theologians and spiritual writers showed a new fascination with the nature and structure of the soul, and with the God present within it;[81] and the journey inwards, supremely exemplified in the *Confessions* of St Augustine, came to embody the spirit of the age. The Cistercian John of Ford wrote:

> Learn to know yourself (*scito teipsam*) and to measure yourself by your own judgment rather than by that of others. Of course, it is good that they should admire you, praise you and reverence you, but if, because of their esteem you have grown even a little in your own eyes, beware that you do not become very much less in [God's] eyes.[82]

And Goscelin of Saint-Bertin, writing to a nun from the convent at Wilton who had left it in order to live the solitary life in France, tells her that she has made her own the journey of Abraham, leaving behind her home and family, in search of the promised land God will give her.[83]

Love Human and Divine: Devotion to the Human Christ

The lives of hermits such as St Godric contain striking differences of emphasis from earlier eremitical texts. The emphasis on severe and lonely spiritual combat remains (like hermits of earlier generations, St Godric revered the uncompromising St John the Baptist[84]); but it is tempered with a new warmth, a new interest in the inner workings of the soul, a new delight in an unforced intimacy with the Virgin Mary and other saints,[85] and above all a new emphasis on union with Christ.[86] Hermits like St Godric sought to make their own the medieval fascination with love human and divine – and with the popular view of life as a quest, or adventure, a journey towards a distant and unimaginably attractive goal.[87] This was not a rejection of the world so much as a challenge to it: a summons to others to make the priorities of the hermit's life their own. And of these priorities, the greatest was love. Thus the God that people discovered within themselves came gradually to be something more than simply the top of the feudal pecking order: he was also a friend, even a lover.[88]

This theological shift is rooted in Christology, and can be seen in contemporary art. Figures in Romanesque sculpture are much more physical than in most previous art: interest in the expression of feelings, especially of suffering, has increased considerably.[89] In the cathedral at Chichester there are two remarkable carvings in Purbeck

limestone from the third decade of the twelfth century, both illustrating scenes from
the story of the raising of Lazarus. They may derive from a contemporary mystery
play,[90] and reflect a distinctively Anglo-Saxon style and intensity (perhaps influenced
by German Romanesque art) that is remarkable in an area of post-Conquest England
so close to the continent.[91] All the figures, above all that of Jesus, are suffused with
emotion: the sense of suffering and tragedy (which, as Henry Moore has stressed, is
represented chiefly through the heads of the participants), is all the more striking in
what is after all a spectacular miracle of resurrection.[92] In the Chichester carvings,
Jesus is seen no longer simply as cosmic victor over the powers of evil, or as judge of
humanity, even when he performs his greatest act of supernatural power. Indeed it is
in the very act of performing it that he becomes also the exemplar of suffering love.[93]
This is not to say that the earlier models, of *Christus victor* and *Christus judex*, were lost
to view: rather, they belonged together. Hence (as we shall see) the immense popularity of pilgrimage to the Holy Land, for 'only by imitating Christ the man could one
placate Christ the judge'.[94]

   In monastic spirituality devotion to the human Christ found its highest expression;
and we shall see, in the writings of Anselm and Aelred, some of the profoundest
examples of that devotion. But the principal aspects of it are worth sketching here.
The thirteenth-century Cistercian monk Stephen, successively abbot of Sawley,
Newminster, and Fountains, was not one of the greatest theologians of his order;[95] but
his 'Meditations on the joys of the blessed and glorious ever-Virgin Mary' reflect a
clear movement in Christian spirituality towards a greater emphasis on the suffering
humanity of Christ:

> Rejoice, most glorious mother of God and most holy ever-Virgin Mary,
> who with holy eyes gazed on your beloved son hanging on the cross – his
> spotless body, conceived in purity in you, a pure virgin, exposed to every
> beating, his precious blood pouring out in abundance from every part of
> his body to cleanse our iniquities, while he undergoes death on the cross of
> his own free will, thereby redeeming the entire world from the power of
> the devil.
>
>   I beseech you, O sweetest lady, through that same precious blood which
> with tearful gaze you saw pour forth from the wounds of your beloved son,
> that you may make me, of your servants the least worthy of that glorious
> redemption, a sharer in your most holy merits, so that I may be purified
> from every taint of sin by the cleansing of that health-giving flow of blood
> and water from his side, and by sharing in that same mystery (*sacramen-*
> *tum*) of the altar, may be found worthy in this life to be united in his
> mystical body, and in the next to be enlightened by the glory of his resur-
> rection, through your constant patronage, O mother of mercy, O clement,
> O gracious, O sweet [Virgin] Mary.[96]

Christ is still the conqueror of death; but whereas Anglo-Saxon spiritual texts invited a
response of wonder at his power, Stephen of Sawley's meditation invites a response of
love at his suffering.[97] The Carthusian monk and bishop St Hugh of Lincoln goes even
further:

How sweet I should have found it to have beheld and kissed his footprints, or, if it had been possible, to have held close to my heart anything which his hands or any part of his body had touched! What shall I say of his excretion, if it is not impious to call an excretion what flowed from the tree of life? What, I say, should I feel about the sweat which perchance flowed from the vessel of such great blessedness, owing to his assumption of our infirmity? Certainly, if I were given the chance, I would not only carefully collect it, but would devour it with my lips and imbibe it as something sweeter than honey.[98]

Such an approach may appear either extravagant or simply gruesome to modern minds. But medieval devotion to the human Christ was not purely imitative. Stephen of Sawley and Hugh of Lincoln were not engaging in a kind of pre-Ignatian imaginative exercise, inserting themselves into the earthly life of Christ as (for example) Margery Kempe was later to do.

The late-twelfth-century English Cistercian Baldwin of Ford (later archbishop of Canterbury 1184–90) wrote a treatise on the Eucharist, *De sacramento altaris*, in which he argued that by receiving Holy Communion we are not only led to imitate Christ's sufferings but also enter into the very presence of the Word himself, becoming united with him in a manner which demands of us a response in love, faith and good works.[99] And the contemporary reverence for relics, which will be discussed below, reflects the manner in which medieval Christians refused to dissociate the physical from the spiritual, the part from the whole, so that, just as a relic actualizes the presence of the dead saint, so meditation on some aspect of the life of Christ (whether eucharistic or purely spiritual) incorporates us into that life, so that he lives in us and we in him.[100] It is this which lies behind Baldwin's near-contemporary and fellow-Cistercian John of Ford's insistence on appropriating the life and work of Christ in prayer: for, in so doing, we become more than *imitators* of Christ – we become *participators*, reproducing in our own lives the dynamic of his dying and rising:

Ponder and ponder again, print it and imprint it, what Christ once did by dying for you, and do it very often in commemoration of him.[101]

In eremitical texts, this eucharistic emphasis would be taken even further still, making the soul into Christ's bride. Thus in the *Ancrene Wisse*, the author gives this advice to the anchoress for whom he is writing:

After the kiss of peace in the Mass, when the priest communicates, forget the world, be completely out of the body, and with burning love embrace your Beloved who has come down from heaven to your heart's bower, and hold Him fast until He has granted all that you ask.[102]

There is an important sense in which this process, of entering into the very life of Christ, is possible only as a *response* to Christ's love for us, by virtue of which the terrible consequences of the original sin we inherit are overcome. The point is made by St Bernard, perhaps the greatest and certainly the most influential of all Cistercian writers of the period, in a letter he wrote to Thomas, Provost of Beverley:

> Already, O loving Father, that most vile worm [i.e. humanity], worthy of
> everlasting hatred, is confident that it is loved because it feels that it is
> loved: or rather because it divines that it is loved, it is ashamed not to love
> in return.[103]

Bernard goes on to say that 'a great secret which from all eternity has remained hidden
. . . has now been revealed' – namely, that God wants the wretched to repent and live;
and they may do this by *responding* to God's love for them. 'Loved, we love in return,
and loving we deserve to be still more loved (*amati amamus, amantes amplius meremur
amari*)'.[104] Through the gift of the Spirit the human beings receive 'both the audacity
to believe themselves loved and the power to love in return, so that they should not be
loved without return'.[105]

This is a confident spirituality, for all the protestations of human wretchedness. So
John of Ford can write: 'We are God's kind (*genus Dei*), we are his noble creation, we
are capable of love (*capax amoris*) and of that love which is directed towards God.'[106]
And it leads to a spirituality of striking intimacy. In another of his sermons, John of
Ford writes:

> It is to be her [the soul's] privilege to kiss at will, not only his mouth and his
> face, but also his head and his hands and his feet and every part of his most
> sacred body. Certainly this is a bold desire (*audax desiderium*), but where
> the Spirit of love is, there is freedom. No law is laid down for lovers
> (*Amantibus lex non posita est*).[107]

Furthermore this inner freedom is something that grows; and John goes on to speak of
the 'growth of freedom in the spouse [of Christ]' (*profectum libertatis in sponsa*),[108] a
spouse whose freedom and confidence are comparable to the breasts of the bride in the
Song of Songs, 'a proud and full bosom that she feels no shame in baring and exposing
relying on her spouse's grace'.[109] In a later sermon, John extends the imagery further,
referring to all that the spouse receives 'from those true motherly breasts which are in
heaven'.[110]

But it was in texts written by, or for, recluses that the full implications of this
devotion to the human Christ are explored. In such texts the commonest metaphor
for union with Christ is a nuptial one: the author of the *Ancrene Wisse* constantly refers
to the anchoress' relationship with Christ as a marriage, at one point using the analogy
of a human marriage.[111] And although, for the recluse Christina of Markyate, Christ
was her king, he was also her spouse. From the start she talks to him intimately:

> as she had heard that Christ was good, beautiful, and everywhere present,
> she used to talk to him on her bed at night just as if she were speaking to a
> man she could see.[112]

Here Christ is not only *human*: he is also *beautiful*, drawing the anchoress to him as
the woman draws the man in the Song of Songs. And this beauty draws Christina, at
the end of her life, into a union which is more than purely marital: it is ecstatic. 'And
when she had gazed on this beauty, she felt herself rapt in some way to another
world.'[113]

And there is a more important point still. By responding to the desire for God (which is present within us by virtue of our creation in God's image), and specifically by responding to the beauty of Christ, we are ennobled.[114] Another anchoritic text, *The Wooing of Our Lord*, makes this point constantly: the beauty of the human Jesus draws us to himself, and thereby changes our entire status; for Jesus is the most *noble* man a woman can possibly want, raising her to a far higher dignity than anything offered by mere men.[115] In rejecting the possibility of even the most socially advantageous of worldly marriages, the anchoress in her cell has surpassed them all; for her husband is the king of kings, and her status is thereby reversed: the hidden recluse has been raised higher than the proudest lady, but only by making her own the self-abasement of the human Christ. The most vivid illustration of all this appears in an early-thirteenth-century text written for female recluses, *Holy Maidenhood*. The writer spares no rhetorical device or image in condemning earthly marriage from the point of view of women:

> Though these are trivial things to speak of, they show all the more what slavery wives who must suffer these same things are in, and what freedom maidens have, who are free from them all. And what if I go on to ask, even if it seems absurd, what life is like for the woman who, when she comes in, hears her children screaming, sees the cat at the bacon and the dog at the rind, her cake burning on the hearth and her calf sucking spilt milk, the pot boiling over in the fire – and the lout grumbles away? Though what I say is comic, maiden, it ought to urge you the more strongly away from it; for it does not seem comic to her who experiences it.[116]

Countless generations of wives could doubtless echo that experience.[117] And the writer offers by contrast a marriage to Christ, a husband who can make even the ugliest bride beautiful and the most barren and oppressed of women fecund and playful:

> If you would be glad of children, give yourself to him by whom you will give birth in your maidenhood to daughters and sons, spiritual children who never die, never can, but who will always play before you in heaven.[118]

Spirituality of this kind is subversive in a double sense. The woman who, in a male-dominated feudal world might otherwise expect nothing but subjection, is in the seclusion of the recluse's cell raised to royalty. And the means by which this happens is precisely the voluntary self-abasement of Christ, who for Christina of Markyate becomes not only human, but childlike too: after she has endured a prolonged period of struggle against temptation, Christ appears to her in the guise of a small child,

> and remained with her a whole day, not only being felt but also seen. So the maiden took him in her hands, gave thanks, and pressed him to her bosom. And with immeasurable delight she held him at one moment to her virginal breast, at another she felt his presence within her even through the barrier of her flesh.[119]

The celibate woman becomes not only a queen but a mother; and Christ is both lord, lover, and child. In the thirteenth-century eremitic text *An orison to God Almighty* these roles too are reversed: Jesus is the mother, and the woman recluse is the child:

> Why do I not throw myself between those arms spread so very wide, and opened like a mother does her arms to enfold her darling child?[120]

There is an intensely introspective quality to this kind of spirituality which reflects its strongly monastic context. Yet that is not the whole story. There is much dispute about the extent to which the spirituality of the regular canons differs from that of the conventional black monks.[121] What is certain is that, in canonical texts above all, love of both God *and* neighbour are enjoined. Thus Robert of Bridlington, prior of a community of Augustinian canons in the mid-twelfth century, follows (appropriately enough) Augustine himself in declaring that

> the one who lives an upright and holy life is the one who sees things whole (*qui rerum integer estimator est*); such a one has an ordered love, not loving what ought not to be loved.[122]

He goes on to say that 'every human being, inasmuch as he is human, is worthy to be loved for God's sake'; and that, although the love of God takes priority over love of neighbour, the latter must be performed first, for

> you yourself, who do not yet see God, become worthy to see Him through loving your neighbour. By loving your neighbour you purge your sight, so that you can see God.[123]

This love of neighbour is very precisely defined. Elsewhere in the same work Robert tells his fellow-canons that they are to love (say) a woman, but hate that which ties her to the world – in other words, her status as a wife (*Diligit in ea quod homo est, odit autem quod uxor est*), justifying this in a typically medieval manner by saying that 'we must surely hate a thing concerning which we honestly desire that some day it may not exist': here too the perspectives of eternity are determinative of the way this world is seen, and the understanding of love is thoroughly Augustinian.[124]

However, it was only with the coming of the friars to England in the early thirteenth century that, as we shall see, a less rigorously interior spirituality of love came to develop. For St Francis, the whole of life was a direct and unmediated *imitatio Christi*: the human life of Christ was at once the centre of history and the centre of what it was to be human.[125] The love of God embraced the whole of creation, whose beauty in turn pointed to its creator;[126] and Christ is the appearance of absolute beauty, made incarnate. For the great thirteenth-century Franciscan theologian St Bonaventure, 'to look on the nature of the world in the [light of the] *Verbum incarnatum* means to understand this nature for the first time genuinely as an expression [of the divine reality], and so to see it in its own proper beauty',[127] which is what St Francis did in his 'Canticle of the Sun'.

The Growth of Lay Spirituality

For much of the Middle Ages, lay piety remained firmly dominated by those who had embraced the religious life. Thus those of aristocratic status (many of whom would have either endowed, or at least generously contributed to, monastic houses) were sustained spiritually by private prayers written or collected together by monks: those of Anselm, which we shall explore later, exerted a particularly important influence on this pattern of spirituality.[128] Many monasteries had confraternities, comprising lay supporters and benefactors, most of whom would have been wealthy, and who would have been rewarded for their gifts by having prayers offered for them: indeed, until the late twelfth century such people might even receive the monastic habit on their deathbed in order to ensure salvation.[129] Others, known as 'corrodians', received either an income from, or actual residence in, a monastery, normally in return for some kind of endowment or grant of land.[130] These relationships between laypeople and monasteries fitted well into a feudal world, for it was based on the familiar feudal practice of 'gift-exchange', i.e. gifts made in expectation of a return;[131] and the return came gradually to be more clearly specified: lay benefactors might expect anything from the saying of some prayers for a departed relative to the recitation of masses for the dead in perpetuity.[132] But they would certainly also expect the monks they were endowing to live lives appropriate to their vocation, not least for fear that otherwise their prayers might not prove efficacious.

Gradually, however, parish (i.e. secular) clergy came to assume a greater importance in the pastoral and spiritual guidance of laypeople. The role of parish churches and clergy in fostering the spiritual life of their parishioners is very hard to calculate, though it is clear that from the eleventh century onwards local secular clergy were gradually replacing those who had embraced the religious life as the primary agents in this regard.[133] There is no reason to assume that all parish clergy were uneducated, especially as the influence of the Gregorian reform increased; and the major overhaul of canon law wrought by Gratian's *Decretum* of 1140, together with the decrees of the Fourth Lateran Council in 1215, seems to have given the secular clergy an enhanced sense of belonging to a corporate body with its own rules and identity.[134] At the very least it can safely be argued that the twelfth- and thirteenth-century English parish church represented a focus for prayer for the souls of both the living and the dead, for a good harvest and protection from evil, and a place where the Gospel was taught in both Latin and the vernacular.[135]

Many parish clergy clearly concerned themselves with the moral and spiritual development of those entrusted to their care. In the middle of the twelfth century one Jeremy, archdeacon of Cleveland and formerly a canon of Rouen, compiled a kind of manual designed to assist laypeople in praying during the liturgy: this manual was translated from French into English as the *Lay folks' Mass book* at the end of the thirteenth century.[136] It provides guidance to assist in focused devotion throughout the Mass – paternosters, personal prayers in simple rhyming style, and so on – for use while the priest recited the liturgy itself in Latin. It was of course accessible only to those who were literate, and written for people with servants and tenants rather than for those at the lower end of the feudal spectrum:[137] one modern author says that 'this is not so much a lay spirituality, as a clerical one reduced for laymen'.[138] In the following extract from a prayer for the church militant, it is worth noting the order of priority: the petitioner begins with him or herself, then prays for church and country, and only then is he or she permitted to express what must presumably have been the primary concern – seasonable weather and a good harvest. It is worth noting, too, the reference to merchants and craftsmen:

> I have done against thy will
> sins many, great and ill;
> thou art ready, of thy goodness,
> for to grant me forgiveness
> For these good things, and many more
> I thank thee, Lord, I pray also
> that all my guilt thou me forgive,
> and be my help while I shall live;
> And give me grace for to eschew
> to do that thing that I should rue;
> And give me will aye well to work.
> Lord, think on the state of holy kirk,
> And on the bishops, priests and clerks,
> That they be kept in all good works,
> The king, the queen, the lords of the land,
> that they may be well maintaining
> their estates in all goodness,
> and rule the folk in righteousness;
> Our kinsmen and our well-wishers,
> Our friends, tenants and servants,
> Old men, children and all women,
> Merchants, men of craft, and husbandmen,
> Rich men and poor, great and small,
> I pray thee, Lord, for them all,
> that they be kept especially
> in good health and holy life.
> To them that are in ill-health,
> In slander, discomfiture, or strife,
> Sick or in prison, or upon the sea,
> poor, exiled, dispossessed, if (any) there be,
> to all men may thou send succour,
> to thy worship and honour.
> All that are in good standing today,
> and cleanly living to thy pleasure,
> keep them, Lord, from all folly,
> and from all sin for thy mercy,
> and give them grace to endure and abide,

in thy service to their end.
This world that turns in many ways,
make thou good for us in all our days;
the weather stormy and unstable,
Lord, make good and seasonable;
the fruits of the earth make plenteous,
as thou sees best, ordain for us,
such grace to us may thou send,
that in our last day, at our end,
when this world and we shall sever,
Bring us to the joy that lasts for ever. Amen.[139]

Two other ways in which twelfth-century secular clergy concerned themselves with lay piety are also worth mentioning: preaching, and the sacrament of penance. Surviving Old English homilies of the period give us some insight into contemporary preaching and moral attitudes. Thus one sermon warns against eating at unseasonable hours in alehouses, and lying-in in the mornings;[140] another criticizes priests who have concubines;[141] another strikes a modern note in its disapproval of those whose motive for worship is social rather than spiritual ('They go to church, not for the love of God, but to preserve their neighbours' [good] report');[142] and yet another inveighs against the perils of spending too much time in idle play.[143] One of the sermons contains a vigorous criticism of the clergy:

> The fourth lair of this wilderness is the church, in which the devil setteth up the snare of pride, and entraps therein, sometimes the clergy, and sometimes the laity, and sometimes both. The clergy he catcheth in this snare, sometimes single and sometimes double, when he causeth the clerk to let his church stand without a service when it is time to perform the services; and as often as he speaketh in church what he ought not, or is silent about what he ought not, that is to teach well the sinful and to admonish those that are slow to church and to good works to be diligent thereto, and those that lie in sin to forsake their wickedness, and to comfort them with kind words, and on each 'high day' to feed with God's word the hungry souls whom he hath to protect . . . And if he sing with voice to be well-pleasing to women or directeth willingly his eyes to them to seek their looks, then shall he be caught and be led to hell.'[144]

Some of the sermons of Herbert de Losinga, bishop successively of Thetford and Norwich (1091–1119), reveal a real concern to foster a theology of the spiritual life suitable for laypeople. In a sermon for Ash Wednesday he declares that 'those who abide not in the sound Faith, and wander, as it were, out of the country of the Image and Likeness of God, miserably afflict their own souls by their banishment, that is to say, by being unlike Him (*suas animas exilio dissimilitudinis infeliciter affligunt*)';[145] and elsewhere he strikingly states that, by means of Christ's harrowing of hell on Holy Saturday, 'the prison-house of perdition is made the house of prayer'.[146] Herbert also warns his hearers to serve the poor, calling them 'the very saints whose feast you celebrate today'.[147] Here, as so often in medieval sermons, the perspectives of the next world crucially determine people's attitudes to this one; and in one contemporary poem the point is vividly expressed:

> Each man with what he has may purchase the kingdom of heaven,
> He who hath more and he who hath less, both alike may;
> He even so with his penny, as the other with his pound.
> This is the most marvellous bargain that any man ever might find,
> And he who may not do more, he may do it with his good-will,
> As well as he that hath of gold many a heap.[148]

Heaven is accessible to all; but (as the poet goes on to make clear) no amount of money will extricate someone from hell.[149]

Penance

The development of the theology and practice of penance reflects another area in which the secular clergy influenced lay piety. The Fourth Lateran Council of 1215 laid down that the laity must follow monks in confessing their sins to their parish priest at least once each year; and the growth of the mendicant orders both supported and often supplanted parochial clergy in enforcing the use of the confessional.[150] The introspection which was so characteristic of the twelfth century was not a kind of neo-Romantic triumph of the individual: rather it was a view of holiness in which no detail of personal life or thought was irrelevant; and the importance of guilt as an objective, ecclesiastically-determined and controlled state exemplifies the way in which medieval spirituality reflected feudal society around it.[151] A sin against God, however slight or secret, represented an infringement of one's obligations to God no less objective or definable than a sin against one's liege lord; and both guilt and expiation became primary themes in the spirituality of penance during the Middle Ages.[152] In sacred as in secular society, gestures conveyed power; and the sign of the cross made by the priest at the moment of bestowing absolution restored the penitent's relationship with God by objectively remitting his or her guilt.[153] The role of the priest as confessor was at once powerful and pastoral, as the decrees of the Fourth Lateran Council illustrate:

> The priest [who hears confessions] should be discreet and cautious, that, like a skilful physician, he may pour oil and wine into the wounds of the injured person, carefully inquiring into the circumstances of the sinners and the sin, by which he may understand how to give such counsel to the person confessing as he ought to receive, and to apply some kind of remedy, making divers experiments, to heal the sick person. He must, however, take all possible care that he do not by word or sign, or in any way whatever, betray the sinner; but if he, the priest, needs advice from any wiser person, let him ask it carefully without mentioning the man's name; and whoever shall presume to disclose any sin revealed to him at the penitential tribunal, shall not only be deposed from his sacerdotal office, but shall also be immured in some strict monastery, to undergo perpetual penance.[154]

The intense seriousness of sin recurs constantly in contemporary sermons: one sin will undo all the goodness of almsgiving;[155] and the threat of eternal damnation must have concentrated the mind of many otherwise reluctant penitents.[156]

Pilgrimage

Another important aspect of lay spirituality in the Middle Ages, an aspect which reflects not only clerical influence but also the gradually broadening physical and mental horizons of the age, is the practice of pilgrimage. Medieval devotion to the humanity of Jesus prompted a new interest in pilgrimage to the place of his birth, though the practice itself went back to the days of St Jerome, if not earlier; and pilgrims had been travelling to Rome and elsewhere since St Augustine of Canterbury first came to England in 597.[157] But, as we have already seen, emphasis on the humanity of Christ in the eleventh and twelfth centuries did not so much supplant the earlier emphasis on Christ the judge as enlarge it; and the two together provided the practice of pilgrimage with a formidable theological impetus.

The fact that, for most of the twelfth century, Jerusalem was in Christian hands, inevitably increased the frequency of pilgrims travelling there;[158] though the development (much assisted by the crusades) of the doctrine of indulgences, whereby the faithful were assured of remission of time spent in purgatory on successful completion of a pilgrimage in expiation of some sin or sins, transformed the pilgrim's journey into a ritual, with a less personal and subjective quality than the pilgrimages of the eleventh century.[159] The pilgrim did not travel in order to see the world: he or she went in order symbolically to reject it, and for both those within and outside the cloister the practice of pilgrimage (whether literal or metaphorical) represented a conscious decision to journey away from the world towards God.[160] More common still, of course, was the practice of pilgrimage as a penance: early Irish penitentials prescribe lifelong exile (in other words, a pilgrimage of penance) for sins such as murder;[161] and an early-eleventh-century penitential thought to have been written by Oswald, nephew of the eponymous bishop of Worcester, goes even further:

> If anyone in any way breaks into the place of keeping of the chrismal of any saint, or a place of keeping for staves or cymbals, or takes away anything by robbery, or in any way injures someone, he shall make sevenfold restitution and remain through five years in hard penance on pilgrimage abroad. And if his penance is commendable, let him afterwards come to his own country; but if not, let him remain in perpetual exile.[162]

Even so, the practice of pilgrimage must still have helped enormously to widen both physical and spiritual horizons at a time when most people lived in villages largely closed off from the world outside.[163] The eleventh-century monk Goscelin of Saint-Bertin, who spent most of his life in England, followed St Augustine (of Hippo) in describing Cain as symbolizing this world in being the founder of the first city, whilst Abel symbolized the next in living as a pilgrim.[164]

The pervasive influence of monasteries and clergy does not mean that all magical or pre-Christian elements in the lay *mentalité* disappeared with the Norman Conquest. For many, religion, magic and medicine must have remained inextricably linked and the boundaries between them still blurred.[165] The ancient demons of the night might be driven away by prayer; but they were no less real than they had been a few centuries earlier. Saints' names were given to herbs believed to possess magical properties; and the sign of the cross was erected above cow byres and invoked as protection against elves and other maleficent phantoms.[166] Yet, even if prayer for protection and deliverance from evil remains a crucial ingredient of lay spirituality, prayer for healing assumes a new significance. St Apollonia would be invoked in cases of toothache;[167] and one medieval manuscript contains an extended charm or prayer for use with a sick horse.[168]

The Thirteenth Century: The Spirituality of the Friars

All that has been said so far suggests that medieval lay spirituality was dominated by, if not entirely determined by, those who had embraced either the priestly or the religious life. Gradually, however, this picture changed; and the old threefold structure of *oratores*, *bellatores*, and *laboratores* began to break down. In the mid-thirteenth century, more as a result of fundamental economic and social changes than of any theological development, the laity came to be regarded as an *ordo* in their own right: Jacques de Vitry can include married people, widows, soldiers and (significantly) also merchants as belonging to an *ordo* whose rule is the Gospel.[169] As the structures of feudal society gradually crumbled or became blurred, and as culture and education developed away from the old monastic schools to the new universities, so there arose a burgeoning middle class no longer satisfied simply with patterns of spirituality provided *de haut en bas* by those who belonged to the monastic orders.[170]

The growth of towns led to the corresponding growth of gilds and confraternities. We have already seen that confraternities linked to monasteries formed an important part of medieval lay piety. But with the growing search for a recovery of the pristine apostolic life, the thirteenth century in particular saw the growing number of lay-led gilds, confraternities, and the like, creating their own spiritual rules of life: churches came to be furnished with gild altars at which masses would be offered for members, gild festivals of various kinds were organized, and there was a new stress not only on regular penance, but on fraternal charity and public morality as well.[171]

The response of the organized church to this new emphasis on municipal life and love of neighbour was supremely exemplified in the ministry and spirituality of the friars. The first Dominicans reached England in 1221,[172] and the first Franciscans in 1224.[173] Like St Godric, Francis of Assisi was part of the fabric of a thriving mercantile and urban society, and like Godric he rejected it in response to what he believed to be a vocation to a more spiritual life. But where Godric's response to that vocation took the traditional form of the eremitic life, that of Francis was something quite new. With the growth of a more economically and socially mobile society, the spiritual life of the laity could never again be simply regarded as the preserve of monks and priests alone: the vow of stability and the emphasis on the journey inward were not enough to meet the needs of a mobile, articulate and outward-looking society.[174]

The appearance of the friars on the scene was not universally appreciated: both the monastic orders and the secular clergy understandably felt threatened by them. The Benedictine chronicler Matthew Paris was definitely not impressed:

With an insolent bearing . . . they [the Preachers] were continually asking every one, and even religious men, 'Have you been confessed?' and if they answered in the affirmative, the Preachers asked them, 'By whom?' and on the reply being given, 'By my priest', they added, 'Who is that idiot? he has never listened to theology, he has never studied the decrees; he has never learnt to unravel any one question. They are blind, and leaders of the blind'.[175]

But the influence of the friars on medieval spirituality was nonetheless immense. The development of moral theology, and a concern to apply it to every aspect of human life and behaviour, received a vital new impetus and flexibility from them.[176] As confessors, educators, and above all as preachers, the friars were able to address themselves to a range of issues which had never much troubled the monks: private property, money, usury, and much else besides.[177] Like the old monastic orders, the friars soon developed confraternities: St Francis drew up a rule for groups of lay people in 1221, based on penance;[178] and the Dominicans did the same.[179] Thomas of Eccleston describes one layperson, William Joynier (Sheriff of London in 1216 and 1222) as someone who 'remained in close spiritual friendship (*in spiritualitate fratrum*) with the brethren until his death, and made them frequent gifts':[180] the early use of the term 'spirituality' here is noteworthy. The concluding story in Thomas' chronicle of the first Franciscans in England catches the new emphasis on the fostering of an active love of neighbour which both Franciscans and Dominicans were to make so much their own:

A certain John, a man of influence in the world, tall, wealthy, but with very little education, later joined the [Franciscan] Order as a novice and was professed, holding the office of door-keeper until he grew old. Shortly before he died, he accurately foretold the hour of his death. He said that one night he dreamed that he had to climb a high mountain. But when he had scrambled up halfway on hands and feet, he became exhausted and despaired of getting any further. Then several active boys with eager faces called down to him from the summit, saying, 'Hullo, Brother John! Why are you stopping down there? Climb up to us.' And immediately some grasped him by the arms, while others lowered a rope and hauled him joyfully to the top of the mountain. 'I believe,' he said, 'that the little boys and poor folk whom I fed in Genoa with the food left over from the brethren will help me to reach heaven very soon.' And with these words he surrendered his soul into the hands of his Saviour.[181]

Saints, Shrines, and Miracles

'To everyone who has shall be given and he shall have abundance, but from him who has not shall be taken away even what he seems to have.' I think, serene judge, that this formula applies to all of us, late in time and furthest in place, present in the flesh and English by race, whom God in His goodness has led, though most recent, into equality with the ancients, making people all but cut off from the world equal to the glory of the eastern world.[182]

Those nurtured in a feudal society had no difficulty in conceiving of the communion of the saints: for the saints were the members of God's court, as influential in putting in a word for lesser mortals as members of the king's court were on earth.[183] This spiritual world-view is exemplified in the following extract from the Cistercian Stephen of Sawley's *Joys of the Virgin Mary*:

> Picture to yourself the Queen of Heaven sitting in the flesh on the right hand side of her Son and dispatching with clearcut efficiency, in the presence of the highest Judge, the pleas and complaints of her clients as they continue to flood her with their requests day and night from this valley of tears. See how she moves her Son's mind towards mercy with a mother's love, pointing out to him the chaste bosom on which she fondled and rested him, and the breast filled with the milk of heaven with which she nourished him; see how she faithfully acts as faithful mediatrix pleading for the salvation of her people.[184]

This conception is not new: we have already seen it at work in Anglo-Saxon spirituality, and the cult of the saints goes back to the earliest Christian centuries.[185] Nor is the gradual shift in hagiography from seeing the saints as heroes to seeing them as exemplars new: that too had begun in Anglo-Saxon times. But, as that shift of emphasis gathered momentum, it was accompanied by a changing approach to miracles: as people came increasingly to question the arbitrary and chaotic nature of life, so miracles were seen less as demonstrations of outright power, and more as evidence of an interior sanctity.[186] This is not to say that miracles or other apparently supernatural phenomena – portents, eclipses and so on – mattered less (if anything, they came to matter more[187]): rather it is to see a change in the way people responded to them. Such things were no longer simply, or even primarily, signs of the spiritual combat engaged in by heroic individuals on our behalf: they were signs of objective holiness which were the fruit of a costly inner journey undertaken by the soul in partnership with the grace of God. As such, they were not just intended to be wondered at: they were intended to be imitated, too.[188] We have seen already that St Godric deals with the huntsmen not by *force majeure* but by his transparent holiness; and that holiness is intended to be within the grasp of us all.

This is not to say that the saints were no longer powerful. William of Malmesbury describes St Wulfstan stilling a storm that threatened a ship travelling between Bristol and Ireland;[189] and the anonymous thirteenth-century author of the *vita* of St Gilbert of Sempringham tells this story about a miracle wrought by 'our master' (Gilbert):

> A man from Stamford had lived a long time with a wife without having children. It happened that Father Gilbert stopped at their house to spend the night. The discreet lady of the household put her trust in the holiness of the guest she had conceived, and prepared a place for him on her own couch so that through his merits she might be found worthy to bear a son, as the Shunammite did through Elisha. It turned out just as she believed.

For when her husband came home to sleep he before long fathered a son upon her, and they named him after Father Gilbert. When Our Lord's servant heard what had happened, being a cheerful and generous person he sent the boy a cow to supply him with food, acting just as if the boy had been his own son.[190]

But the story underlines the fact that the miracles wrought by the saints were no longer intended simply to impress, or even merely to protect. Ward has shown that, as society became relatively more stable, the need for protection came gradually to be outweighed by the need for healing.[191] And it has been argued that over nine-tenths of the miracles claimed for English and European saints' shrines between the twelfth and the fifteenth centuries were cures of human illness.[192]

The miracles also had a valuable role in combating heresy. Thus in a letter dated 1202 to Hubert Walter, archbishop of Canterbury, Innocent III can say that God,

wishing to manifest wonderfully the might of His power and mercifully to effect our salvation, not only does He always crown His faithful ones in heaven but also often honours them on earth – at their tombs doing signs and marvels which will confound the perversity of heretics and strengthen the catholic faith.[193]

One of the major consequences of the improvements in travel, and of the close relationship between England and the continent, was the growth in the number and importance of shrines associated with particular saints, most of whom were contemporaries.[194] Devotion to some saints was strongly influenced by Roman practice: thus 'Roman' saints like Peter, Andrew and Paul all had strong cults in eleventh-century England.[195] Not all such devotion was well motivated: as monasteries became richer, they found the observance of more saints' days a convenient excuse for seasonable changes to their normal diet.[196] Monasteries of course stood to gain considerably by fostering the cult of their own saint: thus the Chronicle of Jocelin of Brakelond describes how St Edmund, whose remains were interred at the monastery of what is now Bury St Edmunds, 'desired to terrify our Convent and to teach it that his body should be guarded with greater reverence and care'; so in 1198 he caused a fire, as a result of which Abbot Samson felt obliged to rebuild the shrine on a much grander scale.[197] And an early-twelfth-century illuminated manuscript of Abbo of Fleury's *Passio sancti Edmundi* contains a gruesome illustration of the agonizing death by hanging of eight thieves who had tried to plunder the saint's shrine: a clear deterrent to any others who failed to treat the saint or his shrine with sufficient respect.[198]

The great English shrines of saints attracted vast numbers of pilgrims, of widely differing social backgrounds. The murder of Thomas Becket, in his cathedral at Canterbury in 1170, rapidly led to the development of a shrine in his honour which became a centre of international pilgrimage.[199] The majority of the pilgrims to the shrine of St Godric at Finchale were local people, most of them women.[200]

One of the crucial means by which a saint's shrine drew pilgrims was by the possession of relics. This too was in no sense a medieval invention,[201] though its importance in the Middle Ages must have been massively increased by the flow of relics from the

East after the sack of Constantinople by the crusaders in 1204. In one sense the power of relics as a focus for devotion underlines the power of those who possessed them, in other words of the monasteries;[202] and the fact that King Harold lost both his throne and his life after breaking the oath he had sworn on the relics in Bayeux Cathedral doubtless concentrated innumerable medieval minds.[203]

In another sense, though, relics stress the *bodiliness* of much medieval religion: not only could a piece of the saint provide healing or protection – it also represented the whole body of the dead person, one part standing for the whole.[204] Two illustrations may underline this: Benedict of Peterborough describes the faithful rushing to scoop up some of the blood of Thomas Becket as soon as he was murdered, on 29 December 1170, so as to possess for themselves 'the precious treasure of the martyr's body'.[205] And Adam of Eynsham's life of St Hugh, bishop of Lincoln, describes the great man biting off two small pieces of the bone of the arm of St Mary Magdalene as a relic while visiting the abbey of Fécamp in Normandy.[206] The local abbot is outraged:

> What terrible profanity! We thought that the bishop has asked to see this holy and venerable relic for reasons of devotion, and he has stuck his teeth into it and gnawed it as if he were a dog.

But the saint answers:

> If . . . I handled the most sacred body of the Lord of all the saints with my fingers, . . . why should I not venture to treat in the same way the bones of the saints for my protection, and by this commemoration of them increase my reverence for them, and without profanity acquire them when I have the opportunity?[207]

Devotion to Angels

There is one portion of the communion of saints which appears to have had a particular appeal to the English: the angels. We have already seen that the hunters drew back when they saw in St Godric's face 'the beauty of an angel'. Medieval architecture reflects this interest, frequently representing in sculpture their presence at the Mass.[208] English medieval embroidery is also noteworthy for the frequency with which angels are represented,[209] something which is all the more striking in view of the fact that such embroidery was executed by people of both genders and of every class.[210] Angels appear with great frequency in spiritual texts, including the works of Anselm[211] and the spirituality of Stephen of Sawley;[212] and Aelred conceives of the Cistercian monastery as an imitation of the common life of the angels.[213] More generally, the cult of St Michael the Archangel was immensely popular in medieval England.[214]

It is also worth noting that almost all extant prayers to a guardian angel come from England.[215] One such prayer, from the twelfth century, vividly evokes the sense of the one praying being surrounded by both angels and demons, in an intensely active cosmic context in which the possibility of eternal damnation is uncomfortably real ('may the gehenna of inextinguishable flame be hateful to you, O my soul, where there is weeping and gnashing of teeth').[216] Another prayer, written by Eadmer, the biographer of St Anselm, is directed to the archangel Gabriel, and ends with a prayer to be set free from the snares of the devil and an expression of confidence in Gabriel's protective powers:

> O my surest advocate, by that glory which you possess forever in the sight of God; I pray you to assist me, that I may be freed from the snares of the devil by which I know myself to be utterly trapped – lest, through their grip, I live in immediate fear of the abyss of eternal death. For what hope or counsel have I? Seeing that my sins are more than the hairs of my head, indeed undoubtedly innumerable, yet if those saints whom I commemorate were willing readily to aid me for love of you, then may that sweet mercy of God, which knows no limit, have mercy on me unrestrainedly.
>
> So rejoice, O my soul, rejoice and have hope in your rejoicing, never doubting that if your most powerful guide – I mean the archangel Gabriel – were to devote himself at once to your salvation, nothing could separate you from eternal salvation . . .[217]

Spirituality and death

We have already seen that the medieval *mentalité* was powerfully influenced by a belief in the power and closeness of the saints, supremely in shrines associated with them.[218] And this reverence for the holy dead was increased by the proliferation of relics, reverence for which must for many have offered an alternative to pilgrimage,[219] as well as reproducing for medieval people something of the closeness to heaven earlier Christians experienced at the actual graves of saints and martyrs.[220]

In more general terms, 'the dead played a very active part in the religious sentiment of the late Middle Ages', as Christopher Brooke has written.[221] Medieval cemeteries, invariably set around parish churches, seem to have been meeting-places as well as memorials to the dead.[222] And the anxiety which, as has already been mentioned, is evident in so much medieval spirituality, affected this area more than any other: the serene confidence of earlier Christians that their departed fellow-believers were in heaven had by the eleventh century largely vanished. Whereas a minority Church, competing against other faiths in the late Roman Empire, could offer the virtual guarantee of eternal life to any prospective adherents, the Church of medieval Christendom had to find some other means of concentrating the minds of its faithful, who might otherwise be prone to *acedia* (melancholy or torpor), or (still worse) to heresy. The result was the increasing prominence of hell in preaching and art, the increasing belief in purgatory as a place of purification prior to admission to heaven, and the consequent increase in prayer for the dead.[223]

These developments affected every part of medieval society. The proliferation of masses for the dead continued in both monastic and parish churches: at Westminster Abbey, the anniversaries of royal deaths were marked with immensely elaborate ceremonies; and a substantial proportion of the monastery's income (as well as their resources for almsgiving) came from the endowments established for these.[224] St Anselm said a mass every day for a year for the soul of a dead monk;[225] and St Hugh of

Lincoln would even inconvenience royalty in order to attend to someone's burial, justifying his action in these words:

> Renew the acceptable sacrifice of my son and prepare a magnificent feast, that the panting soul still restless and weary from the struggles of its ingrained but now cast off mortality may recover its breath and vigour. Let the body, now abandoned by its former inmate, be cherished for a time in the lap of mother earth, be watered by these holy rites, that on the last day, once more happily united with its former companion, it may blossom gaily anew, clad in the brilliant verdure of eternity.[226]

Nor did this vivid sense of the immediacy of death and judgement affect only monks.[227] The liturgy used to mark the enclosure of anchorites stressed the belief that they were in effect being buried alive, at least to all the concerns of this world, when they embraced the life of a recluse;[228] and one of the English exemplars of this way of life, Christina of Markyate, imagined herself on her deathbed while still a young maiden.[229] So far as the laity were concerned, it is instructive to trace the development of the monastic *libri vitae*: these books had their origins in prayers for both living and dead Christians which were inserted in the canon of the mass until they became too lengthy to be used at this point; but during the medieval period they grew in both length and scope to include both monks from other religious houses and laity as well, reflecting the concern of layfolk for what happened after death, and the importance of religious as intercessors for the dead.[230] The twelfth-century *Lay folks' Mass book* (translated into English in the late thirteenth century) contains this passage in one of its bidding prayers:

> And specially [pray] for all those souls
> that have most need to be prayed for
> and have the fewest friends.[231]

But perhaps the most vivid illustration of the importance of this theme is found in contemporary art. On one of the capitals on the main arch of the apse in Hereford Cathedral is an early-twelfth-century representation of the harrowing of hell, a theme that became very popular in the medieval period. Christ, with a banner and dressed as a priest, with the hand of God reaching towards him from above, takes Adam's hand to draw him out of hell. Other naked figures are also emerging from the mouth of hell, which is depicted upside-down; and the devil is at the bottom with his hands bound. On the other face of the same capital is another devil, holding instruments of torture. The implications must have been obvious: both the terrors of hell and the rescue wrought by Christ are simultaneously emphasized.[232]

INDIVIDUAL STUDIES

The Cost of Conscience: Anselm of Canterbury (1033–1109)

Introduction

Anselm of Canterbury stands classically at the heart of what today might be regarded as the most conservative tradition within English spirituality: western, monastic, and male, he emerges from the pages of Eadmer's *Life* as firm, serious, of unimpeachable integrity, with a particular horror of sin and a vivid and immediate sense of eternity. Yet few writers on the spiritual life have a more intense (and intensely *creative*) self-knowledge, and even fewer are able to allow that self-knowledge to become the seedbed for a spirituality of universal significance. In part this was the consequence of his pastoral wisdom and long experience of spiritual direction, reflected in his extensive extant correspondence: the Burgundian chronicler Guibert of Nogent says that Anselm

> readily offered to teach me to manage the inner self, how to consult the laws of reason in the government of the body.[233]

The essential heart of Anselm's life, the focus and context of his spirituality, was the monastery. Religious communities were

> the mother-churches, shrines, burial places, refuges in old age and adversity, for widely dispersed family and feudal groups. To Anselm, the monasteries were this, and a great deal more than this. They were in principle, intention, and possibility, the perfect form of Christian life, giving the best opportunity for the exercise of Christian virtues in a tumultuous world, and for eternal salvation hereafter.[234]

We cannot enter, still less understand, Anselm's spiritual world-view unless we see that for him monastic life *was* Christianity in its idealized form: in a stormy and dangerous world, monasteries were the safest place to be, and the best in which to grow to the full stature of the Christian life. His own life story is relevant here: he was born in Aosta in 1033, and his biographer Eadmer tells us how he was persecuted by his father after the death of his mother, causing him to leave home (in 1056) and to embark on a journey which would lead him eventually to the abbey of Bec in Normandy, where at last he felt at home.[235] Thereafter his career marched in tandem with that of Lanfranc, abbot of Bec on Anselm's arrival there in 1059: when Lanfranc moved to Caen in 1063, Anselm became first prior and later abbot (1078) in his place; and when Lanfranc died after nineteen years as archbishop of Canterbury, Anselm eventually (in 1093) agreed to succeed him, leaving with the utmost reluctance the monastic life he loved.

The Prayers and meditations

The starting-point for an understanding of Anselm's spirituality is the collection of *Prayers and meditations* which he wrote between 1070 and 1075, some twenty years before he came to England as archbishop of Canterbury. They comprise a number of prayers, most of which are directed either to God or to individual saints, and three meditations, the last of which (the *Meditation on human redemption*) was written in 1099, soon after Anselm (now archbishop of Canterbury) had completed his *Cur Deus homo*. Since these texts circulated as an integral collection during Anselm's own lifetime, it seems that (like St Augustine before him, and countless others since) he was not unaware of the didactic and spiritual value of his own seemingly introspective reflections.[236] The practice of recording such reflections were not new: Anselm followed Augustine in combining personal and spiritual experience with theological argument; and, although he never directly quotes Augustine, he wrote the *Prayers and meditations* after intensive study of the earlier master (especially his *De Trinitate*), combining something of the precise introspection of Augustine's *Soliloquies* with the intensely personal fervour of the *Confessions*.[237] The debt Anselm owed to Augustine was immense: where he differed from him was in the fact that, whilst Augustine wrestled constantly with heresy and unbelief, neither was a serious problem for Anselm: doubt and anxiety are the enemies that stalk his pages. It is in this respect that Anselm's spirituality is very much more intra-Christian than that of his Anglo-Saxon predecessors, for whom the threat of paganism remained a real one. Anselm sought to deepen a faith that was itself unquestioned, and above all to enable the individual to appropriate it for his own self-understanding and spiritual journey.[238]

The Prayer to St Paul: Jesus as Mother

The best point of entry into his spirituality is gained by exploring in more detail an extract from his *Prayers and Meditations*. What follows is from the first part of his *Prayer to Saint Paul*:

> St Paul, great Paul: one of the great apostles of God. You followed after all the rest in time, but you surpassed them in labours and in effect in the husbandry (*in agricultura dei*) of God. While you were still weighed down by the flesh you were rapt 'even to the third heaven', and 'being rapt into paradise' heard 'things that cannot be spoken by human beings'. Among Christians you were like a nurse who not only cared for her sons, but in some way brought them forth a second time, with careful and marvellous tenderness. You were 'made all things to all people' so that 'you might gain all'. Sir, you are known to the world by these and many other words and deeds to be of great power before God and of immense pity towards humanity: to you I come, certainly a very great sinner and greatly accused before God, the powerful and strict judge . . .

> Unhappy little man (*infelix homuncio*) that I am! What has become of my prayer? Where have my hope and faith vanished to? I began to pray with the hope of rashness, and despair soon made me understand the truth of my state; my prayer itself slackened out of despair of anyone being well-disposed towards me . . .[239]

It is worth noting first of all the pervasive influence of the Bible: medieval *meditatio* consisted of a regular and focused reflection on scripture as it was heard daily in the liturgy and offices of the monastery, ruminated upon and *appropriated* for the monk's own life.[240] The Bible is rarely cited exactly: thus the references to the saint's rapture are a loose adaptation of 2 Corinthians 12.2–4; and Anselm cites St Paul's reference to himself as an 'unhappy man' (*infelix homo*) in Romans 7.24, but alters the biblical *homo* to the self-deprecating diminutive *homuncio*.[241] He also changes the context: where Paul was concerned with the grand themes of sin and redemption ('Wretched man that I am, who will liberate me from this body of death?'), Anselm's concern is more narrowly spiritual ('Unhappy little man that I am, what has become of my prayer?'). The biblical texts are reflected on and appropriated for the meditator's own spiritual life.

More interesting still is the way Anselm meditates on St Paul's own reference to himself as a nurse caring for her children (from 1 Thessalonians 2.7). This is significantly developed, so that the saint becomes a mother as well as a nurse ('brought them forth a second time'), an idea absent from the biblical text. Later in the same prayer Anselm takes up this theme again, praying to Paul as his mother:

> Dear mother (*dulcis mater*), recognize your son by the voice of his confession . . . O mother, you who again give birth to your sons, offer your dead son again, to be raised up by him who by his death gives life to his servants.

Here Anselm clearly has in mind Galatians 4.19 ('My little children, for whom I am again in the pain of childbirth until Christ is formed in you'): though it is not quoted explicitly, the twin themes of motherhood and reformation recur throughout the prayer. Having reflected on the theme of Paul as mother, Anselm proceeds to apply this theme to Jesus too:

> And you, Jesus, are you not also a mother? . . . Truly, Lord, you are a mother; for those to whom others have given birth are in fact received from you. You died before they did, and what they brought forth by their labours you yourself brought forth by your death. For if you had not been in labour, you could not have borne death; and if you had not died, you would not have given birth. For, longing to bear sons into life, you tasted of death, and by dying you begot them. So you, Lord God, are the great mother.

After this, Anselm implicitly introduces St Paul's reference to himself in 1 Thessalonians 2.11 as a father, and brings his prayer to a climax by combining all four possibilities – both saint and Christ are at once mother and father:

> Then both of you are mothers. Even if you are fathers, you are also mothers. For you have brought it about that those born to death should be reborn to life – you [Christ] by your own act, you [Paul] by his [Christ's] power. So you are fathers by your effect and mothers by your affection. Fathers by your authority, mothers by your kindness. Fathers by your teaching, mothers by your mercy.

This careful schematizing is classically medieval. The prayer ends by incorporating Jesus' own reference to himself, in Matthew 23.37, as a mother-hen gathering her chickens beneath her wings; and again the biblical text is appropriated for Anselm's own personal experience:

Christ, my mother, you gather your chickens under your wings; this dead chicken of yours puts himself under your wings. For by your gentleness the badly frightened are comforted, by your sweet smell the despairing are reformed, your warmth gives life to the dead, your touch justifies sinners. Mother, know again your dead son, both by the sign of your cross and the voice of your confession. Warm your chicken, give life to your dead man, justify your sinner. Let your terrified one be consoled by you; despairing of himself, let him be comforted by you; and in your whole and unceasing grace let him be reformed by you. For from you flows consolation for sinners; to you be blessing for ever and ever. Amen.

The references to Jesus as mother need to be seen in the context of the prayer as a whole. We have already seen that Anselm refers to God as 'the powerful and strict judge', and himself as a wretched and unworthy sinner. St Paul is addressed as 'Sir' (*domine*), and later, as Anselm's confidence grows, as a nurse and a mother too. The implication is clear. Like any suppliant seeking a hearing before a feudal monarch, Anselm needs friends at court to intercede for him; and having persuaded himself, on the basis of both the biblical texts and his own sense of intimacy with his chosen intercessor, that he may reasonably address the saint as his mother, he comes to see that he may legitimately do the same with Jesus. Jesus is his mother, in part because Jesus himself spoke of gathering his chicks under his protective wings, and in part because, like St Paul, Jesus gives birth spiritually to Christians. As mothers, both Paul and Jesus might be expected to have compassion on their sinful child (Anselm describes himself in the prayer as dead through his sins, and begs Paul to offer him up to Jesus as a mother might lay her lifeless child before a great doctor). But Jesus' motherhood goes beyond that of Paul, as Anselm makes clear elsewhere in the same prayer: as mother Jesus brings forth children through his own death – Anselm is making a theological point here, but may also be reflecting the frequency with which contemporary women died during childbirth:

Truly, Lord, you are a mother; for both those who were in labour and those who gave birth are accepted by you. You died before they did, and what they brought forth after being in labour you brought forth by your death. For if you had not been in labour, you could not have borne death; and if you had not died, you would not have given birth.

The death of Jesus on the cross is as intensely painful as contemporary childbirth must have been for any mother. But (and this is the point) both are procreative: Jesus is our mother not simply because he evinces a mother's compassion and so softens the Father's heart, not even because like a mother he suffers with and for his offspring, but supremely because he gives his life for his offspring, and thereby restores theirs to them.

It is important to be clear about what Anselm is and is not saying here. He does not describe God as mother – indeed in his *Monologion* he argues specifically against so doing on the twofold grounds that male is superior to female and that in any case the man contributes more than the woman in the creation of a new child (which was the medical view of the time).[242] And elsewhere in his *Prayer to Saint Paul*, as we have seen, he makes it clear that Jesus is our father by virtue of his authority, and our mother by virtue of his kindness. Furthermore, Anselm has none of St Bernard's confidently affective and often erotic emphasis on the breasts of Jesus as nurturing his spiritual off-spring.[243] But what we do see in this remarkable (and entirely characteristic) text is the careful process, at once personal and theological, by which Anselm's meditation leads him to develop an original (and highly influential) spirituality which interweaves both scripture, prayer and personal experience. It is not surprising to find his biographer describing him in similar terms to those Anselm uses of Christ and St Paul:

> While he was a father to those who were well, he was a mother to the sick:
> or rather, he was both father and mother to the sick and the sound alike.[244]

Spirituality and the self

Two other fundamental aspects of Anselm's spirituality are reflected in his *Prayer to Saint Paul*, and both need briefly to be explored. The first is his thoroughgoing intro-spection. As the prayer unfolds, it becomes clear that Anselm's own dictum about 'faith seeking understanding' begins unequivocally with himself; and that his own self-understanding requires much more than a purely rational process. Thus he writes:

> Certainly neither could I pray, nor did I know how. This was so because I understood that I was cursed by all things, and I did not grieve, as if unfeel-ing. I understood through my rational nature, but I did not become aware because of the insensibility of death. Indeed I was dead, and as a dead person I have come to you; it is only now that I know I am dead.

For Anselm, 'understanding' appears to be close to the Old Testament concept of knowledge as both intellectual and affective; and it is not the least of Anselm's contri-butions to the history of spirituality that he refuses to separate the two. Even when he appears to be most effusively emotional, his intellect is never left behind.[245] And this all-pervasive understanding is first directed towards himself, with terrifying results: he sees himself to be, not just sinful, but effectively dead.[246] And what saves him is not that he proceeds to discover new and more hopeful aspects of himself, nor even the fact that he becomes aware of his need for redemption, but precisely the free gift of God's grace. Nowhere is this more vividly described than in the opening section of the greatest of all Anselm's prayers and meditations, the *Meditation on human redemption*:

> O Christian soul, brought to life again out of the heaviness of death, redeemed and set free from wretched servitude by the blood of God, rouse yourself (*excita mentem tuam*) and remember that you are risen, realize that you have redeemed and set free. Consider again the strength of your salvation, and where it is found. Meditate upon it, delight in the contem-plation of it. Shake off your lethargy and set your mind to thinking over these things.[247]

Anselm goes on to reflect on the strength of Christ revealed precisely in his weakness, and in so doing gives the popular contemporary theme of the harrowing of hell a characteristic twist: it is not the *triumphant* but the *tormented* Christ who draws the damned forth from the underworld:

> There is something mysterious in this abjection. O hidden strength: a man hangs on a cross and lifts the load of eternal death from the human race. O mysterious strength: one soul coming forth from torment draws countless souls with him out of hell, a man submits to the death of the body and destroys the death of souls.[248]

This is not the affirmative humanism of later twelfth-century writers, though Anselm's writings were to contribute significantly (and ironically) to the twelfth-century 'discovery of the individual'.[249] Nor is it a rhetorical artifice, though Anselm's writings are clearly the product of very careful planning and high literary skill.[250] Yet neither is it an exclusively introverted spirituality, though many of both Anselm's predecessors and successors were to produce precisely that by retaining his emotional intensity and omitting his theological rigour.[251] Rather what we find in Anselm is a new and remarkable form of the traditional monastic virtue of *compunctio cordis* (compunction), the acute awareness of our own sinfulness,[252] which for Anselm becomes simultaneously an awareness of our terrible predicament and a recognition that we are already saved, if only we can accept it.[253] Self-knowledge becomes the only means to a proper apprehension of what it means to be saved in Christ, not least because it reveals to us a saviour whose own power is itself made manifest in the furthest extremities of human weakness.

Spirituality and atonement

And this brings us to the other vital aspect of Anselm's spirituality, much of which has already been hinted at: his focus on the cross of Christ. In his *Meditation on human redemption*, Anselm engages with the subject which was to occupy him yet more fully in his theological treatise *Cur Deus homo* – why God became human. God became human because humanity could not be restored unless human beings first made entire satisfaction for their sins (*quae non fit nisi praecedente integra satisfactione*).[254] The effect of sin is to *dishonour* God (*si enim peccare est deum exhonorare*): now plain reason demands that sinners should give something better to God in return for the honour of which God has deprived them; and since human beings could not do this, God took on human nature and did it for them; and in Christ's free obedience (*liberrima oboedientia*) to the Father's will humanity is both restored and exalted.[255]

Such an argument may sound strange to modern ears; but its strength is precisely its rootedness in the values of its time. Honour was a fundamental ingredient in feudal society: in Anglo-Saxon times, as in (say) twentieth-century Sicily, a person's honour could be damaged by the infidelity of his closest kinsfolk, entitling him to wreak vengeance on them if satisfaction were not forthcoming. Above all, honour was the sign of a person's status, which was why human sin, by dishonouring God, did far more than hurt God's feelings or even wound God's dignity. It challenged God's position:

To be dishonoured is to be rejected from the role to which one aspired. 'I am who I am' is answered: 'You are not who you think you are.'[256]

Hence in the *Cur Deus homo* Anselm asserts

> that God cannot allow even the slightest violation of his honour because that would disturb the order and beauty of the universe.[257]

And there is more. In a feudal society, a person's honour, together with his place in the structures of that society, depended ultimately on the person at the top of the hierarchy: the maintenance of the king's honour preserved the fabric of society as a whole, which was why whole wars might be fought if that honour were impugned. And, if the king's honour and status were in turn derived from those of God, it followed that everyone else's honour derived from God's. Thus human sin, if not atoned for, threatens the entire structure of society because it subverts the honour of the one who maintains that structure in being.

And the means by which God's honour may be restored is also thoroughly feudal in conception. Humanity has to offer satisfaction to God; and, in medieval times, that means

> doing as many and as great good works by way of repentance, as you did many and great sins when you were leading a bad life.[258]

By performing this satisfaction for us, Christ does what we must but could not do; and in making this point, Anselm puts the emphasis not so much on the divinity of the Son as on

> the covenant between God and man and on the obligation God has placed on himself by his decision that man should remain an authentic partner.[259]

Finally, in performing this satisfaction on our behalf, Christ manifests supremely the virtue of obedience, a virtue which was fundamental not only to feudal society but to monastic society as well.[260] And Christ's obedience ensures the restoration not only of God's honour but also of our place in his presence. The intimacy of Eden, for which we were created, is ours once more; and Anselm concludes his grandest meditation with a prayer of peroration worthy of its theme, once again seeking to appropriate for himself (and his readers) the fruits of our redemption:

> Lord, make me taste by love what I taste by knowledge; let me know by love what I know by understanding . . . Draw me to you, Lord, in the fullness of love. I am wholly yours by creation; make me all yours, too, in love. Admit me into the inner room of your love (*intra cubiculum amoris tui*) . . . Lord, do not reject me; I faint with hunger for your love; refresh me with it. Let me be filled with your love, rich in your affection, completely held in your care. Take me and possess me wholly, who with the Father and the Holy Spirit are alone blessed to ages of ages. Amen.[261]

Conclusion

A final question needs to be asked: to what extent was this Italian-born Norman monk replacing the wider perspectives of Anglo-Saxon spirituality with something as foreign as it was narrow? It is certainly true that Anselm's *Prayers and meditations* reflect the influence of Carolingian (i.e. continental French) patterns of devotion, though Anselm far exceeded his forebears, both in stylistic subtlety and theological depth.[262] But it is also clear that eleventh-century England reflected considerable interest in the kind of devotion (including prayer to individual saints) which Anselm was to make so much his own.[263] There is little reason to suppose that he was importing something that was foreign to English patterns of devotion, save only inasmuch as his florid and sophisticated style did go far beyond anything English writers had hitherto produced.

Yet that is also part of his greatness. Anselm's unflinching self-exploration, and his willingness constantly to reflect on the fact that a soul like his deserved damnation and avoided it only through the loving generosity of God, offered his contemporaries a spirituality for an anxious age, in which the unpredictability of one's feudal lord was no greater than that of one's creator. That anxiety seems to have burdened Anselm throughout his life: in an early letter he tells two friends that

> nobody, looking behind him, should contemplate how many he outstrips on the road to the celestial country, but continually looking ahead, let him consider anxiously whether he is advancing in the same way as those whose election none of the faithful doubts.[264]

And Eadmer describes Anselm as comparing the soul, hemmed in after death by demons, to a hare trapped by dogs beneath a horse's legs.[265] In the end, though, Anselm's recurrent anxiety (which must have been as much a personal characteristic as a *point-de-départ* for his theology) only leads him to contrast the more sharply what humanity deserves and what, through Christ, it can receive. It is precisely his achievement to bequeath to the world a spirituality in which painful realism about human nature is counterpointed by a hope that is all the greater for being so utterly undeserved. In a magnificent letter to Hugh, a hermit in Normandy, written in c.1086, Anselm expressed this with all the considerable force at his command:

> Dearest brother, God proclaims that he has the kingdom of heaven up for sale. For the kingdom of heaven is such that neither the eye of mortal man can see, nor his ear hear, nor his heart imagine (*cogitare*) its blessedness and glory. So that you may be able to imagine it [I say this]: if anyone deserves to reign there, whatever he wills shall be done in heaven and on earth; whatever he does not will shall be done neither in heaven nor on earth. For so great shall be the love (*dilectio*) between God and those who shall be there, and between themselves, that they shall all love each other as they love themselves but all shall love God more than themselves. And because of this, no one there shall will anything but what God wills; and what one wills, all shall will. Wherefore, whatever anyone individually wills, shall come about for himself and for all the others, for the whole of creation,

and for God himself. And thus they shall each be perfect kings, because what they will individually, shall come about; and all of them shall at the same time be one king with God and, as it were, one person . . . From heaven God proclaims that he has such merchandise for sale . . . Yet God does not give so great a gift for nothing, for he does not give it to anyone who does not love . . . Give love, therefore, and receive the kingdom; love and possess (*ama et habe*).

Moreover, since reigning in heaven is nothing but being so welded (*conglutinari*) through love into one will with God and all holy angels and human beings, that all at the same time experience one power: love God more than yourself and you will already begin to hold what you want to have there in perfection.[266]

In heaven, our deepest and most individual aspirations will be fulfilled, precisely because they will become identical with God's. And when that happens, we shall become kings and queens. It is tempting to see in this letter, written well before Anselm became archbishop, a foretaste of his later battles with English royalty over the liberty of the church. But that would be naïve. In the final analysis, feudal structures are for Anselm not so much subverted as transfigured: post-Conquest kingship, whose power and religious mystique had been considerably enhanced, and which must have appeared both unattainable and magically attractive to many who heard of it only through rumours and stories, was accessible to all, not just to courtly grandees[267] – all, that is, who were prepared (ideally in the monastic life) to make Anselm's lonely courage and integrity their own: 'Give love, therefore, and receive the kingdom: love, and possess.'

From Image to Likeness: Aelred of Rievaulx (1110–67)

Introduction

Aelred was born in the year after Anselm died, and on paper appears to have had a far more insular life than the latter: born at Hexham, and probably educated at Durham (though he describes himself as a graduate of the kitchen, rather than of the schools[268]), he spent about ten years in the household of King David of Scotland before becoming a monk at the Cistercian abbey of Rievaulx in 1134: thereafter he was successively novice master at Rievaulx, abbot of the daughter house of Revesby, and abbot of Rievaulx itself from 1147 until his death in 1167.[269] But the bare account is deceptive: apart from Scotland, Aelred visited Rome in 1142 and several general chapters of the Cistercian Order at Cîteaux; and his work is a major part of the astonishing spread of Cistercian influence and spirituality at the time. His writings include a history of the kings of England, a set of homilies on Isaiah, and lives of St Ninian and St Edward the Confessor, as well as the five most important spiritual texts: the 'Mirror of charity' (*Speculum caritatis*); the rule of life Aelred wrote for female recluses (*De institutione inclusarum*); the 'Treatise concerning Jesus as a boy of twelve' (*Tractatus de Jesu puero duodenni*); the study of Christian friendship (*De spiritali amicitia*); and 'On the soul' (*De anima*), which was almost certainly finished only shortly before his death.[270]

Aelred's world-view is that of Cîteaux, and supremely that of St Bernard, from whose monastery of Clairvaux Rievaulx was founded. This gave Aelred a particularly close link with French Cistercian spirituality. We should not underestimate his Englishness: quite apart from his *vitae* of Edward the Confessor and Ninian, he evidently had a special fondness for St Cuthbert.[271] But it is perfectly true that many of his works contain little that could not have come from a French Cistercian pen: this is perhaps particularly true of the *De Iesu puero*, with its characteristically Cistercian combination of rhetorical exuberance, intensely scriptural texture, and affective meditation on the humanity and human life of Jesus.[272] It is also true that Aelred is an unequivocally monastic writer, not only in that he wrote above all for the edification of his brethren and of fellow-religious, but also in his stout espousal of conservative Augustinian theology: in all his works, but above all in the *De anima*, Aelred's reliance on and defence of St Augustine, whom he called 'that man of inimitable subtlety',[273] is unwavering, though that in no way prevents his writings from exuding a character and clarity of their own. Indeed it could be said that Aelred, like Bernard, gave Augustine's spirituality a less generally ecclesial, more sharply monastic content and focus.

Aelred and Cistercian spirituality

The most attractive aspects of Aelred's spirituality are usually regarded as those found in his *Speculum caritatis* and in his *De spiritali amicitia*. But if we are really to enter, as far as we are able, into his spiritual worldview, we might do best to begin with his last work (the *De anima*), which reflects his lifelong interest in psychology and the inner workings of the soul,[274] and which opens up to us his understanding of the human person as someone created in the image and likeness of God. For Aelred, this understanding was no speculative analysis. Rather, as Dom Odo Brooke put it,

> his main purpose is to show how this theme with its foundation in the objective history of salvation is reflected in the journey of the individual soul to God within the whole formation of the monastic experience.[275]

So the spiritual journey of the (monastic) soul becomes the paradigm of the whole history of salvation. Hence the stress on *experience* of God, so crucial in both Aelred and other Cistercian writers like St Bernard: what interested the Cistercians was how we come to know the mystery of salvation through our own experience, precisely by living it;[276] and it is this appropriating of objective truth as both a mainspring and a metaphor for the interior life which forms the essential heart of Cistercian spirituality. This approach was to have a long history: the stress on the experience of the trinitarian life within the soul was to be extensively developed by the Rhineland mystics – Eckhardt, Ruusbroec and Tauler.[277] But it was lived first in the cloisters of Clairvaux and Rievaulx.

Spiritual anthropology

Aelred follows Augustine in arguing that God is unchanging being, present in everything he has made, and that the relationship of the soul to the body is analogous to that of God to creation: thus he writes that 'the human soul, made in the image of its creator, acts in its own body in somewhat the same fashion as does God in all his creatures'.[278] By acting in this way the soul is 'imitating the likeness of him who is everywhere in all his creatures'.[279] Like Augustine, Aelred conceived of human beings as midpoints in creation, halfway between angel and beast, consisting not merely of a soul imprisoned in a body (as in much Platonism), but of a combination of both soul and body in one person.[280]

And the crucial point about the human soul is that (because it is made in God's image) its primary attribute is reason. Aelred describes the soul as 'a kind of rational life, changeable in time but not in place, immortal in its own way, and capable of being either happy or miserable'.[281] It is our rational attributes (such as our memory) which, for Aelred, distinguish us from animals, who only have irrational souls.[282] And, because these attributes are also attributes of God, they are eternal, whereas the irrational soul of an animal dies when it does.

It is crucial to see that for Aelred this distinction is a theological one (indeed for him it was doubtless a physiological one too): we are different from animals not quantitatively, as a modern evolutionist might argue, but qualitatively. So Aelred can happily agree with Augustine that in terms of the senses animals are often our superiors: they can see further, run faster, and have a stronger sense of smell.[283] But it is reason, not the senses, which is the highest creaturely attribute, not simply (as we might say) because it enables us to use our senses shrewdly, but because it is part of the soul and thus on an altogether higher level of creation. Each human soul, created in God's image, is eternal; and because body and soul form one person, the human body must be eternal too. So, even though in many respects the bodies of animals are better than ours, in the final analysis ours are more holy than theirs, for ours (unlike theirs) will rise again.[284]

It should already be clear how utterly different Aelred's view of human beings is from ours. We are likely to conceive of human beings, animals and even trees as parts of a single chain of being, or evolutionary process, each stage shading imperceptibly into the next. But Aelred does not see creation like that at all. Trees have life, but only of a vegetative kind: animals possess in addition the life of the senses; but human beings alone possess reason, a divine attribute, and so are destined for eternity. So, although Aelred affirms the natural goodness of the whole created order, declaring that no one 'may consider any of God's creatures impure without impious sacrilege',[285] this reflects more his reverence for the providential *ordo* of the creation, whereby everything has its place in the divine scheme of things (just as everyone has their place in a feudal society or Cistercian monastery), rather than any interest in creatures in their own right.[286]

A number of important principles follow from this view. First, the senses have a real but limited role: they can be put to good use by the rational soul[287] (we shall see below how this happens), but they remain potentially earthbound and distracting. Secondly, the entire preoccupation of the human being should be with the salvation of his or her own soul, and with those of others: for Aelred, human beings will end up either infinitely better off or infinitely worse off than animals – either damned or saved.[288] Confronted by so terrifying a choice, we might be tempted to envy the easy vacuity of an animal's life, with only mindless extinction to look forward to. But we would do so in vain: we are created with an eternal destiny, for the sabbath of infinite love or the torment of infinite condemnation. Thirdly, the logical consequence of such a view of human nature is the life of the cloister. The monastery is, for Aelred as for Anselm, the natural (and ideally the normative) place in which to spend this life;[289] and its entire purpose is to create a situation in which human beings may best seek (and proclaim to others) the eternal fulfilment for which they were made.

The 'land of unlikeness'

Now the fact of being created in the image of God endows us with the capacity to share the life of God, the *beatitudo* which he supremely enjoys, as well as with a longing to share it. Alas, human beings missed their chance: by trying to steal the likeness of God (in Eden) – that is, by trying to make themselves godlike by their own efforts and for their own ends – Adam and Eve achieved instead the reverse: the 'unlikeness of beasts' (and were thus clothed in animal skins).[290] The result of the Fall is that we dwell in this 'land of unlikeness', a common theme in patristic and medieval literature and described by Aelred as being like the experience of the Prodigal Son far from home.[291] Thus the image of God within us was disfigured (*corrupta*), but not wholly destroyed: we still possess within ourselves a trinity which is a faint but real imprint of the divine Trinity: memory (but now subject to forgetfulness), knowledge (but prone to error), and love (but tempted towards cupidity).[292] Indeed, because of our creation in the image of God, there is no human being who does not seek happiness – everyone has an *appetitus beatitudinis*. The trouble is that most seek it in the wrong places – in worldly pleasures, or in association with creatures that belong beneath us in the *ordo* of the world.[293]

The remedy is, first, like the Prodigal Son, to come to our senses: that is, to see the truth about our selves and our condition if we are to find our way home (to 'return to your heart', as Aelred puts it);[294] and, secondly, to seek the recovery of our lost happiness, in other words of the divine likeness which we were made to share, by directing our divinely given longings towards God. Again, the ideal place to do this is the monastery, where the monk can share in the virtue and goodness which befit one dwelling in the 'land of likeness' (the *regio similitudinis*).[295]

Spirituality and desire

One of the most positive aspects of Aelred's theology is the dynamism that it imparts to the spiritual life. Like Augustine, Aelred has a high doctrine of desire, for it is precisely in virtue of our being created in God's image that there exists within us an infinite desire that God alone can satisfy.[296]

Aelred speaks of 'a desire born deep within us' (*innatum desiderium internis visceribus*) which must be rightly ordered and directed if it is not to lead us astray.[297] Thus he can declare that:

Love arouses desire, desire obtains access, access prepares the way for consent [between God and his spouse], and so the wedding feast is celebrated.[298]

But the effort involved in ensuring that this desire is indeed directed aright was clearly for Aelred a continual, even desperate, struggle: Walter Daniel describes him periodically plunging into a cold water tank to quench the heat of every vice;[299] and Aelred advises nuns to fast in order to dampen physical longings,[300] recalling in times of temptation the communion of saints (especially those female saints whose heroic chastity they should imitate),[301] and reflecting in the process on his own long and often agonizing struggle to remain chaste:

> Frequently . . . when he felt forbidden movements he rubbed his body with nettles . . . When all this proved of no avail and the spirit of fornication still harassed him, he prayed . . . He was granted some temporary relief but refused lasting tranquillity. My God, what crosses, what tortures, that wretched man then endured, until in the end he came to find such joy in chastity that he conquered all the pleasures of the flesh that can be experienced or imagined. But then also it was only for a time that he was delivered, and now when sickness is added to old age he still cannot flatter himself that he is safe.[302]

It is language of this kind, and the experiences which gave rise to it, that underline the immense difference of perspective between Aelred's world-view and ours. To modern minds, outward happiness is likely to conduce to inward happiness too, and outward suffering to inward suffering. Nonsense, says Aelred: it is precisely the other way round. If your intention is rightly directed – in other words, if you are genuinely seeking to do God's will, then outward suffering will actually increase inward consolation provided it is undertaken as a conscious *imitatio Christi*.[303] Where a twentieth-century spiritual writer might be expected to argue that true happiness derives from the *integration* of physical and spiritual needs, Aelred in effect argues that it comes from their uncompromising *separation*: and the more we suffer in this world, the more we shall be consoled in the next.[304] But all of this makes clear sense if we set it in the context of Aelred's view of the human person, with which we began. The enormous cost of either repressing altogether or redirecting the promptings of the flesh is infinitely worthwhile – literally so, for it is precisely such promptings that are most likely to divert us from our eternal vocation and draw us down to a life dominated by sensuality and thus little different from that of animals. And for Aelred that would be both catastrophic (in view of its ultimate consequences) and tragic: for we are created with infinite longings, and will be happy only when those are infinitely satisfied.

This is not to say that Aelred has an entirely negative view of sensuality and the emotions, for they too are eternal. On the contrary: his spirituality is infused with a warm affectivity. He writes of the 'attachment of charity' (*affectus caritatis*), defining *affectus* as 'a kind of spontaneous, pleasant inclination of the spirit toward someone';[305] and although he stresses that the surest criterion for sound spiritual progress is the alignment of our will with God's rather than the experience of these 'attachments',[306] it is clear that he sees a positive role for spontaneous and affective impulses in the spiritual life as a whole. In particular he encourages us to reflect on the human Christ with 'tender attachment' (*pium affectum*) precisely in order to turn away from carnal delights.[307] Aelred, like both Anselm and Bernard, encourages his readers to contemplate the motherhood of Jesus, though this time the focus is not so much Anselm's view of Christ's self-giving love but an intensely intimate personal union with Jesus – that 'oneness which is found only in the One . . . in whom there is no change'.[308]

Divine and human love

So love, for Aelred, is at once affective and rational, the fusion of will and desire;[309] and he defines it as 'a wonderful delight of the spirit' (*mira delectatio animi*). [310] Here too, what matters is that our love is rightly ordered, which means that it must be directed outside ourselves;[311] and he follows both St Bernard and St Augustine in dwelling on the importance of *amor ordinatus* – loving what one ought to love, and to the extent that it should be loved.[312] This right ordering is not something we can achieve unaided: we need the work of divine grace, a grace which 'does not take away free will'[313] (though Aelred embraces what to modern minds is one of the least attractive aspects of Augustinian theology by emphasizing that God owes no one salvation and inscrutably saves and condemns whom he wills[314]).

But how are we to know whether or not our love is rightly directed? Aelred describes love (*amor*) as 'capable of either charity or cupidity' (*capax etiam caritatis sive cupiditatis*);[315] and his suggestion as to how we may distinguish the one from the other reflects his acute pastoral sense. Charity leads to tranquillity, which is not some introspective quietism but rather a situation in which the mind does not allow itself to be upset by any disturbing events, but is able to make everything that happens contribute to its spiritual progress.[316] Cupidity, on the other hand, causes relentless anxiety,[317] which seems to have been as much a problem for Aelred as it was for Anselm.

And the tranquillity of spirit which is the fruit of a rightly ordered love is precisely a foretaste of paradise, and specifically of that sabbath rest which God enjoyed both before and after the work of creation.[318] Here too the doctrine of image and likeness is crucial; for although Aelred maintains that all creatures can experience (and indeed seek) repose, that sought by human beings is of an altogether different and higher character, because only an infinite repose can satisfy our infinite desires.[319]

The heavenly sabbath

The true sabbath is not temporal but eternal:[320] it is the 'mutual delight of Father and Son', by which each reposes in the other.[321] And its essential character is charity, *caritas*, the love which orders and enfolds all things:[322] and that love itself has a threefold character, for the tranquillity of the seventh day is not attainable without the labours and good deeds of the first six.[323] First comes a proper love of self, for without that there can be no real love of anyone else;[324] secondly, love of neighbour, for which Aelred sets out a sixfold structure, corresponding to the first six days of creation: we begin with love of our immediate family, then with love successively of our special friends, our fellow-religious, our fellow-Christians, those outside the church, and finally of our enemies (the latter constituting that virtue by which a person is made a son or daughter of God[325]).

Above them both, though, is the love of God, when the soul, purified and prepared first by a properly ordered love of neighbour and of self, and 'inflamed with utmost desire' (*nimio desiderio succensa*), goes beyond the veil of the flesh and enters the sanctuary where Christ is present: here, in the ultimate leisure of eternity (the *Sabbatum sabbatorum*), it sees and knows God in all his fullness:[326] its restless desires are satisfied, and its mutable nature transformed into that Being which is by nature unchangeable.[327] Aelred's vision of the eternal sabbath reflects the anthropology with which we began: he believes that, in heaven, our senses will (so to speak) be put to sleep, thus enabling the soul to contemplate what is above it in a manner which is impossible while it is distracted by earthly needs and images.[328] He clearly envisages a state in which his own long struggle against wrongly directed desires will at last be over – not a chilly, dispassionate objectivity, but an active repose, absorbed and cradled in the divine love:

> If love of the flesh has been thoroughly lulled to sleep or really absorbed (*absorptus*) by the fire of divine love, there will be no toil over outward things, because the mind will not be able to be vexed by any affliction which cannot be melted by love.[329]

This progression from love of self, via love of neighbour, to love of God marks the rhythm of all spiritual progress for Aelred. The movement is always *ad se . . . extra se . . . supra se*, first inward, then outward, then upward.[330] And the three forms of love (of self, neighbour, and God) belong together: 'none of them can be possessed without all. And when one wavers they all diminish'.[331] In the monastery, where an accurate self-love, practical and enduring love of neighbour, and unconditional love of God can be synthesized, the fullness of each can be sought and (to the extent that it is possible in this life) attained.

It is important to set Aelred's conception of the sabbath against its background in Augustine if we are to see clearly what he means. In his extended treatment of the sabbath in Book IV of the *De Genesi ad litteram*, Augustine emphasizes that God's sabbath rest implies not a *withdrawal* from the creation but rather its continuing oversight,[332] and that we begin to experience that sabbath rest now, not by abstaining from good works, but by doing them in the hope of what is to come.[333] And that experience is not simply an *imitation* of God's rest, but a *participation* in it, for it is precisely in the eternal sabbath that our changeable natures are transfigured by our sharing in God's unending changelessness, in which our lost likeness to him is recovered in its entirety at last.[334]

Spiritual friendship

It is within the context of this spirituality – rooted in the inner workings of the human person, dynamic in its analysis of how the soul may recover its lost likeness to God, but sternly ascetic in its application – that the other aspects of Aelred's spirituality need to be seen. The 'humanism' with which Aelred is associated, in particular because of his delight in human friendship, is nothing remotely like the humanism of Cicero or Petrarch, for all his citations of classical authors:[335] his consists in a sharply focused fascination with human beings made in God's image, with their fearful potential for both paradise and perdition, and rooted in his ascetic psychology. It is true that for Aelred friendship is one of the distinguishing marks of human beings.[336] But it is clear that he cannot conceive of a genuine spiritual friendship existing outside the church,[337] and perhaps not even outside the cloister.[338] What he surely has in mind is rather the unselfish, disinterested mutual love of two people vowed to the religious life, each of whom can be a *custos animi* for the other,[339] and whose friendship enables each to despise the world and experience something of the first-fruits of eternity.[340]

A final point remains to be made. For Aelred, as for so many of his monastic contemporaries, the religious life is a *solitudo pluralis*, a shared solitude, because God made all his creatures (even trees) to share in his essential oneness, and thus to enjoy one another's company;[341] and even those vowed to physical separation from others are never alone: indeed the monastic community forms one body.[342] Aelred cites Augustine's attractive notion of the communion of saints: they cannot have any direct knowledge of what happens on earth (for otherwise they would not be happy in heaven); but they receive from those who die an up-date on the latest situation so as to enable them to pray for us![343] He ends his last work by declaring that the saints care and pray for us 'all the more devoutly as they realize that their own supreme happiness is unattainable without us'.[344] This approach is characteristic of medieval monastic spirituality at its best: for all its inwardness, the infinite potential that exists within the soul is to be developed within a community of love, where monks or nuns, freed from both the constraints and the delusions of life in the world, may offer their fellow human beings outside the cloister a blueprint for living, to be imitated as best they may.

Conclusion

Aelred died at Rievaulx on 11 January 1167, finally released from the terrible arthritis that overshadowed his last years.[345] His character emerges fitfully from his writings. He was clearly a person of great personal warmth and affection, capable of both the heights of spiritual intensity and of bleak despair[346] – but capable too of bringing both extremes into his prayer:[347] there is in his own life of prayer not just an affective intimacy but also a robust integrity, even courage, and a determination to bring the needs of the whole world before God.[348] He is instinctively introspective: he occasionally celebrates the beauty of nature, but not nearly as often as the intrinsic beauty of the human being, made in God's image.[349] He admires the majesty of London, but only in order to emphasize that the human soul is far greater than any city.[350] Like any good Cistercian he has no time for ornate display in music[351] or architecture,[352] let alone any kind of 'inquisitive restlessness to know about events and things in the world'.[353] Above all, though, his long experience as novice master seems to have shaped his writings, giving all of it (even the histories, with their fascination with individual characters[354]) a strongly pastoral edge.[355] He loved his brethren, and saw the cloister at Rievaulx not as an escape from the world so much as a vantage point from which it could best be served: so he tells the recluse to whom he writes to embrace the whole world with her love, and especially the afflicted and poor:

> Open the heart of your love to them all, bestow your tears upon them, pour out your prayers for them.[356]

Like St Bernard's, his spirituality is more affective than scholarly;[357] and it lacks the rigorous theology of Anselm's. But that was not Aelred's fault, nor even his concern. He sought instead to give to those within the cloister a perspective and a programme which could lead them to eternity, and to those outside it the best of all possible reasons for joining them:

> The whole strength of his mind was poured out like a flood upon God and His Son – it was as though he had fastened to the crucified Christ a very long thread whose end he had taken back as far as the seat of God the Father. By this thread I mean the strain and concentrated vigour of his mental being. He always remembered and strove after that which made us when we were not and, when we were evil, made us over again to be good. Whenever he considered the beauty, order or worth of creatures, he saw in the transitory him who is not able to pass away . . . In his reflections about the world of material creation and its agreement in variety he realized how wonderful was the Creator of beings which, weak and beyond counting, yet possess to the utmost, throughout and in their totality, the grace of harmonious beauty.[358]

CONCLUSION: THE WALL PAINTINGS OF HARDHAM

In the tiny eleventh-century church at Hardham, near Pulborough in West Sussex, there is a collection of wall paintings which date from c.1120. The church itself came under the jurisdiction of the Cluniac priory at Lewes after the Conquest; and the paintings may well have been executed by someone from there. They exhibit a remark-able stylistic eclecticism: Anglo-Saxon figures, Byzantine iconography (such as the crossed arms of the angel Gabriel), Norman motifs. Nature and supernature, patristic theology and contemporary daily life, are intertwined: after the Fall, Adam and Eve are shown sitting glumly back-to-back, peeking at each other over their shoulders; and Eve is shown not (as usually) spinning, but milking a huge cow, while Adam watches from a tree. The walls of the nave tell the story of the birth of Christ, with a number of unusual or continental details (such as the wise men wearing brimmed hats in one scene, and in another sleeping under a single coverlet while they dream). At the west end (largely indecipherable) is hell: at the east, the Majesty: in the centre, above the chancel arch, the Agnus Dei. Angels appear frequently throughout the cycle.[359]

In its eclecticism, its depiction of the human Christ, its deceptive simplicity, its sturdy originality, the Hardham design catches exactly the character of medieval English spirituality. Life is a journey, a movement from birth to death through conflict, temptation and labour: the final goal is damnation or joy, and unquestion-ably judgement. But the journey is travelled in company – with the angels and saints, and with Christ, whose humanity is our constant example. It is an anxious journey, but never a lonely one. Taken as a whole, the paintings (which cover the entire church) are overwhelmingly moving; and that for one reason above all others. Enter the church door, and they surround you. You are no longer a spectator, or even an imitator. You are a participant. Like the mystery plays, the gilds and confraternities, the lives of monks and recluses, the stories of saints like Godric – yet perhaps more vividly than all of them – the paintings at Hardham offer us a priceless point of entry to the troubled but transforming beauty of the medieval vision.

NOTES

1. From Geoffrey of Durham, *Vita S. Godrici* 2, in *Acta Sanctorum*, May, vol. 5 (Antwerp, 1685), pp. 74–5 (my trans.).

2. Ward (1982) p. 78. For an exploration of similar contemporary stories about hermits and hunters, see Brian Golding, 'The hermit and the hunter', in J. Blair and B. Golding (eds.), *The cloister and the world: essays in medieval history in honour of Barbara Harvey* (Oxford: Clarendon, 1996), pp. 95–117: Golding makes the fascinating point that, at a time when royal forests were being inexorably extended, the hermits' sanctuaries in their midst were defiant symbols of divine (and ecclesiastical) authority, safe places for humans and animals alike where royal and baronial power was stopped in its tracks.

3. Reginald of Durham, *Libellus de vita et miraculis S. Godrici*, pp. 152–8, and cf. p. 31. There is a long and rich Christian tradition regarding the capacity of wild animals to recognize and venerate (and be transformed by) the power of the holy. See, e.g., St Jerome's very popular *Life of St Paul the first hermit*, in which Paul welcomes a thirsty she-wolf to his lonely cave, and two fierce lions appear to mourn his death (*Life*, chapters 9 and 16); and Sr Mary Donatus, *Beasts and birds in the lives of the early Irish saints* (Philadelphia, 1934).

4. This is not to argue that belief in the power of the saint to work miracles disappeared; but it is to emphasize that the *life* of the saint, both as miracle-worker and as exemplar, came to take precedence over the manner of the saint's dying or the power of his or her relics, however sig-nificant these remained. See below; and also Vauchez (1997) p. 434.

5. William of Newburgh, who visited Godric, describes him as *rusticanus et idiota, nihilque sciens nisi Christum Jesus et hunc crucifixum* (rustic and stupid, knowing nothing save Christ Jesus and him crucified); *Historia rerum Anglicarum* 2.20, p. 149. For the striking proportion of medieval saints to be born of noble lineage, see Murray (1978) part IV and appendix I.

6. Strictly speaking, an 'anchorite' or 'anchoress' is enclosed for life in a particular dwelling, whereas a 'hermit', though living in solitude, may move about: some acted as bridge-keepers.

7. The notion of hermits living in inaccessibly beautiful and solitary places is often as much a spiritual as a physical affair: the celebration of natural beauty in such contexts was often part of a desire to see the solitary life as recovering the pristine purity of Eden rather than any delighting in nature for its own sake. See Constable (1996) p. 140.

8. He was, though, under the auspices of the prior of Durham: see Reginald, *Libellus de vita et miraculis S. Godrici*, Prologue, pp. xviii–xix.

9. See Ward (1982) pp. 76–82. The capacity of animals to recognize what human beings often missed appears in other medieval saints' lives: in the eleventh-century *vita* of the child martyr St Kenelm (probably written by Goscelin of Saint-Bertin), a white cow persists in continuing to graze at the place where Kenelm's body has been secretly buried: this, and the fact that the

grass kept growing and her milk supply was twice that of the entire herd, drew people's attention to what had happened: 'that which bright lights from heaven made known, and on earth mute animals, as it were, spoke of, human cowardice did not dare to mutter'. See chapter 9 of the *vita* in Love (1996) pp. 63–5 (and for the question of authorship see pp. xcvii–ci).

10. See Douglas (1964) p. 7, though it is important to remember that Scandinavian culture and migrations had had a major effect on Normandy as on England (p. 21). See also on this subject Chibnall (1986) Part 1, Ortenberg (1992), Fleming (1993), and Stafford (1989) pp. 114–28. Several authors stress the important fact that pre-Conquest England already enjoyed very close links with continental Europe (see, e.g., Ortenberg (1992) p. 264). For an excellent exposition of English history in the period covered by this chapter, see Bartlett (2000) (pp. 102–3 deal with the shift from a Scandinavian to a Franco–German perspective for England during this period).

11. Feudalism 'involved a far-reaching restriction of social intercourse, a circulation of money too sluggish to admit of a salaried officialdom, and a mentality attached to things tangible and local. When these conditions began to change, feudalism began to wane' (Marc Bloch, *Feudal society*, vol. 2 (ET by L. A. Manyon of *La société féodale*), 2nd edn (London: Routledge & Kegan Paul, 1962), p. 443.

12. See Benson and Constable (1982) and Constable (1996). The language and imagery of renewal occurs frequently in texts from this period: thus Gilbert of Hoyland can declare that the God who remains unchanged in himself 'renews all other things' (*in se manens unus, innovat omnia*) and explores the implications of this for the spiritual life: *Sermons on the Song of Songs* 15.1, ET in CF 14, p. 178; PL 184:74.

13. On the Gregorian reform movement, see Southern (1953) chapter 3; Knowles (1963) chapter 11; Morris (1989) pp. 79–173. On the three orders, see Duby (1980), esp. pp. 102–5, and Constable (1995) pp. 279–88 (noting the references in the work of Alfred the Great and St Ælfric). There were other ways of 'ordering' medieval society: St Anselm (*De similitudinibus* 131(127), PL 159:679) classifies the three orders slightly differently as *oratores, defensores,* and *agricultores.* Alfred the Great was the first in England, and perhaps in Europe, to use the concept of the three orders: see J. E. Powell, 'The "Three Orders" of society in Anglo-Saxon England', in Lapidge et al. (eds.), *Anglo-Saxon England* 23 (Cambridge UP, 1994), pp. 103–32. See also Constable (1995), section III, esp. pp. 252–3 and 257–8. No one expressed the power of the medieval concept of *ordo* better than Shakespeare (see Ulysses' speech in *Troilus and Cressida*, Act I Scene 3: 'The heavens themselves . . .').

14. See R. W. Southern, 'Ranulf Flambard and early Anglo–Norman administration', in *Transactions of the Royal Historical Society,* 4th series, 16 (1933), pp. 95–128.

15. Fleming (1991) p. 144. Bolton (1980, pp. 37–8) also underlines the much greater insecurity of tenure brought about by the change of land ownership after the Norman Conquest.

16. Morris (1989) pp. 154–73. On the investiture contest in England, see N. F. Cantor, *Church, kingship and lay investiture in England 1089–1135* (Princeton UP, 1958); on the pivotal role played in it by Anselm, see Southern (1963) pp. 163–80 and (1990) pp. 232–4 and 264–6.

17. See especially Little (1978), Murray (1978), and Bolton (1980) pp. 73–81.

18. The *Peterborough Chronicle*, p. 160. For a brief description of this chronicle, and its relationship with the other MSS of what is collectively known as the Anglo-Saxon Chronicle, see F. M. Stenton, *Anglo-Saxon England* (Oxford history of England), 2nd edn (Oxford: Clarendon, 1947), pp. 679–83.

19. It is worth bearing in mind a point made by Frank (1995, pp. 14–15): there was no separate church community in the early Middle Ages. The whole parish, or town, or manorial estate, constituted what was assumed to be a Christian community, and people would feel they belonged to that rather than to an ecclesial community within it.

20. William the Conqueror at least facilitated (if he did not actively encourage) the advent of Jews from Normandy into England (Douglas (1964) p. 314). See also Little (1978) chapter 3, Bartlett (2000) pp. 346–60; and the Chronicle of Matthew Paris, which contains numerous references to Christian antisemitism. Ward (1982, pp. 68–76) describes the cult of St William

of Norwich (d.1144), who was believed to have been murdered by Jews.

21. Jocelin of Brakelond, *Chronicle*, p. 46.

22. *Chronicle of Matthew Paris*, trans. Giles, vol. III, p. 280.

23. Boase (1953) p. 89. On bestiaries, see also F. McCulloch, *Medieval Latin and French bestiaries* (1960).

24. On the relationship between monks, hermits and poverty, see Leyser (1984) pp. 52–6; M. Mollat, 'Les moines et les pauvres', in *Il monachesimo e la riforma ecclesiastica (1049–1122)* (Milan: Università Cattolica del Sacro Cuore, 1971), pp. 193–227; and Little (1978). Constable (1996, p. 30) points out that, for many in this period, material prosperity represented a blessing, as much for those in religious communities as for those 'in the world'. See also p. 34 for the hermit Robert of Arbrissel's espousal of voluntary poverty; pp. 125ff and 283–4 for the notion of imitating the poor and naked Christ in this period; and Constable (1995) section II for the imitation of Christ in general during this period. For the relationship between saint-hood and the imitation of Christ, see also Vauchez (1997) pp. 439–40.

25. Douglas (1964) pp. 249–55 and p. 286. On the means by which William the Conqueror presided over a considerable increase in royal power at the cost of the major landowning barons (at least partly the effect of winning England by military victory rather than on the terms previously offered and rejected by King Harold), see Fleming (1991), esp. chapter 7. For the religious nature of medieval kingship, see Erickson (1976) pp. 129–34 and Bartlett (2000) pp. 125–7.

26. Duby (1981) p. 33.

27. Duby (1981) pp. 44–5.

28. Duby (1981) p. 45.

29. It is important, though, to stress that even for systematic scholastic writers like Aquinas, God remained, either directly or indirectly, the cause of all that happened: see Brian Davies, *The thought of Thomas Aquinas* (Oxford: Clarendon, 1992), esp. chapter 9.

30. For the treatises, such as those of Vincent of Beauvais (d.1264) and others, see E. Mâle, *The Gothic image* (trans. D. Nussey) (London: Dent, 1913; repr. Fontana, 1961), esp. pp. 23–7; Chenu (1968) pp. 99–145; Duby (1981) pp. 136–65; Hamilton (1986) pp. 94–5. For the cathedrals, see N. Pevsner, *An outline of European architecture,* 7th edn (Harmondsworth: Penguin, 1963), esp. pp. 114–18; Mâle, esp. pp. 390–9; and Southern (1995) p. 35.

31. Hugh of St Victor, *Didascalicon* 6.5; trans. Jerome Taylor, *The Didascalicon of Hugh of St Victor* (New York: Columbia University Press, 1961); cited in M. K. Lafferty, *Walter of Châtillon's Alexandreis* (Publications of the Journal of Medieval Latin 2) (Turnhout: Brepols, 1998), p. 142 (chapter 4 of Lafferty's book contains an excellent study of twelfth-century attitudes to nature).

32. See Southern (1970) pp. 171ff and (for the shrines of saints) Nilson (1998). There is a fasci-nating passage in William of Newburgh's *Historia rerum Anglicarum* (I.28) where he describes certain spectacular events (*prodigiosi*) and then proceeds to ponder their causes.

33. Chenu (1968) p. 46. See also C. S. Lewis, *The discarded image: an introduction to medieval and Renaissance literature* (Cambridge UP, 1964), pp. 152–3.

34. Cited in Southern, *Robert Grosseteste: the growth of an English mind in medieval Europe*, 2nd edn (Oxford: Clarendon, 1992), p. 216. See also Grosseteste's *On the six days of creation* (*Hexaemeron*), trans. C. F. J. Martin (Auctores Britannici Medii Aevi VI(2)) (Oxford UP for the British Academy, 1996).

35. See the remarks of Lewis Mumford, in *Technics and civilization* (1934), quoted in Chenu (1968) p. 39: 'By a slow natural process, the world of nature broke in upon the medieval dream of hell and paradise and eternity. In the fresh naturalistic sculpture of the thirteenth-century churches one can watch the first uneasy stir of the sleeper, as the light of morning strikes his eyes . . . The interest in nature steadily broadened and became more consuming.'

36. The classic study of English medieval monasticism remains Knowles (1963), though he has little to say on the regular canons. See also Dickinson (1950), Leclercq (1978), Duby (1980), Bolton (1983), Hamilton (1986), Constable (1996), and (for a graphic description of the practice of medieval monasticism) Harvey (1993). See also the articles in *Il monachesimo e la*

Riforma ecclesiastica (1049–1122) (Milan: Università Cattolica del Sacro Cuore, 1971). Constable (1996, p. 35) reminds us that most of the extant textual material from this period was itself written by clerics and religious involved in the process of reform and renewal: this needs to be taken into account in assessing its objectivity. For a much more negative view about the significance of monasticism, see L. Milis, *Angelic monks and earthly men: monasticism and its meaning to medieval society* (Woodbridge: Boydell, 1992).

37. *A short history of England* (1917), chapter 6 ('The Age of the Crusades').

38. Quoted in Baker (1973) pp. 50–1. Constable (1996, p. 297) points out that in the twelfth century the term *religio* meant not a body of personal beliefs but a way of life through which people expressed their commitment to God.

39. Constable (1996, p. 87) points out that acceptance of a rich diversity of forms of religious life was one of the key characteristics of twelfth-century monastic reform.

40. See Elkins (1988) for a comprehensive exploration of this phenomenon; also Thompson (1991) and Vauchez (1997) pp. 371–2. For Cistercian opposition to women's religious houses, see Thompson (1991), esp. pp. 94 and 213.

41. Cîteaux, though, was itself founded from Molesme, a centre of reformed monasticism established by St Robert in 1075. It is a mistake to assume too sharp a distinction between the various monastic orders in this period: see J. Haseldine, 'Friendship and rivalry: the role of *amicitia* in twelfth-century monastic relations', *Journal of Ecclesiastical History* 44 (1993), pp. 390–414.

42. William of Malmesbury, *Gesta Regum Anglorum* II.380, trans. Giles in EHD vol. II, p. 694. The phrase cited comes originally from Juvenal, *Satires* I.38.

43. See Knowles (1963) chapters XIII–XIV.

44. St Bernard of Clairvaux.

45. William of Newburgh, *Historia rerum Anglicarum* I.14.

46. John of Ford, *Sermons on the final verses of the Song of Songs* 96.4, CCCM 18, p. 651; ET in CF 46, p. 168. For John's spirituality, see Holdsworth (1959) and (1961), Costello (1972), McCorkell (1985), and Costello and Holdsworth (1996). Gilbert was abbot of the Cistercian monastery of Swineshead in Lincolnshire: he followed St Bernard in writing a series of sermons on the Song of Songs, though he does not appear to regard himself as in any formal sense responsible for continuing the series that Bernard began. For Gilbert, see Braceland (1982), Holman (1984), and Braceland's introduction to the English translation of the Sermons (CF 14) (Kalamazoo, 1978), pp. 3–40. For John's predecessor Baldwin of Ford, who became archbishop of Canterbury, see Knowles (1963) pp. 316–27, Bell (1980), and Holman (1988). His sermons are printed in PL 204 and have been translated by Bell (see Bibliography).

47. See Cowdrey (1986) pp. 345–6.

48. For the Carthusians, see Knowles (1963) chapter XXII (which includes some of Knowles' purplest prose); and Thompson (1930), still an essential study and reference work. Her earlier work, *A history of the Somerset Carthusians* (London: John Hodges, 1895), though less critical and comprehensive, contains some vivid portrayals of early English Carthusian life. For St Hugh, see the *Vita* by Adam of Eynsham. See also Knowles (1963) pp. 381–91, and Mayr-Harting (1987).

49. Adam of Eynsham, *Magna vita* II, pp. 188–9.

50. It is noteworthy, though, that many hermitages became houses of Augustinian canons – not primarily (as on the continent) because of the infectious fervour of the original hermit or hermits, but because of the extent to which secular lords whose families had patronized the original hermits sought to enhance their reputations by enlarging the original foundation. See Herbert (1985).

51. Dickinson (1950) p. 26.

52. Notably in exhorting canons to return to the common life, rather than living alone, and to give up what had become an increasing practice of owning property: see Damian's letter of 1051 to the canons of Fano Cathedral (Ep. 39, in *Die Briefe des Petrus Damiani*, ed. K.

Reindel (MGH) vol. I (Munich, 1983), pp. 373–84); and his letter of 1063 to Pope Alexander II (Ep. 98, in vol. 3 (Munich, 1989), pp. 84–97). English translations by Owen J. Blum OFM, *The Letters of Peter Damian* (The Fathers of the Church: mediaeval continuation, vol. 2) (Washington DC: Catholic University of America Press, 1990), pp. 98–110. Both letters give valuable insights into the canonical reform movement of the eleventh century. See also Dickinson (1950) pp. 34–5.

53. For the spirituality of the order in general, see Petit (1947). For a brief account of their arrival in England, see Knowles (1963) pp. 360–2.

54. Brooke (1985) p. 115. Webber (1992, pp. 113–39) shows how the regular canons at Salisbury Cathedral during this period drew heavily, but not uncritically, on monastic texts in order to fashion a pattern of spirituality appropriate to their own manner of life.

55. For Gilbert see Foreville (1986), Elkins (1988), and Golding (1992); for the order, see Thompson (1991) pp. 73–9.

56. There was an abortive attempt, though, in the first decade of the thirteenth century, to establish a foundation of Gilbertine nuns in Rome; see Golding (1992) pp. 259–61.

57. Golding (1992) pp. 7–33. Brooke (1985, pp. 114–15) and Knowles (1963, pp. 205–7) suggest that the reason why the Cistercians refused to allow Gilbert to affiliate was because they wanted nothing to do with a community of women: Golding (1992, pp. 26–8) argues convincingly that the real reason had to do with the poverty and remoteness of Sempringham.

58. *The Book of St Gilbert*, chapter 18, pp. 50–1; Golding (1992) pp. 28 and 31–3.

59. Golding (1992) pp. 78–90. Golding points out that Gilbert's rule was firmly authoritarian, and that the women enjoyed almost no say in decision relating to their lives (see esp. p. 135). For Gilbert's tendency to authoritarianism, see pp. 14 and 69–70.

60. *The Book of St Gilbert*, chapter 25, pp. 76–85; see also Knowles, 'The revolt of the lay brothers of Sempringham', in *English Historical Review* 50 (1935), pp. 465–87; D. M. Smith, 'Hugh's administration of the diocese of Lincoln', in Mayr-Harting (1987), pp. 19–47, esp. p. 35; Golding (1992) pp. 40–51. Elkins (1988, pp. 130–4) stresses the apocalyptic dimension of Gilbertine spirituality.

61. 'Ascetics, like hippies, flourish in a successful materialist society where there are the resources and surpluses to sustain and indulge them' (Baker (1993) p. 211).

62. For the best recent exploration of this theme in English, see Leyser (1984). See also Murray (1978), esp. Part IV; and the series of articles in *L'eremitismo in Occidente nei secoli XI e XII* (Miscellanea del Centro di Studi Medioevali 4) (Milan: Università Cattolica del Sacro Cuore, 1965). For medieval emphasis on imitating the human Christ, see Constable (1995), esp. pp. 169–93.

63. Reginald, *Libellus* 9, p. 41. The biblical text is Matthew 19.2.

64. See B. Ward, 'The desert myth: reflections on the desert ideal in early Cistercian monasticism', in Pennington (1976) pp. 183–99. It is worth noting that terms like 'solitude' or 'wilderness' in this period could have a spiritual rather than primarily geographical meaning: many solitaries lived close to, or even in, centres of population (see Constable (1996) p. 120).

65. Constable (1987) points out how twelfth-century writers affirmed the value of an inner solitude whereby the external isolation of the hermit might be imitated by any devout Christian willing to practise an interior withdrawal in order to contemplate Christ.

66. Compare the arguments of Baker (1970 and 1973) with Leyser (1984) pp. 36–7.

67. Mayr-Harting (1975), Herbert (1985). For the general social and economic context to medieval eremitism, see L. Genicot, 'L'érémitisme du XIe siècle dans son contexte economique et social', in *L'eremitismo in Occidente nei secoli XI e XII* (Milan: Università Cattolica del Sacro Cuore, 1965), pp. 45–69.

68. Warren (1985) pp. 19–20.

69. Savage and Watson (1991) pp. 15–16. The term 'recluse' is used as a generic term comprising both 'hermits' (men or women living the solitary life but not necessarily in one place all the time) and 'anchorites' or 'anchoresses' (men and women respectively living the solitary life in one place, having normally been formally enclosed by a bishop or other dignitary).

70. For Christina, see Holdsworth (1978) p. 187, Elkins (1988) pp. 27–38, and Thompson (1991) pp. 16–23.

71. Christie (1938) p. 33. This was an art-form at which England excelled at the time: see p. 2.

72. Talbot (1959) p. 29.

73. Holdsworth (1978) p. 192.

74. Mayr-Harting (1975).

75. Reginald, *Libellus* 26, p. 74.

76. John of Ford, *Life of Wulfric of Haselbury*, chapter 30, pp. 46–7.

77. See above, p. 126 ; Constable (1996) pp. 125–6.

78. See Erickson (1976) chapter 8 ('The vision of women') and Dyan Elliott, 'The physiology of rapture and female spirituality' (full ref. in the Bibliography to Chapter 4), p. 157 and n75.

79. See successively Morris (1972), Bynum (1980), Morris (1980), and Constable (1996, pp. 293–4). See also the perceptive comments of D. Elliott in *Spiritual marriage: sexual abstinence in medieval wedlock* (Chichester: Princeton UP, 1993), pp. 183–94.

80. See, e.g., Pauline Matarasso, *The redemption of chivalry: a study of the 'Queste del Saint Graal'* (Histoire des idées et critique littéraire 180) (Geneva: Droz, 1979). See also Southern (1953) pp. 209–44.

81. See Benton (1982); Southern (1995), esp. pp. 26–7; and Constable (1996) pp. 275–6.

82. *Sermons on the final verses of the Song of Songs* 101:1, CCCM 18, p. 683; ET in CF 47, p. 2.

83. Goscelin, *Liber confortatorius*, p. 37: 'egressa es cum Abraham de terra et de cognatione tua, ut uenias in terram quam Dominus Deus tuus dabit tibi.'

84. 'whom he particularly loved', writes William of Newburgh, *Historia rerum Anglicarum* 2.20, p. 150.

85. Reginald describes the Virgin and St Mary Magdalene appearing to St Godric and teaching him a song; *Libellus* 50, p. 119.

86. Thus Southern writes (1990, p. 31): 'Nothing is more characteristic of the time than the new light in which hermitages were beginning to be viewed: instead of being seen as battlefields in a savage war against demons and evil spirits, we begin to hear of the sweetness of solitude, the pleasing springs and refreshing breezes, and the unhindered communion with God which these surroundings afforded.' See also Southern (1966) p. 28 and Leyser (1984), esp. p. 21.

87. It is worth recalling here Pauline Matarasso's point: the medieval *aventure*, on which legends such as the Arthurian romances are based,

> has a much wider connotation than its modern English equivalent . . . In a general way the adventure represents the random, the gratuitous, the unpredictable element in life; often it is the challenge which causes a man to measure himself against standards more than human, to gamble life for honour or both for love. To this the author of the *Quest [of the Holy Grail]* adds a further dimension. For him the adventure is above all God working and manifesting himself in the physical world. To accept an adventure is to accept an encounter with a force which is in the proper sense of the word supernatural, an encounter which is always perilous. (P. M. Matarasso, introduction to *The Quest of the Holy Grail* (Harmondsworth: Penguin, 1969, p. 293)

88. On this subject, see especially Morris (1972), Bynum (1980), Benton (1981), and Constable (1996) p. 263. Richard Southern expressed the point with compelling simplicity: 'the greatest triumph of medieval humanism was to make God seem human' (1970, p. 37). See also Southern (1995) pp. 22–8 and 44.

89. Zarnecki, Holt, and Holland (1984) p. 84.

90. Zarnecki (1953) p. 117.

91. See Zarnecki (1953), and also the moving description of the carvings by Ian Nairn in *Sussex* (The buildings of England) (Harmondsworth: Penguin, 1965), pp. 157–8.

92. Henry Moore, in *Chichester 900* (Chichester Cathedral, 1975), p. 11. This emphasis on emotional display in contemporary art is underlined in ivory carving: the twelfth-century *Adoration of the Magi* in the British Museum reflects an emotional intensity not normally found in comparable continental works (see Dean A. Porter, *Ivory carving in later medieval*

England, 1200–1400 (unpublished D.Phil. thesis, State University of New York (Binghamton, NY, 1974), p. 50).

93. It is possible that English devotion to the human Christ was influenced by traditions even further afield than Ottonian Romanesque: Ortenberg (1992, p. 208) argues for Greek influence as well as that of Carolingian spirituality. Cf. also the prayer of Tovi in the *Waltham Chronicle*, which emphasizes the bitterness of Christ's suffering on the cross and thanks God 'that you have deemed me worthy of sharing in such blessings' (*The Waltham Chronicle*, pp. 14–15).

94. Sumption (1975) p. 135.

95. See the remarks of Wilmart (1932, p. 321). For Stephen, see also Hugh Farmer, 'Stephen of Sawley', in J. Walsh (ed.), *Pre-Reformation English spirituality* (London: Burns & Oates, 1965), pp. 93–103.

96. The eleventh Joy and Petition, from the *Meditationes de gaudiis beate et gloriose semper virginis Marie* of Stephen of Sawley, ed. Wilmart (1932) p. 352.

97. On these Meditations, see Baker (1973).

98. Adam of Eynsham, *Magna vita*, pp. 14–15.

99. Baldwin of Ford, *De sacramento altaris*, ed. J. Morson, pp. 270, 214–16, and 368. See also G. Macy, *The theologies of the eucharist in the early scholastic period* (Oxford: Clarendon, 1984), pp. 98–9.

100. See Bynum (1991), esp. p. 183.

101. John of Ford, *Sermons on the final verses of the Song of Songs* 105.9, CCCM 18, p. 714; ET in CF 47, p. 63; cf. Gilbert of Hoyland, *Sermons on the Song of Songs* 8.2: 'We cannot change [the divine nature] but only share in it, by participation certainly but not by essence' (ET in CF 14, p. 119, rendering the Latin '*Non commutare, sed communicare illam possumus, fruendo certe non existendo*', PL 184:49; see Braceland's textual note in CF 14, p. 126 n. 4; cf. Gilbert, 16.1, CF 20, p. 205). Note too the emphasis on perseverance ('Ponder and ponder again'), a point often made by Cistercians: thus John of Ford elsewhere speaks of the disturbing propensity for his and his fellow-monks' harps to fall silent in the middle of their chant (12.2, CF 29, p. 219); and Gilbert of Hoyland says that 'dogged prayer reaches its goal' (*pertinax oratio pertingit ad finem*), *Sermons on the Song of Songs* 6.1, ET in CF 14, p. 98; PL 184:38.

102. ET by Salu, p. 14. On this passage, see Savage and Watson (1991) pp. 345–6, and Bynum (1987). Underlying this kind of passage is a philosophical conviction, deriving originally from Platonic thought, that true love unites the lover with the object of his or her love: hence Gilbert of Hoyland can say that 'to love is already to possess; to love is also to be assimilated and united' (*nam amare, jam tenere est; etiam assimilari et uniri est*), *Sermons on the Song of Songs* 8.6, ET in CF 14, p. 123; PL 184:51. The *Ancrene Wisse* (= guide for anchoresses) is also known as the *Ancrene Riwle* (for a discussion of the title, see Wada (1994) pp. xiii–xviii). See references in the Bibliography, and also Elkins (1988) pp. 156–60, Thompson (1991) pp. 31–5, and the article by L. Johnson and J. Wogan-Browne in Wallace (1999), esp. pp. 110–19.

103. St Bernard, Letter 107, vol. 7 p. 272; ET p. 162.

104. St Bernard, Letter 107, vol. 7 p. 273; ET p. 163. Cf. Gilbert of Hoyland: 'He forestalled me . . . in finding me when I was lost. He anticipated (*pravenit*) me, though I deserved nothing . . . He found me not that I might choose him but that he might choose me. He anticipated me that he might love me before I loved him' (*Sermons on the Song of Songs* 8.8, ET in CF 14, p. 125; PL 184:52).

105. St Bernard, Letter 107, vol. 7 p. 274; ET p. 163 (slightly altered). This is not to exclude the need for human beings to take initiatives in responding to God's love, as Gilbert of Hoyland makes clear: 'a holy love promotes much personal initiative' (*multum sibi fiduciae sanctus amor assumit*), *Sermons on the Song of Songs* 1.3, trans. Braceland, CF 14, p. 71; PL 184:25. For devotion to the Holy Spirit in this period, see Constable (1996) p. 40.

106. *Sermons on the final verses of the Song of Songs* 107.7, CCCM 18, p. 726; ET in CF 47, p. 85. Another manifestation of the confident nature of this spirituality is the willingness of Cister-

cian writers to acknowledge the integrity of other ways to Christ than their own: see Gilbert of
Hoyland, *Sermons on the Song of Songs* 5.5, CF 14, p. 89; PL 184:34.

107. *Sermons on the final verses of the Song of Songs* 94.3, CCCM 18, p. 636; ET in CF 46, pp.
137–8. Cf. Gilbert of Hoyland, *Sermons on the Song of Songs* 11.5, ET in CF 14, p. 145; PL
184:60–1.

108. *Sermons on the final verses of the Song of Songs* 94.3, CCCM 18, p. 636; ET in CF 46, pp.
137–8. Cf. Gilbert of Hoyland, *Sermons on the Song of Songs* 5.6, ET in CF 14, p. 90; PL
184:35.

109. *Sermons on the final verses of the Song of Songs* 86.6, CCCM 18, p. 589; ET in CF 46, p. 42. For
John's view of freedom, see H. Costello, in Costello and Holdsworth (1996) pp. 108–9. Is it
possible that the sharp (and in some respects increasing) differences between the free and the
unfree, the *liberi homines* and the villein tenants, which characterized medieval English
society (see, e.g., Bolton (1980) p. 31) helped to foster this concern for a pervasive interior
freedom?

110. *Sermons on the final verses of the Song of Songs* 115.5, CCCM 18, p. 777; ET in CF 47, p. 184.

111. ed. Salu, p. 97 (Wada, pp. 47–8).

112. *The Life of Christina of Markyate*, pp. 36–7. Prayer during the night, both for personal spiritual growth and in order to combat the demons of darkness, is a crucial dimension of
monastic spirituality: see, e.g., John of Ford's *Life of Wulfric of Haselbury* 31, p. 48. Gilbert
of Hoyland commends the night, 'which in discreet forgetfulness disguises all things
ephemeral, scheduling a time and providing an occasion to seek him who is eternal' (*Sermons
on the Song of Songs* 1, trans. Braceland, vol. 1 p. 48; PL 184:15).

113. *The Life of Christina of Markyate*, pp. 186–7. Cf. the vivid description, in the late-twelfth-
century *Waltham Chronicle*, of the finding of a stone image of the crucified Christ, *imago
inestimabilis decoris* (an image of inestimable beauty) (*Waltham Chronicle*, pp. 8–11).

114. Gilbert of Hoyland eloquently expresses the fruits of our desire for God:

    The man who prays and desires (*optat*) seems to me to offer perfume. But he is then steeped
    in ointment when he gains access to the one he loves and takes delight in his presence. It is
    good indeed to pray and to long for (*desiderare*) the Lord but to love him and hold him and
    enjoy him is better . . . If you can love someone in his absence, how much more when he is
    present, when he grants you his company, when sweet experience *dulcis experientia*) serves
    food for love. Then indeed the soul is anointed more spiritually and more profusely when it
    is more closely joined with him. (*Sermons on the Song of Songs* 32.8, CF 20, p. 393; Migne,
    PL 184:170)

115. *The wooing of our Lord*, p. 250. For the theme of spiritual marriage, and its implications for
Christina and the writer of *Holy maidenhood*, see Elliott (1993), esp. pp. 208–9 and 224.
Elliott stresses (p. 73) the growing early medieval belief that spiritual marriages (i.e. chaste
and unconsummated ones) were eternal, whereas physical ones probably were not. She also
underlines the Gregorian church's encouragement of the cult of the virginal king, which may
in turn have encouraged the notion that true royalty was the prerogative, not of the hereditary
monarch, but of the chaste spouse of Christ (see p. 125).

116. *Holy maidenhood*, p. 239 (original in *Hali meidhad*, p. 19).

117. As Elkins (1988, p. 11) points out, many medieval women must have found the convent
infinitely preferable to matrimony.

118. *Holy maidenhood*, p. 240; *Hali meidhad*, p. 20 (and see the note on spiritual pregnancy on p.
50).

119. *The Life of Christina of Markyate*, pp. 118–19.

120. *An orison*, p. 323. The theme of Jesus as mother will be explored more fully in our treatment of
Anselm below.

121. Bynum (1984, pp. 22–58) argues that the difference consists above all in the much greater
concern, on the part of the canons, for love of both God and neighbour. But Brooke (1985, p.
121) questions whether the evidence bears this out. Since it is in any case very hard to discern
a consistently distinctive identity on the part of any given order of either monks or canons in

this period, it is likely that Brooke is correct in arguing for a difference of gradation rather than of substance here.

122. Robert of Bridlington, *The Bridlington dialogue* (ET slightly altered), 2, pp. 18–18a. The authorship of this work is disputed; and more important than the author's name is the fact that much of the text is borrowed from a slightly earlier work which is almost certainly the work of Richard of St Victor, one of the most important medieval writers on the spiritual life and one who was firmly in the Augustinian tradition. See Marvin L. Colker, 'Richard of Saint Victor and the Anonymous of Bridlington', *Traditio* 18 (1962), pp. 181–227.

123. *The Bridlington dialogue* 2, pp. 20–20a.

124. *The Bridlington dialogue* 6, pp. 69–69a.

125. Although Francis himself nowhere specifically proposes the imitation of Christ, his writings are filled with references to Christ's life and teachings and example, and his followers conceived of his own life as a model of the imitation of Christ. See Knowles (1948) vol. 1, p. 122, and Constable (1995) pp. 192–3.

126. On Francis' intuitive sense of the beautiful, see Knowles (1948) vol. 1, pp. 122–3.

127. Balthasar (1984) p. 347.

128. See Bestul (1977), and his introduction to the *Durham book of devotions*.

129. Knowles, *The religious orders*, II pp. 282–6; Morris (1989) pp. 310–12. For an example of a medieval confraternity, see the description in Meersseman (1977, pp. 50–4) of the confraternity of St Peter at Abbotsbury, Dorset, established by Orcey, a military companion of William I, after the Conquest, and consisting entirely of laity: it was self-governing.

130. For a detailed picture of how the corrodies worked, see Harvey (1993) chapter VI.

131. See Thompson (1991).

132. Thompson (1991) p. 251. The signifance of religious houses as sources of effective intercession, for laypeople in general and the gentry in particular, appears to have increased during the early thirteenth century: A. D. Brown (*Popular piety in late medieval England: the diocese of Salisbury 1250–1550* (Oxford: Clarendon, 1995), p. 33) suggests that this may reflect the growing influence of the doctrines of penance and purgatory.

133. Dickinson (1950) pp. 23–4 and 92.

134. Clanchy (1979) p. 192, Brett (1975) pp. 219–21. For Gratian's *Decretum* (its full title was *Concordia discordantium canonum*) and its influence on the English clergy, see C. Duggan, *Twelfth-century decretal collections and their importance in English history* (London: Athlone Press, 1963), Warren (1973) pp. 418–20, and Southern (1995) pp. 283–318.

135. It is worth noting that thirteenth-century canon law required parishioners to engage in duties connected with their own pastoral welfare (Brown (1995) p. 90).

136. *The Lay folks' Mass book*, introduction, pp. xxxii, li, xxxv.

137. *The Lay folks' Mass book*, introduction, pp. xxvii–xxviii.

138. Morris (1989) p. 300.

139. *The Lay folks' Mass book*, Text B, pp. 32–6.

140. Sermon for the Third Sunday in Advent, EETS s.s. 53, pp. 10–11.

141. Sermon on the Assumption, EETS s.s. 53, p. 164.

142. Sermon for Mid-Lent Sunday, EETS s.s. 53, pp. 82–3.

143. Sermon on Psalm 119.110, EETS s.s. 53, p. 210.

144. Sermon on Psalm 119.110, EETS s.s. 53, p. 214.

145. Herbert de Losinga, Sermons, vol. 1, pp. 96–7.

146. Herbert de Losinga, Sermons, pp. 240–1.

147. Herbert de Losinga, Sermons, pp. 426–7. Provision for the poor was, as canonists had emphasized since the twelfth century, an essential part of the penitential process of making satisfaction for sin (Brown (1995) p. 180 and n. 2).

148. *Poema morale*, EETS o.s. 28/34, p. 162.

149. *Poema morale*, EETS o.s. 28/34, p. 176.

150. Dickinson (1979) pp. 201–2.

151. See Frank (1995) pp. 17–19. For concepts of the holy in this period, see Bartlett (2000) pp. 180–1 and 442–9.

152. See esp. Benton (1982).

153. Duby (1981) p. 46.

154. From the Decrees of the Fourth Lateran Council (1215), cited in the Chronicles of Matthew Paris, vol. II, p. 140.

155. From an Old English Homily for Lent, ed. R. Morris, EETS o.s. 29/34, p. 22.

156. From an Old English Homily for Lent 1, ed. R. Morris, EETS o.s. 29/34, p. 36.

157. See Ortenberg (1992), esp. pp. 148–50; and W. J. Moore, *The Saxon pilgrims to Rome and the Schola Saxonum* (Fribourg: Society of St Paul, 1937).

158. Morris (1989) p. 278.

159. Sumption (1975) p. 137.

160. 'A pilgrimage was the most thorough and most acceptable form of asceticism that the hero-conscious Christianity of the eleventh century could offer to knights fearing for their salvation' (Duby (1981) p. 50). For the characteristically monastic emphasis on seeking an 'interior' Jerusalem, see Constable (1987); C. Cummings, *Monastic practices* (Cistercian Studies 75) (Kalamazoo: Cistercian Publications, 1986), pp. 174–5); and Constable (1996) p. 151.

161. See McNeill and Gamer (1938), p. 34. The theme of exile was crucial in medieval monastic spirituality: the monk embarked upon a form of spiritual exile no less real than the different forms of physical exile that many experienced.

162. Cited in McNeill and Gamer (1938) p. 425. For pilgrimage as penance, see also Sumption (1975) p. 101.

163. Sumption (1975) p. 11.

164. 'Cain in typo secularium iam pullulantibus multis millibus humani generis condidit civi-tatem: Abel in typo regnum Dei expectantium peregrinus erat' (*Liber confortatorius*, p. 37). Cf. St Augustine, *De civitate Dei* XV.1: 'we read in Scripture that Cain founded a city; but Abel, being a sojourner (*peregrinus*), founded none. For the city of the saints is above.'

165. Gray (1974) p. 60.

166. Gray (1974) p. 58.

167. Gray (1974) p. 63.

168. British Library MS Sloane 962, fol. 135; cited in Gray (1974) p. 64.

169. S. Tugwell, 'Friars and canons: the earliest Dominicans' in J. Loades (ed.), *Monastic Studies: the continuity of tradition*, II (Bangor: Headstart History, 1991), pp. 193–208; Duby (1980) p. 73; Chenu (1968) pp. 221–4. It is possible that the development of a more distinctively lay spirituality was, at least indirectly, encouraged by the Gregorian church: Dyan Elliott (*Spiri-tual marriage: sexual abstinence in medieval wedlock* (Chichester: Princeton UP, 1993), p. 141) points out that the stress on a clerical celibate elite in turn required a conventionally married laity if boundaries were not to be blurred and the elite lose its status: hence a monastic pattern of lay piety eventually came to be depreciated even by the hierarchy of the church.

170. See Chenu (1968) pp. 228–9 for a brief summary of what this meant for the development of lay spirituality.

171. See Chenu (1968) pp. 261–2.

172. Knowles (1948) vol. 1, chapter 14; Dickinson (1979) p. 211.

173. Knowles (1948) vol. 1, chapter 12; Dickinson (1979) p. 209.

174. Chenu (1968) pp. 243ff; Little (1978) p. 176; Georgianna (1981) p. 33. See also J. R. H. Moorman, *The Franciscans in England* (London: Mowbray, 1974). Elliott (1993, p. 203) points out, however, that the friars themselves became swiftly clericalized. The friars appear to have been more popular as intercessors with less prosperous laypeople than the monastic orders: see A. D. Brown, *Popular piety in late medieval England: the diocese of Salisbury, 1250–1550* (Oxford: Clarendon, 1995), p. 44.

175. Matthew Paris, *Chronica maiora*, vol. 2, p. 138, for the year 1246.

176. See, e.g., Robert Mannyng's *Handling Sin*, a translation of an Anglo-Norman manual for con-fessors based on William Peraldus' *Summa on Vices and Virtues* (mid-C13), and S. Tugwell,

Ways of imperfection: an exploration of Christian spirituality (London: DLT, 1984), chapter 14.

177. Little (1978) p. 176.
178. Little (1978) p. 207.
179. The Congregation of St Dominic, for laity, was organized in Bologna within the decade following Dominic's canonization: Little (1978) p. 208.
180. Thomas of Eccleston, *De adventu* 4, p. 21; ET p. 16.
181. Thomas of Eccleston, *De adventu* 15, p. 104; ET p. 81.
182. *The Book of St Gilbert*, Prol., p. 3.
183. See esp. Duby (1981) pp. 47–8, and Vauchez (1997) pp. 444–62, esp. pp. 461–2.
184. *Meditationes de gaudiis beate et gloriose semper virginis Mariae*, XV Meditatio, ed. Wilmart (1932) p. 356; ET (slightly altered) in CF 36, p. 57.
185. See Brown (1981). For the way in which the Norman church took up and adapted for its own purposes the Anglo-Saxon cults of royal saints, see S. Ridyard, *The royal saints of Anglo-Saxon England* (Cambridge UP 1988), esp. pp. 251–2.
186. See Chenu (1968), esp. pp. 41–2; and Ward (1981), esp. pp. 3–19 and 166–91.
187. A point made by Southern (1970, pp. 171ff).
188. See the remarks of Constable (1996, p. 269).
189. *Vita Wulfstani*, pp. 42–3.
190. *The Book of St Gilbert*, chapter 47, pp. 112–15. St Gilbert seems to have had a particular gift for making barren women fecund: see the same book, pp. 114–15 and 300–1.
191. Ward (1981), esp. pp. 67 and 215.
192. Finucane (1977) p. 59.
193. Innocent III, *Selected Letters* 10, p. 26.
194. Nilson (1998, pp. 9–10) points out the advantages for cathedrals of creating shrines in honour of a former bishop: their relics would already be in the cathedral's possession; and episcopal wealth helped meet the increasing costs of the long canonization process.
195. Ortenberg (1992) pp. 160–84.
196. Harvey (1993) p. 39.
197. Jocelin of Brakelond, *Chronicle*, pp. 106–11; and note the detailed and vivid description of how Samson reverently touches the body of the saint after rebuilding the shrine (pp. 111ff).
198. The illuminated manuscript, which dates from c.1130, is in the Pierpont Morgan Library, New York, MS M736; see Zarnecki, Holt and Holland (1984) p. 95.
199. For the shrine of St Thomas Becket, the principal sources are the accounts kept at Canterbury by two monks, Benedict and William, from 1171 to c.1184. See Benedict of Peterborough, *Miracula S. Thomas Cantuariensis*; and William of Canterbury, *Miracula S. Thomae Cantuariensis*. See also Ward (1982) pp. 89–109; and Nilson (1998) (who argues that in many instances the shrine was conceived of as an inner sanctum, a place of mystery and awe; see p. 91).
200. Ward (1982) p. 80; Finucane (1977) pp. 126–7 and 167ff.
201. See Brown, *The cult of the saints* (1981) pp. 78 and 88–94.
202. Finucane (1977) chapter 9.
203. Finucane (1977) p. 26.
204. See Vauchez (1997) pp. 427–33 and, for the devotions of pilgrims at saints' shrines, Nilson (1998) pp. 99–105.
205. Benedict of Peterborough, *Miracula S. Thomae Cantuariensis* II.15, ET in EHD, II, no. 153, p. 768.
206. See Ortenberg (1992) pp. 250–6 (esp. p. 255) for Carthusian, and general English, devotion to St Mary Magdalene.
207. Adam of Eynsham, *Magna Vita,* II, pp. 169–70. On this story, see Bynum (1991) p. 185. A similar point is made in Eadmer's *Life of St Anselm*: Eadmer breaks off a piece of a relic of St Prisca and is disappointed at its smallness; but Anselm says to him, 'If you have treated it with proper reverence, that will be as acceptable to her [to St Prisca] as if you had done so to her whole body' (*Vita Anselmi* II.55, p. 134).

208. Brieger (1957) pp. 125–6; in the thirteenth century, angelic choirs appeared at Wells, Lincoln, Salisbury, Chichester, and Westminster Abbey, among others.

209. Christie (1938) pp. 5 and 12.

210. Christie (1938) pp. 17–18.

211. See the index to his works in PL 159:1047–9.

212. In his *Threefold Exercise* (Wilmart (1930) pp. 355–74; ET in CF 36, pp. 73–4), Stephen reflects on the distinctive threefold role of angels as helpers, protectors and fellow-citizens. He clearly loved meditating on angels (see CF 36, p. 120 n. 6).

213. *Serm. in festo omnorum sanctorum II*, PL 195:347. See also Dumont (1961) pp. 535–6. This stress on the monastic life as an imitation of that of the angels appears in Alcuin's letters, and earlier still in those of St Basil: see Constable (1995) p. 175 and n. 183.

214. Ortenberg (1992) pp. 108–9. The anchorite Wulfric of Haselbury was accustomed to attending the night office in the nearby church dedicated to St Michael: his biographer John of Ford describes an angel coming to him one evening, and drawing his soul out of his body for long enough for him to see the glory of God and the hope of the saints (*Life* 18, p. 35). Interest in fallen angels was similarly extensive: thus, in attempting to explain the cause of a group of extraordinary events, including the discovery of two fierce and odoriferous greyhounds inside a huge rock, the twelfth-century historian William of Newburgh puts the blame on wicked angels (*Historia rerum Anglicarum* I.28).

215. Wilmart (1971) p. 538.

216. Wilmart (1971) p. 458. For medieval belief in a cosmos actively peopled by spiritual beings, see the first chapter of Erickson (1976).

217. Latin text in Wilmart (1935) pp. 371–9. See also Southern (1963) pp. 296–7.

218. Barrow (1956) p. 98.

219. See Ariès (1981) p. 35.

220. See Brown (1981) p. 2.

221. Brooke (1984), p. 110.

222. Ariès (1981) pp. 64–5.

223. Ariès (1981), esp. pp. 147–57.

224. Harvey (1993) pp. 24–30. Anniversary services for the dead were celebrated in parish churches as well as monastic houses from the thirteenth century onwards: see Brown (1995) pp. 93 and 96.

225. Eadmer, *Vita Anselmi* I.10, p. 19.

226. Adam of Eynsham, *Magna vita* II, pp. 75–6. The same work also includes a striking eye-witness account, obviously experienced by Adam personally, of Hugh officiating at the burial of a prelate whose body had become blackened and stinking after death (pp. 81–3).

227. Ariès (1981, esp. p. 161) argues, however, that it was not until the thirteenth century that this concern began to influence lay piety as well as that of the monasteries.

228. Warren (1985) pp. 98–9.

229. *The life of Christina of Markyate*, pp. 38–9.

230. See the introduction of A. Hamilton Thompson to his edition of the *Liber vitae ecclesiae Dunelmensis* (Surtees Society 136 (1923)), and Knowles (1963) pp. 473–6.

231. *The Lay folks' Mass book*, Bidding Prayer IV.

232. See Zarnecki, Holt and Holland (1984) p. 157; N. Pevsner, *Herefordshire* (The buildings of England) (Harmondsworth,: Penguin, 1963; repr. 1973), p. 155). The capitals date from c.1100–1110, but were moved in 1842 to various other parts of the cathedral, being replaced *in situ* by copies. There is an even more impressive representation of the harrowing of hell in the church at Quenington in Gloucestershire, for which see C. E. Keyser, 'Supplementary notes on the Norman tympanum at Quenington church', in *Archaeological Journal* 62 (1905), pp. 155–6; and J. Knowles, 'Symbolism in Norman sculpture at Quenington', in *Archaeological Journal* 62 (1905), pp. 147–54.

233. Guibert de Nogent, *De vita sua* XVII, ed. Labande (Les Classiques de l'Histoire de France au Moyen Age) (Paris: Société d'Édition Les Belles Letres, 1981), p. 140; trans. C. C. Swinton

Bland, *The autobiography of Guibert* (London: Dutton, 1925) p. 70.

234. Southern (1990) p. 182.
235. Eadmer, *Vita Anselmi* I.4–5, pp. 6–10.
236. Bestul (1988) p. 600.
237. See esp. Bestul (1988) pp. 597–9.
238. See Southern (1990) pp. 133–4.
239. *Oratio ad sanctum Paulum*, ed. Schmitt, vol. 6, pp. 33–41 *passim*. The translation is based on that of Benedicta Ward, pp. 141–56 *passim*, but has been altered by me in a number of places.
240. Southern (1990) pp. 77–8. The difference between Anselm's *Prayers* and his *Meditations* is, as Southern points out (1990, p. 103), that the *Prayers* are petitions to the saints which then lead to introspective reflection, whereas the *Meditations* 'are inward-looking acts, in which the soul examines itself, and seeks God in humiliation and supplication'. But Southern is surely wrong in arguing (1990, p. 94 and n. 7) that St Benedict, under whose Rule Anselm lived, conceived of meditation only as a kind of practical preparation for the liturgy. See A. de Vogüé, *The Rule of Saint Benedict: a doctrinal and spiritual commentary* (Cistercian Studies 54) (Kalamazoo: Cistercian Publications, 1983), pp. 242–7 and the patristic references cited therein. Mary Carruthers (1998, pp. 104–5) argues that 'rumination' is too peaceful a word to describe Anselm's meditation: he is engaging in something far more emotionally demanding.
241. i.e. the Latin Vulgate text of the Bible known to Anselm. Anselm uses *homuncio* elsewhere as a means of self-deprecation: see, e.g., the opening of his *Proslogion* ('Eia nunc, homuncio . . . ').
242. *Monologion* 42, ed. Schmitt, vol. 1, p. 58.
243. For this, see Bynum (1982) pp. 115–19 and Constable (1996) p. 281 and n. 125.
244. Eadmer, *Vita Anselmi* I.13, p. 23. For the medieval devotion to Jesus as mother in general, see Bynum (1982), and the article by A. Cabassut in *Revue d'ascétique et de mystique* 25 (1949), pp. 234–45 (ET by G. Arsenault, 'A medieval devotion to "Jesus our mother"', in *Cistercian Studies* 21 (1986), pp. 345–55). There is an important text in Augustine which may well have influenced Anselm in this respect; Augustine describes Christ as both teacher and nurse, cherishing her children, and calls upon the catechist to be the mother-hen together with Christ, defending her brood (*De catechizandis rudibus* 10.15). See also Constable (1996) p. 183.
245. On this, see esp. Southern (1990) pp. 84–7. Anselm's *Proslogion* can be seen as either a work of prayer, or a philosophical treatise; but best of all as both (see Aidan Nichols OP, 'Anselm of Canterbury and the language of perfection', *Downside Review* 103 (1985), pp. 204–17, esp. p. 209). This careful holding-together of intellect and devotion is not unique to Anselm, even though his was the outstanding contribution to it: see Gillian R. Evans, '*Mens devota*: the literary community of the devotional works of John of Fécamp and St Anselm', *Medium Ævum* 43 (1974), pp. 105–15.
246. Here Anselm goes even further than Augustine, refusing to acknowledge even implicitly any value in himself other than that self-disgust can lead him towards God. See Southern (1990) pp. 71–87, esp. p. 81; and Balthasar (1984) p. 218.
247. *Meditatio redemptionis humanae*, ed. Schmitt, vol. 3, p. 84; ET p. 230.
248. *Meditatio redemptionis humanae*, ed. Schmitt, vol. 3, pp. 84–5; ET p. 231.
249. Southern (1990) p. 86.
250. Southern (1990) p. 101; Southern (1966) p. 44.
251. Southern (1966) p. 42; Ward (1983) pp. 180–1.
252. For this, see Leclercq (1978) pp. 37–41.
253. See the important article of Pouchet (1959), though he is surely wrong in accusing Anselm of 'une certaine prolixité, qui correspond à son tempérament italien' (p. 502). Anselm's seeming prolixity is precisely the means by which he can plumb the depths of his own fallenness and thus comprehend the magnitude of his rescue.
254. Schmitt edn, vol. 3, p. 86.
255. Schmitt edn, vol. 3, pp. 87–8.
256. Pitt-Rivers (1965) p. 72. The whole of his essay is illuminating on this subject, even though his focus is not that of Anselm's day. See also J. K. Campbell's fascinating study of the Sarakat-

sani peoples in modern Greece: he makes the point that, for them, honour means something very different for men from what it means for women, but also that any impugning of anyone's honour demands an immediate (and usually violent) response: *Honour, family and patronage: a study of institutions and moral values in a Greek mountain community* (Oxford: Clarendon, 1964), esp. pp. 268–74.

257. *Cur Deus homo*, ed. Schmitt, vol. 1, p. 15; Evans (1980) p. 172. See also Southern (1990) pp. 225–7.

258. Robert of Bridlington, *The Bridlington dialogue* 5, pp. 61–61a.

259. Balthasar (1984) p. 250.

260. Balthasar (1984) p. 252; Southern (1990) p. 217.

261. *Meditatio humanae redemptionis*, ed. Schmitt, vol. 3, p. 91; ET p. 237.

262. Southern (1966) pp. 42–3. On the influence of the eleventh-century monastic writer Jean of Fécamp (1078) on Anselm, see Ward (introduction to ET of *The Prayers and Meditations*), pp. 47–50.

263. See Bestul (1983).

264. Ep. 2 (to Odo and Lanzo), ed. Schmitt, vol. 3, pp. 98–101; ET p. 77. On Anselm's stress on anxiety, see Southern (1990) p. 85.

265. Eadmer, *Vita Anselmi* II.18, pp. 89–90.

266. Anselm, Letter 112 (to Hugh the Hermit), ET pp. 269–70 (translation slightly altered); ed. Schmitt, vol. 3, pp. 244–6.

267. Douglas (1964) pp. 249–55 and p. 286.

268. *Qui de coquinis, non de scholis ad eremum veneris'* was the description of him by his fellow-Cistercian abbot Gervase: see his letter to Aelred, PL 195:501–2. The same point is made by St Bernard in his letter to Aelred, which acts as a preface to Aelred's *Speculum caritatis* (Preface, 3; CCCM 1, pp. 3–4; ET by E. Connor in CF 17, p. 70).

269. The primary source for Aelred's life is the *Vita Ailredi* by Walter Daniel, and Powicke's introduction to it. There is an immense secondary literature on Aelred: the two essential reference points are: A. Hoste, *Bibliotheca Aelrediana* (Turnhout: Brepols, 1962) (for all works written before 1962); and P.-A. Burton, *Bibliotheca Aelrediana secunda: une bibliographie cumulative (1962–1996)* (Louvain: FIDEM, 1997).

270. See C. H. Talbot, introduction to the ET of the *De anima*, p. 8. His argument is much more convincing than those of Squire (1969, pp. 130–1), who follows Walter Daniel in arguing that the work remained unfinished. For the works in general, see Powicke's introduction to his edition of Walter Daniel's *Vita Ailredi*, pp. xcv–cii.

271. See Powicke, introduction to the *Vita Ailredi*, p. xxxvii.

272. The manuscript history of the *De Iesu puero* shows that it had much popularity also in fifteenth-century Germany, where preoccupation with the human life of Christ was also to be prominent. See CCCM 1, p. 247.

273. *ille inimitabilis subtilitatis vir . . .* , *De anima* I.19, CCCM 1, p. 691; ET p. 44.

274. For this, see Talbot's introduction to *Sermones inediti*, p. 23. Squire (1969, pp. 130–1) is surely wrong in suggesting that in the *De anima* Aelred 'seems to get lost in his own puzzles and questions'; on the contrary – to this writer at least the work reads as an impressive and thoroughly coherent treatise, conservative in theology but always pastoral and sensitive in application.

275. Brooke (1980) p. 220. Note this stress on the corporate nature of experience: in the medieval monastic tradition, 'experience' was always essentially a communal, not a private, reality.

276. In one of his sermons, Aelred cites St Bernard's injunction to 'read from the book of our own experience' (*Serm. in Ypapanti Domini de diversis moribus*, in *Sermones inediti*, pp. 48–9).

277. Brooke (1980) p. 222.

278. *De anima* I.4, CCCM 1, p. 686; ET p. 37. For the same point in Augustine, see his *De Genesi ad litteram* VII.3.4, BA 48, p. 514.

279. *De anima* I.4, CCCM 1, p. 686; ET p. 37.

280. See the introduction by C. H. Talbot to the ET of the *De anima*.

281. *De anima* I.12, CCCM 1, p. 688; ET pp. 39–40.
282. *De anima* I.12, CCCM 1, p. 688; ET p. 40.
283. *De anima* II.18–19, CCCM 1, pp. 712–3; ET p. 81.
284. *De anima* II.20, CCCM 1, p. 713; ET p. 82.
285. *Spec. car.* III.32.78, CCCM 1, p. 143; ET p. 275.
286. Aelred's thought here is both Augustinian and deeply conservative, showing no interest in contemporary discussion about the nature and status of the creation. But that is in any case not his concern.
287. *De anima* I.62–3, CCCM 1, p. 705; ET p. 68.
288. *De anima* II.32, CCCM 1, pp. 718–19; ET pp. 90–1.
289. 'Si, dans notre société déchristianisée, le monachisme est assez peu compris, au XIIe siècle la situation était tout autre; c'était en effet la vie laïque qui faisait problème, car on identifiait communément fidélité à l'Évangile et vie religieuse sans guère se soucier de justifier une telle position' (Dumont (1961) p. 528).
290. *Spec. car.* I.4.11, CCCM I, p. 17; ET p. 93. In one of his sermons, Aelred says that the three sins Adam committed in paradise were curiosity, vanity, and the pursuit of pleasure (*In annunciatione beatae Mariae*, in *Sermones inediti*, p. 84). Aelred goes on to describe the Virgin Mary as *mulier fortis* whose three distinctive virtues are the mirror-opposite of Adam's vices – seriousness instead of curiosity, humility instead of vanity, virginity instead of the pursuit of pleasure (p. 85).
291. Serm. 8, PL 195:391. On the *regio dissimilitudinis*, see E. Gilson, '*Regio dissimilitudinis* de Platon à Saint Bernard de Clairvaux', in *Mediaeval Studies* 9 (1947), pp. 108ff; and other refs. listed in B. McGinn, *The golden chain: the theological anthropology of Isaac of Stella* (Cistercian Studies 15) (Washington: Cistercian Publications 1972), pp. 133–4 n. 132.
292. *Spec. car.* I.4.12–13, CCCM I, p. 17; ET p. 93. From the time of Augustine, *memoria* was associated with the doctrine of the image and likeness: see Costello (1976) p. 337. It is also important to realize that by 'memory' Aelred, once more following Augustine, means not just the capacity to recall experiences or facts but an inherited recollection in our minds of the 'highest good' (*summum bonum*) from which our forebears were expelled and towards which we are summoned to return: see, e.g., Aelred's *Serm. de quadragesimali ieiunio*, in *Sermones inediti* p. 53: 'Necesse primum (=heaven) est, ut memoria summi boni a cordibus nostris non recedat . . .' (We need the first of these [heaven], so that the memory of the highest good may not withdraw from our hearts).
293. There is nothing wrong with these creatures, as Aelred stresses (he says that no one 'may consider any of God's creatures impure without impious sacrilege', *Spec. car.* III.32.78, CCCM 1, p. 143; ET p. 275): indeed in some respects they are actually superior to us (*De anima* II.18–19, CCCM 1, pp. 712–13; ET p. 81). It is simply that we are created for something infinitely greater than they are: to be like God, and to live with him for ever.
294. *Spec. car.* I.6.21, CCCM I, p. 20; ET p. 98; Hallier/Heaney (1969) p. 15.
295. *De oneribus* 8, PL 195:391; Javelet (1967) I, p. 341.
296. For this idea in Augustine, see G. Bonner, 'The desire for God and the need for grace in Augustine's theology', in *Atti del Congresso Internazionale su S.Agostino nel XVI Centenario della Conversione*, I (Studia Epheridis 'Augustinianum' 24) (Rome: Institutum Patristicum 'Augustinianum', 1987), pp. 203–15, esp. p. 204; and, more generally, Isabelle Bochet, *Saint Augustin et le désir de Dieu* (Paris: Études Augustiniennes, 1982), esp. chapter 8.
297. *Spec. car.* III.17.40, CCCM 1, p. 124; ET p. 248.
298. *Serm. de adventu Domini*, in *Sermones inediti*, p. 40.
299. *Vita Ailredi*, p. 25.
300. *De inst. inclus.* 15, CCCM 1, p. 651; ET p. 64.
301. *De inst. inclus.* 16, CCCM 1, p. 652; ET pp. 65–6.
302. *De inst. inclus.* 18, CCCM 1, pp. 653–4; ET pp. 66–7. Despite the use of the third person, Aelred appears almost certainly to be writing here about himself.
303. *Spec. car.* II.5.9, CCCM 1, p. 71; ET p. 170; *Serm. 'Tempus est'* (for Advent), PL 184:819. See

Constable (1995) pp. 211–12. For the importance of intention in twelfth-century spirituality, see Constable (1996) pp. 269–70.

304. *Spec. car.* II.6.16, CCCM 1, p. 73; ET p. 174: Aelred here cites 2 Corinthians 4.16–17.

305. *Spec. car.* III.11.31, CCCM 1, p. 119; ET p. 241.

306. *Spec. car.* II.18.53, CCCM 1, p. 91; ET p. 200.

307. *Spec.car* III.5.13, CCCM 1, pp. 111–12; ET p. 230. On this text Squire (1969, p. 47) comments: 'Entering into the scenes of his [Jesus'] life as vividly as if we were present at them, we can spontaneously react with our whole being to him who became man that we might, as St John insists, see and touch him, and hence express our affection for him in an ordinary human way. This is a complete *ascesis* in itself.' See also Dumont (1961) p. 532.

308. *De inst. inclus.* 26, CCCM 1, pp. 658–9; ET pp. 73–4. See also *Spec. car.* II.12.30, CCCM 1, p. 79; ET p. 183; and II.19.59, CCCM 1, p. 94; ET p. 204.

309. 'If the mind chooses something for its enjoyment, then reaches out to it by a kind of inward desire (*quodam interno desiderio*), and finally does what will enable it to attain what it desires, this should without any doubt be called "to love"' (*Spec. car.* III.21.49, CCCM 1, p. 128; ET p. 254).

310. *Spec. car.* I.1.2, CCCM 1, p. 13; ET p. 88.

311. *Spec. car.* III.8.22, CCCM 1, p. 115; ET p. 235.

312. *Spec. car.* III.18.41. For this idea in Augustine, see his *De civitate Dei* 15.22, CCSL 48, pp. 487–8; for St Bernard, see his Letter 11.7, *Sancti Bernardi Opera*, vol. 7, p. 58.

313. This theme is explored in *Spec. car.* I.11.31–4.

314. *Spec. car.* I.15.46, CCCM 1, p. 31; ET p. 112.

315. *Spec. car.* I.9.27, CCCM 1, p. 23.

316. *Spec. car.* II.3.6, CCCM 1, pp. 68–9; ET p. 167.

317. *Spec. car.* II.4.7, CCCM 1, p. 69; ET p. 168.

318. See Brooke (1980) p. 222.

319. *Spec. car.* I.22.62, CCCM 1, p. 38; ET pp. 122–3.

320. *Spec. car.* I.19.54, CCCM 1, pp. 34–5; ET pp. 117–18.

321. *Spec. car.* I.20.57, CCCM 1, p. 36; ET p. 120.

322. *Spec. car.* I.21.59, CCCM 1, p. 37; ET p. 121.

323. *Spec. car.* III.3.6, CCCM 1, p. 108; ET p. 225.

324. *Qui vero semetipsum non amat, alium amare qui potest* (*De spir. amicit.* III.128, CCCM 1, p. 348).

325. *Spec. car.* III.4.10, CCCM 1, p. 110; ET p. 228. The stress on love of family as the essential starting-point is noteworthy; and family piety will play an increasingly large part in the story of English spirituality as time passes. Owen Chadwick noted that 'the base of Christianity lay . . . in the family . . . Religion was at its most powerful when men stood by the open graves of their father or their mother in a churchyard' (*The secularization of the European mind in the nineteenth century* (Cambridge UP, 1975), pp. 113–14).

326. *Spec. car.* III.6.17, CCCM 1, p. 113; ET p. 232.

327. *De anima* II.51, CCCM 1, p. 725; ET p. 101. See also *Spec. car.* I.19.56, CCCM 1, p. 35; ET p. 119.

328. *De anima* I.17, CCCM 1, p. 690; ET p. 43; I.29, CCCM 1, p. 693; ET p. 49. Aelred stresses that the senses, as part of our physical selves, will be resurrected at the last day (*De anima* III.7, CCCM 1, p. 734; ET p. 114), though it is difficult to resist the impression that he would have preferred life in heaven without them.

329. *Spec. car.* II.22.66, CCCM 1, p. 97; ET p. 209. See also *Spec. car.* I.31.87–8, CCCM 1, pp. 51–2; ET p. 140; I.23.67, CCCM 1, p. 41; ET p. 126; and I.33.95, CCCM 1, pp. 55–6; ET p. 146. It is worth comparing this approach to the sabbath with that of Aelred's fellow-Cistercian Gilbert of Hoyland: 'if you are free [i.e. free from earthly cares for the enjoyment of God], you have a sabbath; if you are free and have eyes to contemplate the delights of the Lord, then your sabbath is delightful and holy, a glorious sabbath of the Lord; a sabbath within a sabbath, that is freedom in freedom' (*sabbatum ex sabbato, ide est vacatio de vacatione*)

(*Sermons on the Song of Songs* 11.5, ET in CF 14, p. 145; PL 184:61).

330. *In primo colligitur ad se; in secundo extenditur extra se; in tertio rapitur supra se* (*Spec. car.* III.6.19, CCCM I, p. 114).

331. *Spec. car.* III.2.3, CCCM 1, pp. 107–8; ET p. 223.

332. *De Genesi ad litteram* IV.12.22, BA 48, p. 308.

333. *De Genesi ad litteram* IV.13.24, BA 48, p. 312.

334. For Augustine's extended treatment of the sabbath theme, see the whole of Book IV of the *De Genesi ad litteram* (BA 48, pp. 276–370, and the *Note complémentaire* ('Le repos de Dieu au septième jour'), in the same volume, pp. 639–44. See also Augustine's *Tractatus in Iohannis Evangelium* 20:2, BA 72, pp. 226–7 with refs., and the *Note complémentaire* ('Le sacrament du sabbat, figure du repos éternel'), in the same volume, pp. 749–51.

335. McGuire (1988, p. 298) says that 'Aelred's christian neoplatonism envisaged a continuous movement, from physical loves to those of the mind and heart and thence to the threshold of God. Even Augustine, the great model for Aelred's thought and life, separated decisively the love of one's fellow human beings from the love of God. Aelred saw no gap.' But this is surely nonsense. Aelred is as careful as Augustine is, and for the same reasons, to distinguish with the utmost care between rightly and wrongly directed aspects of human love, and went even further than Augustine did in setting his entire conception of love within an unequivocally ascetic and eschatological perspective. Squire (1969, p. 103) is much closer to the mark in arguing that we see in Aelred a *monastic* Christian humanism, closer to Cassian than Cicero in spirit. Similarly Dumont (1961, p. 537) writes that 'on ne comprend pleinement cette doctrine de l'amitié qu'à condition de ne pas la séparer du système ascétique et théologal dont elle est la couronnement.' For an opposing view, see (as well as McGuire) C. S. Jaeger, *The envy of angels: cathedral schools and social ideals in medieval Europe, 950–1200* (Philadelphia: Pennsylvania UP, 1994), pp. 279–80 and refs.

336. *De spir. amicit.* II.10, CCCM 1, p. 304.

337. *De spir. amicit.* II.35–6, CCCM 1, p. 309.

338. Note his definition of *amicitia spiritalis* as something based on a community of lifestyle and interests, *De spir. amicit.* I.38, CCCM 1, p. 295, and his declaration that those without material wealth are more capable of lasting friendships than the rich (III.70, CCCM 1, p. 331). Elkins (1988) underlines the significance of friendship for medieval recluses: see, e.g., Goscelin of Saint-Bertin's *Liber confortatorius*, written for Eve of Wilton c.1082, when she left Wilton to live as a recluse in France; and Elkins, pp. 21–7.

339. *De spir. amicit.* I.20, CCCM 1, p. 292.

340. *De spir. amicit.* III.127, CCCM 1, p. 348.

341. *De spir. amicit.* I.53–4, CCCM 1, p. 298. For this conception of *solitudo pluralis*, see André Louf, 'Solitudo Pluralis', in A. M. Allchin (ed.), *Solitude and communion: papers on the hermit life given at St David's Wales in the Autumn of 1975* (Oxford: Fairacres, 1977), pp. 17–29.

342. *De inst. inclus.* 5, CCCM 1, p. 641; ET p. 50 (and see the latter, p. 50 n. 5, for patristic precedents). See also *Serm. in assumptione*, PL 195:360; *Serm. III in natale sancti Benedicti*, PL 195:249.

343. *De anima* III.24, CCCM 1, p. 741; ET p. 126.

344. *De anima* III.51, CCCM 1, p. 754; ET p. 149.

345. Walter Daniel describes him as frail and 'twisted like a piece of parchment' (*quasi membrane folium*): *Vita Ailredi*, p. 49. On his death see also the closing pages of Knowles' classic discussion of his life and works (1963, pp. 257–66, esp. pp. 265–6).

346. Walter Daniel describes him in old age as often plunged into the *abysso contemplationis*: *Vita*, p. 50.

347. Walter Daniel goes on to describe Aelred as wrestling in prayer (*saepe in oratione agonizans*), the one praying being on the mountain 'suspended, as it were, between heaven and earth': *Vita Ailredi*, p. 21. Prayer was effortful, tiring; 'after such prayer he would be tired and sad, as though he had come from great toil, and lament the hurt of the descent [from the mountain of prayer] and sigh as he reflected on the glory of the assumption' (p. 21).

348. See in particular *De Jesu puero* 22–4, CCCM 1, pp. 269–71; ET pp. 29–32.
349. Thus in one sermon he celebrates the divine majesty that is at once revealed and concealed in all created things (*Serm. in annunciatione beatae Mariae*, in *Sermones inediti*, p. 86); but in another he writes that 'the beauty of the rational creature consists not in colours but in virtues': the three ingredients of the rational soul are memory ('the capacity for both images and forms'), reason and will (*Serm. in die Pentecosten*, in *Sermones inediti*, p. 107).
350. 'Do you remember London and how vast it is? Do you call to mind how the river Thames flows past it, how Westminster Abbey beautifies its western side, how the enormous Tower stands guard over the east and how St Paul's Cathedral rises majestically in the middle?' (*De anima* II.6, CCCM 1, p. 708; ET p. 73).
351. *Spec. car.* II.23.67, CCCM 1, pp. 97–8; ET pp. 209–10.
352. *Spec. car.* II.24.70, CCCM 1, pp. 99–100; ET pp. 212–13.
353. *Spec. car.* II.24.72, CCCM 1, p. 100; ET p. 213.
354. Squire (1969) p. 78.
355. There is much wisdom in the original French title of Fr Hallier's study of Aelred (*Un éducateur monastique, Aelred de Rievaulx*), which is unfortunately lost in the title chosen for the English translation (. . . *an experiential theology*).
356. *De inst. inclus.* 28, CCCM 1, pp. 661–2; ET pp. 77–8. On Aelred's conception of love of neighbour, Dumont (1961, p. 534) says 'Ce que l'amour fraternel perd en universalité, lorsqu'il se limite aux frères avec lesquels le moine passe sa vie, il le gagne en profondeur et en fidélité.'
357. In his letter to Aelred, St Bernard distinguishes the knowledge that comes from the school of the Holy Spirit from that which comes from the schools of rhetoric (Ep. 177, trans. B. S. James (1953), pp. 246–7).
358. *Vita Ailredi*, p. 19.
359. For the paintings at Hardham, see P. M. Johnston, 'Hardham church and its early paintings', in *Sussex Archaeological Collections* 44 (1901), pp. 73–115; E. W. Tristram, *English medieval wall painting: the twelfth century* (London: Oxford UP, 1944; repr. New York: Hacker, 1988), pp. 27–8 and 128–33; the description by Ian Nairn in Nairn and Pevsner, *Sussex* (The buildings of England) (Harmondsworth: Penguin, 1965), pp. 234–5; and (best of all) the article by John Wyatt in C. Aggs and J. Wyatt, *The wall paintings at Hardham* (Otter Memorial Papers 2) (Chichester: Bishop Otter College, 1987; available from Hardham House near the church and from Bishop Otter College, Chichester, PO19 4PE).

BIBLIOGRAPHY

Primary Works

Adam of Eynsham: see Hugh of Lincoln

Aelred of Rievaulx, *De anima*, CCCM 1 (Turnhout, 1971) pp. 683–754; ET by C. H. Talbot, *Dialogue on the soul* (CF 22) (Kalamazoo: Cistercian Publications, 1981)

Aelred of Rievaulx, *De Iesu puero*, CCCM 1 (Turnhout, 1971) pp. 247–78; ET by T. Berkeley, *Jesus at the age of twelve* (CF 2) (Kalamazoo: Cistercian Publications, 1971), pp. 1–39

Aelred of Rievaulx, *De institutione inclusarum*, CCCM 1 (Turnhout, 1971) pp. 636–82; ET by M. P. Macpherson, *A rule of life for a recluse* (CF 2) (Kalamazoo: Cistercian Publications, 1971), pp. 41–102

Aelred of Rievaulx, *Oratio pastoralis*, CCCM 1 (Turnhout, 1971) pp. 757–63; ET by R. P. Lawson, *The pastoral prayer* (CF 2) (Kalamazoo: Cistercian Publications, 1971), pp. 103–18

Aelred of Rievaulx, *Sermones de oneribus*, PL 195:363–500

Aelred of Rievaulx, *Sermones inediti*, ed. C. H. Talbot (Series Scriptorum S.Ordinis Cisterciensis 1) (Rome, 1952)

Aelred of Rievaulx, *Speculum caritatis*, CCCM 1 (Turnhout, 1971) pp. 2–161; ET by E. Connor, *The mirror of charity* (CF 17) (Kalamazoo: Cistercian Publications, 1990)

Aelred of Rievaulx, *De spiritali amicitia*, CCCM 1 (Turnhout, 1971) pp. 286–350; ET by M. E. Laker, *Spiritual friendship* (CF 5) (Kalamazoo: Cistercian Publications, 1974)

[Aelred of Rievaulx.] Walter Daniel, *Vita Ailredi* (*Life of Aelred of Rievaulx*), ed. and ET by F. M. Powicke (London: Nelson, 1950; repr. 1963)

Albert the Great, *Albert and Thomas: selected writings* ed. S. Tugwell (Classics of western spirituality) (New York and Mahwah: Paulist Press, 1988)

The Ancrene Wisse (Riwle), ET by M. B. Salu, *Ancrene Riwle* (London: Burns & Oates, 1955); repr. in Exeter Medieval English texts and studies (Exeter UP, 1990); ET by A. Savage and N. Watson, *Anchoritic spirituality: Ancrene Wisse and associated works* (Classics of western spirituality) (New York: Paulist Press, 1991); Middle English text with modern ET by Yoko Wada, *'Temptations' from Ancrene Wisse*, vol. 1 (Kansai University Institute of Oriental and Occidental Studies, sources and materials series 18) (Osaka: Kansai UP, 1994)

Anselm, *Opera omnia*, ed. F. S. Schmitt, 6 vols (Edinburgh: Nelson, 1946–61)

Anselm, *Anselm of Canterbury* (selected works in ET by J. Hopkins and H. Richardson), 4 vols (Toronto and New York: Edwin Mellen, 1964–6; London: SCM Press, 1974–)

Anselm, *Letters*, ed. Schmitt, vol. 3; ET by W. Fröhlich (Cistercian Studies 96) (Kalamazoo: Cistercian Publications, 1990)

Anselm, *The Prayers and Meditations*, ed. Schmitt, vol. 3, pp. 76–91; ET by B. Ward (Harmondsworth: Penguin, 1980)

Anselm, *Proslogion*, ed. Schmitt, vol. 1; ET by M. J. Charlesworth, *St Anselm's Proslogion* (Oxford UP, 1965)

[Anselm.] Eadmer, *The Life of St Anselm* (*Vita S.Anselmi archiepiscopi Cantuariensis*), ed. R. W. Southern (Oxford medieval texts) (Oxford, 1963)

[Anselm.] *Memorials of St Anselm*, ed. R. W. Southern and F. S. Schmitt (Auctores Britannici Medii Aevi, i) (London: British Academy, 1969)

Aquinas, Thomas: see Albert the Great

Augustine, *De Genesi ad litteram libri XII*, ed. and French trans. by P. Agaësse and A. Solignac, *La Genèse au sens littéral* (Bibliothèque Augustinienne 48–9) (Paris: Desclée de Brouwer, 1972)

Baldwin of Ford, Sermons, in PL 204; ET by D. N. Bell, *Baldwin of Ford, Spiritual Tractates* (CF 38 and 41) (Kalamazoo: Cistercian Publications, 1986)

Benedict of Peterborough: see Thomas Becket

Bernard of Clairvaux, Letters, in *Sancti Bernardi opera*, ed. J. Leclercq et al., 8 vols (Rome: Editiones Cistercienses, 1957–78); ET by B. S. James, *The letters of St Bernard of Clairvaux* (London: Burns & Oates, 1953)

Brook, G. L., *The Harley Lyrics*, 2nd edn (Manchester, 1956)

Capgrave, John, *Vita S. Gilberti* (EETS o.s.140) (1910), pp. 61–142

[Christina of Markyate.] *De S. Theodora, virgine, quae et Christina dicitur* (The life of Christina of Markyate), ed. and ET by C. H. Talbot, *The life of Christina of Markyate* (Oxford: Clarendon, 1959)

The Chronicle of Bury St Edmunds (1212–1301), ed. A. Gransden (London: Nelson, 1964)

Councils and Synods, with other documents relating to the English Church, vol. 1 (871–1204) ed. D. Whitelock, M. Brett, and C. N. L. Brooke (Oxford: Clarendon, 1981); vol. 2 (1205–1313), ed. F. M. Powicke and C. R. Cheney (Oxford: Clarendon, 1964)

Distinctiones monasticae. Parts only published in A. Wilmart, 'Un répertoire d'exégèse composé en Angleterre vers le début du XIIe siècle', in *Mémorial Lagrange* (1940), pp. 307–46

A Durham book of devotions, ed. T. H. Bestul (Toronto medieval Latin texts 18) (Toronto, 1987)

[Durham.] *Liber vitae ecclesiae Dunelmensis*, ed. A. Hamilton Thompson (Surtees Society 136) (1923)

Eadmer: see under Anselm

Edmund of Abingdon, *Speculum religiosorum*, ed. H. P. Forshaw (London: Oxford University Press, 1973)

English historical documents vol. 2 (1042–1189), ed. D. C. Douglas and G. W. Greenway, 2nd edn
     (London: Methuen, 1981)
Gilbert of Hoyland, *Sermones in Canticum Salomonis* (Sermons on the Song of Songs), PL
     184:11–252; ET by L. Braceland (CF 14, 20, 26 and 34) (Kalamazoo: Cistercian Publica-
     tions, various dates)
Gilbert of Hoyland, Letters, PL 184:292–8
[Gilbert of Sempringham.] *The Book of St Gilbert*, ed. and ET by R. Foreville and G. Keir (Oxford
     medieval texts) (Oxford: Clarendon, 1987)
Goscelin of Saint-Bertin, *Liber confortatorius*, ed. C. H. Talbot (Studia Anselmiana 37) (Rome:
     1955), pp. 1–117
Goscelin of Saint-Bertin: see also under Hamilton (1973), and Kenelm (below)
Hali meidhad, ed. Bella Millett (EETS 284) (Oxford UP, 1982); ET by A. Savage and N. Watson as
     Holy maidenhood in *Anchoritic spirituality: Ancrene Wisse and associated works* (Classics of
     western spirituality) (New York: Paulist Press, 1991)
Harley lyrics: see under Brook, G. L.
Herbert de Losinga, Sermons, ed. E. M. Goulburn and H. Symonds, *The life, letters and sermons of
     Bishop Herbert de Losinga*, 2 vols (London, 1878)
Herbert de Losinga: see also under Alexander in Secondary Works below
Hugh Candidus, *The Chronicle of Hugh Candidus, a monk of Peterborough*, ed. W. T. Mellows, rev.
     A. Bell (London: Oxford UP, 1949); rev. edn (Peterborough: Museum Society, 1966)
[Hugh of Lincoln.] Adam of Eynsham, *The 'Magna Vita' of St Hugh of Lincoln* (ed. Douie & Farmer,
     2nd edn, 2 vols (Oxford medieval texts) (Oxford: Clarendon, 1989)
Hugh the Chanter, *History of the church of York*, ed. C. Johnson (London: Nelson, 1961)
Innocent III, Pope, *Selected letters concerning England*, ed. C. R. Cheney and W. H. Semple (London:
     Nelson, 1953)
Jocelin of Brakelond, *Chronicle*, ed. H. E. Butler (London: Nelson, 1949)
John of Ford, *Super extremam partem Cantici Canticorum Sermones CXX* (120 Sermons on the final
     part of the Song of Songs), ed. Mikkers and Costello, CCCM 17–18 (Turnhout, 1970); ET
     by W. Beckett (CF 29, 39, 43–7) (Kalamazoo: Cistercian Publications, various dates)
John of Ford: see also under Wulfric
John of Salisbury, Letters, vol. 1 ed. W. J. Millor and H. E. Butler (London: Nelson, 1955); vol. 2 ed.
     W. J. Millor and C. N. L. Brooke (Oxford UP, 1979)
[Katherine.] *St Katherine*; ET by A. Savage and N. Watson in *Anchoritic spirituality: Ancrene Wisse
     and associated works* (Classics of western spirituality) (New York: Paulist Press, 1991)
[Kenelm.] *The life and miracles of St Kenelm* (probably by Goscelin of Saint-Bertin), ed. R. C. Love,
     in *Three eleventh-century Anglo-Latin saints' lives* (Oxford: Clarendon, 1996), pp. 49–90
The Lay folks' Mass book, ed. T. F. Symons (EETS 71) (1879)
McNeill, J. T., and Gamer, H. M. (eds.), *Medieval handbooks of penance: a translation of the principal
     Libri poenitentiales* (Records of western civilization) (New York: Columbia UP, 1938;
     repr.1990)
Marsh, Adam, Letters, ed. J. S. Brewer, in *Monumenta Franciscana* I (1858)
Old English homilies of the twelfth century, ed. and modern ET by R. Morris (EETS, s.s. 53) (1873)
Old English homilies and homiletic treatises of the twelfth and thirteenth centuries, ed. and modern ET
     by R. Morris (EETS o.s. 28 & 34) (1868; repr. New York: Greenwood, 1969)
Osbert of Clare, *De armatura castitatis*, ed. E. W. Williamson, *The Letters of Osbert of Clare* (Oxford:
     publisher unknown, 1929)
Paris, Matthew, *Chronica majora*, ET by J. A. Giles as *Matthew Paris's English history*, 3 vols.
     (London, 1852–4)
The Peterborough Chronicle, ET by H. A. Rositzke (Records of civilization, sources and studies 44)
     (New York: Columbia UP, 1951)
Philip, Prior of St Frideswide's, *Miracula S. Frideswidae*, in Acta SS, Oct 8, pp. 567–90
Reginald of Durham, *Libellus de vita et miraculis S. Godrici, heremitae de Finchale; appendix miraculo-
     rum*, ed. J. Stevenson (Surtees Society 20) (London, 1847)

Robert of Bridlington, *The Bridlington dialogue: an exposition of the Rule of St Augustine for the life of the clergy*, ET by a Religious of CSMV (Sr Penelope) (London: Mowbray, 1960)

Sawles warde; ET by A. Savage and N. Watson in *Anchoritic spirituality: Ancrene Wisse and associated works* (Classics of western spirituality) (New York: Paulist Press, 1991)

The South English legendary (collection of saints' lives probably compiled by a 13th-century English Dominican) (EETS o.s. 87)

The Southern Passion, ed. B. D. Brown (EETS o.s. 169)

Stephen of Sawley, *Meditationes de gaudiis beate et gloriose semper virginis Marie*, in 'Les méditations d'Étienne de Salley sur les Joies de la Vierge Marie', in Wilmart (1971) pp. 317–60; ET by J. O'Sullivan in Stephen of Sawley, *Treatises* (CF 36) (Kalamazoo: Cistercian Publications, 1984), pp. 25–62

Stephen of Sawley, *Speculum novitii*, in E. Mikkers, 'Un *Speculum novitii* inédit d'Étienne de Salley', in *Collectanea OCR* 8 (1946), pp. 17–68; ET by O'Sullivan in Stephen of Sawley, *Treatises* (CF 36) (Kalamazoo: Cistercian Publications, 1984), pp. 83–122

Stephen of Sawley, *Threefold exercise*, in A. Wilmart, 'Le triple exercice d'Étienne de Sallai', in *Revue d'ascétique et de mystique* 11 (1930), pp. 355–74; ET by J. O'Sullivan in Stephen of Sawley, *Treatises* (CF 36) (Kalamazoo: Cistercian Publications, 1984), pp. 63–82

[Thomas Becket.] *Materials for the history of Archbishop Thomas Becket*, ed. J. C. Robertson, 7 vols (Rolls series) (London, 1875–85). Includes the *Miracula S. Thomas Cantuariensis* of Benedict of Peterbrough (vol. 2, pp. 21–281) and the *Miracula S. Thomae Cantuariensis* of William of Canterbury (vol. 1, pp. 137–546)

Thomas of Chobham, Sermons, ed. F. Morenzoni, CCCM 82A (Turnhout, 1993)

Thomas of Eccleston, *Tractatus de adventu Fratrum minorum in Angliam*, ed. A. G. Little (Manchester UP, 1951); ET by L. Sherley-Price, *The coming of the Franciscans* (London: Mowbray, 1964)

Thomas of Monmouth: see under William of Norwich

The Waltham Chronicle, ed. and trans. L. Watkiss and M. Chibnall (Oxford medieval texts) (Oxford: Clarendon, 1994)

William of Canterbury: see under Thomas Becket

William of Malmesbury, *Miracles of the Virgin*, ed. P. Carter, 2 vols (Oxford University DPhil thesis, 1959)

William of Malmesbury: see also under Wulfstan; also under Thomson in Secondary Works below

William of Newburgh, *Historia rerum Anglicarum*, ed. R. Howlett in *Chronicles of the reigns of Stephen, Henry II and Richard I*, 4 vols (Rolls Series) (London, 1884–9); ET (of Book I) by P. G. Walsh and M. J. Kennedy, *William of Newburgh: The history of English affairs* (Warminster: Aris & Phillips, 1988)

[William of Norwich.] Thomas of Monmouth, *The life and miracles of St William of Norwich*, ed. A. Jessopp and M. R. James (Cambridge, 1896)

The wooing of our Lord; ET by A. Savage and N. Watson in *Anchoritic spirituality: Ancrene Wisse and associated works* (Classics of western spirituality) (New York: Paulist Press, 1991)

Wulfric of Haselbury. (De vita beati Wulrici anachoretae Haselbergiae), by John, Abbot of Ford, ed. Maurice Bell (Frome: Somerset Record Society, 1933)

[Wulfstan.] *Miracula S. Wulfstani*, ed. R. R. Darlington (Camden Society, 3rd series 40) (London, 1928), pp. 115–80

[Wulfstan.] William of Malmesbury, *Vita Wulfstani*, ed. R. R. Darlington (Camden Society, 3rd series 40) (London, 1928), pp. 1–110

Secondary Works

Alexander, J. W., 'Herbert of Norwich 1091–1119; studies in the history of Norman England', in *Studies in Medieval and Renaissance History* 6 (1969), pp. 115–232

Ariès, P., *The hour of our death*, ET by A. A. Knopf (Harmondsworth: Penguin, 1981)

Ault, W. O., 'The village church and the village community in medieval England', in *Speculum* 45 (1970), pp. 197–215

Baker, D., 'The desert in the north', in *Northern History* 5 (1970), pp. 1–11

Baker, D., '"The surest road to heaven": ascetic spiritualities in English post-Conquest religious life', in D. Baker (ed.), *Sanctity and secularity: the church and the world* (Studies in church history 10) (Oxford: Blackwell, 1973), pp. 45–57

Baker, D. (ed.), *Medieval women* (Studies in church history, subsidia 1) (Oxford: Blackwell, 1978)

Baker, D., '"The whole world a hermitage": ascetic renewal and the crisis of western monasticism', in M. A. Meyer (ed.), *The culture of Christendom: essays in medieval history in commemoration of Denis L. T. Bethell* (London: Hambledon, 1993)

Baldwin, Mary, *Ancrene Wisse and its background in the Christian tradition of religious instruction and spirituality* (Toronto University dissertation, 1974)

Baldwin, Mary, 'Some difficult words in the *Ancrene Riwle*', in *Mediaeval Studies* 38 (1976), pp. 268–90

Balthasar, Hans Urs von, *The glory of the Lord; a theological aesthetics*, vol. 2: *Studies in theological style: clerical styles* (ET of *Herrlichkeit: eine theologische Ästhetik*, vol. 2) (Edinburgh: T. & T. Clark, 1984)

Barlow, F., *William I and the Norman Conquest* (London: English Universities Press, 1965)

Barlow, F., *The English Church 1000–1066*, 2nd edn (London: Longman, 1979)

Barlow, F., *The English Church 1066–1154: a history of the Anglo-Norman Church* (London: Longman, 1979)

Barrow, G. W. S., *Feudal Britain* (London: Edward Arnold, 1956)

Bartlett, Robert, *England under the Norman and Angevin kings, 1075–1225* (Oxford: Clarendon, 2000)

Bell, D. N., 'The ascetical spirituality of Baldwin of Ford', in *Cîteaux* 31 (1980), pp. 227–50

Bennett, J. A. W., and Gray, D., *Middle English literature 1100–1400* (Oxford history of English literature) (Oxford: Clarendon, 1986)

Benson, R. L. and Constable, G.(eds.), *Renaissance and renewal in the twelfth century* (Oxford: Clarendon, 1982)

Benton, John F., 'Consciousness of self and perceptions of individuality', in Benson and Constable (1982), pp. 263–95

Bestul, T. H., 'St Anselm and the continuity of Anglo-Saxon devotional traditions', in *Annuale mediévale* 21 (1977), pp. 167–70

Bestul, T. H., 'St Anselm, the monastic community at Canterbury, and devotional writing in late Anglo-Saxon England', in *Anselm Studies* I (Millwood NY: Kraus International, 1983), pp. 185–98

Bestul, T. H., 'St Augustine and the *Orationes sive Meditationes* of St Anselm', in *Anselm Studies* II (White Plains NY: Kraus International, 1988), pp. 597–606

Bethune, Brian, 'Personality and spirituality: Aelred of Rievaulx and human relations', in *Cistercian Studies* 20 (1985), pp. 98–112

Bloomfield, M. W., *The seven deadly sins* (Michigan: Michigan State College Press, 1952)

Boase, T. S. R., *English art, 1100–1216* (Oxford: Clarendon, 1953)

Boase, T. S. R., *Death in the Middle Ages* (London: Thames & Hudson, 1972)

Bolton, Brenda, 'Mulieres sanctae', in Baker (1973) pp. 77–85

Bolton, Brenda, *The medieval reformation* (Foundations of medieval history) (London: Edward Arnold, 1983)

Bolton, J. L., *The medieval English economy, 1150–1500* (London: Dent, 1980)

Braceland, L., 'The honeycomb in Gilbert of Hoyland', in *Cistercian Studies* 17 (1982), pp. 233–43

Brett, M., *The English church under Henry I* (Oxford UP, 1975)

Brieger, P., *English art 1206–1307* (Oxford: Clarendon, 1957)

Brooke, C. N. L., 'Gregorian Reform in action', in *Cambridge Historical Journal* 13 (1956), pp. 1–21; repr. in *Medieval church and society* (London: Sidgwick & Jackson, 1971)

Brooke, C. N. L., 'Monk and canon: some patterns in the religious life of the twelfth century', in W.

J. Sheils (ed.), *Monks, hermits and the ascetic tradition* (Oxford: Blackwell, 1985), pp. 109–30

Brooke, C. and R., *Popular religion in the Middle Ages: western Europe 1000–1300* (London: Thames & Hudson, 1984)

Brooke, C. N. L., and Keir, G. *London 800–1216: the shaping of a city* (London: Secker & Warburg, 1975)

Brooke, Odo, 'Monastic theology and St Aelred', in *Studies in monastic theology* (Cistercian Studies 37) (Kalamazoo: Cistercian Publications, 1980), pp. 219–25

Brooks, N., *The early history of the church of Canterbury* (Leicester UP, 1984)

Brown, A. D., *Popular piety in late medieval England: the diocese of Salisbury 1250–1550* (Oxford: Clarendon, 1995)

Brown, P., *The cult of the saints* (London: SCM Press, 1981)

Bynum, C. W., 'Did the twelfth century discover the individual?' in *Journal of Ecclesiastical History* 31 (1980), pp. 1–17

Bynum, C. W., *Jesus as mother: studies in the spirituality of the high Middle Ages* (London: California UP, 1982)

Carruthers, Mary, *The craft of thought: meditation, rhetoric, and the making of images, 400–1200* (Cambridge studies in medieval literature 34) (Cambridge UP, 1998)

Chenu, M.-D., *Nature, man and society in the twelfth century: essays on new theological perspectives in the Latin West*, ed. and ET by J. Taylor and L. K. Little (Chicago and London: Chicago UP, 1968)

Chibnall, Marjorie, *Anglo-Norman England, 1066–1166* (Oxford: Blackwell, 1986; repr. 1993)

Christie, A. G. I., *English medieval embroidery* (Oxford: Clarendon, 1938)

Clanchy, M. T., *From memory to written record: England 1066–1307*, rev. edn (Oxford: Blackwell, 1993)

Constable, G., *Medieval monasticism: a select bibliography* (Toronto medieval bibliographies 6) (Toronto UP, 1976)

Constable, G., 'The ideal of inner solitude in the twelfth century', in H. Dubois et al., *Horizons marins, itinéraires spirituels, I: Mentalités et sociétés* (Paris: Publications de la Sorbonne, 1987), pp. 27–34

Constable, G., *Three studies in medieval religious and social thought* (Cambridge UP, 1995)

Constable, G., *The reformation of the twelfth century* (Cambridge UP, 1996)

Costello, Hilary, 'John of Ford and the quest for wisdom', in *Cîteaux* 23 (1972), pp. 141–59

Costello, Hilary, 'Hesychasm in the English Cistercians of the twelfth and thirteenth centuries', in Pennington (1976), pp. 332–51

Costello, Hilary, and Holdsworth, C. (eds.), *A gathering of friends: the learning and spirituality of John of Forde* (Cistercian Studies 161) (Kalamazoo: Cistercian Publications, 1996)

Courcelle, P., 'Aelred de Rievaulx à l'école des Confessions', in *Revue des Études Augustiniennes* 3 (1957), pp. 163–74

Cowdrey, H. E. J., 'Unions and confraternity with Cluny', in *Journal of Ecclesiastical History* 16 (1956), pp. 152–62

Cowdrey, H. E. J., 'The Carthusians in England', in *La naissance des Chartreuses* (VI Colloque international d'histoire et de spiritualité Cartusiennes) (Grenoble: Éditions des Cahiers de l'Alpe, 1986), pp. 345–56

Cramer, Peter, *Baptism and change in the early Middle Ages, c.200–c.1150* (Cambridge studies in medieval life and thought 20) (Cambridge UP, 1993)

Cuming, G. J., and Baker, D., *Popular belief and practice* (Studies in church history 8) (Cambridge UP, 1972)

Dauphin, H. H., 'L'érémitisme en Angleterre aux XIe et XIIe siècles', in *L'eremitismo in Occidente nei secoli XI e XII* (Atti della seconda Settimana internazionale di studio, Mendola 1962) (Miscellanea del Centro di Studi Medioevali 4) (Milan: Università Cattolica del Sacro Cuore, 1965), pp. 271–310

Dickinson, J. C., *The origins of the Austin Canons and their introduction into England* (London: SPCK, 1950)

Dickinson, J. C., *The later Middle Ages: from the Norman Conquest to the eve of the Reformation* (Ecclesiastical history of England) (London: A. & C. Black, 1979)

Dobson, E. J., *Moralities on the Gospels: a new source of Ancrene Wisse* (Oxford: Clarendon, 1975)

Dobson, E. J., *The origins of Ancrene Wisse* (Oxford: Clarendon, 1976)

Douglas, D. C., *William the Conqueror: the Norman impact upon England* (London: Eyre & Spottiswoode, 1964)

Douie, L., 'Archbishop Pecham's sermons and collations', in *Studies in mediaeval history* (Oxford: Oxford University Press, 1948), pp. 269–82

Duby, Georges, *Rural economy and country life in the medieval West* (London: Edward Arnold, 1968)

Duby, Georges, *The three orders: feudal society imagined* (ET by A. Goldhammer of *Les trois ordres ou l'imaginaire du féodalisme*) (Chicago UP, 1980)

Duby, Georges, *The age of the cathedrals: art and society 980–1420* (ET by E. Levieux & B. Thompson of *Les temps des cathédrales: l'art et la société 980–1420*) (London: Croom Helm, 1981)

Dumont, C., 'Aelred de Rievaulx', in *Théologie de la vie monastique: Études sur la tradition patristique* (Paris: Aubier, 1961), pp. 527–40

Dumont, C., 'L'équilibre humain de la vie cistercienne d'après le Bx.Aelred de Rievaulx', in *Collectanea OCR* 18 (1965), pp. 177–89. (ET 'St Aelred: the balanced life of a monk', in *Monastic Studies* 1 (1963), pp. 25–38)

Dumont, C., 'Personalism in community according to Aelred of Rievaulx', in *Cistercian Studies* 12 (1977), pp. 250–71

Erickson, C., *The medieval vision: essays in history and perception* (New York: Oxford UP, 1976)

Elkins, Sharon K., *Holy women of twelfth-century England* (Chapel Hill: North Carolina UP, 1988)

Elliott, Dyan, *Spiritual marriage: sexual abstinence in medieval wedlock* (Chichester: Princeton UP, 1993)

Evans, G. R., '*Mens devota*: the literary community of the devotional works of John of Fécamp and St Anselm', in *Medium Ævum* 43 (1974) pp. 105–15

Evans, G. R., *Anselm and talking about God* (Oxford UP, 1978)

Evans, G. R., *Anselm and a new generation* (Oxford UP, 1980)

Finucane, R. C., *Miracles and pilgrims: popular beliefs in medieval England* (London: Dent, 1977)

Fiske, A., 'Aelred of Rievaulx', in *Cîteaux* 13 (1962), pp. 5–17 and 97–132

Fleming, R., *Kings and lords in Conquest England* (Cambridge studies in medieval life and thought, 4th series) (Cambridge UP, 1991)

Flint, Valerie, *The rise of magic in early medieval Europe* (PrincetonUP, 1990)

Frank, I. W., *A history of the mediaeval church* (ET by John Bowden) (London: SCM Press, 1995)

Fredeman, J. C., 'John Capgrave's Life of St Gilbert of Sempringham', in *Bulletin of the John Rylands Library* 55 (1972) pp. 112–45

Georgianna, Linda, *The solitary life: individuality in the Ancrene Wisse* (London: Harvard UP, 1981)

Gray, Douglas, 'Notes on some Middle English charms', in B. Rowland (ed.), *Chaucer and Middle English studies in honour of Rossell Hope Robbins* (London: Allen & Unwin, 1974), pp. 56–71

Hallier, A., *The monastic theology of Aelred of Rievaulx: an experiential theology* (ET by C. Heaney of *Un éducateur monastique, Aelred de Rievaulx*) (Cistercian Studies 2) (Shannon: Irish UP, 1969)

Hamilton, Bernard, *Religion in the medieval West* (London: Edward Arnold, 1986)

Hamilton, T. J., *Goscelin of Canterbury: a critical study of his life, works and accomplishments* (University of Virginia PhD thesis, 1973)

Harding, Alan, *England in the thirteenth century* (Cambridge medieval textbooks) (Cambridge UP, 1993)

Harvey, Barbara, *Living and dying in England 1100–1540: the monastic experience* (Ford Lectures 1989) (Oxford: Clarendon, 1993)

Heaney, C., 'Aelred of Rievaulx: his relevance to the post-Vatican II Age', in M. B. Pennington (ed.), *The Cistercian Spirit: a symposium in memory of Thomas Merton* (Cistercian Studies 3) (Shannon: Irish UP, 1970), pp. 166–89

Henderson, G., 'Narrative illustration and theological exposition in medieval art', in K. Robbins (ed.), *Religion and humanism* (Studies in church history 17) (Oxford: Blackwell, 1981), pp. 19–35

Herbert, Jane, 'The transformation of hermitages into Augustinian priories in twelfth-century England', in W. J. Sheils (ed.), *Monks, hermits and the ascetic tradition* (Studies in church history 22) (Oxford: Blackwell, 1985), pp. 131–45

Hill, B. D., *English Cistercian monasteries and their patrons in the twelfth century* (Chicago: Illinois UP, 1968)

Hinnebusch, W. A., *The Early English Friars Preachers* (Rome: Institutum Historicum FF. Praedicatorum, 1952)

Holdsworth, C., *The learning and literature of the English Cistercians 1167–1214 with special reference to John of Ford* (Cambridge University PhD thesis, 1959)

Holdsworth, C., 'John of Ford and English Cistercian writing', in *Transactions of the Royal Historical Society* 5th series 11 (1961), pp. 117–36

Holdsworth, C., 'Christina of Markyate', in D. Baker (ed.), *Medieval women* (Studies in church history, subsidia 1) (Oxford: Blackwell, 1978), pp. 185–204

Holman, Jean, 'Monastic joyfulness in Gilbert of Hoyland', in *Cistercian Studies* 19 (1984), pp. 319–35

Holman, Jean, 'Stephen of Sawley: man of prayer', in *Cistercian Studies* 21 (1986), pp. 109–22

Holman, Jean, 'The Cistercian spirituality of Baldwin of Ford: a review article', in *Cistercian Studies* 23 (1988), pp. 355–64

Javelet, R., *Image et ressemblance au XIIme siècle,* 2 vols (Paris: Letouzey & Ané, 1967)

Knowles, David, *The religious orders in England,* 3 vols (Cambridge UP, 1948–59)

Knowles, David, *The monastic order in England: a history of its development from the times of St Dunstan to the Fourth Lateran Council, 940–1216,* 2nd edn (Cambridge UP, 1963)

Lackner, Bede, *The eleventh-century background of Cîteaux* (Cistercian Studies 8) (Washington: Cistercian Publications, 1972)

Lebreton, M. M., 'Recherches sur les principaux thèmes théologiques traités dans les sermons du XII siècle', in *Recherches de théologie ancienne et médiévale* 23 (1956), pp. 5–18

Leclercq, J., 'Écrits spirituels d'Elmer de Cantorbéry', in *Studia Anselmiana,* 2nd series 31 (1953), pp. 45–117

Leclercq, J., 'La lettre de Gilbert Crispin sur la vie monastique', in *Studia Anselmiana,* 2nd series 31 (1953), pp. 118–23

Leclercq, J., *The love of learning and the desire for God: a study of monastic culture* (ET by C. Misrahi of *L'amour des lettres et le désir de Dieu*), 2nd edn (London: SPCK, 1978)

Le Goff, Jacques, *Medieval civilization, 400–1500* (ET by J. Barrow of *La civilisation de l'occident médiéval*) (Oxford: Blackwell, 1988)

Little, L. K., *Religious poverty and the profit economy* (London: Elek, 1978)

Leyser, Henrietta, *Hermits and the new monasticism: a study of religious communities in Western Europe, 1000–1150* (New studies in medieval history) (London: Macmillan, 1984)

Lesyer, Henrietta, 'Hugh the Carthusian', in Mayr-Harting (1987), pp. 1–18

Loades, J. (ed.), *Monastic studies II* (Bangor: Headstart History, 1991)

Mayr-Harting, H., 'Functions of a twelfth-century recluse', in *History* 60 (1975), pp. 337–52

Mayr-Harting, H. (ed.), *Saint Hugh of Lincoln* (Oxford: Clarendon, 1987)

McCorkell, E., 'Herald of the Holy Spirit: John of Ford's Sermons on the Song of Songs', in *Cistercian Studies* 20 (1985) pp. 303–13

McGinn, B., 'Pseudo-Dionysius and the early Cistercians', in Pennington (1976) pp. 200–41

McGuire, B., *Friendship and community* (Cistercian Studies 95) (Kalamazoo: Cistercian Publications, 1988)

Meersseman, G., *Ordo fraternitatis: confraternite e pietà dei laici nel medioevo,* 3 vols (Rome: Herder, 1977)

Mikkers, Edmund, 'Image and likeness: the doctrine of John of Ford', in Pennington (1976) pp. 352–6

Morris, C., *The discovery of the individual 1050–1200* (London: SPCK, 1972)

Morris, C., 'Individualism in twelfth-century religion: some further reflections', in *Journal of Ecclesiastical History* 31 (1980), pp. 195–206

Morris, C., *The papal monarchy* (Oxford history of the Christian Church) (Oxford: Clarendon, 1989)

Murray, A., *Reason and society in the Middle Ages* (Oxford: Clarendon, 1978)

Nilson, Ben, *Cathedral shrines of medieval England* (Woodbridge: Boydell, 1998)

Ortenberg, V., *The English Church and the continent in the tenth and eleventh centuries: cultural, spiritual and artistic exchanges* (Oxford: Clarendon, 1992)

Owst, G. R., *Literature and pulpit in medieval England* (Oxford UP, 1961)

Pächt, O., Dodwell, C. R., and Wormald, F., *The St Albans Psalter* (London: Warburg Institute, 1960)

Pächt, O., 'The illustrations of Anselm's Prayers and Meditations', in *Journal of the Warburg and Courtauld Institutes* 19 (1956), pp. 68–83

Pearsall, D., and Salter, E., *Landscapes and seasons of the medieval world* (London: Elek, 1973)

Pennington, M. B. (ed.), *One yet two: monastic tradition East and West* (Cistercian Studies 29) (Kalamazoo: Cistercian Publications, 1976)

Petit, F., *La spiritualité des Prémontrés aux XIIe et XIIIe siècles* (Études de théologie et d'histoire de la spiritualité 10) (Paris: Vrin, 1947)

Pitt-Rivers, J., 'Honour and social status', in Jean G. Peristiany, *Honour and shame: the values of Mediterranean society* (The nature of human society) (London: Weidenfeld & Nicolson, 1965), pp. 19–78

Pouchet, Jean-Marie, 'La componction de l'humilité et de la piété chez saint Anselme', in *Spicilegium Beccense* 1 (Congrès international du IXme centenaire de l'arrivée d'Anselme au Bec) (Paris: Vrin, 1959), pp. 489–508

Pouchet, Jean-Marie, *La 'rectitudo' chez saint Anselme: un itinéraire augustinien de l'âme à Dieu* (Études Augustiniennes 1) (Paris, 1964)

Raw, Barbara, 'The prayers and devotions in the *Ancrene Wisse*', in B. Rowland (ed.), *Chaucer and Middle English studies in honour of Rossell Hope Robbins* (London, 1974), pp. 260–71

Rigg, A. G., *A history of Anglo-Latin literature 1066–1422* (Cambridge UP, 1992)

Salzman, L. F., 'Some Sussex miracles', in *Sussex Archaeological Collections* 66 (1925), pp. 62–82

Southern, R. W., *The making of the Middle Ages* (London: Hutchinson, 1953)

Southern, R. W., 'St Anselm and Gilbert Crispin, Abbot of Westminster', in *Medieval and Renaissance Studies* 3 (1954), pp. 78–115

Southern, R. W., 'The English origins of the "Miracles of the Virgin"', in *Medieval and Renaissance Studies* 4 (1958), pp. 176–216

Southern, R. W., 'The place of England in the twelfth-century renaissance', in *History* 45 (1960), pp. 201–16

Southern, R. W., *St Anselm and his biographer* (Cambridge UP, 1963)

Southern, R. W., *Medieval humanism* (Oxford: Blackwell, 1970)

Southern, R. W., *Saint Anselm: a portrait in a landscape* (Cambridge UP, 1990)

Southern, R. W., *Scholastic humanism and the unification of Europe* vol.1: *Foundations* (Oxford: Blackwell, 1995)

Squire, A., 'Aelred and the northern saints', in *Collectanea OCR* 23 (1961), pp. 58–69

Squire, A., 'The composition of the *Speculum caritatis*', in *Cîteaux* 14 (1963), pp. 135–46 and 219–33

Squire, A., *Aelred of Rievaulx: a study* (London: SPCK, 1969); repr. as *Cistercian Studies* 50 (Kalamazoo: Cistercian Publications, 1981)

Stafford, Pauline, *Unification and conquest: a political and social history of England in the tenth and eleventh centuries* (London: Edward Arnold, 1989)

Sumption, J., *Pilgrimage: an image of medieval religion* (London: Faber & Faber, 1975)

Thompson, Benjamin, 'From "Alms" to "Spiritual Services": the function and status of monastic property in medieval England', in Loades (1991), pp. 227–62

Thompson, E. Margaret, *A history of the Somerset Carthusians* (London: Hodges, 1895)

Thompson, E. Margaret, *The Carthusian Order in England* (London: SPCK, 1930)

Thompson, Sally, *Women religious: the founding of English nunneries after the Norman Conquest* (Oxford: Clarendon, 1991)

Thomson, R. M., *William of Malmesbury* (Woodbridge: Boydell, 1987)

Vauchez, André, *Sainthood in the later Middle Ages* (ET by J. Birrell) (Cambridge UP, 1997)

Vaughan, R., *Matthew Paris* (Cambridge: Cambridge University Press, 1958)

Vaughan, R., *Chronicles of Matthew Paris: monastic life in the thirteenth century* (Gloucester: Sutton, 1984)

Wallace, David (ed.), *The Cambridge history of medieval English literature* (Cambridge UP, 1999)

Ward, B., 'Faith seeking understanding: Anselm of Canterbury and Julian of Norwich', in A. M. Allchin (ed.), *Julian of Norwich* (Oxford: SLG Press, 1973)

Ward, Benedicta, *Miracles and the medieval mind: theory, record and event, 1000–1215* (London: Scolar Press, 1982)

Ward, Benedicta, '"Inward feeling and deep thinking": the Prayers and Meditations of St Anselm revisited', in *Anselm Studies* I (Millwood NY: Kraus International, 1983), pp. 177–84

Warren, Ann K., 'The nun as anchoress: England 1100–1500', in Nichols and Shank (eds.), *Distant echoes: medieval religious women* 1 (Cistercian Studies 71) (Kalamazoo: Cistercian Publications, 1984), pp. 197–212

Warren, Ann K., *Anchorites and their patrons in medieval England* (Berkeley: California UP, 1985)

Warren, W. L., *Henry II* (London: Eyre Methuen, 1973)

Watson, Nicholas, 'The methods and objectives of thirteenth-century anchoritic devotion', in M. Glasscoe (ed.), *The medieval mystical tradition in England* (Exeter Symposium IV) (Cambridge: D. S. Brewer, 1987), pp. 132–54

Williams, David, 'Layfolk within Cistercian precincts', in Loades (1991), pp. 87–118

Wilmart, A., 'L'instigateur du *Speculum caritatis*', in *Revue d'ascétique et de mystique* 14 (1933), pp. 369–94

Wilmart, A., 'Edmeri Cantuariensis cantoris nova opuscula de sanctorum veneratione et obsecratione', in *Revue des sciences religieuses* 15 (1935), pp. 184–219 and 354–79

Wilmart, A., 'Le manuel de prières de saint Jean Gualbert', in *Revue Bénédictine* 48 (1936), pp. 259–99 (on Carolingian spirituality)

Wilmart, A., *Auteurs spirituels et textes devots du moyen âge latin* (Paris, 1932; repr. in Études Augustiniennes, 1971)

Wilson, Katharina M., *Medieval women writers* (Manchester UP, 1984)

Wilson, R. M., *The lost literature of medieval England* (London: Methuen, 1952)

Zarnecki, G., 'The Chichester reliefs', in *Archaeological Journal* 110 (1953), pp. 106–19

Zarnecki, G., Holt, J., and Holland, T., *English Romanesque art 1066–1200* (Catalogue of an Exhibition at the Hayward Gallery, London, 1984) (London: Weidenfeld & Nicolson, 1984)

Collected Studies

L'eremitismo in Occidente nei secoli XI e XII (Atti della seconda Settimana internazionale di studio, Mendola 1962) (Miscellanea del Centro di Studi Medioevali 4) (Milan: Università Cattolica del Sacro Cuore, 1965)

Ilaici nella 'societas christiana' dei secoli XI e XII (Atti della terza Settimana internazionale di studio, Mendola 1965) (Miscellanea del Centro di Studi Medioevali 5) (Milan: Università Cattolica del Sacro Cuore, 1967)

Il monachesimo e la Riforma ecclesiastica (1049–1122) (Atti della quarta Settimana internazionale di studio, Mendola 1968) (Miscellanea del Centro di Studi Medioevali 6) (Milan: Università Cattolica del Sacro Cuore, 1971)

4

The Quest for the Suffering Jesus

Late Medieval Spirituality (1300–1500)

I wandered through the desire of riches, and I did not find Jesus. I walked through the abyss of delights, and I did not find Jesus. I ran through the lust of the flesh, and I did not find Jesus. I sat with a crowd of revellers, and I did not find Jesus. In all these places, I sought Jesus and did not find him; for he revealed to me through his grace that he was not to be found on earth living in comfort. So I turned aside by another way, and wandered through poverty; and I found Jesus born a pauper into the world, laid in a manger, and wrapped in swaddling bands. I walked through the endurance of hardships; and I found Jesus worn out by the journey, hungry, thirsty, afflicted with cold, made weary by abuses and insults. I was sitting alone, making myself solitary; and I found Jesus fasting in the desert, praying alone on the mountain. I ran through suffering and penitence; and I found Jesus bound, scourged, wounded, given gall to drink, nailed to the cross, hanging on the cross, dying on the cross. So Jesus is not found among the rich but among the poor; not with the pleasure-seekers but with the penitent; not among the lustful and the revellers but the bitter and the weeping; not in the crowd, but in solitude. The wicked person certainly does not find Jesus, because he does not seek him where he is; for he strives to seek Jesus amidst the joy of the world, where he is never found.[1]

This is an extract from Richard Rolle's Latin commentary on the Song of Songs. Even in English, its rhetorical power is immediately apparent: the careful structure and repeated verbs, the vivid contrasts, the allegorizing of virtues and vices, the description of an individual's journey or quest in search of an elusive goal. All these are characteristic of much late medieval English literature. But there are three aspects of the text which are worthy of further comment.

First, there is an implicitly subversive quality to Rolle's writing. Jesus is not to be found amongst the rich and powerful. Why not? For Rolle the answer is simple: because he told me so. Rolle not only challenges any equation of Christianity with power and wealth (a challenge also made by others in the period, both orthodox and Lollard): he does so on the authority of his own experience. Secondly, the journey that Rolle describes is a solitary one: no echo here of Chaucer's cheery group of pilgrims assembling at a Southwark inn. It is a journey, but a journey rooted in the experience of one individual: a journey inwards. Thirdly, and most important of all, attention is focused on the suffering Christ. Rolle says nothing about Jesus' divinity, his teaching, his miracles, or his resurrection, though it is nonetheless the divine Son of God (not a charismatic human being) of whom he writes. He tells us of his birth among the poor, his weariness and unpopularity, his solitary prayer, his suffering and dying. This is a Christ whose divinity is undoubted, yet whose presence is manifested in poverty and solitude, and above all in the individual's intimate experience. But above all it is a Christ who bleeds.[2]

These three themes – the turning upside-down of many traditional assumptions as lay spirituality acquired a new maturity and confidence; the interior journey; and the suffering Christ – will be found in effect to be *leitmotiven* in our exploration of late medieval spirituality. First, however, something needs to be said about the context in which Rolle and others like him lived and wrote.

THE CONTEXT OF LATE MEDIEVAL
ENGLISH SPIRITUALITY

Introduction: Late Medieval Life and Thought

Rolle was born at Thornton-le-Dale in North Yorkshire in or around 1305. He went to Oxford, but failed to complete his degree: the anonymous late-fourteenth-century compiler of *The Officium and Miracula of Richard Rolle of Hampole,* which is our primary source of information about his life, tells us that this was because of his acute sense of *brevitas vitae.*[3]

Whether or not this is true, Rolle was certainly born into an anxious age. The English translator of a French spiritual text written not long before Rolle's birth declared that the person is not alive who does not live each day in busyness, cares and anxieties;[4] and by the end of the century a chronicler lamented that 'almost all the lamps have gone out in the Church of God'.[5] High inflation, the sharply divergent fortunes of towns (inevitably affected by major economic fluctuations[6]), an expanding middle class together with an enlarged bureaucracy (royal, ecclesiastical, and municipal), and a steady movement in the structure of society away from serfdom and hierarchy and towards what would later be called a cash-based economy eroded the stable structures and (as it seemed to many) God-given *ordo* of the feudal state;[7] and that erosion inevitably affected (in many and different ways) people's relationships with God, who must for so long have represented the highest level of the feudal hierarchy.

William of Ockham

One major manifestation of this process can be found in the writings of the great Franciscan theologian William of Ockham, who was at Oxford at the same time as Rolle and whose life reflects even more than Rolle's the upheavals and uncertainties of the period.[8] William sought to restore the biblical emphasis on God's freedom to do whatever he wanted, an emphasis he believed to have been perilously diminished by the influence of Aristotle and the assumption that faith and knowledge were one and the same.[9] Thus William distinguished between God's *potentia absoluta* (his utter freedom to do what he wants) and his *potentia ordinata* (what he actually does) in order to stress that the observable laws of the universe are the consequence, not of an iron necessity which binds even the Creator, but of that Creator's unconditioned choice to commit, or covenant, himself, to this world and this particular way of acting, when he could equally have chosen another quite different one.[10] William writes:

> I claim that God is able to do certain things by his ordained power (*potentia ordinata*) and certain things by his absolute power (*potentia absoluta*) . . . The distinction should be understood to mean that 'power to do something' is sometimes taken [to mean] 'power to do something in accordance with the laws that have been ordained and instituted by God' . . . [and sometimes taken to mean] 'power to do anything such that its being done does not involve a contradiction', regardless of whether or not God has ordained that he will do it.[11]

The academic precision of William's language conceals its spiritual significance. The effect of the distinction for which he argues is further to undermine the assumption that God is (in effect) a part, albeit the principal part, of his own creation – the topmost rung in a feudal order, or the unmoved mover in a chain of being. William wants to argue that everything which God does is done freely, and is done within the context of the covenant relationship he has established with humanity; and it is in terms of this covenant with God that we must seek to understand all that befalls us. God created this world, and us, when he could have created a quite different world and put quite different people into it. Hence we matter, as individuals and not just as participants in a hierarchy of being reaching (as Augustine saw it) from the lowest levels of plant life to the Creator himself.[12] And if God is free, so are we: free to choose salvation rather than damnation; and if we choose the latter rather than the former, we have only ourselves to blame.[13]

It is precisely this radical individualism that we find in the work of Richard Rolle, and not least in the text with which this chapter began: it is at least possible that the young Rolle was familiar with the ideas and emphases that William was later to express so forcefully. Where people in the twelfth century could think of themselves as dwarves standing on the shoulders of giants, those in the fourteenth were more likely to adopt a critical attitude to the past, and to see the present (especially their own experience) as possessing an *auctoritas* of its own.[14]

The Black Death
The process whereby hitherto accepted assumptions came to be challenged was accelerated by a series of events whose influence upon contemporaries ranged from the critical to the cataclysmic: of these, the first was the most terrible of all. The 'Black Death' is a name given later to the plague that swept through England from Europe, killing nearly half the population in about eighteen months in 1348 and 1349 and causing profound economic and social instability. The reaction to it varied: some blamed the plague on moral laxity:[15] others, in a response which anticipates that of

many to the Holocaust, believed that 'God is deaf now-a-days and deigneth not to hear us / And prayers have no power the Plague to stay'[16] – though this did not prevent a vast effusion of prayer from being offered and new prayers specially written, including the *Stella coeli extirpavit* to the Virgin:

> Star of Heaven, who nourished the Lord and rooted up the plague of death which our first parents planted; may that star now deign to counter the constellations whose strife brings the people the ulcers of a terrible death. O glorious star of the sea, save us from the plague. Hear us: for your Son who honours you denies you nothing. Jesus, save us, for whom the Virgin Mary prays to you.[17]

Three other major events of the fourteenth century were scarcely less dramatic and far-reaching in their effects. In 1337 the Hundred Years War with France began, the effect of which remains a matter of debate but which must certainly have contributed both to national xenophobia and to social and economic dislocation.[18] In 1381 England was shaken by the Peasants' Revolt, in which both country and townsfolk rebelled against unprecedented taxation (itself substantially the consequence of having to finance the war), as well against attempts by the government to force them back into their old static subservience to feudal serfdom. Though brief and swiftly suppressed, it may well have assisted in ensuring the steady but definitive erosion of the practice of villeinage or serfdom.[19] In both theory and practice, the old certainties and the hierarchical world-view that supported them were no longer accepted without question.

Many of them were yet further undermined as a result of the papal schism which began with the establishment of a rival papacy at Avignon in 1378 and ended after the Council of Constance in 1414. For the ordinary Christian, imbued with a pervasive sense of the God-given importance of order and hierarchy, the effect of this split at the highest level of the Church must have been profoundly disorientating, raising fundamental questions about people's political and religious allegiances, and unleashing a degree of anxiety and dissent which significantly affected the course of English spirituality.[20]

The changing spiritual landscape: Geoffrey Chaucer

All this might suggest a society plunged into gloomy and uncertain introspection; but the reality is inevitably more complex. Anyone interested in obtaining a vivid perception of the colour and texture of late medieval England could scarcely do better than read the General Prologue of the most famous literary work to emerge from these centuries: Geoffrey Chaucer's *Canterbury tales*. From its opening pages tumble a throng of varied characters, each with a tale to tell: a knight, a squire, a yeoman, a prioress, a merchant, and many others. Each is a real person, not a pale stereotype. The sheer variety reflects a society with a very different make-up from that of Anselm or Aelred. And the characters are described with neither apology nor qualification. The Wife of Bath who had travelled across Europe; the skinny Oxford Clerk with many books but no money; the Monk who 'let old things pass away / And held after the new world', the 'wanton and merry' Friar and devious Pardoner, the gentle Prioress who abhorred cruelty to animals – these and their fellow-pilgrims breathe a new kind of world, in which old certainties and structures were no longer set in stone. One of the positive consequences of so much social and religious upheaval, combined with the rapid growth of the universities and the spread of literacy, was the rise of a new and more confident laity whose spiritual (not to mention other) needs were no longer to be satisfied by unquestioning acceptance of what was handed to them by others.

Two responses to this situation may serve to illustrate the point. The first comes from one of the great spiritual texts of the period, the *Scale of perfection* by Walter Hilton, whose contents will be explored later. Writing to an anchoress, Hilton tells her firmly:

> Although if you are saved you will have such great and special reward for your state of life, nevertheless it may be that many a wife, and many a woman living in the world, shall be nearer God than you are and will love God more and know him better than you do, for all your state.[21]

The second illustration is from Chaucer's *Canterbury tales*. In the Knight's tale, Palamoun, still in prison after Arcite's unexpected release, challenges the gods in one of the most powerful thunderbolts to be hurled at the gates of heaven since the seventy-third Psalm:

> O crueel goddes that governe
> This world with byndyng of youre word eterne,
> And written down in adamantine stone
> Is all your will and youre fixèd decree,
> How is mankynde more by you held
> Than is the sheep, that cowers in the field?
> For slayn is man right as another beest,
> And dwelleth too in prison and arreest,
> And hath siknesse, and greet adversitee,
> And ofte tymes guiltless, indeed.
> What governance is in this prescience,
> That thus tormenteth guiltless innocence?
> And yet my suffering is increased by this:
> That man is bounden to his observaunce,
> For Goddes sake to conquer al his wille,
> Whereas a beest may al his lust fulfille.
> And when a beest is dead, he hath no peyne;
> But man after his deeth must wepe and pleyne,
> Though in this world he have care and woe.
> Without a doute it must indeed be so.
> The answer of this leve I to divinis,[22]
> But wel I know, that in this world greet pyne is.
> Allas, I see a serpent or a theef,
> That hath to many a trewe man done mescheef,
> Go at his large, and where he will may turne.
> But I must be in prisoun.[23]

Chaucer might leave the answer to Palamoun's question to divines. But in framing the question he must have articulated the puzzlement of countless faithful Christians whose experience of terrible suffering, whether in war, plague, schism or personal tragedy, must have led them, as it led the psalmist, to challenge the God who was supposed to be responsible for all that happened.

The Growth of Lay Spirituality (1): Prayer and the Liturgy

Certainly there are many indications of lay people taking the initiative in aspects of church and social life which impinged significantly upon spirituality.[24] By the fourteenth and fifteenth centuries, English church life was far less static and stable than in earlier periods, for reasons which have already been mentioned.[25] In practice the medieval parish always admitted of a variety of patterns of religious activity:[26] the growth of local shrines, side chapels and chantries, private chapels belonging to the gentry, hermitages, and centres catering for seasonal workers[27] (not to mention the itinerant teaching and sacramental ministry of the friars), all increased the number of options open to local laypeople – and their options would of course have been increased further still if they lived in a town with a number of different parish churches available to them. This local diversity is matched by a new recognition on the part of many monastic and clerical writers of the value in more general terms of different states of life within the church: thus the fourteenth-century monastic scholar Uthred of Boldon commends *diversitas vivendi*, citing examples from scripture, and arguing that it is not diversity but contentiousness that causes strife and envy.[28]

The growing diversity and confidence of lay Christianity presented the late medieval church with a major challenge, to which it responded with all the energy and resources at its disposal. The decrees of the Fourth Lateran Council in 1215 and the activities of thirteenth-century English bishops (particularly the Council of Lambeth in 1281) stimulated the production of numerous orthodox liturgical and spiritual texts designed to instruct and edify laypeople, and to encourage a fuller participation in the liturgy:[29] devotion to the Eucharist was a major characteristic of this period, and both complements and counteracts the pervasive individualism we have already noted.[30] The later Middle Ages saw an emphasis on the power of the holy as insistent as anything from Anglo-Saxon England, as in this story from a sermon for Corpus Christi:

> In Devon, near Axbridge, there dwelt a holy curate one of whose parishioners, a woman, lay sick at the point of death in a town half a mile from where he lived. At midnight this woman sent for him to administer the [last] rites to her. Then this man rose up as fast as he could, went to the church, and took God's body in an ivory box, and put it in his pocket (for in those days men had pockets). And he rode towards this woman, and went across a meadow that was the shortest route. Then, as he hastened on his way as fast as he could, the box was jerked from his bosom and fell to the ground; and as it fell the box opened, and the host trundled out onto the grass. Then, after he had shriven this woman, he asked her if she

wanted to receive Holy Communion, and she said 'Yes.' Whereupon he put his hand into his bosom to seek the box. When he did not find it, he was highly afraid, and said to the woman, 'Lady, I shall fetch God's body and come back again as quickly as I can.' And so he came to a willow-tree, and made himself a good scourge from it, and stripped himself naked, and beat himself with all his might, so that the blood ran down his sides; and he said to himself 'You foul thief, who has lost your creator: you shall pay for it.' And when he had beaten himself in this way, then he put his clothes on and ran forth. And then he became aware of a pillar of fire that went all the way from earth to heaven. At first he was aghast, but afterwards he blessed God and rode towards it, and saw all the animals in the field encompassing it. So when he came to this pillar, it shone as bright as any sun. Then he perceived God's body lying on the grass, and the pillar of fire reaching up from it to Heaven. He sank to his knees and asked for mercy with all his heart, weeping sorely for his negligence. But when he had finished his prayer, he rose up and looked about him, and saw all the animals kneeling on both their knees and worshipping God's body, save only one black horse which knelt on only one knee. Then this good man said to the horse 'If you are an animal that can speak, I bid you by the power of this body that lies here, that you speak and tell me why you are kneeling on only one knee, while all these other animals kneel on both their knees.' Then it answered and said: 'I am a fiend from hell, and would not willingly kneel on either knee, yet am I made to do so against my will; for it is written that every man of Heaven, and of earth, and of hell, shall bow to him.' Then he said to the horse: 'Why are you like a horse?' And it replied 'I go thus like a horse, so as to make men steal me. And a man of such-and-such a town was hanged for doing this, and later another, and at such-and-such a town a third.' Then said this curate: 'I command you, by the power of this body that is here, that you go into the wilderness where no one dwells, and stay there till Doomsday!' And so at once it vanished. And with all the reverence he could show, he took up the host and put it into the box, and so rode again to the woman, and gave her the sacrament therewith. And so he returned home, thanking God with all his heart for showing him this miracle.[31]

In addition to the increasing elaboration of liturgy, there is also a discernible desire to foster a devotion to the sacrament that is inward as much as outward.[32] Thus the Carthusian Nicholas Love's defence against the Lollard view of the Eucharist is based not on the doctrine of transubstantiation but on personal experience: he condemns Lollards for assuming that, just because they experience nothing on receiving the sacrament, neither does anyone else; and he goes on to say, speaking with an unusually personal voice, that

> I am sure that no one may tell or speak of it [the presence of Christ in the sacrament], and that no one may fully and truly know it other than the person who experiences it for himself.[33]

Devotion to the Eucharist was above all reflected in the feast of Corpus Christi, which was introduced to England by 1318, having originated in Liège, and with its colourful processions and associated mystery plays became a major feature of liturgical and social life in both monasteries and parishes.[34] Such devotion was directed to both external and internal impulses in its participants: thus Corpus Christi processions could be spectacular affairs, such as the one in York (from 1449 onwards) in which a magnificent silver shrine to house the sacrament was carried through the streets;[35] and the elevation of the host in the Eucharist became (as much as many a saint's miracle) the moment at which God became visible:

> And now we can say that this is our God, and no other can compare with him, he is seen here on earth everyday when he is elevated by the hands of the priest, and comes into the company of human beings . . . And the host is thus raised high so that it can be contemplated by all surrounding believers. And by this the devotion of believers is excited, and an increase in their faith is effected . . . Not only should they bow with respect but kneel and adore their creator with all devotion and reverence.[36]

One Thomas Goisman, an alderman of Hull, left £10 in his will of 1502 to build a machine by which angels would descend from the roof at the elevation, and ascend after the Paternoster.[37] Yet this was not simply the admiration of a great spectacle. The author of the *Lay folks' Mass book* encourages people to use this climactic point in the liturgy for prayer, telling them that they may 'pray for anything between the sanctus and the sacring'.[38]

Books such as this reflect the church's concern to foster interior devotion at each point of the Eucharist,[39] and doubtless also to discourage inattention. The anonymous fifteenth-century author of instructions for a devout and literate layperson offers this advice:

> When you hear Mass, do not by any means engage in talk with other people; but while the clerks are singing, look at the books of the church; and on every feast day, look at the Gospel and the exposition of it and at the Epistle. There is a certain Legenda Sanctorum which is very old; look at that and especially at the Common of Saints at the end of the book.[40]

We have seen already that late medieval religion was already increasingly pluralist in its different manners of expression; and this is reflected in liturgical spirituality. More prosperous laity with their own private chapels received communion much more frequently than everyone else, though many parishes seem to have attempted to maintain a daily Mass.[41] The author of *Dives and Pauper* encourages both private and public prayer, commending the former when attendance at church is impossible but clearly preferring the latter:

> Prayer is good in chamber and in oratory, but it is better in holy church with the community when it is time for common prayer and when people may come and attend.[42]

In a perspective that carried over into the Reformation with even greater force, common prayer is seen as better than prayer alone because Christ commended it; and even those with private oratories or chapels are exhorted to go to the church on major feasts. The author warns his readers that those who pray alone are more vulnerable to deception by the illusions and tricks of the devil, which is what often happens to those who flee company and spend much time on their own,[43] an attitude to which Richard Rolle would certainly have taken exception.[44]

What is reflected here is surely the fact that, as both liturgy and people's understanding of it developed, a diversity of approaches to it was inevitable: Bossy, arguing for a wide variety of patterns of prayer used at Mass, makes the point well: 'Liturgists and reformers rarely like it, but pluralism in prayer is one of the advantages of a relatively non-participatory rite'.[45]

The Growth of Lay Spirituality (2): Private Prayer

The burgeoning lay interest in the spiritual life was met by the Church in various ways. The production of spiritual texts increased enormously, even before the invention of printing. The use of illustrations extended the scope of such texts beyond aristocratic and Latinate circles: vivid depictions of hell, or of demons and angels hovering at a deathbed scene, must have concentrated the wavering mind significantly;[46] and even in poor households where there were no books there may well have been an increased concern to teach children the basic prayers and other ingredients of an informed religious observance.[47] Much of the material produced by the church during this period consisted of translations of spiritual texts originally written in Latin or French, and drawn from a wide range of European sources.[48] These were not, however, absorbed neat: the English church seems to have gone to some lengths to ensure that only texts of unimpeachable orthodoxy became available to nourish the growing appetites of an increasingly literate laity, carefully revising or diluting material where necessary.[49]

Much of the material produced in order to foster lay spirituality is clearly written by religious for those living *in seculo,* and reflects the generally depreciatory attitude to this world of those who have chosen to leave it. Thus the anonymous author of the late-fourteenth-century *Contemplations of the dread and love of God* tells his readers to love 'the flesh' only as a source of sustenance, and in no way for its own sake, and warns them to be satisfied with their present social station.[50] Perhaps the most characteristic example of this kind of text is *The abbey of the Holy Ghost,* a fourteenth-century translation of a French original. The author interiorizes the various architectural features of the monastery: penance represents the chapter-house, preaching the frater, prayer the chapel, contemplation the dormitory, pity the infirmary, devotion the cellar, and meditation the granary. For all their conservatism, manuals of this kind do encourage a progressive view of the spiritual life, exhorting their readers to grow spiritually rather than to settle for a lower level than they need.[51] Much of the material they contain is standard Augustinian spirituality.[52]

By the late fourteenth century books of hours and primers (lay prayer books), usually rich elaborations of the psalms and other scriptural texts, had become the primary devotional material used by prosperous and literate people in secular life, a process which in turn reflects the growing importance of the family and household as the primary focus of piety.[53] The primers originated in monastic offices, and since their essential core was liturgical they enabled laypeople to share the regular prayer of clergy and religious:[54] one illustration shows a layman with a book, seated in the church near the officiating priest, engaged in his devotion.[55] But they also included extra-liturgical devotions, affective and penitential prayers to Jesus, the office of the dead, prayers for different times of the day, and familiar scriptural texts such as the prologue to St John's Gospel.[56] Some households also created their own 'common-place book', a pattern of devotion which remained popular from the fifteenth until the eighteenth centuries, and might include poems, songs, and sayings considered worth preserving.[57]

We know something of the spirituality of pious noble women from contemporary or near-contemporary descriptions. Thus Cecily, duchess of York and mother of Edward IV, is described as being accustomed to rise at seven o'clock and to say matins of the day and of Our Lady with her chaplain: she used to hear at least three masses daily and would listen to readings from Walter Hilton, St Bridget's *Revelations* and similar spiritual texts during meals. Yet she was no religious prude: 'after supper she spends time with her gentlewomen in the enjoyment of honest mirth'.[58]

The Growth of Lay Spirituality (3): Gilds and Confraternities

One of the most significant manifestations of increasing lay initiative in church and spiritual life is the growth of the gilds and confraternities.[59] These gilds (in origin mostly craft gilds) became increasingly religious in character, and as they grew in number and size came to challenge the old static structures of ecclesiastical life in two ways: first, by cutting across geographical boundaries; secondly, in the fact that they were (to a greater extent than on the continent) led by laypeople.[60] It is striking that the language adopted by gilds when drawing up their statutes was that of kinship: indeed they may often have functioned as though they were a second set of kin, the members praying for each other as though they were all related:[61] this in itself points to the importance of gilds in the spiritual lives of their members.

Membership of most gilds was open to men and women alike: thus the Gild of the Blessed Virgin Mary in Hull was founded on 23 July 1357 by 22 people of whom 10 were men and 12 women, 9 of the latter being wives of the men;[62] and one scholar has calculated that, of the 500-odd gilds whose records are extant, no more than five excluded women.[63] Nevertheless, in contrast to some continental centres, there were no exclusively female gilds in England; and it was certainly men for whom member-ship mattered most, since the gilds will have functioned as work-based organizations whilst the parish churches drew worshippers on the basis of where they lived and may thus have acquired relatively greater importance in the spiritual lives of women (whose work was more often centred on the home) than of men.[64] The fact that the majority of twentieth-century organizations whose functions most closely resemble the medieval gilds (freemasons, Rotarians and the like) are either predominantly or exclusively male in membership prompts a further question: did the kind of corporate, structured, practical, convivial and 'club-like' pattern of life characteristic of medieval gilds (similar in many respects to that of their twentieth-century successors), together with the twin sense of solidarity and secrecy that seems often to have been attached to membership, appeal more to men than to women?[65]

Gilds exerted a considerable influence on the spiritual lives of their members. Some actively encouraged private as well as corporate prayer: thus members of the Gild of Our Lady at Maldon in Essex were bound to say the Psalter of the Virgin three times each year for living and dead members of the fraternity and for all Christian souls.[66] Others expected members to pray for more than simply themselves and their fellow-members: the members of the York Gild of the Lord's Prayer were bound to meet together every six weeks, and at that time to pray 'for the welfare of our lord the King and for the good governance of the kingdom of England', as well as for gild members living and departed and their benefactors;[67] the members of the Carpenters' Gild at Norwich prayed for 'peace and unity in the land';[68] and the Gild of the Assumption at Wyggenale (Wiggenhall) in Norfolk prescribed prayer for the Church, the King and Queen, the nobility, the Pope, the Patriarch of Jerusalem, the Church, the conversion of the Holy Land, the harvest, those who travel, and the departed, as well as the gild's own members.[69] Some gilds showed an interest in praying for wider issues, such as the healing of the Schism or the recovery of the true Cross.[70] The Gild of St Benedict at Lincoln required every member to give a penny to any member wishing to go on pilgrimage to the Holy Land, and a halfpenny to any wishing to go to Compostela or Rome.[71]

It is also fascinating to see how spiritual and social activities intermingle in gild meetings:

> On feast days, the brethren and sisters shall have three flagons and six tankards, with prayers [i.e. said over the flagons and tankards]; and the ale in the flagons shall be given to the poor who most need it. After the feast, a mass shall be said and offerings made for the souls of those who are dead.[72]

Finally it is worth noting that gilds may well have exerted some influence upon the spiritual lives of young people, a subject on which clear evidence is particularly difficult to locate. Possibly the first Christian young people's organization appears in the survey of religious gilds carried out during the reign of Richard II in 1389: it was the gild of St William (believed to have been martyred in childhood) at King's Lynn, which was founded in 1388, consisting 'of younge scolers to mayntene and kepen an ymage of seynt Wylyam standyng in a tabernakle in the chirche of seynt Margarete of Lenne'.[73]

Confraternities existed in a vast variety of forms, some of which have been explored in Chapter 3. In part religious fraternities were poor people's chantries, benefits normally comprising payment in full of the member's funeral expenses, together with an annual dinner and requiem mass.[74] Some, however, especially civic fraternities, became wealthy organizations, endowing numerous priests and holding splendid annual celebrations.[75] Their primary purpose was prayer for the dead, though they also provided material support for members and widows.[76]

Evidence of a particular kind of confraternity exists in a manuscript in Lichfield which contains over 50,000 names of families and clergy in the archdeaconry of Stafford in the 1530s, many of whom were dead.[77] It appears to have been a prayer list of some kind,[78] somewhat similar to the *libri vitae* (such as that of Durham, though that lists only prominent benefactors and is on a much smaller scale) and the *libri fraternitatis* of monastic confraternities. This may have been linked to a local example of a particular kind of confraternity, the fabric confraternity, whose members will have been people who contributed to the fabric of a cathedral or monastic house (in this case to Lichfield Cathedral) and had their names inscribed on the roll with the promise that they would be prayed for.[79] Each area's entries are normally listed in order of social hierarchy: thus gentlefolk and clergy come first (some members of religious houses are also included).

The Growth of Lay Spirituality (4): John Wyclif and the Lollard Movement

One of the most important signs of the increased questioning both of established authority and of patterns of religious life inherited from the past is the rise of heterodox spirituality, and specifically of the Lollard movement. We enter here upon an area fraught with hazard: recent authors have rightly warned that we too easily underestimate both the importance and the vitality of heterodox spirituality in the later Middle Ages,[80] not least because the transmission of texts and other essential materials remained largely in the hands of those who longed to see heresy extirpated.[81] The result is that few Lollard texts survive – other than a substantial collection of 294 Lollard sermons which points to the extent of Lollard ideas and influence.[82] There are other problems too: few will have admitted voluntarily to being a member of a heterodox group, and some may have espoused some heterodox views whilst remaining orthodox in practice.[83] Nor did Lollard ideas form a single indivisible set of beliefs that had to be accepted or rejected in their entirety.[84] Furthermore it is hard to estimate the effects of a movement whose originating impulse was in the world of academic debate, not of social and political revolt: one of the commonest misunderstandings about late medieval heterodoxy seems to be the assumption that it represents what happens when ill-educated layfolk appropriate for themselves what ought to remain under the watchful eye of monks and priests.[85]

Lollardy was not the only manifestation of dissent in the fourteenth century (though it was the most substantial); and many of its ideas were not new:[86] only gradually did the full impact of ideas drawn partly from earlier heterodox movements, partly from the rich legacy of Franciscan piety, but mainly from the writings of the Oxford theologian John Wyclif, become clear.[87] It flourished primarily between 1381 and 1413, the term 'Lollard' first appearing in 1382.[88] The relationship between Wyclif's theological ideas and the popular movement which was inspired by them is complex and elusive:[89] what is clear is the paradox of a movement drawn from academic circles, and fuelled by the spread of literacy, and yet accompanied by widespread anti-intellectualism.[90] Wyclif himself, who died in 1384, was a philosopher and biblical scholar, almost all of whose works are prolix and highly complex;[91] but he stood firm on a number of central convictions, three of which are worth noting here – the belief that all goods ought to be held in common and that therefore the Church should spurn worldly wealth;[92] the belief that the Bible should be accessible to and read by everyone (i.e. that it should be translated into the vernacular);[93] and (most controversially of all among contemporaries) the belief that Christ is present in the sacrament of the Eucharist but without annihilating the bread and wine.[94]

But what made Wyclif in particular, and Lollardy in general, so suspect in the eyes of contemporary churchmen was their shared emphasis on the importance and integrity of the individual over against the church: personal re-formation is the essential means to corporate reform, and the private conscience of the true Christian, conformed to the authority of Scripture, a surer guide to truth than the dictates of popes. This principle is not exclusive to Wyclif: it is found in Langland's *Piers Plowman*,[95] in the closing pages of which Piers becomes a pope, the successor of Peter, presiding over a radically reformed church.[96] And in many respects it is merely a logical extension of the kind of spirituality reflected in the text from Rolle with which this chapter began. But it did present a clear challenge to the church as a whole, and to the clergy in particular, partly because Lollard emphasis on the primacy of conscience led them to disapprove of oral confession,[97] and partly because their views on eschatology and predestination caused them to conceive of themselves as a church within a church, the true Christians being those who belong to the *congregatio omnium predestinatorum* and who alone will withstand the coming apocalypse.[98] Extant Lollard texts are full of anticlerical satire and withering attacks on clerical abuses, though not (significantly) on the principle of priesthood itself.[99] One Lollard writer criticizes priests who

> commonly . . . sleep in soft beds when other men rise to their labour, and blabber out mattins and the mass like huntsmen without devotion and contemplation.[100]

Another describes priests as God's pantrykeepers who often behave as stepmothers rather than as true mothers;[101] and in a text attributed to Wyclif the author declares that 'a simple paternoster of a ploughman that is [said] in charity is better than a thousand masses of covetous prelates and vain religious full of envy and pride and false flattery and nourished by sin'.[102]

It is this stress on personal integrity, and on the fact that for Lollards God prefers inward holiness to social status,[103] which provides the key to Lollard spirituality: the Lollard knight Sir John Clanvowe (who died in 1391) spoke of those whom the world regards as 'lollers' and whom God regards as wise and honourable.[104] On the Lollard view, which is strikingly close to that of Richard Rolle, true holiness is an interior reality, not ostentatiously public;[105] and what matters above all else is not conformity to church law and practice but true Christian love, which is itself the fruit of an inner apprehension of divine truth as revealed in scripture, so that preaching and practice, theology and ethics, become perfectly one:[106]

> Only these be chosen who endure in love of God until their dying day, for
> to all such and only such has God ordained bliss.[107]

> A person [who wishes to practise true penance] should believe that every
> sin comes principally from the devil, and not from God; for those who sin
> excuse themselves by saying, 'It was my destiny, or the star I was born
> under; it was devised for me before any clothes.'[108]

Lollard spirituality was in many respects a family-based affair, not only because
public ecclesial practice of it was impossible, but also because of this insistent
emphasis on the individual's relationship with God. Hence Lollards disapproved of
prayer to the saints (one Lollard, Agnes Ward, when asked by her brother to seek the
help of the Virgin and other saints, is said to have replied, 'What need is it to go to the
feet, when we may go to the head?'[109]). But this did not completely reduce prayer to a
narrowly private affair: in one Lollard sermon the preacher declares that, when we
pray as we should, the saints in heaven pray with us even though we do not (and
should not) pray to them.[110]

In a Lollard sermon for the Epiphany, the preacher stressed three aspects essential to
true prayer: it must be in conformity with God's will (a theme close to that of both
William of Ockham and of Julian, as we shall see); it must be persevering, even when it
is not answered at once; and it must be 'made in charity'.[111] Each of these forms a significant strand in Lollard spirituality. Conformity to God's will meant avoiding
spurious religious practices:

> Some be led by the way of exceptional fastings; some by multiplying of
> many prayers; some by hearing of many masses; some by false religion;
> some by worthless vows of their false pilgrimages; some by creating abbeys,
> and some houses of friars; some by colleges; and some by chantries.[112]

Perseverance was crucial because commended in scripture. Another Lollard sermon
describes the upright person persisting in prayer, and saying

> the perfect Paternoster, for that prayer pleases God. But then comes his
> trivia (literally 'muck') into his mind and hinders him in the midst [of his
> prayer], and says: 'Leave your labour for a little while, and go and attend to
> what is neglected, or you may regret it for ever, and do your duty on
> another day, and double it.' And thus the word of God is strangled.[113]

The Paternoster was the primary prayer for Lollards, 'of more authority than is prayer
made by other men, even if their prayer be good'.[114] In a Lollard sermon for Quinquagesima, the preacher quotes St Augustine, describing every man as 'the beggar of God',
like Bartimaeus by the roadside, whose prayer is the Paternoster, seeking daily bread.
And if the prayer is not answered, the Christian should go and do good:

> Right so, you Christian man who prays, when you see that your prayer is
> not at once heard as you wanted, go and worship the Lord with works of
> mercy ('almesdede') for the poor members of his body, and then your
> prayer shall be heard.[115]

Hence the link between prayer and active love, a link that is fundamental to Lollard spirituality. 'Devout and effectual prayer must be knitted to mercy', wrote one Lollard preacher.[116] In a splendid Christmas sermon, the preacher uses material from the thirteenth-century Golden Legend to describe the stable at Bethlehem as a meeting-place in the heart of Bethlehem with roof but no walls, so that all could gain access. The preacher lays constant stress on the gospel being preached for the poor and humble, declaring that the angel brought the news of Christ's birth not to the powerful but to poor and simple shepherds; and that these shepherds, though poor, were hardworking, caring for their sheep.[117]

There is much that Lollardy has in common with contemporary orthodox spirituality (such as its stress on the importance of preparing for death,[118] or its traditional depreciation of the flesh, or its emphasis on devotion to the Passion of Christ). Furthermore Wyclif's stress on the primacy of the individual's relationship with God is fascinatingly close to that of Rolle on the one hand and of Hilton on the other, despite Wyclif's disavowal of both the eremitic and the religious states of life.[119] At the same time it could be argued that Lollard spirituality is a pale, one-dimensional affair when compared with that of Rolle or Hilton, showing little interest in the idea of prayer other than as one (admittedly vital) ingredient in active Christian discipleship.

Yet that is also precisely its strength. Wyclif's major achievement from the perspective of the history of English spirituality was surely to advance yet further the development of a genuinely lay pattern of spiritual life, in which the authenticity of any progress towards holiness is measured by the best and highest criterion of all: the quality of love and goodness to which it gives rise. There is a fascinating Lollard version of the *Ancrene Wisse*, the thirteenth-century guide for anchoresses, in which the original is subtly adapted to apply to laypeople; at one point the Lollard reviser actually reverses the meaning both of the original and of the New Testament and declares that Martha (symbol of the active life) has chosen the higher part, not her contemplative sister Mary.[120] In the final analysis, the spirituality of Lollardy is much more corporate, more richly inclusive, than it is often given credit for, as their view of heaven makes clear:

> The third thing of which this joy principally consists is the worshipful, blessed and comfortable company that shall be in that place [heaven]. That comprises, first, the fellowship, mirth and melody of angels and archangels in their nine orders, into which company of orders human beings shall be received at one level or another, as they have deserved on earth . . . The will of one is the will of another. The more they have been, the more is their bliss. There no one is hurt, no one is angry. No one is envious of another's good. There no envy burns in human hearts, for they have more joy than they can desire, for love is their law and leads everyone. There no one seeks to be worshipped, or seeks higher rank, but each man is content with the state that he is in. There is one peace, one accord, and everlasting gladness . . . There shall be youth without any age. There shall be beauty without any spot of filth. There shall be health without any sickness. There shall be riches without any poverty. There shall be

knowledge without any ignorance. There shall be rest without any weariness. There shall be fullness without any want. There shall be worship
without any villainy. There shall be generosity without any thirsting. And
soon all who are good shall be among that company.[121]

Carthusian Spirituality

One of the subversive aspects of Lollard thought was their hostility to the monastic
life: where Chaucer and Langland derided the foibles of individual monks, nuns and
friars, Lollards went further, criticizing the very existence of what they called 'private
religions' because they were not legitimated by scripture.[122] It is true that none of the
outstanding spiritual figures of this period was a monk or nun: Rolle and Julian were
recluses, Walter Hilton a regular canon, Margery Kempe a married woman, and the
author of *The cloud of unknowing* anonymous.[123] The mainstream male monastic
orders did not so much decline as stagnate during this period:[124] there is evidence to
suggest that the Cistercian Order experienced a slow but inexorable loss of control
over its own affairs, first to the papacy and thereafter to the crown, with a consequent
sad decline in standards of life and spirituality.[125] Women's religious communities
appear generally to have maintained exemplary standards of piety, in part because they
were less wealthy than those of men.[126]

In general, however, the initiative among religious passed from the black (Benedictine) and white (Cistercian) monks to the strict enclosed orders, especially the
Carthusians, whose expansion during this period reflects the extent of royal and aristocratic support for the order as much as any flowering of its own spiritual life.[127] The
contrast between the life of the charterhouse and that of many of the nobility who
sponsored them must have been striking;[128] but that in itself hints at the reason why
they did so – in an age still haunted by the imminence of death, an enclosed religious
order of impeccable integrity must have provided the surest source of prayer for those
anxious about their own salvation.[129]

The importance of the Carthusians in transmitting spiritual texts, especially those
imported from the continent, has already been referred to: it reflects not only their
own vocation as 'heralds of the truth',[130] but also their keen interest in continental
spirituality, an interest strikingly absent from most of the older and larger orders, most
of whose libraries seem to have contained scarcely any texts of this kind.[131] Mount
Grace in Yorkshire played a key role in this respect, propagating the works of Richard
Rolle as well as those of continental writers such as Suso;[132] and the Carthusians in
general, like Walter Hilton and the author of *The cloud of unknowing*, were particularly concerned to foster spiritual orthodoxy and to protect ordinary layfolk from
anything that might have seemed questionable in its theology or possible effect.

Of Carthusian writers in this period, perhaps the most significant is Nicholas Love,
prior of Mount Grace from 1409 or 1410 until 1421, whose work will be considered
below.[133] In terms of original work, however, the major figure is Richard Methley
(1451–1528), who produced, in addition to careful Latin translations of *The cloud of
unknowing* and of Marguerite Porete's *Mirror of simple souls,* a letter on the solitary life
(*To Hew Heremyte: a pystyl of solytary lyfe nowadayes*[134]) which strongly reflects the

influence of Richard Rolle.[135] His autobiographical works describe his own intensely affective mystical experiences in the charterhouse, most of which took place during the liturgy; and they give a vivid picture both of life in a late medieval charterhouse and of someone endeavouring to put the teaching of *The cloud of unknowing* into practice.[136] Methley's affective spirituality has rendered him suspect to those who are similarly censorious of Margery Kempe (and marginal notes in the original manuscript of Kempe's *Book* suggest similarities between the two authors).[137] But the theme of *amor sensibilis* which runs through his works is frequently found among late medieval authors; and much of Methley's work is firmly rooted in the Bible and in the spirituality of Augustine, Gregory and Bernard.[138]

Spirituality and the Solitary Life

The most obvious manifestation of interest in the journey inwards was the practice of the eremitic life, which continued to flourish during the later medieval period, stimulated both by the crises afflicting contemporary society and by the growth of individualism already noted.[139] In part this may reflect the conservative temper of much late-medieval English spirituality: where contemporary continental practice witnessed a wide diversity of experiments in religious life such as beguinages and other groups of lay people living together under a common rule, in England solitaries were far more common.[140] Some recluses (like John Whiterig, the 'Monk of Farne') were closely linked with religious communities in the manner recommended by Aelred of Rievaulx;[141] others were formally authorized by the local bishop and lived under the rule attributed to St Paul the first hermit;[142] but many (like Rolle) resisted the constraints imposed upon them by institutions and put themselves under the patronage of local secular lords,[143] incurring considerable opposition in the process.[144] What such recluses gained in autonomy they tended to lose in security, however, as Rolle was to discover in 1322 when his patron John de Dalton was imprisoned;[145] and even the new-found autonomy was not always an advantage. The anonymous author of the early-fifteenth-century text *Dives and Pauper* declared that the reason women lasted longer as recluses than men was because the latter tended to trust too much in themselves and not in God, and indeed often became solitaries because they wanted to be able to do exactly what they liked, whereas women embraced solitude for the sake of God alone.[146]

Why did secular lords like John de Dalton patronize recluses? Partly because they valued their prayers, seeing them as crucial intermediaries between this world and the next: it was no coincidence that recluses were often to be found as bridge-keepers, safeguarding vital connections both literally and spiritually.[147] But we have seen already that holiness was increasingly seen not simply in terms of power but also in terms of wisdom: recluses came more and more to be consulted by their contemporaries as sources of spiritual guidance, and those who acted as their patrons would of course have had the most immediate access to them.[148] In Julian's Norwich recluses like her were clearly held in high esteem by clergy and laity alike.[149] In an age in which only the grandest of lords enjoyed any kind of privacy or solitude in their lives, the proximity of someone who had opted for both to the most extreme extent imaginable may well have served not only to provide a powerful and effective advocate at the heavenly court but also to exemplify a level of holiness which those 'in the world' seem constantly to have aspired after even when they could not attain it.[150]

Hence recluses were not seen to engage in the spiritual quest so that everyone else did not have to, nor simply in order to inspire many more to embrace the solitary life (though Rolle certainly hoped to achieve this): rather they were seen to have a number of significant roles – as protectors, intercessors (for both living and departed), spiritual guides and confidants, teachers, but perhaps supremely as being in some sense incarnate reminders of the primacy of the spiritual life even for those who were busy *in seculo*.

Late-medieval people of every social background still conceived of themselves as engaged upon a hazardous pilgrimage through life surrounded by hostile forces both natural and supernatural; and for such a journey they needed all the support they could find. The 'journey inwards' was not a cosy escape-route for the pious, but an essential dimension of everyone's lives if they were to survive the rigours of the outward journey. And if late-medieval people appear to twentieth-century observers as enjoying a peculiarly lively and varied form of spiritual life, that was (at least in large part) because they believed themselves to be ranged against foes and hazards no less peculiarly lively and varied. Spells, ghosts, and the lures of the devil remained real and active features of the cosmic landscape.[151] Prayer for deliverance from evil remained fundamental to every kind of spirituality, from the Rogationtide processions designed to drive out evil spirits[152] to Julian of Norwich's terrifying encounter with the devil.[153] Both the interior piety of the recluse and the highly visual, exterior, public piety of the church as a whole alike testify to the continuing perception of the cosmos as intensely alive, a world in which both the mysterious love of God and the insidious promptings of the devil were apprehensible at every turn of the road.[154]

This point becomes at once evident on even the most cursory inspection of the classic spiritual and literary texts of the period. Many of these (most obviously *The Canterbury tales*, the anonymous *Sir Gawain and the Green Knight,* Langland's *Piers Plowman,* and the dreamlike poem *Pearl*) are explicitly conceived as journeys, allegories of the journey inward though with much to say also about contemporary life and values.[155] The same is of course true of the great continental works of the period, such as Dante's *Divina commedia* or the various retellings of the legend of Tristan and Ysolt (of which the early-thirteenth-century version by the German Gottfried von Strassburg appeared also in English[156]). The journeys described in works such as these could be seen as metaphors for everyone else's human journey: we shall see below how Margery Kempe's account of her own life operates in this manner.

THEMES IN LATE MEDIEVAL SPIRITUALITY

Penance

The importance of the interior journey in late-medieval spirituality has already been noted with reference to our opening text from Richard Rolle. We shall see shortly that another of the great figures of the period, the Augustinian Walter Hilton, articulated perhaps the most coherent and nuanced account of what this entailed. First, however, it is worth noting some of the principal themes and spiritual virtues believed by contemporaries to be essential items of equipment for those desirous of embarking upon the hazardous journey of the soul towards God. It will come as little surprise to discover that one of them is the practice of penance. Chaucer concluded his most famous work with the Parson's tale (a stern reminder of the importance of penance and forgiveness) with good reason: the stories of his pilgrims, whether intended as satire, allegory, or entertainment, were not designed to distract his readers from the hazards of their own pilgrimages, but rather to equip them with the wisdom and resources they urgently required.[157] Hence he wrote:

> Many be the spiritual ways that lead folk to our Lord Jesus Christ, and to the reign of glory; of which ways, there is a full noble way and a full suitable, which may not fail to man nor to woman, who through sin have departed from the right way of Jerusalem celestial; and this way is called Penitence.[158]

The late-medieval Church sought both to deepen the spiritual lives of its members and to assure their adherence to orthodoxy by the promotion of regular confession; and this period witnessed a flood of penitential literature and devotion,[159] the purpose of which was to ensure the healing of the soul in the same way as a knight in an Arthurian romance would seek the healing of his wounds.[160] Indeed one contemporary sermon compares sins that are forgiven to the wounds inflicted on a knight during battle: they become a source of honour,[161] a point also made by Julian of Norwich.[162]

Perhaps the most attractive and original example of this kind of literature is the *Livre de seyntz medicines* written by Henry, duke of Lancaster (1310–61) in 1354, probably for a small circle of his friends. Henry was a diplomat and military leader during the Hundred Years War, and his work reflects his experience: he explores in some detail his 'wounds' (represented by his five senses, his limbs, and his heart), which need healing by Christ just as physical wounds need the ministrations of the physician. Using contemporary military images, he compares his body with a castle and the inmost part of it with his soul: the enemies are his sins.[163] The use of such imagery is a commonplace in spiritual literature, and some of Henry's extended similes become wearisome; but he has an eye for fresh and vivid parallels from everyday life: thus the Devil is compared to a cat who sneaks back onto its master's chair once he has left the house, which is what will happen in our hearts if God does not continue to dwell there.[164]

In the practice of penance the emphasis on the journey inwards is manifested in a heightened sense of personal sinfulness, and a greater concern on the part of spiritual writers to contrast a formal and perfunctory confession with a searching inner self-exploration. Thus the fifteenth-century *Instructions for a devout and literate layman* contain this admonition:

> At the door [of your house] when you go out say: 'All the men of this city or town from the greater to the less are pleasing to God, and only I am worthy of hell. Woe is me. Welawey'; let this be said from all your heart so that the tears run; you need not always say it with your mouth; it is sufficient to say it with a groan . . . Sometimes if you meet a dog or other beast, you may say: 'Lord, let it bite me, let it kill me; this beast is much better than I; it has never sinned.'[165]

But it was in the writings of Walter Hilton himself that the theory and practice of penance received its most significant exploration. Hilton described penance as 'a great courtesy of our Lord's', a kind of divine *acte gratuite* comparable to the unmerited clemency shown by a 'courteous' knight to his foe.[166] He goes on to describe penance as a second baptism: it was commonly argued in the Middle Ages that the two sacraments of baptism and penance were 'sacraments of the dead' – without receiving both, the person was spiritually dead. For Hilton, the practice of penance and the free gift of God's forgiveness allows the image of Christ within each of us to be reformed. As a shrewd spiritual guide, he is well aware that even after penance a person may 'feel' no different,[167] for (as we have seen) this re-formation is objective, independent of feeling, and does not dispose of the promptings to sin:

> My dear friends, we are even now, while we live here, the sons of God, for we are reformed by faith in Christ to his likeness; but what we are does not yet show: it is all hidden.[168]

The crucial priority is to examine your will: if it is turned away from all mortal sin and towards God, 'your soul is reformed in faith to the likeness of God'.[169] Hilton sees penance as part of a progressive view of the spiritual life, rather than as a mechanical obliterating of immediate sins. We grow, slowly and in a largely hidden manner, as we allow ourselves to be remade in the image of Christ.

Humility and Self-knowledge (1): Walter Hilton

Progress on the spiritual journey demanded other virtues as well as penance, of which two deserve some mention here: humility and patience.[170] Both are traditional virtues in monastic spirituality; and humility is linked in the Neoplatonic (and particularly the Augustinian) tradition with self-knowledge: by learning to apprehend the truth about yourself, you are able to value yourself as you really are and to embrace that humility which is proper to the role and status of the human being made in God's image but deformed through sin.[171]

Again it is Walter Hilton who develops this theme most fully. He begins his *Scale of perfection* by exhorting the anchoress to whom he is writing to turn to God inwardly so that her inner life may conform with her outer one.[172] He goes on to emphasize the need for a sense of self-abasement and self-negation;[173] but even here humility is linked with self-knowledge: 'you must know [your own soul] first if you are to come to the knowledge of God';[174] and he explicitly cites Augustine in this regard.[175]

This brings Hilton to the heart of the matter. In his *Scale of perfection* he tells his anchoress that

> through looking inward you will be able to see the honor and dignity it
> [the soul] ought to have from the nature of the first making . . . [i.e. its
> original creation].[176]

A humility which allows her to see both this dignity and the wretchedness which is the result of sin will lead to a 'great desire with great longing' to recover that lost dignity, which in turn will require striving against 'the ground of all sins' which is 'a false disordered love of a person for himself'.[177] Hilton is writing in the tradition of St Augustine and St Bernard here;[178] and for him, as for them, humility is a virtue that is both theological (not simply moral) and dynamic: theological because it is grounded in an accurate apprehension of the truth of our nature as beings created by God, gone astray through sin, and redeemed by God in Christ; and dynamic because it is precisely the twin awareness both of our infinite potential as creatures and of our present wretchedness which should lead us to co-operate unconditionally with the grace of God and allow ourselves to be re-formed in the divine likeness.[179]

And it is this re-formation through the working of God's grace which is the ultimate fruit of humility, provided we do not transmogrify that humility by turning it into a kind of subtle pride (here, as so often in his work, Hilton reveals his exceptional wisdom as a spiritual director). Hilton argues that the problem with heresy is that it presupposes *pride*:

> A heretic sins mortally in pride, because he chooses his resting place and
> his delight in his own opinion.[180]

Heresy thus involves putting your will before that of God, which is precisely the sin of pride, the mirror opposite of humility. But heretics have no monopoly of pride: those called to the religious life are vulnerable to it too, and for them it clearly means a smug sense of superiority over those still living *in seculo*[181] (elsewhere Hilton describes pride as stealing someone else's honour[182]). Pride means setting yourself in God's place: whereas humility *is truth*, as Hilton explicitly says,[183] because it allows you to see yourself as you truly are. In the end (as we have seen) the spiritual journey of re-formation is a work of grace with which you co-operate, not a personal achievement;[184] and in this context humility becomes more even than the essential starting-point for the spiritual journey – it becomes the fruit of God's self-disclosure, for only when we see God as God really is can we see ourselves as we really are.[185]

Humility and Self-knowledge (2): William Langland

An equally important exploration of the theme of humility and self-knowledge is made by William Langland in *Piers Plowman*. Like Hilton, Langland is heir to the Neoplatonic and Augustinian stress on knowledge of self as the fundamental starting-point for the spiritual journey; and in Passus VIII to XII of his great poem the central character, Will, encounters a whole series of characters – Thought, Wit, Study, Imaginatif (= imagination) et al. who in effect represent dimensions of the self.[186] But for Langland self-knowledge is also the starting-point for a different process: the reform of society. The re-forming of the individual, oriented to the truth and dignity of his or her condition as someone created and restored by God, is the key to this larger social re-formation; and in this perspective the inward journey of the individual person, as microcosm of the world as a whole, assumes a new and vital significance: inward and outward journeys, spirituality and the renewal of society, become inseparably linked.[187]

It is in *Piers Plowman* that we also find a fascinating reflection on the importance of that other primary virtue for the spiritual journey: patience. In traditional medieval moralizing, patience was the principal remedy against anger;[188] but in the history of western spirituality its etymological links with suffering (both 'patience' and 'passion' derive from the Latin *patior*) caused many late medieval writers to follow their forebears in conceiving of patience not merely as the endurance of suffering in anticipation of the world to come, but as a loving imitation of the suffering Christ, and sometimes of his mother too.[189] Thus medieval theologians conceived of patience as possessing a twofold value: first, the patient endurance of suffering was a means of doing satisfaction for sin; and secondly, it was the virtue which *par excellence* caused the practitioner to imitate the redemptive suffering of Christ.[190]

Both of these attributes of patience appear in Langland's *Piers Plowman*;[191] but its real importance soon becomes apparent when it is personalized, and declared by Conscience to be the crucial companion for Will's pilgrimage.[192] Together the two go off in search of the fullness of truth, an interior journey of self-exploration: it is clear that Patience represents both steadfast trust and the capacity to suffer.[193] It is thus a source of true wisdom (*sapientia*) rather than of narrow book-learning (*scientia*), which Langland deprecates.[194] But it is also much more: patience effects change, both by being a protection against sin, a means of converting unmerited suffering into a penance for the sin we have committed, and thus also by being a means of attaining heaven.[195]

Such a view of patience acquires much greater force when we recall the generally accepted medieval assumption that God was the cause of all that happened: in such a context, patience becomes one of humanity's surest companions for the spiritual journey, allowing us to respond creatively to whatever befalls us: small wonder that Rolle included impatience (*untholmodnesse*) among the sins of human hearts.[196]

For Langland, as for Chaucer, patience was closely linked with poverty, a subject which was prominent in late medieval theological debate, particularly (though not only) among Franciscans: Pope John XXII's condemnation in 1323 of the Franciscan *spirituales*, who had advocated extreme poverty by rejecting even communal property, reflects the intensity of this debate; and the extent to which this debate, focussing as it did upon two factions within the Franciscan order, attracted widespread interest outside the order, in turn reflects the prominence of that order in the late medieval period.[197] It was not only Franciscans, however, who were concerned about poverty. In his monastic treatise *De substancialibus regulae monachalis*, the English Benedictine monk Uthred of Boldon commends poverty as (in varying degrees) a priority for all Christians, on the grounds that all goods belong ultimately to God alone, man being only a *villicus Dei* (steward of God).[198] But Langland went further, in effect making poverty an essential precondition of contemplation in *Piers Plowman*: in Passus XI, referring to the story of Martha and Mary, Trajan declares that it was Mary's poverty, not her holiness, which caused her to be esteemed more highly than Martha.[199] Trajan continues:

> And all the wise that ever were, by aught I can espy,
> praise poverty as best in life if Patience is followed too:
> both better and more blessed are than the pursuit of wealth.
> Though sour it be to suffer, there cometh sweetness after.
> As on the outside the walnut bears a bitter bark,
> and after that bitter bark, once take the shell away,
> is a kernel of comfort to nourish and restore.
> So when poverty or penance are with patience undertaken,
> they make a man have mind of God and summon a great will
> to weep and wail, from which waxeth Mercy
> (whose kernel is Christ) to comfort the soul.
> And well secure he sleepeth, the person that is poor,
> and less he feareth death, or robbery in the dark,
> than he that is right rich.[200]

Langland is criticizing Christians who do not practise what they preach. The external observance of the Christian (or even the religious) life is not enough: only those whose spirituality is incarnated in a life of patient poverty in imitation of the suffering Christ can truly expect mercy.[201] And the reason why this is so is declared by Patience herself with bold clarity in Passus XIV:

> So may beggars, like beasts, await their recompense
> Who all their lives have lived in hunger and lack.
> Yet God sends them at some time some manner of Joy
> either here or elsewhere, for nature would not allow it to
> be otherwise.[202]

Humility and Patience (3): Richard Rolle

Richard Rolle makes his own distinctive contribution to this subject. Many of his works, as well as the text with which this chapter began, evince his concern for the poor and his prophetic critique of worldly wealth. But it is crucial to see this in the context of his thoroughgoing asceticism: it is *because* the poor have so little in this world that they are much more likely to inherit eternal life in the next one. Thus, commenting on Psalm 22, he writes

> The poor love God, the rich love themselves; for although the bodies of the poor die, their hearts live for ever; whilst the rich live in joy in this world, and therefore die in endless pain.[203]

He goes on to say that the rich, who 'love earthly good, shall fall; for they take the sacrament unworthily in the sight of God. For he alone knows how they fall, and whither; in another world, we shall know too'.[204]

Pilgrimage

True poverty, then, patiently borne, becomes a primary attribute of those who seek to progress on the spiritual journey, whatever their state of life. It leads us to (and indeed is often closely connected with) another public manifestation of this emphasis on the journey inwards in the late (as indeed in the earlier) Middle Ages: the practice of pilgrimage.[205]

There is some evidence that the great saints' shrines at Durham, Canterbury and the like experienced some decline during the fourteenth and fifteenth centuries, though this is uncertain.[206] What is unquestionable is that pilgrimage, both within and beyond the realm, remained a major part of contemporary spiritual life, with considerable social and economic implications as well.[207] Pilgrimages to distant shrines such as Rome, Jerusalem, and Compostela became relatively common: Margery Kempe managed all three, and a good many others besides, as we shall see. Surviving medieval wall paintings reflect this: above an altar in the parish church of Wisborough Green in Sussex there is a thirteenth-century representation of St James welcoming pilgrims to Compostela.[208] Numerous surviving wills contain bequests for people to make pilgrimages on behalf of the testators: sometimes hermits were paid to do this.[209] Thus Nicholas Lathe, a parchmenter of Norwich, left money in his will dated 1499 to pay for a priest to 'sing and pray' for a year for his and his wife's souls, during which time the priest was to go to Rome and 'go the Stations' for Nicholas and his friends.[210]

The reference to the Stations of the Cross is significant for another reason. The practice of pilgrimage came increasingly to be linked with devotion to the Passion of Christ: from the late thirteenth century onwards the standard tour of Jerusalem focused on a number of 'stations' which by the fifteenth century had increased to over a hundred.[211]

But it is in the masterpieces of two of the greatest late medieval English writers that the significance of pilgrimage is most fully explored. The interpretation of Geoffrey Chaucer's *Canterbury tales* is much controverted and the subject of a vast secondary literature. For our purposes it is important only to draw attention to the point firmly made in the concluding Parson's tale: that pilgrimage is something we all undertake by journeying through life towards a longed-for goal, and that it demands the utmost integrity, both personal and corporate, on the part of the pilgrims. In *Piers Plowman* William Langland makes this point more clearly still: we are all pilgrims;[212] and the primary focus of our pilgrimage is the interior journey towards Truth.[213] Thus in Passus VI Piers' ploughing turns out to be the most authentic kind of pilgrimage, in which the person stays at home and seeks to grow in understanding of (and manifestation of) Truth. This is genuinely lay spirituality: the real satisfaction required in the performance of penance consists not only, or even primarily, in a sacramental action, however powerful, but in right living and right relationships in the context of an agrarian society.[214]

Spirituality and Buildings

At the heart of everyone's spiritual journey, whether literal or interior, stood the church building; and the later Middle Ages witnessed a remarkable interest in their erection, embellishment or enlargement.[215] Much of this, of course, was the work of wealthy patrons anxious to ensure permanent memorials to themselves.[216] But this was not the whole picture: a study of the diocese of Salisbury has shown that many poorer churches were also significantly altered during the fifteenth century;[217] medieval penitentiaries showed that a contribution to the building of churches was one form of penance;[218] and in cathedrals the number and variety of daily services increased dramatically, thereby ensuring that there would always be a mass which workmen, travellers or others could attend, at almost any time between dawn and mid-morning.[219] The result was that the church building became, as Colin Richmond puts it, 'an ante-chamber of purgatory', crammed with expressions of gratitude to benefactors in search of prayer for their souls, thereby articulating a sense of community that encompassed not only present local inhabitants but all who had gone before them.[220] The universal belief in the physical presence of Christ in the eucharistic sacrament also led to an increasing propensity for enclosing the high altar, above all by the erection of chancel screens, at once heightening and privatizing the sense of the holy.[221]

Companions on the Journey: The Cult of the Saints

For most late medieval Christians, whether living in solitude or in the world, the spiritual journey was in one important respect a corporate one. We have already noted, in examining earlier medieval spirituality, the gradual process whereby the saints came to be viewed as much as companions and exemplars as spiritual heroes.[222] This process is continued during this period: late medieval art abounds with representations of the saints, often as part of a catechetical programme.[223] But the old fascination in exotic and heroic hagiography did not disappear: indeed it grew. Jacobus de Voragine's *Legenda aurea* (or Golden Legend), which is full of material of this kind, was as popular in England as everywhere else, even in the centuries before Caxton produced his English version in 1483.[224] The Augustinian friar Osbern Bokenham (c.1392–1447), from Stoke Clare in Suffolk, produced the *Legendys of Hooly Wummen*, much (though not all) of which is derived from the *Legenda aurea*, and which (like Jacobus' work) is designed to provide encouragement as well as wonder among its readers.[225]

It may seem strange that in an age of ever-increasing theological precision, an age moreover in which the role of priest and sacrament as mediators between heaven and earth came to equal (if not to exceed) that of the saints, seemingly extravagant stories about early Roman virgin martyrs should arouse such interest.[226] In part this may be, as Eamon Duffy suggests, that it was precisely the exceptional quality of such saints which increased their power as intercessors;[227] in part it was doubtless the consequence of the church's concern to evoke among pious laypeople patterns both of *admiratio* and of *imitatio* for the nourishment of their own spiritual lives.[228]

Yet there was another factor at work too. The fourteenth century saw a new interest in spiritual autobiographies and in other quasi-autobiographical works, many of which took Augustine's *Confessions* as their model, a subject we shall explore more fully in the case of Margery Kempe.[229] These works, together with their Augustinian precedent, reflect a new concern with the inner life of the saint, with his or her personality and with the (often luridly extravagant) struggles against evil and temptation which tended to characterize such accounts.[230] The terrible sufferings and persecutions experienced by many of these saints, together with the constant emphasis on the divine protection that surrounded them, must have afforded powerful comfort both to those afflicted by plague and to those whose faith (for whatever reason) came under severe self-questioning. The message of such hagiographical texts was unambiguous: fear not, for others have trodden this path before you.

The Middle English version of Thomas de Cantimpré's life of the memorable Christina of Saint-Trond (better known as St Christina the Astonishing) underlines this point.[231] Christina (1150–1224) is presented as a contemporary manifestation of the desert fathers and mothers. She is a laywoman, belonging to no order, and hailing from a mercantile centre. Her longing for solitude and asceticism is matched only by her striking capacity for self-advertisement, which culminates in her death, vision of purgatory, and amazing return to life during her own funeral service.[232] But this restoration to earthly existence is vouchsafed so that she might deliver through her exemplary suffering the souls she had seen in purgatory, and save others through her example and holy life.[233] For all her modernity, however, her ascetic values are as uncompromising as any in the age of St Antony or St Pachomius:

> Therefore after this [after her return to her body at her own funeral] when Christina fled from the presence of folk with a wonderful longing into the wilderness and into trees, into the tops of towers or churches or of other high things, her friends, assuming that she was filled with devils, eventually with great labour took her and bound her with chains of iron. And when she, being bound, had suffered many penuries and pains, above all in suffering the smell of men: one night she was helped by Our Lord, and her bonds and fetters undone, she escaped and fled far into the desert to woods, and there she lived as birds do, in trees.[234]

Stories of this kind are common (though Christina the Astonishing outdoes everyone else in spectacular spiritual exploits), and exerted a powerful influence on individuals like Margery Kempe, as will be seen. But is it not possible that they also influenced others precisely through their subtle combination of the holy and the everyday? Christina came from an ordinary town in an age not far distant from that in which her story was told. Part at least of the effect of that story must surely have been to instil in its readers the sense, not only that St Christina was praying for them, or that their sufferings were shared by her and others like her, but also the thought that if she could overcome such terrible experiences, lesser mortals ought surely to be able to endure theirs.[235] In a manner as vivid and exciting as any chivalrous quest, the life of Christina the Astonishing must have served both to warn the new mercantile rich not to rely on their wealth, and to transform for others the grim realities of everyday life with a piercing vision of how things could be.[236]

Lives such as this served other purposes too, not least the concern of particular towns or areas to obtain the canonization of 'their' saint.[237] Despite the warnings of some spiritual writers not to set devotion to a saint before devotion to Christ,[238] it is clear both from the quantity of late-medieval feast days dedicated to the saints and from the number of bequests made in favour of lights before images of saints in parish churches that the cult of the saints remained a vital part of late-medieval piety.[239]

The Cult of the Virgin

Devotion to the Virgin Mary continued to grow throughout the late medieval period:[240] the four early medieval feasts of the Virgin (the Purification, Annunciation, Assumption, and Nativity) were increased by the addition of the Visitation (in 1389) and the Presentation of the Temple (in the fourteenth century). The Office of the Blessed Virgin became the principal liturgical complement to the ordinary monastic Hours, ousting the older Office of All Saints even in the monasteries.[241]

In private prayer the Five Joys of Mary became very popular, especially in the north of England, and the rosary even more so;[242] and the equally popular Marian prayer *Obsecro te* neatly incorporates much of the catechetical programme of the late medieval Church into devotion to Our Lady.[243] The Virgin became the queen of chivalry: one story in the *Legenda aurea* describes a knight who missed a tournament because he was hearing masses in honour of the Virgin, only to be told that he had been victorious in the tournament in his absence: he saw that 'the courtly Queen had honoured him in a courtly way'.[244] But she was also the patron saint of all, particularly of lay women: St Bridget of Sweden hears Mary saying that she is particularly ready to help wives, widows and maidens, inasmuch as in a sense she was herself all three.[245] In an early-fifteenth-century hymn to the Virgin, probably from the north of England, she is described not only as Our Lady but as our sister, and Christ as our brother.[246]

The Virgin was above all the protectress of those who prayed to her. John Mirk, in a sermon for the Conception of the Virgin, tells this story:

> I read that there was a lord who had a rent-collector: he had collected his master's rent and hastened to bring it to him. And there were some thieves who waited for him in a wood through which he had to pass. But when he entered the wood, he remembered that he had not said Our Lady's Psalter, which he used to say daily. So at once he knelt down, and began to recite it. Then immediately Our Lady appeared like a fair maiden, and set a garland on his head; and at each 'Ave' she set a rose in the garland that shone as bright as a star. Thus the garland was made as a result of the words he spoke: it was so bright that it lit up the entire wood. Thus, when he had finished, he kissed the earth and went his way. And the thieves took him and brought him to their master, who had seen all that had taken place. And the thief said to him: 'I know you are lord N.'s servant and have his money with you. But tell me: what woman was that, who set this garland

upon your head?' 'Truly, I saw no woman, nor have any garland that I know of. But because I had forgotten to say Our Lady's Psalter and was frightened of you, I knelt down and said it, praying to her to help me in my need.' Then the thief said: 'For love of her, go your way, and pray to her for us.' And so he hastened on his way, safe and sound, by the help of Our Lady.[247]

Such devotion could become extravagant even by medieval standards. In his Meditation on the Virgin, John Whiterig (the 'monk of Farne') goes so far as address her thus: 'O wondrous woman, whose flesh may be adored without blame'.[248] In the following chapter he makes it clear that Mary's flesh is to be seen as divine only insofar as the Word was made flesh from within her; but even so it is a startling indication of the extent to which such devotion could go.[249] In the Prioress's tale, Chaucer draws upon the liturgy of the feast of the Holy Innocents together with an ancient legend of a miracle of Our Lady to create the grim story of a little Christian boy who is murdered by Jews because (seduced by Satan) they believe he is lampooning their faith by singing the *Alma Redemptoris* in the streets of their ghetto. The intended message is that those who, like the child, do honour to Mary not just by singing her praises but by making their own her humility and poverty of spirit will, like her, be exalted; and the story ends with the dead boy continuing to sing the *Alma Redemptoris* and being honoured as a martyr.[250] But the antisemitism of the story is disturbing to modern readers, and unfortunately by no means rare in medieval Christian spirituality;[251] it serves to remind us that sometimes fervent devotion and virulent scapegoating can go hand in hand.

Yet the heart of late-medieval Marian devotion is surely to be found in texts such as this exquisite fifteenth-century poem, in which Mary's suffering love is second only to that of her son:

> In a small chamber of a tower,
> As I stood gazing at the moon,
> A crownèd queen of great honour
> I saw there, sitting on a throne.
> She made her cómplaint on her own,
> For man's soul is all wrapped in woe:[252]
> 'I may not leave mankind alone,
>> *Quia amore langueo.*
>
> Wretch, in this world I look on thee
> I see thee trespass day by day,
> With lust against my chastity,
> with pride against my meek array.
> My love abides: wrath hast away;
> My love calls, yet thou fleest from me;
> Pursue me, sinner, I thee pray,
>> *Quia amore langueo!*

My son was outlawed for thy sin,
His body beaten for thy trespass.
It pricked my heart that my own kin
Afflicted is, my son, alas!
My son's thy father: his mother I was,
He sucked my breasts; he loved thee so,
He died for thee; my heart thou hast
    Quia amore langueo.

My son is dead all for thy love,
His heart was piercèd with a spear,
to bring thy soul to heaven above,
For love of thee so died he here.
So thou must be to me most dear,
seeing my son hast loved thee so;
Thou pray'st not to me, yet I am here,
    Quia amore langueo.

My son hath granted me, for thy sake,
Each merciful prayer that I will have;
For he will no indulgence take
if I seek thy mercy, that I shall have.
So seek it, and I shall thee save,
With pity I weep upon thee so,
I long for mercy, that thou should'st crave,
    Quia amore langueo.'[253]

Devotion to the Angels

The angels remain a significant part of English piety during this period as in previous centuries. They appear in vast profusion in medieval wall-paintings and manuscripts – swinging censers, holding draperies, bearing shields of arms, sitting or even dancing in heaven with Christ, playing musical instruments, and bearing departed souls heavenward.[254] Their role as protectors is evident in John Whiterig's meditation addressed to them,[255] in which he agrees with Gregory the Great that some angels remain in perpetual contemplative attendance on God rather than acting as messengers. He is in no doubt about their power as guardians of humanity ['It is through our most noble patrons, the angels, that God daily works out the salvation of men throughout the whole world, even the islands afar off, – on one of which I myself dwell – and in the distant sea'];[256] and pays grateful tribute to his own guardian angel:

> On another occasion when I was walking carelessly on a plank bridging the river Cherwell, I was very nearly drowned. I had completely lost my balance and was on the point of falling in, when you suddenly lifted me up and set me upright on my feet . . . How often would I have fallen into a

> pond or down a well, had you not placed your hand upon me . . . How often when hewing wood with axe or hatchet would I have maimed myself, had you not turned aside the implement as it struck, and thus averted the danger . . . How often you have taught me in my ignorance, brought me back when I had taken a wrong turning, roused me when I was all too ready to go on sleeping, consoled me when I was sad and overcome with grief, steadied me with the thought of death and the last judgement when I was dissipated with laughter and foolish joy, healed me when sick; in short whenever human counsel or aid have been of no avail, you have come hastening with all speed to my assistance.[257]

The naïveté here may be unappealing; but the profound sense of being accompanied through life by a protector, and of never taking for granted experiences of rescue or consolation, is impressive nonetheless. Nor was this interest in angels restricted to the relatively unsophisticated: the author of *The cloud of unknowing* translated a text of Pseudo-Dionysius (*Deonise hid divinite*), and in so doing added 'or to aungel' to the Latin text (which has only 'to man') at one point,[258] at another changing the Latin 'anima neque mens' (neither soul nor mind) to 'neither soule ne [nor] aungel'.[259] The author follows Pseudo-Dionysius in drawing out the importance of angels within the celestial hierarchy, though not forgetting to remind readers of the need eventually to pass beyond angels in order to attain to God alone.[260] Above all, angels represent friends at court (John Mirk describes them as 'friends and servants to all good men and women'[261]); and the Carthusian Nicholas Love describes the angels as the heavenly equivalent of minstrels, keeping us company with their music whenever we eat alone.[262]

The Suffering Christ

The third ingredient in the text from Rolle's commentary on the Song of Songs with which this chapter started was his stress upon the search for the suffering Jesus, whose suffering is not only redemptive but exemplary too. Few aspects of late medieval spirituality more palpably reflect the experience of the age, even though (as we have seen) devotion to the human and suffering Christ was a prominent feature of early medieval piety too. But later writers went further: their presentation of Christ strove to maximize the extent both of his sufferings and of our participation in them (and thus, by implication, of his in ours). Consider this extract from the anonymous fifteenth-century text *Dives and Pauper*:

> Take heed by means of the image how his head was crowned with the garland of thorns till they went into the brain and the blood burst out on every side so as to destroy the high sin of pride that is revealed most in men's and women's heads, and make an end of it.[263]

The gruesome description has theological significance in each particular here. And Dives is counselled not to pray *to* the image, any more than a priest worships his prayer book, but to the person it represents.[264] Devotion to the wounds of Christ was a prominent theme in late medieval art.[265] In the church of Breage in Cornwall there is a late-fifteenth-century wall painting of the wounded Christ, almost naked, surrounded by implements such as knives, combs, dice and fish-hooks: the intention seems to have been not only to portray in more detail the biblical account of Christ's passion and crucifixion, but also to emphasize in symbolic form our responsibility for it.[266] Such visual representation thus has a twofold purpose: to foster contrition for our part in, or responsibility for, Christ's death; and also to lead us to enter more fully into the sufferings of Jesus and thus to discover meaning and value in our own.[267]

This theme became the source of a veritable torrent of devotion in the later middle ages – innumerable meditations on the life of Christ, sermons, plays, poems, images, books of hours, altarpieces and wall paintings alike sought to encourage people to reflect on this theme to an extent far beyond that sought by writers of an earlier age. The general approach can be illustrated by an extract from a text of monastic spirituality by St Edmund of Abingdon, a thirteenth-century archbishop of Canterbury whose *Speculum ecclesiae* seems only to have become popular in the second half of the fourteenth century:[268]

> With regard to the Passion, you should reflect on how at this hour [sext] Jesus was crucified between two thieves, one on the right and the other on the left, as their master. Here I do not know what to say. For if all the diseases and pains of this world were contained in the body of a single human being, and if that person could conceive of all the suffering and pain that everyone in the world undergoes, it would be as nothing in comparison to the pain that he endured for us in one hour of the day. And if I could live for a hundred thousand years, and on any day die a thousand times the same death for him by which he died once for me, it would be nothing in comparison to the pain he experienced.[279]

This is not simply monastic hyperbole. Edmund, like many medieval writers, saw the events of Good Friday not simply as the story of the Son of God enduring human suffering, but as his endurance of that suffering to a literally superhuman extent. As human, Christ could and did suffer with and for us: as divine, he could and did do that to a superhuman extent. Julian of Norwich makes a similar point, describing Christ as leading her into his body through a wound, 'and there he showed a fair and delectable place, and large enough for all mankind that shall be saved'.[270] Hence there is no earthly suffering which can compare to his: hence, too, meditation on Christ's suffering humanity leads to meditation on his divinity, the latter being revealed through the former; and although hitherto meditation on Christ's humanity had been seen as a concession to those unable to meditate on his divinity, it came increasingly to be seen either as the appropriate starting-point for meditation on his divinity, or as a legitimate form of devotion in its own right.[271]

The forms which this devotion took were immensely varied. For William Langland, with characteristic originality, Christ became the ideal knight enlisting, in unprotected flesh, against the powers of evil and calling to his side a new spiritual nobility who represent the purified, reborn church of Langland's ideal.[272] Piers begins as a ploughman and ends as becoming, or at least becoming *like*, Christ the noble knight, illustrating the central patristic conviction that human beings may become like God because God has become like them.[273] The image of Christ as a knight, suffering but ultimately victorious, was predictably popular, though none brought to it the subtlety and allusive richness of Langland.[274]

Others took a quite different approach. The monastic writer John Whiterig (alias the Monk of Farne) encouraged devotion to the wounds of Christ thus:

> Study then, O man, to know Christ; get to know your Saviour. His body, hanging on the cross, is a book, open for your perusal. The words of this book are Christ's actions, as well as his sufferings and passion, for everything that he did serves for our instruction. His wounds are the letters or characters...[275]

He goes on to criticize those who possess all kinds of other knowledge, arguing that if they lack knowledge of Christ crucified all their other knowledge is worthless.[276] Devotion to Christ's wounds was popular across Europe, especially in Franciscan spirituality, and in England remained so until the Reformation.[277] For Whiterig, the wounds have a didactic value, instructing learned and unlettered alike about the nature of Christ's suffering: devotion to his wounds is encouraged in manuals of instruction intended for parish clergy.[278] For the mystics, however, and particularly for Rolle and Julian of Norwich, the wounds become points of entry into an intimate identification with the suffering Jesus.[279]

Jesus as Mother

Perhaps the most interesting manifestation of late medieval English devotion to the suffering Jesus was in the image of Jesus as mother, a theme which played a significant part in the spirituality of St Anselm.[280] The importance of this theme in the work of Julian of Norwich will be explored below; but it is worth drawing attention now to its presence in other contemporary texts. The Carthusian Nicholas Love describes Jesus' motherly love for his disciples, picturing the disciples like chickens behind the hen, following Jesus down the hill after the Sermon on the Mount, jostling each other for pride of place at his side.[281] And the Benedictine John Whiterig speaks of Christ's soul being 'knit with ours by thy love for man which exceeds that of a mother for her only son', and goes on:

> Even so is it with mothers who love their little children tenderly; if these happen to be at a distance from them, and want to run to them quickly, they are wont to stretch out their arms and bend down their heads. Then the little ones, taught in a natural way by this gesture, run and throw themselves into their mothers' arms, and the latter bestows trinkets on them, or, if they are not yet weaned, gives them the breast.
>
> Christ our Lord does the same with us. He stretches out his hands to embrace us, bows down his head to kiss us, and opens his side to give us suck; and though it is blood which he offers us to suck, we believe that it is health-giving and sweeter than honey.[282]

Such devotion did not originate in England; and the theme of Jesus' motherhood was extensively developed in the writings of late medieval women mystics on the continent, who themselves were heavily influenced by the affective Cistercian spirituality of St Bernard.[283] It is at least worth considering the possibility that a society in which most men were away from the home working for six days out of seven, and in which childhood was thus often dominated by mothers, may have lent wing to a devotional approach which conceived of Jesus in this way.[284]

Devotion to the Name of Jesus

Not all late medieval devotion to Jesus concentrated upon his passion and death. Devotion to the name of Jesus was another universally popular theme; and Richard Rolle in particular waxed lyrical about it, following Henry Suso in propagating the cult of the Holy Name in England.[285] The name was believed by Rolle to contain intrinsic and awesome power, in a manner not entirely dissimilar to the Old Testament reverence for the divine name (YHWH):

> If you think (on the name of) Jesus continually, and hold it stably, it purges your sin and kindles your heart, it clarifies [= purifies] your soul, it removes anger, it does away slowness, it wounds (you) with love, fulfils (you) in charity, chases away the devil and puts out dread, it opens heaven and makes a contemplative man.[286]

Rolle waxes even more eloquently about it in his commentary on the Song of Songs (from which the opening text in this chapter is taken):[287] the Song had similarly inspired St Bernard two centuries earlier. Hope Emily Allen has argued that 'concentration on the thought of Jesus, the Divine Person, seems to fulfil what [Rolle] means by devotion to the Name';[288] but it is also possible that Rolle was here consciously following Bernard and other recognized authorities in an attempt to establish his own spiritual credentials.

Devotion to the Christ Child

One of the other manifestations of the late medieval fascination with all aspects of Jesus' human life was devotion to the Christ Child: we shall see below how this included a new interest in the Gospels' infancy narratives.[289] Henry of Lancaster believed that in some sense Jesus always remained a child, and for three reasons: first, because the longer a person's life, the longer his childhood is – a fact which (he argues) must have been true of our forebears, who lived to a great age because they were not as wicked as we are; hence, and secondly, Christ, being eternal, must have remained a child for infinitely longer than even our forebears did. Thus, and finally, we need have no fear of speaking with so great a *seigneur* since he is also a child: indeed we could hardly dare to be so bold as to speak with him at all unless that were the case.[290] Henry concludes that Christ pardons us when we seek mercy in the way a child would; and, like a child longing for a red apple, he longs for our hearts.[291]

The Harrowing of Hell

This charming but quaint approach reflects, like Edmund of Abingdon's view of Christ's suffering, the idea that Christ's divinity is reflected not only in the fact of Christ's humanity (i.e. in the fact that he took human flesh at the Incarnation), but also in the kind of humanity he took. It is as though Christ becomes *more than human*, far exceeding ordinary human experience in the extremity of his suffering or (as with Henry of Lancaster) in the extent of his childlikeness. And this stress on Christ's superhuman nature and attributes finds expression in another focus for late medieval devotion: the harrowing of hell.

The semi-biblical story of Christ descending to hell in order to rescue the souls of the just featured in many medieval plays, and formed the main subject of one of them, dating from the mid-thirteenth century.[292] The theme was prominent in Anglo-Saxon drama and poetry,[293] though it did not fit so well with late medieval emphasis on a suffering and human Christ. But it does find fascinating expression in *Piers Plowman*: in his presentation of it, Langland represents Christ out-arguing the devil in a long address[294] in which what is made clear to the reader is the legality, the necessary triumph, of Christ over the devil and thus of good over evil.[295] But Langland also stresses something else here. At one point Peace declares:

> Thus God in his goodness took the first man, Adam,
> set him in solace and in sovereign mirth,
> and soon he suffered him to feel both sin and sorrow,
> that he might know in his own nature what well-being was.
> And later God adventured himself and took Adam's nature
> to see what he had suffered, and in three different places,
> both in heaven and on earth, and finally in hell he thought
> to know what all woe is, who knoweth of all joy.[296]

Langland here goes well beyond the traditional representation of the harrowing of hell as the triumphant action of a victorious lord. His description of Jesus as entering hell in order to experience the furthermost extremity of human suffering is much more characteristically medieval in its concern to demonstrate that no experience of pain or evil is unreached by the love of Christ.

Spirituality and the Visual Imagination

Much of the material designed to foster devotion to the suffering Christ during this period was of a highly affective and visual nature (as indeed is Rolle's approach in the text which begins this chapter).[297] The graphic fifteenth-century wall-painting of Doomsday in St Thomas' church Salisbury is set above the chancel arch for good reason: it implicitly reminds worshippers that the movement from earth (represented by the nave) to heaven (represented by the chancel, where the Eucharist was celebrated) was possible only by passing through the ordeal of Judgement first.[298] And nothing could emphasize the importance of the visual in late medieval spirituality

more than the fact that after the Reformation wall-paintings of this kind were systematically replaced by edifying scriptural texts: the word replaced the imagination as *the*
normative medium for spiritual truth.

Visual representations of this kind were common in the earlier Middle Ages too, as
we have seen:[299] what was new in this period was the increasing interest in individualism: thus where the bell-founders' fourteenth-century stained-glass window in York
Minster is 'formalized and abstract', fifteenth-century glass reflects a new emphasis on
the actual events of the New Testament and on the characters who participated in
them – and particularly (though not only) on events relating to suffering.[300] In the
fourteenth-century psalter of Robert de Lisle, the biblical characters are represented as
individuals, each with their own personality; whereas the settings and backgrounds
are invariably flat, patterned with abstract motifs.[301]

The part played by the senses and the imagination in such devotion is worth noting.
In the De Lisle Psalter the story of the resurrection of Lazarus is depicted with the
onlookers holding their noses at the smell, graphically illustrating the scriptural
text.[302] Edmund structures the contemplation of God's humanity according to the
sevenfold monastic office: each should comprise a twofold meditation, one on Christ's
passion and the other on some other aspect of his life. Thus at Mattins the meditator
should reflect on Christ's nativity before the office and on his passion after it:

> With regard to the nativity, you should attentively reflect on the time,
> place and hour in which our dear lord Jesus Christ was born. The time was
> midwinter, when the cold is at its greatest; the hour was midnight, which is
> the hardest hour; the place was in the middle of the road, in a house
> without walls which is called an inn for travellers; for thither people were
> diverted because of rain and other storms. In this house he was wrapped in
> the most wretched clothes, bound in swaddling-cloths and laid in a crib,
> with an ox and ass next to him, because there was no room in the inn. Here
> you should reflect on the attentive care of blessed Mary for her child Jesus,
> and on Joseph her husband, and on his great joy.[303]

In itself, this kind of devotion is not new: Aelred of Rievaulx had already developed,
in his *De Iesu puero*, the technique of visualizing mentally a scriptural event and then
dwelling upon it meditatively. But 'meditation' in the late medieval period was
extended in meaning, and in three respects: in its subject matter, its scope, and its
audience. In terms of subject matter, interest extended beyond Christ's suffering and
death to encompass the whole of his earthly life, and many of the other biblical characters who participated in it: Edmund's text, with its detailed and imaginative depiction
of the Christmas story, is typical of this new interest.[304] The scope of meditation was
broadened to include a wide range of material, from poems to broader didactic texts
like Chaucer's Parson's tale (which is explicitly described as a 'meditacioun'[305]),
designed to foster self-examination as a prelude to penance.[306]

Furthermore, where the meditations of Anselm's age were directed to devout
nobility, those of the later medieval period had a far wider lay audience in view. A
good example of this broader approach appears at the end of the anonymous

late-fourteenth-century (or early-fifteenth-century) *Contemplations of the dread and love of God*: after recommending a suitable place for prayer, the author says

> You may imagine there in your heart, as you see your Lord taken by his enemies with many reproofs and insults, brought before a judge . . . See how they do not cease from their angry strokes until they see him stand in his own blood up to his ankles, sparing none of his skin from the top of his head to the sole of his foot, his flesh they cut to the bone, and for weariness of himself they leave him almost for dead.

This part of the meditation ends:

> Take heed of the comfort of his apostle Saint John, to the tears of Magdalene and of his other friends, and I believe among all these you will have compunction and plenty of tears. When such devotion comes, then is the time for you to speak for your own need, and for all other living and dead people who trust to your prayer. Cast your body down to the ground, lift up your heart on high, with doleful cheer then make your prayer.[307]

By comparison with Anselm, the approach is literal, less richly theological, homely rather than rhetorical. Such meditation is designed to evoke a threefold response: first, intense visualization of Jesus' sufferings; secondly, a response of compunction to that suffering; and, thirdly, appropriate prayer for oneself and for others.

The writer who may be said to exemplify this kind of highly visual and affective spirituality is perhaps the Carthusian Nicholas Love, who defined meditation as imagining oneself to be present at the various events in Christ's life, and wrote

> If the great mysteries and all that follows from them were inwardly considered with all the inner mind and beholding of man's soul, I believe they would bring that beholder into a new state of grace, for to him who would search the passion of Our Lord with all his heart and all his inner affection, there would come many devout feelings and stirrings that he never experienced before.[308]

Much of Love's piety is of a moralizing and frankly simplistic kind. Thus he concludes from the story of the Visitation that young people ought to visit older ones for their mutual edification;[309] he speculates on what it was that the angels brought Jesus to eat after his forty days in the wilderness before eventually deciding that Jesus must have sent them off to fetch food from his mother, because he liked her cooking best;[310] and he declares that Joseph's tolerant attitude to his unexpectedly pregnant partner is a reproof to jealous husbands tempted to leave their wives at even the slightest hint of an encounter with another man.[311] His reflections on the life of the Holy Family are characteristic of his style:

> Let us behold the manner of living of that blessed company [=the Holy Family] in poverty and simplicity together; and how that old man Joseph wrought as he might in his craft of carpentry; our Lady also with distaff and needle, and therewith making meals and doing other tasks that belong

to a household, in divers manners as we may imagine; and how our Lord Jesus meekly helped them both when needed, and also in laying the table, making the beds and such other chores, ministering gladly and lowly, and so fulfilling in deed what he said of himself in the Gospel: That the Son of Man came not to be served, but to serve.[312]

The thought of meditating on Jesus making the beds in a clean and cosy home may appear to smack more of the worst excesses of Victorian children's piety than of serious spiritual endeavour. But, again, appearances can be deceptive. The purpose of such meditation is not only, or even primarily, to encourage a prim and unquestioning conformity to contemporary social norms. Rather it is to locate the life of Jesus within our own experience and world-view, and vice versa; and thus to make the dynamic of his life ours too, not only in his attention to domestic detail but in his self-giving and outgoing love. The result is both to consecrate and to challenge human experience by laying alongside it the life of Christ; and the aim and fruit of such meditation, as Love writes, is not simply the discovery of Christ in one's own life but 'a new compassion and a new love'.[313]

Love and Knowledge of God

But texts of this kind raise a larger issue. Earlier generations viewed this form of highly affective and literalist meditation, focusing on the humanity of Christ, as only the starting-point for a much higher form of contemplation in which both the senses and the humanity of Jesus are left behind in a more intellectual, more strictly mystical, vision. But by the time writers like Rolle came to put pen to paper there were already many who were challenging the classic Thomist assumption that union with God is supremely achieved through the intellect (though it is crucial to remember that for St Thomas the ascent to God must be motivated by love and never altogether loses its affective dimension).[314] Late medieval thinkers had found in Augustine an important distinction between two kinds of knowledge: *scientia*, knowledge of practical things, and *sapientia*, the contemplation of eternal things;[315] and this distinction was heightened in an age which saw thinkers like William of Ockham clearly separating the knowledge accessible to reason and the senses from the knowledge or wisdom revealed in scripture.

The advantage of such an approach was obvious: it made the spiritual life as a whole accessible to those who had little or no intellectual ability by stressing instead the use of the senses and of the imagination. But (as we have already seen) it carried with it an ominous price tag: knowledge and love, intellect and emotion, theology and spirituality, began, slowly but surely, to be prised apart. In Langland's *Piers Plowman*, Patience becomes a more reliable guide for Piers than Clergy – the former incorporates all the elements of affective, experiential knowledge, the latter of hypocritical and vain learning that has no impact on one's behaviour.[316] And there is a powerful moment in the poem when Will asks a mysterious stranger what love is:

> 'What is charity? said I then. 'A childish thing,'
> he said. '*Nisi efficiamini sicut parvuli non intrabitis*
> *in regnum celorum.*'[317]

For Richard Rolle there could be no doubt that *scientia* was irreducibly inferior to *sapientia*, and that love was superior to both. So he writes:

> It is clear that Christ does not give his grace equally to all the saints. For to one he gives speech filled with wisdom (*sermo sapientiae*), to another speech filled with knowledge (*sermo scientiae*). Some of these he chooses more particularly for himself, whom he further endows inwardly with the greater grace and sweetness of fruitful love.[318]

It is true that Rolle elsewhere concedes that 'the more learned [people] are, the more they are by right capable of loving (*Quo enim scientiores sunt, eo de iure aptiores sint ad amandum*)'.[319] And he follows Aquinas in stressing both that God is essentially mysterious, beyond all knowing[320] and that what matters is to know *that* God is rather than struggle unavailingly to find out *what* God is.[321] But he makes it quite clear that it is love of God, not any kind of knowledge, which alone conduces to salvation: he contrasts the *sapientia* which the simple-hearted may receive as a gift from God with the *scientia* that is laboriously acquired by learned scholars who foolishly disdain the higher wisdom;[322] and, at the beginning of the *Form of living*, he warns of the perils awaiting those, whether in vows or not, who do not love him.[323]

We can see the effects of this process in the career and writing of the fourteenth-century English Benedictine monk Uthred of Boldon: he produced numerous works, many of which form serious contributions to the major theological issues of his day (Franciscan poverty, grace and justification, the relationship of ecclesiastical and civil power, the Eucharist and others). Yet this only makes the more disappointing his principal spiritual text, the long and rambling *Meditacio devota*, which, although well-received in the later middle ages,[324] is (by comparison with the meditations of Anselm, whom Uthred explicitly cites) notably lacking in theological depth. To read Uthred's *Meditacio* alongside any of the works of William of Ockham is to become aware of a new and (for the historian of spirituality) depressing phenomenon: where Anselm had held theology and spirituality together to the advantage of both, late medieval writers allowed them to diverge, so that theology became an arcane scholastic discipline, and spirituality a perilously subjective affair in which personal experience is less often submitted to the rigours of theological scrutiny.

It reflects the vitality and diversity of late medieval English piety that many sought to resist this process. Some (especially monastic) writers endeavoured to cling to the old and well-tried patristic formula which sought actually to identify love and knowledge (*amor ipse notitia est*), among them John Whiterig, the Monk of Farne:

> Let the meek hear it [this teaching] . . . , and rejoice that there is a knowledge of holy Scripture which is to be learnt from the Holy Ghost and is manifested in good works. Often enough a layman has it while a cleric has not, a fisherman has it but a rhetorician knows naught of it, an old woman has acquired it but not a doctor of theology. Its name is love or charity, for according to Gregory: 'Love itself is knowledge' – that is, knowledge of the one towards whom the love is directed. The measure of your love is the measure of your knowledge: if you love greatly, you know a great deal.[325]

Others sought different ways of holding together the affective and the intellectual in contemplating God. Julian of Norwich laid particular stress on the practice of beholding God as precisely the appropriate response to God's *shewing* of himself in the suffering Jesus.[326] Her 'beholding' is strongly influenced by Augustine;[327] and what is striking about it is that it is as much an intellectual as an affective process: 'beholding' for Julian seems close in this respect to St Bernard's definition of *consideratio* as 'thought searching for truth, or the searching of a mind to discover truth'.[328] Even more strikingly, for Julian (as for Aquinas) 'beholding' the image of the soul as a city ruled over by Christ makes us 'like to him that is beholden, and one in rest and in peace'.[329] Despite Julian's description of such a soul as Christ's 'homeliest home', we have travelled far here from Nicholas Love's homely meditations: this is a visual (more strictly a contemplative) spirituality in which the practice of seeing the truth as manifested in Christ becomes precisely the means to union with him, a union which would already be ours in virtue of our humanity were it not for the consequence of sin which occludes our vision of God.[330]

'Seeing' of this kind is far more than mere moralizing, however imaginative. It is an act of the mind as much as of the imagination or the senses. Thus Walter Hilton writes:

> He [the soul] does not see *what* he [God] is, for no created being can do that in heaven or earth; and he [the soul] does not see him as he is, for that sight is only in the glory of heaven. But he sees *that* he is.[331]

And the soul sees God with a depth and warmth of spiritual understanding which is much deeper than the cool reason of the scholar – 'more clearly and more fully than it may be written or told'.[332] For Hilton, as for Julian, this seeing has a transforming effect: he says that what Jesus most loves in the soul is that

> it might be made divine and spiritual through seeing and loving, to be through grace like what he is by nature – for that shall be the aim of all lovers.[333]

For him, meditation on the humanity of Christ is an essential stepping-stone on the way to contemplation of his divinity;[334] and he explicitly commends the former, provided that it leads to the latter.[335] He stresses the limitations of the former in an important passage:

> This kind of practice is good and comes of grace, but it is much less and lower than the practice of understanding: that is when the soul by grace beholds God in man. For in our Lord Jesus there are two natures: the manhood and the divinity. Then just as the divine nature is more excellent and honourable than the manhood, so the spiritual consideration of the divinity in Jesus the man is more honourable, more spiritual and more deserving of reward than the consideration of the manhood alone, whether one beholds the manhood as mortal or as glorified. And just so, for the same reason, the love that a soul feels in considering and thinking of the divinity in man, when it is shown by grace, is more honourable,

spiritual and deserving of reward than the fervour of devotion that the soul feels by imagining only the manhood, however much it shows outwardly. For in comparison with that, this is only human, since in the imagination our Lord does not show himself *as* he is, or *that* he is; for the soul could not at that time bear such a thing, because of the frailty of the fleshly nature.[336]

For Hilton the human always remains inferior to the divine, even in Christ: the incarnation was a concession to human need, albeit a means of raising us much higher than we would otherwise have been able to attain. And to behold something of Christ's divinity is a much more difficult process than mere imaginative introspection: the soul has to see the truth about its own ontological status, to see the Christ within it, beginning with but eventually leaving behind all imaginative aids and processes.[337] It is above all a work of grace, and what is required is clarity of sight:

This is another work of contemplation: to see Jesus in the scriptures after the opening of the spiritual eye. The purer the sight as it gazes, the more comfort is given to the affection as it tastes.[338]

Here, as so often, Hilton represents the quintessence of Augustinian spirituality: the beauty of God draws us to himself in a process which begins with the capacity to see God in everyday life, and everyday life in God, but culminates in a vision which has both the crystalline clarity of the mountain-top –

It is beautiful to look with the inner eye on Jesus in bodily creatures, to see his power, his wisdom and his goodness in ordaining their nature; but it is much more beautiful to look at Jesus in spiritual creatures [i.e. rational souls].[339]

– and the passionate intensity of love:

Truly grounded in grace and humility, these contemplations make a soul wise, burning in desire for the face of Jesus. These are the spiritual things I spoke of before; they can be called new gracious feelings, and I touch on them only a little for the instruction of your soul: for a soul that is pure, stirred by grace to the practice of this work, can see more of such spiritual matter in an hour than could be written in a great book.[340]

Spirituality and Death

Perhaps the combination of orthodox and critical spirituality which so characterizes late-medieval England can be seen in the relationship between spirituality and death in late-medieval England. The omnipresence of death remained a key feature of the late (as of the early) medieval world-view, expressed with exquisite simplicity in this tiny poem scrawled on the fly-leaf of a manuscript:

> For under the sunne a man may se
> Thys warld ys butte a vanyte.
> Grace passeth gollde
> And precyous stoon,
> And god schal be god
> When goolde ys goon.[341]

But there were changes. Death was not simply seen as something to be embraced in the hope of heaven, but as a hard and painful reality requiring explanation as much as passive acceptance. In the Middle English version of the *Revelations* of St Bridget of Sweden, God tells the saint:

> What is Christian death, if not to die as I died, innocently, willingly, and patiently? Am I therefore to be despised because my death was despicable and hard? Or are my chosen ones fools, because they suffered despicable torments? Or is this the result of fortune, or wrought by the course of the planets and stars? No: the reason I and my chosen suffered hard passion was to show in word and example that the way to heaven is hard.[342]

There is an increasing emphasis on the importance of contemplating one's own death. In a sermon on marriage, John Mirk says that the cloth held over the couple's thighs at the high altar symbolizes the skins with which God clothed Adam and Eve, and encourages the couple to contemplate their own deaths.[343] In the fifteenth century John Lydgate visited Paris and translated into English the French poem *Danse macabre* which he found in the church of the Holy Innocents, Paris: it consists of a series of brief dialogues between Death and various characters from the pope downwards.[344] *The book of the craft of dying*, a fifteenth-century translation made from an anonymous Latin (or perhaps a French) original which reflects contemporary interest in the *ars moriendi*, contains a prayer for use when dying:

> Holy angels of Heaven, I beg you to assist me who am about to pass out of this world, and strongly preserve and keep me from all my enemies, and receive my soul into your blessed company; and particularly you, the good blessed angel which has been my continual guardian, appointed by God.[345]

Prayer for the dead remained universally popular in this period, though priests who spent more time praying for the souls of the powerful rather than caring for their parishes were sometimes criticized.[346] Religious communities attracted huge incomes in return for saying countless requiem masses: the fact that in general nunneries seem to have been less well-endowed than monasteries (especially contemplative male orders like the Carthusians) may be because women, not being priests, could not say mass for the souls of those who had endowed them.[347] Sometimes a monk could be, so to speak, hired in perpetuity to pray for someone's soul. Thus the Carthusians at Hull received benefactions from one John Colthorpe in return for which they agreed to assign a cell in their great cloister to be known henceforth as 'The Cell of John Colthorpe', and would assign a monk chaplain to inhabit this cell continuously and to be called 'the monk of the sins of John Colthorpe and Alice his wife' – another monk would replace him when he died, and so on.[348]

But the most common manifestation of prayer for the dead in this period was through the endowment of a chantry, or provision of masses offered in prayer for the soul or souls of the dead.[349] Such prayer was not simply disinterested: John Bossy has argued that it could have been a means of enlarging one's circle of kinship, grounded in the belief that one's own chance of eternal life, as well as one's present fortunes, could be ameliorated by generous endowment of prayer for someone else.[350] Certainly the amounts left in wills to endow prayers for their souls reflects the very strong belief in, and anxiety about, life after death in the period,[351] an anxiety which may well have increased sharply after the Black Death.[352]

Chantries normally took the form of endowing land and property sufficient to provide an income for a priest whose primary duty would be to pray for the souls of whoever had endowed it: a fully-fledged perpetual chantry might cost at least £200;[353] but those with less means could pay for a specific number of masses rather than for the stipend of a priest. Some endowers of chantries hoped to obtain the prayers of the poor by offering them alms if they attended masses said for the endower's soul.[354] The will of Lady Jane Strangweys in 1500 contains this:

> I bequeath and leave to every person (man and woman) within the four leper houses 1d., to pray for my soul.[355]

One fifteenth-century Sussex gentleman's will reflects the spirit of the time:

> Sir John Atkins, 30 January 1487, to be buried in the Cathedral cloisters. To the Cathedral fabric 20s., to the Subdean for tithes forgotten 3s.4d., to his parish clerk 4d. For five years after my death a priest is to celebrate for me, saying on Sundays the Mass of the Trinity, on Mondays, Tuesdays, Wednesdays and Thursdays that of the Holy Ghost, on Fridays that of Requiem, on Saturdays that of the Commemoration of Our Lady, to be paid £33.6s.8d. The Warden of the Friars Minor is to say the same Masses for two years, and to be paid £12. Mr John Kyng to celebrate for me for one year with the same masses, to have £5. On the day of my burying the Dean to have 12d., each Canon 8d., each Vicar 6d., likewise on my trental. to each chorister 2d., thurifer 2d., sacrist 4d., bellringer 2d., 26s. 8d. in all. The same sum is to be spent at my trental, and at my year's mind; on each of these days 20s. is to be given to the poor, £3 in all; for 40 years my anniversary is to be kept with a payment of 6s. 8d., £13. 6s. 8d. in all . . . To William Atkyns a silver-gilt cup with a figure of St George on the cover, . . . also 12 silver spoons, a feather-bed and £5 in cash, for him to pray daily for my soul . . . On the days of my burial and trental each of six poor men is to have a gown of white frieze down to the feet with a hood, and to hold in his hand on each day a 4lb. candle; at my burial 60 shirts and smocks to be given to the poor. To the four priests carrying my body to church 16d. for their pains. The priest who celebrates for me for five years is to do so in the Subdeanery, and is to pray for my father and mother, my brother, Sir William Lucy, and Mr John Plente; these names are to be written on a list and put on the altar, lest they be forgotten . . .[356]

In 1495 Geoffrey Downes, a gentleman from Pott Shrigley in Cheshire, established a trust of a hundred cows, to be individually rented to the local poor, the rent being the commitment of those who hired the cows to pray for his soul and for those of all in purgatory: when one cow died or became ill, it was replaced by another, and similarly with the hirers.[357]

The endowment of chantries might appear to be no more than a reflection of the neurotic anxieties of the worried rich in the middle ages. Yet, however mixed the motives of those who endowed them, the chantry certainly reflects the profound sense of *continuity* that is an essential part of late medieval spirituality: living and dead, rich and poor, individual and society, lay and religious, were bound together in the face of death. The thirteenth-century Flemish story of the three kings, a precursor of the *Danse macabre*, was popular in England too.[358] Three young kings went hunting and encountered three corpses, who said to them 'As you are, so once we were. As we are, so shall you be.' But the response to death was increasingly positive: the *ars moriendi*, or art of dying, had implications for the whole of one's life; and the endowment of chantries provided parishes with priests who appear to have made a substantial contribution to parochial life.[359] Above all, the practice reflects a new stress on personal identity, and a new confidence (perhaps the result of an increasingly mercantile economy) that even the Grim Reaper could be, if not cheated of his goods, at least persuaded to agree more favourable terms.

The *Lay folks' prayer book*, a late medieval compilation including a number of offices which seem to have become part of the pattern of daily common prayer in cathedrals by the first half of the thirteenth century,[360] contains in the *Dirige*, or Office for the Dead, a number of the great psalms of lament (6–7, 40–2 and 51) and lessons from the Book of Job which include some powerful challenges to any placid acceptance of the reality or imminence of death.[361] One of the lessons from Job includes this passionate plea:

> Why dost thou hide thy face, and count me as thy enemy? Wilt thou frighten a driven leaf and pursue dry chaff? For thou writest bitter things against me (Job 13.24–6a, RSV).

It is striking to notice that the famous passage from Job 19 ('For I know that my Redeemer lives'), which in the seventeenth-century Book of Common Prayer is separated from its context, thereby becoming an expression of serene trust in God, is retained within it in the *Dirige*, thereby restoring its original force as part of an angry assault on God ('Have pity on me, have pity on me, O you my friends, for the hand of God has touched me!' Job 19.21). The final extract from Job in the *Dirige* is the most terrible of all, and underlines the severe honesty with which late medieval English folk wrestled with God in the face of death:

> Why did you bring me forth from the womb? Would that I had died before any eye had seen me, and were as though I had not been, carried from the womb to the grave. Are not the days of my life few? Let me alone, that I may find a little comfort before I go, never to return, to the land of gloom and deep darkness.[362]

INDIVIDUAL STUDIES[363]

The Solitary Lover: Richard Rolle

Introduction

The second fundamental ingredient of the text from Richard Rolle with which this chapter began was its stress on a journey, and a journey inwards. Our attention is focused upon one individual's quest for (and experience of) Jesus, both in order to introduce us to Rolle himself, and in order to apostrophize the kind of life he had made his own – that of the solitary. It is this which gives the passage its peculiarly late-medieval tone. The theology is Catholic and medieval, the subjectivity a harbinger of later Protestantism, the emphasis on a Christ of the poor not dissimilar from that of Third World theologians of today. But the style, the rhetoric and (above all) the aim of the passage set Rolle in the grand tradition of western apologists for the ascetic and solitary life: it is St Jerome, St Peter Damian, St Bernard, not Bunyan, Wesley, or the liberation theologians whose company we keep as we read it.

Spirituality and personal experience

There is nothing new about this emphasis on personal experience in Christian spirituality: it is found in many of the classic accounts of the spiritual life, not least in the Cistercian tradition examined in Chapter 3. It is within this tradition that the anonymous author of the *Instructions for a devout and literate layman* writes:

> When you are in bed, go back to the beginning of the day, and look diligently in your heart: if you have done any evil, and there be sorry; if any good, and there give thanks to God, always in fear and trembling, and do not think it certain that you will survive till the morrow.[364]

What is distinctive about Rolle is the strong sense of his own experience as self-authenticating. Where (say) Jerome or Peter Damian constantly stress the relationship of the solitary life to that of the church as a whole, Rolle not only exalts solitude above all other forms of life but (as we have seen) makes his own experience the litmus test of his authority.[365] It is of course arguable that he had little choice in the matter: how else is he to explain the fact that scarcely anyone before him had spoken of the spiritual life in anything like the way that (as we shall see) he does? Either he is obliged to deny the validity of what he has experienced on the grounds that it has little precedent in the Christian tradition, or he is obliged to take that very experience as the basis for its own legitimacy.[366] It is the latter course that he chooses:[367] and no Christian writer since St Augustine, almost a thousand years earlier, had made his own life and experience so crucial in authenticating his spirituality.[368]

The asceticism of love

None of this is to suggest that for Rolle the journey towards God was in any way easy. It requires an unequivocal turning away from this world, as he makes clear again and again.[369] One of his most popular works, the commentary on the readings in the office of the dead taken from the Book of Job (*Expositio super novem lectiones mortuorum*), combines a celebration of the delights of heavenly song, or *canor*, with a bleak and unforgiving emphasis on the universality of death: indeed Rolle's response to the question 'why?' raised by Job is simply that suffering is a necessary condition of virtuous living, because it teaches us to despise this world and long for death. Rolle's prayer in the same work is revealing:

> So, Lord, let me not be among those whom you spare in the present and punish in the future, whom you spare from present suffering and torment in future burning, whom you spare temporarily and punish eternally. But, O good Jesus, cut me, burn me, scourge me, castigate me here, that you may spare me in the future; here cut a rotten, burn a mangy, scourge a sinful, castigate a negligent person, and spare him in the future.[370]

And yet Rolle's great achievement is to render this sternly ascetic manner of living almost irresistibly attractive. He does this in a manner similar to earlier apologists for the solitary life, such as St Peter Damian and St Bernard: he lays great stress on the importance of desire, arguing that our innate desires must be purified and redirected away from worldly things towards the only object capable of fulfilling them beyond our furthest imaginings: the God who is revealed in Jesus Christ.[371] And with great skill he accepts the reality of physical beauty, but only in order to draw us beyond it, in classic Augustinian fashion, to the infinitely more attractive beauty of the Creator. In *Incendium amoris* he says that God gives man and woman beauty, not so that they should delight in each other's beauty but so that they might yearn for the divine beauty which never fades. He goes on to ask: if the loveliness of the form is apparent in the servants of the world, what will the beauty of the sons of God in heaven be like? (*si amabilis forma apparet in servis mundi, quae erit pulchritudo in filiis Dei in coelo constitutis?*).

One of his lyrics catches perfectly the striking combination of passionate love, fierce asceticism, and longing for death that characterizes Rolle's spirituality:

> Therefore, I advise, love thou Christ, as I thee tell.
> With angels take thy place, that joy thou dost not sell.
> In earth hate thou no ill but that thy love might fell;
> For love is strong as death, love is hard as hell.
>
> Love is a burden light, love gladdens young and old;
> Love is free of pain, as lovers have me told;
> Love is a ghostly wine, that maketh big and bold;
> Of love nothing shall lose that in its heart shall hold.
>
> Love is the sweetest thing that man on earth hath ta'en;
> Love is God's darling; love bindeth blood and bone;
> In love be our dwelling, I know no better home;
> For me and my loving, love maketh both be one.

But fleshly love shall fare as doth the flower in May;
and lasting be no more than it were but a day;
And sorroweth after that full sore their proudhood and their play
When they be cast down in despair to the pain that lasteth aye.

When earth and air shall burn, then may they quake and dread,
And up shall rise all men to answer for their deed.
If they be seen in sin, as now their lives they lead,
They shall sit hell within, and darkness have as mede.

Rich men their hands shall wring, and wicked works shall bye;[372]
In flame of fire knight and king with grief and shame shall lie.
If thou wilt love, then may thou sing to Christ in melody;
The love of him o'ercomes all things; in love live well and die,
    Amen.[373]

And it is this rich interplay of love and death, rooted in the Song of Songs, the late medieval celebration of courtly love, and the Augustinian tradition of apologists for the solitary life, which lies at the heart of all that Rolle wrote. In *The commandment* Rolle defines love as 'a wilful stirring of our thought in to God':[374] it is an act of human will (literally 'a work of man's will'). Rolle's thought is unsystematic, and he offers various ways of classifying different levels of love, of which the account given in *Ego dormio* is perhaps as illuminating as any other.[375] There he delineates three degrees of love: the first is moral rectitude, consisting of keeping the Ten Commandments and avoiding sin; the second is renouncing the world, and seeking 'to desire burningly the light of heaven with angels and saints',[376] so that the person may be 'God's lover . . . Christ's dear maiden and spouse in heaven' – this will however involve 'ever fighting', a constant struggle, throughout this life;[377] and the third is 'contemplative life, which loves to be solitary without ringing or din or singing or crying'.[378] In this degree of love

> you will have no need afterward of any liking [= affection], of no lying down, not even of a bed, nor of this world's solace, but you will ever love sitting, that you may be ever loving your Lord. In this degree of love you will long for your death.[379]

Much that is characteristic of Rolle's spirituality may be found here. The emphasis on desire; the close interrelation of love and death, and the consequently strong eschatological element in Rolle's writing; the vivid and highly original style, together with the references to sounds, sitting, and solitude, all of which figure prominently in his work – all these are important. But what matters most is the single most prominent characteristic of everything he wrote: the unrelenting focus on love of God, to the exclusion not only of knowledge but even of neighbour. It may be this which underlies his curious fascination with sitting, for elsewhere he writes

> I loved for to sit, not for any penance or any speculation (fantasie) that I wanted men to have about me, nor for any pain, but only because I knew that I loved God more, and the comfort of God lasted longer with me than going (about) or standing or kneeling. For when I sit I am most at rest, and

my heart is most upward. But perhaps, therefore, it is not the best (thing) for someone else to stay sitting as I have done, and will do until my death, unless he were disposed in his soul as I was.[380]

This absence of interest in love of neighbour is not as common as might have been expected among classic eremitical texts of the western spiritual tradition, most of which stoutly refuse to separate the two great love commandments from one another. It is true that on occasions Rolle does praise love of neighbour:

I . . . love always and unceasingly. For indeed I am delighted to love the agreeable and disagreeable, my friend and my enemy, for Christ's sake.[381]

But texts like this have a somewhat formulaic ring to them; and it is hard to escape the conclusion that loving others mattered little to Rolle, except in one crucial respect: his longing for them to share the life and experience he had made his own.[382] Hence the recurrent stress on preaching in his work, which might have been thought odd or even self-regarding in a hermit:[383] in *Melos amoris* Rolle describes the only kind of 'mixed life' he saw as authentic, which was that of the contemplative-preacher.[384] Yet what really animates him is the life of the recluse, and the joy to which it leads:

He who does not do outward works is filled with the splendour of eternal light.[385]

The solitary life

Much of what Rolle has to say about love of God is derived from Augustine, either directly or indirectly.[386] He also stands within the classic western eremitical tradition in implicitly declaring that true solitude is a corporate experience because it is an anticipation of heaven:

[The faithful one remains in solitude] because in his heavenly conversation he stands far apart from men. Neither is he able to mingle in worldly partnership who only delights in the joys of angels.[387]

Real loneliness is to be without God, not to live without other people;[388] and to live in solitude is no excuse for feeling superior to those who do not.[389] The originality of Rolle's work is to be found in the way in which he writes about his experience in solitude, and the richly affective style and imagery he employs in doing so.

Rolle divides the contemplative (i.e. solitary) life into two parts: the lower consists of

meditation of holy writing, that is God's word, and in other good and sweet thoughts that men have of the grace of God about the love of Jesus Christ.[390]

The higher is 'beholding and desire of the things of heaven'.[391] He tells us little about what he actually does during the long hours of solitude, and shows little or no interest in liturgy or the recitation of the office.[392] But in his English commentary on the Psalter, he gives us a hint of what matters most:

> When all the powers of my heart are raised into the sound of heaven, then I can sing with joy and with the wonderful crying that marks the contemplative life.[393]

The song of the heart

The individualism is worth noting: this is Rolle the hermit, singing alone to the praise of God.[394] And it introduces us to the heart of his spirituality. What is distinctive about it is the priority he accords to three key mystical experiences, all of which he has directly experienced himself. Rolle's account of these is not systematic, and he does not even always refer to the three by the same names; but it is clear that together they constitute the highest reaches of intimacy with God accessible in this life.

The three experiences are usually called by Rolle *fervor, dulcor* (sweetness), and *canor* (song);[395] and it is fairly (though not conclusively) evident that none can be experienced outside the solitary life.[396] In the *Incendium amoris* Rolle defines *fervor* as being 'when the mind is truly kindled by eternal love':[397] he seems to have in mind an experience at the end of a long period of prayer, when he was suddenly granted a powerful sense of the love of God in response to God's love for him. *Dulcor* is less precisely defined than the others, and can appear to be almost interchangeable with *fervor*:[398] in *Melos amoris* Rolle describes it a blend of longing and fulfilment ('eager for heavenly things alone, they are set alight in love of the Creator').[399]

But the highest and most distinctive of the three experiences is *canor* (song). In *Incendium amoris* Rolle describes it as being that moment when 'in the mind, abounding in ardour, is received the sweetness of eternal praise: thought is turned into song, and the mind dwells in mellifluous song (*melos*)'.[400] Rolle is clear about why this *canor* cannot be experienced outside solitude:[401] the clamour of everyday life renders inaudible the inner music of heaven, which only those who have heard it can possibly know.[402]

Musical imagery recurs throughout Rolle's writing; and there is no doubt that singing came naturally to him, as a spontaneous response to the love of God.[403] He is heir to patristic precedents in seeing musical instruments as symbols for spiritually transformed souls;[404] and he describes a person ascending 'like the notes of an organ (*quasi in organo*)' towards what he longs to contemplate.[405] But it is fairly clear that by *canor* he means something more: there is a moving moment in the *Incendium amoris* when he describes how his solitary recitation of the psalms appointed for the night office seemed to be caught up in the chorus of angelic praise above and around him.[406] He began to sing inwardly; and this singing is itself the result of feeling himself to be lifted into the corporate praise of heaven. Later he says that the heavenly music has a seductive, siren-like quality that draws the soul towards eternity.[407] And in the fullness of eternity the redeemed discover that their own individual song 'is absorbed into the most splendid praise'.[408]

Imagery of this kind is not unknown among Rolle's contemporaries: indeed the fifteenth-century music theorist Johannes Tinctoris quoted a popular saying that '[the English] jubilate, whereas the French sing' – to 'jubilate' meant to vocalize in the florid melismatic style of liturgical alleluias.[409] The writer of the thirteenth-century text *Hali Meidhad* (Holy Maidenhood) eloquently describes the singing and dancing of holy maidens in heaven.[410] Margery Kempe hears heavenly music 'in her bodily hearing';[411] and Julian of Norwich refers to the marvellous melody emanating from the friends of God who dwell in his presence.[412] The monastic writer Dan Michel compares the Our Father with a song of seven notes, each representing one of the gifts of the Holy Spirit, and describes its first line as being 'like an overture of the fiddle'.[413]

But Rolle goes much further than all of them in describing the highest mystical experience as being an interior song by which the soul is caught up into the music of heaven; and his source (directly or indirectly) is surely Augustine.[414] In his commentary on Psalm 33, Augustine interprets 'jubilation' as meaning

> to be unable to understand, to express in words, what is sung in the heart. For they who sing, either in the harvest, in the vineyard, or in some other arduous occupation, after beginning to manifest their gladness in the words of songs, are filled with such joy that they cannot express it in words, and turn from the syllables of words and proceed to the sound of jubilation. The *jubilus* is something which signifies that the heart labours with what it cannot utter. And whom does jubilation befit but the ineffable God?[415]

There is an important sense in which for Rolle *canor* represents the synthesis of interior spiritual experience, liturgical singing (specifically the singing of the psalms in the Office), and the music of heaven.[416] He insists that the first two of these must be attuned to each other.[417] And he hints at the fact that the ensuing experience of *canor* is not just a momentary perception of the heavenly music: at one point he says that that music is 'continually with us'.[418] In his commentary on Psalm 150, he writes:

> 'Praise him on the timbrel'; that is, in flesh changed into immortality and impassibility; for the timbrel is made of a dried skin; and 'in chorus', that is, in harmonious fellowship and concord of voices; 'praise him on the strings', that is, in flesh free of all corruption; for the strings represent all musical instruments that sound through strings; and with the strings he puts organs, which are made like a tower of different whistles, not so that each can sound by itself but so that they all sound together in concordant discord, as organs do.[419]

What is clear is that this, the highest level of the spiritual life attainable in this life, is above all a matter of love and experience, rather than of knowledge and intellect. For Rolle the affective dimension of love is not suppressed or left behind but transformed into the object of its love.[420] It is true that Rolle refers frequently to the act of thinking: he says that what will stir up a person's heart to long for God's love and to desire heaven is 'steadfast thinking of the mischievous and grievous wounds and of the death of Jesus Christ';[421] and elsewhere he says that while the essential condition of 'cleanness of heart' is 'conscious (waking) and steadfast (*stabil*) thought of God',[422] the essential condition of 'cleanness of work' (by which he means integrity of action) is 'assiduous thought of your death'.[423] But 'thought' for Rolle clearly meant careful, single-minded attention, not dissimilar from the *Cloud* author's 'naked intent', rather than any distinctively intellectual process.

Conclusion

There is much in Rolle's spirituality that resembles and anticipates that of the great twentieth-century monastic writer Thomas Merton. Rolle's life, like Merton's, was insecure and unsettled:[424] like Merton, Rolle exhibited an overriding concern with his own spiritual status and with the authenticity of his experiences of God, which make his work apologetic (even self-justificatory) rather than didactic in tone. Like Merton, Rolle was a master of literary style and rhetoric. He did not achieve this without experiment, but at his best was capable of expressing in words of rhapsodic beauty the essence of an almost incommunicable experience.[425] More striking still, Rolle anticipates Merton in his intriguing ambivalence about women: many of his works were written for them, and it has been argued that in his role as a spiritual director he showed a remarkable willingness to respect the integrity and autonomy of those he advised;[426] and, for all his occasionally vituperative bursts of misogyny, there may be something in Watson's suggestion that he was always seeking a woman to play Clare to his Francis.[427]

Rolle also resembles Merton in his strong emphasis on the equality of all human beings, rejecting nobility of birth or wealth and presenting the eremitic life as precisely the reversal of this world's values;[428] and, although he does not share Merton's concern for social issues, he does in effect democratize the spiritual life by representing its loftiest levels as being accessible to all.[429] Perhaps most striking of all, however, Rolle shares with Merton (and with many other great apologists for the solitary life) a curious inability to avoid the perils of activity even in the midst of solitude: both resemble in this regard St Bernard's description of 'a holy man violently tossed between the fruit of action and the quiet of contemplation'.[430] The author of the Office prepared for the cause of Rolle's canonization writes of him thus:

> It seems worthy of great wonder that once, when he was seated in his cell (one day, after dinner), the lady of the house came to him, and many other persons with her, and found him writing very quickly. And they besought him to leave off writing and speak a word of edification to them, which he immediately did, exhorting them most eloquently to virtue and to renounce worldly vanities and stablish the love of God in their hearts. Yet in no way on account of this did he cease from writing for two hours without interruption, but continued to write as quickly as before.[431]

The Interior Re-formation: Walter Hilton

Introduction

The spirituality of Richard Rolle raised a number of serious questions, both for his contemporaries and for later generations. The thoroughgoing relegation of *amor proximi* (love of neighbour) in Rolle's work leaves his accounts of the highest reaches of the spiritual life open to the serious charge of being unverifiable: the primacy of personal experience over everything else brings him dangerously close to pure subjectivity. For contemporaries his affective and highly subjective form of piety, based as it was so unequivocally on his own personal experience, and coupled with severe criticisms of book-learning, came perilously close to heterodox movements such as Lollardy and the continental 'Free Spirit' movement.[432] The latter was identified particularly with a work entitled *The mirror of simple souls*, originally written in French by Marguerite Porete, who was condemned as a heretic and burned in 1310.[433] The work was translated into Middle English by someone known only by his (or her) initials M. N.: the person inserted glosses into the text; but rather than seeking thereby to respond to criticisms of the text's doctrinal contents (as has until very recently been assumed), M. N. appears simply to be attempting (perhaps not very successfully) to elucidate a work whose orthodoxy and spiritual significance he or she does not question.[434]

Marguerite's work, even with glosses added, has much in common with that of Rolle. Both exalt love over knowledge, personal experience over theology; both consistently minimize the importance of love of neighbour and the practice of good works; and neither is altogether clear about whether union with God is in the end something attainable by one's own efforts or solely through the workings of grace. As a result both aroused the suspicions of some contemporaries, and both attracted the attention of perhaps the greatest contemporary exponent of orthodox Augustinian spirituality, Walter Hilton, whose account of the 'journey inwards' deserves particular attention, even though some aspects of his spirituality have already been explored.

Hilton was a Yorkshireman, educated in canon law at Cambridge before entering the priory of Augustinian canons at Thurgarton in Yorkshire, probably in 1386.[435] He died in 1396. Of the canonical orders, whose spirituality was discussed in the previous chapter, he was unquestionably the outstanding figure during this period. Thurgarton was in the diocese of York; and Hilton played a significant part in furthering the aims of Archbishop Thomas Arundel, who sought to counter the influence of Lollardy by regulating and renewing both lay piety and the eremitical movement.[436] It is thus not surprising to find Hilton defending the authenticity of the religious life against the criticisms of Wyclif,[437] and presenting the traditional Augustinian view of the veneration of images against Lollard attacks.[438] Hilton's most important works, however, were those he wrote as spiritual direction: his *Epistle on the mixed life* was addressed to a wealthy layman, and exerted considerable influence on both secular clergy and laity alike;[439] and he may well have been responsible for *The prickynge of love*, an expanded Middle English version of the popular *Stimulus amoris*, itself a much enlarged version of an eponymous text by the thirteenth-century Franciscan writer James of Milan, but attributed in Hilton's day to St Bonaventure.[440]

The Scale of perfection

Hilton's greatest work, however, was a substantial treatise which came to be known as *The ladder* [or *scale*] *of perfection*, a text which Martin Thornton justly described as a minor *summa* of the spiritual life.[441] It was written in English but translated into Latin in 1400 by a Carmelite, Thomas Fishlake: both Carmelites and Carthusians held Hilton in high esteem not only as a spiritual writer but as a stern defender of orthodoxy against the Lollards.[442] The *Ladder* is in two parts: Hilton wrote Book I for an anchoress, either real or representative; and his rich and mature Augustinian theology is firmly rooted in the practicalities of the eremitic life. Book II is more advanced in teaching, but paradoxically addressed to all Christians, because for Hilton the contemplative life represents the authentic fullness of what it means to be a baptized Christian.[443]

The *Ladder* is a substantial work, similar in literary genre to the *Ancrene Wisse* and evidently influenced by monastic writers like Gilbert of Hoyland and Bernard of Clairvaux.[444] As an Augustinian canon, however, it should not perhaps be surprising to find that Hilton's major source was Augustine, as will become clear when we explore some aspects of his spirituality below.[445] This is no slavish dependence: Hilton clearly had a thorough grasp of medieval theologians such as Aquinas as well as of Augustine. Rather it represents Hilton's belief that, in an intellectual climate in which theology and spirituality were beginning to diverge as the former became more speculative and the latter more affective and inward, one appropriate response was to offer a reasoned and balanced but primarily experiential approach to the spiritual life in which traditional Augustinian principles could be retained as sound building-blocks. This runs the risk of giving Hilton's spirituality a slightly old-fashioned feel; but it also allows him to develop an approach to the subject in which a warm and pastoral affectivity is moderated by a firm grasp of theological principle.

The image and likeness

In our earlier exploration of the spirituality of Aelred of Rievaulx, we saw a strongly Augustinian theology, grounded in the conviction that the human soul is created in the image of God the Trinity but in need of re-formation by grace in view of the soul's inherited predisposition to sin. It is exactly this kind of theology we find in the writings of Walter Hilton two hundred years later, though with a number of significant differences. For Hilton, as for Aelred and Augustine, the image of God within each one of us has been overlaid by this inherited (or 'original') sin: Hilton goes so far as to describe this as the 'image of sin'. He tells us that this image is 'nothing';[446] but that does not imply a vacuous non-existence. Hilton has in mind here Augustine's notion of sin as *privatio boni*, the active lack of what is good: thus he tells us that 'this nothing is no other than a lack of love and of light, as sin is nothing but an absence of good'.[447]

If we are to dispose of the 'image of sin' we must first of all recognize that it is there; and this requires a measure of humility and self-knowledge, a subject we have already explored. It also requires entering the darkness that is within the soul: although Hilton speaks of a 'good night, and a luminous darkness',[448] he does not have in mind the mysterious darkness which (according to the *Cloud of unknowing*) surrounds the transcendent mystery of God: rather it is a metaphor for the stripping-off of worldly entanglements,[449] and whilst within it the soul must cleave to its desire for God[450] in order to discern Jesus, 'who is both love and light' and who 'is in this darkness'.[451] Hilton describes this darkness within the soul as a 'rich nothing';[452] and what he has in mind is something akin both to the inner detachment or 'night' of St John of the Cross and the 'indifference' of St Ignatius of Loyola: 'we may not', he writes, 'suddenly start out of this dark night of this fleshly corruption into that ghostly [= spiritual] light'[453] because we could not bear to do so. Hence we must begin with what he calls 'bodily working' before we can proceed to 'ghostly working'. The former means

> all manner of good works that your soul does by [means of] the wits and members of your body, to yourself, as in fasting, waking, and in restraining of fleshly lusts by doing penance, or to your fellow-christian (evencristen) by fulfilling your deeds of bodily or spiritual mercy, or to God by enduring all bodily mischiefs for the sake of righteousness.[454]

Note Hilton's characteristic concern with love of neighbour. He tells the lawyer to whom he addresses his 'Letter to someone wanting to renounce the world' that he must love his neighbour (which means everyone) – his friends in God, and his enemies for God's sake; and he must suffer with all who are sinful, ignorant or infirm, and comfort them, if not in deed than at least by his goodwill.[455] This 'bodily working' is the essential preliminary to the re-formation of ourselves as images of God; but it does not of itself achieve that re-formation, which is unequivocally the work of grace. Hilton's theology of atonement is clearly influenced by that of St Anselm:

> This [our restoration] could be done by no man who was man alone and had come from Adam by natural generation, for the reason that this trespass and dishonour was infinitely great, and therefore it surpassed the power of man to make amends for it.[456]

He also takes a positive view of Adam's Fall: as a result of it humanity, now restored, attains to much greater glory and joy than if it had never fallen.[457] That restoration has taken place in and through the work of Christ: everything, however, depends on the human will as to whether or not we benefit from its fruits.[458] Thus Hilton declares that

> He [Christ] forms and reforms: he forms by himself alone, but he reforms us with us; for all this is done by the giving of grace, and by applying our will to grace.[459]

This is of crucial importance. We cannot achieve our own reformation: there is no hint of Pelagianism here. But we can (indeed we must) co-operate with Christ in effecting it. Hilton calls this process 'reformation in feeling': early in his *Ladder of perfection* he tells his addressee that she must

> always seek to come to the spiritual feeling of God: and that is to know and experience the wisdom of God.[460]

But faith must come first:

> Our Lord said . . . to a man who was paralyzed, when he healed him: '*Confide fili, remittuntur tui peccata tua*'. That is, Son, believe steadfastly, your sins are forgiven you. He did not say to him, 'See or feel how your sins are forgiven you' – for forgiveness of sin is done spiritually and invisibly through the grace of the Holy Spirit – but *believe* it.[461]

Even so, feeling is important: God can transmute our human affections into spiritual ones;[462] and God sends such 'stirrings' as ways of inciting many souls to shake off worldly entanglements.[463] But the crucial point is that 'feeling' is not for Hilton something separate from 'understanding': rather it is, as Clark says, 'the realisation of our adoption in Christ, a supernaturally given awareness of the life of grace'.[464] Hilton is here very close to the Cistercian tradition exemplified in England by Aelred and considered in Chapter 3: personal experience, or 'feeling', is not some autonomous and self-authenticating department of our relationship with God which overrules all others: rather it is that intimate process by which we make our own both the awareness of our need for reformation and the faith that such re-formation is already accomplished in Christ.[465] It thus becomes the springboard for our sharing with Christ in restoring our lost likeness to him.

God in the Darkness: *The Cloud of Unknowing*

Introduction
Both the text with which this chapter began and much of what followed reflects the affirmative, even visual character of late medieval spirituality, rooted as it is in the classic western theological tradition which culminated in the monumental *Summa theologiae* of St Thomas Aquinas. In this tradition God is Being itself, the cause of all that is, the unmoved Mover who alone moves all things. God is present to us in creation, in our own inner selves, in our neighbour; and countless anguished crucifixes, combined with any number of processions of the eucharistic Sacrament, proclaimed a God who had made himself available, even visible, to his suffering creatures. The Benedictine Uthred of Boldon follows the teaching of Aquinas when he declares in his *Meditacio devota* that the most terrible punishment for anyone is to be deprived of that vision of God which

> just as it satisfies every possible longing of the blessed, so too it tortures by
> its absence beyond any conceivable torment.[466]

A fourteenth-century English encyclopaedia contains a fascinating illustration of the face of God, who is represented as a young bearded man with close-set eyes: groups of men and women, in discreetly separate groups, gaze directly at God.[467] The English theologian Richard Fitzralph, whose teaching was accepted by Pope John XXII, argued that souls destined for salvation were granted the direct vision of God once they had been purified after death, and before the general resurrection. There could be no more graphic illustration of the visual nature of late medieval spirituality.

Apophatic spirituality: Pseudo-Dionysius
Yet there was another important but quite different strand in late medieval spirituality, which centred upon the influence, often indirect, of a fifth-century writer known as Pseudo-Dionysius (but universally assumed in the middle ages to be Dionysius the Areopagite, the convert of St Paul mentioned in Acts 17.34, and thus to have quasi-apostolic authority).[468] In his *Divine names* he wrote:

> We cannot know God in his nature, since this is unknowable and is
> beyond the reach of mind or of reason. But we know him from the

arrangement of everything, because everything is, in a sense, projected out from him, and this order possesses certain images and semblances of his divine paradigms. We therefore approach that which is beyond all as far as our capacities allow us and we pass by way of the denial and the transcendence of all things and by way of the cause of all things. God is therefore known in all things and as distinct from all things. He is known through knowledge and through unknowing . . . He is all things in all things and he is no thing among things. He is known to all from all things and he is known to no one from anything.

This is the sort of language we must use about God . . . The most divine knowledge of God, that which comes through unknowing, is achieved in a union far beyond mind, when mind turns away from all things, even from itself, and when it is made one with the dazzling rays, being then and there enlightened by the inscrutable depths of Wisdom.[469]

Part of this passage is quoted directly by the author of the *Cloud of unknowing*:[470] indeed it is the only text from Pseudo-Dionysius that is directly quoted in the *Cloud*. Dionysius is arguing that God can indeed be known through his works, but that he is always infinitely more than anything we can see or understand.[471] Dionysius is often misunderstood: he is not speaking of a knowledge that is mere cerebration, but of a profound participation in what is known. Nor is he saying that we can apprehend God more through darkness and negation than through vision and affirmation. Rather he is saying that God is infinitely beyond both, so that we experience him not so much in *nothingness* as in *mystery*, and supremely in the mystery of the liturgy.

Unlike William of Ockham, Pseudo-Dionysius does not simply place the stress on revelation rather than reason in our search for God: he says that God may be known in and through any created thing, but that that knowledge takes us only a short distance towards him: his work is a constant corrective to those who would seek to domesticate God in man-made systems or insist that theirs is the only true way to encounter him.[472]

Two other points about Pseudo-Dionysius' thought are worth mentioning here. First, his theology is intensely and dynamically hierarchical: the entire cosmos comprises a series of ascending hierarchies of being, each level having its own place yet each unceasingly drawn towards what is above it, so that all creation both proceeds from the Trinity and longs to return to it. Dionysius applied this rich Neoplatonic approach both to the universe as a whole, to each level of being within the human person, and to the hierarchies of the church: each of these was inseparable from the others.[473] The relevance of this approach to a socially hierarchical age must have been apparent to many who drew on his thought for their own understanding of the spiritual life.

Secondly, Pseudo-Dionysius laid especial stress on the beauty of God, and on the importance of desire or longing in our relationship to him. God is absolute beauty, and 'any thinking person realizes that the appearances of beauty are signs of an invisible loveliness'.[474] Yet they are only signs: there is no Wordsworthian celebration of natural beauty for its own sake. Rather Dionysius expects the beauty we see around us to kindle within us a desire for the infinitely and incomparably greater beauty which is both its source and ours. When directed towards God, this desire effects our participation in God: it helps to make us godlike and to draw others to him as well.[475] It does this because our desire for God is literally ecstatic, lifting us up out of ourselves into unity with God.[475] And, by a mysterious paradox, what happens to us also happens to God in what Christians call the Incarnation. Dionysius writes:

> He is, as it were, beguiled by goodness, by love, and by yearning and is enticed away from his transcendent dwelling place and comes to abide within all things, and he does so by virtue of his supernatural and ecstatic capacity to remain, nevertheless, within himself.[477]

Few theologians evoked a more literally *attractive* God, and fewer still integrated theology and spirituality, the life of the cosmos and the interior life of the individual, more seamlessly than did Dionysius – to the extent that, as Hans von Balthasar puts it, 'theology is exhausted in the act of wondering adoration'.[478]

The influence of Pseudo-Dionysius in the Latin West is an immensely complex subject. What is important for our purposes is to see that medieval writers did not simply swallow him whole, so to speak. Influenced by St Bernard and others in setting love of God above knowledge of him (and Christ's suffering humanity as the primary focus for that love), they took Dionysius' imagery of darkness to mean that in order to draw near to God we must renounce our intellect and rely only on love. For Pseudo-Dionysius the divine darkness lies beyond the farthest effort of the mind, though it is still the mind that enters it: for his medieval disciples, we enter the darkness when we leave all mental activity behind and rely only on the impulse of love that draws us towards God. Thus Dionysius follows St Gregory of Nyssa in using the ascent of Moses on Mount Sinai as a metaphor for the ascent of all things towards God:

> He [Moses] breaks free . . . from what sees and is seen, and he plunges into the truly mysterious darkness of unknowing. Here, renouncing all that the mind may conceive, wrapped entirely in the intangible and the invisible, he belongs completely to him who is beyond everything. Here, being neither oneself or someone else, one is supremely united by a completely unknowing inactivity of all knowledge, and knows beyond the mind by knowing nothing.[479]

The spirituality of the Cloud

Pseudo-Dionysius has in mind here the immense and mysterious 'return' of all things to the Creator who made them, the cosmic longing which gives the universe its meaning and dynamism. His conception of union with God is entirely to do with knowing and unknowing: he has adapted the Neoplatonic dynamic of procession from God and returning to God, changing it from a description of objective, external reality (represented, for example, by the Incarnation and Ascension) into a subjective, cognitive process. He certainly also has in mind the approach of the human creature to its Creator as the creature assents to the infinite desire for God that stirs within it. But this desire is above all ontological, the result of the kind of being which human creatures possess: it is much nearer the Platonic *eros* than the Christian *agape*.[480] For

Dionysius it finds its most concrete expression neither in moral action nor in personal spiritual growth but in liturgy, in which the divine power is released so that earthly worship becomes an anticipation of the heavenly liturgy, divinizing those who take part in it.[481]

Here, by contrast, is a passage from the fourteenth-century English text the *Cloud of unknowing*:

> Lift up your heart unto God with a meek stirring of love; and focus intently upon (lit. *mene*) himself, and not on his goods. And thereto be loth to think on anything but himself, so that nothing works upon your knowledge nor your will but only himself. And do all you can to forget all the creatures that ever God made, and their works, so that neither your thought nor your desire be directed or reach towards any of them, neither in general or in particular. Let them be, and be not mindful of them.
>
> This is the work of the soul that most pleases God. All the saints and angels have joy from this work, and make haste to help it with all their strength. All fiends are enraged when you do this, and try to destroy it in every way they can. All people living on earth are wonderfully helped by this work, though you do not know how. Yes, the souls in purgatory are eased in their pain by virtue of this work. You yourself are cleansed and made virtuous by no work so much as by this. And yet it is the lightest work of all, and the soonest done, when a soul is helped by grace with a perceptible desire – for otherwise it is hard and miraculous for you to accomplish.
>
> Do not delay, then, but work therein until you experience that desire. For the first time you do it, you find only a darkness, and as it were a cloud of unknowing, which you do not understand, save that you feel in your will a naked aspiration (lit. *nakid entent*) towards God.[482]

The parallels with Pseudo-Dionysius are clear: the significance of darkness, the process of renunciation and the movement (or aspiration)[483] towards God alone, the need to reach out beyond all knowledge towards the mysterious God. But there are also major differences. The movement the *Cloud* author has in mind is not the cognitive (or perhaps supra-cognitive) flight of the soul towards its origin so much as the costly moral and spiritual journey that takes us close to God. And its primary dynamic is not the dialectic of knowing and unknowing, but the impulse of love. It is more practical, more moral, and much harder work. Where Pseudo-Dionysius describes with grandiloquent splendour the dazzling beauty of the universal Creator hidden in the mists on the mountain-top, the *Cloud* author prescribes with careful precision the only route he knows that will enable us to get there.[484]

It is not the least of the similarities between these two great spiritual writers that their identities remain as mysterious as the God they wrote about. The author of the *Cloud of unknowing* wrote a number of other spiritual works, including a translation of Pseudo-Dionysius' *Mystical theology*: there is some evidence to suggest that the person was a Carthusian;[485] and everything he or she wrote indicates a high degree of skill and experience as a spiritual director. Beyond that, we know nothing; and that may well have been the author's intention. The Prologue to the *Cloud* suggests that the addressee was in religious orders; but much of what the author writes could have been profitably studied by a wide range of people.[486] What is crucial is that the *Cloud* is not an academic exercise in mystical theology, but a practical yet serious manual of spiritual direction.[486]

In seeking to understand the *Cloud* author's spirituality we may return to the extract from the *Cloud* cited above. The addressee is instructed to lift up his or her heart to God 'with a meek stirring of love', and to focus intently on him and not on his 'goods' or gifts. This 'stirring' is the action of God upon our wills, not something we generate by ourselves:[488] the entire process by which we draw near to God is the work of grace, even though it requires hard labour on our part in co-operating with God.[489] Our 'werk' consists first of all in actively renouncing, indeed 'forgetting', anything but God; and the author tells us to set a 'cloud of forgetting' beneath us, as a climber ascending above the cloud level might do: this is, of course, not some kind of willed amnesia but a deliberate setting of a distance between ourselves and all other creatures in order to ascend towards God.[490]

Yet (and this is crucial) the act of 'forgetting' is not a deliberate rejection of the world but precisely the means by which we are of most use to it. In the text cited above, the author stresses the fact that this 'werk' is of inestimable value to others, and that far from being an experience of destructive loneliness we find ourselves accompanied by the communion of saints. Later the author writes:

> For Christ is our head, and we are his limbs, if we are in charity; and whoso will be a perfect disciple of our Lord, let him strain up his spirit in this spiritual work (*werk*) for the salvation of all his brothers and sisters in kind, as our Lord did his body on the cross. And how? Not for his friends and his family and his homely lovers, but generally for all mankind, without any special beholding more to one than to another.[491]

The *Cloud* author is closer here to the mainstream eremitical tradition than was Richard Rolle, and close too to traditional Augustinian theology: by seeking to love God for his own sake, above all else, we discover the means of loving everyone for God's sake, and thus to love them as we should, unpossessively. It is this focused yet inclusive love which is the fruit of the ascetic spiritual journey: the addressee seeks freely to renounce the love of any one in particular in order to learn how to love everyone in particular. And we achieve this only by first loving God, again in particular (for the Christian, rooted in the Incarnation, there can be no such thing as a 'general' love).

But how do we achieve this? Later in the *Cloud* the author sets out the essential physical and spiritual conditions for setting about our 'werk': 'a full great restfulness, and a full whole and clean disposition, as well in body as in soul'.[492] The language may again suggest the would-be mountaineer; but the author has in mind a quality of inner repose which is itself the fruit of a freely-willed renunciation of 'the world.' Later still we are warned not to rely on over-exertion: 'work more with a zest than with any brute strength'.[493] And it is this almost playful zest, or divinely given desire, which is fundamental.[494] This is the 'naked aspiration' towards God referred to in our earlier extract from the *Cloud*. It denotes a singleminded direction of the whole person (not just the mind or the affections) towards God;[495] and it is itself a gift of God, the result of his having 'kindled [our] desire full graciously, and fastened by means of it a leash of longing' to us even while we were lost through the fall of Adam.[496] To this gentle leading on God's part we are to respond by learning 'to lift up the foot of [our] love' and to 'step towards that state and degree of living which is perfect, and the highest state of all'.[497] And our response is not a once-for-all decision, but something that needs to be continually renewed, and that demands of us a radical unpossessiveness, an ability to travel light, as any mountain-walker knows well:

> Go on, then, I pray you, quickly. Look now ahead of you, and let go what is behind. See what you lack, not what you possess . . . All your life now you must always remain in desire, if you will profit in the way of perfection.[498]

This desire grows as its goal draws closer, particularly if that goal is God himself:

> For not what you are, nor what you have been, does God behold with his merciful eyes, but what you want to be. St Gregory is witness that 'all holy desires grow by delay; and if they diminish by delay, they were never holy desires'. For he that feels less and less joy in new discoveries and sudden presentations of his original (old) purposed desires, though they may all be called natural desires conducing to the good, nevertheless they were never holy desires. Of this holy desire St Augustine speaks and says that 'the whole life of a good Christian is nothing but holy desire'.[499]

The Divine Compassion: Julian of Norwich

Introduction

If we know nothing at all about the author of the *Cloud of unknowing*, we know little more about Julian of Norwich. The first and shorter version of her *Showings* begins:

> Here is a vision shown by the goodness of God to a devout woman, and her name is Julian, who is a recluse at Norwich and still in this life, in the year of our Lord 1413.[500]

We have seen earlier in this chapter that there were many varieties of recluse in late medieval England, some attached to religious communities but others living more or less autonomously. Norwich was one of the wealthiest and most populous cities in England at the time, and with extensive mercantile links with continental Europe.[501] But it was from East Anglia that the Peasants' Revolt originated; and Julian is unlikely to have been unacquainted with the upheavals taking place in society around her. We do not know whether or not she was a nun: Benedicta Ward argues convincingly that she had been married and widowed before becoming a recluse.[502]

Beyond that, all we can conclude from her own writings is that she was born in 1342 or 1343, fell sick at the age of 30, and that just when she thought she was dying her pain vanished and she was granted sixteen revelations, or *shewings* (in May 1373).[503] These formed the basis of what has come to be called the Short Text; but Julian tells us that she spent almost twenty years seeking to understand the meaning of the revelations before writing the second and much fuller version of them which is now known as the Long Text.[504] There are various scattered references in contemporary wills to recluses called Julian in Norwich at the time;[505] but none of them can be conclusively identified with our author. Beyond this, there is only silence about Julian's identity and life; and since (as with the *Cloud* author) it is entirely possible that this obscurity is a deliberate intention on the author's part, it seems better to respect it rather than to indulge in unverifiable speculation.[506]

The dates of the two versions of Julian's *Showings* are uncertain. The only surviving manuscript of the Short Text dates from the mid-fifteenth century.[507] There are three extant copies of the Long Text; but these date from the late sixteenth century at the earliest.[508] Such a modest manuscript history suggests that the influence of Julian was (until very recently) very slender.[509] There is even uncertainty about the title: the only one to appear in the texts themselves is *A revelation of love*: all other titles are later editorial inventions.[510] It is almost universally agreed that the Short Text represents an earlier work (rather than an abridgement of the Long Text); but we do not know when either was actually composed. There is much to be said for the theory that even the Short Text was written some years after the experiences which gave rise to it, perhaps as late as between 1385 and 1388: it is possible that she wrote it down soon after being enclosed as a recluse.[511] If this were so, the Long Text will have been written in the second decade of the fifteenth century, which would increase the probability of Julian having become acquainted with some of the themes and ideas then current in fourteenth-century spirituality, such as those of Rolle and Hilton.[512]

The relationship between Short and Long Texts has been much discussed.[513] The fact that the two references in the Short Text which appear to suggest that it was directed to those in the religious life are omitted from the Long Text may argue for an intended wider audience for the latter; but this too is uncertain.[514] What can be affirmed with reasonable confidence is that the Long Text reveals a Julian at once more confident and more searching, concerned to probe difficult theological issues more intensively than in the earlier version, and in the process articulating a more systematic Trinitarian theology than appears in the Short Text.[515]

Julian's style has given rise to controversy: one scholar, aware of her use of Latin rhetorical devices, nonetheless argues that she uses them 'sparingly and perhaps rather amateurishly'.[516] Others have gone to great lengths to establish the stylistic sophistication of her work, reflected in particular in her extensive use of rhetoric, which in their view points to the extent of her academic learning.[517] But again it must be emphasized that we have no sure evidence: her style is certainly fluent and assured; but her use of rhetorical devices, like her references to subjects or ideas explored in earlier theologians, need not imply any direct borrowings. What we see in Julian's work is surely the result of a formative religious experience which has been deeply pondered in the light not just of her personal faith but of some of the largest of all theological questions: why did Christ undergo passion and death? Why is there sin and suffering? What difference does belief in God make? It is time to explore in more detail how Julian sets about both asking her questions, and seeking her answers.

The suffering Christ

The Short Text begins with Julian's desire to enter into Christ's suffering.[518] She does not begin with her own experience, but with her desire to share Christ's experience: a quite different thing. Her own experience is always theologically interpreted: indeed it is precisely lived theology – her theology determines her experience, rather than (as we might expect) the other way round.[519]

Thus the beholding of Christ's suffering enables Julian to behold accurately the meaning of this life in general, and of her own suffering in particular.[520] It is also worth noting that, as one scholar has pointed out, Julian's visions of Christ are of Christ alone: unlike most contemporary artists or meditators, she scarcely has eyes for the other participants in the drama of the Passion.[521] When Julian sought truth and wisdom, she did not begin with herself, or even with 'the world.' She began with Christ, and Christ *crucified*. For her, it seems, there could be no other possible place to start.[522]

The implications of this approach become clear if we consider Julian's view of self-knowledge and knowledge of God. In the Long Text she writes:

> It belongs to us to have three kinds of knowledge. The first is that we know our Lord God. The second is that we know ourselves, what we are through him in nature and in grace. The third is that we know meekly what our self is with regard to our sin and feebleness.[523]

Julian's teaching on self-knowledge is not always consistent: thus at one point she insists that self-knowledge comes only after knowledge of God, only to state the opposite shortly afterwards.[524] But in general she does not do what many in the classic Augustinian tradition do, which is to begin with self.[525] Rather she begins with God, and seeks to understand herself in the light of God, rather than the other way round.

Spirituality and creation

This is not to say that Julian has a negative view of creation. God shows her 'a little thing, the size of a hazelnut', and tells her that it is all that is made. She goes on to say:

> In this little thing I saw three parts. The first is that God made it, the second is that he loves it, the third is that God keeps it. But what is that to me? Truly, [that God is] the maker, the lover, the keeper. Until I am united (lit. *oned*) in my substance to him, I may never have love, rest nor true bliss; that is to say, that I be so fastened to him that there be nothing at all that is made between my God and me.[526]

Julian enlarges and reflects on this vision in the Long Text:

> For this is the cause why we be not all in ease of heart and of soul, for here we seek rest in this thing that is so little, where no rest is, and we know not our God, who is almighty, all-wise and all-good, for he is true rest.[527]

Creation is infinitely precious to God: indeed she follows St Thomas in saying that all things have their being through the love of God.[528] At one point Julian describes

God as arranging even our excretion.[529] We are *clothed* in God's goodness: the thought here is very Pauline.[530] Yet we shall find our rest in none of the creation: only in its creator. The hazelnut may be infinitely precious to God; but it is also infinitely small.[531] She may echo Augustine implicitly; but the thought and the manner of its expression is entirely her own.

Spirituality and the passion

Julian believes that we are loved from all eternity, and that from all eternity the Trinity had conceived of the incarnation, so that Christ would be the midpoint, the mediator, between us and God.[532] But his work of mediation is carried out supremely on the cross, and it is this which forms the heart of her theology. This is contemplative prayer at its most honest, costly and revealing:

> After this Christ showed me a part of his Passion close to the time of his dying. I saw that sweet face as it were dry and bloodless with the pallor of dying, then yet more dead, pale and languishing, and then turning blue (lit. 'more dead to the blue'), and yet more blue, as the flesh turned more deep dead . . . This long torment (lit.'pining') seemed to me as though he had been dead for seven nights and yet still suffering pain, and I thought the drying-up of Christ's flesh was the greatest pain of his Passion and the last . . . Herein I saw in part the compassion of Our Lady Saint Mary; for Christ and she were so oned in love that the greatness of her love was the cause of the greatness of her pain . . . And so all his disciples and all his true lovers suffered pains greater than their own physical death. For I am certain by my own experience that the least of them loved him more than they did themselves. Here I saw a great oneing between Christ and us; for when he was in pain we were in pain, and all creatures that might suffer pain suffered with him.[533]
>
> I thought: is any pain in hell like this? And I was answered in my reason: Hell is a different pain, for that is despair. But of all pain that led to salvation, this is the worst, to see one's lover suffer.[534]
>
> Then said our good Lord asking: Are you well pleased that I suffered for you? I said, Yes, good Lord, all thanks to you! Then said Jesus our good Lord, If you are pleased, I am pleased. It is a joy, a bliss, an endless delight to me that ever I suffered the Passion for you; and if I could suffer more, I would suffer more.[535]

Again, this is a striking inversion of what we might expect: instead of saying that Christ suffers when we do, she says that we suffer when he does, and that this is the greatest pain imaginable. Elsewhere she develops the argument somewhat: we are suffering now because it is Christ's suffering, not his bliss, that he shows us; and 'for this little pain that we suffer here we shall have a high endless knowing in God, which we might never have without that'.[536]

So creaturely suffering is taken up into the suffering of Christ. The passion of Christ is, literally, the crux of Julian's theology. But how does his suffering help us? Julian believed, like other medieval authors, that Christ suffered unimaginably more than any human being, precisely because he is also divine – if he could have suffered more, he would have.[537] Hence his suffering is victorious over evil, not merely exemplary.[538] And the result of his suffering love is that

> we are not only his through our being but also by the courteous gift of his Father. We are his bliss, we are his reward, we are his worship, we are his crown.[539]

The lord and the servant

Julian articulates the heart of her thought in the parable of the lord and the servant:

> And then our courteous Lord answered in a very hidden way (lit. 'full mystely') by showing a marvellous story of a lord who had a servant . . . The Lord sits solemnly in rest and in peace. The servant stands before his lord, reverently ready to do his lord's will. The lord looks upon his servant very lovingly, sweetly and gently. He sends him to a certain place to do his will. The servant not only goes, but suddenly leaps up and runs very quickly for love of doing his lord's will. And soon he falls in a dell, and suffers terrible pain; and then he groans and moans and tosses about and writhes, but he cannot rise or help himself in any way. And in all this the greatest hurt that I saw in him was absence of consolation (lit. 'comfort'), for he could not turn his face to look upon his loving lord . . . And all the time his loving lord beholds him most tenderly . . . For in all this our good Lord showed his own son and Adam as but one man. The virtue and the goodness that we have is of Jesus Christ, the feebleness and blindness that we have is of Adam, both of whom were revealed in the servant.[540]

The servant is Christ, compared in the parable to a gardener, 'delving and dyking, toiling and sweating and turning the earth upside-down', and suffering the ultimate pain imaginable by being deprived of the vision of God.[541] Yet even then God still 'beholds' him. The crucial point is that the servant is also Adam, indeed both Christ and Adam (here Julian recapitulates St Paul's teaching in Romans 5 and 1 Corinthians 15): when God looks on Adam, he 'sees' Christ. So too, by virtue of the incarnation, when God looks on us and our sins, he 'sees' only Christ.[542] Thus we are ourselves both Adam and Christ:

> For the duration of this life we have in us a marvellous mixture (lit. 'medley') both of well-being and of woe. We have in us our lord Jesus Christ up-rising, and we have in us the wretchedness and mischief of Adam falling.[543]

Much of Julian's teaching is either summarized or adumbrated here. We are both Adam and Christ: Julian uses, not St Paul's language of 'flesh' and 'spirit' to describe our two natures, but 'sensuality' and 'substance'.[544] Yet it is again Paul's theology that she reflects here: our sensuality represents that which constitutes our separatedness from God, or the whole of our lives conceived of in a narrowly this-worldly perspective.[545] Our substance is our human nature conceived of in the light of eternity: it is what we are by virtue of being created in the image of God. Thus Julian says that our substance was united to God in our first making (i.e. at the creation), our sensuality in our second making (i.e. through Christ's work of redemption).[546] In the Incarnation and Passion, our sensuality is united (or, to use Julian's word, 'oned') to our substance because Christ embraced both.[547] Here too we only understand ourselves in the light of Christ, for Christ is perfect human nature.[548]

Christ as mother

It is within this context that we need to see Julian's stress on Christ as our mother, a theme which appears only in the Long Text, where it is firmly set within the much more fully developed trinitarian theology which Julian articulates there. It first appears in the context of a reference to the divine *mercy*, a key attribute of God for Julian.[549] She goes on to say that the 'almighty truth' of the Trinity is our father, its 'deep wisdom' is our mother, and its 'high goodness' is our lord (i.e. the Holy Spirit).[550] She then proceeds to develop her view of divine motherhood by understanding it in three ways: God is our mother because he created us ('ground of our natural making'): he is our mother because he redeemed us ('taking of our nature'); and he is our mother because he ceaselessly cares for us (what Julian calls a 'motherhood of working').[551]

The result is a love of infinite fecundity: there is 'a forth-spreading by the same grace of length and breadth, of height and of depth without end; and all is one love'.[552] And it is precisely through this love that we are made and remade. Thus Julian writes:

> I saw and understood that the high might of the Trinity is our father, and the deep wisdom of the Trinity is our mother, and the great love of the Trinity is our lord; and all these we have by nature and in our substantial creation. And furthermore I saw that the second person, who is our mother, in substance the same beloved person, has now become our sensual mother, for we are made by God to be twofold, that is to say both substance and sensuality. Our substance is the higher part, which we have in our father, almighty God; and the second person of the Trinity is our mother in nature in virtue of our substantial creation, in whom we are grounded and rooted, and he is our mother of mercy by taking upon himself our sensuality.[553]

We should note that, here as elsewhere, Julian begins with the Trinity and proceeds to humanity, rather than the other way round. She does not begin with earthly concepts of motherhood and then apply them to God: nor does she ever say that Christ is like an earthly mother. On the contrary, earthly mothers are like Christ, albeit less satisfactory, since Christ never allows his children to perish.[554] In speaking of the second person of the Trinity as our mother, Julian seeks to give expression to her conviction that the divine love is at once procreative, compassionate (in the sense of sharing our sufferings), and protective.[555] Julian has much to say about the *homeliness* of God's love, of which the ultimate manifestation is the Incarnation, through which God condescends to enter the heart of human experience.

Thus it is precisely in a vision of Christ's terrible sufferings that she perceives 'that our good lord, that is so reverent and dreadful, is so homely and courteous';[556] and she goes on to draw out the contemporary social context of such an image: the greatest honour a great lord may do to a poor servant is to be homely with him, though this homeliness must never be taken for granted.[557] But this homeliness also has an eschatological dimension, echoing the rich theme of the sabbath which we saw in the spirituality of Aelred of Rievaulx: Julian says that in heaven love and fear will be united: we shall be 'homely and near to God'.[558] Fear? Yes; but this fear is

> that fear that makes us hastily flee from all that is not good and fall onto our lord's breast, as the child into its mother's arms, with all our intent and with all our mind, knowing our feebleness and our great need, knowing his everlasting goodness and his blessed love, only seeking him for salvation, cleaving to him with faithful trust. That fear that brings us to do this is natural and gracious and good and true; and all that is contrary to this is either wrong or mixed with wrong. This, then, is the remedy: to know them both, and refuse the wrong.[559]

Where does Julian get her notion of motherhood from? We have already considered Anselm's exploration of this theme, though Julian goes far beyond both Anselm and contemporary writers already noted in this chapter in applying motherhood to the Trinity.[560] Modern scholars have noted both Augustinian and Thomist presuppositions in the light of which such a notion of motherhood might appear both appropriate and logical, though still highly original.[561] In the final analysis, however, none of the texts in either earlier or contemporary literature in which this image is found are sufficiently close to Julian to argue for any direct borrowing on her part from any of them.[562] For Julian, the image of God as mother articulates more powerfully than any other image could the crucial fact that the essence of the outgoing love of the Trinity is that of the mother for her children: costly, nurturing, self-giving and literally life-giving too.[563]

The meaning of sin

The notion of God's suffering love brings us to the hardest question Julian addresses: how can we reconcile human wickedness with the divine love? We have seen that in the parable of the lord and the servant Julian brings both Fall and Incarnation together. But although she takes a view similar to that of St Irenaeus in seeing the Fall as a *felix culpa*, this in no way causes her to minimize the seriousness of sin.[564] At one point she says that in this world 'man shall do right nought but sin'.[565] She describes with terrible clarity her own encounter with the devil:[566] only if evil is taken seriously can redemption be too.[567]

The difficulty, for Julian as for all theologians before her, consists in taking sin seriously enough to do justice to the reality of evil, yet not so seriously as to end up with effectively a dualist view of reality. In the Short Text she sees God 'in a point', or moment of time, and beholds that he does all that is done.[568]

But this only begs a further question: if God does all that is done, what is sin? The answer she receives at this point is that 'sin is nought'.[569] She returns to the question a little later, when she sees that the only thing that hindered her (and thus also our) longing for God was sin, which again begs the question of why God allows it.[570] She is told that 'sin is behovely [= necessary]':[571] it is all that is not good, both the shame and 'despite' of Christ, and our own suffering. It becomes clear that, for Julian as for Augustine and Aquinas before her, sin is more than simply a *privatio boni*: it is a destructive nothingness[572] – and her description of sin as 'nought' inescapably calls to modern minds the use by the Nazis of the German word *vernichten* (= to annihilate, reduce to nought) to indicate their intention towards the Jews.[573] We may not be able to see sin, but we can see the effect it has.[574] Towards the end of the Long Text she says that the fact of our being strangers to God through our sin means that we 'let my lord stand alone',[575] a vivid image of the destructive power of sin in damaging the essential oneness of creation and creator. Sin *separates*, tears apart, what should be 'oned'; and it is by taking upon himself the excruciating pain of the cross that Jesus, both divine and human, 'ones' us to God again.

But if sin is so destructive, why is it 'necessary'? Once again Julian looks for the answer not in us, but in Christ:

> In this word 'sin' our Lord brought to my mind generally all that is not good: the shameful despite and the utter noughting that he bore for us in this life and in his dying, and all the pains and passions of all his creatures, spiritual and bodily.[576]

We need to remember here Julian's conviction that the suffering of Christ was the greatest 'pain' the world had ever known, or could ever know. When she thinks of sin, she sees at once its terrible consequences: first on Christ, then on all creatures. And she sees that our response must be a costly one:

> For we are all in part noughted, and we should be noughted, following our master Jesus, until we be fully purged, that is to say until we be fully noughted of our own deadly flesh, and of all our inward affection(s) which are not good.[577]

In the Long Text she replaces 'noughted' by 'troubled';[578] but she clearly has in mind the need for us to set at naught all that caused Christ to suffer.

There is a threefold process, then: our sin and consequent suffering causes Christ to suffer, infinitely more than we have; and our response to the appalling spectacle of his suffering must be to suffer yet more. But this latter suffering has positive value: it purges us, 'makes us to know ourselves and ask for mercy',[579] indeed annihilates all within us that was itself the cause of Christ's passion. Thus by his suffering ours is redeemed. Sin is 'necessary' because without it Christ would never have suffered; and without that we would never have been restored to an incomparably more wonderful union with God than we would have had if Adam had never eaten the forbidden fruit. This does not make sin good: it means that for Julian, as for Irenaeus centuries earlier, it is an inevitable consequence of our being the kind of people God made us to be. As Tugwell puts it, Julian has no doubt about the fact that 'what God wants is precisely saints who have been sinners'.[580]

The Christian hope

This brings us to the question of salvation. Julian never doubted the fact that the revelations she has received are intended for all Christians: they are not some private experience that she may (if she so chooses) share with others. She explicitly says that all that she saw she saw on behalf of, or standing in the place of, 'all my even-Christians'.[581] She makes it clear that she writes for all Christians, 'as we are all one'.[582] And she emphasizes the inseparability of the two kinds of Christian love: love of neighbour and love of God.[583] But it is precisely this conviction of our solidarity with one another which causes Julian to wonder whether anyone could not be saved. At one point Julian concedes the orthodox view that some will be damned, but only in order to challenge it at once.[584] The answer she receives is that what is impossible to us is not impossible to God,[585] and that there are limits to what we may presume to know.[586] She sees that 'sin is no shame, but worship to man': great sinners like David, St Peter and St Paul and others, are all in heaven; and in heaven 'the betokening of sin is turned into worship'.[587] Sins become wounds, in the sense of Francis' stigmata, *provided we have contrition for them*,[588] and allow ourselves to suffer 'noughting' as Christ did; and just as our sins have 'defiled the fair image of God', so our contrition and penance enables us to be healed, so that the sinner's 'wounds are seen before God not as wounds but as worships'.[589]

Julian's theology of atonement is thoroughly Pauline: just as all humanity fell through Adam, so all humanity is redeemed through Christ, the second Adam; and grace abounds through Christ to a far greater extent than did sin through Adam.[590] At its heart is the conviction that, as we are separated from God through sin, so we are 'oned' with God though the redeeming work of Christ.[591] Whether this means that at the universal judgement all will finally be saved is something that by definition we cannot know in this life.[592] What is clear is that for Julian the love of God extends far further than is implied (for example) in the gloomy Augustinian teaching about the *massa damnata*. She refuses to distinguish 'ordinary' salvation from a perfection that belongs exclusively to contemplatives.[593] And she has no doubt about the transforming power of the ultimate vision of God:

> Our faith is a light, [the] natural command of our endless day, that is our father, God; in which light our mother, Christ, and our good lord, the Holy Spirit, lead us in this passing life. This light is measured discreetly, needfully standing [close] to us in the night. The light is the cause of our life, the night is the cause of our pain and of all our woe, in which we deserve reward and thanks of God; for we, with mercy and grace, willingly know and believe [in] our light, going therein wisely and mightily. And at the end of woe, suddenly our eyes shall be opened, and in clarity of light our sight shall be full; which light is God our maker and the Holy Spirit in Christ Jesus our saviour. Thus I saw and understood that our faith is our light in our night; which light is God, our endless day.[594]

The theology and practice of prayer

It remains to consider Julian's understanding of prayer.[595] This too is God-centred before it is human-centred: it consists in aligning ourselves with God's will.[596] Hence God declares 'I am the ground of your beseeching':[597] if our prayer is the alignment of our wills with his, we cannot not want what he wants; so we shall obtain whatever we ask. Understood in this light, prayer is precisely the mirror-opposite of sin, restoring what had been sundered.[598] So Julian writes

> Prayer ones the soul to God, for though the soul be always like God in nature and in substance, it is often unlike in condition through sin on man's part. Then prayer makes the soul like God, when the soul wills as God wills, and then it is like God in condition as it is in kind.[599]

Prayer 'makes the soul homely with God', so that we co-operate with God: it makes us *buxom* (obedient, pliant, *disponible*) before God.[600] Julian echoes St Thomas' theology of petitionary prayer when she writes that

> in this word ['If you ask for it'] God showed such great pleasure and such great liking, as [though] he were much beholden to us for each good deed that we do; and yet it is he that does it.[601]

For her, the highest kind of prayer consists in seeking nothing other than to be 'oned into the sight and the beholding of him to whom we pray'.[602] The more we see God, the more we desire him; and when we do not see him we must make our selves 'supple and buxom'.[603] But when, by the working of his grace, we do behold him, we are filled with 'a high mighty desire to be all oned into him, centred to his dwelling, and enjoy his loving and delight in his goodness';[604] and we shall see God face to face, 'homely and fulsomely'.[605]

All true prayer, then, is designed to 'one' us with God by conforming our wills entirely with his. And such prayer, together with the strong trust in God that must underlie it, needs to be 'large',[606] as it will be if we recognize that our Lord is the ground from which our prayer springs.[607] The implication of this recognition is that prayer becomes primarily a *response* to what God has already done for us, in virtue of our making and remaking: hence too its primary attributes are *beholding* and *thanksgiving*:[608] we have both to see what God is doing to redeem us, and to pray for it.[609] In this context prayer has an eschatological dimension: it is 'a rightwise understanding of that fullness of joy that is to come, with true longing and true trust'.[610] Prayer is always forward-looking, seeking to behold God's future for the world as well as for ourselves. And this beholding makes us like the one we are beholding, and united to him in rest and peace:[611] through it the terrible distance between the Lord and the Servant, as a result of which the Servant can no longer 'behold' his Lord, is overcome, and humanity is at last oned with its creator.

Julian's view of prayer may be directed towards a profound conformity of our own wills with God's; but it does not lack fire and spirit either. We have already seen that she brings into her relationship with God some of the deepest and most difficult questions humanity can ask: this is part of what 'large' prayer involves. For Julian, prayer is never merely an affective activity, not something we engage in if or when we 'feel' like it: she says that we are to

> pray wholeheartedly, though you feel nought, though you see nought, yes, though you think you cannot, for in dryness and barrenness, in sickness and in feebleness, then is your prayer full pleasant to me.[612]

She is alert to the reality of evil even when we pray: whilst in church she 'heard a bodily jangling and talking . . . as if [the demons] had held a parliament with great busyness, and all was soft muttering', an experience which leads her close to despair[613] and which is uncomfortably close to what happens in many churches. But we are not to suppose that barrenness in prayer is a sign of God's absence: it is merely a sign of the transient nature of our feelings.[614] And if our prayer, like our lives, is marked by suffering, it does not undermine God's ultimate assurance:

> He [God] did not say, You shall not be tempted, you shall not be belaboured, you shall not be disquieted; but he said, You shall not be overcome.[615]

Conclusion

What are the sources of Julian's remarkable presentation of Christian faith and spirituality? The two texts contain virtually no explicit references to any other author; and modern scholars have suggested a wide range of possible source material.[616] The general influence of Franciscan piety is unmistakable:[617] visual imagery relating to the suffering Christ was particularly popular in Franciscan spirituality; and Julian's desire to participate in Christ's passion, and specifically to experience the three wounds of contrition, compassion and 'wilful longing towards God',[618] is very close to much devotion associated with St Francis (notably of course to the saint's own experience of the Stigmata).[619] There are also similarities between Julian and continental female spiritual writers, many of whose works were beginning to appear in England by the last decade of the fourteenth century at the latest:[620] thus Julian's request for a physical sickness echoes that of Margaret Ebner, who in 1312 received a preparatory sickness before embarking on the contemplative life;[621] and Angela of Foligno's *Book* contains an exploration of theodicy very similar to that of Julian.[622] But none of these parallels need suggest any direct influence.

The matter is further complicated by Julian's own reference to herself as 'a simple unlettered creature'.[623] There has been much debate about what this means, and many ingenious suggestions designed to render it compatible with the vast scholarship many modern authors discern in Julian's work.[624] And it is of course possible that she is merely being self-deprecating, a not uncommon trait among female spiritual writers at the time.

But let us suppose for a moment that Julian was telling us the truth. Is it remotely conceivable that she could have produced so remarkable and original a work of theology whilst relying on a scribe to set down her thoughts and without having read even (say) Augustine or Aquinas? The answer is surely: yes. She tells us herself that she took twenty years to set down the longer version of her work. As a recluse, and perhaps as a shrewd, devout, and attentive laywoman before that, Julian would have had the opportunity to discuss her beliefs with a wide range of people, including scholars. And she would have had a familiarity with scripture no less intimate for being based upon attentive listening rather than reading.[625] The theologian who most influenced Julian was one whose work she will have pondered constantly in public and private prayer, St Paul: we have seen at various points the ways in which she articulates his theology in her own distinctive manner, and there are many other fascinating resonances between them.[626]

If this is so, the implications are immensely important. At the very point in the history of English religion at which theology and spirituality, the intellectual and the affective, were (as we have seen) inexorably being prised apart, we see in Julian of Norwich precisely the reconciliation of both. Her vision of God is grounded in both intellect and love; her evaluation of personal experience is rooted in firm theological truth as rigorous as any found in the work of more widely-read writers. This is not conventional scholarship. It is wisdom, the fruit of an extraordinary process of attentive reflection on the deepest questions of life itself. We should take seriously Julian's own presentation of herself as a child, but a child secure in the all-embracing assurance of parental love:

> Fair and sweet is our heavenly mother in the sight of our soul, precious and lovely be the gracious children in the sight of our heavenly mother, with mildness and meekness and all the fair virtues that belong to children by nature. For the natural child does not despair of its mother's love, the natural child does not rely upon itself, the natural child loves its mother and each of them the other.
>
> These fair virtues, with all others that are like them, are those with which our heavenly mother is served and pleased. And I understood that there is no higher stature in this life than childhood, in feebleness and lack of strength and knowledge until the time that our gracious mother brings us up to our father's bliss. And there it shall truly be made known to us his meaning in the sweet words which he said: All shall be well, and you shall see it yourself, that all manner of thing shall be well. And then shall the bliss of our motherhood in Christ be to begin anew in the joys of God our Father; and this new beginning shall endure, a new beginning without end.[627]

The quest for the spiritual marriage: Margery Kempe

Introduction

Perhaps no English spiritual author has evoked such sharply divergent reactions as has Margery Kempe. The *Book* that bears her name was not written by her, for she tells us herself that she was illiterate: it was written down by someone (perhaps her son), and later rewritten by a priest who needed some persuading to do so, took many years over the task, and was shortsighted.[628] The book, which is a kind of spiritual autobiography, was (by Margery's own admission) not written in order and was in any case set down in writing so long after the events it describes that its historicity must remain an open question. After it was written (in 1436) the substance of it was lost until the discovery of the fifteenth-century manuscript containing it in 1934. Extracts from it had been published in the early sixteenth century by Wynkyn de Worde, whose compilation was carefully arranged to present a 'safe' selection of innocuous meditative passages with little hint of the formidable personality who inspired them.[629]

After the discovery of the full text, the reaction of most male scholars was dismissive, even vituperative: some criticized her for not living the hidden life of an anchoress, and thus drawing attention to herself rather than to Christ;[630] Edmund Colledge and James Walsh, noting that (by her own admission) Margery's conversion began in mental illness, refer to her 'morbid self-engrossment' and her 'babblings';[631] François Vandenbroucke says that 'her excited tone awakens distrust and makes the reader wonder whether she is not a case for a psychiatrist rather than a theologian'.[632] Only with the more recent, sensitive and nuanced treatment accorded her by (mainly women) scholars such as Bynum, Fries and Staley has Margery begun to receive her due.[633]

It is not altogether surprising that Margery attracted such opprobrium. She lacked a formal education (which leads another modern scholar to describe her as possessing a faith that was 'frustrated for lack of doctrinal content'[634]); she conformed neither to standard expectations of holiness by living as an anchoress, nor to standard expectations of domestic rectitude by living submissively with her husband; she could be extremely rude to interlocutors, especially to senior male clerics, who were rarely amused; she manifested highly emotional behaviour, often in public and sometimes in the liturgy, thereby exposing her (among other things) to suspicion of Lollardy;[635] she describes her own and other people's sexual inclinations with extraordinary frankness, whilst claiming (much as Rolle did) to have had many intimate conversations with Christ; and she was a wife and a mother at a time and in a place where holiness was still almost invariably associated with cloistered chastity.

If we are to understand Margery we clearly need to pay careful attention both to her own life and to the spiritual context of her *Book*. She lived from c.1373 until c.1438: she was the daughter of a prosperous burgess and prominent citizen in King's Lynn (then Bishop's Lynn), and married to John Kempe (described in the *Book* as a 'worshipful burgess'[636]). Soon after her marriage, and having given birth to her first child, Margery suffered from some kind of depressive illness which was triggered partly by her sense of guilt arising from an unconfessed (and unspecified) sin and partly by the severity with which her confessor responds when she tries to confess it.[637] The illness lasted for over six months, during which time Margery was forcibly restrained in a locked room: she associated her recovery with an appearance of Jesus, who said to her, 'Daughter, why have you forsaken me, and I never forsook you?'[638] This powerful conviction that her sense of guilt and fear of damnation were misconceived led both to her ensuing recovery, and to the beginning of her personal and intimate relationship with Christ.

It did not, however, either in her own eyes or in anyone else's, lead to an immediate transformation of her character. In the second chapter of the *Book* she describes with great honesty her love of fine dresses and her envy of other people's, together with her two failed attempts to set up her own business; and in the fourth chapter she reveals her willingness to commit adultery when accosted by someone she knew. It is only after this catalogue of failure and shame that Margery comes to discover in her relationship with Christ the fulfilment she could find nowhere else. Not the least of reasons for supposing her religious experiences to be genuine is that they lead, not to some surgical alteration in her personality but rather to a lifelong pilgrimage involving profound personal change in the face of considerable hostility and incomprehension. It is not insignificant that the four saints she invokes during the long prayer that concludes her *Book* (Saints Mary Magdalene, Mary of Egypt, Paul, and Augustine) experienced similarly costly spiritual conversions in the light of which Margery may well have sought to interpret her own.[639]

The Book as quest

Margery's relationship with Christ is no easy or cosy affair, even though like Julian she marvels at 'how homely our Lord was' in her soul:[640] rather it has the character of high adventure, with heights of excitement and depths of suffering at every turn. But it does not lead to self-absorption: later in her story Margery is able to comfort another woman who is troubled in the same way as she was.[641] She bears her husband fourteen children before persuading him (with great difficulty) to let her live a life of chastity.[642] She embarks on a series of ambitious (indeed astonishing) journeys or pilgrimages, visiting the Holy Land, Rome, Santiago de Compostela, Danzig and Aachen (among other places), as well as Canterbury and York and other English towns. She is arrested (in Leicester and later in Yorkshire) on suspicion of heresy. The *Book of Margery Kempe* is perhaps best read as a quest, the dramatic tale of someone seeking God with the fervour and determination of an Arthurian knight or an amorous troubadour – except that in this story the hero has far less romantic attributes: a history of psychiatric illness and failed business ventures, together with marital and family commitments.[643] And she is a woman.

Yet throughout she reveals a personality as close to an Arthurian hero as to conventional patterns of hagiography. She has enormous energy, is convinced of her vocation to the kind of life she adopts, and (whilst reflecting a serious concern to preserve an orthodox faith) has no hesitation in answering back to her (predominantly male) critics. When a rich man refuses to let her sail in a ship to Santiago, she replies

> Sir, if you put me out of the ship, my Lord Jesus shall put you out of Heaven, for I tell you, sir, our Lord Jesus has no liking for a rich man unless he will be a good man and a meek man.[644]

When the Mayor of Leicester threatens her with prison, she responds in a manner entirely worthy of John Bunyan:

> I am as ready, sir, to go to prison for God's love as you are ready to go to church.[645]

And when the Archbishop of York tells her that people have described her as a wicked woman, she delivers a ferocious riposte:

> Sir, and I hear it said that you are a wicked man. And if you are as wicked as people say, you shall never come to Heaven unless you amend now while you are here.[646]

Above all, she has a kind of indestructible spiritual merriment which frequently breaks out spontaneously, often upsetting bystanders. On one occasion she announces to those around her that 'It is full merry in heaven!', causing them to be angry not only because they cannot believe she knows anything at all about heaven but also because 'she would not hear nor speak of worldly things as they did, and as she did previously'.[647] After her ordeal before the Archbishop of York, his household ask her to pray for them:

> but the steward was wroth, for she laughed and made good cheer, and he said to her, 'Holy folk should not laugh.' She said, 'Sir, I have good cause to laugh, for the more shame I suffer and scorn, the merrier may I be in our Lord Jesus Christ.'[648]

Not the least of the reasons for the uncomprehending hostility she arouses among neighbours is the difficulty of believing that the housewife next door has suddenly become someone special; yet Jesus is recorded as having suffered from a similar lack of recognition, as Margery was doubtless aware.[649]

Late medieval women's mystical writings

It is impossible to evaluate this extraordinary person without taking some account of the movement of late medieval women's mysticism within which she certainly saw herself. Much work has recently been done on this subject, especially on the flowering of spirituality associated with late medieval holy women on the continent.[650] Yet it remains a subject fraught with interpretative pitfalls. A few general comments might be made before we consider Margery in more detail.

First, the contemporary English view of women was not as negative as is sometimes supposed.[651] Thus the (almost certainly male) author of *Dives and Pauper* declared that God made women from Adam's rib because the rib is next to the heart:

> God did not make woman from the foot, to be man's servant, nor did he make her of the head, to be his master, but from his side and from his rib, to be his fellow in love and helper in need.[652]

It was only as a result of Eve's sin that woman was made subject to man.[653] In that Christ became a man, he honoured men; but in that he received his manhood from a woman alone, he honoured women.[654]

In another contemporary text, closer in genre to Margery, it is worth noting the covert robustness of the presentation of women saints: in his Middle English life of St Christina, Osbern Bokenham represents the saint as a strong woman who not only defies her father and other pagan persecutors with vigour but sees each successively fall dead when they try to kill or torture her. Texts of this kind may well have influenced Margery, directly or indirectly.[655]

Secondly, a number of distinctive features recur in spiritual texts written by women during this period. Women tend to have far more visions than men (most of which are duly condemned by male authority figures): in an age when few women could read, it is not surprising to find their reputation for holiness based more on visions and charismatic character than on scholarship or a cloistered life.[656] Women are often described (or describe themselves) as possessing a special capacity for a quality of supernatural attentiveness to what God is saying, or to what will happen:[657] where men possess power, women possess vision.[658] Furthermore, and for the same reasons, women often experience ecstasy in spiritual union with Christ: Bynum points out that this experience represents for women what priesthood and preaching came increasingly to represent for men.[659] Descriptions of paramystical phenomena recur more often in writings about women than in those about men.[660] Women are described as experiencing a much higher degree of suffering in the later medieval period. They become ill more often.[661] They engage in a degree of penitential asceticism which (however bizarre to modern ears) underlines their claims to be taken seriously as icons of holiness. The Middle English life of St Christina the Astonishing describes the following incident:

> And another time about midnight she rose and provoked and called forth
> all the dogs of the city of Saint-Trudous to bark, and ran quickly before
> them like an animal, and they followed after her and drove and chased her
> through busks and briars and thick thorns, so that no part of her body
> remained unhurt; yet nevertheless, when she had washed away the blood,
> there appeared no sign of hurt nor sores.[662]

Finally, eucharistic devotion plays a particularly prominent part in the lives of holy women, underlining their experience of physical intimacy with Christ, whose body and blood they thereby venerated.[663] Devotion to the humanity of Christ was (as we have seen) a common feature of all spirituality in this period: it is perhaps not surprising to find that, where male writers tend to stress feminine aspects of this devotion (such as Jesus as mother), female writers saw Jesus as their spouse or even as their child.[664]

Margery Kempe and continental women's spirituality

It is against this general background that we may set Margery's own self-perception. The direct sources for her *Book* remain much controverted: she explicitly refers to Walter Hilton and to Rolle's *Incendium amoris*.[665] She also explicitly cites St Bridget of Sweden (who was canonized in 1391, and whose cult in England during Margery's lifetime was extensive)[666] and Mary of Oignies,[667] and will almost certainly have experienced at first hand the cult of Blessed Dorothea of Montau (1347–94) when visiting Danzig.[668] But far more important than direct references is the pervasive influence of continental female spiritual writers, many of whose works were widely available in England during Margery's lifetime,[669] and the similarities of whose lives and writings with those of Margery are worth briefly noting.[670]

The *lives* of many of these continental women show clear parallels with that of Margery: thus Angela of Foligno, like Margery, married at the age of about 20, and it appears that her sons and husband all died early in her conversion process, allowing her to respond unconditionally to what she perceived to be God's call to holiness.[671] Furthermore it is clear that the extraordinary lives of several of these women are the key to understanding their writings.[672] Thus many of them share Margery's determination to live chastely despite being married;[673] and embarked on pilgrimages to the Holy Land and elsewhere.[674]

Many specific aspects of Margery's spirituality are also found in the lives and writings of continental women. Her *devotion to, and identification with, the sufferings of Christ* is in many respects similar to those of her continental counterparts;[675] and she shares with most of them the experience of being reviled and misunderstood.[676] The frequency with which Margery received *Holy Communion*, and her experiences in the presence of the eucharistic host, echo the eucharistic devotion of Angela of Foligno and others.[677] Margery's combination of *intense experiences of Jesus and concern for the needs of the poor* is comparable to that of St Catherine of Siena, Mary of Oignies, and Christina the Astonishing, not to mention St Francis of Assisi.[678] Margery's *gift of tears* and propensity to 'roar', which we shall consider more fully below, is found among other holy women, most strikingly in descriptions of Angela of Foligno.[679] Margery also shared with Julian of Norwich and others a *longing for universal salvation*.[680] At one point Margery refers to dancing in heaven, when Christ tells her that

> because you are a maiden in your soul, I shall take you by the one hand in heaven, and my mother by the other, and so you shall dance in heaven with other holy maidens and virgins.[681]

There are earlier English references to mystical dance in the writings of Aelred of Rievaulx and the anonymous *Holy maidenhood*,[682] as well as in continental women's writings.[683] And many of the great continental writers share Margery's belief that Christ had espoused himself to her in a spiritual marriage.[684] Finally, Margery's view of herself as being in some sense a redemptive figure finds echoes in other women's texts.[685]

There are many other parallels between Margery and continental female spiritual writers; and it would be tedious if not impossible to list or locate them all.[686] There is, however, one striking dissimilarity: in contrast to most of those cited above, no cult of Margery ever developed, and (as we have seen) her book was effectively buried for four centuries. Even in the company of other holy women, Margery seems to have been too controversial a figure to inspire devotion in late medieval England.[687] Less surprising, but no less important, are the aspects of Margery's indebtedness to other writers and traditions: thus her emphasis on the importance of a right intention is strongly Augustinian;[688] her *Book* reflects the influence of the friars as spiritual guides, and much of her affective response to Christ may be said to be within the Franciscan spiritual tradition;[689] and there is a fascinating connection between Margery and the Carthusian Order, one of whose members (Richard Methley) appears to have read the *Book* at Mount Grace[690] – at one point in the manuscript, where Margery describes herself as falling down in a field among the people while meditating on the life of Christ, a fifteenth-century hand has added in red ink 'father M. was wont so to doo', which almost certainly refers to Methley.[691] Methley was known to be an advocate of intensely affective devotion to Christ, but even so it is striking to note this reference to Carthusians engaging in experiences similar to those of Margery.[692]

Devotion to the human Christ

Several of the principal features of the *Book* deserve some comment in their own right. Much of Margery's devotion to the human Christ reflects, as we have seen, contemporary patterns of piety. Her spirituality, involving as it does the *making present* of Christ's life, and entering imaginatively into the events of that life, is similar to much of what we saw in the work of the Carthusian Nicholas Love. Thus Margery says to a priest, 'Sir, [Christ's] death is as fresh to me as if he had died this same day';[693] and she comes very close to Love's pattern of homely piety when she makes Our Lady 'a good caudle and brought it to her to comfort her'.[694] But before dismissing such piety as maudlin we should note what follows: Our Lady refuses Margery's hot drink, saying 'Give me no meal but my own child.' The context is the intense suffering of Mary at the death of her son; and it is precisely that experience of suffering into which Margery seeks imaginatively to insert herself. Furthermore, she combines this approach with an intimate devotion to Christ's human body which echoes the most affective – indeed erotic – aspects of earlier Cistercian spirituality: thus Jesus tells her

> I must needs be homely with you and lie in your bed with you. Daughter, you desire greatly to see me, and you may boldly, when you are in your bed, take me to yourself as for your wedded husband, as your dearest darling, and as your sweet son, for I want to be loved as a son should be loved [by] the mother and want you to love me, daughter, as a good [wife] ought to love her husband. And therefore you may boldly take me in the arms of your soul and kiss my mouth, my head, and my feet as sweetly as you want.[695]

Such intensely erotic devotion may have raised eyebrows among contemporaries, not least Margery's long-suffering husband; and, although there are both parallels and precedents for it, they are rare with regard to the experience of married Christians like Margery.[696] Some have criticized this kind of devotion either for its naïveté or for its apparent inability to see beyond the concrete to some higher spiritual level behind it.[697] But Margery's experience is surely that it is precisely in the concrete, in directly personal incarnational terms, that Christ relates to her. Thus she is caught in a dilemma whose pain she feels keenly: she longs for Christ to be her spouse, yet he keeps sending her back to her own husband.[698]

It is precisely this paradox which marks her importance as an exemplar for lay spirituality, seeking to hold together both love of God and love of neighbour without compromising either. It cannot be said that Margery succeeds fully in achieving this; but it cannot be denied that she tries.

The God within

It is with this in mind that we should see Margery's emphasis on the indwelling God. At one point she hears Christ say to her

> I am a hidden God in you . . . wheresoever God is, Heaven is; and God is in your soul, and many an angel is about your soul to keep it both night and day. For when you go to church, I go with you; when you sit at your meal, I

sit with you; when you go to your bed, I go with you; and when you go out of town, I go with you.[699]

This interior presence has to be consciously adverted to: thus Christ warns her

And, daughter, if you will be high in Heaven with me, keep me always in your mind as much as you may, and forget me not at your meal, but think always that I sit in your heart and know every thought that is therein, both good and ill, and that I perceive the least thinking and twinkling of your eye.

And Margery beautifully responds:

Now truly, Lord, I wish I could love you as much as you might make me love you.[700]

This emphasis on the need to be attentive to the presence of Christ at every moment is traditional in much monastic spirituality, but striking nonetheless in the life of a busy laywoman. It is worth noting the prominent part played by the Holy Spirit in the *Book*: she hears

a manner of sound as [if] it had been a pair of bellows blowing in her ear. She, being abashed thereof, was warned in her soul to have no fear, for it was the sound of the Holy Spirit. And then our Lord turned that sound into the voice of a dove, and afterwards he turned it into the voice of a little bird which is called a redbreast that often sang full merrily in her right ear.[701]

She tells some lawyers interrogating her that she obtained her knowledge 'from the Holy Spirit';[702] and on a number of occasions her interlocutors recognize that she speaks on the Spirit's authority.[703] When Margery goes to visit Julian of Norwich, the latter confirms the authenticity of her spiritual experience and says:

Any creature that has these tokens must steadfastly believe that the Holy Ghost dwells in his soul. And much more, when God visits a creature with tears of contrition, devotion, or compassion, he may and ought to believe that the Holy Spirit is in his soul. Saint Paul says that the Holy Spirit asks for us with mourning and weeping unspeakable (Rom. 8.26); that is to say, he makes us ask and pray with mourning and weeping so plenteously that the tears may not be numbered. There may no evil spirit give these tokens, for (Saint) Jerome says that tears torment the Devil more than do the pains of Hell.[704]

The gift of tears

In the concluding prayer, Margery begins by praying the *Veni creator spiritus* and invoking the Spirit, which features prominently in the prayer itself: Margery believes that it is the Spirit alone which grants her the gift of tears, one of the most prominent features of the *Book*.[705] We have already seen that this aspect of Margery's behaviour has aroused the greatest criticism amongst modern commentators, and has given rise to suspicions of hysteria or of emotional self-indulgence. It also gave rise to much hostility amongst her contemporaries, as she herself tells us.[706] Yet such criticism misses the point. Margery did not weep during her illness, nor when her businesses failed, and begins to do so only in response to the experience of God revealing himself within her.[707] Her 'roaring' only began after her pilgrimage to Jerusalem, and again as a response to her heightened sense of identification with the suffering Christ; and 'she could not weep but when God gave it to her': the tears were an involuntary gift.[708]

It is thus as a theological, not psychological, phenomenon that we should see the gift of tears; and as such it is part of the long spiritual tradition of compunction and the 'baptism of tears'.[709] Margery's tears often had a redemptive or intercessory value.[710] The first specific reference to them within the *Book* itself (other than in the Prologue) occurs after she hears what she believes to be the music of heaven; and then she specifically relates them to contrition and compunction.[711] In the concluding prayer Margery makes it clear that she believes her tears to be at once an act of contrition for her sins, a means of increasing both her own and other people's love for Jesus, and an instrument for the conversion of others: indeed the bulk of the prayer is an extended act of intercession for a wide variety of people from the Pope to heretics, Saracens, lepers, her own enemies, and many others as well.[712] Earlier in the *Book* Christ tells her that

> I have ordained you to be a mirror amongst them [those who do not respond to God's word], to have great sorrow, so that they should take example from you . . . that they might through that be saved.[713]

Earlier still, we are told that

> The said creature was desired by many people to be with them at their dying and to pray for them, for, though they loved not her weeping nor her crying in their lifetime, they desired that she should both weep and cry when they were dying, and so she did.[714]

The powerful sense in which contemporaries recognized and valued Margery as an intercessor whose vocation was to participate in the redemptive work of Christ is reflected in texts such as these.

The Book as lay spirituality

Yet the crucial point was that Margery was to exercise this role in the world, as a lay and married woman. It was precisely this which clearly perplexed many of her contemporaries. At one point, after she had wept greatly, a monk declares that she should be shut up in a house of stone,[715] enclosure being the traditional solution to the problem of articulate spiritual women.[716] Margery always took great care to consult clerics, confessors and other male authority figures.[717] Nonetheless hostility to her does not diminish: at one point some men say to her

> Damsel, forsake this life that you have, and go and spin and card as other women do, and suffer not so much shame and so much woe.[718]

She replies that her suffering is as nothing in comparison with Christ's. At no point does she appear to consider withdrawing altogether from the secular world:[719] instead she seeks intimacy with Christ as a married person living in the world. Christ tells her that

> though the state of maidenhood be more perfect and more holy than the state of widowhood, and the state of widowhood more perfect than the state of wedlock, yet, daughter, I love you as well as any maiden in the world.[720]

Later Christ describes her as 'a maiden in your soul'.[721]

Margery is thus called to holiness, to radical identification with (and imitation of) Christ, yet within the constraints of domestic and married life. True, she struggles against those constraints all the time. She has a confidence and a capacity for individual initiative which reflects not just her prosperous background but something of the mercantile values of contemporary East Anglia; and she can and does bargain and argue with God as much as with archbishops and others. Towards the end of the *Book* she loses both her husband and her son; and her determination (despite her own advanced age) to accompany her bereaved daughter-in-law back home to Prussia causes her effectively to invert the story of Ruth and Naomi, and to display something of the resourcefulness of both.[722]

Conclusion

In the end Margery has to live with the tensions her vocation involves. The cost become clearest a little earlier in the *Book*, when Margery's husband falls down the stairs, injuring himself seriously, and Margery finds herself torn between her life of prayer and her responsibility to care for him. Christ says to her

> You shall have as much reward for looking after him and helping him in his need at home as if you were in church to say your prayers. And you have said many times that you would gladly look after me. I pray you now, look after him for love of me.[723]

This passage represents a major development in authentic lay spirituality. Rather than adapt religious life to lay conditions, here we see someone trying (albeit reluctantly and with great difficulty) to live a lay life religiously. And it is precisely the difficulties she experiences in so doing that underline her importance. As Bynum notes, Margery 'cannot write her own script',[724] or walk away from her domestic commitments as St Francis did so memorably at Assisi. She remains a woman in a man's world; she cannot in the final analysis control all that happens to her. Like the psalmist, struggling to make some spiritual sense out of what he or she cannot control or comprehend, Margery Kempe lays bare the cost and implications of seeking God in the midst of the world. And that is precisely her enduring value.

CONCLUSION: WALTER FRYE'S ANTIPHON

Towards the middle of the fifteenth century the English composer Walter Frye (d.1475) wrote a setting of the Marian antiphon *Ave regina celorum* (Hail, Queen of Heaven).[725] Little is known about Frye's life; but his music became popular across Europe, the *Ave regina celorum* alone surviving in almost twenty continental manuscripts (some from as far away as Hungary). The music will have been used for private devotion (perhaps in a merchant's or nobleman's household) rather than in public liturgy: its notes are also depicted in panel- and wall-paintings of the Assumption of Our Lady, which suggest that it was performed by confraternities dedicated to the Virgin, perhaps as a votive antiphon in their own chapels.[726] It is an exquisitely simple three-part piece; yet it is also intensely individual, reflecting melodic and rhythmic patterns used in continental courtly songs, and subtly highlighting in short quaver runs the repeated reference to Mary as *flos virginum* (flower of virgins).

In its international milieu, its delicate beauty, its intercessory prayer to Our Lady, but above all in its genuinely individual character, Frye's antiphon is characteristic not only of fifteenth-century sacred music but of the world of late medieval spirituality, both of which reflected a new interest in the private life and experience of the individual, whether as composer or listener to music, or as seeker after God.[727] Both the angels' song beloved of Richard Rolle and haunting motets such as those of Frye reflect something not to be found in earlier centuries: a new preoccupation with the self, a new confidence that even in the midst of terrible suffering individuals are not beyond the reach of a loving God, a tentative but unmistakable conviction that the quest for the suffering Jesus was a high adventure demanding all that the searcher had to give. Both Rolle's opening soliloquy and Frye's concluding motet breathe, in the dark perspectives of the later middle ages, the new air of the Renaissance:

> Hail, Queen of Heaven,
> mother of the king of angels!
> O Mary, flower of virgins,
> like a rose, like a lily,
> Pour forth your prayers to your Son
> for the salvation of the faithful.[728]

NOTES

1. *Super Canticum Canticorum,* ed. Murray, p. 45 lines 5–24, my translation.
2. For an excellent summary of this approach to Jesus, see J. L. Houlden, *Jesus: a question of identity* (London: SPCK, 1992), chapter 7. See also Constable (1995) pp. 194–248.
3. *Officium,* trans. Comper, p. 301. The *Officium* was written in c.1380 as part of an (unsuccessful) attempt to secure Rolle's canonization; but its existence reflects the popularity of Rolle soon after his death.
4. Dan Michel of Northgate, a black (=Benedictine) monk from Canterbury, who in 1340 translated (or possibly only copied) the French *Somme le Roi* (written in 1279 by Brother

Lorens, a Dominican) as *Ayenbite of Inwyt*, or 'Remorse of Conscience'. The reference is to p. 93 of the edition cited in the Bibliography. See also Pantin (1955) pp. 225–6.

5. L. C. Hector and B. Harvey (Oxford: Clarendon, 1982), pp. 84–5.

6. For summaries see A. Dyer, *Decline and growth in English towns 1400–1640* (London: Macmillan, 1991; repub. by Cambridge UP, 1995), esp. chapters 1–5; and D. M. Palliser, 'Urban society', in Horrox (1994ii) pp. 132–49.

7. For a general survey of late medieval England, see Thomson (1983).

8. The two make a fascinating comparison. William was a southerner, from Ockham (near Guildford), whilst Rolle was a Yorkshireman. William became deeply involved in contemporary political and ecclesiastical issues, in particular advocating poverty against a papacy anxious to defend church wealth: Rolle showed little interest in external issues at all. William's writing is immensely difficult, couched in the arcane formulae of late scholastic thought and eschewing all rhetoric and personal reflection: Rolle's is suffused with the passion of one who writes of what he has himself experienced. Yet both were at Oxford at the same time, and may even have met there: the academic careers of both were interrupted, Rolle's by his own choice and William's when he moved to London before being summoned to defend his opinions before the Pope at Avignon in 1324: both spent much of their lives in semi-itinerant obscurity; and both fell victim to the Black Death in the same year (1349), Richard in Yorkshire and William in Munich. For William's life, see Knowles (1962) chapter 27, and M. M. Adams, *William Ockham* (Indiana: Notre Dame UP, 1987).

9. See Leff (1975) p. 359.

10. See Oberman (1974).

11. William of Ockham, *Quodlibeta Septem,* VI q.1 a.1 in *Guillelmi de Ockham Opera Theologica,* ed. J. C. Wey, vol. 9 (St Bonaventure, NY: Franciscan Institute Press, 1967–86), p. 586; ET by A. J. Freddoso, *William of Ockham: Quodlibetal Questions,* vol. 2 (New Haven and London: Yale UP, 1991), pp. 491–2.

12. Thus Oberman (1986, p. 29) writes: 'Nominalism [the term frequently applied to the thought of William and his followers] did call traditional truths and answers into question in order to replace them with a new vision of the relationship between the sacred and the secular by presenting coordination as an alternative to subordination and partnership of persons instead of the hierarchy of being.'

13. 'Man's merits and demerits usually decide his eternal fate, although positive exceptions may be made, as in the case of the Virgin Mary and St. Paul. Even faith in Christ may not be necessary; if a person lived according to right reason, God might ordain his salvation. Reprobation results only from sin in time' (C. T. Davis (1974) p. 63).

14. This point is vividly made by the anonymous late-fourteenth- or early-fifteenth-century author of *Contemplations of the dread and love of God.* The author begins by describing 'our holy fathers in old time that for love of God forsook the world and everything worldly, and lived in the desert on grass and roots. Such men were fervent in the love of God, but I believe there be few if any who follow them now, for we do not find by God's commandment that we should live thus' (p. 5, my transliteration).

15. See the extracts from contemporary texts in Horrox (1994i).

16. Quoted in Briggs (1983) p. 86.

17. Quoted and trans. Horrox (1994i) p. 124.

18. Knowles (1955, vol. II, p. 74) argues that it contributed significantly to isolating England from currents of continental thought, though in view of the continued inflow of texts and ideas from continental sources during this period his view should be treated with caution. McKisack (*The fourteenth century, 1307–1399* (The Oxford history of England) (Oxford: Clarendon, 1959), pp. 149–51) argues that the war massively increased English xenophobia. See also B. C. Keeney, 'Military service and the development of nationalism in England, 1272–1327', in *Speculum* 22 (1947), esp. pp. 536–7; and Thomson (1983) pp. 65–72.

19. For the Peasants' Revolt see Fryde (1981); Thomson (1983) pp. 25–31; Poos (1991) pp. 231–49; Swanson (1993ii) pp. 101–2.

20. Hence the vigorous denunciations of cardinals in Langland's *Piers Plowman,* B-text, Prologue and Passus XIX. See also Oberman (1986) p. 22, and Harper-Bill (1989). Huizinga (1924, p. 21) describes the fanatical hatreds engendered by the schism. Telesca (1971) underlines its destructive impact on the life of the Cistercian order.

21. *Scale of perfection* I.62, p. 133.

22. Literally 'dyvynys', i.e. theologians.

23. Chaucer, The Knight's Tale (1 (A) 1303–28), text slightly modernized.

24. Brown (1995, p. 4) points out that, in response to the decrees of the Fourth Lateran Council of 1215, bishops of Salisbury in this period 'began to show an unprecedented interest in laying down the responsibilities of lay people to their local churches'. See also Mason (1976), and Poos (1991) p. 275. Kümin (1996, p. 119) points to the evidence of laypeople having a greater understanding of the Church's teaching than is often supposed.

25. See also Bossy (1973), esp. pp. 140–2. Note however that the geographical pattern of the parochial system was largely fixed by the end of the twelfth century (Brown (1995) p. 70 and n. 12).

26. Rosser (1991) p. 174; P. Collinson, *The Religion of Protestants: the Church in English society 1559–1625* (Oxford: Clarendon, 1982) p. 281.

27. In Great Yarmouth by the twelfth century there was a chapel on the seashore open during the herring-season for fishermen (Rosser (1991) p. 178 and n. 22).

28. Pantin (1948) p. 374.

29. The Council of Lambeth drew up a schema of instruction for the laity, usually known as the *Ignorantia sacerdotum,* which was to be expounded in the vernacular to parishioners four times a year (Duffy (1992) p. 53): it was adapted and versified by Archbishop Thoresby of York in 1357 as the *Lay folks' catechism* (Duffy (1992) pp. 53–4; Pantin (1955) pp. 211–12). In late medieval Norwich the existence of standard liturgical books in lay wills suggests that at least some laypeople had a great interest in liturgy (Tanner (1984) p. 111). Nichols (1994, p. 259 and n. 54) suggests that the consistent presence of laypeople in contemporary iconography of the Eucharist argues that the sacrament was conceived of not only in terms of clerical power but as being 'the work – the liturgy – of all the people'.

30. It is important to note that eucharistic devotion could have unattractive implications: Miri Rubin has pointed out the link between reverence for the Eucharist and active persecution of the Jews because of their presumed irreverence for the sacrament: *Gentile tales: the narrative assault on late medieval Jews* (Yale UP, 1999).

31. Mirk, *Festial,* EETS e.s. 96, pp. 173–5.

32. Hughes (1988) pp. 240–1.

33. Love, *Myrrour,* ed. cit., pp. 208–9.

34. See Rubin (1991), esp. chapter 3; and D. M. Palliser ('Urban Society', in Horrox (1994ii) p. 147), who suggests that Corpus Christi plays and processions were important in fostering a sense of civic harmony (and perhaps identity too).

35. Johnson (1976) p. 378.

36. Statutes of Coventry (1224–37), quoted by Rubin (1991) p. 57.

37. Rubin (1991) p. 62.

38. *The lay folks' Mass book,* EETS o.s. 105/109, p. 141, quoted in Rubin (1991) p. 105.

39. See Duffy (1992) pp. 118–19.

40. ed. Pantin (1976) p. 399.

41. Duffy (1992) p. 99. Duffy offers no evidence for his suggestion that 'many lay people, perhaps even most of them', attended weekday masses regularly; see p. 112. Colin Richmond makes an interesting suggestion: that the increasing preference among the gentry for their own private religion, with their own chapel and priest and perhaps even their own reliquary, crucially helped to point the way forward to the Reformation – which was unquestionably facilitated by the increasing role of the gentry ('Religion and the fifteenth-century gentleman', in Dobson (1984) pp. 193–208, esp. p. 198).

42. EETS 275, p. 196. Norman Cohn (*The pursuit of the millennium* (London, 1957; Paladin,

1970) p. 200) points out that *Dives and Pauper* stressed the common and egalitarian nature of all God's creation.

43. EETS 275, p. 202.

44. The author of *The chastising of God's children* (see note 49) warns of the perils of giving preference to one's own private prayers over public ones simply because one feels more spiritually uplifted by the former (chapter 21, ed. Bazire & Colledge, p. 220).

45. Bossy (1991) p. 148.

46. See Driver (1989). The author of *Dives and Pauper* defends the use of imagery as 'a book to lewd folk' (EETS 275, p. 2) and a means of stirring people's affections and their hearts to devotion more effectively than books could do (p. 82).

47. Orme (1994) p. 566.

48. Sargent (1983) p. 303, Swanson (1993ii) p. 91. On this subject, see especially Lovatt (1965), Riehle (1981), Lovatt (1982), and Sargent (1983). In terms of the transmission of texts, Sargent (1983, p. 303) argues that England received far more from the continent than it gave in return; though the influence of Wyclif on the continent was considerable (Kenny (1985) p. 102). It is striking that the reception of ideas and material from Europe had a strongly regional bias: continental spiritual texts circulated much more extensively in eastern England, from Yorkshire to London, than elsewhere, reflecting both the mercantile prosperity of towns like Norwich and the religious vitality of areas like Yorkshire (Lovatt (1965) p. 365). For Norwich, see Tanner (1984); for Yorkshire, see Hughes (1988). All new charterhouses (Carthusian monasteries) in this period were founded on or near the east coast.

49. A good example of this is *The chastising of God's children*, which appeared in English soon after 1382 and became very popular throughout the fifteenth century: it is a Middle English devotional compilation of texts by various authors, of whom the principal one was the Flemish mystical writer Jan van Ruusbroec (or Ruysbroeck) (1293–1381); but the meaning of the original writers is often extensively altered to suit the compiler's intended audience (it was probably designed to be read in refectory in a religious community of women) and to serve his particular orthodox interests. Bazire and Colledge (*The chastising*, p. 78) arguably exaggerate the extent to which the compiler adapted his material because he was writing for 'simple-minded women' who needed protecting from the higher reaches of contemplative prayer: it is much more likely that the compiler was not at ease with these higher reaches himself, as he suggests in his Prologue (p. 95).

50. pp. 12–13.

51. See the article by Carruthers (1996), in which he explores how the author of *The abbey* seeks to commend monastic patterns of holiness to a lay audience.

52. E.g. in *Contemplations of the dread and love of God*, where Augustine is constantly quoted implicitly or explicitly. Elliott (1993, p. 189) points out the extent to which clerical confessors and spiritual guides encouraged laypeople, especially women, to foster patterns of piety which made no reference to their physical or familial contexts, thereby encouraging a 'detached' form of spirituality. But cf. this argument with that of Nicholas Watson (1997), who argues convincingly that texts like *Pearl* and *Sir Gawain and the Green Knight* were written precisely to offer spiritual reassurance to aristocratic readers by insisting that those living *in mundo* were no less lofty in spiritual terms than recluses or virgins: they thereby present a more outward-centred pattern of piety.

53. Harper-Bill (1989) p. 86, Rubin (1991) p. 156. For this subject in general see Duffy (1992) pp. 209–98, Rosser (1991), and Mertes (1987).

54. Duffy (1992) p. 231.

55. Littlehales, introduction to *The lay folks' prayer book*, p. xlviii.

56. Many believed that those who crossed themselves during this recitation would be protected from harm that day; Duffy (1992) p. 215. The seven 'Penitential Psalms' were particularly popular: see, e.g., the translation in EETS o.s. 155 (1921), of which numerous different versions survive (probably reflecting individual taste), and the more liturgical translation attributed to Thomas Brampton (1402), in 'A paraphrase of the seven penitential psalms', ed.

W. H. Black, in Percy Society 7 (London, 1842); cf. also 'Thomas Brampton's metrical paraphrase of the seven penitential psalms', ed. J. R. Kreuzer, in *Traditio* 7 (1949), pp. 359–403, and Kuczynski (1995) pp. 124–35.

57. One of these, in a sixteenth-century manuscript, was produced by one Richard Hill; and its contents give a fascinating insight into the seriousness with which devout and literate families sought to foster a pattern of spirituality suitable for their own particular circumstances and character: see Mertes (1987).

58. See the extract from *A collection of ordinances and regulations for the government of the Royal Household* (London: Society of Antiquaries, 1790, pp. 37–9), cited in J. Ward (ed.), *Women of the English nobility and gentry, 1066–1500* (Manchester medieval sources) (Manchester UP, 1995), pp. 217–18. This text has been much discussed: for a succinct summary, see Leyser (1995/6) pp. 232–3.

59. The fifteenth century has been called the 'golden age' of gilds (G. Rosser, 'The Anglo-Saxon gilds', in J. Blair, *Minsters and parish churches: the local church in transition 950–1200* (Oxford UP, 1988), pp. 31–5; Brown (1995) p. 132 and n. 2. See also Phythian-Adams (1979) chapters 7 and 8; and Kümin (1996) pp. 149–59, esp. pp. 153–4.

60. See the ordinance of the Gild of Holy Trinity Cambridge in Toulmin Smith (1870/92) pp. 264–5; Tanner (1984) pp. 67–8; Rosser (1988) pp. 32 and 40. For parish-based craft gilds and fraternities see Brown (1995) pp. 132–58 and 179.

61. Fleming (1991) p. 10. Gilds also had a gerontocratic dimension, seniority and age being virtually synonymous (Phythian-Adams (1979) p. 114).

62. Toulmin Smith, in EETS o.s. 40 p. 155.

63. Toulmin Smith, introduction to EETS o.s. 40, p. xxx. See also Rosser (1988) p. 34.

64. See P. J. P. Goldberg, 'Women', in Horrox (1994ii) pp. 115–16. Phythian-Adams (1979, p. 88) points out that most late medieval women were kept busy working at home all day: legally inferior to men, 'a woman's main weapon remained her tongue' (p. 89).

65. Gilds were restricted to those who had some means (Rosser (1988) p. 35), though the ordinance of the Gild of St Michael-on-the-Hill Lincoln states that membership should be restricted to 'the rank of common and middling folks' (*de statu communum et mediocrum virorum*), Toulmin Smith edn, EETS o.s. 40, p. 178). People had to be financially (and thus socially) respectable (Rosser (1988) p. 36). Membership of a gild was felt to be superior to mere membership of a parish and in many ways anticipates membership of a 'sect' after the Reformation (Rosser (1988) p. 37). There was also doubtless a fair measure of secrecy about them (the ordinance of the Gild of the Blessed Virgin at Chesterfield specifically proscribes those who reveal its affairs to outsiders: Toulmin Smith edn, EETS o.s. 40, p. 167).

66. Rosser (1988) p. 44.

67. Ordinance cited in Toulmin Smith, EETS o.s. 40, p. 139.

68. Ordinance cited in Toulmin Smith, EETS o.s. 40, p. 37.

69. Ordinance cited in Toulmin Smith, EETS o.s. 40, pp. 111–12.

70. See Tanner (1984) p. 74, on Norwich gilds.

71. Ordinance cited in Toulmin Smith, EETS o.s. 40, p. 172.

72. Ordinance of the Gild of Taylors at Lincoln, cited in Toulmin Smith, EETS o.s. 40, p. 183.

73. Orme (1994) p. 583.

74. Both gilds and fraternities frequently took responsibility for organizing the funerals of their members. See J. Litten, *The English way of death: the common funeral since 1450* (London: Robert Hale, 1992), pp. 9–11.

75. Scarisbrick (1984) p. 23.

76. Scarisbrick (1984) pp. 20–1. Fraternities may also have helped to create a sense of devotional identity in large parishes (Brown (1995) p. 143).

77. Text in Kettle (1976).

78. Kettle (1976) p. viii.

79. See Edwards (1967) pp. 318–19.

80. See especially P. Sheldrake, *Spirituality and history* (London: SPCK, 1991).

81. At the same time we need to recall that the late medieval growth in personal piety and in what we might call lay spiritual confidence did not necessarily lead to heterodox beliefs: see, e.g., Brown (1995) p. 208 and n. 36.

82. Hudson (1988) p. 10. For these sermons see Spencer (1993), esp. pp. 257–8 and 277–80.

83. Recent scholarship has, however, demonstrated the remarkable extent to which Lollardy came to penetrate the whole of local society in areas where it took root. See D. Plumb, 'The social and economic status of the later Lollards' and 'A gathered church? Lollards and their society', in M. Spufford (ed.), *The world of rural dissenters, 1520–1725* (Cambridge UP, 1995), pp. 103–63. On the nature of the Lollard movement, see Margaret Aston, 'Were the Lollards a sect?', in P. Biller and B. Dobson (eds.), *The medieval Church: universities, heresy and the religious life (Essays in honour of Gordon Leff)* (Studies in church history, subsidia 11) (Woodbridge: Boydell, 1999), pp. 163–92.

84. Hudson (1988) p. 116; Catto (1999).

85. See McLaughlin (1973) for a discussion of how this assumption has affected our understanding of the continental 'Free Spirit' movement. The majority of Lollards were in any case from the middle ranks of society (Hudson (1988) pp. 128–34). For a nuanced discussion of the relationship between the spread of Lollard ideas and widespread existing (or latent) antinomianism, each feeding the other, see Poos (1991) pp. 231–79.

86. Swanson (1993ii) p. 330.

87. Hudson (1988) p. 393. For the influence of Franciscan spirituality on Wyclif, see Wilks (1994).

88. Kenny (1985) pp. 95–6; Hudson (1988) pp. 2 and 117.

89. See Hudson (1985) pp. 85–110; Kenny (1985) pp. 95–6, 101–2; Hudson (1988) p. 2; Swanson (1993ii) p. 332; Catto (1999).

90. McFarlane (1952) p. 13; Cross (1976/87) p. 15; Hudson (1988) p. 225. Ronald Knox (*Enthusiasm* (Oxford: Clarendon, 1950), p. 114) argues, not unreasonably, both that the ever-increasing obscurity of contemporary academic debate encouraged an anti-intellectual reaction, and that such a reaction inevitably carried the risk of becoming dangerously irrational.

91. For an excellent summary of his life, see Hudson (1988) pp. 1–13. For the complexity of his works, see p. 104. Wyclif's sermons, however, which he edited and published towards the end of his life, are much more accessible, and may have been intended as model sermons for sympathetic preachers (see Kenny (1985) p. 96).

92. 'All the goods of God should be common. This is proved thus. Every man should be in a state of grace; and if he is in a state of grace, he is lord of the world and all it contains. So every man should be lord of the universe. But this is not consistent with there being many men, unless they ought to have everything in common. Therefore all things should be in common.' (Wyclif, *De civili dominio,* trans. and cited in Kenny (1985) p. 47).

93. McFarlane (1952) p. 118; Kenny (1985) pp. 64–6.

94. Wyclif, *Confession on the Eucharist,* in Hudson (1978), p. 17. Nichols (1994, p. 91) argues that the Church sought to erase the Lollard attack on the sacraments by a vigorous deployment of art representing orthodox teaching on the seven sacraments, especially in East Anglia: though Claire Cross (review of Nichols in *History* 81 (1996) p. 254) queries how far it really was Lollardy, rather than fashion and imitation, which caused this deployment.

95. See especially Passus XIX, where it becomes clear that the purification of the church is inseparable from personal sanctity, the former depending on the latter; see also Simpson (1990). On the relationship between Langland and Lollardy, see Hudson (1988) pp. 401–8; Anna P. Baldwin, 'The historical context', in Alford (1988) p. 73; and Wilks (1994).

96. Passus XIX–XX; Simpson (1990) p. 222.

97. Hudson (1988) pp. 21–2.

98. Kenny (1985) pp. 68–79; Hudson (1988) p. 169; Wilks (1995).

99. Wyclif was, however, opposed to both the ideal and the practice of monasticism: see Hudson (1988) pp. 22 and 349–50. For Wyclif's own views on priesthood, see his *De officio pastorali*

(original Latin version, ed. G. V. Lechler (Leipzig & London: Wyclif Society, 1863); Middle English version in F. D. Matthew (ed.), *The English works of Wyclif hitherto unprinted* (EETS o.s. 74) (1880; repr. 1975), pp. 405–57; extracts in modern English in Jeffrey (1988) pp. 295–9.

100. *The order of priesthood* 4 (attributed to Wyclif), in EETS o.s. 74, p. 168.

101. Sermon for Lent 4 in *Lollard Sermons*, EETS 294, pp. 185–6.

102. *How Satan and his priests* chapter 4, EETS o.s. 74, p. 274.

103. 'Highness of state maketh not evermore a man better to God', Sermon for Trinity 3, in *English Wycliffite sermons* (1983) p. 233.

104. ET in Jeffrey (1988) pp. 282–3. For Clanvowe, see Cross (1976/87) pp. 19–22.

105. See Sermon for Trinity 8, in *English Wycliffite sermons* (1983) p. 253.

106. Hence the characteristic Lollard stress on, and love of, preaching; see Hudson (1988) p. 197.

107. Sermon for Trinity 2 in *English Wycliffite sermons* (1983) p. 228.

108. Sermon for Lent 2, *Lollard sermons*, EETS 294, p. 159.

109. Quoted by Foxe in *Acts and Monuments* (ed. S. R. Cattley) vol. 4, p. 229; Hudson (1988) p. 313.

110. Sermon for Lent 2, *Lollard sermons*, EETS 294, p. 161. There is some evidence for the idea of Lollard saints (including Wyclif himself; Hudson (1988) p. 171), and for Lollards praying at their places of martyrdom (p. 172).

111. Sermon for Epiphany, *Lollard sermons*, EETS 294, pp. 77–8.

112. Sermon for Advent 2, *Lollard sermons*, EETS 294, p. 15.

113. Sermon for Sexagesima, *Lollard sermons*, EETS 294, p. 98.

114. The Paternoster (text attributed to Wyclif), in EETS o.s. 74 p. 201. For the importance of the Paternoster in this period, see V. Gillespie, 'Thy will be done: Piers Plowman and the Paternoster', in A. J. Minnis (ed.), *Late-medieval religious texts and their transmission: essays in honour of A. I. Doyle* (Cambridge: D. S. Brewer, 1994), pp. 95–120.

115. Sermon for Lent 2, *Lollard sermons*, EETS 294, p. 162. The citation of Augustine is from his *Sermones de scripturis* 16, PL 38:381.

116. Sermon for Advent Sunday, *Lollard sermons*, EETS 294, p. 4. The author of *Of prelates*, a text attributed to Wyclif, declares that 'Prayer standeth principally in a good life' (chapter 11, EETS o.s. 74, p. 76).

117. Sermon for Christmas Day, *Lollard sermons*, EETS 294, pp. 54–65. The reference to the Golden Legend is to the description therein of 'The birth of Our Lord Jesus Christ according to the flesh', trans. W. G. Ryan, vol. 1, pp. 37–43. Texts such as this should not, however, lead us to assume that Lollardy flourished only among the poor: Derek Plumb points out ('The social and economic spread of rural Lollardy: a reappraisal', in W. J. Sheils and D. Wood (eds.), *Voluntary religion* (Studies in church history 23) (Oxford: Blackwell, 1986), pp. 111–30) that many relatively prosperous folk, some of them holding recognized offices such as local bailiff or churchwarden, were Lollards.

118. Sermon for Septuagesima, EETS 294, pp. 86–7, quoting St Bernard; or the 'Sermon of Dead Men', in the same volume.

119. See Hughes (1988) pp. 218–19.

120. The English text of the *Ancrene Riwle* (Pepys MS 2498), ed. A. Zettersten (EETS o.s. 274, 1976), pp. 27–8. See E. Colledge, 'A Lollard interpolated version of the Ancren Riwle', in *Review of English Studies* 15 (1939), pp. 1–15 and 129–45, esp. pp. 7–8.

121. 'Sermon of Dead Men', in *Lollard sermons*, EETS 294, pp. 238–9.

122. See, e.g., this extract from a Lollard sermon: 'It were wonderful that these sinful fools [monks, canons etc.] should find a better rule than Christ himself founded' (Sermon for Trinity 11, ed. Hudson (1983) p. 265). See also Hughes (1988) p. 115 and refs; Hudson (1988) pp. 27 and 349–50. There is a Lollard version of the *Ancrene Riwle* (ed. in EETS 274 (1976)). It is possible that this version was designed to adapt the spirituality of the *Ancrene Riwle* for lay Lollards, but unlikely – Hudson (1988, pp. 27–8) argues instead that it was originally an orthodox version clumsily or perfunctorily revised by a Lollard.

123. Colin Richmond ('Religion', in Horrox (1994ii) p. 192) goes further, arguing that there were virtually no outstanding figures in the fifteenth-century church apart from Henry V: people of exceptional ability were drawn to practise law rather than religion.

124. Power (1922, pp. 288–9) argues that, once the crucial Benedictine balance of prayer, work, and study was lost by the omission of the latter two, the entire spirit of the order went with it: she cites fifteenth-century episcopal injunctions against nuns who wandered idly in the garden instead of coming to compline, or overslept and missed mattins as a result of sitting up drinking and gossiping after compline the night before (pp. 291–2). See also Thomson (1983) pp. 335–6.

125. See Desmond (1971).

126. See the study by Marilyn Oliva, *The convent and the community in late medieval England: female monasteries in the Diocese of Norwich, 1350–1540* (Studies in the history of medieval religion 12) (Woodbridge: Boydell, 1998), esp. p. 212. Some women's communities showed signs of decay as well: the visitation of the Bishop of Lincoln to Elstow Abbey in 1421–2 revealed 'grave shipwreck' in the purity of the religious life there, especially (in the Bishop's view) because of 'the stay of visitors in the said monastery, especially of married persons' (see the extract printed in Goldberg (1995) pp. 266–71).

127. See Knowles, *Religious Orders* II (1955) pp. 129–38; Hogg (1980); Hogg (1989). The chartas of the Carthusian general chapter and their dealings with the English province during the fifteenth century give the impression of a serious and committed order with only minor abuses disturbing the even tenor of its enclosed and ordered life. Catto (1999, pp. 147–8) points out that some prominent Lollards defected from the movement and became Carthusians, which testifies to their influence at the time.

128. Salter (1974) p. 26; though Lovatt (1984, p. 183), exploring John Blacman's description of the spirituality of Henry VI, stresses the impact of the Carthusians on the former, and perhaps on both. See also Ann Hutchison, 'Devotional reading in the monastery and in the late medieval household', in Sargent (1989, pp. 215–27) for the influence of the Carthusians on the spirituality of aristocratic women in this period.

129. On the enthusiastic support of the nobility for the Carthusians, see Hughes (1988); see also Knowles, *Religious Orders* II (1955) p. 134, and Tanner (1984) pp. 124–5.

130. See the Carthusian Customs (*Consuetudines Cartusiae*) of Prior Guigo I, in *Guigues Ier: Coutumes de Chartreuse* (Sources Chrétiennes 303) (Paris: Editions du Cerf, 1984), 28:4, p. 224.

131. Lovatt (1965) p. 395. The new Carthusian communities in eastern England were linked to their continental houses and were a key link with Rhineland spirituality: in 1415 Henry V made provision for seven monks from Germany in his monastery at Sheen (Hughes (1988) p. 104). Although Carthusian houses tended to become more insular after the creation in 1369 of the Carthusian Provincia Angliae, contacts with the continent remained considerable (Hogg (1983i) p. 257). It is important to note, however, that the influence of the *devotio moderna* on English Carthusian life was relatively slight, due in part at least to the conservatism of the order as a whole (Hogg (1983i), esp. p. 268). For the significance of the Carthusian practice of copying spiritual texts for wider dissemination, see L. Cox Ward, 'The e Museo 160 manuscript: writing and reading as remedy', in J. Hogg (ed.), *The mystical tradition and the Carthusians* vol. 4 (Analecta Cartusiana 130) (Salzburg: Institut für Anglistik und Amerikanistik, 1995), pp. 68–86.

132. Hughes (1988) p. 104; Hogg (1978).

133. Nothing is known about him before his appointment first as rector and then as prior. He died in 1424. For Love, see Salter (1974); Hogg (1980); and Spencer (1993) pp. 186–8.

134. ed. J. Hogg, Analecta Cartusiana 31 (Salzburg, 1977), pp. 91–119. References to some of Methley's other works will be found in the Bibliography to this chapter.

135. See Hughes (1988) p. 104. For Methley's translation of Porete, see Watson (1996), esp. pp. 48–9.

136. See Hogg (1980).

137. See Knowles (1962) p. 151; but see also Knowles' typically evocative description of Methley in *Religious orders* II (1955), pp. 225–6.
138. Hogg (1980) p. 37. Hogg (p. 31) suggests that Methley's later work reflects a more serene, less exuberantly enthusiastic, spirituality; but Lochrie (1991, pp. 216–17) argues that the aim of his later works was quite different than that of the earlier ones.
139. Knowles (1955) vol. II, p. 222.
140. Tanner (1984) p. 64. In the same way the continental *devotio moderna* movement (itself a reaction against what was perceived to be the unfettered speculativeness of the Dominican Meister Eckhart) had only a limited influence in England: its adaptation of monastic piety for lay purposes, together with its stress on imitation of Christ and on seeking union with God through conformity with his will, are echoed in much late medieval English piety. Here too, however, English readers and compilers seem to have stressed the more conservative characteristics of the movement (such as its anti-intellectualism), avoiding its more innovative ideas (such as its approach to community life). Thus the anonymous Middle English version of Henry Suso's *Horologium*, entitled *The treatise of the seven points of true love and everlasting wisdom,* drastically alters the original, whose elevated rhetoric is replaced by practical and prosaic piety. See Lovatt (1965) pp. 330–1; and (for the *devotio moderna* in general) Hogg (1983i) and Gründler (1988).
141. See esp. Aelred's *De institutione inclusarum* (refs. in the Bibliography to Chapter 3).
142. See Davis (1985). The life of St Paul (of Thebes), by tradition the first Christian hermit, was written by St Jerome (ET in W. H. Fremantle (trans.), *St Jerome: Letters and select works* (Nicene and Post-Nicene Fathers, 2nd series, vol. 6), pp. 299–303. A summary of it, popular in the late middle ages, appears in *The golden legend of Jacobus de Voragine* (trans. cit. in Bibliography), vol. 1, pp. 84–5.
143. Hughes (1988) p. 80.
144. This opposition was caused partly by the intemperate manner in which Rolle defended his chosen way of life by exalting it above all others and by criticizing those who embraced the monastic life in letter but not in spirit (see above all his *Emendatio vitae*); partly by the fact that Rolle's life as a recluse was in many respects irregular (he seems to have made no attempt to have gained episcopal permission, nor was he under the authority or guidance of a religious community); and partly by his frequent changes of location: the author of the *Officium* significantly defends him against charges of instability, undoubtedly reflecting the seriousness of such an accusation ('Frequent change of place does not always come from inconstancy', Comper trans., pp. 306–7).
145. Allen (1927) pp. 449–58. John lost his lands because of his support for Thomas, earl of Lancaster, whose revolt against Edward II ended in defeat in 1322. See also M. McKisack, *The fourteenth century (1307–1399)* (The Oxford history of England V) (Oxford: Clarendon, 1959), pp. 64–7.
146. *Dives and Pauper,* VI.13, EETS 280, pp. 92–3.
147. On the role of recluses as keepers of bridges, see esp. Kerry (1892). One document from c.1490 calls on people to give alms to one John Ferrour, a hermit on the bridge between Oxford and Abingdon, in return for which he would both undertake to keep it in good repair and pray for those who contributed (text in Swanson (1993i) pp. 204–5). See also Thomson (1983) p. 59; Tanner (1984) p. 62; Duffy (1992) p. 367.
148. Hughes (1988) pp. 77–8.
149. Tanner (1984) p. 63.
150. The 'solitude' of the recluse was a manner of life objectively demarcated (and usually given formal episcopal sanction); but it did not necessarily involve total separation from other people, recluses being much in demand as spiritual guides. See Jantzen (1987) pp. 28–50.
151. The anonymous author of the early-fifteenth-century treatise *Dives and Pauper* argues that witchcraft and invocation of the devil are very widespread, particularly among older people, who then lead the young astray (EETS 275, p. 165; see also p. 163). Pantin argues (1955, p. 209 n. 1) that fear of witchcraft seems to have been less prominent in the fourteenth century

than it became later; but Duffy has recently and convincingly argued against the theory that such a world-view was held only by the unlettered and the credulous (1992, pp. 277–9).

152. Duffy (1992) p. 136.
153. *Showings,* LT (Long Text) 67, ed. cit., pp. 635–6.
154. See Erickson (1976) chapter 1.
155. For Gawain see esp. Watson (1997) (and see n. 52 above), and the remarks of Andrew and Waldron (*The poems of the Pearl manuscript* (1996), pp. 36–43). For *Pearl* see pp. 29–36 of the same work.
156. D. D. R. Owen, *Noble lovers* (London: Phaidon, 1975), pp. 78–9.
157. For the Parson's tale see Bestul (1989).
158. The Parson's tale (from *The Canterbury tales*), ed. cit., X (I), pp. 78–80.
159. Kieckhefer (1988) pp. 102–3; Pantin (1955) p. 192. See also Nichols (1994) for the influence of font carvings in conveying the Church's teaching on penance.
160. See Rubin (1991) p. 84; Duffy (1992) p. 60; Hughes (1988) pp. 120–1.
161. Mirk's *Festial*, ed. cit. p. 2.
162. *Showings* (ed. cit.), LT 24, pp. 394–5; LT 39, p. 452.
163. *Livre de seyntz medicines*, ed. cit., pp. 65–6. For other examples of late medieval use of the image of an interior castle, see Hamburger (1997), esp. pp. 168–75; for the importance of the heart in late medieval monastic piety, see Hamburger (1997) chapter 4.
164. p. 101.
165. Pantin (1976) pp. 398–9.
166. Walter Hilton, *Scale of perfection* II.7, p. 201.
167. *Scale of perfection* II.8, pp. 203–4.
168. *Scale of perfection* II.9, p. 205.
169. *Scale of perfection* II.9, p. 205. Cf. also II.12, where Hilton argues that even those whose images are reformed must carry within themselves the potential for sin (p. 213).
170. On the relationship between them, see Kieckhefer (1984) pp. 64–5; Elliott (1993) p. 241 n. 173.
171. Hence the traditional role of humility as the *radix virtutum*, the root of all other virtues (e.g. in the fourteenth-century de Lisle Psalter; see Sandler (1983) p. 50 and adjacent plate). For humility in the Augustinian tradition, see J. M. Rist, *Augustine: ancient thought baptized* (Cambridge UP, 1994), pp. 158 and 188–91.
172. *Scale of perfection* I.1, p. 77.
173. *Scale of perfection* I.16, p. 88.
174. *Scale of perfection* I.16, p. 89.
175. *Scale of perfection* I.40, p. 111.
176. *Scale of perfection* I.42, p. 112.
177. *Scale of perfection* I.42, p. 112.
178. Clark (1990) pp. 126–7.
179. See *Scale of perfection* II.21 and Clark (1990) pp. 128–9.
180. *Scale of perfection* I.58, p. 128.
181. See *Scale of perfection* II.37, p. 273.
182. *Scale of perfection* II.34, p. 266.
183. *Scale of perfection* II.20, p. 225.
184. See especially *Scale of perfection* II.20, a balanced account of this.
185. See Clark (1990) p. 131. *Scale of perfection* II.20 is again the key chapter in regard to this theme; and it is worth noting Clark's point that Hilton's Trinitarian emphasis is strongest from this chapter onwards (Clark (1990) p. 126). For Hilton, imitation of, or identification with, Jesus involves being caught up in the life of the Trinity, for the Trinity is wholly realized in Jesus (Kennedy (1982) p. 292).
186. See Simpson (1990) and Wittig (1972) for detailed explorations of this theme. Langland certainly knew the pseudo-Bernardian *Meditationes piissimae de cognitione humanae conditionis*, which is a late medieval compilation of Augustinian reflection on the importance of

self-knowledge (rather than worldly *scientia*) as the key starting-point for the ascent of the soul to God (Wittig (1972) pp. 212–14; Kerby-Fulton (1990) p. 68).

187. Hence Wittig: 'Witte [a character in *Piers Plowman*] shows how the renewal of the kingship, Christian society, and marriage interlocks with the renewal of the internal, microcosmic society – the individual person. If reform occurs there, it will accordingly be manifested not only in society's smallest unit, marriage, but also in the larger *civitas*' (Wittig (1972) p. 228). Wittig argues that these central passus of Langland's poem 'are the nub of Langland's rhetorical address, that his concern with the reform of society gradually closes its focus to the individual human will, and that it finally expands the implications of individual reform to embrace the universal Church and its history' (p. 280). See also Kuczynski (1995) pp. 189–215 for an exploration of how Langland uses the Psalter in order to articulate the essence of his reforming vision.

188. So Chaucer, in the Parson's tale, ed. cit., p. 488.

189. Kieckhefer (1984) p. 11. For the importance of patience in late medieval hagiography (esp. in Suso and St Catherine of Siena), see Kieckhefer (1984) pp. 50–88. The author of *Contemplations of the dread and love of God* sees patience in precisely this way (ed. cit., pp. 36–9). For patience as imitative of the Virgin, see the Middle English text of the *Revelations* of St Bridget, EETS 178 p. 12.

190. Baldwin (1990) p. 76. For a straightforward account that exemplifies the latter approach see Rolle, *Emendatio vitae* 6.

191. See Baldwin (1990) p. 83.

192. Passus XIII.

193. Passus XIV; Simpson (1990) p. 148. It represents something similar in Chaucer's Nun's Priest's tale, with the description of Chauntecleer's owner, the 'povre wydwe [poor widow]' who 'in pacience ladde [led] a ful symple lyf', VII.2825.

194. Alford (1988) p. 51.

195. See Baldwin (1990) *passim*.

196. *The form of living*, EETS 293, p. 11.

197. Oberman (1986, p. 22) argues that the Franciscans were more in tune with the contemporary *Zeitgeist* than the other orders, and that consequently late medieval spirituality was dominated by them.

198. Pantin (1948) p. 348.

199. Passus XI, l. 255; ed. cit., p. 452. For the importance of poverty for Langland, and his position in relation to contemporary debates between mendicants and others, see Kerby-Fulton (1990), esp. pp. 140–53 and 192–3. For an absorbing exploration of the way medieval people variously interpreted the story of Mary and Martha (though he does not mention Langland), see G. Constable, 'The interpretation of Mary and Martha', in *Three studies in medieval religious and social thought* (Cambridge UP, 1995), pp. 1–141.

200. Passus XI ll .257–69, ed. cit., pp. 452–3.

201. See Wittig (1972) pp. 260–1.

202. Passus XIV ll. 117–20, ed. cit., pp. 519–20.

203. *English Psalter*, p. 82 (on Psalm 22.27).

204. *English Psalter*, p. 82 (on Psalm 22.31).

205. See Erickson (1976) pp. 84–7.

206. See Swanson (1993ii) pp. 225–6 and 295. The vicissitudes of the different shrines is complex, and the attraction of many lesser ones was short-lived: see R. C. Finucane, *Miracles and pilgrims: popular beliefs in medieval England* (London: Dent, 1977).

207. For the economic implications, see Swanson (1993ii) p. 247. For the social ones, Chaucer's work is the obvious starting-point.

208. Tristram (1955) p. 92.

209. Tanner (1984) p. 85. For the value of wills in general as sources of lay piety, see M. Spufford, *Contrasting communities* (Cambridge UP, 1974), pp. 320–2, and C. R. Burgess, 'Late medieval wills and pious convention: testamentary evidence reconsidered', in M. Hicks (ed.),

Profit, piety and the professions in later medieval England (Gloucester: Alan Sutton, 1990), pp. 14–33.

210. Tanner (1984) pp. 101–2.

211. Kieckhefer (1988) p. 84.

212. See Passus XI l. 242 '. . . and patient as pilgrims, for pilgrims are we all'; ed. cit., p. 451.

213. See Passus V.

214. See the beginning of Passus VII, where Truth sends merchants a letter urging them to do good works to the poor and sick if they wish to obtain a full remission of punishment for their sins (ed. cit., pp. 370–1). See also Simpson (1990) pp. 69–71.

215. For this subject see esp. Brown (1995) pp. 122–3. The fifteenth century was particularly notable for 'the time, energy and money [parishioners] contributed to the maintenance, renovation and reconstruction' of the fabric of their local churches (Colin Richmond, 'Religion', in Horrox (1994ii) p. 184).

216. In East Anglia, for example, prosperous laypeople gave thanks for their wealth by building or extending churches on a grand scale (Nichols (1994) p. 3); and Brown (1995, p. 51) shows that most benefactors to Salisbury Cathedral during this period were aristocratic, and most chantries within it were founded by clergy (p. 53).

217. Brown (1995) p. 121.

218. McNeill and Gamer, p. 354; Brown (1995) p. 124 and n. 44.

219. Brown (1995) p. 56 and n. 37. Edwards (1967, pp. 59–67) shows that cathedral canons were obliged to offer regular hospitality to the entire cathedral community (junior clergy, choir, vergers, etc.) and sometimes to visitors too.

220. Horrox (1994ii) p. 186. The artistic representations of (e.g.) memorials to local gentry reflected carefully both earthly and heavenly hierarchies (for an interesting example of this see Saul (1986) pp. 148–52).

221. See Brooke (1971) for a fascinating exploration of this point.

222. See pp. 109–12 above.

223. Caiger-Smith (1963) p. 73.

224. *The Golden Legend or Lives of the Saints as Englished by William Caxton*, 7 vols (London: Dent, 1931), Caxton omits some of Jacobus' saints and adds a number of English and Irish ones.

225. See A. S. G. Edwards, 'The transmission and audience of Osbern Bokenham's *Legendys of hooly wummen*, in A. J. Minnis (ed.), *Late-medieval religious texts and their transmission: essays in honour of A. I. Doyle* (Cambridge: D. S. Brewer, 1994), pp. 157–68.

226. See esp. Winstead (1997), a fascinating exploration of precisely this question: she shows how the editors or compilers of early saints' lives adapted their material to help it address their intended audiences and to make specific points.

227. Duffy (1992) p. 175.

228. See Elliott (1993) pp. 176–83. Cramer (*Baptism and change in the early Middle Ages* (Cambridge, 1993) pp. 107–8) makes the point that the character and powers of a particular saint are adapted to the community's needs, but 'then turn back to shape the community', supremely through liturgy.

229. Kieckhefer (1984) pp. 6–7.

230. Kieckhefer (1984) p. 10.

231. Ed. cit. in Bibliography to this chapter. For Christina see also Bolton (1978), Stargardt (1985), and Elliott (1997) p. 162.

232. *Life* (Middle English version), chapters 2–3.

233. Chapter 3, pp. 120–1. Note her compassion for the Jews (chapter 18, p. 126).

234. Chapter 4, p. 121.

235. Hence Kieckhefer's point (1984, p. 14): 'if a saint is able to overcome lust even to this heroic degree, then an ordinary Christian should all the more be capable of normal chastity.' See also Colin Richmond ('Religion', in Horrox (1994ii), p. 188): 'By the later middle ages it was for exhibiting human values to a super-human degree that men and women were regarded as saints.'

236. Cf. Duffy's remark (1992, p. 198) about the manner in which saints' miracles 'opened a window of hope on a daunting world'. See also Kieckhefer (1984) pp. 192–3.

237. There was a dramatic increase in the volume of hagiographical material during this period, partly caused by papal centralization of canonization procedures (Kieckhefer (1984) p. 5), and partly also fuelled by local cults, such as the veneration in late medieval Yorkshire of Saxon and Norman saints such as St Cuthbert and St William of York (Hughes (1988) p. 299).

238. John Whiterig (*Meditations*, ET 1961, p. 56) warns against setting love of the saints above love of Jesus: 'I do not forbid the love of saints, but I do desire that right order should be kept in loving them.'

239. For late-medieval feast days see Duffy (1992) p. 156. For bequests in favour of lights see Tanner (1984) p. 84. For local devotion to the saints in general, see Swanson (1993ii) pp. 287–91.

240. Kieckhefer (1988) p. 89.

241. Bishop (1897) p. xxvi.

242. See Mirk's *Festial*, EETS e.s. 96, p. 109 and (for the Seven Joys) pp. 232–3; Evans (1949) p. 88; Duffy (1992) pp. 257–9. Tanner (1984, p. 90) points out that surviving bequests in wills reflect the popularity of religious objects like rosaries, images of saints, Paxes etc. For the rosary, see also Erickson (1976) p. 83, Hamburger (1997) p. 75 and A. Winston-Allen, *Stories of the rose: the making of the rosary in the Middle Ages* (University Park: Pennsylvania State UP, 1997).

243. Duffy (1992) p. 265.

244. *Legenda aurea*, trans. cit. in Bibliography, vol. 2, p. 154.

245. 'There is . . . no widow that stably prays after the help of God to stand firm in her widowhood to the worship of God until death, but that I am at once ready to fulfil her will with her. For I was as a widow, in that I had a son on earth who had no physical father', *Revelations* (Middle English version, my transliteration), EETS 178, p. 100.

246. Prayer to the Blessed Virgin, ll. 309–14, in *The Wheatley Manuscript (from British Museum Add.Ms.39574)*, ed. Mabel Day, EETS o.s. 155 (1921), p. 14.

247. *De Concepcione beate Marie*, in Mirk's *Festial* (ed. cit. in Bibliography), 1, p. 17. For Mirk, see Spencer (1993), esp. pp. 62 and 277–8. For the enormous significance of the rose in late medieval spirituality, see Hamburger (1997) chapter 2.

248. *Meditations* 5, ET (1961) p. 122.

249. See Farmer's comments in his Introduction to the ET of Whiterig's *Meditations*, pp. 23–4. The holiness of Mary is sharply contrasted, in much late medieval iconography, with the character of St Joseph, who is frequently represented as a quasi-comical character, and even as a grumpy old cuckold with a crutch and a drink problem. See Walsh (1986).

250. For the Prioress's tale see Chaucer, *The Canterbury tales,* pp. 209–12; and Russell (1969) pp. 211–27.

251. This can hardly refer to Chaucer's England, since Jews had been expelled from the country at the end of the thirteenth century. But it is a part of a wider European antisemitism, particularly evident in eucharistic piety: see Miri Rubin, *Gentile tales: the narrative assault on late medieval Jews* (Yale UP, 1999). Antisemitic remarks, often directly based on New Testament references, appear almost casually in late medieval English devotional literature: see, e.g., the anonymous late-fourteenth-century untitled poem about the life and passion of Jesus, which describes the Jews as 'cruel dogs' (*hondes felle*) and 'hungry wolves' (*Meditations on the life and passion of Christ*, ed. Charlotte d'Evelyn, EETS o.s. 158 (1921), esp. p. 38).

252. Literally 'sin'.

253. Part 1 of *Quia amore langueo*, from Lambeth MS. 853, c.1430, in *Political, religious and love poems*, EETS o.s. 15 (1866), pp. 177–9 *passim*, my transliteration. Reflection on *Quia amore langueo* appears also in Rolle's *The form of living*, 7.

254. Tristram (1955) p. 25. See Nichols (1994) pp. 175–6 for representations of angels in font art.

255. *Meditations*, ET (1961) pp. 127–36.

256. *Meditations*, §7, p. 132.
257. *Meditations*, §§8–10, ET (1961) pp. 133–6.
258. Hodgson (1982) chapter 1, p. 122 and note on p. 191.
259. Hodgson (1982) chapter 5, p. 127.
260. Hodgson (1982) p. 158.
261. *Festial* (Sermon for Christmas Day), EETS e.s. 96, p. 22.
262. Love, *Myrrour*, p. 98.
263. *Dives and Pauper*, EETS 275, p. 83, text modernized.
264. *Dives and Pauper*, EETS 275, pp. 85–6.
265. Davidson (1976) pp. 144–6; Nichols (1994) pp. 14–15.
266. Evans (1949) pp. 225–6; Caiger-Smith (1963) pp. 55–7. Representations of the implements of the Cross are fairly common in English art.
267. For some fascinating examples of the use of images of the suffering Christ in late medieval monastic piety, see Hamburger (1997), esp. pp. 102–28
268. The *Speculum ecclesiae* has survived in two Latin versions, one French (Anglo-Norman) and one Middle English (the latter a loose translation omitting sections of the original). The manuscript evidence in general suggests that the work enjoyed little popularity in the first 50 years after its composition (see Forshaw, Introduction to ed. cit. in Bibliography, p. 16). It is hard to explain the gap between its original composition in the early thirteenth century and its eventual appearance in the second half of the fourteenth (Forshaw, pp. 15–16): the English version dates from the fifteenth century. The work (whose earliest manuscripts in England were found in Augustinian religious houses) contains much standard Augustinian theology. See also Nichols (1994) pp. 151–5.
269. *Speculum ecclesiae* 23, Latin ed. p. 91 (my translation).
270. *Showings*, LT 24, pp. 394–5.
271. Baker (1994) p. 30.
272. See especially Passus XVIII; see also Alford (1988) pp. 53–4 and (for the important links between this theme and medieval apocalyptic theory) Kerby-Fulton (1990).
273. Alford (1988) p. 55.
274. See, e.g., Alexander Nequam's story charming but not very profound story of the knight and the lion, retold by John Mirk in a sermon for Holy Week; Mirk's *Festial*, EETS e.s. 96, pp. 119–20.
275. *Meditations*, ET (1961) p. 76.
276. *Meditations*, ET (1961) p. 77.
277. Rubin (1991) p. 303; Duffy (1992) p. 238. Such devotion was not new: see (e.g.) St Bernard of Clairvaux, Sermon 61 on the Song of Songs (ET by Walsh and Edmonds, *Bernard of Clairvaux: On the Song of Songs III* (Cistercian Fathers 31) (Kalamazoo: Cistercian Publications, 1979), pp. 140–48).
278. such as the *Oculus sacerdotis* of William of Pagula, cited in Pantin (1955) pp. 200–1, in a passage taken from the thirteenth-century *Stimulus amoris* of James of Milan.
279. For Rolle, see his *Meditations on the Passion*, (trans. R. Allen, *The English Works*, p. 97), where Rolle prays for 'wounds of deep remorse' in a manner which may well have influenced Julian's similar suffrage. Later in the same text, Rolle compares Christ's wounds to the stars (p. 112) – and, in a quaint analogy, compares Christ's wounded body to a dovecote through whose openings we can find refuge, and a honeycomb packed with sweet cells (p. 113). For Julian, see ST (Short Text) 1, ed. cit., pp. 205–6; see also below.
280. See Chapter 3.
281. *Myrrour*, pp. 103 and 115.
282. *Meditations*, ET (1961), pp. 44–5.
283. For this theme, see Bynum (1984); Baker (1994) pp. 107–34.
284. For the dominance of mothers in the home, see Phythian-Adams (1979) p. 96.
285. Catto (1985ii) p. 109; Allen (1927) p. 72; R. W. Pfaff, *New liturgical feasts in late medieval England* (Oxford, 1970), pp. 62–83. Brown (1995, p. 86) shows that in the diocese of

Salisbury the cult of the Holy Name flourished more in urban than in rural areas.

286. *Form of living*, EETS 293, p. 18; cf. Walter Hilton, *Qui habitat* 13, ed. D. Jones, pp. 159–62. For one of many similar passages on this theme, see the section on the Circumcision of Jesus in Jacopus de Voragine's *Legenda aurea* (trans. Ryan, vol. I, pp. 73–4), which cites St Bernard.

287. See esp. the section in Boenig's translation, pp. 99–107.

288. Allen (1927) p. 76.

289. This kind of devotion was especially associated with the Franciscans, and its most famous manifestation was perhaps the wooden image (originally c.1500) of the infant Jesus (*Il Bambino*) in the Franciscan church of S.Maria d'Aracoeli in Rome. Margery Kempe has 'high meditations on the birth and the childhood of Christ' (*The Book of Margery Kempe* I.30, EETS 212 p. 78).

290. Coment donqes oserons estre si hardis de toutes noz foliez et malveisteez de parler a cest grant seignur, s'il ne fust une humble et douce enfant? (*Livre de seyntz medicines*, p. 37).

291. *Livre de seyntz medicines*, pp. 36–7.

292. See Hulme, introduction to EETS o.s. 100, pp. vii–viii.

293. See Chapter 2, n. 56.

294. This has no counterpart in the prototypical *Gospel of Nicodemus*, though there is such an address in the vernacular Middle English version of it, EETS o.s. 100, pp. 6–13.

295. See Waldron (1986).

296. Passus XVII, ll.218–25 (ed. cit., p. 619).

297. Lovatt, reflecting on the highly visual, Christocentric spirituality of Henry VI as described in John Blacman's *Collectarium mansuetudinum et bonorum morum Regis Henrici VI*, points to the link between this kind of piety and that of Richard Rolle (1984, p. 175). See also Nichols (1994) p. 157 on the importance of fifteenth-century provincial art in catechesis.

298. Davidson (1976) p. 144. There is evidence to suggest that many medieval laypeople took home cheap single-sheet woodcuts of devotional subjects, perhaps especially depictions of the *pietà*: see T. Watt, *Cheap print and popular piety 1550–1640* (Cambridge UP, 1991), p. 131.

299. See Chapter 3.

300. Davidson (1976) pp. 128–9.

301. Sandler (1983) pp. 14–15.

302. Sandler (1983) p. 56 and adjoining plate. The text from scripture is John 11.39b: 'Martha, the sister of the dead man, said to him, "Lord, already there is a stench because he has been dead four days."'

303. Edmund of Abingdon, *Speculum ecclesiae* 20, Latin edn, pp. 83–4, my translation. There is a fascinating illustration in Robert de Lisle's Psalter (Sandler (1983) p. 62 and adjacent plate) of the Seven Acts of the Passion (Christ before Pilate, the Flagellation, Christ bearing the Cross, Christ nailed to the Cross, Christ giving up the Spirit, the Deposition, and the Entombment). Each of these is linked with one of the seven canonical hours (respectively Matins, Prime, Terce, Sext, None, Vespers, and Compline) and with one of the seven gifts of remembrance (respectively hearing, sight, smell, taste, touch (the five senses), empathy, and freewill). This careful interrelation between monastic offices, Christ's suffering and death, and the individual's senses is highly characteristic of late medieval piety.

304. A growing interest in the early episodes of Christ's life is characteristic of this period and complements its preoccupation with the Passion. See (e.g.) the charming Christmas scene in the fourteenth-century English de Lisle Psalter (Sandler (1983) p. 54 and adjoining plate). Margery Kempe has 'high meditations on the birth and the childhood of Christ' (*The Book of Margery Kempe*, I.30, EETS 212, p. 78). See also note 289.

305. The Parson's tale, ed. cit., X(I) 69.

306. 'Its purpose came to be more precisely understood as leading beyond the arousal of emotions of fear of God's judgment and love for Christ toward systematic self-examination as a prelude to penance' (Bestul (1989) p. 604).

307. *Contemplations of the dread and love of God*, pp. 42–3.

308. Nicholas Love, *Myrrour*, p. 217.

309. *Myrrour*, p. 39.
310. *Myrrour*, pp. 96–8.
311. *Myrrour*, p. 41.
312. *Myrrour*, p. 83.
313. *Myrrour*, p. 217.
314. For this subject see above all the texts assembled, together with an excellent introduction, by Simon Tugwell, in *Albert and Thomas: selected writings* (Classics of western spirituality) (New York: Paulist Press; London: SPCK, 1988).
315. Augustine, *De trinitate* XII.14.22: 'But there is a difference between the contemplation of eternal things and the action by which we use temporal things well: the former is called wisdom, the latter science.' ET by S. McKenna (Fathers of the Church 45) (Washington DC: Catholic University of America Press, 1963), p. 363.
316. See Alford (1988) p. 50. In *Piers Plowman* it is arguable that Piers himself is made by Langland into 'a remarkable example of the authority that could be accorded experiential knowledge, even when it was unsupported by any large measure of *scientia*' (Watson (1991) p. 24).
317. 'Unless you become like little children you shall not enter into the kingdom of heaven' (Passus XV ll.149–50, ed. cit., p. 543.
318. *Super Canticum Canticorum,* p. 70, my trans.
319. *Incendium amoris*, Prologue, ed. cit., p. 147, my trans.
320. 'He knows God perfectly who recognizes that he is beyond our comprehension and capacity' (*Ille autem Deum perfecte cognoscit, qui ipsum incomprehensibilem et incognoscibilem esse deprehendit*) (*Incendium amoris* 6, ed. cit., p. 161; ET p. 62). For Aquinas' view on this subject, see Davies (1992) chapter 3.
321. 'It is enough for you to know *that* God is: to want to know *what* he is will only hinder' (*Sufficit ergo tibi ut cognoscas quod Deus est, et oberit tibi si scire velis quid Deus est*) (*Incendium amoris* 6, ed. cit., p. 162; ET p. 63). For Aquinas' view on this subject, see Davies (1992) p. 40, with refs.
322. *Incendium amoris* 33; see also Clark (1983i) p. 113.
323. *Form of living*, EETS 293, p. 4. Walter Hilton makes a similar point in *Bonum est* 5 (ed. D. Jones, pp. 185–7), though his authorship of this text remains disputed.
324. Pantin (1955) p. 174; Farmer, introduction to the *Meditacio devota* (1958) p. 193; for its manuscript tradition, see pp. 191ff.
325. *Meditations* ('Meditation addressed to Christ crucified' §63), ET (1961), p. 85. The reference to St Gregory is to his *Homiliae XL in Evangelia* 27, PL 76:1207. Another approach to this question is that of Edmund of Abingdon, who uses this kind of affective meditation as a means of encouraging devotion to both the human and the divine Christ. In his *Speculum ecclesiae* Edmund uses the terms *meditatio, contemplatio,* and *consideratio* interchangeably (Forshaw, introduction to the Latin edn, p. 18); and he defines contemplation as 'the vision of God in creatures' (*visio Dei in creaturis,* or (in the Middle English version) 'thought of God in great liking in soul'(*Speculum,* ed. cit., pp. 45 and 21 respectively). Although he distinguishes this form of contemplation from two others (the contemplation of God in the Bible, and the contemplation of God in himself, both outwardly in his humanity and inwardly in his divinity), this highly visual, Thomist approach to the subject, much influenced by the twelfth-century writers Hugh and Richard of St Victor is characteristic of much late medieval spirituality (especially in its stress on the proper use of the imagination in meditation and contemplation; see Forshaw, introduction to the *Speculum,* pp. 20–24). Note that St Thomas defined contemplation as 'the simple gazing on the truth' (*contemplatio pertinet ad simplicet intuitum veritatis*): *Summa theologiae* II.II q.180 art.3 ad.1.
326. Riehle (1981) p. 125.
327. Julian follows Augustine in distinguishing three kinds of seeing, hers being 'bodyly syght' (cf. Augustine's *visio corporalis*), 'goostely syght' (cf. Augustine's *visio intellectualis*), and 'gostly in bodely lycknesse' or 'more gostly withoute bodely lycknes'. Julian's use of these terms does not

completely correspond to Augustine, and is not very systematic (Riehle (1981) pp. 125–6).

328. Bernard of Clairvaux, *De consideratione* II.5, trans.J. D. Anderson and E. T. Kennan (Cistercian Fathers 37) (Kalamazoo: Cistercian Publications, 1976), p. 52. Phyllis Hodgson, in her edition of the *Cloud of unknowing* and other works (Analecta Cartusiana, 1982, p. 189), says that the Middle English *beholde* means also 'keep' and its extension 'keep in view, consider'. In the *Ancrene Riwle*, to behold ('bihalden') means to consider, in the sense of to meditate, 'using the imagination to present events in Christ's life to the mind as subjects of meditation' (Baldwin (1976) p. 269). Thus to 'bihald inward' means to turn your attention inwards, and meditate devoutly. 'Beholding' certainly signified an effort of the imagination inextricably linked with the process of meditation itself (Baldwin (1976) p. 272).

329. Julian of Norwich, *Shewings* (ST) 22, p. 268. See also St Thomas Aquinas, *Summa theologiae* II.II q.180 a.7; ET by S. Tugwell, *Albert and Thomas: selected writings* (Classics of western spirituality) (New York: Paulist Press, 1988), esp. p. 560.

330. Something similar is described in *The Book of Margery Kempe* I.57, when Margery's mind is drawn

> wholly into the Passion of our Lord Christ Jesus, whom she beheld with her spiritual eye in the sight of her soul as verily as if she had seen his precious body beaten, scourged and crucified with her bodily eye; which sight and spiritual beholding wrought by grace so fervently in her mind, wounded her with pity and compassion, so that she sobbed, roared and cried and, spreading her arms wide said with loud voice, "I die, I die".' (EETS 212, p. 140)

Margery's is an intensely affective response to the death of Jesus, rather than Julian's clear-eyed contemplative union. But it would be inappropriate to regard the one as superior to the other.

331. *Scale of perfection* II.32, p. 259.

332. *Scale of perfection* II.32, p. 259.

333. *Scale of perfection* II.42, p. 292. Cf. *Qui habitat* 8, ed. D. Jones, pp. 140–3.

334. 'For a person shall not commonly come to spiritual delight in the contemplation of Christ's divinity unless he first comes in imagination by anguish and compassion for his humanity' (*Scale of perfection* I.36, p. 106). It should be noted that in *Qui habitat*, his commentary on Psalm 91, Hilton commends meditation on the humanity of Christ in its own right as a means of quieting fleshly impulses (*Qui habitat* 4, ed. D. Jones, pp. 125–8).

335. *Scale of perfection* II.30, p. 253.

336. *Scale of perfection* II.30, p. 254.

337. *Scale of perfection* II.33, p. 262.

338. *Scale of perfection* II.43, p. 286.

339. *Scale of perfection* II.45, p. 299.

340. *Scale of perfection* II.46, p. 302.

341. Cambridge University Library, MS Dd.VI.1, f.142b; quoted by Caiger-Smith (1963) p. 46. For an excellent survey of contemporary attitudes to death, see Margaret Aston, 'Death', in Horrox (1994ii) pp. 202–28.

342. *Revelations* IV.40, EETS 178, p. 11.

343. EETS e.s. 96, p. 291.

344. F. Warren (ed.), *The Dance of Death*, EETS o.s. 181 (1931). See also J. M. Clark, *The Dance of Death in the Middle Ages and the Renaissance* (Glasgow: Jackson, 1950). The church in Paris was destroyed in 1669. Clark points out (p. 11) that Lydgate's verses originally accompanied a representation of the Dance of Death in the cloister of the original St Paul's Cathedral, London. Late medieval artistic representations of the Dance of Death can still be found in Hexham Abbey and in the Markham Chapel of St Mary Magdalene, Newark-on-Trent.

345. Modern translation in Swanson (1993i) p. 138; full refs. in Bibliography.

346. See the comments of Thomas Brinton, bishop of Rochester, in a sermon of 1375, quoted in Horrox (1994) p. 143.

347. Tanner (1984) p. 122.

348. Wood-Legh (1965) pp. 132–3.

349. For the history and meaning of the chantry see Wood-Legh (1965), esp. pp. 1–2; Edwards

(1967) pp. 285–303; and Kümin (1996) pp. 159–67. Another manifestation of prayer for the dead was the extensive rebuilding or enlargement of parish churches by local gentry or nobility during the later Middle Ages; see Saul (1986) chapter 5 for a fascinating example of this.

350. Bossy (1973), esp. pp. 132–6. Edwards (1967, p. 287) makes the point that the provision of chantries may in part reflect 'the natural desire of people to have something private in religion'.

351. Tanner (1984) pp. 104–5.

352. Hughes (1988) p. 39.

353. Wood-Legh (1965) p. 46.

354. Tanner (1984) p. 97. This has caused some historians to conclude that concern for the poor in this period was motivated less by compassion than by a desire to accumulate spiritual merit for oneself. See esp. M. Rubin, *Charity and community in medieval Cambridge* (Cambridge UP, 1987); P. W. Fleming, 'Charity, faith and the gentry of Kent 1422–1529', in A. J. Pollard (ed.), *Property and politics: essays in late medieval English history* (Gloucester: Alan Sutton, 1984), esp. pp. 45–6; Brown (1995) chapter 8.

355. Text in Swanson (1993i) p. 251.

356. Cited in Peckham (1948) pp. 6–7.

357. Richmond (1991) p. 122 and n. 3.

358. It appears in the de Lisle Psalter (c. 1339) and in church wall paintings, of which 12 survive, the best at Pickforth in Lincolnshire and Widford, near Burford (Evans (1949) p. 94). See also Caiger-Smith (1963) p. 45.

359. Burgess (1985); Brown (1995) pp. 106–7. Brown points out (p. 127) that in many churches chantries were also used as Easter sepulchres, thereby increasing their role in corporate devotional life.

360. Bishop (1897) p. xxxiv. For the spiritual life of cathedrals in the later Middle Ages, see Edwards (1967).

361. The *Dirige* was recited at funerals; and both gilds and parishes used it as a form of corporate prayer for departed members or parishioners. See Duffy (1992) pp. 220–1.

362. Job 10.18–21.

363. For an important overview of the so-called 'Middle English Mystics', and a critique of the notion of these writers (Rolle, Hilton, the *Cloud* author, Julian, and Margery Kempe) forming some kind of school, see Watson (1999).

364. *Instructions for a devout and literate layman*, ed. cit., p. 400.

365. See Clark (1983i) pp. 119–20. For Jerome's concern for ecclesiology, see Y. Bodin, *Saint Jérôme et l'église* (Théologie Historique 6) (Paris: Beauchesne, 1966), esp. pp. 281–357; for Peter Damian, see above all his *Liber qui dicitur 'Dominus vobiscum'*, in which he sets the eremitic life in an unambiguously ecclesial context; in *Die Briefe des Petrus Damiani* (Monumenta Germaniae Historica), ed. K. Reindel (Munich, 1983), no. 28, pp. 248–78; ET by O. J. Blum OFM, *The Letters of Peter Damian, 1–30* (Fathers of the Church, Mediaeval Continuation 28) (Washington: Catholic University of America, 1989), pp. 255–89.

366. Watson (1991) p. 166. The whole of Watson's book explores this theme with careful and nuanced analyses of individual texts from Rolle's works.

367. 'Certainly I knew this better, because I experienced it myself' (Hoc utique melius cognovi, quia illud expertus sum); *Super Cantica Canticorum*, p. 60 (my trans.).

368. For a superb exposition of this theme in Rolle's writing, see Watson (1991).

369. See, e.g., *The Commandment*, in which he tells the addressee to take such delight in Jesus that 'thy heart receive neither the world's joy nor the world's sorrow' (EETS 293, p. 37).

370. *Expositio super novem lectiones mortuorum*, ed. cit., II.127, my trans. This was the first of his works to be printed (at Oxford in 1483), and one of his most popular, especially among secular clergy (Watson (1991) pp. 198–9).

371. For a classic presentation of this approach, see St Bernard, Sermon 83 on the Song of Songs; ET by Irene Edmonds, *Bernard of Clairvaux: On the Song of Songs IV* (CF 40) (Kalamazoo:

Cistercian Publications, 1980), pp. 180–7.

372. pay for.

373. *Lyrics* 1, EETS 293, pp. 43–4.

374. EETS 293, p. 34.

375. For other accounts, see *Incendium amoris* 17 and *Emendatio vitae* 11.

376. *Ego dormio*, EETS 293, p. 29.

377. *Ego dormio*, EETS 293, p. 29.

378. *Ego dormio*, EETS 293, p. 31.

379. *Ego dormio*, EETS 293, p. 31.

380. *Form of living*, EETS 293, pp. 23–4.

381. *Contra amatores*, ed. cit., pp. 75 and 157. See also *Incendium amoris* 13, where he refers in passing to the fact that the primary aim of the eremitical life is to live in love of God and neighbour (ed. cit., p. 180).

382. Vauchez (1997, pp. 411–12) goes so far as to suggest that late medieval mystical sanctity was profoundly elitist, its practitioners being really interested only in political and religious leaders and in fellow-aspirants after perfection, not in the generality of Christians.

383. See Watson (1991) p. 17. The link between preaching and the contemplative life is made by many earlier authors, among them St Bernard (Sermon 57:9 on the Song of Songs, ET by Walsh and Edmonds, *Bernard of Clairvaux: On the Song of Songs III* (CF 31) (Kalamazoo: Cistercian Publications 1979), p. 103.

384. Watson (1991) p. 185.

385. *Super canticum canticorum*, trans. Boenig, p. 62.

386. Such as his references to 'ordered love', *amor ordinatus* (*Incendium amoris* 1, p. 148 and 4, p. 154) (though in *Emendatio vitae* 11 he declares that 'truly Christ's lover keeps no order in his loving'), and to the importance of loving creatures for God's sake, and God for his own sake alone (4, p. 155).

387. *Super Psalmum vicesimum*, trans. Boenig, p. 41.

388. *Incendium amoris* 13, ed. cit., p. 180.

389. *Incendium amoris* 14, ed. cit., p. 183.

390. *Form of living*, EETS 293, p. 24.

391. *Form of living*, EETS 293, p. 24. Note the absence of any reference to knowledge or the intellect here.

392. Watson (1991) p. 65.

393. English commentary on Psalm 12(13).6, ed. cit., p. 47.

394. This kind of individualism, if taken to extremes, can of course become dangerous, and justifies Evelyn Underhill's description of Rolle as 'something of a free lance' (*The mystics of the Church* (London: J. Clarke, 1925), p. 120). Jonathan Hughes has studied the piety of King Richard III and argued that, far from a superficial matter, Richard was deeply influenced by the northern English spirituality of people like Rolle, a spirituality 'not designed to achieve a state of detachment and reconciliation with fortune, but to convince the worshipper of his special relationship with a divinity that would actively intervene to fulfil his individual destiny' (*The religious life of Richard III: piety and prayer in the north of England* (Stroud: Sutton Publishing, 1997), p. 63).

395. In the *Melos amoris* the three are usually *calor* (or *melos*), *dulcor* and *canor* (Arnould, introduction to ed. cit., p. xxxv).

396. In *Incendium amoris* 13 (ed. cit., p. 185) Rolle says that none of the three can exist *sine magna quiete* (see also Watson (1989) p. 130). Yet there are hints, especially in *Emendatio vitae*, that Rolle did come to accept the possibility of a non-eremitic life being compatible with perfection and contemplation (Watson (1991) p. 215). John A. Alford ('Biblical *Imitatio* in the writings of Richard Rolle', in *English Literary History* 40 (1973), pp. 1–23) points out how Rolle invariably refers to particular biblical texts when referring to *dulcor, calor,* and *canor*.

397. *quando mens amore eterno veraciter incenditur* (*Incendium amoris* 13, ed. cit., p. 185).

398. Clark (1983i) p. 112. In *Incendium amoris* 13, *dulcor* appears to be the product of *fervor* and *canor* (ed. cit., p. 185).

399. Cited in Allen (1927), p. 84. Sweetness (*dulcor*) is a common term in medieval mysticism, but less appealing to modern minds: it may be said to represent the emphasis on experiencing God, on spiritual love as affective (rather than purely intellectual) union, so characteristic of (among others) the Cistercian school. See Chapter 3 and the articles on *Douceur* (by André-Ignace Mennessier) and *Dulcedo* (by Jean Chatillon) in *Dictionnaire de spiritualité* (Paris: Beauchesne, 1957), vol. 3, cols. 1674–85 and 1777–95 respectively. Both Mennessier and Chatillon cite various Augustinian texts which may well have influenced Rolle: see, e.g., Augustine's *Sermon* 159.4, PL 38:869, where he affirms the value of the senses in interior prayer.

400. '*iam in animo, abundante ardore, suscipitur suavitas laudis aeternae, ac cogitatus in canticum convertitur, et mens in mellifluum melos immoratur*' (*Incendium amoris* 13, ed. cit., p. 185).

401. 'All [lack *canor*] who have not the courage to break away from everyone' (*Melos amoris* 4, cited and trans. Watson (1991) p. 176).

402. Thus he writes 'Those in the active life indeed rejoice in external songs, while we, kindled by divine contemplation, fly away from earthly things to the sound of (heavenly) feasting, (*Contra amatores* 4, ed. cit., p. 80). In *Emendatio vitae* 12 he again explicitly links contemplation with song.

403. Those who have much love often want to sing of it (*Form of living*, EETS 293, p. 15).

404. English commentary on Psalm 150, trans. R. Allen, p. 84. Cf. Pseudo-Origen, *Selecta in Psalmos* 150, PG 12:1684–5.

405. *Incendium amoris* 4, ed. cit. p. 156.

406. '*quasi tinnitum psallentium vel potius canentium supra me ascultavi*' (ed. cit., p. 189). Rolle elsewhere makes it clear that the gift of song can be granted during personal prayer (*Emendatio vitae* 7).

407. Cf. *Incendium amoris* 16.

408. '*concinentes cum choris clarissimis*' (*Incendium amoris* 5, ed. cit., p. 159).

409. Tinctoris, *Opera theoretica*, vol. IIa, 10; cited in Strohm (1993) p. 377.

410. *Holy maidenhood* (ed. cit. in Bibliography to Chapter 3) pp. 231–3.

411. *The Book of Margery Kempe*, I.36, EETS 212, p. 90. See also I.3, p. 12, where she jumps out of bed at the sound of heavenly music; and I.17, p. 39, where she 'heard so hideous a melody that she might not bear it'.

412. Riehle (1981) p. 119.

413. *Agenbite of Inwyt*, EETS o.s. 23, p. 105. Hilton also uses musical imagery: see, e.g., *Bonum est* 3, ed. D. Jones, pp. 179–81.

414. See R. Boenig, 'St Augustine's *jubilus* and Richard Rolle's *canor*', in A. C. Bartlett (ed.), *Vox mystica: essays on medieval mysticism in honor of Professor Valerie M. Lagorio* (Cambridge: D. S. Brewer, 1995), pp. 75–86.

415. *Enarr. in psalmum 32:2*, CCSL 38:254, cited and trans. J. McKinnon, *Music in early Christian literature* (Cambridge readings in the literature of music) (Cambridge UP, 1987), pp. 156–7.

416. See Watson (1999) p. 549.

417. '*non valeat sustinere clamorem psallentium nisi canor eius interior ad cogitatum redigatur*' (*Incendium amoris* 33, ed. cit., p. 238).

418. *Super canticum canticorum*, trans. Boenig, p. 132. Rolle thus goes well beyond the medieval tradition, exemplified by St Bernard and the Cistercians, in which any experience approximating to *deificatio* can only be transitory in this life.

419. *English Psalter*, p. 493 (on Psalm 150.4).

420. Thus he writes: 'For what is love if not the transformation of the feeling (*affectus*) into the thing that is loved?' (*Incendium amoris* 17, ed. cit., p. 195).

421. *The commandment*, EETS 293, p. 38.

422. *Form of living*, EETS 293, p. 13.

423. *Form of living*, EETS 293, pp. 13–14.

424. See, above all, Watson (1991).

425. For important reflections on Rolle's style, see Watson (1991); Theiner (introduction to the *Contra amatores*), pp. 29–38; Arnould (introduction to the *Melos amoris*); Riehle (1981).

426. So Beer (1992) p. 118, on the *Ego dormio*. But note the remarks of Watson (1991) pp. 229–32: the *Ego dormio* communicates Rolle's sense of himself as an authoritative spiritual guide for women.

427. Watson (1991) p. 224. Rolle's attitude to women is perhaps best expressed in this extract from his *Incendium amoris*, beautifully caught in Wolters' translation: 'When women love, they love without reserve, because they do not know how to restrain their manner of loving. On the other hand loving them can be a very tricky and prickly business!' (*Feminae, si viros ament, insaniunt, quia modum amando tenere non sciunt. Quando autem amantur amarissime pungunt* (*Incendium amoris* 29, ed. cit. p. 228; trans. Wolters, p. 136).

428. See, e.g., *Incendium amoris* 7, ed. cit., p. 164; and 14, p. 184.

429. See Watson (1999) pp. 550–1.

430. Sermon 57:9 on the Song of Songs; ET by Walsh and Edmonds, *Bernard of Clairvaux: On the Song of Songs III* (CF 31) (Kalamazoo: Cistercian Publications, 1979), p. 104.

431. *The Officium and Miracula of Richard Rolle*, trans. Comper, pp. 304–5.

432. For this movement see McLaughlin (1973).

433. See Clark (1978i) p. 63; Watson (1996) (who includes a fascinating account of the reception given to Porete's work in the centuries since it was written); McGinn (1998) pp. 244–65.

434. Porete (1968) p. 245; Clark (1978i, p. 64) believes that much of Hilton's *Scale* 2 touches on points raised by M. N.'s glosses. Despite the fact that all three extant manuscripts of the English translations of 'M. N.' beonged to the Carthusians (College and Guarnieri, in Porete (1968) p. 358), there is no reason to assume that 'M. N.' is necessarily a Carthusian. Watson (1996) convincingly disposes of Colledge's and Guarnieri's view of 'M. N.' as an orthodox English scholar prudently pasteurizing Porete's heterodoxies, arguing instead that 'M. N.' reflects a distinctively English preoccupation with the *language* of mystical union.

435. For Hilton at Cambridge see Clark (1992). Clark and Dorward (1991, p. 16) argue that his preference for the Augustinian canons as opposed to the Carthusians suggests that he felt more at home in a 'mixed life', revealing a range of sympathies wider than that of the author of the *Cloud*.

436. For this subject see above and Hughes (1988), esp. p. 249; see also Spencer (1993) pp. 163–88. In *The Scale of perfection* I.21, Hilton stresses the need for a 'firm belief in all articles of the faith and sacraments of holy church'. See also Clark (1978i).

437. See especially his letter *De utilitate et prerogativis religionis* (1384–5) to Adam Horsley, encouraging him to become a Carthusian and defending the religious life: ed. cit., esp. pp.141–2 and 170–1; see also Clark (1985) p. 4; Hughes (1988) p. 209.

438. Hilton almost certainly wrote *Conclusiones de imaginibus* (or *De adoracione ymaginum*), defending the orthodox position on the veneration of images (again against the Lollards): see Clark and Dorward (1991, p. 16), Clark (1985), Hussey (1995) p. 48. This is a defence of the church's traditional teaching on the subject, written after Hilton entered Thurgarton. It is influenced by Augustine's *De trinitate* (Clark (1985)). It is also a strongly Thomist work, clearly favouring the concrete over the abstract (Kennedy (1982) p. 291). Hilton himself used verbal images with great effect in his own work: see Hussey (1995), esp. pp. 54–6.

439. Ed. cit. in Bibliography. See also Hughes (1988), esp. pp. 215 and 256–8.

440. Kane (1983) is very uncertain of Hilton's authorship on external grounds. Clark (1984ii, pp. 105–6) concludes that the internal (part theological, part stylistic) evidence is in favour of Hilton's authorship of the English text, as is Hussey (1995, pp. 58–9): both tentatively date it after the composition of *Scale* I. For the *Prickynge* see Bibliography to this chapter under James of Milan.

441. Thornton, *English spirituality*, p. 176. The work is more commonly known as *The scale of perfection*, though 'ladder' is surely more accessible today. The title is in any case editorial rather than authorial: see Janel Mueller, in *Walter Hilton: The scale of perfection*, trans. Clark and Dorward (Classics of western spirituality) (SPCK, 1991) pp. 5 and 19. For the sake of clarity,

'Scale' will be used in all bibliographical references here.

442. Clark and Dorward (1991) pp. 18–19. For Fishlake's translation see Clark (1982ii).

443. Judging by MS distribution, Book I was more popular and widely known than Book II: see Clark and Dorward (1991) p. 33.

444. For Hilton's sources in general, see the brief account in Clark and Dorward (1991) pp. 21–7. For Gilbert's influence, see Clark (1990) p. 128.

445. For Augustine's influence on Hilton, see Clark (1982ii). Augustine is explicitly cited at various points in the *Scale* (e.g. I.18, I.40, I.71).

446. *Scale of perfection* I.53, p. 124.

447. I.53, p. 124. See the discussion of Julian of Norwich below for a fuller treatment of sin as *privatio boni*.

448. II.24, p. 235.

449. 'This dying to the world is this darkness, and it is the gate to contemplation and to reforming in feeling' (II.27, p. 245).

450. II.25, pp. 238–9.

451. II.24, p. 237.

452. II.24, p. 236. Cf. the description of the spiritual night which the soul must endure in *Bonum est* 2, ed. Jones, pp. 176–8.

453. *Mixed life*, p. 265.

454. *Mixed life*, p. 265.

455. *Epistola ad quemdam seculo renunciare volentem*, ed. cit. p. 297: 'Disce etiam proximum diligere. Per proximum intellige omnem hominem. Diliges amicos in Deo et inimicos propter Deum. Disce neminem odire, neminem spernere nec ledere verbo vel facto, sed omnibus compati paccatoribus ignorantibus et infirmis, omnes velle iuvare, confortare, etsi non actu, saltem bona voluntate.'

456. *Scale of perfection* II.2, p. 194.

457. II.4, p. 198. This is the classic theme of the *felix culpa*, or 'happy fault': in medieval England it found expression in the theology of Robert Grosseteste (c.1170–1253), for which see R. Southern, *Robert Grosseteste: the growth of an English mind in medieval Europe*, 2nd edn (Oxford: Clarendon, 1992), pp. 220ff. There is a vast literature on the relationship between Genesis 2–3 and the notion of the *felix culpa*: see esp. R. W. L. Moberly, 'Did the serpent get it right?', in *Journal of Theological Studies* n.s. 39 (1988) pp. 1–27, and (more accessibly) Trevor Dennis, *Lo and behold! The power of Old Testament storytelling* (London: SPCK, 1991), pp. 7–23.

458. II.2, p. 196. Hence the importance of intention, for Hilton as for Augustine: see Hussey (1995) pp. 47 and 50.

459. II.28, p. 247.

460. I.12, p. 86.

461. II.11, p. 210. Hilton makes the same point to the lawyer who is the addressee of his *Epistola ad quemdam seculo renunciare volentem* (Letter to someone wanting to renounce the world), ed. cit., esp. pp. 265–7.

462. Hilton describes this as 'a great courtesy of our Lord' (II.35, p. 268).

463. II.29, p. 250.

464. Clark (1982ii) p. 116.

465. Riehle (1981, p. 110) says that, whereas for Rolle *sentire*, or *feling*, means 'to savour', in the sense of sharing the experience of, for example, the Passion of Christ, for Hilton it means 'the ability which man has as a gift of divine grace, to experience God through the powers of his soul'.

466. Ed. cit., p. 201, my trans. For Aquinas' teaching on the vision of God, see *Summa theologiae* II.II q.175 a.3–5.

467. See Sandler (1986).

468. On the identity of Pseudo-Dionysius, and the history of how his pseudonym came to be unmasked, see Rorem (1993) pp. 13–18. Rorem concludes: 'The most we can say with

confidence is that the author reflects a mixture of late fifth-century Syrian Christianity and Athenian Neoplatonism' (p18).

469. *The Divine names* 7.3, pp. 108–9. All references to Pseudo-Dionysius's works are to the English translation cited in the Bibliography to this chapter.

470. *Cloud* 70, p. 70 (all references are to the edition by P. Hodgson, *The cloud of unknowing and related treatises*, cited in the Bibliography).

471. Simon Tugwell offers the analogy of speaking about both the music student next door and Mozart as 'being musical': the word applies to both, but there is an almost unimaginable difference between the two, so that the ascription of 'musical' to Mozart if based solely on the analogical knowledge gained by meeting the student next door will give us only a minute insight into the nature of Mozart's musical genius (Introd. to *Albert and Thomas: selected writings* (Classics of western spirituality) (New York: Paulist Press, 1988), pp. 42–3).

472. See especially the comments of Tugwell in his excellent introduction to *Albert and Thomas: selected writings* (Classics of western spirituality) (New York: Paulist Press, 1988); and also Louth (1989); Rorem (1993, pp. 156–7); and Turner (1995) pp. 19–49.

473. 'For Denys the individual and social orders are inseparable' (Balthasar, *The glory of the Lord*, vol. II p. 161). See Rorem (1993, esp. pp. 30–6 and 57–9). For an important feminist critique of Pseudo-Dionysius, see Jantzen (1995) pp. 95–109: Jantzen points out that women nowhere feature in his writing, and certainly not in his hierarchical schemas.

474. *The Celestial hierarchy* 1.1, p. 146. For the influence of Dionysius' aesthetics on the Middle Ages, see Rorem (1993) pp. 77–83.

475. *Celestial hierarchy* 1.3; *Divine names* 5.3.

476. Dionysius says that the effect of this divine yearning is to bring us *ecstasy* (in Greek *ekstasis*, or 'standing outside'), 'so that the lover belongs not to self but to the beloved' (*Divine names* 4.13). We are lifted up out of ourselves towards our Source and Goal. 'Love is ecstatic, because it is unitive: the lover is united to the beloved, who is, for him, a manifestation of beauty' (Louth (1989) p. 94). 'The essence of each being is ecstatic towards God' (Balthasar, *The glory of the Lord,* vol. II p. 205). We should however note that for Pseudo-Dionysius this ecstasy was primarily a supramental, rather than an affective, reality – it was the result of the mind being lifted up above itself into a union beyond all knowing or unknowing, rather than the mystical union of love propounded by many medieval writers.

477. *The Divine names* 4.13, p. 82. See Rorem (1993) p. 156.

478. Balthasar, *The glory of the Lord,* vol. II p. 170.

479. *The mystical theology* I.3, p. 137.

480. See Walsh (1988) pp. 58–9.

481. See *The Ecclesiastical hierarchy* 1.3, p. 198.

482. *Cloud* 3, p. 9. All references to the *Cloud* are to the edition of Phyllis Hodgson (cited in Bibliography). Bruce Norquist has pointed out (1995, p. 25) that 'experience' (i.e. 'affeccion', 'felyngs' and related words) in the *Cloud* denotes not simply subjective feelings but an encounter with the objective reality of God, 'a true knowing and feeling of God as he is in himself'. J. P. H. Clark (*Analecta Cartusiana* 119:5, p. 93) suggests, in relation to one text in the *Cloud*, that '"felyng" answers to that awareness of God by love which in the conditions of this life takes the place of open vision'.

483. The Middle English *entent* (modern 'intention') catches the dynamism implicit in the Latin *intentio*, literally a straining towards something: it denotes an act of the will moved by love and directed by reason (Hodgson (1982) p. 159).

484. The *Cloud* author almost certainly did not know Pseudo-Dionysius's original texts, which were written in Greek: he had access to them via the Latin translation of John Sarracenus (1167). The *Cloud* author's understanding of the Dionysian original was also profoundly influenced by a western school of Dionysian interpretation whose principal figure was Thomas Gallus, a regular canon from the Abbey of Saint-Victor in Paris, and thus himself heir to the Victorine school of twelfth-century spirituality, which gave precedence to love over knowledge. Gallus' overriding concern was thus to modify Dionysius' emphasis on knowing

and unknowing by giving a higher place to love as the primary means of union with God. He became abbot of Vercelli in northern Italy c.1220 and died in 1246. He wrote a paraphrase of the whole Dionysian corpus, based on John Sarracenus' Latin translation, and an extended commentary on all of it. (See also Hodgson (1982) p. 188, Walsh (1988) pp. 63–8, Rorem (1993) pp. 216–9, Turner (1995) pp. 186–210.) The *Cloud* author was almost certainly also influenced by the Carthusian spiritual writer Hugh of Balma, prior of the charterhouse of Meyriat from 1289 until his death in 1304: Thomas Gallus' work (which had a very wide circulation in England from the mid-thirteenth century onwards) strongly influenced works of affective piety like Hugh of Balma's *De mystica theologia* and *Viae Sion lugent*: (see Walsh (1981) pp. 19–23; Minnis (1982) p. 65; Hodgson (1982) p.xi; Lees (1983) p. 192; Rorem (1993) p. 221; Clark (*Analecta Cartusiana* 119:4, pp. 53–76). Balma went further than Gallus had in giving priority to love over knowledge in the ascent to God, yet nonetheless without devaluing the importance of the latter: see Dennis D. Martin's introduction to his translation of works by Hugh of Balma and Guigo de Ponte: *Carthusian spirituality: the writings of Hugh of Balma and Guigo de Ponte* (Classics of western spirituality) (New York: Paulist Press, 1997), pp. 19–34.

485. Hodgson (1982 p. ix) suggests his anonymity is deliberate. This of course could argue in favour of Carthusian authorship, as Hodgson herself points out (p. xii). Hogg (1984, p. 106) points out that the Carthusian Richard Methley (of Mount Grace charterhouse) translated the *Cloud* into Latin (now in Pembroke College Cambridge MS. 221); and this ms. strengthens the possibility (though it is only a possibility) that the *Cloud* was written by a Carthusian of Beauvale, a theory also supported by J. P. H. Clark (*Analecta Cartusiana* 119:4, pp. 13–19). Riehle (1981, p. 25) points out that the work of the Franciscan Rudolf of Biberach, which has great similarities with the works of the *Cloud* author, was disseminated mainly through Augustinian and Carthusian houses, strengthening the possibility that the *Cloud* author came from one of these orders. But no conclusive evidence has ever been established.

486. J. P. H. Clark (*Analecta Cartusiana* 119:5, p. 9) notes a movement in the textual tradition of the *Cloud* towards a wider readership than the exclusively monastic.

487. It is clear from *Cloud* 26 that the work is intended for contemplatives, i.e. those in religious orders. The author does however make clear in the Prologue (p. 2) that those living 'in the world' may make use of the teaching in the book to the extent that they can.

488. *Cloud* 34, p. 39.

489. The *Cloud* author here reflects Aquinas' distinction between 'operating' and 'co-operating' grace: the former is the direct initiative of God in influencing us; the latter is our own action or initiative which is assisted or affirmed by God, who thus co-operates with us (see *Summa theologiae* I II.111.2; and B. Davies, *The thought of Thomas Aquinas* (Oxford: Clarendon, 1992), pp. 270–2). It is this second kind of grace that the *Cloud* author has in mind here.

490. 'But in what does this travail consist, I ask you? Surely this travail is all in treading down of the thought of all the creatures that ever God made, and in holding of them under the cloud of forgetting' (*Cloud* 26, p. 34). For an analysis of the different connotations of the 'cloud of forgetting', see Norquist (1995) pp. 40–2. The notion is not original: within the English tradition, it is found in the sermons of Gilbert of Hoyland (1172): 'consider the night to be a kind of forgetfulness (*oblivionem quamdam intellige in nocte*)', *Sermons on the Song of Songs* 1, trans. L. Braceland (Kalamazoo, 1978), p. 47; Latin text in PL 184:14. The fundamental image of ascending towards the vision of God through cloud derives from St Gregory the Great: see Cuthbert Butler OSB, *Western mysticism* (London: Constable, 1922), pp. 127–8.

491. *Cloud* 25, p. 33.

492. *Cloud* 41, p. 44.

493. *Cloud* 46, p. 48.

494. Simon Tugwell, commenting on this theme in the *Cloud*, writes: 'The most typical evidence of grace being at work in us is not that we find ourselves aware of a duty, but that we find ourselves aware of a desire' (Preface to Walsh's translation of *The cloud of unknowing* (Classics of western spirituality) (New York: Paulist Press) p. xii). Cf. also *The book of privy counselling*, p.

75, Norquist's remarks on the meaning of *list* in the *Cloud* (1995 p. 27), and Turner (1995) p. 195. For the significance of play in the *Cloud* author's corpus, see J. P. H. Clark (*Analecta Cartusiana* 119:5 pp. 175–8 and 119:6 pp. 56–7) and René Tixier, "'Good Gamesumli Pley": games of love in *The cloud of unknowing*', *Downside Review* 108 (1990), pp. 235–53.

495. See esp. *Cloud* 34, pp. 38–9. J. P. H. Clark (*Analecta Cartusiana* 119:5 p. 26) suggests that the use of the term 'naked' (*nakid*) in the *Cloud* is intended to resonate with the common monastic emphasis on following the naked (i.e. poor) Christ.

496. *Cloud* 1, p. 8. This is St Thomas's 'operating grace' (see above, n. 489). The *Cloud* author may also have had in mind here Hosea 11.4, where God speaks of drawing his people towards him 'with leading-strings of love'.

497. *Cloud* 1, p. 8.

498. *Cloud* 2, pp. 8–9.

499. *Cloud* 75, p. 74.

500. Short Text (hereafter ST) 1, p. 201. All references to both Short and Long Text are to the edition by E. Colledge and J. Walsh (1978). For an excellent recent summary of the history of editions of Julian, as well as some critical comments on Colledge and Walsh's edition, see Barratt (1995).

501. Tanner (1984) p. xvi. See also Bolton (1980) chapter 9.

502. Ward (1988) and (1993) pp. 49–51. Colledge and Walsh (1978 p. 43) argue that she became an anchoress only after completing the LT, and that until then she had been a nun. Tanner (1984 p. 60) points out that some of the medieval anchoresses in Norwich were given the title 'domina' or 'dame', but that this title was also accorded to laypeople.

503. ST 2, p. 207; LT 2, p. 285.

504. LT 51, p. 520. The Long Text is six times the length of the Short Text.

505. Summarized in Colledge and Walsh (1978) pp. 33–4.

506. Julian explicitly asks her readers to 'leave the beholding of the wretched worm and sinful creature that it was shown to', and instead behold God (ST 6, p. 219). For the relationship between Julian's *Showings* and autobiography, see Abbott (1999).

507. Its provenance is uncertain; but it was certainly at one time in the care of the Carthusian scholar/scribe James Grenehalgh, so it may come from a Carthusian monastery. The manuscript is an anthology of spiritual texts. See Colledge and Walsh (1978) pp. 1–5.

508. For the details of the manuscripts, see Colledge and Walsh (1978) pp. 1–10; Glasscoe (1986) pp. vii–x.

509. Colledge and Walsh (1978) p. 25.

510. LT 1, p. 281.

511. See Watson (1993), esp. pp. 667–72.

512. Watson (1993) p. 682. An alternative chronology is proposed by Ward (1992) pp. 61–2.

513. There is a good deal to be said for Hussey's argument (1989, pp. 116–17) that Julian, like William Langland, never completely let go of what she had written, constantly revising and rethinking it.

514. So Baker (1994) pp. 33 and 176 n. 57: see also Jantzen (1995) p. 167. The two references are ST 4, p. 215; and ST 13, p. 243.

515. See Tugwell (1984), and Watson (1993), esp. pp. 669–71.

516. Wilson (1956) p. 97.

517. Colledge and Walsh (1978) pp. 45 and 735–48.

518. ST 1, p. 202. She reflects something of the Franciscan spirituality of her day with remarks like 'I thought I would have been that time with Mary Magdalene and others that were Christ's lovers' (ST 1, p. 201). See Colledge and Walsh (1978) p. 202 n. 23.

519. See, e.g., her description in ST 9, pp. 231–2 (cf. LT 15, p. 355) of a striking alternation of consolations and desolations, which she believes we experience in order to apprehend the nature of eternal, unchanging bliss.

520. See ST 10, p. 233.

521. Baker (1994) p. 49. The exception is Our Lady (see esp. ST 10, p. 235).

522. Jantzen (1995, p. 159) makes the telling point that, for many women, experience (both Christ's and their own) was effectively the *only* place to start, since conventional education and intellectual study was often not available to them.

523. LT 72, p. 665. The reading from the two Sloane manuscripts seems better than that of the Paris one, despite Colledge and Walsh's comments in their modern English version (1978ii, p. 321 n353).

524. LT 56, pp. 570 and 573 respectively.

525. E.g. Walter Hilton: ('you must know [your own soul] first if you are to come to the knowledge of God', I.16, p. 89). Hilton cites Augustine in this regard (I.40, p. 111).

526. ST 4, p. 213. Compare Julian's vision of the hazelnut with that of Angela of Foligno:

> Afterward he [God] added: 'I want to show you something of my power.' And immediately the eyes of my soul were opened, and in a vision I beheld the fullness of God in which I beheld and comprehended the whole of creation, that is, what is on this side and what is beyond the sea, the abyss, the sea itself, and everything else. And in everything that I saw, I could perceive nothing except the presence of the power of God, and in a manner totally indescribable. And my soul in an excess of wonder cried out: 'This world is pregnant with God!' Wherefore I understood how small is the whole of creation . . . but the power of God fills it all to overflowing.' (*The Book of Blessed Angela (Memorial)*, 6, pp. 169–70)

527. LT 5, p. 301.

528. ST 4, p. 213. Cf. Davies (1992) p. 35.

529. LT 6, pp. 306–7.

530. See Colledge and Walsh (1978) p. 307 n44.

531. Kenneth Leech (1988) stresses the simplicity and earthiness of the hazelnut, but misses the thoroughgoing ascesis that is essential to Julian's view of creation, a view that is much more Augustinian than Leech allows.

532. LT 53, p. 557. Her thought here is very similar to St Paul in Colossians 1.13–20; cf. Colledge and Walsh (1978) p. 557 n. 32.

533. ST 10, pp. 233–5.

534. LT 17, p. 365. Other mss. of the LT here have 'to see thy love suffer' (Colledge and Walsh (1978) p. 20).

535. LT 22, p. 382.

536. LT 21, pp. 380–1.

537. 'Love gave strength to the manhood [of Christ] to suffer more than all men might', ST 11, p. 237. See also ST 12, p. 240. The same point is made in the *Revelations* of St Bridget of Sweden, where God says 'yet I love your soul with charity, that rather than that I should fail it, I would be crucified again, if it were possible' (EETS 178, p. 37).

538. ST 8, p. 227.

539. ST 12, p. 240.

540. LT 51, pp. 513–34 *passim*. There is an interesting precedent to this story in the writings of Robert Grosseteste, Bishop of Lincoln (c.1170–1253), in which he stresses the importance of human beings recognizing their dependence on a divine Saviour:

> Let us imagine a man fallen into a deep pit. And let us imagine that there is one alone who can get him out without any other aid. And let us assume that the whole happiness of the man in the pit lies in recognizing the full extent of his debt and loving his rescuer accordingly. This requires time: if he were rescued at once he would think that, given time, or a lamp, or a rope, or a ladder he could have got out by his own efforts. In order to disabuse him, he is given each one of these in turn – time, the light of natural law, the rope of the Commandments, the ladder of the ceremonial law. All to no avail. Now at last he knows that, even with every possible aid, he can do nothing by his own efforts. If his rescuer now appears and pulls him out without any extraneous aid, the rescued man will recognize that he owes everything to his Saviour, and his devotion to him will be immeasurably increased by this knowledge. Will not his happiness in devotion to his Saviour be correspondingly greater? (*De cessatione legalium* I.8.7–13, trans. R. W. Southern, *Robert Grosseteste: the*

growth of an English mind in medieval Europe, 2nd edn (Oxford: Clarendon, 1992), p. 224)

541. LT 51, p. 530. There is an interesting analogue to Julian's parable in the anonymous late-fourteenth-century untitled poem usually called *Meditations on the life and passion of Christ* (ed. Charlotte d'Evelyn, EETS o.s. 158 (1921)), in which God is described as a king who makes himself into a page 'to bring his servants out of servitude' (p. 27, lines 1011–12).

542. LT 51, p. 533. See also Clark (1984iv) p. 83.

543. LT 52, pp. 546–7.

544. See Pelphrey (1982, pp. 89–91) for the medieval context of this terminology.

545. Baker (1994) argues that Julian's distinction of substance and sensuality is based on Augustine' distinction between the higher and lower reason, basing her argument on the ME definition of *sensualite* as 'the natural capacity for receiving physical sensation understood as an inferior power of the soul concerned with the body' (quoted p. 193 n. 57). But there is no reason why Julian should not simply have developed her own theological terminology as she sought to apply biblical (and especially Pauline) theology to the mystery of suffering and human redemption.

546. LT 55, p. 568.

547. Palliser (1992) p. 45.

548. Pelphrey (1982) p. 164; Palliser (1992) p. 54. Jantzen (1995, p. 150) is surely correct in emphasizing the originality of Julian in affirming our 'sensuality' as well as our 'substance': the body is inherently good, and is to be taken up and redeemed with all the rest of us.

549. This theme is developed by Palliser (1992, esp. pp. 25ff), who shows that mercy is an exclusively divine attribute for Julian, rooted in the 'rightfulness' (fullness of right) of the Trinity. Evelyn Underhill (*Mysticism* (1911), chapter 5) justly says that Julian 'treats this austere and subtle dogma [of the Trinity] . . . with an intimacy and vigour which carry with them a conviction of her own direct and personal apprehension of the theological truth she struggles to describe'. See also Underhill's essay 'Julian of Norwich' (repr. in her *The essentials of mysticism* (1920), pp. 183–98), esp. pp. 195–6).

550. LT 54, p. 563.

551. LT 59, p. 593.

552. LT 59, p. 593.

553. LT 58, pp. 585–6.

554. LT 61, pp. 604–5.

555. As Palliser (1992) has shown, a key theme for Julian is God's protective love. Thus in LT 71 Julian writes 'This he showed to all his lovers who have need of his mercy, with security of keeping' (p. 657). 'Keeping' means 'the working of mercy, our oneing in Christ, as experienced in time' (Palliser (1992) p. 69). It is our personal, existential experience of the divine mercy (cf. Romans 8), the unconditional security of a mother's love as we experience it (Palliser (1992) p. 222).

556. LT 7, p. 313.

557. LT 77, p. 695. Hence the complementary stress Julian always places on God's *courtesy*, his divine condescension in taking upon himself human nature. See esp. LT 7, pp. 313–14; and Riehle (1981) p. 99; Pelphrey (1982) p. 196 n. 2; Jantzen (1987) p. 133; Palliser (1992) p. 173 and n. 41. There is a sociological point here too: Norbert Elias has suggested that 'one of the most decisive transitions' in the civilizing process of Western Europe 'is that of *warriors* to *courtiers*', the strategies of military belligerence gradually replaced by those of courtly etiquette and power (*Power and civility*, (New York: Pantheon Books, 1982) p. 259; quoted in M. C. Schoenfeldt, *Prayer and power: George Herbert and Renaissance courtship* (Chicago UP, 1991), p. 207).

558. LT 74, p. 676.

559. LT 74, pp. 675–6.

560. For Anselm see Chapter 3 above.

561. Clark (1982v) points out that Julian implicitly follows Augustine in using the doctrine of 'appropriation' (identifying particular virtues with individual members of the Trinity, though

without over-schematizing them). In such a context, the idea of God as mother can be seen as one such appropriation. Tugwell (1984, p. 191) argues that she has in mind the Thomist assumption that God is involved in every human action, in which context the image of God as mother intimately concerned with every aspect of human life would seem particularly appropriate.

562. In addition to the texts discussed earlier in this chapter, see the references in Margaret of Oingt (1310), quoted by Cabassut (1949, p. 240) and Colledge and Walsh (1978, p. 616 n.). Mechthild of Hackborn seems to have been a significant possible influence, even if indirectly (Colledge and Walsh (1978) p. 152). Colledge and Walsh also suggest (1978, p. 152) important precedents for her teaching in the *Ancrene Riwle*, and in a homily *An Bispel* (in *Old English Homilies* I, pp. 233–5). But none of these references, nor any of the numerous other references suggested by other modern authors in this connection, is particularly close to Julian in either style or substance.

563. For the latter point, see Pelphrey (1982) p. 188.

564. Palliser (1992, p. 94 and n. 233) rightly argues that Julian does not take sides in contemporary debates about the Fall and the incarnation; rather she is close to Irenaeus' 'Verbum Dei, Jesum Christum Dominum nostrum . . . propter immensam suam dilectionem factus est quod sumus nos, uti nos perficeret esse quod est ipse' (Adv. Haer. V, *praef.*, PG 7:120). Baker (1994, p. 92) stresses the fact that in LT 51 the servant's fall is neither deliberate nor voluntary, unlike Anselm's interpretation of the Fall (in *Cur Deus homo*). Julian does, however, make use of the medieval stress on the *regio dissimilitudinis* by emphasizing that Adam fell into a place ontologically separated from God (medieval theologians referred to both creation and transgression as a fall into the 'region of unlikeness', Baker (1994) p. 94). Nonetheless, for Julian the servant's sin is one of ignorance, rather than of depravity (p. 99).

565. LT 36, p. 438; and cf. LT 64, where she speaks of the 'great wretchedness of our deadly flesh', p. 623.

566. LT 67, pp. 635–6.

567. See the comments of Palliser (1992) p. 93.

568. ST 8, p. 226.

569. ST 8, p. 226.

570. ST 13, pp. 243–4.

571. ST 13, p. 244.

572. 'It (sin) has no manner of substance', ST 13 p. 245. Cf Augustine's statement:

> And to you, therefore, evil is no thing (*non est malum*), and not only to you, but to your whole creation . . . When I asked what wickedness was, I discovered that it was nothing substantial (*Et quaesivi quid esset iniquitas, et non inveni substantiam*), but a perversion of the will and its distortion towards lower things, away from you, O God, who are the highest substance, so that it [the will] throws away what is closest to it and grasps greedily for outward things. (*Confessions* VII.13.19 and VII.16.22)

See also Augustine, *Enchiridion* XI: 'For what is that which we call evil but the absence of good (*privatio boni*)?' Cf. Clark (1981, p. 101); and Aquinas, *Summa theol.* 1a.q.48.a.1 & 3) (Palliser (1992) p. 95 and n. 234). Herbert McCabe OP famously expresses the heart of Aquinas' view of sin as the absence of good:

> If I have a hole in my sock, the hole is not anything at all, it is just an absence of wool or cotton or whatever, but it is a perfectly real hole in my sock. It would be absurd to say that holes in socks are unreal and illusory just because the hole isn't made of anything and is purely an absence. *Nothing* in the wrong place can be just as real and just as important as *something* in the wrong place. If you inadvertently drive your car over a cliff, you will have nothing to worry about; it is precisely the nothing that you will have to worry about. (*God Matters* (London, 1987), p. 29; quoted in Davies (1992), p. 91)

Palliser (1992, p. 97 n253) puts Julian's view well: 'Evil is not merely the neutral absence of a good but the absence of a good which ought to be there.'

573. 'Die Juden würden bei uns vernichtet', remarked Hitler to Czech Foreign Minister František

Chvalkovsky on 21 January 1939, quoted in Introd. (by Antony Polonsky) to Abraham Lewin, *A cup of tears: a diary of the Warsaw Ghetto* (Oxford: Blackwell, 1988), p. 3.

574. See ST 13, p. 245, and ST 14, p. 247.
575. LT 80, p. 712.
576. ST 13, p. 244.
577. ST 13, pp. 244–5.
578. LT 27, pp. 405–6.
579. ST 13, p. 245.
580. See LT 38, and Tugwell (1984) p. 197.
581. e.g. ST 6, p. 219.
582. ST 6, p. 220.
583. 'The more I love with this loving [of my fellow-Christians] while I am here, the more I am like the bliss that I shall have in heaven without end' (ST 6, p. 221). Cf. LT 65 'The charity of God makes in us such a unity that when it is truly seen, no man can part himself from others' (p. 629). See also ST 13, p. 246.
584. 'Methought it was impossible that all manner of thing should be well', LT 32, p. 425.
585. LT 32, p. 426.
586. LT 33, p. 429.
587. ST 17, p. 255.
588. ST 17, p. 256.
589. ST 17, p. 256.
590. Cf. Romans 5.12–21 with ST 14, p. 247.
591. LT 46, p. 493.
592. By definition, because our sensuality precludes us from such knowledge: LT 46, p. 490.
593. As the *Cloud* author does; see Colledge and Walsh (1978) p. 492 n. 18 and Baker (1994) p. 82.
594. LT 83, following the text in the Sloane MSS in Glasscoe (1986) p. 100; cf. with the Paris text in Colledge and Walsh (1978) pp. 723–5.
595. For this subject, see especially the treatment in Molinari (1958).
596. ST 19, p. 258; cf. also LT 2 'Lord, you know what I would, if it be your will that I might have it, and if it be not your will, good lord, be not displeased, for I will not but as you will' (p. 288), and LT 30, where the saints will nothing but what our Lord wills (pp 415–16); cf.also Colledge and Walsh (1978) p. 117.
597. ST 19, p. 259.
598. Julian's view of prayer is close to William of Ockham's *conformitas voluntatis* ('the act of adapting one's will to the will of God' (Oberman (1963) pp. 463–4). For Ockham, as for Julian, sin was essentially nothing, a lack of that conformity of our wills with God's, or rather a deformity of our will: 'Sin lies in the will's refusal to do what it knows should be done' (Leff (1975) pp. 501–8, esp. p. 505). Prayer thus has a moral as well as a spiritual value: by freely conforming our wills with God in prayer, we help to undo the damage wrought by sin.
599. ST 19, p. 260; cf. LT 41, p. 464.
600. ST 19, p. 262. In LT 49 (p. 507) this word is also used of God.
601. LT 43, p. 476. Cf Aquinas, '[Divine providence] does not merely arrange what effects are to occur; it also arranges the causes of these effects and the relationships between them. And among other causes, some things are caused by human acts. So human beings have to do certain things, not so as to change God's plan by their acts, but in order to bring about certain effects by their acts, according to the pattern planned by God. The same thing applies also to natural causes. Similarly in the case of prayer we do not pray in order to change God's plan, but in order to obtain by our prayers those things which God planned to bring about by means of prayers, in order, as Gregory says, that our prayers should entitle us to receive what almighty God planned from all eternity to give us' (*Summa theologiae* II.II q.83 a.2, quoted Davies (1992) p. 180). On the importance of petitionary prayer in Aquinas' thought, see Tugwell, *Albert and Thomas: selected writings* (Classics of western spirituality) (New York:

Paulist Press, 1988), pp. 271ff.
602. LT 43, p. 477: the point is clearer in the Sloane text, ed. Glasscoe (1986) p. 46.
603. LT 43, p. 478.
604. LT 43, following the Sloane texts (Glasscoe (1986) p. 46; the Paris MS has 'entende to his motion'; Colledge and Walsh (1978) p. 480.
605. LT 43, p. 481.
606. LT 42, p. 469.
607. LT 42, p. 469.
608. LT 42, p. 471.
609. LT 42, pp. 471–2.
610. LT 42, p. 473.
611. ST 22, p. 268.
612. LT 41, pp. 464–5.
613. ST 23, p. 270.
614. See ST 19, p. 259, and the development of this passage in LT 41, p. 460.
615. ST 22, p. 269.
616. Among the wide range of opinions on this matter, see Colledge and Walsh (1978) pp. 43–59; Ward (1989); Palliser (1992), esp. p. 5 n. 21; Baker (1994), esp. p. 8.
617. One modern author (Palliser (1992) p. 6) has suggested that Julian moves beyond the (relatively unsophisticated Franciscan) piety of the Short Text to a far surer theology in the Long Text; but this surely undervalues the theological importance of the Short Text, which is conclusively demonstrated by Ward (1992).
618. ST 1, pp. 205–6.
619. See also Colledge and Walsh (1978) pp. 52–3. The fact that, as they point out on p. 40, Benedict XII established one of the Franciscan Order's *studia generalia* in Norwich in the early fourteenth century may also be worth noting.
620. Watson (1993) p. 653. It is however perilous to assume too great a traffic in ideas between Norwich and the continent at the time: see Clark (1992) for the most balanced view on this matter. For differing views see Jantzen (1987) pp. 19–20; Davies (1988) p. 186.
621. Riehle (1981) p. 28.
622. Angela asks God why he created us and why he allowed us to sin (*The Book of Blessed Angela* 6, p. 177). It is striking that it is precisely within the state of prayer that Angela is moved to ask such searching questions, as with Julian. Julian's interest in univeral salvation is similar to that of St Bridget of Sweden (see the Middle English version of St Bridget's *Revelations*, where God says 'But now I, God, who am in the mother [= Mary] and the mother in me, send my messenger to the king: all is well for them that are now living as for those who are not yet born. For righteousness and mercy are endless in God . . . '; EETS 178, p. 65). St Bridget is also close to Julian in stressing not Adam's depravity but God's mercy:
> man was made perfect . . . but consenting to the suggestion of the fiend, he trespassed, saying 'Let us eat of the tree of life, and we shall know all things good and evil.' Thus Adam and Eve did not wish to do harm to God, as the fiend did; nor did they want to be above God, but they did want to be as wise as God. And they fell, but not as the fiend did; for the fiend was envious of God, and his wretchedness shall never have an end. But man willed other than God wanted him to will, and therefore he deserved and suffered righteousness with mercy. (EETS 178, pp. 65–6)
623. LT 2, p. 285.
624. Pelphrey (1982, p. 20) suggests that she could have been able to read but not write, a not unlikely possibility at a time when English was only just emerging as a written language. Tugwell suggests (1984, p. 188) that her reference to herself as 'unlettered' could be seen as a 'modesty formula' which in fact allows her to pass on what has been revealed to her with the more authority since she can hardly claim any of it as her own. Colledge and Walsh (1978, pp. 43–59) argue at length for Julian's intellectual sophistication. Ward (1989) suggests that 'unlettered' denotes the absence of a university education. Others have suggested that Julian

could not read Latin, or even that she was unlettered when she actually experienced the revelations, in which case she would still have had plenty of time to acquire the wisdom which both versions certainly reveal.

625. Colledge and Walsh (1978, pp. 37 and 45) show that Julian usually quotes the Bible from memory, often making her own translations directly from the Vulgate. For the little that we know of the education of girls in this period, see P. J. P. Goldberg ('Women') in Horrox (1994ii), esp. pp. 122–5.

626. A few deserve mention here. (1) While reflecting on her second showing (of the suffering Christ), Julian concludes that this showing 'was a figure and a likeness of our foul black deed, which our fair bright blessed lord bore for our sin' (LT 10, pp. 327–8). As Colledge and Walsh suggest (1978, p. 327), this admirably conveys the sense of Romans 1.23, 'They exchanged the glory of the immortal God for images resembling a mortal human being'. Cf. also 2 Corinthians 5.21, 'For our sake he made him to be sin who knew no sin, so that in him we might become the righteousness of God.'

(2) In the ninth 'showing', Julian rejoices when she realizes that 'we are now in our Lord's meaning on his cross with him in our pains and in our passion dying, and we freely abide on the same cross with his help and his grace' (LT 21, pp. 379–80). Compare, not the actual words, but the underlying theology, with Galatians 2.19 ('I have been crucified with Christ; and it is no longer I who live, but it is Christ who lives in me') and Colossians 1.24 ('I am now rejoicing in my suffering for your sake, and in my flesh I am completing what is lacking in Christ's afflictions for the sake of his body, that is, the church') (Colledge and Walsh (1978) p. 379 n. 11).

(3) There are a number of more general resonances, most of them pointed out by recent authors. The manner in which Julian argues not that we are guiltless, but rather that God does not judge us as our guilt deserves, is clearly Pauline (Palliser (1992) p. 101). The relationship (especially in LT 29 and LT 51) between Adam, Christ, and ourselves is unmistakably derived from Romans (see above and also Jantzen (1987) p. 99, Clark (1982iv), and Baker (1994) pp. 111 and 116. Colledge and Walsh argue (1978, pp. 150–1) that the whole of the fourteenth 'Showing' reflects someone whose mind and heart are 'impregnated with the wealth of Paul's Christological insights'. Palliser (1992, p. 59) suggests that Julian's approach collapses the usual categories of time and eternity: for her as for St Paul the 'already' and the 'not yet' co-exist in tension; and this tension is (at least in part) what we experience as sin (p. 92). Baker (1994, p. 86) points out that, where Augustine focuses his theodicy on Romans 5.12–14, Julian focuses hers (and specifically her story of the lord and the servant) on Romans 5.15–21. There is a key difference.

627. LT 63, pp. 617–18.

628. *The Book of Margery Kempe* (hereinafter called the *Book*), Proem, EETS 212, p. 5; Windeatt (1985) p. 37. All references are to the critical edition by S. B. Meech in EETS 212 (1940) and to the (excellent) modern translation by Barry Windeatt (1985). Bhattacharji (1997, pp. 6 and 102) suggests that the anonymous priest-scribe could easily have added didactic passages to Margery's script: though one wonders why, if he had done so, he did not proceed to censor or homogenize the entire book.

629. For de Worde's extracts, see S. B. Meech (EETS 212) pp. xlvi–xlvii; Stargardt (1985) p. 278; Glasscoe (1993) p. 269; Holbrook (1987); Lochrie (1991) pp. 220–5.

630. Herbert Thurston SJ, in 'Margery the Astonishing' (*The Month*, November 1936, pp. 446–56) and *The Tablet* (review in 24 October 1936).

631. Introduction to their edition of Julian of Norwich's *Showings*, vol. 1 p. 38.

632. Vandenbroucke (1968) p. 426. Knowles (1955, vol. II, p. 198) describes her as someone 'who combined great determination and native wit with the psycho-physical characteristics of an hysteric, and a liability to fits in public of loud sobbing and crying'.

633. See especially Bynum (1988 and 1991), Fries (1984), and also Dickman (1980, 1983 and 1984), Stargardt (1985), Beckwith (1986), Lochrie (esp. 1991), Johnson (1992), Staley (1994) and Bhattacharji (1997). Hope Allen, who made the first (unfortunately never com-

pleted) serious study of Margery's spirituality (in her extensive notes to Meech's edition in EETS 212), describes Margery as 'petty, neurotic, vain, illiterate, physically and nervously over-strained; devout, much-travelled, forceful and talented' (EETS 212, p. lxiv). Not all male scholars dismissed Margery: Martin Thornton (1963, p. 222) describes her *Book* as containing 'the solid core of English spirituality vividly alive'; see Thornton (1960); and note the sensitive response of W. A. Pantin (1955, pp. 256–61).

634. Jeffrey (1988) p. 20.

635. For the subtle way the *Book* negotiates the dangerous divide between orthodoxy and Lollardy, see Staley (1994) pp. 5–11.

636. I.1, EETS 212 p. 6, Windeatt p. 41.

637. I.1, EETS 212 p. 7, Windeatt p. 41. The nature of this illness is much controverted: Fries (1984 p. 355 n8) points out that most male writers on Margery have described this illness as hysteria, and wonders whether such a judgement would have been applied to a male mystic. Depressive illness consequent upon childbirth is much likelier (though it is noteworthy that it does not seem to have recurred after subsequent childbirths). See also Atkinson (1983) p. 209. It should also be noted that the experience of illness is not uncommon among continental female mystics (see Riehle (1981) p. 30; Bynum (1991) p. 188), not to mention Julian of Norwich.

638. I.1, EETS 212 p. 8, Windeatt p. 42.

639. II.10, EETS 212 p. 253, Windeatt p. 297. See Allen, EETS 212 p. 350. There are a number of similarities between the lives of these saints as described in the *Legenda aurea* (which Margery may well have known) and Margery's own life, such as the gift of tears and the hostility of contemporaries. See Jacopone da Voragine, *The Golden Legend*, vol. I pp. 227–9, 350–64, 374–83; vol. II pp. 116–32. For the relationship between Margery and early virgin martyrs, see Winstead (1997) chapter 2.

640. Proem, EETS 212 p. 3, Windeatt p. 34.

641. *Book* I.74, EETS 212 p. 177; Windeatt p. 217.

642. *Book*, I.48, EETS 212 p. 115, Windeatt p. 143; I.3, EETS 212 pp. 11–12, Windeatt pp. 46–7.

643. On the *Book* as quest, see Fries (1984) p. 219. It is worth noting Pauline Matarasso's comments on the Quest of the Holy Grail: 'Its author certainly propounds a hierarchy in which love of God takes precedence over human ties, whether of blood or of friendship, and in so doing treads a path worn smooth by many twelfth century religious writers and leading back to the Gospel itself. But so long as there is no conflict of interest divine and human loves can flourish side by side, the latter purified and strengthened by the former.' (*The redemption of chivalry: a study of the Queste del Saint Graal* (Geneva: Droz, 1979) p. 160).

644. *Book* I.45, EETS 212 p. 108; Windeatt p. 146.

645. I.46, EETS 212 p. 112; Windeatt p. 149.

646. I.52, EETS 212 p. 125; Windeatt p. 163.

647. I.3, EETS 212 p. 11; Windeatt p. 46.

648. I.54, EETS 212 pp. 134–5, Windeatt p. 173. Lochrie (1991, p. 136) writes: 'Kempe uses laughter and what she calls "good game" to mock, disperse, and subvert the culture which excludes her'. Note especially her disagreement with the Archbishop of York on the matter (I.54). It is important to note that Kempe's laughter is not only culturally subversive: it also springs from an intimacy with Jesus, as does Rolle's *iocunditas*, a quality often disapproved of in the mystical tradition but ably defended by Rolle himself (in *Incendium amoris* 26). See Lochrie (1991) pp. 135–63.

649. See I.30 (EETS 212 p. 75, Windeatt p. 111), where Margery says she 'found all people good to her and gentle, save only her own countrymen'.

650. See esp. Bolton (1978) and Bynum (1988 and 1991).

651. P. J. P. Goldberg, however, ('Women', in Horrox (1994ii) pp. 112–31) reminds us that fifteenth-century England's dominant patriarchalism sharply restricted the activities of women outside the home; and Dyan Elliott (1997, p. 157) points out that 'the negative assessment of

women's physiology . . . received new purchase in the late twelfth century with the reintroduction of Aristotle and the ensuing rhetoric of woman as a deformed male'.

652. EETS 280, p. 66.

653. EETS 280, p. 66.

654. VI.10, EETS 280 p. 84. Pauper condemns women whose clothes are so short that the contours of their bodies are visible, thus tempting men (VI.13, EETS 280 p. 91)!

655. *Vita S. Christianae*, in Bokenham, *Legendys of hooly wummen*, pp. 58–86. The immediate source has not been determined (so Serjeantson, Introd. to Bokenham, p. xxii), though it is close to the life of the same saint in Jacobus da Voragine's *Legenda aurea*.

656. See Lagorio (1986); Jantzen (1995), esp. pp. 161–71.

657. St Bridget of Sweden is a particularly fascinating example of this: the theme of attention recurs frequently throughout her *Revelations*. See the comments by Kezel (1990, p. 265).

658. Thus St Bridget describes Christ saying to her: 'To these things that you have now seen and to the other things that I endured, the world's princes are not attentive' (*Revelations*, trans. Kezel (1990) p. 191). NB here the contrast between the attentiveness of the mystics and the inattentiveness of the powerful.

659. Bynum (1991) pp. 135 and 155.

660. This becomes clear on any reading of medieval female hagiography, such as Thomas de Cantimpré's *vitae* of women saints or Bokenham's *Legendys*. On this subject with regard to Margery, see Hirsh (1989). In his magisterial *Western mysticism*, Dom Cuthbert Butler OSB comments on the fact that the kind of spiritual experience that finds expression in divine communications, messages, and pictorial visions occurs almost exclusively among women, and is entirely alien to the classical Christian 'mystical' writers like SS Augustine, Gregory the Great, and Bernard. His conclusion, though cautious, shows that he does not see women mystics as comparable in quality with male ones: 'it is not suggested that the visions [of such women] are any the worse for that; but it does seem that there is something in the mental or psychic make-up of women that renders them susceptible to this kind of quasi-mystical experience' (1922, p. 184). His Downside near-contemporary Dom John Chapman suggests a different explanation: 'contemplation . . . is subconscious, like the circulation of the blood, but quite as real. It is deep down at the root of the intellect, and, in unimaginative and unemotional people, has absolutely *no effect* on the imagination and emotions. In imaginative and emotional people it *does translate* itself into *phantasmata*, and the imagination (and emotions) may be full of joy . . . or of visions and locutions, etc.' (*The spiritual letters of Dom John Chapman* (London: Sheed & Ward, 1935), p. 57).

661. See above, with regard to Margery.

662. Thomas de Cantimpré, *Life* (Middle English version), chapter 9 p. 123. For both Thomas and Christina, see McGinn (1998) pp. 160–2. See also Bynum (1988 p. 131) on the significance of physical suffering in the stories of female saints.

663. Bolton (1978); Bynum (1991). Christina the Astonishing, like many others, received Holy Communion frequently (Thomas de Cantimpré, *Life* (ME version), cap. 15 p. 125). For eucharistic spirituality among the nuns of Helfta, see Bynum (1984), pp. 170–262, esp. pp. 256–7.

664. Where female writers do speak of Jesus as mother (as Julian does) they tend to stress the costliness of motherhood, not its tender affectivity; Bynum (1991) pp. 161 and 164. See also Bynum (1984).

665. Riehle (1981, p. 11) argues that the *Incendium amoris* may be her primary source, but unconvincingly: both the genre and the nature of their respective spiritual experiences diverge. But Rolle's influence was considerable at the time Margery was writing; and she may well have been indebted to it, e.g. in her ability to hear heavenly music, in her confidence in the authenticity of her own spiritual experience, and in her predilection for screaming: for the latter, see Bhattacharji (1997) pp. 30 and 144 n4. For Hilton's influence, see Bhattacharji (1997) p. 45.

666. See Allen (EETS 212, pp. 304–5) and Kezel (1990). References to Bridget in the *Book* include I.20, EETS 212 p. 47, Windeatt p. 83; I.39, EETS 212 pp. 94–5, Windeatt p. 132.

667. I.62, EETS 212 p. 153, Windeatt p. 191; I.68, EETS 212 pp. 165–6, Windeatt p. 205.

668. See Allen in EETS 212 pp. lix, 258, 342–3, 378–80.

669. St Bridget's *Revelations* were translated from the Latin in the fifteenth century (now in EETS o.s. 178), though we cannot be certain that Margery knew them. St Catherine of Siena's *Dialogue* was translated into English in the early fifteenth century for the nuns of the Bridgettine convent at Syon (which Margery visited), and was entitled *The orcherd of Syon* (see references in the Bibliography under Catherine). Angela of Foligno's writings appear in a late-fourteenth-century Oxford manuscript together with Margaret Porete's *Mirror of simple souls*. Jacques de Vitry's life of Mary of Oignies was translated into Middle English in 1213: the prologue to it describes a small group of holy Lotharingian women from his own diocese of Liège whom he sought to commend to the church, advocating their spirituality as a modern form of that of the desert fathers (see Bolton 1978): these women included Mary of Oignies herself (1177?–1213), Christina of St Trond ('the Astonishing', or Christina Mirabilis) (1150–1224), Ivetta of Huy (1157–1228), Margaret of Ypres (1216–37), and Lutgard of Aywières (1182?–1246). The MS that contains the English translation of Jacques' Latin *vita* also contains translations of the Latin *vitae* of St Elizabeth of Spalbeck (1266) and of Christina – the latter an exact translation of Thomas of Cantimpré's *vita* (full details in Bibliography), though we cannot know for certain whether Margery knew these (Stargardt (1985) p. 285).

670. On the influence of continental women mystics on Margery, see H. E. Allen in EETS 212 pp. liii–lxii; Dillon (1996).

671. See Lachance (1993) p. 85; McGinn (1998) p. 143. Dorothea of Montau spent most of her life living as a layperson in Danzig before becoming an anchoress at a nearby Dominican house (Stargardt (1985) p. 307).

672. 'Her revelations as she wrote or dictated them comprise a record of her experiences, exterior and interior. It is her life that is the key to the understanding of her revelations' (Harris, introduction to Kezel (1990), on St Bridget, p. 2).

673. See I.9, and Windeatt (1985) p. 304; cf. Bridget, who was betrothed at the age of 13, bore eight children, and after her husband's death underwent the profound conversion of being a bride of Christ; and Dorothea of Montau. For Angela of Foligno her experience of human love allowed her to enter more deeply later into love of Christ (Lachance (1993) p. 101). She also underwent (as did Margaret of Cortona) a profound conversion after the death of her husband (*The Book of Blessed Angela (Memorial)*, 1, ed. cit. p. 126 and p. 367 n. 11). Mary of Oignies was also married and yet came to be described as one of Christ's chosen brides (Stargardt (1985) p. 280; Jacques de Vitry, *Vita b. Mariae Oigniacensis*).

674. St Bridget moved from being a noble Swedish lady to a pilgrim, visiting the Holy Land and seeing visions based on the lives of Christ and Mary (Nyberg, introduction to Kezel (1990), p. 30; Windeatt (1985) p. 313). Margery follows Angela of Foligno in weeping at the church at Assisi (I.31, and Windeatt (1985) p. 314). See also I.82. On Angela's pilgrimages to Rome and Assisi, see her *Book* (ed. cit. pp. 139ff). The pilgrimage to Aachen (in Margery's case, en route home from accompanying her daughter-in-law back to Prussia): Bridget of Sweden and Bl. Dorothea of Montau also went on pilgrimage to venerate the relics there (Windeatt (1985) p. 329). Margery wanted to see them when they were exposed to the faithful on St Margaret's day, which may have had a special meaning for her as St Margaret was patron of her church in Lynn (Allen, EETS 212 p. 348). Santha Bhattacharji (1997) offers some illuminating insights into Margery's spirituality by examining some contemporary accounts of pilgrimage. Chaucer's Wife of Bath has some interesting parallels with Margery here: see Staley (1994) p. 125, and Wayne Shumaker, 'Alisoun in Wander-Land: a study in Chaucer's mind and literary method', *English Literary History* 18 (1951), pp. 77–89.

675. Margery reflects the characteristic contemporary concern with counting the wounds of Christ (I.80), a concern which was also found among women continental mystics (St Bridget, St Mechthild of Hackborn, et al.; Allen, EETS 212 pp. 334–5; Bynum (1984) p. 192). Cf. Angela of Foligno, *The Book of Blessed Angela (Memorial)*, 1 (ed. cit.) p. 127.

676. St Bridget was recorded as 'patiently enduring, for the sake of Christ's name, the reproaches and affronts of many', *Life* §43, trans. Kezel (1990) p. 84. Margery follows St Bridget in being accused of laughing (I.54 and Allen, EETS 212 p. 317) and defending herself. Angela shares the terrible abandonment of Christ on the cross (see Lachance (1993) p. 85). Angela is also taunted while married and says so explicitly (*The Book of Blessed Angela (Memorial)*, 1, ed. cit. p. 126). Angela is reassured by God when she feels abandoned by him (6, p. 172).

677. I.20, EETS 212 p. 47, Windeatt p. 83; I.72, EETS 212 p. 172, Windeatt p. 212. Angela of Foligno had visions of the suffering Christ during the Eucharist (*The Book of Blessed Angela (Memorial)*, 9, ed. cit. pp. 208–11; Lachance (1993) p. 87; Bynum (1987) chapters 3–5; McGinn (1998) p. 145). St Elizabeth of Spalbeck experienced swoonings and moanings while observing the mass from a cot in her cell (Stargardt (1985) p. 286). See also n. 33 above.

678. I.20, EETS 212 p. 48, Windeatt pp. 83–4; I.74, EETS 212 pp. 176–7, Windeatt pp. 216–17 and 325.

679. Mary of Oignies also wept frequently, e.g. during mass (texts quoted in Stargardt (1985) p. 282), and was often chastised by clergy for so doing (p. 283). When Angela of Foligno experienced Christ betrothing himself to her, she 'began to shout and shriek almost inarticulately as she rolled on the pavement at the entrance to the basilica' – this was the cry of the wounded lover as Christ withdrew himself from her (Lachance (1993) p. 61; *The Book of Blessed Angela (Memorial)*, 3, ed. cit. p. 142). Angela screams when she hears anyone speak about God (because she loves him so much; 1, p. 131). Cf also *Angela*, 2, p. 136 (in this passage, note the embarrassment of male onlookers; the man goes on to suspect that Angela's screaming might be diabolically inspired; see p. 137). The similarities with Margery's experiences are striking. St Bridget's biographer(s) describe her thus: 'the bride of Christ [= Bridget] was so very fervent in prayer and tears that when her husband was away, she passed almost whole nights in vigil' (*Life* chapter 15, in Kezel (1990) p. 75). Bridget also describes herself as being at Mount Calvary, 'most mournfully weeping' (*Revelations* 7, in Kezel (1990) p. 188). Kezel points out (p. 295) that the reason for this weeping is not given: it is simply juxtaposed with the vision of Christ's passion). St Catherine of Siena (*Dialogue* 89, in Noffke (1980) p. 164) situates tears within the context of an integrated love of God and neighbour, a love that derives from God's prior love of the soul (and cf. *Dialogue* 95: 'Such is the glorious fruit that comes of tears joined with charity for others', p. 179). Later (*Dialogue* 92, p. 170) she says that tears are the fruit of our infinite desire ('Thus are fire and tears made one in burning desire. And because desire has no end it cannot be satisfied in this life'). She distinguishes tears of death from tears of life: 'tears are the messenger that lets you know whether life or death are in the heart' (*Dialogue* 94, p. 175). See also Thomas de Cantimpré's description of Christina the Astonishing, who 'wept and tormented herself' when anyone in the city whom she knew to be a sinner died; *Life* (ME version), chapter 17 p. 126.

680. I.59, EETS 212 p. 144, Windeatt p. 183; for Julian, see *Showings*, LT 25 (ed. cit. vol. 2 pp. 398–401); Allen notes that St Catherine of Siena had argued with God against the existence of hell, and that contemporary continental heretics were denying the existence of it too (EETS 212 p. 321).

681. I.22, EETS 212 p. 52, Windeatt p. 88.

682. Aelred, *De institutione inclusarum* 15; *Holy maidenhood* (ed. cit. in Bibliography to Chapter 3), p. 233.

683. Mechthild of Hackborn had a vision of the Lord in heaven taking her by the hand for a dance (Allen, EETS 212 p. 283). Allen may be wrong here. Hamburger (1990, pp. 58–9) quotes the *Das fliessende Licht der Gottheit* of Mechthild of Magdeburg (not of Hackborn) in this respect.

684. The most important text is I.35, where 'the Father took her by the hand in her soul before the Son and the Holy Ghost and the Mother of Jesus . . . saying to her soul, "I take thee, Margery, for my wedded wife, for fairer, for fouler, for richer, for poorer"' (EETS 212 p. 87, Windeatt p. 123). A similar passage occurs in the Middle English version of St Bridget's *Revelations*: 'I have chosen and take thee to me to be my spouse for to show thee my privy counsels, for so it pleases me' (Revelations I.2, EETS 178 p. 1). This reflects the ceremonious description of

spiritual marriage within the mystic's heart in Bl. Dorothea's experience (see Allen, EETS 212 p. 301). For St Catherine's 'mystical espousal' to Christ in 1368, see Noffke (1980) p. 4. Angela of Foligno hears Christ say to her: 'You are holding the ring of my love. From now on you are engaged to me and you will never leave me' (*The Book of Blessed Angela (Memorial)*, 3, ed. cit. p. 143). The stress on taking Christ as one's husband is common to all the women described by Jacques de Vitry and others, and is characteristic of contemporary Cistercian and Dominican (as well as of contemporary beguine) spirituality (Bolton (1978) p. 267). Elliott (1993, p. 254) points out that the stress on spiritual marriage among the married female mystics of the late Middle Ages hardly ever seems to have led to a deepening of their own earthly marriages. It certainly did not do very much for the marriage of Margery and John.

685. Angela seems to have conceived a kind of priestly role for herself: she is told that the blessing she performs over food and drink will take away not only her sins but those of others too (Lachance (1993) pp. 88–9). Margery, like Christina the Astonishing and Mary of Oignies, is anxious both to avoid the pains of purgatory and try to help those who are already there (Stargardt (1985) p. 288).

686. A few others may be briefly noted. Like Margery, Mary of Oignies wears white clothing, as does Christina the Astonishing (Thomas de Cantimpré, Life of Christina (Middle English version), EETS cap. 17 p. 126. See also Stargardt (1985) p. 287; and D. Elliott, 'Dress as mediator between inner and outer self: the pious matron of the High and later Middle Ages', in *Mediaeval Studies* 53 (1991), pp. 279–308). Margery's capacity to foretell future events is similar to that of Christina the Astonishing, who prophesies the capture of Jerusalem by Moslems (Thomas de Cantimpré, op. cit., cap. 25 p. 128). Margery's capacity for laughter and mirth echoes a reference in Julian of Norwich's *Showings*, where she comments, after a vision of Christ: 'I understood that we may laugh to comfort ourselves and rejoice in God, because the devil is overcome', LT 13); and Bokenham describes St Elizabeth of Hungary as having a vision of heaven, to which her response is to laugh ('I thought I could no better express it than with laughing') (quoted Lochrie (1991) p. 147).

687. See Kieckhefer (1984) pp. 188–9, and Colin Richmond ('Religion') in Horrox (1994ii) p. 195. Was this because her personality was unsuitable (unlikely), or because she had no clerical associates to sponsor her (more likely), or because she had no links with any religious order (possible), or because of something that happened during the last years of her life, not covered by her Book (conceivable)? Or was it because late medieval English religion was altogether too cool and rational in tone to provide fruitful soil for the flowering of Margery's 'enthusiastic' spirituality?

688. Margery says 'I receive every good will as for the deed [itself]', I.86, EETS 212 p. 212, Windeatt p. 253. See also Allen, EETS 212 pp. 339–40.

689. See Knowles (1955) vol. II pp. 198–9. Margery's devotion to the childhood of Christ (I.30, EETS 212 p. 78, Windeatt p. 113) may have originated with Francis (Allen, EETS 212 p. 297), though it is common among continental women mystics (Bynum (1984) p. 173).

690. The only extant manuscript of it comes from this.

691. I.73, EETS 212 p. 174 and n. 5, Windeatt p. 214; Allen, in EETS 212 p. 330.

692. Lochrie (1991) pp. 210–20. As Lochrie points out (p. 215), Methley's experiences would of course be less public than those of Margery.

693. I.60, EETS 212 p. 148, Windeatt p. 187.

694. I.81, EETS 212 p. 195, Windeatt p. 236.

695. I.36, EETS 212 p. 90, Windeatt pp. 126–7. See Allen's references to Cistercian and other writers in EETS 212 p. 302.

696. For this kind of devotion, see Bynum (1987) pp. 246ff.

697. Thus Dickman (1980, p. 165) charmingly comments that 'for Margery Kempe, Christ has become the boy next door', and that Margery is 'too fascinated with the concrete to search for what is hidden within it'.

698. At one point (I.35, EETS 212 p. 87, Windeatt p. 123) Margery experiences God the Father taking her as his wife.

699. I.14, EETS 212 pp. 30–1, Windeatt p. 66. See also I.84, where Christ says: 'I am as a hidden God in your soul', EETS 212 p. 205, Windeatt p. 246.
700. I.77, EETS 212 p. 184, Windeatt p. 224. Hamburger (1997, esp. p. 157) shows that late medieval nuns used the image of the heart as a bridal chamber or home for Christ to dwell in.
701. I.36, EETS 212 pp. 90–1, Windeatt p. 127. Cf. also I:89, EETS 212 p. 219, Windeatt p. 260. The stress on the Holy Spirit is particularly pronounced in the Proem.
702. I.55, EETS 212 p. 135, Windeatt p. 174.
703. E.g. I:15, EETS 212 p. 34, Windeatt p. 69; I.27, EETS 212 p. 64, Windeatt p. 100.
704. I.18, EETS 212 pp. 42–3, Windeatt p. 78. The reference to one of St Jerome's writings has not been traced. Bhattacharji (1997, pp. 41–2) points out the significance of Jerome for Margery as a precedent for the gift of tears.
705. II.10, EETS 212 pp. 248ff, Windeatt pp. 292ff.
706. She was greatly despised and reproved because she wept so much – both by the monks and priests, and by secular men (I.13, Windeatt p. 62). In I.44 many concluded that she had a devil within her. Yet Atkinson (1983, p. 64) points out that almost every spiritual guide or authority to whom Margery turned for advice understood and respected her tears – including of course Julian of Norwich. See also Bhattacharji (1997) p. 43.
707. Atkinson (1983) p. 60; Bhattacharji (1997) p. 122; and see the Proem, EETS 212 p. 2, Windeatt p. 34.
708. I.40, EETS 212 p. 98, Windeatt p. 135. In I.28 Margery says she holds back the tears for as long as she can: the body is 'overcome with the unspeakable love that wrought so fervently in her soul' (EETS 212 pp. 69–70, Windeatt p. 105). See also I.40: 'she could not weep but when God gave it to her, and often he gave it so plenteously that she could not withstand it' (EETS 212 p. 98, Windeatt p. 135).
709. See Adnès (1976). A key precedent for Margery is clearly St Anselm's *Oratio* XVI (to St Mary Magdalene), where tears (both hers and the supplicant's) are treated in *extenso* (Allen, EETS 212 p. 272). One of the earliest mentions of them (in I.5) may imply a kind of *baptisma lacrimarum*, since she claims a plenary indulgence was granted her at that moment (Allen, EETS 212 p. 262). The distinctive theological ingredients of compunction as understood by St Gregory the Great (true contrition, compassion, and desire for God) are found in Margery's spirituality as much as in that of Julian (see Colledge and Walsh in Julian, *Showings*, p. 72; and J. Leclercq, *The love of learning and the desire for God* (trans. C. Misrahi) (London: SPCK, 1978), pp. 37–41).
710. See, e.g., I.6, EETS 212 p. 19, Windeatt p. 53; I.12, where she weeps amazingly for a monk's sins, EETS 212 p. 26, Windeatt p. 61; and I.57, where she weeps for the souls in purgatory, for the poor, for Jews, Saracens and heretics, that they might become Christians, EETS 212 pp. 140–1, Windeatt p. 179.
711. I.3, EETS 212 p. 13, Windeatt p. 48.
712. II.10, EETS 212 pp. 248–54, Windeatt pp. 292–7.
713. I.78, EETS 212 p. 186, Windeatt p. 226.
714. I.72, EETS 212 pp. 172–3, Windeatt pp. 212–13.
715. I.13, EETS 212 p. 27, Windeatt p. 63.
716. Allen points out, though (EETS 212 p. 270) that this passage may refer to imprisonment.
717. Thus, as Allen points out (EETS 212 p. 257) avoiding the mistake and the consequent fate of St Joan of Arc. For the significance of confessors for medieval women mystical writers, see Dillon (1996).
718. I.53, EETS 212 p. 129, Windeatt p. 168.
719. Dickman (1980) p. 169.
720. I.21, EETS 212 p. 49, Windeatt pp. 84–5.
721. I.22, EETS 212 p. 52, Windeatt p. 88.
722. II.2, EETS 212 p. 225, Windeatt p. 269.
723. I.76, EETS 212 p. 180, Windeatt p. 220.
724. Bynum (1991) pp. 41–3.

725. For Frye see S. Kenney, *Walter Frye and the Contenance Angloise* (New Haven and London: Yale UP 1964). For the *Ave regina celorum* see Strohm (1993) pp. 394–8.
726. An exquisite painting of Mary Queen of Heaven (by the Master of the Saint Lucy Legend, active in Bruges c.1480–1510), now at the National Gallery of Art, Washington DC, includes a representation of the score of what appears to be a variation on Walter Frye's motet. The painting (c.1485–1500) comes from the convent of Santa Clara, near Burgos in Spain, and depicts simultaneously the Immaculate Conception, the Assumption and the Coronation of Mary.
727. See Christopher Page, 'Music in the rise of Europe', in *Musical Times* 136 (1995), pp. 127–34.
728. For the pervasive influence of the rose as an image of late medieval spirituality, see Hamburger (1997) chapter 2.

BIBLIOGRAPHY

Primary Works

The Abbey of the Holy Ghost (trans. from the French), ed. N. F. Blake in *Middle English religious prose* (York medieval texts) (London: Edward Arnold, 1972); ET in Swanson (1993i) pp. 96–103

Angela of Foligno, *Book*: trans. P. Lachance in *Angela of Foligno: Complete works* (Classics of western spirituality) (New York: Paulist Press, 1993)

Bokenham, Osbern, *Legendys of hooly wummen*, ed. M. S. Serjeantson (EETS o.s. 206) (1938)

The book of prive counseling, A pistle of preier, A pistle of discrecioun of stirings, Deonise hid divinite, A tretys of the stodye of Wysdome that men clepen Beniamyn, A tretis of discrescyon of spirites (all by the *Cloud* author), ed. P. Hodgson, *The cloud of unknowing and related treatises* (Analecta Cartusiana 3) (Salzburg: Institut für Anglistik und Amerikanistik, 1982); P. Hodgson (ed.), *Deonise hid divinite and other treatises on contemplative prayer related to The cloud of unknowing* (EETS o.s. 231) (1955); modern ET by James Walsh, *The pursuit of wisdom and other works by the author of The cloud of unknowing* (Classics of western spirituality) (New York: Paulist Press, 1988)

The book of the craft of dying, ed. C. Horstman, *Yorkshire writers: Richard Rolle of Hampole and his followers* (London: Sonnenschein, 1895–6), vol. 2, pp. 406–20; modernized by Swanson (1993i), pp. 125–47

The book of vices and virtues, ed. W. N. Francis (EETS o.s. 217) (1842)

Bridget of Sweden (Birgitta), *Revelations* (Middle English translation): *The Revelations of Saint Birgitta*, ed. W. P. Cumming (EETS o.s. 178) (1929); modern ET of Books V and VII by A. R. Kezel, *Life and selected revelations* (Classics of western spirituality) (New York: Paulist Press, 1990)

Catherine of Siena, *Dialogue*, trans. S. Noffke (Classics of western spirituality) (New York: Paulist Press, 1980); anonymous fifteenth-century ET *The orcherd of Syon* ed. P. Hodgson and G. M. Liegey (EETS 258) (1966) (see also under Hodgson below)

The chastising of God's children, ed. J. Bazire and E. Colledge (Oxford: Blackwell, 1957)

Chaucer, Geoffrey, *The Riverside Chaucer*, ed. L. D. Benson, 3rd edn (Oxford UP, 1987)

Clanvowe, John, *Works*, ed. V. J. Scattergood (Cambridge: D. S. Brewer, 1975)

Clanvowe, John, *The two ways* trans. in Jeffrey (1988) pp. 272–90

The cloud of unknowing, ed. P. Hodgson, EETS 218 (1944); English text in BL MS Harley 959, ed. J. P. H. Clark (6 vols with commentary) (Analecta Cartusiana 119) (Salzburg: Institut für Anglistik und Amerikanistik, 1989–96); ed. P. Hodgson (Oxford UP, 1958); ed. J. McCann (London: Burns Oates, 1952); ed. P. Hodgson, *The cloud of unknowing and related treatises* (Analecta Cartusiana 3) (Salzburg: Institut für Anglistik und Amerikanistik, 1982); Latin versions ed. J. P. H. Clark and J. Hogg, *The Latin versions of the Cloud of unknowing*, 4 vols. (Analecta Cartusiana 120) (1989–90); modern ET by James Walsh (Classics of western spirituality) (New York: Paulist Press, 1981)

Contemplations of the dread and love of God, ed. M. Connolly (EETS 303) (Oxford UP, 1993)

De gracia Dei, in Lincoln Cathedral Library, Thornton MS (Cat.A.1.17); trans. in Jeffrey (1988) pp. 265–71

Dives and Pauper, ed. P. H. Barnum (EETS 275 and 280) (1976 and 1980)

Edmund of Abingdon (Edmund Rich), *Speculum ecclesiae*, in Edmund of Abingdon, *Speculum religiosorum and Speculum ecclesiae* ed. H. P. Forshaw (Auctores Britannici Medii Aevi 3) (London: British Academy, 1973), pp. 29–111; Middle English version (*The mirror of St Edmund*) in G. G. Perry (ed.), *Religious pieces in prose and verse* (EETS o.s. 26) (1867, rev. 1913), pp. 16–50

English Wycliffite sermons, 3 vols (Oxford UP, 1983–90)

Froissart, *Chronicles*, abridged and trans. G. Brereton (Harmondsworth: Penguin, 1968)

Furnivall, F. J. (ed.), *The fifty earliest English wills* (EETS o.s. 78) (1882)

Henry, Duke of Lancaster, *Le Livre de seyntz medicines*, ed. E. J. Arnould (Anglo Norman Text Society 2) (Oxford: Blackwell, 1940; repr. Johnson Reprint Company, 1967)

Hilton, Walter, *The scale of perfection*: modern ET by J. P. H. Clark and R. Dorward (Classics of western spirituality) (New York: Paulist Press, 1991)

Hilton, Walter, *Epistola ad quemdam seculo renunciare volentem* (Letter to someone seeking to renounce the world), in *Walter Hilton's Latin writings*, vol. 2, ed. J. P. H. Clark and Cheryl Taylor (Analecta Cartusiana 124/2) (Salzburg: Institut für Anglistik und Amerikanistik, 1987), pp. 243–98

Hilton, Walter, *Epistola de lectione &c* (Letter on reading, &c), in *Walter Hilton's Latin writings*, vol. 2, ed. J. P. H. Clark and Cheryl Taylor, (Analecta Cartusiana 124/2) (Salzburg: Institut für Anglistik und Amerikanistik, 1987), pp. 215–43; ET by Joy Russell Smith ('Letter to a hermit'), in *The Way* 6 (1966), pp. 230–41

Hilton, Walter, *Epistola de utilitate et prerogativis religionis* (Letter on the usefulness and privileges of religion), in *Walter Hilton's Latin writings*, vol. 1, ed. J. P. H. Clark and Cheryl Taylor (Analecta Cartusiana 124/1) (Salzburg: Institut für Anglistik und Amerikanistik, 1987), pp. 103–73

Hilton, Walter, Epistle on the *Mixed Life*, ed. C. Horstman in *Yorkshire writers: Richard Rolle of Hampole, an English father of the Church, and his followers*, vol. 1 (London: Sonnenschein, 1895), pp. 264–92; ed. S. J. Ogilvie-Thompson in *Salzburg Studies in English Literature* (Elizabethan and Renaissance studies 92:15) (Salzburg, 1986); ed. and modernized D. Jones, *Minor works of Walter Hilton* (London, 1929); trans. in Swanson (1993i), pp. 104–24

Hilton, Walter, *Benedictus*, ed. and modernized D. Jones in *Minor works of Walter Hilton* (London: Burns, Oates & Washbourne, 1929), pp. 217–31

Hilton, Walter, *Bonum est*, ed. and modernized D. Jones in *Minor works of Walter Hilton* (London: Burns, Oates & Washbourne, 1929), pp. 171–213

Hilton, Walter, *Of angels' song*, ed. C. Horstman in *Yorkshire writers* (London: Library of Early English Writers, vol. 1, 1895), pp. 175–82; ed. T. Takamiya (Studies in English Literature) (Tokyo: English Literary Society of Japan, 1977); ed. and trans. R. Dorward in *Eight chapters on perfection and Angels' song* (Fairacres, Oxford: SLG Press, 1983)

Hilton, Walter, *The prickynge of love*: see under James of Milan

Hilton, Walter, *Qui habitat*, ed. B. Wallner (Lund Studies in English 23) (Lund, 1954); ed. and modernized D. Jones in *Minor works of Walter Hilton* (London, 1929), pp. 115–68

The holy boke Gratia Dei, ed. M. L. Arntz, in *Elizabethan and Renaissance Studies*, ed. J. Hogg (Salzburg: Institut für Anglistik und Amerikanistik, 1981)

Jacobus de Voragine, *Legenda aurea* (The Golden Legend), ed. T. Graesse (Leipzig, 1850); ET by W. G. Ryan, *The golden legend: readings on the saints*, 2 vols. (Princeton UP, 1993)

Jacques de Vitry, *Vita b.Mariae Oigniacensis*, in *Acta SS* June vol. 5; ET *The lyf of S.Marye of Oegines*, ed. C. Horstmann, in *Anglia (Zeitschrift für englische Philologie)* 8 (1885)

James of Milan, *Stimulus amoris*: Middle English trans. (attrib. to Walter Hilton) *The prickynge of love*, ed. H. Kane, 2 vols (Salzburg studies in English Literature: Elizabethan and Renaissance studies 92:10) (Salzburg, 1983); lightly modernized edn as *The goad of love*, ed. C. Kirchberger (London: Faber & Faber, 1952)

Jeffrey, D. L. (ed. and trans.)., *The law of love: English spirituality in the age of Wyclif* (Grand Rapids: Eerdmans, 1988)

Julian of Norwich, *A book of showings to the anchoress Julian of Norwich*, ed. E. Colledge and J. Walsh, 2 vols (Toronto: Pontifical Institute of Mediaeval Studies, 1978); *A revelation of love*, ed. M. Glasscoe (Exeter UP, 1986); modern ET *Showings*, ed. E. Colledge and J. Walsh (Classics of western spirituality) (New York: Paulist Press, 1978) (1978ii)

Kempe, Margery: *The Book of Margery Kempe*, ed. S. B. Meech and H. B. Allen (EETS o.s. 212) (1940); ed. Lynn Staley (Kalamazoo, Mich.: TEAMS Mediaeval Institute Publications, 1996); trans. B. A. Windeatt (Harmondsworth: Penguin, 1985)

A ladder of foure ronges by the whiche men mowe wele clyme to heven, ed. P. Hodgson in *Deonise hid divinite* (EETS o.s. 231) (rev. edn, Oxford UP, 1958)

Langland, William, *Piers Plowman* (B text), ed. Kane and Donaldson: *Piers Plowman: the B version* (Piers Plowman: the three versions, vol. II) (London: Athlone, 1975)

Lay folks' Mass book ed. T. F. Simmons (EETS 71 or 118) (1879)

Lollard sermons, ed. G. Cigman (EETS 296) (1989)

Love, Nicholas, *The mirrour of the blessed lyf of Jesu Christ*, ed. J. Hogg and L. F. Powell, 3 vols (Analecta Cartusiana 91) (Salzburg: Institut für Anglistik und Amerikanistik, 1989–95)

Lydgate, John, *The minor poems of John Lydgate* vol. 1, ed. H. N. MacCracken (EETS e.s. 107) (London, 1911)

The pilgrimage of the life of man (trans. by Lydgate from the French), ed. F. J. Furnivall and K. B. Locock (EETS e.s. 77, 83, and 92) (London, 1899–1904; repr. as 1 vol., New York, 1975)

Pilgrimage of the soul (c.1413) (EETS e.s. 69, 84 and 89)

Mannyng, Robert (of Brunne), *Handlyng synne* ed. I. Sullens (Medieval and Renaissance studies 14) (Binghamton, NY, 1983); ed. F. J. Furnivall (EETS 119, 123) (London, 1901–3)

McNeill, J. T., and H. M. Garner, *Medieval Handbooks of Penance* (New York: Columbia UP, 1938, repr. 1990)

The meditations on the life and passion of Christ, ed. C. d'Evelyn (EETS o.s. 158) (London, 1921)

Methley, Richard, *To Hew heremyte: a pystyl of solytary lyfe nowadayes*, ed. J. Hogg (Analecta Cartusiana 31) (Salzburg: Institut für Anglistik und Amerikanistik, 1977), pp. 91–119

[Methley, Richard.] Hogg, J., 'A mystical diary: the *Refectorium Salutis* of Richard Methley of Mount Grace Charterhouse', in *Kartäusermystik und -mystiker* 2 (Analecta Cartusiana 55/1) (Salzburg: Institut für Anglisitik und Amerikanistik, 1981), pp. 208–38

[Methley, Richard.] 'The *Scola Amoris Languidi* of Richard Methley of Mount Grace Charterhouse transcribed from the Trinity College Cambridge ms. 0.2.56', in *Kartäusermystik und -mystiker* 2 (Analecta Cartusiana 55/2) (1981), pp. 138–65

[Methley, Richard.] 'The *Dormitorium Dilecti Dilecti* of Richard Methley of Mount Grace Charterhouse', transc. by J. Hogg, in *Analecta Cartusiana* 55/5 (1982), pp. 79–103

Michel, Dan, *Ayenbite of inwyt or Remorse of conscience*, ed. P. Gradon; vol. 1 (text) (EETS o.s. 23) (1866); vol. 2 (notes) (EETS 278) (1979) (ET of *Somme le roi*)

The Middle-English Harrowing of hell and Gospel of Nicodemus, ed. W. H. Hulme (EETS o.s. 100) (1907, repr. 1961)

Mirk, John: *Mirk's Festial: a collection of homilies by Johannes Mirk*, ed. T. Erbe (EETS e.s. 96) (1905)

Myers, A. R. (ed.), *English historical documents* vol. 5 (1485–1558) (London: Eyre & Spottiswoode, 1967)

Our daily work: a mirror of discipline, in Lincoln Cathedral Library, Thornton MS (Cat. A.1.17); trans. in Jeffrey (1988) pp. 236–64

Pecock, Reginald, *The reule of Crysten religioun*, ed. W. C. Greet (EETS o.s. 171) (1927)

Pearl, ed. E. V. Gordon (Oxford: Clarendon, 1953); M. Andrew and R. Waldron, *The poems of the Pearl manuscript* (Exeter UP, 1996)

Political, religious and love poems, ed. F. J. Furnivall (EETS o.s. 15) (1866)

Porete, Marguerite, *The mirror of simple souls*, CCCM 59; ME trans. ed. M. M. Doiron, in *Archivio Italiano per la storia della pietà* 5 (Rome: Edizioni di Storiae Letteratura, 1968), pp. 241–382 (with Appendix on 'M. N.'s glosses by E. Colledge and R. Guarnieri)

The Prymer or Lay folks' prayer book, ed. H. Littlehales (EETS o.s. 105 and 109) (1895 and 1897) [includes article by Edmund Bishop (q.v.), 'The origin of the Prymer']

Rich, Edmund: see Edmund of Abingdon

Richard of St Victor, *Beniamin minor* (Middle English version): *Richard of St Victor's Benjamin minor, englished*, ed. C. Horstman in *Yorkshire writers: Richard Rolle of Hampole, an English father of the Church, and his followers*, vol. 1 (London: Sonnenschein, 1895), pp. 162–72

Rolle, Richard, *English writings of Richard Rolle, hermit of Hampole*, ed. H. E. Allen (Oxford: Clarendon, 1931; repr. Gloucester: Sutton, 1988)

Rolle, Richard, *Liber de amore Dei contra amatores mundi*, ed. P. F. Theiner, *The Contra amatores mundi of Richard Rolle of Hampole* (Berkeley: California UP, 1968)

Rolle, Richard, *English Psalter*, ed. H. R. Bramley, *The Psalter or Psalms of David and certain canticles, with a translation and exposition in English by Richard Rolle of Hampole* (Oxford: Clarendon, 1884)

Rolle, Richard, *Emendatio vitae*: Latin text ed. N. Watson (with *Orationes ad honorem nominis Ihesu*) (Toronto medieval Latin texts 21) (Toronto: Pontifical Institute of Mediaeval Studies, 1995); ME translation, *The mending of life* (by R. Misyn); modern ET by F. M. M. Comper in R. C. Petry, *Late medieval mysticism* (The library of Christian classics) (Philadelphia: Westminster Press, 1957), pp. 208–44

Rolle, Richard, *Expositio super novem lectiones mortuorum*: Moyes, M. (ed.), *Richard Rolle's Expositio super novem lectiones mortuorum: an introduction and contribution towards a critical edition*, 2 vols. (text in vol. II pp. 122–283) (Salzburg Studies in English Literature: Elizabethan and Renaissance Studies, 92:12) (Salzburg: Institut für Anglistik und Amerikanistik, 1988)

Rolle, Richard, *Incendium amoris*, ed. M. Deanesly, *The Incendium amoris of Richard Rolle of Hampole* (Manchester UP, 1915); ME trans. *The fire of love*, ed. R. Harvey (EETS o.s. 106) (1896); ET by Clifton Wolters, *The fire of love* (Harmondsworth: Penguin, 1972)

Rolle, Richard, *Melos amoris*, ed. and trans. Vandenbroucke in *Le chant d'amour*, SC 168–9; ed. E. J. F. Arnold (Oxford: Blackwell, 1957)

[Rolle, Richard.] *The Officium and Miracula of Richard Rolle of Hampole*, ed. R. Woolley (London: SPCK, 1919); ET in F. M. M. Comper, *The life of Richard Rolle together with an edition of his English lyrics* (London: Dent, 1928), pp. 305–14

Rolle, Richard, *Super Canticum Canticorum*, ed. E. M. Murray, *Richard Rolle's Comment on the Canticles, edited from MS. Trinity College Dublin 153* (New York: Fordham University dissertation, 1958); trans. R. Boenig, *Richard Rolle: Biblical commentaries* (Elizabethan and Renaissance studies 92:13) (Salzburg, 1984)

Rolle, Richard, *Super Psalmum vicesimum*, ed. J. C. Dolan (Lewiston: Edward Mellon, 1991); trans. R. Boenig, *Richard Rolle: Biblical commentaries* (Elizabethan and Renaissance studies 92:13) (Salzburg, 1984)

Rolle, Richard, *Tractatus super Apocalypsim*: *Richard Rolle de Hampole: vie et oeuvres, Tractatus super Apocalypsim*, ed. N. Marzac (Paris: Vrin, 1968); trans. R. Boenig, *Richard Rolle: Biblical commentaries* (Elizabethan and Renaissance studies 92:13) (Salzburg, 1984)

Rolle, Richard, *The English writings*, ed. and trans. R. S. Allen (Classics of western spirituality) (New York: Paulist Press, 1989)

Rolle, Richard, English works, in *Prose and verse*, ed. S. J. Ogilvie-Thompson (EETS o.s. 293) (1988)

Ruusbroec, Jan van: J. Bazire and E. Colledge (ed.), *The chastising of God's children and The treatise of perfection of the sons of God* (Oxford: Blackwell, 1957)

Selections from English Wycliffite writings, ed. Anne Hudson (Cambridge UP, 1978)

Sir Gawain and the Green Knight, ed. I. Gollancz (EETS o.s. 210); M. Andrew and R. Waldron, *The poems of the Pearl manuscript* (Exeter UP, 1996)

Songs, carols and other miscellaneous poems from the Balliol MS.354 (Richard Hill's Commonplace-Book), ed. R. Dyboski (EETS e.s. 101) (1907)

Suso, Henry, *Orologium sapientiae*: ME version *The seven points of trewe wisdom*, in C. Horstmann (ed.), '*Orologium sapientiae* or *The seven points of trewe wisdom* aus MS. Douce 114', in *Anglia*

(Zeitschrift für englische Philologie) 8 (1888)

Thomas de Cantimpré, *Vita S.Christinae Mirabilis*, in AA.SS July 1868 vol. 5, pp. 650–60; ME version *The lyfe of seinte Cristin the mervelous of the towne of seinte Trudous in Hasban*, ed. C. Horstmann, in *Anglia (Zeitschrift für englische Philologie)* 8 (1885), pp. 119–33

Tracts on the Mass, ed. J. W. Legg (Henry Bradshaw Society 27) (1904)

Transcripts of Sussex wills as far as they relate to ecclesiological and parochial subjects, up to the year 1560, ed. R. G. Rice and W. H. Godfrey (Sussex Record Society vols. 41–43 and 45) (1935–41)

Uthred of Boldon: H. Farmer, 'The *Meditacio devota* of Uthred of Boldon', in *Analecta Monastica* 4 (Studia Anselmiana 43) (Rome: Pontifical Institute of St Anselm, 1958), pp. 187–206

The vision of Orm, ed. Hugh Farmer, in *Analecta Bollandiana* 75 (1957), pp. 72–82

Whiterig, John, *Meditationes cuiusdam monachi apud Farneland quondam solitarii*, ed. H. Farmer (Studia Anselmiana 41) (*Analecta Monastica* 4) (Rome, 1957), pp. 141–245; ET *The monk of Farne: the meditations of a fourteenth century monk*, ed. H. Farmer, trans. by a Benedictine of Stanbrook (London: DLT, 1961)

Windeatt, B. (ed.), *English mystics of the Middle Ages* (Cambridge UP, 1994)

Wyclif, John (attrib.), *Unprinted English works of Wyclif*, ed. F. D. Matthew (EETS o.s. 74) (1880)

Secondary Works

Abbott, Christopher, *Julian of Norwich: autobiography and theology* (Studies in medieval mysticism 2) (Woodbridge: D. S. Brewer, 1999)

Adnès, P., 'Larmes', in *Dictionnaire de spiritualité* 9 (1976)

Alford, J. A. (ed.), *A companion to Piers Plowman* (Berkeley: University of California, 1988)

Allen, H. E., *Writings ascribed to Richard Rolle, hermit of Hampole, and materials for his biography* (New York: D. C. Heath, 1927)

Astell, Ann, 'Feminine *figurae* in the writings of Richard Rolle', in *Mystics Quarterly* XV:3 (Sept 1989)

Aston, Margaret, 'Lollardy and sedition, 1381–1431', in *Past and Present* 17 (1960), pp. 1–37

Atkinson, C. W., *Mystic and pilgrim. The 'Book' and the world of Margery Kempe* (Ithaca, NY: Cornell UP, 1983)

Baker, D. N., *Julian of Norwich's Showings: from vision to book* (Princeton UP, 1994)

Baldwin, A. P., 'The tripartite reformation of the soul in *The scale of perfection*, *Pearl*, and *Piers Plowman*', in Glasscoe (1982), pp. 136–49

Baldwin, A. P., 'The triumph of patience in Julian of Norwich and Langland', in H. Phillips (ed.), *Langland, the mystics and the mediaeval English tradition: essays in honour of S. S. Hussey* (Woodbridge: Boydell, 1990), pp. 71–83

Balthasar, Hans Urs von, *The Glory of the Lord*, vol. 2 (ET of Herrlichkeit), trans. A. Louth et al. (Edinburgh: T&T Clark, 1984)

Barratt, A., 'How many children had Julian of Norwich? Editions, translations, and versions of her *Revelations*' in A. C. Bartlett (ed.), *Vox mystica: essays on medieval mysticism in honor of Professor Valerie M. Lagorio* (Cambridge: D. S. Brewer, 1995), pp. 27–40

Beckwith, S., 'A very material mysticism: the medieval mysticism of Margery Kempe', in D. Aers (ed.), *Medieval literature: criticism, ideology and history* (Brighton: Harvester, 1986), pp. 34–57

Beer, Frances, *Women and mystical experience in the Middle Ages* (Woodbridge: Boydell, 1992)

Bestul, Thomas H., 'Devotional writing in England between Anselm and Richard Rolle', in Lagorio (1986), pp. 12–28

Bestul, Thomas H., 'Chaucer's Parson's Tale and the late-medieval tradition of religious meditation', in *Speculum* 64 (1989), pp. 600–19

Bhattacharji, Santha, *God is an earthquake: the spirituality of Margery Kempe* (London: DLT, 1997)

Bishop, Edmund, 'The origin of the Prymer', in *The Prymer or Lay folks' prayer book*, ed. H. Little-hales, II (EETS 109) (London, 1897), pp. xi–xxxviii

Le Blevec, D., and Girard, Alain, *Les Chartreux, l'art et la spiritualité, XIV–XVIIIme siècles* (Xme Colloque International) (Paris: Éditions du Cerf, 1989)

Blenkner, L., 'The theological structure of *Pearl*', in *Traditio* 24 (1968), pp. 43–75

Bolton, Brenda, '*Vitae matrum*: a further aspect of the *Frauenfrage*', in D. Baker (ed.), *Medieval women* (Oxford: Blackwell, 1978), pp. 253–73

Bolton, J. L., *The medieval English economy, 1150–1500* (London: Dent, 1980)

Bossy, John, 'Blood and baptism: kinship, community and christianity in western Europe from the fourteenth to the seventeenth centuries', in D. Baker (ed.), *Sanctity and secularity: the Church and the world* (Studies in church history 10) (Oxford: Blackwell, 1973), pp. 129–43

Bossy, John, 'Social history of confession', in *Transactions of the Royal Historical Society* (1974)

Bossy, John, *Christianity in the West 1400–1700* (Opus books) (Oxford UP, 1985)

Bossy, John, 'Holiness and society', in *Past and Present* 75 (1977)

Bossy, John, 'The Mass as a social institution, 1200–1700', in *Past and Present* 100 (1983)

Bossy, John, 'Prayers' (Christian life in the later Middle Ages), in *Transactions of the Royal Historical Society* 6th series, I (1991), pp. 137–48; and V. Reinburg, 'Note on John Bossy, "Prayers"', pp. 148–50

Bradley, Ritamary, 'Julian of Norwich on prayer', in *Analecta Cartusiana* 106:1 (1983)

Bradley, Ritamary, 'Julian of Norwich: writer and mystic', in *An introduction to the medieval mystics of England*, ed. P. E. Szarmach (Albany NY: State University of New York Press, 1984), pp. 195–216

Brieger, P., *English Art 1216–1307* (Oxford: Clarendon Press, 1957)

Brooke, Christopher, 'Religious sentiment and church design in the later Middle Ages', in *Medieval church and society: collected essays* (London: Sidgwick & Jackson, 1971), pp. 162–82

Brown, A. D., *Popular piety in late medieval England: the diocese of Salisbury 1250–1550* (Oxford: Clarendon, 1995)

Bühler, C. F., 'Prayers and charms in certain Middle English scrolls', in *Speculum* 39 (1964), pp. 270–78

Burgess, Clive, '"For the increase of divine service": chantries in the parish in late medieval Bristol', in *Journal of Ecclesiastical History* 36 (1985), pp. 46–65

Butler, Cuthbert, *Western mysticism*, 2nd edn (London: Constable, 1951)

Bynum, C. W., *Jesus as mother: studies in the spirituality of the High Middle Ages* (London: California UP, 1984)

Bynum, C. W., *Holy feast and holy fast: the religious significance of food to medieval women* (London: California UP, 1987)

Bynum, C. W., 'Religious women in the later Middle Ages', in Raitt (1988) pp. 121–39

Bynum, C. W., *Fragmentation and redemption: essays on gender and the human body in medieval religion* (New York: Zone, 1991)

Cabassut, A., 'Une dévotion médiévale peu connue: la dévotion à Jesus notre mère', in *Revue d'asceticisme et de mysticisme* 25 (1949), pp. 234 ff.

CaigerSmith, A., *English medieval mural paintings* (Oxford: Clarendon, 1963)

Carpenter, C., 'The religion of the gentry of fifteenth–century England', in D. Williams (ed.), *England in the fifteenth century: proceedings of the 1986 Harlaxton Symposium* (Woodbridge: Boydell, 1987), pp. 53–74

Carruthers, Leo, 'In pursuit of holiness outside the cloister: religion of the heart in *The abbey of the Holy Ghost*', in B. M. Kienzle (ed.), *Models of holiness in medieval sermons: proceedings of the International Symposium at Kalamazoo, 47 May 1995* (Textes et études des instituts d'études du Moyen Age 5) (Louvain-la-Neuve: Fédération Internationale des Instituts d'Études Médiévales, 1996), pp. 211–27

Catto, J., 'Wyclif and the cult of the Eucharist', in K. Walsh and D. Wood (eds.), *The Bible in the Medieval World* (Studies in church history, subsidia 4) (Oxford: Blackwell, 1985), pp. 269–86 (1985i)

Catto, J., 'Religious change under Henry V', in D. L. Harriss (ed.), *Henry V: the practice of kingship* (Oxford UP, 1985), pp. 97–115 (1985ii)

Catto, J., 'Fellows and helpers: the religious identity of the followers of Wyclif' in P. Biller and B. Dobson (eds.), *The medieval Church: universities, heresy, and the religious life: essays in honour of*

Gordon Leff (Studies in church history, subsidia 11) (Woodbridge: Boydell, 1999), pp. 141–62

Chambers, R. W., *On the continuity of English prose* (London: Oxford University Press, 1932)

Clark, J. P. H., 'Walter Hilton and "Liberty of Spirit"', in *Downside Review* 96 (1978), pp. 61–78 (1978i)

Clark, J. P. H., 'The "Cloud of Unknowing", Walter Hilton and St John of the Cross: a comparison', in *Downside Review* 96 (1978), pp. 281–98 (1978ii)

Clark, J. P. H., 'Intention in Walter Hilton', in *Downside Review* 97 (1979), pp. 69–80 (1979i)

Clark, J. P. H., 'Action and contemplation in Walter Hilton', in *Downside Review* 97 (1979), pp. 258–74 (1979ii)

Clark, J. P. H., 'Sources and theology in *The cloud of unknowing*', in *Downside Review* 98 (1980), pp. 83–109

Clark, J. P. H., '<u>Fiducia</u> in Julian of Norwich', in *Downside Review* 99 (1981), pp. 97–108, 214–29

Clark, J. P. H., 'English & Latin in the *Scale of perfection*: theological considerations', in *Analecta Cartusiana* 35:1 (1982), pp. 167–212 (1982i)

Clark, J. P. H., 'Augustine, Anselm and Walter Hilton', in Glasscoe (1982), pp. 102–27 (1982ii)

Clark, J. P. H., 'Walter Hilton and the Psalm commentary *Qui habitat*', in *Downside Review* 100 (1982), pp. 235–62 (1982iii)

Clark, J. P. H., 'Predestination in Christ according to Julian of Norwich', in *Downside Review* 100 (1982), pp. 79–91 (1982iv)

Clark, J. P. H., 'Nature, grace and the Trinity in Julian of Norwich', in *Downside Review* 100 (1982), pp. 203–20 (1982v)

Clark, J. P. H., 'Richard Rolle: a theological reassessment', in *Downside Review* 101 (1983), pp. 108–39 (1983i)

Clark, J. P. H., 'The problem of Walter Hilton's authorship: *Bonum est, Benedictus* and *Of Angels' Song*', in *Downside Review* 101 (1983), pp. 15–29 (1983ii)

Clark, J. P. H., 'Some monastic elements in Walter Hilton and in the "Cloud" Corpus', in *Die Kartäuser und die Reformation* vol. 1 (*Analecta Cartusiana* 108:1) (1984) (1984i)

Clark, J. P. H., 'Walter Hilton and the *Stimulus Amoris*', in *Downside Review* 102 (1984), pp. 79–118 (1984ii)

Clark, J. P. H., 'Walter Hilton in defence of the religious life and of the veneration of images', in *Downside Review* 103 (1985), pp. 1–25

Clark, J. P. H., 'The Trinitarian theology of Walter Hilton's *Scale of perfection, Book II* ', in *Langland, the mystics and the mediaeval English tradition: essays in honour of S. S. Hussey*, ed. H. Phillips (Woodbridge: Boydell, 1990), pp. 125–40

Clark, J. P. H., 'Late fourteenth-century Cambridge theology and the English contemplative tradition', in Glasscoe (1992) pp. 1–16

Clark, J. P. H., 'The *cloud of unknowing* and the contemplative life', in *Die Kartäuser und ihre Welt-Kontakte und 'gegenseitige Einflüsse'* 1, Analecta Cartusiana 62 (1993), pp. 44–65

Clark, J. P. H.: see also *Cloud of unknowing* in Primary Works above

Clark and Dorward (1991): see under Hilton, Walter

Cleve, Gunnel, 'Margery Kempe: a Scandinavian influence in medieval England?', in Glasscoe (1992) pp. 163–78

Colledge and Walsh (1978): see Julian of Norwich among Primary Works above

Colledge and Walsh (1978ii): see Julian of Norwich among Primary Works above

Courtenay, W. J., 'Nominalism and late medieval religion', in Trinkaus and Oberman (1974) pp. 26–58

Cowdrey, H. E. J., 'The Carthusians in England', in *La naissance des Chartreuses* (VI Colloque International d'histoire et de spiritualité cartusiennes) (Grenoble: Editions des Cahiers de l'Alpe, 1986), pp. 345–56

Cross, C., *Church and people 1450–1600: the triumph of the laity in the English church* (Oxford: Blackwell Publishers Ltd, 1976; rev. edn 1987)

Davidson, C., 'Northern spirituality and the late medieval drama in York', in E. R. Elder (ed.), *The spirituality of western Christendom* (Cistercian Studies 30) (Kalamazoo: Cistercian Publications, 1976), pp. 125–51

Davies, Brian, *The thought of Thomas Aquinas* (Oxford: Clarendon, 1992)

Davies, Oliver, *God within: the mystical tradition of northern Europe* (London: DLT, 1988)

Davis, C. T., 'Ockham and the Zeitgeist', in Trinkaus and Oberman (1974) pp. 59–64

Davis, C. T., *Schools and scholars in fourteenth-century England* (Princeton UP, 1987)

Davis, N. Z., 'Some tasks and themes in the study of popular religion', in Trinkaus and Oberman (1974) pp. 307–36

Davis, V., 'The Rule of Saint Paul, the first hermit, in late medieval England', in W. J. Sheils (ed.), *Monks, hermits and the ascetic tradition* (Studies in church history 22) (Oxford: Blackwell, 1985), pp. 203–14

Desmond, L. A., 'The Statute of Carlisle and the Cistercians 1293–1369', in *Studies in medieval Cistercian history presented to Jeremiah F. O'Sullivan* (Cistercian Studies 13) (Spencer, Mass.: Cistercian Publications, 1971), pp. 138–62

Dickman, Susan, 'Margery Kempe and the English devotional tradition', in Glasscoe (1980) pp. 156–72

Dickman, Susan, 'Julian of Norwich and Margery Kempe: two images of fourteenth-century spirituality', in J. Hogg (ed.), *Spätmittelalterliche geistliche Literatur in der Nationalsprache*, 1 (*Analecta Cartusiana* 106) (Salzburg, 1983), pp. 178–94

Dickman, Susan, 'Margery Kempe and the continental tradition of the pious woman', in Glasscoe (1984), pp. 150–68

Dillon, Janette, 'Holy women and their confessors or confessors and their holy women? Margery Kempe and the continental tradition', in R. Voaden (ed.), *Prophets abroad: the reception of continental holy women in late-medieval England* (Cambridge: D. S. Brewer, 1996), pp. 115–40

Doiron (1968); see under Porete among Primary Works above

Doyle, A. I., 'Carthusian participation in the movement of works of Richard Rolle between England and other parts of Europe in the 14th and 15th centuries', in *Analecta Cartusiana* 55:2 (1981), pp. 109–20

Driver, M. W., 'Pictures in print: late fifteenth- and early sixteenth-century English religious books for lay readers', in M. G. Sargent (ed.), *De cella in seculum: religious and secular life and devotion in late medieval England* (Cambridge: D. S. Brewer, 1989), pp. 229–44

Duffy, Eamon, *The stripping of the altars* (Yale UP, 1992)

Dunn, E. C., 'Popular devotion in the vernacular drama of medieval England', in *Medievalia et Humanistica* n.s. 4 (1973), pp. 55–68

Edwards, Kathleen, *The English secular cathedrals in the Middle Ages: a constitutional study with special reference to the fourteenth century* (Manchester UP, 1967)

Ellis, R., 'Viderunt eam filie Syon: the spirituality of the English house of a medieval contemplative order from its beginnings to the present day', in *Analecta Cartusiana* 68:2 (1984)

Elliott, Dyan, *Spiritual marriage: sexual abstinence in medieval wedlock* (Chichester: Princeton UP, 1993)

Elliott, Dyan, 'The physiology of rapture and female spirituality', in P. Biller and A. J. Minnis (eds.), *Medieval theology and the natural body* (York studies in medieval theology 1) (Woodbridge: York Medieval Press, 1997), pp. 141–74

Englert, R. W., *Scattering and oneing: a study of conflict in the works of the author of the Cloud of unknowing* (*Analecta Cartusiana* 105) (Salzburg, 1983)

Erickson, C., *The medieval vision* (New York: Oxford UP, 1976)

Erskine, J. A., 'Margery Kempe and her models: the role of the authorial voice', in *Mystics Quarterly* 15 (1989), pp. 75–85

Evans, J., *English art 1307–1461* (Oxford: Clarendon, 1949)

Farmer, H. (1957) and (1961): see under Whiterig, John, among Primary Works above

Farmer, H. (1958): see under Uthred of Boldon among Primary Works above

Fleming, P. W., 'Charity, faith, and the gentry of Kent 1422–1529', in Tony Pollard (ed.)., *Property and politics: essays in later medieval English history* (Gloucester: Sutton, 1984)

Fries, M., 'Margery Kempe', in *An introduction to the medieval mystics of Europe*, ed. P. E. Szarmach (Albany: New York State UP, 1984), pp. 217–36

Foster, Frances A., *Legends of the after-life*, in *A manual of the writings in Middle English: 1050–1500*, ed. J. Burke Severs and A. E. Hartung (Hamden, Conn., 1967–), vol. 2 pp. 452–57 and 645–49

Fryde, E. B., *The Great Revolt of 1381* (General series pamphlets 100) (London: Historical Association, 1981)

Galbraith, M. E., *The figure of Piers: the image on the coin* (Cambridge: D. S. Brewer, 1981)

Gatta, Julia, *A pastoral art: spiritual guidance in the English mystics* (London: DLT, 1987)

Gillespie, Vincent, 'Strange images of death: the passion in later medieval English devotional and mystical writing', in J. Hogg (ed.), *Zeit, Tod und Ewigkeit in der Renaissance Literatur* 3 (*Analecta Cartusiana* 117) (Salzburg, 1987), pp. 111–59

Gillespie, Vincent, 'Vernacular books of religion', in J. Griffiths and D. Pearsall (eds.), *Book production and publishing in Britain, 1375–1475* (Cambridge: Cambridge University Press, 1989), pp. 317–44

Glasscoe, Marion (ed.), *The medieval mystical tradition in England* (Exeter: University of Exeter, 1982)

Glasscoe, Marion (ed.), *The medieval mystical tradition in England* III (Cambridge: D. S. Brewer, 1984)

Glasscoe, Marion (ed.), *The medieval mystical tradition in England* IV (Cambridge: D. S. Brewer, 1987)

Glasscoe, Marion (ed.), *The medieval mystical tradition in England* V (Cambridge: D. S. Brewer, 1992)

Glasscoe, Marion, 'Means of showing: an approach to reading Julian of Norwich', in *Analecta Cartusiana* 106:1 (1983)

Glasscoe, Marion, *English medieval mystics: games of faith* (Longmans medieval and Renaissance library) (London: Longmans, 1993)

Glasscoe, Marion (1986): see Julian of Norwich among Primary Works above

Goodman, A., 'The piety of John Brunham's daughter, of Lynn', in D. Baker (ed.), *Medieval women* (Oxford: Blackwell, 1978), pp. 347–58

Gougaud, L., *Devotional and ascetic practices in the Middle Ages*, trans. G. C. Bateman (London: Burns, Oates, 1927)

Gray, Douglas, *Themes and images in the medieval English religious lyric* (London: Routledge & Kegan Paul, 1972)

Gründler, Otto, 'Devotio moderna', in Raitt (1988) pp. 176–93

Haas, Alois Maria, 'Schools of late medieval mysticism', in Raitt (1988) pp. 140–75

Hackett, B., *The spiritual life of the English Austin friars of the fourteenth century* (Studia Augustinia: Vita Spiritualis Magister 11) (Rome, 1959), vol. 2, pp. 471–92

Hackett, B., 'William Flete and the *De remediis contra temptaciones*, in *Mediaeval studies presented to Aubrey Gwynn SJ* (Dublin: Colm O Lochlainn, 1961), pp. 330–48

Hamburger, J. F., *The Rothschild Canticles: art and mysticism in Flanders and the Rhineland circa 1300* (London and New Haven: Yale UP, 1990)

Hamburger, J. F., *Nuns as artists: the visual culture of a medieval convent* (Berkeley: California UP, 1997)

Hanawalt, B. A., 'Keepers of the lights: late medieval English parish gilds', in *Journal of Medieval and Renaissance Studies* 14 (1984)

Harding, Alan, *England in the thirteenth century* (Cambridge medieval textbooks) (Cambridge UP, 1993)

Harper-Bill, C., *The Pre-Reformation Church in England, 1400–1530* (London: Longman, 1989)

Harper-Bill, C. (ed.), *Religious belief and ecclesiastical careers in late medieval England* (Woodbridge: Boydell, 1991) (articles by Swanson, Dunning, and Richmond)

Harriss, G. L., *Henry V: the practice of kingship* (Oxford UP, 1985)

Hausherr, Irénée, SJ, *Penthos: the doctrine of compunction in the Christian East*, trans. A. Hufstader OSB (Cistercian Studies 53) (Kalamazoo: Cistercian Publications, 1982)

Heath, P., 'Urban piety in the later Middle Ages: the evidence of Hull wills', in *The church, politics and patronage in the fifteenth century*, ed. B. Dobson (Gloucester: Sutton, 1984), pp. 209–34

Hicks, M. A. 'The piety of Margaret, Lady Hungerford (d.1478)' in *Journal of Ecclesiastical History* 38 (1987), pp. 19–38

Hirsh, J. C., 'Prayer and meditation in late medieval England: MS Bodley 789', in *Medium Ævum* 48 (1979), pp. 55–66

Hirsh, J. C., *The revelations of Margery Kempe: paramystical practices in late medieval England* (Medieval and Renaissance authors 10) (Leiden: Brill, 1989)

Hodgson, Phyllis, *The Orcherd of Syon and the English mystical tradition* (London: Oxford University Press, 1964)

Hodgson, Phyllis, *The fourteenth century mystics* (London: Longmans, 1967)

Hodgson (1982): see *The cloud of unknowing* among Primary Works above

Hogg, James, 'Mount Grace Charterhouse and late medieval English spirituality vol. 2: the Trinity College Cambridge ms. O.2.56', in *Analecta Cartusiana* 64 (1978)

Hogg, James, 'Mount Grace Charterhouse and late medieval English spirituality' (Collectanea Cartusiensia 3), *Analecta Cartusiana* 82:3 (1980), pp. 1–43

Hogg, James, 'English charterhouses & the Devotio Moderna', in *Acta colloquii quarti internationalis Cartusiensis*, ed. J. de Grauwe (Destelbergen, 1983) (1983i)

Hogg, James, 'The contribution of the Brigittine Order to late medieval English spirituality', in *Analecta Cartusiana* 35:3 (1983), pp. 153–74 (1983ii)

Hogg, James, 'The Latin *Cloud*', in Glasscoe (1984), pp. 104–15

Hogg, James, 'Everyday life in a contemplative order in the 15th century', in *Analecta Cartusiana* 116:4 (1989), pp. 95–109

Hogg, James, 'Richard Whytford', in *Studies in St Birgitta and the Brigittine Order* 2 (*Analecta Cartusiana* 35:19) (Salzburg, 1993), pp. 254–66

Holbrook, S. E., 'Margery Kempe and Wynkyn de Worde', in Glasscoe (1987), pp. 27–46

Horrox, Rosemary, *The Black Death* (Manchester medieval sources) (Manchester UP, 1994) (1994i)

Horrox, Rosemary (ed.), *Fifteenth-century attitudes: perceptions of society in late medieval England* (Cambridge UP, 1994) (1994ii)

Hudson, Anne, *Lollards and their books* (History series 54) (London and Ronceverte: Hambledon Press, 1985)

Hudson, Anne, 'A new look at the Lay folks' catechism', in *Viator* 16 (1985), pp. 243–58

Hudson, Anne, 'The Lay folks' catechism: a postscript', in *Viator* 19 (1988), pp. 30–79

Hudson, Anne, *The premature Reformation: Wycliffite texts and Lollard history* (Oxford UP, 1988)

Hughes, Jonathan, *Pastors & visionaries: religion and secular life in late medieval Yorkshire* (Woodbridge: Boydell & Brewer, 1988)

Huizinga, J., *The waning of the Middle Ages* (1924; ET by F. Hopman: Harmondsworth: Penguin, 1955)

Hussey, S. S., 'Walter Hilton: traditionalist?', in Glasscoe (1980), pp. 1–16

Hussey, S. S., 'Editing the Middle English mystics', in *Analecta Cartusiana* 35:2 (1983), pp. 160–73

Hussey, S. S., 'The audience for the Middle English mystics', in M. G. Sargent (ed.), *De cella in seculum: religious and secular life and devotion in late medieval England* (Cambridge: D. S. Brewer, 1989), pp. 109–22

Hussey, S. S., 'From *Scale* I to *Scale* II', in *The mystical tradition and the Carthusians* 4 (*Analecta Cartusiana* 130:4) (Salzburg: Institut für Anglistik und Amerikanistik, 1995), pp. 46–67

Inge, W. R., *Studies of English mystics* (London: Murray, 1906)

Jantzen, Grace, *Julian of Norwich* (London: SPCK, 1987)

Jantzen, Grace, *Power, gender and Christian mysticism* (Cambridge studies in ideology and religion 8) (Cambridge UP, 1995)

Johnson, A. F., 'The Guild of Corpus Christi and the procession of Corpus Christi in York', in *Mediaeval Studies* 38 (1976), pp. 372–84

Johnson, L. S., 'Margery Kempe: social critic', in *Journal of Medieval and Renaissance Studies* 22 (1992), pp. 159–84

Johnston, William, *The mysticism of the Cloud of unknowing* (Wheathampstead: Anthony Clarke, 1974)

Jolliffe, P. S., *A checklist of Middle English prose writings of spiritual guidance* (Toronto: Pontifical Institute of Mediaeval Studies, 1974)

Jones, M. K., and Underwood, M. G., *The king's mother: Lady Margaret Beaufort, Countess of Richmond and Derby* (Cambridge: Cambridge University Press, 1992)

Kahrl, S. J., 'Secular life and popular piety in medieval English drama', in T. J. Heffernan (ed.), *The popular literature of medieval England* (Tennessee studies in literature 28) (Knoxville: Tennessee UP, 1985), pp. 85–107

Kane, H. (1983): see under James of Milan among Primary Works above

Keiser, G. R., 'The Holy Boke Gratia Dei', in *Viator* 12 (1981)

Keiser, G. R., 'Noght how lang man lifs; bot how wele": the laity and the Ladder of perfection', in M. G. Sargent (ed.), *De cella in seculum: religious and secular life and devotion in late medieval England* (Cambridge: D. S. Brewer, 1989), pp. 145–59

Kennedy, D. G., *Incarnational element in Hilton's spirituality* (Salzburg studies in English literature, Elizabethan and Renaissance studies 92:3) (Salzburg, 1982)

Kenny, Anthony, *Wyclif* (Past masters) (Oxford UP, 1985)

Kerby-Fulton, K., *Reformist apocalypticism and 'Piers Plowman'* (Cambridge studies in medieval literature) (Cambridge UP, 1990)

Kerry, C., 'Hermits, fords and bridge-chapels', in *Derbyshire Archaeological and Natural History Journal* 14 (1892), pp. 54–71

Kettle, Ann J. (ed.), 'A list of families in the archdeaconry of Stafford 1532–3', in *Collections for a History of Staffordshire* (Staffordshire Record Society), 4th series, 8 (1976)

Kezel (1990): see Bridget of Sweden among Primary Works above

Kieckhefer, Richard, *Unquiet souls: fourteenth-century saints and their religious milieu* (Chicago UP, 1984)

Kieckhefer, Richard, 'Major currents in late medieval devotion', in Raitt (1988) pp. 75–108

Kleinberg, Arvaid M. *Prophets in their own country: living saints and the making of sainthood in the later Middle Ages* (Chicago UP, 1992)

Knight, S., 'Chaucer's religious Canterbury Tales', in G. Kratzmann and J. Simpson (eds.), *Medieval English religious and ethical literature: essays in honour of G. H. Russell* (Cambridge: D. S. Brewer, 1986), pp. 156–66

Knowles, David, *The religious orders in England II: The end of the Middle Ages* (Cambridge UP, 1955)

Knowles, David, *The English mystical tradition* (London: Burns & Oates, 1962)

Knowles, David, 'The influence of Pseudo-Dionysius on western mysticism', in P. Brooks (ed.), *Christian spirituality* (London: SCM Press, 1975)

Kuczynski, Michael P., *Prophetic song: the Psalms as moral discourse in late medieval England* (Philadelphia: Pennsylvania UP, 1995)

Kümin, B. A., *The shaping of a community: the rise and reformation of the English parish c.1400–1560* (Aldershot: Scolar Press, 1996)

Lachance (1993): see Angela of Foligno among Primary Works above

Lagorio, V. M., 'The medieval continental women mystics: an introduction', in P. Szarmach (ed.), *An introduction to the medieval mystics of England* (Albany NY: New York State UP, 1984), pp. 161–93

Lagorio, V. M. (ed.), *Mysticism medieval and modern* (Salzburg studies in English literature, Elizabethan and Renaissance studies 92:20) (Salzburg, 1986)

Leech, Kenneth, 'Hazelnut theology: its potential and perils', in *Julian reconsidered* (Oxford: Fairacres, 1988), pp. 1–9

Lees, R. A., *The negative language of the Dionysian school of mystical theology: an approach to the Cloud of unknowing*, 2 vols. (*Analecta Cartusiana* 107) (Salzburg, 1983)

Leclercq, J., Vandenbroucke, F. and Bouyer, L. *The spirituality of the Middle Ages* (vol. 2 of *A history of Christian spirituality*) (London: Burns & Oates, 1968)

Leff, Gordon, *Bradwardine and the Pelagians: a study of his 'De causa Dei' and its opponents* (Cambridge studies in medieval life and thought, new series 5) (Cambridge UP, 1957)

Leff, Gordon, *Heresy in the later Middle Ages*, 2 vols (Manchester UP, 1967)

Leff, Gordon, *William of Ockham: the metamorphosis of scholastic discourse* (Manchester UP, 1975)

Leff, Gordon, *The dissolution of the mediaeval outlook* (New York, London: Harper and Row, 1976)

Lewis, C. S., *The allegory of love* (Oxford UP, 1958)

Llewelyn, R., *With pity not with blame* (London: DLT, 1982)

Llewelyn, R. (ed.), *Julian: woman of our day* (London: DLT, 1985)

Lochrie, Karma, '*The Book of Margery Kempe*: the marginal woman's quest for literary authority', in *Journal of Medieval and Renaissance Studies* 16 (1986), pp. 33–55

Lochrie, Karma, *Margery Kempe and translations of the flesh* (Philadelphia: Pennsylvania UP, 1991)

Lossky, V., "Les éléments de 'Théologie négative' dans la pensée de saint Augustin", in *Augustinus Magister: Congrès international augustinien: Paris, 21–24 Septembre 1954*, 3 vols (Paris: Études Augustiniennes, 1954) vol. 1, pp. 575–81

Louth, Andrew, *Denys the Areopagite* (London: Geoffrey Chapman, 1989)

Louth, Andrew, 'Platonism in the Middle English mystics', in Anna Baldwin and Sarah Hutton (eds.), *Platonism and the English imagination* (Cambridge UP, 1994), pp. 52–64

Lovatt, R., *The influence of religious literature of Germany and the Low Countries on English spirituality c1350–1475* (Oxford University DPhil thesis, 1965)

Lovatt, R., 'The imitation of Christ in late medieval England', in *Transactions of the Royal Historical Society*, 5th series, 18 (1968), pp. 97ff.

Lovatt, R., 'Henry Suso and the medieval mystical tradition', in Glasscoe (1982), pp. 47–62

Lovatt, R., 'A collector of apocryphal anecdotes: John Blacman revisited', in T. Pollard (ed.), *Property and politics: essays in later medieval English history* (Gloucester: Sutton, 1984), pp. 172–97

Lovatt, R., 'The library of John Blacman and contemporary Carthusian spirituality', in *Journal of Ecclesiastical History* 43 (1992), pp. 195–230

McFarlane, K. B., *John Wycliffe and the beginnings of English Nonconformity* (London: English Universities Press, 1952)

McGinn, Bernard, *The flowering of mysticism* (The Presence of God, 3) (New York: Crossroad, 1998)

McKenna, J. W., 'Piety and propaganda: the cult of Henry VI', in B. Rowland (ed.), *Chaucer and Middle English studies* (London: Allen & Unwin, 1974), pp. 72–88

McLaughlin, E., 'The heresy of the Free Spirit and late medieval mysticism', in *Medievalia et Humanistica* n.s. 4 (1973), pp. 37–54

McNamer, Sarah, 'The exploratory image: God as mother in Julian of Norwich's *Revelations of Divine Love*', in *Mystics Quarterly* 15 (1989), pp. 21–8

Madeleva, M., *Pearl: a study in spiritual dryness* (New York: D. Appleton, 1925)

Maisonneuve, R., 'Margery Kempe and the eastern and western tradition of the "perfect fool"', in Glasscoe (1982), pp. 1–17

Manning, R. B., *Religion and society in Elizabethan Sussex: a study of the enforcement of the religious settlement, 1558–1603* (Leicester UP, 1969)

Mason, E., 'The role of the English parishioner, 1100–1500', in *Journal of Ecclesiastical History* 27 (1976), pp. 17–29

Meersseman, G., *Ordo fraternitatis: confraternite e pietà dei laici nel medioevo*, 3 vols (Rome: Italia Sacra, 1977)

Mertes, R. G. K. A., 'The household as a religious community', in J. Rosenthal and C. Richmond (eds), *People, politics and community in the later Middle Ages* (Gloucester: Sutton, 1987), pp. 123–39

Milosh, J. E., *The scale of perfection and the English mystical tradition* (University of Wisconsin Press, 1966)

Minnis, A. J. (ed.), 'The sources of *The cloud of unknowing*: a reconsideration', in Glasscoe (1982), pp. 63–75

Minnis, A. J., *Gower's Confessio Amantis: responses and reassessments* (Cambridge: Brewer, 1983)

Minnis, A. J., *Medieval theory of authorship: scholastic literary attitudes in the later Middle Ages*, 2nd edn (Aldershot: Scolar Press, 1988)

Minnis, A. J. and Scott, A. B. (eds.), *Medieval literary theory and criticism c.1100–c.1375: the commentary-tradition* (Oxford: Clarendon, 1988)

Molinari, P., *Julian of Norwich, the teaching of a 14th century English mystic* (London: Longmans, Green, 1958)

Mountney, J. M., *Sin shall be a glory* (London: DLT, 1992)

Murtaugh, D. M., *Piers Plowman and the image of God* (Gainesville: University Presses of Florida, 1978)

Nichols, A. E., *Seeable signs: the iconography of the seven sacraments 1350–1544* (Woodbridge: Boydell, 1994)

Noffke (1980): see Catherine of Siena under Primary Works above

Norquist, Bruce, 'Glossary of certain key theological terms in the *Cloud*', in *The mystical tradition and the Carthusians* vol. 1 (*Analecta Cartusiana* 130:1) (Salzburg: Institut für Anglistik und Amerikanistik, 1995), pp. 23–59

Oberman, H. A., *The harvest of medieval theology: Gabriel Biel and late medieval nominalism* (Cambridge, Mass.: Harvard UP, 1963)

Oberman, H. A., 'The shape of late medieval thought: the birthpangs of the modern era', in Trinkaus and Oberman (1974) pp. 3–25

Oberman, H. A., *The dawn of the Reformation: essays in late medieval and early Reformation thought* (Edinburgh: T. & T. Clark, 1986)

O'Connell, R., *Art and the Christian intelligence in St Augustine* (Oxford: Blackwell, 1978)

Orme, Nicholas, 'Children and the Church in medieval England', in *Journal of Ecclesiastical History* 45 (1994), pp. 563–87

Owen, D. D. R., *The vision of hell* (Edinburgh and London: Scottish Academic Press, 1970)

Owst, G. R., *Literature and pulpit in medieval England* (Oxford: Blackwell, 1961)

Ozment, Steven, 'Mysticism, nominalism and dissent', in Trinkaus and Oberman (1974), pp. 67–92

Palliser, M. A., *Christ our mother of mercy: divine mercy and compassion in the theology of the Shewings of Julian of Norwich* (Berlin: Walter de Gruyter, 1992)

Pantin, W. A., 'Two treatises of Uthred of Boldon on the monastic life', in *Studies in medieval history presented to F. M. Powicke* (Oxford: Clarendon, 1948), pp. 363–85

Pantin, W. A., *The English Church in the fourteenth century* (Cambridge UP, 1955; repr. Toronto, 1980)

Pantin, W. A., 'The monk-solitary of Farne: a fourteenth-century English mystic', in *English Historical Review* 59 (1944), pp. 162–86

Pantin, W. A., 'Instructions for a devout and literate layman', in J. J. G. Alexander and M. T. Gibson (eds.), *Medieval learning and literature: essays presented to R. W. Hunt* (Oxford UP, 1976), pp. 398–422

Patterson, L. W., 'The "Parson's Tale" and the quitting of the "Canterbury Tales"', in *Traditio* 34 (1978), pp. 331–80

Peckham, W. D., 'Some Chichester wills, 1483–1504', in *Sussex Archaeological Collections* 87 (1948), pp. 1–27

Pelphrey, Brant, *Love was his Meaning. The theology and mysticism of Julian of Norwich* (Salzburg studies in English Literature. Elizabethan and Renaissance studies 92:4, 1982)

Pelphrey, Brant, *Christ our mother* (London: DLT, 1989)

Peters, Brad, 'The reality of evil within the mystic vision of Julian of Norwich', in *Mystics Quarterly* 13 (1987), pp. 195–202

Pfaff, R. W., *New liturgical feasts in later medieval England* (Oxford UP, 1970)

Phythian-Adams, Charles, *Desolation of a city: Coventry and the urban crisis of the later Middle Ages* (Cambridge UP, 1979)

Pollard, Tony (ed.)., *Property and politics: essays in later medieval English history* (Gloucester: Sutton, 1984)

Poos, L. R., *A rural society after the Black Death: Essex, 1350–1525* (Cambridge UP, 1991)

Power, Eileen, *Medieval English nunneries c.1275–1535* (Cambridge UP, 1922)

Powicke, F. M. and Cheney, C. R. (eds.), *Councils and synods*, vol. 2 (Oxford: Clarendon, 1964)

Pseudo-Dionysius: *The Complete Works*, trans. C. Luitheid (Classics of western spirituality, London: SPCK, 1987)

Raitt, J. (ed.), *Christian spirituality II: High Middle Ages and Reformation* (World spirituality) (New

York: Crossroad, 1988; London: SCM Press, 1989)

Raw, B., 'Piers and the image of God in man', in S. S. Hussey (ed.), *Piers Plowman: critical approaches* (London: Methuen, 1969), pp. 143–79

Richmond, C., 'The English gentry and religion, c.1500', in C. Harper-Bill (ed.), *Religious belief and ecclesiastical careers in late medieval England* (Woodbridge: Boydell, 1991), pp. 121–50

Riddy, Felicity, 'Women talking about the things of God: a late medieval subculture', in C. Meale (ed.), *Women and literature in Britain, c.1150–1500* (Cambridge: Cambridge University Press, 1993), pp. 101–27

Riehle, R., *The Middle English mystics* trans. Standring (London: Routledge & Kegan Paul, 1981)

Rorem, Paul, *Pseudo-Dionysius: a commentary on the texts and an introduction to their influence* (New York: Oxford UP, 1993)

Rosser, Gervase, 'The town and guild of Lichfield in the late Middle Ages', in *Transactions of the South Staffordshire Archaeological and Historical Society* 27 (1987), pp. 39–47

Rosser, Gervase, 'Communities of parish and guild in the late Middle Ages', in S. J. Wright (ed.), *Parish, church, and people: local studies in lay religion, 1350–1750* (London: Hutchinson, 1988), pp. 29–55

Rosser, Gervase, 'The Guild of St Mary and St John the Baptist, Lichfield: ordinances of the late fourteenth century', in *Staffordshire Record Society*, 4th series (1988), pp. 19–26

Rosser, Gervase, 'Parochial conformity and popular religion in late medieval England', in *Transactions of the Royal Historical Society*, 6th series, I (1991), pp. 173–89

Rubin, M., 'Corpus Christi fraternities and late medieval piety', in D. Baker (ed.), *Sanctity and secularity: the church and the world* (Studies in church history 10) (Oxford: Blackwell, 1973)

Rubin, M., *Corpus Christi: the Eucharist in late medieval culture* (Cambridge UP, 1991)

Russell, G. A., 'Chaucer: the Prioress's Tale', in D. A. Pearsall and R. A. Waldron (eds.), *Medieval literature and civilization: studies in memory of G. N. Garmonsway* (London: Athlone, 1969), pp. 211–27

Salter, Elizabeth, *Nicholas Love's 'Myrrour of the Blessed Lyf of Jesu Christ'* (*Analecta Cartusiana* 10) (1974)

Sandler, L. F., *The Psalter of Robert de Lisle* (London: Harvey Miller, 1983)

Sandler, L. F., 'Face to face with God: a pictorial image of the Beatific Vision', in W. M. Ormrod (ed.), *England in the fourteenth century: proceedings of the 1985 Harlaxton Symposium* (Woodbridge: Boydell, 1986), pp. 224–35

Sargent, Michael, 'The transmission by the English Carthusians of some late medieval spiritual writings', in *Journal of Ecclesiastical History* 27 (1976), pp. 225–40

Sargent, M. G., 'Contemporary criticism of Richard Rolle', in *Analecta Cartusiana* 55:1 (1981)

Sargent, M. G., 'The self-verification of visionary phenomena: Richard Methley's *Experimentum veritatis*', in *Analecta Cartusiana* 55:2 (1981), pp. 121–37

Sargent, M. G., 'Ruusbroec in England: *The Chastising of God's Children* and related works', in *Historia et spiritualitas Cartusiensis: acta Colloquii Quarti Internationalis*, ed. J. de Grauwe (Destelbergen, 1983), pp. 303–12

Sargent, M. G., 'Minor devotional writings', in A. S. G. Edwards (ed.), *Middle English prose: a critical guide to major authors and genres* (Brunswick, NJ: Rutgers UP, 1984), pp. 147–75

Sargent, M. G. (ed.), *De cella in seculum: religious and secular life and devotion in late medieval England* (Cambridge: D. S. Brewer, 1989)

Saul, Nigel, *Scenes from provincial life: knightly families in Sussex 1280–1400* (Oxford: Clarendon, 1986)

Schmidt, A. V. C., 'The treatment of the Crucifixion in Piers Plowman and in Rolle's Meditations on the Passion', *Analecta Cartusiana* 35:2 (1983)

Simpson, James, *Piers Plowman: an introduction to the B-text* (Longman medieval and Renaissance library) (London: Longmans, 1990)

Spencer, H. Leith, *English preaching in the late Middle Ages* (Oxford: Clarendon, 1993)

Staley, Lynn, *Margery Kempe's dissenting fictions* (University Park, PA: Pennsylvania State UP, 1994)

Stargardt, U., 'The beguines of Belgium, the Dominican nuns of Germany, and Margery Kempe', in

T. J. Heffernan (ed.), *The popular literature of medieval England* (Tennessee studies in literature 28) (Knoxville: Tennessee UP, 1985), pp. 277–313

Stokes, M., *Justice and mercy in Piers Plowman* (London: Croom Helm, 1984)

Strohm, Reinhard, *The rise of European music, 1380–1500* (Cambridge UP, 1993)

Swanson, R. N., 'The origins of the *Lay folks' catechism*', in *Medium Ævum* 60 (1991), pp. 9–27

Swanson, R. N., *Catholic England: faith, religion and observance before the Reformation* (Manchester medieval sources) (Manchester UP, 1993) (1993i)

Swanson, R. N., *Church and society in late medieval England* (Oxford: Blackwell, 1989; repr. with extended bibliography 1993) (1993ii)

Tanner, Norman P., *Popular religion in Norwich with special reference to the evidence of wills, 1370–1532* (Oxford University DPhil. thesis, 1973)

Tanner, Norman P., *The Church in late medieval Norwich 1370–1532* (Studies and texts 66) (Toronto: Pontifical Institute of Mediaeval Studies, 1984) (review in *Journal of Ecclesiastical History* 36 (1985), pp. 312–13)

Telesca, W. J., 'The Cistercian dilemma at the close of the Middle Ages: Gallicanism or Rome', in *Studies in medieval Cistercian history presented to Jeremiah F. O'Sullivan* (Cistercian Studies 13) (Spencer, Mass.: Cistercian Publications, 1971), pp. 163–85

Thomson, J. A. F., 'Piety and charity in late medieval London', in *Journal of Ecclesiastical History* 16 (1965)

Thomson, J. A. F., *The transformation of medieval England 1370–1529* (Foundations of modern Britain) (London: Longman, 1983)

Thompson, E. Margaret, *The Carthusian Order in England* (London: SPCK, 1930)

Thornton, M., *Margery Kempe: an example in the English pastoral tradition* (London: SPCK, 1960)

Toulmin Smith, J. and L., *English Gilds* (EETS o.s. 40) (1870 and 1892)

Trinkaus, C., and Oberman, H. A. (eds.), *The pursuit of holiness in late medieval and renaissance religion* (Studies in medieval and Reformation thought 10) (Leiden: Brill, 1974)

Tristram, E. W., *English wall painting of the fourteenth century* (London: Routledge & Kegan Paul, 1955)

Tugwell, Simon, *Ways of imperfection* (London: DLT, 1984)

Tugwell, Simon, 'The spirituality of the Dominicans', in Raitt (1988) pp. 15–30

Turner, Denys, *The darkness of God: negativity in Christian mysticism* (Cambridge UP, 1995)

Underwood, Malcolm G. 'Politics and piety in the household of Lady Margaret Beaufort', in *Journal of Ecclesiastical History* 38 (1987), pp. 39–52

Vandenbroucke, François (1968): see Leclercq (1968)

Vauchez, André, *Les laics au moyen âge: pratiques et expériences religieuses* (Paris: Éditions du Cerf, 1987)

Waldron, R. A., 'Langland's originality: the Christ-Knight and the harrowing of hell', in G. Kratzmann and J. Simpson (eds.), *Medieval English and religions and ethical literature: essays in honour of G. H. Russell* (Cambridge: D. S. Brewer, 1986), pp. 66–81

Walsh, J., *Pre-Reformation English spirituality* (London: Burns & Oates, n.d. [1965])

Walsh, J.: see also under *The cloud of unknowing* and *The book of prive counselling* among Primary Works above

Walsh, M. W., 'Divine cuckold/holy fool: the comic image of Joseph in the English "Troubles" play', in W. M. Ormrod (ed.), *England in the fourteenth century: proceedings of the 1985 Harlaxton Symposium* (Woodbridge: Boydell, 1986), pp. 278–97

Ward, B., 'Faith seeking understanding: Anselm of Canterbury and Julian of Norwich', in A. M. Allchin (ed.), *Julian of Norwich* (Oxford: Fairacres, 1973; repr. 1978)

Ward, B., 'Julian the solitary', in *Julian reconsidered* (Oxford: Fairacres, 1988), pp. 11–35

Watkin, E. I., 'In defence of Margery Kempe', in *Downside Review* 69 (1941), pp. 243–63 [paper originally printed in *Poets amd mystics* (London: Sheed & Ward, 1953) on Julian]

Watson, Nicholas, 'Richard Rolle as elitist and as popularist', in M. G. Sargent (ed.), *De cella in seculum: religious and secular life and devotion in late medieval England* (Cambridge: D. S. Brewer, 1989), pp. 123–43

Watson, Nicholas, *Richard Rolle and the invention of authority* (Cambridge studies in medieval literature 13) (Cambridge UP, 1991)

Watson, Nicholas, 'The composition of Julian of Norwich's *Revelation of Love*', in *Speculum* 68 (1993), pp. 637–83

Watson, Nicholas, 'Melting into God the English way: deification in the Middle English version of Marguerite Porete's *Mirouer des simples âmes anienties*', in R. Voaden (ed.), *Prophets abroad: the reception of continental holy women in late-medieval England* (Cambridge: D. S. Brewer, 1996), pp. 19–50

Watson, Nicholas, 'The *Gawain*-poet as a vernacular theologian', in D. Brewer and J. Gibson (eds.), *A companion to the* Gawain-*poet* (Arthurian studies) (Cambridge: D. S. Brewer, 1997), pp. 293–313

Watson, Nicholas, 'The Middle English mystics', in D. Wallace, *The Cambridge history of medieval English literature* (Cambridge UP, 1999), pp. 539–65

Weissman, Hope, 'Margery Kempe in Jerusalem: *Hysteria compassio* in the late Middle Ages', in M. J. Carruthers and E. D. Kirk (eds.), *Acts of interpretation: the text in its context, 700–1600: essays in honor of E. Talbot Donaldson* (Norman, Oklahoma: Pilgrim, 1982), pp. 201–17

Westlake, H. F., *The parish gilds of mediaeval England* (London: SPCK, 1919)

Wieck, R. S., *The book of hours in medieval art and life* (London: Sotheby's, 1988)

Wilks, M., 'Wyclif and the Great Persecution', in M. Wilks (ed.), *Prophecy and eschatology* (Studies in church history; subsidia 10) (Oxford: Blackwell, 1994), pp. 39–64

Wilmart, A. 'Auteurs spirituels et textes devots du moyen age latin' (Paris: 1932; repr. in Études Augustiniennes, 1971)

Wittig, J. S., 'Piers Plowman B, Passus IX–XII: elements in the design of the inward journey', in *Traditio* 28 (1972), pp. 211–80

Wilson, R. M., 'Three Middle English mystics', in *Essays and Studies* n.s. 9 (1956), pp. 87–112

Winstead, Karen A., *Virgin martyrs: legends of sainthood in late medieval England* (Ithaca: Cornell UP, 1997)

Wood-Legh, K. L., *Perpetual chantries in Britain* (Cambridge UP, 1965)

Wright, S. J. (ed.), *Parish, church, and people: local studies in lay religion, 1350–1750* (London: Hutchinson, 1988)

5

The Fellows of St Antony

Spirituality, Reformation and Revolution (1500–1700)

INTRODUCTION

I read once a story of a holy man, (some say it was St Anthony), which had
been a long season in the wilderness, neither eating nor drinking any thing
but bread and water: at the length he thought himself so holy, that there
should be nobody like unto him. Therefore he desired of God to know
who should be his fellow in heaven. God made him answer, and commanded him to go to Alexandria; there he should find a cobbler which
should be his fellow in heaven. Now he went thither and sought him out,
and fell in acquaintance with him, and tarried with him three or four days
to see his conversation. In the morning his wife and he prayed together;
then they went to their business, he in his shop, and she about her house-
wifery. At dinner time they had bread and cheese, wherewith they were
well content, and took it thankfully. Their children were well taught to fear
God, and to say their *Paternoster*, and the Creed, and the Ten Commandments; and so he spent his time in doing his duty truly. I warrant you, he
did not so many false stitches as cobblers do nowadays. St Anthony per-
ceiving that, came to knowledge of himself, and laid away all pride and
presumption. By this ensample you may learn, that honest conversation
and godly living is much regarded before God; insomuch that this poor
cobbler, doing his duty diligently, was made St Anthony's fellow. So it
appeareth that we be not destituted of religious houses: those which apply
their business uprightly and hear God's word, they shall be St Anthony's
fellows; that is to say, they shall be numbered amongst the children of
God.[1]

These words are taken from one of the sermons of Hugh Latimer, the stoutly Protes-
tant Bishop of Worcester, later to be one of the martyrs of the Marian persecutions.[2]
With characteristic rhetorical panache, Latimer adapts a story from the age of the early
Church to suit his purposes.[3] It is worth comparing his version with the original:

St Anthony had prayed to the Lord to be shown to whom he was equal.
God had given him to understand that he had not yet reached the level of a
certain cobbler in Alexandria. Anthony left the desert, went to the cobbler

and asked him how he lived. His answer was that he gave a third of his income to the Church, another third to the poor, and kept the rest for himself. This did not seem a task out of the ordinary to Anthony who himself had given up all his possessions and lived in the desert in total poverty. So that was not where the other man's superiority lay. Anthony said to him, 'It is the Lord who has sent me to see how you live.' The humble tradesman, who venerated Anthony, then told him his soul's secret: 'I do not do anything special. Only, as I work I look at all the passers-by and say, "So that they may be saved, I, only I, will perish."'[4]

Latimer's changes are striking. St Antony's prayer for a clear awareness of his spiritual state is turned into an arrogant self-deception. The cobbler who reveals a Christlike willingness to die for the sake of others is replaced with a paradigm of Protestant family piety: happily married, with a safely domestic wife and dutiful children, all content with their lot and going about their godly duties.[5] The ascetic renunciation and self-sacrifice that mark out both monk and cobbler in the early text are replaced by a study in contrasts: the old monastic view of holiness as separation *from* the world is supplanted by the new Protestant view of the godly life *in* the world.[6]

This tendency to exalt lay piety over that of the cloister did not begin with Latimer, or even with the Reformation. The late medieval Dominican John Tauler tells of

a man who has the closest walk with God of any I ever saw, and who has been all his life a husbandman . . . and is so still. This man once asked the Lord in prayer if he should give up his occupation and go into the Church; and it was answered him, No; he should labour, earning his bread by the sweat of his brow, to the glory of Christ's precious blood, shed for him.[7]

Latimer makes this point even more explicitly in his second narration of the story of St Antony and the cobbler, preached a few months after the first. Latimer introduces it by reference to the story of shepherds at Bethlehem

where we learn every man to follow his occupation and vocation, and not to leave the same, except God call him from it to another: for God would have every man to live in that order that he hath ordained for him.[8]

There are, then, significant continuities between this view and that of the late Middle Ages: the bold critique of the old monastic spiritual ideal, the celebration of honest labour, the stress on good religious instruction – all these have late-medieval precedents, both orthodox and Lollard. But there is something new in the atmosphere, the tone, the world-view, of Latimer's writing. The old religion, like the old religious houses to which Latimer refers, is not only worthless, but powerless too: it is, after all, hard to imagine St Antony returning to his bread and water after encountering Latimer's cobbler, but entirely possible to imagine him doing so after his experience with the original one. It is not only St Antony who has 'come to knowledge of himself': in Latimer's mind, half of Christianity has done so too.

And we can see in Latimer's versions of the story of St Antony and the cobbler the outlines of some of the fundamental changes wrought in the texture of English spirituality by the Reformation, changes which will be explored in more detail in the rest of this chapter. It is worth noting first the role of God in the story. There is no hint of any aspiration to ontological union with him in Latimer's presentation of either saint or cobbler: the movement towards a covenantal view of the relationship of God and humanity began, as we have seen, with William of Ockham and other late-medieval thinkers; but it was given further impetus by the Protestant reformers.[9] Yet God remains in absolute control, and the cobbler and his family go about their lives and duties in full awareness of this: not for nothing do words like 'godly' and 'God-fearing' appear so often in accounts of reformed piety;[10] and we are a long way here from any Renaissance or Shakespearean celebration of Fortune.[11]

Latimer's reference to St Antony 'coming to himself' could echo the experience of the Prodigal Son in Tyndale's translation;[12] but it could also reflect the pervasive Reformation emphasis on the individual opting for or against faith in Christ, and first accepting his or her own inherent sinfulness ('he laid away all pride and presumption').[13] In this respect Latimer's presentation of the cobbler's piety reflects the spirituality of the great German reformer Martin Luther: the latter did not deny the genuine holiness of some Catholic ascetics, but he did argue that that alone is not enough. In one of his works which was most often translated into English, Luther wrote:

> If ye have nothing but this holiness and chastity of life to set against the wrath and judgment of God, ye are in very deed the sons of the bond-woman which must be cast out of the kingdom of heaven and be damned.[14]

Hence the contrast Latimer implies between the anxiety of St Antony and the assurance of the cobbler, a contrast that (as we shall see) runs through the whole texture of Reformation spirituality. The cobbler lives his godly life, not in order to achieve salvation, but precisely because he is already assured of it: he is already a child of God. It is the saint, exemplar of the old monastic way, whose spiritual state proves defective. Nothing in reformed theology did more to gnaw at the foundations of medieval Catholic piety than Luther's doctrine of justification.[15]

This is not to suggest that Latimer regarded himself and his Protestant co-religionists as creating something entirely new: an irreducibly historical religion like Christianity has always reformed itself by seeking some kind of 'return to sources'; and the Protestant reverence for *sola scriptura* is extensively indebted to the Renaissance humanist reverence for ancient Greece and Rome,[16] as well as having precedents in the twelfth century.[17] But by the time Latimer came to preach his sermon, Pandora's box had been opened too widely and for too long for the world ever to be quite the same again. The invention of printing and the rapid dissemination of vernacular religious texts, above all of the Bible; the new awareness of lands and peoples far removed from European Christianity;[18] the inexorably widening split between academy and pew, theology and spirituality, within the Christian church;[19] and the seismic implications of Henry VIII's rejection of papal authority and appropriation of monastic lands without appearing to suffer divine retribution as a consequence – all these things introduced Latimer's contemporaries into an alarmingly unsettled new age.

No longer, then, could English spirituality be primarily something infused or imposed from above and beyond, from texts or people of unimpeachable authority: now people had to decide for themselves. Religious faith and experience was to become rather less a matter of culture, context or conditioning, and rather more a matter of *choice*.[20] Truth was no longer something 'out there', declared and policed by ecclesiastical authority: it had to be appropriated in (and authenticated by) the individual's own spiritual life and journey.

REFORMATION, REVOLUTION AND RESTORATION: THE CONTEXT OF SIXTEENTH- AND SEVENTEENTH-CENTURY ENGLISH SPIRITUALITY

Spirituality and the Reformation

In 1510, aged about twenty-five, Hugh Latimer was elected a Fellow of Clare Hall, Cambridge, and later almost certainly became a member of a small group of thinkers known to its critics as 'Little Germany' because of their enthusiasm for the thought of Martin Luther – neither the first nor the last time that narrow xenophobia was to be directed at those open to intellectual developments across the English Channel.[21]

The course of the Reformation in England, the state of religion immediately prior to its impact, and the reasons for the almost total replacement of medieval Catholicism with the new Church of England by the end of Elizabeth's reign, are all the subjects of immense study and dispute among modern scholars.[22] Three facts appear to be winning general acceptance: first, that pre-Reformation English piety was broadly speaking in a healthy state (insofar as such things are susceptible of assessment);[23] secondly, that the changes wrought by the Reformation were imposed from above, the consequence of political decisions and leadership;[24] and, thirdly, that within half a century the Reformation settlement had been accepted in almost all of the country.[25]

Exactly how these facts are interpreted remains a matter of immense debate, though some of the factors which helped ensure the success of the Reformation settlement are clear: the great increase in centralized royal power under the Tudors, together with a shift of power from clergy and episcopacy to gentry;[26] the extent to which the soil had already been fertilized by the activities and teaching of the Lollards;[27] an increasingly educated and articulate ordained ministry;[28] and Mary Tudor's early death and with it the failure of her revisionist policy.[29] Three more general considerations, not easy to assess, seem worth adding to these: the extent to which increasing levels of literacy gave Protestant emphasis on the Word of God a particular purchase in towns and universities;[30] the shift in perspective from the next world to this one, especially with regard to spirituality: thus prayer for the dead, albeit not expressly banned, declined rapidly once bequests for mass endowments or chantries could no longer be assured of enactment, and tended to be replaced by a growing mercantile this-worldly individualism more characteristic of the age of Michelangelo and Columbus;[31] and the almost incalculable effect on people of the powerlessness of the old faith to protect itself or its sacred property, especially in an age in which religion was conceived of in terms of power to a far greater extent than is the case now.[32]

This last point is especially significant with regard to the dissolution of the monasteries under Henry VIII. There is little evidence to suggest that contemporary laypeople thought ill of the monks, or thought them less efficacious as intercessors, which only makes the relatively modest level of reaction to their disappearance all the more astonishing, even if some allowance is made both for the lack of any outstanding monastic leaders in the period and for much opportunistic human greed once open season was declared on the riches of the monastic houses.[33] It is true that some reaction was more forthright: Sir Simon Degge, a Staffordshire gentleman (1612–1703), argued that the change of ownership of former monastic properties, which affected half of Staffordshire within a mere sixty years, was God's just punishment of the gentry of Henry VIII's reign for appropriating monastic properties for themselves;[34] and Latimer himself boldly criticized the king to his face for stabling horses in monasteries that were built 'for the comfort of the poor'.[35]

What was the effect of the Reformation on English spirituality? The question is large, and much of the rest of this chapter will in effect attempt to offer an answer. But some important points need to be made at the outset. First, piety became more secular in two particular ways: first, insofar as religious authority was now exercised by a monarch and parliament with both the means and the motive for enforcing it to an extent impossible for medieval popes; secondly, insofar as this helped to pave the way for the eventual secularization of England once religious toleration allowed for a plurality of differing beliefs.[36]

Secondly, there was an immense visual and architectural change. By the 1570s the bishops had carried out a successful programme of reform of church buildings: pictures and images were replaced with words (painted texts, from which Latimer's cobbler and his devout family will have learned the Creed, the Commandments, and the Lord's Prayer).[37] Royal coats of arms, often set above chancel arches, replaced the rood – one king was effectively supplanted by another, a point reinforced by the replacement of elaborate chantries with splendid monuments effectively glorifying the local gentry or aristocracy.[38] Church interiors were less colourful and atmospheric: candles, painted glass, statues and vestments were replaced by solid pews and lofty pulpits.[39] Underpinning this change was of course a profound shift in the idea of the holy: where late-medieval Catholic spirituality conceived of church buildings as holy because they contained holy things and were the scene of holy and powerful rituals, Protestant spirituality saw them only as meeting-places for the godly. There was, in other words, a clear movement from the public towards the interior: from the corporate towards the individual.[40]

Thirdly, there was an important change in the role and significance of the clergy. Chantry priests and other unbeneficed clergy vanished, to be replaced by graduate clergy preachers. Some scholars have argued that this entailed a shift of power upwards, as the old gilds were abolished and effectively replaced by a new alliance of parson and squire.[41] But this may be too simplistic: while the status of the clergy almost certainly rose, the confidence and authority of some lay people rose too.[42] Anticlericalism, and in particular vigorous criticism of erring priests, was an important feature of sixteenth-century church life – though this was accelerated, not initiated, by the Reformation.[43]

Post-Reformation piety reflected a pervasive concern to encourage people to pray and worship with the mind as well as with the heart, though in many respects (as we shall see) Protestantism further accentuated the fissure between theology and spirituality already present in the later medieval period. Piety became more didactic and prosaic: word prevailed over sacrament, scholarship over mystery.[44] None of this was conceivable without the great increase in literacy and education,[45] which in turn provided the ecclesiastical authorities with a massive challenge: how to help form people in the new perspectives and principles of Protestant piety?[46] For all their reverence for *sola scriptura*, sixteenth-century English church life witnessed a large-scale concern on the part of those authorities to adapt Catholic spiritual texts for post-Reformation purposes, a project significantly assisted by the proliferation of English printing houses.[47]

Spirituality in the seventeenth century
If the sixteenth century witnessed major changes in thought and piety, the seventeenth century witnessed revolution on a far greater scale, a revolution whose political and religious dimensions have been charted by many modern scholars.[48] The execution of a king, and the huge social dislocation involved in the Civil War;[49] the changes in the Church of England's dominant ideology from a Calvinist stress on human depravity and God's absolute power, first to a gentler and more inclusive theological tone in the earlier part of the century, then to a sharply Arminian outlook under William Laud, and eventually to a more positive post-Restoration evaluation of reason and freewill;[50] the progress made in both philosophy and scientific thought, with the inevitable consequence that the part played by religion in public life began, albeit slowly, to diminish;[51] the sudden though short-lived explosion of both political and religious freedom of thought during the Commonwealth; all these and many other factors played their part in determining the course of English spirituality. John Milton was scarcely typical of the century as a whole; but his transformation of Psalm 8 from a celebration of the dignity of the human condition into an anguished lament about the sufferings of the righteous must, consciously or not, have articulated the spiritual experience of millions who struggled to make some sense of the ways of God in so disordered an age:

> God of our fathers, what is man!
> That thou towards him with hand so various,
> Or might I say contrarious,
> Temper'st thy providence through his short course,
> Not evenly, as thou rul'st
> The angelic orders and inferior creatures mute,
> Irrational and brute.
> Nor do I name of men the common rout,
> That wandering loose about

Grow up and perish, as the summer fly,
Heads without name no more remembered,
But such as thou hast solemnly elected,
With gifts and graces eminently adorned
To some great work, thy glory,
And people's safety, which in part they effect:
Yet toward these thus dignified, thou oft
Amidst their height of noon,
Changest thy countenance, and thy hand with no regard
Of highest favours past
From thee on them, or them to thee of service.
Nor only dost degrade them, or remit
To life obscured, which were a fair dismission,
But throw'st them lower than thou didst exalt them high,
Unseemly falls in human eye,
Too grievous for the trespass or omission,
Oft leav'st them to the hostile sword
Of heathen and profane, their carcases
dogs and fowls a prey, or else captived:
Or to the unjust tribunals, under change of times,
And condemnation of the ingrateful multitude.
If these they scape, perhaps in poverty
With sickness and disease thou bow'st them down,
Painful diseases and deformed,
In crude old age;
Though not disordinate, yet causeless suffering
The punishment of dissolute days, in fine,
Just or unjust, alike seem miserable,
For oft alike, both come to evil end.[52]

The impact of all these changes on the course of English spirituality will be considered in more detail below. It is worth noting here the extent of the evidence that suggests a greater level of continuing conformity and active worship among laypeople during the seventeenth century than has often been supposed.[53] The disappearance of gilds may well have caused the family to become more important as a centre for lay piety: the 'godly household' is a phrase characteristic of much Protestant spirituality. Within that household, women's piety acquired a greater prominence than hitherto, and not only in aristocratic circles, as literacy increased, and their role in the administration of the home and the education of children increased.[54]

SPIRITUALITY AND THE BIBLE

Introduction

The influence of the Bible on English spirituality of the sixteenth and seventeenth centuries can hardly be overestimated. We have already noted the part it played in the spiritual life of the Lollards; but the invention and development of printing rendered it more accessible still, especially since this coincided with a concern to make the scriptures available in the vernacular. This concern was was rooted in two things: the humanist commitment to returning *ad fontes*, to the pristine purity of early Christianity;[55] and the concern of both Catholics and Protestants to foster lay education and piety. Hence it is not surprising to find both Protestants and Catholics seeking to make the Bible available in the vernacular.[56] In England it was Thomas Cromwell, in 1536, who arranged for an English Bible to be made available in every parish church for the laity to hear and read;[57] during Mary's reign, Cardinal Pole sought to make use of the vernacular Bible in his plans for the education of the clergy;[58] and exiled Jesuits took advantage of its availability for their own work of catechesis and spiritual formation:[59] indeed in 1582 the first Catholic English version of the New Testament appeared at Reims.[60] By the early seventeenth century, cheap Bibles, Psalters, catechisms and Prayer Books were all widely available.[61]

William Tyndale

The central figure in sixteenth-century English biblical spirituality was William Tyndale (?1491–1536), whose own roots were in strongly Lollard areas:[62] he spent much of his life in exile in northern Europe before being arrested as a result of a cruel stratagem and executed in 1536. Copies of his translation of the New Testament began arriving secretly in England in 1526;[63] and its influence was immense.[64] For Tyndale the scriptures had a self-authenticating power: hence the overriding need to make them available in the vernacular.[65] And his own words may serve to express the heart of what biblical spirituality meant for him: commenting on the contrast between Simon the Pharisee and the woman who anointed Jesus in Luke 7, he wrote:

> Simon believed and had faith, yet but weakly; and, according to the proportion of his faith, loved coldly and had deeds thereafter: he bade Christ unto a simple and bare feast only, and received him not with any great humanity. But Mary had a strong faith and therefore burning love and notable deeds, done with exceeding profound and deep meekness. On the one hand she saw herself clearly in the law, both in what danger she was in . . . and also the fearful sentence and judgment of God upon sinners. On the other side, she heard the gospel of Christ preached; and in the promises she saw with eagles' eyes the exceeding abundant mercy of God, that passeth all utterance of speech; which is set forth in Christ for all meek sinners, which knowledge their sins; and she believed the word of God mightily . . . and being overcome and overwhelmed with the unspeakable . . . riches of the kindness of God, did inflame and burn in love; yea, was so swollen in love, that she could not abide, nor hold, but must break out; and was so drunk in love, that she regarded nothing, but even to utter the fervent and burning love of her heart only: she had no respect to herself, though she was never so great and notable a sinner . . . but with all humbleness did run unto his feet, washed them with the tears of her eyes, and wiped them with the hairs of her head, and anointed them with her

precious ointment; yea, and would no doubt have run into the ground under his feet, to have uttered her love toward him; yea, would have descended down into hell, if it had been possible. Even as Paul, in the ninth chapter of his Epistle to the Romans, was drunk in love, and overwhelmed with the plenteousness of the infinite mercy of God, which he had received in Christ unsought for, wished himself banished from Christ and damned, to save the Jews, if it might have been. *For as a man feeleth God in himself, so is he to his neighbour.*[66]

Spirituality and the King James Bible

The influence of the Authorized (or King James) Version of the Bible is equally hard to calculate, but unquestionably immense. Despite its unequivocal support for royal authority,[67] Puritan hostility to it gradually waned;[68] and there may well be force in the argument that the stately and luminous simplicity of its language led to its being accorded a reverence proper to the truth it sought to convey.[69] Yet reverence was not the only ingredient of the new biblical spirituality: scholarship, and a desire better to understand the message of scripture, were vitally important too;[70] one of their consequences was the decision by Oliver Cromwell to readmit Jews to England, partly in order to help foster Hebrew studies.[71]

But in what ways did the Bible help to shape the character of English spirituality in this period? In 1618 Nicholas Byfield published his *Directions for the private reading of the Scriptures*; and there is some evidence of individuals engaging in systematic personal study of scripture.[72] We shall explore later the practice of scriptural meditation, in both Catholic and Protestant traditions; but it is worth noting now the encouragement given to this practice by Cranmer's homily *A fruitful exhortation to the reading and knowledge of holy Scripture*:

> let us night and day muse, and have meditation and contemplation in them; let us ruminate, and, as it were, chew the cud, that we may have the sweet juice, spiritual effect, marrow, honey, kernel, taste, comfort, and consolation of them.[73]

And the author of the Elizabethan homily *An information for them which take offence at certain places of the holy Scripture* argues that 'the more obscure and dark the sayings [of scripture] be to our understanding, the further let us think ourselves to be from God, and his holy Spirit, who was the author of them. Let us with more reverence endeavour ourselves to search out the wisdom hidden in the outward bark of the scripture.'[74]

Spirituality and the Psalms

This has particular implications for the Psalms, perhaps the most used and studied book in the Bible during this period:[75] the same author argues that we should not be offended when David prays for the destruction of his adversaries: for David

> spake not of a private hatred, and in a stomach against their persons: but wished spiritually the destruction of such corrupt errors and vices, which reigned in all devilish persons set against God . . . And when David did

profess in some places, that he hated the wicked, yet in other places of his Psalms [Psalm 139.21–2] he professeth, that he hateth them with a perfect hate, not with a malicious hate, to the hurt of the soul. Which perfection of spirit, because it cannot be performed in us, so corrupted in affections as we be, we ought not to use in our private causes the like words in form, for that we cannot fulfil the like words in sense. Let us not therefore be offended, but search out the reason of such words before we be offended, that we may the more reverently judge of such sayings, though strange to our carnal understandings, yet to them that be spiritually minded, judged to be zealously and godly pronounced.[76]

We may use the Psalms as a case study for some of the ways in which the Bible was appropriated for the spiritual life, both individual and corporate. William Perkins suggests that we use the cursing psalms such as Psalm 109 not 'as prayers against the persons of our enemies, but onely as prophesies [sic] against the enemies of God'.[77] In his defence of the Prayer Book, Antony Sparrow develops this point: we are to work at the Psalms if we are to recover their primitive power:

If any man thinks these Psalms too hard for him to understand, and apply to his several needs, let him make trial a while, and spend that time in them, which he spends in humane compositions; let him study them as earnestly, as he does books of less concernment; let him pray the Holy Spirit that made them, to open his eyes, to see the admirable use of them; let him intreat holy and learned guides of souls to direct him in the use of them, and by the grace of God, in the frequent use of them he may attain to the Primitive fervour, and come to be a Man, as holy David was, after God's own heart.[78]

How was the spirituality of the Psalter appropriated to contemporary life and experience during this period? When English Protestants, exiled during Mary Tudor's reign, returned after her death, they brought with them from the continent the custom of singing the Psalms, a custom which spread rapidly.[79] We have noted already the way in which individuals used psalm-texts to articulate the depths of their own experience, particularly in times of suffering. Sternhold and Hopkins, authors of the most popular of many contemporary renderings of the psalms in metrical form suitable for congregational singing, preface the bleakest of all the psalms, Psalm 88, thus:

A grievous complaint of the faithfull sore afflicted by sicknesse, persecution and adversitie, being as it were left of God without any consolation: yet hee calleth upon God by faith, and striveth against desperation complaining himselfe to be forsaken of all earthly helpe.[80]

In 1568 there appeared a version of fifteen psalms oriented especially towards combatting one's enemies, and also including some loosely scriptural prayers directed to the same end[81] – another example of an attempt to apply the Psalms to contemporary experience. Henry Howard, Earl of Surrey, was imprisoned five times between 1537 and 1547, when he was executed, and his metrical versions of some of the great lament psalms (55, 73 and 88) are usually attributed to his final imprisonment in the Tower, which may well explain the small but subtle ways in which he appropriates them to his personal situation, something which other prisoners (notably Sir Thomas More, as we shall see) were also to do.[82]

John Hooper, the Protestant bishop of Gloucester who was executed in 1555, wrote to his wife Ann from the Fleet prison, commending the use of the psalms:

> When ye find yourself too much oppressed (as every man shall be sometime,) with the fear of God's judgment, use the 77th psalm, that beginneth – I will cry unto God with my voice, and he shall hearken unto me. In which psalm is both godly doctrine, and great consolation unto that man or woman that is in anguish of mind.

He had this to say to her about Psalm 88:

> Use also in such troubles the 88th psalm, wheerein is contained the prayer of a man that was brought into extreme anguish and misery, and, being vexed with adversaries and persecutions, saw nothing but death and hell; and although he felt in himself, that he had not only man but also God angry towards him, yet he by prayer humbly resorted unto God as the only port of consolation, and, in the midst of his desperate state of trouble, put the hope of his salvation in him whom he felt his enemy. Howbeit no man of himself can do this; but the Spirit of God, that striketh the man's heart with fear, prayeth for the man stricken and feared, with unspeakable groanings. And when you feel yourself, or know any other, oppressed after such sort, be glad: for after that God hath made you to know what you be of yourself, he will doubtless show you comfort, and declare unto you what you be in Christ, his only Son: and use prayer often; for that is the means whereby God will be sought unto for his gifts.[83]

An equally interesting application of a psalm-text is that of John Bradford, another Protestant martyr, who used prayers either directly from, or very similar to, the lament psalms in his letters from prison, crying passionately to God both for deliverance and for vindication.[84] His version of Psalm 79, written during his final imprisonment, applies its dramatic description of the appalling state of Jerusalem to the present state of England, so that the 'defilement' described by the psalmist is explained with regard to the use of Latin, invocation of the saints, adoration of the eucharistic elements, and so on; and the second and third verses of this psalm are applied to the burning of the Protestant martyrs. Bradford catches the spirit of the psalm well, applying it directly though not unthinkingly to his own situation, and appropriating for himself finally the concluding act of praise:

> This is the end why we crave thy help. This is the end why we desire to live, that, as we have been negligent, we might become diligent, to serve, love, laud, and magnify thy holy name in all our thoughts, words, and deeds, publicly and privately, when we shall perceive and feel how good thou our

God art; when we shall see how thou art merciful and mindful of goodness towards them that put their trust in thee. O dear Father, so be it, so be it, so be it, so be it.[85]

It is important to note another way in which the psalms were appropriated to experiences of suffering. In his classic *Anatomy of melancholy*, Robert Burton attacked the Calvinist doctrine of double predestination, citing a number of texts from lament and other psalms to stress that experience of sorrow or even despair need not imply abandonment by God or the certainty of ultimate condemnation:

> as a mother doth handle her childe sicke and weake, not reject it, but with all tendernesse observe and keep it, so doth God by us, not forsake us in our miseries, or relinquish us for our imperfections, but with all pitty and compassion, support and receave [sic] us; whom he loves, he loves to the end. *Whom hee hath elected, those hee hath called, justified, sanctified, and glorified.* Thinke not then thou hast lost the spirit, that thou art forsaken of God, be not overcome with heavinesse of heart, but as *David* said, *I will not feare though I walke in the shadowes of death* . . . David in his misery prayed to the Lord, remembring how he had formerly dealt with him, and with that meditation of Gods mercy confirmed his faith, and pacified his owne tumultuous heart in his greatest agony. *O my soule, why art thou so disquieted within me?* &c. Thy soul is Eclipsed for a time, I yeeld, as the Sunne is shadowed by a clowd, no doubt but those gratious beames of Gods mercy will shine upon thee againe . . . we must live by faith, not by feeling.[86]

The Puritan tradition saw, as might be expected in view of their reverence for scripture, much use of the psalms and encouragement to Christians to pray with them.[87] In his influential work *The practice of piety*, Lewis Baily encourages the householder to lead his household in singing a psalm after supper, as our Lord did at the Last Supper.[88] Psalms are to be sung spiritually, as befits God's word, and with understanding; reverently, with uncovered heads; 'be sure that the Matter make more melody in your hearts, than the Musick in your ear';[89] and he sets out a table of individual psalms for use at different times of day and on different occasions.[90] Richard Baxter specifically commends the use of psalms for family prayer,[91] and wrote a number of hymns that are in fact centos of psalm-texts,[92] one of which, *Ye holy angels bright*, is a loose adaptation of Psalm 148.[93] The Lancashire Puritan Roger Lowe, an apprentice mercer from Ashton-in-Makerfield, left a diary whose entries are steeped in references to the psalms, both explicit and half-remembered, including a personal lament in the manner of the psalms written when 'in a troubled condition' after leaving his job in Ashton.[94]

Use of the psalms in domestic circumstances was not only commended by dissenters. John Donne gives us tiny vignettes in his sermons about the use of the psalms in lay piety: thus in his funeral sermon for Lady Danvers in 1627 he says that she, 'with her whole family, (as a Church in that elect Ladie's house, to whom John writ his second Epistle), did, every Sabbath, shut up the day, at night, with a generall, with a cheerfull singing of Psalmes; This Act of cheerfulnesse, was still the last Act of that family, united in it selfe, and with God'.[95] Mary Sidney Herbert clearly envisaged her translation of the psalms to be sung, and danced to, with instrumental accompaniment. This is her exuberant rendering of part of Psalm 149:

> Play on harp, on tabret play:
>> daunce Jehova publique daunces.
> he their state that on him stay,
>> most afflicted, most advaunces.
>> O how glad his saincts I see!
>> ev'n in bed how glad they be!
> heav'nly hymnes with throat unfolding,
> swordes in hand twice-edged holding.[96]

Jeremy Taylor not only created general prayers out of psalm-verses in *Holy living*, and provided other psalm-verses for use as short prayers during the day:[97] he also wove psalm-texts into prayers directed to immediate contemporary concerns: thus he uses parts of Psalms 144 and 147 for 'time of Drought, immoderate Rain, or Scarcity or Death of Cattle, &c'.[98] In the same work there is 'An Office in time of Persecution' which includes centos of psalm-texts for use in times of affliction,[99] of persecution,[100] 'in the public or private Calamities of a Church, of a Family, of a single Person, under Persecution or Oppression, false Imprisonment, unjust and vexatious Lawsuits, &c',[101] and 'A Hymn consolatory and petitory for the Church and Clergy, in Times of Persecution'.[102]

There is also a cento of psalm-texts for the use of prisoners, which has a strongly praise-centred, future-oriented tone.[103] All these include extensive texts from lament psalms, including questions directed at God. Finally, there is a powerful psalm-cento based on Psalms 22, 32, and 39 in his 'A form of devotion to be used and said in the days of sorrow and affliction of a family, or of private persons'.[104] Taylor affirms the potential importance of the psalms as ecumenical prayer in a bitterly divided age:

> This manner of devotion might be a good symbol and instrument of communion between Christians of different persuasion: for if we would communicate in the same private devotions, it were a great degree of peace and charity. The Nicene fathers, in their zeal against heresy, forbade their people to be present at the prayers of heretics: and they had great reason, so long as they derived their heresy into their liturgy, into their very forms of baptism. But I am much scandalized, when I see a man refuse to communicate with me in my prayers, even such as are in his own Breviary or Manual.[105]

Conclusion

It might be well to conclude with a moving example of the use of the psalms in a moment of terrible sorrow. Ralph Josselin, vicar of Earls Colne in Essex from 1641 to 1683, records that when his little daughter Mary was terminally ill 'divers texts in the psalmes I read this day cheered my heart, the lord I hope speaking those things to mee my faith endeavoured to lay hold on them psal. 27.v.1.5.10' (entry for 22 May 1650). As he watched by her bedside ('my duty is to waite'[106]), he also recited a number of other psalm-texts – 'these texts spoke to mee'.[107] On 24 April he wrote

> I went to bed at night, but was raised up, with the dolour of my wife, that Mary was dying, she was very neare death, but the lord preserved her this night also, oh lord suite my heart unto all thy dealings, shewe mee why thou dost contend with mee, oh mother saith shee if you could but pull out something hansomely here, (and layes her hand on her stomacke) I should bee well, lord doe it beyond all meanes, thou alone art more then all.[108]

Mary died on 27 May 1650 at 2.15 p.m. A few days later Josselin wrote, following the death of a close friend and of another of his own children, 'when Mrs Mary dyed, my heart trembled, and was perplexed in the dealings of the lord so sadly with us, and desiring god not to proceed on against us with his darts and arrowes, looking backe into my wayes, and observing why god had thus dealt with mee, the lord followed mee with that sin no more lest a worse thing happen unto thee, and the intimacion of god was he would proceed no farther against mee or mine . . . if I clave to him with a full purpose of heart'.[109]

SPIRITUALITY AND THE CHURCH OF ENGLAND

Latimer, Cranmer, and the Book of Common Prayer

Introduction

It was the accession of Edward VI in 1547 that saw the beginning of a concerted national policy of making England Protestant, a policy principally directed by Edward Seymour, the Lord Protector, and by Thomas Cranmer, Archbishop of Canterbury. But the process had begun much earlier: Latimer, as we have seen, was actively discussing Luther's works while at Cambridge in the second decade of the century, and was preaching in Cambridge about the corruption of the late-medieval church as early as 1525. On several occasions he was suspected of heresy and in 1552 tried for it, though without suffering excommunication (perhaps at the king's own request);[110] but he succeeded in navigating the dangerous currents of royal opinion, and in 1531 was given the living of West Kington in Wiltshire. He was appointed Bishop of Worcester in 1535, perhaps partly through the influence of Queen Anne Boleyn, but principally because his reformist views were congenial at court following the royal divorce.[111] He held the post for four years.

Despite his increasing involvement in the life of the national church, Latimer was an active diocesan bishop, both reformer and scholar, and a vigorous defender of the poor in an age of grasping landlords and gentry;[112] but he was even more active, indeed (at least by modern standards) intemperately violent, in espousing the Protestant cause.[113] He followed Cranmer in preaching at St Paul's Cross in London against Rome and Roman beliefs in 1536, and supported the attack on the monasteries;[114] but, together with Cranmer and Cromwell, he received a setback with the promulgation of the Six Articles of 1539, which enshrined Catholic doctrines (and particularly belief in the real presence of Christ in the Eucharist) on pain of burning.[115] He survived Henry VIII's death to become a major figure in the Edwardian Protestant reform, preaching regularly before the king and embarking on preaching tours of the country in 1550 and 1552.[116]

Unfortunately for Latimer, however, Edward's early death in 1553 and the accession of Mary saw an uncompromising (though ultimately unsuccessful) attempt to restore the Catholic faith. Imprisoned at Oxford in 1555, and awaiting execution, he wrote 'to all the unfeigned lovers of God's truth':

> Read the tenth Psalm, and pray for me your poor brother and fellow-sufferer for God's sake: his name therefore be praised! And let us pray to God that he of his mercy will vouchsafe to make both you and me meet to suffer with good conscience for his name's sake. Die once we must; how and where, we know not. Happy are they whom God giveth to pay nature's debt (I mean to die) for his sake.[117]

He may have recalled his own words, at the climax of one of his finest and most moving sermons, preached on Good Friday 1549 before Edward VI, in which he had reflected on the terrible experience of Christ's suffering, both in Gethsemane and at the descent into hell:

> He would not only suffer bodily in the garden and upon the cross, but also in his soul when it was from the body; which was a pain due for our sin . . . He suffered in the very place, and I cannot tell what it is, call it what ye will, even in the scalding-house . . . such pain as our capacity cannot attain unto . . . We must have this continually in remembrance: *Propter te morti tradimur tota die*, 'For thee we are in dying continually.' The life of a christian man is nothing but a readiness to die, and a remembrance of death . . . If ye will believe and acknowledge your sins, you shall come to the blessed communion of the bitter passion of Christ worthily, and so attain to ever-lasting life: to the which the Father of heaven bring you and me! Amen.[118]

After finally refusing to recant, Hugh Latimer, aged about sixty-four, was burned at the stake at Oxford together with Ridley on 16 October 1555.[119]

If we allow Latimer and Cranmer to be our principal guides in a brief exploration of the spirituality they helped so much to foster, it will not be for want of other authoritative figures, but because these two represent something close to the heart of the Church of England's nascent identity in those formative decades. This is not to suggest that there were no tensions between the approaches they espoused: on the contrary, it will be to argue that it was precisely those tensions which, albeit capable of tearing the fledgling church apart, in fact provided it with a creative identity of its own.[120]

Justification by faith

Latimer's starting-point is unequivocally Protestant. In one sermon he describes himself, and his fellow Christians, thus:

> I am of myself, and by myself, coming from my natural father and mother,
> the child of the ire and indignation of God, the true inheritor of hell, a
> lump of sin, and working nothing of myself but all towards hell, except I
> have better help of another than I have of myself.[121]

But this bleak recognition of personal sinfulness leads, for both Latimer and
Cranmer, to an urgent recognition of our need for salvation, a recognition which in
turn makes possible a true act of faith:

> The answer of this question ['Who art thou?'] is, when I ask it unto myself,
> I must say that I am a christian man, a christian woman, the child of ever-
> lasting joy, through the merits of the bitter passion of Christ. This is a
> joyful answer.[122]

Of myself, then, I am nothing; but by faith in the merits of Christ's saving death,
and by that alone, I am justified. In his homily on justification by faith, Cranmer distinguishes three key ingredients within it: God's mercy and grace; Christ's justice, in
making full satisfaction for our sins by shedding his blood; and our faith, which is
itself the work of God within us.[123] Thus justification is exclusively and absolutely the
work of God, who elects and saves whom he chooses.[124]

The implications of this great Protestant principle for the spiritual life are considerable. In the first place it means that the starting-point for Christian spirituality is not
so much our creation as our redemption, not our nature as human beings but our
status as Christians, not our participation in the common life of the Church but our
individual relationship with God.[125] Both Latimer and Cranmer distinguish between
a general faith (such as the Devil might have) and a special one, which distinguishes
the Christian, and which is bound to be manifested in a changed pattern of life.[126] The
person who lives by this faith is like the tree in Psalm 1, firmly rooted in a deep trust in
God which bears fruit in good works.[127]

Thus faith becomes the absolute precondition for any prayer worthy of the name, as
Latimer emphatically underlines:

> It is not the babbling of our lips, nor dignity of our words, but the prayer of
> the heart is the offering that pleaseth, through the only means of his Son.
> For our prayer profiteth us, because we offer Christ to his Father. Whoso-
> ever resorteth to God without Christ, he resorteth in vain. Our prayer
> pleaseth because of Jesus Christ, whom we offer. So that it is faith, faith,
> faith is the matter. It is no prayer that is without faith, it is but a lip-
> labouring and mockery, without faith; it is but a little babbling.[128]

Children and servants

But there is an even more important point still. The *Articles of Religion* articulate the
classic Pauline principle that those who are justified by God through Christ are
adopted by God as children, not servants.[129] This does not preclude the importance of
reverence and obedience in the Christian's approach to God.[130] But it does mean that
prayer is not only, or even primarily, the language of courtiers: it is the language of
children addressing a loving parent who has called them to share his life, his inheritance and his kingdom. Thus Latimer can say that

our Saviour, when he teacheth us to call God 'Father', teacheth us to understand the fatherly affection which God beareth towards us; which thing maketh us bold and hearty to call upon him, knowing that he beareth a goodwill towards us, and that he will surely hear our prayers.[131]

Cranmer is noticeably less at ease with any suggestion of intimacy or childlike boldness in approaching God. One of the nineteenth-century English Tractarian scholars noted how the Prayer Book translations of older Latin prayers frequently interpose the word 'servant' where it is not found in the Latin, whilst otherwise tending to follow strictly the language of the original.[132] The Puritan Thomas Cartwright noticed this tendency in the Prayer Book, though the examples he cited in his controversy with Archbishop Whitgift are in fact unaltered from the medieval Latin. Citing the Collect for the Twelfth Sunday after Trinity (which in Cranmer's original ran '. . . giving unto us that, that our prayer dare not presume to ask; through Jesus Christ our Lord'), Cartwright wrote

> This request carrieth with it still the note of the popish servile fear, and savoureth not of that confidence and reverent familiarity that the children of God have through Christ with their heavenly Father.[133]

In his *Laws of ecclesiastical polity*, Hooker made a spirited defence against Cartwright's criticism, arguing that it is precisely the combination of boldness and humility found in the best prayer which most exactly articulates the correct manner of our approach to God:

> The knowledge of our own unworthiness is not without belief in the merits of Christ. With that true fear which the one causeth there is coupled true boldness, and encouragement drawn from the other . . . Looking inward we are stricken dumb, looking upward we speak and prevail. O happy mixture . . . ![134]

Hooker's defence was impressive; but Cartwright had a point; and the nineteenth-century author of Tract 86 both agreed with him and went further: 'this "note of servile fear" is one peculiarly our own, as differing from the forms of prayer which we have in common with the Church of Rome.'[135] The noble spirit of the Church of England's *via media* cannot always disguise a tendency to retreat to the language of courtiers and servants, implying a meekness in the face of the *status quo* which can translate into a hushed and even servile reverence in approaching God.[136]

The theology and practice of prayer

For both Latimer and Cranmer, however, prayer is an active and vigorous engagement of the whole person with the God who in Christ has delivered us from the consequences of our sins; and it is inseparable from the practice of a moral life – indeed both are themselves the fruits of our redemption. Latimer makes this point with rhetorical vigour:

> you must not take my sayings after such sort, as though you should do nothing but sit and pray; and yet you should have your dinner and supper

made ready for you. No, not so: but you must labour, you must do the
work of your vocation.[137]

We must work for that which we pray for, even though it is God who brings about
what ensues.[138] And we must do this because prayer is also a constant engagement with
the Devil, who tries to stop us praying by reminding us of our sinfulness, and who
becomes progressively stronger each time we admit him.[139] The practice of prayer
demands perseverance even when no answer is received, as with Christ in Gethsemane:

> Christ had been with his Father, and felt no help: he had been with his
> friends, and had no comfort: he had prayed twice, and was not heard: what
> did he now? Did he give prayer over? No, he goeth again to his Father, and
> saith the same again: 'Father, if it be possible, away with this cup.' Here is
> an example for us . . . We must be importune upon God. We must be
> instant in prayer. He prayed thrice, and was not heard: let us pray three-
> score times.

Latimer proceeds to articulate his anxiety about a falling-off in attendance at worship:
evidently people were less attracted to the word-based liturgy of Protestantism:

> Folks are very dull now-a-days in prayer, to come to sermons, to resort to
> common prayer.[140]

And the boldness that should mark our approach to God should also find expression in our approach to our fellow human beings. Latimer's unquestioning emphasis
on the overwhelming priority of what God has done for us does not reduce him to a
dim or silent cypher in God's service. His sermons (especially those preached during
the reign of Edward VI) are full of passionate pleas for social justice and moral reform:
this refusal to separate private from public morality, notwithstanding the emphasis on
individual faith, is one of the most striking characteristics of Latimer's spirituality; and
it is rooted in scripture: 'When I say, "Give every one of us our daily bread", I pray not
for myself only, if I ask as he biddeth me; but I pray for all others.'[141] Hence we are to
pray for our enemies as well as our friends or fellow Christians.[142]

For Latimer, as for any Protestant, the *source* of our prayer is exclusively the act of
faith in Christ as redeemer and Saviour: the *scope* of our prayer must extend to
embrace the world. Why? Partly because this is Christ's teaching; but primarily
because, in Latimer's Protestant piety, the fact that Christians are justified through
their faith gives them the courage, the boldness (the New Testament *parrhesia*) to
speak out against wickedness and to proclaim the Gospel; and he notes that it was
precisely this boldness for which St Paul prayed.[143]

Spirituality and the state

This approach is rooted in a further implication of the Protestant emphasis on justification by faith alone: all who are saved are equal in Christ, all alike children of the one
heavenly Father. Latimer makes this point more forcefully than Cranmer, inhibited as
the latter was both by his role as archbishop and by an innate caution. Thus Latimer

can tell Edward VI to his face that 'they in Christ are equal with you . . . The poorest ploughman is in Christ equal with the greatest prince that is'.[144] By contrast Cranmer's writing can reveal another aspect of English Protestant piety: a strongly conformist, even nationalist, obedience to secular law. In his homily on good works, Cranmer compares the (wholly misplaced) obedience rendered by monks to their superiors with the (wholly legitimate) obedience due to the secular ruler.[145]

Latimer is as assiduous as Cranmer in emphasizing the obligation of Christians to obey the monarch; but he is much bolder in developing the implications of their shared Protestant faith. In his famous sermon to Convocation in 1536, Latimer denounces his fellow Christians for clothing religious images in silk and jewellery while the poor, Christ's 'faithful and lively images, bought with no less price than with his most precious blood', live in hunger and cold.[146] In his second telling of the story of St Antony and the cobbler, Latimer uses it to emphasize the fact that God 'is not partial: he hath not respect to any person, neither to the rich, wise, nor mighty; but he delighteth in those which are meek, and lowly in spirit'.[147] And his uncompromisingly Protestant faith leads him to a striking boldness before Henry VIII: in Christ, all alike are sinners in need of salvation.[148]

The Book of Common Prayer: introduction

It is within this general theological perspective that we need to see the Book of Common Prayer, perhaps the proudest single achievement of the Church of England during this period. Its history has been told many times, and is an involved and complex one. Notwithstanding the firmly Protestant tone of its final (1662) version, this too (as with so many 'new' developments associated with the Reformation), had its roots in the medieval past; and the immediate causes of its appearance were as much secular (the rapid spread of the vernacular, together with the invention of printing[149]) as theological. In 1544 Henry VIII, at war with France, requested general processions and prayers in the vernacular to be instituted throughout the country;[150] and in the following year the first official Primer of the Church was produced.[151]

Primers had their origins in late-medieval piety;[152] and the increase in both lay literacy and lay confidence during the early sixteenth century helped to foster an increasing demand for them.[153] Henry's 1545 Primer was reproduced unaltered in 1547 as the First Primer of Edward VI: it alone was authorized for use as a substitute for the Latin one.[154] As successive versions of the Primer were published, so the increasing influence of Protestant teaching became apparent.[155] The primers produced during Mary's reign inevitably reflected Catholic revisionism, though on a moderate scale;[156] and in 1560 the markedly Protestant 1553 Primer was reprinted.[157]

As might be expected, then, the first primers of the Reformation era reflected the growing confidence of the new Protestant leaders: devotion to Mary diminished, indulgences and other spiritual benefits were excised, non-scriptural material severely pruned, and the vernacular became ubiquitous. Prayers for the dead disappeared: prayers for the king, however, became a regular feature.[158]

What were the contents of these primers? Broadly speaking, their *aim* was to provide a complete catechetical and spiritual framework for daily life as a lay

Christian:[159] their *effect* was (among other things) greatly to increase the influence of the printed page on people's devotional lives. The Edwardian Primer of 1553 omitted the hours of the Virgin and several other hitherto standard Catholic devotional texts, replacing them with grace for use before and after meals, a simple form of daily office for personal use, collects for Sundays and feast days, and prayers for the king, parliament, judges, labourers, parents, and others, including a prayer for landlords which includes the following:

> We heartily pray thee, to send thy holy Spirit into the hearts of them that possess the grounds, pastures, and dwelling places of the earth, that they, remembering themselves to be thy tenants, may not rack and stretch out the rents of their houses and lands, nor yet take unreasonable fines and incomes after the manner of covetous worldlings, but so let them out to other, that the inhabitants thereof may both be able to pay the rents, and also honestly to live, to nourish their families, and to relieve the poor.[160]

The 1549 Book

It was during the 1540s that, at Cranmer's instigation, two schemes for a reformed version of the Latin breviary were prepared.[161] The accession of Edward VI accelerated the process of liturgical reform,[162] resulting in the appearance of the first Book of Common Prayer in 1549. The title of this book is significant:

> The Booke of the Common Prayer and Administracion of the Sacramentes and other Rites and Ceremonies of the Churche: after the Use of the Churche of England.

Note the claim to unique authorization ('the' Booke): this was, from the start, a prayer book for the entire English nation.[163] Note too that this is a book of *common prayer* – neither simply a manual for private devotion, nor a collection of service orders in the manner of the Church of England's Alternative Service Book 1980. From the start, the Prayer Book was conceived as a book whose aim was to furnish basic patterns of common prayer that would sustain and underpin the spiritual life of the nation.[164]

From 1549 to 1662

Much (probably too much) has been made of the differences between this 1549 Prayer Book and its successor in 1552, for which Cranmer was also primarily responsible. The 1549 Book, which reflects a more Catholic theological tone, is best seen as a means of reassuring traditionalists whilst still shifting the Church of England inexorably towards a more thoroughgoing Protestantism:[165] indeed there are many continuities between the liturgy of even the 1552 Prayer Book and that of the Roman Mass that preceded it.[166] And, although the 1662 Book incorporates a number of further changes, that essential tone remains.

The spirituality of the Prayer Book

What were the means by which its compilers sought to achieve this aim, and how far did they succeed? First, and to some extent foremost, Cranmer and his colleagues (like many other Reformers) sought a recovery of what they considered to be the original purity and simplicity of Christian spirituality.[167] They criticized what they saw as the accretion of unnecessary ceremonies in late-medieval Catholic religion.[168] The lectionary, largely the work of Cranmer in 1549, almost entirely follows the working year, with minimal alterations for major feasts, setting simplicity and continuity above seasonal or ceremonial considerations.[169] The Commination service is based on 'the godly discipline' of the Primitive Church. And numerous apologists for the Prayer Book cited patristic texts as warrant for both its theology and its liturgy.[170]

Yet this return to the past was no academic exercise, nor even simply a desire to remove what was perceived as obfuscation and distracting detail. Rather it was a part of a far deeper concern: to produce, as the title suggests, a book of prayer for everyone, not only (or even primarily) for clergy or theologians. This is, above all else, a manual of lay spirituality, as one of its greatest seventeenth-century apologists pointed out:

> It [the Prayer Book] is not only all in English, but in common and plain
> English, such as we use in our common Discourse with one another . . . So
> that the meanest person in the Congregation that understands but his
> Mother Tongue, may be Edified by it, as well as the greatest Scholar.[171]

One of the most obvious indications of this is the subject matter of the Prayers and Thanksgivings, which is firmly rooted in the immediate concerns of contemporary English people. The secular and the sacred are integrated: the prayers provided are for rain, for fair weather, in time of dearth and famine, in time of war and tumults, in time of any common plague or sickness, for those to be ordained, for Parliament, and 'for all sorts and conditions of men'. The subjects themselves are not particularly original, though the prayers are; and some of them reflect a (now) disquieting tendency to connect sin and suffering.[172] But a comparison with the prayers provided in the Alternative Service Book 1980 is instructive: in the later book the subject index of prayers is dominated by the church's life and concerns, whereas the priorities of the Prayer Book reflect the needs of the entire nation, seen as coterminous with those of the church. In this respect the earlier book is far closer to the spirit of biblical texts such as Leviticus 19 or the Sermon on the Mount, in integrating sacred and secular, individual and corporate, the ethical and the spiritual.[173]

Yet that comparison should not be pressed too far. One of the most significant dimensions of Cranmer's theology was his wholehearted concern to replace allegiance to the Pope with obedience to the King; and this gives the Prayer Book an unequivocally English identity which can occasionally veer perilously close to what might now be considered mere nationalism. Religious feasts are replaced with national days commemorating Queen Elizabeth's accession, the victory over the Spanish Armada, the martyrdom of Charles I, 'the day of the Papists' Conspiracy' (5 November), and the restoration of Charles II.[174]

It is true that this gave English spirituality a strong sense of identity in an age when foreign threats were both apparent and real;[175] and nationalism is hardly surprising in an age in which almost everyone conceived of the secular order as divinely ordained. But the absence of any real emphasis either on the *parrhesia* with which the elect may address God, or on that prophetic boldness with which they may denounce wicked-ness even in the highest places, robs the Book of Common Prayer of one of the most dynamic ingredients of both biblical and Protestant spirituality. It is a serious defect.

Yet there are major compensations, no less firmly rooted in the Book's Protestant parentage. The Churching of Women was the title given in the 1552 Book to what in the 1549 Book was called 'The Order of the Purification of Women', following its medieval antecedent: the new title omits any reference to the need for purification. The rite itself is distinctive in placing the woman at the centre of what is taking place, and there is evidence of the occasion becoming a popular focus for female piety and festivity.[176]

The Commination service (in 1549 prescribed for the beginning of Lent only, but in 1552 and 1662 permitted for use on other occasions as well) is intended to move people to 'earnest and true repentance', so that they 'may walk more warily in these dangerous days'. The series of solemn curses is based upon a medieval original;[177] but its subject matter is rooted in contemporary moral concerns such as the expropriation of land ('Cursed is he that removeth his neighbour's land-mark'), and its character is derived ultimately from the ethical teaching of Deuteronomy.[178] This service, together with the Exhortations at Holy Communion and many other texts, underline the Protestant concern to connect justification, piety and moral integrity referred to above. Obliged for theological reasons to abandon medieval Catholic rituals or anath-emas in which power was conveyed through ritual, the compilers of the Prayer Book produced a firmly biblical service in which that power was instead conveyed through words.[179]

And it is in the deployment of both Word and words that Cranmer's finest achieve-ment is found. The language of the Prayer Book, much of it almost certainly the achievement of Cranmer himself, has been almost universally praised.[180] The poetic simplicity of some of the common texts; the strong sense of rhythm in Cranmer's translations of medieval responses;[181] and the effective deployment of scriptural image-language wherever opportunity allowed, thereby heightening the impact of the vernacular, are all noteworthy.[182] Sometimes a Protestant desire to set the didactic above the symbolic leads to a heavy-handedness: many have noted Cranmer's curious propensity for doubling words, both in texts he wrote himself ('erred and strayed', 'declare and pronounce', 'absolution and remission', 'pardoneth and absolveth') and in his translations from the Latin ('sins and wickedness', 'let and hindered', 'supplica-tions and prayers', 'church and household', 'power and might', and so on), which can become tedious with frequent use.[183]

And yet, in true Protestant fashion, Cranmer makes the Word primary: for him, as for the writer of Genesis, God's Word precedes everything else that is, and the essence of all true prayer consists both in our attentiveness to that Word and in God's willing-ness to hear our response. In his eucharistic prayer of consecration, Cranmer makes this explicit in a superbly crafted sentence in which the long-delayed principal verb finally crowns both the prayer itself and the entire theology that underlies it:

> Almighty God our heavenly Father, which of thy tender mercy didst give thine only Son Jesus Christ, to suffer death upon the cross for our redemp-

tion, who made there (by his one oblation of himself once offered) a full, perfect and sufficient sacrifice, oblation, and satisfaction for the sins of the whole world, and did institute, and in his holy Gospel command us to continue, a perpetual memory of that his precious death, until his coming again: *Hear* us, O merciful Father, we beseech thee . . .[184]

There are other important strengths too. Cranmer really did believe common prayer to be the bedrock of all true Christian piety: thus in 1552 he altered the titles of the morning and evening offices from 'Matins' and 'Evensong' to 'Morning Prayer' and 'Evening Prayer' respectively, changed the opening versicle of both from singular to plural ('O Lord, open thou our lips'), made their daily recitation obligatory for priests and deacons, and insisted that they be recited wherever they may best be heard, in the hope that lay Christians would indeed come to recite them with their priest.[185]

Nor was this hope merely a pious aspiration. Cranmer clearly envisaged the Book as both a standard manual for liturgy and a compendium of spiritual guidance;[186] and this latter character is evident in many places: the encouragement of communicants to replace auricular confession with the 'opening of grief' to a wise and discreet minister of the word;[187] the characteristic concern with both spiritual and practical aspects of life reflected in the rubrics for the Visitation of the Sick;[188] and the stark recognition of death's ineluctable reality.[189] Martin Thornton may overstate somewhat the greatness of the Prayer Book in this and other regards.[190] But what is incontestable is its importance in bequeathing to subsequent generations of worshippers a norm, a pattern, and a rhythm of 'practicall divinitie' which is accessible to all.[191]

Conclusion

Protestant piety, rooted as it is in the individual's free and undeservable justification and articulated in word rather than symbol or ritual, at first sight lends itself far less easily than Catholic spirituality to the process of assimilation into every aspect of a country's life and concerns. Yet it is precisely in fostering that process that Cranmer's achievement lies. His Book tells us far more than most comparable texts about *both* the theology that underlies it *and* the vivid and specific contemporary context for which it was written. Thus his Visitation of the Sick reflects a significant theological shift away from its medieval predecessor, with its vigorous prayers for recovery from sickness, towards a much more passive acceptance of sickness as being the will of God and the just punishment for our sins.[192] But it also encourages people to keep their affairs in order even when healthy, and (in 1549) tells the minister to encourage them to give generously to the poor.[193]

The God of Protestant piety is to be found in the midst of every aspect of human life, though in Cranmer's view he is best approached with circumspection and fear rather than intimacy or boldness: reserve, and a clear preference for thought over emotion, characterizes much of the Prayer Book's piety. There is little celebration of the created order,[194] little emphasis on the presence of Christ in the sacrament even in the attenuated manner in which Protestants like Cranmer believed in this,[195] little to nourish the spirituality of those for whom words alone fail to satisfy. Yet, given the difficulty of fostering a genuinely enduring spiritual identity for the Church of England during the terrifying central decades of the sixteenth century, Cranmer's achievement is extraordinary, and Antony Sparrow's defence of his Book's overall rationale both compelling and just:

> A wise Constitution of the Church it is, thus to mingle Services of several sorts, to keep us from wearisomness. For whereas devout Prayer is joyned with a vehement intention of the inferior powers of the Soul, which cannot therein continue long without pain, therefore holy Church interposes still somewhat for the higher part of the mind, the understanding to work upon, that both being kept in continual exercise with variety, neither might feel any weariness, and yet each be a spur to the other. For Prayer kindles our desire to behold God by speculation; and the mind delighted with that speculation, takes every where new inflammations to pray; the riches of the mysteries of heavenly Wisdom continually stirring up in us correspondent desires to them; so that he which prays in due sort, is thereby made the more attentive to hear, and he which hears, the more earnest to pray.[196]

Participation in God: Hooker, Andrewes, and the Patristic Tradition

Introduction

About two years before Latimer's grisly end, another giant of the Church of England's early years was born. Unlike Latimer, Richard Hooker was educated at Oxford: he never attained episcopal office, becoming successively Master of the Temple (1585) and Rector of Bishopsbourne in Kent (1595), where he remained until his death in 1600. His death, like most of his life, took place during the long reign of Elizabeth I, during which the Church of England acquired much of its distinctive identity. Izaak Walton describes him thus:

> an obscure, harmless man; a man in poor clothes, his loins usually girt in a coarse gown, or canonical coat; of a mean stature, and stooping, and yet more lowly in the thoughts of his soul; his body worn out, not with age, but with study.[197]

Yet this unprepossessing rural parson produced, in his monumental *Laws of Ecclesiastical Polity*, not only an apology but an identity for the Church of England, an identity rooted in the wisdom and theology of the best patristic and medieval scholarship,[198] yet centred upon the Prayer Book and rooted in the realities of the Elizabethan settlement.[199]

Hooker represents, in his judicious critique both of Roman dogmas and of Protestant fundamentalism, and his espousal of a theological method based on scripture and reason, something that later generations will rightly recognize as distinctively Anglican.[200] On subject after subject he calmly and carefully develops his own view, scorning easy conformity with Rome and Geneva alike, and producing as a consequence not only, or even primarily, a *via media*, but a genuinely independent theology[201] in which a proper reverence for tradition is never allowed to degenerate into supine subservience,[202] and in which the pastoral and practical are always held together with the search for truth. Hooker exerted little influence in his own day: much of his great work was published long after his death and not read until later in the seventeenth century. But his combination of scholarship, spirituality, common sense, and gentle wit bequeathed to his successors not only a distinctively Anglican religious identity, but a distinctively English one, too. He is the implacable enemy of the intransigent, intolerant, irrational, totalitarian mind.

Three years after Hooker's birth, another major theologian of the Church of England was born: like Latimer, Lancelot Andrewes (1556–1626) was formed by his years at Cambridge at a time when it was still predominantly Calvinist in orientation.[203] Andrewes was a scholar of prodigious ability, and his ecclesiastical career was distinguished: he became Master of Pembroke College, Cambridge in 1589, Dean of Westminster in 1601, and Bishop successively of Chichester (1605–9), Ely (1609–19) and Winchester (1619–26). He played a significant part in the life of James I's court, and many of his works are ferocious polemical texts written at the king's request against the great Roman Catholic theologian St Robert Bellarmine.[204] Unlike Latimer, Andrewes seems to have shown little interest in social or political affairs other than as a relatively uncritical supporter of the existing *status quo*;[205] and his life has been well described by one of his modern biographers as one 'of profound routine',[206] rooted in an ordered pattern of scholarly piety.

Spirituality and law

Where Latimer could be said to have begun his exploration of Christianity with sin, Hooker began with law. Near the start of his great work he wrote

> That which hath greatest force in the very things we see is notwithstanding itself oftentimes not seen. The stateliness of houses, the goodliness of trees, when we behold them delighteth the eye; but that foundation which beareth up the one, that root which ministereth unto the other nourishment and life, is in the bosom of the earth concealed.[207]

The same is true of the laws which govern all life, for everything works according to a law:[208] there is a reason for everything God does, even if we cannot always see what it is.[209] Hooker is more Thomist than Ockhamist, conceiving of the laws which govern the universe as deriving from God's sovereign will and as discernible, to some extent at least, by human reason and aspiration.[210] But, as always, Hooker's approach is both nuanced and eclectic. He balances this stress on the divine law with an insight drawn from the Dionysian tradition of 'negative theology':

> Our soundest knowledge is to know that we know [God] not as indeed he is, neither can know him: and our safest eloquence concerning him is our silence, when we confess without confession that his glory is inexplicable, his greatness above our capacity and reach. He is above, and we upon earth; therefore it behoveth our words to be wary and few.[211]

Hooker also insists that the *individual* natural law working in each creature towards its appointed end is overruled by a higher natural law by means of which individual creatures are constrained to work for the good of all: hence the logic of neighbourly love,[212] and hence too the nature of both religion and virtue as objective realities, not simply the outworkings of our subjective consciences or personal experiences of God.[213] Hence the importance of reason as well as scripture in theology, liturgy and spirituality: the one is not sufficient without the other.[214] And even law is inferior, in the final analysis, to equity, which is the highest court of appeal in determining whether particular laws are just or unjust.[215]

This emphasis on law may appear to give Hooker's thought a rigid or authoritarian tone. But it does nothing of the sort. For him the divine law, like the *torah* of the Jews, is a providential gift, enabling us not only to discern meaning and pattern and purpose in our lives and our world, but also to participate in the very life of God (a point to which we shall return), and to recognize his presence. Hooker has a profound reverence for God's *glory*:[216] when we cannot by our own ability discern God in the world around us, he grants us a special vision of his glory:

> Sith God in himself is invisible, and cannot by us be discerned working, therefore when it seemeth good in the eyes of his heavenly wisdom, that men for some special intent and purpose should take notice of his glorious presence, he giveth them some plain and sensible token whereby to know what they cannot see. For Moses to see God and live was impossible, yet Moses by fire knew where the glory of God extraordinarily was present.[217]

For Hooker, God is far more than merely the *fons et origo* of the law that governs all things: Olivier Loyer, in a magnificent study of his thought, stresses what he calls Hooker's *principe de extériorité*, his stress on the grandeur and glory of God, which prevents his spirituality from becoming too inward and too 'straitened'.[218]

Hooker and Andrewes on justification by faith

It is when we come to the central theological issue of the Protestant Reformation, the doctrine of justification by faith, that the rich diversity which comprises the spirituality of the Church of England in its early years becomes apparent. In his homily on the subject, Thomas Cranmer describes the nature of our justification through Christ in classically Protestant terms, presenting it as an event absolutely extrinsic to Christians[219] and Cranmer is at pains to stress that even the faith by which we accept our justification is in itself a gift of God.[220] Luther had gone on to argue that the spiritual and moral life of Christians in no way contributes to their salvation: rather it is a sign that they are already saved.[221] Thus, in Protestant theology, we are saved by something that happens 'out there'; and the spiritual life is a response, itself actuated by God's grace, to what has already happened.

But both Hooker and Andrewes refuse to separate the outward from the inward process of justification, just as they also refuse to separate God's action from human response. For Hooker, the doctrine of justification by faith is integrally related to the notion of *participation* in God through Christ. He defines participation as 'that mutual inward hold which Christ hath of us and we of him, in such sort that each possesseth other by way of special interest, property, and inherent copulation'.[222] Since all things receive their being from God, all are partakers in him;[223] and, furthermore, since God in Christ became human, humanity participates in the life of God.[224] Christians are saved not simply by God's external action in Christ but also by

> our actual and real adoption into the fellowship of his saints in this present world. For in him we actually are by our actual incorporation into that society which hath him for their Head, and doth make together with him one Body, (he and they in that respect having one name,) for which cause, by virtue of this mystical conjunction, we are of him and in him even as though our very flesh and bones should be made continuate with his. We are in Christ because he knoweth and loveth us even as parts of himself . . . We are therefore adopted sons of God to eternal life by participation of the only-begotten Son of God, whose life is the well-spring and cause of ours.[225]

The language is ponderous, but the point fundamental. Being justified is not simply an external act of God's gratuitous love to which we then respond, though it *is* that. It is something else too – it is our adoption as Christ's children, and our invitation to participate in his very being by a profound mutual indwelling,[226] just as (for Lancelot Andrewes) humanity participated in the incarnation.[227] Although all creatures participate in God by virtue of their being, only those who are justified become 'partakers of that grace whereby he inhabiteth whom he saveth'.[228] And the implications of this are important:

> The participation of Christ importeth, besides the presence of Christ's Person, and besides the mystical copulation thereof with the parts and members of his whole Church, a true actual influence of grace whereby the life which we live according to godliness is his.[229]

We participate in Christ partly by imputation, when what he did and suffered for us is imputed to us for righteousness; and partly by 'habitual and real infusion', when grace is bestowed on us both here and (more fully) in the world to come.[230] The extent to which we participate in him depends not on the imputation of righteousness (by which we are adopted as God's children), but on how far we allow his grace to be infused into our lives: 'we have hereby only the being of the Sons of God, in which number how far soever one may seem to excel another, yet touching this that all are sons, they are all equals, some haply better sons than the rest are, but none any more a son than another'.[231] Note the plural here: Hooker, like Andrewes, stresses strongly the corporate nature of our participation in Christ:

> they which belong to the mystical body of our Saviour Christ, and be in number as the stars of heaven, divided successively by reason of their mortal condition into many generations, are notwithstanding coupled every one to Christ their Head, and all unto every particular person amongst themselves.[232]

Eucharistic spirituality

Hooker argues for a view of the Eucharist based on this notion of participation, which Loyer defines as a 'reciprocal presence', a mutual indwelling.[233] This leads him to argue that 'the real presence of Christ's most blessed body and blood is not therefore to be sought for in the sacrament, but in the worthy receiver of the sacrament'.[234] We are capable of being transformed or transfigured only to the extent to which we are united with Christ,[235] because the eucharistic presence is always primarily personal.[236]

Lancelot Andrewes, by contrast, does not restrict the presence of Christ in the Eucharist to the worshipper, though for him as for Hooker what matters is the reality of that presence; and, here as elsewhere, Andrewes stresses the transforming action of the Holy Spirit, whom we really receive at the Eucharist as at Pentecost, and who makes us participants in the very life of God.[237] And it is this participation, this becoming God-like (to the extent that is possible in this world) which is the ultimate object of all prayer, personal or corporate: '*Summa religionis est, assimilari Ei quem colis*, to become like to Him we worship is the pitch of all religion'.[238]

Andrewes further develops this emphasis on human redemption as being the fruit of the co-operation of God and humanity in his understanding of faith: for him Christian faith, though invariably a response to God's own initiative, is in effect worthless unless it evokes an active response; and for him the quintessential response is in loving and costly adoration of God. In his sermon on the Epiphany, made famous through its citation in a poem of T. S. Eliot, he expresses this in his characteristically scholarly and yet vivid prose:

> It is not commended to stand 'gazing up into Heaven' too long; not on Christ Himself ascending, much less on His star. For they sat not still gazing on the star. Their *vidimus* begat *venimus*; their seeing made them come, come a great journey. *Venimus* is soon said, but a short word; but many a wide and weary step they made before they could come to say *Venimus*, Lo, here 'we are come'; come, and at our journey's end. To look a little on it. In this their coming we consider, 1. First, the distance of the place they came from. It was not hard by, as the shepherds – but a step to Bethlehem over the fields; this was riding many a hundred miles, and cost them many a day's journey. 2. Secondly, we consider the way that they came, if it be pleasant, or plain and easy; for if it be, it is so much the better. 1. This was nothing pleasant, for through deserts, all the way waste and desolate. 2. Nor secondly, easy neither; for over the rocks and crags of both Arabias, specially Petraea, their journey lay. 3. Yet if safe – but it was not, but exceeding dangerous, as lying through the midst of the 'black tents of Kedar,' a nation of thieves and cut-throats; to pass over the hills of robbers, infamous then, and infamous to this day. No passing without great troop or convoy. 4. Last we consider the time of their coming, the season of the year. It was no summer progress. A cold coming they had of it at this time of the year, just the worst time of the year to take a journey, and specially a long journey in. The ways deep, the weather sharp, the days short, the sun farthest off, *in solstitio brumali*, 'the very dead of winter.' *Venimus*, 'we are

come', if that be one [thing], *venimus*, 'we are now come', come at this time, that sure is another.[239]

Andrewes goes on to compare the *venimus* ('we are come') of the Magi with the *veniemus* ('we may come') of most Christians: we are 'ever coming, never come. We love to make no great haste. To other things perhaps; not to *adorare*, the place of the worship of God.'[240] Fortunately for us, God's faithfulness is more enduring than ours:

> There is in God that faithfulness that is in a mother towards her children,
> for as a woman cannot but pity her own child and 'the son of her womb,'
> so the Lord 'will not forget' His own people.[241]

Spirituality and ecclesiology

The way in which Hooker and Andrewes draw out the Protestant doctrine of justification into a rich understanding of Christian life as participation in the life of God, and of co-operation with God, is crucial to an understanding of their spirituality, because it means that 'spiritual life' is very much more than discipleship with Christ: it is, in some sense at least, union with him – or, perhaps more precisely, a being-present with him.[242] Thus the church is Christ's mystical body, invisibly yet really united to him;[243] and in the last part of his great work Hooker argues (against the Protestant notion of the gathered church) for the Church of England as established, and thus in effect coterminous with the nation, because he refuses to take it upon himself to cut off anyone from union with Christ.[244] And he passionately defends the rhythm of the liturgical year with its mix of feasts and fasts thus on the grounds that only by making our own such a rhythm can we participate in the fullness of life which is Christ's pledge and promise to us:

> Our life is a mixture of good with evil. When we are partakers of good
> things we joy, neither can we but grieve at the contrary. If that befall us
> which maketh glad, our festival solemnities declare our rejoicing to be in
> him whose mere undeserved mercy is the author of all happiness; if any
> thing be either imminent or present which we shun, our watchings,
> fastings, cries and tears are unfeigned testimonies, that ourselves we
> condemn as the only causes of our own misery, and do all acknowledge
> him no less inclinable than able to save. And because as the memory of the
> one though past reneweth gladness; so the other called again to mind doth
> make the wound of our just remorse to bleed anew, which wound needeth
> often touching the more, for that we are generally more apt to calendar
> saints' than sinners' days, therefore there is in the Church a care not to
> iterate the one alone but to have frequent repetition of the other.[245]

There is in the spirituality of Hooker and Andrewes what we might today call an integrating concern, a longing to bring together discordant dimensions of human life and experience and unite them to the life of Christ as it is lived in his Church. Hooker is compassionate towards those whose faith is mingled with doubt, distinguishing between 'doubting through Infidelity' and 'doubting through Infirmity', the latter being something even Abraham did.[246] He sees the suffering that tests faith as an integral part of that faith:

> The light would never be so acceptable, were it not for that usual intercourse of darkness. Too much honey doth turn to gall; and too much joy even spiritually would make us wantons . . . Better it is sometimes to go down into the pit with him, who, beholding darkness, and bewailing the loss of inward joy and consolation, crieth from the bottom of the lowest hell, 'My God, my God, why hast thou forsaken me?' than continually to walk arm in arm with angels, to sit as it were in Abraham's bosom, and to have no thought, no cogitation, but 'I thank my God it is not with me as it is with other men.' No, God will have them that shall walk in light to feel now and then what it is to sit in the shadow of death. A grieved spirit therefore is no argument of a faithless mind.[247]

In a superb passage later in the same sermon, Hooker develops this point: we so easily forget the evidence of God's love for us, as a result of which we are quick to complain when evil befalls us. We have lost that deep intuitive sense of our unity with one another in the life of Christ which should distinguish the Christian:

> Yet if we could reckon up as many evident, clear, undoubted signs of God's reconciled love towards us as there are years, yea days, yea hours, past over our heads; all these set together have not such force to confirm our faith, as the loss, and sometimes the only fear of losing a little transitory goods, credit, honour, or favour of men, – a small calamity, a matter of nothing, – to breed a conceit, and such a conceit as is not easily again removed, that we are clean crost out of God's book, that he regards us not, that he looketh upon others, but passeth by us like a stranger to whom we are not known. Then we think, looking upon others, and comparing them with ourselves, Their tables are furnished day by day; earth and ashes are our bread: they sing to the lute, and they see their children dance before them; our hearts are heavy in our bodies as lead, our sighs beat as thick as a swift pulse, our tears do wash the beds wherein we lie: the sun shineth fair upon their foreheads; we are hanged up like bottles in the smoke, cast into corners like the sherds of a broken pot: tell us not of the promises of God's favour, tell such as do reap the fruit of them; they belong not to us, they are made to others. The Lord be merciful to our weakness, but thus it is.[248]

Thus the effect of sin is precisely to divide us from God, a point Andrewes makes in one of his sermons on prayer:[249] hence the crucial need for contrition, for a repentance that is real and deep, if we are to be both forgiven and healed.[250]

The theology and practice of prayer

It is this pervasive emphasis on integrity, on unity with one another in Christ, on the participation by the Christian in the eternal *circumincessio* of the Trinitarian life,[251] that characterizes Hooker's approach to the spiritual life. It should not therefore surprise us that he begins his treatment of prayer by emphasizing the inseparability of prayer and theology, a principle already effectively abandoned by theologians of a previous generation. Divine truth, or doctrine, is delivered to us by angels descending, whilst prayer is 'the sending of Angels upward', a beautiful idea;[252] and since we know that the saints pray in heaven, our prayer is a participation in the life of heaven, a communion or mutual indwelling with the church both triumphant and militant.[253]

And prayer itself is, for Hooker, a holding-together, a 'happy mixture', of two polar opposites: a clear awareness of our own unworthiness, and an equally clear confidence in Christ's mercy:

> The knowledge of our own unworthiness is not without belief in the merits of Christ. With that true fear which the one causeth there is coupled true boldness, and encouragement drawn from the other. The very silence which our unworthiness putteth us unto, doth itself make request for us, and that in the confidence of his grace. Looking upward we are stricken dumb, looking upward we speak and prevail. O happy mixture, wherein things contrary do so qualify and correct the one the danger of the other's excess, that neither boldness can make us presume as long as we are kept under with the sense of our own wretchedness; nor, while we trust in the mercy of God through Christ Jesus, fear be able to tyrannize over us![254]

Hooker reproduces here Julian of Norwich's understanding of human beings as having in themselves a 'marvellous medley' both of well-being and of woe: 'We have in us our lord Jesus Christ uprising, and we have in us the wretchedness and mischief of Adam falling.'[255] This is a crucial point: where the reformed tradition seeks to separate the state of sinfulness from the condition of redemption, God's free act of justification in Christ forming the point of separation, Hooker, following the medieval Catholic tradition, seeks to hold both together. For him, it is not that we were once sinners and are now saved: rather it is that we are still both, at the same time.[256] Where holiness in the Protestant tradition is a process of *separation* from the world into a gathered church, holiness in the tradition of the Church of England is better seen as a process whereby all of our selves is brought into unity with the redeeming Christ, in a church virtually coterminous with society around it.[257]

Both Hooker and Andrewes approach the subject of prayer ontologically, that is to say from the perspective of our very nature as human beings. Hooker follows St Augustine in conceiving of that nature as rooted in a desire for what we do not have, for God, who alone is unchangeable goodness,[258] for everything necessarily desires the highest good of which it is capable (in our case, felicity).[259] So pain and difficulties are to be endured for the sake of a greater good, by comparison with which they pale into insignificance,[260] for the higher ought always to rule the lower, as the soul the body.[261] Hence, as Olivier Loyer points out, the importance of sacrifice in this regard: if we are truly to desire God, we must renounce our own will and insistent longings, as Christ had to do in Gethsemane.[262]

This emphasis on desire is characteristic of Neoplatonic, Augustinian spirituality. God alone is to be desired, infinitely, as an end:[263] hence the real motivation of repentance is not fear of God but desire for union with him – or, to be more accurate, the first leads organically to the second.[264] And Hooker asks, with characteristic pragmatism: what is the point of giving human beings a desire unless you also give them the means of satisfying it?[265] He stands in the classical tradition of western Christian spirituality by insisting on holding together goodness and beauty, ethics and aesthetics; for the ultimate object of our desires and our love is beauty, 'that incomprehensible Beauty which shineth in the countenance of Christ the Son of the living God'.[266] Thus the fact that our natural desire has a supernatural end has firmly ethical as well as spiritual consequences;[267] and, again like Augustine, Hooker insists that our desire must be rightly ordered and directed, by the rational will, not just the appetite.[268]

It thus follows that for Hooker prayer is by nature rooted in human desire:

> Every good and holy desire though it lack the form, hath notwithstanding
> in itself the substance and with him the force of a prayer, who regardeth
> the very moanings, groans, and sighs of the heart of man.[269]

Yet we are not only human beings. We are also Christians; and consequently Hooker at once insists that the one absolute condition of prayer is that it be 'joined with belief in Christ'.[270] Our spirituality is rooted both in our humanity and in our faith; and characteristically Hooker refuses to separate them. We articulate our desires in prayer, not because God does not already know what they are, 'but because we this way shew that we honour him as our God, and are verily persuaded that no good thing can come to pass which he by his omnipotent power effecteth not'.[271] And the purpose of such prayer is not only to enable us to procure what God is willing to grant us, but also to articulate the desires we feel, provided that they are not 'in themselves unholy or unseemly'.[272] We may not obtain what we desire, if what we desire is unworthy or inappropriate.[273]

Lancelot Andrewes' nineteen sermons on the Lord's Prayer constitute a major contribution to English spirituality in their comprehensiveness, their mix of scholarship and pastoral sense and their careful interweaving of theology and spirituality.[274] They deserve a much wider audience than they have hitherto had. For Andrewes, as for Hooker, prayer is not only a religious impulse but a natural one too, rooted in our innate need for what is good: hence even the ravens call upon God, albeit without knowing it.[275] And Andrewes is too shrewd a pastor not to be aware that the prayer of petition is for many, as for animals and birds, the only possible starting-point in the spiritual life.[276]

But prayer is not only asking God for things: it is also that means by which we discover meaning and purpose in both our thoughts and our desires, and order both appropriately; Andrewes describes it as both 'the interpreter of our mind' and 'the interpreter of our desire'.[277] As such it is animated by the Holy Spirit (here again the significance of the Spirit for Andrewes is worth noting).[278] Hence prayer reflects the dignity of our human nature, that action by which

> a man doth abstract himself from the earth, and by often prayer doth grow
> into acquaintance and familiarity with God; for this is a great dignity, that
> flesh and blood shall be exalted so much as to have continual conference
> with God.[279]

And, as such, prayer must be the work of the whole person, not of either mind or emotions alone, a point Andrewes makes frequently.[280]

Hooker, like Andrewes, refuses to separate the private from the public elements of prayer, though the latter takes precedence over the former.[281] As by now we might expect, Hooker's view of common prayer is rooted in his understanding of the church;[282] and he defends the use of the Prayer Book litany in the worship of the Church, on the grounds that

> what dangers at any time are imminent, what evils hang over our heads, God doth know and not we. We find by daily experience that those calamities may be nearest at hand, readiest to break in suddenly upon us, which we in regard of times or circumstances may imagine to be furthest off. Or if they do not indeed approach, yet such miseries as being present all men are apt to bewail with tears, the wise by their prayers should rather prevent. Finally, if we for ourselves had a privilege of immunity, doth not true Christian charity require that whatsoever any part of the world, yea any one of all our brethren elsewhere doth either suffer or fear, the same we account as our own burden?[283]

He stresses the need for public as well as private penance, for sin damages the whole body.[284]

But it is in Andrewes' *Preces privatae* ('Private prayers') that we encounter the fullest expression of this rich and integrated spirituality so characteristic of both these writers. Compiled for his own use and unpublished until some years after his death, they are drawn from a wide variety of sources[285] and written in a mixture of Hebrew, Greek, and Latin, the three languages consecrated on the cross.[286] Yet they reflect far more than Andrewes' prodigious scholarship: they reveal his fascination with the world around him, and his determination to hold together the corporate and the personal, religious faith and every aspect of human experience. What Andrewes does is to draw together material from a wide variety of sources, which is then assimilated and appropriated as his personal prayer; and this is designed to issue in practical action and concern for the world outside his study. An occasional note of what (to modern minds) may hint of smug complacency jars, as when Andrewes, adapting a sixteenth-century prayer, thanks God that he was not born a barbarian, or illegitimate, or a dullard, or disabled, or rude and unlettered.[287] Nonetheless it is an outstanding example of a particular kind of prayer – meditative, scholarly, comprehensive, structured, scriptural, measured (almost leisured), nothing left to chance or spontaneous impulse, yet as a result nothing excluded: the world and its needs are drawn into Andrewes' prayer through the prism of a rich inheritance of spiritual texts.

Conclusion

Andrewes' spirituality stands in sharp contrast to much reformed theology, not least to the Calvinist orthodoxy which dominated the Church of England in the latter part of his life. He valued learning and scholarship, preferred a pattern of prayer that was ordered and methodical, and emphasized in a way Calvin or (say) Latimer never could the part played by humanity, co-operating with God, in the work of our redemption. Yet there are interesting similarities between Andrewes and Protestant spirituality, not least in his emphasis on the work of the Holy Spirit; and, for all his splendid prose, he himself declares, in words that Bunyan could have echoed, that 'it is not fine phrases and goodly sentences that commend our prayer but the fervency of the Spirit from whom it proceeds'.[288]

He constantly stresses the importance of human *response* to the divine action: it is not enough to 'sit still, and hear a Sermon and two Anthems, and be saved'.[289] And he tells us why all prayer is ultimately corporate, for when our own prayer is weak and lacking in fervour, those lacks are made up for by others who pray for us, 'so that the weakness of one member is supplied by the fervent and earnest prayer of the other'.[290]

And yet, for all his wisdom, there is something missing from his spirituality: a prophetic edge, a spontaneity, a passion, that might effectively complement his massive scholarship. It may be significant that the most conspicuous manifestation of such features in his writings comes in his rant against Cardinal Bellarmine; and that, trotted out obediently at the behest of his king, does him little credit. His work is all somehow too *safe*, too structured, too densely and allusively patristic, too comfortable even for it to be able to capture the hearts and minds of many, either in his day or in ours.

But Hooker's still can. For all his reverence for the Christian spiritual tradition, there is a hint of the pioneer and the pilgrim in his work, a glint of adventure in his eye which augured well for the future of the Church whose spiritual and theological foundations he helped so much to lay. He declared that 'constitutions and canons made for the ordering of church affairs are dead taskmasters'; he excoriates with humour as well as rhetorical skill those nonconformists whose worship was (in his view) hopelessly disorderly and emotive:

> Suppose that the people of a whole town with some chosen man before them did continually twice or thrice in a week resort to their king, and every time they come first acknowledge themselves guilty of rebellions and treasons, then sing a song, after that explain some statute of the land to the standers-by, and therein spend at the least an hour, this done, turn themselves again to the king, and for every sort of his subjects crave somewhat of him, at the length sing him another song, and so take their leave. Might not the king well think that either they knew not what they would have, or else that they were distracted in mind, or some other such like cause of the disorder of their supplication? This form of suing unto kings were absurd. This form of praying unto God they allow.[291]

And he inveighs against the appalling triviality of so much religious disputation, asking (in regard to the question of whether the minister should face the people during services) 'whether it be not a kind of taking God's name in vain to debase religion with such frivolous disputes, a sin to bestow time and labour about them. Things of so mean regard and quality, although necessary to be ordered, are notwithstanding very unsavoury when they come to be disputed of'.[292] 'No practice', he later wrote, 'is so vile, but pretended holiness is made sometime as a cloak to hide it.'[293] Hooker knew that true holiness is the fruit of a painful struggle between ourselves and God, between our own wills and our deepest and most hidden longings; and sometimes, like Christ in Gethsemane, all we can do is to lay before God our raw and confused aspirations and ask him to make of them what he will:

> We are therefore taught by [Christ's] example, that the presence of dolorous and dreadful objects even in minds most perfect, may as clouds overcast all sensible joy; that no assurance touching future victories can make present conflicts so sweet and easy but nature will shun and shrink from them . . . [and] desire ease and deliverance from oppressive burdens; that the contrary determination of God is oftentimes against the effect of this desire, yet not against the affection itself, because it is naturally in us; that in such case our prayers cannot serve us as means to obtain the thing we desire; that notwithstanding they are unto God most acceptable sacrifices, because they testify we desire nothing but at his hands, and our desires we submit with contentment to be overruled by his will.[294]

The Seventeenth Century and the Art of Meditation

Introduction

The seventeenth century was an age of immense, indeed volcanic, change; but it was also an age of remarkable fecundity in almost every aspect of life; and both of these features are reflected in the development of the spiritual life within the Church of England. For adherents of the episcopal church, this century was far more than a period of consolidation after its painful birth at the Reformation: it was a period in which it all but disappeared, and in which almost every aspect of its doctrine and practice was subject to strenuous and passionate criticism. Even so, it proved to be the most fertile and creative period in the Church of England's history thus far, producing many of its most significant figures. Some of the greatest of these (Donne, Herbert, and Taylor) will occupy our attention at the end of this chapter; and it must suffice at this point to highlight a few of the main themes and movements within the spiritual life of the Church of England during this period.

Spirituality and the Prayer Book in the seventeenth century

The violent upheavals in both state and church during the seventeenth century did have one consequence which Cranmer could hardly have foreseen, yet would certainly have rejoiced at: the Prayer Book became a symbol of all that was most enduring and characteristic in the established episcopal church, and above all of the piety that was designed to underpin it.[295] In 1549 Cranmer had offered the fledgling Church 'an order for prayer . . . much agreeable to the mind and purpose of the old fathers',[296] rooted in the Word of God and written in the vernacular which he hoped would furnish English Christians with a rhythm and pattern of piety that was comprehensive in scope, accessible in character, and Protestant in theology.

The compilers of the revised 1662 Book confronted what was if anything an even more daunting challenge than that faced by Cranmer: a church and country still bitterly divided by the experience of civil war and the uneasy equilibrium of the Commonwealth, and anxiously awaiting the outcome of the monarchy's restoration in 1660. Their amendments to the 1552 Book were relatively modest: language was modernized in places;[297] the latest translation of scripture was adopted;[298] and a number of services were adapted or inserted to meet contemporary needs.[299]

The resulting book rapidly became the rallying-point for all concerned to defend the integrity and piety of the Restoration Church and its sixteenth-century forebears. Numerous bishops (among them Jeremy Taylor of Down and Connor, Antony Sparrow of Norwich, William Beveridge of St Asaph) wrote extensive treatises defending the Prayer Book not only on the grounds that formal liturgical prayer was inherently superior to its extemporary equivalent, but also as the coping-stone of a complete and systematic pattern of piety. Thus Taylor declared that

> there is no part of religion, as it is a distinct virtue, and is to be exercised by interior acts and forms of worship, but is in the offices of the church of England.[300]

The fundamental ingredients of this pattern were set out by John Cosin in 1627: observance of the Prayer Book's calendar of festivals and holy days, together with the fast days designed to precede many of them; regular, if possible daily, attendance at Morning and Evening Prayer and the occasional offices; and receiving Holy Communion at least three times each year, always preparing by confessing one's sins.[301] This fundamental spiritual diet was to be supplemented by other seasonable nourishment provided by the Prayer Book: notably by the Litany (one of Cranmer's finest compositions, albeit itself extensively based on earlier texts[302]) and the sermon. The Eucharist too may have played a more significant part in contemporaries' spirituality than we might suppose from the relative infrequency with which they received Communion.[303]

The question how far this pattern was both observed and internalized by members of the Church of England in the seventeenth century is not easy to answer. Martin Thornton argues that it was comprehensively observed, though the examples he adduces are all either aristocrats or divines;[304] and certainly the Prayer Book appears to have remained largely in use throughout the Commonwealth period, despite having been formally unauthorized.[305] Much recent scholarship has argued both for a high level of regular attendance at church,[306] and for the pervasive and formative impact on worshippers of hearing the vernacular liturgy and scriptures week by week, year by year.[307] But issues of this kind are not easily assessed by those living several centuries later;[308] and we might do well to bear in mind two remarks made by the seventeenth-century priest and diarist Ralph Josselin: reflecting on the lack of interest shown by his parishioners in a fast day proclaimed by the state for observance on 25 September 1644, he says sadly that it would make a man bleede to see how regardles people are of the same(.) nothing moves them. [It] affect[s] me that others are not affected.[309]

And he makes an obvious but crucial point in his diary entry for 21 April 1650: "tis very hard to bee at rest to outward things when wee have never so many [i.e. so few] of them'.[310] Much of his diary is filled with concern about his and his children's recurrent illnesses and fear of death or bereavement. People whose lives are dominated by such preoccupations (and there will have been thousands of them in seventeenth-century England[311]) may have not found always regular attendance at lengthy Prayer Book services as easy or satisfying as we suppose.[312]

Spirituality and women

Women's piety during this period took a wide variety of forms, which is not surprising given both the diversity of spiritual traditions but also the common contemporary assumption that 'the weaker sexe, to piety more prone'.[313] In addition to the keeping of spiritual journals (where literacy and leisure time allowed), many sought to introduce a spiritual dimension into their everyday lives, singing psalms or meditating as they worked; others chose biblical scenes for their needlework patterns.[314] Most of these scenes were of Old Testament stories about women, and among the commonest seems to have been the grim tale of Abraham and Hagar.[315] In one such, preserved at the Victoria and Albert Museum, there are two scenes: in the first, Abraham (dressed as a prosperous seventeenth-century gentleman) is holding little Ishmael's hand; in the other, Hagar (having been driven out of the household by the jealous Sarah) is praying alone in the wilderness by a bush, while the tiny baby Ishmael lies alone and exposed with a lion uncomfortably close by.[316]

Not all such embroidery depicts the sufferings of women: some playfully depict Esther appearing before King Ahasuerus; Esther (usually presented in gorgeous robes) is unquestionably the principal character.[317] In a (rarer) depiction of a New Testament scene from the late sixteenth or early seventeenth century, Veronica is shown holding her cloth with Christ's face imprinted on it and emblems of the passion surrounding it: the inscription reads IHESU FILI DEI MISERERE ME, PRAYE FOR ME ANNE INGLEBYE.[318]

Aristocratic women like Anne Lady Halkett (1622–99) could enjoy the benefits of a household with its own chaplain, 'who preached twice every Sunday in ye chapell, and dayly prayers morning and evening';[319] she also used to enjoy retiring after dinner to read sermons.[320] Yet even upper-class ladies were not immune from tragedy: when Lady Joan Barrington's husband Francis died in 1628, she seems to have experienced a deep crisis of faith; and a clergyman named Roger Williams wrote her a moving letter of spiritual consolation, acknowledging her terrible suffering, and advising her to 'cry hard, and the lord helpe me to cry for you'.[321]

It is important also to note the existence of prophetic texts written by women, or based on their experience. Although most such texts were produced by Quakers, some came from members of the Church of England, such as the appeal for peace directed by Elinor Channel from Cranleigh in Surrey to Oliver Cromwell in 1654. It begins with all the immediacy and directness of an Old Testament prophet's experience of divine vocation:

> May it please your highness to understand that your petitioner is an inhabitant at Cranley in Surrey, who upon a Sabbath-day about two months agone, at night, as she was in bed in a slumber, had a blow given her upon her heart, which blow awaked her. And immediately with that, the thoughts of her heart were changed, and all the corruption thereof taken away, that from that day to this, she could think of no evil. And then she heard an audible voice, which said unto her, 'Come away, I will send thee on my message to London, fear not to go, for I thy Lord am with thee.'[322]

The art of meditation: Joseph Hall (1574–1656)

The Prayer Book, and the kind of piety which came to be associated with it, was not, of course, all that the established church had to offer to contemporary spiritual needs. In 1606 Joseph Hall, bishop of Norwich, published *The arte of divine meditation*, which rapidly became both popular and influential within and beyond the episcopal tradition.[323] Hall was a scholar-pastor of a kind that was very common in this first century of the Church of England; and, like Cranmer, he drew extensively on earlier sources – monastic spirituality both patristic and medieval, and fifteenth- and sixteenth-century continental Catholic writers – in order to offer contemporaries a pattern of prayer designed to foster personal spiritual growth.[324]

Hall describes meditation as 'the ladder of heaven and . . . the best improvement of Christianity',[325] and defines it as 'the bending of the mind upon some spiritual object, through divers forms of discourse, until our thoughts come to an issue'.[326] Although it is directed primarily to the mind, it is no narrow intellectual endeavour: it can be concerned either with knowledge ('for the finding out of some hidden truth') or with affection ('for the enkindling of our love to God'), and it is the latter which Hall regards as being most needful for his own age:

> for if there be some, that have much zeal, [but] little knowledge; there are more, that have much knowledge, without zeal.[327]

It would be easy to dismiss Hall as a kind of mild-mannered English version of St Ignatius of Loyola; and it is true that he lacks the great Spaniard's overriding emphasis on an ethical and unconditional response to the will of God as it is revealed in meditation. Yet Hall is important, not so much because he restored the practice of a strongly scriptural, meditative form of prayer to the mainstream episcopal tradition of English spirituality, but because he drank deeply of the waters of contemporary continental piety and thereby helped to ensure (as Cranmer, in a very different manner, had done earlier) that the Church of England's spiritual life drew upon rich eclectic resources for its nourishment.

Even so, it is at least worth wondering how many of Josselin's parishioners, buffeted successively by ill-health, civil war and economic deprivation, would have found time or inclination to practise meditation of this kind. Hall knew that any Christian spirituality worthy of the name needed to nourish both head and heart together: yet the characteristically English (and particularly Anglican) fondness for balance, prudence and reserve could have the effect of anaesthetizing anything that smacked of the passionate or the prophetic if taken too far. Robert Burton, a near-contemporary of Joseph Hall and the author of the astonishingly erudite *Anatomy of melancholy*, is in many respects a typically Renaissance figure: yet he too manifests this suspicion of extremes which was characteristic of the spirituality of the Church of England at the time. Reflecting on spiritual ecstasy, he wrote:

> *Extasis is a taste of future happinesse, by which we are united unto God, a divine melancholy, a spirituall wing*, Bonaventure tearms it, to lift us up to heaven: But as it is abused, a mere dotage, madnesse, a cause and symptome of *Religious melancholy. If you shall at any time see* (saith *Guianerius*) *a Religious person over superstitious, too solitary, or much given to fasting, that man will certainly bee melancholy, thou maist boldly say it, he will be so.*[328]

The Beauty of Creation: The Platonic Tradition

Introduction: the 'Latitude-Men'

We shall see, in exploring the spirituality of Jeremy Taylor, the way in which the great figures of the Restoration period sought to foster a pattern of piety which would be rooted in the exigencies of daily life; and we shall also consider how the spirituality of dissent addressed the questions raised above. But there was another movement within the Church of England in the seventeenth century which sought to foster moral and spiritual renewal in a manner which would be genuinely accessible and yet rooted in sound learning. They came to be described pejoratively as the 'Latitude-Men' or 'Latitudinarians' by hostile contemporaries because of their desire to reduce the Christian religion to a few plain but essential fundamentals that could be easily assimilated, and because they were happy to accommodate themselves within the established church.[329]

The Latitudinarians were strongly influenced by classical (especially Platonic) thought as well as by the concept of natural law inherited from Aquinas; and they were vehemently opposed to any kind of irrational 'enthusiasm'.[330] Since in addition most of them wrote in a consciously elevated, even highly rhetorical, style, it might have been supposed *prima facie* that their contribution to the mainstream of English spirituality could only be minimal. Yet they bequeathed to the Church of England a vitality and imaginativeness of thought and spiritual depth which remains remarkable to this day.

Peter Sterry (1613–72)

One of the most interesting of those associated with the Latitudinarians (though never properly speaking a Latitudinarian himself) was Peter Sterry, son of a merchant and clerical protégé of Cromwell: he was not a priest of the Church of England so much as a dissenting clergyman and influential preacher during the Commonwealth – which in itself may remind us that the eleven years from the execution of Charles I to the restoration of his son were not as grim and barren a period in the spiritual life of the Church of England as some have supposed.[331]

Sir Thomas Browne (1605–82)

There were other important contributors to the spiritual life of the Church of England in the second half of the seventeenth century, whose thought may appropriately be considered together with that of Sterry and the Latitudinarians. Sir Thomas Browne was a medical doctor from Norwich, whose wide learning and experience of life are reflected in his writings: his *Religio medici* (1635) must rank among the finest works of English literature in what was a golden age. Like Sterry and the Latitudinarians, he owed a great debt to Plato and other classical texts.[332]

Thomas Traherne (1637–74)

Thomas Traherne, an Oxford-educated priest, was for many years Rector of Credenhill in Herefordshire before becoming domestic chaplain to Sir Orlando Bridgman at Teddington in 1667.[333] He was little known in his day; the majority of his work was only recently discovered, and much of it remains unpublished: his *Commentaries of heaven* is a massive, unfinished torso of a work (perhaps 350,000 words long), rescued from a burning rubbish tip in Lancashire in 1967. It was intended to be a kind of encyclopaedic commonplace book comprising articles on various subjects considered in the light of Traherne's favourite theme, 'Felicitie';[334] but he completed only the entries from 'Abhorrence' to 'Bastard'. Traherne is as profoundly indebted to Plato as Browne and Sterry, and his writing is more visionary, imaginative and rhapsodic even than theirs.[335]

The image and likeness

The world-view of the Latitudinarians was much more affirmative than that of the Protestant Reformers, albeit tinged with Plato's suspicion of all things corporeal; and the Latitudinarian view of the human condition was a more positive one than theirs, albeit with reservations. We are very far here from the theology of Latimer or Cranmer, Luther or Calvin. Browne says that 'there is another man within mee that's angry with mee, rebukes, commands, and dastards mee';[336] and Sterry speaks of 'this Mixture in thee', declaring that 'thy Life will be like an April day; which hath far more Showers than Sunshines in it'.[337] Traherne, typically more optimistic still, declares simply that we are created in the image of God, so that we might 'becom Divine'.[338] Hence the importance of self-knowledge: 'You never Know your self, till you Know more then [= than] your Body. The Image of God was not seated in the features of your face, but in the Lineaments of your Soul'.[339] As images of God, we are mirrors;

and, as such, what matters is what people see in us,[340] and the fact that 'We were made in his Image that we might liv in His similitud'.[341]

The image, then, though obscured, is still present and active within us.[342] And for Sterry Christ is the divine image dwelling within us, summoning us to co-operate with the work of grace in conforming image to likeness.[343] The theology is Augustinian and classically western, though the language (with its characteristic inter-play of light and darkness) is more Neoplatonic, closer to Pseudo-Dionysius than Augustine:

> Natural Joy is the Dilatation, or Enlargement of the Heart. Spiritual Joy is the Dilatation, or Enlargement of the Holy Spirit in man. When the Divine Principle in the Soul breaks out of the Darkness of our Nature, when it breaks forth from the Bonds of Flesh into its own Liberty, and Freedom: this is the Kingdom of God, and the Joy thereof in the Soul.[344]

Sir Thomas Browne also echoes Pseudo-Dionysius in his description of what the latter called 'dissimilar similarities':[345]

> even in things alike, there is diversitie, and those that doe seeme to accord, doe manifestly disagree. And thus is Man like God, for in the same things that wee resemble him, wee are utterly different from him.[346]

All this leads both Browne and Sterry to a rich and nuanced view of human beings. On the one hand we are deeply mysterious creatures, as Browne declares in *Religio medici*:

> No man can justly censure or condemne another, because indeed no man truely knowes another. This I perceive in my self, for I am in the darke to all the world, and my nearest friends behold mee but in a cloud.[347]

On the other hand we are microcosms of the universe, carrying the entire cosmos about within ourselves,[348] and also vessels for the indwelling Christ, who for Sterry as for Thomas Traherne is the divine seed within us, the dynamic principle of fruitfulness and procreation:

> As every creature hath this Seed in it, so it hath lying in it the Eternal Beauty of the Divine Nature, the Immortal Beauty of the Spiritual Creature, which both are wrapt up together, in this Seed.[349]

Traherne goes even further: the human soul ('This busy, vast, enquiring Soul'[350]) is infinitely greater than the cosmos ('The World was more in me, then I in it'[351]). In the extraordinary poem *My Spirit* he says 'all my Mind was wholy Evry where';[352] and in *Fullnesse*, a kind of postcript to *My Spirit*, he speaks of the soul as

> A Spiritual World Standing within,
> An Univers enclosd in Skin.[353]

The divine beauty

The consequence of this combination of divinity and mystery is a profound fascination not only with the inner self and the God who dwells there, but also with the world around us. Browne reflects here not just the long Platonic tradition of aesthetics but also the scientific outlook of his own age:

> The world was made to be inhabited by beasts, but studied and contemplated by man . . . The wisedome of God receives small honour from those vulgar heads, that rudely stare about, and with a grosse rusticity admire his workes; those highly magnifie him whose judicious enquiry into his acts, and deliberate research into his creatures, returne the duty of a devout and learned admiration.[354]

Browne even compares Christians unfavourably with pagans, since the former 'disdain to suck Divinity from the flowers of Nature'.[355] This is not to say unequivocally that creation is entirely good; and Sterry sometimes follows Plato in conceiving of the physical body as a shadow or prison.[356] But it is to say that, again following Plato, God draws us towards himself through his creation, Beauty manifested through the Beautiful. For Sterry, then, we can delight here and now at finding ourselves in so wonderful a world:

> This World is indeed a Deep of Darkness, yet it hath the Wonders of God in it (Ps 107:24). The Soul sports itself, and plays with the Miserablest Things of the World, when she perceives herself to be in them, as in the midst of the Mystery of God, and among his Wonders . . . Faith and Joy are like the Sun, and Light. Joy is the Daughter of Faith, but ever as old, and strong, as the Mother.[357]

Traherne again goes further still. For him, reflecting as he does a spirituality of creation that is closer to St Francis and St Bonaventure than Pseudo-Dionysius or St Augustine, the universe is his precisely because he does not and must not seek to possess it (a point to which we shall return):

> From Dust I rise,
> And out of Nothing now awake,
> These Brighter Regions which salute mine Eys,
> A Gift from GOD I take.
> The Earth, the Seas, the Light, the Day, the Skies,
> The Sun and Stars are mine; if those I prize . . .
>
> A Stranger here
> Strange Things doth meet, Strange Glories See;
> Strange Treasures lodg'd in this fair World appear,
> Strange all, and New to me.
> But that they mine should be, who nothing was,
> That Strangest is of all, yet brought to pass.[358]

Narrow Souls seldom Consider all thy Glories. Even Ants can see the splendor of this world, the Glory of the Heavens, Gr[ass] Trees, and flowers, the Brightnes of the Sun, and Beauty of the Day. Bli[nd] men Seldom See them.[359]

What is it about beauty that draws us? Sterry represents classical Christian Platonism when he declares that Christ is himself Beauty made manifest, drawing us towards him:

Jesus Christ is Beauty in its Original . . . the Perfection of Beauty . . . All Beauty is derived from him . . . The True Beauty [= Christ] calls, and allures all hearts to it. The True Good gives them rest in the bosom of that Beauty. Beauty is Goodness visible.[360]

And he stands here in the grand tradition of Western Platonism in binding together two of the great transcendentals, beauty and goodness.

The attractiveness of Christianity

It is crucial to see that this is far more than a speculative exercise, or some kind of wishful thinking.[361] Sterry's unique blend of the Puritan, the Platonic, and the rational is ordered to a pastoral end: he wants to make Christianity attractive, and he wants to integrate spirituality and ethics, the practice of prayer and the love of neighbour, the worship of God and the scientific study of the world around us, which so many of his contemporaries sought to prise apart. Here he is, applying his rich Platonic metaphysics to the harsh reality of grief:

Grief is then alone a Grace in thy soul, when the Sun shines upon the watery Cloud. When the Glory of Christ mingles its sweet Beams with thy Grief, and makes a Spiritual Rain-bow in thy Soul. Then is there the Covenant of God in the Cloud of thy Grief. This Over-spreading of a Spiritual chearfulness upon thy Sorrows is a Sign from Heaven, that the waters of Sin, Despair, and Wrath shall never quite cover the Image of God in thee.[362]

It is true that all the Latitudinarians tended to undervalue the seriousness of evil and suffering: like Augustine, though in very different ways, they longed to proclaim a goodness that was more attractive, more real, than its opposite, and in the process ran the inevitable risk of minimizing evil's destructive power.[363] But they did this because they wanted above all else to bolt together faith and morality, beauty and ethics: without moral goodness, religious knowledge was worthless, and they made this point constantly.[364]

This is why Sterry and others spoke so often about the reality of Christ as the divine principle living within us, thereby incarnating religious truth in the heart of human life. The result was a relative devaluing of doctrine in favour of living a moral and spiritual life, an emphasis which was closer to Quaker than to either Catholic or Puritan spirituality, and which spoke to a post-Restoration England hungry for reconciliation and weary of empty religious speculation. Another Latitudinarian, Ralph Cudworth, knew that religion detached from morality simply divided people:

> Christ came not into the world to fil [*sic*] our heads with mere Speculations; to kindle a fire of wrangling and contentious dispute amongst us, and to warm our spirits against one another with nothing but angry & peevish debates, whilst in the mean time our hearts remain all ice within towards God.[365]

And in this context even prayer was not enough on its own: 'you may pray, and hear the Word, and receive the Sacrament, and be wicked still'.[366]

Spiritual childhood

This is not to say that faith and revealed religious truth held little or no importance for the Latitudinarians: it is rather to say that they are inseparable from the moral life which they animate. It is in this context that their optimistic view of human nature needs to be seen: it is not a celebration of human potential or achievement in their own right, but a theological affirmation of the divine within each of us and of its profound implications. Peter Sterry, in a superb section of his extended compilation of sermons on Jesus' exhortation to his followers to become 'as little children' (*The rise, race, and royalty of the kingdom of God in the soul of man*, 1683) grounds this affirmation in our nature as children, not slaves, of God. Where servility is characterized by fear, immature dependence, a preoccupation with outward things, and a pervasive anxiety, the Christian state of childlikeness has four fundamental properties. The first is love, the deep awareness of God's love for us which imparts a boldness to all our dealings with our heavenly Father:

> A Saint, that is, a Son, knows, and feels God to be *Love* . . . He knows himself to be in this *Love*, to be One with God in his Heavenly Glory . . . He knows this *Love* to be in him, God to be one with him in his worldly Disguise: *We have boldness, because as he is, so are we* in this World.[367]

The second is life itself, for by virtue of being adopted as children we become partakers of the divine life and nature (this is what Sterry means by living 'in a Divine Principle').[368] The third is 'spirituality', which is nourished by the divine life and conduces towards 'the Unity of things, 1 Cor. 3:7':

> A *Spiritual* man takes not away the Differences of things, he allows, owns them in their utmost variety, latitude, and distance. But he tunes them, and attones [*sic*] them, 1 Cor. 12:23, 25.[369]

Thus the truly spiritual person is in himself or herself a promoter of harmony and reconciliation: 'He makes, or finds a Unity everywhere'.[370] Such a person is able to do this by virtue of the fourth property of childlikeness: resignation, or *trust*, which brings us to the heart of the spiritual life:

> There is nothing so natural, as for a Child to run to the lap of its Parents in extremities, and to have a Confidence in them. It is as natural for a Child of God in pains, or griefs to cast itself into the arms of God, and there to breathe forth its sorrows.[371]

For Sterry, God is even more than a natural father because we have our being not only of, but in him.[372] And he concludes:

> There is no Earthly Relation, or Form, which more sets out the Spiritual, Evangelical, Eternal Union between God, and Man, than this of a *Father.* Trace it, apply it from the beginning to the end, and it will lead you into all the *Mysteries* of Eternity. Only remember these *two Cautions.* 1. Take away all the *Imperfection*, which this Relation hath in the Creature. 2. *Add* to it all *Perfection*, that it is capable of, or can be imagined. So apply it to God, and a Saint. For the Brightest Beauty in Nature, is but a Shadow of Spiritual Glories.[373]

The interrelation of the spiritual and the moral in this analysis is clear. Sterry's view of spiritual life is dynamic because it is supremely the life of a child, growing up not into barren rational autonomy but precisely from a helpless childishness into a mature childlikeness. Sterry offers four tests by which we may know if we are growing as we should: have I seen a resurrection, a change, in myself – or (as he puts it in typically Platonic language) 'am I awakened into the light?' Can I distinguish between what is of the flesh and what is of the spirit? Am I aware of the limitations of this world, considered purely on its own terms? ('have I seen a Night come upon this World?') And 'have I tasted the Sweetness of a Life within, in my own spirit?'[374]

For Traherne too, childlikeness is a fundamental (perhaps the fundamental) virtue; but his approach to it is different, and his starting-point is not the teaching of Jesus but the Garden of Eden.[375] Thus he writes in *Eden*:

> Those Things which first his Eden did adorn,
> My Infancy
> Did crown. Simplicitie
> Was my Protection when I first was born.
> Mine Eys those Treasures first did see,
> Which God first made. The first Effects of Lov
> My first Enjoyments upon Earth did prov.[376]

He returns to this theme constantly: for him, as for Sterry, childlikeness is the central condition, the mainspring, of the spiritual life: 'I must becom [*sic*] a Child again';[377] God 'in our Childhood with us walks';[378] and

> To Infancy, O Lord, again I com,
> That I my Manhood may improv:
> My early Tutor is the Womb;
> I still my Cradle lov.
> 'Tis strange that I should Wisest be,
> When least I could an Error see.[379]

In *Centuries*, Traherne explains what he means, this time reflecting on the same text as had inspired Sterry:

Our Saviors Meaning, when He said, He must be Born again and becom a little Child that will enter into the Kingdom of Heaven: is Deeper far then is generaly believed. It is not only in a Careless Reliance upon Divine Providence, that we are to becom Little Children . . . but in the Peace and Purity of all our Soul . . . all our Thoughts must be Infantlike and Clear: the Powers of our Soul free from the Leven of this World, and disentangled from mens conceits and customs. Grit in the Ey or the yellow Jandice [*sic*] will not let a Man see those Objects truly that are before it. And therfore it is requisit that we should be as very Strangers to the Thoughts Customs and Opinions of men in this World as if we were but little Children. So those Things would appear to us only which do to Children when they are first Born. Ambitions, Trades, Luxuries, inordinat Affections, Casual and Accidental Riches invented since the fall would be gone, and only those Things appear, which did to Adam in Paradise, in the same Light, and in the same Colors.[380]

For Traherne, then, spiritual childlikeness means, first, a stripping-off of all evil habits and worldly customs; secondly, a valuing only of those things which we valued as children (wonder, awe, and a sense of the whole world being ours) and which Adam valued in Eden (such as God, light, and glory);[381] and, thirdly, being clothed with the virtues which we were created to make our own.[382] Like Sterry, he conceives of spiritual childhood as a state we experience in virtue of our creation, not in virtue of our redemption, so that although he praises St Paul's 'divine philosophy' he makes little reference to Paul's teaching on our status as children by adoption.[383] Like Sterry, but unlike Browne, his view of childlikeness imparts a naïveté to his thought, a naïveté which is the more marked in Traherne's case because he makes less of the relationship of the spiritual with the moral that is so important to Sterry. One is tempted to speculate that, confronted (say) with a pocket-watch, Sterry would have rhapsodized about Time and Eternity as Platonic Ideas and then exhorted us to use both well,[384] Traherne would have praised the Christ who died to give us eyes to behold such wonders, whilst Browne (no less admiring) would have wanted to know how it worked.

Deification

Now this pervasive emphasis on childlike wonder does not just draw us closer to God: it makes us like him, indeed unites us with him. In using the language of deification, the Latitudinarians do not attempt to distinguish between a union of wills and a union of being, and thus go far beyond what Protestant spirituality could accept. This process is, however, not simply the result of their high view of human nature: union with God is attainable only through Christ, who in himself unites the divine and the human both as a person in history and as a living principle indwelling each of us.[385] When we allow Christ's life to become ours, and yield ourselves entirely to the life he longs to bring to fruition within us, we become divine, a point the Latitudinarians constantly make.[386] But this process is no exercise in self-glorification or even (as it might today be understood) in self-fulfilment: it is profoundly costly, as Sterry points out:

The Love of a Saint to Jesus Christ is a Daily Death; a Separation from all Created Objects, a Retirement out of this whole World visible, or invisible, into the World of the Blessed, that World of Eternal Light, and Beauty.[387]

We become Christ-like only by becoming less self-centred, more able to see the divine that lies beneath the surface: Sterry's 'retirement' is close to Traherne's quasi-Franciscan celebration of creation – both involve a deliberate and ascetic refusal to possess what can only be enjoyed when it is seen in God, and seen to belong to all.[388]

And yet, though costly, this process of deification is (especially for Traherne) the only conceivable way of becoming fully human, because part of what makes us human is our longing for the divine. Traherne describes desire, in a poem entitled simply *Desire*, as a 'restlesse longing Heavenly Avarice',[389] and elsewhere he describes it as 'insatiableness':[390] it is precisely this insatiability which derives from the nobility, the divine nature, of our souls.[391] 'Want' is 'the Parent of Celestial Treasure', he writes, adding that 'It is very Strange; Want it self is a Treasure in Heaven', because there we both desire and are satisfied infinitely.[392] Here Traherne is at his most intensely Augustinian:

To be Holy is so Zealously to Desire, so vastly to Esteem, and so Earnestly to Endeavour it [the end for which we were created], that we would not for millions of Gold and Silver, Decline, nor fail, nor Mistake in a Tittle. For then we Pleas God when we are most like Him. We are like Him when our Minds are in Frame. Our Minds are in Frame when our Thoughts are like his.[393]

The reference to 'thoughts' is very characteristic of Traherne: indeed he gives that name to three of his poems. In one he writes:

Thoughts are the Angels which we send abroad,
To visit all the Parts of Gods Abode.
Thoughts are the Things wherin [*sic*] we all confess
The Quintessence of Sin and Holiness
Is laid. All Wisdom in a Thought doth Shine,
By Thoughts alone the Soul is made Divine.[394]

And elsewhere he says that it is only by means of our thoughts that we *see* anything.[395] Traherne's writing is penetrated with the notion of vision and the imagery of light; but we need to see that his understanding of vision is primarily intellectual, close to that of Aquinas: the contemplation of God is something that involves the mind more than any other faculty.[396] When we think as God thinks, we become as he is;[397] because for Traherne, as for Aristotle and Aquinas, it is our thoughts that make us superior to animals and thus capable of participation in the life of God.[398] Peter Sterry is much less rigorously intellectual, more Dionysian, in his exploration of union with God, using (like Traherne) the imagery of light in his description of the Trinity:

The Lord Jesus cometh in the Glory of all the Three Persons; the Father shineth in the Person of the Son; the Son shineth in the Person of the

Spirit; all Three in One shine together in the glorified Humanity of the Lord Jesus, all three glorifie that with themselves; Inhabiting, and shining forth round about with a full Light of glory in it, Figuring themselves in their Divinest Forms upon it; overshadowing it, and cloathing [*sic*] it with the Brightnesses of their own, most entire, and most naked Appearances.[399]

The divine presence

But Sterry too is insistent that spirituality must be more than simply something we experience: if we seek God only in our own experience or feelings, we soon encounter the terrible dereliction of Psalm 77: the divine absence. So we must 'make God, as He is in Himself', the object of our joy and of our thoughts, indeed of our entire lives.[400] And we do this by walking in the way of Christ ('Tread in the Steps of this Shepherd of the Flock. Go by the Cross'[401]). Sterry cites the example of St Paul in 2 Corinthians, not boasting in his spiritual experience but in his Christlike weakness;[402] and he follows in the tradition of St Anselm and Julian of Norwich in describing Jesus as our mother, who will 'dandle you in all your Motions with dances of love'.[403]

Again Traherne goes further, pressing Platonic thought to its furthermost point compatible with Christian theology. 'Then [i.e. before my birth] was my Soul my only All to me, /A Living Endless Ey'.[404] Traherne's spirituality has a pervasively Greek quality to it in setting vision before hearing.[405] He says that with 'Cleerer Eys' we can 'see all Creatures full of Deities; Especialy Ones self'.[406] And, just when we begin to wonder exactly where Christ fits in to his soaring Platonizing metaphysics, Traherne makes the bold claim that, if we could but see it, the entire creation is praising Christ, and Christ *crucified*:

> With all their Eys behold our Savior, with all their Hearts Adore Him, with all their Tongues and Affections praise him. See how in all Closets, and in all Temples; in all Cities and in all feilds; in all Nations and in all generations they are lifting up their hands and Eys unto his Cross; and Delight in all their Adorations. This will Enlarge your Soul and make you to Dwell in all Kingdoms and Ages . . . Men do mightily wrong themselvs: when they refuse to be present in all Ages: and Neglect to see the Beauty of all Kingdoms, and Despise the Resentments of evry Soul, and Busie them selvs only with Pots and Cups and things at home, or Shops and Trades and things in the street. But [they] do not liv to God Manifesting Himself in all the World, nor care to see, (and be present with Him, in) all the Glory of his Eternal Kingdom. By seeing the Saints of all Ages we are present with them. By being present with them we becom too Great for our own Age, and near to our Savior.[407]

Yet how can we be present in other ages, or other people? Traherne explores in some detail the theme of 'being-in'. He argues that, when we see something, it exists within the faculty seeing it, and thereby in the soul of the person seeing. Lifeless objects existing in a room are valueless 'unless they are Objectively in the Soul of a Seer', and the pleasure (and consequent joy and wisdom) of the person who enjoys them is the reason for the things being there anyway. It is in this way that all things are present in my soul, and Christ with them, and in this way also that 'the Kingdom of God (as our Savior saith, this Way) is within you':[408] it is in this way too that Traherne can appropriate the events and truths of the Bible for himself.[409] It allows us to possess all things without owning anything: precisely the experience of Adam and Eve in Eden. Hence Traherne's exquisitely simple summary of all he wrote:

> All Bliss
> Consists in this,
> To do as Adam did.[410]

And in paradise, we shall do precisely that. A longing for heaven is a rich and common theme in both Platonic and Christian spirituality; but all three of these remarkable writers have their own contribution to make to the subject.[411] For Sir Thomas Browne, death is an extraordinary challenge to the lofty view of human nature he has himself espoused: indeed it is

> the very disgrace and ignominy of our natures, that in a moment can so disfigure us that our nearest friends, Wife, and Children stand afraid and start at us. The Birds and Beasts of the field that before in a naturall feare obeyed us, forgetting all allegiance begin to prey upon us.[412]

Indeed it makes sense only in the light of what follows it; and hence, he declares that as doctors 'we all labour against our owne cure, for death is the cure of all diseases. There is no Catholicon or universall remedy I know but this, which thogh nauseous to queasie stomachs, yet to prepared appetites is Nectar, and a pleasant potion of immortality';[413] and elsewhere he declares that 'were the happinesse of the next world as closely apprehended as the felicities of this, it were a martyrdome to live'.[414]

For Browne, as for Traherne, it is precisely our desires and restless hopes of a reality beyond ourselves that argue for the existence of a life after this one, which in turn allows us to see this one in its only true perspective:

> It is the heaviest stone that melancholy can throw at a man, to tell him he is at the end of his nature; or that there is no further state to come, unto which this seemes progressionall, and otherwise made in vaine . . . But the superiour ingredient and obscured part of our selves, whereto all present felicities afford no resting contentment, will be able at last to tell us we are more than our present selves; and evacuate such hopes in the fruition of their own accomplishment.[415]

This 'superiour ingredient and obscured part of our selves' is deeply mysterious: Browne the doctor can affirm only that it is certainly inorganic;[416] and he goes on to say

> There is surely a peece of Divinity in us, something that was before the Elements, and owes no homage unto the Sun. Nature tels me I am the Image of God as well as Scripture; he that understands not thus much,

hath not his introduction or first lesson, and is yet to begin the Alphabet of man.[417]

For Browne this leads to a deep moral sensibility:

I cannot behold a Begger without relieving his necessities with my purse, or his soule with my prayers; these scenicall and accidentall differences betweene us cannot make mee forget that common and untoucht part of us both; there is under these Centoes and miserable outsides, these mutilate and semi-bodies, a soule of the same alloy with our owne.[418]

And, like many of the Latitudinarians, he edges towards universalism:

I doe desire with God, that all, but yet affirme with men, that few shall know salvation, that the bridge is narrow, the passage straite unto life; yet those who doe confine the Church of God, either to particular Nations, Churches, or Families, have made it farre narrower than our Saviour ever meant it . . . I believe many are saved who to man seeme reprobated, and many are reprobated, who in the opinion and sentence of man, stand elected; there will appear at the last day, strange, and unexpected examples, both of his justice and his mercy, and therefore to define either is folly in man.[419]

Although Traherne has less to say than either Browne or Sterry about love of neighbour, he does not neglect it altogether:

There is a certain kind of sympathy that runs through the universe, by virtue of which all men are fed in the feeding of one. Even the angels are clothed in the poor and needy. All are touched and concerned in every one.[420]

It is a pleasant thing to enjoy Heaven and Earth, but much more pleasant to Lov a man, that is possessor of it . . . O give me more of that Spirit, wherby we strongly Lov and Delight each in other, wherby we Liv in each other[s] soul, and feel our Joys and sorrows![421]

And in one of the poems in *Commentaries of heaven* he comes close to articulating the heart of his spirituality:

In useless Glory, tho tis in the Sun,
To stand, in truth's inglorious: But to run
A Race of Service, and to Minister
Unto the World; its Profit to prefer
Abov ones own; to stoop even down to Hell.
Tho once we did abov the Heavens dwell;
In many glorious things beneath to serv,
To purifie, to Quicken, to preserv,
To shine on Things, to help make a Day
That all might see; this is the Noble Way,

> Whereby like Jesus Christ, Descending so,
> As Sons, unto the Throne of God we go;
> Who coming down did greater Glory gain,
> Then in the Throne, where he of old did reign.[422]

The implicit reference to our heavenly pre-existence ('Tho once we did abov the Heavens dwell') is characteristic: Traherne's Platonism is constantly threatening to break out of the firm parameters of Christian orthodoxy, as is Sterry's. Taken as a whole, these three writers articulate a view of spiritual life which is too unequivocally positive to do full justice to the realities of human sin and evil: Traherne in particular is vulnerable to the charge of undervaluing both of these. Yet he is arguably in good company in this respect; and his view of evil is not too far distant from the *privatio boni* of Aquinas, and of Augustine before him. Like them, he wants to present the good as more enduringly attractive, more *real*, than the evil.[423] He will have none of the grim deterministic view of the Fall so beloved of some Calvinists, and says so emphatically:

> Our Misery proceedeth ten thousand times more from the outward Bondage of Opinion and Custom, then from any inward corruption or Depravation of Nature . . . it is not our Parents Loyns, so much as our Parents lives, that Enthrals and Blinds us.[424]

It is our capacity for being distracted and enslaved by external lures, rather than a fundamental corruption in our nature, that constitutes the effect of the Fall: 'Natural Things are Glorious'.[425] Even so, evil is real and active: if it is essentially negation, the absence of a positive reality, it is a deeply destructive absence: 'Souls to Souls are like Apples to Apples, one being rotten rots another'.[426] Traherne expresses this in a wonderful image: sin 'breeds a long Parenthesis in the fruition of our Joys'.[427] And, memorably reflecting on a vivid image from the Psalms, he declares that 'Gods Eternitie is a Bottle like the Heavens Wherein the Tears of Penitents Glitter like the Stars'.[428]

Conclusion

And it must be with this profound and pervasive sense of joy that we conclude our exploration of these three remarkable and original Christian thinkers. If they stand accused of underplaying the seriousness of evil, and thereby of minimizing the role of Christ in working human redemption, it is in the interests of reminding human beings of the infinite wonder of their own potential in virtue of their creation in God's image. There is of course a risk here too, and one to which all Christian Platonists are vulnerable: that of overlooking the beautiful in the search for Beauty, dematerializing Christianity in the interests of a 'pure' spiritual world-view that does no justice to the Gospel. But all three of these writers are writing for pastoral purposes, and out of long pastoral experience. Traherne echoes Augustine in reminding us that what matters is a right use of the Eden which is both around us now and yet always in the future, drawing us home:

> You never Enjoy the World aright, till you see how a Sand Exhibiteth the Wisdom and Power of God: And Prize in evry Thing the Service which

they do you, by Manifesting His Glory and Goodness to your Soul, far more then the Visible Beauty on their Surface, or the Material Services, they can do your Body. Wine by its Moysture quencheth my Thirst, whether I consider it or no: but to see it flowing from his Lov who gav it unto Man, Quencheth the Thirst even of the Holy Angels. To consider it, is to Drink it Spiritualy. To Rejoice in its Diffusion is to be of a Publick Mind. And to take Pleasure in all the Benefits it doth to all is Heavenly for so they do in Heaven. To do so, is to be Divine and Good and to imitat our Infinit and Eternal Father.[429]

And Peter Sterry reminds his congregation that only a religion which attracts and delights and transforms us is ultimately credible: here is Cromwell's favourite cleric in ebullient form, happily subverting all who have maintained that the great Protector was no more than a grim and gloomy Calvinist:

Do not think Religion, or Holiness a Melancholy thing. Do not fear to be Religious, as if then you must part with all your Delights, and put your self into the perpetual Desert of a solitary, sad sour Conversation. Holiness, and Religion have their own Joy . . . Religion is a Discovery in the Soul, of God, as the Eternal Spirit, the Quicking [sic] Spirit; as bringing forth Himself, as working his own works, as fulfilling his Joy, as setting up his Kingdom in the Soul. 'He hath shined into our Hearts the Glory of the Knowledge of God', (2 Cor 4:6). Religion is a Drawing of the Soul up to God, into the Glory of God . . . Can this be a Melancholy thing?[430]

CATHOLIC SPIRITUALITY IN THE SIXTEENTH AND SEVENTEENTH CENTURIES

Introduction

For Roman Catholics, the move from establishment to recusancy (and, briefly, back again during the reign of Mary Tudor) could not be anything but traumatic, and has been extensively studied.[431] There will have been many who might have echoed the words Shakespeare sets on the lips of the stalwart Catholic bishop of Winchester, Stephen Gardiner, in *King Henry VIII*:

> If we suffer,
> Out of our easiness and childish pity
> To one man's honour, this contagious sickness,
> Farewell all physic – and what follows then?
> Commotions, uproars – with a general taint
> Of the whole state.[432]

Many now argue that the so-called Counter-Reformation is misleadingly named, since it began before Luther's famous protest;[433] and since both Protestant and Catholic Reformations took place within continental Europe and within distinctively European contexts, the difficulties involved in communicating their essential ideas to

England were considerable. Mary's reimposition of Catholicism was inevitably frustrated by her early death; but she in any case faced a country that was already extensively permeated by Protestant belief and practice;[434] and, although Cardinal Reginald Pole did attempt to improve the educational and spiritual formation of the priesthood in accordance with Counter-Reformation principles, it could be said that the really important decision made by him and his queen was the decision not to withdraw the vernacular Bible, a decision which in fact reflects the scriptural nature of Counter-Reformation spirituality.[435]

After Mary's death, Catholicism had perforce to become an underground movement, sustained partly by missionary clergy trained in continental seminaries, and partly by recusant[436] gentry whose strength was concentrated in particular regions, notably Lancashire. Thus English Catholicism became a complex and sometimes combustible mix of foreign-trained priests, who had to be both sponsored and hidden by conservative landed gentry, together with (in some areas) poor recusants often attached to those gentry.[437] What is crucial is that all these groups depended for their lives on one another; and the result was a piety which combined some features of contemporary continental Catholicism with the rich inheritance of the later Middle Ages. Despite the risks of discovery and imprisonment (or worse), some Catholics managed to sustain a rich spiritual life. Thus Dorothy Lawson (1580–1632), a Catholic widow, made her house near Newcastle-on-Tyne into a spiritual oasis for Catholics, with a chapel and resident chaplain, sung masses on feast days which were well attended by local Catholics, and even retreats for clandestine Jesuit visitors in defiance of the penal laws:

> Half a dozen of the Society [of Jesus] made each year the spirituall exercises in her house for eight days with collegiall form and discipline; for which shee provided gowns, a refectory, glasses for bear [sic], dishes for antipasts, portions . . . At night shee made a feast for the whole house, and the next morning they departed with the apostolicall salutation or farewell, *Pax huic domui*, 'Peace be to this house.'[438]

Monastic Spirituality

The general state of monastic life in England before the Dissolution has also been much studied, and might be summarized as routine but generally healthy.[439] The energetic Premonstratensian Richard Redman, abbot of Shap from 1458 until 1505 and successively bishop of St Asaph, Exeter and Ely, carried out a series of comprehensive visitations of his own order; and these reflect an order whose vitality and fidelity to its observance is impressive.[440] The register of Butley Priory in Suffolk, one of the last such records prior to the Dissolution, tells us that on 21 May 1531 the abbot of Leyston, John Grene (or Green), gave up his office and became an anchorite in a former monastery by the sea:[441] scarcely a sign of an order facing or anticipating imminent extinction.

One of the most important features of sixteenth-century English monastic spirituality was the close interaction between those within the cloister and those outside it.

The practice, already noted in the previous century, of producing spiritual texts within monasteries for the benefit of those outside it, continued apace: one such, *The pomander of prayer*, was published on the eve of the Reformation by an anonymous (probably Carthusian) author, and went through four editions in as many years (1528–32): it seems to have been primarily directed to those responsible for lay formation and catechesis, one of the fundamental themes of continental Counter-Reformation spirituality.[442]

Richard Whytford (c.1478–1543) was successively an academic, a monk of the Brigittine house at Syon, and (in all probability) a layman who accepted the Act of Supremacy; and this chequered career seems to have given him a profound concern for the spiritual life of those both within and outside the cloister. *A werke for housholders*, which he wrote just before he entered Syon, contains detailed spiritual guidance for laypeople much of which is based on scriptural texts such as the Ten Commandments and Lord's Prayer.[443] But this process was a two-way affair: the London Charterhouse in particular, given its urban location, developed a very close relationship with local laypeople, many of whom lived (and were buried) within its grounds, attended its services, and endowed its liturgy and consequent architectural extensions.[444]

Both Carthusians and Brigittines also wrote books for the benefit of their fellow religious. Whytford adapted a work of St Bernard's in order to produce an extended exploration of the monastic life organized around the vows taken by religious:[445] in it he shows himself to be fully aware of the looming threat of the Reformation, comparing its effects to the people of Israel being faced with a return to Egyptian bondage after the Exodus,[446] and criticizing disagreements between religious orders as becoming more important for religious themselves than their life in Christ.[447] John Norton, prior of the charterhouse of Mount Grace from 1509 until his death in 1522, produced several works of highly affective devotion:[448] it was Norton who is said by the sixteenth-century commentator on Margery Kempe's *Book* to have fallen down and roared in response to the Passion of Christ 'in hys excesse', just as Margery herself had done.[449] This highly emotional spirituality should not mislead us into assuming a lack of resilience or deep roots in those living the monastic life at this time, however. The terrible suffering of the Carthusian martyrs under Henry VIII is heightened not only by the courage and determination of the monks themselves but also by their austere, in some cases scholarly, characters.[450]

John Colet, John Fisher, Robert Southwell

Apart from Sir Thomas More, the three principal figures in sixteenth-century English Catholic spirituality were John Colet (1467–1519), St John Fisher (1469–1535), and the young poet and martyr St Robert Southwell (1561–95). Colet, who became Dean of St Paul's Cathedral, London, was an old-fashioned ascetic:[451] his work was characterized by both his reverence for patristic scholarship and his antipathy towards non-Christian classical sources. He stands firmly in the Platonizing, Augustinian, deeply conservative strand of early sixteenth-century thought, taking from Pseudo-Dionysius an interest in hierarchical *ordo* and a richly symbolic cosmology but reflecting a world-view far more radically ascetic even than Dionysius;[452] and standing in the tradition of St Bonaventure in arguing for the primacy of love and will over reason and knowledge, which were by contrast stressed by St Thomas Aquinas.[453] His biblical exegesis, though informed by this already old-fashioned theology, did however reflect contemporary Renaissance fascination with 'hidden meanings' accessible only to the spiritual and the scholarly.[454]

John Fisher was educated at Cambridge and became successively Vice-Chancellor and Chancellor: he was bishop of Rochester from 1504, resigning because of the royal divorce in 1534, a decision which swiftly led to his imprisonment and (in 1535, soon after Paul III had made him a cardinal) execution.[455] He too was a deeply Augustinian, conservative writer, albeit one actively concerned with educational and moral reform:[456] his published sermons were influential,[457] not least because of his vivid and lively style.[458]

Robert Southwell was born long after Fisher had died; and everything he wrote (including his poetry) was designed to console and strengthen English Catholics in their faith.[459] He was born of a Norfolk Catholic family in 1561, was educated at the Jesuit school at Douai in Belgium, entered the Jesuit novitiate in 1578 and in 1586 returned secretly to England to begin proselytizing and engaging in pastoral work for the beleaguered Catholic community: during the next few years he was constantly on the move, publishing books, devotional tracts and poems from his own secret press,[460] until his arrest and imprisonment in 1592. He was tortured terribly during the last three years of his life, and was executed at Tyburn on 21 February 1595. Like Colet, his was a deeply world-renouncing spirituality, though there are hints in his work that this thoroughgoing asceticism was not achieved without great personal cost.[461]

The spirituality of these three Catholic writers is firmly ascetic, rooted in Plato's and Pseudo-Dionysius' stress on the material acting only as a pointer towards, or symbol of, what lies beyond it. They can sometimes employ images of mystical intimacy; but it has to be said that their use of these images lacks the affective warmth of their late-medieval predecessors. Thus Colet says that

> if we wish to be linked and joined (*coniungi et copulari*) to God, who is spirit, we must needs mortify the flesh and become wholly spirit, utterly renewed in Christ and living in Christ after the pattern (*formam*) of him who gave the example that we might follow in his footsteps; for this purpose only did he become human, to show people the spiritual and divine life in humanity and to teach them what wedding garment human beings must put on if they would be taken to wife by God.[462]

Christ thus came in order to rescue us not only from the terrible consequences of the Fall but also from physical life altogether, for (as Colet elsewhere notes)

> Human beings, placed midway between things pertaining to the senses and things pertaining to the understanding, may be led by the body to the spirit, by the senses to the understanding, by the shadow to the light, by the image to the truth; that finding truth at length, he may then wholly despise the flesh, and striving after the spirit may rest in spiritual truth alone.[463]

It is not surprising to find Colet giving a high place both to the sacraments, conceived of in a Platonic manner as signs pointing to higher spiritual realities,[464] and to the priesthood.[465] Nor is it surprising to find both him and Fisher stressing a view of *imitatio Christi* which is pervasively ascetic: we follow Christ by making our own the purity and radical otherworldliness which in their view characterized the whole of his earthly life. Thus Colet can go so far as to say that

> The whole life, in truth, of Jesus Christ on earth was nothing else than a continual ascending to heaven; its whole aim being there, and not here . . . that as many as possible might make haste to depart hence and follow him.[466]

The positive aspect of this kind of writing is the strong emphasis given to human potential as spiritual beings. Colet speaks at several points about deification, defining 'to deify' as what 'to animate' means when God is the subject, and pointing out that God can accomplish our deification in diverse ways,[467] one of which is precisely by our imitation of Christ:

> By such means and for such fitting reasons [the imitation of Christ], by the marvellous goodness and kindness of God towards humanity, there is a recalling and drawing back to heavenly things; from the body to the spirit, from the spirit to God; that human beings, being in this life made spiritual in Christ, out of what is corporeal and carnal, may hereafter be most blessedly made godlike (*deificentur*) in God himself.[468]

The negative aspect of such piety is the fierce asceticism, characterized both by Colet's radical depreciation of marriage (if no one had married, the kingdom of heaven would simply have come that much sooner[469]), and by Southwell's longing for death as the only proper fulfilment of our capacity for love:

> Where love is hot, life hateful is,
> Their groundes doe not agree:
> Love where it loves, life where it lives,
> Desireth most to be.

> And sith love is not where it lives,
> Nor liveth where it loves:
> Love hateth life, that holdes it backe,
> And death it best approves.[470]

This allows Southwell to give a strong emphasis to the need for patient endurance during suffering in the hope of ultimate joy, a point he makes with particular power in *Scorne not the least*. This is the spirituality of the *Benedicite*, where Nebuchadnezzar's victims celebrate their God's ultimate victory over evil:

> Where wards are weake, and foes encountring strong:
> Where mightier doe assault, then [= than] do defend:
> The feebler part puts up enforced wrong,
> And silent sees, that speech could not amend.

Yet higher powers must thinke, though they repine,
When sunne is set: the little starres will shine.

While Pike doth range, the silly Tench doth flie
And crouch in privie creekes, with smaller fish:
Yet Pikes are caught when little fish goe bie:
These, fleet aflote [swim freely]; while those, doe fill the dish.
There is a time even for the worme to creepe:
And sucke the dew while all her foes doe sleepe.

The Marlyne [merlin] cannot ever sore [soar] on high,
Nor greedie greyhound still pursue the chase:
The tender Larke will find a time to flie,
And fearefull Hare to runne a quiet race.
He that high growth on Ceders did bestow:
Gave also lowly mushrumpes leave to grow.

In Hamans pompe poore Mardocheus [Mordechai] wept;
Yet God did turne his fate upon his foe.
The Lazar [Lazarus] pinde, while DIVES feast was kept,
Yet he, to heaven; to hell, did Dives goe.
We trample grasse, and prize the flowers of May:
Yet grasse is greene when flowers doe fade away.[471]

And it also enables Fisher, less uncompromisingly otherworldly than Colet, to offer some wise pastoral guidance on the theme of sin and forgiveness. He tells his hearers that the more sinners remember their sins, the more God forgets them.[472] And he movingly reflects his awareness that the kind of piety which meant so much to him appeared to be in irreversible decline:

I fere me, many now a dayes be of that condicyon they wyll not wepe, they wyll not sorowe, they wyll not abstayne from theyr olde customes and use, leest it sholde be thought that they had done amysse. Dere bretherne let not us do so, let us appere and shewe our selfe even as we be.[473]

He suggests as a result that

it semeth almyghty god to be in maner in a deed slepe, suffrynge these grete enormytees so longe. No we must do as the dyscyples dyd than [= then] in the shyppe, they awaked Ihesu theyr mayster from slepe with cryenges and grete noyses that they made . . . In lyke maner let us reyse up almighty god by our prayers.[474]

In *A vale of teares*, Southwell conceives of the individual's sorrow affecting the natural landscape, and of the individual's terror in the face of wild untamed nature. This is important: he is, after all, writing for those who may well experience martyrdom; and he wants to subvert the evil of persecution by assuring those who suffer for their faith that the very stones and trees will articulate their anguish even if they can no longer do so themselves:

> To plaining thoughts this vaile a rest may bee,
> To which from worldly joyes they may retire.
> Where sorrow springs from water, stone and tree,
> Where everie thing with mourners doth conspire.[475]

It is hard to see many reading Colet for spiritual benefit today: those who do read him are likely to find him of more narrowly intellectual than spiritual interest; and his relentlessly antifeminine style and entire lack of interest in major theological debates of the period will not encourage many to make the attempt.[476] But Fisher's pastoral warmth and Southwell's ascetic but vivid poetry, together with the martyrdom both experienced, imparts to their work and achievement a deeper quality: in both, the intensely personal love of God is of enduring and transforming power. Fisher wrote that, unlike mothers, who will suffer for their children but forget them when their children are unkind in return, God will never forget us: 'therefore we be more derely beloved of god than chyldren ben of theyr moders' and 'no carnall fader may love his chylde better than our hevenly fader loveth us'.[477] 'Truly all we ben chyldren of the hevenly fader': all of us are prodigal children gone astray and summoned to make the journey home.[478]

Spirituality and Exile: Augustine Baker and Continental Recusant Women

Most of the principal figures in seventeenth-century English Catholic spirituality spent much of their lives on the continent. There were two attempts at restoring the Roman hierarchy in England during the century, both short-lived;[479] and Charles II's 1672 Declaration of Indulgence, tolerating Catholic and nonconformist worship, was even more short-lived, as were those of the Catholic monarch James II. Furthermore, political events like the Gunpowder Plot and the Thirty Years War, together with the frequent risk (whether real or imagined) of war with Spain, fuelled sporadic but intense periods of anti-Catholicism.[480]

Dom Augustine Baker

In this atmosphere the life of Dom Augustine Baker may have been typical of many.[481] Born in Abergavenny in 1575 (as David Baker), he studied law at Oxford (though left without a degree): in 1603 he became a Roman Catholic after a miraculous rescue from near-drowning, and in 1605 entered the Benedictine abbey of St Justina at Padua. Thereafter his career alternated between England and Europe: he was chaplain to the household of Sir Nicholas Fortescue in Worcestershire for a while; but most of the rest of his life was spent on the continent, in particular as spiritual director to the English Benedictine nuns at Cambrai (now at Stanbrook). Here his methods as director caused controversy:[482] the dispute was resolved in Baker's favour in 1633, though Baker himself was moved to Douai. In 1638 he was sent to England as a missionary priest, despite increasing ill-health: he was arrested in 1641, and died in the same year.[483]

Baker produced a number of works, some of which are only now appearing in modern editions.[484] They include his *Secretum*, ostensibly an extended commentary on the *Cloud of unknowing*, though in the process revealing much about the uneven development of Baker's own spirituality,[485] and works concerned with the Catholic mission to England. But his most famous work was *Sancta Sophia* (Holy Wisdom), which is a compilation of his writings made by Fr Serenus Cressy OSB, a monk of Douai. The question of how much Cressy altered Baker's original teaching remains an open one;[486] and in any case *Holy wisdom* itself is a long, repetitive and ill-organized work giving us only a second-hand glimpse of Baker's methods as a spiritual director of nuns. Even so, it remains a substantial and important text in its own right, reflecting Baker's own spiritual maturity and the rich Catholic heritage, both European and English, on which he was able to draw.[487]

Holy wisdom begins with a distinctly Platonic view of human beings ('man . . . consisting of a frail earthly body, which is the prison of an immortal, intellectual spirit');[488] but he immediately proceeds to say that human beings are created with a supernatural light which gives them the potential to attain 'to such a measure of perfection of union with God in this world, as without dying to merit a translation from hence to heaven'.[489] Baker makes the traditional distinction between active and contemplative lives, giving precedence to the latter (though he does remark that a contemplative whose life lacks any interior spiritual depth is quite likely to be worse than someone living in the world).[490] Union with God is attainable 'almost only with the heart and blind affections of the will pouring themselves upon God apprehended only in the obscure notion of faith, not inquiring what He is'.[491] Note the absence of any stress on the mind or the understanding here: we are far from any Thomist view of contemplation, though this does allow Baker to declare that 'simple unlearned women are more frequently graced by Almighty God with the gift of high contemplation than men, and especially such men as are much given to sublime speculations'.[492]

The whole of *Holy wisdom* is of course oriented towards spiritual guidance; and its essential concern is with advising individual souls about how to discern and obey divine inspiration and guidance, whether received directly or mediated by means of a spiritual director or religious supervisor.[493] Baker declares that 'God alone is our only master and director', and that all directors must conform with the dictates of the Holy Spirit: he tells his nuns to avoid those who say you must 'take all your instructions from without',[494] and later says that God

> deals with an humble soul as a writing-master with his scholar, who at first moves and directs his hand to form and join letters, but afterwards directs him only with his eye and tongue; or as a father that carries his child over a ditch or stile, but lets him go alone in the even plain way.[495]

This approach inevitably exposes both Baker and his nuns to the risk of a kind of spiritual subjectivism, despite his stress on the interior divine light that guides the Christian seeking union with God.[496] But Baker warns his nuns against excessive reliance either on themselves or on their director, telling them that the director's 'principal care must be to set them in such a way as that they may not need to have much recourse unto him afterward'.[497] He also stresses the extent to which individuals should monitor their own spiritual growth ('by observing their own abilities and inclinations, and by marking what more particular forms of prayer, &c., suit best with them and do them most good').[498] It is a sign of a lack of progress if the person is constantly troubling her director 'with a multiplicity of questions and doubts'.[499]

Baker also has much wise pastoral advice for the would-be contemplative: for all his uncompromising stress on obedience, interiority, and asceticism, he tells her not to engage in excessive mortifications,[500] and reminds her that no amount of devout practices will compensate for factiousness or a love of speaking critically about others.[501] More positively, he tells her that prayer is the opposite of food: whereas the one who fasts soon finds she has a greater appetite for food, the one who stops praying will soon 'have a less stomach and disposition to it, and so in time will come willingly and even with pleasure to starve in spirit';[502] and he warns that 'those who in religion are sluggish and indevout do grow continually worse and worse'.[503]

Even so, there is a significant degree to which the individual is left to climb the mountain of contemplative union alone. Baker stresses that a soul can attain to perfection without the benefit of any books or directors at all;[504] in the last analysis, the Holy Spirit remains the only indispensable director.[505] He stresses love ('an affection rather of the will than the sensitive faculties'),[506] and the action of grace,[507] as crucial ingredients in any genuine spiritual progress. But the most crucial ingredient of all is a radical openness to the free and unconditioned work of the Holy Spirit: Baker defines this openness as 'a free indifferency and suppleness of spirit';[508] and later he says that

> a spiritual life is subject to many and wonderful changes, interior as well as exterior, and all are according to the mere will and good pleasure of God, who is tied to no methods or rules.[509]

Hence the importance of total resignation to his will, an approach which gives his teaching both a refreshing openness to the Spirit and a genuine sense of change and adventure. He stresses that resignation requires 'intending purely the love of God, and seeking His glory'.[510] Its positive strength is that it allows the soul to make use indifferently of both prosperity and adversity:[511] indeed 'the sufferings of our Lord are never as perfectly understood by reading or meditation, as when devout souls themselves taste of the like'.[512] Resignation means remaining in the presence of God as a petitioner, but without making any requests, so that God may entirely possess her.[513] We empty ourselves for his sake.[514]

This state of absolute resignation to the will of God is quite different from the reformed doctrine of assurance. Baker says that

> the point of resignation lies in this, that a soul ought to content herself not to know how and in what manner God will dispose of her after death. Her anchor is hope, which she ought to cherish and fortify all she can, and the best way for souls to fortify that is to make as few reflections on themselves as may be, and to employ all their thoughts and affections directly upon God. It is divine love alone that is at least the principal virtue that brings souls to beatitude, and therefore fearful souls, though they were in as dangerous a state as they suspect, must needs rationally argue thus: that the way to procure and strengthen love is by fixing their minds upon the mercies, goodness, and perfections of God, and to contradict or forget all

arguments or motives of servile fear, the greatest enemy of love . . . Surely, at the close of our lives we ought to practise after the best manner we can the best actions, and most acceptable to God, which is to relinquish ourselves, and to contemplate, trust, rely, and roll ourselves upon Him . . . Let the soul withal consider that He which hath denied unto her an assurance and forbidden her to presume, hath yet commanded her to hope.[515]

Baker's teaching on prayer follows organically from his overall spiritual theology. He sees prayer as the highest of all spiritual virtues or actions because it alone is proof against sin:

We may, lying in our sins, give alms, fast, recite the Divine Office, communicate, obey our superiors, &c.; but it is impossible to exercise true prayer of the spirit and deliberately continue under the guilt of sin, because by prayer, a soul being converted and united to God, cannot at the same time be averted and separated from Him.[516]

That is why prayer is so exposed to assaults from the devil,[517] and why it must be continual.[518] Baker follows traditional teaching in distinguishing three stages of prayer (the practice of discursive meditation, affective prayer, and contemplative prayer), though he does acknowledge that the three may merge at times.[519] Taken as a whole, he sees prayer (as we might by now expect) in primarily affective, not intellectual, terms. He allows for discursive meditation, on some suitable religious subject, for spiritual beginners;[520] but is conscious of the twin dangers of a wandering imagination and of empty speculation.[521] He encourages the person to persevere, arguing in prayer for

an importunate earnestness, a resolution to take no denial nor to stand upon nice civilities, but rather than to return empty, to force out a grant even by wearying out the person to whom we address ourselves.[522]

In God's good time this will bring her to affective prayer (which for Baker corresponds with the traditional 'illuminative way'): the soul will 'find in herself a certain motion or inward invitation to enter into some other new exercise, as yet not clearly known to her':[523] this is the sign for her to move on from discursive meditation. She will experience 'certain painful yet delightful longings after God; certain languishing elevations of spirit towards an unknown, dark, Divine Object'.[524] This kind of prayer may begin, like meditation, by the soul representing to herself a specific theme such as the Incarnation or Passion, but without discursive reflection on it: instead there should be simple acts of the will, seeking what God wants unconditionally.[525] Baker appends lengthy lists of such acts[526] and refers to the many that appear in the Psalms and scripture generally,[527] as well as the Lord's Prayer.[528]

Thus the Christian enquires and learns in meditation, wills actively and perseveringly to be one with God in affective prayer, and (again in God's good time) spontaneously experiences union with him as a free gift in the highest form of prayer accessible in this life, contemplative prayer. Baker defines contemplation as

> a clear, ready, mental seeing and quiet regarding of an object, being the
> result and effect of a precedent diligent and laborious inquiry and search
> after the nature, qualities, dependencies, and other circumstantial condi-
> tions of it.[529]

In this kind of prayer there is no longer any need for the soul 'to produce good affections to Him',[530] because it is a state in which 'it is not she that lives, but Christ and His
Holy Spirit that lives, reigns, and operates in her'.[531] In contemplative prayer, unlike
meditation, no images are needed: the soul 'contents herself with the only general
obscure notion of God which faith teaches her'.[532] Baker uses the analogy of playing a
musical instrument or writing poetry: eventually the skills are sufficiently mastered, so
that they can be employed quite unconsciously.[533] The soul accomplishes a union
beyond words, 'knowing [God] most perfectly by ignorance ... and conversing with
Him ... by silence ... remaining in this silent busy idleness and negative knowledge,
more full of fervour and light than all the speculations of the schools or studious meditations of cloisters', like a mother directing all her love to her child (an unusual image
of the soul towards God, rather than vice versa).[534]

This union with God is not absorption, though 'so far is the soul from reflecting on
her own existence, that it seems to her that God and she are not distinct, but one only
thing'.[535] In it the will becomes 'deiform, and in a manner deified, for it is so closely
united and hidden in the Divine Will, that God may be said to will and do all things in
and by her'.[536] It is (as Thomas Traherne might have said) a recovery of Eden, a restoration of our lost innocence,[537] and on the face of it entirely useless since it involves
leaving behind all exterior concerns. And yet

> those inexpressible devotions which [contemplatives] exercise, and in
> which they tacitly involve the needs of the whole Church, are far more
> prevalent with God than the busy endeavours and prayers of ten thousand
> others. A few such secret [lit. 'secrets'] and unknown servants of God are
> the chariots and horsemen, the strength and bulwarks of the kingdoms
> and churches where they live.[538]

Such experiences of union with God will alternate with experiences of God's withdrawal: at such times the soul 'complains in her prayers to God for deserting her'; but
all she can do is to await his return.[539] Such experiences are in themselves an experience
of the cross, and of Christ's cry of despair upon it.[540]

Baker stood accused of a form of quietism inasmuch as his stress on resignation in
prayer, albeit an inevitable consequence of his entire spirituality, exposed him to the
risk of an interiorized subjectivism insufficiently challenged by either external activity
or serious intellectual study.[541] This is undoubtedly a serious weakness in his thought,
and one which is accentuated by the absence of any serious engagement with scripture
(here, as in many respects, he is far from the spirituality of St Ignatius Loyola or St
François de Sales, let alone that of Protestantism). His is a highly intense, inward form
of piety, lacking any of the colourful and externalizing features of continental Baroque
spirituality. But he is, after all, writing for enclosed nuns; and he remains an important
figure, not only for his achievement in preserving and building on the rich vernacular

tradition of medieval English spirituality,[542] but also in his own right. For him the spiritual life is a movement of love in response both to the divine love and to the divine
beauty; in one of his works he goes so far as to say that God cannot help but love us:

> Thereupon I say first, that the love of God towards man is so great that it
> exceedeth all speech & understanding of man or angel, and it is unsepara-
> ble [*sic*] from God, (I mean, his love towards man is), and is as it were so
> naturall & inherent to him, that so far as lyeth in him & belongeth to him,
> he cannot chose [*sic*] but love man. And this proceedeth out of this, that he
> made man according to his own image, by which man doth in some
> manner participate of the divinity, and is thereupon capable (by way of
> participation or communication) of that felicity which is proper &
> naturall only to God himselfe.[543]

Those who make this love their own become both free from servile fear, and filled
with love of all people alike in God,[544] partakers of the divine nature,[545] attaining as
near as is possible in this life 'unto the top of the mountain, where God is seen: a
mountain, to us that stand below, environed with clouds and darkness, but to them
who have their dwelling there, it is peace and serenity and light'.[546]

Catholic meditation

One more manifestation of the elusive but real impact of Counter-Reformation spirituality on England is in the area of meditation.[547] There are many examples of this
impact: the Spanish Carthusian Antonio de Molina wrote *A treatise of mental prayer*
(1617), which was translated into English by a Jesuit and published with another spiritual text in a book addressed to Mother Mary Wiseman, prioress of the English
Augustinian house at Louvain.[548] Molina's understanding of meditation is in some
respects more balanced than Augustine Baker's, enlisting more fully the services of the
understanding,[549] and reflecting clearly the influence of St Ignatius of Loyola:[550] he
stresses the importance of *admiratio* (wonder), so characteristic of Baroque piety, and
seems to share with John Fisher an interest in animals:

> Consider the love that a dogge, and other beasts do beare to their maisters,
> how they follow them whither soever they go, and never part far from them,
> and being absent, they (as it were) complaine and howle, and seeke to find
> them, and shew great joy when they find them . . . Remember this well, and
> be ashamed, that a brute beast gets such love, and keeps such lealty [*sic*] with
> one who gives him but a peace [*sic*] of bread; and thou dost not get this love
> towards him, that hath done thee so many and so great favours.[551]

Continental recusant women's spirituality

The women's Benedictine community at Cambrai was important for other reasons
than the teaching of Augustine Baker. Together with its sister community in Paris, it
became a centre for the dissemination of Catholic ideas and spirituality both within
Europe and across the Channel.[552] Cambrai was also something of a family affair: four

of Thomas More's great-great-granddaughters were professed at Cambrai early in the seventeenth century.[553] One of these remarkable women, Dame Gertrude More (1606–33), left England to enter the religious life aged 18 and was directed by Baker at Cambrai, where she died of smallpox in 1633.[554] Since she and her cousins were also cousins of John Donne, who travelled extensively on the continent, there may well be grounds for Latz' suggestion that they acted as crucial intermediaries between continental Catholic spirituality and England.[555] Her cousin Dame Agnes (1591–1655/6) translated all or part of *La ruine de l'amour propre et bâtiment de l'amour divin*, a mystical study of the Song of Songs composed in 1622–3 by the French recluse Jeanne de Cambry (1581–1639), rendering it into English as *The building of divine love*, 'a mystick explycation of the Canticle of Canticles of Solomon' and intending it for married and single, lay and religious alike.[556]

Another Cambrai nun, Dame Lucy Magdalena Cary (1619–50) was one of four daughters who entered the convent.[557] She wrote a biography of her mother, Elizabeth Cary, Lady Falkland,[558] whom she describes as being influenced in her own conversion to Roman Catholicism by reading Hooker's *Laws*.[559] One of her sisters, Dame Clementina Cary, wrote a beautiful poem which has survived in a manuscript at Lille:

> You blessed Soules, who stand before
> Th'Eternall King, and so long see
> His glory that you changed be
> Into that Glory you adore,
> Prayse that great Founder, and above,
> Admire His Power, and blesse His Love …
>
> Thou, too, who with a borrowed ray,
> When all the Lamps of Heaven hang out,
> In the Night's silence walkst about,
> And when the torch restorest the Day,
> Fair Noon and Stars, extol God's Name,
> And in your dance His Power proclaim.[560]

An even more remarkable figure in this period was Mary Ward (1585–1645): daughter of a recusant gentry family from Yorkshire, she first experienced a vocation to the religious life at the age of 15, went to the Netherlands in 1605 and spent two years there with the Poor Clares. In 1609 she established a school for young ladies in exile at Saint-Omer, where they lived a semi-religious life,[561] and later founded the Institute of the Blessed Virgin Mary, which was intended to support the work of Catholic married women in England in and around the home, and to help in the religious instruction of their households.[562] Ward was an extraordinary woman: very widely read, and undoubtedly influenced by (among others) St Ignatius of Loyola and St Angela Merici,[563] she encountered much opposition within continental Catholicism; and her courageous attempt to establish schools in England was thwarted by the Civil War, during which she died in Yorkshire. She was herself a person of exceptional spiritual maturity: here she describes an experience of the glory of God which directly influenced her vocation:

> One morning, making my meditation coldly and not at all to my satisfaction, at the end of it I resolved to assist a person to be accepted in some convent . . . And then going to dress myself according to the fashion of the country and other circumstances, whilst I adorned my head at the mirror, something very supernatural befell me . . . I was abstracted out of my whole being and it was shown to me with clearness and inexpressible certainty that I was not to be of the Order of St Teresa, but some other thing was determined for me, without all comparison more to the glory of God than my entrance into that holy religious Order. I did not see what the assured good thing would be, but the glory of God which was to come through it, showed itself inexplicably and so abundantly as to fill my soul in such a way that I remained for a good space without feeling or hearing anything but the sound 'GLORY, GLORY, GLORY'. All appeared to last but a moment, even at those times when afterwards I made a computation and found it to have been about two hours.[564]

It is worth noting here the vital link between spiritual experience and costly vocational direction, so characteristic not only of Ignatius' *Spiritual exercises* but of the whole biblical tradition of theophanies: worth noting, too, is the close similarity with the auditory and ecstatic experience of St Paul (in 2 Corinthians 12).

Conclusion

It has to be said that, taken as a whole, English Catholic spirituality in this period is scarcely comparable with the riches of its continental counterparts in Spain and France, though given the political circumstances this is scarcely surprising. What we do find, again unsurprisingly, is a pervasive sense of *separation* in Catholic piety of this period in the sense which is so significant in (say) the spirituality of the Book of Leviticus: this is a community surrounded by enemies, and holiness is experienced above all by withdrawal from the world into the clearly defined milieu of the convent, or the Catholic family household.[565] The terrible experience of exile marks the lives of almost all English Catholic writers after the accession of Elizabeth;[566] yet many of them, like Augustine Baker, followed the people of Israel in nurturing a spiritual life which would sustain their years 'by the waters of Babylon' and put their adversity to good use:

> Such an *exilium cordis*, such a desertion and internal desolation is a mortification to the purpose; yet, as of extreme bitterness, so of unexpressible efficacy to the purifying and universal perfecting of the soul and spirit.[567]

Baker is writing here about mortification; but his words could appropriately be taken to articulate the spiritual experience of an entire community. And at its heart was the fundamental conviction that the Christ whose real presence was encountered in every Eucharist would never desert his people. The poet Richard Crashaw, whose wonderful collection *Steps to the temple* reflects some of the most distinctive features of contemporary Catholic piety, expresses this with exquisite simplicity:

On Matt. 8

'I am not worthy that thou should'st come under my roofe.'

Thy God was making hast into thy roofe,
Thy humble faith and feare keepes him aloofe:
Hee'l [*sic*] be thy Guest, because he may not be,
Hee'l come – into thy house? no, into thee.[568]

PURITAN SPIRITUALITY

Introduction

We have already seen, in exploring the spirituality of the Church of England during this period, how the great principles of the Protestant Reformation were brought to bear, and what influence they exerted. Yet that Reformation did not bequeath a single, coherent Christian church to England, but a vastly complex constellation of Protestant groupings existing both inside and outside the established church, and in differing kinds of uneasy relationship with it. It is difficult to describe, or even to give accurate names to, these groups. What all of them shared was a deep dissatisfaction with the visible and episcopal church, though not all felt this sufficiently strongly to be obliged to leave it.[569] And yet to refer to them generically as 'dissenters' would be to risk tarring them with an unattractively (and unfairly) negative brush.

The term still most commonly used to describe them is 'Puritan', a term that was used (initially as an insult) to refer to Christians, both within and outside the established church, who sought to emphasize the purity of scriptural religion, and who thus dissented in varying degrees from ecclesiastical ceremonies and government. Richard Baxter refers to those who criticized his 'puritanical, precise way of serving God which only deserves the name of holiness':[570] what he means by this is a comprehensive pattern of godly living (and the term 'the Godly' was commonly used by Puritans to describe themselves) which should distinguish all who believed they were members of the elect and who accepted a scripture-based faith kept 'pure' from ecclesiastical accretions.[571] Most Puritans were broadly Calvinist in theology; and it is vital to remember that until the ascendancy of William Laud in the late 1620s episcopal Calvinism was the dominant orthodoxy in the Church of England.[572] Thus a Puritan could be either a nonconformist or an Anglican, though both of these terms only became common near the end of our period:[573] what he or she could not be, however, was an Arminian.

Arminius was a Dutch theologian who opposed Calvin's doctrine of predestination, instead giving a significant role to human free will in determining whether someone was saved or not: this approach in turn led to a greater emphasis upon the sacraments, and on human co-operation with God in the spiritual life. It was rejected by the Dutch church in 1618 at the Synod of Dort, but (although only a minority grouping within the Church of England) became dominant in England once Laud became archbishop in 1633, a development which duly led to a powerful reaction among dissenters and would-be dissenters.[574]

'Puritan' and 'Arminian' are not the only terms in need of clarification. The term 'separatist' is often used as a synonym for 'dissenter', denoting those who worshipped and conducted their Christian lives separately from the established church. Among the separatists were a number of smaller groups. 'Baptists' (often described by contemporaries as 'Anabaptists', or rebaptizers), rejected infant baptism on scriptural grounds.[575] 'Presbyterians' sought to replace an episcopal church with a Geneva-style ecclesial system (though they did sometimes work within the established church), retaining university-trained ministers not chosen exclusively by their congregations, and a firm emphasis on spiritual discipline imposed on local churches by the elders of the presbytery.[576] 'Independents', or 'Congregationalists', disliked both episcopal and presbyteral government with their accoutrements of synods and courts, preferring to concentrate authority in the local congregation: their ministers were still often university-educated but were chosen exclusively by their congregations.[577] Quakers and a number of radical sectarian groups will require separate treatment.

The origins of sixteenth- and seventeenth-century English religious dissent did not lie only in the theological writings of Luther and Calvin. John Wyclif's own thought may not have been vastly influential in the period; but his achievement in challenging the church of his day unquestionably was[578] – and some have traced Puritanism further back than him.[579] Many Puritan scholars were immensely learned, deeply influenced by early Christian authorities and supremely by Augustine, whose writings on personal experience, predestination, and grace were of critical importance.[580] It is important to remember that, notwithstanding the longing (virtually universal among dissenters) to recover the pristine purity of apostolic Christianity, not every pre-Reformation author or movement was regarded as worthless: both Luther and Calvin themselves have been shown to be significantly indebted to St Bernard of Clairvaux;[581] many Catholic texts were translated (often carefully adapted in the process) for the use of devout dissenters;[582] and the association among some Puritan thinkers of the Holy Spirit with human reason is one reflection of the indebtedness of the dissenting movement as a whole to the values of the Renaissance.[583] Latimer was not the only Protestant writer to discover riches in the Christian tradition to be quarried from the deep mines of the Catholic centuries.

The God of Puritan Spirituality

In a major recent study, John Stachniewski has argued that the darker side of the English Puritan *mentalité* has been underplayed by historians.[584] The God of English neo-Calvinism was supremely a God of power, the God who, freed by William of Ockham from the fetters of scholasticism, could and did elect and damn as he pleased; and the incidence of despair among English people (especially women) of this period testifies to the grim and unrelenting nature of the God they were encouraged to worship.

There is some truth in Stachniewski's argument, though it is of course extremely hard to calculate how much.[585] Yet there are important and positive dimensions to this picture of God, unpredictable and authoritarian as he might well have appeared to be:

many contemporary Puritans, for example, both continental and English, stressed the significance of the biblical theme of the covenant in their understanding of the way in which God freely bound himself into an enduring mutual relationship with his people.[586] And the doctrine of predestination, whereby God is held to choose, for his own inscrutable reasons, who are to be saved and who to be damned, did not only generate despair: John Bradford (c.1510–55), one of those martyred during Mary's reign, believed that it did the opposite:

> it provoketh to piety . . . by teaching us of what dignity we be . . . It engen-
> dereth a true desire of our home in heaven . . . It maketh man wholly and
> continually to give over himself to be careful, not for himself, but for his
> brethren and for those things that make to God's glory.[587]

Furthermore, this emphasis on the power and unpredictability of God led to a far greater reverence for the natural world than Puritans are usually given credit for. In his immensely popular manual of devotion *The practice of piety* (1612), Lewis Baily encourages the godly to take Sunday evening walks in the fields, meditating on God's works, 'for in every creature thou may'st read, as in an open Book, the Wisdom, Power, Providence, and Goodness of Almighty God'.[588] Richard Baxter goes further, conceiving of human beings as priests of the creation in a manner strikingly similar to that of eastern Orthodox theology:

> What an excellent book is the visible world for the daily study of a holy
> soul! . . . O wonderful wisdom, and goodness, and power which appeareth
> in every thing we see! . . . Every creature silently speaks his praise, declaring
> him to man, whose office is, as the world's high-priest, to stand between
> them and the great Creator, and expressly offer him the praise of all.[589]

And the Baptist John Smyth says that

> he that cannot see and acknowledge the glory of God in the heavens, and
> the interchangeable course of day and night, Summer, Harvest, Spring,
> and winter [sic], &c. is as blinde in not seeing Gods providence, as the
> mote is to the Sunne . . . whereas in them all the attributes of God shine
> most cleerely, as his power, mercie, wisedome, iustice: and to this purpose
> the Prophet hath composed whole Psalmes (104 and 136).[590]

Puritans naturally argued that the beauty of creation should lead us to contemplate the infinitely greater beauty of heaven.[591] But we are far here from any narrow moralizing: if God's self-revelation in Christ and scripture remains absolutely primary, we may still discern God's presence and purpose by looking around us.[592]

The Doctrine of the Holy Spirit

But there was an even more important way in which the awesome power of the God whom Puritans worshipped was manifested in human life. Nothing more distinguishes Puritan spirituality than the major part played within it by the Holy Spirit, and the sense that the Protestant Reformation had been a second Pentecost, allowing that Spirit to break forth from the rigid chains of ecclesial control and flood Christendom anew with its power and joy.[593] John Calvin, so often himself seen as a theologian of rigid dogma, wrote:

> The beauty which the world displays is maintained by the invigorating power of the Spirit, but . . . even before this beauty existed the Spirit was at work cherishing the confused mass [of creation; cf. Genesis 1.1] . . . But the best proof to us [of the Spirit's divinity] is our familiar experience. For nothing can be more alien from a creature, than the office which the Scriptures ascribe to [the Spirit], and which the pious actually feel him discharging – his being diffused over all space, sustaining, invigorating, and quickening all things, both in heaven and on the earth. The mere fact of his not being circumscribed by any limits raises him above the rank of creatures, while his transfusing vigour into all things, breathing into them being, life, and motion, is plainly divine . . . By means of him we become partakers of the divine nature, so as in a manner to feel his quickening energy within us. Our justification is his work; from him is power, sanctification, truth, grace, and every good thought, since it is from the Spirit alone that all good gifts proceed.[594]

This uninhibited celebration of the Third Person of the Trinity appears only rarely in the spirituality of Catholicism or of the Church of England, in which the Spirit's work (at best) is held in creative tension with human reason and divine order, and (at worst) is stifled by the dead weight of ecclesiastical authority. But Calvin had a different vision; and in the (often anarchic diversity) of English Puritanism the fire and power of the Holy Spirit that Calvin passionately described was given full rein. No one explored this subject more comprehensively than John Owen (1616–83), perhaps the greatest theologian of the Cromwellian period, whose magisterial work on the subject (the *Pneumatologia*) reflects his indebtedness to Calvin, and fills two stout volumes: a brief examination of his thought will give us a clear view of the theological foundations of Puritan piety.[595]

Owen accepts the description of the Spirit 'moving on the face of the waters' in the opening verse of Genesis as suggesting a procreative force at work at the dawn of creation, which in turn argues for a particular intimacy in his view between Creator and creatures.[596] All created things 'in their first production had darkness and death upon them'; and this primal gloom described in Genesis 1.2 is for Owen analogous to the spiritual darkness and death which came by sin on all humanity; so, just as the Spirit brought new life to birth from the first creation, so it does the same out of the second.[597] This spiritual darkness is both subjective (within us) and objective (a darkness that hangs upon us). 'It is the work of the Holy Spirit to remove and take away this darkness; which until it is done no man can see the kingdom of God, or enter into it.'[598] And the Spirit's work is above all procreative: just as the natural body of Christ is formed in the womb, so his mystical body (the Church) is formed in his saints through regeneration; and both are the work of the Spirit.[599]

How does the Spirit work in human beings? All life is from God; and we share that life with all other creatures. We also possess a life which they do not share, the life which belongs to the union of the rational soul with the body (cf. Genesis 2.7; Job 10.12). But neither of these is ever called 'the life of God' in the Bible; the life that is so called is 'that life which God worketh in us, not naturally by his power, but spiritually by his grace', the life by which Christ himself dwells in us.[600]

Owen thus distinguishes natural life (which he calls the 'life of power', and which is simply the way we live as creatures possessing both a body and a soul) from life in the Spirit (which he calls the 'life of God'): the latter consists of the life of soul and the 'quickening principle of spiritual life' combined.[601] This quickening principle is communicated to us through Christ as mediator by the Holy Spirit:[602] it is unattainable by human beings on their own; and the principal means by which this happens is through the Word of God which we receive through the ministry of the church.[603]

The idea of a 'principle of spiritual life' dwelling within us may at first appear a thin and unimaginative way of describing the presence of the Holy Spirit. But Owen wants to emphasize that the work of the Spirit is *both* an objective reality (the life of the risen and ascended Christ communicated to us) *and* an apprehensible and transforming experience accessible to every Christian.[604] Thus (as we might expect) Owen argues, against the Catholics, that regeneration is not just a participation in the sacrament of baptism and a profession of repentance: it must be more than an objective, external action, and (against the Socinians) more too than a purely moral reformation.[605] Rather it must consist of

> the infusion [by the Spirit] of a new, real, spiritual principle into the soul and its faculties, of spiritual life, light, holiness, and righteousness, disposed unto and suited for the destruction or expulsion of a contrary, inbred, habitual principle of sin and enmity against God.[606]

This infusion makes us a new creature with 'renewed faculties' and 'new dispositions, power, or ability to them and for them' recreated in righteousness and true holiness;[607] and it renews the image of God within us.[608] This infusion is, again, more than a moral operation: it is a physical, immediate one, working on our minds and souls:[609] and it is above all a process of allurement God draws us to himself, allowing us by his grace to live to and for him.[610]

We are, then, transformed, our minds renewed, and our wills set free, 'by an effectual implantation in [them] of a principle of spiritual life and holiness in the room of that original righteousness which [they] lost by the fall'.[611] All this is the work of the Holy Spirit; but it is the direct consequence both of Christ's saving work, and of our faith in him; and it is that faith which begins the process of conforming our wills to that of God, and thus to renewing our natures in his image,[612] thereby allowing God to establish in us this vital 'principle of holiness'.[613] And the result is *sanctification* – 'of the whole spirit, soul, and body (1 Thessalonians 5.23)':[614] Puritan piety constantly stresses the total transforming of the whole person, not some narrowly religious process. Where regeneration is instantaneous, 'consisting in one single creating act',[615] sanctification is a continual process of growth, involving the transformation of the whole person and nature of the believer because the whole person was created in the image of God.[616] And the Spirit *assists* in the continuing process of sanctification ('continually to be renewed and gone over again, because of the remainder of sin in us and the imperfection of our grace'),[617] by preserving that vital 'principle of spiritual life and holiness communicated unto us in our regeneration';[618] by exciting us to good actions, both morally and 'really and internally'; by granting us experiences of the truth; and by increasing the presence of grace within us.[619] This is crucial, for 'grace gives beauty'; and 'the spiritual beauty and comeliness of the soul consists in its conformity unto God'.[620]

In order to describe the process of sanctification, Owen uses the analogy of trees, which 'have the principle of their growth in themselves' – they grow primarily (though not entirely) through 'their own seminal virtue and radical moisture' – in other words, from within. All grace 'is immortal seed, and contains in it a living, growing principle'; but it needs to be 'watered from above' – God works on the soul from both inside and outside.[621] Our role in this process is by removing hindrances to growth in sanctification, and simply by awakening to its reality at work in us.[622] This latter point underlines Owen's insistence that sanctification is only possible for believers:[623] whereas for nonbelievers afflictions simply deaden their lusts and emotions, for true believers afflictions have a positive value, leading them to become partakers of God's holiness (2 Corinthians 4.16–18).[624]

And this holiness is accessible to everyone: 'much of the glory of heaven may dwell in a simple cottage, and poor persons, even under rags, may be very like unto God'.[625] It is infused by the Spirit: sometimes Owen speaks of the Holy Spirit as *being* the 'principle of holiness' within us.[626] But it needs *cherishing* and preserving.[627] And it brings with it the power and ability to live by it:[628] 'to discern spiritual things in a spiritual manner', and freely to choose and embrace them.[629] It also 'gives an insight into the beauty . . . and glory of holiness'.[630] It is, then, both this- and next-worldly: it allows us to experience 'spiritual and heavenly glory' in this world:

> There is in this holiness . . . a ray of eternal light, a principle of eternal life, and the entire nature of that love whereby we shall eternally adhere unto God . . . It represents unto God the glory of his own image renewed in us.[631]

It is thus all that God requires of us; yet he knows that we cannot attain to it by our own efforts; and so he accomplishes it for us by the Holy Spirit, 'the immediate peculiar sanctifier of all believers, and the author of all holiness in them'.[632] We shall know it is the Spirit at work because the graces of holiness will increase and grow, and because we shall find ourselves 'stirred up' to good works, 'out of a sense of that electing love from whence all grace doth proceed'[633] – which is a very different thing from mere religious busyness.[634]

If this holiness is genuine, then, it will grow, and so will our capacity to do good. Owen suggests further tests: we will find that none of the commands of the gospel will be grievous or burdensome, and that none of the truths of the gospel will be strange or uncouth.[635] But, most important of all, we will become Christlike: in the fostering of holiness, Christ is both our 'idea and exemplar' and the means by which holiness is possible at all.[636] Thus by beholding him, as in 2 Corinthians 3.18 we are changed into his image, 'or made holy, and therein like unto him';[637] and this likeness to Christ is the sole cause of our usefulness to anyone else.[638] Thus Owen declares that 'there is no greater evidence that whatever we seem to have of any thing that is good in us is no part of evangelical holiness, than that it doth not render us conformable to Christ' – a convoluted but crucial point.[639] We are united to him 'by a participation of his Spirit. And hereby Christ himself is in us'.[640] Christ's holiness is profoundly *attractive* to the believer, alluring us and drawing us towards him;[641] and it works in us in three ways: by *contemplation* (by which we are changed into his likeness); by *admiration* ('that beauty of God which attracts the love of a believing soul, and fills it with a holy admiration of him'), and by granting us *delight* in obedience to Christ.[642]

The Doctrine of Preparation

For Owen, as for many other Puritans, sanctification is 'the universal renovation of our natures by the Holy Spirit into the image of God, through Jesus Christ';[643] and in his view the Holy Spirit prepares us for regeneration by its work of illumination of the mind, and by convicting mind, conscience and affections of the reality of sin,[644] as well as by reforming our lives and bringing about a change in our affections.[645] Now in strict predestinarian thought, religious conversion took place entirely by means of God's overriding grace, unilaterally transforming the sinner from a state of damnation to one of grace, as in the conversion of St Paul. However the idea that the Spirit helped to prepare or dispose the soul in advance, and the consequent image of 'the heart prepared', became prominent in late-sixteenth-century and early-seventeenth-century Puritan thought.[646] Not everyone accepted this notion: Luther, famously, did not;[647] but others, for whom the experience of conversion was less instantaneous than that on the Damascus road, did. Thus Richard Sibbes said that the fear of God first breaks the heart and prepares it for tenderness:[648] indeed to be *aware* of your hardness of heart and to want it changed is enough to distinguish you from the true reprobate.[649] And, even more importantly, a real concern for the reprobate is in itself the mark of a true tender heart.[650] Furthermore, if these first stirrings of God's regenerating work within us do not lead to a complete transformation, we must hammer on heaven's doors until they do:

> We must with boldness and reverence challenge the Covenant of grace: for this is the Covenant that God hath made with us, to give us tender hearts, hearts of flesh, Ezek.11:19 . . . Now seeing this is a Covenant God hath made, to give us fleshly hearts, and to take away our stony; let us challenge him with his promise, and go to him by prayer: intreat him to give thee a fleshly heart; go to him, wait his time, for that is the best time; therefore wait, though he do not hear at first.[651]

Puritan Conversion Narratives: Hannah Allen

As Puritans reflected more extensively on their own spiritual journeys, the practice of writing a spiritual autobiography or conversion narrative became more common.[652] Hannah Allen wrote a journal which gives important insights into the spiritual world of a Puritan woman, insights which give uncomfortable support to Stachniewski's thesis about the impact of the Calvinist God on many people, especially women: there is a pervasive sense in it of utter self-contempt and worthlessness.[653]

Allen describes her religious upbringing, and tells us that her father died while she was very young.[654] From an early age she was afflicted by 'horrible blasphemous thoughts and injections into my mind', and came to believe she had committed the unforgivable sin against the Holy Spirit.[655] She dared not tell anyone about this. These attacks, exacerbated by the fact of her being 'much inclined to melancholy, occasioned by the oft absence of my dear and affectionate Husband', persisted into adulthood.[656] The melancholy worsened after her first husband died abroad; and prayer provided no comfort, though she did at least manage to keep a journal.[657] The attacks seem above all to have been temptations to despair;[658] and eventually she tried to commit suicide.[659] The melancholy gradually wore off after her second marriage, and thanks in part to the kindness and hospitality of friends.[660] In the depths of her despair, on 26 May 1664, she wrote this deeply moving prayer of lament:

> I desire . . . exceedingly to bless and praise thy Majesty that hath yet in some measure supported me under these dreadful trials and temptations, which do yet continue and have been woful [sic] upon me, for almost four Months together; For Christ's sake pity my case, or else I know not what to do; and do not deny me strength to bear up under my burthen; and for the Lord's sake grant, whatever thou dost with me, that one Sin may not be in me, unreported of or unmortified; Do with me what thou wilt as to the Creature, so thou wilt subdue my sins, and chain up Sathan, and smile upon my Soul; Lord, I know not what to do, only mine Eyes are up to thee, the Devil still keeps me under dreadful bondage, and in sad distress and wo, but blessed be my God, that he doth not lay upon me all afflictions at once; that my Child is so well, and that I have so many other mercies, which the Lord open my Eyes to see; especially that Christ is mine, for the Lord's sake, and then I have enough.[661]

This stress on desire is important; and the sixteenth-century Protestant William Tyndale (who may count early in the Puritan lineage) among others, maintains that the very fact that we long for assurance of salvation is in itself a sign of election:

> Mark this then: To see inwardly that the law of God is so spiritual, that no flesh can fulfil it; and then for to mourn and sorrow, and to desire, yea, to hunger and thirst after strength to do the will of God from the ground of the heart, and . . . to cleave yet to the promises of God, and to believe that for Christ's blood sake thou art received to the inheritance of eternal life, is a wonderful thing, and a thing that the world knoweth not of; but whosoever feeleth that, though he fall a thousand times in a day, doth yet rise again a thousand times, and is sure that the mercy of God is upon him.[662]

Assurance and Faith

Once membership of the visible church is discounted as a sign of election, anxieties about whether one is saved or not are inevitable, and for some Puritans like Hannah Allen these could be terrifyingly strong. But Richard Baxter, characteristically moderate in tone, warned against an unhealthy preoccupation with doubt on this matter:

> A sincere Christian may attain to an infallible knowledge of his own sincerity in grace, or his performance of the conditions of the covenant of life, and consequently of his justification, adoption, and title to glory; and this without any extraordinary revelation.[663]

Baxter explores in great detail the 'marks of grace' by which this knowledge can be tested, and has no doubt that the central such mark is our willingness 'to love Christ savingly, that is . . . sovereignly, or chiefly',[664] which involves both loving our fellow Christians for Christ's sake,[665] and those who may not be saved in the hope that thereby they may be brought to salvation.[666] We cannot do this, of course, until we both believe in and experience God's love for us, as John Owen points out.[667] And Thomas Brooks (1608–80), a Puritan who remained within the established church, wrote a treatise on Christian assurance (*Heaven on earth*, 1654) in which he reminded his readers that not all Christians possess assurance, or possess it continually,[668] and that (like many biblical figures, from the psalmist to Simeon in the Temple) we must be prepared to wait in hope for God to manifest signs of our election:

> After God had exercised David's patience in waiting, he sweetly breaks in upon him, and knocks off his bolts, and opens the prison doors, and takes him by the hand, and leads him out of the pit of noise and confusion [cf Psalm 40.2], in which he was, and causes his love and goodness so to beam forth upon him as causes his heart to rejoice, and his tongue to sing.[669]

And the essential sign of election is faith: William Tyndale defines true faith, by which alone we are justified, as 'a spiritual light of understanding, and an inward knowledge or feeling of mercy'.[670] He distinguishes between what he calls a 'historical faith' (what we believe as a result of others' testimony), and a 'feeling faith' (what we believe as a result of personal experience).[671] Faith in God is both a rational decision and a profound personal experience; and it issues in a change of life.[672]

Puritan theologians disagreed about whether the effects of faith, rather than simply faith itself, are evidence of election,[673] though John Owen speaks for many in saying that sanctification is what makes us beautiful – 'not only accepted, but also acceptable'.[674] What all agree on is that both the gift of faith itself and the fruits of it in sanctification are alike gifts of God; and John Owen criticizes those in the Arminian and Catholic traditions who 'would spin a holiness out of their own bowels'.[675] Most Puritans would have accepted Calvin's distinction between the action God takes to justify us through Christ, an action essentially external to anything we do or are, and the subsequent work of God within us to deepen our faith and awareness of him, which is sanctification.[676]

The Godly Life

Now it is within this context that we need to see what Puritans meant by 'godly life'. One of the greatest Elizabethan Puritans, William Perkins (1558–1602), who was not a separatist, elaborated the connection between faith and sanctification, saying that faith works two things in the believer: first, it deepens our memory, 'whereby Gods word is laid up in the heart, that it may be drawne out to use, when occasion shall be offered'; and secondly, it deepens our capacity for attention, that process by which we apply God's word to specific situations.[677] For Perkins,

> Spirituall life, which is the beginning of eternall life, stands specially in foure things. Reconciliation with God, peace of conscience, joy of the holy Ghost, and newnesse of life.[678]

Reconciliation with God is the direct result of faith, and becomes self-evident to us: 'He that truely beleeves hath his minde and conscience supernaturally inlightned to discerne that hee beleeves', and this is 'the foundation of all our joy and spirituall comfort'.[679] Peace of conscience is the peace of Psalm 3.5: 'I lay myself down and sleep' – serenity in danger.[680] Newness of life is that whereby we are made new creatures, 'not because the substance of body and soule is changed, but because the image of God is restored'.[681] It comprises 'true wisdome', 'good affections' and 'good workes'.[682] And the acid test of this spiritual life is its capacity to sustain us in affliction and temptation: if it is genuine, it will make us dependent on God's promises and able to trust him unconditionally precisely in our misery, and it will assure us of his presence with us, just as Elisha opened the eyes of his servant to see that those who were with them were more than those who were against them.[683]

But this still begs the question of what exactly Puritans meant by 'the godly life'. No one wrote more eloquently on this subject than Richard Baxter, for whom godliness (or holiness: he does not distinguish between the two) denotes a total Christian life, in which family piety, worship, moral uprightness and good relations with others are inseparably bound together:[684] hence it is not only important for the individual, but brings peace and harmony to an entire nation:

> Godliness takes away the ball of the world's contention, that sets men every where together by the ears ... If all the ambitious climbers and state-troublers were truly godly, they would quietly seek for higher honours. If all the covetous noblemen, soldiers, landlords, and rich men were truly godly, they would never set both city and country into combustions, and poor oppressed families into complaints, for the love of money. If thieves turned godly you might travel safely, and spare your locks and keep your purses ... What is there for societies to strive about, when the bone of contention is taken away, and godliness hath cast down the idol of the world, that did disturb them?[685]

And Baxter responds to the argument that religion is the cause of so much disunity in the world by passionately asserting that holiness of this kind is precisely the key to Christian (and hence human) unity:

Objection. 'But do we not see that the main divisions of the world are about religion?' *Answer.* It is true; but not by the truly religious. The great quarrel of the world is against religion in the life and practice of it. It is unholy men that cannot abide to be accounted unholy, that are the chief dividers. Among the truly godly, there is no division in the main, but only differences about the smaller branches of religion, which are numerous, and less discernible, and less necessary than the common truths. They are all agreed of truth enough to bring them to heaven; and therefore enough to unite them in dear affection upon earth. Nay, there is not one of them that hath not a special love to all that he discerneth to be the servants of the Lord. If any be without this, he is ungodly. And we are not to answer for the miscarriages of every infidel or ungodly man, that will put on the name of Christianity and godliness. If there should be fallings out among the godly, they cannot rest till they are healed and set in joint again. But you must not then be so unjust as to conclude, that we can have no unity, till we are in all things of a mind. May not men of various complexions be of one society? Are not the multitudes of veins and arteries in your bodies, united in the trunks and roots? Is not the tree one, that hath many branches?[686]

This approach is characteristic of Baxter, and one wishes those Christians of his own and earlier generations, who seemed to have no difficulty in combining profound wisdom about the spiritual life with vituperative attacks on their opponents, had taken his words to heart. Godliness teaches rulers to resist temptations and personal gain and govern wisely; it teaches people to know themselves and their place, and to dispose people to unity and concord.[687] It may be an idealistic view of the world; but at least Baxter had dreams to dream, and a vision to proclaim that was far wider than the concerns of individual or private holiness. For Baxter, holiness not only brought security and happiness: it also brought honour,[688] the only honour that endures, because it consists in recognizing our true dignity as those who are created and renewed in the image of God himself.[689] Last but not least, godliness makes us happy, here and now:[690] our holy desires for others' good, albeit unfulfilled, bring us happiness:[691]

How pleasant it must be to a believing soul, to have this Spirit of adoption, this childlike love and confidence, and freedom with the Lord, methinks you might conjecture though it is sensibly known by them only that enjoy it.[692]

Godliness makes prayer and worship a pleasure ('Is it grievous for a child to speak to his Father? or are you weary of the presence of your dearest friend?'[693]), and the praise of God a joy:

Be acquainted with his praise. Is there not a better cure for melancholy here among the servants of the Lord, than in an alehouse, or in the company of transgressors?[694]

It makes works of justice a pleasure too, both private and public;[695] and although it is true that the godly sometimes appear gloomy and sad, this is because of their acute awareness of their sin,[696] for 'the joy of a believer is intimate and solid', and a cause for unending rejoicing.[697]

This heartwarming vision of the godly life is among the best things in Puritan spirituality. But it brings us to a crucial question: is holiness, in the Puritan vision, primarily a matter of walking with Christ,[698] or does it imply some measure of intimacy with, even union with, Christ? Or (to put it another way) is there such a thing as 'Puritan mysticism'?

Union with Christ[699]

Puritan writers certainly conceived of an intimate and personal union between the individual Christian and Christ, though a union that never dissolved each other's identity. Thus John Owen argues for a union between the Christian and Christ that is similar to that of the union of diverse natures *within* Christ: 'There may be a manifold union, mystical and moral, of divers, of many persons, but a personal union there cannot be of any thing but of distinct natures.'[700] We always remain distinct persons in our relationship with God.[701] Richard Baxter, speaking of our communion with Christ in heaven, puts it thus:

> What can you desire yet more? Except you will, as some do, abuse Christ's expression of oneness, to conceive of such a union, as shall deify us; which were a sin one step beyond the aspiring arrogancy of Adam; and, I think beyond that of the devils. A real conjunction, improperly called union, we may expect; and a true union of affections. A moral union, improperly still called union, and a true relative union, such as is between the members of the same politic body and the head: yea, such as is between the husband and the wife, who are called one flesh. And a real communion, and communication of real favours, flowing from that relative union. If there be any more, it is acknowledged unconceivable, and consequently unexpressible, and so not to be spoken of.[702]

This use of marital imagery is employed by Puritan writers just as it was by medieval and later Catholic ones. John Owen, commenting on the Song of Songs (which was of course the favourite mystical text for Catholic theologians of the spiritual life), comes very close to identifying the spouse in the Song with the individual Christian, not simply (as is commonplace) with the Church as a whole:

> The spouse is quite ravished with the sweetness of this entertainment, finding love, and care, and kindness, bestowed by Christ in the assemblies of the saints. Hence she cries out, verse 5, 'Stay me with flagons, comfort me with apples; for I am sick of love.' Upon the discovery of the excellency and sweetness of Christ in the banqueting-house, the soul is instantly overpowered, and cries out to be made partaker of the fulness of it. She is 'sick of love:' not (as some suppose) fainting for want of a sense of love, under

the apprehension of wrath; but made sick and faint, even overcome, with the mighty actings of that divine affection, after she had once tasted of the sweetness of Christ in the banqueting-house.[703]

What is important here is to note the interrelation of the individual and the corporate: the soul is Christ's spouse, yet experiencing his intimate love not in the bedroom (as with St Bernard) but 'in the assemblies of the saints', in the heavenly banquet. Thus Owen can speak at one point as though Christ were married to all Christians at once (in other words, to the church),[704] and at another as though he were married to each individual Christian:

> Christ gives himself to the soul, with all his excellencies, righteousness, preciousness, graces, and eminencies, to be its Saviour, head, and husband, for ever ... in carrying on this union, Christ freely bestoweth himself upon the soul ... And this is the soul's entrance into conjugal communion with Jesus Christ as to personal grace, the constant preferring him above all pretenders to its affections, counting all loss and dung in comparison of him.[705]

The seeming paradox is resolved later in the same work (*Of communion with God the Father, Son, and Holy Ghost*): commenting on the text in the Song of Songs which describes the spouse seeking her bridegroom in the streets of the city, Owen says that this represents the soul which 'when it finds [Christ] not in any private endeavours, it makes vigorous application to the ordinances [= sacraments] of public worship'.[706] We are created and predestined for a relationship of intimate union with God in Christ; but we experience the fullness of that union not in some private encounter but precisely within the worshipping life of the godly.[707]

How does this union come about? John Owen has no doubt about that: it is the fruit of Christ's death, in which we participate by faith. This participation is no mere intellectual assent: it is a sharing in Christ's dying and rising, for 'there is almost nothing that Christ hath done ... but we are said [in scripture] to do it with him'.[708] By this participation we die to sin as Christ did, though this is hard spiritual work: Owen notes that

> sin is never more alive than when it is thus dying. But there is a dying of it as to the root, the principle of it, the daily decaying of the strength, power, and life of it; and this is to be had alone in Christ.[709]

And the reason we seek this union with Christ through his death is because Christ draws us, attracts us by his intrinsic beauty, transforming us into his own likeness, and making us his marriage partner.[710] So Richard Sibbes (1635), one of the most remarkable Puritan writers on the spiritual life, says that

> you may know by this altering, changing, transforming power, whether he be in you or not. He alters and changes us to his own likenesse; that as he is set down in the Gospel in his life, conversation, and disposition; so (if we have entertained him, and he be in us) we should have the same disposition, the same mind, and the same will with him.[711]

We become Christlike as we respond to Christ's call: and then (as Owen puts it), for the Christian 'every day whilst we live is his wedding-day', and every day Christ shares his secrets with us.[712]

This kind of spirituality may be termed 'mysticism' if by that is implied a direct and unmediated experience of God that is vouchsafed to the individual Christian, provided we remember three things: first, that this experience happens within the context of a personal intimacy, for which marriage is the natural analogy, which is itself the result of God's election of the individual and the individual's response in a commitment of faith; secondly, that this intimacy has nothing to do with 'deification' of the kind described by some thinkers in the Arminian and Catholic traditions – there is no suggestion of an ontological union, a mutual absorption of the soul into the Godhead; and, thirdly, that the natural context for the development of this intimacy is not on a private retreat, so to speak, or in the monastic life, but precisely in the midst of the Christian community, and supremely in its worship.

It is true that some broadly within the Puritan tradition went much further still. John Everard (c.1575–1640) translated the *Theologia Germanica* and a number of other continental mystical and esoteric texts, as well as some of the writings of Pseudo-Dionysius.[713] Everard goes much further than Tyndale had in stressing the experiential, subjective dimension of faith: for him knowledge of Christ through scripture is essential, but what really matters is 'a Christ begotten within thee, a Christ in experience':[714] we must 'touch Christ inwardly'.[715] This really is a mystical, hidden, knowledge, rooted in mystery:

> Thou saist thou Readest it [the Scriptures] in the Church, and in thy family twice a day, and thou delightest to be exercised therein, and to see that others do so; Thou doest well, it is good in its place: but what good doth it convey to thy soul? what refreshment and nourishment dost thou find by this thou so delightest in, and so boastest of?[716]

> If there be not in every one of us something of Jesus Christ that is of his own nature, the same mind, the same quickning [*sic*] Spirit, the same disposition, and the same new nature, something of his own offspring, we are but in a dead and perishing condition.[717]

Christ must live within us spiritually:[718] he must be born in us as he was in Mary: we must become the Virgin, feeling the child beginning to be conceived in us.[719] For Everard, Christ is in us already, in virtue of our creation;[720] but his coming-to-birth in us must be the beginning of a conscious, and costly, process, whereby he grows up to full manhood within us.[721] Everard expounds the life of Christ in terms of our own spiritual lives and growth: thus the twelve-year-old Christ preaching to the doctors of the Law represents Christ putting to flight our various sins (Doctor Pride, Doctor Arrogance, etc[722]). Christ was conceived in us when we were born; but he must be *manifested* in us, be born *again*.[723]

Everard constantly stresses the two-stage nature of the spiritual life: we begin by studying the letter of scripture, but must continue by appropriating for ourselves its spirit: we must learn to break open the shell in order to claim the kernel or oyster within.[724] This process has six stages, beginning with condemnation of self,[725] continuing with conformity to Christ as head, and concluding with *deiformity* ...

> not, that is, when we act no longer ourselves, but God acts in us; that if we do anything, yet we see and feel, and confess it is God that doth it; that if we speak, it is Christ that speaks; if we think, it is Christ that thinks.[726]

This is still not ontological union: rather it is Christ living in us, making us Christlike. Later in the same work Everard says that, once this process takes place, we become like someone who suddenly recognizes the King sitting in a room with him: we become changed, aware of our own inadequacies, like Jacob at Bethel:[727] like St John the Baptist, God must increase in us and we must decrease, as the vision of God's glory transforms us entirely into the people God calls us to become.[728]

Everard does not develop this idea further: perhaps he could not, for his work could be said to represent a kind of *terminus ad quem*, one very particular peak, of Puritan spirituality. The route to this peak lies through vastly different terrain from (say) the route required for travellers along the way of Everard's Catholic contemporary Dom Augustine Baker: Everard lived in the midst of this world's clamour, not in the cloister, and devoted his life and preaching above all to the poor and humble of city and countryside. Yet there are similarities: both Everard and Baker, the Puritan and the Catholic, suffered interrogation and imprisonment for their beliefs; both strayed perilously close to the boundaries of what their co-religionists considered orthodox; both sought successfully to convey something of the cost and the excitement of the Christian's spiritual journey; and although their maps and itineraries differed, the view from the summits they finally reached was unmistakably the same.

The Fruits of Sanctification

Fasting

It remains to consider some of the main implications of this theology for the practice of the spiritual life. Some of the devotional customs of late medieval piety continued to flourish after the Reformation even among radicals and later dissenters, though with a different emphasis.[729] Thus dissenters encouraged fasting, but insisted on trying to combine outward physical fasting with the cultivation of inward virtues.[730] One prominent Elizabethan dissenter, Thomas Becon, wrote *A treatise of fasting* in which he commends the practice in what he conceives of as its true scriptural character. But, crucially, he emphasizes that fasting is not to be engaged upon as a means of obtaining salvation: rather it is a response to having already obtained it.[731] Theologically this is part of the process of sanctification, which is always (in Reformed piety) the result of having already been justified. For Becon, there are four reasons why good Protestants should fast: first, in order to become more obedient to the Spirit than to the flesh; secondly, in order to give more generously to the poor and hungry;[732] thirdly, as a preparation for prayer; and, fourthly, in order to make us more clear-headed and responsive to the word of God.[733] And another dissenter, Richard Rogers (1551–1618), describes in his diary a group of clergy fasting, 'to the stirringe upp of our selves to greater godlines [*sic*]'.[734]

Boldness

We have already seen how the Protestant doctrine of assurance logically led to a pervasive emphasis on spiritual boldness in Reformed piety, and a new interest in its New Testament roots. Thus John Owen can say that the Old Testament characters who walked intimately with God nonetheless lacked the boldness which belonged only to those who had communion through Christ;[735] and he stresses that this boldness is the consequence of Christ's saving death, not of any achievement of ours.[736] Thomas Brooks makes the same point: assurance produces 'holy boldness':

> Assurance makes the soul converse with God as a favourite with his prince, as a bride with her bridegroom, as a Joseph with a Jacob . . . You will not then stand at the door of mercy with a *may I knock?* with a *may I go in?* with a *may I find audience and acceptance?* but you will, with Esther, boldly adventure yourselves upon the mercy and goodness of God.[737]

This boldness is not presumptuous; and John Smyth cautions against barging into the presence of God like a horse rushing into battle.[738] Rather we should, as the writer of the Letter to the Hebrews reminds us, approach with confidence to the throne of grace, 'hoping assuredly to obtaine mercie (Heb. 4:16)'.[739] And the reason why we should do this is made clear by John Owen, citing Ephesians 6.19:

> where this Spirit of liberty and boldness is, the heart is enlarged with a true, genuine openness and readiness to express all its concerns unto God as a child unto its father . . . The whole of our concerns in this world is to be committed unto God in prayer, so that we should not retain any dividing cares in our own minds about them. And herein the apostle would have us to use a holy freedom and boldness in speaking unto God, as one who concerns himself in them; to hide nothing from God . . . but use a full, plain-hearted, open liberty with him.[740]

The analogy of the child with its father is significant; and Pauline teaching about our adoption as children through the work of the Holy Spirit is a major theme in Puritan spirituality.[741] Thus Owen can say that

> If the love of a father will not make a child delight in him, what will? . . . In all the hard censures and tongue-persecutions which the saints meet withal in the streets of the world, they may run with their moanings unto their Father, and be comforted.[742]

This is the source of our boldness,[743] and of that fundamental freedom which psychologists now argue to be the fruit of unconditional parental love. But it is a boldness, and a freedom, which paradoxically finds expression precisely in doing God's will: true freedom, for Owen, consists not in doing what we want but in doing what God wants.[744] And it is only when we apprehend God as our father that we can pray as we ought.[745]

Nonetheless this boldness, for Owen as for Latimer, has an important social dimension too:

> All the story of the church is filled with instances of persons mean in their
> outward condition, timorous by nature, and unaccustomed unto dangers,
> unlearned and low in their natural abilities, who, in the face of rulers and
> potentates, in the sight of prisons, tortures, fires, provided for their
> destruction, have pleaded the cause of the gospel with courage and success,
> unto the astonishment and confusion of their adversaries.[746]

And Owen defines faith as

> that *parrhesia en pistei*, that freedom, confidence, and 'boldness in the
> faith' or profession of the faith, 'which is in Christ Jesus', mentioned by the
> apostle, 1 Tim. 3:13 . . . And there is no more certain sign of churches
> being forsaken of Christ in a time of trial than if this gift be withheld from
> them, and pusillanimity, fearfulness, with carnal wisdom, do spring up in
> the room of it.[747]

Hence *parrhesia* (literally 'freedom of speech'), or spiritual boldness, is an essential gift
for all ministers.[748] And not only for them: it is worth noting the extent to which
devout Puritan women acted with a boldness and independence of spirit regardless of
attempts by clergy to maintain them in submission.[749]

Christian hope

An active expectation of the second coming of Christ is a characteristic feature of
much Puritan piety; and this expectation was fuelled by historical events such as the
Civil War. After the Restoration, with the disappearance of their hopes for a Christian
commonwealth in this world, Puritan spirituality became both more inward and
more eschatological, as hopes came to be pinned more on the next world.[750] Both their
expectancy and their vision of heaven profoundly affect their perspective on life in this
world.[751] Thus Richard Baxter, for whom heaven will be something like soldiers
returning home when their work is done,[752] writes:

> A heavenly mind is a joyful mind; this is the nearest and the truest way to
> live a life of comfort . . . Can a man be at the fire, and not be warm; or in
> the sunshine, and not have light? Can your heart be in heaven, and not
> have comfort? . . . When the sun in the spring draws near our part of the
> earth, how do all things congratulate its approach! The earth looks green,
> and casteth off her mourning habit: the trees shoot forth; the plants revive;
> the pretty birds, how sweetly do they sing! the face of all things smiles upon
> us, and all the creatures below rejoice.[753]

Many Puritans emphasize the egalitarian nature of the Christian hope. For Lewis
Baily life in heaven will be

> Light without Darkness; Mirth, without Sadness; Health, without
> Sickness; Wealth, without Want; Credit, without Disgrace . . . Let us not
> then dote so much upon these wooden Cottages, and Houses of
> mouldring clay . . . but let us look rather, and long for this heavenly City.[754]

Everyone in heaven will be kings and priests, keeping perpetual sabbath, enjoying 'all the goodness, beauty, glory, and perfection of all creatures (in all the World) united together'.[755] This dramatic exaltation of the humble is a characteristic theme in Puritan spirituality.[756]

This vision should not lead to some kind of passive quietism: 'Sitting still', says Baxter, 'will lose you heaven, as well as if you run from it'.[757] We must desire this rest, and make it our true end.[758] Baxter even declares that 'violence and laborious striving for salvation, is the way that the wisdom of God hath directed us to as best'.[759] 'If you knew that this were the last day you had to live in the world, how would you spend this day?'[760]

Not all Puritan visions of life beyond death are as appealing as this. Richard Sibbes, with uncharacteristic understatement, describes hell fire as 'that greatest of inconveniences';[761] and some Puritans, notably Bunyan, envisage life in heaven as including an active delighting in the sufferings of the damned, though Baxter characteristically takes a more temperate view.[762] His own view of heaven is at one point disconcertingly close to an assembly of learned divines: 'will it be nothing conducible to the completing of our comforts, to live eternally with Peter, Paul, Austin, Chrysostom, Jerome, Wickliffe, Luther, Zwinglius, Calvin, Beza, Bullinger . . . Hooper, Bradford, Latimer' and many others?'[763] But he has a vivid sense of the reality of the saints and angels accompanying us on our journey heavenwards:

> Pray for the protection and help of angels, as part of the benefits procured for the saints by Christ; and be thankful for it as a privilege of believers, excelling all the dignities of the ungodly. And walk with a reverence of their presence, especially in the worshipping of God.[764]

This is not of course prayer *to* the saints, of which all Protestants disapproved: it is prayer to God for the privilege of sharing their company.[765] The Puritan heaven was nothing if not warmly sociable,[766] as was the Christian life now, for the true church 'is nothing else but a communion and society of saints'.[767] And in heaven we shall become at last partakers of the divine nature, and become the people God from all eternity created us to be. Baxter told his friends what he believed that final consummation would be like:

> Then, dear friends, we shall live in our element. We are now as the fish in some small vessel of water, that hath only so much as will keep him alive; but what is that to the full ocean? . . . To be locked up in gold, and in pearl, would be but a wealthy starving; to have our tables with plate and ornaments richly furnished without meat, is but to be richly famished; to be lifted up with human applause, is but a very airy felicity; to be advanced to the sovereignty of all the earth, would be but to wear a crown of thorns; to be filled with the knowledge of arts and sciences, would be but to further the conviction of our unhappiness; but to have a nature like God's very image, holy as he is holy; and to have God himself to be our happiness, how well do these agree? Whether that in 2 Pet.1:4 be meant, as is commonly understood, of our own inherent renewed nature, figuratively

called divine, or rather of Christ's divine nature without us, properly so called, whereof we are also relatively made partakers, I know not; but certainly were not our own in some sort divine, the enjoyment of the true divine nature could not be to us a suitable rest.[768]

The firmly corporate nature of Puritan spirituality is frequently forgotten: despite their emphasis on individual salvation and their suspicion of the visible, institutional church, Puritans in general attached primary importance to worship, and in particular to the 'ordinances' or sacraments, above all to the Lord's Supper,[769] and saw the gathered church as a family.[770] Solitude was not impossible for the Christian; and John Owen acknowledged that someone who is 'a great proficient in spirituality' might dare to venture on 'an absolute retirement from the world'; but it was not normative.[771]

Hence the pervasive stress on *praise* in so much Puritan piety: because it is the defining activity of those experiencing eternal rest, we should make it a priority now.[772] Baxter declared that

> The liveliest emblem of heaven that I know upon earth is, when the people of God, in the deep sense of his excellency and bounty, from hearts abounding with love and joy, do join together, both in heart and voice, in the cheerful and melodious singing of his praises.[773]

Praise is 'soul-raising'.[774] Praise with the heart as well as the voice is 'reviving and exhilarating';[775] and it is the fundamental duty of true Christians gathered together in worship.

The Theology and Practice of Prayer

This brings us to the Puritan understanding of prayer; and here, as in so much else, the role of the Holy Spirit is vital. It seems to have been characteristic of much Puritan spirituality to base true prayer on St Paul's letters, especially on Romans and the First Letter to the Corinthians. Thus John Owen cites 1 Corinthians 12.3 in saying that the very fact of praying for the Holy Spirit is impossible without his assistance.[776] As we might expect, the work of the Spirit in prayer is crucial for Owen, first in articulating the 'groanings that cannot be uttered' (Romans 8.26), and secondly in making manifest to believers the reality of 'spiritual, mysterious things' so that they have 'a real and experimental sense' of them.[777] It also reveals to us what we should pray for, and how[778] – and what we want (though we may not all know it) is 'the inward sanctification of all our faculties'.[779] Owen is making a polemical point here: those who pray aimlessly (which is how he regards those who pray using 'devised aids of prayer') are not praying at all, unless they have some understanding of what God has promised, so that our prayer can conform to that.[780]

True prayer, then, is itself a gift of the Holy Spirit,[781] and the fruit of faith in Christ.[782] Tyndale defines it as

> either a longing for the honour and name of God, that all men should fear him, and keep his precepts . . . [or] prayer is, to give God thanks for the benefits received [as opposed to thanking God for what they think they

have obtained by their own efforts] . . . [or] prayer is a complaining and a shewing of thine own misery and necessity, or of thy neighbour's before God; desiring him, with all the power of thine heart, to have compassion and to succour.[783]

And he stresses that a prayer unaccompanied by active and costly good works is hypocrisy:

If I stick up to the middle in the mire, like to perish without present help, and thou stand by and wilt not succour me, but kneelest down and prayest, will God hear the prayers of such an hypocrite? God biddeth thee so to love me, that thou put thyself in jeopardy to help me; and that thine heart, while thy body laboureth, do pray and trust in God that he will assist thee, and through thee to save me. An hypocrite, that will put neither body nor goods in peril for to help me at my need, loveth me not, neither hath compassion on me; and therefore his heart cannot pray, though he wag his lips never so much.[784]

Negatively, this leads to a depreciation of any kind of formal or liturgical prayer (especially, though not only, that of the cloister[785]). In extreme cases this could include a refusal even to say the Psalms or the Lord's Prayer;[786] but most Puritans took a far more nuanced view than that, Baxter among them:

The heavy charge and bitter, scornful words which have been too common in this age, against praying without a set form by some, and against praying with a book or form by others, is so dishonourable a symptom or diagnostic of the church's sickness, as must needs be matter of shame and sorrow to the sounder, understanding part. For it cannot be denied, but it proveth men's understandings and charity to be both extremely low. [787]

And sixteenth-century Protestants like Bradford commended the Lord's Prayer as the exemplar of all common prayer:

This prayer . . . [the *Paternoster*] is a common and general prayer, serving for the use of the whole church or congregation of God, in the which we pray one for another, the prince for the subject, and the subject for the prince . . . and not every man for himself only; yea, and that both in spiritual and corporate things . . . that as we be members all of one body, and children of one heavenly Father, so are we careful one for another, gentle and loving one to another, and pray generally one for another, wishing indifferently all good things to all men without exception, and without any respect had to private profit and singular commodity.[788]

Positively, Puritans wanted to stress that the way we pray affects the kind of people we are;[789] and the risk of set forms is that they do the work for us, preventing the truthful articulation in our own words of the feelings and experiences we both want and need to express.[790] Prayer, then, is hard work; but (and this is crucial) it is the action of the child who knows that he or she is already loved and accepted, and who in response longs to bring the whole of life into a living relationship with the Father. Thomas Brooks makes the point that assurance of salvation allows us to believe that we shall receive the things we pray for *as though we had already received them*,[791] and encourages us to persevere in prayer:

> A dog, of all creatures, is best able to endure hunger; he will run from place to place, and never leave off till he hath got his prey. So a child of God in his hunting after God, Christ, grace, peace, mercy, glory, never gives over till he hath found his heavenly prey. Song of Solomon 3:4, 'At length I found him whom my soul loved; I held him, and would not let him go.' The spouse never left hunting after her beloved till she had found him.[792]

The implications of this are important. Most Puritans would have agreed with Thomas Becon that the primary ingredient of prayer, after praise and thanksgiving, is petition;[793] but it belongs to the child to ask anything it needs, however mundane or secular.[794] Wakefield compares the narrow range of Puritan intercessory prayer with the wider scope of, say, Lancelot Andrewes' *Preces privatae*;[795] and it is true that some Puritans bear out this argument.[796] But this is only partly true. Richard Sibbes commends intercessory weeping, as Christ did for Jerusalem, and stresses that this requires a desire to see and respond to the miseries of others.[797] John Bradford says that

> The mind of man hath so large room to receive good things, that nothing can fully fill it but only God; whom then thy mind fully possesseth, when it fully knoweth him, it fully loveth him, and in all things is framed after his will. They therefore, dear Lord God, that are thy children and have tasted somewhat of thy goodness, do perpetually sigh, that is, do pray, until they come thereto: and, in that they love thee also above all things, it wonderfully woundeth them that other men do not so, that is, love thee, and seek for thee with them. Whereof it cometh to pass, that they are inflamed with continual prayers and desires that thy kingdom might come every where, and thy goodness might be both known, and in life expressed, of every man.[798]

And William Tyndale says that the Christian when praying

> feeleth other men's need, and no less commendeth to God the infirmities of other than his own . . . His neighbour is no less care to him than himself: he feeleth his neighbour's grief no less than his own. And whensoever he seeth occasion, he cannot but pray for his neighbour as well as for himself: his nature is to seek the honour of God in all men, and to draw (as much as in him is) all men unto God.[799]

The question inescapably arises of whether the prayers of those who are not assured of salvation will be heard: some English Puritans argue that they will not, though Baxter and Calvin himself maintain that they will.[800] But the really important point is that those who have faith endeavour to bring the whole of their lives into their prayers, so that prayer consists both of our deepest desires and of their honest articulation,[801] and can be engaged in wherever we happen to find ourselves.[802]

Prayer is not simply the expression of an individual's relationship with God through Christ. For Puritans the family is the primary focus for prayer, and ought to meet for this purpose twice daily: for Baxter,

> holy families are the seminaries of Christ's church on earth, and it is very much that lieth upon them to keep up the interest of religion in the world . . . Oh, that God would stir up the hearts of people thus to make their families as little churches, that it might not be in the power of rulers or pastors that are bad to extinguish religion, or banish godliness from any land![803]

Married couples are to take every opportunity 'to be speaking to each other about the matters of God';[804] and the head of the household is to have a special concern to pray for its members:

> He must be as it were the priest of the household; and therefore should be the most holy, that he may be fit to stand between them and God, and to offer up their prayers to him.[805]

Prayer is not only something that should integrate individual and community: it should also integrate mind and heart; and, for all their emphasis on the importance of the affective dimension of prayer, Puritans had a healthy concern for the involvement of the intellect too. John Smyth, the great Baptist theologian, offered a thoughtful approach to the relationship of prayer and healing:

> God never appointed prayer to be a meanes to cure diseases or such like, being applied to the sore or disease or atch [sic]: for although it be neede-full that we pray to God for the removing of paines and sicknes [sic] from us and ours; yet it doth not follow thereupon that God appointed prayer for a medicine, which being applied to diseases shall cure them: for then every man would be a physition to himselfe whatsoever disease he had, by his prayers. Prayer doth sanctifie physicke unto us, it is no physicke it selfe.[806]

In contrast to what they perceive as semi-magical spirituality, unrelated to holiness of life, Puritans stress the need for knowledge (understanding what you pray), faith (assurance of obtaining what is asked), repentance and devotion in the one praying.[807] No one articulated this essential integration in the matter of prayer more eloquently than John Owen:

> It is from God's institution and blessing that the mind and will of praying do lead unto the words of prayer, and the words of prayer do lead on the mind and will, enlarging them in desires and supplications. And without this aid many would oftentimes be straitened in acting their thoughts and affections towards God, or distracted in them, or diverted from them. And we have experience that an obedient, sanctified persistency in the use of gracious words in prayer hath prevailed against violent temptations and injections of Satan, which the mind in its silent contemplations was not

able to grapple with. And holy affections are thus also excited hereby. The very words and expressions which the mind chooseth to declare its thoughts, conceptions, and desires about heavenly things, do reflect upon the affections, increasing and exciting of them.[808]

Owen is here directing his criticisms at Catholics and Quakers alike – all who in his view set 'mental' (i.e. non-verbal) prayer above vocal prayer. Spiritual ecstasies which cannot be understood lead us to 'the old question, *cui bono?*'[809] Even apparent holiness of life is inadequate as a justification for such a form of prayer: 'prayer without an actual acknowledgment of God in all his holy excellencies, and the actings of faith in fear, love, confidence, and gratitude, is a monster in nature, or a by-blow of imagination, which hath no existence in *rerum natura*'.[810] Even more seriously, such prayer takes little or no regard for Christ and his mediating work.[811]

And it is in this context that we need to consider the Puritan practice of meditation, a subject which has aroused considerable scholarly debate, and which may be instructively compared with the approach of Bishop Hall discussed earlier.[812] Attentive and meditative private reading of scripture, enlarged by discussion with fellow believers, was the foundation of much Puritan spirituality;[813] and the absolute authority of scripture was accepted by almost (though not quite) all Puritan writers.[814] Baxter defines meditation in its wider sense as 'thinking on things spiritual',[815] distinguishing between the meditation proper to the soul, and the mere cogitations of the senses.[816] He defines the former thus:

> I call it the acting of 'all' the powers of the soul, to difference it from the
> common meditation of students, which is usually the mere employment
> of the brain. It is not a bare thinking that I mean, nor the mere use of
> invention or memory, but a business of a higher and more excellent nature.
> When truth is apprehended only as truth, this is but an unsavoury and
> loose apprehension; but when it is apprehended as good, as well as true,
> this is a fast and delightful apprehension. As a man is not so prone to live
> according to the truth he knows, except it do deeply affect him, so neither
> doth his soul enjoy its sweetness, except speculation do pass to affection.
> As God hath made several parts in man to perform their several offices for
> his nourishing and life, so hath he ordained the faculties of the soul . . . the
> understanding must take in truths, and prepare them for the will, and it
> must receive them, and commend them to the affections.[817]

Note the integrated approach here, and the reference to several of the great transcendental realities of scholastic thought (truth, goodness, and delight or beauty).[818]

The subject matter of Puritan meditation tended to be Christocentric, though with far more interest shown in the saving work of Christ than in the details of his human life.[819] In this sense it differs significantly from medieval *meditatio*, though in other respects it is strikingly similar; and there are very close parallels between Puritan meditation and the *consideratio* taught and practised by St Bernard of Clairvaux: both involve a careful and ruminative process by which the person seeks to appropriate, from a given passage of scripture or reflection on one's own experience or both, what

God is seeking to say in the present.[820] Puritans could and did also follow Bernard in meditating on heaven but the commonest form of meditation involved seeking to discern God's will for oneself or for others.[821] In his *Diary* Richard Rogers recalls times

> when I was not sooner risen from bedde and board but I was immed[iately] with the lorde [*sic*] in med[itation] about my self, or seeking the good of others.[822]

Underlying this practice is the central Puritan conviction of the active work of grace in the life of the soul, and thus of the importance of reflecting both on how and when grace has been at work in one's own life, and on 'redeeming the time' as St Paul commended in Ephesians 5.16.[823] It can be engaged in anywhere, though Baxter and others commend regular daily periods of meditation, preferably in solitude.[824] Thus Lewis Baily recommends, for daily evening prayers:

> Sit down a while before thou goest to bed, and consider by thy self, what memorable thing thou hast seen, heard, or read that day, more than thou sawest, heardst, or knewest before; and make the best use of them.[825]

Note the stress on profiting from personal experience. Samuel Ward's *Diary* contains much appealing reflection on his sense of personal sinfulness:

> My to [*sic*] much drinking after supper, my idle talk with Tunstal of Durham matters . . . My immoderate dyet in eating chese, very hurtful for my body att 3 oclock . . .[826] My anger att Mr. Newhouse after dinner for singing so long a Psalme, and my unwillingness to sing any.[827]

Spiritual Direction

Given their preoccupation with the way in which God manifests his election of an individual in that person's own life, it is not surprising to find Puritans attaching as much importance to spiritual direction as those in the Catholic or Anglican traditions: Puritans too stressed the role of the minister in guiding people and helping them to resolve cases of conscience:[828] John Owen spoke of the need for 'faithful watchmen' to guide the soul that is troubled at losing contact with Christ;[829] and elsewhere he stresses the importance of waiting patiently for God to act.[830] Puritan texts are full of wise guidance for the practice of the Christian spiritual life, ranging from simple apophthegms (like Lewis Bayly's 'Make not a Jest of another Man's infirmity' and 'Ever think him a true friend, who tells thee secretly and plainly of thy faults'[831]) to vast compendia of practical guidance in cases where the conscience is likely to be troubled.[832] As so often, Baxter's work is crammed with practical wisdom on this subject: 'Lothness to displease men, makes us undo them';[833] 'neglect not the due care for the health of thy body, and for the maintaining a vigorous cheerfulness in thy spirits';[834] the best way of teaching people to pray is to pray with them;[835] married couples are not to conceal the state of their souls from one another[836] and to 'join together in frequent and fervent prayer';[837] and, above all, learn to know yourself:

Labour for a constant acquaintance with yourselves, your sins and manifold wants and necessities; and also to take an actual, special notice of your case, when you go to prayer.[838]

Quaker Spirituality

The term 'Quaker' was first used in 1650: George Fox describes Justice Bennet of Derby as being the first to call his fledgling movement 'Quakers' 'because I bid them tremble at the word of the Lord';[839] and Fox himself affirms the accuracy of this derisory term.[840] Fox also describes the movement as Friends, or 'the free ministry of Jesus'.[841] But the original and more famous term is significant: this was, from the start, a movement that was radical in theory and practice.[842]

George Fox (1624–91) was the most prominent, though by no means the only, architect of Quaker piety.[843] His great colleague William Penn (1644–1718) described him as 'a man that God endued with a clear and wonderful depth, a discerner of others' spirits, and very much a master of his own',[844] and as someone with an outstanding gift for prayer: 'The inwardness and weight of his spirit, the reverence and solemnity of his address and behaviour, and the fewness and fulness of his words, have ofen struck, even strangers, with admiration'.[845] Fox was an energetic proselytizer for the movement in the manner of St Paul, criss-crossing the British isles continually for decades, enduring imprisonment and persecution, and eventually (1669) marrying a fellow-Quaker, Margaret Fell;[846] he crossed the Atlantic to the West Indies and North America, and also visited Europe.[847] His tireless itinerant ministry and organizational skills welded together groups of what might otherwise have been entirely disparate Christians: the vision he experienced on Pendle Hill in Lancashire in 1652, when he 'felt the throb of an unstoppable spiritual movement' animated all his work thereafter.[848]

The spirituality of the Quaker movement owes its origins in part to a longing, widespread at the time, to rediscover the original purity of apostolic Christianity.[849] The German spiritual writer Jakob Boehme (1575–1624) is a possible source of Fox's writings, though no direct parallels have been discerned;[850] and the notion of an invisible, gathered church, which was to become fundamental (though by no means unique) to Quakers, may be indebted to the writings of Sebastian Franck (1499–1542).[851] More generally, and characteristically, Quakers had a wide and eirenic appreciation of spiritual texts from a range of sources: thus the Quaker Robert Barclay spoke warmly of Augustine Baker's *Holy wisdom*.[852]

The Quakers incurred heavy opposition and sustained persecution from the start because they refused to pay tithes to the established church, thereby sharpening the difference between them and other dissenting communities. But there were other, theological, differences too, notably over their understanding of the church. In his Preface to Fox's *Journal*, William Penn criticizes the early Protestant reformers for being too ready to take up worldly arms and seek worldly power, and for the fact that there was too much of human invention, tradition, and art, that remained both in praying and preaching . . . especially in this kingdom, Sweden, Denmark, and some parts of Germany. God was therefore pleased among us, to shift from vessel to vessel . . .[853]

As a result, Penn believed, God 'was pleased . . . to honour and visit this benighted and bewildered nation with his glorious dayspring from on high . . . so what people had been vainly seeking without, with much pains and cost, they by this ministry found *within* . . . viz., the right way to peace with God'.[854]

This conviction of the essential interiority of the church was reinforced by Fox.[855] Like other Protestants, Quakers viewed the story of the church as a progressive degeneration from the pristine purity of the apostles.[856] Instead, Quakers stressed the gathered church: Fox writes of the first Yearly Meeting of the Society of Friends (in 1658), at which 'the Lord's power came over all, and a glorious meeting it was'.[857]

Penn sets out simply and clearly the principal doctrines of the Friends, all deriving from 'the Light of Christ within'. He sets first the need for repentance from 'dead works' to serve the living God, which must include 'a sense and godly sorrow' for one's sins.[858] This repentance leads to justification, which comprises both 'justification from the guilt of the sins that are past, as if they had never been committed, through the love and mercy of God in Christ Jesus' and 'the creature's being made inwardly just through the cleansing and sanctifying power and Spirit of Christ revealed in the soul which is commonly called sanctification':[859] the careful holding-together of the *extrinsic* process of justification with the *intrinsic* process of sanctification is noteworthy. This in turn issues in regeneration (being perfectly set free from sin, and in belief in 'eternal rewards and punishments').[860]

From these fundamental theological principles Penn and Fox drew out a number of spiritual and ethical implications. Stress on love and service of neighbour, rooted in the loving mutual support of the apostolic community, was primary;[861] and this rapidly extended to a passion for social justice.[862] A refusal to take oaths, especially oaths of allegiance, and a concomitant commitment to 'not fighting but suffering', was also primary,[863] as was their refusal to finance the national church by paying tithes.[864] The emphasis on the value of silence and solitude was also significant from the start, as was the rejection of any kind of organized ministry and the replacement of infant baptism with parental naming ceremonies:[865] in general they minimized or even avoided altogether any kind of sacramental worship, eschewing formal rites even at burial.

This doctrinal foundation was in turn based upon another distinctive Quaker belief: the conviction that God was present within every person. Thus Fox wrote

Christ [*sic*] blood being shed for every man, he tasted death for every man, and enlighteneth every man that cometh into the world; and his grace that brings salvation having appeared to all men, there is no place or language where his voice may not be heard.[866]

The presence of Christ in the believer's life is for Friends precisely his second coming, an event which they believed both to be already happening and to be imminent.[867]

As a result, the 'seed' of the Sower is an image often used by them.[868] The term might be used to denote the people of God,[869] or (as in Jesus' parable) the raw potential of humanity awaiting reaping; [870] or it might be applied to Christ, 'the Seed':

> The promise of God being to the Seed, which is one, Christ Jesus, every man and woman must come to witness this Seed, *Christ in them*, that they may be heirs of the promise.[871]

As a result Fox denied Puritan belief in double predestination,[872] though later he did write of 'the seed which the curse remains upon'.[873] More generally, the 'seed' is an image which implies growth; and Isaac Penington, another early Quaker, stressed that growth in the Christian life required that we become like children.[874]

But the central ingredient of Quaker spirituality, as with that of Puritanism in general, was the doctrine of the Holy Spirit, and the consequent stress on the primacy of spiritual experience over any kind of reason-centred, externally-constructed, faith. Fox believed that 'every [person] was enlightened by the divine light of Christ', though only those who believed in it emerged from condemnation into the light of life.[875] It is instructive that he came to believe this through a direct revelation of the Spirit: only later did he find it in scripture.[876] As we might expect, then, Quakers believed that even the wicked possess the Holy Spirit.[877] This 'light of Christ' is an essential manifestation of the Holy Spirit, and by it alone can the scriptures (or any other text) be truly understood;[878] and Fox often stresses that the gift of the Spirit is now, as it was at Pentecost, an essentially corporate one.

But the gift of the Spirit was much more than a means of enlightenment. Friends believed that God could and did vouchsafe profound spiritual experiences to any of them (indeed to anyone) at any time. In his Journal, Fox describes his profound sense of God's love for him:

> Passing from thence, I heard of a people that were in prison in Coventry for religion. And as I walked towards the jail, the word of the Lord came to me saying, 'My love was always to thee, and thou art in my love.' And I was ravished with the sense of the love of God, and greatly strengthened in my inward man. But when I came into the jail, where the prisoners were, a great power of darkness struck at me, and I sat still, having my spirit gathered into the love of God.[879]

And the Quaker Sarah Chevers, questioned by Roman Catholic inquisitors in Malta about how she knew it was the Lord who had told her go 'to over the Seas to do his Will', replied

> he bid her go, and his living presence should go with her, and he was faithful that had promised, for she did feel his living presence.[880]

It is worth noting here how the intense experience of God's love offers no insurance against an immediate sense of being assailed by the power of darkness: worth noting too that for Fox 'experience' meant more than emotion: 'he knew that in real experience the will must be involved'.[881] The Friends valued a deep personal identification with Christ in his sufferings more than eucharistic communion with him; and this identification was not only an inward one. In defending the Friends against charges of denying the reality of the Eucharist, Fox says

> Now ye that eat and drink this outward bread and wine in remembrance of Christ's death, and have your fellowships in that, will ye come no nearer to Christ's death, than to take bread and wine in remembrance of it? After ye have eaten in remembrance of his death, ye must come into his death, and die with him, as the apostles did, if ye will live with him. This is a nearer and further advanced state, to be with him in the fellowship of his death, than only to take bread and wine in remembrance of his death. You must have fellowship with Christ in his sufferings.[882]

This argument is worth noting because it controverts the charge that Quakers believed only in an interior, inward union with Christ. Indeed Penington explicitly addresses this charge:

> That charge of thine on us, that we deny the person of Christ, and make him nothing but a light or notion, a principle in the heart of man, is very unjust and untrue; for we own that appearance of him in his body of flesh, his sufferings and death, and his sitting at the Father's right hand in glory: but then we affirm, that there is no true knowledge of him, or union with him, but in the seed or principle of his life in the heart, and that *therein* he appears, subdues sin, and reigns over it, in those that understand and submit to the teaching and government of his Spirit.[883]

The point is that intellectual faith must be incarnated, or appropriated, in inward personal experience for it to have any value at all.[884] This emphasis could lead to some suspicion of intellectual study in its own right:[885] like the Puritan mystics, the Friends interpreted even the most historical parts of the Bible in terms of its impact within the individual human soul. But Isaac Penington sets out clearly its central implication:

> It is not enough to hear of Christ, or read of Christ; but this is the thing to feel him my root, my life, my foundation; and my soul engrafted into him, by him who hath power to engraft.[886]

The combination of *experience* and of *being engrafted into Christ* is striking. In another letter (to 'S. W.', 1678), Penington develops this theme, combining it with the image of the seed mentioned above: God alone sows the seed; we are to allow our hearts to be 'ploughed up by the Lord', and experience them as gardens, 'more and more enclosed, watered, dressed, and delighted in by him'.[887] When this happens 'there is an ingrafting into Christ, a being formed and new created in Christ, a living and abiding in him, and a growing and bringing forth fruit through him unto perfection' – and we can *feel* this happening within us.[888]

The Friends' attitude to prayer and worship also controverts any suggestion that their spirituality is essentially individualist. Unsurprisingly, they conceived of prayer as conducted 'in the Spirit' – spontaneous, not based on formularies,[889] and as efficacious when consisting of groans and sighs as when it is verbal.[890] Katharine Evans and Sarah Chevers told the friars who interrogated them in Malta that 'we could not pray

but as we were moved of the Lord';[891] and Mary Penington recalls the time when she
had no idea that people could pray other than by reading something out of a book.[892]
Her husband Isaac Penington wrote that

> Prayer is a gift, and he that receiveth it, must first come to the sense of his
> own inability; and so wait to receive; and perhaps begin, but with a groan
> or sigh from the true Spirit.[893]

For Penington, Christ is the true teacher of prayer, and all prayer must be according to
his leading: 'a little praying from God's spirit and in that which is true and pure is
better than thousands of vehement desires in one's own will and after the flesh';[894] 'The
troubled soul is not only to go to the Lord, but it must be taught by him *how* to go to
him. The Lord is the teacher.'[895] In another letter, and writing on prayer in families,
Penington writes

> Ye must come out of your knowledge, into the feeling of an inward princi-
> ple of life, if ever ye be restored to the true unity with God, and to the true
> enjoyment of him again. Ye must come out of the knowledge and wisdom
> ye have gathered from the Scriptures, into a feeling of the things there
> written of, as it pleaseth the Lord to open and reveal them in the hidden
> man of the heart.[896]

Here too the Friends believed they were following the example of the early apostles:

> as the apostles and saints did, so do we; we pray in secret, and we pray in
> public, as the Spirit gives us utterance, which helps our infirmities, as it did
> the apostles and true Christians; after this manner we pray for ourselves,
> and for all men both high and low.[897]

It is vital to see here that for the Friends, as for those in the Orthodox tradition,
worship is *the* primary source of spiritual growth and formation.[898]

The characteristic Quaker emphasis on the presence of God within the person,
often referred to as an 'inward principle' or 'seed', has important implications for their
attitude to suffering.[899] Fox frequently counsels his fellow-Friends to be patient in
affliction;[900] and his *Journal* includes the text of a letter he wrote to Lady Claypole,
Cromwell's daughter, when she was sick: he advises her to 'be still and cool in thy own
mind and spirit from thy own thoughts, and then thou wilt feel the principle of God
to turn thy mind to the Lord': this inner stillness and freedom from imaginations and
thoughts allows the mind to be 'stayed on God', and the person to 'feel the power of
God' and receive the wisdom of God, 'which is Christ, by which all things were made
and created, and thou wilt thereby be preserved and ordered to God's glory'.[901]
Another prominent early Quaker, James Nayler (1618–60), wrote in a letter from
Appleby prison:

> Dear hearts, you make your own troubles, by being unwilling and disobe-
> dient to that which would lead you. I see there is no way but to go hand in
> hand with him in all things, running after him without fear or consider-
> ing, leaving the whole work only to him. If he seem to smile, follow him in

fear and love; and if he seem to frown, follow him, and fall into his will, and you shall see he is yours still.[902]

Here too spirituality is much more than feeling, though it includes that: rather it has to do with focused and alert attentiveness to that interior principle of life which is God's gift to every human being. Such attentiveness is not only a priceless source of enduring strength in times of suffering: it is also the reason for the equality of all human beings, and the inspiration for the passionate Quaker concern for justice and moral reform. Quakers may be associated with silence: but this radical attention to the presence and call of God is precisely the clarion-call for action in the world; and in this respect the Quakers stand in the classic Christian tradition of contemplative prophets. There are striking similarities between the *Journal* of George Fox and the *Book* of Margery Kempe: each engaged in peripatetic ministries, each boldly denounced any who do not conform to their view of Christianity, each encountered formidable opposition virtually everywhere they went: yet each exhibited an enduring and infectious confidence which is all the more striking given their lack of ecclesiastical status or power. 'We can challenge all the world,' said George Fox:[903] and, in effect, that is exactly what he did.

Radical Spirituality

Introduction

Quakers were far from the only people to believe in a universal presence of the Holy Spirit. Consider this extract from *The light and dark sides of God* (1650), a treatise written by Jacob Bauthumley (or Bottomley):

> I see that God is in all Creatures, Man and Beast, Fish and Fowle, and every green thing, from the highest Cedar to the Ivey on the wall; and that God is the life and being of them all, and that God doth really dwell, and if you will personally; if he may admit so low an expression in them all, and hath his Being no where else out of the Creatures.[904]

Bauthumley was a Ranter, a group of antinomian Christians who believed themselves to be at one with God both morally and ontologically: sin did not exist for the believer, enabling the Ranters to indulge in behaviour which would have shocked most Christians.[905] It is almost impossible to reconstruct the sense of both exhilaration and fear which must have characterized the middle decades of the seventeenth century, when an undreamed-of freedom of belief existed: the need for clergy, sacraments, church buildings and structures, or even any but the most rudimentary form of religious authority, was abandoned; and a vast range of sects flourished, most of them enjoying a brief if spectacular efflorescence.[906] No longer did it appear necessary to many to approach God through some form of mediator: access to, and experience of, the divine was available to everyone, irrespective of learning or status. But this was no easy or tolerant pluralism: events as unprecedented as the execution of a king caused many to fear or anticipate an imminent second coming of Christ, who for many would reign in person and dispense for ever with the need for earthly monarchs.[907]

The Family of Love

There is space for only a brief reflection on three of these radical groupings.[908] The *Family of Love* was (like many of these sects) founded from the continent: Hendrik Niclaes (c.1502–c.1580) was a prosperous German merchant living in the Netherlands, one of several messianic leaders to have appeared there in the mid-sixteenth century, but the only one to have had a significant following in England.[909] Niclaes claimed to have received direct revelations from God, many of a strongly apocalyptic kind. His teaching reached England during Elizabeth's reign, or perhaps slightly earlier.[910]

Sects of this kind cannot be seen simply as direct offshoots of continental Anabaptism: the writings of Niclaes also reflect the late medieval mystical tradition both in England and on the continent, not least in their emphasis on experience and their latent anti-intellectualism.[911] Nor should they be seen as no more than a motley group of landless and uneducated folk: many English Familists (as members of the Family of Love came to be called) were prosperous merchants like Niclaes himself.[912] The Family of Love attracted sufficient public attention to be banned by royal proclamation on 3 October 1580, the only sect in Elizabethan England to be the exclusive subject of a banning order of this kind.[913] Thereafter, apart from a brief resurgence during the early years of James I, Familism waned, though Niclaes' works continued to be influential.[914]

The heart of Niclaes' spirituality is a process whereby the godly undergo a spiritual transformation or divine illumination which leads them into becoming eventually one of the 'elders': the individual becomes united with God ('godded with god'[915]), the key feature of this unity being a profound *imitatio Christi* based on an identification between the believer and Christ.[916] It is a highly interiorized, subjective process, without which (according to Niclaes) the death of Christ has little effect. The Family of Love stood out, then, by virtue of their insistence on the intimate inward union between the believer and Christ as an essential part of the process of salvation. The events at Calvary were not enough on their own:[917] hence the need for a new prophet, Niclaes.[918]

To this interior spirituality Niclaes adds a fiercely apocalyptic urgency ('we witnesse and set forth the wonderfull Acts of God, which are revealed and manifested unto us in these last daies, according to the foretelling of the Prophets'[919]) and radical expectation – salvation and honour for believers ('we may all obtain Kingly Crowns . . . and be all Priests and Kings'[920]), and doom for the reprobate.[921] Furthermore this inward union with Christ is an absolute condition of salvation,[922] as is submission to the elders of the Family of Love,[923] who alone can offer an authentic interpretation of the scriptures.[924]

In general, Niclaes' teaching on the spiritual life is vague: the true believer is to learn true godly wisdom (as opposed to the 'witty dexterity' and 'letter-learned wisdom' of the established church)[925] and

> suck also . . . all gentlenesse out of the brests [*sic*] of the Love, and seek the peace of concord. And when ye have gotten all this same, then play, sing, and praise the Lord as his little lambs, and as the sheep of his pasture, and as little children.[926]

The Behmenists

Other Familists stressed the theme of exile as an image for the life of members during this world,[927] a theme that was to reappear in the thought of many seventeenth-century radical movements, imbued with a powerful millennial sense that led them to pore over the Book of Revelation and other apocalyptic texts as a means of deciphering the strange times they lived in.[928] Some of these movements were essentially introspective, like the Behmenists, a small group of adherents of the teaching of the German spiritual writer Jakob Boehme:[929] one of his disciples, John Pordage, rector of Bradfield, wrote a *Theologia mystica* (published posthumously in 1683) and assembled around him a group of devotees to live the spiritual life as he conceived of it.[930] The group came to be known as the Behmenists, and continued for a while in London after Pordage was ejected from his living in 1654: one of its members, and easily the most interesting of the English Behmenists, was Jane Lead (1624–1704), who had the first of several visions of 'Virgin Wisdom' after the death of her husband in 1670.[931] Thereafter she devoted herself to a life of chastity, still working with Pordage: after his death she, together with other former members of Pordage's group, began to hold public meetings, calling themselves the Philadelphian Society: it attracted much public hostility, and collapsed soon after Lead's death.[932]

Boehme's work is dense, highly speculative, and shot through with astrological and alchemical theories and imagery.[933] At heart, however, he was a Lutheran: his writing is rooted in scripture, albeit subject to highly esoteric interpretation; and his spirituality is indebted to a particular strand of German Reformation thought in its emphasis on the renunciation of self-will and a turning inwards towards God.[934] He laid great stress on the need for a second, spiritual, birth; and both this and much of his rich and imaginative cosmology exerted a considerable influence on English eighteenth-century writers, notably William Law, as we shall see. What seems particularly to have attracted his small group of seventeenth-century English disciples was his notion of Sophia, or Virgin Wisdom, through which God sees the wonders of his own Trinitarian being in the form of seven 'fountain-spirits', which provide the structure of the created world and are described in detail in Boehme's early treatise *Aurora*:[935] the creation in general, and human beings in particular, are thus our point of access to the hidden God.[936] But in order to find God, and our own true identities, we must renounce self-will and be reborn spiritually[937] – though for Boehme this does not involve a monastic withdrawal from the world: indeed he stresses the importance of neighbourly love and compassion for the poor.[938]

The indebtedness of John Pordage to Boehme, and of Jane Lead to both, is unquestionable;[939] and Lead's cosmology in her *The wonders of God's creation* is clearly derived from Boehme, though she adds what appear to be original reflections of her own.[940] Lead and other English Behmenists lay great stress on the Holy Spirit, which Lead believed to have been lost to the church since Pentecost and now 'to be revived again'.[941]

But it is Boehme's notion of Virgin Wisdom, appropriated by the English Behmenists, which is perhaps of greatest interest. Pordage writes of 'Divine Wisdom' in his *Theologia mystica*, using the kind of highly visual imagery beloved of Boehme himself.[942] Jane Lead describes her visions of 'Virgin-Wisdom' (which took place first in April 1670) in *A fountain of gardens*.[943] In *The wonders of God's creation* Lead sets out at length what she understands by it:

> God created *Adam* at first to bear his own image and figure, who was to represent God himself, the High and Divine Masculine, Male and Female; so that *Adam* had his virgin in himself in imitation of his Creator, which in time was brought forth in a distinct figure. And this was a type of the Eternal Virgin Mother that lay hid in God, the Centre and Heart of Flaming Love; from whence the production of a Glorious Female Figure was brought forth; that was so commixed and mingled with Deity, as she became God's Spouse and Bride, being Spirit of his Spirit. Now be it known unto all, that from this Eternal Virgin Wisdom a new generation of Virgin spirits shall be born to make up the glory of the New *Jerusalem*, JESUS CHRIST being the head, and the first-born of this royal and princely generation, who was after the way and manner of human nature conceived in the womb of that virgin *Mary*, that was but a type of the Eternal Virgin.[944]

The speculative theology, the references to a virginal (indeed to an androgynous) Adam before the Fall, the interrelation of Wisdom, Eve, and the Virgin Mary, are all found in Boehme.[945] What is worth noting is not only Lead's determination (again from Boehme) to identify and emphasize a feminine dimension of God's own nature, but her application of this to the contemporary church: in her *Second message to the Philadelphian Society* she conceives of the church as a virginal community, describing it later in the same work as the 'new modelled church', perhaps the spiritual equivalent of Cromwell's famous army. Within it there are to be

> spiritual fathers and spiritual mothers, which will be true fathers and mothers indeed, in this church of the first born, that shall generate and bring forth births in the Spirit and after the will of God.[946]

And she tells her companions that they are to be deified, transformed into pure musical instruments on which the Holy Spirit can play 'Triumphant Sounds, and teach such new Lessons as have not hitherto been understood'.[947] On 2 January 1682 God told her

> that *those who were taken into the Glory, had finished their inward Transformation, to the utmost Perfection, waiting only for the Confirmation of the Nuptial Glory*.[948]

In Paradise there will be no distinction between male and female, 'though the Typical Priesthood admitted none but Males in its day: All of that is done away . . . Male and Female are alike here'.[949] Lead was well aware of St Paul's strictures upon the place of women within the church; but for her, as for Margery Kempe, she had no option but to declare what had been revealed to her: 'Christ being my head-covering, I have both commission and munition-strength, upon which I shall proceed, and go forward'.[950] Her society might have been short-lived; but both its aims and its name were significant: the Philadelphians stood for spiritual renewal and internationalism in a turbulent and sectarian age.[951]

Gerrard Winstanley and the Diggers

Other sects were as much concerned with this world as with the next; and of these one of the most interesting was a group that came to be known as the Diggers. Their founder, Gerrard Winstanley, was born in Lancashire in 1609, and is unlikely to have had more than a rudimentary education: much of his early life is unknown, though he may have been a tradesman in the cloth industry before launching his political programme in 1649.[952] Winstanley was one of many who could not find spiritual fulfilment in any organized religious body: he described his mystical revelation from God, which he took to be self-authenticating, in *The new law of righteousness*, written at the same time as he and William Everard were bringing together a small group of poor men at St George's Hill in Surrey, with the intention of digging and cultivating the common land for the benefit of the poor. The Diggers were variously arrested and released, before the movement finally collapsed in the spring of 1650.

Winstanley's mysticism has been variously seen – either as a cloak for political revolution or an immature and secondary stage in his thought (as with, e.g., C. Hill). Thus, although the famous digging experiment has been interpreted as straightforward political radicalism, for Winstanley it was the outworking, within a community of like-minded people, of a shared experience of the Spirit:[953] Winstanley's political actions were derived from his intense religious experience and the conclusions he drew from it.[954]

Winstanley describes God as 'the incomprehensible spirit, Reason'.[955] He appears to call God 'reason' because he discerns a purpose of some kind in everything that happens.[956] Only when a person 'feels and sees, by experience' God as Spirit ruling as king over his or her flesh, however, can God be proclaimed and believed in: until that time the believer must simply 'wait upon him till he teach thee'.[957] Winstanley defines the Spirit thus:

> The spirit of the Father is pure Reason: which as he made, so he knits the whole creation together into a one-nesse of life and moderation; every creature sweetly in love lending their hands to preserve each other, and so upholds the whole fabrique.[958]

Reason, then, is the simple sensation of God, whereas Spirit represents the effects of that sensation on others.[959] In common with most other radicals, Winstanley argues that the Spirit is not restricted to the scholarly,[960] nor to the written scriptures, which are only testimony to the fact that the Spirit was poured out:[961] personal experience, not written authority, is primary.

It is also not surprising to find Winstanley maintaining that 'a Christ within is thy Saviour':[962] we know that Christ dwells in us by the testimony of the Spirit, for which however we have to be prepared to wait.[963] Less common is Winstanley's doctrine of redemption: he argues that Christ purified the whole of creation through his death: by lying dead within the earth, he redeemed the corruption of the created order, and now through his Spirit 'drawes up Sonnes and daughters; yea, the whole Creation into himselfe'.[964] Nonetheless, 'every creature in its place, and stature, is a son to the Father'.[965]

Winstanley maintains that both the first (fallen) Adam and the second (Christ) are visibly present in every human being, and shall be so until the end of time:[966] the first Adam is manifested in greedy landlords;[967] and the poor are to await with patience the time when the 'Law of Righteousnesse draws up all in himself'.[968] The second Adam (Christ) is in every creature that exists too, present in our poverty or our experience of persecution.[969] Thus there is war within us:

> In every condition you are in, this law of the Spirit meets with the powers of your own flesh fretting and fighting against him: For envy, froward-nesse, self-love, covetousnesse are the power of darkness in you, that fights against the Spirit, that sweetly seeks the preservation and peace of all. But that opposing power in you is the devil, serpent and power of dark-nesse, which Christ the power of light, rising up in you, will destroy; and so *mortality shall be swallowed up of life.*[970]

The crucial thing is for human beings to realize this; to name the two warring powers within us, and to decide whose side we are on;[971] for the presence of the old Adam within us does not allow us any determinist fatalism or complacency:

> when a man fals, let him not blame a man that died 6000 years ago, but blame himself, even the powers of his own flesh, which lead him astray; for this is *Adam* that brings a man to misery.[972]

It is striking to note Winstanley's rejection of the Augustinian view of original sin:

> This Law of darknesse in the members is not the state of Nature; for nature, or the living soule is in bondage to it, and grones under it, waiting to be delivered from it, and is glad to heare of a Savioure. Looke upon a childe that is new borne, or till he growes up to some few yeares, he is innocent, harmelesse, humble, patient, gentle, easie to be entreated, not envious; And this is *Adam*, or mankinde in his Innocency; and this continues till outward objects intice him to pleasure, or seeke content without him.[973]

But the spiritual struggle is not only an interior one: it concerns justice in society as well. A person 'walks righteously' when he or she acts justly towards fellow human beings, living 'in the knowledge and love of the Father, seeing the Father in every creature', and exercising his or her 'spiritual senses' so as to be able to do this, and to live 'in love and cheerfull obedience to the Spirit'.[974]

Like that of all radical sects in the period, Winstanley's thought is uncompromis-ingly future-oriented: he predicts the end of wars, violence, privilege and wealth, because the earth is the Lord's, and

> as the inclosures are called such a mans Land, and such a mans Land; so the Commons and Heath, are called the common-peoples, and let the world see who labours the earth in righteousnesse, and those to whom the Lord gives the blessing, let them be the people that shal [*sic*] inherit the earth.[975]

Winstanley's writings are suffused with an intense expectancy: the restoration of creation under the 'new law of righteousnes' is already under way:[976] it will bring with it an end to all bondage and poverty ('That al man-kinde ought to have a quiet substance and freedome, to live upon earth; and that there shal be no bond-man nor begger [sic] in all his holy mountaine'[977]).

All this has important implications for Winstanley's understanding of prayer, which is integrally related to the search for justice. He says that prayer is that means by which we seek 'to pay the king of righteousnesse his due',[978] by which he means that every person should 'act according to the creation of a man, which is to do righteously to all fellow creatures'.[979] Prayer is thus concerned with justice and right actions, with regard both to the interior struggle within the self (in, say, avoidance of gluttony) and to one's relations with one's fellow creatures ('use the labour of your cattell with Reason . . . doe to men and women, as you would have them doe to you').[980]

Furthermore, prayer 'lies in the Reasonings of the heart':[981] that is, in a rigorous self-examination in order to see whether one's actions conform to one's prayers:

> Words and actions going together are the declaration of a sincere heart; but words in prayer, without acting according to creation, as the generall practise is, are declarations of hypocriticall and deceived flesh: let his profession be what it will be.[982]

In this context, the specific words used in prayer are 'the remotest part of prayer', since words are valueless unless they issue in right actions, and so should be 'few and faithfull'.[983]

What is especially notable in Winstanley's spirituality is its firmly corporate nature: all humanity forms Christ's mystical body;[984] and the appearance of many different kinds of worship and religious customs is for him only a sign of the gradual return of all creation to true worship of the Father in spirit and truth: 'that is, to walk righteously in the Creation'.[985] But even more impressive is his conviction that the entire cosmos is both fallen with Adam and redeemed with Christ: he had a strong sense of the intimate relationship between God, humanity and all other creatures, which appears regularly in his writings, and is rooted, loosely but unmistakably, in the theology of St Paul's Letter to the Romans. His writing is intensely biblical, the exegesis highly personal and sometimes extremely odd.[986] Yet the fierce integrity of his works is palpable, with the clear single-minded vigour of an Old Testament prophet:

> This is the shame and misery of our age, That every one professes Christ and the spirit, and they will preach of, and pray to the Spirit; And yet they know not inwardly, by what spirit or inward power they are ruled; Every one lookes upon a God and a ruler without him, as the Beast of the field does, few sees their Ruler within.[987]

> These professors will still confine Christ to a private chamber, and to particular bodies, and restraine him, who is the universall power of Love and peace. They owne him in words, but they denie him in power; they worship God at a distance, not knowing where he is, nor what they

worship; And they call this blasphemie, to say Christ is in you, though the Scriptures which they professe say the same . . . Love your enemies, and doe as you would be done by, in actions and not in words only.[988]

Conclusion

Puritanism has often been accused by its detractors, both contemporary and modern, as pervasively gloomy because fatalist: you were either elected or not, and you could do nothing whatever to alter the fact. It was a charge the Puritans themselves were aware of; and no one did more to controvert it than arguably the greatest of all Puritan theologians, Richard Baxter. He vigorously exhorted his fellow-Christians to be cheerful, for 'there is more matter of delight in the face and love of God, than in all the things in the world besides'. And, in a moment of piercing vision, he declared that

> the very business of a Christian's life and God's service, is rather taken to be scrupling, quarrelling, and vexing ourselves and the church of God, than to be in love and gratitude, and a delighting our souls in God, and cheerfully obeying him. And thus when Christianity seems a thraldom and torment; and the service of the world, the flesh, and the devil, seems the only freedom, and quiet, and delight, no wonder if the devil have more unfeigned servants than Christ . . . God calls men from vexation and vanity, to high delights and peace . . . O what blessed lives might God's people live, if they understood the love of God in the mystery of man's redemption, and did addict themselves to the consideration and improvement of it, and did believingly eye the promised glory, and hereupon did make it the business of their lives to delight their souls in him that hath loved them! And what a wonderful success might we expect to our preaching, if the holy delights and cheerful obedience of the saints did preach, as clearly to the eyes of the world, as we preach loudly to their ears.[989]

Here is Puritan spirituality at its best, as relevant today as when it was first written. But Stachniewski's question remains: how easy was it for the godly to practise 'cheerful obedience' when anxious doubts about their own election, and the terrible possibility of predestined damnation, remained?[990] Certainly Hannah Allen, one of the few women writers to appear here, would have found it hard to share Baxter's vision. And there are other difficulties too: the piety of the Puritans, for all Baxter's warmth, is exclusively (and designedly) word-centred, lacking the colour and diversity of materials found in its late medieval Catholic equivalent. Godliness can elide too easily with smugness; the stress on interior experience of the Spirit can be subtly subverted into elitism; the high moral seriousness can eventually become wearisome, unrelenting, even dull.

Yet it would be unfair to end on such a note. There is a prophetic fire, as well as an inward warmth, about Puritan spirituality; and the emphasis on predestination allows the least and the lowliest in secular terms to become priests and kings. God may be grim and fearsome at times; but he never forsakes his own, and is as capable of dethroning the powerful and sustaining the poor as he was in the Magnificat or the preaching of Amos. Furthermore, because those he has called are his *children*, not his servants, they can challenge him boldly, and all the world in his name. Nor is Puritan thought nearly as narrowly exclusive as is sometimes supposed: not all Christians, now or then, would agree with Tyndale in declaring that 'I am bound to love the Turk with all my might and power; yea, and above my power, even from the ground of my heart, after the ensample that Christ loved me';[991] and any tempted to accuse Puritans of arrogance should read John Smyth's *Retractation*, his last (and probably unfinished) work, which breathes a spirit of eirenic generosity and regret for earlier intolerance that could be profitably studied by many Christians today.[992]

Puritanism faded after the Restoration in 1662; and of the radicals only the Quakers endured.[993] Yet the stress on choice and on a personal commitment of faith; the emphasis on a pilgrim people who devote their lives to practical holiness as a grateful response to all that God in Christ has done for them; the recognition that not even scripture can ultimately bind a God who must always remain free from human (even ecclesiastical) control – all these and many other features of Puritan spirituality may speak eloquently to an uncertain, mobile and pluralist age. William Tyndale's stirring challenge to his fellow-Christians from a century earlier may breathe the air of controversy; but that, given his tragic life, is scarcely surprising; and, long after the battles he fought are over, the power and vision that sustained him remains:

> And remember that Christ is the end of all things. He only is our resting-place, and he is our peace . . . Thou shalt never have rest in thy soul . . . till thou come at Christ . . . If thou trust in thy works, there is no rest. Thou shalt think, I have not done enough. Have I done it with so great love as I should do? Was I so glad in doing, as I would be to receive help at my need? I have left this or that undone; and such like. If thou trust in confession, then shalt thou think, Have I told all? Have I told all the circumstances? Did I repent enough? Had I as great sorrow in my repentance for my sins, as I had pleasure in doing them? Likewise in our holy pardons and pilgrimages gettest thou no rest. For thou seest that the very gods themselves, which sell their pardon so good cheap, or some whiles give them freely for glory sake, trust not therein themselves . . . As pertaining to good deeds therefore, do the best thou canst, and desire God to give strength to do better daily; but in Christ put thy trust . . . And the God of all mercy give thee grace so to do, unto whom be glory for ever! Amen.[994]

INDIVIDUAL STUDIES

The King's Good Servant: Thomas More (1478–1535)

Introduction

Thomas More, Lord Chancellor of England and canonized saint, stands in a long tradition of aristocratic sanctity, and in particular of those who found the conflict between secular status and spiritual integrity irresolvable other than by drastic action.[995] But he was more than a statesman and a saint: he was also a lawyer, a layperson, a family man, a career politician, an historian, a humanist, a poet, a fierce controversialist, an ascetic, a martyr, and a wit. As if all that were not enough, his early works reflect a capacity for severe melancholy and even for cynicism, and reveal tensions which underlie the complexities of this extraordinary man.

There was, first of all, the tension between the lover of Carthusian asceticism on the one hand, and of the humanist learning of Erasmus on the other, a tension which is explicit in More's early *Life of John Picus*: the latter, whose real name was Giovanni Pico della Mirandola, was a Renaissance figure who, like More, struggled to hold together humanist and monastic values.[996] During his mid-twenties More was simultaneously pursuing a legal career and adopting ascetic devotions at the London Charterhouse:[997] it is almost as though he already realized what he felt to be the only legitimate spiritual ideal for the devout Catholic, while also recognizing his certain inability ever to attain it.[998] He may well have been influenced in this regard by his confessor, John Colet, Dean of St Paul's Cathedral and a rigorously ascetic man.[999]

Then there was the tension between the private and the public More, the family man and the furious polemicist. We shall return to this subject below; but with regard to the former it is worth recalling now the heightened sense of the self which Renaissance humanism fostered, together with the growing interest within Catholic circles of formulating patterns of piety explicitly designed for people in public life.[1000]

The latter is more complex. In 1520 Luther challenged the church with his *De captivitate Babylonica ecclesiae* (The Babylonian Captivity of the Church), to which Henry VIII himself responded.[1001] Luther answered this with a ferocious attack on Henry;[1002] and it was this second work to which More was either asked or volunteered to reply. But More's *Responsio ad Lutherum* is a depressing mix of routine theology and violent personal abuse;[1003] and his later, even more massive, diatribe against Tyndale (the *Confutacyon of Tyndales answere*, 1532–3) is if anything even more legalistic and malevolent in tone.[1004] It may well be, as modern scholars have noted, that More was so acutely conscious of the tension between good and evil that existed within himself and (in his view) every other Christian that he denounced with all the ability he could command the Protestant notion of an absolute disjunction between the elect and the fallen, the 'pure' church and the *massa damnata*.[1005] And could there also be an anger born of the frustration caused by being drawn ineluctably into disputes he would have preferred to avoid?[1006] Whatever the explanation, it would be more profitable to remember only More's own conclusion to his attack on Luther:

> My most earnest prayer is that I may sometime see the day in which all
> mortals will cast aside both these trifles of mine and all the insane heresies
> of that fellow [Luther], so that, with the pursuit of the worst things con
> signed to oblivion, with the incitements to railing buried, and the memory
> of contentions wiped out, the serene light of faith may shine into souls,
> sincere piety and truly Christian harmony may return; and I pray that He
> who came into the world to bring peace from heaven may one day bring
> back and restore that harmony to the world.[1007]

Thirdly, there was the tension between the humorist and the martyr. Some commentators have seen this as characteristic of the true saint, for whom the grim realities of this world are happily transient in the light of the next.[1008] But More's humour is intensely this-worldly and satirical, and bubbles irrepressibly throughout his work: thus in *Utopia* he tells us that

> They [the Utopians] have priests of exceeding holiness and therefore very few . . . The priests, unless they be women (for that kind is not excluded from priesthood, howbeit few are chosen, and none but widows and old women), the men priests, I say, take to their wives the chiefest women in all their country.[1009]

And it appears that he himself decided to omit from the *De tristitia Christi* (one of the works he wrote in the Tower) a sentence in which, commenting on St Peter's action in cutting off Malchus's ear without waiting to hear an answer to his question 'Shall we strike with the sword?', More had written 'just as mendicant friars ask the bishop's permission to preach but go ahead and preach anyway even before they have gotten it'.[1010] This is not the humour of a St Francis: its presence here, in one of More's last works, suggests that it represents an aspect of his character that was never fully integrated with the rest,[1011] though we should remember that More's combination of scholarship, rhetoric, religious devotion, virulent polemic, and sharp wit is entirely typical of other Renaissance writers, among them More's own friend Erasmus.[1012]

More was born in 1478, the son of a judge;[1013] and he himself became a brilliantly successful lawyer: indeed it is precisely his qualities as a lawyer which are reflected in the verve and vituperation of his anti-Protestant polemics.[1014] He rose steadily in Henry VIII's court, succeeding Wolsey as Lord Chancellor in 1529, but resigned in 1532, thereafter engaging in his literary battles with Tyndale. Though willing to swear fidelity to the Act of Succession, More refused to take any oath which might impugn the pope's authority or justify the royal divorce: he was therefore imprisoned in the Tower in 1534, indicted of high treason, found guilty, and beheaded in 1535. He was canonized in 1935.

The spirituality of Thomas More

The heart of More's spirituality is found in his 'Tower works', composed during his final imprisonment; and it is in these that one senses someone discovering, as though for the first time, a faith that goes far deeper than polemic. What is fascinating about these works is their lack of personal introspection: it is as though More encounters, in his exploration of Christ's suffering, the surest possible means of coping with his own. Thus his *Dialogue of comfort against tribulation* stands in the classical tradition of St Paul, Boethius and others; and his *De tristitia Christi* (The Grief of Christ), far from being an explicitly autobiographical work written in the shadow of execution, is more like a collection of sophisticated essays. But we should not be deceived: this approach represents the epitome of Renaissance classicism, in which private emotion is articulated precisely through public rhetoric: in later centuries Mozart will reveal himself as surely as More does, through the form and restraint of the string quartet or concerto.

And it is exactly this restraint which makes the conclusion of the *De tristitia* all the more moving: it ends, not with a personal expression of faith, but with the noble words of Psalm 119: *tribulatio et angustia invenerunt me: mandata tua meditatio mea est* (Trouble and anguish have taken hold of me: but your commandments are my delight).[1015]

Spirituality and ecclesiology

This points to an important dimension of More's spirituality: his emphasis on the church, its shared truth and common life. His reverence for the Carthusians was not uncritical;[1016] and in *Utopia* we are given a vital clue to his priorities: in that country,

> the people and the priest together rehearse solemn prayers in words expressly pronounced, so made that every man may privately apply to himself that which is commonly spoken of all.[1017]

Hence his preference for the form and language of scripture and his deep reverence for the Eucharist:[1018] hence too his passionate hatred of those who, like Henry VIII and (in his view) Luther and Tyndale, opted for their own interests rather than submitting to the truth: heresy (from the Greek *hairesis*, the act of choosing for oneself) horrified More as it had John Fisher, because it subverted the unity and authority of the Church at the whim of the individual.[1019] For More, as for the twentieth-century Pope John Paul II, religious truth was nothing if not universal, catholic, all-embracing; and in the light of the church's overriding obligation to save souls, teach the faith, and serve the poor, tolerance of individual dissent was at best an indulgent luxury and at worst a challenge to the rich mutual interdependence of the entire system.[1020]

More and the spirituality of the Psalms

More's deeply Catholic spirituality is best illustrated by reference to his use of the Psalms, which for him (as, ironically, for Luther and many great Protestants) represented one of the most precious and enduring jewels of scripture.[1021] One of his Tower works (the *Imploratio divini auxilii contra tentationem*, or 'Prayer for divine help against temptation'), is a cento of psalm-texts fashioned into a single coherent prayer; and both this and More's own prayer book (consisting of a book of hours and psalter) need to be studied together with the Latin marginalia written by More alongside the texts he chose.[1022] The verses in the *Imploratio* are chosen from a number of Psalms (between Psalm 3 and Psalm 67), and include the whole of the great lament Psalms 38 and 39, and the passionate articulation of longing for God that forms Psalm 42.[1023] The unexpected conclusion with Psalm 67 could be another example of More's deliberate identification of his own prayer and personal situation with that of the whole church.[1024]

Some of More's choice of psalm-texts reveal the violent changes of mood to which he, imprisoned on a capital charge, must have been subject. Thus the vivid expressions of hope in Psalms 16.8–9 and 18.30–31 are immediately followed by the despair of Psalm 22.6–7 ('I have set the Lord always before me: he is at my right hand and I shall not fail . . . with the help of my God I can leap a city wall. But as for me I am a worm and no man . . .').[1025] In his own Prayer Book, More has written alongside verses

12–20 of Psalm 38 ('My friends and my neighbours have approached and stood against me . . .') the words:

> A meek man ought to behave in this way during tribulation; he should neither speak proudly himself nor retort to what is spoken wickedly, but should bless those who speak evil of him and suffer willingly, either for justice's sake if he has deserved it or for God's sake if he has deserved nothing.[1026]

And he has written against the beautiful opening verses of Psalm 84 ('How lovely is your dwelling place: O Lord God of hosts!') the words 'a prayer of someone who is imprisoned, or of one who lies sick in bed, yearning to go to church, or of any faithful person who yearns for heaven'.[1027]

More's predilection in his spiritual writings for expressing his inmost convictions not in personal prayers but in psalms and other liturgical formularies confirms Kenny's view that More does not put self first in opposing the King; rather, he sets fidelity to the law of God above his or anyone else's inclinations.[1028] This is not, of course, a *suppression* of self: it is an *articulation* of self.[1029]

The theology and practice of prayer

None of this makes prayer easy: exactly the opposite is true. In the *De tristitia* More several times stresses the importance of attentiveness in prayer,[1030] and asks whether it is surprising that God refuses to take our prayer seriously when it is so obvious that we don't do so ourselves:[1031] we should persevere in our prayers even if we do not obtain what we ask, mindful that Christ in Gethsemane did not obtain what he wanted either;[1032] for prayer is a costly conformity to God's will, entrusting the whole outcome to him.[1033] Furthermore, it is precisely the unity of the church in common obedience to the truth that demands of Christians an active concern for those threatened by seemingly distant enemies such as the Turks:

> Whenever we see such things or hear that they are beginning to happen, however far away, let us think that this is no time for us to sit and sleep but rather to get up immediately and bring relief to the danger of others in whatever way we can, by our prayers at least if there is no other way.[1034]

It is important to see that sincerity and integrity in prayer are as important for More as they are for (say) Latimer, commending his cobbler's godliness: both condemn what they perceive as mindless or formulaic repetition. In another of his works, More points out that the prayers of Christ in the depths of his Passion were the holiest he ever spoke:

> And these prayers of our Saviour at his bitter passion and of his holy martyrs in the intensity of their torment shall serve to make us see that there is no prayer made at leisure so strong and effectual as in tribulation.[1035]

And the prayers of Gethsemane form a constant reference point for true Christian piety:

I wish that sometime we would make a special effort, right after finishing our prayers, to run over in our minds the whole sequence of time we spent praying. What follies will we see there? How much absurdity, and sometimes even foulness will we catch sight of? Indeed we will be amazed that it was at all possible for our minds to dissipate themselves in such a short time among so many places at such great distance from each other, among so many different affairs, such various, such manifold, such idle pursuits.[1036]

More and the Carthusians: spirituality and martyrdom

More's preoccupation with the suffering Christ is, like much of his spirituality, late-medieval in tone: for him, as for Erasmus, mere contemplation of the Passion in words or paintings was not enough unless it led to an uncompromising identification of the person with Christ. Here is the other dimension of More's seeming displacement of self: he finds his own deepest meaning not only by submitting himself to the forms of liturgical prayer, but by conforming himself to the life of the suffering Jesus.

But this did not lead More to some glad embracing of a martyr's death, even though he was certainly profoundly affected by both the courage and the horrifying suffering of the monks from the London Charterhouse, the first of whom (including the prior, St John Houghton), were hung, drawn and quartered at Tyburn on 4 May 1535.[1037] In his De tristitia More wonders why it is that Christ should have been filled with fear in Gethsemane when most early Christian martyrs appear to have gone joyfully to their deaths.[1038] He concludes that Christ's fear should both dissuade those over-eager for martyrdom and comfort those fearful of it,[1039] provided we make his prayer and experience our own.[1040] And, if we do so, we may also experience the striking transformation in Christ from the anguish of his solitary prayer to the boldness of his confrontation with Caiaphas' soldiers:[1041] it is exactly both of these together that comprise the spirituality of the martyr.

Here, ironically, More is strikingly close to Hugh Latimer, who makes a complementary point: bravery in the face of death need not imply authentic martyrdom, since 'our Saviour Christ was afraid of death himself';[1042] and death is a terrifying experience even for the elect.[1043] Christ did not die so that we need not do so, but precisely in order to give us courage to do the same:

> He did not suffer, to discharge us clean from death, to keep us clean from it, not to taste of it. Nay, nay, you must not take it so. We shall have the beholding of this ugsome [sic] face every one of us; we shall feel it ourselves. Yet our Saviour Christ did suffer, to the intent to signify to us that death is overcomeable.[1044]

And More maintains that we are not expected to rush headlong into martyrdom, since Christ himself encouraged us to avoid it if we can (cf. Matthew 10.23); but we should not avoid it either if by doing so we deny Christ and thereby forfeit eternal life:

it must be stressed again and again that no one should pray to escape danger so absolutely that he would not be willing to leave the whole matter up to God, ready in all obedience to endure what God has prepared for him.[1045]

More noted, as he awaited his own doom, that Christ's suffering was the consequence of his *anticipation* of what lay ahead,[1046] and commends those who 'go on in spite of their fearful anxiety and face the terrible prospect [of martyrdom] out of love for Christ',[1047] for 'almost all of us are fearful in the face of death'.[1048]

What More is seeking to do is to find spiritual sustenance from the freely-embraced suffering and sacrifice of Christ in order to cope, and to help others cope, with that suffering and those sacrifices over which we have no control at all.[1049] He expresses this graphically in another work, his *Treatise upon the Passion*:[1050]

> And here it is good to consider, that as our Saviour knew when he should die . . . and yet nevertheless diligently performed those things that he had to do before his death, albeit he might have deferred his death until whatever time he wanted, and have done in the meantime everything at ease and leisure, how much need have we poor wretched who will die before we want to, and cannot tell when, but peradventure this very day, what need have we, I say, to make haste about those things that we must do, so that we may have nothing left undone when we are suddenly sent for and must go? For when death comes, the dreadful mighty messenger of God, no king can command him, no authority constrain him, no riches hire him, to delay past his appointed time one moment of an hour. Therefore let us consider well in time, what words we are bound to speak, and what deeds we are bound to do, and say them, and do them apace; and leave unsaid and undone all superfluous things, and even more all damnable things, knowing well that we have no empty time allowed to us for them.[1051]

This approach, unsurprisingly, marks his last work, the *Devout prayer* almost certainly composed just before his death. It includes a prayer to be freed from 'all appetite of revenging',[1052] and this request:

> Good Lord, give me the grace in all my fear and agony to have recourse to that great fear and wonderful agony, that you my sweet Saviour had at the mount of Olivet before your most bitter passion, and in meditating on it to conceive spiritual comfort and consolation profitable for my soul.[1053]

Conclusion

We should not be surprised to find in these last works the best of More: medieval Catholic piety, Renaissance rhetoric and style, scriptural devotion pierced with shafts of the old mordant wit, imitation of Christ and submission to a higher Law – the latter representing the last great decision of this brilliant legal mind.[1054] It is no surprise either to find that More's *Dialogue of comfort against tribulation* should have sustained his Protestant opponent Thomas Cranmer while he himself awaited death.[1055] But what is so desperately tragic is to find in all these men – More and Fisher, Cranmer, Latimer, and Tyndale – the same mix of frenzied vitriol and passionate devotion, the same identification with the suffering Christ, the same spirituality in the face of the imminent and horrible deaths each sought to inflict upon the other, the same terror honestly acknowledged and bravely embraced, the same hope in everlasting life, the same submission to the overriding dictates of the truth as they perceived it: *tribulatio et angustia invenerunt me: mandata tua meditatio mea est.*

Shaking the Foundations: John Bunyan (1628–88)

Introduction

Of all the figures to appear in this most crowded chapter of the history of English spirituality, John Bunyan's is the most widely known; and his famous allegory *The pilgrim's progress* has become one of the classic texts of English literature. Yet in the context of Christian spirituality he has still not received the attention he deserves. Louis Bouyer devotes one page to him in his study of Orthodox, Protestant, and Anglican spirituality: he declares that *The pilgrim's progress* is 'childish and tedious and has contributed not a little to Puritanism's reputation as being the quintessence of boredom'.[1056] Martin Thornton's *English spirituality* does not mention him at all. He receives only the slightest of attention in the more recent *World spirituality* series.[1057] And, two centuries ago, Lord Macaulay dismissed Bunyan's autobiographical work *Grace abounding to the chief of sinners* with these words:

> It is a full and open confession of the fancies which passed through the mind of an illiterate man, whose affections were warm, whose nerves were irritable, whose imagination was ungovernable, and who was under the influence of the strongest religious excitement.[1058]

It is George Bernard Shaw who gets closer than any of them to the heart of the matter; in a letter to Max Beerbohm he explains his inability to appreciate the elegant stylist Walter Pater:

> The reason Bunyan reached such a pitch of mastery in literary art . . . whilst poor Pater could never get beyond a nerveless amateur affectation . . . was that it was life or death with the tinker to make people understand his message and see his vision, whilst Pater had neither message nor vision and only wanted to cultivate style . . . Pater took a genteel walk up Parnassus: Bunyan fled from the wrath to come: that explains the difference in their pace and in the length they covered.[1059]

We know little of Bunyan's early life;[1060] but he does tell us that he used to enjoy 'drinking, dancing, playing, pleasure with the wicked ones of the world'.[1061] Bunyan was born in 1628 in Bedfordshire, a stronghold of religious and political dissent:[1062] his father was moderately poor and illiterate, though he sent his son to school:[1063] later, Bunyan was to boast of not having had a classical education, because the lack of it made him more dependent on scripture and experience.[1064] A tinker by trade, Bunyan

served in the parliamentary army from 1644 until 1647, when he returned to a Bedfordshire ablaze with religious and political controversy and an unprecedented
freedom of thought and debate.[1065] Yet within a few years this ferment of
undreamed-of possibilities for the poor was gradually to be replaced by the old dominance of aristocracy and gentry. In 1655 Bunyan became a member of a separatist
congregation in Bedford, and was soon active as a preacher, his first and favourite
ministry.[1066] But after the Restoration Bunyan's position outside the established
church became impossible: he refused to submit, was imprisoned in 1661 and (apart
from a short period in 1666) remained in prison until 1672. He spent the rest of his
life either preaching or again in prison (1676–7) until James II's Declaration of Indulgence in 1687 suspended penal laws against all dissenters.

The formative influences on his life, then, are clear: the brief but thrilling period in
English life when those who could not accept established Christianity were given their
head; the suffering and subsequent disappointment of so many among the poor; his
own long imprisonment, which deeply affected his thought;[1067] the atmosphere of
alternating fear and widespread acclaim in which he preached; and, above all else, the
huge uncertainties that gnawed at him and at so many others: what must I do to be
saved?[1068] His abiding relevance consists both in his incessant concern with this
question, and with his discovery, at once fleeting and transforming, that he was loved
even – indeed precisely – as he was.[1069]

Bunyan's conversion

Bunyan's religious conversion was really a lifelong process: *Grace abounding* reflects his
awareness of God's providential guidance in his early life in a manner not dissimilar
from that of Augustine's *Confessions*,[1070] as well as qualities often associated with the
Puritan notion of 'preparation': 'a very great softness and tenderness of heart' and 'a
great bending in my mind to a continual meditating' on scripture.[1071] Like Augustine,
Bunyan's progress towards a full Christian faith was as much social as personal, deeply
influenced by friends and by fellow Christians in the Bedford congregation:[1072] like
Augustine again, Bunyan never altogether achieved the inner assurance and definitive
certainty for which he longed so much.[1073]

Bunyan wrote a great deal, much of it directly arising out of his preaching ministry
and addressing specific theological controversies in which he was involved. In general
terms, it is true to say that his earlier, more confident and often highly polemical,
theology was gradually replaced by a more introspective tone: with the slow erosion of
hopes in an enduring political and religious transformation of England, Christians
like Bunyan began to take refuge in a more inward, but still markedly political,
eschatology.[1074]

Spirituality and the covenant

We need to begin this brief exploration of Bunyan's spirituality with his theology of
the covenant, a coping-stone of Calvinist thought.[1075] The first covenant (the
'covenant of works', summarized in the Ten Commandments) was between God and
Adam:[1076] Bunyan compared it to 'ten great guns', because its primary aim was to

convince humanity of sin, and of its need for the second covenant (the 'covenant of grace').[1077] This second covenant had nothing directly to do with humanity: it was a covenant between Christ and the Father, 'before man was in being'.[1078] Christ offered himself as a sacrifice to appease the wrath of God by taking upon himself the sins of Adam and his posterity. In an early work Bunyan describes this covenant thus:

> God having thus purposed in himself that he would save some of them that by transgression had destroyed themselves, did with the everlasting son of his love make an agreement, or bargain, that upon such and such terms, he would give him a company of such poor soules as had by transgression fallen from their own innocency and uprightnesse, into those wicked inventions that they themselves had sought out [Ecclesiastes 7.29]. The agreement also how this should be, was made before the foundation of the world was laid [Titus 1.2] . . . Now this promise, or covenant, was made with none but with the Son of God, the Saviour.[1079]

Note the reference to 'bargain': this mercantile language may have had a particular appeal to those unaccustomed to theological niceties.[1080] This second covenant could be said to represent Protestant theology in its most extreme form, in the sense that the process by which we are saved is absolutely extrinsic to anything we do or are: it is grounded not on our obedient response, but entirely on the utterly free and gratuitous love of God,[1081] which is constantly being conveyed to us through Jesus' intercession as priest at God's right hand, through which souls are won and those already won are 'preserved'.[1082] Human participation in the process of salvation is non-existent: we are saved or damned by decisions taken in the heart of God, entirely independently of us.[1083]

This uncompromising theology has some significantly positive implications. It means that salvation has nothing to do with status or attendance at church or even with evident holiness of life. It means too that those most acutely conscious of their ignorance or sin are more open to the gift of God's free love than those who may covertly believe they deserve it.[1084] It appealed most of all to those who had little to look forward to in this life, and even less once the restoration of the monarchy doomed Puritan hopes of a new social order. So the true church subverts worldly order (and even that of the established church):

> This place, as *Hospitals*, will entertain
> Those which the lofty of this World *disdain*:
> The *Poor*, the *Lame*, the *Maimed*, *Halt* and *Blind*,
> The *Leprous*, and *Possessed* too, may find
> Free welcome here, as also such relief
> As ease them will of Trouble, Pain and Grief.[1085]

Bunyan himself tells us that the effect of the covenant of grace is that 'the divine nature is conveyed from heaven into [the elect]' and 'the human nature . . . is received up, and entertained in, and hath got possession of heaven'.[1086] 'All who go to heaven will be kings and be crowned'.[1087] Holiness, the spiritual life of the elect, is our response to what God in Christ has done for us.[1088] And what he has done for us is unimaginably costly:

Christ . . . died, or endured the Wages of Sin, and that without an Intercessor, without one between God and he: He grappled immediatly [sic] with the Eternal Justice of God, who inflicted on him Death, the Wages of Sin: there was no man to hold off the Hand of God; Justice had his full blow at him, and made him a Curse for Sin. He died for sin without a Mediator, he died the Cursed Death . . . Never was poor mortal so beset with the apprehensions of approaching death as was this Lord Jesus Christ; *Amazement beyond measure, Sorrow that exceeded* seized upon his Soul. *My Soul,* saith he, *is exceeding sorrowful even unto Death. And he began,* saith Mark, *to be sore amazed, and to be very heavy,* Mat. 26:38, Mk 14:33.[1089]

Worse, Christ experienced the full measure of God-forsakenness: 'God now becomes as an Enemy to him. He forsakes him. *My God, my God, why hast thou forsaken me?* Yea, the Sence [sic] of the Loss of God's comfortable Presence abode with him even till he gave up the Ghost.'[1090] Christ's suffering is important for Bunyan, not as an example to follow, but as act of free self-offering in our place to which we must respond.[1091]

The Intercession of Christ

And Christ's primary role for Bunyan now that the work of salvation is accomplished is as intercessor, a theme to which he constantly returns. In *The advocateship of Jesus Christ,* a late work, he produces a long and rather odd piece of apologetic about how Jesus as advocate pleads with the Father in the face of our sins, presenting Christ as a kind of high-powered lawyer who acts only on behalf of the elect.[1092] Yet this idea too has positive implications: Bunyan argues that the fact of Christ's advocacy should be a strong stimulus to our prayer, especially if or when we feel like giving it up;[1093] and it is through Christ's continuing intercession on our behalf that we are delivered from the evil of the sins that even the elect continue to commit,[1094] and are thus encouraged to *persevere* (a crucial virtue for Bunyan, doubtless reflecting his own terrible struggles against doubt[1095]). More important still, the intercession of Christ imparts a dynamism to the spiritual life of the Christian, which might otherwise have appeared as a static affair since the entire work of salvation is accomplished already, and externally: Christ's continuing prayer on our behalf is what leads us on beyond the cross to behold the glory of God in the face of the risen Jesus:

> Since Christ is an Intercessor, I infer that Believers should not rest at the Cross for Comfort; Justification they should look for there; but, being justified by his Blood, they should ascend up after him to the Throne: at the Cross you will see him in his sorrows and humiliations, in his tears and blood; but follow him to where he is now, and then you shall see him . . . wearing the Breastplate of Judgment, and with all your Names written upon his heart. Then you shall perceive that the whole Family in Heaven and Earth is named by him, and how he prevaileth with God, the Father of Mercies, for you. Stand still awhile, and listen, yea, enter with boldness into the Holiest, and see your Jesus, as he now appears in the presence of God for you; what work he makes against the Devil and Sin, and Death, and Hell for you (Heb. 10:9).[1096]

Assurance and doubt

Yet this theological schema posed a massive question, for Bunyan as for so many others: how can I know whether or not I am one of the elect? We have already noted that Bunyan remained unsure about the answer to this question throughout his life: thus, in *The pilgrim's progress*, Christian fears he is drowning at the very moment of crossing over to the Celestial City, and (in the second part) Christiana and her band have to avoid the Sleepy Arbour shortly before arriving at their destination:[1097] we walk with doubt until the very moment of death. Bunyan's own seminal experience in this regard forms one of the most graphic moments in *Grace abounding*: deeply worried that he has committed the unpardonable sin against the Holy Spirit, he is 'walking to and fro in a good mans Shop', when

> suddenly there was as if there had rushed in at the Window, the noise of Wind upon me, but very pleasant, and as if I had heard a Voice speaking, *Didst ever refuse to be justified by the Blood of Christ?* and withal my whole life of profession past, was in a moment opened to me, wherein I was made to see, that designedly I had not; so my heart answered groaningly *No*. Then fell with power that Word of God upon me, *See that ye refuse not him that speaketh*, Heb.12.25. This made a strange seisure [*sic*] upon my spirit; it brought light with it, and commanded a silence in my heart of all those tumultuous thoughts that before did use, like masterless hell-hounds, to roar and bellow, and make a hideous noise within me. It showed me, also, that Jesus Christ had yet a work of Grace and Mercy for me, that he had not, as I had feared, quite forsaken and cast off my Soul; yea, this was a kind of chide for my proneness to desparation [*sic*] . . . it commanded a great calm in my Soul, it perswaded me there might be hope.[1098]

Note the vivid description of the wind, the irresistible force of God's words, the sense of inner calm, the stirring of the senses, and the vision of one's whole life revealed in a single moment. But we should also note Bunyan's own self-confessed proneness to despair, and the absence of any kind of certainty: this is both a religious and an emotional experience, but not at all an indulgent one. The God who spoke to Bunyan here was emphatically not one to trifle with, and the encounter with him brought temporary relief rather than enduring assurance.[1099]

What, then, were the authentic signs of election? The first, as we have seen, was conviction of sin, which has implications for the practice of prayer:

> A good sense of sin, and the wrath of God, with some encouragement from God to come unto him, is a better Common Prayer-Book than that which is taken out of the Papistical Mass-Book; being the Scraps and Fragments of the devices of some Popes, some Friars, and I wot not what.[1100]

This is Bunyan in typically combative mood: it is as though the only way he can cope with his own terrifying anxieties about salvation is by hammering the easy religiosity of others who slept more easily in their beds than he ever could. Hence his hostility towards set forms of prayer, which is manifested in a striking exchange between Bunyan and the judge at his trial:

KEELIN [= John Kelyng]: But saith Justice *Keelin* (who was the judge in that court) Do you come to church (you know what I mean) to the parish church, to hear divine service?

BUNYAN: I answered, no, I did not.

KEELIN: He asked me, why?

BUNYAN: I said, because I did not find it commanded in the Word of God.

KEELIN: He said, we were commanded to pray.

BUNYAN: I said, but not by the Common Prayer-book.

KEELIN: He said, how then?

BUNYAN: I said with the Spirit. As the apostle saith, *I will pray with the Spirit and with understanding* (1 Cor. 14:15).

KEELIN: He said, we might pray with the spirit, and with understanding, and with the Common Prayer-book also.

BUNYAN: I said that those prayers in the Common Prayerbook, was such as was made by other men, and not by the motions of the Holy Ghost, within our Hearts; and as I said the Apostle saith, he will pray with the Spirit and with understanding; not with the Spirit and the Common Prayerbook.

ANOTHER JUSTICE: What do you count prayer? Do you think it is to say a few words over before, or among a people?

BUNYAN: I said, no, not so; for men might have many elegant, or excellent words, and yet not pray at all: But when a man prayeth, he doth through a sense of those things which he wants (which sense is begotten by the spirit) pour out his heart before God through Christ; though his words be not so many, and so excellent as others are.

JUSTICES: They said, that was true.[1101]

This conviction of sin, then, can be creative, if it leads us to call upon God:

The sweetest frame, the most heart-indearing frame, that possibly a Christian can get into, while in this World, is to have a warm sight of sin, and of a Saviour upon the heart at one time.[1102]

It can awaken people spiritually: 'so awakned [*sic*] as to be made to see themselves, what they are; the World, what *it* is; the Law, what *it* is; Hell, what *it* is; Death, what *it* is; Christ, what *he* is; and God, what *he* is; and also what Judgment is'.[1103] It can cause us to desire God whole-heartedly, itself a sign of election.[1104] This desire too is wholly a gift of God, reflecting the sheer *attractiveness* of Christ; and here we begin to glimpse a different face of the awe-inspiring, inscrutable divinity that dominated Bunyan's life. At the splendid conclusion of *Come, and welcome, to Jesus Christ*, Bunyan addresses the 'coming sinner' (the person who is drawing closer to God):

All thy strange, passionate, sudden rushings forward after Jesus Christ (coming Sinners know what I mean), they also are thy helps from God. Perhaps thou feelest at sometimes, more than at others, strong stirrings up of heart, to fly to Jesus Christ; now thou hast at this time a sweet, and stiff gale of the Spirit of God filling thy sails with the fresh gales of his good Spirit; and thou ridest at those times, as upon the wings of the wind, being carried out beyond thy self, beyond the most of thy prayers, and also above all thy fears and temptations. Coming Sinner, hast thou not, now and then, a kiss of the sweet lips of Jesus Christ? I mean, some blessed word droping [sic] like an Honey-Comb upon thy Soul to revive thee, when thou art in the midst of thy dumps. Does not Jesus Christ sometimes give thee a glimps [sic] of himself . . . Hast thou not sometimes as it were the very warmth of his wings over-shadowing the face of thy Soul, that gives thee as it were a gload [=warming sensation] upon thy Spirit, as the bright beams of the Sun do upon thy body, when it suddenly breaks out in the midst of a cloud, though presently all is gone again?

Well, all these things are the good hand of thy God upon thee, and they are upon thee to constrain to provoke and to make thee willing, and able to come (coming Sinner) that thou mightest in the end be Saved.[1105]

Christ draws us to himself, or (to use the imagery of the Song of Songs, one of Bunyan's favourite books[1106]) taps on our windows, inviting us to come away with him. Beauty places an important part in Bunyan's spirituality: the Delectable Mountains encourage the pilgrims on their approach to the Celestial City;[1107] and it is through the Holy Spirit that 'we come to see the Beauty of Christ, without a sight of which, we should never desire him, but should certainly live in the neglect of him, and perish'.[1108] The true beauty of Christianity is a holy life; so Bunyan entitled one of his later works 'A holy life, the beauty of Christianity'. For Bunyan, as for Calvin, holiness, or sanctification, is not the *cause* of our salvation, but the *fruit* of it.[1109]

The nature of holiness

But what is a holy life? it does not mean living *like* Christ: rather it means responding through faith to what Christ has already done for us.[1110] Holiness for Bunyan is always God's holiness imputed to us, not our own intrinsic capacity to be holy.[1111] And the crucial reason why this matters is because true holiness confers freedom, that enduring inner freedom which is wholly God's gift, and which derives from committing one's soul unconditionally into God's hands.[1112] This is a freedom no secular power can take from us, a freedom rooted in our personal union with God:

Further, The Lord did also lead me into the mystery of Union with this Son of God, that I was joyned to him, that I was flesh of his flesh, and bone of his bone.[1113]

Yet such a union is available only in the life of heaven: we have only glimpses of it here below. Bunyan's spirituality is always future-oriented, and like much millenarian religion it seeks to offer a sense of spiritual hope to those who have seen their worldly hope cruelly disappointed. This is spirituality for the disillusioned and the desperate: a vision for those betrayed by the powerful, or simply by life itself. Pilgrims become princes; the hard and lonely struggle wins ultimate vindication, *and we don't have to deserve it.* Bunyan had no time for the Quaker belief in the second coming of Christ as an interior spiritual experience:[1114] for him, the only second coming worth believing in was a coming in fire and judgement, an overturning of this world's bitter injustices, and the inauguration of a new kingdom of righteousness. Hence his gruesome descriptions of the torments of the damned,[1115] by comparison with which the present sufferings of the elect are utterly trivial:

> 'I have a cross husband and that's a great grief to mee [*sic*].'
> 'It is like so, but thou shalt be troubled with him no longer than thy life time, and therefore be not dismaid.'[1116]

Hence too the imagery associated with the Celestial City – music, vineyards and gardens, and sweet fresh air.[1117] And this is not simply a prospect to entice us: it is a reminder that we are already one with those who are enjoying it now:

> The difference then betwixt us, and them, is, not that we are really two, but one body in Christ, in divers places. True, we are *below* stairs, and they *above*; *they* in their *holy-day*, and *we* in our *working-day* cloaths; *they* in *harbour*, but we in the *storm*; they at *rest*, and *we* in the Wilderness: They *singing*, as *crowned* with Joy; we *crying*, as *crowned* with *thorns*. But I say, we are all of one house, one family, and are all the Children of one father.[1118]

The theology and practice of prayer

Bunyan's teaching on prayer contains much that will be familiar to those acquainted with any of the other major figures in Puritan spirituality: it is the fruit of our justification[1119] the work of the spirit of Christ in the soul,[1120] demanding the involvement of the whole person;[1121] and what matters is sincerity, not formal correctness.[1122] But (as we might by now expect) he stresses more than most others the ever-present possibility of despair: right prayer 'bubleth [*sic*] out of the heart when it is over-pressed with grief and bitterness' because of the danger of sin[1123] – hence the urgent need to pray through Christ, and Bunyan's grim conclusion that any prayer not so directed is useless.[1124] Hence too the need to recall our true status as adopted children of God, a theme to which he frequently returns.[1125] Prayer is a deeply serious business:

> I once met with a poor Woman, that, in the greatest of her Distresses, told me, she did use to rise in the Night, in cold Weather, and pray to God while she sweat with Fears of the loss of her prayer, and desires that her Soul might be saved. I have heard of many that have *played*, but of few that have *prayed* till they have sweat, by reason of their wrestling with God for mercy in that duty.[1126]

This is not to say that we must struggle to pray alone and unaided: God sees 'the brokenness of thine heart, and that it is, that makes the very bowels of the Lord run over'.[1127] But it is to say that for Bunyan prayer is far more than the child's cry to its father: it is spiritual combat, another theme to which Bunyan constantly returns. Christian struggles with Apollyon in *The pilgrim's progress*,[1128] and finds All-prayer an indispensable weapon when he approaches the mouth of Hell.[1129] He and Hopeful spend a whole night in prayer in Giant Despair's dungeon, as a result of which he remembers the key called Promise he has in his bosom.[1130] There is an intriguing passage in *The holy war* in which Emanuel invents an instrument

> that was to throw stones from the Castle of *Mansoul*, out at *Mouth-gate*; an instrument that could not be resisted, nor that would miss of execution; wherefore for the wonderful exploits that it did when used, it went without a name, and it was committed to the care of, and to be managed by the brave Captain, the Captain *Credence*, in case of war.[1131]

This instrument is, almost certainly, the prayer of the Christian, and it can be used not only against enemies but even against God.[1132] But the really important point is that without this capacity to wage war against evil such prayer is not really prayer at all:

> About this time I took an opportunity to break my Mind to an Antient [*sic*] Christian; and told him all my case. I told him also that I was afraid that I had sinned the sin against the Holy Ghost; and he told me, *He thought so too*. Here therefore I had but cold comfort, but, talking a little more with him, I found him, though a good man, a stranger to much Combate [*sic*] with the Devil. Wherefore I went to God again as well as I could, for Mercie still.[1133]

Spirituality and suffering

And this brings us to the question of suffering, and of how to use it positively, one of the richest dimensions of Bunyan's spirituality.[1134] We have already noted some of the suffering he himself had to undergo; and his *Prison meditations* are among his most moving works:

> Thou they say then, that we are Fools
> Because we here do lye,
> I answer, Goals [= jails] are Christ his Schools,
> In them we learn to dye.[1135]

He suffered from the random tragedies of fate too: his first child, Mary, was blind, and predeceased him.[1136] He never ceased to ponder how the Christian should respond to such events. In one of his most brilliant passages, he illustrates through the story of St John the Baptist's martyrdom the appalling suddenness of so much human suffering:

> *And immediately the King sent an Executioner, and commanded his head to be brought* (Mk 6:27). The story is concerning *Herod* and *John* the Baptist. *Herod's* dancing girl had begged *John Baptist's* head: and nothing but his head must serve her turn; well girl, thou shalt have it. Have it? I, but it will be long first. No, thou shalt have it now, just now, immediately, *And immediately he sent an executioner, and commanded his head to be brought.*

> Here is sudden work for sufferers; here is no intimation beforehand. The
> executioner comes to *John*; now, whether he was at dinner, or asleep, or
> whatever he was about, the bloody man bolts in upon him, and the first
> word he salutes him with, is, Sir, strip, lay down your neck; *For I come to*
> *take away your head.* But hold, stay, wherefore? pray, let me commit my
> Soul to God. No, I must not stay, I am in haste; slap, says his sword, and off
> falls the good mans head. This is sudden work, work that stays for no
> man.[1137]

This passage comes from *Seasonable counsel*, one of his finest works, in which
Bunyan provides much pastoral wisdom for those who suffer, even though he
unhesitatingly accepts the traditional Calvinist view that all suffering (indeed everything that happens) is directly willed by God.[1138] He distinguishes between passive
and active suffering: both can be redemptive.[1139] He acknowledges that 'the people
of God are a suffering people, a people subject to trouble for their faith and profession'.[1140] He advises all who suffer to commit their souls into God's keeping, even
though they may have no idea of what will ensue. It is true that this leads him to an
unexpected analogy:

> We should be like the *Spaniel-dogg*, even lie at the foot of our God, as he at
> the foot of his Master: yea, and should be glad, could we but see his face,
> though he treads us down with his feet.[1141]

But it is also true that he acknowledges how desperately hard that is, envisaging
someone's objection to it:

> *But I am in the Dark.*
> I answer, never stick at that. 'Tis *most* bravely done, to trust God with my
> soul *in the dark*, and to resolve to serve God for *nothing*, rather than give
> out. *Not to see*, and *yet to believe*, and to be a follower of the Lamb, and yet
> to be at uncertainty, what we shall have at last; argues Love, Fear, Faith,
> and an honest mind, and gives the greatest sign of one that hath true
> sincerity in his soul.[1142]

'To be a follower of the Lamb, and yet to be at uncertainty' – this is Bunyan at his
best, turning his own gnawing anxieties to good spiritual account. He argues that God
can *change* the person who acts thus ('He can turn thee into another man, and make
thee that which thou never wast'[1143]): hence 'I have often thought that the best Christians are found in the worst of times'.[1144] What matters is how we respond to what
happens to us:

> God sends his Love Tokens to his Church two ways, sometimes by her
> Friends, sometimes by her Enemies . . . They bring them of Malice, God
> sends them of Love.[1145]

And there is more. The effect of committing one's soul to God in the midst of
darkness is the gift of a new spiritual boldness, which is precisely the fruit of this sober
Calvinist theology – it is *because* we are saved by a process entirely external to

ourselves, a process that in no way requires achievement or initiative on our part, that we may apprehend God's free gift of life and hope in the midst of our utter despair:[1146] 'Pray God grant us boldness to come to him as the Publicane did, and also in that trembling Spirit as he did, when he cried in the Temple before him, "God be merciful to me a sinner."'[1147] And the person who has in this way entrusted all that happens to God discovers, in the very act of doing so, a new and indestructible inner peace; and this too elicits some of Bunyan's finest writing:

> No *suffering*, no *inflicter* of suffering, can reach the peace of the sufferer without his own consent . . . The body is Gods, and he gives that to them to destroy; the spirit is Gods, and he keeps that to himself: to shew that he has both power to do with us what he pleases, and that he will recover our body also out of their hand; for if the spirit lives, so must the body, when men have done what they can therewith.[1148]
>
> Wherefore, as I said, be always dying; die dayly: he that is *not only ready to be bound, but to die,* is fit to encounter any amazement.[1149]

The Christian's adventure

The journey through the Valley of the Shadow of Death is one of Christian's hardest challenges in *The pilgrim's progress*: it is 'a very solitary place', and Christian finds the experience of going through it harder than his battle with Apollyon.[1150] Its worst aspect is the total darkness.[1151] What keeps him going is, first, a sense of life as *pilgrimage*, with a definite goal in view ('Then again he thought he might be half way through . . . '); secondly, memories of the past ('he remembred [sic] also how he had already vanquished many a danger'[1152]); and, thirdly, the discovery that he is not alone after all:

> When *Christian* had travelled in this disconsolate condition some considerable time, he thought he heard the voice of a man, as going before him, saying, *Though I walk through the valley of the shaddow [sic] of death, I will fear none ill, for thou art with me.*
>
> Then was he glad . . . because he gathered from thence, that some who feared God were in this Valley as well as himself.[1153]

John Bunyan died on 31 August 1688: by the end of the year William of Orange was in London, and within months the passing of the Toleration Act exempted dissenters from the drastic penalties from which Bunyan himself had suffered so much. That suffering, as we have seen, indelibly marked his view of the spiritual life. In *The pilgrim's progress*, Mr Worldly-Wiseman tries to tempt Christian to get rid of his burden by calling on Legality, saying

> I could direct thee to the obtaining of what thou desirest, without the dangers that thou in this way wilt run thyself into: yea, and the remedy is at hand. Besides, I will add, that instead of those dangers, thou shalt meet with much safety, friendship, and content.[1154]

Christian was not impressed; and later Evangelist criticized Mr Worldly-Wiseman as favouring only the doctrines of this world, 'for it saveth him from the Cross'.[1155] For Bunyan, the trouble with the religion of Mr Worldly-Wiseman, Mr Facing-Bothways, and all his other splendid caricatures (many of them uncomfortably credible), is that it had no depth, no power to change either individuals or society. He needed something far more radical, something that could offer hope in a way that would not depend on either social position or personal confidence. He found it in the deep soil of English Calvinism; and, more than any other English writer, he managed to transmute the inheritance of the great Swiss Reformer from something like a theory into something more like a friend: 'Righteousness', he once wrote, 'is the only intimate that a Christian has'[1156] – and, in the final analysis, the only one he needs.

And he did something even more remarkable. The problem with Calvinist theology was that, even assuming the assurance of salvation could be believed with certainty, the life of the Christian could thereafter become a frankly dull affair, with all the real choices and high drama reserved for what God had already done in Christ, leaving the believer with little to do but persevere.[1157] What Bunyan did was to turn the sombre perspectives of covenant theology and justification by faith into a thrilling *adventure* – not in the sense of a jolly outing for the leisured, but in the far deeper medieval sense of a way of viewing the whole of life's unpredictable prospects as a pilgrimage in response to the call of God.

This adventure is not an option: all of us must embark upon it, as Formalist and Hypocrisy discover when they try to take a short cut, because it is part of what it means to be human.[1158] But it is a way of seeing reality which allows us to subvert it from within: it is, precisely, play, in the classic sense of the Song of Songs, the love-ballads of the troubadors, the dreams and stories of Chaucer's pilgrims and Langland's Piers Plowman.[1159] One way to read *The pilgrim's progress* is as a protest against the seeming triumph of all that Bunyan had fought against, and a protest that is all the more potent precisely because it is playful. Like the polar bear in a zoo, continuing to rehearse its young in the techniques they once made use of in the wild, or children in school grounds and housing estates dreaming in their play of how things could be, Bunyan offers us a pattern of spirituality that challenges every impulse to despair or collude in a dreary *status quo*.[1160] On this matter at least, Lord Macaulay was absolutely right, when he said of Bunyan's work:

> This is the highest miracle of genius, that things which are not should be as though they were, that the imaginations of one mind should become the personal recollections of another.[1161]

And Bunyan himself, in his *Book for boys and girls*, invited his fellow-Christians to consider the spider: it was better off than them, for it had no need to fear hell, no anxiety to oppress it on its journey through life. Yet, for all the hazards of the human condition, those prepared to embark upon it as Christians could attain to realms which spiders could not even dream of:[1162]

I am a Spider, yet I can possess
The Palace of a King, where Happiness
So much abounds. Nor when I do go thither,
Do they ask what, or whence I come, or whither
I make my hasty Travels, no not they;
They let me pass, and I go on my way.
I seize the Palace, do with hands take hold
Of Doors, of locks, or bolts; yea I am bold,
When in, to Clamber up unto the Throne,
And to possess it, as if 'twere mine own. Nor is there any Law forbidding me
Here to abide, or in this Palace be . . .
Nor, my Reproacher, I do by all this
Shew how thou may'st possess thy self of Bliss:
Thou art worse than a Spider, but take hold
On Christ the Door, thou shalt not be controul'd.
By him do thou the Heavenly Palace enter,
None chide thee will for this thy brave Adventure.[1163]

The Weight of Glory: John Donne (1572–1631)

Introduction

We conclude this chapter with a brief exploration of the spirituality of three towering giants of the Church of England in the seventeenth century: John Donne, George Herbert, and Jeremy Taylor. Donne's life, like Bunyan's, was marked with tragedy: born in London of a well-to-do Catholic family, he studied at Oxford and in Europe before training as a lawyer; but his burgeoning legal and political career (he became MP for Brackley in 1601) was interrupted by his clandestine marriage to Ann More, whose outraged father procured Donne's imprisonment. Subsequently a series of children were born, several of whom died young; and in 1615 Donne was ordained in the Church of England, becoming rector of both Keyston and Sevenoaks in 1616 and Dean of St Paul's Cathedral in 1621. He died on 31 March 1631.

The process by which Donne moved from Catholicism to the Church of England (and, in some respects, as we shall see, to Calvinism) is complex and uncertain, and may well have been influenced both by the heavy penalties attaching to recusant Catholics in Elizabethan England and by the fate of his brother Henry in 1593 (who died of the plague in Newgate Prison, where he was incarcerated for harbouring a seminary priest). What is noteworthy is, first, Donne's later refusal either to encourage others to convert as he had done, or to believe that salvation was only possible within the church he had joined; and, secondly, his passionate concern for the union of Christians, one of the primary themes in his work.[1164] Nor did conversion offer any easy buoyancy of spirit: Donne seems to have suffered from a persistent melancholy that was doubtless accentuated by the death of his beloved wife in 1617, and may well, as Carey suggests, have involved both a lack of a sense of self-worth and an anxiety about future damnation:[1165] in his *Devotions*, Donne prays for protection against 'an inordinate dejection of spirit'.[1166] Both these themes, a longing for unity, and a deep inner melancholy, will recur frequently in what follows.[1167]

Donne's literary works reflect, unsurprisingly, both his considerable learning and the chequered story of his life. His great religious poetry, written after his wife's death, is suffused with the melancholy already noted, and with a sense of anxiety far more pervasive than the dominant Anglo-Catholic historiographical tradition of interpretation seems to have allowed for.[1168] He wrote a number of polemical religious works, some of them reflecting the vituperative tone so sadly common among deeply spiritual writers of all traditions during this period.[1169] He also wrote *Biathanatos*, virtually an apologia for suicide;[1170] *Essays in divinity* (1614–15, written before his ordination); and *Devotions upon emergent occasions* (1624), which forms an excellent introduction to his somewhat melancholy piety.[1171] But best and most important of all are his vast collection of Sermons:[1172] more personal, though no less learned, than those of Lancelot Andrewes, they also reflect his love of legal, mercantile, and marine images. The influence of Augustine is prominent, as with so many writers of this and nearly every period;[1173] and so is that of Calvin.[1174] Donne's prose style is magnificent: long and sweeping sentences combining rhetorical flourish with lightly-worn learning, personal reflection and vivid aphoristic illustration. From the point of view of Christian spirituality, his sermons on the Psalms are outstanding: as one of thirty prebendaries at St Paul's (where many of his sermons were delivered), Donne had to recite his five psalms (62–6) daily and was expected to meditate on them: hence their appearance as subjects of sermons.[1175]

The character of Donne's spirituality

For all his personal melancholy, Donne has a positive (and very Augustinian) view of this world:

> There is not so poore a creature but may be thy glasse to see God in . . . all things that are, are equally removed from being nothing; and whatsoever hath any beeing [*sic*], is by that very beeing, a glasse in which we see God, who is the roote, and the fountaine of all beeing.[1176]

But the real point here is his underlying sense of the unity of all things in God, which for Donne was rooted in the Trinitarian life of God (he once refers to the Trinity as a 'holy and whole Colledge'[1177]). He loves to stress 'the *sociablenesse*, the *communicablenesse* of God; He loves holy meetings, he loves the *communion of Saints*':[1178] God the Trinity created us because he longed to share his life with his creatures.[1179] If we are, as Latimer said, the 'fellows of St Antony', it is not because of the godliness of our lives but because of the generosity of our God.

In contrast, Donne had little time for solitude or the monastic life; and this at first sight gives his spirituality not only a corporate but also a cheerful tone: 'Be not apt to think heaven is an *Ermitage*, or a *Monastery*, or the way to heaven a sullen *melancholy*; Heaven, and the way to it, is a *Communion of Saints*, in a holy cheerfulnesse.'[1180] 'God loves not singularity; The very name of Church implies company . . . It is not any one man'.[1181] Christ too 'loves not singularity' – he chose his disciples in pairs.[1182] This has implications for every aspect of our lives: 'The root of all societies is in families, in the relation between man and wife, parents and children, masters and servants'.[1183] And it elicits from Donne one of his most eloquent and justly famous utterances:

> The *Church* is *Catholike, universall,* so are all her *Actions; All* that she does, belongs to *all*. When she *baptizes a child,* that action concernes mee; for that child is thereby connected to that *Head* which is my *Head* too, and engraffed into that *body,* whereof I am a *member.* And when she *buries a Man,* that action concernes me: All *mankinde* is of one *Author,* and is one *volume;* when one Man dies, one *Chapter* is not *torne* out of the *booke,* but *translated* into a better *language;* and every *Chapter* must be so *translated; God* emploies severall *translators;* some peeces are translated by *Age,* some by *sicknesse,* some by *warre,* some by *justice;* but *Gods* hand is in every *translation;* and his hand shall binde up all our scattered leaves againe, for that *Librarie* when every *booke* shall lie open to one another . . . No Man is an *Iland,* intire of it selfe; every man is a peece of the *Continent,* a part of the *maine;* If a *Clod* bee washed away by the *Sea, Europe* is the lesse, as well as if a *Promontorie* were, as well as if a *Mannor* of thy *friends,* or of *thine owne* were; Any Mans *death* diminishes *me,* because I am involved in *Mankinde;* And therefore never send to know for whom the *bell* tolls; It tolls for *thee.*[1184]

The point is that anyone's death is an occasion for me to draw closer to God because it reminds me of my indissoluble solidarity with all humanity. Later in the same work Donne praises God 'that in this sound and voice [that of the funeral bell] I can hear thy instructions, in another man's to consider my own condition; and to know, that this bell which tolls for another, before it come to ring out, may take in me too'.[1185] And in one of his sermons he criticizes those who think the world is 'a great and har- monious Organ, where all parts are play'd, and all play parts; and must thou only sit idle and hear it?'.[1186] Everybody needs the help and company of others: after all, as Donne notes, there were only married people in the Ark![1187]

This richly corporate view of human life has important positive consequences. In characteristically masterly fashion he sets out what it means to be created in God's image, and how easily we forget this: since we are all created in the image of God,

> we should wonder to see a Mother in the midst of many sweet Children passing her time in making babies and puppets for her own delight. We should wonder to see a man, whose Chambers and Galleries were full of curious master-peeces [*sic*], thrust in a Village Fair to looke upon sixpenny pictures, and three farthing prints. We have all the Image of God at home, and [yet] we all make babies, fancies of honour, in our ambitions. The master-peece is our own, in our own bosome; and we thrust in countrey Fairs, that is, we endure the distempers of any unseasonable weather, in night-journies, and watchings: we indure the oppositions, and scornes, and triumphs of a rivall, and competitor, that seeks with us, and shares with us . . . we endure the decay of fortune, of body, of soule, of honour, to possesse lower Pictures; pictures that are not originalls, not made by that

hand of God, nature; but Artificiall beauties. And for that body, we give a soule, and for that drugge, which might have been bought, where they bought it, for a shilling, we give an estate. The Image of God is more worth then all substances; and we give it, for colours, for dreames, for shadowes.[1188]

Yet (and this is crucial) this view of human life has important negative consequences too. Precisely because of our greatness, we are less able to heal ourselves than simpler creatures are: 'It is too little to call *Man* a *little World*; Except *God*, Man is a *diminutive* to nothing. Man consists of more pieces, more parts, then the world . . . [yet] Heere [i.e. in sickness] we shrinke in our proportion, sink in our dignitie, in respect of verie meane creatures, who are *Phisicians* to themselves'.[1189] This points up the essentially paradoxical nature of human beings, as the Book of Genesis makes clear: we are *both* spirit *and* flesh, both heavenly and earthly;[1190] and Donne's description of original sin catches this with extraordinary vividness:

> in the very first minute of our life, in our quickning in our mothers womb, wee become guilty of *Adams* sin done 6000 years before, and subject to all those arrows, *Hunger*, *Labour*, *Grief*, *Sicknesse*, and *Death*, which have been shot after it. This is the fearfull swiftnesse of this arrow, that *God himself* cannot get before it. In the first minute that my soul is infus'd, the Image of God is imprinted in my soul; so forward is God in my behalf, and so early does he visit me. But yet *Originall* sin is there, as soon as that Image of God is there. My soul is capable of *God*, as soon as it is capable of *sin*; and though sin doe not get the start of God, God does not get the start of sin either.[1191]

The reality and effect of sin is a constant theme of Donne's.[1192] He has some graphic images for evoking the corrosive power of sin: repeated sins create 'a spunginesse in the soul, an aptnesse to receive any liquor, to embrace any sin, that is offered to it'[1193] – a vivid description, as apt today as in Donne's day, for all that leads to addiction of any kind.[1194] Sin is heavy, a dead weight,[1195] a *conversio ad creaturam* in Augustine's words – a turning towards creatures.[1196] Hence the need to throw off every weight of sin:[1197] hence too the fact that God became man ('They [sins] were heavy, they weighed him down from his Fathers bosome, they made God Man'[1198]). For the ultimate effect of sin is to *separate* us from God. Donne describes how religion can effect this by a vivid personal recollection:

> Lying at *Aix*, at *Aquisgrane*, a well known Town in *Germany*, and fixing there some time, for the benefit of those *Baths*, I found my self in a house, which was divided into many families, and indeed so large as it might have been a little Parish, or, at least, a great lim of a great one; But it was of no Parish: for when I ask'd who lay over my head, they told me a family of *Anabaptists*; And who over theirs? Another family of *Anabaptists*; and another family of *Anabaptists* over theirs; and the whole house, was a nest of these boxes; severall artificers; all *Anabaptists*; I ask'd in what room they met, for the exercise of their Religion; I was told they never met: for,

though they were all *Anabaptists*, yet for some collaterall differences, they detested one another, and, though many of them, were near in bloud, and alliance to one another, yet the son would excommunicate the father, in the room above him, and the Nephew the Uncle . . . And I began to think, how many roofs, how many floores of separation, were made between God and my prayers in that house.[1199]

Sin (in this case false religion) divides what should be united, fractures what ought to be one. We are, then, caught in an iron paradox; and the way out of this dilemma, the achievement of our restoration and wholeness, is God's alone.[1200] But here Donne distances himself from classic Calvinist theology: there is something *we* can do as well:

How long shall we make this bad use, of this true doctrine, that, because we cannot doe *enough*, for our salvation, therefore we will doe *nothing*?[1201]

The process of conversion has various stages, all of them fundamentally gifts of God: he gives us resurrection from superstition and ignorance; from sin, and a love of sin; from sadness, and spiritual dejection.[1202] God has given us the means of salvation, then; but the responsibility of using them is ours, precisely because we are made like him:

Put not God to save thee by miracle; God can save an Image by miracle; by miracle he can make an Image a man; If man can make God of bread, certainly God can make a man of an Image, and so save him; but God hath made thee his own Image, and afforded thee meanes of salvation: Use them. God compels no man.[1203]

How are we to do this? The first step on the road to faith is a sense of wonder, because until we grasp the astonishing mystery of our nature and of God's, we will be unable to understand anything:

The first step to faith, is to wonder, to stand, and consider with a holy admiration, the waies and proceedings of God with man: for, Admiration, wonder, stands as in the midst, betweene knowledge and faith, and hath an eye towards both.[1204]

And the first and primary object of our wonder should be the fact that God became human.[1205]

The second step, as with Luther or Augustine, is to recognize the serious reality of sin, and to know ourselves to be sinners: 'firste the prisoner must knowe himselfe to be in prison, and send forth a voyce of mourninge'.[1206] Donne points out that true knowledge of Christ crucified involves appropriating his cross for ourselves, and not just as individuals:

I know nothing, if I know not Christ crucified, And I know not that, if I know not how to apply him to my selfe, Nor doe I know that, if I embrace him not in those meanes which he hath afforded me in his Church, in his Word, and Sacraments.[1207]

To this end Donne commends sacramental confession, provided it does not lead to 'that torture of the Conscience, that usurpation of Gods power, that spying into the counsails [sic] of Princes, and supplanting of their purposes, with which the Church of Rome hath been deeply charged.'[1208]

But the crucial resource God has given us, the real source of our potential transformation, is love: Donne defines it as 'a transmutatory Affection, it changes him that loves, into the very nature of that that he loves, and he is nothing else'.[1209] Love is 'a holy impatience in being without [purity of heart]';[1210] and the love of that purity 'is both the ballast and the frait [freight], to carry thee steadily and richly too, through all storms and tempests, spiritual and temporal in this life, to the everlasting Jerusalem'.[1211] Unexpectedly, this leads to a bleak and urgent reminder, which surely reflects Donne's own terrible experience of bereavement:

> All the sunshine, all the glory of this life, though all these be testimonies of Gods love to us, yet all these bring but a winters day, a short day, and a cold day, and a dark day, for except we love too, God doth not love with an everlasting love: God will not suffer his love to be idle, and since it profits him nothing, if it profits us nothing neither, he will withdraw it.[1212]

So we return to the paradox we encountered earlier. Like the late quartets of Shostakovich, or the closing movement of Tchaikovsky's *Pathétique* symphony, there is a persistent sense in Donne's work of an inability to sustain the optimism or high view of human nature which he sometimes introduces. Melancholy constantly breaks through the slender carapace of confidence: 'Fire and Aire, Water and Earth, are not the Elements of man; Inward decay, and outward violence, bodily pain, and sorrow of heart may be rather styled his Elements'.[1213] What Donne seeks to do is to turn this melancholy to creative spiritual effect. Thus:

> Heare us, O heare us Lord; to thee
> A sinner is more musique, when he prayes,
> Then spheares, or Angels praises bee,
> In Panegyrique Allelujaes,
>   Heare us, for till thou heare us, Lord
>   We know not what to say.
> Thine eare to'our sighes, teares, thoughts gives voice and word.
> O Thou who Satan heard'st in Jobs sicke day,
> Heare thy selfe now, for thou in us dost pray.
>
> That wee may change to evennesse
> This intermitting aguish Pietie,
> That snatching cramps of wickednesse
> And Apoplexies of fast sin, may die;
>   That musique of thy promises
>   Not threats in Thunder may
> Awaken us to our just offices;
> What in thy booke, thou dost, or creatures say,
> That we may heare, Lord heare us, when wee pray.[1214]

Donne's famous 'A Hymne to God the Father' reflects in full flower his 'intermitting aguish Pietie':

> Wilt thou forgive that sinne where I begunne,
> Which was my sin, though it were done before?
> Wilt thou forgive that sin through which I runne,
> And doe run still: though still I doe deplore?
>   When thou hast done, thou hast not done,
>   For, I have more.
>
> Wilt thou forgive that sinne which I have wonne
> Others to sinne? and, made my sinne their doore?
> Wilt thou forgive that sinne which I did shunne
> A yeare, or two: but wallowed in, a score?
>   When thou hast done, thou hast not done,
>   For, I have more.
>
> I have a sinne of feare, that when I have spunne
> My last thred, I shall perish on the shore;
> Sweare by thy selfe, that at my death thy sonne
> Shall shine as he shines now, and heretofore;
>   And, having done that, Thou hast done,
>   I fear no more.[1215]

Yet we have seen already that Donne believed God to have given him the means of transmuting dejection into joy. He asks God why he does not manifest his joy in the midst of his (Donne's) sickness – Donne suffered from illness from various kinds almost throughout his life:

> Pardon, O *God*, this *unthankfull rashnesse*; I that aske why thou *doest not*, finde even now in *my selfe*, that thou *doest*; such *joy*, such *glory*, as that I conclude upon *my selfe*, upon *all*, They that finde not *joy* in their *sorrowes*, *glory* in their *dejections* in this *world*, are in a fearefull *danger* of missing both in the *next*.[1216]

Then he recognizes that the paradox goes deeper: it is precisely in our suffering that we experience the deepest possible kind of joy:

> This . . . is not a collaterall joy, that stands by us in the tribulation, and sustaines us, but it is a fundamentall joy, a radicall joy, a viscerall, a gremiall joy, that arises out of the bosome and wombe and bowels of the tribulation it selfe. It is not that I rejoyce, though I be afflicted, but I rejoyce because I am afflicted; It is not because I shall not sink in my calamity, and be buried in that valley, but because my calamity raises me, and makes my valley a hill, and gives me an eminency, and brings God and me nearer to one another, then without that calamity I should have been [because I am counted worthy to suffer for Christ's sake].[1217]

Here we find ourselves closer to the perspectives of Calvinism.[1218] Donne is clear that 'there is no joy in the suffering it self', nor is it to be over-valued: rather it is only when I acknowledge that all my sufferings can be directed to God's glory can I (so to speak) own my own sufferings and find joy through them, because only then am I able to throw myself utterly upon God.[1219]

The theology and practice of prayer

And it is here that Donne's teaching on prayer is relevant.[1220] He seeks to set suffering in a Pauline context: if we can, like St Paul, glory in the cross of Christ (Galatians 6.14), then

> I may come to God, reason with God, plead with God, wrastle [*sic*] with God, and be received and sustained by him.[1221] The Lord, and onely the Lord knowes how to wound us, out of love; more then that, how to wound us into love; more then all that, to wound us into love, not onely with him that wounds us, but into love with the wound it self, with the very affliction that he inflicts upon us.[1222]

Donne follows Augustine in distinguishing between a purely physical complaint at our suffering, and a genuinely spiritual lament (what he calls 'a hearty groaninge'[1223]). And it must be 'a groaninge not a roaringe, the voice of a Turtle not of a Lyon' – we mustn't be complaining at every worldly adversity, as though we could not be happy unless we were rich.[1224] Furthermore, we must remember Christ's experience in Gethsemane: as he had to wait for his lament to be answered, so must we.[1225] The trouble is, as he has doubtless discovered himself, that 'the best men have had most laid upon them'.[1226] What alone makes this bearable is the *pondus gloriae*, the 'exceeding waight of eternall glory, and that turnes the scale'[1227] – if, as we have seen, the weight of sin drags us down, then glory ultimately outweighs it.[1228]

Donne tells his congregation to lament and weep, as Christ did over the death of Lazarus, when people refuse to hear their preaching or despise their prayers.[1229] This kind of prayer is our response to those situations we cannot control, just as Christ wept over Jerusalem because 'he had rather it were not so'.[1230] But, here as always, he rejects any self-absorbed individuality: if we are truly to weep for our brethren, we must be close to them, as Christ was to Jerusalem: 'If we will not come neare the miseries of our brethren, if we will not see them, we will never weep over them, never be affected towards them.'[1231] Recalling the patristic tradition of the gift of tears, Donne goes on to say that

> as God sees the water in the spring in the veines of the earth, before it bubble upon the face of the earth; so God sees teares in the heart of a man, before they blubber his face; God heares the teares of that sorrowfull soule, which for sorrow cannot shed teares.[1232]

Joy and sorrow are integral to one another: 'they doe not onely touch and follow one another in a certaine succession, Joy assuredly after sorrow, but they consist together, they are all one'.[1233]

And this brings us back to where we started. Just as sin separates us from God, so prayer seeks to restore that common unity of all creatures (and especially of all human beings) with the Creator which was lost at the Fall. Hence, unsurprisingly, Donne sets common above private prayer:

> I can build a Church in my bosome; I can serve God in my heart, and never cloath my prayer in words. God is often said to *heare*, and *answer* in the Scriptures, when they to whom he speaks, have said nothing. I can build a Church at my beds side; when I prostrate my selfe in humble prayer there, I do so . . . But yet, I finde the highest exaltations, and the noblest elevations of my devotion, when *I give thanks in the great Congregation, and praise him among much people* [Psalm 35.18], for so, me thinks, I come nearer and nearer to the Communion of Saints in Heaven.[1234]

And he advances a fascinating reason for this: we must speak aloud when we pray, because that is what God did in creating the universe:

> God had conceived in himselfe, from all eternity, certaine Ideas, certaine patterns of all things, which he would create. But these Ideas, these conceptions produced not a creature, not a worme, not a weed; but then, *Dixit, et facta sunt*, God spoke, and all things were made. Inward speculations, nay, inward zeale, nay, inward prayers, are not full performances of our Duty. God heares willingliest, when men heare too; when we speake alowd in the eares of men, and publish, and declare, and manifest, and avow our zeale to his glory.[1235]

This is not to say we may not pray alone, or without words: 'A man may pray in the street, in the fields, in a fayre . . . in our Chamber . . . But the greatest power of all, is in the publique prayer of the Congregation.'

It can be seen here that Donne's understanding of prayer is very wide, integrating words and actions.[1236] What is needed is *both* an upright sentiment (*pius affectus*) – after all, as he points out, the Devil prayed, but without this – *and* a willingness to pray for appropriate ends.[1237] Prayer must be serious: 'a prayer must be with a serious purpose to pray; for else, those fashionall and customary prayers, are but false fires without shot, they batter not heaven'.[1238] What matters above all is simply that it happens: 'whosoever thou be, that canst not readily pray, at least pray, that thou mayst pray. For, as in bodily, so in spirituall diseases, it is a desperate state, to be speech-lesse'.[1239] Prayer breaks the silence: as Shakespeare put it

> Give sorrow words. The grief that does not speak
> Whispers the o'er-fraught heart and bids it break.[1240]

We need, and are given, a holy boldness (a characteristic of so much Protestant spirituality), itself the consequence of being accepted and justified: 'when thou are established in favour, thou maist make any suit'.[1241] Preaching on the story of Abraham interceding with God for the people of Sodom, Donne says that

The words of man, in the mouth of a faithfull man, of *Abraham*, are a Canon against God himselfe, and batter down all his severe and heavy purposes for Judgements. Yet, this comes not, God knows, out of the weight or force of our words, but out of the easinesse of God. God puts himself into the way of a shot, he meets a weak prayer, and is graciously pleased to be wounded by that: God sets up a light, that we direct the shot upon him, he enlightens us with a knowledge, how, and when, and what to pray for; yea, God charges, and discharges the Canon himself upon himselfe.[1242]

But, if boldness is needed in prayer, something else is needed too, something that runs like a thread through Donne's spirituality and keeps reminding us of its ineradicably Calvinist base, even when he deviates from it: a pervasive sense of our unworthiness. The 'Center and Basis' of all true prayers is to begin by saying, like Jacob in Genesis 32, 'I am not worthy.' Paradoxically this is precisely the source of our nobility: 'It is a degree of spiritual exaltation, to be sensible of our lowness; I am not worthy to stoop down, and unloose his shoe latchet, says John Baptist'.[1243] It is because we are aware of our predicament, of the terrible paradox that cleaves us in half, that we can hope, because only then can we entrust ourselves unconditionally to God.

The significance of praise

And the natural manifestation of that trust is praise, which plays a vital part in Donne's spirituality. Prayer and praise are our two 'incomparable duties': prayer *besieges* God;[1244] but praise *presses* him by reminding him of former mercies. 'By Prayer we incline him, we bend him, but by praise we bind him.'[1245] This is the true value of liturgical praise; and when God hears praises, he translates them into prayers:

> The way of prayer, prayer so elemented and constituted . . . that consists rather of praise and thanksgiving, then supplication for future benefits, God shall infuse into us, a zeale of expressing our consolation in him, by outward actions, to the establishing of others.[1246]

Hence praise leads to an inner and indestructible joy. Citing the different Hebrew words for joy, Donne says that we may lose our *Ranan* ('our outward declarations of Rejoycing'), 'yet God shall never take from me, my *Shamach*, my internall gladnesse and consolation, in his undeceivable and undeceiving Spirit, that he is mine, and I am his; And this joy, this gladnesse, in my way, and in my end, shall establish me'[1247] – it will sustain us in old age. Praise makes us like angels because we are doing what they do.[1248] It is thus oriented towards the future, a crucial point: Donne cites the rabbis who said that whoever recites Psalm 145 three times daily is a *filium futuri seculi*, a son of the future age, because 'he is a child of the next World, that directs his Praise every day, upon three objects, upon God, upon himselfe, upon other men'.[1249] Praise alone can subvert the grim perspectives of this world's sorrows by lifting God's future into our present and celebrating it now: indeed it recognizes the fact that God's work has already collapsed the barriers between past, present, and future.[1250] 'Creatures of an inferiour nature are possest with the present; Man is a future Creature. In a holy and usefull sense, wee may say, that God is a future God'.[1251] Hence we should be *expectant* people, sustained in our dejections of spirit by all that is yet to come.[1252] And this really is a cause for joy:

> There are many *tesserae externae*, outward badges and marks, by which others may judge and pronounce mee to bee a true Christian; But the *tessera interna*, the inward badge and marke, by which I know this in my selfe, is joy . . . Essentiall blessednesse is called so, *Enter into thy Masters joy*, that is, into the Kingdome of heaven; and accidentall happinesse added to that essentiall happinesse is called so too: There is joy in heaven at the conversion of a sinner . . . As that man must never look to walk with the Lamb wheresoever he goes in heaven, that ranne away from the Lamb whensoever he came towards him, in this life; so he shall never possesse the joyes of heaven hereafter, that feels no joy here . . . For heaven and salvation is not a Creation but a Multiplication; it begins not when wee dye, but it increases and dilates it self infinitely then . . . Hee that looks for the fulnesse of the joyes of heaven hereafter, will have a taste, an insight in them before he goe.[1253]

Conclusion

It is time to sum up. The dark anxiety about salvation, the constant presence of an underlying melancholy, mark Donne's writing, and were clearly evident to his contemporaries as well as to himself ('they tell me that it is my *Melancholy*', he once wrote[1254]). It is tempting to ascribe this to the many tragedies, both private and public, that afflicted him. But that would be simplistic: Donne was a prominent public figure supremely versed in the art of rhetoric, fully capable of suppressing his personal feelings if it suited him to do so. It is far more likely that, once he had forsaken the Catholic orthodoxy into which he was born, he entered a spiritual world fraught with uncertainty; and the greatness of his poems and his preaching consists precisely in his struggle to hold that in tension with the stubborn religious hope, and the deep sense of a communion existing between all God's people, which never left him. Such a struggle allows him to speak to our day because it first allowed him to speak to his: we too easily forget the effects on people of the unprecedented and terrifying changes through which Donne and his contemporaries lived. For many, these must have led either to apathy, to prudent acquiescence, to introspection or to despair. For Donne they led first to a determination to make something of what was happening to him and around him, and to apply the great truths of moderate Calvinist Christianity to himself in a manner which is the very opposite of self-absorption:

> The hidinge of our groaninges in our desires (cf. Ps 38:9) is to wrap up all sorrowe for sinne in a verball confession and enumeration of our sinnes, without any particular contrition for the sinne, or detestation of it. We must hide neither; but anatomize our soule in both, and find every sinnewe, and fiber, every lineament and ligament of this body of sinne, and then every breath of that newe spirit, every drop of that newe bloud

that must restore and repayre us. Study all the history, and write all the progres [*sic*] of the Holy Ghost in thy selfe. Take not the grace of God, or the mercy of God as a meddall, or a wedge of gold to be layd up, but change thy meddall or thy wedge into currant money, find this grace and this mercy applyed to this and this action . . . Hide nothinge from God, neyther the diseases thou wast in, nor the degrees of health that thou art come to, nor the wayes of thy fallinge or risinge; for *Dominus fecit, et erit mirabile*. If I mistake not the measure of thy conscience, thou wilt find an infinite comfort in this particular tracinge of the Holy Ghost, and his workinge in thy soul.[1255]

The crucial thing is to appropriate the great mystery of our redemption in Christ for ourselves; and we can do this only through the most costly and honest self-reflection.[1256] Donne acknowledges, in another marvellous passage from one of his sermons, how this will mean different things for different people:

The ordinary way, even of the *holy Ghost*, for the conveying of *faith*, and supernaturall graces, is (as the way of worldly knowledge is) by the *senses*: where his way is by the *eare*, by hearing his word *preached*; do not thou crosse that way of his, by an inordinate delight, in hearing the eloquence of the preacher; for, so thou hearest the man, and not *God*, and goest *thy way*, and not *his*. God hath divers wayes into divers men; into some he comes at noone, in the sunshine of prosperity; to some in the *dark* and *heavy* clouds of adversity. Some he affects with the musick of the Church, some with some particular Collect or Prayer; some with some passage in a Sermon, which takes no hold of him, that stands next him. Watch the way of the Spirit of God, into thee; that way which he makes his path, in which he comes oftnest to thee, and by which thou findest thy self most affected, and best disposed towards him, and pervert not that path, foule not that way.[1257]

And yet such reflection is never solitary. Donne's enduring sense of the unity of all creatures in the life of their Creator triumphed in the end over everything else. Not for him the stern solitude of the Carthusians: 'think not heaven a Charter-house, where men, who onely of all creatures, are enabled by God to speak, must not speak to one another. The Lord of heaven is *Verbum*, The word, and his servants there talk of us here, and pray to him for us.'[1258] No man is an island; and since, as he declared in one of his last sermons, that great truth is rooted in the nature of God himself, it will not only sustain us in our darkest sorrows: it will encourage us in turn to sustain others in theirs:

The master beleeved, and the servant was healed. Little knowest thou, what thou hast received at Gods hands, by the prayers of the Saints in heaven, that enwrap thee in their generall prayers for the Militant Church. Little knowest thou, what the publique prayers of the Congregation, what the private prayers of particular devout friends, that lament thy careless-nesse, and negligence in praying for thy selfe, have wrung and extorted out of Gods hands, in their charitable importunity for thee. And therefore, at last, make thy selfe fit to doe for others, that which others, when thou wast unfit to doe thy selfe that office, have done for thee.[1259]

'Engine Against th'Almightie': George Herbert (1593–1633)

Introduction

If there remains much argument about the precise extent of John Donne's indebtedness to Protestant theology, there ought to be less about that of Herbert. This is the closing stanza of 'Judgement':

> But I resolve, when thou shalt call for mine,
> > That to decline,
> And thrust a Testament into thy hand:
> > Let that be scann'd.
> There thou shalt finde my faults are thine.[1260]

It is hard to think of a more pithy account of classic Protestant atonement theology than this.[1261] There is much good sense in Robert Shaw's remark that, while Donne's central question, like that of Bunyan's pilgrim, was 'what shall I do to be saved?', Herbert's was rather 'since I am saved, what must I do now?'[1262] Few (perhaps no) others explored the question of what might constitute 'spiritual life' for a devout Protestant with anything like the sharpness and breadth of vision as he did.

Herbert was born in 1593 of 'an ancient, distinguished and martial family of the Welsh border',[1263] the seventh of ten children. He won distinction in his studies at Westminster School and Trinity College Cambridge (becoming in 1620 Public Orator to the University); he served briefly in Parliament as member for Montgomeryshire before being ordained deacon in 1624.[1264] Five years later he married Jane Danvers, and in the following year was ordained priest and appointed to the benefice of Fuggleton-with-Bemerton, just outside Salisbury. He died there, aged only 39, in 1633.

All Herbert's work was published posthumously. The collection of poems entitled *The temple* was produced in 1633, shortly after his death.[1265] There are various theories both about its provenance and about the organization of the collection:[1266] what matters for our purpose is simply that the collection forms one of the greatest poetic achievements in English, and one of the peaks of English spiritual writing. In 1652 a work entitled *The country parson* was published (this title is Herbert's: the other title, *A priest to the temple*, may have been added by Herbert's literary executors). Herbert tells us that he wrote it so that he 'may have a Mark to aim at':[1267] it embodies his own theology of priesthood. Herbert is also probably responsible for a collection of apophthegms,[1268] and for some Latin works firmly in the European Renaissance tradition;[1269] and he seems also to have translated into English a treatise on the medicinal and spiritual benefits of fasting by the Italian Luigi Cornaro.[1270]

The literary arguments about Herbert's principal sources extend far beyond the scope of this book, though some reflections will be found in the notes to this chapter.[1271] There can be no question about his knowledge of, and indebtedness to, the

Bible: of the scriptures, he says, the country parson 'sucks, and lives';[1272] and he expresses his own attitude in 'The H. Scriptures 1':

> Oh Book! infinite sweetnesse! let my heart
> Suck ev'ry letter, and a hony gain,
> Precious for any grief in any part;
> To cleare the breast, to mollifie all pain . . .
> thou art heav'ns Lidger here,
> Working against the states of death and hell.
> Thou art joyes handsell: heav'n lies flat in thee,
> Subject to ev'ry mounters bended knee.[1273]

More specifically, Herbert's fondness for the Book of Common Prayer, a pattern of worship he will have experienced at school and at Cambridge (and very possibly when a child at home), and which clearly became even more central to his life after his ordination, is important.[1274] The same is true of the Psalms: one modern author has suggested that a way of conceiving of *The church* (which forms the major part of the collection of poems in *The temple*) is as a book of personal psalms,[1275] a common seventeenth-century view of the collection as a whole.[1276] A number of commentators have discerned illuminating resonances between the Psalms and Herbert's poetry;[1277] and he himself alludes to them frequently, often citing the psalm proper to a particular feast in a poem on the same theme.[1278] We shall see below how he fashions both the structure and the theology of the lament psalms to his own purposes.

Spirituality and ministry

Given Herbert's own vocation and preoccupations, it seems appropriate to begin our exploration of his spirituality with his reflections on ministry. He describes the pastor as 'the Deputy of Christ for the reducing [= bringing back] of Man to the Obedience of God';[1279] and among his primary tasks are catechizing[1280] and preaching.[1281] The latter will be conducted in a manner suited to 'Countrey people; which are thick, and heavy, and hard to raise to a poynt of Zeal',[1282] and will move them not by wit or learning but by holiness – 'For there is no greater sign of holinesse, then the procuring, and rejoycing in another's good.'[1283] But his primary resource for the conversion of parishioners to the true faith will be through his prayers, 'beseeching the Father of lights to open their eyes, and to give him power so to fit his discourse to them, that it may effectually pierce their hearts, and convert them'.[1284]

More generally, but with great shrewdness, Herbert stresses the value of an integrated ministry of pastoral work and scholarship:

> Country people are full of these petty injustices [as, e.g., coveting their neighbours' spades], being cunning to make use of another, and spare themselves: And Scholers ought to be diligent in the observation of these, and driving of their generall Schoole rules ever to the smallest actions of Life; which while they dwell in their bookes, they will never finde; but being seated in the Countrey, and doing their duty faithfully, they will soon discover: especially if they carry their eyes ever open, and fix them on their charge, and not on their preferment.[1285]

There is nothing very original in this approach: it is a kind of adaptation to the Church of England's rural ministry of St Bernard's remark to Aelred of Rievaulx five centuries earlier.[1286] What is interesting is the way in which Herbert encourages his fellow-clergy to appropriate the truths of the Gospel for the lives of their parishioners, by an integrated ministry of scholarship rooted in the realities of rural life. Hence he can say that 'the Countrey Parson's Library is a holy life: for besides the blessing that that brings upon it, there being a promise, that if the Kingdome of God be first sought, all other things shall be added, even it selfe is a Sermon'.[1287] He tells parsons not to frequent inns, to keep their word and to wear plain clothing.[1288] They must invite *all* their parishioners to the rectory for hospitality, 'because countrey people are very observant of such things, and will not be perswaded, but being not invited, they are hated'.[1289] 'The Countrey Parson is generally sad, because hee knows nothing but the Crosse of Christ . . . Nevertheless, he somtimes refresheth himselfe, as knowing that nature will not bear everlasting droopings, and that pleasantnesse of disposition is a great key to do good.'[1290] He articulates the heart of the spirituality of ministry in 'The Church-porch':

> Pitch thy behaviour low, thy projects high;
> So shalt thou humble and magnanimous be:
> Sink not in spirit: who aimeth at the sky,
> Shoots higher much then he that means a tree.
>   A grain of glory mixt with humblenesse
>   Cures both a fever and lethargicknesse.[1291]

Spiritual anthropology

All this might appear to imply a view of human nature that was at best patronizing and at worst dismissive. But Herbert is not being élitist. He is being truthful. He wants to argue, like all devout Protestants, for a radical disjunction between human nature and divine love. First, he expresses the intimacy of human beings with the creation, and the medieval notion of the individual as a microcosm of the universe:

> Nothing hath got so farre,
> But Man hath caught and kept it, as his prey.
>   His eyes dismount the highest starre:
>   He is in little all the sphere.
> Herbs gladly cure our flesh;
>   because that they finde their acquaintance there . . .
>   The starres have us to bed;
> Night draws the curtain, which the sunne withdraws;
>   Musicke and light attend our head.
>   All things unto our flesh are kinde
> In their descent and being; to our minde
>   In their ascent and cause . . .

> Since then, my God, thou hast
> So brave a Palace built; O dwell in it,
> That it may dwell with thee at last!
> Till then, afford us so much wit;
> That, as the world serves us, we may serve thee,
> And both thy servants be.[1292]

So far, so good. But in another poem he articulates the dichotomous nature of humanity: we touch both heaven and earth, which is at once privilege and problem:

> But as his joyes are double;
> So is his trouble.
> He hath two winters, other things but one:
> Both frosts and thoughts do nip,
> And bite his lip;
> And he of all things fears two deaths alone.
>
> Yet ev'n the greatest griefs,
> May be reliefs,
> Could he but take them right, and in their wayes.
> Happie is he, whose heart
> Hath found the art
> To turn his double pains to double praise.[1293]

The problem is that the art of turning our double pains to double praise is beyond us: and Herbert expresses this with exquisite brevity in the closing lines of 'A true hymne':

> Whereas if th'heart be moved,
> Although the verse be somewhat scant,
> God doth supplie the want.
> As when th'heart sayes (sighing to be approved)
> *O, could I love!* and stops: God writeth, *Loved.*[1294]

Spirituality and creation

Herbert's view of the creation is as delicate and subtle as his view of human beings within it. In a superb poem ('The pearl. Matt. 13.45'), he explores one of his primary themes, the importance of relinquishing the creation for the Creator: whilst not rejecting the creation or scorning it, he makes it clear which matters more.[1295] In the equally wonderful 'Dulnesse' he goes further, stressing the beauty and attractiveness of God which confers beauty on his creation:

> Thou art my lovelinesse, my life, my light,
> Beautie alone to me:
> Thy bloudy death and undeserv'd, makes thee
> Pure red and white.

> When all perfections as but one appeare,
> That those thy form doth show,
> The very dust, where thou dost tread and go,
> Makes beauties here.[1296]

There is no romantic or even sacramental celebration of natural beauty here. In 'The forerunners', Herbert writes:

> True beautie dwells on high: ours is a flame
> But borrow'd thence to light us thither.[1297]

This is not a negative view; but neither is it a symbolic one.[1298] Instead it is a view of creation close to that of Calvin, who told his reader to understand

> that he has a genuine apprehension of the character of God as the Creator of the world; first, if he attends to the general rule, never thoughtlessly or obliviously to overlook the glorious perfections which God displays in his creatures; and, secondly, if he makes a self-application of what he sees, so as to fix it deeply on his heart.[1299]

Thus our response to the creation must be to seek to discern what God is doing within it, as Herbert points out in *The country parson*: the pastor labours with country people in order

> to reduce them to see Gods hand in all things, and to beleeve, that things are not set in such an inevitable order, but that God often changeth it according as he sees fit, either for reward or punishment.[1300]

God exercises a threefold power in all that he does: a sustaining, a governing and a spiritual power. The first keeps the universe in being: 'Preservation is a Creation; and more, it is a continued Creation, and a creation every moment'.[1301] The third 'is observable in this, how Gods goodnesse strives with mans refractorinesse. Man would sit down at this world, God bids him sell it, and purchase a better'.[1302] And Herbert articulates the proper role of human beings in 'Providence':

> Man is the worlds high Priest: he doth present
> The sacrifice for all; while they below
> Unto the service mutter an assent,
> Such as springs use that fall, and windes that blow . . .

> Wherefore, most sacred Spirit, I here present
> For me and all my fellows praise to thee:
> And just it is that I should pay the rent,
> Because the benefit accrues to me.[1303]

This view of humanity as priests of the creation may, as F. E. Hutchinson suggests, be close to that of the Latitudinarian Henry More, and even of Orthodox theology.[1304] But it is perfectly compatible with Calvin:

For we, though in ourselves polluted, in [Christ] being priests (Rev.1:6), offer ourselves and our all to God, and freely enter the heavenly sanctuary, so that the sacrifices of prayer and praise which we present are grateful and of sweet odour before him.[1305]

It leads Herbert to emphasize the value of praise as the natural response of human beings to the wonder of the creation and the even greater wonder of its Creator.[1306]

The Christian's spiritual life

Yet Herbert's primary interest is elsewhere: in the way in which we live as Christians in response to God's saving work in Christ, and in how we articulate that in our prayer. In 'The glance' he describes how he felt when God, as he believed, set him free from sin, and how he held onto that deep apperception in later trials.[1307] In another poem ('The temper (1)'), Herbert explores the variety of experiences, some good and some terrible, which the soul undergoes; and this leads him to complain bitterly to God for 'stretching' him too far:

> O rack me not to such a vast extent;
>   Those distances belong to thee:
> The world's too little for thy tent,
>   A grave too big for me.

> Wilt thou meet arms with man, that thou dost stretch
>   A crumme of dust from heav'n to hell?
> Will great God measure with a wretch?
>   Shall he thy stature spell?

He asks God for shelter:

> O let me, when thy roof my soul hath hid
>   O let me roost and nestle there:
> Then of a sinner thou art rid,
>   And I of hope and fear.

But finally he submits himself to God's will in a superb conclusion:

> Yet take thy way; for sure thy way is best:
>   Stretch or contract me, thy poore debter:
> This is but tuning of my breast,
>   To make the musick better.

> Whether I flie with angels, fall with dust,
>   Thy hands made both, and I am there:
> Thy power and love, my love and trust
>   Make one place ev'ry where.[1308]

In this last verse, Herbert submits himself into God's hands in a manner that transcends even experience and feeling: this is, as Strier points out, Calvin's 'firm and stable constancy of heart which is the chief part of faith'.[1309]

And this profound and personal assurance of salvation allows him to offer wise advice in a letter to Arthur Woodnoth, a goldsmith considering ordination:

> Though you want all success either in inclining or restraining, To desire good & endeavour it when we can doe no more, is to doe it. Complaine not of ye want of success, when you have the fruit of it. In Gods accepting you have done ye good you intended, & whom serve you? or whom would you please? David built the temple as much as Solomon because he desired it, & prepared for it. Doe this & be a man as David, after Gods hart.[1310]

Once God has accepted us, and we have accepted our acceptance, our longings are as fruitful as our achievements, precisely because neither count towards our justification. So Herbert can quip: 'Hee begins to die, that quits his desires'.[1311] Herbert here shows a degree of assurance that neither Donne nor Bunyan could ever quite attain, though this does not lead him to complacency: on the contrary, many of his poems are concerned to banish the terrible anxiety that Calvinist belief in predestination sowed in so many. Thus he writes:

> Away distrust:
> My God hath promis'd; he is just.[1312]

More generally, he reflects a constant concern with lay spiritual formation. He stresses the importance of regular self-examination:

> By all means use sometimes to be alone.
> Salute thy self: see what thy soul doth wear.
> Dare to look in thy chest, for 'tis thine own:
> And tumble up and down what thou find'st there.
>> Who cannot rest till hee good-fellows finde,
>> He breaks up house, turns out of doores his minde.
>
> Summe up at night, what thou hast done by day;
> And in the morning, what thou hast to do.
> Dresse and undresse thy soul: mark the decay
> And growth of it: if with thy watch, that too
>> Be down, then winde up both; since we shall be
>> Most surely judg'd, make thy accounts agree.[1313]

He also reminds the parson of the essential purpose of catechizing: 'to multiply, and build up this knowledge [of salvation] to a spirituall Temple' and 'to inflame this knowledge, to presse, and drive it to practice, turning it to reformation of life, by pithy and lively exhortations'.[1314] He warns his parishioners not to bicker fruitlessly: 'Contentiousnesse in a feaste of Charity [i.e. at the Eucharist] is more scandall then any posture';[1315] and when the parson encounters this, 'he either prevents it judiciously, or breaks it off seasonably by some diversion'.[1316] And he evinces a deep Protestant reverence for the church building: the parson is to ensure that it is free of dust or cobwebs, 'and at great festivalls strawed, and stuck with boughs, and perfumed with incense', with texts of scripture painted everywhere, 'and that all the painting be grave, and reverend, not with light colours, or foolish anticks,' with clean furnishings and a 'seemly Carpet of good and costly Stuffe':[1317]

> When once thy foot enters the church, be bare.
> God is more there, then thou: for thou art there
> Onely by his permission. Then beware,
> And make thy self all reverence and fear.
> > Kneeling ne're spoiled silk stocking: quit thy state.
> > All equall are within the churches gate.[1318]

Spirituality and liturgy

This is no doctrine of the real presence; but it is a reminder that all true worship both demands reverence of worshippers, and reminds them of their fundamental equality before God.[1319] And this makes demands on the parson too. He should lead divine services 'as being truly touched and amazed with the Majesty of God, before whom he then presents himself; yet not as himself alone, but as presenting with himself the whole Congregation',

> by no means enduring either talking, or sleeping, or gazing, or leaning, or halfe-kneeling, or any undutifull behaviour in them, but causing them, when they sit, or stand, or kneel, to do all in a strait, and steady posture, as attending to what is done in the Church, and every one, man, and child, answering aloud both Amen, and all other answers, which are on the Clerks and peoples part to answer; which answers also are to be done not in a hudling [sic], or slubbering fashion, gaping, or scratching the head, or spitting even in the midst of their answer, but gently and pausably, thinking what they say.[1320]

The picturesque language reflects a serious concern for worship to engage the whole person, neither simply heart nor head. And for Herbert public prayer took precedence over private:

> Though private prayer be a brave designe,
> Yet publicke hath more promises, more love:
> And love's a weight to hearts, to eies a signe.
> We all are but cold suitours; let us move
> Where it is warmest. Leave thy six and seven;
> Pray with the most: for where most pray, is heaven.[1321]

The theology and practice of prayer

This brings us to Herbert's understanding of prayer itself. We should note first a quality not so far in evidence in extracts from *The country parson*: boldness. He says that parsons 'are not to be over-submissive, and base, but to keep up with the Lord and Lady of the house, and to preserve a boldness with them and all, even so farre as reproofe to their very face, when occasion cals, but seasonably and discreetly'.[1322] And he will sometimes achieve his ends 'by a bold and impartial reproof, even of the best in the Parish, when occasion requires: for this may produce hatred in those that are reproved, but never contempt either in them, or others'.[1323] Herbert articulates this virtue with characteristically exquisite precision in 'The Church-porch':

> Dare to be true. Nothing can need a ly:
> A fault, which needs it most, grows two thereby . . .
>   all may have,
> If they dare try, a glorious life, or grave.[1324]

This boldness is matched, as in the New Testament and in much Protestant spirituality, with a boldness towards God that (as we have seen elsewhere) is the fruit of our assurance of salvation.[1325] The principal expression of this theme is in 'Prayer (1)':

> Prayer the Churches banquet, Angels age,
>   Gods breath in man returning to his birth,
>   The soul in paraphrase, heart in pilgrimage,
> The Christian plummet sounding heav'n and earth;
> Engine against th'Almightie, sinners towre,
>   Reversed thunder, Christ-side-piercing spear,
>   The six-daies world transposing in an houre,
> A kinde of tune, which all things heare and fear;
> Softnesse, and peace, and joy, and love, and blisse,
>   Exalted Manna, gladnesse of the best,
>   Heaven in ordinarie, man well drest,
> The milkie way, the bird of Paradise,
>   Church-bels beyond the starres heard, the souls bloud,
>   The land of spices; something understood.

This tremendous poem deserves a book to itself. The first line tells us that prayer is a participation in the life of heaven; the second, that it is wholly a gift of God; the third, that it encapsulates and enlarges the whole life of the soul on its journey towards heaven.[1326] But the fifth line is more interesting still: prayer is an 'Engine against th'Almightie', a dramatic and boldly secular image appropriate both to the sinner's struggles with an unmanageable God and to a country soon to experience the eruptions of civil war.[1327] It is perfectly true that in 'Artillerie', where Herbert employs a similar image, the fierce boldness of the language used towards God gives way at the end to submission ('There is no articling with thee'), as happens also in 'The collar'.[1328]

The prayer of lament

But this is no meek surrender: rather, as in the Psalms (which must surely have powerfully influenced Herbert here), it is precisely the bold willingness to confront God, reflecting the bafflement of the child whose loving parent appears to have abandoned her, which alone leads to a new sense of meaning and acceptance in the very midst of the bafflement.[1329] Elsewhere Herbert stresses how confident and intimate prayer can gain access to God in a manner that makes it worth far more than 'wealth, fame, endowments, vertues, all.'[1330] We are close here to the teaching of St Paul on prayer in the eighth chapter of his Letter to the Romans; but we are closer still to the great lament psalms, all of which Herbert will have known and prayed, and most of which catch exactly the combination of fury and intimacy, of doubt and faith, which Herbert so powerfully incarnates here.[1331]

In another wonderful poem, 'Affliction (3)', Herbert describes the presence of God in the life of someone who suffers. That presence is not static but dynamic: God 'guides and governs' the person's grief, gently transforming it from within:

> My heart did heave, and there came forth, *O God!*
> By that I knew that thou wast in the grief,
> To guide and govern it to my relief,
>> Making a scepter of the rod:
>>> Hadst thou not had thy part,
> Sure the unruly sigh had broke my heart.
>
> But since thy breath gave me both life and shape,
> Thou knowst my tallies; and when there's assign'd
> So much breath to a sigh, what's then behinde?
>> Or if some yeares with it escape,
>>> The sigh then onely is
> A gale to bring me sooner to my blisse.
>
> Thy life on earth was grief, and thou art still
> Constant unto it, making it to be
> A point of honour, now to grieve in me,
>> And in thy members suffer ill.
>>> They who lament one crosse,
> Thou dying dayly, praise thee to thy losse.[1332]

The poet's prayer ('O God!'), at once tiny and vast, is enough to assure him of God's presence. Had it not been, 'the unruly sigh' would indeed have broken his heart; but it is, because Herbert's sigh is Christ's prayer in him, his once-for-all dying ('They who lament one crosse') appropriated for the life of the suffering Christian, who does not simply pray *like* Christ, or even *with* Christ: rather, Christ prays in him, making the Christian's suffering his own, turning his sigh into 'a gale to bring me sooner to my blisse'.

In another poem, 'Sion', Herbert contrasts the glory of Solomon's Temple with the inward encounter between God and the soul:

> There thou art[1333] struggling with a peevish heart,
> Which sometimes crosseth thee, thou sometimes it:
>> The fight is hard on either part.
>> Great God doth fight, he doth submit.
> All Solomons sea of brasse and world of stone
> Is not so deare to thee as one good grone.[1334]

God is more concerned with the agonized cry of one of his children than with all the architectural splendour of the Temple. The real Temple is the human being, Herbert here capturing in glorious poetry Christ's bold identification of the Temple with himself (John 2.21), and perhaps also suggesting that God cares more about the cries of one poor Christian than about all the grandeur of an earthly monarch:[1335]

> And truly brasse and stones are heavie things,
> Tombes for the dead, not temples fit for thee:
>   But grones are quick, and full of wings,
>   And all their motions upward be;
> And ever as they mount, like larks they sing;
> The note is sad, yet musick for a King.[1336]

Elsewhere Herbert goes further still. In 'The storm', perhaps the most vivid of all examples of his emphasis on a God who freely puts individual cries of pain before everything else, he stresses the urgent desperation of so much authentic human prayer, and the need for an immediate response from God:

> If as the windes and waters here below
>   Do flie and flow,
> My sighs and tears as busie were above;
>   Sure they would move
> And much affect thee, as tempestuous times
> Amaze poore mortals, and object their crimes.
>
> Starres have their storms, ev'n in a high degree,
>   As well as we.
> A throbbing conscience spurred by remorse
>   Hath a strange force:
> It quits the earth, and mounting more and more
> Dares to assault thee, and besiege thy doore.
>
> There it stands knocking, to thy musicks wrong,
>   And drowns the song.
> Glorie and honour are set by, till it
>   An answer get.
> Poets have wrong'd poore storms: such dayes are best;
> They purge the aire without, within the breast.[1337]

Here it is a 'throbbing conscience spurred by remorse' which batters on heaven's door. In 'Affliction (4)', suffering is itself a cause for wonder ('Once a poore creature, now a wonder'); and Herbert catches with great force the experience of interior suffering ('My thoughts are all a case of knives/ Wounding my heart'). He prays to God to scatter those interior aspects of himself (in effect the 'enemies' of the Psalms) which cause him such distress:

> Then shall those powers, which work for grief,
>   Enter thy pay,
>   And day by day
> Labour thy praise, and my relief:
>   With care and courage building me,
>   Till I reach heav'n, and much more, thee.[1338]

In 'Deniall', Herbert explores the dilemma of those whose prayers go unanswered:

> When my devotions could not pierce
> Thy silent eares;
> Then was my heart broken, as was my verse:
> My breast was full of fears
> And disorder:
>
> My bent thoughts, like a brittle bow,
> Did flie asunder:
> Each took his way; some would to pleasures go,
> Some to the warres and thunder
> Of alarms.
>
> As good go any where, they say,
> As to benumme
> Both knees and heart, in crying night and day,
> *Come, come, my God, O come,*
> But no hearing.
>
> Therefore my soul lay out of sight,
> Untun'd, unstring:
> My feeble spirit, unable to look right,
> Like a nipt blossome, hung
> Discontented.
>
> O cheer and tune my heartlesse breast,
> Deferre no time;
> That so thy favours granting my request,
> They and my minde may chime,
> And mend my ryme.[1339]

Note the musical imagery, here as so often in Herbert's poetry: this is another of the many parallels between the Psalms and his poems, singing forming a means both of articulating the suffering and of transcending it, universalizing it, lifting it into the heart of God.[1340] The same theme of unanswered prayer, with a corresponding emphasis on the need both to 'know oneself to be a sinner' and to persevere, appears powerfully in *The method*:

> Poore heart, lament.
> For since thy God refuseth still,
> There is some rub, some discontent,
> Which cools his will.
>
> Thy Father could
> Quickly effect, what thou dost move;
> For he is *Power*: and sure he would;
> For he is *Love*.

> Go search this thing,
> Tumble thy breast, and turn thy book.
> If thou hadst lost a glove or ring,
>   Wouldst thou not look?
>
> What do I see
> Written above there? *Yesterday*
> *I did behave me carelessly,*
>   *When I did pray.*
>
> And should Gods eare
> To such indifferents chained be,
> Who do not their own motions heare?
>   Is God lesse free?
>
> But stay! what's there?
> *Late when I would have something done,*
> *I had a notion to forbear,*
>   *Yet I went on.*
>
> And should Gods eare,
> Which needs not man, be ty'd to those
> Who heare not him, but quickly heare
>   His utter foes?
>
> Then once more pray:
> Down with thy knees, up with thy voice.
> Seek pardon first, and God will say,
>   *Glad heart rejoyce.*[1341]

In 'Longing', Herbert approaches most closely to the style and manner of a psalm of lament, with his vivid imagery, use of vigorous questions, and the dialectic of despair and intimacy:

> To thee help appertains.
> Hast thou left all things to their course,
>   And laid the reins
>   Upon the horse?
> Is all lockt? hath a sinners plea
>   No key? . . .
>
> My love, my sweetness, heare!
> By these thy feet, at which my heart
>   Lies all the yeare,
>   Plucke out thy dart,
> And heal my troubled breast which cryes,
>   Which dyes.[1342]

But it is in the exquisite miniature 'Bitter-sweet' that Herbert encapsulates to perfection the spirituality of the lament-psalms:

Ah my deare angrie Lord,
Since thou dost love, yet strike;
Cast down, yet help afford;
Sure I will do the like.

I will complain, yet praise;
I will bewail, approve:
And all my sowre-sweet dayes
I will lament, and love.[1343]

Here Herbert answers the God of Calvin (and also, let it be remembered, the God of the Bible) with his own medicine: he gives as good as he gets, not simply out of some desire to get even with God, but because such an attitude is of the very essence of an authentic Christian spiritual life. Here is the quiet but strong inner confidence of the one who knows himself to be adopted as a child of God, to be loved for all eternity, and who thereafter may bring before God every possible aspect not only of his own life and experience, but of all the world's.[1344]

Conclusion

In the final analysis, George Herbert sidesteps the terrible implications of Calvin's grisly belief (itself inherited from Augustine) that most of humankind forms a *massa damnata*. Instead he builds on his own profound but never uncritical religious faith to fashion a relationship with a God whose gentle but irresistible grace offers, not just a glimpse of the 'land of spices', but an invitation to a party.[1345] There is no more subtle, more economical, more sheerly attractive, presentation of the epicentre of Protestant spirituality than this:

Love bade me welcome: yet my soul drew back,
        Guiltie of dust and sinne.
But quick-ey'd Love, observing me grow slack
        From my first entrance in,
Drew nearer to me, sweetly questioning,
        If I lack'd anything.

A guest, I answer'd, worthy to be here.
        Love said, you shall be he.
I the unkinde, ungratefull? Ah my deare,
        I cannot look on thee.
Look took my hand, and smiling did reply,
        Who made the eyes but I?

Truth Lord, but I have marr'd them: let my shame
        Go where it doth deserve.
And know you not, sayes Love, who bore the blame?
        My deare, then I will serve.
You must sit down, sayes Love, and taste my meat.
        So I did sit and eat.[1346]

'Practicall Divinitie': Jeremy Taylor (1613–67)

Introduction

Jeremy Taylor is both the best-known and arguably the greatest of the Caroline theologians, a group of Church of England scholars generally associated with the Arminian or Laudian tradition, decidedly royalist and ready to defend episcopal order in the church, but interested above all in fostering 'an exact and careful piety aiming at bringing all daily life under the lordship of Jesus Christ'.[1347] Most of them practised their ministry outside the universities; but all of them were learned, drawing upon a vast and catholic range of sources in order to produce a genuinely comprehensive view of the Christian life, and all shared English worship when England was at war with itself.[1348] Their methods in bringing to birth this 'practicall divinitie' included worship, preaching, catechesis, and spiritual guidance, each informing the other. It was this kind of religion which prevailed in the England of Charles II; and it found its *locus classicus* in the revised and reissued Book of Common Prayer of 1662, of which Taylor himself wrote:

> there is no part of religion, as it is a distinct virtue, and is to be exercised by interior acts and forms of worship, but is in the offices of the church of England.[1349]

It is a large claim; and Taylor set about defending it in a substantial body of works, and with a learning and a style virtually unequalled even in this most golden of ages. His scholarship is not only classical and patristic:[1350] it included a knowledge of Judaism, a vast familiarity with medieval theology, and an amazing Renaissance-style fascination with almost every aspect of life, from elderly women dancing in Lapland[1351] to the dietary idiosyncrasies of the Greek goat.[1352] His literary style is superb, measured but not pompous, extended and rhetorical but crammed with images drawn from everyday life and seasoned with apposite aphorisms, some grave ('*Baldnesse* is but a dressing to our funerals'[1353]), some witty ('I desire to *dye a dry death*, but am not very desirous to have a *dry funeral*: some flowers sprinkled upon my grave would do well and comely'[1354]), almost all thought-provoking ('Marriage . . . is the seminary of the church';[1355] 'be governed by your needs not by your fancy'[1356]).[1357]

Taylor's own life was far from easy. He was one of a group of firmly royalist Church of England clergy who were sequestered from their livings by Parliament for joining the King's forces, finding protection and shelter as chaplains in royalist households.[1358] Sent by William Laud to Oxford after having first been educated at Cambridge, Taylor became in 1636 a Fellow of All Souls: it was while at Oxford that he came in contact with William Chillingworth and the circle of scholars associated with Great Tew.[1359] He married in 1639, a year after becoming Rector of Uppingham, where he remained until his ejection in 1642. During the Civil War he was attached to the royal household as a chaplain, but in 1645 was captured by parliamentary troops: after his release he went to live as chaplain to Lord Carbery's household at Golden Grove in Carmarthenshire for nearly ten years; and it was here that he wrote many of his major works. In 1658 he was given a lectureship at Lisburn, and two years later became Bishop of Down and Connor (to which the see of Dromore was subsequently added).

He combined his episcopal duties with the role of Vice-Chancellor of the University of Dublin: neither task was easy, and in both he encountered a good deal of vigorous opposition. He died in 1667 and was buried in the cathedral at Dromore which he was himself responsible for building.

Taylor's works include some polemic (his *Dissuasive from Popery* of 1664–7), a long *History of the life and death of the Holy Jesus* (usually called *The great exemplar* and published in 1649), which combines theological and devotional reflection with a great deal of moral guidance, and the even larger *Ductor dubitantium* of 1660, a comprehensive guide to every conceivable aspect of Christian ethical behaviour.[1360] His most famous works are *The rule and exercises of holy living* (1650) and *The rule and exercises of holy dying* (1651), both written at Golden Grove and both designed 'to sustain afflicted members of the Church of England' after the execution of Laud and Charles I.[1361]

Spirituality and creation

Where Herbert's view of the creation was entirely compatible with Calvin's, reflecting a desire to discern the will of an omnipotent God by seeking its manifestation among his creatures, Taylor's was more sacramental:

> If God is glorified in the sun and moon, in the rare fabric of the honeycombs, in the discipline of bees, in the economy of pismires [= ants], in the little houses of birds, in the curiosity of an eye, God being pleased to delight in those little images and reflexes of Himself from those pretty mirrors, which, like a crevice in the wall, through a narrow perspective transmit the species of a vast excellency: much rather shall God be pleased to behold Himself in the glasses of our obedience, in the emissions of our will and understanding; these being rational and apt instruments to express Him, far better than the natural, as being nearer communications of Himself.[1362]

Note the characteristically vivid but long-breathed sentence; but note too the clear recognition that creation is only a starting-place for the spiritual life: human behaviour and morality is an altogether higher priority for him. One of the reasons why this is so is evident here too: our will and understanding, being 'rational and apt instruments to express him', come far closer to the nature of God than anything else in the created order. We are a long way from Calvinism here: for Taylor, reason and revelation balance and fulfil one another: 'God's Spirit does not destroy reason, but heightens it'.[1363] He is not keen on disorder and enthusiasm: his entire spirituality is *reasonable*; and he criticizes a piety that lacks this vital foundation.[1364]

'Practicall divinitie'

For Taylor, the spiritual life is a careful fusion of reason and experience of a kind which alone conduces to wisdom: 'into the greatest mysteriousness of our religion, and the deepest articles of faith, we enter by our reason'.[1365] He objects to transubstantiation because it involves a deliberate suspension of our reason.[1366] On the other hand, empty intellectual speculation is useless because it has no power to change lives:[1367] this leads

Taylor to a clear preference for 'those old wise spirits, who preserved natural reason and religion in the midst of heathen darkness' (by which he means classical Latin and Greek authors) over 'the triflings of many of the later Schoolmen, who promoted a petty interest of a family, or an unlearned opinion . . . but added nothing to Christianity but trouble, scruple, and vexation'.[1368] In short, learning is no substitute for holiness:

> Want of learning and disability to consider great secrets of Theology does not at all retard our progresse to spirituall perfections; love to JESUS may be better promoted by the plainer understandings of honest and unlettered people, then by the finer and more exalted speculations of great Clerks, that have lesse devotion.[1369]

What we find in Taylor's work, then, is an *integrated* view of spiritual life ('God requires of us to serve him with an integral, entire, or a whole worship and religion'): to serve God without both body and soul is worthless.[1370] Hence his strictures on a compartmentalized religion – reproving a sinner, but pompously, or giving to the poor while not forgiving our enemies;[1371] or praying all day and behaving intemperately at night.[1372] Faith and charity are mutually inseparable:[1373] those who never seek to bring about in action what they asked for in prayer are 'deceitful workers'.[1374] Religion, in short, has to become the mainspring of the business of our lives;[1375] and Taylor's entire work was consecrated to helping people make it so.

This crucial point underlies the whole of his spirituality. He has no interest in a narrowly academic theology: he readily acknowledges that we are justified not by works and merit but 'by mercy and the faith of Jesus Christ';[1376] but instead of warning of the perils attending those who believe otherwise, he castigates those who insist on 'disputing about the philosophy of justification':

> These things are knotty, and too intricate to do any good; they may amuse us, but never instruct us; and they have already made men careless and confident, disputative and troublesome, proud and uncharitable, but neither wiser nor better. Let us therefore leave these weak ways of troubling ourselves or others, and directly look to the theology of it, the direct duty, the end of faith, and the work of faith, the conditions and the instruments of our salvation, the just foundation of our hopes, how our faith can destroy our sin, and how it can unite us unto God; how by it we can be made partakers of Christ's death, and imitators of His life.[1377]

He refuses to separate justification from sanctification in the manner of Calvin: 'no man is actually justified, but he that is in some measure sanctified'.[1378] This is 'practicall divinitie' again: faith cannot be reduced to acceptance of a proposition. 'The act of believing propositions is not for itself, but in order to certain ends; as sermons are to good life and obedience'.[1379] Hence too 'justification and sanctification are continued acts: they are like the issues of a fountain into its receptacles; God is always giving, and we are always receiving'.[1380]

Taylor appears to have little doctrine of assurance: in his examination of the theme of repentance in *Holy living*, he warns people against assuming that they are forgiven the moment they repent: 'a true penitent must all the dayes of his life pray for pardon, and never think the work completed till he dyes'.[1381] 'Whether God hath forgiven us or no, we know not'.[1382] But he does lay great stress on Christ's intercession for us ('Consider that as it cost Christ many millions of prayers and groans, and sighs, so he is now at this instant and hath been for these 1600 years night and day incessantly praying for grace to us that we may repent'[1383]). Again and again, however, he returns to his principal theme: the fact of our salvation is inseparable from the way in which we make that salvation a reality in our lives. Imputed, external righteousness of the Calvinist kind is not enough:

> The righteousness evangelical is [not an intermittent or partial goodness but] another kind of thing: it is a holy conversation, a god-like life, an universal obedience, a keeping nothing back from God, a sanctification of the whole man, and keeps not the body only, but the soul and the spirit, unblamable to the coming of the Lord Jesus.[1384]

This 'sanctification of the whole man' necessarily involves addressing the reality of sin, a reality which directly challenges the integrated view of religion Taylor champions:

> It is so little we spend in religion and so very much upon ourselves, so little to the poor and so without measure to make ourselves sick, that we seem to be in love with our own mischief, and so passionate for necessity and want, that we strive all the ways we can to make ourselves need more than nature intended.[1385]

To do this is to forget our own nature. Taylor argues that from the beginning humanity's first appetite was to be like God.[1386] 'From this first appetite of man to be like God, and the first natural instrument of it, love, descend all the first obligations of religion.'[1387] Humanity's second appetite was 'to beget one like himself'.[1388] From these two primary appetites flow the twofold commandment to love God and neighbour, for 'a man came to have a neighbour, by being a husband and a father'.[1389] Hence

> Man who was designed by GOD to a happy life, was fitted with sufficient meanes to attain that end, so that he might, if he would, be happy; but he was a free agent, and so might choose. And it is possible, that man may faile of his end, and be made miserable by God, by himselfe, or by his Neighbour. Or by the same persons he may be made happy in the same proportions, as they relate to him. If God be angry or disobeyed, he becomes our enemy, and so we faile: if our neighbour be injured or impeded in the direct order to his happy living, he hath equall right against us, as we against him, and so we fail that way: and if I be intemperate, I grow sick and worsted in some faculty, and so I am unhappy in my self. But if I obey God, and doe right to my neighbour, and confine my selfe within the order and designe of nature, I am secured in all ends of blessing, in which I can be assisted by these three, that is, by all my relatives, there being no end of man designed by God in order to his happinesse, to which

these are not proper and sufficient instruments. Man can have no other relations, no other discourses, no other regular appetites, but what are served and satisfied by religion, by sobriety, and by justice. There is nothing, whereby we can relate to any person, who can hurt us, or doe us benefit, but is provided for in these three. These therefore are all, and these are sufficient.[1390]

The luminous and ordered vision of life, the clear-headed emphasis on human freewill, the refusal to separate theology from ethics, and the unadorned beauty of the prose, are all characteristic of Taylor. And they underpin his understanding of the spiritual life. He sees this in a dynamic way: 'our holiness must persevere to the end. But . . . it must also be growing all the way';[1391] and the person who is 'grown in grace' as the one who 'hath made religion habitual to his spirit'.[1392] Such a person will manifest certain signs of that spiritual growth: regular reception of Holy Communion;[1393] an active *disponibilité* for the service of God;[1394] an equally active concern for justice and charity;[1395] and a persistent concern for repentance, which 'is a rough and a sharp virtue, and like a mattock and spade breaks away all the roughnesses of the passage, and hinderances of sin'.[1396]

Elsewhere he suggests three more signs of spiritual growth: a willingness to endure persecution (and if necessary to be obedient 'unto death'); a capacity to be merciful and generous to others; and a willingness to love one's enemies.[1397]

The work of the Holy Spirit

Now all this might seem to imply that spiritual progress is primarily to be achieved by human effort; but Taylor has no intention of suggesting such a thing. In his two Whitsun sermons he argues that those who are 'in the Spirit' hand over their wills to the Spirit, into a *libera custodia*, 'a holy and amiable captivity to the Spirit', in which 'we are free as princes within the circle of their diadem, and our chains are bracelets, and the law is a law of liberty'.[1398] The Spirit gives us *discernment* ('a man that hath tasted of God's Spirit, can instantly discern the madness that is in rage'[1399]), and an appetite for spiritual things.[1400] The Spirit does not stop us from sinning: it makes sin unnatural, unappealing ('so all spiritual men, all that are born of God, and the seed of God remains in them, "they cannot sin;" cannot *without trouble*, and doing against their natures, and their most passionate inclinations'[1401]). The Spirit *inoculates* us against worldly pleasures and comforts us in times of sorrow.

But it does more as well. By the work of the Spirit we become tripartite: body, soul, and spirit; we become sons and daughters of God by adoption, and new creatures, 'capable of a new state, entitled to another manner of duration, enabled to do new and greater actions in order to higher ends; we have new affections, new understandings, new wills'.[1402] We discover that we have 'passions and desires of things beyond and contrary to our natural appetites', especially for that sanctity that makes us like God.[1403] What the Spirit does, then, is to create a new nature within us and to animate us with a new life, which needs to bear fruit in holy living.[1404]

Holy living

This brings us to the heart of Taylor's spirituality: the practice of holy living and holy dying. One of the reasons we find these difficult is because we do not begin to acquire wisdom until we are already half-dead with gout and other disabilities:[1405]

> Old age seizes upon most men while they still retain the minds of boyes and vitious youth, doing actions from principles of great folly, and a mighty ignorance, admiring things uselesse and hurtfull, and filling up all the dimensions of their abode with businesses of empty affairs, being at leasure to attend no vertue: they cannot pray, because they are busie, and because they are passionate: they cannot communicate because they have quarrels and intrigues of perplexed causes, complicated hostilities, and things of the world; and therefore they cannot attend to the things of God, little considering, that they must find a time to die in; when death comes, they must be at leisure for that.[1406]

Taylor is acutely aware of how little time we end up devoting to 'religious walking with God' because of all the time we spend on eating, sleeping, ill company, worldly civilities and so on.[1407] Fortunately for us, God has enabled us to make the necessities of nature into parts of our religious duty, and thereby 'he, by adopting them into religion may turn our nature into grace, and accept our natural actions, as actions of religion'[1408] – as Elisha stretched himself upon the child, breathing new life into him.[1409] Thus 'strive not to forget your time, and suffer none of it to passe undis-cerned'.[1410] He offers a range of ways in which we can exercise 'care of our time':[1411] we should avoid idleness, 'the greatest prodigality in the world'[1412] (though he acknowl-edges that due relaxation is vital[1413]). He encourages us to intersperse our busy work with ejaculatory prayers, and warns against useless busyness ('there are some people, who are busie, but it is as Domitian was, in catching flies'[1414]). More positively, we need to set appropriate priorities in our lives, putting religious obligations first,

> not like the Patriarch who ran from the Altar in S. *Sophia* to his stable in all
> his Pontificals, and in the midst of his office, to see a Colt newly fallen
> from his beloved and much valued Mare *Phorbante*.[1415]

Above all we must seek to 'redeem the time', ending each day by examining carefully but without fussiness all that we have done.[1416]

But holy living involves much more than good use of time. We must aspire to purity of intention,[1417] doing all for the glory of God. Taylor has no shortage of vivid illustra-tions to make his point: 'if a man visits his sick friend, and watches at his pillow for charitys sake, and because of his old affection we approve it: but if he does it in hope of legacy, he is a Vulture, and onely watches for the carkasse'.[1418] Instead Taylor recom-mends beginning each action in the name of the Father, the Son and the Holy Spirit;[1419] and he offers a shrewd way of discerning whether or not we have yet made this purity of intention our own:

> He that does his recreation, or his merchandise cheerfully, promptly,
> readily and busily, and the works of religion slowly, flatly, and without

appetite, and the spirit moves like *Pharaohs* chariots when the wheels were off, it is a signe, that his heart is not right with God, but it cleaves too much to the world.[1420]

Taylor proposes three 'general instruments of holy living': care of our time, purity of intention, and the practice of the presence of God:[1421]

God is wholly in every place, included in no place, not bound with cords (except those of love) . . . we may imagine God to be as the Aire and the Sea, and we all inclosed in his circle, wrapt up in the lap of his infinite nature, or as infants in the wombs of their pregnant Mothers: and we can no more be removed from the presence of God, than from our own being.[1422]

And the process of fostering a conscious awareness of God's presence allows us to experience more directly its blessings:

In the face of the Sun you may see Gods beauty: In the fire you may feel his heat warming, in the water, his gentleness to refresh you: he it is that comforts your spirit when you have taken Cordials: it is the dew of Heaven that makes your field give you bread; and the breasts of God are the bottles that minister drink to your necessities.[1423]

But this is not just a matter of *discerning* God's presence: it is a matter of *reverencing* it:

God is in every creature: be cruel towards none, neither abuse any by intemperance. Remember that the creatures and every member of thy own body is one of the lesser cabinets and receptacles of God. They are such which God hath blessed with his presence, hallowed by his touch, and separated from unholy use by making them to belong to his dwelling.[1424]

And this brings Taylor to his sonorous and splendid summary:

He that can look upon death, and see its face with the same countenance with which he hears its story . . . he that does nothing for opinion sake, but every thing for conscience, being as curious of his thoughts, as of his actings in markets and Theaters, and is as much in awe of himself, as of a whole assembly; he that knows God looks on, and contrives his secret affairs as in the presence of God and his holy Angels; that eats and drinks because he needs it, not that he may serve a lust or load his belly; he that is bountifull and cheerfull to his friends, and charitable and apt to forgive his enemies; that loves his countrey and obeyes his Prince, and desires and endeavours nothing more than that he may do honour to God, this person may reckon his life, to be the life of a man, and compute his moneths, not by the course of the sun, but the Zodiac and circle of his vertues: because these are such things which fools and children and birds and beasts cannot have: These are therefore the actions of life, because they are the seeds of immortality. That day in which we have done some excellent thing, we may as truly reckon to be added to our life, as were the fifteen years to the dayes of *Hezekiah*.[1425]

Here indeed is a charter for spiritual citizenship, a balanced and practical wisdom for ordered and peaceable living. But holy living involves much more than this: it includes sobriety ('all that duty that concerns our selves in the matter of *meat* and *drink* and *pleasures* and *thoughts*'[1426]), justice (which extends from the responsibilities of parents to their children to the workings of the civil law[1427]), and the practice of religion and the duties incumbent upon all Christians in respect of their faith.[1428] It also requires of us the capacity to face death, for 'it is a great art to dye well, and to be learnt by men in health, by them that can discourse and consider . . . [for] he that prepares not for death, before his last sicknesse, is like him that begins to study Philosophy when he is going to dispute publikely in the faculty.'[1429] Taylor articulates the essence of 'holy dying' in yet another superlative piece of prose:

> If we could from one of the battlements of Heaven espie how many men and women at this time lie fainting and dying for want of bread, how many young men are hewn down by the sword of war, how many poor orphans are now weeping over the graves of their father by whose life they were enabled to eat: if we could but hear how many mariners and passengers are at this present in a storm, and shriek out because their keel dashes against a rock, or bulges under them, how many people there are that weep with want, and are mad with oppression, or are desperate by too quick a sense of a constant infelicity; in all reason we should be glad to be out of the noise and participation of so many evils. This is a place of sorrows and tears, of great evils and a constant calamity: let us remove from hence, at least in affections and preparation of mind.[1430]

It is by meditating soberly on death that we 'make death safe and friendly' and free ourselves from its terrors.[1431] He exhorts daily self-examination with some vivid contemporary images: 'the computations of a mans life are buisie as the Tables of Signes and Tangents, and intricate as the accounts of Eastern Merchants: and therefore it were but reason we should summe up our accounts at the foot of every page, I mean, that we call our selves to scrutiny every night when we compose our selves to the little images of Death.'[1432] We should thereby 'dash our sins against the stones, that we may go to God, and to a spirituall Guide, and search for remedies and apply them'.[1433]

Taylor's piety is directed to people who had to try to find God, and meaning, and hope in the midst of social upheavals which subverted all older certainties. So although on occasions he commends a holy boldness,[1434] it is perhaps not surprising that he is inclined to give modesty and gentility a higher place;[1435] and he admits winningly that 'he hath need be a bold man that shall tell his Patron, he is going to Hell'!'[1436] His attitude in this regard is well reflected in his long treatise on the life of Jesus: he typically describes Christ's piety as 'even, constant, unblameable, complying with civil society'.[1437] There is an ordered serenity about Taylor's Christ, free of extravagant ecstasies or irrational behaviour.[1438] But he does stress that seeking to imitate Christ has a profound effect on us:

> JESUS becomes the fountain of spiritual Life to us, as the Prophet *Elisha* to the dead childe: when he stretched his hands upon the childes hands,

laid his mouth to his mouth, and formed his posture to the boy, and breathed into him, the spirit returned again into the childe at the prayer of *Elisha*: so when our lives are formed into the imitation of the life of the holiest JESUS, the spirit of God returns into us, not onely by the efficacy of the imitation, but by the merit and impetration of the actions of JESUS.[1439]

He heart-warmingly acknowledges that this imitation must not be over-literal:

We never read that JESUS laughed, and but once that he rejoyced in spirit; but the declensions of our Natures cannot bear the weight of a perpetual grave deportment, without the intervals of refreshment and free alacrity.[1440]

And he commends the prayer of Christ in Gethsemane as a normative model for our own:

There is not in the world any condition of prayer which is essential to the duty, or any circumstances of advantage to its performance, but were concentred in this one instance: Humility of spirit, lowlinesse of deportment, importunity of desire, a fervent spirit, a lawful matter; resignation to the will of GOD, great love, the love of a Son to his Father.[1441]

The theology and practice of prayer

This brings us finally to Taylor's understanding of prayer. Here too he takes a balanced, integrated view: 'our prayers must be fervent, intense, earnest, and importunate';[1442] and prayer without a deep inner affection is worthless.[1443] He emphasizes the importance of right desires in relation to prayer, and with great sensitivity acknowledges how difficult this is:

They only can be confident that their desires are right, who feel sharpnesses and zeal in their acts of love . . . Great desires are a great pain; and the spouse in the Canticles complains that she is 'sick of love' . . . In all spiritual progressions we are sure that our desires shall never cease growing, till they be full of God, and are swelled up to immensity; and till they come to some greatness, that they are like hunger and thirst, or like the breasts of a fruitful nurse, full and in pain till they be eased, we cannot be so confident that things are well with us in this particular.[1444]

This is a vital point: true devotion comprises both prayer and a willingness to rejoice in God, to make God the centre of our lives.[1445] Once tasted, this spiritual rejoicing and delight increases the soul's appetite for them, 'and cannot become a weariness, because they satisfy all the way, and only increase the desire, because themselves grow bigger and more amiable', thereby excluding all other desires:

If you can once obtain but to delight in prayer, and to long for the day of a communion, and to be pleased with holy meditation, and to desire God's grace with great passion, and an appetite keen as a wolf upon the void plains of the north; if you can delight in God's love, and consider concerning His providence, and busy yourselves in the pursuit of the affairs of His kingdom, then you have the grace of devotion, and your evil nature shall be cured.[1446]

Taylor returns to this point frequently, and with characteristic eloquence.[1447] And he agrees with Bunyan in insisting that our prayers will be judged and heard in accordance with the sincerity of our desire and the fervour of spirit with which they are offered.[1448] But what this means is that prayer is not only integrating, demanding the fullest use of both head and heart: it is also hard work. Intercessions for others requires 'a great stock of [personal] piety':[1449]

He that prays to recover a family from an hereditary curse, or to reverse a sentence of God, to cancel a decree of heaven gone out against his friend; he that would heal the sick with his prayer, or with his devotion prevail against an army, must not expect such great effects upon a morning or evening collect.[1450]

Yet, paradoxical as it might appear, Taylor wants to insist that prayer is not only costly and effortful: it is also profoundly invigorating ('our duty to God should be hugely pleasing, and we should rejoice in it'[1451]); and this conviction elicits from him a passage that is memorably eloquent and deeply felt even by his Olympian standards:

If a man goes to his prayers as children go to school . . . 'he acts a part' which he cannot long personate, but will find so many excuses and silly devices to omit his duty, such tricks to run from that which will make him happy; he will so watch the eyes of men, and be so sure to do nothing in private; he will so often distinguish and mince the duty into minutes and little particles, he will so tie himself to the letter of the law, and be so careless of the intention and spiritual design, he will be punctual in the ceremony and trifling in the secret, and he will be so well pleased when he is hindered by an accident not of his own procuring, and will have so many devices to defeat his duty, and to cozen himself, that he will certainly manifest, that he is afraid of religion, and secretly hates it; he counts it a burden and an objection, and then the man is sure to leave it when his circumstances are so fitted. But if we delight in it, we enter into a portion of the reward as soon as we begin the work . . . But this delight is not to be understood as if it were always required that we should feel an actual cheerfulness and sensible joy . . . our joy must be a joy of hope, a joy at the least of confident sufferers, the joys of faith and expectation; 'rejoicing in hope'.[1452]

It is no surprise to find that for Taylor prayer is inseparable from action, and in particular from love of neighbour: we cannot expect God to listen to our prayers if we show no concern whatever for those around us who are afflicted; and for him it is not surprising that so few prayers are answered when so few people live lives worthy of what they are praying.[1453] This was precisely the Pharisees' weakness; and Christians are all too often no different:[1454]

> Some men talk like angels, and pray with great fervour, and meditate with
> deep recesses, and speak to God with loving affections, and words of
> union, and adhere to Him in silent devotion, and when they go abroad are
> as passionate as ever, peevish as a frighted fly, vexing themselves with their
> own reflections: they are cruel in their bargains, unmerciful to their
> tenants, and proud as a barbarian prince.[1455]

Prayer offers us a priceless opportunity to transmute the dross of our lives into gold:
to 'convert our very scorpions into the exercise of virtues'.[1456] 'Do not trouble yourself
by thinking how much you are afflicted, but consider how much you make of it.'[1457]
Taylor speaks eloquently about prayer 'in the Spirit', and describes it thus:

> we speak His sense, we live His life, we breathe His accents, we desire in
> order to His purposes, and our persons are gracious by His holiness, and
> are accepted by His interpellation and intercession in the act and offices of
> Christ: this is 'praying with the Spirit'.[1458]

Yet he insists that public and formal prayer should take precedence over extempore
and private prayer. He does allow that 'sometimes an exuberant and active affection
and overflowing of devotion may descend like anointing from above, and our cup run
over, and is not to be contained within the margent of prescribed forms',[1459] though
he thinks this should happen in private, not in public prayer, as with Christ in
Gethsemane:

> in these prayers [of Christ in Gethsemane] the spirit was bound up with
> the strictness and violence of intention, but could not ease itself with a
> flood of language and various expression. A great devotion is like a great
> grief, not so expressive as a moderate passion; tears spend the grief, and
> variety of language breathes out the devotion; and therefore Christ went
> thrice, and said the same words; He could just speak His sense in a plain
> expression, but the greatness of His agony was too big for the pleasure of a
> sweet and sensible expression of devotion.[1460]

But Taylor criticises extemporary prayer on the grounds that it is so often unpre-
pared and therefore ill-considered:[1461] the Spirit comes to assist us in our labours, not
to remove the need for them altogether.[1462] By contrast, prayer in the Bible is essentially liturgical – the Psalms, the Lord's Prayer, and so on.[1463] Liturgical prayer unites
us with the whole church, allows us to appropriate for ourselves articles of faith, is
reliable because rooted in proper authority;[1464] and 'there may be great liberty in set
forms' just as there can be severe restriction in extempore prayer – the latter can lead to
the tyranny of the subjective – no one regards the singing of a psalm as a restriction on
the spirit.[1465]
It is important to note Taylor's own reminder that true prayer in the Spirit is not
only, or even primarily, a matter of words:

> for the words of prayer are no part of the spirit of prayer; words may be the
> body of it, but the spirit of prayer always consists in holiness, that is, in
> holy desires and holy actions. Words are not properly capable of being

holy; all words are in themselves servants of things; and the holiness of a prayer is not at all concerned in the manner of its expression, but in the spirit of it, that is, in the violence of its desires, and the innocence of its ends, and the continuance of its employment. This is the verification of that great prophecy which Christ made, that 'in all the world the true worshippers should worship in spirit and in truth;' that is, with a pure mind, with holy desires, for spiritual things, according to the mind of the Spirit, in the imitation of Christ's intercession, with perseverance, with charity or love. That is the Spirit of God, and these are the spiritualities of the Gospel, and the formalities of prayers as they are christian and evangelical.[1466]

Yet, by the same token, those who regard true prayer as nothing more than emotional vapourings, and who pour out words without stopping to consider what they mean, are dangerously misguided.[1467] And he concludes with a noble and comprehensive summary:

Prayer is one of the noblest exercises of christian religion, or rather it is that duty in which all graces are concentred. Prayer is charity, it is faith, it is a conformity to God's will, a desiring according to the desires of heaven, an imitation of Christ's intercession, and prayer must suppose all holiness, or else it is nothing; and therefore all that in which men need God's spirit, all that is in order to prayer. Baptism is but a prayer, and the holy sacrament of the Lord's supper is but a prayer; a prayer of sacrifice representative, and a prayer of oblation, and a prayer of intercession, and a prayer of thanksgiving. And obedience is a prayer, and begs and procures blessings: and if the Holy Ghost hath sanctified the whole man, then He hath sanctified the prayer of the man, and not till then.[1468]

This sane and integrated approach to prayer leads Taylor to warn against any form of spiritual elitism, as though familiarity with God might be enjoyed only by a privileged few: for such familiarity,

which is an affection of friendship, is the entercourse of giving and receiving blessings and graces respectively: and it is produced by a holy life, or the being in the state of grace, and is part of every mans inheritance that is a friend of GOD. But when familiarity with GOD shall be esteemed a priviledge of singular and eminent persons not communicated to all the faithfull, and is thought to be an admission to a neerer entercourse of secrecy with GOD, it is an effect of pride.[1469]

True familiarity with God is accessible to all; but it remains that of a servant 'or a son in minority', implying obedience, duty and fear, not 'the impudence of proud equals'.[1470] It is difficult to disagree with his principal point here; but it runs the risk of removing almost any possibility of spontaneous intimacy from the experience of prayer. Taylor believes, for example, that anger invalidates prayer;[1471] and his reflections on prayer in times of suffering, though deeply eloquent, carry little hint of any

stress on intimacy with God of the kind so powerfully expressed in the Psalms of
lament:

> Sighs and groans, sorrow and prayers, humble complaints, and dolorous
> expressions are the sad accents of a sick mans language . . . Therefore,
> silence and still composures, and not complaining, are no parts of a sick
> mans duty; they are not necessary parts of patience. We find that *David*
> *roared for the very disquietnesse of his sicknesse*; and he lay *chattering like a*
> *swallow*, and his *throat was dry* with calling for help upon his God. Thats
> the proper voice of sicknesse: and certain it is, that the proper voyces of
> sicknesse are expressly *vocal*, and *petitory* in the eares of God, and call for
> pity in the same accent, as the cryes and oppressions of Widows and
> Orphans do for vengeance upon their persecutors, though they say no
> Collect against them. For there is *the voyce of man*, and there is *the voice of*
> *the disease*, and God hears both . . . when a man cries out, and complains
> but according to the sorrowes of his pain, it cannot be any part of a
> culpable impatience, but an argument for pity.[1472]

In his eucharistic spirituality, Taylor avoids language of ontological union with
Christ (though he does use Johannine language of incorporation or engrafting into
Christ[1473]). But he stresses, yet again, the interrelationship of our worship with the rest
of our lives;[1474] and, although his treatise on the Eucharist is immensely long and
repetitive, there is at its heart a teaching at once simple and profound: 'Worship Jesus:
love him; dedicate thyself to him; recollect what he hath done for thy soul.'[1475]

Conclusion

Jeremy Taylor's work is suffused with wise pastoral and spiritual advice. He wrote, or
adapted, a great number of prayers for almost every conceivable occasion, all of them
reflecting both the breadth of his concerns and the careful and sensitive way he seeks
to integrate theology, spirituality and Christian living ('The natural order of theology
is by faith to build up good life'[1476]). More generally, his vision of 'holy living' is rooted
in the ancient practical divinity of the Holiness Code in Leviticus, or the Sermon on
the Mount in the Gospel of St Matthew. He lacks the spontaneity of the Puritans, and
the ecstatic exuberance of some of the Counter-Reformation Catholics. But he offers
something which is absolutely their equal in depth and maturity, and perhaps their
superior in allowing the whole of life to become prayer. No one in the life of the
Church of England commands greater eloquence and sensitive, pastoral scholarship:
in so doing, he did more than offer a rich and sustaining spirituality for his own day;
he also laid enduring foundations for the modern age. Taylor's work is the quintessence of Anglican piety, and every word of his vast *oeuvre* is charged with his passionate
longing to renew the church he loved:

> We make religion to be the work of a few hours in the whole year; we are
> without fancy or affection to the severities of holy living; we reduce
> religion to the believing of a few articles, and doing nothing that is consid-
> erable; we pray seldom, and then but very coldly and indifferently; we

communicate not so often as the sun salutes both the tropics; we profess Christ, but dare not die for Him; we are factious for a religion, and will not live according to its precepts; we call ourselves Christians, and love to be ignorant of many of the laws of Christ, lest our knowledge should force us into shame, or into the troubles of a holy life.[1477]

Do not instantly upon your return from Church, return also to the world, and secular thoughts and imployments; but let the remaining parts of that day be like a *post-Communion* or an *after-office*, entertaining your blessed Lord with all the caresses and sweetnesse of love and colloquies, and enter-courses of duty and affection, acquainting him with all your needs, and revealing to him all your secrets, and opening all your infirmities; and as the affairs of your person or imployment call you off, so retire again with often ejaculations and acts of entertainment to your beloved Guest.[1478]

CONCLUSION: THE REBUILDING OF PETWORTH

In 1688, the same year that Bunyan died and William of Orange arrived at Torbay to claim the throne of England, Charles Seymour, 6th Duke of Somerset and descendant of Edward VI's Lord Protector, began to rebuild his country house at Petworth, set in rolling parkland a few hundred yards from the town centre, on a gentle sandstone ridge four miles north of the South Downs. A few parts of the old thirteenth-century castle, the Sussex seat of the proud Percy family, were retained, of which the most important was the chapel: the Duke had this refitted in 1690–2, and its liturgical design, with prominent carved pews and pulpit and no chancel or other 'holy' area reserved for the plain altar, reflects the triumph of Reformation theology over the undoubtedly ornate medieval original. Latimer's cobbler, and all the other 'fellows of St Antony', would have felt at home here – if they had been admitted to so aristocratic a residence.

The rest of the rebuilt mansion, however, is a different matter. The rebuilding was conceived on the grandest scale, befitting someone who was to be remembered as the 'Proud Duke'.[1479] The architect of the monumental west front is unknown, but his indebtedness to French influence is unquestionable:[1480] it exudes a kind of opulent reticence – Versailles with an English accent. The tension between the wings and the centre, between the vast width (320 feet) and the three-storey vertical rows of windows, between the whole composition and the sweeping landscape of Lancelot 'Capability' Brown in which it now stands, is the tension of reason and emotion, rhythm and rhetoric, order and freedom, that suffuses the toccatas and fugues of J. S. Bach.[1481] Inside, the astonishing wood-carvings created by Grinling Gibbons in 1692 evoke something quite different again: the rich imaginative wonder of the Baroque, recreating in playful vernacular style the primal innocence of Eden.[1482] And even in that sober Protestant chapel something new is stirring amidst the grave and elegant woodwork: the local estate woodcarver John Selden created a profusion of cherubs' heads, each one, as Ian Nairn put it, 'a roaring cantankerous epitome of babyhood'.[1483] Latimer would never have approved of *that*.

In its rich blend of the medieval, the reformed, and the rococo, with its continental style, its celebration of natural beauty, its careful fusion of the classical and the Baroque, Petworth both encapsulates and points beyond the two centuries we have just explored. The wars of More and Tyndale, the sufferings of Bunyan and Taylor, the martyrdoms of Cranmer and Latimer, were over: though none of them lived to enjoy it, the 1689 Toleration Act, passed in the teeth of opposition from the Anglican hierarchy, permitted the creation of non-Anglican churches and chapels, and thereby (though unintentionally) tolerated non-attendance at any place of worship as well. The coming decades would see the rise, not just of tolerance, but of agnosticism, rationalism and scepticism too. The legacy of the past endured; and the spirituality of the eighteenth and nineteenth centuries was incalculably indebted to the faith of its Tudor and Stuart forebears. But a new spirit was in the air, and not only among the wealthy; and those who walked from the chapel at Petworth to gaze from the windows of the Proud Duke's noble façade looked out upon a different world.

NOTES

1. Latimer, Sermon 5 on the Lord's Prayer, in *Sermons* (1844), pp. 392–3.
2. The sermon (one of a series on the Lord's Prayer) was given in the form of a lecture to the household of Katherine, Duchess of Suffolk at Grimsthorpe Castle, Lincolnshire, in 1552. See Latimer's own dedication (*Sermons*, 1844, p. 326) and Chester (1954) pp. 185ff.
3. C. S. Lewis (1954, p. 193) celebrates Latimer's rhetorical abilities.
4. From the sayings of the monk Silvanus, quoted in Archimandrite Sophrony, *Staretz Silouane* (Paris: Sisteron, 1973, p. 203), and repr. in O. Clément, *The roots of Christian mysticism* (ET of *Sources* by T. Berkeley and J. Hummerstone) (London: New City, 1993), p. 302: the original is in Jerome (attrib.), *Vitae patrum: de vita et verbis seniorum*, ed. by H. Rosweyde (Antwerp: De officina Plantiniania, 1615), L.vii, p. 510. The story appears in various subsequent works: E. B. Pusey cites two versions of it in a sermon, and traces it back to a Greek text translated by Paschasius (died 512 CE): Pusey, *Parochial and cathedral sermons* (London: Walter Smith, 1887), no. 11, p. 156 and note o. In Charles Kingsley's version of the story, the cobbler has become a goldsmith: Kingsley, *The hermits*, in *Works*, vol. 12 (London: Macmillan, 1879), pp. 97–8.
5. It should be noted that Latimer goes on to affirm the single life as well as the married one: see Sermon 5 on the Lord's Prayer, in *Sermons* (1844), pp. 393–4. The long-held assumption that Protestantism somehow created, or fitted most naturally, the modern nuclear family is not well founded: see Collinson (1988) pp. 60–93, esp. p. 84; Watt (1991) p. 225.
6. Latimer makes this point explicit in one of his sermons: he criticizes those who have embraced the monastic life because they 'ran out into the wilderness; where they fell into great inconveniences . . . We are born into this world, not for our own sakes only, but for our even [=fellow] Christians' sake' (Sermon 42 (Epiphany 5 1552), *Sermons and remains* pp. 196–7). Compare this approach with the traditional monastic perspective of (say) St Jerome, who describes St Antony, hitherto convinced that he was the most perfect monk dwelling in the desert, being shown in a vision that there was one yet more holy: the venerable Paul, himself a hermit in a remote desert cave (Jerome, *The life of Paul the first hermit*, chapter 7).
7. From a sermon trans. by S. Winkworth and cited in Shaw (1981) p. 11. In his *Lectures on Romans* (trans. W. Pauck; Library of Christian classics 15) (London: SCM Press, 1961), p. 227), Luther describes St Antony bemoaning the temptations of the world and being told that only humility can avoid them.
8. Sermon 34 (Christmas 1552), *Sermons and remains* pp. 94–5. Latimer makes the same point

frequently: see Sermon 38 (Epiphany 1 1552), *Sermons and remains* pp. 154–5 and 158–9; and Sermon 44 (Sexagesima 1552), *Sermons and remains* pp. 214–15. Elsewhere Latimer says that Christ called fishermen because they take infinite trouble over their craft, and he wanted them to do the same with catching men (Sermon 31 (Feast of St Andrew 1552), *Sermons and remains* p. 24). See also Calvin, *Institutes* 3.10.6, pp. 34–5, and the interesting discussion of sixteenth-century views on vocation in Shaw (1981).

9. See McGrath (1987) p. 82.
10. See, e.g., the titles of innumerable Protestant texts such as Thomas Becon's *The flower of godly prayers* or John Bradford's *Godly meditations on the Lord's prayer*; and the excellent pamphlet by MacCulloch, *Building a godly realm* (1992).
11. See Thomas (1971) p. 79.
12. Cf. Tyndale's 1534 translation of this passage in Luke 15: 'Then he came to himself and said: how many hired servants at my father's, have bread enough, and I die for hunger' (*Tyndale's New Testament*, p. 117).
13. Cf. Luther, *Commentary on Galatians* 3.6, p. 226; Calvin's *Institutes of the Christian religion* begins 'True and substantial wisdom principally consists of two parts, the knowledge of God and the knowledge of ourselves' (I.1.1). It is this true knowledge which leads to *pietas*, a central ingredient of authentic spirituality for Calvin; see Gründler (1976) p. 172.
14. *Commentary on Galatians* 4.30, p. 439. On its English versions see Rupp (1984) p. 166.
15. Cf. Luther's ringing assertion: 'I have used many words to declare that a Christian must assure himself that he is in the favour of God, and that he hath the crying of the Holy Ghost in his heart. This have I done, that we may learn to reject and utterly to abandon that devilish opinion of the whole kingdom of the Pope, which taught that a man ought to be uncertain and to stand in doubt of the grace of God towards him. If this opinion be received, then Christ profiteth nothing' (*Commentary on Galatians* 4.6, p. 370). 'Let us therefore give thanks unto God, that we are delivered from this monstrous doctrine of doubting, and can now assure ourselves that the Holy Ghost crieth and bringeth forth in our hearts unspeakable groanings. And this is our anchor-hold, and our foundation: the Gospel commandeth us to behold, not our own good works, our own perfection, but God the promiser, and Christ the mediator' (p. 371). For its importance see McGrath (1993) pp. 102–5; Loades (1996) pp. 4–5.
16. For the main similarities between reformed and Renaissance thought, see especially McGrath (1987 and 1993).
17. See Chapter 3. It is important to recall that at the dawn of the sixteenth century 'humanism' pertained to the critical study of classical texts and thought, and as such greatly influenced the new Protestant concern for the study and authority of scripture.
18. In c.1504, Bishop John Fisher bewails the fact that enemies of Christianity now control Asia and Africa, 'two the gretest partes of the worlde. Also they holde from us a grete porcyon of this parte called Europe whiche we now inhabyte, soo that scante the syxth parte of that we had in possessyon before is lefte unto us' (*Penytencyall Psalmes*, EETS 27, p. 171). C. S. Lewis, however, warns against exaggerating the extent to which this awareness affected most people's mental horizons (1954, pp. 16 and 63).
19. In the mid-fifteenth century the Carthusian Vincent of Aggsbach said that 'mystical theology and scholasticism are no more related than the art of painting and shoemaking' (*Tractatus de mystica theologia*, ed. E. Vansteenberghe; cited in O. Steggink, 'Study in spirituality in retrospect: shifts in methodological approach', in *Studies in Spirituality* 1 (1991), p. 5.
20. On this, see esp. Sommerville (1992). Choice in most areas of life was of course infinitely more restricted in the sixteenth than (say) in the twentieth century, even allowing for wide variation between rich and poor. It is worth recalling that legal divorce was introduced in England only in 1857.
21. Chester (1954) pp. 14–22; Haigh (1993) p. 58; MacCulloch (1996) p. 25. On the importance of Cambridge in fostering Reformation thought, see Porter (1972), Watts (1978, p. 72), and others. McGrath (1993, p. 13) points out that Cambridge was nearer the east coast than Oxford: hence its greater exposure to reformed and Lutheran ideas. For a vivid contemporary

account of Protestantism at Cambridge, see Robert Browne's *A True and Short Declaration* of 1584, in *The writings of Robert Harrison and Robert Browne*, pp. 396–429, esp. pp. 397–405. On the relationship between English and continental Protestantism, see esp. Collinson (1985).

22. See esp. Collinson (1982), Scarisbrick (1984), Fleming (1984), Rupp (1984), Tanner (1984), Davies (1985, esp. pp. 84–8), the contributors to Haigh (ed.) (1987), Dickens (1987i and 1989), Richmond (1991), Duffy (1992), Sommerville (1992), Haigh (1993), and Loades (1996). Those new to the subject could profitably begin with the excellent Historical Association pamphlet by MacCulloch (1992). Those interested in the way in which the course of events in local areas illuminates the entire subject will be greatly helped by Manning (1969), Wrightson and Levine (1979/95), Davis (1983), Fleming (1984), MacCulloch (1986), Palliser ('Popular reactions to the Reformation during the years of uncertainty', in Haigh (ed.) (1987) pp. 94–113), Whiting (1989), and Brown (1995). Among earlier scholars mention must be made of the important studies by Helen White (1951), Gordon Rupp (*The righteousness of God* (London: Hodder & Stoughton, 1953), esp. chapter 2), and David Knowles (1971).

23. See esp. the evidence amassed by Scarisbrick (1984), Tanner (1984), Hutton ('The local impact of the Tudor reformations', in Haigh (ed.) (1987) pp. 114–38), and Duffy (1992) as well as Whiting (1989, esp. p. 23) and Christine Carpenter (quoted in Richmond (1991) p. 131). See also Collinson (1988, p. 39) and Kümin (1996, p. 257). One of the signs of the health of pre-Reformation piety is the evidence of continuity of some elements of it into the reign of Elizabeth I: in a study of contemporary 'godly ballads', Tessa Watt has shown how some late-medieval traditions persisted, notably the emphasis on death and judgement, and a mental framework which still allowed room for the saints and the seven deadly sins (1991, esp. pp. 86, 111, 229, 327).

24. Collinson (1988, p. 41); Duffy (1992, esp. pp. 386 and 573); McGrath (1993, p. 5); Brown (1995, p. 247); Loades (1996, p. 7). Richmond (1991, pp. 135ff) argues for the seminal importance of the gentry in achieving the change, though see Fleming (1984, esp. p. 41) for an opposing view. MacCulloch (1996, p.41 and n. 2) underlines the extent to which Henry VIII's campaign to divorce Queen Catherine of Aragon occupied some of the best minds in Europe and was productive of many major developments in the history of ideas.

25. Some regions, however, Lancashire in particular, stood out for the old faith, while others sought a far more thoroughgoing Protestantism. One of the sources of evidence for major changes in popular religious belief is the piety revealed in wills: though these have to be treated with caution because of their formulaic nature, they can still help us to chart the clear movement towards widespread acceptance of Protestant faith: see esp. Spufford (1974, esp. pp. 320–2 and 336–7), Cross (1984), and Marsh (1990).

26. See esp. Cross (1976/87, esp. chapter 3); Duffy (1992, pp. 415, 453, 478, 591 &c). Kümin (1996, p. 231) argues that the distinctive feature of mid-sixteenth-century English parish life was not the role of the gentry, which remained stable during this period, but the increasingly active part played by the 'common people', not least in virtually monopolizing the office of churchwarden. Hill (1964, p. 446) makes the important point that the decline in the power of the clergy after the Reformation gave more responsibility to the lay heads of households for the promotion of family piety.

27. See Cross (1975); and Cross (1976/87, pp. 30–52); Dickens, *Lollards and Protestants in the diocese of York* (2nd edn, London, 1982); Martin (1989) pp. 14–18; Acheson (1990) pp. 1–2; D. Plumb, 'The social and economic status of the later Lollards', in Spufford (ed.) (1995), pp. 103–31 and 'A gathered church? Lollards and their society' in the same volume, pp. 132–63. The Protestant writer and polemicist John Foxe remarks in his *Actes and monuments* (vol. 4, p. 241) that Lollardy had flourished during the first two decades of the sixteenth century: see D. Plumb, *John Foxe and the later Lollards of the mid Thames Valley* (Cambridge PhD thesis, 1987). Plumb demonstrates convincingly that the later Lollards included many prosperous and prominent citizens in the particular localities where they thrived; that their religious convictions in no way prevented them from playing an active part in the life of these localities; and that they were willing to travel considerable distances in order to keep in

touch with, to worship with, and to support, one another.

28. See esp. Collinson (1967, 1982, and 1988 pp. 41–7), Spufford (1974, pp. 175–6) and MacCulloch (1992, p. 15). Manning (1969, p. 36) concludes that traditional Catholic piety persisted in Sussex until the coming of a learned Protestant ministry in the 1570s. Changes to Protestant piety were carefully policed, as Visitation records reflect: e.g., among Bishop Hooper's Interrogatories for Gloucester and Worcester dioceses 1551–2:

> whether the midwives at the labour and birth of any child do use any prayers or invocations unto any saint, saying to God in Christ, for the deliverance of the woman. (Frere & Kennedy, vol. 2, p. 292)

> whether any man do occupy any such Primers or books of prayers in Latin as be forbidden by the laws of the realm, or any beads, knots, relics, or any such other superstition, or whether any man pray in the church his private and own prayer whiles the Common Prayer is a-saying, to the trouble and hindrance of the understanding thereof. (Frere & Kennedy, vol. 2, p. 293)

or, from Bishop Bentham's instructions to every clergyman and churchwarden of Coventry and Lichfield diocese in 1565:

> *Item*, that you do call upon the people daily that they cast away their beads with all their superstitions that they do use praying upon them, and to follow the right use of prayer, which doth consist in lifting up the mind unto Almighty God, calling for mercy and grace, and not in numbering of their beads, prating with their lips, their hearts and minds in the meantime being occupied about their worldly business. (Frere & Kennedy, vol. 3, p. 165)

29. See esp. Loades (1996) and R. H. Pogson, 'Revival and reform in Mary Tudor's church: a question of money' in Haigh (ed.) (1987) pp. 139–56.

30. Spufford (1974, pp. 171ff and 1981, pp. 19–44) charts the educational expansion in this period. See also Collinson (1988, pp. 28–59) for the relationship between the Reformation and the development of English towns. For the growth of literacy, and for the many ways in which Protestant teaching and piety were disseminated across the community (e.g. by the composition of 'godly ballads'), see the excellent studies by Spufford (1981, esp. pp. 194–218) and Watt (1991). We need to remember, however, that immense progress in extending lay literacy had already taken place in the two centuries up to the Reformation: see J. A. Hoeppner Moran, *The growth of English schooling, 1340–1548: learning, literacy, and laicization in pre-Reformation York Diocese* (Princeton NJ and Guildford: Princeton UP, 1985). As Moran suggests (p. 226), this may have helped the progress of the Reformation by loosening the levers of clerical control.

31. See esp. Scarisbrick (1984, p. 4), Brown (1995, pp. 234 and 246), Richmond (1991, p. 144), Loades (1994) and Whiting (1998, pp. 71–7). For the impact of mercantilism for the new Protestant spirituality, see, e.g., G.Starr, *Defoe and spiritual autobiography* (Princeton UP, 1965) pp. 10–13.

32. This point is well made by Sommerville (1992, p. 63). See also Duffy (1972), esp. pp. 394, 439, 444, and 586.

33. See esp. Knowles (1971), Scarisbrick (1984, pp. 70ff), and the conclusions of MacCulloch (1986, p. 133) on the state of monasticism in Suffolk before the Reformation. Knowles' picture (1971, pp. 6–7) of the monasteries surrounded by a sea of selfish and hostile indifference in early Tudor England is not sufficiently borne out by the evidence to be convincing. In general terms Knowles paints a generally unexciting, though far from depressing, picture of early sixteenth-century English monasticism: there was a lack of major spiritual figures or writers, but not much evidence of widespread decline or failures in monastic observance, and some clear evidence of the influence of Renaissance humanism on monastic scholarship (see e.g. pp. 100–7).

34. Letter to George Digby of Sandon, 1669, in Sampson Erdeswicke, *A survey of Staffordshire* (first published posthumously in 1717); ed. T. Harwood (London: Nichols, 1844), p. lv.

35. Sermon preached before Edward VI in 1549, in *Sermons* (1844) p. 93; Chester (1954) p. 127. Latimer's words may also reflect the increasing economic divergence, in sixteenth-century England, between rich and poor (see, e.g., Spufford (1974) pp. 47–9 and 118–19).

36. See esp. Sommerville (1992). There is much good sense in Robert Southey's remark that 'in this country the best people and the worst combined in bringing about the Reformation, and in its progress it bore evident marks of both' (*Life of Wesley*, chapter IX).

37. In his visitation articles for the formal visitation of ten diocese in 1605, Archbishop Richard Bancroft included a question for every parish about 'whether are the tenne commaundements set upon the east ende of your church or chappell, where the people may best see and reade them' (Fincham (1994) p. 10); many other visitation articles contained similar questions. See also Watt (1991) pp. 217–18. Watt emphasizes (pp. 134ff) that it would be rash to assume that this meant the visual element disappeared altogether from English spirituality in the Reformation period: many images, for example, remained in church buildings, often because of the high cost of removing them. Neither Luther nor Calvin disapproved altogether of the use of visual material for didactic and devotional purposes; and the Puritan William Perkins allowed its use in domestic settings (Watt, pp. 185–6).

38. Collinson (1988) pp. 9 and 55. Often it was not only the rood, but the entire chancel screen, which was removed, an act which was motivated by a desire to dispose of any separation between chancel and nave, and thus any sense of a sanctuary exclusively restricted to monks or priests. Not all contemporaries shared this view: see Addleshaw and Etchells (1948) pp. 25, 30–1, 34–5, and 40ff.

39. See Yates (1991, pp. 2304), MacCulloch (1992), and Summerson (1993, pp. 157–60) for summaries of this process, and Davies (1985, p. 79), Spufford (1974, pp. 239–41) and Marsh (1998, pp. 56–69) for some reflections on its impact. The immense length of the (Elizabethan) *Homily against peril of idolatry, and superfluous decking of churches* – far longer than any of the others in the collection – reflects the government's concern to erase everything connected with images. It is based on a *theological* shift of emphasis: the true image of God is in human beings, and the writer argues that generosity to the poor and homeless is much more spiritually profitable than the purchase of images or the gilding of churches; ed. cit. p. 238.

40. Calvin, *Institutes* 3.20.30, p. 180: 'If this [common prayer] is the legitimate use of churches (and it certainly is), we must, on the other hand, beware of imitating the practice which commenced some centuries ago, of imagining that churches are the proper dwellings of God, where he is more ready to listen to us, or of attaching to them some kind of secret sanctity, which makes prayer there more holy'. Article XXI of the Westminster Assembly includes the declaration that 'Neither Prayer, nor any other part of Religious Worship, is now, under the Gospel, either tyed unto, or made more acceptable by any place in which it is performed . . . but God is to be Worshipped every where' (p. 35). See also Sommerville (1992) pp. 18–19. It is of course no coincidence that for a hundred years at this time almost no churches were built in Britain (N. Pevsner, *An outline of European architecture*, 7th edn (Harmondsworth: Penguin, 1963, p. 310). A good example of Protestant attitudes to buildings can be found in the sixteenth-century Robert Harrison's *A little treatise upon the firste verse of the 122 Psalm* (1583), in which he argues that 'Christe dwelleth not, where he ruleth not': the true beauty of a sanctuary is to be found in the Christian's own life, not in any church building (text in *The writings of Robert Harrison and Robert Browne*, pp. 70–123, esp. p. 115).

41. So Scarisbrick (1984) p. 169.

42. See Spufford (1974, p. 247), Davis (1983, p. 91), and Collinson (1982, p. 96). Alldridge (1988, esp. p. 104) and E. Carlson ('The origins, function, and status of the office of churchwarden, with particular reference to the diocese of Ely', in Spufford (ed.) (1995) pp. 164–207) show how the growth of elected lay officers tempered the authority of the clergy. Prayers for the clergy, which appear in many sixteenth-century collections, reflect this new confidence: thus the Protestant Edward Dering includes a prayer that asks God to 'place over every Church a painfull watchman, remove all idle Lubbers, and confound the power of Antichrist' (*Godly private prayers*, 'Morning prayer for private houses and families' (page unnumbered)).

43. See Cross (1976/87, pp. 53–80), Dickens (1987ii), and (for a very different view) Haigh, 'Anticlericalism and the English Reformation', in Haigh (ed.) (1987) pp. 56–74. As an example of anticlericalism, note the complaints made during Warham's visitation in Kent, 1511–12:

[at the church of Sturry]

It is alleged: that mass is sung no more than once or twice at most in the week in the said church; we have asked the vicar for masses to be sung more frequently, and he answers: Would you have me sing masses when I don't feel like it?')

[at the church of Swalecliffe]

Item, Sir James, the parish priest, pesters the wife of John Potters, and she cannot be rid of him.

Item, the said Sir James stands listening under people's windows at 10 o'clock at night [full references in Swanson (1993) p. 262].

44. See esp. Duffy (1993).

45. See the Preface to the 1562 edition of *Certain homilies,* ed. cit. p. xiv; Sommerville (1977, pp. 22–32); Tanner (1984, p. 170); McGrath (1987, p. 11). Spufford (1995, p. 74) points to the crucial link between religious formation and education: 'if you could read, you were also religiously indoctrinated'.

46. See the remarks of White (1951) p. 173.

47. See esp. White (1951), Scarisbrick (1984, pp. 15–16), Duffy (1992, p. 86), and McGrath (1993, p. 13). A good example of this is *The first booke of the Christian exercise, appertayning to resolution,* produced (probably at Rouen) in 1580–1 by the Jesuit Robert Persons to assist the inchoate Jesuit mission to England. When this book appeared in England it was seized upon by a Calvinist clergyman of the Church of England called Edmund Bunny, who duly adapted it to suit Protestant beliefs (*A booke of Christian exercise, appertaining to resolution* (London, 1584)). Both Persons' and Bunny's Resolution became immensely popular. Bunny's version even influenced Richard Baxter, who attributed his conversion to reading an old torn copy of what was then known as '*Bunny's Resolution*' (White (1951) p. 171). For more recent critiques of White's conclusions about the original work, see V. Houliston, 'Why Robert Persons would not be pacified: Edmund Bunny's theft of *The book of resolution*', in T. M. McCoog (ed.), *The reckoned expense: Edmund Campion and the early English Jesuits: essays in celebration of the first centenary of Campion Hall, Oxford (1896–1996)* (Woodbridge: Boydell, 1996), pp. 159–77 and B. S. Gregory, 'The "True and Zealouse Seruice of God": Robert Parsons, Edmund Bunny, and the *First booke of the Christian exercise*', in *Journal of Ecclesiastical History,* 45 (1994), pp. 238–68. Such adaptations reflect fundamental theological shifts: thus the Protestant version of the popular late-medieval spiritual text *The fifteen Oes* reflects a movement away from stress on the suffering humanity of Jesus towards his redemptive work, from God the Son to God the Father, from a desire to enter into the experience of the Passion itself to a concern to ponder its saving significance for the redeemed (see White (1951, chapter 13), Duffy (1992, pp. 249–56), and Barnes (1994, p. 155)).

48. An indispensable starting-point for the enquirer are the works of Christopher Hill (see Bibliography).

49. Not to mention the already increasing fragmentation of landholding, as difficult economic circumstances at the end of the sixteenth century force many tenants from their lands (see Spufford (1974), esp. p. 137).

50. For succinct and penetrating analyses, see esp. Stachniewski (1991) for the former and Rivers (1991i) for the latter. Spufford (1974, p. 272) notes that about 30 per cent of English livings were under sequestration at some time between 1643 and 1660, and that 20 per cent of the clergy intruded under the Commonwealth were ejected at the Restoration.

51. See, e.g., Sommerville (1977) pp. 1–8. Even so, it is unquestionable that the seventeenth century remained a deeply religious age for England, the growth of literacy allowing Christian (especially Protestant) apologists to reach an unprecedentedly wide audience (though that very growth also allowed satirical and other critical ideas to be widely disseminated): see Watt (1995). For a good introduction to this theme, see Duffy (1986).

52. *Samson Agonistes,* ll. 652–704, pp. 368–70. The opening line echoes Psalm 8.4 (KJV): 'What is man, that thou art mindful of him?' See ed. cit. p. 368 and note to l. 667.

53. For this subject see esp. Maltby (1998), Acheson (1990, p. 49), Morrill (1982), and Marsh

(1998).

54. See Crawford (1993), and Marsh (1998, p. 127).

55. See Daniel (1994, p. 61) (and p. 66 on the significance in this regard of Erasmus' *Enchiridion*); McGrath (1993) pp. 138–9.

56. Catholic attitudes to the use and availability of scripture in the vernacular were more ambivalent, however: see Marsh (1998) pp. 140–1.

57. Dickens (1989) p. 134; Sommerville (1992) p. 45; MacCulloch (1996) p. 166 and n. 95 and pp. 196–7. Hall (1993, p. 28) wants to give Cranmer, not Cromwell, the primary credit for this. This Bible, *The Byble in Englyshe* or 'Great Bible', was compiled by John Rogers from William Tyndale's and Miles Coverdale's translation of the Old Testament and Tyndale's New Testament, and then revised by Coverdale. See Brightman and Mackenzie, in Lowther Clarke (1964) p. 147. For the enormous influence of the Bible on almost every aspect of sixteenth- and seventeenth-century life, see Hill (1993).

58. Loades (1996) p. 14.

59. See O'Malley (1990) pp. 10–11; Hill (1993) p. 14.

60. Hill (1993) p. 11. Thomas More, horrified at the thought of scripture being translated by heretics, suggested that the Bible 'myght be wyth dylygence well and truely translated by some good catholyque and well lerned manne or by dyvers dyvydynge the laboure amonge theym' (*A dialogue concerning heresies* III.16, ed. T. M. C. Lawler et al., *The complete works of St Thomas More* (New Haven: Yale UP, 1981), vol. 6, p. 341.

61. See Marsh (1998) pp. 142–3.

62. There is some dispute among scholars about whether Tyndale originated from Gloucestershire (so Daniell (1994) p. 17) or the Forest of Dean (so A. J. Brown, *William Tyndale on priests and preachers, with new light on his early career* (London: Inscriptor Imprints, 1996), though since both were known for their strongly Lollard sympathies the question may not matter much.

63. Daniell (1994) p. 190.

64. Bush (1945) p. 68. Daniell (1994, p. 1) points out that nine-tenths of the Authorized Version rendering of the New Testament is in fact by Tyndale.

65. See Williams (1975) p. 126.

66. *The parable of the wicked mammon*, pp. 57–8 (my italics).

67. See Hill (1993) p. 635. See Collinson (1988, p. 10) on the link between the availability of the vernacular Bible and the growth of nationalism.

68. G. Campbell, in Keeble (1988) p. 139. It was some forty years after its publication before the King James Version supplanted the Geneva Bible in popular affection.

69. See Sommerville (1992) p. 54, and G. Hammond, 'English translations of the Bible', in R. Alter and F. Kermode (eds.), *The literary guide to the Bible* (London: Collins, 1987), pp. 647–66.

70. Not least, for both dissenters and establishment Christians, in locating precedents for their own theological convictions: see Yule (1984) p. 188; Hill (1993) pp. 8, 55 &c.

71. The decision for readmission was taken at the 1655 Whitehall Conference. See Katz (1994) pp. 107ff.

72. While an undergraduate at Cambridge, Isaac Archer records in his diary that he devoted himself 'to many chapters [of the Bible] a day according to Mr Bifield's book . . . though I thinke it was not very good for my eyesight' (*Diary* 27/1657, ed. cit. p. 55). Two years later he noted that 'I was diligent in reading the scriptures every day, and read them once through in a yeare for the 3 first yeares according to Mr Bifield's directions; yet gate I not much good for want of due meditation' (*Diary* 38/1659, ed. cit. p. 60).

73. *Certain homilies*, p. 8. This stress on ruminative familiarity with scripture recurs regularly: George Wither, in his *A preparation to the Psalter*, says that 'I would advise evry man (in his prosperity, and whilst he hath meanes) to store up, in his heart, some sweete and necessary sentences of the *Psalmes*; and he shall at some time or other finde admirable comfort in them: as it hath beene apparant in many godly Martyrs, who have not onely lessened their torment by the repetition of them; but many times by a sentence out of them, have strucken shame and confusion into the persecutors, and put even the Devils to flight' (1619, p. 131).

74. *Certain homilies*, p. 337.

75. For the influence and use of the Psalms during this period, see the introduction to *The collected works of Mary Sidney Herbert, Countess of Pembroke. Volume II: The Psalmes of David*, ed. M. P. Hannay, N. J. Kinnamon and M. G. Brennan (Oxford: Clarendon, 1998), pp. 3–33; also Marsh (1998) pp. 38–9 (with refs.). Luther himself produced metrical versions of the Psalter, which were introduced to England by Protestant exiles returning after the death of Mary Tudor. Arthur Golding translated Calvin's Commentary on the Psalms into English in 1571: in his dedicatory preface, he argued that 'next untoo [Calvin's] Institutions [sic], this presente volume beareth the Bel, bothe for varietie of matter, substantialnes of doctrine, depth of iudgement, and perfectnesse of penning' (Dedication, in Calvin Society edition, p. 23, Ages Digital Library CD-ROM 1998). It should be noted that, although the translation of the Psalms included in the Book of Common Prayer is that of Coverdale (originally published in 1535 and revised by Coverdale for the Great Bible of 1540), it was not printed as a constituent part of the Prayer Book until 1662 (E. C. Ratcliff, 'The choir offices', in W. K. Lowther Clarke (ed.), *Liturgy and worship: a companion to the Prayer Books of the Anglican Communion* (London: SPCK, 1932; repr. 1964), p. 289.

76. *Certain homilies*, pp. 338–9.

77. *Cases of conscience* 2.6, in *Works* vol. 2, p. 66.

78. *A rationale upon the Book of Common-Prayer*, ed. cit., p. 31.

79. See the introduction by Hannay et al. to Mary Sidney Herbert's translation of the Psalms, pp. 4–6.

80. Sternhold and Hopkins, p. 85. Cf. the remark of the Puritan Walter Marshall on this Psalm (*The Gospel-mystery of sanctification*, p. 185): 'The most mournful Psalm in Scripture begins with an Expression of some Assurance.' For the work of Sternhold and Hopkins and that of (near-)contemporaries, see Le Huray (1967) chapter 11. In the eighteenth century John Wesley wrote of their 'miserable, scandalous doggerel' (*Letters*, ed. J. Telford (London: Epworth, 1931), vol. 3, p. 227). It used to be thought that one of the aims of the composers and compilers of metrical psalmody was to combat the growing popularity of secular ballads: now many scholars recognize that the two had a good deal in common, some writers composing both. By the end of the sixteenth century, however, even the so-called 'godly' ballad was declining in popularity by comparison with the Psalms (see Watt (1991) pp. 40–1; Spufford (1995) pp. 81–5). For a vigorous contemporary apologia for the production of verse translations of the Psalter, see George Wither's *A preparation to the Psalter* (1619), chapter 2 (pp. 6–13).

81. *The Kynges Psalmes*; see White (1951) pp. 48–9.

82. For Howard, see Zim (1987) pp. 89ff.

83. *An exhortation to Patience*, October 1553, in *The letters of the martyrs*, pp. 115–16.

84. See, e.g., his *Letter to Master Warcup and his wife Mistress Wilkinson*, ed. cit. p. 218; or his letter to 'a faithful Woman, in her heaviness and trouble', in which he reminds her of the number of times David 'saw God's sweet love' while reading the Psalms 'in the shadow of death' (p. 249). Writing to Augustine Berneher soon before he died, Bradford cited Psalm 102 in the Vulgate: 'Factus sum sicut nycticorax in domicilio, et passer solitarius in tecto' (p. 360).

85. p. 291.

86. *Anatomy of melancholy* 3.4.2, vol. 3, pp. 440–2.

87. Spufford (1974, pp. 208–9) describes devout laity arriving for the Puritan conferences at Wisbech in the last two decades of the sixteenth century, with 'their horses and pack-animals burdened with a multitude of Bibles', diligently looking up, and arguing over, each text cited by the preachers: a vivid reflection both of rural literacy and of Puritan devotion to scripture. Sommerville (1977, p. 67) points out that Church of England writers were more likely to cite the Psalms than Puritans, although the book as a whole was immensely influential for all Christian denominations. Watt (1991, p. 218) points out that psalm-texts were particularly popular for use as inscriptions on the interior walls of domestic houses. See also Scholes (1934) pp. 270–4 (with his charming description of Cromwell, 'pious yet practical', choosing the shortest psalm in the collection (117) for recitation after the victory at Dunbar); Rupp (1977) p. 119 and Tripp (1991) pp. 98–104.

88. *The practice of piety*, p. 207.
89. p. 208. For the different ways in which the psalms were sung in churches during this period, see Le Huray (1967) pp. 157–63.
90. p. 209.
91. *Christian directory* 2.3, vol. 4, pp. 67 and 73.
92. *Works* vol. 19, pp. 646–55.
93. vol. 19, pp. 652–5. The original is far longer, with 16 verses, than the version in general use today.
94. *Diary*, ed. cit., pp. 62–3. References to the Psalms recur throughout: see, e.g., pp. 2, 5, 13 (where it is worth noting that Lowe records singing a psalm on his own in his shop by candle-light 'with a lusty heart chearfullness'), 16, 19, 212, 25, 29, 32, 33, and 52. Lowe was no narrow Puritan: he enjoyed both his ale and the assiduous courtship of various local ladies.
95. Sermon 8.2, p. 86.
96. Mary Sidney Herbert, *Psalmes* p. 252. See also the introduction, pp. 27–8.
97. See e.g. *Works* vol. 4, pp. 46–8; cf. *A collection of offices,* vol. 15, pp. 246–9 and 258–60, the morning prayers more anticipatory and the evening ones ruminative.
98. *A collection of offices*, pp. 268–9.
99. 'A Hymn petitory and complaining', comprising texts from Psalms 74, 77, and 79; *Works* vol. 15, pp. 332–3.
100. 'A Hymn consolatory, in Time of Persecution', *Works* vol. 15, pp. 334–5.
101. pp. 335–6.
102. pp. 336–8.
103. pp. 344–6.
104. *A collection of offices*, pp. 371–2.
105. *The Psalter of David*, Preface, in *Works* vol. 15, p. civ.
106. *Diary*, pp. 201–2.
107. p. 202. The psalm texts cited are 28.1, 67; 30.23, 10–12; 31.15; 22.24; 32.1, 6, 7; and 33.18–19.
108. p. 202.
109. Entry for 4 June 1650; p. 205.
110. Chester (1954) pp. 76–81.
111. Chester (1954) pp. 55, 102, 111–13; Haigh (1993) p. 124; MacCulloch (1996) p. 139.
112. Witness his Visitation of his cathedral monastery at Worcester in 1537; Knowles (1971) pp. 346–7. Latimer's visitation injunctions to convents and parishes clearly reflect his pastoral priorities: good catechesis and preaching (which is better than reciting the Rosary), accessibility of the scriptures in English, &c (*Injunctions*, pp. 240–4). See also Mackie (1952) pp. 456 and 458; Chester (1954) pp. 106–10 and 134–44.
113. In 1538 Latimer personally attended the ceremonial burning of the Observant friar John Forest, preaching a long sermon immediately before it took place (Cranmer was there too; Chester (1954) pp. 131–3; MacCulloch (1996) pp. 214 and 408). The sermon does not survive; but Latimer himself says that his purpose in preaching was the conversion, not simply the denunciation, of Forest (Letter 30, to Thomas Cromwell, 18 May 1538, *Sermons and remains*, pp. 391–3).
114. He appears to have sought their reform, though, rather than their dissolution: see Chester (1954) pp. 122–9; Haigh (1993) pp. 128 and 131.
115. Chester (1954) pp. 148–9; Haigh (1993) pp. 152–3; MacCulloch (1996) pp. 251, 254.
116. Chester (1954) pp. 162–82; Haigh (1993) p. 189.
117. Letter 51 (1555), in *Sermons and remains* (1845), pp. 443–4.
118. Sermon 13 (19 April 1549), *Sermons,* pp. 235–8 passim. In general, Protestant writers stressed the saving work of Christ on the cross rather than the exemplary value of his human life as a focus for spirituality: it is the former, not the latter, which underlies Latimer's emphasis here.
119. The exact date of Latimer's birth is uncertain.
120. We need to note Spufford's important point (1974, p. 319) that it is extraordinarily hard to

calculate the nature of 'established', orthodox piety in this (or any) age.

121. Sermon 1 (c.1529), in *Sermons*, p. 4.

122. Sermon 1 (c.1529), in *Sermons*, p. 7. Cf. the sober beginning of Cranmer's homily on salvation (*A sermon of the salvation of mankind*, in *Certain homilies*, p. 17):

> it is our parts and duties ever to remember the great mercy of God, how that (all the world being wrapped in sin by breaking of the law) God sent his only son our saviour Christ, into this world, to fulfil the law for us, and, by shedding of his most precious blood, to make a sacrifice and satisfaction, or (as it may be called) amends to his Father for our sins, to assuage his wrath and indignation conceived against us for the same.

123. *A sermon of the salvation of mankind*, in *Certain homilies*, p. 19.

124. pp. 22–3; cf. *Articles of Religion* XI ('that we are justified by Faith only is a most wholesome Doctrine, and very full of comfort'). For the influence of Luther on Cranmer's doctrine of justification, see Hall (1993).

125. Latimer, however, does use our common and fallen human nature as an argument for caring about the poor: 'seeing then that we are all but beggars, why should we then disdain and despise poor men?' (Sermon 21 (1552), in *Sermons*, p. 397).

126. Latimer, Sermon 30 (Advent 1552), in *Sermons and remains*, p. 10; Cranmer, *A sermon of the salvation of mankind*, in *Certain homilies*, p. 26; for Cranmer's approach to this, see MacCulloch (1996) p. 210. Cf. Calvin, *Institutes* 3.24.8, p. 247; and see also Latimer, Sermon 29 (for Trinity 24), in *Sermons*, pp. 537–8.

127. Cranmer, *Sermon of faith*, in *Certain homilies*, p. 32.

128. Sermon 11 (5 April 1549), in *Sermons*, p. 172; cf. Sermon 40 (24 January 1552), in *Sermons and remains*, p. 180; Sermon 21 (1552), in *Sermons*, p. 389; and the *Homily concerning prayer*, in *Certain homilies*, p. 284; and cf. Calvin, *Institutes* 3.20.12, p. 157, and 3.20.31, p. 180. The same point is made by many contemporaries: thus the Independent Robert Browne compares worship in the Catholic tradition to a game of tennis: 'Their tossing to & fro of psalms and senteses [sic], is like tenisse plaie' (*A true and short declaration, in the writings of Robert Harrison and Robert Browne*, p. 415).

129. See esp. *Articles of Religion* XVII and XXVII.

130. In the Homily *Concerning Prayer*, prayer is itself a means of encouraging us to acknowledge God:

> to the intent we might acknowledge him to be the giver of all good things, and behave ourselves thankfully towards him in that behalf, loving, fearing, and worshipping him sincerely and truly, as we ought to do, he hath profitably and wisely ordained, that in time of necessity we should humble ourselves in his sight, pour out the secrets of our heart before him, and crave help at his hands, with continual, earnest, and devout prayer (*Certain homilies*, p. 284).

131. Sermon 17 (1552), in *Sermons*, p. 328; cf. the *Homily concerning prayer*, in *Certain homilies*, p. 289 (quoting St Isidore).

132. The author of Tract 86 ('Indications of a superintending Providence in the preservation of the Prayer Book and in the changes which it has undergone' (1839)) cites the Collects for Lent 3 (where 'humilium', lit. 'humble people', is rendered as 'humble servants'); for Trinity 10 (where 'supplicantium', lit. 'those who supplicate', is rendered as 'humble servants'); for Easter 5 and in the daily Collect for grace (in each of which 'thy supplicants' is rendered as 'thy humble servants'); in the Litany, where 'we Thy servants' is simply added in to the original; and the Collect for Trinity 20, where the original reference to 'free hearts' is rendered 'cheerfully', so that the idea of freedom is lost altogether (*Tracts for the times*, vol. 5, Tract 86, pp. 14–15).

133. Cartwright, *Second reply to an answer made of Mr Dr Whitgift* (1575), 1.136, cited in Hooker, *Laws* 5.47.1 (ed. cit., p. 198 and n. 4). For Cartwright, see A. F. Scott Pearson, *Thomas Cartwright and Elizabethan Puritanism 1535–1603* (Cambridge UP, 1925), and A. Peel and L. H. Carlson (eds.), *Cartwrightiana* (Elizabethan Nonconformist texts, 1) (London: Allen & Unwin, 1951). The original Latin collect for Trinity 12 (from Leo's Sacramentary) had 'O God . . . who bestowest more than we seek or deserve, grant, we beseech Thee, that by Thy mercy that may be bestowed on us which confidence in our deserts does not allow us to ask'; see E. Daniel,

The Prayer-Book: its history, language and contents, 22nd edn (London: Wells Gardner, Darton, 1909), pp. 298–9).

134. Hooker, *Laws* 5.47.4, in *Works*, vol. 2, p. 200.

135. Tract 86, p. 16.

136. Adrian Hastings, in his *A history of English Christianity 1920–1985* (London: Collins, 1986, p. 32), acutely describes the sixteenth-century Church of England as 'intellectually one of the freest of Christian churches, [but] socially . . . one of the most subservient'. And the Methodist Leslie Weatherhead was not wide of the mark in suggesting in 1965 that 'Cranmer's God was like Cranmer's schoolmaster' – a person to inspire fear (*The Christian agnostic* (London: Hodder and Stoughton, 1965), p. 156).

137. Sermon 21 (1552), in *Sermons*, p. 402.

138. Sermon 23 (1552), in *Sermons*, p. 433. Latimer also argues here that we must learn to turn the commandments of God into a prayer so as to appropriate them for ourselves. So the process is: faithful obedience to God's commandments, which are appropriated in prayer, and then issue in action.

139. Sermon 17 (1552), in *Sermons*, pp. 329–30; Sermon 27 (Trinity 21 1552), in *Sermons*, pp. 506–10; Sermon 30 (1552), in *Sermons and remains*, p. 12. Note that Latimer, unlike some Protestant thinkers, maintained that even the elect were quite capable of sinning even after having received the Spirit: Sermon 13 (19 April 1549), in *Sermons*, p. 229.

140. Sermon 13 (19 April 1549), in *Sermons*, p. 229.

141. Sermon 21 (1552), in *Sermons*, p. 398; see also Sermon 17 (1552), in *Sermons*, pp. 337–8; and cf. Calvin, *Institutes* 3.20.39, p. 187, though Latimer explores this point at far greater length. For Latimer's commitment to social justice, see Chester (1954) pp. 171–6.

142. Sermon 20 (1552), in *Sermons*, p. 388.

143. Sermon 27 (for Trinity 21 1552), in *Sermons*, p. 507. This emphasis on biblical boldness recurs frequently in sixteenth-century Protestant spirituality: see, e.g., Edward Dering's collection *Godly private prayers, for housholders to meditate upon, and to say in their families* (1600), in which the opening prayer on the first petition of the Lord's Prayer declares that 'as a pledge thou hast given us thy Holy Spirit of adoption, whereby we may with boldness and full trust and confidence come to thee by harty [*sic*] prayer, as unto a loving and merciful Father, being assured that thou wilt not deny us any thing which thou knowest shall be expedient for us' (page unnumbered: the same point is made in later prayers).

144. Sermon 14 (Lent 1550), in *Sermons*, p. 249.

145. *Sermon of good works*, in *Certain homilies*, p. 51. For the relationship between nationalism and the new Protestant ascendancy, see Collinson (1988) pp. 1–27.

146. Sermon 4 (9 June 1536), in *Sermons*, pp. 36–7.

147. Sermon 34 (Christmas 1552), in *Sermons and remains*, p. 93.

148. Letter 3, to King Henry VIII (1 December 1530), in *Sermons and remains*, p. 299. Cf. Sermon 13 (19 April 1549), in *Sermons*, pp. 231–2; and Latimer's last sermon preached before Edward VI (Lent 1550), in *Sermons*, p. 249: 'They in Christ are equal with you. Peers of the realm must needs be. The poorest ploughman is in Christ equal with the greatest prince that is.'

149. Barnes (1994, p. 150) notes the fact that printers and publishers came to exert a significant influence on the course of English spirituality as they sought both to respond to rapidly-changing royal policy and to supply (and to some extent shape) the needs of laypeople for an adequate spiritual diet.

150. Brightman and MacKenzie (1964) p. 148; MacCulloch (1996) p. 329. This *Exhortation unto prayer* included prayers and suffrages and in particular a litany written by Cranmer and based on the Sarum Processional, Luther's litany, and the Orthodox Greek Liturgy: it also included some Rogation prayers and the 'Prayer of Chrysostome' from the Greek – a characteristic example of Cranmer's eclectic genius in producing superb and coherent prose out of a strange cocktail of ingredients.

151. Barnes (1994) pp. 148–50. The primer was part-Latin, part-English, with much traditional (i.e. Catholic) material but reflecting some strong Protestant influence.

152. See Chapter 4, pp. 167–8. For a succinct guide to sixteenth-century primers, see esp. Barnes (1994).

153. See White (1951), esp. p. 69. Barnes (1994, p. 141) suggests that, until vernacular Bibles were allowed or became available, laypeople had recourse to English-language primers as the most obvious means of enriching their devotional lives, though the effect of this was further to interiorize that devotion.

154. See the Royal Articles of Edward VI (1547), 67, in Frere and Kennedy, vol. 2, p. 112; cf. Royal Injunctions of Edward VI, 34, on p. 129.

155. Thus the 1549 Primer omitted invocations to the Virgin, angels and patriarchs from the Litany; further Catholic devotions were dropped in the 1551 version; and the 1553 Primer had no hours of the Virgin or prayers for the dead, containing instead a morning and evening office for lay use (Mattins and Evensong) with readings for the days of the week, and a large collection of 'Sundry godly prayers for divers purposes' including prayers for masters and servants, landlords and tenants, and others: see Duffy (1992) pp. 537–8.

156. See Duffy (1992) pp. 540–1 and p. 563; White (1951) p. 76.

157. It was further reprinted in 1560 and 1568. In 1566 another primer was published, similar to the 1551 version, but including the Catechism and with John Fisher's translations of fifteen Psalms replacing the old Commendations.

158. White (1951) p. 97.

159. The preface to Henry VIII's Primer (reprinted in the 1559 version) says that the book is principally designed so that people may pray with both mind and heart; so that they may pray in their own tongue; and so that everyone may have a uniform pattern for prayer. See also White (1951) p. 105 and Barnes (1994), esp. p. 151.

160. *The two liturgies*, p. 458.

161. See the detailed descriptive history by Brightman and MacKenzie (1964).

162. Brightman and MacKenzie (1964) pp. 151ff.

163. The compilers themselves stress this: 'And in these our doings we condemn no other Nations, nor prescribe any thing but to our own people only. For we think it convenient that every country should use such ceremonies as they shall think best to the setting forth of God's honour and glory, and to the reducing of the people to a most perfect and godly living, without error or superstition.'

164. It is of course arguable how far the lack of variety and of alternatives was not ultimately an impoverishment; at the time, national religious unity seemed an overriding requirement.

165. See Beckwith (1992) pp. 102–3; Loades (1996) p. 9; MacCulloch (1996) pp. 391 and 486. The latter argues (pp. 392, 405, 441 &c) that Cranmer's eucharistic theology was already firmly Protestant by 1548: he had already rejected belief in the real presence by then, preferring belief in a vaguely-defined 'spiritual presence'; and see Cranmer's own *A defence of the true and Catholic doctrine of the sacrament of the body and blood of our saviour Christ* (1550).

166. See Marsh (1998), esp. p. 37.

167. MacCulloch (1996, p. 180) quotes a letter from Cranmer to the Swiss reformer Joachim Vadianus which underlines his concern to recover the pristine purity of apostolic Christianity. The extent of Cranmer's learning was vast: his library, long since dispersed, was rich in both patristic and medieval scholastic texts (see D. G. Selwyn, 'Cranmer's library: its potential for Reformation studies', in P. Ayris and D. Selwyn (eds.), *Thomas Cranmer: churchman and scholar* (Woodbridge: Boydell, 1993), pp. 39–72). This emphasis on the Church of England's loyalty to the perceived purity of early Christianity while Roman Catholicism was held to have departed from it is common among apologists for the new Church: see, e.g., William Laud's critique of Roman Catholicism in *A relation of the conference between William Laud . . . and Mr Fisher the Jesuit*, 6th edn, in *The works of . . . William Laud* (Oxford: Parker, 1849), vol. 2, sect. 38, pp. 363ff.

168. See, e.g., *Of ceremonies*, BCP (1549) p. 156. All references to the Book of Common Prayer are to the Parker Society edition of the 1549 and 1552 texts (*The two liturgies, A.D. 1549 and A.D. 1552, with other documents*, ed. J. Ketley (Cambridge UP, 1844)) unless otherwise indicated. It should be noted that this stress on simplicity is found in the *Breviarium Romanum nuper*

reformatum of Cardinal Francisco de Quiñones (Brightman & MacKenzie (1964) p. 138). For Cranmer's hostility to ceremonies, see Duffy (1993) pp. 202–4.

169. Collinson (1988) pp. 54–5. For some perceptive remarks on the significance of the calendar and the particular commemorations selected for inclusion, see Barnes (1994) pp. 152 (with n. 68) and 157.

170. See, e.g., Sparrow, *Rationale* (1661).

171. Beveridge, *A sermon concerning the excellency and usefulness of the Common-Prayer* (London, 1681, printed 1687), p. 12.

172. See Ratcliff, 'The choir offices', in Lowther Clarke (1964) p. 277. Ratcliff points out that in the older Sarum use prayers and thanksgivings of this kind and with these subjects are included within the Eucharist; the fact that Cranmer sets them apart in an independent section of the new Prayer Book underlines his concern to minimize the role of the Eucharist as an intercessory sacrifice.

173. Jeremy Taylor (*An apology for authorized and set forms of liturgy*) commends, characteristically, the integrity of the Prayer Book: every possible need is catered for ('there is no part of religion, as it is a distinct virtue, and is to be exercised by interior acts and forms of worship, but is in the offices of the church of England', Preface 37, *Works* vol. 7, p. 303).

174. Collinson (1988) p. 9. Bishops' visitation articles indicate that serious attempts were made to enforce the observance of these days; see Fincham (1994).

175. See MacCulloch (1992) pp. 11 and 18; Collinson (1988) pp. 1–27; Kishlansky (1996) p. 98.

176. For the history of the rite, see E. Daniel, *The Prayer-Book: its history, language and contents*, 22nd edn (London: Wells, Gardner, 1909), pp. 515–16; W. K. Lowther Clarke, *Liturgy and worship* (London: SPCK, 1964), pp. 425–6; for its relevance to sixteenth-century women's piety, see D. Cressy, 'Purification, thanksgiving, and the churching of women in post-Reformation England' in *Past and Present* 141 (1993), and Marsh (1998) p. 30.

177. See Procter and Frere (1949) p. 641 and n. 3; Lowther Clarke (1964) pp. 856–7.

178. See the Preface to the Commination, and Deuteronomy 27. How much the Commination was actually used is hard to determine: only a relatively small number of bishops' visitation articles in the period enquire about whether it is ever said; see Fincham (1994) pp. 42 and 188.

179. See Sommerville (1992) pp. 50 and 141.

180. See the remarks of C. S. Lewis (1954), who describes the collects, mostly translated from Latin medieval originals, as 'perhaps the supreme example of the virtues required for translating highly-wrought Latin' (pp. 217, 221). MacCulloch (1996) notes the beginning of the long process during which Cranmer's literary skills developed (p. 54; see also p. 417). For the extent and the manner of Cranmer's borrowings from others, see G. J. Cuming, 'Thomas Cranmer, translator and creative writer', in D. and R. C. D. Jasper (eds.), *Language and the worship of the church* (London: Macmillan, 1990), pp. 110–19.

181. Note, for example, the threefold pulse in the versicle 'O *Lord*, open *thou* our *lips*' and correspondingly in the response 'And our *mouth* shall shew *forth* thy *praise*' (BCP 1552, p. 219). BCP 1549 retains the medieval Latin singular 'O Lord, open my lips' (p. 29).

182. 'We have erred and strayed from thy ways like lost sheep' (BCP 1552, p. 218) is infinitely more effective than most modern equivalents.

183. See Cuming (1983) p. 58.

184. BCP 1552, p. 279. The 1549 Rite continues 'and with thy Holy Spirit and word vouchsafe to bless and sanctify these thy gifts, and creatures of bread and wine, that they may be unto us the body and blood of thy most dearly beloved Son Jesus Christ' (p. 88).

185. BCP 1552, p. 217; MacCulloch (1996) pp. 224 and 510–11. Cuming (1983, p. 66) points out that the phrase 'daily throughout the year' recurs three times in Mattins, beside two occurrences each of 'daily' and 'throughout the year'; and the 1552 Preface explicitly indicates his hope that laypeople would be there with the clergy.

186. For this, see G. Mursell, 'Traditions of spiritual guidance: The Book of Common Prayer', in *The Way* 31 (1991), pp. 163–71.

187. BCP 1552, p. 274. Pastoral guidance and skilled listening replaces sacramental absolution: word takes precedence over ritual.

188. BCP 1552, pp. 313–14.
189. See, e.g., the first rubric in *The communion of the sick*, BCP 1552, p. 316. The importance of reflecting on death was one of a number of continuities between late-medieval and Reformation spirituality: Tessa Watt has shown (1991, p. 113) how some of the 'godly ballads' which focused on this theme had the same function as the visual *memento mori* of the pre-Reformation era.
190. Thornton (1963), esp. pp. 257ff.
191. The term recurs frequently during this period. Thus the seventeenth-century clergyman Isaac Archer records in his diary: 'My father in his letters grounded mee in practicall divinity; and when by dutyes I strived to worke out salvation, and by strict observing God's law, and the sabbath day I thought to please God, he beat mee of from a resting in any thing I did, and sent mee higher then all such performances' (25/1657, ed. cit. p. 54; cf. also 87/1663: 'my father . . . wished mee to study that practicall divinity which no books could teach', ed. cit. p. 92).
192. The BCP (1549) Visitation of the Sick is derived from the Sarum *Ordo ad visitandum infirmum*. This began with nine 'earnest and confident prayers for recovery', alluding to the raising of Tabitha, and the healing of Tobias and Sarah and of Hezekiah. Only one of these (the least confident one) was retained in 1549, which clearly made the emphasis on suffering as divine punishment for sin the primary one, relegating expectation of recovery to the background. 1549 also reduced the seven penitential psalms to Psalm 143, which in 1662 was replaced by Psalm 71: whereas the former explicitly prays for restoration from the edge of death, the latter prays simply that God will not forsake the psalmist, and continues 'As for me, I will patiently abide alway: and will praise thee more and more.' Patient acceptance replaces prayer for a recovery of health; and by 1662 all references to healing which had appeared in 1549 and 1552 had been removed. See also C. Harris, 'Visitation of the sick', in Lowther Clarke (1964), esp. pp. 514–15, and Loades (1994) pp. 209–10.
193. BCP 1549, p. 138. On the significance of will-making for personal piety, see Marsh (1990).
194. A small but significant indicator of Cranmer's relative lack of interest in a theology of creation can be seen in his translation of the Latin collect for Pentecost 5 (Trinity 6): where the original reads 'that we, loving thee in all things and above all things (*in omnibus et super omnibus*)', Cranmer removes 'in all things', removing any reference to the presence of God in the created order.
195. See Cuming (1983) p. 111. On Cranmer's theology of eucharistic presence, see MacCulloch (1996) pp. 392, 405, 441, &c), and the famous 'Black Rubric' (BCP 1552, pp. 282–3) which excludes any possibility of belief in the real presence of Christ in the Eucharist. This rubric was retained but modified in 1662 (see Brightman and Mackenzie, in Lowther Clarke (1964), pp. 195–6).
196. Sparrow (1661) pp. 34–5.
197. Walton, *Life*, p. 77.
198. Hooker constantly quotes patristic sources, especialy Augustine, as well as Aristotle and Aquinas, but also Greek sources like St Basil. The range of his reading is remarkable. For all his Aristotelian/Thomist roots, there is a humanist breadth about Hooker as well: thus he commends foreign travel and getting to know distant peoples, just as the Queen of Sheba visited Solomon (*Laws* 1.10.12, in *Works* vol. 1, pp. 250–1).
199. Hence the centrality of the massive Book 5 (Loyer (1979) p. 445). The story of the production and publication of the *Laws* is complex (see Lewis (1954) pp. 452–3). Books 1–4 of the *Laws* were written by 1592 and published in 1594 (Walton, *Life*, pp. 70–1), while Hooker was incumbent of Boscombe, near Salisbury. Book 5 was printed in 1597. Books 6–8 did not appear until 1648–62. The whole work appears authentic, even though Book 6 is only a fragment and 7–8 are unlikely to be in the finished form Hooker would have wanted for them (on the compilation and authenticity of Book 6, see Loyer (1979) pp. 637–8). It may well be that Lancelot Andrewes played a key role in preserving the later parts of the work for posterity (see Welsby (1958) pp. 70–1).
200. For Hooker's rejection of Roman dogmas 'not . . . only because they are not in the Scripture, but

because they are neither in Scripture, nor can otherwise sufficiently by any reason be proved to be of God', see *Laws* 1.14.5, in *Works* vol. 1, p. 272. In Book 2 he argues vigorously against biblical fundamentalism (e.g. 2.4.5, in *Works* vol. 1, pp. 297–8; 2.4.7, in *Works* vol. 1, p. 299, where he quotes Augustine's Ep. 19; and 2.7.3, in *Works* vol. 1, pp. 320–1).

201. It is worth noting that he defends the God-given independence of each human being as lord of himself (*Laws* 8.2.5, in *Works* vol. 3, pp. 343–4), whilst allowing for human societies to develop in which some lord it over others.

202. *Laws* 7.18.5, in *Works* vol. 3, p. 267.

203. Welsby (1958) p. 15; Porter (1958); Lossky (1991) pp. 91–3.

204. See Lossky (1991) p. 23 and Peter E. McCulloch, *Sermons at court: politics and religion in Elizabethan and Jacobean preaching* (Cambridge UP, 1998), esp. pp. 147–54. These works, of which the most significant are *Tortura torti* (1609) and the *Responsio ad apologiam Cardinalis Bellarmini* (1610), can be found in *Works* vols 7 and 8. Welsby (1958, p. 149) points out that *Tortura torti* 'is marred by a facetiousness and smart cleverness . . . and by a certain unscrupulousness'. For Andrewes' confrontation with the Jesuit missionary Fr William Weston, see the latter's *Autobiography* pp. 128–9, where he describes Andrewes as 'one of those Puritans who allow some form of [sacramental] confession . . . his frame of mind, as some held, was not altogether opposed to the Catholic faith'.

205. This point has been much disputed by recent scholars. Welsby (1958, esp. pp. 13, 34, and 223–43) and Reidy (1955, esp. pp. 25 and 178) are severely critical of Andrewes, whilst Lossky (1991, esp. pp. 22, 29 and 289–325) defends him. But Lossky's defence is only intermittently convincing. Thus he argues (1991, p. 29) that Andrewes' political sermons (commemorating 5 August, the failed Gowrie conspiracy, and 5 November, the Gunpowder Plot, respectively) reflect not so much his uncritical adulation of James I as his view of liturgical prayer, as being where time and eternity meet: 'he interiorizes this spirit to such a point that he interprets these two political events in these sermons as manifestations of the divine mercy'. This scarcely fits with the polemical tone of his controversial works; and there are many occasions on which his praise of the sovereign is unquestionably both verbose and sycophantic (e.g. Sermon 4 for Lent, vol. 2, pp. 76–7, on which see Lossky (1991) pp. 106–7). In fairness, he elsewhere says that 'as we may not usurp God's honour for ourselves, so we may not deify princes' (Sermon 9 on Prayer, vol. 5, p. 388), and he sometimes denounces human pride ('by . . . seeking glory, glory is lost'; Sermon 13 on the Nativity, vol. 1, p. 226; on which see Lossky (1991) p. 90). In general, however, Welsby's and Reidy's criticisms remain valid.

206. Reidy (1955) p. 1.

207. *Laws* 1.1.2, in *Works* vol. 1, pp. 198–9.

208. *Laws* 1.2.2, in *Works* vol. 1, p. 200.

209. *Laws* 1.2.4, in *Works* vol. 1, p. 203.

210. Though only to some extent; Hooker says that it would be impossible for nature to work as it does if it were not guided by God, i.e. subject to the higher eternal Law. And we are no more able to understand the workings of this Law than natural creatures can understand the workings of human law (*Laws* 1.3.4, in *Works* vol. 1, pp. 210–11). See the remarks of Bouyer (1969, pp. 110–11) and of McAdoo (1949, pp. 18–25).

211. *Laws* 1.2.2, in *Works* vol. 1, p. 201.

212. *Laws* 1.3.5, in *Works* vol. 1, pp. 211–12; *Laws* 1.8.7, in *Works* vol. 1, pp. 230–2; see also 1.10.6, in *Works* vol. 1, p. 244.

213. *Laws* 1.10.1, in *Works* vol. 1, p. 239.

214. *Laws* 3.8.11, in *Works* vol. 1, p. 374.

215. *Laws* 5.9.3, in *Works* vol. 2, pp. 39–40.

216. See Loyer (1979) p. 450.

217. *Laws* 5.57.3, in *Works* vol. 2, p. 257.

218. Loyer (1979, p. 449) uses the word *dépouillée*; cf. Hooker, *Laws* 5.6.2. Hence the need for ritual, externalizing spiritual truth. Loyer's study urgently deserves translation into English.

219. See *A sermon of the salvation of mankind*, in *Certain homilies*, p. 17; cf. *Articles of Religion* XI.

220. p. 19.
221. See, e.g., *Commentary on Galatians* 2.16, p. 141, and 3.10, pp. 247–8: 'Christians are not made righteous in doing righteous things, but being now made righteous by faith in Christ, they do righteous things.'
222. *Laws* 5.56.1, in *Works* vol. 2, p. 245. It is worth noting the echoes of Pseudo-Dionysius here: cf., for example, *The divine names* 1.2: 'The Good . . . draws sacred minds upward to its permitted contemplation, to participation and to the state of becoming like it': trans. C. Luibheid, *Pseudo-Dionysius: the complete works* (Classics of western spirituality) (Mahwah, NJ: Paulist Press, 1987), p. 50.
223. *Laws* 5.56.5, in *Works* vol. 2, pp. 247–8.
224. 'The union therefore of the flesh with Deity is to *that flesh* a gift of principal grace and favour. For by virtue of this grace, man is really made God, a creature is exalted above the dignity of all creatures, and hath all creatures else under it' (*Laws* 5.54.3, in *Works* vol. 2, p. 233). 'Sith God hath deified our nature, though not by turning it into himself, yet by making it his own inseparable habitation, we cannot now conceive how God should without man either exercise divine power, or receive the glory of divine praise. For man is in both an associate of Deity' (*Laws* 5.54.5, in *Works* vol. 2, p. 235). This is classical patristic theology.
225. *Laws* 5.56.7, in *Works* vol. 2, pp. 249–50.
226. Loyer describes participation in Hooker's theology as 'reciprocal presence' (1979, p. 485). See also Lossky (1991) p. 268; Allchin (1988) pp. 72–3; Stevenson (1994) pp. 26–7. The Pauline doctrine of adoption is affirmed in *Articles of Religion* XVII and XXVII. Andrewes also speaks of human beings as having been *adopted* by the Holy Spirit. Because God is our Father, his love for us is immutable – we may offend him grievously, but we never cease to be his children (Sermon 7 on Prayer, vol. 5, pp. 366–7). And it is the dignity of our sonship which leads us to participation in the divine nature:
   If we consider the dignity whereunto we are exalted, we shall see on earth, *Si filii Dei, quodammodo dii sumus*, 'If we be sons, we are after a sort gods;' *et divinae participes naturae*, 'partakers of the divine nature,' as the sons of men are men. (Sermon 7 on Prayer, vol. 5, p. 369)
227. See, e.g., Sermon 9 on the Nativity, vol. 1, pp. 139ff, and Sermon 12 on the Nativity, vol. 1, pp. 196f, and Lossky (1991) pp. 48 and 86 n. 164.
228. *Laws* 5.56.10, in *Works* vol. 2, p. 253.
229. *Laws* 5.56.10, in *Works* vol. 2, p. 253.
230. Hooker is here consciously synthesizing the Reformed stress on righteousness as *imputed* with the Catholic stress on righteousness as *imparted* and grace as *infused*; Stevenson (1994) p. 27; Loyer (1979) p. 489.
231. *Laws* 5.56.12, in *Works* vol. 2, p. 255.
232. *Laws* 5.56.11, in *Works* vol. 2, p. 254.
233. Loyer (1979) p. 485. See also *Laws* 5.67.5, in *Works* vol. 2, p. 352: 'the bread and cup are his body and blood because they are causes instrumental upon the receipt whereof the *participation* of his body and blood ensueth'.
234. *Laws* 5.67.6, in *Works* vol. 2, p. 352. Stevenson (1994, p. 29) underlines the fact that there is some confusion in Hooker's eucharistic theology, describing it as 'an astonishing and impressive tightrope walk' (p. 30).
235. See Loyer (1979) pp. 480–1.
236. Loyer defines this view as 'principe essentiel, qui permet à la fois de repousser la présence substantielle du corps et d'affirmer sa présence réelle' (1979, p. 484).
237. 'And it is not in the power of nature to elevate and lift itself up to conceive hope of being partakers of the blessedness of the life to come, to be made "partakers of the Divine Nature", and of the heavenly substance; if men hope for any such thing, it is the Spirit of God that raiseth them up to it' (Sermon 1 on Prayer, vol. 5, p. 306). Andrewes distinguishes here between what comes from ourselves naturally, and what comes from ourselves by virtue of having been engrafted into us (p. 307): thus 'the power wherewith we are endued from above to the doing of heavenly and

spiritual things, is of ourselves but not from ourselves' (p. 308). See also Lossky (1991), esp. chapter 6. Andrewes describes the Spirit as 'the essential love of God' (Sermon 18 on Prayer, vol. 5, p. 459). For Andrewes' view of the Eucharist, see pp. 96–100 (esp. n. 194) and 340–5. Note too the prominence of the Holy Spirit in some sections of Andrewes' *Preces privatae*, especially in 'The Creed Meditated' (ed. cit., p. 185).

238. Sermon for Easter 13, vol. 2, p. 407; Sermon for Christmas 13, vol. 1, p. 230; Reidy (1955) pp. 75 and 153. Lossky argues (1991, p. 268) that, whereas Hooker stresses participation as his central theme in response to the debate on justification, Andrewes instead stresses deification.

239. Sermon 15 on the Nativity, vol. 1, pp. 256–7.

240. Sermon 15 on the Nativity, vol. 1, p. 258.

241. Sermon 19 on Prayer, vol. 5, p. 472; cf. Sermon 3 on Repentance and Fasting, vol. 1, pp. 345f.

242. See, as well as Loyer, the interesting discussion of Hooker's understanding of participation and presence in Shaw (1981) pp. 79–81.

243. *Laws* 3.1.2, in *Works* vol. 1, p. 338.

244. 'In a word, our estate is according to the pattern of God's own ancient elect people, which people was not part of them the commonwealth, and part of them the Church of God, but the selfsame people whole and entire were both under one chief Governor, on whose supreme authority they did all depend' (*Laws* 8.1.7, in *Works* vol. 3, p. 340).

245. *Laws* 5.72.2, in *Works* vol. 2, pp. 409–10.

246. See Genesis 17.17; Sermon 1, *Of Faith in the Elect*, in *Works* vol. 3, p. 472.

247. Sermon 1, *Of Faith in the Elect*, in *Works* vol. 3, pp. 474–5.

248. Sermon 1, *Of Faith in the Elect*, in *Works* vol. 3, p. 479.

249. 'Our sins do make a partition between God and us', Sermon 14 on Prayer, vol. 5, p. 425.

250. John Booty, in an important article (1982), underlines the importance of this theme, not only in Hooker, Donne, and Herbert, as a development of the late medieval awareness of sin and penance; but also in any healthy contemporary spirituality, if we are truly to become aware (e.g.) of how far we have failed to care for our planet (p. 44).

251. See Loyer (1979) p. 485.

252. *Laws* 5.23, in *Works* vol. 2, p. 115; see Booty (1978) pp. 33–4. On the inseparability (for Hooker) of prayer and doctrine, as of law and the authority on which it rests, see Loyer: 'Doctrine, c'est-à-dire la prédication ou l'enseignement ['preaching or teaching'] dans la célébration liturgique, mouvement de Dieu vers l'homme; Prière, c'est-à-dire adoration, action de grâce, demande, mouvement de l'homme vers Dieu; Sacrement enfin, rencontre de Dieu et de l'homme, présence de Dieu en l'homme et de l'homme en Dieu par participation réciproque' (1979, pp. 446–7).

253. *Laws* 5.23, in *Works* vol. 2, p. 116.

254. *Laws* 5.47.4, in *Works* vol. 2, p. 200.

255. Julian of Norwich, *Showings*, Long Text 52, ed. cit. in Chapter 4 pp. 546–7. See Chapter 4 p. 221.

256. The same point is made in *Articles of Religion* XVI.

257. Duffy, though (1993, p. 215), argues that, by comparison with late medieval piety, Cranmer's liturgical reforms introduced a much more sharply individualist stress, in particular by obliterating any sense of communion between the living and the dead; and in this sense it is true that the holiness of the Church of England is a less inclusive thing than that of late medieval Catholicism. But Duffy's argument does no justice to those aspects of the spirituality of the Prayer Book which do seek to integrate the individual within a wider social and spiritual environment.

258. *Laws* 1.5.1, in *Works* vol. 1, p. 215.

259. *Laws* 1.8.1, in *Works* vol. 1, p. 225 – desire for Hooker is, in Loyer's phrase, 'le mouvement spontané de la nature vers sa fin' (1979, p. 469).

260. *Laws* 1.8.5, in *Works* vol. 1, pp. 228–9.

261. *Laws* 1.8.6, in *Works* vol. 1, p. 230.

262. See the fascinating discussion in Loyer (1979) pp. 469–71. Loyer discerns both Platonic and Thomist roots in Hooker's view of prayer as desire: 'il est orienté vers Dieu, mais il est enraciné

dans les forces obscures de la sensibilité. Le supérieur s'appuie sur l'inférieur. *L'affection*, le mouvement des parties cachées de l'âme, nourrit la prière' (p. 471). But Hooker is more Augustinian than he is either Platonic or Thomist. He says that desire 'tendeth unto union with that it desireth' (*Laws* 1.11.2, in *Works* vol. 1, p. 255); and he goes on to say, quoting Augustine, that whereas now we only love what is good *for us*, in heaven we shall love what is good *in itself*, absolutely, which is the source of true felicity. Lower creatures cannot attain to this because they are incapable of loving what is good in itself, and can only love what is good *for them* (*Laws* 1.11.3, in *Works* vol. 1, pp. 255–6).

263. 'What is love towards God but a desire of union with God?', *Laws* 6.3.3, in *Works* vol. 3, p. 9.

264. 'The well-spring of repentance is faith, first breeding fear, and then love' (*Laws* 6.3.4, in *Works* vol. 3, p. 11). On this, see also Booty (1982).

265. *Laws* 1.11.4, in *Works* vol. 1, p. 257; see also *Laws* 1.12.3, in *Works* vol. 1, p. 264.

266. *Laws* 1.11.6, in *Works* vol. 1, p. 261. It is interesting to compare this view with the celebration of the divine beauty in Burton's *Anatomy of melancholy*, 3.4.1, vol. 3, pp. 332–4.

267. See *Laws* 1.6.2–3, in *Works* vol. 1, pp. 217–18.

268. *Laws* 1.7.3–4, in *Works* vol. 1, pp. 221–2.

269. *Laws* 5.48.2–3, in *Works* vol. 2, p. 201. See Loyer (1979, p. 467): for Hooker, 'la prière est désir'. It is also offering – 'une offrande, une sacrifice . . . L'expression du désir est offrande; quand l'objet du désir est refusé, l'offrande est sacrifice. Paradoxalement, la prière atteint à sa perfection quand Dieu la repousse. Elle est ramenée à sa fin propre, à ce qu'elle est réellement. Elle est sacrifice, elle est don, non pas un don restreint mais un don de tout l'homme à Dieu' (1979, pp. 468–9). The seventeenth-century French Reformed pastor Charles Drelincourt (1595–1669), whose *Christian's defence against the fears of death* had many editions in contemporary England, wrote in it that 'A groan of an oppressed soul, and a sigh from us by necessity . . . are far more acceptable to [God] than prayers of forty hours, that come forth of an hypocritical mouth' (trans. M. D'Assigny (London, 1814), p. 242; cited in Tripp (1991) p. 91 n. 48.

270. *Laws* 5.48.3, in *Works* vol. 2, p. 201.

271. *Laws* 5.48.2, in *Works* vol. 2, p. 201.

272. *Laws* 5.48.4, in *Works* vol. 2, p. 202. Hooker here argues against his old Puritan adversary Thomas Cartwright, who maintained that 'we ought not to desire to be free from all adversity if it be his will', citing at length the conflict within Christ between his human desire to avoid a painful death and his divine desire to do his Father's will. In particular Hooker argues against an 'over-restrained consideration of prayer', restricting it to what the will resolves to seek as a result of the understanding knowing the object sought will be obtained. Rather, for us as for Christ, prayers are 'as well sometime a presentation of mere desires, as a mean of procuring desired effects at the hands of God' – *Laws* 5.48.11, in *Works* vol. 2, p. 209.

273. 'We pray and obtain not, because he which knoweth our hearts doth know our desires are evil. In like manner we give and we are not the more accepted, because he beholdeth how unwisely we spill our gifts in the bringing. It is to him which needeth nothing all one whether any thing or nothing be given him. But for our own good it always behoveth that whatsoever we offer up into his hands we bring it seasoned with this cogitation, "Thou Lord art worthy of all honour."' (*Laws* 5.79.8, in *Works* vol. 2, pp. 490–1).

274. Reidy (1955, p. 172) describes them as forming 'a fairly complete treatise', and Andrewes himself seems to have conceived of them thus: see Sermon 15 on Prayer. The sermons can be found in volume 5 of the collected *Works*, pp. 362–476.

275. Psalm 147.9; Sermon 4 on Prayer, in *Works* vol. 5, pp. 334–5.

276. See Sermon 6 on Prayer, in *Works* vol. 5, p. 353.

277. *Pattern of catechistical doctrine* 3.6, p. 97; Sermon 5 on Prayer, in *Works* vol. 5, p. 346.

278. The Spirit kindles within us the desires that should cause us to pray (Sermon 4 on Prayer in *Works* vol. 5, p. 338). Wrongly-directed desires can lead our prayer to be wrongly directed too (Sermon 5 on Prayer, in *Works* vol. 5, p. 346); but the Spirit of grace inspires us with holy desires which are recognized and interpreted by the act of prayer (Sermon 6 on Prayer, in *Works* vol. 5, p. 351). Andrewes maintains that the work of the Spirit does not just inspire in us desires for

God, but also desires for all that is good (Sermon 6 on Prayer, in *Works* vol. 5, p. 352).

279. Sermon 5 on Prayer, in *Works* vol. 5, p. 345.

280. 'When we come to pray to God the whole man must be occupied, and all the members of the body employed in the service of God' (Sermon 3 on Prayer, in *Works* vol. 5, p. 325), making our own the three virtues of confidence, diligence and perseverance (p. 326). 'Both our heart, our understanding, our affection must concur in making intercession to God' (Sermon 4 on Prayer, in *Works* vol. 5, p. 335).

281. See *Laws* 8.2.18, in *Works* vol. 3, pp. 359–60: 'The good which is proper unto each man belongeth to the common good of all, as a part of the whole's perfection; but yet these two are things different; for men by that which is proper are severed, united they are by that which is common. Wherefore, besides that which moveth each man in particular to seek his private, there must of necessity in all public societies be also a general mover, directing unto the common good, and framing every man's particular to it.' See also 5.23, in *Works* vol. 2, pp. 113–14, where he says that the devotion of others inspires us when our own flags.

282. See Loyer (1979) p. 454.

283. *Laws* 5.41.4, in *Works* vol. 2, p. 175. Hooker warns that our prayers will not always bring the answer we expected: 5.48.3, in *Works* vol. 2, pp. 201–2; cf. *Luther, Lectures on Romans* trans. W. Pauck (Library of Christian classics 15) (London: SCM Press, 1961), pp. 240–1.

284. 'No doubt but penitency is as prayer a thing acceptable unto God, be it in public or in secret. Howbeit as in the one if men were wholly left to their own voluntary meditations in their closets, and not drawn by laws and orders unto the open assemblies of the Church that there they may join with others in prayer, it may be soon conjectured what Christian devotion that way would come unto in a short time' (*Laws* 5.72.13, in *Works* vol. 2, p. 241).

285. Notably the Bible (with which Andrewes had a familiarity remarkable even for that scripturally saturated age), existing devotional collections, and an eclectic variety of other sources. See Brightman's introduction to his edition, esp. pp. xlii ff.

286. Brightman, introduction to ed. cit., p. xli.

287. It is interesting to compare Andrewes' *Confessio laudis* with its principal source, the *Hortulus animae* (Lyons, 1516). Andrewes sharpens the contrast his source makes between himself, as a literate Christian, and other people, thanking God for making him *literatus* and *non mechanicus*, a free man and not a slave, and omits his source's glad acceptance of his 'simple and poor parents'; *Preces privatae*, Parker edn, pp. 345–6; ed. Brightman, p. 346, ET p. 231; the *Hortulus* is in Brightman, p. 368.

288. Sermon 4 on Prayer, in *Works* vol. 5, p. 340.

289. Sermon 11 for Whitsun, vol. 4, pp. 318–19; see Lossky (1991, p. 284).

290. Sermon 4 on Prayer, vol. 5, p. 339; see also Sermon 7 on Prayer, vol. 5, p. 370.

291. *Laws* 5:34:2. *Works* 2:150–1. It is not surprising to find spiritual writers of this period using the analogy of petitioning the king for prayer: John Fisher does it in comparing the Psalms to the way someone seeking something from the king might solicit a wise person to compose a suitable letter on his or her behalf (*English works*, EETS 27, p. 73, quoted in Chambers 1955, pp. 21–2).

292. *Laws* 5:30:1, *Works* 2:138.

293. *Laws* 7:15:7, *Works* 3:242.

294. *Laws* 5:48:11, *Works* 2:209–10.

295. For the attempts by Parliament to suppress the Prayer Book between 1643 and 1649, see Morrill (1982).

296. BCP 1549, pp. 18–19.

297. BCP 1662, Preface, p. 14.

298. 'A more perfect rendering', BCP 1662, Preface, p. 14. The Authorized Version was used throughout apart from the Psalter, offertory sentences and 'Comfortable Words'.

299. Such as prayers for those at sea, and provision for adult baptisms, partly as a result of the growth of the (adult) Baptist movement and 'for the baptizing of Natives in our plantations, and others converted to the Faith'.

300. *An apology for authorized and set forms of liturgy,* Preface 37, in *Works* vol. 7, p. 303.

301. See Cosin, *Devotions*; and Thornton (1963) p. 263. Cosin's *Devotions* are rooted in the tradition of the medieval primers, and were designed to provide a supplement to the common prayer of the church. See also G. Cuming, 'The Anglicanism of John Cosin', in (1983) pp. 123–41; Stevenson (1994), esp. p. 91; McAdoo (1949) p. 145.

302. See Brightman and MacKenzie, in Lowther Clarke (1964); MacCulloch (1996) p. 328.

303. In 1663 Isaac Archer, then incumbent of Chippenham in Cambridgeshire, noting that 'there had not bin a sacrament in Chippenham for about 20 yeares last past', records that 'I gave the sacrament, and found the people very serious and reverent, and loving to one another' (*Diary* 812/1663, ed. cit. p. 89). See the remarks of the diary's editor, Matthew Storey, ed. cit. p. 37. The Suffolk farmer and churchwarden William Coe (1662–1729) gives extensive evidence of genuine eucharistic piety in his *Diary*, frequently preparing for Holy Communion by fasting and self-examination (see, e.g., *Diary* fol. 8r, ed. cit. p. 208; fol. 10r, p. 210). He normally received the sacrament at or near Easter, Whitsun and Christmas each year. See also Morrill (1982) pp. 103–12. See also Maltby (1998), pp. 46–52.

304. Thornton (1963) p. 265.

305. Thornton (1963) p. 262; MacCulloch (1996) pp. 627–8.

306. Alldridge (1988, pp. 98–9) suggests that in sixteenth- and seventeenth-century Chester something between 51% and 83% of parishioners attended church regularly (figure arrived at through calculations of pew rents); and see also Spaeth (1988), esp. pp. 132–3 and references given at n. 35.

307. Spaeth (1988) p. 146, and (more generally) Thornton (1963). See also the research undertaken by Maltby (1998) in assessing the level of use of the Prayer Book in Elizabethan and early Stuart England.

308. See the important points made in this regard by Spufford (1985i and 1995, p. 7).

309. Josselin, *Diary* p. 22. Matters were of course very different when disaster struck: in his memoirs of the Great Plague of London, Daniel Defoe noted how the people of London 'flock'd to the Churches and Meetings, and they were all so throng'd, that there was often no coming near, no, not to the very Doors of the largest Churches; Also there were daily Prayers appointed Morning and Evening at several Churches, and Days of private praying at other Places; at all which the People attended, I say, with an uncommon Devotion' (*A journal of the plague year*, Shakespeare Head edn (Oxford: Blackwell, 1928), pp. 34–5).

310. *Diary*, p. 197.

311. Spufford (1981, p. 203) points out that a fifth of the 'godly chapbooks' published during the period for devout laypeople, and later collected by Samuel Pepys, are concerned specifically with death and judgement.

312. In his *Diary*, the East Anglian clergyman Isaac Archer records his difficulties in trying to decide whether to submit to hearing (and later reading) the Prayer Book when his formidable nonconformist father warned him against it (Archer senior 'never thought that one sprung from his loynes would plead for Baal'; *Diary* 54/1661, ed. cit. p. 72; see also 52–3/1660–1, ed. cit. p. 69). The Suffolk farmer William Coe frequently acknowledges in his diary his inability to remain awake during long church services (thus, 24 March 1699: 'Slept att church forenoon and afternoon, and dull and heavy att my devotions' (*Diary* fol. 24r, ed. cit. p. 219).

313. The Earl of Stirling (1637); cited in Mendelson and Crawford (1998) p. 226.

314. Mendelson and Crawford (1998) p. 228. In the seventeenth century, needlework was the most important aspect of a girl's education, involving among other things the careful study of scripture: for women, the leisure to practise fine embroidery could be a sign of status.

315. Other stories embroidered, of which extant examples may be seen at the Victoria and Albert Museum, include the marriage of Isaac and Rebekah (T.45–1937, early eighteenth century); the judgement of Solomon (T.17–1946; 1686, a raised work-picture); the story of David and Bathsheba (T.253–1927, c.1630–70: a wonderful presentation of Bathsheba taking a bath on the rooftop while David ogles her from the roof of his palace at the top left); Jacob meeting Rachel at the well (T.225–1968, an exquisite wooden casket of c.1650–75 with several other scenes represented as well); and the story of Ruth (e.g. T.45–1973, an embroidered casket of

c.1650–75, showing inter alia Ruth sitting at Boaz's feet, and Ruth and Boaz in splendid wedding garments).

316. Victoria and Albert Museum, ref.1741–1869.

317. See, e.g., Victoria and Albert Museum embroideries, Morshead Loan 6 (G36), mid-seventeenth-century English; 892–1864, a raised work-picture of c.1670, with Esther splendidly attired.

318. Victoria and Albert Museum T.101–1915; embroidered panel, perhaps originally a book cover. Cf. ibid. 1415–1874 (second half of sixteenth century): a linen embroidered chalice veil with an inscription; in the centre is UNTO GOD GIF PRIS; and round the edge

    O LORD CONSIDER MI DISTRES

    AND VTH SPED SOME PETE [= pity] TAK

    MI SIN DEFAC MI FALT REDRES

    LORD FOR THI GREAT M[ercy] SAK

(the opening of W. Whittingham's metrical translation of Psalm 51). The embroiderer is anonymous.

319. *Autobiography of Anne Lady Halkett*, p. 31.

320. *Autobiography of Anne Lady Halkett*, p. 35. She was a passionate royalist who described the execution of Charles I as 'the greatest murder [that] was committed . . . except the Crucifying of our Saviour' (p. 109), and could not understand why Presbyterians did not kneel to pray ('Lord convince them of the evil of this way that are guilty off itt', p. 116).

321. *Barrington family letters*, p. 67. See also the letter to Lady Barrington from Thomas Bourchier, 2 March 1629 (pp. 60–1).

322. From *A message from God, by a dumb woman* (1654), reproduced in Hinds (1996) pp. 219–21. See pp. 11–12 of the same volume for contemporary women's prophetic literature.

323. For its influence on Richard Baxter's *The saints everlasting rest*, see below. The *Arte* was first published in 1606 and quickly went through two more separate editions (1607, 1609), then appearing in Hall's collected works, of which there were at least 13 editions by 1650 (Martz (1954) p. 332). For an excellent introduction, see Booty (1984); for a fuller exploration of Hall's thought, stressing his Calvinist theology, see R. A. McCabe, *Joseph Hall: a study in satire and meditation* (Oxford: Clarendon, 1982).

324. Hall himself cites Gerson (*Arte* 8, p. 50), St Bernard and St Jerome (9, p. 51), Denys the Carthusian (11, p. 53) and many others. He does not explicitly name his principal sources in his own Foreword (*Arte*, p. 43): they were Johan Wessel Gansfort's *Scala meditatoria* (c.1487) and a subsequent text, John Mombaer's *Rosetum exercitiorum spiritualium et sacrarum meditationum* (1494) (Martz (1954) p. 332; Booty (1984) p. 203). Both Gansfort and Mombaer belonged to the Brethren of the Common Life (Booty (1984) p. 204). Mombaer's *Rosetum* was very popular in the sixteenth century, and strongly influenced García de Cisneros and thus indirectly St Ignatius's *Spiritual exercises* (Martz (1954) p. 331).

325. *Arte* 1, p. 44.

326. *Arte* 2, p. 45.

327. *Arte* 12, p. 53.

328. *An anatomy of melancholy* 3.4.1, vol. 3, p. 361. Stachniewski (1991, p. 222) suggests that Burton was, in an idiosyncratic way, representative of the dominant episcopalian Calvinist orthodoxy of his day.

329. For their origins and nature, see especially Rivers (1991i), pp. 25ff; for their influence, see Patrides (1969) pp. 39–41; for a detailed bibliographical survey, see Rivers in Keeble (1988) pp. 45–69; for their indebtedness to classical philosophy see Dominic Scott, 'Reason, recollection and the Cambridge Platonists' in Baldwin and Hutton (1994) pp. 139–50. The first generation of Latitudinarians (Whichcote, More, Smith, and Cudworth) have since the nineteenth century been called the 'Cambridge Platonists'; but this is not a term contemporaries used; it draws attention to one particular strand in their thought at the expense of others; and it obscures the continuity of interest between the first and second generations of Latitudinarians (Rivers (1991i) p. 28). Those who do try to distinguish between Latitudinarians and Cam-

bridge Platonists either suggest that the former lack the mysticism of the latter (e.g. Wakefield (1992) p. 63), or point out that some at least of the former were not strictly Platonists at all (e.g. Rupp (1986) p. 30). Thomas Traherne was a stout defender of the established church: 'The Government of a church Established by Laws is a Great fortress in which the welfare of Millions is concerned' (*Select meditations* 3.24, p. 63).

330. Bush (1945) p. 340. Benjamin Whichcote associates enthusiasts ('who know not to day what they shall think to morrow') with atheists, self-flatterers and hypocrites (Sermon on the Unity of the Church, in Patrides (1969) p. 89).

331. For Sterry, see Pinto (1934), still an excellent introduction to his life and thought, and Matar's introduction to his edition of some of Sterry's writings, though the reader can inevitably only obtain a sense of the breadth and range of Sterry's thought by reading one of his own works *in extenso* rather than in small extracts. For Sterry's relationship with the Latitudinarians, see Matar's introduction (1994, p. 13). After the Restoration, Sterry established a small lay community of fellow Puritans at West Sheen in Surrey, not dissimilar in nature to that of Church of England members at Little Gidding.

332. For Browne, see the memoir by Dr Johnson (followed by that of the editor) in Simon Wilkin's edition of Browne's works (*The works of Sir Thomas Browne* (London: Henry Bohn, 1852), vol. 1 pp. ix–lxvii), and J. F. S. Post, *Sir Thomas Browne* (Boston, 1987).

333. For Traherne's political context and views (he was basically a conformist), see Smith 1988.

334. The term recurs constantly in Traherne's work. See, e.g., *Select meditations* 3.65: 'Felicity is a Bird of Paradice So Strang, that it is Impossible to flie a mong men without Loseing some feathers were She not Immortal' (p. 91); and 4.18, p. 123, where he describes felicity as 'the Queen of Heaven'. This stress on 'Felicitie' as essentially a heavenly, not earthly, experience is taken from Augustine: see (e.g.) Augustine's *Sermon* 19.4, where he says that 'happiness (*felicitas*) is not to be found here [on earth]' (*The works of Saint Augustine*, vol. 3:1 (Brooklyn, NY: New City, 1990), trans. by Edmund Hill OP, p. 381).

335. For Browne, see Bush (1945), esp. pp. 149 and 332ff; Salter (1964, esp. her comments on Bush, pp. 103–4); for the story of the discovery of Traherne's works, see Ridler, ed. cit. of the Poems etc., pp. xiii–xiv; J. J. Smith, 'Traherne from his unpublished manuscripts', in A. M. Allchin et al. (eds.), *Profitable wonders*, pp. 38–51); and Smith and Yeandle (1997) (in which they describe the discovery of yet another Traherne work, the unfinished poem *The Ceremonial Law*, consisting of about 1,800 lines based on Genesis and Exodus). Much of Traherne's work has never been published: for extracts and analysis, see (in addition to works cited under Traherne in the Bibliography) A. Pritchard, 'Traherne's *Commentaries of Heaven* (with selections from the manuscript)', in *University of Toronto Quarterly* 53 (1983), pp. 1–35; and Carol L. Marks, 'Traherne's Church's Year Book', in *Papers of the Bibliographical Society of America* 60 (1966), pp. 31–72 as well as the articles in Allchin et al., *Profitable wonders*. For Traherne's Platonism, see S. Hutton, 'Platonism in some Metaphysical poets', in Baldwin and Hutton (1994), pp. 167–77. See also Martz (1964) and Wolf (1982). Traherne explicitly acknowledges his debt to Plato in *Select meditations* 2.49, p. 30, and 3.16, pp. 57–8; but it is succinctly encapsulated in a single sentence: 'Deep Misteries are beneath the Surface of common works' (*Select meditations* 3.20, p. 61).

336. *Religio medici* II.7, p. 64.

337. *The rise, race, and royalty,* p. 145; cf. p. 185.

338. *Centuries* 1.15, p. 171; *The Designe* vv. 5–6, p. 39.

339. *Centuries* 1.19, p. 173; cf. *Select meditations* 1.81, p. 1; 4.6, pp. 117–18; 4.66, p. 149: 'Till we see our nothing, we cannot understand the value of our Being.'

340. *Centuries* 2.78, p. 249.

341. *Centuries* 3.58, p. 294; *Christian ethicks* 1, p. 25 and 18, p. 152. The idiosyncrasies of spelling and orthography are Traherne's own.

342. Thus Sterry: 'Man fallen from God in Adam is banished out of the Garden. He hath lost the pleasant, and glorious Appearances of God in him, by the Natural Image. Yet he hath the Field left in him still, the Natural Image itself: which though it be beset, over-grown, shut up with

Bryers, and Thorns from the Earth, corruptions, cares, miseries from the Image of the Creature; yet it affords us some low, weak Strength, and Sweetness for man to feed upon' (*The rise, race, and royalty*, pp. 109–10).

343. In *A discourse* (p. 32), Sterry speaks of the image of the Trinity (which he describes as 'the first Marriage, and glorious Prototype of all Marriages') existing within each soul, so that 'Love is their Spring and their Spirit'. See also *A discourse* pp. 35 and 50 and Sterry's letter to 'Scipio' (*Select writings*, pp. 144–50). The part played by grace in the theology of the Latitudinarians is modest (by comparison with the Reformers) but nonetheless important. The Latitudinarians eschewed the characteristic Protestant antithesizing of grace and nature, which involved height-ening the significance of the former and stressing the radical fallenness of the latter. Yet they did not go as far as some Christian Platonists (e.g. Plotinus) in believing that human beings could achieve union with the Divine unaided. Instead, they sought (rather as Aquinas had) to inte-grate both divine grace and human freewill in formulae such as this: 'No man is truly free, but he that hath his will enlarged to the extent of Gods [*sic*] own will, by loving whatsoever God loves, and nothing else' (Ralph Cudworth, *A sermon preached before the House of Commons*, in Patrides (1969) pp. 125–6; see also Patrides (1969) pp. 17–18 and Rivers (1991i) pp. 74–5). Traherne, characteristically, went further in the direction of Plotinus; and he often gives the impression that human beings can come close to union with God by their own efforts, and their own exercise of freewill: see, e.g., *Christian ethicks* 3, p. 36, and 4, p. 40; and *Centuries* 1.93 'let my Will becom Conformable to thine: that thy Will and mine, may be united, and made one for evermore', p. 210): this is because for Traherne what is compelled is spoiled – the very antithesis of Calvinism (see *Christian ethicks* 4, p. 40, and 12, p. 104). Yet even Traherne envis-aged the spiritual life as the co-operation of God and human beings, and for that process grace was indispensable: 'The World', he wrote, 'is a Pomgranat . . . becaus it containeth the Seeds of Grace and the Seeds of Glory' (*Centuries* 2.96, p. 259).

344. *The rise, race, and royalty*, p. 109. Sterry explicitly quotes Pseudo-Dionysius on occasions (see, e.g., *A discourse*, p. 158). The influence of the German mystic Jakob Boehme on Sterry is also important, though Sterry was far from uncritical of Boehme: see N. I. Matar, 'Peter Sterry and Jacob Boehme', in *Notes and Queries* 33 (1986), pp. 33–6; Gibbons (1996) pp. 124 and 133.

345. See Pseudo-Dionysius, *The celestial hierarchy* 2.4.

346. *Religio medici* II.2, p. 58.

347. Browne, *Religio medici* II.4, pp. 60–1.

348. Browne, *Religio medici* I.34, p. 33, and II.10, p. 69.

349. *The rise, race, and royalty*, p. 36; cf. pp. 111, 147 &c.; *A discourse*, p. 59; Letter 1 to Morgan Llwyd (1651), ed. Matar (1994) p. 39. Elsewhere Sterry stresses the importance of retiring 'into the Seede of God in you, till that open itselfe as a heavenly eye in you': we must learn to see with the eyes of Christ' (Letter to his son, ed. Matar (1994) p. 130).

350. *Insatiableness* II, l.1, p. 134.

351. *Silence* l.81, p. 27.

352. vol. 4, p. 29.

353. vol. 1, p. 31. See also *The circulation*, vol. 6, p. 47; *Centuries* 2.83, p. 251; and *Thanksgivings for the soul*, pp. 390–403.

354. *Religio medici* I.13, p. 13. For the Platonic tradition in England, see the series of essays in Baldwin and Hutton (1994). Traherne also celebrates the human capacity to know, to be insa-tiably curious, and to be ambitious (*Centuries* 3.42, p. 285).

355. *Religio medici* I.16, p. 15. He goes on to declare forcefully that 'there is a generall beauty in the works of God, and therefore no deformity in any kind or species of creature whatsoever' (p. 16). Cf. John Smith: 'Thus may a Good man walk up and down the World as in a Garden of Spices, and suck a Divine Sweetness out of every flower' (*Select discourses* 9, in Patrides (1969) p. 186).

356. e.g. 'when the Spirit, which is the Head, and the Man in us, withdraws itself from its Shadowy Image, the Body, which is as the Woman, it finds itself in the Form of an Angel, and in the Society of Angels' (*The rise, race, and royalty*, p. 194); in his first Letter to Morgan Llwyd (1651), in which he describes the creation as 'a shadowy Image of God, & of Christ' (ed. Matar (1994)

p. 39). He begins a letter to his son by saying that 'A cheife thing in life is to understand, that wee are hee in A land of Shadows, and dreams' (*Select writings* ed. Matar (1994) p. 95); 'God is the *Light*, the Creature the *Shadow*' (*The clouds in which Christ comes*, p. 4); 'The Body is esteem'd a Prison or Grave to the Soul, because it tyes the Soul up into One Particular Appearance' (*The clouds in which Christ comes*, p. 48). See also his short treatise *The state of a saints soul and body in death* (in *Select writings*, pp. 204–14), in which Sterry's attitude to the prison-house of the flesh as uncompromisingly Platonic.

357. *The rise, race, and royalty*, pp. 132–3; cf. *A discourse*, p. 95.

358. *The salutation*, vv. 5, 7, p. 6; cf. *Centuries* 3.16, p. 271. In *Select meditations* Traherne says 'Wise and Holy must man be to all the Creatures in Heaven and Earth' (1.92, p. 10).

359. *Select meditations* 1.87, p. 5. Cf. 2.42 'O what could this world be, but a silent chaos, a Dull and Empty wilderness, were [it] not for the Invisible Things of His Eternal Kingdom!' (p. 28); cf. also 2.94, p. 45; 4.30, p. 130; and 3.83, p. 100, a beautiful reflection on looking at 'a Little Church Environed with Trees' and seeing all the love and labour which created it.

360. *The rise, race, and royalty*, pp. 206–7; cf. *A discourse*, p. 45.

361. Sterry is very conscious that 'we easily believe that which we desire' (*A discourse*, p. 45).

362. *The rise, race, and royalty*, p. 168. Cf. *The clouds in which Christ comes*, p. 30: 'If you will touch the Heart of God with your Prayers and Sorrowes, it must be by a union between Him and you, in One Universall, Common Person, the Lord Jesus, God-Man.'

363. e.g. Ralph Cudworth: 'there is a weaknesse and impotency in all Evil, a masculine strength and vigour in all Goodnesse' (*A sermon preached before the House of Commons*, in Patrides (1969) p. 106). For the Latitudinarians virtue is natural (not supernatural), vice unnatural (Benjamin Whichcote, Sermon 1.3, in Patrides (1969) p. 49). Virtue is an integrating, vice a disintegrating, force (John Smith, *Select discourses* 9, in Patrides (1969) p. 179).

364. See, e.g., Cudworth: 'Inke and Paper can never make us Christians, can never beget a new nature, a living principle in us' (*A sermon preached before the House of Commons*, in Patrides (1969) p. 92; or John Smith: 'To seek our Divinity meerly [*sic*] in Books and Writings, is to seek the living among the dead' (*Select discourses* I, in Patrides (1969) p. 129). The way to be sure of knowing Christ is to be obedient to his commandments, not to read books about him (Cudworth, p. 108). 'That is not the best & truest knowledge of God which is wrought out by the labour and sweat of the Brain, but that which is kindled within us by an heavenly warmth in our Hearts' (Smith, *Select discourses* I, in Patrides (1969) p. 129). See also Traherne: 'Philosophers are not those that Speak, but Do great Things' (*Centuries* 4.2, p. 316); and 'To return to the Living waters, and leave sophisticat puddles, is to Returne to the simple Treasures of Eden' (*Select meditations* 3.13, p. 56; cf. 3.30, p. 68).

365. Cudworth, *A sermon preached before the House of Commons*, in Patrides (1969) p. 96.

366. Benjamin Whichcote, Sermon 2.3, in Patrides (1969) p. 69.

367. *The rise, race, and royalty*, p. 65.

368. p. 70.

369. p. 71. Sterry writes of 'the Spirituality of our Saviour's [second] Comming', as distinct from the carnal nature of his first coming (*The clouds in which Christ comes*, p. 13).

370. p. 72. This is a rich theme in Sterry's writing. In his *The consort of musicke* he describes Christ as the 'Chiefe Musitian', the mediator who unites all things in a universal harmony: we are called to play our parts in his consort, each with his or her own unique contribution to make, so that all may 'flow divinely into the all Ravishing Unity of the whole Lesson' (text in *Select writings*, pp. 168–75).

371. p. 73.

372. p. 75.

373. p. 77.

374. pp. 23–5. In one of the letters he wrote to his son, Sterry says 'I have read of a Person, who wearied with travaile in a forest, leans himself against a Rock in the side of a mountain. As he leans a barre of stone in the rocke gives way, and opens; He enters, meets with a stately palace, pleasant Gardens, in which he finds a beautifull young Princesse with her attendance. Thus

when our wearied Soules touch upon any forme of things in the forest of this world; Christ in the spirit is both the rocke, and the doore in every state in every Appearance, who opens in every Darknesse, Herb or dust, and lets us into a new heaven, where wee meete with the divine beauty' (ed. Matar (1994) p. 80).

375. The theme of Eden recurs frequently also in Henry Vaughan's devotional cycle of poems *Silex scintillans* ('He sighed for *Eden*, and would often say *Ah! what bright days were those?'*: *Corruption* ll.19–20, ed. cit. p. 197; and cf. Vaughan's famous *Peace* ('My soul, there is a country Far beyond the stars', pp. 185–6).

376. *Eden* v. 6, p. 10. Cf. his fuller exploration of all that we once enjoyed in Eden in *Select meditations* 3.11, pp. 54–5.

377. *Innocence* v. 5, p. 12; cf. *Centuries* 3.3, p. 264.

378. *The Approach*, v. 2, p. 21.

379. *The Return*, v. 1, p. 79.

380. *Centuries* 3.5, p. 266.

381. See, e.g., *Select meditations* 3.98, p. 111.

382. *Christian ethicks* 4, pp. 39–40.

383. *Centuries* 4.4, p. 317; but note *Select meditations* 4.4, p. 116: 'we are made his Sons, we are made his Heirs'.

384. Sterry does expatiate at length on the superior reality of Ideas: see his letter to 'Scipio' in *Select writings*, p. 149.

385. See Sterry, *The rise, race, and royalty*, pp. 147ff.

386. Whichcote, citing 2 Peter 1.4, links deification with the total transformation that occurred in the first disciples of Christ, concluding from this 'that nothing of the Natural State is base or vile' (Sermon 2.3, in Patrides (1969) p. 70). Participation in the divine nature is the truest source of human pleasure and satisfaction (p. 72). For Whichcote deification is the process whereby Christ works in man to repair his ruined nature (Rivers (1991i) p. 83). John Smith wrote:

> it is most God-like and best suits with the Spirit of Religion, for a Christian to live wholy [*sic*] to God, to live the life of God, having his own life hid with Christ in God; and thus in a sober sense he becomes Deified. (*Select discourses* 9, in Patrides (1969) p. 167)

And he goes on to say that when 'the frame of [someone's] Mind and Life is wholly according to that Idea and Pattern which he receives from the Mount [Sinai]', the divine Shekinah dwells in that person: 'we best glorifie him when we grow most like to him'(*Select discourses* 9, in Patrides (1969) p. 168). Smith says that for someone to be wholly devoted to the will of God 'bestows a kind of Immortality upon these flitting and Transient acts of ours' (p. 189). Ralph Cudworth draws on the patristic theology of St Athanasius in declaring that 'the Gospel is nothing else, but God descending into the World in Our Form, and conversing with us in our likeness; that he might allure, and draws us up to God, and make us partakers of his Divine Form' (*A sermon preached before the House of Commons*, in Patrides (1969) p. 101, quoting the famous formula from Athanasius' *De incarnatione* 54). Cf. also Traherne: 'Snatch the occasion [*sic*]: become Divine: do Him good [by doing good works] and Liv sweetly in thy Grave' (*Select meditations* 3.56, p. 86); and '[God] Deifieth us in makeing us the End of all His Doings' (*Select meditations* 4.7, p. 118).

387. *The rise, race, and royalty*, p. 232; cf. *A discourse*, p. 131. Poor Sterry was devastated when his own son, also named Peter, abandoned his parents' devout piety for the pleasures of the world (see esp. the letter Sterry wrote to his son in Matar (ed.), *Select writings* (1994) pp. 102–4 and Matar's comments on pp. 104–5.

388. Sterry was obliged to make a literal retirement after the Restoration, withdrawing to West Sheen in Surrey where he established a 'lovely Society' of fellow Puritans: see Matar's introduction to his edition of Sterry's works (1994).

389. *Desire*, l.8, p. 70.

390. *Insatiableness*, pp. 133–4.

391. *Centuries* 1.22, p. 174; cf. *Select meditations* 1.83, where Traherne speaks of God having 'made

every Soul almost a God, Like God unto Thee' (p. 2).

392. *Centuries* 1.41, p. 182.

393. *Centuries* 1.13, p. 171. Traherne's Augustinianism is evident in his use of the term 'enjoy' or 'enjoyment' to denote a delighting in something for its own sake: see, e.g., *Select meditations* 2.29, p. 23: 'And God wholy in every thing to be enjoyed'.

394. *Thoughts III* ll.1–6, p. 67. Cf. *Select meditations* 2.92, p. 44 and 4.12, pp. 121–2.

395. *The Inference*, l.21, p. 128; cf. *Select meditations* 2.82, p. 39.

396. See, e.g., *Select meditations* 2.27, p. 23: 'The Reason why man is a Feeble worm is because He DeSpiseth [*sic*] His understanding, and lives onely by His Fleshly Body'. But note also 4.22, pp. 124–5: 'Knowledg is a rare Accomplishment, and they who undervalue it betray their want of it . . . Yet it is not a Star of the first magnitude nor the one Thing needful . . . Grace and vertue must Carry us to Heaven.'

397. *Centuries* 1.13, p. 170; cf. *Christian ethicks* 10, pp. 87–8; *Select meditations* 3.5, p. 51.

398. *Centuries* 5.3, p. 368; *Christian ethicks* 1, p. 21. For a summary of Aristotle's and Aquinas' views on the intellectual nature of contemplative vision, see Simon Tugwell OP (ed. and trans.), *Albert and Thomas: selected writings* (Classics of western spirituality) (Mahwah NY: Paulist Press, 1988), pp. 281–6. Note that for Traherne thoughts in themselves are wholly inadequate: they must be turned to praise:

> Words are but feeble Barren Things,
>
> Worlds, Hearts, Arts, praises to the king of Kings.
>
> He onely Blessed is that praises Sings,
>
> That sees with Angels Eys, Soares on the wings. (*Select meditations* 1.100, p.13)

399. *The rise, race, and royalty*, p. 210.

400. p. 136.

401. p. 137.

402. p. 143.

403. Letter to his son Peter, in *Select writings* (1994) p. 111; and Matar's introduction to the same book, pp. 16–17 and nn. 30–1. By comparison, Traherne describes love as 'this Masculine Perfection' (*Select meditations* 2.76, p. 37).

404. *The Preparative* v. 2, p. 12. This is probably not a reference to Platonic notions of the preexistence of the soul so much as a recollection of antenatal experience (cf. v. 4, where the soul is again described as 'all Sight, or Ey' (p. 13).

405. See, e.g., *Dumnesse* ll. 59ff, where Traherne depreciates hearing 'No Ear,/But Eys them selvs were all the Hearers there' and 'A Nois [*sic*] Disturbing all my Songs and Prayers', and 'these will whisper if I will but hear,/And penetrat [*sic*] the Heart, if not the Ear', p. 24; and *Christian ethicks* 20: 'The eye . . . is of far greater value than if a man had no other member but an eye alone' (p. 171). Note, though, that in *Select meditations* he declares that 'the ear is a more noble Being then the Harp or Organ' (4.33, p. 131).

406. *Dumnesse* ll.39–40, p. 23; cf. *Centuries* 1.38: 'a clear Eye able to see afar off' (p. 181), and 3.44, where he celebrates the capacity of natural philosophy to clear and prepare 'the Ey of the Enjoyer' (p. 287). Hence 'the Atheist is . . . a walking carcase in the Land of the Living, a monstrous Lump of Darkness in the Light of Glory' (*Select meditations* 4.34, p. 132), because atheists see only what is before their eyes, not the invisible spiritual realities Christians see.

407. *Centuries* 1.85, p. 205. In *Select meditations* (1.91, p. 9) Traherne describes Jesus as 'my Elder Brother', yet also the one by whom the divine image in him is restored 'to its first power'.

408. *Centuries* 1.100, p. 214. Cf. Peter Sterry's description of how, at his second coming, Christ will re-open the divine eye, hitherto closed in the soul since the Creation, 'by setting Himselfe in it' (*The clouds in which Christ comes*, p. 26).

409. See, e.g., *Centuries* 3.24, p. 276; and 3.27–35, pp. 278–8; *Select meditations* 3.87, pp. 102–3.

410. *The Apostacy* ll. 37–9, p. 87.

411. For eschatology among the Latitudinarians, see Sarah Hutton, 'Henry More and the Apocalypse', in M. Wilks (ed.), *Prophecy and eschatology* (Studies in church history, subsidia 10) (Oxford: Blackwell, 1994), pp. 131–40. Hutton shows that More's view of the apocalypse was

carefully tempered to fit with the restoration of the monarchy. Eschatology remained a crucial dimension of Sterry's thought throughout his life, albeit acquiring a much more interiorized focus after the Restoration: he frequently refers to the 'Paradise within' – see, e.g., a letter to his son (1658), ed. Matar (1994) p. 55; and Matar (1989). Sterry conceived of his little Puritan community at West Sheen as a *hortus conclusus*, an enclosed garden, in the manner of much spiritual writing in the tradition of the Song of Songs (see his letter to his daughter (1660), ed. Matar (1994) p. 67).

412. *Religio medici* I.40, pp. 38–9; cf. *Hydriotaphia* 5: 'The long habit of living indisposeth us for dying' (p. 119). This is a far cry from Sterry's 'O you, that are Christes, Love Death. Death is now become but a Shadow of Death, and true Life with all the Joyes of life veiles Itselfe beneath that Shadow' (*The state of a saints soul and body in death*, in *Select writings*, p. 213).

413. *Religio medici* II.9, p. 68.

414. *Hydriotaphia* 4, p. 116.

415. *Hydriotaphia* 4, pp. 117–18.

416. *Religio medici* 1.36, p. 36.

417. *Religio medici* II.11, p. 70.

418. *Religio medici* II.13, p. 74.

419. *Religio medici* I.55–7, pp. 52–3.

420. *Christian ethicks* 30, p. 261.

421. *Select meditations* 2.44, p. 29, and 2.72, pp. 35–6.

422. 'Atom', p. 98, ll. 23–36. Cf. *Select meditations* 2.15, where Traherne says that 'God hath use now for an Holy man' – in recalling his fellow human beings 'to the Enjoyment of God, to their Inheritance of the world, to the Recovery of their Blessedness, and to the Similitude of God in the possession of Greater Things then Adam Enjoyd' (p. 17).

423. See the acute remark of Salter (1964, p. 29): 'evil for Traherne is not real; it is the result of an imperfect realization of the world and of the nature of man. It lies in an insensitivity, in a refusal to see.'

424. *Centuries* 3.8, p. 268. In *Select meditations* he argues for the view of the Fall as a *felix culpa*: 'Had not man Sinned there had been neither Place nor roome for the Incarnation of God' (3.80, p. 98; cf. 3.81, p. 99).

425. *Centuries* 3..9, p. 268; cf. 1.8, p. 169; *Select meditations* 3.3, where he summons people to praise God 'for the Advantage of our Disadvantages', conceiving of a positive value of human weakness and failure not dissimilar to that of Julian; and 3.52, pp. 81–2, where evil is clearly a consequence of human freedom.

426. *Centuries* 3.10, pp. 268–9. Note though that even sin can have positive value for Traherne: 'even vanities them selves may be made Enjoyments, when by courage and wisdom we overcome them' (*Select meditations* 2.12, p. 16).

427. *Centuries* 3.51, p. 290. Cf. *Select meditations* 4.50: 'every Sin is an Infinit Poyson' (p. 140).

428. *Select meditations* 1.93, p. 11. Cf. 3.1, p. 49, where he argues that in heaven we must not and should not forget our past sorrows: rather we shall have our spiritual sight cleansed so that we 'might See the Beauties and the Jewels concealed under that rough and Shell'.

429. *Centuries* 1.27, p. 177.

430. *The rise, race, and royalty*, p. 107.

431. See esp. Bossy (19750; Haigh ('The continuity of Catholicism in the English Reformation', in Haigh (ed.) (1987) pp. 176–208).

432. *King Henry VIII (All is true)*, Act V Scene 2.

433. See Loades (1996).

434. See esp. Bossy (1975) chapter 1; R. H. Pogson ('Revival and reform in Mary Tudor's church: a question of money', in Haigh (ed.) (1987) pp. 139–56); Acheson (1990) pp. 5–9, with bibliographical references; Loades (1996). Martin (1989, pp. 107–23, originally published in 1981) explores the failure of the government during Mary's reign to take advantage of printing in order to disseminate Catholic teaching.

435. O'Malley (1990) pp. 10–11; Loades (1996) p. 14. Hill (1993, p. 14) points out that Protestant

devotion to scripture, and its universal availability, affected Catholics too. The spiritual exercises of the Dominican priest William Perin (1557) are an interesting example of Marian Catholic spirituality (even though the work is in large part a translation from a Flemish original).

436. The commonest contemporary term for Catholics was 'Papist': see the useful article by Clancy (1976).

437. There is much debate about the relative strengths, within English Catholicism during this period, of the religion of the gentry and the continental piety introduced by the missionary priests. See esp. Bossy (1975); Scarisbrick (1984, p. 150) stresses the major role played by women (and layfolk in general) in sustaining recusancy, often at great risk, and adduces evidence of poorer Catholics imprisoned for their faith (p. 156). For a succinct summary of the situation, see MacCulloch (1992), esp. pp. 20–4.

438. From the memoir of Dorothy Lawson, written shortly after her death by her last chaplain, the Jesuit William Palmes (who was himself arrested in 1650); printed in B. C. Foley, *Some other people of the penal times: aspects of a unique social and religious phenonemon* (Lancaster Cathedral Bookshop, 1991), pp. 44–6.

439. Kenny (1983, p. 11) points out that no English person had been canonized since Thomas of Hereford, who died in 1282. Knowles (1971, pp. 6–7) describes the age of the Tudors as 'an earthy, selfish, grasping age', which was highly unpropitious for the flourishing of the monastic life: for a more general picture, see pp. 100–7. Local studies have added depth to our knowledge of the overall situation: Heath (1979) describes late-sixteenth-century Lichfield as 'a city of perfunctory conformity and lively Catholic non-conformity'. MacCulloch (1992, p. 133) says of early-sixteenth-century monasticism in Suffolk that 'the general picture is one of conscientious if uninspired and pedestrian observance of the Rule, marred by occasional minor scandal and a good deal of run-of-the-mill ill-nature in the cloister'. However there was no falling-off in numbers until the dissolution was clearly inevitable. Brown (1995, p. 29) points out that almost as many gentry left bequests to the religious in the early sixteenth century as before.

440. Knowles (1971) pp. 39–51; B. Ardura, *Prémontrés: histoire et spiritualité* (CERCOR Travaux & Recherches, 7) (Saint-Etienne UP, 1995) pp. 205–7.

441. *Register of Butley Priory*, ed. Dickens, p. 59. The last monasteries closed in 1540.

442. For the *Pomander*, see Horsfield (1989).

443. See the introd. by J. Hogg in vol. 2 of the ed. cit., pp. 140–89, and also White (1951) pp. 157–61, Duffy (1989) p. 224 and Duffy (1992) p. 86.

444. See esp. McConica (1981) p. 59, and Gribbin (1996) and the references he cites.

445. *The pype or tonne of the lyfe of perfection* is a version of St Bernard's *De praecepto et dispensatione*.

446. 1.1, pp. 8–9.

447. 1.1, p. 9.

448. One of these works (the autobiographical *Devota lamentacio devoti Iohannis Norton prioris*) reflects Norton's deep devotion to the Virgin and his conviction that she had appeared to him robed as a Carthusian nun. See also Hogg (1980).

449. See K. Lochrie, *Margery Kempe and translations of the flesh* (Philadelphia: Pennsylvania UP, 1991), p. 218.

450. See below, p. 398.

451. See Gleason (1989) p. 17. Gleason comments, justly enough, that 'flesh, for Colet, is never rosy, never warm, never comforting, indeed never even neutral; flesh is always the principle opposed to spirit, and therefore always to be crucified' (p. 186).

452. Two of Colet's extant works, the *De caelesti hierarchia* and the *De ecclesiastica hierarchia*, are (as their titles imply) commentaries on Pseudo-Dionysius' eponymous texts, which Colet may have come to know via the continental Neoplatonists Marsiglio Ficino and Pico della Mirandola. The discovery, by the Italian humanist Lorenzo Valla, that the biblical Dionysius could not have written the works attributed to him, did not put an end to his influence, especially with Renaissance Neoplatonic writers like Pico della Mirandola; and Colet was one of many figures, both Catholic and Protestant, who were deeply indebted to the pseudonymous fifth-

century writer: see Froehlich (1987), esp. pp. 36–7. However, Colet makes some important changes to Pseudo-Dionysius' thought: he gives evil a more positive content than his predecessor (see the remarks of Lupton, introduction to ed. cit. of Colet's Dionysian works, p. xlvi), and goes much further than Pseudo-Dionysius in depreciating the material by contrast with the spiritual: see, e.g., his observation that the 'marvellous shining of the divine sun . . . rarefies (so to speak) rational creatures' (*rationales creaturas . . . mirifica illa irradiatio divini solis apprehendens quasi rarifacit*) (*De cel. hier.* I, p. 166, my trans.); his introduction of non-Dionysian terms like 'the naked spirit' (*nudum spiritum* (Lupton translates 'unshrouded spirit'!), *De cel. hier.* I, p. 168), for which enfleshed human beings are not yet ready; and his description of the role of the angels as being to 'spiritualize' (*spiritifacio*) human beings, working first through bishops and priests (*De cel. hier.* V), again using a term unknown to Pseudo-Dionysius. On other occasions Colet explores issues which his predecessor appears not to be interested in, such as the relationship of grace and freewill (*De cel. hier.* IX, p. 183); and, more generally, his work is more Christ-centred than that of Pseudo-Dionysius.

453. Colet's thought was in the line of Bonaventure and the Franciscans, rather than of Thomas: he decried reason (Gleason (1989) p. 131) and natural theology with its Aristotelian influence, diverging even from Augustine in being suspicious of any non-Christian authorities (p. 138). This reflects the influence both of contemporary Italian Benedictine circles (p. 134) and of the anti-scholastic reaction found in late-fifteenth-century and early-sixteenth-century England (p. 142). For Colet's preference for Bonaventure's thought, see Gleason (1989) pp. 197–9, though it should be noted that Colet's theology is far less generous in spirit, far less richly celebratory, than that of Bonaventure and Francis.

454. See Gleason (1989), esp. pp. 162ff.

455. For Fisher in general see Reynolds (1955), Bradshaw (1989), and Rex (1991).

456. See Lewis (1954) pp. 161–2. Augustine is often quoted explicitly in his works: see, e.g., his *Penytencyall Psalmes*, ed. cit. pp. 118, 159, 177, 245, 259.

457. Chambers (1955) pp. 17–23, Rex (1991) p. 34 and n. 25; Duffy (1989) p. 210 and (1992) p. 79.

458. Rex points out two striking images that recur frequently: that of grace as sunlight (e.g. *Penytencyall Psalmes*, p. 82), and that of devotion as a liquid (1991, p. 40). It is also worth noting the frequency with which animals and birds, and especially dogs, feature in Fisher's sermons, either directly or as part of some vivid illustration. Thus he compares the way we are trapped into sin by wicked people to the way hunters catch apes by taking advantage of the fact that apes imitate human beings: so the hunters put on a pair of shoes, having laid out a pair for the apes, who duly put them on and then slip from the trees they try to climb and so are captured (*Penytencyall Psalmes*, p. 79). He begins his sermon on Psalm 51 by comparing the sinner to a man hanging over a pit filled with wild beasts and suspended by a fragile thread held by someone he has grievously offended (p. 91).

459. For his life, see Scallon (1975) pp. 1–61. His poems (compiled by someone else) went through eighteen editions between 1595 and 1636 and were very popular. It is fairly clear that there is an explicitly pastoral and didactic purpose behind all his writings (Brown, introduction to *Poems*, p. xcix; Scallon (1975) p. vi): everything (including the poetry) was written to console, defend and strengthen English Catholics. See the excellent article by G. Hill (1984), esp. pp. 20–7.

460. Martz (1954) pp. 10–11. The press, together with other vivid details from Southwell's time in England, are described in the *Autobiography* of the Jesuit John Gerard (1564–1637), which describes the experiences of the Catholic mission priests in Elizabethan England with the vividness of a detective story.

461. In one short piece of prose, apparently a piece of self-examination (the *Querimonia*), Southwell asks whether the attraction he feels for a handsome youth is purely sexual or a means by which God was enjoining the youth's spiritual welfare on him (ed. cit. of his *Poems*, pp. xxi–xxii) (on Southwell's concern to transmute physical into spiritual love, see Martz (1954) p. 184). See also his *Spiritual exercises* (18.2, ed. cit. p. 54), where he warns himself against 'inordinate affection for the brethren or for any other creature'.

462. *De sacramentis,* pp. 294–5; Gleason's trans. slightly altered.

463. *De cel. hier.* I, p. 167, Lupton's translation (on p. 4) slightly altered.

464. e.g. *De eccles. hier.* II.3 and the whole of Colet's late work *De sacramentis,* for which in general see Gleason (1989) pp. 185ff.

465. e.g. *De eccles. hier.* I, II, III.2–3 and especially V, an extended discussion of priesthood: a good example of his thought may be found in V.3, p. 243, Lupton p. 119. In IV (p. 228) he describes priests as people who keep themselves away from the multitude, preferring solitude. See also *De sacramentis,* pp. 274–5. In fairness it should be pointed out that Colet insists on all power belonging to God, not to his ministers (*De eccles. hier.* VII.3, p. 265); and he also says that 'all who hold authority within Christianity are not *magistri* but *ministri* of the church' (*Enarr. in I Cor.* IV, p. 183).

466. *Enarr. in I Cor.* VII, p. 209; Lupton pp. 71–2. Colet even goes so far as to suggest that we should be 'Jesuits' in our imitation of Christ (*De eccles. hier.* I, p. 200, Lupton p. 53): the name Jesuates was given to a religious order in 1368. See also p. 202, Lupton pp. 54–5. For Fisher, see, e.g., *Penytencyall Psalmes,* pp. 129–31, where he again uses animal images to press home his stress on human sinfulness and Christ's innocence.

467. *Enarr. in I Cor.* I, p. 163.

468. *De cel. hier.* II, p. 171, Lupton's trans. adapted. Note the unequivocally Platonic and world-denying spirituality here. In the *De eccles. hier.* Colet writes 'God deifies, by imparting himself to the angels directly and individually, to human beings indirectly and by a multiple system of likenesses', including scripture (I p. 202, my trans.). Cf. also the *De corpore Christi mystico,* where Colet says 'God, made man, was the means whereby men were to be made gods' (ed. Lupton (1876) pp. 40 and 190; quoted Patrides (1969) p. 19, n. 1).

469. *Enarr. in I Cor.* VII, p. 225.

470. From *Lifes death loves life,* pp. 54–5. Cf. also *The nativitie of Christ,* esp. p. 6, and *I die alive,* p. 53.

471. ed. cit. pp. 69–70. Cf. the remark Southwell makes in his *Spiritual exercises* (39.1, ed. cit. p. 75), which in view of his own impending suffering is profoundly moving: 'When the pain is severe, I will think how great must have been the sufferings of Christ, if my lesser ones are so grievous.'

472. 'The more that they call unto theyr owne mynde and expresse theyr owne trespasses, so moche the more [God] forgeteth and putteth them out of his mynde' (*Penytencyall Psalmes,* p. 25). In his *Prayer,* Fisher acknowledges his propensity for doing virtually the opposite: being quite unable to forget his delight in creatures rather than in their Creator (ed. cit. p. 297).

473. *Penytencyall Psalmes,* p. 31.

474. pp. 170–1. For Fisher's spirituality, see esp. Duffy (1989).

475. ed. cit. p. 42. Could this be a reminiscence of his own Alpine crossing (so Scallon (1975) p. 162), and/or an Ignatian-style determination to discern spiritual meaning within the physical landscape – hence the resonance evoked by the title, from the *Salve Regina* (pp. 165–9)?

476. For Colet's anti-feminine style, see e.g. *Enarr. in I Cor.* VII: 'it ought to be the wish of every one, not to be afflicted with such a disease [i.e. marriage!], but in masculine chastity (*masculina castitate*) to be made more like God, who is chastity itself' (p. 227; Lupton's trans. slightly altered, p. 94). So also, commenting on 1 Corinthians 11: 'God alone, from whom are all things, and who is above all, is absolute male, and unveiled' (*Deus solus, ex quo omnia, et qui omnibus praeest, vir est ipse sine velamine*) (p. 241; Lupton p. 113).

477. *Penytencyall Psalmes,* p. 255.

478. p. 235; cf. also his *Prayer,* ed. cit. p. 298.

479. From 1623 to 1631 William Bishop and Richard Smith successively led the Roman Catholic Church in England as Bishops of Chalcedon; but the latter in particular was a doctrinaire hierocrat whose efforts at imposing his authority failed (Bossy (1975) pp. 49–59). English Catholicism remained a gentry-led movement throughout the seventeenth century (p. 60). The reign of James II, though brief, allowed a new episcopal regime to be successfully launched, and revealed that the Catholic community had a future in towns, even though that future was postponed with his defeat (1975, p. 285).

480. Kishlansky (1996) pp. 102–3.
481. For Baker's life see A. Low, *Augustine Baker* (New York, 1970), Power (1991) pp. 14–33, or (for a succinct and up-to-date summary) Clark (1995).
482. See Clark (1995) p. 94; and Dame Christina Brent, *Some difficulties about the doctrine of verie reverend Father Augustine Baker* (ed. as *A defense of mysticism* in Latz (1989) pp. 61–7). Baker was criticized for not sufficiently emphasizing the duty of obedience to one's religious superior. In fairness to Baker, it is worth noting passages in his work which explicitly stress such obedience: see, e.g., *Holy wisdom* 1.2.9, pp. 129–30 and 2.2.14, p. 323, where he clearly sets the superior's authority over that of the director.
483. Perhaps of plague? So Power (1991, p. 15).
484. J. T. Rhodes has drawn attention to the contents of a large volume (Yale Ms. b.268) containing a number of works by Baker ('Some writings of a seventeenth-century English Benedictine: Dom Augustine Baker OSB', in *Yale University Library Gazette* 67 (1993) pp. 110–17; Clark (1995) pp. 100–1). J. P. H. Clark is editing a number of Baker's major works for the series Analecta Cartusiana, based in Salzburg.
485. For the *Secretum* see Clark (1995). It includes some fascinating material relating to Baker's own spiritual experiences (see the *Confessions* (=extracts from the *Secretum*), esp. chapters 2–8.
486. Knowles (1961) pp. 153ff; Gaffney (1989) p. 15; Clark (1995) p. 97.
487. Knowles (1961, pp. 174–5) suggests, convincingly enough, that Baker was a beneficiary and transmitter of the vast amount of Counter-Reformation spirituality reaching the Low Countries from Spain and Italy, rather than a trained or systematic scholar. Baker himself cites Walter Hilton (1.1.6; Gaffney (1989) p. 51), the *Cloud of unknowing* (1.2.2; Gaffney (1989) pp. 50–1) – was this, as Emery suggests (1995, p. 121), in order to safeguard for posterity these English spiritual texts?), St Bernard and many other Fathers. Augustine's influence is constantly in evidence – e.g. the stress on intention and the will, explicitly citing Augustine (2.2.2, p. 243; see Emery (1995) p. 121). He cites more recent Catholic authors like Cajetan (2.2.10, p. 291), the Jesuit Lessius (a colleague of St François de Sales, and the Franciscan Marchantius (2.2.10, p. 290), St Robert Bellarmine (3.1.3, p. 351), Harphius (=the Franciscan Henry Herp) (passim), Alphonsus (*Method of serving God*, 3.3.3, p. 454), and St Angela of Foligno (3.4.3, p. 526). He also cites Constantin Barbanson's *Secrets sentiers de l'amour divin* (3.2.1, p. 396 &c), which appears to be one of his key sources, and De Ponte's *Meditations* (3.2.3, p. 413), as well as the *Life of the Spirit approved* (*Vita dello Spirito*) of Antonio de Rojas (3.3.7, p. 490), subsequently condemned for quietism (p. 490 n.). The influence of medieval English spirituality is important: like Baker, the English Catholic religious writing or translating texts envisaged 'mystical theology' as being primarily the domain of the affections, following the teaching of Thomas Gallus, Hugh of Balma, the *Cloud* author, Jean Gerson, and Henry Herp (Emery (1995) p. 123).
488. 1.1.1, p. 29. The argument of Power's thesis (1991) is that Baker's anthropology is fatally flawed by a serious undervaluing of the theology of Incarnation.
489. 1.1.1, p. 30.
490. 1.3.4, p. 158.
491. 1.1.3, p. 39.
492. 1.1.3, pp. 39–40.
493. See the comments of Knowles (1961) p. 179.
494. 1.2.1, pp. 68–9.
495. 3.2.5, p. 429.
496. 1.2.1, p. 67.
497. 1.2.2, p. 81; cf. p. 82.
498. 1.2.2, p. 83.
499. 1.2.2, p. 83.
500. 2.1.5, p. 220. In the *Secretum* Baker comments that far too few would-be contemplatives have much idea of what mortification is, or how to practise it appropriately (*The Confessions of Father Augustine Baker*, p. 143).

501. 1.3.9, p. 179.
502. 1.3.8, p. 181.
503. 1.3.8, p. 182; cf. 3.3.4, p. 462. Note too his acknowledgement that almost everyone will experience times of spiritual indisposition, when we experience 'great obscurities in the mind and great insensibility in the affections' (3.1.5, p. 373); but these experiences can help us to grow spiritually provided we stay with them (p. 375). Furthermore, some distractions may be necessary as sources of refreshment (3.1.6, p. 378). His own experience of spiritual darkness and aridity must be relevant here; for its importance in Baker, see Clark (1995) p. 106.
504. 1.2.3, p. 91.
505. 1.2.4, pp. 97–8. Note the importance of the Holy Spirit in John Fisher's *Prayer* (ed. cit. p. 299).
506. 2.2.5, p. 261.
507. He defines this as
    a certain divine principle or faculty, partaking somewhat of the nature of a permanent habit, infused into the spirit of man, by which he is enabled, whensoever the free will concurreth actually, both for knowing, believing, and practising to do the will of God in all things. (1.2.6, p. 105)
    Knowles (*The English mystical tradition* (1933) pp. 183ff) and Clark (1995, p. 99) argue that Baker does not draw out, as Walter Hilton and the *Cloud* author do, the Thomist distinction between 'operant' and 'cooperant' grace.
508. 1.2.5, p. 101. Baker is firmly ascetic in this regard, disapproving of particular friendships (unlike Aelred of Rievaulx) (2.1.6, p. 225; cf. 2.2.2, p. 245).
509. 3.2.5, p. 430.
510. 3.3.3, p. 454.
511. 3.3.3, p. 456.
512. 3.3.5, p. 478.
513. 3.2.7, pp. 492–3. Robert Southwell makes the same point (*Short rules of a good life*, p. 31). Baker warns elsewhere of the threat posed by others, even fellow religious or one's religious superior, who do not esteem a spiritual life rooted in resignation to the will of God (*A secure stay* 2, ed. cit. pp. 93–5).
514. 3.3.7, p. 496.
515. 3.3.5, pp. 471–3.
516. 3.1.1, p. 342. Cf. *A secure stay* 1, ed. cit. p. 24, where Baker encourages the person who has made her confession to aspire 'towards God by means of efficacious mentall prayer' and thus to transcend all 'fears, scruples & intanglements'.
517. p. 343.
518. 3.1.5, p. 366. In *A secure stay* (1, ed. cit. pp. 65–7) he offers a nuanced opinion about the value of the monastic offices, warning against making vocal prayer of this kind take precedence over mental prayer.
519. 3.2.1, p. 404.
520. 3.1.3, pp. 349 and 353; 3.2.1, pp. 399ff.
521. 3.1.3, p. 355; 3.2.2, p. 408; cf. 3.2.5, pp. 422–4.
522. 3.1.5, p. 368, citing the parable of the man seeking bread from his friend in St Luke's Gospel.
523. 3.2.5, p. 428.
524. i.e. something outside the self, 3.3.1, p. 433. For these 'longings', see Baker's comments on the twentieth and thirty-second chapters of the *Cloud of unknowing* (Baker, *The cloud of unknowing . . . with a commentary*, ed. McCann, pp. 194 and 200).
525. 3.3.1, p. 434; cf. 3.3.2, p. 447.
526. ed. cit. pp. 567–662.
527. 3.3.2, p. 443.
528. 3.3.2, p. 445.
529. 3.4.1, pp. 502–3.
530. 3.2.1, p. 401.
531. 3.2.1, p. 402.

532. 3.2.1, p. 403. Note the significance of faith here.
533. 3.2.1, p. 404.
534. 3.3.7, pp. 497–9. For the image of God as mother see Baker, *Secretum* 1, ed. cit. pp. 7–8; *A secure stay* 1, ed. cit. p. 34.
535. 3.4.1, p. 507.
536. 3.4.2, p. 518.
537. 3.4.2, p. 508.
538. 3.4.1, p. 508.
539. 3.4.5, pp. 538–9.
540. 3.4.5, p. 540. It is worth noting the fundamentally passive nature of these religious experiences. Don Cupitt has pointed out (*Mysticism after modernity* (Oxford. Blackwell, 1998) p. 15) that until the seventeenth century 'experience' (both verb and noun) carried a more active meaning than thereafter, the Latin *experiri* meaning 'to experiment' or 'to try out'. Semi-quietist spirituality of this period underlines the movement from an active to a passive notion of 'experience'.
541. In 3.1.7 (pp. 389–94) Baker defends the passive practising of the presence of God advocated by the Jesuit Baltazar Alvarez (1534–80). Alvarez was confessor for six years to St Teresa of Avila (O'Malley (1990) p. 15). His teaching on 'passive' semi-quietist prayer was eventually condemned by the Jesuit general Mercurian in 1577 (O'Malley, pp. 16–17). Baker closely paraphrases two documents in which Alvarez defended himself to the General of the Jesuits, and includes them in his section on prayer (Gaffney (1989) pp. 49–50).
542. Apart from his reflections on the *Cloud of unknowing* and the pervasive influence of Walter Hilton, Baker was also responsible for preserving the Long Text of Julian of Norwich's *Showings* (see Latz (1989) pp. 28 and 55 and Colledge and Walsh's introduction to their modernized version of *Showings* (Classics of western spirituality) (New York: Paulist Press, 1978), pp. 21–2.
543. *A secure stay* 1, ed. cit. p. 34.
544. 3.4.6, pp. 542–3.
545. p. 544.
546. 3.4.6, p. 547.
547. For this subject in general, see especially Martz (1954 rev. 1962, and 1994). In his later work Martz acknowledges the quality and importance of Puritan meditation, and accepts (surely rightly) that he may have exaggerated the extent to which continental (especially Ignatian) texts and practices may have influenced English writers.
548. The other text was by a Jesuit, Francis Arias: his *Treatise of exhortation to spirituall profit*. Molina (c.1550–1612) is not to be confused with Miguel de Molinos (c.1640–97), the Spanish quietist. For a brief summary of his life and work see Hogg (1992).
549. e.g. Molina (1617) 1, pp. 1–2. Baker cites Molina explicitly in his *A secure stay* 2, ed. cit. p. 126 and n. 3.
550. See, e.g., his threefold pattern of meditating on the mysteries of the passion. The person is first to consider the story itself, perhaps imagining yourself to be present within it (1, p. 6); then 'to ponder the circumstances which concurre in it' – i.e. reflect on the context and participating characters; and finally 'to draw the fruite, and actes of vertues, which may be gathered out of them' (1, p. 4). These three stages may be interwoven. Note the strongly Christocentric tone (see, e.g., 2, pp. 33–4).
551. 5, pp. 151–2.
552. Emery (1995), reviewing Latz (1989 and 1992), points to the extensive international network of links between sixteenth-century Catholic reformers, humanists, and religious, centring on Cardinal Reginald Pole and the rapid, widespread communication of spiritual ideas and writings across linguistic (and religious) boundaries in sixteenth- and seventeenth-century Europe. The English convents at Cambrai and Paris became key centres of writing and translating books and manuscripts (Latz (1989) pp. 10–11; Emery (1995) p. 119). Latz (1989) pp. 17–19) points out that the Paris convent library contained a wide range of women's spiritual writings, mostly contemporary but including Julian's *Showings* and part of the *Revelations* of St Bridget of Sweden; the Cambrai library included works by Suso, St John Climacus and many

others (Latz (1989) pp. 20–2 and 137ff: the Renaissance-style breadth of secular learning accessible to these nuns is remarkable: pp. 139–40). The former Cambrai convent (5–27 Rue des Anglaises), now a ruin, is the site of an old people's home (Latz (1992) p. xiii).

553. Latz (1989) p. 10.

554. Latz (1989) pp. 23–5; Crawford (1993) pp. 84–5. For Dame Gertrude, see Marion Norman, 'Dame Gertrude More and the English mystical tradition', in *Recusant History* 13 (1975–6), pp. 196–211.

555. Latz (1989) pp. 28–9. Dame Gertrude's spiritual writings were first published posthumously in 1657–8 and are cited by Evelyn Underhill and Thomas Merton (p. 25). She appears to have been well acquainted with the works of Pseudo-Dionysius (the *Mystical theology*), Hugh and Richard of St Victor, St John of the Cross, St Teresa of Avila, Ruusbroec, Suso, Tauler, St Bridget of Sweden, Walter Hilton, St Gregory the Great, St Bernard of Clairvaux, St Bonaventure, William Fitch, St John Climacus, St Catherine of Siena, the *Vitae patrum* and of course Baker (pp. 27–8). Dame Gertrude's own prose works include *The holy practises of a divine lover or the sainctly ideots devotions* (Paris, 1657) and *The spiritual exercises of the most vertuous of religious D. Gertrude More . . .* (called the *Confessiones amantis* by Augustine Baker) (Paris, 1658; revised and modernized edition by Dom Benedict WeldBlundell, *The inner life and writings of Dame Gertrude More*, 2 vols. (London, 1910–11): see Latz (1989) p. 51.

556. The influence of this substantial spiritual text, extensively permeated with the systematizing, interiorized spirituality of continental writers like St Teresa, St François de Sales and seventeenth-century French mysticism, is hard to calculate. It was completed in 1691 (perhaps finished by Susan Phelype) and evidently intended for publication, but never published. Latz (1992, p. xx) suggests that this was because of contemporary suspicion of quietist-style mystical texts.

557. Latz (1989) pp. 117–18.

558. *Lady Falkland, Elizabeth Cary, her life*; preserved in the Archives du Nord, Lille, MS 20H9. This text was transcribed by Richard Simpson and published in 1861 (Latz 1989, p. 119).

559. Latz (1989) p. 124.

560. The poem is printed in Latz (1989) p. 89. The original is at Lille, Archives du Nord, MS 20H39.

561. Latz (1989) p. 155.

562. Bossy (1975) pp. 160–1. For Ward's life, see Peters (1994). For the role played by Catholic laywomen in the recusant period, see Eales (1998) pp. 93-4.

563. Orchard (1985), esp. p. 38. For the similarities between Ward's plans and those of St Angela Merici see Latz (1989) pp. 166–8.

564. From her *Autobiography*, cited in Orchard (1985) p. 27. The vision took place in 1609: see Peters (1994) pp. 107–9. Ward herself wrote very little.

565. See the acute observations of Bossy (1975) p. 109.

566. And, of course, in a different though no less painful way, for pre-Elizabethan sixteenth-century English Catholics: St John Fisher, in his *Prayer*, asks, 'What is this world but a miserable exile, full of perils and evils?' (ed. cit. p. 297) – and, given his own sufferings, there is no reason to read this simply as conventional asceticism.

567. *Holy wisdom* 3.1.3, p. 354. For Baker's own experience of spiritual desolation, see his *Secretum* (*The confessions of Father Augustine Baker* chapter 4, esp. pp. 78–81); for the spiritual experience of being rejected even by God, see *A secure stay* 2, ed. cit. p. 97.

568. *Steps to the Temple* p. 90: the similarities with George Herbert's poem *Love (III)* ('Love bade me welcome') are striking. Crashaw (1612/13–1649) was born a member of the Church of England, and was for a while a participant in the Little Gidding experiment in semi-monastic living. He was received into the Roman Catholic Church in 1645, dying at Loreto in Italy in 1649. Bush (1945 p. 140) describes him as 'the one conspicuous English incarnation of the "baroque sensibility"'.

569. On the social relationship between communities of dissent and mainstream adherents of the Church of England in the seventeenth century, see Hill (1964) and Bill Stevenson, 'The social integration of post-Restoration dissenters, 1660–1725', in Spufford (ed.) (1995), pp. 360–87:

the latter argues for a far closer relationship between dissenters and others than has hitherto been assumed.

570. *A saint or a brute* 1, in *Works* vol. 10, pp. 110ff. For Baxter, see his *Autobiography*; Nuttall (1965); Keeble (1982); and H. Martin, *Puritanism and Richard Baxter* (London: SCM Press, 1954).

571. John Donne distinguishes between 'true' and 'false' Puritans: 'We finde two sorts of false Puritans then; the *Catharists*, and The *Cathari*', Sermon 3, I p. 186. Donne contrasts these with 'Saint Pauls *Puritan*, Pure in Heart, pure in Hand, pure in Conscience', (p. 189). See also Haller (1938) p. 9 and n. 3; Nuttall (1946), esp. p. 9; Clancy (1976) pp. 238–41; Collinson (1980) and (1987), esp. pp. 7–11; Brachlow (1988), esp. pp. 5–6; Stachniewski (1991) p. 11; Wakefield (1992) p. 4; Durston and Eales (1996) pp. 1–9; Spurr (1998) pp. 1–27; and especially Hall (1990). Kendall (1979) finds the term Puritan 'not very useful'.

572. On this, see the nuanced discussion in Collinson (1985) pp. 213–27.

573. After the Restoration the term 'nonconformist' came to be used specifically to describe those hitherto called 'Puritan'. Recent scholarship has suggested that dissenters were in general tolerated by the remainder of the local community, and integrated into it, to a far greater extent than had hitherto been supposed. See the essays in Spufford (ed.) (1995).

574. See esp. Collinson (1987); a brief and lucid description of Arminianism appears in Kishlansky (1996) pp. 127–9.

575. Rupp (1986) pp. 128–37; Keeble (1987) p. 12; Wakefield (1992) p. 8. Bunyan could properly be regarded as a Baptist, though preferred to be seen simply as a Christian (Greaves (1992) p. 6).

576. Rupp (1986) pp. 108–15; Keeble (1987) pp. 6–8; Acheson (1990) p. 46; Rivers (1991) pp. 91 and 96; Wakefield (1992) p. 7.

577. Rupp (1986) pp. 116–27; Keeble (1987) p. 9. The term 'Congregationalist' first appears in the 1640s (Watts (1978) p. 94; Rupp (1986) p. 116).

578. Note that the early-eighteenth-century Congregationalist historian Daniel Neal began his *History of the Puritans* with John Wyclif (Keeble (1987) p. 4).

579. e.g. Haller (1938) p. 5; Keeble (1987) p. 2.

580. Watkins (1972) p. 59. For the influence of Augustine on Puritan notions of sin and forgiveness, the action of grace, and other themes, see Halewood (1970), esp. pp. 65–70. White (1951, pp. 27–8) points to the enormous popularity during the sixteenth century of works either by or attributed to St Augustine: vast numbers of printed florilegia appeared (see also Halewood (1970), esp. pp. 45–7).

581. For Luther, see C. Volz, 'Martin Luther's attitude toward Bernard of Clairvaux', in *Studies in medieval Cistercian history presented to Jeremiah F. O'Sullivan* (Cistercian Studies 13) (Spencer, Mass.: Cistercian Publications, 1971), pp. 186–204; and D. R. Reinke, 'Martin Luther: language and devotional consciousness', in E. R. Elder (ed.), *The spirituality of western Christendom* (Cistercian Studies 30) (Kalamazoo: Cistercian Publications, 1976), pp. 152–68. For Calvin, see D. E. Tamburello, *Union with Christ: John Calvin and the mysticism of St Bernard* (Columbia series in Reformed theology) (Louisville: Westminster John Knox, 1994).

582. Thomas Rogers translated Thomas à Kempis' *Imitatio Christi* in 1580, censoring it as he did so (White (1951) pp. 28–9).

583. An important point made by both Nuttall (1946), esp. pp. 35–42 and, more generally, by Lewis (1954).

584. See Stachniewski (1991), esp. p. 52.

585. Even if we allow for Stachniewski's argument, that until the ascendancy of Laud Calvinism dominated English religious life (see Stachniewski (1991) p. 158), it is still impossibly hard to determine the extent to which the fear of absolute damnation penetrated all strata of seventeenth-century society, and what impact it had. Even so, the evidence he adduces (see, e.g., p. 27) is certainly compelling. See also Sommerville (1977) pp. 76–9. Spufford (1981, p. 207) points out that over half the extant 'godly chapbooks' published during this period, and later collected by Samuel Pepys, use fear of death and damnation as a deliberate means to excite people to conversion.

586. The doctrine of the covenant is found in late medieval thinkers like William of Ockham as well as in the work of the Protestant reformers, especially Calvin. In England it is explored by (among others) William Tyndale, William Perkins, John Bradford, and Richard Baxter. For English covenant theology, see Møller (1963) and McGiffert (1981). Perkins' *The golden chaine*, Bradford's *Godly meditations*, and Baxter's *The saints everlasting rest* (1.2, in *Works* vol. 22, p. 33) are useful starting points. See also Article VII of the Westminster Assembly of 1648 ('Of God's covenant with man'), ed. cit. pp. 14–16.

587. Bradford, *Defence of election*, p. 308. It may appear anachronistic to include earlier sixteenth-century Protestants like Bradford and Tyndale in an exploration of Puritan spirituality; but it is important to underline the indebtedness of seventeenth-century piety to earlier Protestantism.

588. *The practice of piety* p. 272. For Baily (or Baylie) see Wakefield (1992) pp. 14–15 and Rivers (1991i) pp. 12–13. Cf. the letter of St Bernard to Aelred of Rievaulx, in which he says that 'you will be able to strike something out of those rocks that you have not got by your own wits from the bookshelves of the schoolmen, and . . . you will have experienced sometimes under the shade of a tree during the heats of midday what you would never have learned in the schools' (*The letters of St Bernard of Clairvaux*, trans. B. S. James (London: Burns Oates, 1953), p. 247).

589. *A Christian directory* 1.3, in *Works* vol. 3. pp. 377–8.

590. *A paterne of true prayer*, p. 153; cf. John Bradford, *Godly meditations*, p. 194: 'How fair thou art, the beauty of the sun, moon, stars, light, flowers, rivers, fields, hills, birds, beasts, men, and all creatures, yea, the goodly shape and form of the whole world, doth declare.' For Smyth see Watts (1978), esp. pp. 41–9.

591. See e.g. Baxter, *The saints everlasting rest* 4.11, in *Works* vol. 23, pp. 383–4.

592. See Nuttall (1946) pp. 143–4.

593. Sommerville (1977, p. 80) points out, however, that the Holy Spirit rarely appears in works of contemporary popular piety.

594. Calvin, *Institutes* 1.13.14, pp. 122–3.

595. 'Pneumatologia' was a strange hybrid subject, though centred upon the nature and action of the Holy Spirit: see Rupp (1986) p. 176. For Owen, see Wakefield (1957) pp. 8–9 and (1992) p. 34; Toon (1971); Rupp (1986) pp. 122–3; Ferguson (1987); Rivers (1991i) p. 92; Greaves (1992) pp. 28–30; for the *Pneumatologia*, see Toon (1971) pp. 166–7. Owen remains seriously neglected in general studies of Puritan thought and spiritual life: he receives no mention in Bouyer's survey (*Orthodox spirituality and Protestant and Anglican spirituality* (A history of Christian spirituality 3) (1969), or in *Christian spirituality III: Post-Reformation and modern* (World spirituality series) (1989), and only a very brief entry in F. L. Cross' and E. A. Livingstone's *The Oxford dictionary of the Christian Church*, 3rd. edn (1997).

596. *Pneumatologia* 1.4, in *Works* vol. 3, p. 97.

597. *Pneumatologia* 3.1, in *Works* vol. 3, p. 207.

598. *Pneumatologia* 3.3, in *Works* vol. 3, p. 247.

599. *Pneumatologia* 3.5, in *Works* vol. 3, p. 311.

600. *Pneumatologia* 3.3, in *Works* vol. 3, pp. 256–7.

601. *Pneumatologia* 3.4, in *Works* vol. 3, p. 287. Walter Marshall (*The gospel-mystery of sanctification*, p. 50) speaks of 'a new holy frame and nature'.

602. *Pneumatologia* 3.4, in *Works* vol. 3, p. 292, and 3.5, p. 299.

603. *Pneumatologia* 3.5, in *Works* vol. 3, pp. 302–3. Note the stress on the objective and the corporate here, counterbalancing Owen's earlier stress on experience as an essential counterpart to baptism and repentance. In another work, *The grace and duty of being spiritually minded*, Owen begins with St Paul's distinction between life according to the flesh and life according to the Spirit: although he concedes that both can coexist in the same person at the same time, a different state of being is created where one predominates (1.1, in *Works* vol. 7, pp. 267–8). He argues that St Paul means by 'Spirit' in this context both the person of the Holy Spirit himself, and 'the principle of spiritual life wrought in all that are regenerate by the Holy Ghost' (1.1, in *Works* vol. 7, p. 269).

604. The point is well made by William Tyndale: 'where the Spirit is, there is feeling; for the Spirit

maketh us feel all things. Where the Spirit is not, there is no feeling; but a vain opinion or imagination' (*The parable of the wicked mammon*, p. 78).

605. *Pneumatologia* 3.1, in *Works* vol. 3, pp. 216–17. It is crucial to stress the weakness of the commonly-held assumption that 'Puritanism' consisted of little more than a narrow moralizing imposed on reluctant parishioners. See Spufford (1985ii) for an effective rebuttal of this.

606. *Pneumatologia* 3.1, in *Works* vol. 3, pp. 218–19. Cf. Walter Marshall, *The gospel-mystery of sanctification* p. 122: holiness is not a condition of salvation, but a free gift organically linked with it.

607. *Pneumatologia* 3.1, in *Works* vol. 3, pp. 221–2. This is Owen's description of what Calvin means, citing 2 Peter 1.4, in describing us as 'partakers of the divine nature' in the text cited above.

608. *Pneumatologia* 3.5, in *Works* vol. 3, p. 330.

609. *Pneumatologia* 3.5, in *Works* vol. 3, p. 316.

610. *Pneumatologia* 3.5, in *Works* vol. 3, pp. 318 and 330.

611. *Pneumatologia* 3.5, in *Works* vol. 3, p. 334.

612. *Gospel grounds and evidence of the faith of God's elect*, in *Works* vol. 5, p. 424.

613. *Gospel Grounds* in *Works* vol. 5, p. 426; cf. also p. 429. Walter Marshall (*The gospel-mystery of sanctification* p. 19) describes the image of God within us as 'an actual Bent and Propensity of his [the first Adam's] Heart to the Practice of Holiness, not in a mere Power of Will to chuse Good or Evil'.

614. *Pneumatologia* 3.1, in *Works* vol. 3, p. 223.

615. *Pneumatologia* 4.2, in *Works* vol. 3, p. 387.

616. *Pneumatologia* 4.3, in *Works* vol. 3, pp. 417–19. Elsewhere he defines sanctification as synonymous with inherent righteousness: 'our sanctification is the inherent renovation of our natures exerting and acting itself in newness of life, or obedience unto God in Christ and works of righteousness', *The doctrine of justification* 6, in *Works* vol. 5, p. 155. It is vital here to see that for Owen the process of sanctification is grounded first in the objective fact of our regeneration, and secondly in our own 'relation unto [God], or especial interest in him, or union with him' (*Pneumatologia* 4.3, in *Works* vol. 3, pp. 409 and 414). For a superb and sustained Puritan treatment of the nature and theology of sanctification, see Walter Marshall's *The Gospel-mystery of sanctification*.

617. *Pneumatologia* 3.5, in *Works* vol. 3, p. 325.

618. *Pneumatologia* 4.3, in *Works* vol. 3, p. 409.

619. *Pneumatologia* 4.2, in *Works* vol. 3, pp. 389–91.

620. *Pneumatologia* 4.4, in *Works* vol. 3, p. 429.

621. *Pneumatologia* 4.2, in *Works* vol. 3, p. 396.

622. *Pneumatologia* 4.2, in *Works* vol. 3, pp. 400–1.

623. *Pneumatologia* 4.3, in *Works* vol. 3, p. 407.

624. *Pneumatologia* 4.5, in *Works* vol. 3, p. 448.

625. *Pneumatologia* 5.1, in *Works* vol. 3, p. 583. This is not hyperbole. Spufford (1974, p. 213) underlines the vitality and fervour with which the humblest Christians joined in religious debate in Commonwealth England. See also Duffy (1986).

626. e.g. *Pneumatologia* 8.4, in *Works* vol. 4, p. 385.

627. *Pneumatologia* 4.6, in *Works* vol. 3, p. 482; cf. 7:9, pp. 319 and 322.

628. Owen calls it 'this free, genuine, unforced inclination of the mind and soul, evenly and universally, unto all that is spiritually good, unto all acts and duties of holiness, with an inward labouring to break through and to be quit of all opposition, is the first fruit and most pregnant evidence of the renovation of our natures by the Holy Ghost', (*Pneumatologia* 4.6, in *Works* vol. 3, pp. 490–1).

629. *Pneumatologia* 4.6, in *Works* vol. 3, pp. 493–4.

630. *Pneumatologia* 4.6, in *Works* vol. 3, p. 497.

631. *Pneumatologia* 4.1, in *Works* vol. 3, p. 376.

632. *Pneumatologia* 4.1, in *Works* vol. 3, p. 385.

633. *Pneumatologia* 4.6, in *Works* vol. 3, p. 505.

634. *Pneumatologia* 4.6, in *Works* vol. 3, pp. 506 and 508. Cf. Walter Marshall, *The gospel-mystery of sanctification*, p. 105: 'The difference betwixt the Law and Gospel doth not at all consist in this, that the one requireth perfect doing, the other only sincere doing; but in this, that the one requireth doing, the other no doing, but believing for Life and Salvation. Their terms are different not only in degree, but in their whole nature' – a superb summary of Lutheran doctrine.

635. *Pneumatologia* 4.6, in *Works* vol. 3, pp. 508–9. Cf. Walter Marshall, *The gospel-mystery of sanctification*, p. 109, where he argues that, if you find you want to live by the moral law of the Ten Commandments, it is a clear sign that you are already elected to salvation.

636. *Pneumatologia* 4.6, in *Works* vol. 3, p. 509; cf. 9.4, in *Works* vol. 4, p. 458.

637. *Pneumatologia* 4.6, in *Works* vol. 3, p. 512. Cf. 5.1, in *Works* vol. 3, p. 578: 'Our likeness unto God, that wherein we bear his image, is our holiness.'

638. *Pneumatologia* 5.1, in *Works* vol. 3, p. 583.

639. *Pneumatologia* 4.6, in *Works* vol. 3, p. 513.

640. *Pneumatologia* 4.6, in *Works* vol. 3, p. 516.

641. *Pneumatologia* 5.1, in *Works* vol. 3, p. 570. Cf. Walter Marshall, *The gospel-mystery of sanctification*, p. 253: 'Stir up and strengthen your self to perform the Duties of Holiness, by a firm perswasion of your enjoyment of Jesus Christ.'

642. *Pneumatologia* 5.1, in *Works* vol. 3, p. 586.

643. *Pneumatologia* 4.2, in *Works* vol. 3, p. 386. Note the corporate sense here – Owen frequently stresses the ecclesial dimension of sanctification. Thus 'The Spirit of God is promised and received as to gifts for the edification of the church', though not for those outside it, *Pneumatologia* 4:3, in *Works* vol. 3, p. 410 (and cf. 7.9, in vol. 4, pp. 325–6).

644. *Pneumatologia* 3.2, in *Works* vol. 3, pp. 231–4; cf. Baxter, *The saints everlasting rest* 1.8, in *Works* vol. 22, p. 182.

645. *Pneumatologia* 3.2, in *Works* vol. 3, p. 234.

646. See esp. Pettit (1966) and Cohen (1986).

647. 'Here is no congruence or work done before grace, but wrath, sin, terror and death' (*Commentary on Galatians* 2.16, p. 132).

648. Sibbes, *The saints cordialls*, p. 8.

649. p. 13.

650. p. 16.

651. p. 18.

652. For these, see esp. Haller (1938) pp. 96–8, Watkins (1972), Caldwell (1983), Smith (1989), esp. pp. 23–4, and Spurr (1998) pp. 159–66. These narratives shared some common features: heavy reliance on scripture, some objective self-examination, a conversion experience beginning in sin. They were personal in being profoundly individual in focus; but they were also public in being required of all who would become fully communicant church members: Caldwell (1983) p. 46; Keeble (1987) pp. 209 and 211.

653. *Satan, his methods* (1683). For women's piety in the seventeenth century see Crawford (1993), esp. pp. 73–97; and, for the writings of women in radical sectarian groupings during this period, see H. Hinds, *God's Englishwomen* (Manchester UP, 1996).

654. *Satan, his methods*, pp. 1–2.

655. pp. 3–4.

656. p. 7.

657. pp. 9 and 12.

658. p. 15.

659. p. 32.

660. p. 72.

661. pp. 19–20. Cf. Walter Marshall, *The gospel-mystery of sanctification*, pp. 299–300: 'Complaint and Lamentation are one great part of Prayer, as Lamentations of *Jeremiah*'.

662. *The parable of the wicked mammon*, pp. 75–6. Cf. also John Smyth, *A paterne of true prayer,* pp. 164–5, encouraging us to pray for the imputation of Christ's righteousness to us.

663. *The saints everlasting rest* 3.11, in *Works* vol. 23, p. 2.

664. 3:11, in *Works* vol. 23, p. 15.

665. 3:11, in *Works* vol. 23, p. 42.

666. 3:13, in *Works* vol. 23, pp. 74–114.

667. 'Lay down . . . thy reasonings; take up the love of the Father upon a pure act of believing, and that will open thy soul to let it out unto the Lord in the communion of love' (*Of communion* 1.4, in *Works* vol. 2, p. 37). Cf. Walter Marshall, *The gospel-mystery of sanctification*, pp. 25–6: 'consult your own Experience, if you have any true Love to God, whether it were not wrought in you by a sense of God's Love first toward you'.

668. *Heaven on earth*, p. 49.

669. *Heaven on earth*, p. 63. More generally, Brooks points out that God sustains his people during times of suffering by vouchsafing signs or inner perceptions of assurance (pp. 65–73). Cf. Walter Marshall, *The gospel-mystery of sanctification*, p. 175: 'Beware of thinking so highly of this Assurance, as if it were inconsistent with any doubting in the same Soul.'

670. *Answer*, p. 198.

671. *Answer*, pp. 50–1.

672. 'For I am not come to redeem the world only, but also to change their life. They, therefore, that believe in me shall transform their life after my example and doctrine, and not after any man's traditions' (*The supper of the Lord*, in *Works* vol. 3, p. 238).

673. See the discussion in Kendall (1979) pp. 71–3 (on William Perkins), p. 123 (on John Preston), and pp. 169–70 and 179–80 (on John Cotton).

674. *Of communion* 2.7, in *Works* vol. 2, p. 170.

675. *Of communion* 2.9, in *Works* vol. 2, p. 206.

676. Where Luther never makes the distinction between these two clear, Calvin does (Gründler (1976) p. 180). Justification is a forensic act by which the righteousness of Christ is imputed to us: 'Justification is based on what Christ has done for us; sanctification is based on what he does within us' (L. J. Richard, *The spirituality of John Calvin* (1974), quoted in Gründler (1976) p. 182). The indissoluble connection between justification and sanctification means that 'spirituality' for Calvin is a lifelong process (for the heart of his teaching on this, see *Institutes* 3.6–10).

677. *How to live and that well*, in *Works* vol. 1, p. 478.

678. *How to live and that well*, in *Works* vol. 1, p. 478.

679. p. 418.

680. p. 479.

681. p. 479.

682. p. 479.

683. 2 Kings 6. Perkins, *How to live and that well*, in *Works* vol. 1, p. 480. Cf. Walter Marshall, *The gospel-mystery of sanctification*, p. 15: 'And shall we dare to rush into Battel against all the Powers of Darkness, all Worldly Terrors and Allurements? and our own inbred domineering Corruptions, without considering whether we have sufficient Spiritual Furniture to stand in the Evil day?'

684. For the importance of the family in the spread of dissent, see Spufford (1974), esp. p. 257. For the inextricable link between holiness and morality for Puritans, see Walter Marshall, *The gospel-mystery of sanctification*, esp. p. 145. For women and family piety, see Crawford (1993) pp. 86–91.

685. *A saint or a brute* 2.4, in *Works* vol. 10, p. 186; see also p. 184.

686. p. 185. See also his insistence on the role of the clergy in fostering the unity and peace of the whole Church: *The Reformed pastor*, chapter 3 (ed. cit. pp. 100–1).

687. pp. 188ff.

688. *A saint or a brute* 2.9, in *Works* vol. 10, pp. 258–91.

689. p. 270.

690. *A saint or a brute* 2.10, in *Works* vol. 10, pp. 295–400.

691. p. 305.

692. p. 307.

693. pp. 310, 316–20.

694. p. 315.

695. p. 329.
696. pp. 350–1.
697. pp. 355–6.
698. For this image see esp. Walter Marshall, *The gospel-mystery of sanctification*, pp. 232–6.
699. For this subject see the illuminating discussions in Wakefield (1957, pp. 101–8), and Smith (1989, pp. 107–225). On the Christ-centred nature of Puritan 'mysticism', see Sommerville (1977) p. 79.
700. *Pneumatologia* 8.4, in *Works* vol. 4, pp. 384–5. Walter Marshall (*The gospel-mystery of sanctification*, pp. 45–6 and 77) speaks of a 'mystical union' in the same way, and with the same general meaning.
701. *Pneumatologia* 8.4, in *Works* vol. 4, p. 385.
702. *The saints everlasting rest* 1.4, in *Works* vol. 22, p. 54.
703. *Of communion* 2.1, in *Works* vol. 2, p. 44. For the use of feminine imagery here, and for a comparison between medieval and Puritan exegesis of the Song of Songs, see Susan Hardman Moore, 'Sexing the soul: gender and the rhetoric of Puritan piety', in R. N. Swanson (ed.), *Gender and Christian religion* (Studies in Church History, 34) (Woodbridge: Boydell, 1998), pp. 175–86.
704. 'He [Christ] is married unto us, and we unto him' (*Of communion* 2.3, in *Works* vol. 2, p. 54).
705. pp. 56–8.
706. *Of communion* 2.4, in *Works* vol. 2, p. 130.
707. For this emphasis on the corporate dimension of Reformed piety, see Tripp (1991) pp. 79–86.
708. *Of communion* 2:6, in *Works* vol. 2, p. 155. Cf. Walter Marshall, *The gospel-mystery of sanctification*, pp. 60–1.
709. *Of communion* 2.3, in *Works* vol. 2, p. 100.
710. For this idea among Puritans, see Brauer (1950), esp. p. 152; Brauer, *Francis Rous, Puritan mystic 1579–1659: an introduction to the study of the mystical element in Puritanism* (Chicago University, unpublished diss., 1948); and Gibbons (1996) pp. 66–8.
711. *The saints cordialls*, p. 364. For Sibbes see Haller (1938) pp. 65–7; Wakefield (1957); and Rupp (1977) pp. 122–3.
712. *Of communion* 2.4, in *Works* vol. 2, pp. 118–19.
713. For Everard see Haller (1938) pp. 207–8; Hirst (1964) pp. 137–8; the article by Gordon Wakefield in *A dictionary of Christian spirituality* (London: SCM Press, 1983), p. 140; and Smith (1989), esp. pp. 110–27. The *Theologia Germanica*, a late-fifteenth-century text itself translated by Luther into German in 1518, was a mystical text of great influence in this period (see Smith (1989) p. 118). Everard also translated Nicholas of Cusa's *The vision of God*, Sebastian Franck's *The tree of knowledge of good and evil*, and *The divine pymander of Hermes Trismegistus*. Thomas (1981, p. 270) suggests that Everard became a Familist, but Hamilton (1981, pp. 137–8) argues convincingly that this was unlikely, suggesting a looser link between Everard and the semi-mystical works of the Familist founder Hendrik Niclaes; see also Smith (1989) p. 113. Everard's *The gospel-treasury opened* is a collection of sermons, published posthumously in 1659, and containing Everard's own translation of Pseudo-Dionysius' *Mystical theology* (pp. 415–27). For possible links between Everard and Jakob Boehme, see Gibbons (1996) pp. 5 and 11–12.
714. *The gospel-treasury*, p. 48.
715. p. 335.
716. p. 337.
717. p. 52.
718. p. 53.
719. p. 54.
720. p. 57.
721. p. 63.
722. pp. 64–79.
723. p. 89.
724. pp. 339–41.

725. pp. 221–30.
726. pp. 132–3.
727. pp. 357–9.
728. pp. 361–73. See also Smith (1989, p. 61) on the Ranters and deification.
729. See esp. Rupp (1977).
730. Collinson (1967) p. 214; Tripp (1991) pp. 96–8.
731. *A treatise of fasting*, p. 542; Walter Marshall, *The gospel-mystery of sanctification*, p. 305.
732. Collinson (1985, p. 204) notes the practice of Puritans in Suffolk in 1586, who kept fast days with particular concerns in mind, including 'the state of the Frenche church'.
733. Becon, *A treatise of fasting*, pp. 543–50.
734. *Diary*, 22 December 1587; p. 69.
735. Owen, *Of communion* 1.1, in *Works* vol. 2, pp. 6–7. See also Ferguson (1987) pp. 74–5.
736. The Letter to the Hebrews makes this plain; see also *Of communion* 2.3, in *Works* vol. 2, pp. 110–11, and 2.4, pp. 122–3.
737. *Heaven on earth*, pp. 142–3. Cf. p. 260: 'Verily Jehovah loves to see every one of his petitioners come to him with a steadfast faith, and not with a trembling hand.'
738. *A paterne of true prayer*, p. 124.
739. pp. 124–5; cf. Calvin, 3.20, pp. 155, 161 &c.
740. Owen, *Pneumatologia* 7.6, in *Works* vol. 4, pp. 293–4; cf. 4.5, in *Works* vol. 3, p. 445, and 8.6, in *Works* vol. 4, p. 405.
741. Nuttall (1946) p. 57; Wakefield (1957) p. 81; Tripp (1991) pp. 83–4.
742. *Of communion* 1.4, in *Works* vol. 2, pp. 36 and 38.
743. Owen, *Of communion* 2.10, in *Works* vol. 2, p. 221; cf. Article XII ('Of adoption') of the Westminster Assembly 1648 (p. 22): 'All those that are justified, God vouchsafeth . . . to make partakers of the grace of Adoption: by which they are taken into the number, and enjoy the liberties and priviledges of the children of God, have his Name put upon them, receive the Spirit of Adoption, have accesse to the Throne of Grace with boldness . . .'
744. *Of communion* 2.10, in *Works* vol. 2, p. 214.
745. *Pneumatologia* 7.6, in *Works* vol. 4, p. 293.
746. *Pneumatologia* 8.1, in *Works* vol. 4, p. 363.
747. *Pneumatologia* 9.4, in *Works* vol. 4, pp. 461–2.
748. *Pneumatologia* 9.8, in *Works* vol. 4, p. 512.
749. See Claire Cross, '"He-goats before the flocks": a note on the part played by women in the founding of some Civil War churches', in G. J. Cuming and D. Baker (eds.), *Popular belief and practice* (Studies in church history 8) (Cambridge UP, 1984), pp. 195–202, esp. pp. 197–8.
750. See esp. Nuttall (1946) pp. 102–12; Keeble (1987) p. 192; Brachlow (1988) pp. 78–9 and 88.
751. Sommerville (1977, p. 116) points out the popularity, in post-Restoration popular piety (particularly among dissenters), of the parable of Dives and Lazarus, with its stress on the dramatic reversal of fortunes of rich and poor in the next world. See also Watt (1991) pp. 202 and 209.
752. *The saints everlasting rest* 1.5, in *Works* vol. 22, p. 81.
753. *The saints everlasting rest* 4.3, in *Works* vol. 23, pp. 225–6; cf. *A Christian directory* 1.3, in *Works* vol. 3, p. 452.
754. Bayly, *The practice of piety*, p. 85.
755. pp. 90–5. Isaac Ambrose, more soberly, envisages the joyful meeting-together in heaven of all God's chosen, and a 'heavenly harmony consisting of ten thousand times ten thousand various sorts of Musick!' – a daunting thought (1654–7, Part 3 (*Ultima*), p. 210). The importance of the Christian sabbath in Puritan piety is considerable: though rooted in late-medieval Catholic devotion, Protestants preferred to stress the Christian week where Catholics attended instead to the various feasts of the Christian year. See Collinson (1964) and Parker (1988); see also Bunyan's *Questions about the nature and perpetuity of the seventh-day-Sabbath*, in which he argues against any suggestion of continuity between the Jewish sabbath and the Christian Sunday; and George Herbert's poem *Sunday*, in which he sees that day as both an integral part of the whole cosmic order, and the precursor of the life of heaven ('the fruit of this, the next worlds bud', ed.

cit. p. 75). Lewis Baily (*The practice of piety*, p. 229) describes the Christian sabbath as 'God's Market day, for the weeks Provision; wherein He will have us to come unto him, and buy of him without silver or money, the bread of Angels, and water of life' – this deft use of scriptural language and a contemporary commercial analogy to signal something that altogether transcends it is striking. Baxter's instructions for Sundays are if anything even more sober (*A Christian directory* 2.18, in *Works* vol. 4, pp. 240–51; cf. *The divine appointment of the Lord's-day proved*, in *Works* vol. 13, pp. 369–516, esp.433–5; and *The poor man's family book*, in *Works* vol. 19, pp. 505–28, which includes prescriptions such as 'Rise full as early on that day as on your labouring days; and think not that swinish sloth is your holy rest' (508), and includes recommendations for the rustic poor to spend part of the sabbath reading Baxter's own books (p. 509)!

756. e.g. Baxter 'O fortunate land, where all are kings! O place most holy, where all are priests!' (*The saints everlasting rest* 1.7, in *Works* vol. 22, p. 165); 'That I, a silly, creeping, breathing worm, should be advanced to this high dignity!' (pp. 112–13).

757. *The saints everlasting rest* 1.3, in *Works* vol. 22, p. 40.

758. 1.3, in *Works* vol. 22, p. 44; cf. also 1.7, pp. 136–7.

759. 3.6, p. 465.

760. 3.6, p. 475.

761. *The saints cordialls*, p. 6.

762. 'It must needs affect us deeply with the sense of our mercy and happiness, to behold the contrary condition of others; to see most of the world tremble with terror, while we triumph with joy' (*The saints everlasting rest* 1.5, in *Works* vol. 22, p. 92); though see his more extended reflection on the sufferings of the damned in 3.2, in *Works* vol. 22, pp. 371–95 and 'The torments of the damned must needs be extreme, because they are the effect of the divine revenge. Wrath is terrible, but revenge is implacable . . . Consider, also, how this justice and revenge will be the delight of the Almighty', 3.4, p. 418). Sommerville (1977, p. 84) points out that, in popular religious literature, dissenting writers were far more likely to refer to hell than were writers of the Church of England.

763. *The saints everlasting rest* 1.7, in *Works* vol. 22, p. 122.

764. *A Christian directory* 3.11, in *Works* vol. 5, p. 245.

765. For a vigorous onslaught against prayer to the saints, see Tyndale, *The parable of the wicked mammon*, pp. 66–7.

766. See, e.g., Baxter: heaven 'is not thy joy only; it is a mutual joy as well as a mutual love' (*The saints everlasting rest* 1.4, in *Works* vol. 22, p. 68; cf. 1.7, p. 120).

767. Bradford, *Godly meditations*, p. 146; cf. the Ranter Abiezer Coppe (*A fiery flying roll*, 1649): 'And at this vision, a most strong, glorious voyce uttered these words, *The spirits of just men made perfect*, the spirits &c. with whom I had as absolut, cleare, full communion, and in a two fold more familiar way, than ever I had outwardly with my dearest friends, and nearest relations' (quoted in Cohn (1970) pp. 320–1).

768. *The saints everlasting rest* 1.7, in *Works* vol. 22, pp. 135–6. See also *A saint or a brute* 2.2, in *Works* vol. 10, pp. 161–2, where Baxter argues for the existence of life after death on the grounds of man's *potential* and capacities, by comparison with other animals. The image of heaven as an ocean appears in Ranter spirituality, as in this striking extract from Laurence Clarkson's *The lost sheep found* (1660): 'even as a stream from the Ocean was distinct in it self while it was a stream, but when returned to the Ocean, was therein swallowed and became one with the Ocean; so the spirit of man while in the body, was distinct from God, but when death came it returned to God and so became one with God, yea God it self' (quoted in Cohn (1970) p. 311).

769. See Wakefield (1957) pp. 38ff, Yule (1984) pp. 191–2 and Spufford (1995) pp. 86–102: the latter argues (p. 90) that post-Restoration dissenters exhibited a greater devotion to the sacrament of Holy Communion than mainstream Anglicans. For an excellent study of Puritan ecclesiology and its Calvinist origins see Brachlow (1988).

770. Thus Baxter: 'I say not that a family, formally as a family, is a church; but every family of Christians ought moreover, by such a combination to be a church: yea, as Christians they are so

combined' (*A Christian directory* 2.3, in *Works* vol. 4, p. 75).

771. Owen, *The grace and duty of being spiritually minded* 1.10, in *Works* vol. 7, p. 389. Baxter also commends the converse with God that is possible in solitude; and although he discourages people to withdraw from human society into solitude, he does concede that for those specially called to it there are rich spiritual consolations in enjoying friendship with God (*The divine life* 3, in *Works* vol. 13, pp. 283–361); Baxter says 'My very dog will gladly forsake all the town, and all persons in the world, to follow me alone! And have I not yet found so much love and goodness in thee, my dear and blessed God, as to be willing to converse alone with thee?' (pp. 337–8).

772. Baxter, *The saints everlasting rest* 1.4, in *Works* vol. 22, p. 56.

773. *The saints everlasting rest* 4.5, in *Works* vol. 23, p. 302.

774. p. 303; cf. 4.11, in *Works* vol. 23, pp. 390–1.

775. p. 304.

776. *Pneumatologia* 1.5, in *Works* vol. 3, p. 109.

777. *Pneumatologia* 4:5, in *Works* vol. 3, p. 439. Isaac Ambrose notes the significance of inarticulate prayer ('that which is uttered in sighing, groaning and weeping'), and notes scriptural precedents (1654–7, Part 2 (*Media*), chapter 14 section 4, p. 439).

778. *Pneumatologia* 7.4, in *Works* vol. 4, pp. 272–3.

779. p. 274.

780. p. 276.

781. See Owen, *Pneumatologia* 7.4, in *Works* vol. 4, p. 271.

782. See, e.g., John Bradford, *Preface to Chrysostom on prayer*, in *Works* vol. 1, p. 14; also Thomas Becon, *A new catechism*, p. 132: 'whosoever presumeth to pray without faith, that is to say, without a full and certain persuasion of the mind to obtain the thing which he asketh, he doth none other thing than deride and mock God.'

783. *Exposition*, p. 78.

784. *Exposition*, p. 42. Cf. Walter Marshall's description of prayer as 'chiefly a *heart-work*' (*The gospel-mystery of sanctification*, pp. 294 and 299).

785. See Tyndale's ferocious diatribe against the Carthusians of Sheen and the nuns of Syon 'on the other side of the water' in *Exposition*, p. 81.

786. John Smyth advances the curious argument that, since it is very hard for anyone to pray the Lord's Prayer as it should be prayed, 'there is lesse daunger of sinne in conceiving a prayer agreeable to this prayer, than in using this prayer for a prayer' (*A paterne of true prayer*, p. 104). He surmises that Christ only ever used the prayer twice (p. 245), concluding that 'it is one thing to say the Lords prayer, another thing to pray it' (p. 247; see also pp. 130–1 and Collinson (1967) p. 357).

787. *A Christian directory*, 2.23, in *Works* vol. 4, p. 293. See also 3, in *Works* vol. 5, pp. 41–48. Book 7 of John Owen's *Pneumatologia* (originally published separately as *A discourse of the work of the Holy Spirit in prayer*) is a critique of formal prayer in favour of prayer 'in the Spirit', though Owen does not condemn 'forms of prayer' unequivocally, even allowing that they can be useful (7.11, in *Works* vol. 4, pp. 34–68), only that in his view the Bible commends 'another way of praying' (7.7, in *Works* vol. 4, p. 298, referring to Ephesians 6.18). He simply says that

> if persons are able, in the daily, constant reading of any book whatever, merely of a human composition, to rise up in answer to this duty of 'praying always with all manner of prayer and supplication in the Spirit' . . . I shall say no more but that they have attained what I cannot understand.

The famous prayer of Adam and Eve in Milton's *Paradise lost* (Book 5, lines 144–208) is sometimes seen as a critique of 'formal' prayer; but Carey and Fowler argue convincingly that Milton is really suggesting that prelapsarian prayer embodies the perfection of both formal and informal prayer: see ed. cit. of *Paradise lost*, p. 682. The prayer itself is based on Psalm 19 and the canticle *Benedicite*.

788. *Godly meditations*, p. 160. Cf. p. 177: 'Every godly and charitable person ought to be no less careful for the health and salvation of other than for his own, seeing we are 'members one of

another's body,' and have one heavenly Father, one Saviour, one Redeemer, one Mediator, one Lord; and be baptized with one baptism, profess one gospel, eat and drink of one inheritance of God's most glorious kingdom.' Becon stresses the corporate character of prayer represented by the words 'Our Father': thus prayer without love of neighbour is worthless (*A new catechism*, p. 146; *The pathway unto prayer* 30, p. 166). Bradford makes the same point in *Godly meditations*, pp. 122–3.

789. Thus John Owen: 'He whose prayers are hypocritical is a hypocrite in his whole course; and he who is but negligent in them is equally negligent in all other duties' (*Pneumatologia* 7.8, in *Works* vol. 4, p. 304).

790. 'For it [the use of set forms] takes away the liberty and prevents the ability of framing petitions, or any other parts of prayer, in the mind according to the sense which the party praying hath of them' (Owen, *Pneumatologia* 7.8, in *Works* vol. 4, p. 311. Cf. Walter Marshall, *The gospel-mystery of sanctification* 171, pp. 300–1: 'I do not condemn all Forms [of prayer] . . . better to pray by . . . Forms, than not at all. It is uncharitable to take away Crutches, or Woodden Leggs from lame People, yet none will look upon them *but as dead helps.*'

791. *Heaven on earth*, p. 260.

792. p. 263.

793. 'Prayer . . . is a lifting up of a pure mind to God, wherein we ask somewhat of him' (Becon, *The pathway unto prayer* 1, p. 130) – in fact he explicitly disapproves of prayer which is not designed to ask something urgent and necessary (9, p. 140), desiring something (i.e. not simply desiring God) – *A new catechism*, pp. 125–6. In *The demands of Holy Scripture* (in *Prayers and other pieces*, p. 607), Becon defines prayer as a

> brenning [=burning] desire or petition of the mind, lift up and directed unto God (springing and coming of the need and lack that we find in our self), as far forth as faith and the promise of God suffereth and permitteth us; where mark that we ask such things as be honest and lawful.

794. 'By "bread" [Give us this day our daily bread] I understand not only that which we commonly call bread, but also all other things necessary for the body and for this present life; as meat, drink, apparel, health, peace, tranquillity, strength to labour, wisdom to govern our things, a quiet household, a loving wife, obedient children, faithful servants, a flourishing commonweal, wholesomeness of air, seasonable weather, rain in due time, a fruitful year, abundance of all things, safeguard from enemies, long life, joyful days, house, land, cattle, good magistrats, righteous officers, painful teachers, diligent tutors, and whatsoever is necessary to the mainte-nance and conservation of our life' (Becon, *A new catechism*, p. 166; cf. Bradford, *Godly meditations*, p. 131).

795. 1957, p. 77.

796. See, e.g., John Smyth, *A paterne of true prayer*, pp. 112–13.

797. *The saints cordialls*, pp. 46 and 49.

798. *Godly meditations*, pp. 173–4.

799. *The parable of the wicked mammon*, pp. 93–4.

800. See, e.g., Brooks, *Heaven on earth*, p. 258; Becon, *The pathway unto prayer* 17, p. 149; *A new cat-echism*, pp. 134–6. Baxter believes that God may still hear the prayer of an unbeliever – 'There may be some good desires in unbelievers, which they may express in prayer, and these God may so far hear as to grant them, as he did in part to Ahab' (*The right method for a settled peace of con-science and spiritual comfort*, in *Works* vol. 9, p. 49) – and God may even use their prayers to draw them to true faith (p. 50). Calvin also concedes, on the basis of Psalm 107, that God does hear the prayers of unbelievers, though this only heightens the extent of his mercy rather than remove the need for faith for the rest of us (*Institutes* 3.20, p. 162).

802. Baxter says that 'prayer hath two parts; desire is the soul of it, and expression is the body. The soul can live separated from the body, but so cannot the body separated from the soul. So can desire without expression, but not expression without desire' (*The right method for a settled peace of conscience and spiritual comfort*, in *Works* vol. 9, p. 50; cf. *A Christian directory* 2.23, in *Works* vol. 4, p. 282).

802. Becon argues that we can pray anywhere (*The pathway unto prayer* 22, pp. 156–7), quoting St John Chrysostom:

> Wheresoever thou be, thou mayest make and appoint thine altar . . . Thou mayest, when thou goest unto market, and walkest by thyself alone, make long prayers. Thou mayest also, sitting in thy shop, and sewing skins, dedicate thy soul unto the Lord. The servant also that buyeth, or goeth up and down, and the cook doing his office, when he cannot go to church, may make a prayer long and discreet. For God disdaineth not the place, but requireth one thing, that is to say, a fervent mind and a pure soul (p. 157. Cf. John Smyth, *A paterne of true prayer*, p. 79).

803. *The poor man's family book*, in *Works* vol. 19, pp. 484–5 and 503; cf. *A Christian directory* 2.3, in *Works* vol. 4, pp. 66–90; William Perkins, *A warning against the idolatry of the last times*, in *Works* vol. 1, pp. 714–16; Wakefield (1957) p. 55. For family piety among Puritans in general, see Hill (1964) pp. 443–81 and Tripp (1991) pp. 190–2 and 206–10.

804. Baxter, *A Christian directory* 2.7, in *Works* vol. 4, p. 131; cf. also 2.23, pp. 309–10.

805. *A Christian directory* 2.8, in *Works* vol. 4, p. 144. Baxter goes on to say that 'if this [obligation] be cast on the wife, it will be his dishonour'. However, he advises a godly wife to go to church on Sundays to hear the sermons even if her husband attempts to stop her (2.9, p. 153; cf. John Bunyan, *The life and death of Mr Badman*). This notion of the (patriarchal) head of the household as replacing the priest is of immense importance: Hill (1964, p. 467) argues that the independent congregation is a form of extension of Puritan family prayers.

806. *A paterne of true prayer,* p. 94.

807. Smyth, p. 96.

808. *Pneumatologia* 7.10, in *Works* vol. 4, p. 331.

809. ['For whose good is this?'] p. 332.

810. 7.10, in *Works* vol. 4, p. 336.

811. p. 337.

812. Martz (1954, pp. 156–63) argues that the Puritan theology of grace and predestination effectively prevents the development of a serious theory and practice of meditation because it would appear too much like a 'work'. It certainly must have been the case that the terrible possibility of damnation precluded anything like the complex Catholic systematized forms of meditation, which might have felt for Puritans like rearranging the deckchairs on the *Titanic*; but it didn't preclude a wide-ranging approach to meditation as a desire (a) to discern God's will, and thus one's election, and (b) to reflect on heaven. What *is* true is, as Martz (1954, pp. 163–8) points out, that Puritans attached little importance to the humanity or human life of Christ in their prayer. See also Rupp (1977) pp. 120–1.

813. Wakefield (1957) pp. 14–16. A good example is Richard Rogers' *Diary.*

814. It was not accepted by John Goodwin (noted for his espousal of toleration), nor by John Everard, who says that the words of scripture cannot 'possibly contain the Mighty, Eternal Majesty of the Word of God' which is Christ (quoted Wakefield (1957) p. 19), and who minimizes the historical importance of scripture.

815. *The saints everlasting rest* 4.6, in *Works* vol. 23, p. 310.

816. 'The sensitive soul hath a kind of meditation by the common sense, the fantasy and estimation' (*The saints everlasting rest* 4.6, in *Works* vol. 23, p. 313).

817. p. 313. Baxter regularly returns to the traditional distinction between the two parts of the soul, understanding and will, the former being concerned with truth and the latter with goodness; see *The saints everlasting rest* 4.9, in *Works* vol. 23, p. 344. Note too that Baxter's distinction between understanding and affection, and his preference for the latter, is the same as Joseph Hall, *The art of divine meditation.* John Owen gives meditation a less immediately personal aim, seeing it as 'the thoughts of some subject spiritual or divine, with the fixing, forcing, and ordering of our thoughts about it, with a design to affect our own hearts and souls with the matter of it, or the things contained in it' and its principal aim 'to learn the truth, or to declare it unto others' (*The grace and duty of being spiritually minded* 1.10, in *Works* vol. 7, p. 384).

818. Knappen (introduction to ed. cit. of Rogers' and Ward's diaries) argues, with some justification,

that it was the ethical, 'the good, rather than the beautiful or the true, which occupied the Puritan's mind' (p. 2), though it would be more accurate to say that for Puritans the beautiful and the true had always to be incarnated through the good.

819. Martz (1954) pp. 163–8; Kaufmann (1966) pp. 126 and 140. The fundamental Puritan orientation towards *logos*, the Word, discouraged them from using the imagination, preferring doctrine instead (p. 128), though Baxter did have recourse to imagination and senses only after reason and faith have been exhausted for meditative purposes (p. 147), perhaps because he came to see the fatal weakness of the Puritan approach – once key words had been evacuated of their imaginative content they often lost all their power (e.g. 'Spirit', with its resonance in Hebrew of wind and breath; Kaufmann (1966) p. 148). This Puritan stress on doctrinal reflection led to criticism from, e.g., the Latitudinarians, on grounds of an obsession with vain speculations (Rivers (1991i) p. 54). More generally, the Puritan view of scripture was focused entirely on Christ, seeing every text as a prediction or representation of him (unlike Catholic commentators, with their fourfold medieval exegetical plan). Puritans did however lay stress on the importance of context in reading scripture (Wakefield (1957) p. 21). They envisaged every aspect of scripture being applied to the believer's own moral and spiritual life (p. 25).

820. Walter Marshall describes meditation as 'a Duty whereby the Soul doth Feed and Ruminate upon the Word as its Spiritual Food, and digesteth it, and turneth it into Nourishment, whereby we are strengthened for every good Work.' Baxter explicitly refers to meditation as *consideratio*, and also quotes Bernard's Sermons on the Canticle in this regard; *The saints everlasting rest* 4.8, in *Works* vol. 23, pp. 339–40 and 4.6, p. 314 and note. He cites the example of the Prodigal Son 'considering' whether or not to return home (4.8, p. 341). Isaac Ambrose writes of 'the Sanctification of *Experiences*', and sets in some detail how we may discern an experience of God at work in our lives (1654–7 Part 2 (*Media*) chapter 6, pp. 164ff). He proceeds to set out a method for integrating experience with scripture: in a three-column structure, he describes contemporary events (both individual and collective) in the left-hand column, sets scriptural texts relevant to them in the middle, and in the right-hand column adds further scriptural texts which offer 'Dispositions required in this case, and to be prayed for' (pp. 182–9).

821. See Bernard of Clairvaux, *De consideratione* (ET by J. D. Anderson and E. T. Kennan, *Five books on consideration* (The works of Bernard of Clairvaux vol.13; CF 37) (Kalamazoo: Cistercian Publications, 1976), pp. 146–54. Baxter has a lengthy exploration of meditation on heaven in *The saints everlasting rest* 4, in *Works* vol. 23, pp. 308–450). Isaac Ambrose suggests four subjects for meditation: 'our own unworthinesse'; 'the glorious *majesty* of God our Father'; 'the mediation and intercession of our Saviour Christ' (note again the interest in Christ's saving work rather than in his life); and 'the promises of God in *Christ*, made to our prayers' (1654–7, Part 2 (*Media*), chapter 14 section 2, p. 430).

822. *Diary*, 18 August 1587, pp. 56–7.

823. Hence the importance of Puritan spiritual autobiography; see esp. Kaufmann (1966) pp. 196–7 and G. Starr, *Defoe and spiritual autobiography* (Princeton UP, 1965), esp. pp. 3–50. Kaufmann (1966, pp. 206–7) argues that where Catholic meditation on experience tended to be concerned with recovering the original affective quality of the experience itself, Puritan meditation on experience was more concerned with the evidential value of the experience and of how it reveals God's providential purposes at work. 'Not surprisingly, the austere Calvinistic understanding of the deity as arbitrary sovereign who had voluntarily bound himself by covenant led to a concern to find further evidence of God's beneficent will in acts which confirmed His promises' (Kaufmann (1966) p. 211). Nothing was too trivial to admit of being fruitfully meditated upon (Keeble (1982) p. 111). For 'redeeming the time' see Starr (1965) pp. 9–10.

824. Baxter offers advice on practice in Book 4 of *The saints everlasting rest*: the Christian should try to keep to set times (4.6, in *Works* vol. 23, p. 318; cf. John Owen, *The grace and duty of being spiritually minded* 1.10, in *Works* vol. 7, p. 391), preferably daily (Baxter, op.cit. 4.6, in *Works* vol. 23, p. 320) since otherwise we shall become out of touch with God (p. 321), and especially on Sundays (pp. 324–6: 'I admonish all those that are possessed of the censorious devil, that if they see a poor Christian walking privately in the fields on the Lord's-day, they would not phari-

saically conclude him a sabbath-breaker, till they know more. It may be he takes it as the opportunest place to withdraw himself from the world to God', p. 326). Baxter commends solitude for this practice, though not the solitude of monks or hermits (pp. 333–4); the mind is first to be prepared and cleared of distractions (pp. 335–6; cf. John Owen, op. cit. 1.10, in *Works* vol. 7, p. 392). Material suitable for meditation is to be drawn from the memory, reflected on by the person's judgement, 'till a holy admiration hath possessed thy soul' (Baxter, op. cit. 4.9, in *Works* vol. 23, pp. 346–7), apprehended through faith, and then applied to the affections (pp. 348–50), increasing love, desire, hope, courage or boldness, and joy (pp. 350–64).

825. *The practice of piety*, p. 179.

826. Entries for 21 and 22 June 1595; p. 109.

827. Entry for 31 July 1597; p. 115.

828. See esp. Wakefield (1957) pp. 111ff and, e.g., Baxter, *The saints everlasting rest* 4.5, in *Works* vol. 23, p. 293.

829. *Of communion* 2.4, in *Works* vol. 2, p. 131.

830. 'Waiting is the only way to establishment and assurance; we cannot speed by our own haste . . . No disappointment, then, no tediousness or weariness, should make the soul leave waiting on God, if it intend to attain consolation', *An exposition upon Psalm 130*, verse 4, in *Works* vol. 6, pp. 554–5; cf. Thomas Brooks, *Heaven on earth*, pp. 63–5 and 88–90). This is an active, expectant waiting, modelled on that of the spouse in Song of Songs 3, awaiting the presence of her spouse and eventually going out into the city to look for him – Owen sees this allegory as teaching us the importance of prayer, meditation, reading, hearing of the word, and dispensation of the sacraments, as means of assiduously waiting upon God (verses 5–6, in *Works* vol. 6, pp. 613–14). Owen also compares it to the prophet Habakkuk mounting his watchtower 'and watching to see what God would speak to him [Habakkuk 2.3] – namely, in answer unto that prayer which he put up in his trouble' (p. 615).

831. *The practice of piety*, pp. 167 and 169. Bayly became Bishop of Bangor in 1616, but remained of firmly Puritan views.

832. See, e.g., Baxter's massive *A Christian directory*, esp. 1.3, in *Works* vol. 3, pp. 337–51, and his *The right method for a settled peace of conscience and spiritual comfort*, in *Works* vol. 9, pp. 1–287. William Perkins has much guidance about almost every aspect of the Christian life in *Cases of conscience* (in *Works* 2) and elsewhere. See also Breward's introduction to his ed. cit. of Perkins' works for an extended discussion of this subject.

833. *The saints everlasting rest* 3.13, in *Works* vol. 23, p. 83.

834. *The saints everlasting rest* 4.5, in *Works* vol. 23, p. 307. On the use of the body in Puritan piety, see Tripp (1991) pp. 91–8.

835. *A Christian directory* 2.3, in *Works* vol. 4, p. 77.

836. 2.7, in *Works* vol. 4, p. 133.

837. p. 136.

838. 2.23, in *Works* vol. 4, p. 283; cf. *The poor man's family book*, in *Works* vol. 19, pp. 459–60; Richard Rogers: 'It is an other thing that I desire, to know mine owne hart better, where I know that much is to be gotten in understanding of it, and to be acquainted with the diverse corners of it and what sin I am most in daunger of', *Diary* 30 October 1587; p. 62.

839. *Journal* 1.3, p. 58.

840. Elsewhere in his *Journal* he says that the name indicates those who themselves tremble and quake before the Lord: 'we, whom the world scorns and calls Quakers . . . exalt and honour that power, that makes the devils tremble, shakes the earth, and throws down the loftiness and the haughtiness of man' (*Journal* 1.8, p. 242).

841. *Journal* 1.11, p. 393.

842. This is not to suggest that all Quakers were poor. In an important article, Bill Stevenson argues convincingly that, broadly speaking, early Quakers were drawn from the poorer strata of society, but that as the seventeenth century progressed the number of more prosperous adherents grew (Stevenson (1995), esp. pp. 351–9).

843. As well as Fox's own works, see 'The Testimony of Margaret Fox Concerning her Late Husband

GEORGE FOX' in Garman (1996), pp. 233–43.

844. Penn, Preface to Fox's *Journal*, p. xlvi.

845. p. xlvii.

846. *Journal* 2.3, p. 118. For Fell, see *A relation of Margaret Fell . . . given forth by her self* (1690), in Garman (1996) pp. 244–54.

847. *Journal* 2.4–5, 2.8 and 2.11: the extremely close relationship between England and the continent in terms of the transmission of ideas is a key factor in the development of English spirituality in this period. Fox may well have seen himself as a latter-day St Paul, given the number of his letters to Quakers and others, his ceaseless travels and persecution. There are occasions when he renders the analogy explicit: see, e.g., *Journal* 2.3, p. 124; 2.6, p. 236. He almost certainly also identified himself with early Christian martyrs, and perhaps with persecuted prophets such as Daniel: see, e.g., his recalling of the story of the burning fiery furnace, *Journal* 1.9, p. 273; cf. 2.8, p. 308, and 2.11, p. 385; cf. also Evans and Chevers, *A short relation* p. 9 ('the Lord was as sufficient for us [while in prison], as he was for the children in the fiery Furnace').

848. See Steere (1984) p. 10; for Fox's character, see Nuttall (1967).

849. Steere (1984) p. 42; Nuttall (1967) p. 181.

850. For Boehme, see below. For the question of his connection with English Quakerism, see Thune (1948) pp. 12 and 63ff; Gibbons (1996, pp. 126–9) notes that both Fox and Boehme stressed the olfactory dimension of mystical experience, but without adducing evidence of clear textual indebtedness. Thune points out (1948, pp. 64–5) the difference between Boehme's relatively positive attitude towards the sacraments and the minimizing of these by the Quakers. For Fox's interest in medicine and hermetic writings, see G. Nuttall, '"Unity with the creation": George Fox and the hermetic philosophy', in his *The Puritan spirit* (London: Epworth, 1967), pp. 194–203.

851. Perhaps through Henry Barrowe's *A brief discovery of the false church* (1590).

852. Steere (1984) p. 25.

853. Penn (1902), p. xxiii.

854. pp. xxv–xxvi.

855. Fox describes the true church as 'the pillar and ground of truth, made up of living stones, living members, a spiritual household, which Christ was the head of: but he was not the head of a mixed multitude, or of an old house made up of lime, stones, and wood' (*Journal* 1.2, p. 25; cf. 2.1, p. 65).

856. Fox, *Journal* 1.12, p. 420. It is interesting to note that Catholics at the same time evidently also maintained that their church had recovered the purity of the primitive church (as a Jesuit tells Fox, *Journal* 1.12, p. 428). In another confrontation with a Roman Catholic, Fox argues on scriptural grounds against all who claim theirs is the only 'true church', maintaining that Jerusalem alone can claim to be the mother of Christians (*Journal* 2.2, pp. 101–2).

857. *Journal* 1.12, p. 418; see also 2.9, p. 320.

858. Penn (1902) p. xxviii.

859. p. xxix.

860. p. xxix.

861. See Fox, *Journal* 2.3, p. 119.

862. Penney's historical note on p. 149: it is interesting to note that they were accused of encouraging West Indian blacks to rebel (*Journal* 2:4, p. 157). This deep sense of mutual care and support was characteristic of Quakerism from the start (Steere (1984) p. 22). See also Sommerville (1977, p. 131) for Quaker emphasis on social change.

863. See Fox, *Journal* 1.9, pp. 273–5; 2.1, pp. 27–9, 43–4; 2.6, p. 210. Fox describes them as 'a peaceable people', 2.1, pp. 18 and 39–40; and cf. 2.8, pp. 298–301 and 2.10, p. 364. Quakers, along with other Protestant groups, interpreted Matthew 5.33–7 as explicitly condemning oath-taking.

864. Fox, *Journal* 2.1, pp. 25 and 54–5; 2.7, pp. 262–3.

865. See Fox, *Journal* 2.2, p. 100. The stress on silence is also found among the Ranters: see the texts

cited by Cohn (1970) pp. 307–8, especially the remark of Joseph Salmon: 'I heare much noyse about me, but it serves onely to deafen me into the still slumbers of Divine rest' (from *Heights in depths and depths in heights* (1651), quoted in Cohn (1970) p. 307).

866. *Journal* 2.3, p. 136.

867. 'I do declare the mighty day of the Lord is come and coming', Fox, *Journal* 2.10, p. 351. Fox writes to 'all professors of Christianity' saying that 'Jesus Christ is now spiritually come and made manifest' but 'such as are Christians in outward profession only have the same hard hearts inwardly now, as the Jews had [when he first came]', *Journal* 1.8, p. 216 – by which he clearly means those who fail to recognize the authenticity of Quaker religious experience. The divine indwelling is what Quakers and others meant by 'enthusiasm', a much controverted word in the seventeenth century: see Nuttall (1948), esp. p. 22, and pp. 67–79 and 88–90 for a moving and important account of both its strengths and weaknesses.

868. Fox, *Journal* 1.10, p. 355; see also 1.1, p. 18; 1.4, p. 81, &c; Penn, *Preface*, p. xxix; Fox describes the Quakers as 'the elect seed of God', *Journal* 1.10, p. 343.

869. e.g. Fox, *Journal* 1.11, p. 401.

870. See Isaac Penington, *Letter to Friends of truth in the two Chalfonts* (1666), ed. cit., p. 145. Waiting on God, or on the promptings of the Spirit in worship, was an important dimension of Quaker meetings (Greaves (1992) p. 18).

871. Fox, *Journal* 1.12, p. 420.

872. See *Journal* 2.3, pp. 112–13.

873. *Journal* 2.13, pp. 447–8. Nonetheless for Friends universal salvation is a real possibility, and all should strive for it: 'it was the work of the ministers of Christ, to present every man perfect in Christ' (Fox, *Journal* 2.6, p. 218).

874. *Letter to one under the divine vistation*, undated, ed. cit., pp. 149–50; cf. *Letter to M. Hiorns* (1679), ed. cit., p. 156.

875. *Journal* 1.2, p. 34.

876. *Journal* 1.2, pp. 34–5.

877. See *Journal* 2.1, pp. 34–5: Fox says that 'the least babe might see him'.

878. Fox, *Journal* 1.2, p. 32; see also 2.12, pp. 441–2.

879. 1.3, p. 47. For Fox's *Journal* see esp. Nuttall (1967).

880. Evans and Chevers, *A short relation*, p. 4.

881. Steere (1984) p. 29.

882. *Journal* 1.10, pp. 341–2.

883. Penington, *Letter to the friend of Francis Fines*, undated, ed. cit., p. 144.

884. Thus Penington tells his friend to 'distinguish between words *without* concerning the thing, and the thing itself *within*' (*Letter to a Friend* (1673), ed. cit., p. 145).

885. See, e.g., Fox's *Journal* 1.12, pp. 414–15, where Fox depreciates the learning of Hebrew or other languages as being derived from Babel; cf. *Journal* 2.1, p. 19.

886. *Letter to Thomas Walmsley* (1670), ed. cit. p. 143.

887. Note the reference to the *hortus conclusus* (the enclosed garden), an image from the Song of Songs familiar to innumerable medieval writers on the spiritual life. For this subject, see Emile Bertaud, 'Hortus', in *Dictionnaire de spiritualité* VII (Paris: Beauchesne, 1969), cols. 766–84.

888. ed. cit. pp. 148–9; *Letter to Lady Conway*, undated, ed. cit., p. 149.

889. See, e.g. Fox, *Journal* 1.7, p. 205.

890. *Journal* 1.11, p. 390.

891. *A short relation of some of the cruel sufferings . . . of Katharine Evans and Sarah Chevers* (London: Wilson, 1662), repr. in Garman (1996) p. 183.

892. *Some account of circumstances in the life of Mary Pennington* [sic], in Garman (1996) p. 212.

893. Penington, *Letter to Catharine Pordage* (1671), p. 154.

894. *Letter to Catharine Pordage* (1671), ed. cit., p. 146.

895. p. 154.

896. *Letter on Prayer in Families*, undated, ed. cit., p. 151.

897. Fox, *Journal* 2.8, p. 303.

898. See Steere (1984) p. 28. He also points out (pp. 22–3) the importance of the 'Queries' in Quaker worship: these, somewhat similar to the Catholic practice of examination of conscience, would be read out at meetings [=worship] and used as the basis for personal scrutiny.

899. See Nuttall's study of Thomas Aldam (1948, pp. 25–39).

900. See, e.g., *Journal* 1.12, p. 426: 'Therefore all Friends, keep cool and quiet in the power of the Lord God; and all that is contrary will be subjected; the Lamb hath the victory, in the Seed, through the patience.'

901. *Journal* 1.12, pp. 432–3; see also *Book of miracles* pp. 112–14. For Quaker emphasis on the power of God at work in human lives, see Nuttall (1948) pp. 59–60.

902. The original is in the Swarthmore Hall collection of letters, MS 3.66; cited in Nuttall (1948) p. 73.

903. *Journal* 2.6, p. 200.

904. Quoted in Cohn (1970) p. 304.

905. See, e.g., Cohn (1970) pp. 298–301 for the vivid description of the careers of two other Ranters, William Franklin and Mary Gadbury: the latter believed the former to be 'her Lord and Christ', and slept with him regardless of the fact that he was married. There is much dispute about the nature and even the independent existence of the Ranters: see Nuttall (1948) pp. 80–90; A. L. Morton, *The world of the Ranters* (London: Lawrence & Wishart, 1970), esp. pp. 70–114; J. C. Davis, *Fear, myth and history: the Ranters and the historians* (Cambridge, 1986); Acheson (1990) pp. 65–8; Greaves (1992) pp. 41–2; and B. J. Gibbons et al., 'Debate, Fear, myth and furore: reappraising the Ranters', in *Past and present* 140 (1993) pp. 155–210.

906. Where the relative inclusiveness of the established church during the reign of James I served to dampen the separatist impulse, the much more sharply defined (and vigorously Arminian) religious policy of Charles I and William Laud correspondingly did much to ignite it again. The Restoration saw the demise of nearly all radical sects, partly because the re-appearance of an earthly king diminished expectation of a personal rule by 'King Jesus', partly because of the reinstatement of censorship and strict ecclesiastical control. See Thomas (1971) pp. 142–3; Hill (1972) p. 96; Hill (1975); Keeble (1987) p. 12; and the following note. Hill (1964, pp. 474–4) raises the question of whether the poor attended their parish churches much at all: if (as seems possible) their attendance was at best sporadic, the influence of the sects may have been as significant in christianizing the poorest people as it was in politicizing them. Some radical sects and movements survived the Restoration, among them the Sabbatarians or 'Seventh-day Men', who observed the Christian sabbath on Saturday instead of Sunday, and survived until well into the eighteenth century: see B. W. Ball, *The seventh-day men: sabbatarians and sabbatarianism in England and Wales, 1600–1800* (Oxford: Clarendon, 1994).

907. For this see the previous note. Ralph Josselin speaks in his *Diary* of 'divers men bustle to make Christ king, truly Cromwell will carry it from him at present, but surely there is a time when Christ shall reigne more then inwardly' (Entry for 17 April 1657, pp. 397–8). For the Fifth Monarchists, who went further than others in seeking the overthrow of any earthly monarchy, see Capp (1972).

908. The term 'radical' is used here to denote religious movements whose beliefs or practices challenged contemporary orthodoxy; but it should be noted that many who fall into this category were socially quite conservative – as with the Family of Love.

909. See Moss (1978) p. 187; Hamilton (1981) pp. 24ff.; Dickens (1989) pp. 266–7; Acheson (1990) pp. 14–17.

910. There is no evidence that Niclaes himself visited England (Moss (1975) p. 37). Hamilton (1981, p. 115) suggests that Familist teachings first arrived in England during Mary's reign, soon after 1553. The first record of their presence in England is the 1561 confession of Familists in Surrey (Moss (1978) p. 188). Niclaes' writings were translated and published in England c.1575 and reprinted in 1649 (Haller (1938) p. 205). They were disseminated very rapidly after their first appearance, partly due to the effective propagation undertaken by one of Niclaes' foremost apologists, Christopher Vittels (Marsh (1994) p. 17; Hamilton (1981) pp. 119ff.

911. Marsh (1994, p. 31) argues that English versions of Niclaes' writings may be better seen against

the background of the late-medieval mystical English tradition than against that of Lollardy or Anabaptism. He also sensibly stresses the German late-medieval mystical tradition (the influential *Theologia Germanica*, Sebastian Franck &c) which may have influenced Niclaes (1994, pp. 28–9); Hamilton (1981. pp. 6ff) adds to this the *Imitation of Christ* as a key source, with its hint of anti-intellectual introspection.

912.   Marsh (1994) pp. 252–3; Hamilton (1981, p. 121) points out the curiously large number of mercers like Niclaes who became Familists. See also Spufford (1995) pp. 56–7, Gibbons (1996) p. 13, and Marsh, 'The gravestone of Thomas Lawrence revisited (or the Family of Love and the local community in Balsham, 1560–1630)', in Spufford (ed.) (1995) p. 212.

913.   Moss (1975) p. 42; Martin (1978) p. 90; Hamilton (1981) p. 129–30. In his visitation articles of 1612, Archbishop George Abbot enquired of each parish 'whether there be any . . . that be suspected to be annabaptists [sic], libertines, Brownists, of the Family of Love, or of any other heresie or scisme?' (ed. Fincham (1994) p. 106).

914.   Moss (1975) p. 52.

915.   Marsh (1994) p. 20; Moss (1978) p. 189.

916.   The believer must learn 'to take-upp hys Crosse on hym to followe-after Christ his Saviour in his life Suffering and death of the Crosse' (Niclaes, *Exhortatio* 1 (Cologne 1574), fols. 48v–9r; quoted in Marsh (1994) p. 21).

917.   Marsh (1994) p. 24.

918.   Hamilton (1981) p. 34.

919.   Niclaes, *Glasse of righteousnesse* 1, p. 34.

920.   *Glasse of righteousnesse* 14, p. 194.

921.   *Glasse of righteousnesse* 3, though note the confession of Leonard Romsye, a repentant ex-Familist, who says that for Familists hell is only 'the griefe of conscience in this lyffe' (quoted in Moss (1978) p. 191). In effect Niclaes himself represented the last chance for believers to repent and be saved (Hamilton (1981) p. 34).

922.   *Glasse of righteousnesse* 1, p. 12.

923.   *Glasse of righteousness* 7, p. 86.

924.   See, e.g., *Glasse of righteousnesse* 10, p. 128; for Familists, revelation as experienced by them was superior to scripture or church tradition: Moss (1978) p. 189.

925.   *Glasse of righteousnesse* 5, p. 62.

926.   *Glasse of righteousnesse* 11, p. 130. Music and singing are often referred to in Quaker and other 'radical' spiritual texts, though singing never became an accepted part of Quaker worship (see Nuttall (1948) pp. 57–8).

927.   See esp. *An apology for the service of love* (c.1580); Marsh (1994) pp. 40–1.

928.   Hence the seventeenth-century radical writer Robert Parker calls on 'every Christian man to strive, by prayer, meditation, study, and all other means' to understand the contemporary significance of the fourth vial mentioned in Revelation 16.8–9, which he himself interprets in terms of the downfall of Roman Catholicism (*An exposition*, p. 10). For Parker see also F. B. Carr, *The thought of Robert Parker (1564?–1614) and his influence on puritanism before 1650* (London University PhD thesis, 1964).

929.   For Boehme and the English Behmenists, see Thune (1948), Hirst (1964, pp. 76–109), Smith (1989), Deghaye (1993), and Gibbons (1996). Boehme (correctly Böhme) was a self-taught shoemaker from Alt-Seidenberg in Upper Lusatia: he settled in Görlitz in 1599, where he was converted by the Lutheran pastor there, Martin Møller. He seems to have had his first visionary experience in 1600: while contemplating a pewter vessel he believed he penetrated the mystery of nature (Smith (1989) p. 186; Deghaye (1993) p. 210). Møller's successor Gregory Richter suspected Boehme of heresy, and in 1613 he was told by the town council to stop writing: thereafter he sold his shoemaking business and became a cloth merchant in Silesia and neighbouring Bohemia. He obeyed the injunction to stop writing until 1619, when he resumed with a series of works which were to establish his reputation: when one of these was published by one of his friends, he was again summoned before a court through the agency of Richter, and eventually before the Elector at Dresden, where he seems to have been favourably received; but he fell ill,

returned to Görlitz, and died there in 1624. The influence of Boehme in England reached its height during the Interregnum with the publication and translation of his complete works between 1645 and 1662 (Capp (1972) p. 185; Gibbons (1996) p. 104). For his later influence, see J. F. C. Harrison, *The second coming: popular millenarianism, 1780–1850* (London: Routledge and Kegan Paul, 1979), pp. 19–23.

930. The group attracted some opprobrium: 'Dr Pordage and his family were of this [Behmenist] sect, who lived together in community, and pretended to hold visible and sensible communion with angels, whom they sometimes saw and sometimes *smelt*' (Calamy's *Life of Baxter*, quoted in Southey, *Life of Wesley*, vol. 1, p. 475). There is a delicious description of Dr Pordage and the Philadelphians in the nineteenth-century Congregationalist Robert Alfred Vaughan's *Hours with the mystics,* 5th edn (London: Gibbings, 1891), vol. 2, pp. 142–4).

931. For Lead, see Thune (1948) pp. 61–2, Hirst (1964) pp. 103–9 and 171–2, Smith (1979i and ii), and Gibbons (1996, esp. pp. 106–13 and 143–52). For the place of 'Virgin Wisdom' in Pordage's thought, see Gibbons (1996) pp. 111–13. Gibbons (1996, p. 16) points out that eighteenth-century German interest in Boehme was partly the result of the translation into German of some of Pordage's and his disciples' work: 'English Behmenism was something of an intellectual entrepôt, engaged in the import and re-export of ideas.'

932. Lead was probably seen as leader of the Philadelphian Society, though it appears that she always refused the title of prophetess (Gibbons (1996) pp. 150–1).

933. Gibbons notes (1996, p. 75) Pordage's interest in alchemy.

934. See Gibbons (1996) p. 89.

935. See *Aurora* 8, pp. 127–205, and Gibbons (1996) pp. 90ff. *Aurora* was first published in 1612, and was translated into English by John Sparrow in 1656.

936. 'When we consider the visible world with its essence, and consider the life of the creatures, then we find therein the likeness of the invisible spiritual world, which is hidden in the visible world, as the soul in the body; and see thereby that the hidden God is nigh unto all, and through all; and yet wholly hidden to the visible essence' (Boehme, *Mysterium magnum*, Preface, vol. 1, p. vii).

937. See, e.g., *The way to Christ discovered* 3, esp. pp. 18 and 32; Deghaye (1993) pp. 228–9.

938. e.g., 'Whosoever suffereth the poor and miserable to be in want and distress under his charge, and gathereth into his mind temporal goods for his own property, he is no Christian, but a child of the Serpent' (*Mysterium magnum* 22.81, vol. 1, p. 145; see also 51.46, vol. 2, p. 487).

939. Gibbons argues (1996, p. 151) that Lead's thought was always dominated by Pordage's, 'differing more in emotional expression than in intellectual content' – throughout her religious career, she seems to have worked in a symbiotic relationship with men, and perhaps Gibbons is correct in seeing these relationships as a form of spiritual marriage. Lead acknowledges her link with the *Praefatori Epistl* to Pordage's *Theologia mystica* on the title-page of her *The revelation of revelations*. Pordage in turn acknowledges that the core of his *Theologia mystica* was taken 'out of the Eternal Principle of Pure Nature; according to Jacob Behme's Philosophical Hypotheses and his Theological Maxims' (*Theologia mystica,* p. 2; cf. *A treatise of eternal nature,* p. H3).

940. Compare the cosmology on p. 3 of Lead's *The wonders of God's creation* with that of Boehme in *Mysterium magnum* and *Aurora.* But note that, in discussing the 'Paradisical' world, Lead declares that it is 'very rare that any souls do come up to be with CHRIST the Lord, immediately upon the departing from the body. Though I do not say but some may reach to such a perfect degree of *Christ-likeness* as that when they die, this angelical world may stand open to receive them; and to being admitted into that high glorification, may from glory to glory still be ascending, till at length they arrive to the *New Jerusalem* state' (*The wonders of God's creation,* p. 9) – a reference to some form of purgatorial state which this writer has not been able to discern in Boehme's work.

941. *The messenger of an universal peace,* p. 11. In his lengthy *Praefatori Epistl* (pp. 65–75) to Pordage's *Theologia mystica,* Edward Hooker distinguishes four means by which the Holy Spirit is revealed.

942. See *Theologia mystica,* pp. 66–70. Pordage describes it as 'a flowing, moving power . . . which can

be compared to nothing better, than to a lustrous shining glance' (pp. 66–7); cf. Boehme, *Mysterium magnum* 25.14, where he describes Sophia [=Wisdom] as 'the light's tincture' (vol. 1, p. 167). For Pordage, Wisdom is co-essential and co-eternal with the Trinity (p. 67); it consists of a '*Virgin Purity*, which *consists in this, that she is free from all desire, will and motion of her own*' (p. 68). She is thus utterly passive, transparent to the Eye of Eternity: she 'receives nothing into her self, but this divine Love, from the heart of God' (p. 69). Her office is to be 'a revealer of the Mysteries, and hidden wonders of the Deity', and to be an 'enlightner of the still Eternity' (p. 69) – she gives light to the deep abyss of the 'still Eternity' (p. 70).

943. 1.18–19; see also Gibbons (1996) pp. 144–5. In 1696 she and her companions experienced a collective vision in which Sophia descended accompanied by St Paul, St Elizabeth et al. (*The tree of faith*, p. 105; Gibbons (1996) p. 145).

944. *The wonders of God's creation*, pp. 14–15.

945. For the androgynous prelapsarian Adam, see Boehme, *Mysterium magnum* 18.1–4, vol. 2, p. 103; 41.23, vol. 1, p. 375; 76.11, vol. 2, pp. 775–6; *Concerning the election of grace* 5, p. 51: 'Neither Man nor Woman, but both, viz. a Manly or Masculine virgin, with both Tinctures in the Temperature'; cf. Hirst (1964) p. 93. Gibbons suggests (1996, p. 145) that the figure of Wisdom is as personal for Lead as the Virgin Mary for many Christians, and notes a number of similarities between the two.

946. *Second message to the Philadelphian Society*, pp. 65 and 75–6. For other English writers in the reformed tradition who used feminine imagery and inclusive language, see Tripp (1991) pp. 80–2.

947. *The revelation of revelations* p. 4; cf. p. 31, where she speaks of 'a co-deified operation'; and *The wonders of God's creation*, p. 10: 'Those souls that are born of God, and so renewed in every part, the whole man being changed into a deified nature' need to know and enjoy in this life what state of life they are to be assigned to in the next.

948. *The revelation of revelations*, p. 7.

949. *The revelation of revelations*, p. 105.

950. *The Enochian walks with God*, pp. 4–5.

951. See W. R. Ward, *The Protestant Evangelical awakening* (Cambridge UP, 1992), p. 52.

952. For Winstanley see Baxter (1988), the introduction to Sabine's edition of his works, and C. Rowland, *Radical Christianity* (Cambridge: Polity, 1988), pp. 102–14.

953. Baxter (1988) p. 201; Rowland (1988) p. 110.

954. See Sabine, introduction to ed. cit. of Winstanley, pp. 3 and 6–7.

955. *Truth lifting up its head above scandals*, p. 107.

956. pp. 109–10.

957. p. 108.

958. p. 108.

959. Baxter (1988) p. 188.

960. *Truth lifting up its head*, p. 100.

961. pp. 101, 122: 'the Scriptures were not appointed for a rule to the world to walke by, without the spirit; but were the testimony of the Father in those men that writ them' and passim thereafter. The true 'Law and Testimony' to which each must have recourse is what is revealed within the individual, not the written word of scripture (p. 126).

962. p. 113.

963. p. 115. This emphasis on waiting patiently but expectantly on God, so characteristic of the condition of the poor in Old Testament and other texts, is common in Winstanley.

964. pp. 115–17.

965. p. 131.

966. p. 120.

967. *The new law of righteousnes* 1, p. 158.

968. 1, p. 163.

969. 2, pp. 165–7. The emphasis on the virtue of apostolic poverty and a corresponding abhorrence of owning property is found in many radical texts: see, e.g., Cohn's remarks about the thought

of the Ranter Abiezer Coppe (1970, p. 318).

970. *The new law of righteousnes* 2, p. 167.

971. *The new law* 4, p. 173.

972. *The new law* 5, p. 177. In *Fire in the bush* he offers a different exegesis: in Eden, good and bad plants co-existed. Once man ate of the tree of knowledge, he was driven out of the garden, i.e. out of himself: 'he lives without the true God, or ruler, and is like the Beasts of the field, who live upon objects without them; And does not enjoy the Kingdome within himselfe' (1, p. 452). The tree of life is the source of restoration, which when we eat of 'by experience' will prove to restore us to the garden of God's rest and bring us peace (1, p. 453; for the significance of gardens as images of wealth in seventeenth-century England, see Hill (1993) pp. 126–40). The perverse inclination of human beings to try to possess and keep for themselves land which should properly be shared with others is all the consequence of this Fall, by which we came to ignore the true God within and worship a false God outside ourselves (7, pp. 489–90).

973. *Fire in the bush* 7, pp. 493–4.

974. *Truth lifting up its head,* p. 111.

975. *The new law* 8, p. 196.

976. See, e.g., *The new law* 3, p. 170.

977. *The new law* 6, p. 179; see also 6, p. 183; 7, p. 184; 14, p. 232.

978. *Truth lifting up its head,* p. 136.

979. p. 136.

980. p. 137.

981. p. 137.

982. p. 138. This stress on rigorous self-examination was common among Puritans, and could sometimes becomes excessive: see Greaves (1992) pp. 22–3.

983. p. 139.

984. *The new law of righteousnes* 9, p. 204.

985. 13, p. 120.

986. See, for example, *The new law of righteousnes* 8, p. 202, where he offers an exegesis of Adam as A-dam, 'for indeed he does dam and stop up the streams of the waters of life and libertie.'

987. *Fire in the bush* 2, p. 458.

988. *Fire in the bush* 4, p. 476.

989. *The right method for a settled peace of conscience and spiritual comfort,* in *Works* vol. 9, p. 282–3.

990. Sommerville (1977, pp. 98–104) notes the prevalence of anxiety in popular Puritan works of the Restoration period, but argues that its overall significance in contemporary piety may have been exaggerated.

991. *The parable of the wicked mammon,* p. 96.

992. Smyth, *Retractation,* in *Works* pp. 751–60.

993. Keeble argues (1987), though, for a much more vital post-Restoration Puritan tradition, indeed that the finest Puritan literature was generated precisely by the Restoration experience of persecution and nonconformity (p. 22). See also Greaves (1992) pp. 1–35.

994. *Obedience of a Christian man,* pp. 330–1.

995. See esp. Alexander Murray, 'Nobility and religion', in *Reason and society in the Middle Ages* (Oxford: Clarendon, 1978), pp. 317–415.

996. See Marc'hadour (1972) pp. 129–30; McConica (1981) pp. 65–6; Fox (1982) p. 30; Ackroyd (1998) pp. 102–4.

997. Roper, *Life,* p. 198; Fox (1982) p. 10; Ackroyd (1998) pp. 93–107. Apart from the Carthusians, the main monastic influence on More was the Brigittine community at Syon (Isleworth): see McConica (1981) pp. 60–2.

998. Fox (1982) p. 15, acutely notes that More's 'humanity was too powerful to be effectively sedated by the pious commonplaces he tried to administer to it'. Note the remark Roper ascribes to More when he looked out of his prison window and saw the Carthusian monks going out to Tyburn to die (Roper, p. 242). For the influence of monastic piety on More, see also McConica (1981).

999. Byron (1972) p. 112.
1000. For the latter, see O'Malley (1990) p. 9. Haupt, writing about More's last works, written during
his incarceration, acutely catches the dilemma created by the former:

> [The] predominantly public orientation of the Tower works is richly symbolic of More's
> tenacious commitment to an objective, impersonal, universal order of Christendom. In these
> works of devout exegesis . . . we find an act of public devotion – at a time of personal crisis
> More emerges as the Christian humanist and the Erasmian theologian speaking of the funda-
> mentals of Christianity to a Christian audience. From at least the time of Burckhardt the
> Renaissance has frequently been associated with individualism. But, particularly in thinking
> about northern humanism, a stress on individualism must be replaced with some notion of
> an individual and personal encounter with the impersonal, represented by tradition, the
> church, and the state. It is of the very essence of More's stature as a saint and a man that he
> embodies and lives out this kind of humanism: in his late works the profoundly experienced
> personal element is subsumed within and transcended by an ultimate emphasis upon univer-
> sal Christian experience. (Haupt, introduction to vol. 13 of More's *Works*, p. clxxx)

1001. The king's *Assertio septem sacramentorum*, or Defence of the Seven Sacraments, won him the
title of *Fidei defensor* from a grateful pope.
1002. *Contra Henricum regem Angliae* (1522).
1003. An example:

> If he [Luther] will ever be willing to [retract his heresies], if he will carry on his disputation in
> a serious manner, if he will retract his lies and deceptions, if he will leave off the folly and rage
> and the till-now-too-familiar mad ravings, if he will swallow down his filth and lick up the
> dung with which he has so foully defiled his tongue and his pen, there will not be lacking
> those who . . . will discuss serious matters in a serious way. But if he proceeds to play the
> buffoon in the manner in which he has begun, and to rave madly, to act like a raging
> madman, to make sport with buffoonery, and to carry nothing in his mouth but bilge-water,
> sewers, privies, filth and dung, then . . . we will take timely counsel, whether we wish to deal
> with the fellow thus ranting according to his virtues and to paint with his colours, or to leave
> this mad friarlet (*furiosum fraterculum*) and privy-minded rascal with his ragings and ravings,
> with his filth and dung, shitted and beshitted (*cum suis merdis stercoribus, cacantem caca-
> tumque relinquere*). (*Responsio ad Lutherum*, in *Works* vol. 5, pp. 682–3)

Even the editor accepts that More's treatment of the sacraments in Part II is 'dull and devoid of
any distinction' (p. 745).
1004. See Kenny (1983) p. 61; the remarks of the *Confutacyon's* modern editor, L. A. Schuster, in his
introduction, *Works* p. 1261; and Patrick Collinson (review of Ackroyd (1998) in *The Times
Literary Supplement* 4954 (13 March 1998), p. 4), who remarks that for More 'Tyndale's errors
invited, not persuasive argument, but repression. The only good Protestants were dead ones.'
1005. See the acute observations of Fox (1982, pp. 136–7 and 145–6).
1006. Note too Fox's suggestion (1982, p. 141) that More discerned in Luther the very qualities he was
most ashamed of in himself: the mix of aggression and piety, the sense of personal failure (exacerbated for More by Luther's marriage), the Augustinian revulsion against sensuality combined
with a propensity to indulge in it. See also Ackroyd (1998) p. 225.
1007. *Responsio ad Lutherum*, in *Works* vol. 5, pp. 692–3. It is worth noting C. S. Lewis' eloquent
observation on More's relationship with Tyndale:

> In More we feel all the 'smoke and stir' of London; the very plodding of his sentences is like
> horse traffic in the streets. In Tyndale we breathe mountain air. Amid all More's jokes I feel a
> melancholy in the background; amid all Tyndale's severities there is something like laughter,
> that laughter which he speaks of as coming 'from the low bottom of the heart.' But they
> should not be set up as rivals, their wars are over. Any sensible man will want both: they
> almost represent the two poles between which, here in England, the human mind exists –
> complementary as Johnson and Shelley or as Cobbett and Blake. (1954, p. 192)

1008. So Martz and Manley, introduction to More's *Works*, vol. 12, p. xcviii.
1009. *Utopia* (Everyman edn), pp. 124–5.

1010. Miller, in More's *Works* vol. 14(2), p. 754.

1011. A deeper explanation for the striking interplay of the serious and the humorous in More's work may lie in Auerbach's point about the way reality is seen and represented: during the sixteenth century the conscious distinction between the tragic and the comic in human destiny had come to the fore again, with the recovery of antique drama. Hitherto the medieval 'Christian-figural' manner of representing reality (in which everything was seen in the perspective of Christ, and of the next world) had prevented the development of the tragic (Auerbach, *Mimesis* (Princeton UP, 1952), p. 317). Even in antique drama, the tragic was dominated by what was fated: human destiny was shaped by forces beyond human control, and characterization was developed only insofar as it related to the tragic destiny involved. But in the Renaissance dramas of More's age, individuals exerted much more control over what happened to them, and individual character was far more fully explored, mingling the banal with the sublime, the tragic with the comic – supremely, of course, in Shakespeare (pp. 318–20). On More's humour, John Aubrey in his *Brief lives* says that More's 'discourse was extraordinarily facetious'; and Kenny (1983, p. 3) says 'More was, I believe, the first person systematically to use wit to greet dangerous and desperate situations in a way that was later taken to express a characteristically English sang-froid.' Cf. also Lewis (1954, p. 180): 'Nearly all that is best in More is comic or close to comedy.'

1012. For More's early education in rhetoric, see Ackroyd (1998) pp. 22–4. For Erasmus' sense of humour see M. M. Phillips, *Erasmus and the Northern Renaissance* (London: English Universities Press, 1949), p. 93.

1013. More's exact date of birth is disputed: see Ackroyd (1998) p. 4.

1014. See Kenny (1983) p. 103; Dickens (1989) pp. 164–5.

1015. *Works* vol. 14, p. 681. See also the remarks of Martz and Manley in their introduction to *Works* vol. 12, p. cxlix. In all subsequent references to the 'Tower works', the translations from the Latin originals are by the author except where otherwise indicated.

1016. More seems to have lived as a layperson attached to the London charterhouse for about four years (see McConica (1981) pp. 58–9). He was quite capable of criticizing monks for showing too much attachment to private property; Marc'hadour (1972) pp. 142–3. Marc'hadour may well be right (1972, pp. 146–7) in suggesting that More's closest affinity was with the Franciscans, in their stress on common ownership, poverty, and the centrality of the cross.

1017. *Utopia*, Everyman edn p. 129. See also Fox (1993) pp. 66–76. McConica (1981, pp. 68–9) stresses *Utopia*'s gloomy warning to readers to hold firm to their faith in a dark world.

1018. For the latter, see Marc'hadour (1989) pp. 106–7.

1019. In the *De tristitia* More follows medieval tradition in applying the 'our' of 'Our Father' to the common nature of humanity, and goes on to criticize the Protestant reformers for arrogating to themselves a private access to God which in his view belongs only to Christ: *Works* vol. 14, p. 1017. And Ackroyd (1998, p. 63) is surely correct in arguing that 'the whole of Thomas More's life is caught up in the maintenance of authority'.

1020. Erich Auerbach, commenting on the rich and diverse hinterland of Shakespeare's plays, notes that it reflects the Renaissance sense of the cosmos as 'everywhere interdependent' (*Mimesis*, trans. W. R. Trask (Princeton UP, 1953), p. 323) – a sentiment with which More would certainly have agreed.

1021. For an example of More's use of the Psalms, see Kuhn (1969).

1022. For the marginalia in the *Imploratio*, see Haupt, introduction to *Works* vol. 13, p. cliv. Marc'hadour (1969, vol. 1, p. 103) notes More's preoccupation with devils in his marginalia; Zim (1987, pp. 82–3) points out that More only annotated psalms which contain references to either personal suffering or national calamity.

1023. In his Prayer Book, More has written against the opening verses of Psalm 42: 'Happy the person who can say this from his soul' (*Felix qui istud ex animo potest dicere*) (*Thomas More's Prayer Book*, p. 80).

1024. This seems a likelier hypothesis than Marc'hadour's suggestion (1969, vol. 1, p. 154) that the choice of this psalm as a conclusion means the *Imploratio* is 'obviously unfinished'.

1025. *Imploratio*, in *Works* vol. 13, p. 305.

1026. *Thomas More's Prayer Book,* p. xlii; original on p. 75.

1027. *Oratio vel eius qui in carcere clausus est aut eger recumbit in lecto suspirantis ad templum aut cuiuslibet fidelis suspirantis in celum* (*Thomas More's Prayer Book,* p. 139; trans. on p. xliii, slightly amended).

1028. Kenny (1983) pp. 94–7.

1029. The Renaissance, of course, brought its own distinctive stress on the self into play: see McGrath (1993) p. 48. Kuczynski (*Prophetic song: the Psalms as moral discourse in late medieval England* (Philadelphia: Pennsylvania UP, 1995) p. xxiv) makes the point that 'the Psalms are frequently deployed in Middle English devotional writing for individuals in order to provoke an intense, interior feeling of contrition' – the formal public text is precisely the means of articulating the person's most private feelings. Thus, 'as God's preeminent poet, David takes on *ecclesia's* persona because she is unable to express to God, using her members' language, her own needs and thanks. David's artful arrangements of psalm language are at once distillations of his own subjective emotions, and fictive objectifications of the Christian community's sinful plight' (p. 48).

1030. At one point he mentions the physical manifestations of inattention (*digito purgamus nasum*)! See *Works* vol. 14, p. 127.

1031. *De tristitia*, in *Works* vol. 14, p. 133.

1032. p. 155.

1033. p. 177.

1034. p. 347.

1035. *Dialogue of comfort* 1.19, in *Works* vol. 12, p. 67. Cf. pp. 65–6, where More points out that one short honest prayer arising out of suffering is worth any amount of prayers prayed in ease and leisure.

1036. *De tristitia*, in *Works* vol. 14, pp. 117–19.

1037. Maurice Chauncy, the historian of the Carthusian martyrs, famously described them as going to their deaths *quasi ad epulas . . . alacritate corporis et hilaritate vultus* (as though to a feast, with physical haste and cheerful countenance); quoted in Knowles (1971) p. 233 and Whatmore (1983) p. 94. See Whatmore (1983) for a full account of the Carthusians' terrible suffering.

1038. *De tristitia*, in *Works* vol. 14, p. 55.

1039. pp. 251–3.

1040. p. 255.

1041. p. 415.

1042. Latimer, Sermon 10 (29 March 1549), in *Sermons,* p. 160.

1043. Sermon 13 (19 April 1549), in *Sermons,* pp. 220–1.

1044. Sermon 13 (19 April 1549), in *Sermons,* p. 224.

1045. *De tristitia*, in *Works* vol. 14, p. 217. Byron argues that in More's spirituality the concepts of obedience (1972, p. 64), loyalty (p. 67) and obligation are pre-eminent.

1046. *De tristitia*, in *Works* vol. 14, pp. 233–7.

1047. p. 239.

1048. p. 247.

1049. Note the remarks of More to his children: 'It is now no mastery for you children to go to heaven, for everybody giveth you good counsel, everybody giveth you good example – you see virtue rewarded and vice punished. So that you are carried up to heaven even by the chins. But if you live the time that no man will give you good counsel, nor no man will give you good example, when you shall see virtue punished and vice rewarded, if you will then stand fast and firmly stick to God, upon pain of my life, though you be but half good, God will allow you for whole good' (Roper, *Life,* p. 211). And in his *Treatise upon the Passion*, More notes that it is easy to *say* you are a pilgrim in this world: very hard actually to be one (*Works* vol. 13, p. 99).

1050. The dating of the *Treatise* is uncertain. Haupt (introduction to *Works* vol. 13, p. xliii) argues that part of it seems to have been written in the Tower, i.e. in 1534–5, and the rest shortly before he was imprisoned; but Fox (1982, p. 210) suggests a pre-Tower date of 1534, which would suggest that More had already decided to move away from polemical works even before imprisonment changed his entire perspective (Fox (1982) p. 211).

1051. *Treatise*, in *Works* vol. 13, p. 67; cf. also p. 68. Cf. More's early poem on Fortune, warning the reader to leave as little as possible invested in her arbitrary decisions: in *Songs, carols and other miscellaneous poems from the Balliol MS.354*, ed. Dyboski (EETS 101), pp. 78–9.

1052. *Devout Prayer*, in *Works* vol. 13, p. 22.

1053. p. 229.

1054. For the influence of Thomas à Kempis' *The imitation of Christ* on More and others, see McConica (1981) p. 60.

1055. MacCulloch (1996) p. 595.

1056. L. Bouyer, *Orthodox spirituality and Protestant and Anglican spirituality* (A history of Christian spirituality, 3) (London: Burns & Oates, 1969), p. 160.

1057. *Christian spirituality 3: post-Reformation and modern* (World Spirituality), ed. L. Dupré and D. E. Saliers (London: SCM Press, 1989).

1058. *John Bunyan*, in *Critical and historical essays*, vol. 2, ed. A. J.Grieve (Everyman's Library) (London: Dent, 1907), p. 405.

1059. Letter to Max Beerbohm, 15 September 1903; in Laurence, Dan H. (ed.), *Bernard Shaw: collected letters*, vol. 2 (1898–1910) (London: Max Reinhardt, 1972), pp. 373–4. Note also the comments of Robert Louis Stevenson: 'Throughout his best and worst, in his highest and most divine imaginations as in the narrowest sallies of his sectarianism, the human-hearted piety of Bunyan touches and ennobles, convinces, accuses the reader' (Bagster's 'Pilgrim's Progress', in *The works of Robert Louis Stevenson*, Swanston Edition, vol. 22 (London: Chatto & Windus, 1912), p. 196), and of Coleridge: 'I know of no book, the Bible excepted, as above all comparison, which I . . . could so safely recommend as teaching and enforcing the whole saving truth according to the mind that was in Christ Jesus, as the Pilgrim's Progress' (*Notes on English divines*, ed. D. Coleridge, vol. 2 (London: Moxon, 1853), p. 330).

1060. For this and for Bunyan in general, see the excellent studies by Hill (1989) and Wakefield (1992).

1061. *The doctrine of the law and grace unfolded*, p. 157. See also Mullett (1996), pp. 17–20, on Bunyan's youthful love of sports and athleticism.

1062. Hill (1989) p. 25. Talon (1951, p. 33) argues for the influence of the Bedfordshire countryside on Bunyan's work. For further details about the Bedfordshire of Bunyan's day, see V. Evans, *John Bunyan: his life and times* (Dunstable: Book Castle, 1988).

1063. *Grace abounding* 2–3, p. 5. Bunyan may have gone to school at Houghton Conquest, near Elstow, where he was born. Bunyan almost certainly exaggerated the poverty and lowliness of his background: see Mullett (1996) pp. 10–11.

1064. 'Though I am not skilled in the Hebrew tongue, yet through grace, I am enlightened into the Scriptures' (*Some Gospel-truths opened*, p. 39). Bunyan may well have concealed the extent of his learning, since he (like other Baptists) publicly despised learning and stressed the primacy of the Spirit in opposition to education (G. Campbell, in Keeble (1988), p. 141 and n. 15; Rivers (1991i) p. 111; Greaves (1992) pp. 40–1). In *Grace abounding* he explicitly mentions *The plain mans path-way to heaven* (Arthur Dent) and *The practice of piety* (Lewis Baily), books which his first wife possessed and which he read too (15, p. 8). See also Mullett (1996) pp. 14 and 21–4.

1065. Hill (1989, p. 46) notes that a love for military imagery and language remained with Bunyan throughout his life.

1066. Wakefield (1992) p. 32.

1067. Hill (1989) p. 13.

1068. Hill (1989) p. 59.

1069. *Grace abounding* 91, p. 29.

1070. Talon (1951) pp. 17–18. See also V. Newey, in Keeble (1988).

1071. *Grace abounding* 41, p. 15.

1072. *Grace abounding* 43, p. 16; also 53, p. 19.

1073. Talon (1951) p. 74; V. Newey, in Keeble (1988) p. 195; see also *Grace abounding* 89–106, pp. 29–34, and 131–43, pp. 41–4. Note Bunyan's long struggle with the anxiety that he had committed the sin against the Holy Spirit (148–88, pp. 45–59), and the final spiritual desolation

(333–9, pp. 100–1). Newey (in Keeble (1988) p. 212) notes that the lifelong, unfinished nature of Bunyan's conversion process is reflected in the indecisive endings of both *Grace abounding* and *The pilgrim's progress*: in the latter, Christian achieves admission to the Celestial City but the narrator explicitly does not.

1074. See *A discourse of the house of the forest of Lebanon*, a late work; see also Hill (1989) p. 149; Greaves (1992) pp. 42–50; Mullett (1996) pp. 282–4. On the gradual increase in tolerance in Bunyan's thought as it develops, see also U. M. Kaufmann, in Keeble (1988) p. 180 & n. 22. For the gradual movement in post-Restoration English spirituality towards a more interior, private piety, see Sommerville (1977) pp. 139–42. One of the most striking exemplars of this development is Peter Sterry, for whom see above, pp. 329–42, and Matar's introduction to his edition of some of Sterry's writings (1994, pp. 1, 10 & c).

1075. See Calvin, *Institutes* 2.10.2–7, pp. 370–3; and 2.11.4, pp. 390–1; see also Møller (1963) and McGiffert (1981).

1076. This is the 'ministry of death' of 2 Corinthians 3.7; cf. *The doctrine of the law and grace unfolded*, p. 24, and *Grace abounding* 186, p. 58.

1077. *The doctrine of the law and grace unfolded*, p. 49.

1078. *The doctrine of the law and grace unfolded*, p. 90; this is the 'ministry of the Spirit' of 2 Corinthians 3.8, for which see p. 25.

1079. *Some Gospel-truths opened*, p. 31.

1080. See also *The doctrine of the law and grace unfolded*, pp. 88, 90 &c; Hill (1989) p. 171; Wakefield (1992) pp. 45–52; Mullett (1996) pp. 141–2.

1081. *The doctrine of the law and grace unfolded*, pp. 66, 84 and 161.

1082. pp. 115–16.

1083. This is the significance of Bunyan's stress on righteousness being 'imputed' to us: for this theme see esp. *The desire of the righteous granted*.

1084. Hence the importance of the Slough of Despond for Christian in *The pilgrim's progress* (1, p. 15): awareness of sin was the crucial first step on the journey towards salvation. But Bunyan emphasized that that awareness was not in itself sufficient for salvation: you had to know where to go for help; and this knowing was itself a gift of God, *The doctrine of the law and grace unfolded*, p. 149.

1085. *A discourse of the building*, p. 280.

1086. *The doctrine of the law and grace enfolded*, p. 168.

1087. *Christ a complete Saviour*, p. 22; cf. p. 229.

1088. *The doctrine of the law and grace unfolded*, p. 200.

1089. *Light for them that sit in darkness*, p. 97.

1090. *Light for them that sit in darkness*, p. 99.

1091. See esp. *A defence of the doctrine of justification*. This is why Christ plays so small a part in the story of *The pilgrim's progress*: his role, now that the work of salvation is accomplished, is as intercessor, not exemplar.

1092. The same point is made in *Christ a complete saviour*, p. 259.

1093. *The advocateship of Jesus Christ*, pp. 204–5.

1094. *Christ a complete saviour*, p. 277. Bunyan has some difficulty with the question of whether the elect can sin or not: at one point in *The doctrine of the law and grace unfolded* (p171) he maintains that those who are saved will not sin because they will not want to, whereas a few pages earlier in the same work (p167) he tells us that the individual is certain of salvation even if he or she does continue to sin.

1095. See Talon (1951) p. 73; and *The pilgrim's progress* 1, p. 142, where Hopeful tells Christian he has prayed 'over, and over, and over', and received an answer only after much perseverance, and only after calling to mind Habakkuk 2.3 'If it tarry, wait for it, because it will surely come, and will not tarry'; p. 142.

1096. *Christ a complete saviour*, p. 265.

1097. *The pilgrim's progress* 1, p. 157 and 2, p. 295. See also Hill (1988) p. 239. For a nuanced discussion of Bunyan's presentation of Christiana and his attitude to women, see Mullett (1996) pp.

244–51.

1098. *Grace abounding*, 174, pp. 52–3.

1099. It is worth noting that Bunyan excluded this section from earlier versions of *Grace abounding* and perhaps only finally included it for the sake of completeness (Sharrock (1990) p. 101).

1100. *I will pray with the Spirit*, pp. 238–9. For this work, a key text for Bunyan's spirituality, see Mullett (1996) pp. 151–8. Bunyan's relish for 'a good sense . . . of the wrath of God' was not universally accepted by Puritans: Walter Marshall (*The Gospel-mystery of sanctification*, p. 140) stresses the difference for Christians between 'some holy reverential Fear of God' and 'a panicky tormenting horror'.

1101. *A relation of the imprisonment of Mr John Bunyan*, p. 114. For Bunyan's strictures on formal prayer, see also *I will pray with the Spirit*, p. 247. But note that he did not believe extempore prayer to be *ipso facto* sincere: see *The Pharisee and the publicane*, p. 129. For Kelyng, see Mulett (1996) pp. 77–9.

1102. *The resurrection of the dead*, p. 233.

1103. *Christ a complete saviour*, p. 289; cf. *A confession of my faith*.

1104. See, e.g., *Some Gospel-truths opened*, p. 63. Note that for Bunyan this desire is the consequence of salvation, not of baptism or of creation in the image of God. Once saved, the soul is 'quickened' so that it is no longer satisfied without the joy and peace God alone can give (*The doctrine of the law and grace unfolded*, p. 153).

1105. *Come, and welcome, to Jesus Christ*, p. 392.

1106. Talon (1951) p. 115. It was a sermon on the Song that had a profound effect on the progress of Bunyan's conversion and convinced him of God's love for him (*Grace abounding* 89–90, p. 29). When Christian approaches the Celestial City it is imagery from the Song that dominates the descriptions (*The pilgrim's progress* 1, p. 154; and later 'Christian, with desire fell sick, Hopeful also had a fit or two of the same Disease: Wherefore here they lay by it [the view] a while, crying out because of their pangs, 'If you see my Beloved, tell him that I am sick of love', p. 155).

1107. *The pilgrim's progress*, 1, p. 119.

1108. *Saved by grace*, p. 192.

1109. See *The Pharisee and the publicane*, p. 186. For Calvin, 'justification is based on what Christ has done for us; sanctification is based on what he does within us' (L. J. Richard, *The spirituality of John Calvin* (1974), quoted in Gründler (1976) p. 182).

1110. See *A defence of the doctrine of justification*, esp. p. 330; see also Rivers (1991i) p. 142.

1111. See e.g., *Ebal and Gerizzim* (in *Miscellaneous works* vol. 6) p. 111. In *The pilgrim's progress* (1, p. 83), Faithful speaks of 'a life of holiness; heart-holiness, family-holiness (if he hath a Family) and . . . Conversation-holiness in the world: which in the general teacheth him, inwardly to abhor his sin, and himself for that in secret, to suppress it in his Family, and to promote holiness in the World; not by talk only . . . but by a practical subjection in Faith, and Love, to the power of the word.'

1112. 'Holiness and liberty are joyned together, yea our call to liberty, is a call to holiness' (*Seasonable counsel*, pp. 32–3).

1113. *Grace abounding* 233, p. 73; cf. p. 86.

1114. *A vindication*, p. 176.

1115. *A few sighs from Hell*, pp. 272ff and p. 285; see also, inter alia, *The greatness of the soul*, pp. 166–8, 172–87, 204–10, 217–20 and 239–45; *The resurrection of the dead*, pp. 244–5 and 261ff; *A holy life*, p. 341; *The life and death of Mr Badman*, pp. 168–9.

1116. *A few sighs from Hell*, p. 296.

1117. See also *The holy city*, p. 95: 'Never was fair weather after foul, nor warm weather after cold, nor a sweet and beautiful Spring after a heavy and niping and terrible Winter, so comfortable, sweet, desirable, and welcome to the poor Birds and Beasts of the field, as this day [the day of the Lord] will be to the Church of God.' See also *The holy war*, pp. 115–16, where Emmanuel prepares a wondrous feast for the people; and (on music) p. 110 ('So the Bells did ring, and the people sing, and the musick go in every house in Mansoul'); and pp. 218, 223 and 225. For Bunyan's attitude to music, see Scholes (1934) pp. 154–6.

1118. *Solomon's temple spiritualized*, p. 86.

1119. This is evident even in the early works: see *Some Gospel-truths opened*, pp. 8–9; cf. *A vindication*, p. 196.

1120. *The doctrine of the law and grace unfolded*, p. 156.

1121. *I will pray with the Spirit*, p. 235; *Instruction for the ignorant*, p. 35.

1122. See, e.g., *The Pharisee and the publicane*, p. 234; *The doctrine of the law and grace unfolded*, p. 179.

1123. *I will pray with the Spirit*, p. 237. Cf. also p. 240: 'There is in Prayer, an unbosoming of a man's self, an opening of the Heart to God, an affectionate pouring out of the Soul in requests, sighs, and groans' and p. 258: 'The best Prayers have often more groans than words.' See also *The Pharisee and the publicane*, p. 222. E. Glenn Hinson ('Prayer in John Bunyan and the early monastic tradition', *Cistercian Studies* 18 (1983) pp. 217–30, esp. p. 221) suggests a close correspondence between Bunyan and early monastic theologians in this stress on 'prayer of the heart': both wrote, and prayed, from the depths of their own experience.

1124. *The doctrine of the law and grace unfolded*, p. 180; cf. *I will pray with the Spirit*, pp. 241 and 251.

1125. See, e.g., *Mr Bunyan's last sermon*; *The acceptable sacrifice*; *A treatise of the fear of God*, p. 42, 49–50, and 89; *Grace abounding* 27, p. 12, and 80, p. 26, and 116, p. 36.

1126. *Christ a complete saviour*, p. 279. The reference to play may be autobiographical: see above, for the importance of sports in Bunyan's youth.

1127. *I will pray with the Spirit*, p. 267; cf. *The acceptable sacrifice*, p. 15: 'a broken-hearted sinner ... is of more esteem with God than is either Heaven or Earth'; *Solomon's temple spiritualized*, p. 71: 'right Prayer ... comes from a broken heart.'

1128. *The pilgrim's progress* 1, pp. 56–60.

1129. *The pilgrim's progress* 1, p. 63.

1130. *The pilgrim's progress* 1, pp. 117–18. See also *Grace abounding*, 200–1, p. 63, and 202, p. 64: later (237, p. 74) Bunyan says he should pray not only for the removal of present evils but for protection against future ones.

1131. *The holy war*, p. 117.

1132. See, e.g., George Herbert's 'Engine against th'Almightie'.

1133. *Grace abounding*, 180, p. 55.

1134. See Greaves (1992) pp. 169–83 for a summary of Bunyan's approach to suffering.

1135. *Prison meditations*, p. 45.

1136. See the moving passage about her in *Grace abounding* 327, p. 98, and the comments of Roger Sharrock in ed. cit. p. 156.

1137. *Seasonable counsel*, pp. 25–6. There is an interesting parallel to this passage in Richard Sibbes' *The saints cordialls* (1, p. 4): 'Indeed Herod may have a John Baptist: but what will he do with him in the end, when he doth come to crosse him in his sin? Then off goes his head.'

1138. See, e.g., *Seasonable counsel*, p. 67. For *Seasonable counsel* itself, see Mullett (1996) pp. 264–7.

1139. pp. 41–3.

1140. p. 95.

1141. p. 87.

1142. pp. 18–19.

1143. p. 20.

1144. p. 36.

1145. *The house of the forest of Lebanon*, p. 157.

1146. p. 24.

1147. *The Pharisee and the publicane*, p. 217. Cf. *Seasonable counsel* p. 98.

1148. *Seasonable counsel*, pp. 94–5.

1149. p. 98.

1150. *The pilgrim's progress*, 1, p. 61.

1151. 'The path way was here so dark, that oft times when he lift up his foot to set forward, he knew not where, or upon what he should set it next' (1, p. 62).

1152. For the importance of memory in Bunyan's work, especially in *The pilgrim's progress*, see Knott, in Keeble (1988) pp. 167–8.

1153. *The pilgrim's progress* 1, pp. 63–4.

1154. 1, p. 19.

1155. 1, p. 22.

1156. *Seasonable counsel*, p. 61.

1157. 'O it is hard continuing believing, continuing loving, continuing resisting all that opposeth: we are subject to be weary of well-doing' (*Christian behaviour*, p. 52). Talon (1951, p. 2) makes this point well.

1158. *The pilgrim's progress* 1, p. 40. And is this not also the reason why Christian had no choice but to embark on the pilgrim's progress in the first place? (On this, see Wakefield (1992) pp. 77–8; Mullett (1996) p. 55). For the importance of journey and movement in Bunyan's life, see Mullett (1996) p. 30: for the possible influence of his early reading of medieval romances, see Spufford (1981) pp. 7–8.

1159. See above, and also Mullett (1996) pp. 19–20, for the importance of play in Bunyan's childhood and adolescence. Mullett, arguing for similarities between *The pilgrim's progress* and the medieval allegorical romance (pp. 192–3 and 204), points out that the landscape of the book is deliberately vague, not rooted (as some have suggested) in (say) the Bedfordshire countryside.

1160. See *Seasonable counsel*, p. 62, where Bunyan says that 'A man when he suffereth for Christ, is set upon an Hill, upon a Stage, as in a Theatre, to play a part for God in the World.'

1161. Macaulay, *John Bunyan*, p. 401.

1162. Augustine makes a similar point about animals in general: *Sermons* 8:8, in *The works of Saint Augustine* (ET by Edmund Hill OP) (Brooklyn, NY: New City, 1990), p. 245.

1163. *A book for boys and girls*, p. 219. In *Grace abounding* Bunyan compares his condition unfavourably with that of animals such as the toad or horse, 'for I knew they had no soul to perish' (see, e.g., paras. 104 and 187).

1164. Husain (1938) pp. 1–22; Carey (1990) pp. 15 and 21–2.

1165. Carey (1990) p. 43.

1166. *Devotions*, First Prayer, p. 10.

1167. We should note the interesting argument of Schoenfeldt (1994, esp. p. 79) that Donne explicitly located the sense of the divine, and the imagery used to articulate it, within one's social and personal experience. 'What many of Donne's best religious poems do is explore the profound sociability that links humans and God by addressing God in the deferential language that Donne had come to know so well in his own professional experience' (p. 80). And Stachniewski (1991, p. 291) goes further in suggesting that Donne 'felt his dependence on God to resemble his dependence on secular patronage with its attendant frustration, humiliation and despair'. There may well be some truth in this, and in Stachniewski's further suggestion that Donne learned, from having to deal with his own benefactors, a rhetoric of supplication which he then turned to good effect in dealing with God (though see the points made by Strier (1996)). But we should not press the analogy too far; Donne himself explicitly compares the boldness with which we may approach God with the submissiveness he clearly believes appropriate to addressing an earthly monarch (though we may feel here that Latimer achieves a healthier balance between the two):

> God admits, even expostulation, from his servants; almost rebukes and chidings from his servants . . . If we have an apprehension when we beginne to pray, that God doth not heare us, not regard us, God is content that in the fervor of that prayer, we say with David, *Evigila Domine* and *Surge Domine, Awake O Lord*, and *Arise O Lord* [Psalm 44.23]; God is content to be told, that he was in bed, and asleepe, when he should heare us . . . God is content to be told, that he is slack and dilatory when he should deliver us [Psalm 74.11] . . . Bring a petition to any earthly Prince, and say to him, *Evigila*, and *Surge*, would your Majesty would awake, and read this petition . . . what Prince would not (and justly) conceive an indignation against such a petitioner? (Sermon 3.5, pp. 145–6)

1168. This is a huge subject, beyond the competence of this writer. From the perspective of Christian spirituality, however, we may reasonably assert that the established view of Donne represented by T. S. Eliot, Helen Gardner (introd. to ed. cit. of the *Poems*), Louis Martz (1954) and others underestimates the extent of Donne's Calvinism and thus the impact of his inner anxiety. Carey (1990, p. 32) and Shaw (1981, p. 39) are surely nearer the mark; and Stachniewski (1991, chapter 6) convincingly argues that what Martz (1954, esp. pp. 43–56) sees as Ignatian-style meditation in the *Holy sonnets* is in fact a strongly Protestant understanding of meditation combined with a desperate longing on Donne's part to free himself from the onset of Calvinist anxiety about election. So too, Martz's argument (1954, pp. 55–6) that the last ten lines of *Goodfriday. 1613. Riding westward* is a perfect example of an Ignatian colloquy is not convincing: Donne's conclusion is just as compatible with a more Calvinist spirituality. The significance of the fact that a form of English neo-Calvinism remained the dominant orthodoxy in the Church of England during much of Donne's life is often forgotten. See also the interesting article by Rollin (1986), arguing that the *Holy sonnets* articulate a pervasive religious melancholy which is close to what modern psychiatry would call a form of affective disorder: he suggests that they illustrate Burton's concept of 'religious melancholy' (1986, p. 134), reflected in (e.g.) the frequent and violent alternation of moods within the *Sonnets*. This melancholy was not exclusive to Donne: it formed part of a wider mood during the first half of the seventeenth century, perhaps reflecting a widespread feeling that 'time was running out', and possible too a feeling that Renaissance optimism and confidence had failed to deliver (see Scallon (1975) pp. 155–6).

1169. See esp. the anti-Jesuit treatise *Ignatius his conclave* (1611), and the anti-Protestant treatise *The coutier's library* (1611), which Carey (1990, p. 21) describes as a 'bitter little satire'.

1170. See Carey (1990) p. 41; Booty, introduction to the Classics of Western Spirituality edn, p. 15.

1171. For the *Devotions* see esp. Strier (1996).

1172. All references to these in what follows are from Potter and Simpson's edition, and are given by volume and number: thus 1:5 indicates Sermon no.5 in volume 1.

1173. See Potter and Simpson, introduction to the Sermons, 1:118 and 140, and 10:295 and 345–58; Bush (1945) p. 306; Halewood (1970) pp. 59–60; Patrick Grant, 'Augustinian spirituality and the *Holy sonnets* of John Donne', in *English Literary History* 38 (1971), pp. 542–61. The influence of Augustine on love is particularly evident in Sermon 1:5.

1174. See Veith (1985) pp. 32–3. Strier ('John Donne awry and squint: the *Holy Sonnets*, 1608–1610', in *Modern Philology* 86 (1989), p. 361) argues that Donne is not a convinced Calvinist so much as someone 'who is both unable to be so and unable to admit that he is unable to be so'. Stachniewski (1991, p. 262) goes further and stresses the important influence of Calvin on Donne's poetry, esp. the *Holy sonnets*. Shaw (1981, p. 35) argues that Donne's understanding of vocation is influenced by Calvin, and that, like Calvin, he conceives of it in a twofold manner – God calls Christians to salvation, and he also calls each to a particular station in life.

1175. See, e.g., Sermon 7:9, p. 237, and 7:12, p. 301.

1176. Sermon 8:9, p. 224; cf. Sermon 9:5, p. 137 'Whatsoever is any thing, hath a beeing, and whatsoever hath so, hath in that very beeing some affinity with God, some assimilation to God.'

1177. *Devotions*, Ninth Expostulation, p. 48.

1178. Sermon 6:7, p. 152.

1179. Sermon 6:7, pp. 153–4.

1180. Sermon 3:4, p. 121. Donne has little time for the monastic life, which he considers introspective and selfish: see e.g. Sermon 3:6, pp. 168–9; Sermon 3:10, pp. 233–4; Sermon 3:11, p. 242 'God did not place Adam in a Monastery on one side, and Eve in a Nunnery on the other . . . They that build wals and cloysters to frustrate Gods institution of mariage, advance the Doctrine of Devils in forbidding mariage.' Sermon 6:7 'salvation is a more extensive thing . . . then sullen cloystrall, that have walled salvation in a monastery, or in an ermitage, take it to be' (p. 151). Cf. also Sermon 6:10, p. 215; Sermon 7:3, p. 104, criticizing the monastic life on the grounds that man 'is not sent into this world to live out of it, but to live in it'; and Sermon 7:4, p. 139). His early polemical work *Pseudo-Martyr* is full of anti-monastic sentiment.

1181. Sermon 2:13, p. 279; cf. Sermon 4:7 'Every man is a little world, sayes the Philosopher; Every man is a little Church too' (p. 194); Sermon 6:12 'Every man is a little World' (p. 251); Sermon 6:3 'From the beginning God intimated a detestation, a dislike of singularity; of beeing Alone' (p. 81).

1182. Sermon 2:13, p. 280.

1183. Sermon 2:17, p. 336.

1184. *Devotions*, Seventeenth Meditation, pp. 86–7.

1185. *Devotions*, p. 103. For other references to the bells tolling, see Sermon 4:1, p. 52, where again it is a *memento mori*; Sermon 6:3 'When at any midnight I heare a bell toll from this steeple, must not I say to my selfe, what have I done at any time for the instructing or rectifying of that mans Conscience?'; Sermon 6:8 'A man wakes at midnight full of unclean thoughts, and he heares a passing Bell; this is an occasionall meercy, if he call that his own knell' (p. 171); Sermon 8:7 'Is there any man, that in his chamber hears a bell toll for another man, and does not kneel down to pray for that dying man?' (p. 175); Sermon 10:4, p. 111; Sermon 10:11 (Donne's last sermon), p. 241. For the importance of bells in this context, see Watt (1991) pp. 113–15 and Strier (1996) pp. 106–7 (who notes how Donne's references to the use of bells is directed against the Puritans, who opposed them). John Newton was to make the same point in one of his *Olney hymns* (*The tolling bell*, Book 2 number 74).

1186. Sermon 1:3, p. 207. Cf. also Sermon 3:4 'Because the Lord reigneth, every Island doth rejoice; that is, every man' (p127); Sermon 3:10 'The Holy Ghost in this [text] collects Man, abridges Man, summes up Man in an unity, in the consideration of one, of himselfe. *Oportet hominem fieri unum* (Clement of Alexandria), Man must grow in his consideration, till he be but one man, one individuall man' (p. 227).

1187. Sermon 3:11, p. 246.

1188. Sermon 9:2, pp. 80–1.

1189. *Devotions*, Fourth Meditation, pp. 19–20; see also Eighth Meditation, pp. 40–1; and the sonnet *I am a little world*, where he argues that his 'little world' is pervaded entirely by sin; and the comments of Shaw (1981) p. 47.

1190. 'It is intire man that God hath care of, and not the soule alone' (*Pseudo-Martyr* 3, p. 38).

1191. Sermon 2:1, p. 59, commenting on the 'arrows' of Psalm 38.2 in a manner similar to Shakespeare's 'slings and arrows of outrageous fortune'.

1192. See, e.g., the vivid use of a theme from St Gregory the Great in Sermon 1:4, p. 224. See also Husain (1938) pp. 77–93.

1193. Sermon 2:3, p. 107.

1194. Cf. Sermon 1:2, where he reflects on what it means for someone to set their heart on evil: it is not simply 'a delightful dwelling upon the meditation of that sin' which seduces his imagination; rather 'it is, when by a habitual custom in sin, the sin arises meerly and immediately from my self . . . Such a wilful Madness, and such a voluntary and natural Devil to it self, as that we should be ambitious, though we were in an Hospital . . . This is the evil of the heart, by the mis-use of Gods grace, to devest [sic] and lose all tenderness and remorse in sin' (p179).

1195. Sermon 2:4.

1196. Sermon 2:5, p. 132.

1197. Sermon 2:5, p. 135. The reference is of course to Hebrews12.1.

1198. Sermon 2:5, p. 140.

1199. Sermon 2:3, pp. 112–13.

1200. Sermon 6:13, p. 265.

1201. Sermon 5:8, p. 177.

1202. Sermon 6:13, p. 279.

1203. Sermon 10:1, p. 63.

1204. Sermon 6:13, p. 265. The thought here is not far distant from the famous opening of Calvin's *Institutes* (I.1.1, pp. 36–8), but the implicit evaluation of human nature is more positive than Calvin's. The emphasis on wonder is characteristic of many aspects of Renaissance and Baroque piety: T. G. Bishop reminds us that 'between the efforts of Columbus, Copernicus, and Bruno the dimensions of space expanded, and travellers to undiscovered countries returned with news, words and objects surpassing the dreams of merchants and monarchs – pepper, canaries, comets, and gold. All Europe seemed hungry for amazement' (*Shakespeare and the theatre of wonder* (Cambridge UP, 1996), p. 37).

1205. Sermon 6:13, pp. 265–6.
1206. Sermon 2:6, p. 157. For the importance of contrition in Donne's spirituality, see Booty (1982).
1207. Sermon 5:14, p. 276.
1208. Sermon 9:13, p. 310. For his criticisms of the Roman practice of sacramental confession, see *Pseudo-Martyr* 8, pp. 164–78.
1209. Sermon 1:3, pp. 184–5 – Donne echoes scholastic thought here.
1210. Sermon 1:3, p. 198.
1211. Sermon 1:3, p. 205. Donne writes more extensively about the processes of change in Sermon 1:4, pp. 227–32.
1212. Sermon 1:5, p. 244.
1213. Sermon 2:2, p. 78; cf. Sermon 3:6 'I thinke we find no words in Christs mouth so often, as *vae* [= woe], and *Amen*. Each of them hath two significations: as almost all Christs words, and actions have; consolation, and commination' (p. 163).
1214. *A Litanie*, 23–24, p. 24. Gardner (ed. cit. p. 90) criticizes the excessive stress on the sense of hearing in these stanzas, though the emphasis is effective. Cf. Sermon 2:3: 'The Organ that God hath given the naturall man, is the *eye*; he sees God in the creature. The Organ that God hath given the Christian, is the *ear*; he hears God in his Word' (p. 114).
1215. *Poems*, p. 51, using the 1633 MS text, which seems more satisfactory notwithstanding Gardner's criticisms of it (ed. cit. pp. 109–11).
1216. *Devotions*, Seventeenth Expostulation, p. 89.
1217. Sermon 3:16, p. 343. In his early work *Pseudo-Martyr* Donne, reflecting on the sufferings involved in responding to Christ's call, says that 'Christ promises a reward, but not to take away the persecution; but so to mingle and compound them, and make them both of one taste, and indifferency, that wee shall not distinguish, which is the meate and which is the sauce, but nourish our spirituall growth as well with the persecution, as with the reward' (1, p. 33).
1218. The question of Donne's relationship with Calvinist orthodoxy is complex: the belief of this writer is that it remains his primary reference point after his conversion, even though he did not accept it uncritically. See (among many discussions of this point) Carey (1990) pp. 224–8; Stachniewski (1991) chapter 6; Doerksen (1997), esp. pp. 23–4. It is in any case unlikely that someone who moved from Catholicism to the Church of England at this period would remain broadly Catholic in theology: there would have been little point in the conversion.
1219. Sermon 3:16, pp. 344–5.
1220. For ths subject in general, see Husain (1938) pp. 120–43.
1221. Sermon 2:1, p. 54.
1222. As with the conversion of St Paul; Sermon 6:10, p. 212.
1223. Sermon 2:6, p. 154.
1224. Sermon 2:6, p. 155.
1225. Sermon 2:6, p. 161; cf. Sermon 5:17, p. 363.
1226. Sermon 7:1, p. 54.
1227. Sermon 7:1, p. 55.
1228. This is of course a rich biblical theme: see esp. 2 Corinthians, where St Paul compares the weight of sin (1.8) with the far greater weight of glory (4.17), reflecting the Hebrew word *kabod*, glory, whose root meaning is 'weight'.
1229. Sermon 4:13, p. 335.
1230. Sermon 4:13, p. 337.
1231. Sermon 4:13, p. 338.
1232. Sermon 6:1, p. 49.
1233. Sermon 4:13, p. 343.
1234. Sermon 4:2, p. 84.
1235. Sermon 8:4, p. 120. On this stress on prayer leading to action, see also Sermon 8:15 'The best

words are but words, but they are the fore-runners of Deeds', &c (p. 342).

1236. Sermon 5:12, p. 232.

1237. Sermon 5:12, p. 237.

1238. Sermon 5:17, p. 345. He often notes the dangers of distractions in prayer (see, e.g., Sermon 10:1 'The spirit of slunber closes mine eyes, and I pray drousily; Or *spiritus vertiginis*, the spirit of deviation, and vaine repetition, and I pray giddily', p. 56).

1239. Sermon 5:12, p. 233.

1240. Malcolm, in *Macbeth* Act IV Scene 3.

1241. Sermon 5:17, p. 347.

1242. Sermon 3:5 p. 152; cf. Sermon 7:12, p. 306; cf. also Sermon 7:10, where Donne says that 'God took it not ill, at Davids hands, to be awaked, and to be called up, as though hee were asleepe at our prayers' (p. 269); and Sermon 5:18, p. 364, where he says that 'Prayer hath the nature of Violence.' But cf. also Sermon 7:12, p. 324, where he warns against 'an over-homelines and familiarity with God in the acts of Religion'.

1243. Sermon 1:7, pp. 269 and 271.

1244. So Tertullian; cf. Sermon 7:12, p. 306.

1245. Sermon 5:14, p. 272. See the remarks of Schoenfeldt (1991, pp. 190–1).

1246. Sermon 5:14, p. 289.

1247. Sermon 5:14, p. 291.

1248. Sermon 5:14, pp. 292–3. Donne had an abiding interest in angels (Carey (1990) p. 28): his angelology derived from Aquinas. They recur frequently in his *Devotions* (e.g. Seventh Expostulation, p. 38) and elsewhere (Sermon 1:3, p. 207; Sermon 1:7, pp. 282–4; Sermon 3:9, pp. 215–18; Sermon 4:2, pp. 79–81; Sermon 4:3, pp. 127–8; Sermon 8:3, pp. 105–9; Sermon 8:16, pp. 355–72; Sermon 10:1, pp. 43–64). They are of course another reminder of Donne's emphasis on the common, in this case on the communion of saints.

1249. Sermon 7:9, p. 251.

1250. Hence Donne's recurrent stress on the use of memory: 'The art of salvation, is but the art of memory' (Sermon 2:2, p. 73; cf. p. 74). Hence too his observation that God sometimes speaks of the future, but using the present tense ('Behold I doe come upon thee as a Thiefe') because 'It is so sure, that he will doe it, that he is said, to have done it already' (Sermon 8:2, p. 68).

1251. Sermon 8:2, p. 75.

1252. Sermon 8:2, pp. 77–8.

1253. Sermon 3:16, pp. 339–40; see also Sermon 7:1, pp. 69–71.

1254. *Devotions*, Twelfth Meditation, p. 63.

1255. Sermon 2:6, p. 159.

1256. Donne frequently stresses the spiritual value of rumination, in the manner of cows: Sermon 4:4, p. 136; Sermon 4:12, p. 306; Sermon 6:1, p. 52.

1257. Sermon 4:8, pp. 225–6.

1258. Sermon 3:4, p. 122.

1259. Sermon 10:2, pp. 72–3.

1260. *Poems*, ed. cit., p. 188.

1261. Schoenfeldt (1991, p. 190), in an otherwise absorbing and important study of Herbert, appears to miss the crucial theological point of this poem.

1262. Shaw (1981) pp. 30–1; and see the excellent study by Strier (1983) as well as Doerksen's more recent and wide-ranging work (1997).

1263. Bush (1945) p. 136 n. 1.

1264. It has been argued that his brief political experience was sufficient to propel him into quiet parochial life (so Wall, introd. to Herbert (1981) pp. 12–23, arguing that the warmongering of Prince (later King) Charles in the 1624 Parliament was what made Herbert decide to quit). Herbert's own comment on the matter may appear in *Submission*:

> How know I, if thou shouldst me raise,
> That I should then raise thee?
> Perhaps great places and thy praise
> Do not so well agree. (*Poems*, p. 95)

1265. The edition was master-minded by Nicholas Ferrar, a friend of Herbert, and founder of the religious community at Little Gidding.

1266. Wall (introduction to Herbert (1981)) argues, plausibly enough, that Herbert began work on this substantial collection of poems relatively early in his short life. Freer (1972, p. 40) suggests that the arrangement of *The temple* is the same as that of the Psalter: each has scattered groupings of poems within a larger apparently random one. But, despite Herbert's clear indebtedness to the Hebrew Psalms, his argument is not very convincing.

1267. *The country parson*, p. 224.

1268. *Outlandish proverbs (Jacula prudentum):* see Hutchinson, ed. cit. in Bibliography, pp. 568–71.

1269. Clarke (1992) p. 132.

1270. *Cornaro's treatise of temperance*, ed. Hutchinson pp. 291–303: this was published in 1634 by Nicholas Ferrar. Herbert's translation is based on the Latin version of Cornaro's treatise by Leonard Lessius SJ of Louvain (Hutchinson, p. 564).

1271. Tuve (1952) stresses the medieval poetic and liturgical background to (e.g.) a poem like *The sacrifice* (see esp. 1952, pp. 32–3) – suggesting as model the medieval group of poems of the *O vos omnes qui transitis* genre, which reflect on the Lamentations text in the context of Christ's passion. One wonders whether Tuve is correct in assuming the extensive knowledge of such a background among Herbert's parishioners and first readers as she does (e.g. on p. 70, and again on p. 164) (and see Martz's critical comments (1954, p. 91): he sees the poem more as a meditation on the liturgy (p. 92)). Martz himself (1954 rev.1962, and 1994) argues for St François de Sales as well as Sidney and the Bible as key influences upon Herbert, though Clarke (1997, pp. 71–126) undermines this theory, convincingly showing (see esp. p. 81) that Herbert's use of scripture is not the imaginative meditation favoured by Counter-Reformation figures, but the Protestant approach rooted in the conviction that the living Word can and does speak directly to the believer (not only, or even primarily, through the imagination). Martz also suggests (1989, p. 36) that the early version of *The temple* (pre–1633, and now in Dr Williams's Library, London) is more pervasively Calvinist than the later, more nuanced version, partly because it lacks the strongly eucharistic poems of the later MS. He argues, *contra* Strier (1983), that the later version represents and dramatizes 'the tense and delicate equilibrium that prevailed in the Church of England for most of Herbert's lifetime' (1989, p. 38), and suggests that some of the poems offer a 'generous ambiguity' of interpretation quite deliberately (see 1989, p. 40), though sometimes his argument reads like a rather modern view of a seventeenth-century text. Martz's argument is weakened by his assumption that no Calvinist could be bold or witty in the presence of God (1989, p. 53) – a quite unfounded assumption, as any reading of Bunyan would confirm. Clarke (1992, pp. 139–41 and 1997, pp. 27–70) argues for the influence of the Florentine reformer Savonarola, whose reputation in England during this period was considerable; and she suggests that Savonarola's view of *simplicitas* (in his *De simplicitate Christianae vitae*) as a divinely given principle of inner consistency and integrity which eschews display and ornament seems in particular to have attracted Herbert. From our point of view the important arguments relate to Herbert's theological roots: for which, see esp. Halewood (1970), insisting on 'the essentially Protestant and Augustinian nature of [Herbert's] preoccupations' (p. 89), Strier (1983), Veith (1985) and Clarke 1997: all these offer authoritative and persuasive arguments in favour of the essentially reformed nature of Herbert's theology, Veith and Clarke explicitly and convincingly arguing that Herbert's doctrine and spirituality are thoroughly Calvinist (see e.g. Veith (1985) p. 34 and Clarke (1997) p. 10).

1272. *The country parson* 4, pp. 228–9. For Herbert's indebtedness to the Bible in general, see Bloch (1985).

1273. *Poems*, p. 58. Cf also the opening lines of 'Charms and knots':
      Who reade a chapter when they rise,
      Shall ne're be troubled with ill eyes. (*Poems*, p. 96)

1274. Doerksen, however (1997, pp. 74–5), suggests that the Prayer Book in itself was far less important for Herbert than the Bible itself.

1275. Martz (1954) pp. 280–1. Clarke (1997, pp. 142–3) notes the way Protestant writers interpret scriptural texts (esp. from the Psalms) and apply them to their own experience, and says: 'It is a Protestant article of faith that Scripture is about the Christian's experience: the interpretation of the sacred text involves finding Scriptural parallels for his own circumstances, so that experience acts as a commentary on the text. This is exactly the function of Psalm meditation in English spirituality.'

1276. Clarke (1992) p. 132.

1277. See esp. Asals (1989) who argues that the Christian commentaries on the Psalms represent the chief influence on *The temple*. Thus (e.g.) she notes esp. St Augustine's comment on the first verse of Psalm 22 ('My God, my God, why have you forsaken me?'), quoted in *The sacrifice*, that it is the cry of both our old humanity (*vetus homo noster*) crucified with Christ, and of Christ himself – and suggests that this influenced Herbert's several 'I's' in *The temple* (1989, pp. 515–16): they are all at once Herbert, the church, and Christ. The conflation of individual and corporate is certainly one of the key debts that Herbert owes to the Psalms (1989, p. 516). Cf. also 'Affliction 1' with Psalm 84 (Asals (1989) pp. 519–20). See also Kuczynski (*Prophetic song*; full ref. in the Bibliography to Chapter 4) pp. 219 and 221. Freer (1972, p. 5) argues for the importance of the metrical psalms in understanding Herbert's poetry and piety, not least because of Herbert's love of and interest in music. Freer argues (1972, p. 11)that Herbert probably knew the Sidney psalter, and the 'Old Version' of Sternhold and Hopkins' metrical psalter. He also points out connections of style or imagery between specific psalms and Herbert's poems (e.g. Psalm 103 and 'The flower', p. 222), though these connections are not always well founded (e.g. that suggested by Freer between Psalm 102 and 'The collar', p. 200).

1278. See, e.g., *Easter*, with its reference to Psalm 57 (proper for Easter) (*Poems*, p. 41); or *Whitsunday*, with its reference to the proper Psalm 68 (*Poems*, p. 59).

1279. *The country parson*, 1, p. 225.

1280. *The country parson*, 5, p. 230. Note that this was required of priests in the 1604 Canons Ecclesiastical.

1281. *The country parson*, 6, pp. 232–5.

1282. *The country parson*, 6, p. 233.

1283. *The country parson*, 6, p. 234. Calvinists, and Herbert too, believed holiness to be itself a gift from God, not in any way to the credit of those who manifested it; and one sign of it was precisely this rejoicing in another's good.

1284. *The country parson*, 24, p. 262.

1285. *The country parson*, 26, pp. 265–6.

1286. See Bernard's letter to Aelred in Aelred of Rievaulx, *Mirror of charity*, trans. E. Connor (CF 17) (Kalamazoo: Cistercian Publications, 1990), pp. 70–1 (Latin text in *Corpus Christianorum continuatio mediaevalis* 1) (Turnhout: Brepols, 1971), p. 4); and cf. St Bernard's remark at the beginning of one of his sermons on the Song of Songs: 'Today the text we are to study is the book of our own experience' (Sermon 3:1 in Bernard of Clairvaux, *On the Song of Songs I* (CF 4) (Kalamazoo: Cistercian Publications, 1977), p. 16 (Latin text in Leclercq, J. & Rochais, H. M. (eds.), *Sancti Bernardi Opera* (Rome: Editiones Cistercienses, 1957–77), vol. 1, p. 14)).

1287. *The country parson* 33, p. 278. Strier (1983, p. 198) argues that this reflects a depreciation of the intellect on Herbert's part: experience and feeling always takes precedence for Herbert over learning and artifice; in *A true Hymne* he makes this explicit:
      The fineness which a hymne or psalme affords,
      Is, when the soul unto the lines accords.
      (p168; and see Strier (1983) p. 202)
Technical proficiency is as nothing in comparison with sincerity and love, and from the viewpoint of the Reformation it would in any case be a form of justification by works (Strier (1983) p. 205). Cf. also 'Yeeres know more then bookes' (*Outlandish proverbs* no. 928, p. 351).

1288. *The country parson*, 3, p. 227.

1289. *The country parson*, 11, p. 243. For the significance of hospitality for Herbert, see note 1248 below (to 'Love [III]'.)

1290. *The country parson*, 27, pp. 267–8.

1291. 'The Church-porch' ll.331–6, p. 19. On *Aaron* as embodying the true holiness of the priest which comes from regeneration, see Strier (1983) pp. 127ff and Shaw (1981) p. 95. For the social resonances of Herbert's use of the language and imagery of courtesy and humility, see Schoenfeldt (1991), esp. p. 209.

1292. 'Man', in *Poems*, pp. 90–2.

1293. 'Mans medley', in *Poems*, pp. 131–2.

1294. *Poems*, p. 168.

1295. *Poems*, pp. 88–9.

1296. *Poems*, p. 115.

1297. *Poems*, p. 177. See also the famous 'The elixir' (pp. 184–5).

1298. Notwithstanding the counter-argument of Tuve (1952, p. 103).

1299. *Institutes* 1.14.21, p. 157.

1300. *The country parson* 30, pp. 270–1.

1301. *The country parson*, 34, p. 281. Cf. with the magnificent General Thanksgiving prayer, composed by Bishop Edward Reynolds, in the 1662 version of the Prayer Book: 'we bless thee for our Creation, Preservation, and all the blessings of this life . . .'

1302. *The country parson* 30, p. 272.

1303. *Poems*, p. 117.

1304. See Hutchinson, ed. cit. of the *Poems*, p. 518.

1305. Calvin, *Institutes* 2.15.6, p. 432. For 'Providence,' see Strier (1983) p. 169.

1306. See, e.g., 'Antiphon (2)' (*Poems*, pp. 92–3), an exquisite miniature; and *Praise (2)* ('King of Glorie, King of Peace') (p. 146), and many others above. Shaw (1981, p. 76) suggests that for Herbert the offering of praise is 'the one all-important human action'. For the relationship of prayer and praise in Herbert, see Schoenfeldt (1991) pp. 190–1.

1307. *Poems*, pp. 171–2, and see the analysis in Strier (1983, pp. 136ff).

1308. *Poems*, p. 55.

1309. *Institutes* 3.2.33, p. 499; Strier (1983) p. 233. See also Schoenfeldt (1991) pp. 126–7.

1310. Letter XIX, ed. Hutchinson, p. 381.

1311. *Outlandish proverbs* 2, p. 321.

1312. *Poems*, p. 145. Strier (1983, p. 115) seems a little harsh on this poem, perhaps underrating its primarily pastoral – rather than theological – concern. It is surely right to see both this poem and *Conscience* as directed towards the pastoral experience of anxiety.

1313. 'The church-porch', ll.145–50, p. 12, and 451–6, p. 24.

1314. *The country parson* 21, p. 255.

1315. *The country parson* 22, p. 259.

1316. *The country parson* 18, p. 252.

1317. *The country parson* 13, p. 246.

1318. 'The church-porch', ll.403–8, p. 22.

1319. We must beware of reading too extensive a eucharistic overtone into Herbert's poetry: especially 'Love (3)', which Strier convincingly argues (1983, p. 78) is about true Christian love, not the eucharist, especially in illustrating God's gentle but irresistible grace ('God is a host Who will not take no for an answer', Strier (1983) p. 83). He also argues (p. 191) that 'The altar' is not eucharistic either: the altar referred to is the broken altar of the poet's heart, as in Psalm 51 (p. 192 and, for a different interpretation, Guibbory (1998) pp. 46–50). Herbert's attitude to church buildings becomes clearer if it is compared with a contemporary view by another member of the Church of England: Richard Montagu, in a tract concerned to encourage Roman Catholics to return to the established church, says that the church building 'is most Holy, sacred, holy ground, called, and esteemed by us Gods house, separated and Consecrated to Gods Service, peculiarly to Prayers, and Administration of the holy Sacramentes, used accordingly, and applyed onely to that end' ('Richard Montagu: "Concerning Recusancie of Communion with the Church of England"', ed. A. Milton and A. Walsham, in Taylor, S. (ed.), *From Cranmer to Davidson: a Church of England miscellany* (Church of England Record Society) (Woodbridge: Boydell, 1999), p. 91).

1320. *The country parson* 6, p. 231.

1321. 'The church-porch' ll.396–401 p. 22.

1322. *The country parson* 2, p. 226. In an important exploration of Herbert's work, Schoenfeldt (1991) argues that Herbert employs, in his relationship with God, that subtle rhetorical blend of humility and boldness which is characteristic of the attitude of the seventeenth-century citizen towards his or her sovereign, drawing in particular on the language of Renaissance courtesy as well as on his own experience of public life (for which see, e.g., p. 29).

1323. *The country parson* 28, p. 268. For Herbert's subtle boldness in the face of secular power, see Schoenfeldt (1991) chapter 1, esp. pp. 35–6.

1324. ll. 77–8, *Poems*, p. 9, and ll. 89–90, p. 10. Cf. ibid. ll. 120–6, p. 1; ll. 205–10, p. 15; l.253, p. 16; and ll. 256–7, p. 16. But note that in *Content* he commends gentleness and pliancy (*Poems*, p. 69), though he is here referring to a capacity to sit lightly to worldly status and honours.

1325. Schoenfeldt (1994, p. 77) argues that, in identifying the theological context of Herbert's attitude to supplicatory prayer, we must not lose sight of its indebtedness to 'the language of everyday hierarchical interaction as a dynamic resource of ways for talking to and about God'. This is in striking contrast to the poetry of Herrick, Vaughan and Traherne, who 'deliberately disengage both themselves and their religious poetry from the social drama that Donne and Herbert exploit'. Elsewhere (1989) Schoenfeldt further argues that Herbert's poem 'Dedication' demonstrates his sensitive awareness of how any such act of dedication, indeed any approach to God (as to a secular monarch) combines apparent (and sometimes genuine) humility with a deliberate drawing of attention to oneself. However, a good deal of what he says is as true of the spirituality of the Psalms as of any contemporary secular analogies; e.g. Schoenfeldt's remark that 'In the act of showing how God makes him and his poems . . . Herbert also tries to "make" God behave in a particular way towards him.' This subtlety in dealing with God in what may appear a manipulative way, together with a ready use of secular language in spirituality, may simply be one more reflection of the pervasive influence of the Psalms on Herbert. Schoenfeldt's thesis is in any case not particularly surprising, though it is vigorously controverted by Sister Thekla (*George Herbert – idea and image: a study of The Temple* (Newport Pagnell: Greek Orthodox Monastery of the Assumption, Filgrave, 1974), who declares that: 'He [Herbert] consciously rejects, as far as it was possible, all the words which for him are too grossly associated with sensuality in any form, or with the scintillation of court wit, and he fastidiously selects and preserves a distilled company of words, which he considers the most fitting instrument for his intercourse with God' (p. 13). This is altogether unconvincing. In general, Schoenfeldt's argument simply reflects the theological assumptions Herbert is making: that prayer, as a response to what God has done for us in Christ, may (indeed must) encompass the whole of our lives, and may be offered with a boldness that is itself the consequence of knowing ourselves to be accepted and loved. There need be nothing unhealthily manipulative about that.

1326. Bloch (1985, pp. 87–90) points out the many biblical allusions in this poem. Thus 'reversed thunder' reflects the sense in which, for Herbert, prayer is the bold appropriation of one of God's most powerful weapons, precisely for use against him.

1327. Cf. 'Artillerie': 'Then we are shooters both' (*Poems*, p. 139). Note that Donne speaks of the 'Mercies, Prayers, Sermons, Sacraments, (which are the Engines and Ammunition which God hath put into our hands)' (Sermon 1:3, p. 193). Cf. also Donne, Sermons 3:5, p. 152, and 7:12, p. 306, and Bunyan, *Seasonable counsel*, p. 97, where he says that 'the Artillery of the Christian, is the word, faith, and prayer'. Cf. also Richard Crashaw, *Steps to the Temple*, in which he describes prayer as 'loves great Artillery' (from 'On a prayer book sent to Mrs M. R.', p. 127). Cf. also Milton's 'Lycidas' ll.130–1, where he refers to 'that two-handed engine at the door,/Stands ready to smite once, and smite no more' (p. 249): this may refer to the sword of God which Milton saw as representing Protestantism (see the detailed note in ed. cit. of Milton's poems, pp. 238–9]; and Peter Sterry's letter to his son, in which he exhorts him to 'Let Prayer be the great Engin of your Life' (in Sterry, *Select writings*, ed. Matar (1994) p. 126).

1328. See Clements (1979) p. 34. Clements suggests resonances between the sixteenth-century

Lorenzo Scupoli's treatise *Spiritual combat* and Herbert's approach to God in these poems; but he recognizes (p. 41) that the tone is quite different, and there is no clear evidence tht Herbert was influenced by Scupoli's approach, which is much more sharply directed towards combat with the devil, not an assault on God. Clarke (1997, p. 120) suggests instead Luis de Granada's use of the Augustinian concept of 'jaculatory prayer' – that is, short prayers designed to have the maximum effect on God.

1329. Freer argues (1972, p. 210) that 'Herbert's proclamations of despair are usually supported by a reasoned confidence in, if not a personal cure for, the despair itself. He nearly always intuits a larger controlling purpose within which his despair serves some coherent function' (this is certainly true of 'The collar', which Veith (1985, p. 34) describes as 'the supreme Calvinist poem'). Freer's suggestion of a parallel between 'The collar' and Psalm 102 (1972, p. 200) is far-fetched; but his general point about the similarities between the lament psalms and Herbert's poems is certainly not.

1330. See 'Prayer (2)', in *Poems*, p. 103, and Strier (1983) p. 197; and 'Jordan (2)', in *Poems*, pp. 102–3. Clarke (1997, pp. 39–42) suggests that Herbert was influenced by Savonarola in stressing the dynamism of prayer, and its character of ascent in lifting the soul up towards God: this upward movement is certainly characteristic of Herbert's view of prayer.

1331. These great biblical texts are surely closer to the heart of Herbert's spirituality here than the arguments advanced by Strier (1983, p. 99) and Schoenfeldt (1991, pp. 192–3) in connection with 'Artillerie': Strier argues that Herbert is here attacking the notion that rationalism has any relevance in the practice of religion, whilst Schoenfeldt says that Herbert 'raids the grim world of munitions to find a model for the vehement negotiations that occur between mortals and God'. Schoenfeldt is surely on stronger ground in pointing out that, in poems such as this, Herbert is redirecting the Christian tradition of spiritual combat from sin to God (1991, p. 195). For the influence of the Psalms on Herbert, see Zim (1987), and esp. Clarke (1997), chapter 3. Clarke (p. 140) cites examples of Calvinist use of the Psalms to resonate with contemporary Christian experience.

1332. *Poems*, p. 73.

1333. Strier suggests (1983, p. 181) that there could be a caesura after 'art', so that l.1 reads 'There thou art, struggling . . .'

1334. *Poems*, p. 106.

1335. See Strier (1983) p. 183; see also 'Gratefulnesse', in *Poems*, p. 124. Schoenfeldt's suggestion with regard to 'Sion' (1991, p. 173), that 'it is difficult not to shudder at the spectre of a sovereign who prefers harsh shrieks of pain to harmonious notes of music' surely misses the point: any loving parent would be far more concerned to hear, and far more responsive to, the former than the latter.

1336. 'Sion' (continued), in *Poems*, p. 107. Clarke (1997, pp. 18–19) points out that the word 'motion' was used by the Reformers (especially Calvin) to denote impulses from God vouchsafed to the elect.

1337. *Poems*, p. 132; see Strier (1983) pp. 186–8.

1338. *Poems*, p. 90. See Clarke (1997) p. 153.

1339. *Poems*, pp. 79–80. It is worth comparing the prayer of this poem with Henry Vaughan's fine 'Misery' (in *Silex scintillans*, ed. cit. pp. 234–7), which ends 'Till thou both mend and make me thine'.

1340. Wilcox (1987) suggests that Herbert's musical sympathies were with the older, contrapuntal musical style as against the newer more harmonic one (pp. 42–3). She also points out the evidence which argues for Herbert having a direct personal involvement in music-making (p. 43) and for the fact that he set his own poems to music (pp. 43–4). Here too the influence of the Psalms is important: Herbert was commonly known in the later seventeenth century as a second David, 'that incomparable sweet Singer of our Israel' (so Oliver Heywood, 1672, quoted in Wilcox (1987) p. 55). Wilcox argues that 'Herbert's affinity with music is not only structural but found in the overriding sense of his poems as 'songs' of complaint and praise, bridging by this means the artistic gulf between private and public expression which widened as the seventeenth century progressed' (1987, p. 57) – this too argues for the influence of the Psalms.

1341. *Poems*, pp. 133–4.

1342. *Poems*, pp. 148–50. See Clarke (1997) p. 151.

1343. *Poems*, p. 171. See Bloch (1985) pp. 261–79. Strier argues (1983, p. 167) that in this poem Herbert seeks to integrate God's love and wrath in a manner entirely consonant with that of Luther, for whom God's wrath was the essential concomitant of his love and a fundamental dimension of the 'theology of the cross'. Herbert's orientation here is devotional, and is echoed in 'Praise (3)', in which Herbert contrasts the 'God of the philosophers' fully engaged in ruling the universe with the intimately personal God and Father of Jesus Christ, who (so to speak) drops everything when Herbert (or anyone else) calls upon him. In Lutheran terms here, we move from glory to the cross (Strier (1983) p. 168). But Strier is less convincing when he says that 'Bitter-sweet' illustrates the fact that man's job is not to act in relation to God, but to 'feel': complaining and praising are more than feeling – they both envisage and help to create new and undreamed-of possibilities for the future (1983, p. 165).

1344. 'The strength of the religious poetry of the metaphysical poets is that they bring to their praise and prayer and meditation so much experience that is not in itself religious' (Helen Gardner, introduction to *The metaphysical poets* (Harmondsworth: Penguin, 1957, rev. edn 1966), p. 27). Schoenfeldt (1991, pp. 130–1) and others have pointed out that Herbert never idealizes suffering: rather he laments it; but above all he seeks to discern meaning within it.

1345. Schoenfeldt (1991, pp. 201–2) and others make the point that the imagery of hospitality and a shared table will doubtless have had a particular resonance for Herbert, not only because of their obvious eucharistic associations but because, until he settled at Bemerton for the last years of his short life, he had lived entirely as a guest, dependent on others' favour. Hence 'the contrast between divine hospitality and human poverty [runs] throughout *The temple*' (p. 201). Schoenfeldt argues, *contra* Strier, that Herbert is not concerned with the irresistibility of divine grace here, on the grounds that 'people do turn down invitations to supper; and humans to reject the gracious love of God' (1991, p. 214). But he answers his own objection a few pages later, commenting on the Book of Common Prayer rubrics for the Holy Communion: 'it is an unkind and ungrateful act to refrain from partaking of the rich feast which the Lord has prepared; but it is a perilous venture to approach such a table unworthily' (p. 220). *This* is the context in which to see what the doctrine of irresistible grace must have meant to Herbert.

1346. 'Love (III)', in *Poems*, pp. 188–9.

1347. McAdoo (1949) p. 139.

1348. Thornton (1983, p. 231) points out that they drew from three major sources in particular: first, the primitive and patristic tradition of the Church; secondly, the Protestant Reformers, though their borrowing was never uncritical; and thirdly, contemporary or near-contemporary Catholic devotional writing, such as Thomas à Kempis' *The imitation of Christ* and St François de Sales' *Introduction to the devout life*. The influence of the latter, especially on Taylor's *Holy living* and *Holy dying*, was almost certainly considerable, though Taylor scarcely acknowledges it: see T. K. Carroll's remarks in *Jeremy Taylor: selected works* (Classics of western spirituality) (New York: Paulist Press, 1990), p. 433; and Askew (1997) p. 11.

1349. *An apology for authorized and set forms of liturgy*, Preface 37, in *Works* vol. 5, p. 247.

1350. Askew (1997), in a marvellous study of Taylor's work, underlines the pervasive influence of Taylor's classical education on his work. For a good example of his massive patristic learning, see his arguments against transubstantiation in *The real presence* (e.g. chapter 12, in *Works* vol. 6, pp. 130–62).

1351. *A course of sermons* 1.19, in *Works* vol. 4, p. 237.

1352. *A course of sermons* 2.3, in *Works* vol. 4, p. 365.

1353. *Holy dying* 1.1, p. 21.

1354. *Holy dying* 5.8, pp. 226–7.

1355. *A course of sermons* 1.17, in *Works* vol. 4, p. 210.

1356. *Holy living* 2.6, p. 116.

1357. Coleridge remarks of Taylor's style: 'In all men and in all works of great genius the characteristic fault will be found in the characteristic excellence. Thus in Taylor, fulness, overflow, superfluity' (*Notes on English divines*, vol. 2, ed. D. Coleridge) (London: Moxon, 1853), p. 194).

1358. See Rivers (1991i) p. 18.

1359. Haller (1938) pp. 236–48; Stevenson (1994) p. 111. Chillingworth (1602–44), a friend of William Laud, was in effect the forebear of the Latitudinarians. In his *Brief lives*, John Aubrey describes him as someone who 'would always be disputing . . . he was the readiest and nimblest disputant of his time in the university; perhaps none has equalled him since'.

1360. See esp. Wood (1952). Most of Taylor's work is suffused with a concern for the spiritual guidance of those for whom he wrote; and he is well aware that those who guide others will be accountable for the guidance they give ('they that have the guiding of souls must remember that they . . . must render an account', *Clerus Domini* 3.15, in *Works* vol. 1, p. 23).

1361. See Stranks (1961) p. 69; for the influence of these two works see pp. 93–4. Askew (1997, p. 2) points out that, in writing *Holy living*, Taylor was seeking to offer a guide to holiness for members of the Church of England who could then have had little hope of seeing Prayer Book or monarchy restored to them.

1362. *A course of sermons* 2.5, in *Works* vol. 4, p. 382; see also Stranks (1961) p. 73; Carroll, introduction to *Jeremy Taylor: selected works* (1990), pp. 53–4.

1363. *Miscellaneous sermons* 6, in *Works* vol. 8, p. 376; cf. also *A discourse of the liberty of prophesying* 10, in *Works* vol. 8, pp. 494–9. Note that Taylor does not underestimate the importance of revelation – see, e.g., his sermon on the work of the Spirit in *A course of sermons* 2.1, in *Works* vol. 4, pp. 331–2.

1364. See, e.g., *The great exemplar*, Preface 43 (*Works* vol. 2, pp. 35–6). References to this text are given first to the 1653 edition and secondly (in brackets) to the edition of Taylor's *Works* cited in the Bibliography. The orthography is taken from the 1653 edition.

1365. *Ductor dubitantium* 1.2, in *Works* vol. 9, p. 61.

1366. *Ductor dubitantium* 1.2, in *Works* vol. 9, p. 72; cf. *The real presence* 10–12, in *Works* vol. 6, pp. 85–162.

1367. *Miscellaneous sermons* 6, in *Works* vol. 8, p. 384.

1368. *The great exemplar*, Preface 42 (*Works* vol. 2, p. 36).

1369. *The great exemplar* 1.5, p. 88 (*Works* vol. 2, p. 134); cf. *Miscellaneous sermons* 6: 'Holiness of life is the best way of finding out truth and understanding; not only as a natural medium, nor only as a prudent medium, but as a means by way of divine blessing' (*Works* vol. 8, p. 384).

1370. *A course of sermons* 1.12, in *Works* vol. 4, p. 145. Askew (1997, p. 163) memorably stresses this virtue in respect of *Holy living* and *Holy dying*: 'The two books are about political life, unemployment, market prices, parental anxiety, and terminal illness. Piety gets turned into generosity.'

1371. p. 150.

1372. *A course of sermons* 2.14, in *Works* vol. 4, p. 500.

1373. *A course of sermons* 1.12, in *Works* vol. 4, p. :151.

1374. p. 153.

1375. *A course of sermons* 2.14, in *Works* vol. 4, p. 500.

1376. *A course of sermons* 2.2, in *Works* vol. 4, p. 355.

1377. *Miscellaneous sermons* 3, in *Works* vol. 8, p. 287. Cf. 11, *Works* vol. 8, p. 532: 'What have your people to do whether Christ's body be in the sacrament by consubstantiation, or transubstantiation; whether purgatory be in the centre of the earth or in the air, or any where, or no where? and who but a mad man would trouble their heads with the intangled links of the fanatic chain of predestination?' Hence too Taylor's reiterated insistence on the role of the clergy as teachers and spiritual guides ('Let every minister teach his people the use, practice, methods and benefits of meditation or mental prayer', *Rules and advice to the clergy* 67, in *Works* vol. 1, p. 111).

1378. *Miscellaneous sermons* 3, in *Works* vol. 8, pp. 292 and 293; cf. also pp. 295–6; cf. *Unum necessarium* 1.43, in *Works* vol. 7, p. 389.

1379. *A discourse of the liberty of prophesying* 1, in *Works* vol. 5, p. 370; cf. *Miscellaneous sermons* 3, in *Works* vol. 8, pp. 288–9.

1380. *The worthy communicant* 1:3, in *Works* vol. 8, p. 31.
1381. *Holy living* 4.9, p. 251. For Taylor on repentance, see Hughes (1960) pp. 76–92.
1382. p. 251.
1383. p. 253; see Askew (1997) pp. 116–17. For the relationship between Christ's intercession and that of priests for their people, see *Clerus Domini* 7.5, in *Works* vol. 1, p. 45, and 7.8, pp. 47–8.
1384. *Miscellaneous sermons* 1, in *Works* vol. 8, p. 260.
1385. *A course of sermons* 1.15, in *Works* vol. 4, p. 191. For Taylor's views on original sin, see the succinct summary in Hughes (1960) pp. 31–5.
1386. It was by that appetite that the devil tempted Adam and Eve: *The great exemplar*, Preface 4, (*Works* vol. 2, p. 7).
1387. *The great exemplar*, Preface 7 (*Works* vol. 2, p. 8).
1388. *The great exemplar*, Preface 8 (*Works* vol. 2, p. 8).
1389. *The great exemplar*, Preface 11 (*Works* vol. 2, p. 12).
1390. *The great exemplar*, Preface 13 (*Works* vol. 2, p. 13). The reference here to 'religion, sobriety and justice' here echoes the suffrage in the Prayer Book's General Confession 'that we may hereafter live a godly, righteous and sober life' (I owe this point to Canon Reginald Askew).
1391. *Unum necessarium* 1.44, in *Works* vol. 7, p. 39.
1392. *A course of sermons* 2.14, in *Works* vol. 4, p. 503.
1393. *Holy living* 4.10, p. 262.
1394. *A course of sermons* 2.15, in *Works* vol. 4, p. 507.
1395. *A course of sermons* 2.15, in *Works* vol. 4, pp. 510–12.
1396. *The great exemplar* 3.15, p. 398.
1397. *Unum necessarium* 1.45, in *Works* vol. 7, pp. 39–40.
1398. *A course of sermons* 2.1, in *Works* vol. 4, p. 335. See also Wood (1952) pp. 103–40.
1399. p. 338.
1400. pp. 338–9.
1401. pp. 339–40; cf. also 2.14, *Works* vol. 4, pp. 499–500.
1402. *A course of sermons* 2.2, in *Works* vol. 4, p. 348.
1403. Taylor argues that the reference in 2 Peter 1.3–4 to becoming 'partakers of the divine nature' is mistaken: it is analogical – we become 'partakers of a divine nature, that is, of this new and godlike nature given to every person that serves God, whereby he is sanctified, and made the child of God, and framed into the likeness of Christ' (pp. 348–9).
1404. p. 351.
1405. *Holy dying* 1.3, p. 33.
1406. *Holy dying* 1.3, p. 34.
1407. *Holy living* 1.1, p. 18; cf. 1.3, pp. 33–5.
1408. *Holy living* 1.1, p. 18.
1409. *Holy living* 1.1, p. 19.
1410. *Holy dying* 1.3, pp. 37–8. For Taylor's emphasis on using time well, see Hughes (1960) pp. 119–20.
1411. *Holy living* 1.1, pp. 19–27.
1412. p. 21. He suggests that we should 'sometimes be curious to see the preparation which the sun makes, when he is coming forth from his chambers of the East'.
1413. pp. 24–5.
1414. p. 23; cf. p. 24: 'As much as may be, cut off all *impertinent and uselesse imployments* of your life, unnecessary and phantastick visits, long waitings upon great personages, where neither duty nor necessity, nor charity obliges us, all vain meetings, all laborious trifles, and whatsoever spends much time to no real, civil, religious, or charitable purpose.'
1415. p. 25.
1416. p. 26.
1417. *Holy living* 1.2, pp. 27–34.
1418. p. 28.
1419. p. 29.

1420. p. 32.
1421. *Holy living* 1.3, pp. 35–42. For the eucharistic implications of this in Taylor's work, see McAdoo (1988). Taylor insists on the real presence of Christ in the Eucharist, and that the body of Christ present there is the same body as suffered at Calvary, albeit present in a different manner (*The real presence* 1.11, in *Works* vol. 6, p. 19).
1422. *Holy living* 1.3, p. 35.
1423. p. 39.
1424. p. 40.
1425. *Holy dying* 1.3, p. 40.
1426. *Holy living* chapter 2, pp. 60–140.
1427. *Holy living* chapter 3, pp. 141–73.
1428. *Holy living* chapter 4, pp. 174–299.
1429. *Holy dying*, Epistle Dedicatory, p. 6.
1430. *Holy dying* 1.5, p. 48.
1431. *Holy dying* 2.1, p. 50; cf. 'If we follow Christ, death is our friend', *A course of sermons* 2.3, in *Works* vol. 4, p. 361.
1432. *Holy dying* 2.2, p. 54.
1433. p. 55.
1434. See, e.g., *A course of sermons* 1.13, in *Works* vol. 4, p. 159.
1435. See, e.g., *Holy living* 2.5, p. 102. For the significance of modesty for Taylor, see Askew (1997) pp. 20–2.
1436. *Holy living* 2.6, p. 126. It is worth noting Taylor's argument that God gave 'gifts extraordinary, as boldness of spirit, fearless courage, freedom of discourse, . . . the gift of tongues' at the dawn of Christianity because of the exceptional situation then obtaining; 'but afterward, when all the extraordinary needs were served, the extraordinary stock was spent, and God retracted those issues into their fountaions' (*Clerus Domini* 7.15, in *Works* vol. 1, pp. 51–2).
1437. *The great exemplar*, Exhortation 8, p. 5 (*Works* vol. 2, p. 41).
1438. pp. 8–9 (*Works* vol. 2, pp. 42–3). See Askew (1997, pp. 22–9) for some important reflections on Taylor's view of contentment, or serenity, rooted in classical *apatheia* and in a willingness to let go what cannot be avoided or changed.
1439. *The great exemplar*, Exhortation 10, p. 7 (*Works* vol. 2, p. 43).
1440. *The great exemplar*, Exhortation 11, pp. 7–8 (*Works* vol. 2, p. 44).
1441. *The great exemplar* 3.15, p. 511 (*Works* vol. 2, pp. 661–2).
1442. *Holy living* 4.7, in *Works* p. 213. Cf. William Laud: 'cold prayers are not they which remove the "blasphemy" of enemies. "The prayers indeed of but one righteous man doth [avail] much," but it is when they are "fervent"' (*Sermon preached before His Majesty [Charles I] at Whitehall on 5th July 1626*, in *The works of. . . William Laud* (Oxford: Parker, 1847), vol. 1, p. 143.
1443. cf. *A course of sermons* 1.12, in *Works* vol. 4, p. 147; cf. *A course of sermons* 2.15, in *Works* vol. 4, p. 513, and *The worthy communicant* 2.4, in *Works* vol. 8, p. 75.
1444. *The worthy communicant* 2.2, in *Works* vol. 8, p. 61. The feminine imagery used here is striking. Taylor also provides specific prayers designed to help increase our desires for God (p. 86).
1445. *A course of sermons* 1.11, in *Works* vol. 4, p. 135.
1446. *A course of sermons* 1.11, in *Works* vol. 4, p. 137.
1447. See, e.g., *A course of sermons* 1.4, in *Works* vol. 4, pp. 55–6; *Miscellaneous Sermons* 1, in *Works* vol. 8, p. 254.
1448. *A course of sermons* 1.5, in *Works* vol. 4, p. 66; cf. *Holy dying* 4.1, p. 124.
1449. *Twenty-five sermons* 1.6, in *Works* vol. 4, p. 74.
1450. *A course of sermons* 1.6, in *Works* vol. 4, p. 76 – though note (p. 77) that it is depth of seriousness and commitment rather than sheer length or number of prayers that counts. Cf. also *Holy dying*: 'the growths in grace are long, difficult, uncertain, hindered, of many parts and great variety' (5.6, in *Works* vol. 3, p. 434).
1451. *A course of sermons* 1.13, in *Works* vol. 4, p. 162.
1452. *A course of sermons* 1.13, in *Works* vol. 4, pp. 166–7.

1453. *A course of sermons* 1.4, in *Works* vol. 4, pp. 55–8; cf. *Holy living* 4.7, p. 212.

1454. *Miscellaneous sermons* 1, in *Works* vol. 8, pp. 249 and 252.

1455. *Miscellaneous sermons* 2, in *Works* vol. 8, p. 271.

1456. *A course of sermons* 2.2, in *Works* vol. 4, p. 344.

1457. *A course of sermons* 2.11, in *Works* vol. 4, p. 461.

1458. *A course of sermons* 2.2, in *Works* vol. 4, p. 344. Cf. *An apology* 45 (*Works* vol. 5, p. 276), where Taylor goes so far as to say that praying with the Spirit means 'my co-operation with the assistance of the Spirit of God', rather than the action of the Spirit within me.

1459. *An apology* 58, in *Works* vol. 5, p. 281.

1460. *An apology* 58, in *Works* vol. 5, pp. 281–2.

1461. *An apology* 35, in *Works* vol. 5, p. 272.

1462. *An apology* 25, in *Works* vol. 5, p. 267; and 29, p. 269.

1463. *An apology* 73, in *Works* vol. 5, p. 287.

1464. *An apology* 101, in *Works* vol. 5, pp. 300–1; 107, pp. 302–3; 110, p. 304.

1465. *An apology* 117, in *Works* vol. 5, p. 306; 118, p. 306; 124, p. 308.

1466. *A course of sermons* 2.2, in *Works* vol. 4, p. 345.

1467. *An apology* 37, in *Works* vol. 5, p. 273.

1468. *A course of sermons* 2.2, in *Works* vol. 4, pp. 346–7.

1469. *The great exemplar* 1.5, p. 95 (*Works* vol. 2, pp. 142–3).

1470. *The great exemplar* 1.5, p. 95 (*Works* vol. 2, p. 143).

1471. *A course of sermons* 1.5, in *Works* vol. 4, p. 61. One wonders what he made of Psalm 109! In *Holy living* he commends prayer as 'the great remedy against anger' (4.8, in *Works* vol. 3, p. 196).

1472. *Holy dying* 3.2, pp. 71–2.

1473. 'We must have him within us, and we must be in him: he is our vine, and we are his branches' (*The worthy communicant* 1.3, in *Works* vol. 8, p. 24; cf. also *The real presence* 3, in *Works* vol. 6, pp. 23–40. For Taylor's eucharistic theology, see Hughes (1960) pp. 40–4, and (esp.) McAdoo (1988).

1474. See *The worthy communicant* 2, in *Works* vol. 8, pp. 54–86 and 4–5, pp. 118–208.

1475. *The worthy communicant* 7.1, in *Works* vol. 8, p. 223.

1476. *The worthy communicant* Introd., in *Works* vol. 8, p. 10. Askew (1997, p. 89) makes the point that Taylor's written prayers are often dull: 'it is quite clear that when he prayed he did not intend to show God how eloquent he was'.

1477. *A course of sermons* 2.8, in *Works* vol. 4, p. 425.

1478. *Holy living* 4.10, p. 261.

1479. Kishlansky (1996, p. 25) records the story of the Duke's second wife, who tapped him with a fan to gain his attention only to receive the rebuke: 'Madam, my first duchess was a Percy and she never took such a liberty.' For the sad story of the Duke's first wife, Elizabeth Percy, who inherited Petworth at the age of three and had already been given away in marriage three times by the age of sixteen, see Lady Maxse's *Petworth in ancient times* (Chichester: Moore & Tillyer, 1952), pp. 8–9.

1480. See J. Summerson, *Architecture in Britain 1530–1830*, 9th edn (Pelican history of art) (New Haven and London: Yale UP, 1993, pp. 247–8; G. Jackson-Stops, 'The building of Petworth', in *Apollo* 105 (1977), pp. 324–33; M. Girouard, *The English country house* (New Haven and London: Yale UP, 1978), pp. 146–7 – Girouard includes a wonderful description of the visit of the King of Spain to Petworth in 1703.

1481. Ian Nairn (*Sussex*, in The buildings of England series (Harmondsworth: Penguin, 1965), p. 34), memorably describes the west front at Petworth as feeling 'as strange as one of Purcell's excursions into the minor keys, touched not with anachronism but with a quintessential remote tension'. See also his superb description on pp. 301–3.

1482. See David Green, *Grinling Gibbons: his work as carver and stuary, 1648–1721* (London: Country Life, 1964), esp. pp. 103–9; and David Esterly, *Grinling Gibbons and the art of carving* (London: V&A Publications, 1998).

1483. Nairn, op. cit., p. 307. For Selden see David Green, *Grinling Gibbons* (London: Country Life,

1964) pp. 106–7, though Green is unfairly dismissive of Selden's carvings in the chapel at Petworth, describing them as 'far from Gibbons' standard' (p. 107). Dr Samuel Johnson visited Petworth on 9 November 1782, and noted in his Diary: 'Chappel at Petworth gloomy' (*Works*, Yale edition, vol. 1, p. 349); Horace Walpole, by contrast, visiting Petworthh in August 1749, thought the chapel 'grand and proper' (*The Yale Edition of Horace Walpole's Letters*, ed. W. S. Lewis (London: Oxford UP, 1941), vol. 9, p. 98).

BIBLIOGRAPHY

Primary Works

Allen, Hannah, *Satan, his methods and malice baffled. A narrative of God's gracious dealings with that choice Christian Mrs. Hannah Allen (afterwards married to Mr Hatt)* (London: John Wallis, 1683)

Ambrose, Isaac, *Prima, media & ultima: the first, middle, and last things* (London: Webb & Grantham, 1654–7)

Andrewes, Lancelot, *Preces Privatae*: ed. Wilson and Bliss, in *The works of Lancelot Andrewes* (Library of Anglo-Catholic Theology 10) (Oxford: Parker, 1854); ET by F. E. Brightman, *The Preces Privatae of Lancelot Andrewes Bishop of Winchester* (London: Methuen, 1903)

Andrewes, Lancelot, *Pattern of catechistical doctrine*, in *Minor works of Bishop Andrewes* (Library of Anglo-Catholic Theology) (Oxford: Parker, 1846)

Andrewes, Lancelot, Sermons: ed. J. P. Wilson, *Ninety-six sermons by . . . Lancelot Andrewes*, 5 vols. (Library of Anglo-Catholic Theology) (Oxford: Parker, 1841–3)

Archer, Isaac: Storey, M. (ed.), *Two East Anglian diaries, 1641–1729: Isaac Archer and William Coe* (Suffolk Records Society 36) (Woodbridge: Boydell, 1994)

Baily, Lewis, *The practice of piety, directing a Christian how to walk, that he may please God* (London: Edward Brewster, 1702)

Baker, Augustine, *Holy wisdom*, ed. Serenus Cressy OSB and J. N. Sweeney (London: Burns Oates, 1950)

Baker, Augustine, *Secretum*, ed. J. P. H. Clark (*Analecta Cartusiana* 119:7) (Salzburg: Institut für Anglistik und Amerikanistik, 1997); *The confessions of venerable Father Augustine Baker OSB* [=edited extracts from the *Secretum*], ed. J. McCann (London: Burns Oates & Washbourne, 1922); *The cloud of unknowing and other treatises . . . with a commentary on the Cloud by Father Augustine Baker OSB* [edited extracts from the *Secretum*], ed. J. McCann, 4th edn (London: Burns Oates & Washbourne, 1943)

Baker, Augustine, *A secure stay in all temptations*, ed. J. P. H. Clark (*Analecta Cartusiana* 119:8) (Salzburg: Institut für Anglistik und Amerikanistik, 1998)

Barrington: Searle, A. (ed.), *Barrington family letters, 1628–32* (Camden Society, 4th series, 28) (London: Royal Historical Society, 1983)

Baxter, Richard, *Autobiography (Reliquiae Baxterianae)*, ed. J. M. Lloyd Thomas (London: Dent, 1925)

Baxter, Richard, *A Christian directory* (1673), in *The practical works of the Rev Richard Baxter*, ed. W. Orme (London: James Duncan, 1830), vols. 3–6

Baxter, Richard, *The poor man's family book* (1674), in *The practical works*, vol. 19, pp. 298–642

Baxter, Richard, *The Reformed Pastor (Gildas Salvianus)* (1656), ed. and abridged by J. Wilkinson; 2nd edn (London: Epworth, 1950)

Baxter, Richard, *The right method for a settled peace of conscience and spiritual comfort* (1653), in *The practical works*, vol. 9, pp. 1–287

Baxter, Richard, *A saint or a brute* (1662), in *The practical works*, vol. 10, pp. 1–400

Baxter, Richard, *The saints everlasting rest* (1650), in *The practical works*, vols. 22–3

Becon, Thomas, *A new catechism*, in *The catechism of Thomas Becon with other pieces*, ed. J. Ayre (Parker Society) (Cambridge UP, 1844), pp. 1–410

Becon, Thomas, *The flower of godly prayers*, in *Prayers and other pieces of Thomas Becon*, ed. J. Ayre (Parker Society) (Cambridge UP, 1844), pp. 1–70

Becon, Thomas, *A fruitful treatise of fasting*, in *The catechism*, pp. 523–51

Becon, Thomas, *The fortress of the faithful*, in *The catechism*, pp. 581–619

Becon, Thomas, *The pathway unto prayer*, in *The early works of Thomas Becon*, ed. J. Ayre (Parker Society) (Cambridge UP, 1843), pp. 123–87

Becon, Thomas, *The sick man's salve*, in *Prayers and other pieces*, pp. 87–191

Boehme, Jakob, *Aurora, that is, the day-spring*, trans. John Sparrow (London, 1656)

Boehme, Jakob, *Concerning the election of grace or of Gods will towards man, commonly called Predestination*, trans. John Sparrow (London, 1655)

Boehme, Jakob, *XL Questions concerning the soule* and *The clavis, or key*, trans. John Sparrow (London, 1647)

Boehme, Jakob, *Mysterium magnum*, trans. John Sparrow (London, 1654); 2 vols., ed. 'C. J. B.' (London: John M. Watkins, 1965)

Boehme, Jakob, *Signatura rerum: or the signature of all things* (trans. J. Ellistone) and *Of Christs Testaments, viz. Baptisme and the Supper* (trans. John Sparrow) (London, 1651–2)

Boehme, Jakob, *The way to Christ discovered, by Iacob Behmen*, trans. H. Blunden (London, 1648); trans. P. Erb (Classics of western spirituality) (New York: Paulist Press, 1978)

Bradford, John, *Defence of election*, in *The writings of John Bradford . . . Martyr, 1555*, vol. 1, ed. A. Townsend (Parker Society) (Cambridge UP, 1848), pp. 307–30

Bradford, John, *Godly meditations on the Lord's Prayer, belief, and Ten Commandments, with other exercises* (*Godly meditations*), in *The writings*, vol. 1, pp. 115–20

Bradford, John, Letters, in *The writings*, vol. 2, ed. A. Townsend (Parker Society) (Cambridge UP, 1853), pp. 1–253

Bradford, John, *Meditations and prayers from MSS. in Emmanuel College Cambridge and other sources* (*Meditations and prayers*), in *The writings*, vol. 1, pp. 260–93

Bradford, John, *Preface to Orations of Chrysostom on prayer*, in *The writings*, vol. 1, pp. 13–15

Bradford, John, *Private prayers and meditations, &c.*, in *The writings*, vol. 1, pp. 224–47

Brooks, Thomas, *Heaven on earth: a treatise on Christian assurance* (London: Banner of Truth, 1961)

Browne, Robert: Peel, A., and Carlson, L.H. (eds.), *The writings of Robert Harrison and Robert Browne* (Elizabethan Nonconformist Texts 2); London: Allen & Unwin, 1953

Browne, Thomas, *Religio medici*, in *Religio medici and other works* ed. L. C. Martin (Oxford: Clarendon, 1964), pp. 1–80 (also includes *Hydriotaphia: urn-burial* (1658))

Bunyan, John, *The acceptable sacrifice*, ed. W. R. Owens in *The miscellaneous works of John Bunyan* [hereafter referred to as MW] (Oxford: Clarendon, 1976–), vol. 12, pp. 7–82

Bunyan, John, *A case of conscience resolved*, ed. T. L. Underwood, in MW vol. 4, pp. 293–330

Bunyan, John, *Christ a complete saviour*, ed. W. R. Owens, in MW vol. 13, pp. 257–333

Bunyan, John, *Christian behaviour*, ed. J. Sears McGee, in MW vol. 3, pp. 9–62

Bunyan, John, *A confession of my faith, and a reason of my practice*, ed. T. L. Underwood, in MW vol. 4, pp. 135–87

Bunyan, John, *A defence of the doctrine of justification, by faith*, ed. T. L. Underwood, in MW vol. 4, pp. 7–130

Bunyan, John, *The desire of the righteous granted*, ed. W. R. Owens, in MW vol. 13, pp. 101–59

Bunyan, John, *A discourse of the building . . . of the house of God*, ed. G. Midgley, in MW vol. 6, pp. 271–317

Bunyan, John, *A discourse upon the Pharisee and the Publicane*, ed. O. C. Watkins, in MW vol. 10, pp. 110–235

Bunyan, John, *The doctrine of the law and grace unfolded* and *I will pray with the Spirit*, ed. R. L. Greaves, in MW vol. 2

Bunyan, John, *Good news for the vilest of men*; *The advocateship of Jesus Christ*, ed. R .L. Greaves, in MW vol. 11

Bunyan, John, *Some Gospel-truths opened, A vindication of some Gospel-truths opened* and *A few sighs from Hell*, ed. T. L. Underwood, in MW vol. 1

Bunyan, John, *Grace abounding to the chief of sinners*, ed. R. Sharrock (Oxford: Clarendon, 1962)

Bunyan, John, *The holy city*, ed. J. Sears McGee, in MW vol. 3, pp. 69–196

Bunyan, John, *The holy war*, ed. R Sharrock and J. F. Forrest (Oxford: Clarendon, 1980)

Bunyan, John, *The house of the forest of Lebanon*, ed. G. Midgley, in MW vol. 7, pp. 121–74

Bunyan, John, *Instruction for the ignorant; Light for them that sit in darkness; Saved by grace; Come, and welcome, to Jesus Christ*, ed. R. L. Greaves, in MW vol. 8

Bunyan, John, *The life and death of Mr Badman*, in *Whole works*, ed. J. B. Offor (London: Blackie, 1862), vol. 3, pp. 595–665

Bunyan, John, *The pilgrim's progress*, ed. J. B. Wharey, 2nd. edn rev. R. Sharrock (Oxford: Clarendon, 1960)

Bunyan, John, *Questions about the nature and perpetuity of the seventh-day-Sabbath*, ed. T. L. Underwood, in MW vol. 4, pp. 335–89

Bunyan, John, *The poems*, ed. G. Midgley, in MW vol. 6

Bunyan, John, *A relation of the imprisonment of Mr John Bunyan*, ed. with *Grace abounding* (q.v.) by R. Sharrock, pp. 104–31

Bunyan, John, *The resurrection of the dead*, ed. J. Sears McGee, in MW vol. 3, pp. 203–92

Bunyan, John, *Seasonable counsel*, ed. O. C. Watkins, in MW vol. 10, pp. 5–104

Bunyan, John, *Solomon's temple spiritualized*, ed. G. Midgley, in MW vol. 7, pp. 5–115

Bunyan, John, *A treatise of the fear of God; The greatness of the soul; A holy life*, ed. R. L. Greaves, in MW vol. 9

Burton, Robert, *The anatomy of melancholy* ed. T. C. Faulker, N. K. Kiessling, R. L. Blair; 3 vols. (Oxford: Clarendon, 1989–94)

Butley Priory (Suffolk): Register, in Dickens, A.. G., *Late monasticism and the Reformation* (London: Hambledon, 1994), pp. 1–84

Calvin, John, *Institutes of the Christian religion* (ET by H. Beveridge) (Grand Rapids: Eerdmans, 1989)

Carpenter, Richard, *Experience, historie, and divinitie* (London: Stafford, 1641)

Certain homilies appointed to be read in churches in the time of the late Queen Elizabeth (Oxford UP, 1840)

Coe, William: see Archer, Isaac

Colet, John, *De caelesti hierarchia*, ed. and trans. J. H. Lupton, *Two treatises on the hierarchies of Dionysius* (London: Bell & Daldy, 1869), pp. 1–47 and 165–196

Colet, John, *De ecclesiastica hierarchia*, ed. and trans. J. H. Lupton (1869), pp. 48–162 and 197–272

Colet, John, *Enarratio in primam Epistolam S.Pauli ad Corinthios*, ed. and trans. J. H. Lupton, *An exposition of St Paul's First Epistle to the Corinthians by John Colet M.A.* (London: Bell & Sons, 1874)

Colet, John, *De sacramentis*, in J. B. Gleason, *John Colet* (Berkeley: California UP, 1989), pp. 270–333

Constitutions and canons ecclesiastical . . . agreed upon with the King's Majesty License (1603), in *Certain homilies appointed to be read in churches in the time of the late Queen Elizabeth* (Oxford UP, 1840), pp. 537–600

Cosin, John, *A collection of private devotions* (ed. P. G. Stanwood) (Oxford: Clarendon, 1967)

Cranmer, Thomas: Duffield, G. E. (ed.), *The work of Thomas Cranmer* (Courtenay Library of Reformation Classics 2) (Appleford: Sutton Courtenay, 1964) (with introduction by J. I. Packer)

Crashaw, Richard: Martin, L. C., *The poems (English, Latin and Greek) of Richard Crashaw* (Oxford: Clarendon, 1957)

Dering, Edward, *Godly private prayers, for housholders to meditate upon, and to say in their families* (London: James Roberts, 1600)

Donne, John, *The divine poems*, ed. H. Gardner (Oxford: Clarendon, 1952) (the edition cited here); *The complete English poems*, ed. Smith (Harmondsworth: Penguin Classics, 1971)

Donne, John, *The elegies and The songs and sonnets*, ed. H. Gardner (Oxford: Clarendon, 1965)

Donne, John, *The Epithalamions, Anniversaries and Epicedes*, ed. W. Milgate (Oxford: Clarendon, 1978)

Donne, John, *Essays in Divinity*, ed. E. M. Simpson (Oxford: Clarendon, 1952)

Donne, John, *Devotions upon emergent occasions*, ed. A. Raspa (London and Montreal: McGill-Queen's UP, 1975)

Donne, John, *Pseudo-Martyr*, ed. A. Raspa (Montreal: McGill-Queen's UP, 1993)

Donne, John, *Sermons*: Potter, G. R., and Simpson, E. M. (eds.), *The sermons of John Donne*, 10 vols (Berkeley: California UP, 1953–62)

Donne, John, Selections: Booty, J. (ed.), *John Donne: selections from Divine Poems, Sermons, Devotions, and Prayers* (Classics of western spirituality) (New York: Paulist Press, 1990)

Evans, Katharine, and Chevers, Sarah, *A short relation of some of the cruel sufferings (for the truths sake) . . . in the Inquisition in the Isle of Malta* (London: Robert Wilson, 1662)

Everard, John, *The gospel-treasury opened: or, The holiest of all unvailing* (collection of sermons), 2nd edn (London: R. Harford, 1659)

Evelyn, John, *Diary*, ed. E. S. de Beer (Oxford: Clarendon, 1955)

Fincham, K. (ed.), *Visitation articles and injunctions of the early Stuart Church*, vol. 1 (Church of England Record Society, 1) (Woodbridge: Boydell, 1994)

Fisher, John, *Treatyse concernynge . . . the seven Penytencyall Psalmes*, in *The English works of John Fisher*, ed. J. E. B. Mayor (EETS e.s. 27) (London: Oxford UP, 1876; repr. 1935), pp. 1–267

Fisher, John, Prayer from PRO, State Papers of Henry VIII, 1:93, ff. 99–102; ET in Chambers (1955) pp. 297–9

Fisher, John, *A spiritual consolation and other treatises*, ed. D. O'Connor (London: Burns & Oates, 1935)

Frere, W. H. and Kennedy, W. M., *Visitation articles and injunctions of the period of the Reformation*, 3 vols (Alcuin Club collections 14–16) (London: Longmans, Green, 1910)

Fox, George, *Journal*, ed. N. Penney, 8th edn, 2 vols (London: Society of Friends, 1902)

Fox, George, *Book of miracles*: Cadbury, H. J. (ed.), *George Fox's 'Book of miracles'* (Cambridge UP, 1948)

Foxe, John, *Actes and monuments . . .* , ed. S. R. Cattley and G. Townsend, 8 vols (repr. NY, 1965)

Garman, M. (ed.), *Hidden in plain sight: Quaker women's writings, 1650–1700* (Wallingford, PA: Pendle Hill Publications, 1996)

Gerard, John, *Autobiography*: Caraman, P. (trans.), *John Gerard: the autobiography of an Elizabethan*; 2nd edn (London: Longmans, 1956)

Halkett, Anne (Lady Halkett): Nichols, J. G. (ed.), *The autobiography of Anne Lady Halkett* (Camden Society, n.s.13) (London, 1875)

Hall, Joseph, *The art of divine meditation*, in Pratt, J. (ed.), *The works of Joseph Hall*, vol. 7 (Practical Works) (London: Williams & Smith, 1808), pp. 43–80

Herbert, George, *The works of George Herbert*, ed. F. E. Hutchinson (Oxford: Clarendon, 1941)

Herbert, Mary Sidney (Countess of Pembroke): Hannay, M. P., Kinnamon, N. J., and Brennan, M. G. (eds.), *The collected works of Mary Sidney Herbert, Countess of Pembroke, II: The Psalmes of David* (Oxford: Clarendon, 1998)

Hooker, Edward, Preface (*Praefatori Epistl*) to John Pordage's *Theologia mystica* (London, 1683), pp. 1–95

Hooker, Richard, *Of the laws of ecclesiastical polity*, in *Works*, ed. J. Keble, 3 vols (Oxford UP, 1841)

Hooker, Richard, Sermons, in *Works* vol. 3 (Oxford UP, 1841)

Ignatius of Loyola, *Spiritual exercises*: Puhl, Louis J. (ed.), *The spiritual exercises of St Ignatius* (Chicago: Loyola UP, 1951)

Jewel, John, *A treatise of the sacraments gathered out of certain sermons which the Reverend Father in God, Bishop Jewel, preached at Salisbury*, in *Works*, ed. J. Ayre, vol. 2 (Parker Society) (Cambridge UP, 1847), pp. 1098–139.

Jewel, John, *An apology or answer in defence of the Church of England* (ET of *Apologia ecclesiae Anglicanae*), in *Works*, vol. 3 (Parker Society) (Cambridge UP, 1848), pp. 52–112

Josselin, Ralph *The diary of Ralph Josselin 1616–1683*, ed. A. McFarlane (Records of social and economic history, n.s. 3) (Oxford, 1976)

The kalendar and compost of shepherds, ed. G. C. Heseltine (London: Peter Davies, 1930)

Landor, W. N., *Staffordshire incumbents and parochial records (1530–1680)* (Collections for a history of Staffordshire) (London: St Catherine Press, 1916)

Latimer, Hugh, *Sermons*, ed. G. E. Corrie (Parker Society) (Cambridge UP, 1844); *Sermons and Remains*, ed. G. E. Corrie (Parker Society) (Cambridge UP, 1845)

Lead, Jane, *Ascent to the mount of vision* (London, 1699; ed. W. D. Forsyth (London: Littleborough, 1906)

Lead, Jane, *The Enochian walks with God* (London, 1694; repr. Glasgow: John Thomson, 1891)

Lead, Jane, *A further manifestation concerning this virgin Philadelphian church . . . being a second message to the Philadelphian Society* (London, 1696; repr. in *Three messages to the Philadelphian Society* (Airdrie: Thomson, 1895))

Lead, Jane, *The heavenly cloud now breaking* (London, 1681; repr. Glasgow: John Thomson, 1885)

Lead, Jane, *A message to the Philadelphian Society by Jean [sic] Lead* (London, 1696; repr. in *Three messages . . .* (Airdrie: Thomson, 1895))

Lead, Jane, *The messenger of an universal peace, or a third message to the Philadelphian Society* (London, 1698; repr. in *Three messages . . .* (Airdrie: Thomson, 1895))

Lead, Jane, *The revelation of revelations* (London, 1683)

Lead, Jane, *The wonders of God's creation* (London, 1695; repr. Glasgow: John Thomson, 1887)

The letters of the martyrs: collected and published in 1564, ed. E. Bickersteth (London: Shaw, 1837)

Lowe: Winstanley, I. (ed.), *The diary of Roger Lowe of Ashton-in-Makerfield, Lancashire, 1663–1678* (Ashton-in-Makerfield: Picks Publishing, 1994)

Luther, Martin, *Commentary on St Paul's Epistle to the Galatians* (1575) ET ed. P .S. Watson (London: James Clarke, (1953))

Marshall, Walter, *The gospel-mystery of sanctification* (London: Parkhurst, 1692)

Milton, John: *The poems of John Milton*, ed. J. Carey and A. Fowler (London: Longmans, 1968)

Molina, Antonio, *A treatise of mental prayer (1617)* (English Recusant Literature 1558–1640, 15) (Menston: Scolar Press, 1970)

Molina, Antonio, *A treatise containing some rules and important advices, how to say the Divine Office* (ET by Fr John Thorpe), in *Spiritualität heute und gestern* 16 (*Analecta Cartusiana* 35:16) (Salzburg, 1992), pp. 180–253

More, Dame Agnes: Latz, Dorothy L. (ed.), *'The building of divine love' as translated by Dame Agnes More* (Salzburg studies in English Literature: Elizabethan and Renaissance studies 92:17) (Salzburg: Institut für Anglistik und Amerikanistik, 1992)

More, Thomas, *The confutacyon of Tyndales answere*, ed. L. A. Schuster et al., in *Ccomplete works* (New Haven & London: Yale UP, 1965–), vol. 8:1–3

More, Thomas, *De tristitia Christi*, ed. and trans. C. H. Miller, in *Complete works* vol. 14:1 and 14:2

More, Thomas, *A dialogue of comfort against tribulation*, ed. L. L. Martz and F. Manley, in *Complete works* vol. 12

More, Thomas, *Instructions and prayers* (written in the Tower), ed. G. E. Haupt, in *Complete works* vol. 13

More, Thomas, *Responsio ad Lutherum*, ed. J. M. Headley, in *Complete works* vol. 5:1–2

More, Thomas, *Thomas More's prayer book*, ed. L. L. Martz and R. S. Sylvester (New Haven and London: Yale UP, 1969)

More, Thomas, *A treatise upon the passion*, ed. G. E. Haupt, in *Complete works* vol. 13, pp. 1–177

More, Thomas, *Utopia*, ed. E. Surtz and J. H. Hexter, in *Complete works* vol. 4; ed. and trans. G. M. Logan, R. M. Adams and C. H. Miller (Cambridge UP 1995); trans. R. Robinson (Everyman's Library) (London: Dent, 1910; repr.1994)

Niclaes (Nichols), Hendrik, *An introduction to the holy understanding of the glasse of righteousnesse* (London: Whittington, 1649)

Owen, John, *Works,* ed. W. H. Goold, 24 vols (London and Edinburgh: Johnstone & Hunter, 1850–5, vols 1–16 repr. by Banner of Truth Trust, 1965–8)

Parker, Robert, *An exposition of the powring out of the fourth vial mentioned in the sixteenth [chapter] of the Revelation* (London: Pierrepont, 1650)

Patrides, C. A. (ed.), *The Cambridge Platonists* (Stratford-upon-Avon Library 5) (London: Edward Arnold, 1969)

Penington, Isaac, Letters, in Steere, D. V. (ed.), *Quaker spirituality: selected writings* (Classics of western spirituality) (New York: Paulist Press, 1984), pp. 137–58

Penn, William, Preface ('being a summary account of the divers dispensations of God to men') to the *Journal* of George Fox, ed. N. Penney, 8th edn (London: Society of Friends, 1902), vol. 1, pp. xix–lxii

Perin, William, OP: *Spiritual exercises of a Dominican friar*, ed. C. Kirchberger and F. V. McNabb OP (London: Sheed & Ward, 1929)

Perkins, William, *The foundation of Christian religion gathered into six principles*, ed. Ian Breward in *The work of William Perkins* (Courtenay library of reformation classics 3) (Appleford: Sutton Courtenay, 1970), pp. 138–67

Perkins, William, *The workes of the famous and worthy minister of Christ . . . William Perkins*, 3 vols (London: John Legatt, 1626)

Pordage, John, *Theologia mystica* and *A treatise of eternal nature* (London, 1681–3)

Quaker writings: Garman, M., et al. (eds.), *Hidden in plain sight: Quaker women's writings 1650–1700* (Wallingford, Penn.: Pendle Hill Publications, 1996)

Roper, William, *The life of Sir Thomas More*, in Sylvester and Harding (1962)

Rogers, Richard: *Diary*, in Knappen, M. M. (ed.), *Two Elizabeth Puritan diaries* (London: SPCK, 1933)

Sibbes, Richard, *The saints cordialls* (Selected sermons) (London: Henry Cripps, 1658)

Smyth, John, *A paterne of true prayer*, in Whitley, W. T. (ed.), *The works of John Smyth* (Cambridge UP, 1915), vol. 1, pp. 67–247

Sidney, Sir Philip (and the Countess of Pembroke): Rathmell, J. C. A. (ed.), *The Psalms of Sir Philip Sidney and the Countess of Pembroke* (Stuart editions) (New York UP, 1963)

Southwell, Robert, *Poems*: in McDonald, J. H. and Brown, N. P. (eds.), *The poems of Robert Southwell SJ* (Oxford: Clarendon, 1967)

Southwell, Robert, *Short rules of a good life*: Brown, N. P. (ed.), *Robert Southwell, SJ: Two letters and 'Short rules of a good life'* (Charlottesville: Virginia UP, 1973)

Southwell, Robert, *Spiritual exercises and devotions*, ed. J.–M.de Buck SJ, ET by P. E. Hallett (London: Sheed & Ward, 1931)

Sparrow, Anthony, *A rationale upon the Book of Common-Prayer* (London, 1661; rev. edn 1704)

Sternhold and Hopkins: *The whole booke of Psalmes, collected into English meeter by Thomas Sternhold, John Hopkins and others, conferred with the Hebrue with apt notes to sing them withall . . .* (London: John Windet, for Richard Day, 1599)

Sterry, Peter, *The clouds in which Christ comes* (London: Dawlman, 1648)

Sterry, Peter, *A discourse of the freedom of the will* (London: John Starkey, 1675)

Sterry, Peter, *The rise, race, and royalty of the kingdom of God in the soul of man* (London: Cockerill, 1683)

Sterry, Peter, *Select writings*, ed. N. I. Matar (University of Kansas humanistic studies 60) (New York: Peter Lang, 1994)

Sylvester, R. S., and Harding, D. P. (eds.), *Two early Tudor lives* (Yale UP, 1962)

Taylor, Jeremy, *An apology for authorized and set forms of liturgy*, in *Whole works*, ed. R. Heber, rev. C. P. Eden (London: Brown, Green & Longmans, 1856), vol. 5, pp. 229–314

Taylor, Jeremy, *Clerus Domini, or a discourse of the office ministerial*, in *Whole works* vol. 1, pp. 1–61

Taylor, Jeremy, *A collection of offices or forms of prayer*, in *Whole works* vol. 8, pp. 571–701

Taylor, Jeremy, *A discourse of the liberty of prophesying*, in *Whole works* vol. 5, pp. 341–69

Taylor, Jeremy, *A discourse of the nature and offices of friendship*, in *Whole works* vol. 1, pp. 69–98

Taylor, Jeremy, *A dissuasive from Popery*, in *Whole works* vol. 6, pp. 171–642

Taylor, Jeremy, *Ductor dubitantium; or, The rule of conscience*, in *Whole works*, vols 9–10

Taylor, Jeremy, *Eniautos, or A course of sermons for all the Sundays in the year*, in *Whole works* vol. 4

Taylor, Jeremy, *The golden grove, or a manual of daily prayers and litanies*, in *Whole works* vol. 7, pp. 587–648

Taylor, Jeremy, *The great exemplar of sanctity and holy life* (or *The history of the life and death of the holy Jesus*) (London: James Flesher, 1653); also in *Whole works* vol. 2

Taylor, Jeremy, *Miscellaneous sermons*, in *Whole works* vol. 8, pp. 241–570

Taylor, Jeremy, *The Psalter of David; with titles and collects*, in *Whole works* vol. 15, pp. 93–235

Taylor, Jeremy, *The real presence of Christ in the holy sacrament*, in *Whole works* vol. 6, pp. 1–168

Taylor, Jeremy, *The rule and exercises of holy dying*, ed. P. G. Stanwood (Oxford: Clarendon, 1989)

Taylor, Jeremy, *The rule and exercises of holy living*, ed. P. G. Stanwood (Oxford: Clarendon, 1989)

Taylor, Jeremy, *Rules and advice to the clergy of the diocese of Down and Connor*, in *Whole works* vol. 1, pp. 99–114

Taylor, Jeremy, *Unum necessarium, or, the doctrine and practice of repentance*, in *Whole works* vol. 7, pp. 1–491

Taylor, Jeremy, *The worthy communicant, or a discourse of the nature, effects, and blessings consequent to the worthy receiving of the Lord's Supper*, in *Whole works* vol. 8, pp. 1–241

Taylor, Jeremy, *Selected works*, ed. T. K. Carroll (Classics of western spirituality) (New York: Paulist Press, 1990)

Traherne, Thomas, *Commentaries of Heaven (The Poems)*, ed. D. D. C. Chambers (Salzburg studies in English Literature: Elizabethan and Renaissance studies 92:22) (Salzburg: Institut für Anglistik und Amerikanistik, 1989)

Traherne, Thomas, *Poems, Centuries and three Thanksgivings*, ed. A. Ridler (Oxford UP, 1966)

Traherne, Thomas, *The way to blessedness (Christian Ethicks)*, ed. and modernized M. Bottrall (London: Faith Press, 1962)

Traherne, Thomas, *Select meditations*, ed. Julia J. Smith (Manchester: Carcanet, 1997)

The two liturgies (1549 and 1552) with other documents set forth by authority in the reign of King Edward VI, viz. The Order of Communion (1548), the Primer (1553), the Catechism and Articles (1553), and the Catechismus Brevis (1553), ed. J. Ketley (Parker Society) (Cambridge UP, 1844)

Tyndale, William, *Answer to Sir Thomas More's Dialogue*, in *Works,* ed. H. Walter (Parker Society) (Cambridge UP, 1850), vol. 3, pp. 11–215

Tyndale, William, *An exposition upon the V. VI. VII chapters of Matthew*, in *Expositions and notes*, ed. H. Walter (Parker Society) (Cambridge UP, 1849), pp. 3–132

Tyndale, William, *The obedience of a Christian man* (1527–8), in *Doctrinal treatises . . . by William Tyndale*, ed. H. Walter (Parker Society); Cambridge UP (1848), pp. 127–344

Tyndale, William, *The parable of the wicked mammon* (1527), in *Doctrinal treatises*, ed. H. Walter (Parker Society) (Cambridge UP, 1848), pp. 29–126

[Tyndale, William] *Tyndale's New Testament: a modern-spelling edition of the 1534 translation* ed. D. Daniell (Yale UP, 1989)

Vaughan, Henry, *Silex scintillans*, in Rudrum, A. (ed.), *Henry Vaughan: the complete poems* (Harmondsworth: Penguin, 1983), pp. 135–313

Walton, Izaak, *The life of Mr Richard Hooker*, in *The works of Mr Richard Hooker, with an account of his life and death by Isaac Walton*, ed. J. Keble (Oxford UP, 1841), vol. 1, pp. 1–86

Ward, Samuel, *Diary*, in Knappen, M. M. (ed.), *Two Elizabeth Puritan diaries* (London: SPCK, 1933)

Westminster Assembly (1648), *Articles of Christian religion, approved and passed by both Houses of Parliament, after advice had with the Assembly of Divines by authority of Parliament sitting at Westminster* (London: Husband, 1648)

Weston, William, *Autobiography*: Caraman, P. (trans.), *William Weston: the autobiography of an Elizabethan* (London: Longmans, 1955)

Whitgift, John, *Works*, ed. J. Ayre, 3 vols (Parker Society) (Cambridge, 1851–3)

Whytford, Richard, *The pype or tonne of the lyfe of perfection*, ed. J. Hogg (Elizabethan and Renaissance studies 89) (Salzburg: Institut für Anglistik und Amerikanistik, 1979)

Whytford, Richard, *A werke for housholders*, in J. Hogg (ed.) (Salzburg studies in English literature. English and Renaissance studies 89), vol. 5, pp. 1–62 (with analysis by J. Hogg in vol. 2, pp. 140–89)

Winstanley, Gerrard, *Works*, ed. G. H. Sabine (Ithaca, NY: Cornell UP, 1941)

Wither, George, *The hymnes and songs of the Church* (1623), ed. and introd. by Edward Farr (London: John Russell Smith, 1856)

Wither, George, *A preparation to the Psalter* (1619)

Secondary Works

Acheson, R. J., *Radical Puritans in England 1550–1660* (Seminar studies in history) (London: Longmans, 1990)

Ackroyd, Peter, *The life of Thomas More* (London: Chatto & Windus, 1998)

Addleshaw, G. W. O., and Etchells, F., *The architectural setting of Anglican worship* (London: Faber & Faber, 1948)

Allchin, A. M., *Participation in God: a forgotten strand in Anglican tradition* (London: DLT, 1988)

Allchin, A. M. et al., *Profitable wonders: aspects of Thomas Traherne* (Oxford: Amate, 1989)

Alldridge, N., 'Loyalty and identity in Chester parishes 1540–1640 in S. J. Wright (ed.), *Parish, church and people: local studies in lay religion 1350–1750* (London: Hutchinson, 1988), pp. 85–124 .

Allison, A. F. and Rogers, D. M., *The contemporary printed literature of the English Counter-Reformation between 1558 and 1640*; 2 vols (Aldershot: Scolar Press, 1989 and 1994)

Asals, H., 'The voice of George Herbert's *The Church*', *English Literary History* 36 (1989) pp. 511–28

Askew, Reginald, *Muskets and altars: Jeremy Taylor and the last of the Anglicans* (London: Mowbray, 1997)

Bainton, R. H., 'Feminine piety in Tudor England', in Brooks, P. (ed.), *Christian spirituality: essays in honour of Gordon Rupp* (London: SCM Press, 1975), pp. 183–201

Baldwin, Anna, and Hutton, Sarah (eds.), *Platonism and the English imagination* (Cambridge UP, 1994)

Barnes, G. L., 'Laity formation: the role of early English printed primers', *Journal of Religious History* 18 (1994), pp. 139–58

Baxter, Nicola, 'Gerrard Winstanley's experimental knowledge of God (The perception of the Spirit and the acting of reason)', *Journal of Ecclesiastical History* 39 (1988), pp. 184–201

Beckwith, R. T., 'Thomas Cranmer and the Prayer Book', in C. Jones et al. (eds.), *The study of liturgy*, rev. edn (London: SPCK, 1992), pp. 101–5

Bloch, Chana, *Spelling the word: George Herbert and the Bible* (Berkeley: California UP, 1985)

Booty, John, *Three Anglican divines on prayer: Jewel, Andrewes, and Hooker* (Cambridge, Mass.: Society of St John the Evangelist, 1978)

Booty, John, 'Contrition in Anglican spirituality: Hooker, Donne and Herbert', in William J. Wolf (ed.), *Anglican spirituality* (Wilton, Conn.: Morehouse-Barlow, 1982), pp. 25–48

Booty, John, 'Joseph Hall, *The Arte of Divine Meditation*, and Anglican spirituality', in E. R. Elder (ed.), *The roots of the modern Christian tradition* (The spirituality of western Christendom 2; Cistercian Studies 55) (Kalamazoo: Cistercian Publications, 1984), pp. 200–28

Bossy, John, *The English Catholic community 1570–1850* (London: DLT, 1975)

Brachlow, Stephen, *The communion of saints: radical Puritan and separatist ecclesiology, 1570–1625* (Oxford UP, 1988)

Bradshaw, B., and Duffy, E., *Humanism, reform and the Reformation: the career of Bishop John Fisher* (Cambridge UP, 1989)

Bradshaw, B., 'Bishop John Fisher, 1469–1535: the man and his work', in Bradshaw and Duffy (1989) pp. 1–24

Brauer, J. C., 'Puritan mysticism and the development of liberalism', in *Church History* 19 (1950), pp. 151–70

Brown, A. D., *Popular piety in late medieval England: the diocese of Salisbury 1250–1550* (Oxford: Clarendon, 1995)

Brown, N. P., 'Robert Southwell and the written word' in T. M. McCoog (ed.), *The reckoned expense: Edmund Campion and the early English Jesuits: essays in celebration of the first centenary of Campion Hall, Oxford (1896–1996)* (Woodbridge: Boydell, 1996), pp. 193–213

Burgess, C. R., '"A fond thing vainly invented": an essay on Purgatory and pious motive in late medieval England', in S. J. Wright (ed.), *Parish, church and people: local studies in lay religion, 1350–1750* (London: Hutchinson, 1988), pp. 56–84

Bush, Douglas, *English literature in the earlier seventeenth century* (Oxford history of English literature) (Oxford: Clarendon, 1945)

Byron, Brian, *Loyalty in the spirituality of St Thomas More* (Bibliotheca humanistica et reformatorica IV) (Nieuwkoop: B. de Graaf, 1972)

Caldwell, Patricia, *The Puritan conversion narrative: the beginnings of American expression* (Cambridge UP, 1983)

Capp, B. S., *The Fifth Monarchy men* (London: Faber & Faber, 1972)

Carey, John, *John Donne: life, mind and art* 2nd edn (London: Faber & Faber, 1990)

Chester, Allan G., *Hugh Latimer: apostle to the English* (Philadelphia: Pennsylvania UP, 1954)

Clancy, T. H., 'Papist-Protestant-Puritan: English religious taxonomy 1565–1665', *Recusant History* 13 (1976), pp. 227–53

Clark, J. P. H., 'Father Augustine Baker OSB and his *Secretum*', in James Hogg (ed.), *The mystical tradition and the Carthusians* 1 (*Analecta Cartusiana* 130) (Salzburg: Institut für Anglistik und Amerikanistik, 1995), pp. 91–117

Clarke, Elizabeth, 'George Herbert's *The temple*: the genius of Anglicanism and the inspiration for poetry', in G. Rowell (ed.), *The English religious tradition and the genius of Anglicanism* (Wantage: Ikon, 1992), pp. 127–44

Clarke, Elizabeth, *Theory and theology in George Herbert's poetry* (Oxford: Clarendon, 1997)

Clements, A. L., 'Theme, tone, and tradition in George Herbert's poetry', in J. R. Roberts (ed.), *Essential articles for the study of George Herbert's poetry* (Hamden, Conn.: Archon, 1979), pp. 33–51

Cohen, Charles L., *God's caress: the psychology of Puritan religious experience* (New York: Oxford UP, 1986)

Cohn, Norman, *The pursuit of the millennium* (London: Secker & Warburg, 1957; repr. Paladin, 1970)

Coolidge, J. S., *The Pauline renaissance in England: Puritanism and the Bible* (Oxford: Clarendon, 1970)

Coward, B., *The golden age: a history of England 1603–1714* (London: Longman, 1980)

Collinson, Patrick, 'The beginnings of English Sabbatarianism', in C. W. Dugmore and C. Duggan (eds.), *Studies in Church History* 1 (1964) (London: Nelson, 1964), pp. 207–21

Collinson, Patrick, *The Elizabeth Puritan movement* (London: Cape, 1967)

Collinson, Patrick, 'A comment concerning the name: Puritan', *Journal of Ecclesiastical History* 31 (1980) pp. 483–8

Collinson, Patrick, *The religion of Protestants: the church in English society 1559–1625* (Oxford: Clarendon, 1982)

Collinson, Patrick, 'England and international Calvinism, 1558–1640', in M. Prestwich, *International Calvinism 1541–1715* (Oxford: Clarendon, 1985), pp. 197–224

Collinson, Patrick, 'English Puritanism' (General Series 106) (London: Historical Association, 1983; rev. edn 1987)

Collinson, Patrick, *The birthpangs of Protestant England: religious and cultural change in the sixteenth and seventeenth centuries* (Basingstoke: Macmillan, 1988)

Crawford, Patricia, *Women and religion in England 1500–1720* (London: Routledge, 1993)

Cross, C., 'Popular piety and the records of the unestablished churches, 1460–1660', in D. Baker (ed.), *The materials, sources and methods of ecclesiastical history* (Studies in church history 11) (Oxford: Blackwell, 1975), pp. 269–92

Cross, C., *Church and people 1450–1660: the triumph of the laity in the English church* (Fontana history of England) (London: Fontana, 1976, rev. edn 1987)

Cross, C., 'Wills as evidence of popular piety in the Reformation period; Leeds and Hull, 1540–1640', in D. Loades (ed.), *The end of strife: papers selected from the proceedings of the Colloqium of the Commission Internationale d'Histoire Ecclésiastique Comparée held at the University of Durham, 2 to 9 September 1981* (Edinburgh: T. & T. Clark, 1984), pp. 44–51

Cuming, Geoffrey, '*The Godly Order*': texts and studies relating to the Book of Common Prayer* (Alcuin Club collections 65) (London: SPCK, 1983)

Daniell, David, *William Tyndale: a biography* (New Haven: Yale UP, 1994)

Davie, Donald (ed.), *The Psalms in English* (Penguin classics) (Harmondsworth: Penguin, 1996)

Davies, C. S. L., 'Popular religion and the Pilgrimage of Grace', in A. Fletcher and J. Stevenson (eds.), *Order and disorder in early modern England* (Cambridge UP, 1985), pp. 58–91

Davis, J. F., *Heresy and reformation in the south-east of England 1520–1559* (Studies in history 34)

(London: Royal Historical Society, 1983)

Davis, Walter R., 'Meditation, typology, and the structure of John Donne's Sermons', in C. J. Summers and T.-L. Pebworth (eds.), *The eagle and the dove: reassessing John Donne* (Essays in seventeenth-century literature 1) (Columbia: Missouri UP, 1986), pp. 166–88

Deghaye, Pierre, 'Jacob Boehme and his followers' in A. Faivre and J. Needleman (eds.), *Modern esoteric spirituality* (World spirituality series) (London: SCM Press; New York: Crossroad, 1993), pp. 210–47

Dickens, A. G., 'The early expansion of Protestantism in England, 1520–58', in *Archiv für Reformationsgeschichte* 78 (1987), pp. 187–21; repr. in Dickens, *Late monasticism and the Reformation* (London: Hambledon, 1994), pp. 101–32 (1987i)

Dickens, A. G., 'The shape of anticlericalism and the English Reformation', in E. I. Kouri and T. Scott (eds.), *Politics and society in Reformation Europe: essays for Sir Geoffrey Elton* (London: Macmillan, 1987), pp. 379–410, repr. in Dickens, *Late monasticism and the Reformation* (London: Hambledon, 1994), pp. 151–76 (1987ii)

Dickens, A. G., *The English reformation*, 2nd edn (London: Batsford, 1989)

Doerksen, Daniel W., *Conforming to the Word: Herbert, Donne, and the English Church before Laud* (Lewisburg and London: Associated University Presses, 1997)

Duffy, Eamon, 'The spirituality of John Fisher', in Bradshaw and Duffy (1989) pp. 205–31

Duffy, Eamon, *The stripping of the altars: traditional religon in England, 1400–1580* (New Haven and London: Yale UP, 1992)

Duffy, Eamon, 'Cranmer and popular religion' in P. Ayris and D. Selwyn (eds.), *Thomas Cranmer: churchman and scholar* (Woodbridge: Boydell, 1993), pp. 199–216

Durston, C., and Eales, J. (eds.), *The culture of English Puritanism, 1560–1700* (London: Macmillan, 1996)

Eales, Jacqueline, *Women in early modern England, 1500–1700* (London: UCL, 1998)

Emery, Kent, Jr., 'The story of recusant women exiled on the continent: an essay review of two books by Dorothy L. Latz', in James Hogg (ed.), *The mystical tradition and the Carthusians* 1 (*Analecta Cartusiana* 130) (Salzburg: Institut für Anglistik und Amerikanistik, 1995), pp. 118–34

Ferguson, S. B., *John Owen on the Christian life* (Edinburgh: Banner of Truth, 1987)

Firth, Katharine R., *The apocalyptic tradition in Reformation Britain, 1530–1645* (Oxford UP, 1979)

Fleming, P. W., 'Charity, faith and the gentry of Kent 1422–1529', in A. J. Pollard (ed.), *Property and politics: essays in late medieval English history* (Gloucester: Sutton, 1984), pp. 36–58

Fox, Alistair, *Thomas More: history and providence* (Oxford: Blackwell, 1982)

Fox, Alistair, *Utopia: an elusive vision* (Twayne's masterwork studies 103) (New York: Twayne, 1993)

Freer, Coburn, *Music for a king: George Herbert's style and the metrical Psalms* (Baltimore: Johns Hopkins UP, 1972)

Froehlich, Karlfried, 'Pseudo-Dionysius and the Reformation of the sixteenth century', in *Pseudo-Dionysius: the complete works*, trans. C. Luibheid (Classics of western spirituality) (London: SPCK, 1987), pp. 33–46

Furlong, M., *Puritan's progress: a study of John Bunyan* (London: Hodder & Stoughton, 1975)

Gaffney, James, *Augustine Baker's inner light: a study in English recusant spirituality* (Scranton UP, 1989)

Gibbons, B. J., *Gender in mystical and occult thought: Behmenism and its development in England* (Cambridge UP, 1996)

Gleason, J. B., *John Colet* (Berkeley: California UP, 1989)

Greaves, R. L., *John Bunyan and English Nonconformity* (London: Hambledon, 1992)

Gribbin, Joseph A., '*Ex oblatione fidelium*: the liturgy of the London charterhouse and the laity', in J. Hogg (ed.), *The mystical tradition and the Carthusians* 5 (*Analecta Cartusiana* 130) (Salzburg: Institut für Anglistik und Amerikanistik, 1996), pp. 83–104.

Gründler, Otto, 'John Calvin: ingrafting into Christ', in E. R. Elder (ed.), *The spirituality of western Christendom* (Cistercian Studies 30) (Kalamazoo Cistercian Publications, 1976), pp. 169–87

Guibbory, Achsah, *Ceremony and community from Herbert to Milton* (Cambridge UP, 1998)

Haigh, Christopher, *English reformations: religion, politics and society under the Tudors* (Oxford: Clarendon, 1993)

Haigh, Christopher (ed.), *The English Reformation revised* (Cambridge UP, 1987)

Halewood, W. H., *The poetry of grace: Reformation themes and structures in English seventeenth-century poetry* (New Haven & London: Yale UP, 1970)

Hall, Basil, 'Puritanism: the problem of definition', in *Humanists and Protestants, 1500–1900* (Edinburgh: T. & T. Clark, 1990), pp. 237–54

Hall, Basil, 'Cranmer's relations with Erasmianism and Lutheranism', in P. Ayris and D. Selwyn (eds.), *Thomas Cranmer: churchman and scholar* (Woodbridge: Boydell, 1993), pp. 3–38

Haller, William, *The rise of Puritanism* (New York: Columbia UP, 1938)

Hamilton, Alastair, *The family of love* (Cambridge: James Clarke, 1981)

Heath, P. (ed.), 'Staffordshire towns and the Reformation', in *North Staffordshire Journal of Field Studies* 19 (1979), pp. 1–21

Hill, Christopher, *Society and Puritanism in pre-revolutionary England* (New York: Schocken, 1964)

Hill, Christopher, *A turbulent, seditious and factious people: John Bunyan and his church* (Oxford UP, 1989)

Hill, Christopher, *The world turned upside down* (London: Temple Smith, 1972; repr. Penguin, 1975)

Hill, Christopher, *The English Bible and the seventeenth-century revolution* (Harmondsworth: Penguin, 1993)

Hill, G., 'The absolute reasonableness of Robert Southwell', in *The Lords of limit: essays on literature and ideas* (London: Andre Deutsch 1984), pp. 19–37

Hinson, E. Glenn, 'Prayer in John Bunyan and the early monastic tradition', *Cistercian Studies* 18 (1983), pp. 217–30

Hirst, Désirée, *Hidden riches: traditional symbolism from the Renaissance to Blake* (London: Eyre & Spottiswoode, 1964)

Hogg, James, 'Mount Grace Charterhouse and late medieval English spirituality', *Collectanea Cartusiensia* 3, *Analecta Cartusiana* 82:3 (1980), pp. 1–43

Hogg, James, 'A miscellaneous ms. of Syon Abbey' (on Antonio de Molina), in *Spiritualität heute und gestern* 16 (*Analecta Cartusiana* 35:16) (1992), pp. 177–9

Horsfield, Robert A., '"The Pomander of Prayer": aspects of late medieval English Carthusian spirituality and its lay audience', in M. G. Sargent (ed.), *De cella in seculum: religious and secular life and devotion in late medieval England* (Cambridge: D. S. Brewer, 1989), pp. 205–13

Hughes, H. Trevor, *The piety of Jeremy Taylor* (London: Macmillan, 1960)

Husain, Itrat, *The dogmatic and mystical theology of John Donne* (New York: Haskell, 1938)

Jones, Rufus M., *Mysticism and democracy in the English Commonwealth* (Cambridge, Mass.: Harvard UP, 1932)

Katz, David S., *The Jews in the history of England 1485–1850* (Oxford: Clarendon, 1994)

Kaufmann, U. Milo, *The Pilgrim's Progress and traditions in Puritan meditation* (Yale studies in English 163) (New Haven: Yale UP, 1966)

Keeble, N. H., *Richard Baxter: Puritan man of letters* (Oxford: Clarendon, 1982)

Keeble, N. H., *The literary culture of Nonconformity in later seventeenth-century England* (Leicester UP, 1987)

Keeble, N. H. (ed.), *John Bunyan: conventicle and Parnassus (tercentenary essays)* (Oxford: Clarendon, 1988)

Kendall, R.T., *Calvin and English Calvinism to 1649* (Oxford UP, 1979)

Kenny, Anthony, *Thomas More* (Past masters) (Oxford UP, 1983)

Kishlansky, Mark, *A monarchy transformed: Britain 1603–1714* (Penguin history of Britain 6) (Harmondsworth: Penguin, 1996)

Knowles, David, *The English mystical tradition* (London: Burns & Oates, 1961)

Knowles, David, *The religious orders in England III: The Tudor age* (Cambridge UP, 1959; repr. with corrections 1971)

Kuhn, Joaquin, 'The function of Psalm 90 in Thomas More's *A dialogue of comfort*', in *Moreana* 22 (1969), pp. 61–7

Kümin, B.A., *The shaping of a community: the rise and reformation of the English parish c.1400–1560* (Aldershot: Scolar Press, 1996)

Latz, Dorothy L., *'Glow-worm light': writings of 17th century English recusant women from original man-*

uscripts (Salzburg studies in English Literature: Elizabethan and Renaissance Studies 92:21 (Salzburg: Institut für Anglistik und Amerikanistik, 1989)

Le Huray, Peter, *Music and the Reformation in England, 1549–1660* (London: Herbert Jenkins, 1967)

Lewis, C. S., *English literature in the sixteenth century excluding drama* (Oxford history of English Literature) (Oxford: Clarendon, 1954)

Loades, David, 'Rites of passage and the Prayer Books of 1549 and 1552', in M. Wilks (ed.), *Prophecy and eschatology* (Studies in church history; subsidia 10) (Oxford: Blackwell, 1994), pp. 205–16

Loades, David, 'The spirituality of the restored Catholic Church (1553–1558) in the context of the Counter-Reformation', in T. M. McCoog (ed.), *The reckoned expense: Edmund Campion and the early English Jesuits: essays in celebration of the first centenary of Campion Hall, Oxford (1896–1996)* (Woodbridge: Boydell, 1996), pp. 3–20

Lossky, Nicholas (trans. A. Louth), *Lancelot Andrewes the preacher (1555–1626): the origins of the mystical theology of the Church of England* (Oxford: Clarendon, 1991)

Lowther Clarke, W. K., *Liturgy and worship: a companion to the prayer books of the Anglican Communion* (London: SPCK, 1964)

Loyer, Olivier, *L'anglicanisme de Richard Hooker* (thesis presented at the University of Paris III, 1977) (Lille University III: Atelier de Reproduction des Thèses, 1979)

McAdoo, H. R., *The structure of Caroline moral theology* (London: Longmans, 1949)

McAdoo, H. R., *The eucharistic theology of Jeremy Taylor today* (Norwich: Canterbury Press, 1988)

McConica, James, 'The patrimony of Thomas More', in H. Lloyd-Jones, V. Pearl, and B. Worden (eds.), *History and imagination: essays in honour of H. R. Trevor-Roper* (London: Duckworth, 1981), pp. 56–71

MacCulloch, Diarmaid, *Suffolk and the Tudors: politics and religion in an English county, 1500–1600* (Oxford: Clarendon, 1986)

MacCulloch, Diarmaid, *Building a godly realm: the establishment of English Protestantism 1558–1603* (New appreciations in history 27) (London: Historical Association, 1992)

MacCulloch, Diarmaid, *Thomas Cranmer: a life* (New Haven & London: Yale UP, 1996)

McGiffert, M., 'William Tyndale's conception of covenant', *Journal of Ecclesiastical History* 32 (1981), pp. 167–84

McGrath, Alister, *The intellectual origins of the European Reformation* (Oxford: Blackwell, 1987)

McGrath, Alister, *Reformation thought: an introduction*, 2nd edn (Oxford: Blackwell, 1993)

Mackie, J. D., *The earlier Tudors, 1485–1558* (Oxford history of England 7) (Oxford: Clarendon, 1952)

Maltby, Judith, '"By this Book": parishioners, the Prayer Book and the Established Church', in K. Fincham (ed.), *The early Stuart church, 1603–42* (London: Macmillan, 1993), pp. 115–37

Maltby, Judith, *Prayer Book and people in Elizabethan and early Stuart England* (Cambridge UP, 1998)

Marc'hadour, Gervaise, *The Bible in the works of St Thomas More*, 5 vols (Nieuwkoop: B. de Graaf, 1969–71)

Marc'hadour, Gervaise, 'Thomas More's spirituality', in R. S. Sylvester (ed.), *St Thomas More: action and contemplation* (Proceedings of the Symposium held at St John's University, October 9–10 1970) (New Haven and London: Yale UP, 1972), pp. 123–60

Marc'hadour, Gervaise, 'Fisher and More: a note' in Bradshaw and Duffy (1989) pp. 103–8

Marius, Richard, *Thomas More: a biography* (London: Dent, 1985)

Marsh, Christopher, 'In the name of God? Will-making and faith in early modern England', in G. H. Martin and Peter Spufford (eds.), *The records of the nation: the Public Record Office, 1838–1988; and the British Record Society, 1888–1988* (Woodbridge: Boydell and British Record Society, 1990), pp. 215–50

Martin, G. H., *The Family of Love in English society, 1550–1630* (Cambridge studies in early modern British history) (Cambridge UP, 1994)

Martin, G. H., *Popular religion in sixteenth-century England* (London: Macmillan, 1998)

Martin, J. W., 'Elizabethan Familists and other separatists in the Guildford area', in *Bulletin of the Institute of Historical Research* 51 (1978), pp. 90–3

Martin, J. W., *Religious radicals in Tudor England* (London: Hambledon, 1989)

Martz, Louis, *The poetry of meditation: a study in English religious literature of the seventeenth century* (New Haven: Yale UP, 1954)

Martz, Louis, *The paradise within: studies in Vaughan, Traherne, and Milton* (New Haven and London: Yale UP, 1964)

Martz, Louis, 'The generous ambiguity of Herbert's *Temple*', in M. A. Maleski (ed.), *A fine tuning: studies of the religious poetry of Herbert and Milton* (Medieval and Renaissance texts and studies 64) (Binghamton NY, 1989), pp. 31–56

Martz, Louis, 'The poetry of meditation: searching the memory', in J. R. Roberts, *New perspectives on the seventeenth-century English religious lyric* (Columbia: Missouri UP, 1994), pp. 188–200

Matar, N. I., 'Peter Sterry and the "Paradise Within": a study of the Emmanuel College letters', in *Restoration* 13 (1989), pp. 76–85

Mathew, David and Gervase, *The reformation and the contemplative life: a study of the conflict between the Carthusians and the state* (London: Sheed & Ward, 1934)

Mendelson, Sara, and Crawford, Patricia, *Women in early modern England, 1550–1720* (Oxford: Clarendon, 1998

Miller, C. H., 'The heart of the final struggle: More's Commentary on the Agony in the Garden', in M. J. Moore (ed.), *Quincentennial essays on St Thomas More* (Boone, North Carolina: Albion, 1978), pp. 108–23

Møller, J. G., 'The beginnings of Puritan covenant theology', *Journal of Ecclesiastical History* 14 (1963), pp. 46–67

Morrill, J., 'The church in England, 1642–9', in J. Morrill (ed.), *Reactions to the English Civil War 1642–1649* (Problems in Focus) (London: Macmillan, 1982), pp. 89–114

Moss, J. D., 'The Family of Love and English critics', *Sixteenth Century Journal* 6:1 (1975), pp. 35–52

Moss, J. D., 'Variations on a theme: the Family of Love in Renaissance England', *Renaissance Quarterly* 31 (1978), pp. 186–95

Mullett, M., *John Bunyan in context* (Studies in Protestant Nonconformity) (Keele: Keele UP, 1996)

Nuttall, Geoffrey, *The Holy Spirit in Puritan faith and experience* (Oxford: Blackwell, 1946)

Nuttall, Geoffrey, *Studies in Christian enthusiasm illustrated from early Quakerism* (Pendle Hill, Penn.: 1948)

Nuttall, Geoffrey, *Richard Baxter* (London: Nelson, 1965)

Nuttall, Geoffrey, 'George Fox and his Journal', in *The Puritan spirit: essays and addresses* (London: Epworth, 1967), pp. 177–93

Nuttall, Geoffrey, 'Overcoming the world: the early Quaker programme', in *Sanctity and Secularity: the Church and the World*, ed. D. Baker (Studies in church history 10 (Oxford: Blackwell, 1973), pp. 145–64

O'Day, Rosemary, *The English clergy: the emergence and consolidation of a profession, 1558–1642* (Leicester UP, 1979)

O'Malley, J., 'Early Jesuit spirituality: Spain and Italy', in L. Dupré and D. E. Saliers (eds.), *Christian spirituality III: post-Reformation and modern* (World spirituality series) (London: SCM Press, 1990), pp. 3–27

Orchard, M. Emmanuel IBVM, *Till God will: Mary Ward through her writings* (London: DLT, 1985)

Ozment, S., *Mysticism and Dissent: religious ideology and social protest in the sixteenth century* (New Haven: Yale UP, 1973)

Pettit, Norman, *The heart prepared: grace and conversion in Puritan spiritual life* (New Haven: Yale UP, 1966)

Parker, Kenneth L., *The English sabbath: a study of doctrine and discipline from the Reformation to the Civil War* (Cambridge UP, 1988)

Peters, Henriette, *Mary Ward: a world in contemplation*; ET by H. Butterworth (Leominster: Gracewing, 1994)

Pinto, V. de S., *Peter Sterry: Platonist and Puritan, 1613–1672* (Cambridge UP, 1934)

Porter, H. C., *Reformation and reaction in Tudor Cambridge* (Cambridge UP, 1958); repr. Hamden, Conn.: Shoe String Press, 1972)

Power, D. J., *The Christian anthropology of Augustine Baker's 'Holy wisdom'*, University of London PhD thesis, 1991

Procter, F., and Frere, W. H., *A new history of the Book of Common Prayer, with a rationale of its offices* (London: Macmillan, 1949)

Reidy, M. F. (SJ), *Bishop Lancelot Andrewes, Jacobean court preacher: a study in early seventeenth-century religious thought* (Chicago: Loyola UP, 1955)

Rex, Richard, *The theology of John Fisher* (Cambridge UP, 1991)

Reynolds, E. E., *Saint John Fisher* (London: Burns & Oates, 1955)

Richmond, Colin, 'The English gentry and religion, c.1500', in C. Harper-Bill (ed.), *Religious belief and ecclesiastical careers in late medieval England* (Woodbridge: Boydell, 1991), pp. 121–50

Ridley, Jasper, *Thomas Cranmer* (Oxford UP, 1962)

Rivers, Isabel, *Reason, grace, and sentiment: a study of the language of religion and ethics in England, 1660–1780* (Cambridge studies in eighteenth-century English literature and thought 8), 2 vols (Cambridge UP, 1991)

Rollin, Roger B., '"Fantastique ague": the *Holy Sonnets* and religious melancholy', in C. J. Summers and T.-L. Pebworth (eds.), *The eagle and the dove: reassessing John Donne* (Essays in seventeenth-century literature 1) (Columbia: Missouri UP, 1986), pp. 131–46

Rupp, E. G., 'A devotion of rapture in English Puritanism', in R. B. Knox (ed.), *Reformation, conformity and dissent: essays in honour of Geoffrey Nuttall* (London: Epworth, 1977), pp. 115–31

Rupp, E. G., 'Protestant spirituality in the first age of the Reformation', in G. Cuming and D. Baker (eds.), *Popular belief and practice* (Studies in church history 8) (Cambridge UP, 1984), pp. 155–70

Rupp, E. G., *Religion in England 1688–1791* (Oxford history of the Christian Church) (Oxford: Clarendon, 1986)

Salter, K. W., *Thomas Traherne: mystic and poet* (London: Edward Arnold, 1964)

Scallon, J. D., *The poetry of Robert Southwell SJ* (Salzburg studies in English Literature, Elizabethan and Renaissance studies 11) (Salzburg: Institut für Anglistik und Amerikanistik, 1975)

Scarisbrick, J. J. A., *The Reformation and the English people* (Oxford: Blackwell, 1984)

Schoenfeldt, Michael C., '"Respective Boldnesse": Herbert and the art of submission', in M. A. Maleski (ed.), *A fine tuning: studies of the religious poetry of Herbert and Milton* (Medieval and Renaissance texts and studies 64) (Binghamton NY, 1989), pp. 77–94

Schoenfeldt, Michael C., *Prayer and power: George Herbert and Renaissance courtship* (Chicago UP, 1991)

Schoenfeldt, Michael C., 'The poetry of supplication: toward a cultural poetics of the religious lyric', in J. R. Roberts (ed.), *New perspectives on the seventeenth-century English religious lyric* (Columbia: Missouri UP, 1994), pp. 75–104

Scholes, Percy A., *The Puritans and music* (London: Oxford UP, 1934)

Schwarz, Marc L., 'Some thoughts on the development of a lay religious consciousness in pre-Civil-War England', in G. J. Cuming and D. Baker (eds.), *Popular belief and practice* (Studies in church history 8) (Cambridge UP, 1984), pp. 171–8

Sharrock, Roger, 'Spiritual autobiography: Bunyan's *Grace abounding*', in A. Laurence, W. R. Owens, and S. Sim (eds.), *John Bunyan and his England, 1628–88* (London: Hambledon, 1990), pp. 97–104

Shaw, Robert B., *The call of God: the theme of vocation in the poetry of Donne and Herbert* (Cambridge, Mass.: Cowley Publications, 1981)

Smith, Catherine F., 'Jane Lead: the feminist mind and art of a seventeenth-century Protestant mystic', in R. Ruether and E. McLaughlin (eds.), *Women of spirit: female leadership in the Jewish and Christian traditions* (New York: Simon & Schuster, 1979), pp. 183–204 (1979i)

Smith, Catherine F., 'Jane Lead: mysticism and the woman cloathed with the sun', in S. M. Gilbert and S. Gubar (eds.), *Shakespeare's sisters: feminist essays on women poets* (Bloomington, Ind.: Indiana UP, 1979), pp. 3–18 (1979ii)

Smith, Julia J., 'Thomas Traherne and the Restoration', in *The Seventeenth Century* 3 (1988), pp. 203–22

Smith, Julia J. (with Laetitia Yeandle), 'Felicity disguisd in fiery Words: Genesis and Exodus in a newly discovered poem by Thomas Traherne', in *The Times Literary Supplement* 4936 (7 November 1997), p. 17

Smith, Nigel, *Perfection proclaimed: language and literature in English radical religion 1640–1600* (Oxford: Clarendon, 1989)

Sommerville, C. J., *Popular religion in Restoration England* (Florida University social science monographs 59) (Gainesville: Florida UP, 1977)

Sommerville, C. J., *The secularization of early modern England: from religious culture to religious faith* (New York: Oxford UP, 1992)

Spaeth, D. A., 'Common Prayer? Popular observance of the Anglican liturgy in Restoration Wiltshire', in S. J. Wright (ed.), *Parish, church and people: local studies in lay religion 1350–1750* (London: Hutchinson, 1988), pp. 125–51

Spufford, Margaret, *Contrasting communities: English villagers in the sixteenth and seventeenth centuries* (Cambridge UP, 1974)

Spufford, Margaret, *Small books and pleasant histories: popular fiction and its readership in seventeenth-century England* (London: Methuen, 1981)

Spufford, Margaret, 'Can we count the "Godly" and the "Conformable" in the seventeenth century?', in *Journal of Ecclesiastical History* 36 (1985), pp. 428–38 (1985i)

Spufford, Margaret, 'Puritanism and social control?' in A. Fletcher and J. Stevenson, *Order and disorder in early modern England* (Cambridge UP, 1985), pp. 41–57 (1985ii)

Spufford, Margaret, 'The importance of religion in the sixteenth and seventeenth centuries', in Spufford (ed.) (1995) pp. 1–102

Spufford, Margaret (ed.), *The world of rural dissenters, 1520–1725* (Cambridge UP, 1995)

Spurr, John, *English Puritanism 1603–1689* (Basingstoke: Macmillan, 1998)

Stachniewski, John, *The persecutory imagination: English Puritanism and the literature of religious despair* (Oxford: Clarendon, 1991)

Steere, D. V. (ed.), *Quaker spirituality: selected writings* (Classics of western spirituality) (New York: Paulist Press, 1984)

Stevenson, Bill, 'The social and economic status of post-Restoration dissenters, 1660–1725', in Spufford (ed.) (1995) pp. 332–59

Stevenson, Kenneth, *Covenant of grace renewed: a vision of the Eucharist in the seventeenth century* (London: DLT, 1994)

Stranks, C. J., *Anglican devotion: studies in the spiritual life of the Church of England between the Reformation and the Oxford Movement* (London: SCM Press, 1961)

Strier, Richard, *Love known: theology and experience in George Herbert's poetry* (Chicago UP, 1983)

Strier, Richard, 'Donne and the politics of devotion', in D. B. Hamilton and R. Strier, *Religion, literature, and politics in post-Reformation England, 1540–1688* (Cambridge UP, 1996), pp. 93–114

Summerson, John, *Architecture in Britain 1530–1830* (Pelican history of art) 9th edn (London and New Haven: Yale UP, (1993)

Talon, Henri, *John Bunyan: the man and his work* (ET by B. Wall of *John Bunyan – l'homme et l'oeuvre* (Paris, 1948)) (London: Rockcliff, 1951)

Templeman, G. (ed.), 'The records of the Guild of the Holy Trinity, St Mary and St John the Baptist and St Katherine of Coventry', 2 (Dugdale Society 19) (Oxford UP, 1944) (esp. pp. 152–62, on the religious expenditure of guilds in the early sixteenth century)

Thomas, Keith, *Religion and the decline of magic: studies in popular beliefs in sixteenth- and seventeenth-century England* (London: Weidenfeld & Nicolson, 1971)

Thomson, J. A. F., *The transformation of medieval England 1370–1529* (Foundations of modern Britain) (London: Longman, 1983)

Thornton, Martin, *English spirituality* (London: SPCK, 1963)

Thune, Nils, *The Behmenists and the Philadelphians: a contribution to the study of English mysticism in the seventeenth and eighteenth centuries* (Uppsala: Almquist & Wiksells, 1948)

Toon, P., *God's statesman: the life and work of John Owen, pastor, educator, theologian* (Exeter: Paternoster, 1971)

Trinkaus, C., and Oberman, H. A. (eds.), *The pursuit of holiness in late medieval and renaissance religion* (Studies in medieval and Reformation thought 10) (Leiden, 1974)

Tripp, Diane K., 'Daily prayer in the Reformed tradition: an initial survey', in *Studia Liturgica* 21 (1991), pp. 76–107, 190–219

Tuve, Rosemond, *A reading of George Herbert* (London: Faber & Faber, 1952)

Veith, G. E., *Reformation spirituality: the religion of George Herbert* (Lewisburg: Bucknell UP, 1985)

Wakefield, Gordon S., *Puritan devotion* (London: Epworth, 1957)

Wakefield, Gordon S., *John Bunyan the Christian* (London: HarperCollins, 1992)

Wakefield, Gordon S., *George Herbert and today's church* (Southwell Lecture 6, 1993), privately printed

Wakefield, Gordon S., 'John Milton' ('God and some English poets', 10), in *Expository Times* (1996) pp. 297–301

Watkins, Owen C., *The Puritan experience* (London: Routledge & Kegan Paul, 1972)

Watt, Tessa, *Cheap print and popular piety 1550–1640* (Cambridge studies in early modern British history) (Cambridge UP, 1991)

Watt, Tessa, 'Piety in the pedlar's pack: continuity and change, 1578–1630', in Spufford (ed.) (1995) pp. 235–72

Watts, Michael, *The dissenters* (vol. 1) (Oxford: Clarendon, 1978)

Welsby, P. A., *Lancelot Andrewes 1555–1626* (London: SPCK, 1958)

Whatmore, L. E., *The Carthusians under King Henry the Eighth* (*Analecta Cartusiana* 109) (Salzburg: Institut für Anglistik und Amerikanistik, 1983)

White, Helen C., *The Tudor books of private devotion* (Wisconsin UP, 1951)

White, B. R., *The English separatist tradition* (Oxford UP, 1971)

Whiting, R., *The blind devotion of the people: popular religion and the English Reformation* (Cambridge UP, 1989)

Whiting, R., *Local responses to the English Reformation* (Basingstoke: Macmillan, 1998)

Wilcox, Helen, 'Herbert's musical contexts: Countrey-Aires to Angels Musick', in E. Miller and R. DiYanni (eds.), *Like season'd timber: new essays on George Herbert* (Seventeenth-century texts and studies 1) (New York: Peter Lang, 1987), pp. 37–58

Williams, R. L., 'Patterns of reformation in the theology of William Tyndale', in P. Brooks (ed.), *Christian spirituality: essays in honour of Gordon Rupp* (London: SCM Press, 1975), pp. 119–139

Wolf, William J., 'The spirituality of Thomas Traherne', in William J. Wolf (ed.), *Anglican spirituality* (Wilton, Conn.: Morehouse-Barlow, 1982), pp. 49–68

Wood, T., *English casuistical divinity during the seventeenth century* (London: SPCK, 1952)

Wrightson K. and Levine D., *Poverty and piety in an English village: Terling, 1525–1700* (London: Academic Press, 1979)

Yates, Nigel, *Buildings, faith, and worship: the liturgical arrangement of Anglican churches, 1600–1900* (Oxford: Clarendon, 1991)

Yule, G. S. S., 'The Puritan piety of members of the Long Parliament', in G. J. Cuming and D. Baker (eds.), *Popular belief and practice* (Studies in church history 8) (Cambridge UP, 1984), pp. 187–94

Zim, Rivkah, *English metrical Psalms: poetry as praise and prayer, 1535–1601* (Cambridge UP, 1987)

Index